INTRODUCING COMPARATIVE POLITICS

Examining country case studies within a thematic framework.

The authors introduce the broad debates early to demonstrate how comparativists use various theories and methodologies to understand political phenomena.

Each chapter introduces concepts and then immediately uses these key ideas to examine relevant, topical cases. These case studies are *integrated* into the chapter—not separated from theory—and set within cross-national context.

Eleven Core Cou...

Germany | China | Brazil | United Kingdom
India | Nigeria | Russia | Japan
Mexico | Iran | United States

1 INTRODUCTION

KEY QUESTIONS

- How much power do different people or groups have in different political systems?
- Do self-interest, beliefs, or underlying structural forces best explain how people act in the political realm?
- What kinds of evidence can help us determine why political actors do what they do?
- What can be learned from comparing political behavior and outcomes across countries?

Understanding political developments and disputes around the world has never seemed more important than it does today. The financial crisis that began in 2008 has demonstrated profoundly the interrelationships among countries' and people's well-being across the globe. The crisis began in the United States but ultimately hit Europe at least as hard. Most wealthy countries' relative power and wealth seem to be declining compared with rising powers such as China and India, but China has an authoritarian regime, raising major questions about whether it will move toward a democracy, and if it doesn't what type of global power it will be. The Middle East, meanwhile, has seen upheaval unlike anything in modern history, as long-standing dictators were toppled in Tunisia and Libya, and unrest continues in Bahrain, Egypt, and Syria. These changes threaten to reorient the entire political context of the region, with profound political and economic implications for the United States and other major powers.

Many people now see the world as more complicated and less comprehensible than it was during the post–Cold War era (1989–2001), when the international realm seemed peaceful and stable and foreign politics was of little importance. The end of communist rule in the Soviet Union and Eastern Europe seemed to foreshadow a period in which understanding political differences among countries would be both easier and less important. Instead, the era witnessed dramatic political change: several countries split into two or more new countries, the number of ethnic and religious civil wars increased significantly, and two full-scale genocides have occurred. On the other hand, the number of countries that could claim to have democratic governments also increased substantially, and East Asia, led by China, achieved unprecedented economic growth that lifted more people out of poverty more quickly than ever before in history.

Diversity of political, economic, and social life among nations exists in every period of history. Comparative politics attempts to understand this diversity, assessing current events in the light of fundamental and long-standing questions: Why do governments form? Why does a group of people come to see itself as a nation? Why do nations sometimes fall apart? How can a government convince people that it has the right to rule? Do some forms of government last longer than others? Do some forms of government serve their people's interests better than others? How do democracies form, and how do they fall apart? Can democracy work anywhere or only in particular countries and at particular times? Are certain political institutions more democratic than others? Can government policy reduce poverty and improve economic well-being? This book introduces you to the many and often conflicting answers to these questions that political scientists have proposed by examining these and other questions comparatively. It

CASE Study

RUSSIA: SEMIPRESIDENTIALISM IN A NEW DEMOCRACY WITH WEAK INSTITUTIONS

- **EXECUTIVE POWER**
  Initially strong, now nearly unlimited; appoints and can remove PM

- **LEGISLATIVE POWER**
  Very weak; minimal appointment powers compared with most semipresidential systems; cabinet ministers do not need to be members of legislature

- **ACCOUNTABILITY**
  Minimal

- **VETO PLAYERS**
  None

R ussia is the largest country in the world with a semipresidential system, and it is certainly one of the most important. Its current government demonstrates the worst fears of the system's critics: that in a regime with weak institutions, a powerful presidency can be dangerous to democracy by allowing one official to achieve overwhelming power. This executive dominance is not inherent in all semipresidential systems, as France demonstrates, but Russia is a cautionary case of the problem of a strong presidency in a new democracy with weak institutions.

The Russian constitution adopted in 1993 created a semipresidential system with an exceptionally strong presidency. The president is directly elected to a six-year term (it was a four-year term until a 2012 constitutional amendment), with a maximum of two terms possible. He must be elected by an absolute majority: if no candidate

A quick **Snapshot Overview** helps orient students and encourages critical reading.

Integrated **Case Studies** of eleven core countries are touchstones throughout the text.

A **Case Summary** highlights key lessons.

CASE Summary

Lula came to power as one of the mo[...] bers of the "pink tide." While he i[...] able social programs (see chapter 11), maintaining international i[...] required economic policies that initially gave him few resources to [...] growth, however, allowed the PT government to fund social prog[...] went by, substantially reducing poverty. This growth, though, dep[...] high commodity prices, and when the global market shifted, largely [...] growth in China and Europe, Brazil's model came into question. The [...] claimed it was the champion of the poor, faced massive demonstrati[...]

CASE Questions

1. What are the implications of the Brazilian case for Latin America's "p[...] In the face of globalization, does even a large developing country like [...] the ability to chart its own development policy, or does globalization [...] much?

2. What does a comparison of the Brazilian and Indian cases teach us about[...] over the effect of democracy on economic development? What impor[...] ences and similarities do you see between these two democratic cases [...] how and why democracy affects development?

New **Case Questions** help students apply concepts.

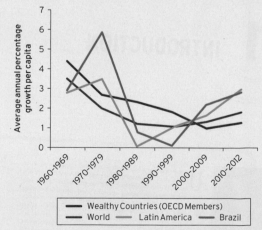

in CONTEXT

Brazilian Economic Growth

Before 1980, the Brazilian economic miracle produced higher economic growth rates than in much of the world. The "lost decades" of the 1980s and 1990s for both Brazil and Latin America as a whole destroyed growth, but they were followed by renewal in the new millennium.

Per capita GDP growth rates (average annual percentages)

Legend: — Wealthy Countries (OECD Members) — World — Latin America — Brazil

Source: Data are from the World Bank, Annual GDP Growth Rate, per capita (http://data.worldbank.org/indicator/NY.GDP.PCAP.KD.ZG).

In Context boxes place case studies and data into instructive regional perspective.

A **Country and Concept** table in each chapter displays key indicators for core countries to offer at-a-glance context and comparison.

COUNTRY AND CONCEPT
Parties, Elections, and Civil Society

Country	Electoral system	Party system	Number of significant parties in legislature[1]	Interest-group system
Brazil	Open-list PR	Multiple	9	Pluralist
China	NA	One	1	State corporatist
Germany	Mixed PR	Two and a half	5	Neocorporatist
India	SMD/FPTP	Multiple	5 (in addition to dozens of minor parties)	Pluralist
Iran	Mixed SMD and multimember districts	None	0[2]	Weak
Japan	Mixed PR	Multiple	4	Pluralist
Mexico	Mixed PR	Multiple	3	Neocorporatist
Nigeria	SMD/FPTP	Dominant	3[3]	Weak
Russia	Mixed PR	Dominant	2	Weak
United Kingdom	SMD/FPTP	Two	3	Pluralist
United States	SMD/FPTP	Two	2	Pluralist

[1] Data on number of parties in legislatures are from *Political Handbook of the World, 2013* (Washington, DC: CQ Press, 2013).

[2] Although political parties are permitted under the constitution, none were recognized following the formal dissolution of the government-sponsored Islamic Republican Party in June 1987, despite Tehran's announcement in October 1988 that such groups would thenceforth be

---

CRITICAL inquiry

Women in Power

Americans are used to considering themselves progressive when it comes to women's rights, yet in 2013 only 17.8 percent of representatives in the House and 20 percent of senators were women. Those numbers put the United States seventy-eighth in the world in 2013, slightly below the global average of 20.8 percent for female representation in national legislatures. As Table 7.1b shows, in some democracies women constitute nearly half of the legislature, while others fare far worse than in the United States. What explains these disparities in how many women achieve power at the national level?

Table 7.1a suggests an initial hypothesis based on political culture, because regional breakdowns seem to suggest that it plays a role. An alternative hypothesis is that the election of women is a case in which institutions matter. Table 7.1b suggests that PR systems are more conducive to electing women than are SMD systems. Because closed PR systems (most PR systems are closed) require parties to submit lists of candidates, more women are nominated. A party may be under some pressure to include at least some women on its list, since an all-male (or even overwhelmingly male) list could provoke negative reaction. Some PR systems include a quota system: parties must include a certain percentage of women candidates on their lists. A third hypothesis is that the longer a country is democratic, the more women will gain office; democracy provides an opportunity for underrepresented and marginalized groups to gain more

influence, and the longer democracy lasts the more likely it will be that such groups will gain influence.

Look at the tables carefully. Based on the data, which of the hypotheses seems to be the best explanation for how many women are elected to national legislatures? Why do you come to the conclusion you do on this question? What implications does your answer have for which electoral system is most democratic?

TABLE 7.1a	Percentage of Seats in Lower House Occupied by Women, Regional Averages
Region	**% women**
Nordic countries	42.0%
Americas	24.4%
Europe, OSCE member countries, including Nordic countries	24.1%
Europe, OSCE member countries, excluding Nordic countries	22.4%
sub-Saharan Africa	21.2%
Asia	19.0%
Arab states	15.7%
Pacific	12.7%

Source: Data are from Interparliamentary Union, "Women in National Parliaments" (http://www.ipu.org/wmn-e/world.htm).

New **Critical Inquiry** boxes invite students to explore a research problem, develop and test a hypothesis with real data, and then answer critical analysis questions.

Elements that help students read, review, research, and study.

KEY QUESTIONS

- Do states continue to have effective economic sovereignty, or does globalization force them to adopt certain economic policies?

- What explains the ability of states to pursue successful development policies in the context of globalization?

- In what ways has globalization affected states' ability to respond effectively to economic crises?

- Why have some countries moved to liberalize their economies in the face of globalization more than others?

- What types of regimes are able to pursue more effective economic policies, and why?

Third, examining politics comparatively helps us develop broad theories about how politics works. A **theory** is an abstract argument that provides a systematic explanation of some phenomenon. The theory of evolution, for instance, makes an argument about how species change over time in response to their environments. The social sciences, including political science, use two different kinds of theories. An **empirical theory** is an argument that explains what actually occurs. Empirical theorists first *describe* a pattern and then attempt to *explain* what causes it. The theory of evolution is an empirical theory in that evolutionary biologists do not argue whether evolution is inherently good or bad; they simply describe evolutionary patterns and explain their causes. A good empirical theory should also allow theorists to *predict* what will happen as well. For example, a comparison of democratic systems in post–civil war situations would lead us to predict that presidential systems are more likely to lead to renewed conflict.

On the other hand, a **normative theory** is an argument that explains what *ought* to occur. For instance, socialists support a normative theory that the government and economy *ought* to be structured in a way that produces a relatively equal distribution of wealth. While comparativists certainly hold various normative theories, most of the discipline of comparative politics focuses on empirical theory. We attempt to explain the political world around us, and we do this by looking across multiple cases to come up with generalizations about politics.

theory
An abstract argument that provides a systematic explanation of some phenomena

empirical theory
An argument explaining what actually occurs; empirical theorists first notice and describe a pattern and then attempt to explain what causes it

normative theory
An argument explaining what ought to occur rather than what does occur; contrast with empirical theory

Marginal Glossary

Chapter-opening
Key Questions

WORKS CITED

Altman, Roger C. 2009. "Globalization in Retreat." *Foreign Affairs* 88 (4).

Cafruny, Alan W., and Leila Simona Talani. 2013. "The Crisis of the Eurozone." In *Exploring the Global Financial Crisis*, edited by Alan W. Cafruny and Herman M. Schwartz, 13–34. Boulder, CO: Lynne Rienner.

Calmes, Jackie, and Jonathan Weisman. 2013. "Economists See Deficit Emphasis as Impeding Recovery." *New York Times.* May 8, 2013 (http://www.nytimes.com/2013/05/09/us/deficit-reduction-is-seen-by-economists-as-impeding-recovery.html?emc=eta1&_r=0).

Crew, David F. 1998. *Germans on Welfare: From Weimar to Hitler.* New York: Oxford University Press.

Cypher, James M., and Raúl Delgado Wise. 2011. *Mexico's Economic Dilemma: The Developmental Failure of Neoliberalism.* New York: Rowman and Littlefield.

Dadush, Uri, and Kemal Derviş. 2013. "The Inequality Challenge." *Current History* 112, no. 750 (January): 13–19 (http://www.brookings.edu/research/articles/2013/01/inequality-challenge-dervis).

Edwards, Haley Sweetland. 2013. "He Who Makes the Rules." *Washington Monthly.* March/April 2013 (http://www.washingtonmonthly.com/magazine/march_april_2013/feature...
ma...
all)

Garret...
in t...
Can...

www.brookings.edu/~/media/research/files/papers/2007/11/generations%20isaacs/11_generations_isaacs.pdf).

Johnson, Chalmers A. 1982. *MITI and the Japanese Miracle: The Growth of Industrial Policy, 1925–1975.* Stanford, CA: Stanford University Press.

Kingston, John. 2013. *Contemporary Japan: History, Politics, and Social Change since the 1980s.* 2nd ed. Malden, MA: John Wiley & Sons.

Lincoln, James, and Masahiro Shimotani. 2009. "Whither the *Keiretsu*, Japan's Business Networks? How Were They Structured? What Did They Do? Why Are They Gone?" Working Paper Series, Institute for Research on Labor and Employment, University of California, Berkeley (http://www.escholarship.org/uc/item/00m7d34g).

Lowrey, Annie. 2013. "The Rich Get Richer through the Recovery." *New York Times,* September 10 (http://economix.blogs.nytimes.com/2013/09/10/the-rich-get-richer-through-the-recovery/?ref=business&_r=0).

Miura, Mari. 2012. *Welfare through Work: Conservative Ideas, Partisan Dynamics, and Social Protection in Japan.* Ithaca, NY: Cornell University Press.

Ocampo, José A...

RESOURCES FOR FURTHER STUDY

Bates, Robert H. 2001. *Prosperity and Violence: The Political Economy of Development.* New York: W. W. Norton.

Friedman, Milton. 1962. *Capitalism and Freedom.* Chicago: University of Chicago Press.

Gilpin, Robert. 2000. *The Challenge of Global Capitalism.* Princeton, NJ: Princeton University Press.

Heilbroner, Robert L. 1985. *The Nature and Logic of Capitalism.* New York: W. W. Norton.

International Monetary Fund. 2007. *Regional Economic Outlook, Sub-Saharan Africa.* Washington, DC: International Monetary Fund (http://www.imf.org/external/pubs/ft/reo/2007/afr/eng/sreo1007.pdf/).

Jameson, Kenneth P., and Charles K. Wilber. 1996. *The Political Economy of Development and Underdevelopment.* 6th ed. New York: McGraw Hill.

Keynes, John Maynard. 1935. *The General Theory of Employment, Interest, and Money.* New York: Harcourt Brace.

The Levin Institute, The State University of New York. "Globalization 101: A Student's Guide to Globalization" (http://www.globalization101.org).

Organization of the Petroleum Exporting Countries. 2006. *OPEC Annual Statistical Bulletin 2006* (http://www.opec.org/opec_web/static_files_project/media/downloads/publications/ASB06.pdf).

Rapley, John. 2007. *Understanding Development: Theory and Practice in the Third World.* 3rd ed. Boulder, CO: Lynne Rienner.

Siebert, Horst. 2005. *The German Economy: Beyond the Social Market.* Princeton, NJ: Princeton University Press.

Woo-Cumings, Meredith, ed. 1999. *The Developmental State.* Ithaca, NY: Cornell University Press.

WEB RESOURCES

Human Development Reports, "International Human Development Indicators"
(http://hdr.undp.org/en/statistics)

International Labour Organization, "LABORSTA Internet"
(http://laborsta.ilo.org)

International Monetary Fund, "World Economic Outlook Database"
(http://www.imf.org/external/pubs/ft/weo/2013/01/weodata/index.aspx)

Organisation for Economic Co-operation and Development, "OECD.Stat Extracts"
(http://www.oecd-ilibrary.org/statistics)

World Bank, Economic Policy and External Debt, Data
(http://data.worldbank.org/topic/economic-policy-and-external-debt)

KEY CONCEPTS

capitalism (p. 198)
codetermination (p. 234)
command economy (p. 199)
comparative advantage (p. 208)
deficit spending (p. 205)
developmental state (p. 238)
externality (p. 201)
fiscal policy (p. 205)
globalization (p. 216)
import-substitution industrialization (ISI) (p. 208)
Keynesian theory (p. 205)

market economy (p. 197)
market failure (p. 201)
monetarist theory (p. 206)
monetary policy (p. 206)
monopoly (p. 202)
natural monopoly (p. 203)
neoliberalism (p. 207)
privatize (p. 210)
public goods (p. 199)
social market economy (p. 232)
structural adjustment programs (SAPs) (p. 210)

SAGE edge for CQ Press — Sharpen your skills with SAGE edge at **edge.sagepub.com/orvis3e.** **SAGE edge for students** provides a personalized approach to help you accomplish your coursework goals in an easy-to-use learning environment.

End-of-Chapter Resources:
key terms, works cited, suggested readings, and web resources lists

Dramatically expanded graphics program and a new full-color interior help students better visualize data and information.

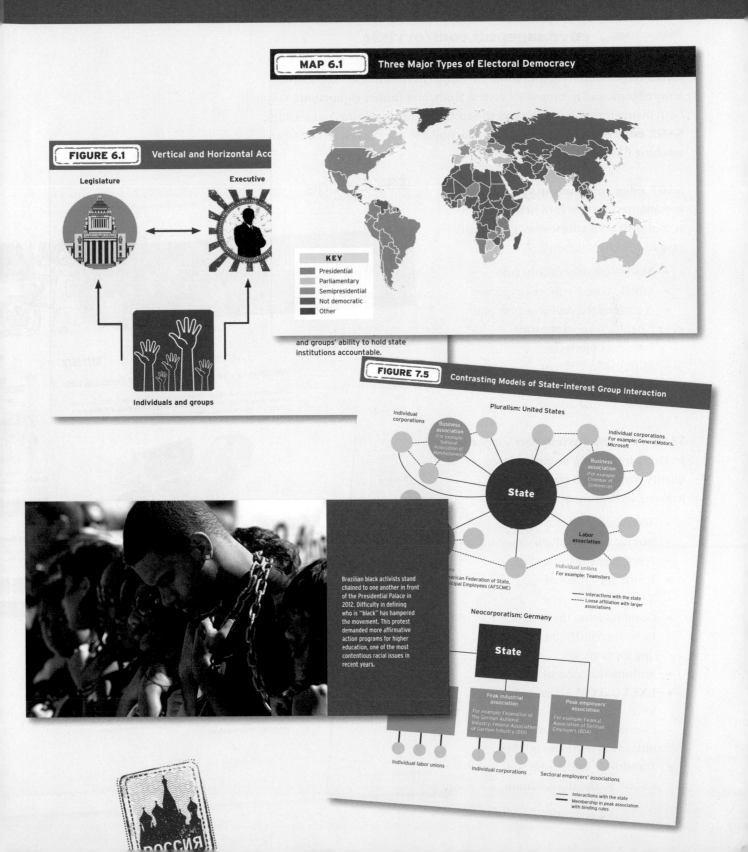

MAP 6.1   Three Major Types of Electoral Democracy

KEY

- Presidential
- Parliamentary
- Semipresidential
- Not democratic
- Other

FIGURE 6.1   Vertical and Horizontal Acc...

Legislature

Executive

Individuals and groups

and groups' ability to hold state institutions accountable.

FIGURE 7.5   Contrasting Models of State-Interest Group Interaction

Pluralism: United States

Individual corporations

Business association (For example: National Association of Manufacturers)

Individual corporations
For example: General Motors, Microsoft

Business association (For example: Chamber of Commerce)

State

Labor association

...merican Federation of State, ...nicipal Employees (AFSCME)

Individual unions
For example: Teamsters

—— Interactions with the state
---- Loose affiliation with larger associations

Neocorporatism: Germany

State

Peak industrial association

For example: Federation of the German Automol Industry; Federal Association of German Industry (BDI)

Peak employers' association

For example: Federal Association of German Employers (BDA)

Individual labor unions

Individual corporations

Sectoral employers' associations

—— Interactions with the state
—— Membership in peak association with binding rules

Brazilian black activists stand chained to one another in front of the Presidential Palace in 2012. Difficulty in defining who is "black" has hampered the movement. This protest demanded more affirmative action programs for higher education, one of the most contentious racial issues in recent years.

$SAGE edge™
for CQ Press

edge.sagepub.com/orvis3e

SAGE edge offers a robust online environment featuring an impressive array of tools and resources for review, study, and further exploration, keeping both instructors and students on the cutting edge of teaching and learning. **SAGE edge** content is open access and available on demand. Learning and teaching have never been easier.

SAGE edge for Students provides a personalized approach to help students accomplish their coursework goals in an easy-to-use environment.

- Mobile-friendly eFlashcards
- Mobile-friendly practice quizzes
- A customized online action plan
- Chapter summaries with learning objectives
- Multimedia content
- **EXCLUSIVE!** Access to full-text SAGE journal articles

SAGE edge for Instructors supports teaching by making it easy to integrate quality content and create a rich learning environment for students.

- Test bank
- Sample course syllabi
- PowerPoint® lecture slides
- Instructor's manual
- TA Guide
- Graphics from the text in PowerPoint®, .pdf, and .jpg formats
- Multimedia content
- **EXCLUSIVE!** Access to full-text SAGE journal articles
- Common course cartridge for uploading resources in LMS
- Transition Guide from the second to the third edition

CQ Press, an imprint of SAGE, is the leading publisher of books, periodicals, and electronic products on American government and international affairs. CQ Press consistently ranks among the top commercial publishers in terms of quality, as evidenced by the numerous awards its products have won over the years. CQ Press owes its existence to Nelson Poynter, former publisher of the *St. Petersburg Times,* and his wife Henrietta, with whom he founded Congressional Quarterly in 1945. Poynter established CQ with the mission of promoting democracy through education and in 1975 founded the Modern Media Institute, renamed The Poynter Institute for Media Studies after his death. The Poynter Institute (*www.poynter.org*) is a nonprofit organization dedicated to training journalists and media leaders.

In 2008, CQ Press was acquired by SAGE, a leading international publisher of journals, books, and electronic media for academic, educational, and professional markets. Since 1965, SAGE has helped inform and educate a global community of scholars, practitioners, researchers, and students spanning a wide range of subject areas, including business, humanities, social sciences, and science, technology, and medicine. A privately owned corporation, SAGE has offices in Los Angeles, London, New Delhi, and Singapore, in addition to the Washington DC office of CQ Press.

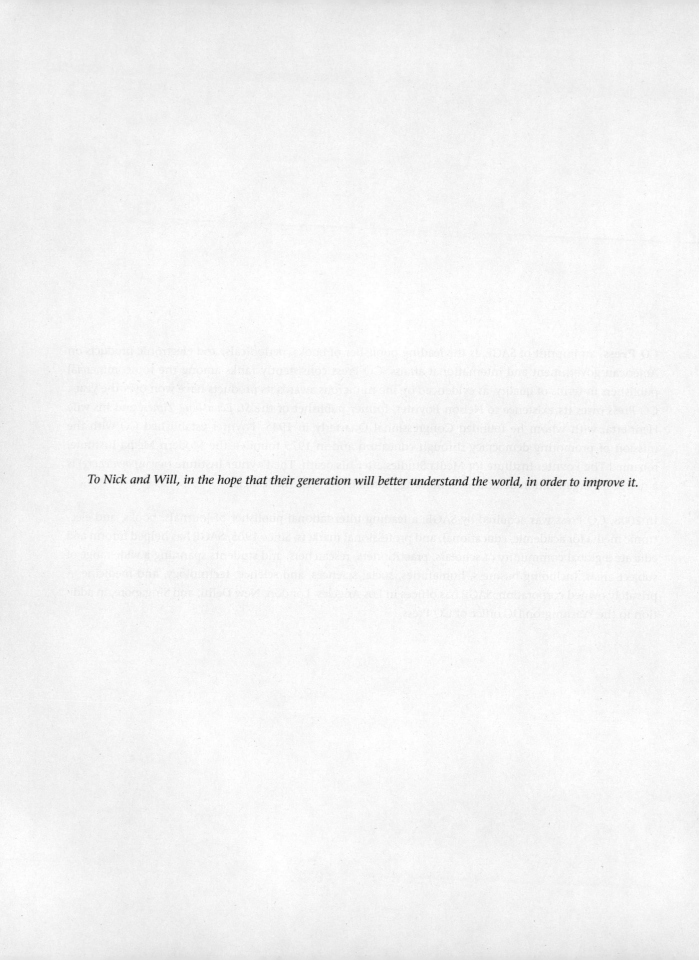

To Nick and Will, in the hope that their generation will better understand the world, in order to improve it.

Introducing Comparative Politics

CONCEPTS AND CASES IN CONTEXT

THIRD EDITION

STEPHEN ORVIS
HAMILTON COLLEGE

CAROL ANN DROGUS
COLGATE UNIVERSITY

Los Angeles | London | New Delhi
Singapore | Washington DC

Los Angeles | London | New Delhi
Singapore | Washington DC

FOR INFORMATION:

CQ Press
An Imprint of SAGE Publications, Inc.
2455 Teller Road
Thousand Oaks, California 91320
E-mail: order@sagepub.com

SAGE Publications Ltd.
1 Oliver's Yard
55 City Road
London, EC1Y 1SP
United Kingdom

SAGE Publications India Pvt. Ltd.
B 1/I 1 Mohan Cooperative Industrial Area
Mathura Road, New Delhi 110 044
India

SAGE Publications Asia-Pacific Pte. Ltd.
3 Church Street
#10-04 Samsung Hub
Singapore 049483

Publisher: Charisse Kiino
Editorial Assistant: Davia Grant
Assistant Editor: Allison Hughes
Developmental Editor: Elise Frasier
Production Editor: Tracy Buyan
Copy Editor: Talia Greenberg
Typesetter: C&M Digitals (P) Ltd.
Proofreader: Lawrence W. Baker
Indexer: Maria Sosnowski
Cover and Interior Design: Auburn Associates
Marketing Manager: Amy Whitaker

Printed in Canada.

Library of Congress Cataloging-in-Publication Data

Orvis, Stephen Walter, 1959–

Introducing comparative politics : concepts and cases in context / Stephen Orvis, Hamilton College. Carol Ann Drogus, Colgate University. — Third edition.

pages cm.
Includes bibliographical references and index.

ISBN 978-1-4522-4152-4 (pbk.)

1. Comparative government.
2. Comparative government—Case studies.
I. Drogus, Carol Ann. II. Title.

JF51.D76 2014
320.3—dc23   2013037023

This book is printed on acid-free paper.

14 15 16 17 18 10 9 8 7 6 5 4 3 2 1

Brief Contents

About the Authors

Stephen Orvis is Professor of Government and Associate Dean of Students for Academics at Hamilton College. He is a specialist on sub-Saharan Africa (Kenya in particular), identity politics, democratic transitions, and the political economy of development. He has been teaching introduction to comparative politics for more than twenty-five years, as well as courses on African politics, nationalism and the politics of identity, political economy of development, and weak states. He has written a book and articles on agricultural development in Kenya, as well as several articles on civil society in Africa and Kenya, and is currently doing research on political institutions in Africa.

Carol Ann Drogus is Senior Associate Director of Off-Campus Study at Colgate University. She is a specialist on Brazil, religion, and women's political participation. She taught introduction to comparative politics for more than fifteen years, as well as courses on Latin American politics, gender and politics, and women in Latin America. She has written two books and numerous articles on the political participation of women in religious movements in Brazil.

Contents

CHAPTER 3. STATES, CITIZENS, AND REGIMES   98

PART II
Political Systems and How They Work

CHAPTER 6. GOVERNING INSTITUTIONS IN DEMOCRACIES   258

CHAPTER 7. INSTITUTIONS OF PARTICIPATION AND REPRESENTATION IN DEMOCRACIES   324

PART III
Issues and Policies

CHAPTER 10. GLOBALIZATION, ECONOMIC SOVEREIGNTY, AND DEVELOPMENT   512

CHAPTER 11. PUBLIC POLICIES WHEN MARKETS FAIL: WELFARE, HEALTH, AND THE ENVIRONMENT   570

CHAPTER 12. POLICIES AND POLITICS OF INCLUSION AND CLASHING VALUES   640

Regional and Country Coverage

Preface

The teaching of introductory comparative politics has long been divided, and to some extent confounded, by the question of "country" or "concept": Should the course be taught, as it traditionally has been, as a series of country studies highlighting the key similarities and differences among political institutions around the world, or should it be focused on the important concepts in the discipline? Throughout twenty-five years of teaching introduction to comparative politics, we have been frustrated by this "either/or" proposition, as well as by the textbooks that have been built upon it. The country approach is far too descriptive, and it is not easy to tease major concepts out of country case studies in any sustained way. This makes it difficult for students to get to the intellectual "meat" of our discipline. A purely conceptual approach, on the other hand, leaves students with little concrete knowledge, even when they're given examples here and there. We want our students to know the difference between a president and a prime minister. We've found that it is impossible for them to assess theories in an empirical vacuum. Students need the context that studying actual country cases provides.

We traded syllabi back and forth over the years, trying to combine the two approaches. Our goal was to introduce a set of related concepts and then immediately examine in some detail how they matter in the real world in a comparative context. To do this, we started using two textbooks, one conceptual and the other country-based, in an iterative fashion. But the parts never fit together well, even if written by the same team. In particular, we found that the conceptual books didn't lend themselves well to connecting key theoretical concepts to case study material. We also found that the case studies in most country-based books were either too detailed, leaving the student overwhelmed by unnecessary information, or too simplistic, leaving the student without adequate knowledge with which to understand the utility of the theoretical concepts.

This textbook tries to resolve this country-or-concept dilemma, using what we've come to think of as a "hybrid" approach. The book is organized conceptually, but each chapter introduces concepts and then immediately uses them to examine a series of topical, interesting, and relevant case studies. For instance, chapter 5, on states and markets, lays out the key concepts in political economy and major economic theories and inserts case studies, where they best fit, of the U.S. laissez-faire model, the German social market economy, the Japanese developmental state, Mexico's history of import substitution industrialization and recent move toward global integration, and Nigeria's underdevelopment and oil dependence.

We use eleven countries throughout the book as "touchstones" (approximately five cases in each chapter), returning to these countries to illustrate the debates we address. The eleven countries—Brazil, China, Germany, India, Iran, Japan, Mexico, Nigeria, Russia, the United Kingdom, and the United States—span the globe, illustrate a wide array of current and past regimes, and avoid a Eurocentrism still too common in the field of comparative politics. Since we know, however, that not all aspects of comparative politics can best be represented by these eleven countries alone, we also feature brief cases of other countries in sidebars, typically classic models such as France's semipresidential system, and we reference dozens of others as examples throughout the text.

By the end of the book, students not only will have been introduced to a wide array of important concepts and theoretical debates but also will have learned a lot about each of the eleven countries. We do not and cannot systematically examine all elements of all eleven as a standard country-by-country book would. Instead, after a brief overview of each country in chapter 2 to give students a basic context, we identify the most conceptually interesting elements of each country. For instance, regarding Japan, we cover the developmental state, the role of that state's bureaucracy and level of corruption, its electoral system, and the country's recent efforts to deal with globalization and resuscitate economic growth. Regarding Germany, we cover the rise and structure of the Nazi regime, Germany's cultural nationalism and citizenship debates, the social market economy, its electoral system, and its efforts to reform the social market economy and welfare state in the face of globalization and European Union integration. The case studies are organized and written in a way that allows students to understand the context of the debates and concepts without having to read an entire "country chapter" on each. And we keep the cases concise, which leaves faculty members the option of lecturing to fill in any additional detail that they may feel important or to provide comparisons with cases not covered in a chapter.

Rather than using any one theoretical or methodological approach, in chapter 1 we introduce students to the broad debates in the field to show how comparativists have used various theories and methodologies to understand political phenomena. We do not generally offer definitive conclusions about which approach is best for understanding a particular issue, preferring instead to show students the strengths and weaknesses of each. Occasionally, we make clear that one approach has become the "conventional wisdom" in the field or that we believe it is the most accurate way to analyze a particular phenomenon, but we do this in the context of a broader debate. Our primary focus on eleven countries gives the book an implicit bias toward comparative case studies over large-N quantitative methodology, but we introduce students to the core ideas and benefits of the latter and refer to large-N studies throughout the book as well. We believe our approach will allow faculty to generate debates among students over key approaches and methodologies. By focusing on the key conceptual debates and illustrating them in the real world, the book enables instructors to move their introductory students beyond the memorization of basic information and toward an ability to assess and debate the real issues in our discipline.

The book also moves firmly away from the traditional Cold War division of the world into first-, second-, and third-world countries. While many textbooks claim to do this, we have found that they typically suffer from a "Cold War hangover," with the old division lurking just beneath the surface. We consciously set out to show that many theoretical concepts in the discipline are useful in a wide array of settings, that political phenomena are not fundamentally different in one part of the world than they are in another. For instance, we illustrate the parliamentary system not only with Britain but also with India, we use both the United States and Brazil to analyze the presidential system, and we examine women's struggle for equality in Russia and Iran. Throughout, we try to show how long-standing concepts and debates in the discipline illuminate current "hot topics."

ORGANIZATION OF THE BOOK

This book is divided into three main parts. It first examines the theories and concepts that inform and drive research as a way to frame our investigation, then moves to a survey of political institutions and institutional change, and, finally, to an examination of several current policy debates. Part I introduces the major theoretical approaches to the discipline and focuses on the modern state and its relationship to citizens and civil society, regimes, identity groups, and the market economy. It provides an introduction to the discipline and its key concepts in the modern world, applying them to case studies throughout. Chapter 1 provides a broad overview of key conceptual debates and divides the field into three broad questions to help students organize these debates: What explains political behavior? Who rules? and Where and why? These orient students by grouping the many debates in the field into broad categories tied to clear and compelling questions. "What explains political behavior?" gets at the heart of the discipline's major disputes, which we divide among rational-actor theories, theories of political culture and ideology, and structural theories. "Who rules?" addresses the dispersion of political power, focusing mainly on the debate between pluralist and elite theorists. While that debate is typically subsumed under the study of American politics, we think it helps illuminate important areas of comparative politics as well. "Where and why?" introduces students to the importance of and approaches to comparison.

The rest of Part I focuses on the modern state and its relationship to other key areas of modern politics. Chapter 2 defines and provides an overview of the modern state and the concept of state strength/weakness, and it uses a brief history of the modern state in our eleven case studies to give students an overview of each. Chapter 3 examines modern states in relation to citizens, civil society, and political regimes, arguing that the latter are based first and foremost on political ideologies that define the relationship between state and citizen. Chapter 4 looks at the debate over political identity and the state's relationship to nations, ethnic and religious groups, and racial groups. Chapter 5 examines the abstract and historical relationship between the state and the market economy, including key concepts in political economy, economic theories, and globalization. Each of these chapters uses case studies to illustrate and assess the concepts and debates it introduces.

Part II examines political institutions in both democratic and authoritarian regimes as well as regime transitions. It is the "nuts-and-bolts" section of the book, providing what traditionally has been a core feature of the course. Chapters 6 and 7 examine political institutions in democratic regimes. Chapter 6 focuses on governing institutions: executive/legislative systems, the judiciary, the bureaucracy, and federalism. The theme throughout is the question of accountability in democracies. Chapter 7 looks at institutions of participation and representation: electoral systems, parties and party systems, and interest groups and social movements. It focuses primarily on how to achieve different kinds of representation and the potential trade-off between active participation and effective governance. Chapter 8 looks at institutions in authoritarian regimes, drawing on the previous two chapters to show how similar institutions function quite differently in nondemocratic regimes, as well as presenting the active debate over authoritarianism over the past decade. Chapter 9, on regime transition, not only focuses on democratic transitions but also sets them in the longer-term debate over regime change, looking first at military coups and social revolutions.

Part III examines some key current policy issues that have been foreshadowed earlier in the book. The conceptual and empirical knowledge that the students have gained in Parts I and II are used to address important current issues. Chapter 10 looks at different states' efforts to respond effectively to globalization, revisiting in a more current context the debates developed in chapter 5. It examines the debate over convergence versus the varieties of capitalism approach in understanding the response to globalization in wealthy countries, as well as developing countries' efforts to respond to globalization; the chapter includes a discussion of the global financial crisis and its implications. The theme of chapter 11 is market failure, examining social policy, health policy, and environmental policy in turn. It draws on chapters 5 and 10, as well as material from Part II, to look at different approaches to current hot topics such as universal health care and climate change. Chapter 12 returns to themes first developed in a theoretical and historical framework in chapter 4 on identity politics. Its theme is how states respond to demands for inclusion in full citizenship by groups typically not included in the past and the clashes of fundamental values those demands raise in the areas of religion, gender, and sexual orientation.

KEY FEATURES

A number of pedagogical features reappear throughout the chapters. Each of them is designed to help students marry the conceptual and country-specific material in the most effective way possible. We think students can manage the concepts without losing sight of the important facts they've learned about the countries if they're given the right tools. Each chapter begins with questions that help students focus on the key issues as they read the chapter, study the cases, and then debate in class. The chapters sometimes provide conclusive answers to some of the key questions, but more often they show students different ways the questions can be answered or approached. New to this edition, students will find "case questions" at the end of each case to help them connect the specifics of the case to the larger thematic points we're making, and to compare cases in the same chapter.

"Country and Concept" tables in each chapter showcase empirical material. These provide key data of relevance for our eleven case study countries. The text refers to the tables at various points, but students and faculty can use these for much more, comparing the countries across the variables and asking questions about what might explain the observable variation.

Most chapters also include one or more "In Context" features that present basic data. These allow students to set a case study or idea into a comparative (and sometimes provocative) context. Students can use these to assess how representative some of our case studies are or to see the distribution of an institution, type of event, or set of factors around the world or within a region. For example, the "In Context" in chapter 4 focuses on identity politics in Latin America and shows racial and ethnic demography across the entire region. This is set next to the case study of race relations in Brazil.

In most chapters, we include a "Critical Inquiry" box, a new feature in which we ask students to think actively about a particular question. Many of these provide students a limited set of data and ask them, simply by visually examining the data, to develop their own hypotheses about key relationships or evaluate competing hypotheses they've studied in the book. Chapter 7, for instance, includes a "Critical Inquiry" box on the question of what explains women's share of legislative seats around the world. It provides data on the number of women in lower houses broken down by region, electoral system, and length of regime, and it asks students to use these data to informally "test" alternative hypotheses about why women gain better representation. A few "Critical Inquiry" boxes direct students toward more normative questions, using the concepts in the chapter to address them.

In addition to these themed features, readers will find many original tables, figures, and maps throughout the book that illustrate key relationships or variables around the world. Students will find end-of-chapter lists of key concepts with page references to help their study and review, as well as a list of works cited and a list of important print and electronic references for further research. We hope the design of the book strikes a balance as well: colorful and well illustrated to help engage student attention, but without adding significantly to cost.

NEW TO THIS EDITION

We're grateful to the many users who have graciously and enthusiastically provided us with feedback over the course of the last two editions. We've done our best to address their suggestions and comments. We've incorporated our own experiences and reactions to using the text in our own classes as well. In addition to thorough updating for recent world events and capturing the latest data points, the majority of our efforts went toward streamlining the text significantly. We heard that students still needed help in finding the forest for the trees—that is, in sorting out the "take-home" points from the details that illustrate them. We made a concerted effort to strike just the right balance between the big-picture thematic content and the nitty-gritty case details. For that reason, we decided to cut the mini-cases (cases on countries not among the eleven "core" countries) and two features, "Where and Why?" and "Methods in Context," to help keep student's attention on the main cases and the key lessons. Several former mini-cases are now incorporated more briefly in the main text. A transition guide is available to instructors at http://introducingCP.cqpress.com (click on "Instructor's Resources"), which details these changes.

Some important new content changes also came as a result of user feedback. We've included more systematic presentation of state strength and weakness in chapter 2; added the "contentious politics" framework in chapters 4, 7, and 9; put greater emphasis on identity-based movements and violence in chapter 4; substantially revised the theoretical treatment of authoritarian regimes, especially via the important new work by Milan Svolik, and improved the context for the study of this regime type in the introduction to the chapter; and substantially revised the treatment of the contemporary development debate in chapter 10, including a full treatment of the leftist development models and governments in Latin America.

Instructors who used the previous edition or two of this book will immediately notice one big change: the book is now in full color! There are significant pedagogical advantages to being able to present the material with color: data in maps, figures, and tables are much easier to comprehend, and images from around the world are more vivid.

Students' access and use of technology today mean that they process information in ways that go beyond reading the printed word on a paper page. To keep up with them and their quickly evolving world, *Introducing Comparative Politics: Concepts and Cases in Context* is now a full-fledged, integrated media experience. When students purchase a new print copy of the book, they receive **free access** to an enhanced e-book. Through a series of annotated icons in the margins, students link to multimedia on the page where a topic is discussed, pointing to articles and background pieces, to audio clips of interviews and podcasts, to video clips of news stories, to *CQ Researcher* policy backgrounder reports, and to important data. This allows students to explore an important concept or idea while reading—a reinforcing exercise as well as vetted content that provides depth and added context.

for CQ Press

edge.sagepub.com/orvis3e

Because we know from experience that making the leap into a new textbook is no small chore, CQ Press offers a full suite of high-quality instructor and student ancillary materials (prepared by Rodrigo Praino at the University of Connecticut and Natalie Wenzell Letsa at Cornell University).

SAGE edge offers a robust online environment featuring an impressive array of free tools and resources for review, study, and further exploration.

SAGE edge for students enhances learning and offers a personalized approach to coursework in an easy-to-use environment.

- Mobile-friendly **eFlashcards** strengthen understanding of key terms and concepts.
- Mobile-friendly practice **quizzes** allow for independent assessment by students of their mastery of course material.
- A customized online **action plan** includes tips and feedback on progress through the course and materials, which allows students to individualize their learning experience.
- **Chapter summaries** with **learning objectives** reinforce the most important material.
- **Multimedia content** includes links to video, audio, web, and data that appeal to students with different learning styles.
- EXCLUSIVE! Access to full-text **SAGE journal articles** have been carefully selected to support and expand on the concepts presented in each chapter.

SAGE edge for instructors supports your teaching by making it easy to integrate quality content and create a rich learning environment for students.

- A comprehensive **test bank** provides more than 700 multiple-choice, fill-in-the blank, and short- and long-essay questions, as well as the opportunity to edit any question and/or insert personalized questions to effectively assess students' progress and understanding. The test bank is available in Word and fully loaded in Respondus, flexible and easy-to-use test-generation software that allows instructors to build, customize, and even integrate exams into course management systems.

- **Sample course syllabi** for semester and quarter courses provide suggested models for structuring one's course, especially if blending country-by-country and thematic approaches and moving to this book's flexible "hybrid" approach.
- Editable, chapter-specific **PowerPoint® slides** offer complete flexibility for creating a multimedia presentation for the course.
- <u>EXCLUSIVE!</u> Access to full-text **SAGE journal articles** have been carefully selected to support and expand on the concepts presented in each chapter.
- An **instructor's manual** features chapter overviews and objectives, lecture starters, ideas for class activities, discussion questions, and country background-ers that offer basic information on all eleven core countries featured in the book.
- A **TA Guide** provides guidance for graduate students and newer instructors who will benefit from a set of goals, points for review, and discussion questions for each chapter.
- A complete set of the **graphics from the text**, including all of the maps, tables, and figures, in PowerPoint, .pdf, and .jpg formats, is available for class presentations.
- **Multimedia content** includes links to video, audio, web, and data links that appeal to students with different learning styles.
- A **common course cartridge** includes all of the instructor resources and assessment material from the student study site, making it easy for instructors to upload and use these materials in LMS, such as Blackboard, Angel, Moodle, Canvas, and Desire2Learn.
- A **Transition Guide** provides a chapter-by-chapter outline of key changes to the third edition.
- **Country by Country Contents** provides the book's table of contents organized by featured countries.

ACKNOWLEDGMENTS

We have developed numerous debts in the process of writing this book. Perhaps the longest standing is to our students over twenty-five years of teaching introduction to comparative politics at Hamilton College. Figuring out how to teach the course in a way that is interesting, relevant, and clear to them led us to develop the approach taken in this book. We kept them in mind as we wrote the book: Will it be clear to them? Will it interest them? Will it help them see the important concepts and how they matter in the real world?

We owe a substantial thank you to the office of the Dean of Faculty at Hamil-ton College as well. It has provided support for research assistants for this project over seven years and three editions, primarily from the Steven Sands Fund for Faculty Innovation. The office also provided sabbatical support for Steve Orvis on Hamilton's program at Pembroke College, Oxford University, where the first elements of this proj-ect were written. Additional thanks go to the fellows and staff at Pembroke College for providing a hospitable venue for a sabbatical leave for research and writing on the first edition. Deep thanks go as well to nine especially talented Hamilton College undergraduates who worked for us as research assistants on the two editions, pulling together vital data and information for many of the book's case studies. They are Charlie Allegar, Henry Anreder, Emily Drinkwater, Luke Forster, Laura Gault, Derek King, Katie McGuire, Joshua Meah, and Natalie Tarallo. They were invaluable help for two faculty members taking on a project of this magnitude. Thanks go also to Andrew Rogan and Dawn Woodward for assistance in preparing the bibliographies in the book. We are very grateful to Rodrigo Praino and Natalie Wenzell Letsa for ably updating and crafting the ancillary materials for this book. Thanks also to Nathan Gonzalez for drafting the initial case studies on Mexico added to the second edition.

The staff at CQ Press have been pleasant, professional, and efficient throughout this process. Our association began with a chance meeting between one of us and a sales representative from CQ Press, in which "complaints were made" about the quality of textbooks in the field and the sales rep asked the inevitable: "So, how would you write one?" A quick response was met with the sales rep's enthusiastic statement: "We're looking for a book just like that! Can my acquisitions editor call you to talk about it?" We said sure, but, to be honest, didn't expect to hear from anyone. A week later the phone rang—Charisse Kiino, now publisher for CQ Press's political science list, was on the line to talk through the ideas further. This led to a long process through which Charisse expertly led us, starting with developing a proposal and draft chapter and responding to the first round of reviews. Charisse patiently walked us through the process with constant good cheer and support. Our development editor for the first and third editions, Elise Frasier, was invaluable, putting forth tremendous ideas for pedagogical elements of the book that we would have never thought of on our own, doing much of the research to develop these elements, and being herself an insightful reader and critic of the text. Of all the people we mention in this preface, she has provided the most valuable input and content for this book.

Finally, our production editor Tracy Buyan and copy editor Talia Greenberg have been fabulous in the final stages of this third edition, improving the prose in innumerable places, pointing out inconsistencies, and working with us in an open, honest, and professional way that has made a tedious process as easy as it could be. We deeply appreciate the work of all at CQ Press who have made the process of writing this book as painless as we could imagine it being.

We wish also to thank the numerous reviewers who read chapters of the book at various stages. Their comments led us to revise a number of elements, drop others, and further develop still others. They have collectively made it a much better book that we hope will serve students well. They are:

William Avilés, *University of Nebraska–Kearney*

Jody Baumgartner, *East Carolina University*

Dilchoda Berdieva, *Miami University*

Michael Bernhard, *University of Florida*

Gitika Commuri, *California State University–Bakersfield*

Jeffrey Conroy-Krutz, *Michigan State University*

Carolyn Craig, *University of Oregon*

William Crowther, *University of North Carolina–Greensboro*

Andrea Duwel, *Santa Clara University*

Clement M. Henry, *University of Texas–Austin*

Eric H. Hines, *University of Montana*

Jennifer Horan, *University of North Carolina–Wilmington*

John Hulsey, *James Madison University*

Christian B. Jensen, *University of Iowa*

Alana Jeydel, *American River College*

Eric Langenbacher, *Georgetown University*

Ricardo René Larémont, *Binghamton University, SUNY*

Carol S. Leff, *University of Illinois at Urbana-Champaign*

Paul Lenze, *Northern Arizona University*

M. Casey Kane Love, *Tulane University*

Mona Lyne, *University of Missouri–Kansas City*

Rahsaan Maxwell, *University of Massachusetts*

Mary McCarthy, *Drake University*

Scott Morgenstern, *University of Pittsburgh*

Stephen Mumme, *Colorado State University*

Nils Ringe, *University of Wisconsin–Madison*

David Sacko, *U.S. Air Force Academy*

Edward Schwerin, *Florida Atlantic University*

Brian Shoup, *Mississippi State University*

Tony Spanakos, *Montclair State University*

Boyka Stefanova, *University of Texas–San Antonio*

Sarah Tenney, *The Citadel*

Erica Townsend-Bell, *University of Iowa*

Kellee Tsai, *Johns Hopkins University*

Dwayne Woods, *Purdue University*

Eleanor E. Zeff, *Drake University*

Darren Zook, *University of California, Berkeley*

Last, but far from least, we have to extend thanks to our children, Nick and Will. They didn't contribute ideas or critique the book, but they showed real enthusiasm for understanding things like who the prime minister of Britain is and why there is a Monster Raving Loony Party, and they endured and even participated in occasional dinner table debates on things like the relative merits of parliamentary systems and different concepts of citizenship. Most of all, they gave of themselves in the form of great patience. This project became more of an obsession, at least at key points, than our work usually is. The first two editions took us away from them more than we like and made our family life rather hectic. They bore it well, going on with their lives in their typically independent way. Now they're older and mostly off on their own, so they don't bear the brunt of it, but we nonetheless preserve our dedication of the book to them and their generation, which gives us great hope.

Introducing
Comparative Politics

THIRD EDITION

1 INTRODUCTION

INTRODUCTION
Comparative Politics
THIRD EDITION

KEY QUESTIONS

- How much power do different people or groups have in different political systems?

- Do self-interest, beliefs, or underlying structural forces best explain how people act in the political realm?

- What kinds of evidence can help us determine why political actors do what they do?

- What can be learned from comparing political behavior and outcomes across countries?

Understanding political developments and disputes around the world has never seemed more important than it does today. The financial crisis that began in 2008 has demonstrated profoundly the interrelationships among countries' and people's well-being across the globe. The crisis began in the United States but ultimately hit Europe at least as hard. Most wealthy countries' relative power and wealth seem to be declining compared with rising powers such as China and India, but China has an authoritarian regime, raising major questions about whether it will move toward a democracy, and if it doesn't what type of global power it will be. The Middle East, meanwhile, has seen upheaval unlike anything in modern history, as long-standing dictators were toppled in Tunisia and Libya, and unrest continues in Bahrain, Egypt, and Syria. These changes threaten to reorient the entire political context of the region, with profound political and economic implications for the United States and other major powers.

Many people now see the world as more complicated and less comprehensible than it was during the post–Cold War era (1989–2001), when the international realm seemed peaceful and stable and foreign politics was of little importance. The end of communist rule in the Soviet Union and Eastern Europe seemed to foreshadow a period in

which understanding political differences among countries would be both easier and less important. Instead, the era witnessed dramatic political change: several countries split into two or more new countries, the number of ethnic and religious civil wars increased significantly, and two full-scale genocides have occurred. On the other hand, the number of countries that could claim to have democratic governments also increased substantially, and East Asia, led by China, achieved unprecedented economic growth that lifted more people out of poverty more quickly than ever before in history.

Diversity of political, economic, and social life among nations exists in every period of history. Comparative politics attempts to understand this diversity, assessing current events in the light of fundamental and long-standing questions: Why do governments form? Why does a group of people come to see itself as a nation? Why do nations sometimes fall apart? How can a government convince people that it has the right to rule? Do some forms of government last longer than others? Do some forms of government serve their people's interests better than others? How do democracies form, and how do they fall apart? Can democracy work anywhere or only in particular countries and at particular times? Are certain political institutions more democratic than others? Can government policy reduce poverty and improve economic well-being? This book introduces you to the many and often conflicting answers to these questions that political scientists have proposed by examining these and other questions comparatively. It will also help you start to assess which of these answers are the most convincing and why.

THE BIG ISSUES

Current "hot-button" political issues around the world are just the latest manifestations of a set of enduring issues that students of comparative politics have been studying for the last half-century. We could list many such issues, but for the moment, let's focus on just five to illustrate the major areas of interest in comparative politics: political development, regime type and change, participation and representation, policy-making processes, and political economy. The logical starting point is the question of **political development.**

political development
The processes through which modern nations and states arise and how political institutions and regimes evolve

Political Development You may be accustomed to seeing development applied to the field of economics, where it relates to the growth of modern industrial economies, but the word has important political dimensions as well. Historically, the biggest political development questions are about how and why modern nations and states arose. Why did the entity now known as France, and a group of people who think of themselves as French, come into existence? Is this process similar for all countries? If not, how and why does it vary?

Political scientists initially thought about these issues in a European context, but since World War II most questions about political development have emerged out of the experiences of former colonies in Latin America, Africa, and Asia. As these colonies gained independence, the relationship between economic and political development came into focus. Most observers assumed that former colonies would go through a process of economic development dubbed **modernization**—the transformation of poor agrarian societies into wealthy industrial societies. Political scientists initially assumed that as this transformation occurred, political systems that were more or less democratic also would emerge.

modernization
The transformation of poor agrarian societies into wealthy industrial societies, usually seen as the process by which postcolonial societies become more like societies in the West

In fact, neither economic nor political development has occurred as planned. Some countries, such as South Korea, have achieved rapid economic transformation and have established electoral democracies. Many others, however, have not. Democracy has emerged in some very poor countries (Ghana), while nondemocratic governments have presided over great economic change in others (Vietnam). In many countries, a sense of being a nation has never fully emerged, and some have even collapsed into civil war (Democratic Republic of the Congo). Even though the assumptions of modernization have not adequately answered the key questions, scholars continue to examine political development because finding an answer remains crucial, as the cases of Afghanistan and Iraq demonstrate so vividly today.

Regime Type and Change Closely related to the issue of political development is the question of regime type and regime change. Americans often use regime to refer to some sort of "bad" government: we (democracies) have governments, whereas they (nondemocracies) have regimes. Political scientists, however, think of regimes in more neutral terms, as sets of political institutions that define a type of government. France has existed as a state and a nation for centuries, but it has had numerous regimes. The long-standing monarchy was overthrown by the world's first modern revolution in 1789 that created a very brief republic, which itself was ultimately overthrown by Napoleon Bonaparte, who created a dictatorship. His regime collapsed and the monarchy was restored in 1815. A different and much more liberal monarchy reigned from 1830 to 1848, when a second revolution proclaimed a second republic. By 1851, though, Louis Bonaparte overthrew the republic and created the "second empire" that lasted until its defeat at the hands of the Prussians in 1870. Finally, a long-lived democracy emerged under the third republic, lasting until it was overthrown by Nazi Germany in 1940. After World War II, the fourth republic was proclaimed, lasting until a constitutional crisis in 1958 led to the creation of the fifth republic, France's current regime. Despite being a state and nation for centuries, France has had (depending on how you count) at least nine regimes.

For greater ease of comparison, political scientists classify regimes into a limited number of categories, or regime types. Two broad categories are democratic and authoritarian regimes. Many definitions of a democracy exist, but for purposes of systematic comparison, most political scientists adhere to what is often called the "minimal definition" of a **democracy** as a regime in which citizens have basic rights of open association and expression and the ability to change the government through some sort of electoral process. This is not to say that democratic regimes are all the same. Besides being "more" or "less" democratic, they are also organized in different ways, for example, as presidential or parliamentary systems (see chapter 6).

Conversely, an **authoritarian regime** is simply a regime lacking democratic characteristics. As is the case with democratic regimes, numerous kinds of authoritarian regimes exist. The most important of these in the twentieth century were fascist regimes such as Nazi Germany, communist regimes such as the Soviet Union, modernizing authoritarian regimes such as the military government in Brazil from 1964 to 1985, and theocratic regimes such as the Islamic Republic of Iran since 1979.

Web link:
Institute for Democracy and Electoral Assistance (IDEA) webpage on political development

A policeman in Vietnam keeps a photographer away from a court building where a politically charged trial was taking place in April 2013. Vietnam's economic success but continued authoritarian government is an interesting case to examine when looking at the relationship between economic and political development, an enduring issue in comparative politics.

democracy
A regime in which citizens have basic rights of open association and expression and the ability to change the government through some sort of electoral process

authoritarian regime
A regime lacking democratic characteristics, ruled by a single leader or small group of leaders

In recent years, a third broad regime category has become more widespread. The semi-authoritarian regime includes some elements of democracy such as elections, but the ruling party has sufficient control over democratic processes to ensure that it remains in power. Most of these regimes have emerged out of attempts to create new democracies during the last two decades. The largest example in the world today is Russia.

Once the various regime categories are identified, we can ask questions about how they differ and how they are similar. On the surface, the answer seems obvious: democracies have elections, and authoritarian regimes have dictators. In fact, the differences and similarities are much more complex. Some formally democratic regimes have significant informal limits on citizen input and participation, whereas some authoritarian regimes allow dissent and even power sharing within certain bounds.

As the French example suggests, we also need to ask questions about regime change, the process through which one regime is transformed into another. This process can take numerous forms. Revolutions, such as the overthrow of Russia's autocratic regime in 1917 and the triumph of Chinese communists in 1949, are violent upheavals of entire societies that result in the creation of new regimes. Military coups d'état also often involve violence, but usually focused only on the old government that the military has chosen to overthrow, such as in many Latin American countries in the 1950s and 1960s and in Mali in West Africa much more recently (2012). The most widespread recent form of regime change, however, has been the spread of democracy since the late 1970s, commonly referred to as democratic transition. Scholars studying democratic transitions ask questions about when and why authoritarian regimes give way to democracies, what kinds of democracies are likely to emerge in particular circumstances, how truly democratic new democracies are, and how likely they are to last.

Participation and Representation Closely related to the issues of regime type and democratization are popular participation and representation. Since Aristotle, if not before, political scientists and political philosophers have sought to understand why and how people participate in the political process, as well as how that participation differs across cultures and regimes. In some countries citizens participate as part of self-conscious identity groups, such as ethnic, religious, or racial groups (see chapter 4). In other countries identity groups have little relevance to politics. When and why do these differences emerge? What are the effects of strong "identity politics" on the stability of democracy? Citizens participate individually by voting or asking their government for assistance, but they may also band together in what is called civil society to pursue common interests via the political process. **Civil society** is defined as the sphere of organized, nongovernmental, nonviolent activity by groups larger than individual families or firms. The most familiar elements of civil society in the United States are interest groups such as the Sierra Club or the U.S. Chamber of Commerce.

Web link:
Institute for Democracy and Electoral Assistance (IDEA) webpage on political participation

civil society
The sphere of organized, nongovernmental, nonviolent activity by groups larger than individual families or firms

Political participation also occurs through the medium of political parties, of course. Different regimes have quite distinct kinds of parties and electoral systems that encourage different kinds of citizen participation. It is no surprise, then, that political scientists want to know which party and electoral systems most accurately represent the interests of citizens in the political process. How can citizens ensure that their representatives actually represent them? Can representation exist in authoritarian regimes? How do different societies conceptualize political representation in different cultural contexts? Each of these questions is an enduring element of comparative politics, and each is discussed in chapters 7 and 8.

Web link:
The UN and civil society

Web link:
The UN's Integrated Civil Society Organizations System

Policymaking Another major issue in comparative politics is policymaking. All governments, whatever the regime, ultimately make policies that govern society. How do different regimes decide which policies to pursue? What role do different political institutions have in the policy-making process? Who is most influential in the process and why? Do the policies that finally gain approval reflect the will of the people? Which decisions should be made at the level of the national government, and which should be delegated to more local governments such as states or provinces? Different regimes provide different answers to these questions.

Political Economy **Political economy** is the study of the interaction of political and economic phenomena. In the modern world, virtually all governments are concerned with and (at least in theory) held responsible for the economic well-being of their people. Political economists try to determine what kinds of economic policies are most likely to prove beneficial in particular cultural, social, and political contexts. They also ask if some types of regimes produce better economic outcomes than others. Many observers have argued, for instance, that modernizing authoritarian regimes can achieve more rapid economic growth in poor countries than democratic regimes can, but in recent years political scientists have found substantial evidence that the relationship is far less black and white. Some authoritarian regimes, such as China's, have been quite capable of achieving growth, whereas others, including Nigeria's, have not. Similarly, some kinds of democratic regimes seem capable of achieving beneficial economic outcomes even as others do not.

political economy
The study of the interaction between political and economic phenomena

These big issues do not encompass all of comparative politics, but they do raise the most prominent questions that comparativists, political scientists who study comparative politics, have been grappling with for the past half-century. Today, these questions are alive and well in the countries making headlines, from Pakistan and Afghanistan to Libya and Egypt. Comparativists try to look beyond the momentary hot topics to examine systematically these enduring questions, seeking ever clearer understanding of how politics works in the world and how it might be made better. Doing this requires some thought about how to study a very complex subject.

Video link:
The Arab Spring in comparative political economic perspective

COMPARATIVE POLITICS: WHAT IS IT? WHY STUDY IT? HOW TO STUDY IT?

politics
The process by which human communities make collective decisions

comparative politics
One of the major subfields of political science, in which the primary focus is on comparing power and decision making across countries

political science
The systematic study of politics and power

first dimension of power
The ability of one person or group to get another person or group to do something it otherwise would not do

second dimension of power
The ability not only to make people do something but to keep them from doing something

third dimension of power
The ability to shape or determine individual or group political demands by causing people to think about political issues in ways that are contrary to their own interests

international relations
The study of politics among national governments and beyond national boundaries

Politics can be defined as the process by which human communities make collective decisions. These communities can be of any size, from small villages or neighborhoods to nations and international organizations. **Comparative politics** is one of the major subfields of **political science,** the systematic study of politics. Politics always involves elements of power, the first concept we need to examine closely.

A definition of power may seem pretty straightforward, but political scientists have long debated its exact meaning. Political theorist Steven Lukes (1974) usefully categorized power into three dimensions. The **first dimension of power** is the ability of one person or group to get another person or group to do something it otherwise would not do. The focus here is on behavior: making someone do something. A **second dimension of power,** first articulated by Peter Bachrach and Morton Baratz (1962), sees power as the ability not only to make people do something but to keep them from doing something. Bachrach and Baratz argued that a key element of political power is the ability to keep certain groups and issues out of the political arena by creating political processes and setting the political agenda to allow certain groups to participate and voice their concerns while preventing others from doing so. A **third dimension of power,** which Lukes contributed, is the ability to shape or determine individual or group political demands by causing people to think about political issues in ways that are contrary to their own interests. The ability to influence how people think produces the power to prevent certain political demands from ever being articulated. We will examine the role of all three of these dimensions of power in this chapter and in the rest of the book.

What Is Comparative Politics? In comparative politics, the primary focus is on power and decision making within national boundaries. This includes the politics of entire countries as well as more local-level politics. Politics among national governments and beyond national boundaries is generally the purview of the field of **international relations,** and while comparativists certainly take into account the domestic effects of international events, we do not try to explain the international events themselves. Perhaps it is self-evident, but comparativists also compare; we systematically examine political phenomena in more than one place and during more than one period, and we try to develop a generalized understanding of and an explanation for political activity that seem to apply to many different situations.

Why Study Comparative Politics? Studying comparative politics has multiple benefits. First, comparativists are interested in understanding political events and developments in various countries. Why did the peaceful regime change happen in Tunisia in 2011 but not in Bahrain and Syria? Why did the Socialist Party win back the presidency in France in 2012 after seventeen years of conservative presidents? Also, as the Middle East example shows, understanding political events in other countries can be very important to foreign policy. If the U.S. government had better understood the internal dynamics of Egyptian politics, it would not have been caught so off guard when regime change happened and perhaps could have shaped that regime change more successfully.

Second, systematic comparison of different political systems and events around the world can generate important lessons from one place that can be applied in another. Americans often see their system of government, with a directly elected president, as a very successful and stable model of democracy. Certainly, it has been used successfully elsewhere as well, but not everywhere. Much evidence suggests that in a situation of intense political conflict, such as an ethnically divided country after a civil war, a system with a single and powerful elected president might not be the best option. Only one candidate from one side can win this coveted post, and the sides that lose the election might choose to restart the war rather than live with the results. A democratic system that gives all major groups some share of political power at the national level might work better in this situation. That conclusion is not obvious when examining the United States alone. A systematic comparison of a number of different countries, however, reveals this possibility.

Third, examining politics comparatively helps us develop broad theories about how politics works. A **theory** is an abstract argument that provides a systematic explanation of some phenomenon. The theory of evolution, for instance, makes an argument about how species change over time in response to their environments. The social sciences, including political science, use two different kinds of theories. An **empirical theory** is an argument that explains what actually occurs. Empirical theorists first *describe* a pattern and then attempt to *explain* what causes it. The theory of evolution is an empirical theory in that evolutionary biologists do not argue whether evolution is inherently good or bad; they simply describe evolutionary patterns and explain their causes. A good empirical theory should also allow theorists to *predict* what will happen as well. For example, a comparison of democratic systems in post–civil war situations would lead us to predict that presidential systems are more likely to lead to renewed conflict.

On the other hand, a **normative theory** is an argument that explains what *ought* to occur. For instance, socialists support a normative theory that the government and economy *ought* to be structured in a way that produces a relatively equal distribution of wealth. While comparativists certainly hold various normative theories, most of the discipline of comparative politics focuses on empirical theory. We attempt to explain the political world around us, and we do this by looking across multiple cases to come up with generalizations about politics.

How Do Comparativists Study Politics? Clearly, political scientists do not have perfect scientific conditions in which to do research. We do not have a controlled laboratory, because we certainly cannot control the real world of politics. Physicists

theory
An abstract argument that provides a systematic explanation of some phenomena

empirical theory
An argument explaining what actually occurs; empirical theorists first notice and describe a pattern and then attempt to explain what causes it

normative theory
An argument explaining what ought to occur rather than what does occur; contrast with empirical theory

can use a laboratory to control all elements of an experiment, and they can repeat that same experiment to achieve identical results because molecules do not notice what the scientists are doing, think about the situation, and change their behavior. In political science, however, political actors think about the changes going on around them and modify their behavior accordingly.

Despite these limitations, comparativists use the scientific method (as explained in the "Scientific Method in Comparative Politics" box) to try to gain as systematic evidence as possible. We use several research methods to try to overcome at least some of the difficulties our complex field of study presents. **Research methods** are systematic processes used to ensure that the study of some phenomena is as objective and unbiased as possible.

One common research method we use is the **single case study,** which examines a particular political phenomenon in just one country or community. A case study can generate ideas for new theories, or it can test existing theories developed from different cases. A single case can never be definitive proof of anything beyond that case itself, but it can be suggestive of further research and can be of interest to people researching that particular country. Deviant case studies that do not fit a widely held pattern can be particularly helpful in highlighting the limits of even widely supported theories. Case studies also deepen our knowledge about particular countries, useful in and of itself. Scholars engaging in case study research search for common patterns within the case or use a method known as process tracing, which involves careful examination of the historical linkages between potential causes and effects. They do this in order to demonstrate as definitively as possible what caused what in the case being studied. Case studies serve as important sources of information and ideas for comparativists using more comparative methods.

Scholars use the **comparative method** to examine the same phenomenon in several cases, and they try to mimic laboratory conditions by selecting cases carefully. Two approaches are common. The **most similar systems design** selects cases that are alike in a number of ways but differ on the key question under examination. For instance, Michael Bratton and Nicholas van de Walle (1997) looked at transitions to democracy in Africa, arguing that all African countries share certain similarities in patterns of political behavior that are distinct from patterns in Latin America, where the main theories of democratization were developed. On the other hand, the **most different systems design** looks at countries that differ in many ways but are similar in terms of the particular political process or outcome in which the research is interested. For instance, scholars of revolution look at the major cases of revolution around the world—a list of seemingly very different countries like France, Russia, China, Vietnam, Cuba, Nicaragua, and Iran—and ask what common elements can be found that explain why these countries had revolutions. Both comparative methods have their strengths and weaknesses, but their common goal is to use careful case selection and systematic examination of key variables to mimic laboratory methods as closely as possible.

research methods
Systematic processes used to ensure that the study of some phenomena is as objective and unbiased as possible

single case study
Research method that examines a particular political phenomenon in just one country or community and can generate ideas for theories or test theories developed from different cases

Web link:
The Society for Political Methodology

Web link:
The Monkey Cage webpage on comparative politics

comparative method
The means by which scholars try to mimic laboratory conditions by careful selection of cases

most similar systems design
A common approach of the comparative method that selects cases that are alike in a number of ways but differ on a key question under examination

most different systems design
A common approach of the comparative method that looks at countries that differ in many ways but that are similar in terms of the particular political process or outcome in which the research is interested

Scientific Method in Comparative Politics

Political science can never be a pure science because of imperfect laboratory conditions: in the real world, we have very little control over social and political phenomena. Political scientists, like other social scientists, nonetheless think in scientific terms. Most use key scientific concepts, including the following:

- Theory: An abstract argument explaining a phenomenon
- Hypothesis: A claim that certain things cause other things to happen or change
- Variable: A measurable phenomenon that changes across time or space
- Dependent variable: The phenomenon a scientist is trying to explain
- Independent variable: The thing that explains the dependent variable
- Control: Holding variables constant so that the effects of one independent variable at a time can be examined

In using the scientific method in political science, the first challenge we face is to define clearly the variables we need to include and measure them accurately. For instance, one recent study of civil wars by Paul Collier and Anke Hoeffler (2001) included, among other variables, measurements of when a civil war was taking place, poverty, ethnic fragmentation, and dependence on natural resources. They had to ask themselves, What constitutes a "civil war"? How much violence must occur and for how long before a particular country is considered to be having a civil war? In 2007 critics of the U.S. presence in Iraq argued

that Iraq was experiencing a civil war, while defenders of the United States denied this, so should the internal conflict in Iraq in 2007 be counted as a civil war or not?

A second challenge we face is figuring out how to control for all the potentially relevant variables in our research. In a laboratory, scientists control many of the variables they work with, holding them constant so that they can examine the effects of one independent variable at a time. Political scientists can rarely do this directly, as we cannot hold variables constant. A common alternative is to measure the simultaneous effects of all the independent variables through quantitative studies, such as Collier and Hoeffler's study of civil wars. Single-case studies and the comparative method attempt to control variables via careful selection of cases. For instance, a comparative case study examining the same questions Collier and Hoeffler studied might select as cases only poor countries, hypothesizing that the presence of natural resources only causes civil wars in poor countries. The question becomes, In the context of poverty, is ethnic fragmentation or the presence of natural resources more important in causing civil war? If, on the other hand, we think poverty itself affects the likelihood of civil war, we might select several cases from poor countries and several others from rich countries to see if the presence of natural resources has a different effect in the different contexts. None of this provides the perfect control that a laboratory can achieve; rather, it attempts to mimic those conditions as closely as possible to arrive at scientifically defensible conclusions.

With about two hundred countries in the world, however, no one can systematically examine every single case in depth. For large-scale studies, political scientists rely on a third method: **quantitative statistical techniques.** When evidence can be reduced to sets of numbers, statistical methods can be used to systematically compare a huge number of cases. Recent research on the causes of civil war, for instance, looked at all identifiable civil wars over several decades, literally hundreds of cases. The results indicated that ethnic divisions, which often seem to be the cause of civil war, are not as important as had been assumed. Although they may play a role, civil war is much more likely when groups are fighting over control of a valuable resource such as diamonds. Where no such resource exists, ethnic divisions are far less likely to result in war (Collier and Hoeffler 2001).

Web link:
Arend Lijphart, "Comparative Politics and the Comparative Method"

quantitative statistical techniques
Research method used for large-scale studies that reduces evidence to sets of numbers so that statistical analysis can systematically compare a huge number of cases

Young men look for diamonds in Sierra Leone. Recent statistical research has supported the theory that conflicts such as the civil war in Sierra Leone in the 1990s are not caused primarily by ethnic differences, as is often assumed, but by competition over control of mineral resources.

Web link:
Five misunderstandings about case-study research

Each of these methods has its advantages and disadvantages. A single case study allows a political scientist to look at a phenomenon in great depth and come to a more thorough understanding of a particular case (usually a country). The comparative method retains some, but not all, of this depth and gains the advantage of systematic comparison from which more generalizable conclusions can be drawn. Quantitative techniques can show broad patterns, but only for questions involving evidence that can be presented numerically, and they provide little depth on any particular case. Case studies are best at generating new ideas and insights that can lead to new theories. Quantitative techniques are best at showing the tendency of two or more phenomena to vary together, such as civil war and the presence of valuable resources. Understanding how phenomena are connected, and what causes what, often requires case studies that can provide greater depth to see the direct connections involved.

No matter how much political scientists attempt to mimic laboratory sciences, the subject matter will not allow the kinds of scientific conclusions that exist in chemistry or biology. As the world changes, ideas and theories have to adapt. That does not mean that old theories are not useful; they often are. It does mean, however, that no theory will ever become a universal and unchanging law, like the law of gravity. The political world simply isn't that certain.

Comparative politics will also never become a true science because political scientists have their own human passions and positions regarding the various debates they study. A biologist might become determined to gain fame or fortune by proving a particular theory, even if laboratory tests don't support it (for instance, scientist Woo Suk Hwang of South Korea went so far as to fabricate stem cell research results). Biologists, however, neither become ethically or morally committed to finding particular research results, nor tend to engage in particular kinds of research because of their moral beliefs. Political scientists, however, do act on their moral concerns, and that is entirely justifiable. Normative theories affect political science because our field is the study of people. Our ethical and moral positions often influence the very questions we ask. Those who ask questions about the level of "cheating" in the welfare system, for instance, are typically critics of the system who tend to think the government is wasting money on welfare. Those who ask questions about the effects of budget cuts on the poor, on the other hand, probably believe the government should be involved in alleviating poverty. These ethical positions do not mean that the evidence can or should be ignored. For example, empirical research suggested that the 1996 welfare reform in the United States neither reduced the income of the poor as much as critics initially feared nor helped the poor get jobs and rise out of poverty as much as its proponents predicted (Jacobson 2001). Good political scientists can approach a subject like this with a set of moral concerns but recognize the results of careful empirical research nonetheless, and change their arguments and conclusions in light of the new evidence.

Normative questions can be important and legitimate purposes for research projects. This book includes extensive discussions of different kinds of democratic political institutions. One of the potential trade-offs, we argue, is between greater levels of representation and participation on the one hand and efficient policymaking on the other. But this analysis is only interesting if we care about this trade-off. We have to hold a normative position on which of the two—representation and participation or efficient policymaking—is more important and why. Only then can we use the lessons learned from our empirical examination to make recommendations about which institutions a country ought to adopt.

Where does this leave the field of comparative politics? The best comparativists are aware of their own biases but still can use various methods to generate the most systematic evidence possible to come to logical conclusions. We approach the subject with our normative concerns, our own ideas about what a "good society" should be, and what role government should have in it. We try to do research on interesting questions as scientifically and systematically as possible to develop the best evidence we can to provide a solid basis for government policy. Because we care passionately about the issues, we ought to study them as rigorously as possible.

An Orientation to Comparative Politics

Although you are only starting your study of comparative politics, it is never too early to start developing the ability to understand and ultimately conduct systematic research in the field. Throughout this book, you'll see boxes labeled "Critical Inquiry." Most of these will present you with some key evidence, such as data on several variables for a select number of countries. We will ask you to use these data to test or challenge other findings, or to develop hypotheses of your own that attempt to answer some of the key questions we address in that particular chapter. We may invite you to use online and other resources for additional research as well, so you can start to formulate conclusions about whether the hypotheses are true or not. In some chapters, we also present normative questions for consideration, as these are also essential to the study of comparative politics. While you won't be able to come to definitive conclusions, these exercises will give you a taste of how comparative politics is done. They will also allow you to think about the limits of the research you've done or encountered, the role of normative questions in the field, and what could be done to answer the questions more definitively.

THREE KEY QUESTIONS IN COMPARATIVE POLITICS

Comparative politics is a huge field. The questions we can ask are virtually limitless. Spanning this huge range, however, are three major questions. The first two are fundamental to the field of political science, of which comparative politics is a part. The third is comparativists' particular contribution to the broader field of political science.

Probably the most common question political scientists ask is, What explains political behavior? The heart of political science is trying to understand why people do what they do in the world of politics. We can ask, Why do voters vote the way they do? Why do interest groups champion particular causes so passionately? Why does the U.S. Supreme Court make the decisions it does? Why has Ghana been able to create an apparently stable democracy, while neighboring Mali had its own democracy overthrown by the military? By asking these questions, we seek to discover why individuals, groups, institutions, or countries take particular political actions. Political scientists have developed many theories to explain various kinds of political actions. Below, we discuss them in terms of three broad approaches that focus on individual motivation, culture and ideology, and underlying structures.

The second large question animating political science is, Who rules? Who has power in a particular country, political institution, or political situation and why? Formal power is often clear in modern states; particular officials have prescribed functions and rules that give them certain powers. For example, the U.S. Congress passes legislation, which the president has the power to sign or veto and which the U.S. Supreme Court can rule as constitutional or not. But does the legislation Congress passes reflect the will of the citizens? Are citizens really ruling through their elected representatives (as the U.S. Constitution implies), or are powerful lobbyists calling the shots, or can members of Congress do whatever they want once in office? The Constitution and laws can't fully answer these broader questions of who really has a voice, is able to participate, and therefore has power.

Virtually all questions in political science derive from these two fundamental questions, and virtually all empirical theories are involved in the debate these two questions raise. Comparativists add a third particular focus by asking, Where and why do particular types of political behavior occur? If we can explain why Americans on the left side of the political spectrum vote for Democrats, can we use the same explanation for the voting patterns of Germans and Brazilians with left-leaning views? If special interests have the real power over economic policy in the U.S. presidential system, is this the case in Britain's parliamentary democracy as well? Why have military coups d'état happened rather frequently in Latin America and Africa but very rarely in Europe and North America? Comparativists start with the same basic theories used by other political scientists to try to explain political behavior and understand who really has power; we then add a comparative dimension to develop explanations that work in different times and places. In addition to helping develop more scientific theories, comparing different cases and contexts can help us determine which lessons from one situation are applicable to another.

What Explains Political Behavior?

The core activity in all political science is explaining political behavior: Why do people, groups, and governments act as they do in the political arena? It's easy enough to observe and describe behavior, but what explains it? In daily discussions we tend to attribute the best of motives to those with whom we agree—they are "acting in the best interests" of the community or nation. We tend to see those with whom we disagree, on the other hand, as acting selfishly or even with evil intent. You can see this tendency in the way Americans use the phrase "special interest." We perceive groups whose causes or ideological leanings we agree with as benevolent and general; those we disagree with are "special interests." Logically, however, any **political actor,** meaning any person or group engaged in political behavior, can be motivated by a variety of factors. Political scientists have developed three broad answers to the question of what explains political behavior: individual motivation, culture and ideology, and underlying structures. Each answer includes within it several theoretical approaches.

political actor
Any person or group engaged in political behavior

Individual Motivation We commonly assume that most people involved in politics are in it for their own good. Even when political actors claim to be working for the greater good or for some specific principle, many people suspect they are just hiding their own self-interested motives. The assumption of self-interest (broadly defined) is also a major element in political science theories about political behavior.

　　Rational choice theory assumes that individuals are rational and that they bring a set of self-defined preferences into the political arena. This does not mean that all people are greedy or selfish, but rather that they rationally pursue their preferences, whatever those may be. The theory borrows heavily from the field of economics, which makes the same assumptions in analyzing behavior in the market. Political scientists use this theory to explain political behavior and its results by making assumptions about political actors' preferences, modeling the political context in which they pursue those preferences, and demonstrating how political outcomes can be explained as the result of the interactions of those actors in that context. For instance, the allocation of money for building new roads is the result of an agreement among members of a congressional committee. All of the members of the committee have certain interests or preferences, based mainly on the stated desires of the voters in the districts they represent as well as the members' own desire for reelection. The committee members pursue those interests rationally, and the final bill is a negotiated settlement reflecting the relative power of the various committee members, as well as their interests within the context of the committee and Congress more broadly.

rational choice theory
An explanation for political behavior that assumes that individuals are rational beings who bring to the political arena a set of self-defined preferences and adequate knowledge and ability to pursue those preferences

Sen. Pat Roberts, R-Kans., discusses the Farm Bill at a news conference in 2012. The proposed legislation—authorizing agricultural subsidies, food stamps, and food aid abroad—represents the type of political conflict based on material interests that lends itself particularly well to analysis via rational choice theory.

Rational choice theorists start their analyses at the level of the individual, but they often seek to explain group behavior. They model group behavior from their assumptions about the preferences of individual members of groups. Group behavior is considered a result of the collective actions of rational individual actors in the group in a particular context. Racial or ethnic minority groups, women's groups, or environmental and religious groups can all be analyzed in this way. Rational choice theorists would argue, for instance, that environmentalists are just as rational and self-interested as oil companies but simply have different preferences. Environmentalists gain benefits from breathing clean air and walking through unpolluted forests; they pursue those preferences in the same way that the oil industry pursues its opposition to environmental regulations. While self-defined preferences may be easier to see when analyzing battles over material goods and money, they exist throughout the political arena. Rational choice theorists thus are not interested in the third dimension of power we mentioned earlier, the ability to influence how people think about politics and thus perhaps change people's preferences. They instead accept people's preferences as given and then ask how those preferences influence political behavior and outcomes.

This raises one of the major criticisms of rational choice theories. Critics contend that rational choice theorists have difficulty explaining outcomes because it is often difficult to know in advance exactly which individuals or groups might be involved in a particular political dispute and exactly how they will define their preferences. When a new political issue arises, individuals or groups have to figure out if they are interested in it and, if so, what preferences they will hold and pursue. In economics, this usually isn't a problem. It's a pretty safe assumption that people engage in economic activity to make money: businesses seek to maximize profits, and workers look for the highest wage. Knowing preferences in advance is much more difficult in political science. For instance, how can a rational choice theorist explain the electoral choice of a voter who is both a devout Catholic and a union member if the two available candidates are (a) a Democrat who favors raising the minimum wage and other workers' benefits but also favors legalized abortion, and (b) a Republican with the opposite views? Will that person vote as a Catholic or as a union member? How can we use rational choice theory to figure out his preferences in this situation?

Many comparativists also ask whether rational choice theories can explain the different political behavior seen around the world. For most of the twentieth century, for example, the most important French labor unions were closely affiliated with the Communist Party and pursued many objectives tied to party beliefs, beyond the basic "shop floor" issues of wages and working conditions. In the United States, by contrast, no major unions were tied to communist or socialist parties, and unions focused much more on improving wages and working conditions with less concern for broader social changes. In Britain, labor unions were not communists, but they created their own party, the Labour Party, to represent their interests in government. Rational choice theorists might be able to explain political outcomes involving these unions after correctly understanding the preferences of each, but they have a hard time explaining why unions in different countries developed strikingly different sets of preferences. Did something about the working conditions of these three countries produce different definitions of "self-interest," or do different workers define their interests differently based on factors other than rational calculation?

Psychological theories also focus on individual motivation but question the assumption of rational action and are particularly interested in how political preferences are formed. They explain political behavior on the basis of individuals' psychological experiences or dispositions. Psychological theories look for nonrational explanations for political behavior. Comparativists who study individual leaders often use this approach, trying to explain leaders' choices and actions by understanding personal backgrounds and psychological states. Psychological theories are also sometimes used to explain group identity and behavior (e.g., strong attachments to racial or ethnic groups) and the willingness to join a group engaging in political actions outside the bounds of social norms (e.g., revolutions, political violence, and genocide). In sharp contrast to rational choice theory, psychological theories are often interested in the third dimension of power: influences on the formation of individual political demands. Critics of the psychological approach argue that the inherent focus on the individual that is fundamental to psychological theories makes them irrelevant to explaining group behavior. If so, their utility in political science is limited. Explanations beyond the level of individual motivation, however, might help explain these situations.

psychological theories
Explanations for political behavior based on psychological analysis of political actors' motives

Culture and Ideology Culture and ideology are probably second only to self-interest in popular ideas about political behavior. If people think a political actor is not simply self-interested, they usually assume she is motivated by a value or belief. Environmentalists care about the environment; regardless of their own personal interests, they think everyone ought to have clean air to breathe and forests to walk through. People who are against abortion believe that life begins at conception and therefore abortion is murder; self-interest has nothing to do with it. Political scientists have developed various formal theories that relate to this commonsense notion that values and beliefs matter. The main approaches focus on either political culture or political ideology.

A **political culture** is a set of widely held attitudes, values, beliefs, and symbols about politics. It provides people with ways to understand the political arena, justifications for a particular set of political institutions and practices, and definitions of appropriate political behaviors. Political cultures emerge from various historical processes

political culture
A set of widely held attitudes, values, beliefs, and symbols about politics

political socialization
The process through which people, especially young people, learn about politics and are taught a society's common political values and beliefs

modernists
Theorists of political culture who believe that clear sets of attitudes, values, and beliefs can be identified in each country that change very rarely and explain much about politics there

typology
A classification of some set of phenomena into distinct types for purposes of analysis

civic culture
A political culture in which citizens hold values and beliefs that support democracy, including active participation in politics but also enough deference to the leadership to let it govern effectively

subcultures
Groups that hold partially different beliefs and values from the main political culture of a country

and can change over time, although they usually change rather slowly as they are often deeply embedded in a society. They tend to endure, in part, because of **political socialization,** the process through which people, especially young people, learn about politics and are taught a society's common political values and beliefs. Theories of political culture argue that the attitudes, values, beliefs, and symbols that constitute a given country's political culture are crucial explanations for political behavior in that country. Widely accepted cultural values, they argue, can influence all three dimensions of power: getting people to do something, excluding them from the political arena, and influencing their political demands.

Two broad schools of thought within political culture theory exist: modernist and postmodernist. **Modernists** believe that clear attitudes, values, and beliefs can be identified within any particular political culture. The best-known example of this approach was presented by Gabriel Almond and Sidney Verba in their 1963 book, *The Civic Culture.* Based on a broad survey of citizens of five countries in North America and Europe, the authors developed a **typology,** or list of different types, of political cultures. They saw each country as dominated primarily by one particular type of political culture and argued that more stable and democratic countries, such as the United States and Great Britain, had a **civic culture.** This meant that their citizens held democratic values and beliefs that supported their democracies; these attitudes led citizens to participate actively in politics but also to defer enough to the leadership to let it govern effectively. On the other hand, the authors described Mexico as an authoritarian culture in which citizens viewed themselves primarily as subjects with no right to control their government, suggesting that these attitudes helped to produce the semi-authoritarian regime that ruled the country until 2000.

Critics of the modernist approach question the assumption that any country has a clearly defined political culture that is relatively fixed and unchanging, and they contest the argument that cultural values cause political outcomes rather than the other way around. They note that **subcultures** (distinct political cultures of particular groups) exist in all societies. Racial or religious minorities, for instance, may not fully share the political attitudes and values of the majority. The assumption that we can identify a single, unified political culture that is key to understanding a particular country can mask some of the most important political conflicts within the country. Furthermore, political attitudes themselves may be symptoms rather than causes of political activity or a governmental system. For example, Mexican citizens in the 1960s may not have viewed themselves as active participants in government for a very rational reason: they had lived for forty years under one party that had effectively suppressed all meaningful opposition and participation. They really did not have any effective voice in government or any chance for effective participation. According to this view, the political institutions in Mexico created the political attitudes of Mexicans, rather than vice versa.

Some political scientists also accuse modernists of ethnocentrism, in that many modernist approaches argue that Anglo-American values are superior to others for

Police confront protesters in Mexico City in 1968. Political culture theory argues that countries like Mexico were not democratic because they did not have a democratic political culture. Critics contend that culture can change quickly, so it isn't a very good explanation of regime type. Mexico transitioned to an electoral democracy in 2000.

establishing stable democracies. Still other critics suggest that political culture is more malleable than *The Civic Culture* assumed. The attitudes that surveys identified in the 1960s were just that—attitudes of the 1960s. Over time, as societies change and new political ideas arise, attitudes and values change accordingly, sometimes with breath-taking speed (Almond and Verba 1989). Many cultural theorists, for instance, have argued that both Arab and Islamic cultures tend to have nondemocratic values that support authoritarian regimes in the Middle East. The revolts in 2011 that toppled regimes in Tunisia and Libya suggest that those theorists either misunderstood the cultures or the cultures changed rapidly.

Some modernist approaches examine change in political culture. Ronald Inglehart (1971) coined the term **postmaterialist** in the 1970s to describe what he saw as a new predominant element in political culture in wealthy democracies. He argued that as a result of the post–World War II economic expansion, by the 1960s and 1970s most citizens in wealthy societies were less concerned about economic (materialist) issues and more concerned about "quality of life" issues. They had become "postmaterial-ist." Economic growth had allowed most citizens to attain a level of material comfort that led to a change in attitudes and values. Individuals had become more concerned with ideas like human rights, civil rights, women's rights, environmentalism, and moral values.

This postmaterialist shift in political culture led to a sea change in the issues that politicians came to care about and the outcomes of elections. It explained, for instance, why many self-identified Catholic voters in the United States shifted from

postmaterialist
A set of values in a society in which most citizens are economically secure enough to move beyond immediate economic (materialist) concerns to "quality of life" issues like human rights, civil rights, women's rights, environmentalism, and moral values

voting Democratic in the middle of the twentieth century to voting Republican by the end of the century. In the 1950s they voted their mostly working-class economic interests, supporting the party that created what they saw as "pro-worker" policies. Later, as they achieved greater economic security as part of an expanding middle class, they came to care more about postmaterial moral values, such as their religious opposition to abortion, and they shifted their party allegiance accordingly. As the bulk of American voters went through this shift in political culture, political battles focused less on economic issues and more on debates over the moral and cultural values that many analysts see dividing the country more recently. Changes like the shift to postmaterialist values in a political culture, though, are still long-term processes. If cultural values are deeply embedded and nearly universal in a society, they can only change slowly. For instance, some might wonder whether the economic crisis that began in 2008 might not shift Western voters away from postmaterialist values and back to more material concerns, but a major shift in this direction will only be apparent over a rather long time period.

Inglehart's (1971) approach, and others like it, shows how political culture can change over time as a result of other changes in society. Nonetheless, Inglehart and others continued to argue that it was useful to think about societies as having identifiable political cultures that explain much political behavior. The **postmodernist** approach, on the other hand, pushes the criticism of modernism further, questioning the assumption that one clear set of values can be identified that has a clear meaning to all members of a society and defines the politics of that society. Postmodernists, influenced primarily by postmodern French philosophers such as Michel Foucault, see cultures not as sets of fixed and clearly defined values but rather as sets of symbols subject to interpretation. When examining political culture, postmodernists focus primarily on **political discourse,** meaning the ways in which a society speaks and writes about politics. They argue that a culture has a set of symbols that, through a particular historical process, has come to be highly valued but is always subject to varying interpretations. These symbols do not have fixed values upon which all members of a society agree; instead, political actors can use them by interpreting them through political discourse. Influencing discourse can be a means to gain power in its third dimension: influencing how people think about politics.

One example of a symbol that political actors use in political discourse is "family values." No American politician would dare oppose family values. In the 1980s Republicans under President Ronald Reagan used this concept in their campaign discourse very effectively to paint themselves as supporters of the core concerns of middle-class families. As a result, Democrats and their policies came to be seen at times as threatening to the ideal of the nuclear family. In the 1990s under President Bill Clinton, Democrats were able to gain back some political advantage by reinterpreting family values to mean what they argued was support for "real" American families: single mothers trying to raise kids on their own, or two-income families in which the parents were worried about the quality of after-school programs and the cost of a

postmodernist
An approach that sees cultures not as sets of fixed and clearly defined values but rather as sets of symbols subject to interpretation

political discourse
The ways in which people speak and write about politics; postmodern theorists argue that political discourse influences political attitudes, identity, and actions

college education. Democrats created a new discourse about family values that allowed them to connect that powerful symbol to the kinds of government programs they supported. Family values, the postmodernists would argue, are not a fixed set of values that all agree on, but rather a symbol through which political leaders build support by developing a particular discourse at a particular time. Such symbols are always subject to reinterpretation in this way.

Critics of the postmodern approach argue that it really cannot explain anything. If everything is subject to interpretation, then how can one explain anything or form any prediction other than "things will change as new interpretations arise"? Postmodernists respond that the discourses themselves matter by setting symbolic boundaries within which political actors must engage to mobilize political support. The ability of political leaders to interpret these symbols to develop support for themselves and their policies is a central element to understanding political activity in any country.

Advocates of political culture, whether modernist or postmodernist, argue that explaining political behavior requires understanding the effects of political culture at the broadest level. A related but distinct way to examine the effect of values and beliefs is the study of **political ideology,** a systematic set of beliefs about how a political system ought to be structured. Political ideologies typically are quite powerful, overarching worldviews that incorporate both normative and empirical theories that explicitly state an understanding of how the political world does operate and how it ought to operate. Political ideology is distinct from political culture in that it is much more consciously elaborated. In chapter 3 we examine the predominant political ideologies of the last century: liberalism, communism, fascism, modernizing authoritarianism, and theocracy.

political ideology
A systematic set of beliefs about how a political system ought to be structured

Advocates of a particular political ideology attempt to mobilize support for their position by proclaiming a vision of a just and good society as a goal toward which political actors should strive. The most articulate proponents of an ideology can expound on its points, define its key terms, and argue for why it is right. Communists, for instance, envision a communist society in which all people are equal and virtually all serious conflicts disappear, meaning government itself can disappear. They appeal to people's sense of injustice by pointing out the inequality that is inherent in a capitalist society, and they encourage people to work with them through various means to achieve a better society in the future.

Web link:
Ideology isn't the natural basis of politics

A political ideology may be related to a particular political culture, but political ideologies are conscious and well-developed sets of beliefs rather than the vague sets of values or attitudes. Some scholars take political ideology at face value, at least implicitly accepting the idea that political leaders, and perhaps their followers as well, should be taken at their word. These scholars believe that political actors have thought about politics and adopted a particular set of beliefs that they use as a basis for their own political actions and for judging the actions of others. Comparativists Evelyne Huber and John Stephens (2001), for instance, argue that the strength of social democratic ideology in several northern European governments partly explains why those states have exceptionally generous welfare policies.

ideological hegemony
The ruling class's ability to spread a set of ideas justifying and perpetuating its political dominance

Web link:
He wears the mask

structuralism
Approach to explaining politics that argues that political behavior is at least influenced and limited, and perhaps even determined, by broader structures in a society such as class divisions or enduring institutions

Marxism
Structuralist argument that says that economic structures largely determine political behavior; the philosophical underpinning of communism

social classes
In Marxist theory, groups of people with the same relationship to the means of production; more generally, groups of people with similar occupations, wealth, or income

bourgeoisie
The class that owns capital; according to Marxism, the ruling elite in all capitalist societies

proletariat
A term in Marxist theory for the class of free-wage laborers who own no capital and must sell their labor to survive; communist parties claim to work on the proletariat's behalf

institutionalism
An approach to explaining politics that argues that political institutions are crucial to understanding political behavior

Critics of this approach point to what they see as the underlying motives of ideology as the real explanation for political behavior. The Italian Marxist Antonio Gramsci (1971) argued that the key element we need to understand is **ideological hegemony,** or the ruling class's ability to propagate a set of ideas that justifies and perpetuates its political dominance. For Gramsci, ideology is a means by which the ruling class convinces the population that its rule is natural, justified, or both (see the "Who Rules?" section in this chapter on page 24 for a discussion of the ruling class). Clearly, this ties directly to the "third dimension" of power. Advocates of rational choice models might argue that a particular leader or group adopts a particular ideology because it is in its own self-interest; for example, business owners support an ideology of "free markets" because it maximizes opportunities to make profits. Similarly, advocates of a political culture approach see cultural values as lying behind ideology. In the United States, for instance, vague but deep-seated American values of individualism and individual freedom may explain why Americans are far less willing to support socialist ideologies than are Europeans. The debate between proponents and critics of political ideology as an explanation for political behavior is about whether scholars should accept political actors' ideological statements at face value or should dig deeper to look for underlying causes of political behavior, including why particular actors adopt particular ideologies.

Underlying Structures The third broad approach to explaining political behavior is **structuralism.** Structuralists argue that broader structures in a society at the very least influence and limit, and perhaps even determine, political behavior. These structures can be socioeconomic or political. An early and particularly influential structuralist argument was **Marxism,** which argues that economic structures largely determine political behavior. Karl Marx contended that the production process of any society creates discrete **social classes**—groups of people with distinct relationships to the means of production. He argued that in modern capitalist society the key classes are the **bourgeoisie,** which owns and controls capital, and the **proletariat,** which owns no capital and must sell its labor to survive. According to Marx, this economic structure explains political behavior: the bourgeoisie uses its economic advantage to control the state in its interest, while the proletariat will eventually recognize and act on its own, opposing interests.

A more recent structuralist theory is **institutionalism.** Institutionalists argue that political institutions are crucial to understanding political behavior. A **political institution** is most commonly defined as a set of rules, norms, or standard operating procedures that is widely recognized and accepted and that structures and constrains individuals' political actions. Major political institutions often serve as the basis for key political organizations such as legislatures or political parties. In short, institutions are the "rules of the game" within which political actors must operate. These rules are often quite formal and widely recognized, such as in the U.S. Constitution.

Other institutions can be informal or even outside government but nonetheless be very important in influencing political behavior. In the United States, George Washington established a long-standing informal institution, the two-term limit on the presidency. After he stepped down at the end of his second term, no other president, no matter how popular, attempted to run for a third term until Franklin Roosevelt in 1940. Voters supported his decision and reelected him, but after his death the country quickly passed a constitutional amendment that created a formal rule limiting a president to two consecutive terms. Informal institutions can be enduring, as the two-term presidency tradition shows. It held for more than 150 years simply because the vast majority of political leaders and citizens believed it should; in that context, no president dared go against it.

Broadly speaking, two schools of thought exist among institutionalists. **Rational choice institutionalists** follow the assumptions of rational choice theory outlined above. They argue that institutions are the products of the interaction and bargaining of rational actors and, once created, constitute the rules of the game within which rational actors operate, at least until their interests diverge too far from those rules. Barry Weingast (1997), for instance, claimed that for democracies to succeed, major political forces must come to a rational compromise on key political institutions that give all important political players incentives to support the system. Institutions that create such incentives will be self-enforcing, thereby creating a stable democratic political system. Weingast applied this argument to several countries, including the United States. He argued that political stability in early U.S. history was due to the Constitution's provision of federalism, a particular separation of powers, and the equal representation of each of the states in the Senate. This gave both North and South effective veto power over major legislation, which enforced compromise and, therefore, stability. The Civil War broke out, in part, because by the 1850s the creation of nonslave states threatened the South's veto power. This changed context meant that Southern leaders no longer saw the Constitution as serving their interests, so they were willing to secede. Rational choice institutionalists argue that political actors will abide by a particular institution only as long as it continues to serve their joint interests. Therefore, a changed context requires institutions to change accordingly or face dissolution.

Historical institutionalists believe that institutions play an even bigger role in explaining political behavior. They argue that institutions not only limit self-interested political behavior but also influence who is involved in politics and shape individuals' political preferences, thus working in all three dimensions of power. By limiting who is allowed to participate, institutions can determine what a government is capable of accomplishing. Stephan Haggard and Robert Kaufman (1995), for example, argued that two key institutions—a strong executive and a coherent party system—shaped political participation in ways that allowed certain countries in Latin America and East Asia to respond positively to economic crises in the 1980s and 1990s, improving their economies and creating stable democracies. Beyond limiting who can participate

political institution
A set of rules, norms, or standard operating procedures that is widely recognized and accepted by the society, structures and constrains political actions, and often serves as the basis for key political organizations

rational choice institutionalists
Institutionalist theorists who follow the assumptions of rational choice theory and argue that institutions are the products of the interaction and bargaining of rational actors

historical institutionalists
Theorists who believe that institutions explain political behavior and shape individuals' political preferences and their perceptions of their self-interests, and that institutions evolve historically in particular countries and change relatively slowly

and what can be accomplished, institutions can create political preferences. Because societies value long-standing political institutions, their preservation is part of political socialization: citizens come to accept and value existing institutions and define their own interests partly in terms of preserving those institutions. Historical institutionalists thus argue that institutions themselves profoundly shape what policies are possible and what political outcomes are likely, independent of people's self-interests or cultural values.

Critics of institutionalism argue that institutions are rarely the actual explanation for political behavior. Skeptics who follow rational choice theory argue that institutions are simply based on rational actions and compromises among elites who will continue to be "constrained" by these only as long as doing so serves their interests. Scholars who focus on political culture or ideology, on the other hand, suggest that institutions are derived from a society's underlying values and beliefs or a more self-conscious ideology. In either case, the real explanation for political behavior and the shape of the institutions is the underlying values, beliefs, or ideology present in a society.

Political scientists look to three sources as explanations for political behavior: rational action, values and beliefs, and structures. Scholars can use each of these approaches to analyze the same political event. For instance, Chile made one of the most successful transitions to democracy in the 1990s. A rational choice institutionalist might argue that this resulted from the strategic interaction of the major political actors, regardless of what they personally believed about democracy. They came to a compromise with the former military regime and with one another around a set of constitutional rules that, given the political context, they thought was better for them than the available nondemocratic alternatives. Therefore, they agreed to act within the democratic "game." A political culture theorist would point to values in Chilean society that favored democracy, values that perhaps derived in part from the European origins of much of the population, as well as the country's past history with democracy. A historical institutionalist, on the other hand, would argue that Chile's prior stable democratic institutions were easy to resurrect because of their past success and that these institutions represented a legacy that many other Latin American countries did not have. So the question becomes, Which of these theories is most convincing and why, and what evidence can we find to support one or another explanation? This is the primary work of much of political science and the kind of question to which we will return frequently in this book. The theories we use are summarized in Table 1.1.

Who Rules?

The second great question in comparative politics is, Who rules? Which individual, group, or groups control power, and how much do they control? At first glance, the answer may seem obvious. In a democracy, legislators are elected for a set term to make the laws. They rule, after the voters choose them, until the next election. Because of elections, it is the voters who really rule. In a dictatorship, on the other hand, one individual, one ruling party, or one small group (such as a military junta) rules. This ruler(s) has all the power and keeps it as long as he pleases, or at least as long as he is able.

Comparativists, however, question this superficial view. Even in democracies, many argue that the voters don't really hold the power and that a small group at the top controls things. Conversely, many argue that dictatorships may not be the monoliths they appear to be in that those officially in charge may have to unofficially share power with others in society in one way or another. Political scientists, in trying to dig beneath the surface of the question, have developed many theories that can be grouped into two broad categories: pluralist theories and elite theories.

Pluralist Theories: Each Group Has Its Voice

Pluralist theories contend that society is divided into various political groups and that power is dispersed among them so that no group has complete or permanent power. This is most obvious in democracies in which different parties capture power via elections. When pluralists look at political groups, however, they look at far more than just parties. They argue that politically organized groups exist in all societies, sometimes formally and legally but at other times informally or illegally. These groups compete for access to and influence over power. Policy is almost always the result of a compromise among groups, and no single group is able to dominate continuously. Furthermore, over time and on different issues, the power and influence of groups vary. A group that is particularly successful at gaining power or influencing government on one particular issue will not be as successful on another. No group will ever win all battles. Pluralists clearly tend to think about power in its first dimension; they do not believe that any one group has the ability to exclude other groups from the political arena or to influence how another group thinks to the extent necessary to gain permanent power over them.

This pluralist process is less obvious in countries that do not have electoral democracies, but many pluralists argue that their ideas are valid in these cases as well. Even in the Soviet Union under Communist rule, some analysts saw elements of pluralism. They believed that for most of the Soviet period, at least after the death of Joseph Stalin in 1953, the ruling Communist Party had numerous internal factions that were essentially informal political groups. These were based on positions in the party and government bureaucracy or on economic position, regional loyalty, or personal loyalty to a key leader. For instance, people in the secret police, the KGB, and the military were each a political group, quietly lobbying to expand the influence and power of their organizations. Leaders of particular industries, such as the oil industry, were a group seeking the ruling party's support for greater resources and prestige for their area of the economy. Leaders of a region or city could also act as a group, seeking greater government spending in their area. In all these cases, pluralist politics were hidden behind a

pluralist theory
Explanation of who has power that argues that society is divided into various political groups and that power is dispersed among these groups so that no group has complete or permanent power; contrast to elite theory

TABLE 1.1	What Explains Political Behavior?			
TYPE	**INDIVIDUAL MOTIVATION** Understanding what internal factors explain political actions		**CULTURE AND IDEOLOGY** Understanding the effect of values or beliefs	
Theory or framework	**Rational choice**	**Psychological theory**	**Political culture**	**Political ideology**
Assumptions	Political actors bring a set of self-defined preferences, adequate knowledge, and ability to pursue those interests and rationality to the political arena.	Nonrational influences explain political behavior.	A set of widely held attitudes, values, beliefs, and symbols about politics shapes what actors do.	Systematic set of beliefs about how the political system ought to be structured motivates political action.
Unit of analysis	Individual actors	Group and individual identity and behavior	Individual actors and groups, political institutions, discourses, and practices	Individual actors and groups
Methods	Observe outcome of political process; identify actors involved, relative power, and preferences; demonstrate how outcome was result of actors' self-interested interactions.	Explain actors' choices and actions by understanding their personal backgrounds and psychological states.	Modernist approach identifies clear attitudes, values, and beliefs within any particular political culture—for example, civic culture or postmaterialist culture. Postmodernist approach holds that cultures do not have fixed and clearly defined values but rather a set of symbols subject to interpretation; focuses primarily on political discourse.	Analyze written and verbal statements of political actors and correlate them with observed behavior.
Critiques	Some difficulty predicting future behavior; hard to explain variation across cases.	Difficult to verify connections between internal state and actions, particularly for groups.	Political culture is not a monolithic, unchanging entity within a given country. Cultural values are not necessarily the cause of political outcomes; the causal relationship may be the other way around. If everything is subject to interpretation, then how can anything be explained or predicted?	Focus on ideology obscures what may be underlying motives, or the real explanation, for political behavior.

UNDERLYING STRUCTURES Understanding how broad structures or forces shape or determine behavior	
Marxism	**Institutionalism**
Economic structures determine political behavior. Production process creates distinct social classes—groups of people with the same relationship to the means of production.	Political institutions are widely recognized and accepted rules, norms, or standard operating procedures that structure and constrain individuals' political actions—the "rules of the game."
Groups and social classes in particular	Interaction of both formal and informal institutions with groups and individuals
Conduct historical analysis of economic systems.	Rational choice institutionalists follow rational choice theory; institutions are products of the interactions and bargaining of rational actors. Historical institutionalists examine the historical evolution of institutions to demonstrate how these institutions limit self-interested political behavior and shape individuals' political preferences.
Ignores noneconomic motives and ignores groups other than social classes.	Difficult to determine if institutions, rather than self-interest or culture, limit behavior.

facade of ironclad party rule in which the politburo, the Communist Party's central decision-making elite, made all decisions and all others obeyed. Dictatorships in postcolonial countries can also be analyzed via pluralism. On the surface, a military government in Africa looks like one individual or small group holding all power for as long as it is able or desires. Pluralists argue, however, that many of these governments have very limited central control. They rule through **patron-client relationships** in which the top leaders, the patrons, mobilize political support by providing resources to their followers, the clients. The internal politics of this type of rule revolve around the competition among group leaders for access to resources they can pass on to their clients. The top clients are themselves patrons of clients further down the chain. Midlevel clients might decide to shift their loyalty from one patron to another if they don't receive adequate resources, meaning those at the top must continuously work to maintain the support of their clients. In many cases, patrons use resources to mobilize support from others in their own ethnic group, so the main informal groups competing for power are ethnically defined (see chapter 4). Various factions compete for power and access to resources, again behind a facade of unitary and centralized power.

Elite Theory While pluralists see competing groups, even in countries that appear to be ruled by dictators, proponents of **elite theory** argue that all societies are ruled by an elite that has effective control over virtually all

patron-client relationships
Top leaders (patrons) mobilize political support by providing resources to their followers (clients) in exchange for political loyalty

elite theory
A theory that all societies are ruled by a small group that has effective control over virtually all power; contrast to pluralist theory

power. Elite theories usually focus on the second and third dimensions of power to argue that certain elites have perpetual power over ordinary citizens. The longest tradition within elite theory is Marxism, mentioned above. Marx argued that in any society, political power reflects control of the economy. In feudal Europe, for instance, the feudal lord, by virtue of his ownership of land, had power over the peasants, who were dependent on the lord for access to land and thus their survival. The peasants were forced to live on the land of the lord under whom they were born, work that land for their own survival and produce a surplus for the lord, and carry out the lord's will in virtually all things. The lord, by virtue of his economic position, had tremendous political power over them. Similarly, Marx contended that in modern capitalist society, the bourgeoisie, by virtue of their ownership of capital, are the **ruling class**, as the feudal lords were centuries ago. The general population, or proletariat, is forced to sell its labor by working in the bourgeoisie's businesses in order to survive and must generally serve the desires of the bourgeoisie. Thus, in *The Communist Manifesto* Marx famously called the modern state "the executive committee of the whole bourgeoisie."

In postcolonial societies, Marxist analysts often argue that at least part of the ruling class is outside the country it rules. With the end of colonialism, a new situation of **neocolonialism** arose. The leaders of the newly independent countries in Africa and Asia benefited politically and economically by helping Western businesses maintain access to their countries' wealth. The new governments came to serve the interests of Western corporations as much as or more than they served their own people.

The Marxist tradition is only one type of elite theory. C. Wright Mills, in *The Power Elite* (1956), argued that the United States was ruled by a set of interlocking elites sitting at the top of economic, political, and military hierarchies. Mills shared with the Marxist tradition an emphasis on a small group controlling all real power, but he did not see the economy as the sole source of this power. He believed that the economic, political, and military spheres, while interlocking, are distinct and that all serve as key elements in the ruling elite. A more recent example of this view was put forward by Charles Lindblom (1977), who referred to the "privileged position of business" in a capitalist society. In his view, government is dependent on business for taxes and the bulk of the population is dependent on business for employment, so business is in a unique position to influence those in power and, therefore, government policy. Lindblom argued that two spheres of power exist in modern democracies: economic and political. The political sphere is subject to democratic control, and the economic sphere is not. Modern democracies, including the United States, are not fully governed by "the people" in any real sense of the word, according to elite theorists, but rather by interlocking elites.

More recently, feminist scholars have also developed elite theories of rule based on the concept of **patriarchy,** or rule by men. They argue that throughout history men have controlled virtually all power. Even though women have gained the right to vote in most countries, men remain the key rulers virtually everywhere. Today, social mores and political discourse are often the chief sources of patriarchy rather

ruling class
An elite who possess adequate resources to control a regime; in Marxist theory, the class that controls key sources of wealth in a given epoch

neocolonialism
A relationship between postcolonial societies and their former colonizers in which leaders benefit politically and economically by helping outside businesses and states maintain access to the former colonies' wealth and come to serve the interests of the former colonizers and corporations more than they serve their own people

Web link:
Joseph Stiglitz on the One Percent

Web link:
David Brooks on inequality

patriarchy
Rule by men

Supporters of the "Occupy Wall Street" movement demonstrate in March 2012. The movement's focus on the political influence of the richest 1 percent of the population in the United States raised serious questions about how truly democratic the U.S. political system is. Elite theorists argue that the Occupy movement is correct: an elite really controls power in spite of the outward appearance of democratic government.

than actual law, but men remain in power nonetheless, and the political realm, especially its military aspects, continues to be linked to masculinity. A leader needs to be able to command a military, "take charge," and "act boldly and aggressively"—all activities most societies associate with masculinity. The second and third dimensions of power help preserve male control despite women now having the same formal political rights as men. Men also continue to enjoy greater income and wealth than women and can translate economic status into political power. According to feminist theorists, men thus constitute an elite that continues to enjoy a near monopoly on political power in many societies.

Similarly, some analysts argue that a racial elite exists in some societies in which one race has been able to maintain a hold on power. Historically, this was done via laws that prevented other races from participating in the political process, such as under apartheid in South Africa or the Jim Crow laws of the southern United States. But, as with feminists, analysts of race often argue that one race can maintain dominance through a disproportionate share of wealth or through the preservation of a particular political discourse that often implicitly places different races in different positions in a hierarchy. Michelle Alexander (2012) argued that laws and discourse around crime, drugs, and "colorblindness" constitute a "new Jim Crow" in the United States; they systemically disempower and disenfranchise black men, in particular, by disproportionately putting a large number of them in the criminal justice system. More generally, race theorists contend that in the United States, cultural attributes associated with being white, such as personal mannerisms and accent and dialect of English, are assumed to be not only "normal" but implicitly superior and are thus expected of those in leadership positions. This gives an inherent advantage to white aspirants for political positions, even when no overt discrimination against others exists.

Web link:
Women's power: a story with sharp divide

Video link:
Racial profiling in Brooklyn

James V. Taylor poses in his home in Park Hills, Missouri. Police found a tiny amount of crack cocaine in his car, which resulted in a fifteen-year prison sentence. Drug laws that give long sentences for possessing even minute amounts of drugs and police who disproportionately patrol in black neighborhoods help create what Michelle Alexander called the "new Jim Crow," a systematic exclusion of a large percentage of black men from full citizenship via imprisonment for minor crimes.

Determining whether pluralist or elite theories best answer the question of who rules requires answering these questions: Who is in formal positions of power? Who has influence on government decision making? Who benefits from the decisions made? If the answer to all of these questions seems to be one or a select few small groups, then the evidence points to elite theory as more accurate. If various groups seem to have access to power or influence over decision making, or both, then pluralism would seem more accurate. Table 1.2 summarizes these theories, which we investigate throughout this book.

Where and Why?

"What explains political behavior?" and "Who rules?" are central questions to all political scientists. The particular focus of comparative politics is to ask these questions across countries in an attempt to develop a common understanding of political phenomena in all places and times. The third major question that orients this book is "Where and why?" Where do particular political phenomena occur, and why do they occur where they do and how they do?

For instance, Sweden is famous for its extensive and expensive welfare state, while the U.S. government spends much less money and attention on providing for people's needs directly via "welfare." Why are these two wealthy democracies so different? Can their differences be explained on the basis of competing rational choices? Did business interests overpower the interests of workers and poor people in the United States, while a large and well-organized labor movement in Sweden overcame a small, weaker business class to produce a more extensive welfare state? Or has the Swedish Socialist Party, which has been dominant over most of the last century, simply been successful at convincing the bulk of the population that its social democratic ideology produces a better society, while Americans' cultural belief in "making it on your own" leads them to reject any form of socialism? Or are the differences because a strong nongovernmental institution, the Landsorganisationen I Sverige (LO), arose in Sweden, uniting virtually all labor unions and becoming a central part of the policy-making process, whereas in the United States the country's more decentralized labor unions were not as capable of gaining the government's ear on welfare policy? Comparative politics attempts to resolve this kind of puzzle by examining the various theories of political behavior in light of the evidence found.

We engage in similar comparative efforts when seeking to understand who rules. A case study of the United States, for instance, might argue (as many have) that a

TABLE 1.2	Who Rules?	

<table>
<thead>
<tr><th></th><th>Pluralist theory</th><th>Elite theory</th></tr>
</thead>
<tbody>
<tr><td rowspan="5">Key arguments</td><td>Society is divided into political groups.</td><td>All societies are ruled by an elite with control over virtually all power.</td></tr>
<tr><td>Power is dispersed among groups.</td><td>Marxism: Political power reflects control of the economy; it is based on the economic power of the bourgeoisie, who owns and controls capital and is the ruling elite in capitalist societies.</td></tr>
<tr><td>No group has complete or permanent power.</td><td>The power elite: Elite consists of military and political elite as well as economic elite.</td></tr>
<tr><td>Even authoritarian regimes have important pluralist elements.</td><td>Patriarchy: The ruling elite is male; social mores and political discourse keep men in power. The political realm, especially the military, is linked to masculinity.</td></tr>
<tr><td></td><td>Critical race theorists: The ruling elite is white; assumed superiority of white cultural characteristics keeps whites in power.</td></tr>
</tbody>
</table>

corporate elite holds great power in American democracy, perhaps so great that it raises questions of how democratic the system actually is. A Marxist might argue that this is due to the unusually centralized and unequal control of wealth in the United States. A political culture theorist would point instead to American culture's belief in individualism, which leads few to question the leaders of major businesses, who are often depicted as "self-made" individuals whom many citizens admire. An institutionalist, on the other hand, would argue that American political institutions allow corporations to have great influence by funding expensive political campaigns and that members of Congress have little incentive to vote in support of their parties and so are more open to pressure from individual lobbyists. A comparativist might compare the United States and several European countries, examining the relative level of corporate influence, the level of wealth concentration, cultural values, and the ability of lobbyists to influence legislators in each country. This study might reveal comparative patterns that suggest, for instance, that corporate influence is highest in countries where wealth is most concentrated, regardless of the type of political system or cultural values. We examine this kind of question throughout the book.

PLAN OF THE BOOK

This book takes a thematic approach to exploring comparative politics. Each chapter examines a set of issues by presenting the major theoretical ideas and debates in that area of comparative politics and then examining how those ideas and issues play out in

COUNTRY AND CONCEPT
Case Study Benchmarks

Country	Population	Age structure	Monetary unit	Major natural resources
Brazil	201,009,622	0-14 years: 24.2%; 15-64 years: 68.5%; 65 years and over: 7.3%	Real	Bauxite, gold, hydropower, iron ore, manganese, nickel, petroleum, phosphates, platinum, timber, tin, uranium
China	1,349,585,838	0-14 years: 17.2%; 15-64 years: 73.4%; 65 years and over: 9.4%	Yuan	Aluminum, antimony, coal, iron ore, lead, magnetite, manganese, mercury, molybdenum, natural gas, petroleum, tin, tungsten, uranium, vanadium, zinc, hydropower potential
Germany	81,147,265	0-14 years: 13.1 15-64 years: 66.1%; 65 years and over: 20.9%	Euro	Arable land, coal, construction materials, copper, iron ore, lignite, natural gas, nickel, potash, salt, timber, uranium
India	1,220,800,359	0-14 years: 29.8%; 15-64 years: 65.5%; 65 years and over: 5.7%	Rupee	Arable land, bauxite, coal (world's fourth-largest reserves), chromite, diamonds, iron ore, limestone, manganese, mica, natural gas, petroleum, titanium ore
Iran	79,853,900	0-14 years: 23.8%; 15-64 years: 71.2%; 65 years and over: 5.1%	Rial	Coal, chromium, copper, iron ore, lead, manganese, natural gas, petroleum, sulfur, zinc
Japan	127,253,075	0-14 years: 13.4%; 15-64 years: 61.7%; 65 years and over: 24.8%	Yen	Negligible mineral resources, fish
Mexico	116,220,947	0-14 years: 27.4%; 15-64 years: 65.7%; 65 years and over: 6.9%	Peso	Petroleum, silver, copper, gold, lead, zinc, natural gas, timber
Nigeria	174,507,539	0-14 years: 43.8%; 15-64 years: 53.2%; 65 years and over: 3%	Naira	Arable land, coal, iron ore, lead, limestone, natural gas, niobium, petroleum, tin, zinc
Russia	142,500,482	0-14 years: 16%; 15-64 years: 70.9%; 65 years and over: 13.1%	Ruble	Broad natural resource base, including major deposits of coal, natural gas, oil, timber, and many strategic minerals
United Kingdom	63,395,574	0-14 years: 17.3%; 15-64 years: 65.4%; 65 years and over: 17.3%	Pound sterling	Arable land, chalk, clay, coal, gold, gypsum, iron ore, lead, limestone, natural gas, petroleum, potash, salt, sand, silica, slate, tin, zinc
United States	316,668,567	0-14 years: 20%; 15-64 years: 66.2%; 65 years and over: 13.9%	Dollar	Bauxite, coal, copper, gold, iron, lead, mercury, molybdenum, natural gas, nickel, petroleum, phosphates, potash, silver, timber, tungsten, uranium, zinc

Source: CIA, *The World Factbook* (https://www.cia.gov/library/publications/the-world-factbook/index.html).

the real world in a set of countries. The rest of Part I looks at a set of key relationships crucial to understanding modern politics. These relationships all involve the modern state (defined fully in chapter 2)—to understand the modern political world, we must first understand what the modern state is, how it functions, and how it arose. We then look at the relationship of states to citizens (chapter 3), group identity (chapter 4), and the market economy (chapter 5). Part II examines the basic institutions of modern politics in both democratic and authoritarian regimes and explores the process of transition from one regime to another. Part III turns to an examination of a set of important policy issues in contemporary politics around the world.

Throughout the book, we draw on a set of eleven countries to illustrate the ideas, debates, institutions, and issues we are examining. Each chapter focuses on a comparison of several of these countries, chosen to illustrate the key ideas and debates in the chapter. The eleven countries include a majority of the most populous countries in the world and provide a representative sample of different kinds of modern political history. They include four wealthy democracies (the United States, Britain, Germany, and Japan), two post-Communist countries (Russia and China), the largest and one of the most enduring democracies in the world (India), the world's only theocracy (Iran), and three examples of countries that have worked to establish democratic systems after lengthy authoritarian regimes (Brazil, Mexico, and Nigeria). Our task is to see what we can learn from a comparative examination of politics in this diverse array of settings.

KEY CONCEPTS

authoritarian regime (p. 5)

bourgeoisie (p. 22)

civic culture (p. 18)

civil society (p. 6)

comparative method (p. 10)

comparative politics (p. 8)

democracy (p. 5)

elite theory (p. 27)

empirical theory (p. 9)

first dimension of power (p. 8)

historical institutionalists (p. 23)

ideological hegemony (p. 22)

institutionalism (p. 22)

international relations (p. 8)

Marxism (p. 22)

modernists (p. 18)

modernization (p. 4)

most different systems design (p. 10)

most similar systems design (p. 10)

neocolonialism (p. 28)

normative theory (p. 9)

patriarchy (p. 28)

patron-client relationships (p. 27)

pluralist theories (p. 25)

political actor (p. 15)

political culture (p. 17)

political development (p. 4)

political discourse (p. 20)

political economy (p. 7)

political ideology (p. 21)

political institution (p. 22)

political science (p. 8)

political socialization (p. 18)

politics (p. 8)

postmaterialist (p. 19)

postmodernist (p. 20)

proletariat (p. 22)

psychological theories (p. 17)

quantitative statistical techniques (p. 11)

rational choice institutionalists (p. 23)

rational choice theory (p. 15)

research methods (p. 10)

ruling class (p. 28)

second dimension of power (p. 8)

single case study (p. 10)

social classes (p. 22)

structuralism (p. 22)

subcultures (p. 18)

theory (p. 9)

third dimension of power (p. 8)

typology (p. 18)

Sharpen your skills with SAGE edge at **edge.sagepub.com/orvis3e.** **SAGE edge for students** provides a personalized approach to help you accomplish your coursework goals in an easy-to-use learning environment.

WORKS CITED

Alexander, Michelle. 2010. *The New Jim Crow: Mass Incarceration in the Age of Colorblindness.* New York: The New Press.

Almond, Gabriel A., and Sidney Verba. 1963. *The Civic Culture: Political Attitudes and Democracy in Five Nations.* Princeton, NJ: Princeton University Press.

———. 1989. *The Civic Culture Revisited.* Newbury Park, CA: Sage.

Bachrach, Peter, and Morton S. Baratz. 1962. "Two Faces of Power." *American Political Science Review* 56 (4): 947–952.

Bratton, Michael, and Nicholas van de Walle. 1997. *Democratic Experiments in Africa: Regime Transitions in Comparative Perspective.* Cambridge, UK: Cambridge University Press.

Collier, Paul, and Anke Hoeffler. 2001. *Greed and Grievance in Civil War.* Washington, DC: World Bank.

Gramsci, Antonio. 1971. *Selections from the Prison Notebooks of Antonio Gramsci.* Edited and translated by Quintin Hoare and Geoffrey Nowell Smith. New York: International.

Haggard, Stephan, and Robert R. Kaufman. 1995. *The Political Economy of Democratic Transitions.* Princeton, NJ: Princeton University Press.

Huber, Evelyne, and John D. Stephens. 2001. *Development and Crisis of the Welfare State: Parties and Policies in Global Markets.* Chicago: University of Chicago Press.

Inglehart, Ronald. 1971. "The Silent Revolution in Europe: Intergenerational Change in Post-Industrial Societies." *American Political Science Review* 65 (4): 991–1017. doi:10.2307/1953494.

Jacobson, Linda. 2001. "Experts Debate Welfare Reform's Impact on Children." *Education Week* 21 (September 19): 1–8.

Lindblom, Charles E. 1977. *Politics and Markets: The World's Political Economic Systems.* New York: Basic Books.

Lukes, Steven. 1974. *Power: A Radical View.* London: Macmillan.

Mills, C. Wright. 1956. *The Power Elite.* New York: Oxford University Press.

Weingast, Barry R. 1997. "The Political Foundations of Democracy and the Rule of Law." *American Political Science Review* 91 (2): 245–263. doi:10.2307/2952354.

RESOURCES FOR FURTHER STUDY

Blank, Rebecca. 2001. "Declining Caseloads/ Increased Work: What Can We Conclude about the Effects of Welfare Reform?" *Economic Policy Review* 7 (2): 25–36.

Dahl, Robert Alan. 1961. *Who Governs? Democracy and Power in an American City*. Yale Studies in Political Science No. 4. New Haven, CT: Yale University Press.

Gaventa, John. 1980. *Power and Powerlessness: Quiescence and Rebellion in an Appalachian Valley*. Urbana: University of Illinois Press.

Katznelson, Ira, and Helen V. Milner, eds. 2002. *Political Science: State of the Discipline*. New York: Norton.

King, Gary, Robert O. Keohane, and Sidney Verba. 1994. *Designing Social Inquiry: Scientific Inference in Qualitative Research*. Princeton, NJ: Princeton University Press.

Landman, Todd. 2003. *Issues and Methods in Comparative Politics: An Introduction*. 2nd ed. New York: Routledge.

Marx, Karl, and Friedrich Engels. 1978. *The Marx-Engels Reader*. Edited by Robert C. Tucker. 2nd ed. New York: Norton.

WEB RESOURCES

CIA, World Factbook
(https://www.cia.gov/library/publications/the-world-factbook)
Organisation for Economic Co-operation and Development (OECD), Data Lab
(http://www.oecd.org/statistics)
Pew Research Center, Pew Global Attitudes Survey 2010
(http://pewglobal.org/2010/?cat=survey-reports)
The World Bank, Data
(http://data.worldbank.org)

2 THE MODERN STATE

KEY QUESTIONS

- What are the common characteristics of all modern states, and how do these characteristics give their rulers power?

- Do the common characteristics of modern states limit power in any way?

- Why are some states stronger than others? Why do some states fail completely?

state
An ongoing administrative apparatus that develops and administers laws and generates and implements public policies in a specific territory

olitical development—the origin and development of the modern state—is the starting point for the study of comparative politics. What do we mean by "the modern state"? In everyday language, *state* is often used interchangeably with both *country* and *nation,* but political scientists use the term in a more specific way. *Country,* the most common term in daily discourse, is not one used in political science because its meaning is too vague. *Nation,* which we discuss in depth in chapter 4, refers to a group of people who perceive themselves as sharing a sense of belonging, and who often have a common language, culture, and set of traditions. *State,* on the other hand, does not refer directly to a group of people or their sense of who they are. One way to think about the state is to ask how and when we "see" or contact the state. Capitols, courts of law, police headquarters, and social service agencies are all part of the state. If you have attended a public school, gotten a driver's license, received a traffic ticket, or paid taxes on something you've purchased, you've come into contact with the state, which provides public goods, enforces laws, and uses public money in the form of taxes to do so. These observations lead to an analytically useful, basic definition of the **state** as an ongoing administrative apparatus that develops and administers laws and generates and implements public policies in a specific territory.

South Sudanese parade their new flag shortly before the referendum in January 2011 that granted them independence from neighboring Sudan at the conclusion of a long civil war. Flags are a universal symbol of modern states. South Sudan is the newest recognized state, and symbols like flags help give it a place and recognition in the world, no matter how poor or weak its state might be.

The *ongoing* nature of the state sets it apart from both a *regime* and a *government*. Regimes are types of government such as liberal democracy or fascism (see chapter 3). Americans use *government* and *state* interchangeably, but "governments" are transient. They occupy and utilize the ongoing apparatus of the state temporarily, typically from one election to the next. Americans often refer to governments as *administrations* (e.g., the Obama administration), but the rest of the world uses the word *government* in this context (e.g., the Cameron government of Great Britain).

Modern states have come to be an exceptionally powerful and ubiquitous means of ruling over people. Any number of groups or individuals, such as dictators, elites, or democratically elected politicians, can rule through the state's institutions. Identifying and understanding the key features of the state help us analyze how those in power rule and how much power they have. Looking at how much institutional apparatus a particular country has developed and how effectively that apparatus can be deployed (Are people really paying taxes? Are neighborhoods run by drug lords or the police?) can help identify the effective limits of official rule. States with stronger institutions are stronger states and give their rules greater power.

In addition to understanding what the state is and how it operates, comparativists study its origins and evolution: Why did modern states emerge at all and become so universal? Where did the modern state first emerge, and why did it develop at different times in different places? Why did strong states develop sooner in some countries and later or not at all in others? A glance at the Country and Concept table on page 57 shows clearly that even within our group of eleven case study countries, the age and strength of the state varies greatly. These states range in age from over three hundred years to just fifty, and they include some of the weakest and strongest (the latter identified by a low number on the Failed States Index), as well as some of the most corrupt and least corrupt of all states worldwide. Though they vary widely, all modern states share some basic characteristics that set them apart from other concepts like nation, government, and regime, as well as from earlier forms of political organization. We will look in turn at the four critical characteristics modern states share: territory, sovereignty, legitimacy, and bureaucracy.

CHARACTERISTICS OF THE MODERN STATE

The first characteristic of the modern state is so obvious that you might overlook it. A state must have **territory,** an area with clearly defined borders to which the state lays claim. In fact, borders are one of the places where the state is "seen" most clearly, not only by the signs that welcome visitors but also by the customs inspectors and immigration officers who patrol and represent it.

territory
An area with clearly defined borders to which a state lays claim

Territory The size of territories varies enormously, from Russia, the largest geographical state at 6,520,800 square miles, to the seventeen states with territories of less than 200 square miles each. The differences between vast Russia and tiny Tuvalu are significant, but territories and borders allow both to claim the status of state.

A glance at any map of the world shows no territories not enclosed by state borders (except Antarctica). Furthermore, many states have inhabited their present borders for so long that we may think of them as being relatively fixed. In truth, the numbers of states and their borders continue to change frequently. The most recent examples are Kosovo's independence from Serbia in 2008 and South Sudan's independence from Sudan in 2011. Border changes and the creation of new states, as both these examples attest, are often attempts to make states coincide more closely with nations; groups with a shared identity (that is, nations) also share or seek to share a distinct territory and government (that is, a state). The lesson of history seems to be that states will continue to change their shapes and borders.

Web link:
List of UN member states

External and Internal Sovereignty In a world of competitive and conflicting states, a state must be able to defend its territory and must not be overly dependent on the resources or decisions of another power. Only in this way can it have real, effective external sovereignty. Governments that lack sovereignty are not

New States and the United Nations

Since 1959, the vast majority of new member states in the United Nations (UN) have been admitted after declaring independence. In the 1960s and 1970s, most newly admitted states were former colonies. In the 1990s, most newly admitted states were the result of the breakup of the Soviet Union and other Eastern-bloc countries. New UN members continue to be added in the twenty-first century.

- **1945–1959:** Eighty-one member states admitted.
- **1960–1969:** Forty-two member states admitted.
- **1970–1979:** Twenty-five member states admitted.
- **1980–1989:** Six member states admitted.
- **1990–1999:** Thirty-one member states admitted.
- **2000–2009:** Five member states admitted.
- **2010– :** One member state admitted.

The example of Kosovo reminds us of another important aspect of territoriality: states exist within an international system of other states (see Table 2.1 on level of state recognition). It is not enough for a state to claim a defined territory; other states must also recognize that claim, even if they dispute a particular border. Political scientists call internationally recognized states **sovereign.** Essentially, a sovereign state is legally recognized by the family of states as the sole legitimate governing authority within its territory and as the legal equal of other states. This legal recognition is the minimal standard for **external sovereignty,** or sovereignty relative to outside powers. Legal external sovereignty, which entails being given the same vote in world affairs as all other states, is vital for sovereignty.

sovereign
Quality of a state in which it is legally recognized by the family of states as the sole legitimate governing authority within its territory and as the legal equal of other states

external sovereignty
Sovereignty relative to outside powers that is legally recognized in international law

truly modern states as comparativists use the term. Examples include the Japanese-backed and -controlled state headed by the Chinese emperor Puyi in Manchukuo (Manchuria) from 1932 to 1945, the collaborationist Vichy government in France during World War II, and all colonial states; although they had a local government, they were not sovereign states because their most crucial decisions were subject to external authority.

Modern states also strive for **internal sovereignty**—that is, to be the sole authority within a territory capable of making and enforcing laws and policies. They must defend their internal sovereignty against domestic groups that challenge it, just as they must defend it externally. Internal challenges typically take the form of a declaration of independence from some part of the state's territory and perhaps even civil war. States rarely are willing to accept such an act of defiance. From the American Civil War in the 1860s to the former Soviet Republic of Georgia in the 1990s when the region of South Ossetia tried to break away, most states use all means in their power to preserve their sovereignty over their recognized territories. Even a relatively insignificant challenge will draw the full attention of a state. In Waco, Texas, in 1993,

internal sovereignty
The sole authority within a territory capable of making and enforcing laws and policies

TABLE 2.1	The Shifting Borders of Modern States: Not Recognized, Limited Recognition, and Majority Recognition States

NOT RECOGNIZED

State	Disputed since	Status
Nagorno-Karabakh	1991	Claimed by Azerbaijan.
Somaliland	1991	Claimed by Somalia.
Transnistria	1990	Claimed by Moldova.

LIMITED RECOGNITION

State	Disputed since	Status
Abkhazia	2008	Recognized by only by 4 countries: Russian Federation, Nicaragua, Nauru, Venezuela.
Kosovo	2008	Recognized by 40 countries.
South Ossetia	2008	Recognized only by Russian Federation.
Palestine	1988	Recognized as a proposed state by 96 UN member states.
Turkish Republic of Northern Cyprus (TRNC)	1983	Recognized only by Turkey.
Sahrawi Arab Democratic Republic (SADR)	1976	Recognized by 45 countries as legitimate government of Western Sahara.
Republic of China (Taiwan) (ROC)	1949	Recognized by 23 countries.

MAJORITY RECOGNITION

State	Disputed since	Status
Czech Republic	1993	Not recognized by Liechtenstein.
Liechtenstein	1993	Not recognized by Czech Republic or Slovakia.
Slovakia	1993	Not recognized by Liechtenstein.
Cyprus	1974	Recognized by all countries except Turkey.
People's Republic of China (PRC)	1949	Not recognized by the Republic of China (Taiwan); the PRC does not accept diplomatic relations with the 22 other UN member states that recognize the ROC.
Israel	1948	Not recognized by Iran or the Sahrawi Arab Democratic Republic (SADR); no diplomatic relations with 34 countries.
North Korea	1948	Not recognized by South Korea.
South Korea	1948	Not recognized by North Korea.

a small religious sect called the Branch Davidians broke various U.S. laws and declared its compound beyond the reach of U.S. authority. Though it was a small and isolated group that most of the country thought was simply "crazy," its direct rejection of U.S. sovereignty ultimately led to high-level government attention. Attorney General Janet Reno was personally involved in the standoff on a daily basis. Even a superpower will react with full force to the smallest threat to its sovereignty.

States try to enforce their sovereignty by claiming, in the words of German sociologist Max Weber, a "monopoly on the legitimate use of physical force" (1970). Put simply, the state claims to be the only entity within its territory that has the right to hold a gun to your head and tell you what to do. Some governments claim a virtually unlimited right to use force when and as they choose. At least in theory, and usually in practice, liberal democracies observe strict guidelines under which the use of force is permissible. For example, law enforcement can be called in when a citizen runs a red light or fails to pay taxes, but not when she criticizes government policy. All states, though, insist on the right to use force to ensure their internal as well as external sovereignty. As one political philosopher reportedly said in response to students who complained about the government calling in police during a demonstration, "The difference between fascism and democracy is not whether the police are called, but when."

Sovereignty does not mean, however, that a state is all-powerful. Real internal and external sovereignty vary greatly and depend on many factors. Because the United States is wealthy and controls much territory, its sovereignty results in much greater power than does the sovereignty of Vanuatu, even though both are recognized as legitimate sovereigns over a clear territory. Wealthier states can defend their territories from attack better than poorer and weaker ones, and they can also more effectively ensure that their citizens comply with their laws. Even the United States, though, cannot completely control its borders, as the undocumented immigrants and illegal narcotics crossing its long border with Mexico attest.

Legitimacy The ability to enforce sovereignty more fully comes not only from wealth but also from legitimacy. Weber argued that a state claims a "monopoly on the *legitimate* use of physical force" [emphasis added]. **Legitimacy** is the recognized right to rule. This right has at least two sides: the claims that states and others make about why they have a right to rule, and the empirical fact of whether their populations accept or at least tolerate this claimed right. All modern states argue at length for particular normative bases for their legitimacy, and these claims are the basis for the various kinds of regimes in the world today (a subject explored in chapter 3).

Weber described three types of legitimate authority: traditional, charismatic, and rational-legal. **Traditional legitimacy** is the right to rule based on a society's long-standing patterns and practices. The European "divine right of kings" and the blessing of ancestors over the king in many precolonial African societies are examples of this. **Charismatic legitimacy** is the right to rule based on personal virtue, heroism, sanctity, or other extraordinary characteristics. Wildly popular leaders of revolutions,

legitimacy
The recognized right to rule

traditional legitimacy
The right to rule based on a society's long-standing patterns and practices

charismatic legitimacy
The right to rule based on personal virtue, heroism, sanctity, or other extraordinary characteristics

such as Mao Zedong in his early years in power, have charismatic legitimacy; people recognize their authority to rule because they trust and believe these individuals to be exceptional. **Rational-legal legitimacy** is the right to rule of leaders who are selected according to an accepted set of laws. Leaders who come to power via electoral processes and rule according to a set of laws, such as a constitution, are the chief examples of this. Weber argued that rational-legal legitimacy distinguishes modern rule from its predecessors, but he recognized that in practice most legitimate authority is a combination of the three types. For example, modern democratically elected leaders may achieve office and rule on the basis of rational-legal processes, but a traditional status or personal charisma may help them win elections and may enhance their legitimacy in office.

Legitimacy enhances a state's sovereignty. Modern states often control an overwhelming amount of coercive power, but its use is expensive and difficult. States cannot maintain effective internal sovereignty in a large, modern society solely through the constant use of force. Legitimacy, whatever its basis, enhances sovereignty at much lower cost. If most citizens obey the government because they believe it has a right to rule, then little force will be necessary to maintain order. This is an example of the third dimension of power we discussed in chapter 1. For this reason, regimes proclaim their legitimacy and spend a great deal of effort trying to convince their citizens of it, especially when their legitimacy is brought into serious question.

Bureaucracy Modern **bureaucracy,** meaning a large set of appointed officials whose function is to implement laws, is the final important characteristic of the state. In contemporary societies, the state plays many complicated roles. It must collect revenue and use it to shore up its legitimacy and monopoly on the use of force. Typically, as discussed further in chapter 5, modern states spend revenues not only on coercive force but also on ways to strengthen the economy within their territory and provide for the well-being of at least some of their citizens in order to enhance legitimacy. Collecting taxes, as well as paving roads, building schools, and providing retirement pensions, all require a bureaucracy. Weber saw bureaucracy as a central part of modern, rational-legal legitimacy, since in theory individuals obtain official positions in a modern bureaucracy via a rational-legal process of appointment and are restricted to certain tasks by a set of laws. Like legitimacy, effective bureaucracy enhances sovereignty. A bureaucracy that efficiently carries out laws, collects taxes, and expends revenues as directed by the central authorities gives the state greater power than it would have otherwise. As we discuss further below, weak legitimacy and weak bureaucracy are two key causes of state weakness in the contemporary world.

From this overview we can enhance our definition of the modern state as an ongoing administrative apparatus that develops and administers laws and generates and implements public policies in a specific territory. We can see that this definition implies internal sovereignty, and we can add that a state must also maintain its external

rational-legal legitimacy
The right of leaders to rule based on their selection according to an accepted set of laws, standards, or procedures

Web link:
Bruce Gilley on state legitimacy

Video link:
Western Sahara: the forgotten struggle

bureaucracy
A large set of appointed officials whose function is to implement the laws of the state, as directed by the executive

sovereignty. We can also add that the distinctive features of modern states include performing these activities not only on the basis of a monopoly on the use of force but also through the cultivation of legitimacy, particularly rational-legal legitimacy. Finally, we can add that bureaucracy is an important and effective tool for carrying out these administrative tasks, thereby potentially enhancing legitimacy.

FIGURE 2.1   The Anatomy of a State

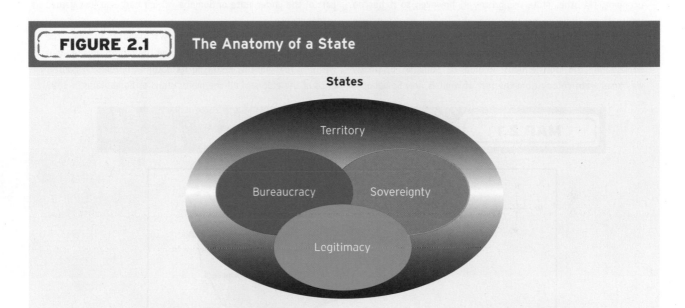

A state is an administrative entity that endures over time, develops laws, creates public policies for its citizens, and implements those policies and laws. A state must have a legitimate and recognized claim to a defined territory that forms its borders and legitimate and recognized authority to govern within its territory. It also must have the institutions needed to administer the state's laws and policies.

Sometimes the people of a nation may also identify as belonging to a particular state and thereby enhance the legitimacy of the state. But states may contain one or more nations, or a national movement or group within a state might contest the state's legitimacy.

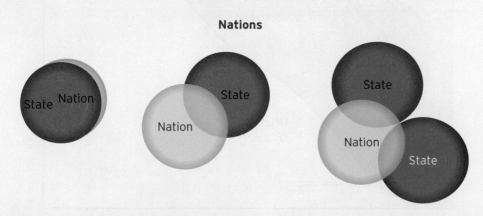

Some nations overlap with states; others exist across borders or may take up only part of a state.

Somaliland: Internal versus External Sovereignty

Somaliland is an interesting recent case of disputed sovereignty. It is a state that has achieved almost unquestioned internal sovereignty, a stable constitutional democracy, and a growing economy. No other state recognizes it, however, so it has no international, legal external sovereignty. This unusual outcome is a result of the collapse of the larger state of Somalia and the international efforts to resolve that country's civil war. Somaliland, the northernmost region of Somalia, originally was a separate colony from the rest of what is now Somalia; it

fell under British control, while the rest of the country was an Italian colony. In 1960 the former British colony gained independence for a few days but then quickly agreed to become part of the larger state of Somalia, which had also just gained independence.

When Somali dictator Siad Barre was deposed in 1991, the rebel movement in Somaliland declared the region independent within a few months, restoring its colonial borders. A conference of the elders of all the major clans of Somaliland in 1993

MAP 2.1

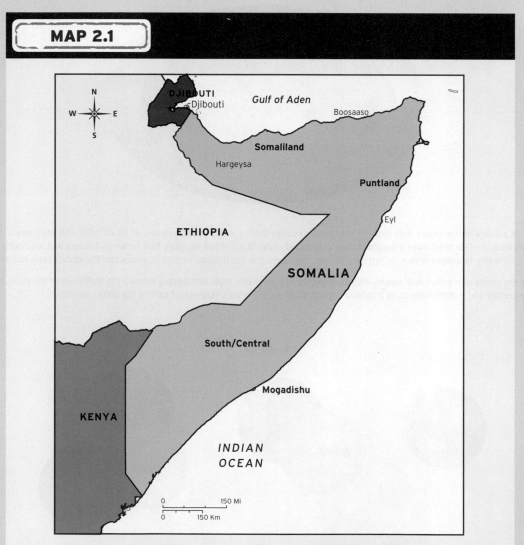

Source: William Clark, Matt Golder, and Sona Nadenichek Golder, Map 4.1, *Principles of Comparative Politics*, 2e. p. 92.

produced a new government with a parliament modeled after traditional Somali institutions, with representation based on clan membership. In 2001 a referendum approved a new constitution that was fully democratic, with a bicameral legislature: one house is filled by directly elected representatives and the other by clan elders. The country held successful democratic elections for president, parliament, and local governments in 2005 and 2010.

Somaliland's economy has grown substantially, based mainly on exports of livestock to the Middle East and money sent home by Somalis living and working around the world. The government has established much better social services and greater security than exist in the rest of war-wracked Somalia. Yet because it has no official recognition from other governments, Somaliland receives no official aid from other countries, has

only one embassy in its capital (that of neighboring Ethiopia), and sends no ambassadors abroad. Unofficially, some Western aid has reached Somaliland via private charities, and the country's leadership has met with representatives from Western countries, including the United States, but Somaliland remains largely on its own.

Most of the world fears that officially recognizing Somaliland's external sovereignty will encourage other regions of Somalia to attempt to break away as well, so recognition of the de facto state, expected eventually by many, awaits resolution of the larger civil war in Somalia. Ironically, it looks far more like a modern state than the official government of neighboring Somalia, which is internationally recognized as a sovereign state but actually controls only a modest portion of the country.

Where modern states overlap with nations, national identity can be a powerful source of legitimacy as well. This is not always the case, however, and most modern states must find other ways to cultivate the allegiance of their inhabitants. They usually do so by attempting to gain legitimacy based on some claim of representation or service to their citizens. The relationship between states and citizens is central to modern politics, and chapter 3 addresses it at length. We explore the contentious relationship among states, nations, and other identity groups more fully in chapter 4.

Video link:
Somalia:
failed state

HISTORICAL ORIGINS OF MODERN STATES

Now that we have clarified what a state is, we need to understand the diverse historical origins of modern states, which greatly influence how strong they are as well as their relationships to their citizens and nations. A world of modern states controlling virtually every square inch of territory and every person on the globe may seem natural today, but it is a fairly recent development. The modern state arose first in Europe between the fifteenth and eighteenth centuries. The concept spread via conquest, colonialism, and then independence for former colonies, becoming truly universal only with the independence of most African states in the 1960s.

Modern States in Europe Prior to approximately 1500, Europe consisted of **feudal states,** which were distinct from modern states in several ways. Most important, they neither claimed nor had undisputed sovereignty. Feudal rule involved multiple and overlapping sovereignties. At the heart of it was the relationship between lord and vassal in which the lord gave a vassal the right to rule a piece of land known as a fief and tax the people living on it, in exchange for political and military loyalty. The

feudal states
Premodern states in Europe in which power in a territory was divided among multiple and overlapping lords claiming sovereignty

The relationship between lord and vassal was the heart of the feudal political order. This fifteenth-century work shows peasants paying taxes in the form of money and livestock to their lord. Peasants were born with duties to their lord, and their legal ties to their land gave them no choice but to obey him.

Web link:
Mutual duties of vassals and lords

absolutism
Rule by a single monarch who claims complete, exclusive power and sovereignty over a territory and its people

system often involved several layers of these relationships, from the highest and most powerful king in a region to the local lord. The loyalty of the peasants—the bulk of the population who had virtually no rights—followed that of their lord. At any given time, all individuals were subject to the sovereignty of not only their immediate lord but also at least one higher lord and often others, and that loyalty could and did change. In addition, the Catholic Church claimed a separate and universal religious sovereignty over all and gave religious legitimacy to the kings and lords who recognized church authority.

By the fifteenth century, feudalism was giving way to **absolutism,** rule by a single monarch who claimed complete, exclusive sovereignty over a territory and its people. Absolutist rulers won battles for power among feudal lords by using superior economic and military resources to vanquish their rivals. Scholars debate the extent to which the absolutist state was a truly modern state, but it certainly introduced a number of the modern state's key elements. Perry Anderson (1974), one of the most influential scholars on the subject, argued that the absolutist state included at least rudimentary forms of a standing army and diplomatic service, both of which are crucial for external sovereignty; centralized bureaucracy; systematic taxation; and policies to encourage economic development. It took centuries for these to develop into fully modern forms, however. Legitimacy remained based largely on tradition and heredity, and most people remained subjects with few legal rights. Perhaps of greatest importance, the state was not conceived of as a set of ongoing institutions separate from the monarch. Rather, as Louis XIV of France famously declared, "*L'état, c'est moi*" (I am the state).

The competition among absolutist states to actualize and preserve external sovereignty helped further the development of the modern state, as well as reduce their number from about five hundred sovereign entities in Europe in 1500 to around fifty modern states today. The states that survived were those that had developed more effective systems of taxation, more efficient bureaucracies, and stronger militaries.

Along the way, political leaders realized that their subjects' loyalty (legitimacy) was of great benefit, so they began the process of expanding public education and shifting from the use of Latin or French in official circles to the local vernacular so that rulers and ruled could communicate directly, thus adding a new dimension to the rulers' legitimacy. This long process ultimately helped create modern nations, most of which had emerged by the mid-nineteenth century.

The truly modern state emerged as the state came to be seen as separate from an individual ruler. The state retained its claim to absolute sovereignty, but the powers of individual officials, ultimately including the supreme ruler, were increasingly limited. A political philosophy that came to be known as liberalism, which we discuss in greater depth in chapter 3, provided the theoretical justification and argument for limiting the power of officials to ensure the rights of individuals. The common people were ultimately transformed from subjects into citizens of the state. Bellwether events in this history included the Glorious Revolution in Great Britain in 1688, the French Revolution of 1789, and a series of revolutions that established new democratic republics in 1848.

Premodern States outside Europe Outside Europe, a wide variety of premodern states existed, but none took a fully modern form. The Chinese Empire ruled a vast territory for centuries and was perhaps the closest thing to a modern state anywhere in the premodern world (including in Europe). African precolonial kingdoms sometimes ruled large areas as well, but their rule was typically conceived of as extending over people rather than a precisely defined territory, having greater sovereignty closer to the capital and less sovereignty farther away. Virtually all premodern empires included multiple or overlapping layers of sovereignty and did not include a modern sense of citizenship.

The Export of the Modern State Europe exported the modern state to the rest of the world through colonial conquest, beginning with the Americas in the sixteenth century. The earliest colonies were ruled by European absolutist states that were not fully modern themselves. European monarchs appointed officials to represent them and rule over newly acquired territories and their populations, both indigenous peoples and European settlers. Over time, settlers began to identify their interests as distinct from the colonizers' interests and began to question the legitimacy of rule by distant sovereigns. The first rebellion against colonial rule ultimately produced the United States. The second major rebellion came at the hands of black slaves in Haiti in 1793, which led to the first abolition of slavery in the world and to Haitian independence in 1804. By the 1820s and 1830s, most of the settler populations of Central and South America had rebelled as well. As in the United States, the leaders of these rebellions were mostly wealthy, landholding elites. This landed elite often relied on state force to keep peasant and slave labor working on its behalf, so while some early efforts at democracy emerged after independence, most Central and South American states ultimately went through many decades of strongman rule. Independence nonetheless began the process of developing modern states.

The colonial origins of early modern states in the Americas created distinct challenges from those faced by early European states. European states went through several centuries of developing a sense of national identity. In the Americas, the racial divisions produced by colonization, European settlement, and slavery meant that none of the newly independent states had a widely shared sense of national identity. Where slavery continued to exist, as in the United States, citizenship was restricted to the "free" and therefore primarily white (and exclusively male) population. Where significant Native American populations had survived, as in Peru and Guatemala, they continued to be politically excluded and economically marginalized by the primarily white, landholding elite who controlled the new states. This historical context would make the ability of the new states to establish strong national identities difficult and would produce ongoing racial and ethnic problems, explored further in chapter 4.

After most of the American colonies achieved independence, growing economic and military rivalry among Britain, France, and Germany spurred a new round of colonization, first in Asia and then in Africa. This time, far fewer European settlers were involved. The vast majority of the populations of these new colonies remained indigenous; they were ruled over by a thin layer of European officials. Colonizers effectively destroyed the political power of precolonial indigenous states and empires but did not exterminate the population en masse. Challenges to this new wave of colonialism, on both the home front and abroad, were quick and numerous. The independence of the first-wave colonies and the end of slavery raised questions about European subjugation of African and Asian peoples. Colonization in this context had to be justified as bringing "advanced" European civilization and Christianity to "backward" peoples. Education, provided primarily by Christian missionaries, was seen as a key part of this "civilizing" mission. It had a more practical aspect as well: with limited European settlement, colonial rulers needed indigenous subjects to

Freed slaves in Zanzibar, off the East African coast, in 1880. One of the stated goals of colonization was ending the slave trade, but it was replaced with complete European political and economic control of the African continent. Colonization created the territories that would later become the independent modern states of Africa.

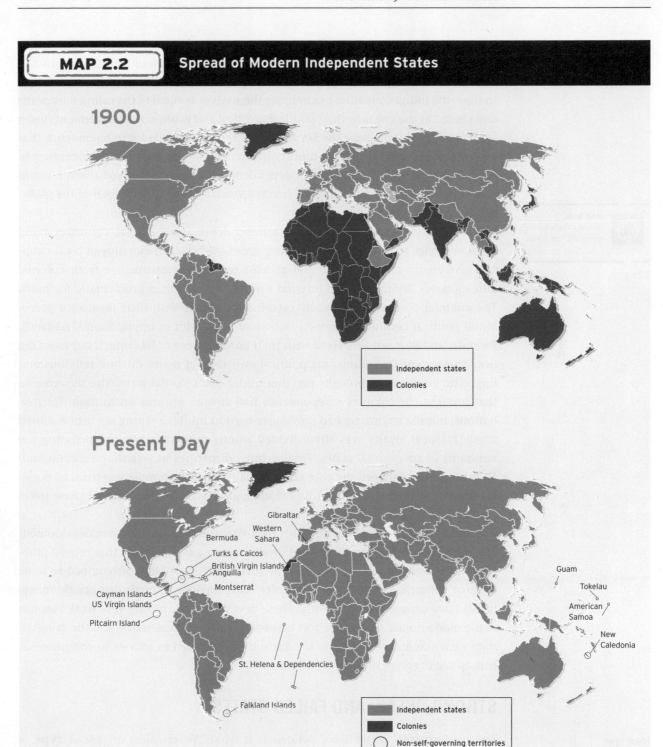

MAP 2.2   **Spread of Modern Independent States**

1900

Independent states
Colonies

Present Day

Gibraltar
Western Sahara
Bermuda
Turks & Caicos
British Virgin Islands
Anguilla
Montserrat
Cayman Islands
US Virgin Islands
Pitcairn Island
Guam
Tokelau
American Samoa
New Caledonia
St. Helena & Dependencies
Falkland Islands

Independent states
Colonies
Non-self-governing territories

serve in the bureaucracies of the colonial states. These chosen few were educated in colonial languages and customs and became local elites, although European officials remained at the top of the colonial hierarchy and exercised nearly unlimited power. In time, the indigenous elites began to see themselves as equal to the ruling Europeans and chafed at the limits to their political position and economic advancement under colonial rule. They became the key leaders of the movements for independence that emerged in the early twentieth century in Asia and by the mid-twentieth century in Africa. This new elite demanded independence and finally received it after World War II. At that point, modern states covered virtually every square inch of the globe, as Map 2.2 demonstrates.

Though successful at achieving independence, postcolonial countries faced huge obstacles to consolidating modern states. Although they enjoyed legal external sovereignty and had inherited at least minimal infrastructure from colonial bureaucracies, legitimacy and internal sovereignty remained problematic for most. The colonial powers had typically established borders with little regard for precolonial political boundaries. Some precolonial states—for example, Siam (Thailand), Rwanda, and Burundi—survived with their borders more or less intact, but most did not. This meant that numerous political entities and many distinct religious and linguistic groups were brought together under one colonial state. The movements that brought the colonies independence had created genuine enthusiasm for new nations, but the colonizers had previously tried to inhibit a strong sense of national unity. Political loyalty was often divided among numerous groups, including the remnants of precolonial states. Finally, huge disparities in wealth, education, and access to power between the elite and the majority of the population reduced popular support for the state. All of this made legitimacy and therefore the new states extremely fragile.

The lasting results of colonial rule for many countries include late development of a modern state and deeply divided loyalties among their citizens that proved problematic for legitimacy, cohesion, and internal sovereignty. Many succumbed to some form of authoritarian rule not long after independence, though democratic movements have emerged more recently. These new states were mostly very weak versions of the modern state. The differences between strong and weak states, and the causes of state weakness and collapse, are the last subjects we need to address to complete our conceptual overview of the modern state.

STRONG, WEAK, AND FAILED STATES

The modern state as we have defined it is what Weber called an **ideal type,** a model of what the purest version of something might be. Nothing in reality perfectly matches an ideal type; no state indisputably enjoys complete external or internal sovereignty, absolute legitimacy and a monopoly on the use of force, and a

Web link:
UN list of non-self-governing territories

ideal type
A term used by Max Weber to denote a model of what the purest version of something might be

completely effective and efficient bureaucracy. Some states, however, are clearly much closer to this ideal than others. States typically use their sovereignty, territory, legitimacy, and bureaucracy to provide what political scientist Robert Rotberg (2004) called "political goods" to their population. Political goods include security; the rule of law; a functioning legal system; and infrastructure such as roads, public education, and health care.

A **strong state** is generally capable of providing adequate political goods to its citizens, while a **weak state** can only do so partially. Obviously, knowing exactly what *adequate* means in this definition is not easy, and an absolutely clear-cut distinction cannot be made between strong and weak states. Rather, all states exist on a continuum of relative strength, with no state being perfectly strong in all conceivable categories. States that seem persistently unable to provide adequate security and other essential political goods are demonstrably weaker than those that can and do. As the Country and Concept table (page 57) shows for our case studies, stronger states tend to be wealthier and consume a larger share of economic resources; they are simply economically bigger than weak states. They also are less corrupt, indicating the presence of stronger bureaucracies, and tend to be more legitimate.

A state that is so weak that it loses effective sovereignty over part or all of its territory is a **failed state.** Failed states make headlines—for example, Sierra Leone, the Democratic Republic of the Congo, Liberia, Sudan, and Afghanistan. In extreme cases, the state collapses totally, as Somalia did in 1991. The total collapse of the Somali state has resulted in two decades of near-total anarchy for much of the population. It became known to many Americans due to the infamous "Black Hawk Down" episode in 1993, in which sixteen U.S. soldiers were killed and dragged through the streets of

strong state
A state that is generally capable of providing adequate political goods to its citizens

weak state
A state that only partially provides adequate political goods to its citizens

failed state
A state that is so weak that it loses effective sovereignty over part or all of its territory

Failed states grab headlines around the world and create havoc for their citizens. A key problem is the state's inability to provide security, which can create scenes like this one of a refugee camp in Afghanistan in 2012.

the capital. State failure, as the case of Somalia suggests, can have effects far beyond the state's borders.

Virtually all elements of state strength are interconnected. If a state lacks the resources to provide basic infrastructure and security, its legitimacy most likely will decline. Lack of resources also may mean civil servants are paid very little, which may lead to corruption and an even further decline in the quality of state services. Corruption in some bureaucracies, such as the military and border patrol, can cause a loss of security and territorial integrity. If the state cannot provide basic services, such as education, citizens will likely find alternative routes to success that may well involve illegal activity (e.g., smuggling), undermining sovereignty that much further. If the state does not apply the rule of law impartially, citizens will turn to private means to settle their disputes, threatening the state's monopoly on the legitimate use of force. Continuing patterns of lawless behavior create and reinforce the public perception that the state is weak, so weak states can become caught in a vicious cycle that is difficult to break.

The question of why some states are strong while others are weak has long been a major subject of political history and development. Several competing arguments have arisen in this debate. Economists Douglass North and John Wallis and political scientist Barry Weingast recently used a rational-choice institutionalist argument to address this question (2009). They argued that the earliest states were based on elite coalitions created to limit violence among themselves. Power remained very personal, as the state was really just a temporary agreement among competing elites, each of whom had control over the means of violence. Because of this, these early states were frequently unstable. Elites abided by the agreements they made with one another in order to gain economic advantages from the absence of warfare and the ability to extract resources. Eventually, some elites negotiated agreements that recognized impersonal organizations and institutions that were separate from the individual leaders. As these developed and functioned credibly, greater specialization was possible, and distinct elites who controlled military, political, economic, and religious power emerged. This required the rule of law among elites. Together with ongoing, impersonal organizations, the rule of law allowed the possibility of a true monopoly over the use of force as individual elites gave up their control of military power. Once established among elites, such impersonal institutions and organizations could expand eventually to the rest of society, typically via the rise of democracy (which we discuss in the next chapter), and a strong modern state was born. Conversely, states that did not arise through this process of elite accommodation are less likely to develop the strong institutions that are the hallmark of strong states.

Comparativists have developed several other arguments to explain in particular why states are weak. A common one is the effects of colonialism. As we've seen, colonial states originated in external conquest. The independent state was created

Web link:
The Economist on state capacity

not by negotiations among local elites but between them and the departing colonial power. Similarly, postcolonial political institutions were often rather hastily copied from the departing colonizers. The kind of elite accommodation that North, Wallis, and Weingast (2009) argued helped create strong states clearly did not occur in these situations. Not having participated seriously in the creation of the new institutions, elites often did not see themselves as benefitting from them. They therefore changed those institutions, used them for their own purposes, or ignored them. This often meant that postcolonial states did not develop the type of impersonal institutions characteristic of strong modern states. Lange (2009) looked at different kinds of colonial rule among British colonies, arguing that the specific type of colonial rule heavily influenced the strength of state institutions. More directly ruled colonies in which the colonizer had built strong bureaucracies early on (e.g., Mauritius) developed stronger bureaucracies after independence than did colonies where the colonizer had relied on local institutions to rule on its behalf (e.g., Nigeria).

Others have looked to the nature of the economy or the modern international system to explain state weakness. Wealth certainly seems to play a role in creating or at least maintaining strong states. States need resources to provide security and other political goods. Resources come from taxation, but to have taxation a state must have some viable economic activity. The poorest states may simply lack the resources to provide the most basic political goods, regardless of the intentions or competence of their rulers. The type of economic activity within a state, however, may make a significant difference. Countries with tremendous mineral wealth, such as oil or diamonds, face a situation known as the **resource curse.** A government that can gain enough revenue from mineral extraction alone does not need to worry about the strength of the rest of the economy or the well-being of the rest of the population. If the asset exists in one particular area, such as the site of a key mine, the government simply has to control that area and export the resources to gain revenue in order to survive. Rebel groups likewise recognize that if they can overpower the government, they can seize the country's mineral wealth, a clear incentive to start a war rather than strive for a compromise with those in power. Once again, in this situation, elite compromise to create stronger institutions seems unlikely.

resource curse
Occurs when a state relies on a key resource for almost all of its revenue, allowing it to ignore its citizens and resulting in a weak state

The neighboring states of Sierra Leone and Liberia in West Africa are a classic case of the worst effects of the resource curse. Ironically, both countries began as beacons of hope. Britain founded Sierra Leone to provide a refuge for liberated slaves captured from slaving vessels, and the United States founded Liberia as a home for former American slaves. Descendants of these slaves became the ruling elite in both countries. Both countries, however, also became heavily dependent on key natural resources. The bulk of government revenue came from diamond mining in Sierra Leone and from iron-mining and rubber plantations owned by the Firestone Tire

Company in Liberia. The ruling elites kept firm control of these resources until rebellion began with a military coup in Liberia in 1980. The new regime was just as brutal and corrupt as its predecessor, leading to a guerrilla war led by the man who became West Africa's most notorious warlord: Charles Taylor. After taking control of a good portion of Liberia, Taylor helped finance a guerrilla uprising in neighboring Sierra Leone. Once the guerrilla forces gained control of Sierra Leone's lucrative diamond mines, Taylor smuggled the diamonds onto the international market to finance the rebellions in both countries. The wars were not fully resolved until 2003, when international sanctions against West African diamonds finally reduced Taylor's cash flow and forced him out of power. Both countries are now at peace and have fragile, elected governments, but they still rely too heavily on key natural resources, so the resource curse could cause further problems.

The contemporary international legal system can have effects similar to the resource curse. Prior to the twentieth century, the weakest states simply didn't last very long; they faced invasions from stronger rivals and disappeared from the map. The twentieth-century international system has fundamentally changed this dynamic. Starting with the League of Nations in 1919 and expanding under the United Nations after 1945, the international system collectively came to an agreement that the hostile takeover of other states was unacceptable. While there have been exceptions, outright invasion and permanent conquest have become rare. This means that weak states are more likely to survive. The result can be what Robert Jackson (1990) called **quasi-states**: states that have legal sovereignty and international recognition but lack almost all the domestic attributes of a functioning modern state. Jackson argued that many postcolonial states, especially in Africa, are quasi-states. Ruling elites in these states often come to rely on external resources, including foreign aid, for their survival. Once again, they have little reason to compromise with their domestic rivals, and their rivals, being cut out of all benefits, often take up arms. During the Cold War, the rivalry between the United States and the Soviet Union led each of the superpowers to back dictators who would support their respective sides in global politics. Both sides provided generous aid to dictators who ruled with little interest in providing political goods to their people. Many of these states failed or became very weak a few years after the end of the Cold War because the elimination of the U.S.-Soviet global rivalry meant that neither side was interested in continuing to support the dictators.

In the post–Cold War era, the international system and major powers have come to see weak and failed states as a significant problem. Weak states produce corruption and illegal activity. They have porous borders through which all manner of illegal arms, contagious diseases, biological and nuclear weapons, and illegal drugs might pass. They undermine economic growth and political stability, and democracy is difficult or impossible to foster when a state is unable or unwilling to

quasi-states
States that have legal sovereignty and international recognition but lack almost all the domestic attributes of a functioning state

CRITICAL inquiry

Measuring State Strength

In response to growing international concern about state failure, the Fund for Peace developed a Failed States Index to highlight countries of imminent concern. In 2013 the seventh annual index ranked 178 countries on twelve factors in three categories considered essential to state strength:

- Social indicators
  - o demographic pressures,
  - o refugees or internally displaced persons,
  - o vengeance-seeking group grievance, and
  - o sustained human flight;

- Economic indicators
  - o uneven economic growth and
  - o poverty/severe economic decline;

- Political indicators
  - o legitimacy,
  - o deterioration of public services,
  - o rule of law/human rights abuses,
  - o security apparatus,
  - o factionalized elites, and
  - o intervention of external political actors.

Tables 2.2 and 2.3 list the weakest and strongest countries and their scores on the indicators listed above.

We can use the Failed States Index to ask a couple of interesting questions. First, what can we argue about why states are weak or strong based on the index? Look at which countries are weakest, strongest, and in between on the index. Based on what you know about the countries (and it never hurts to do a little research to learn more!), what hypotheses can you generate about why states are weak or strong? Do some of these relate to the arguments we outlined above about why states are weak or strong? Can you come up with other arguments that we haven't discussed in this chapter? If so, on what kinds of theories (from chapter 1) are your hypotheses based?

TABLE 2.2	Failed States, 2013
Rank and state	**Total score**
1. Somalia	114.3
2. Chad	113.3
3. Sudan	111.8
4. Zimbabwe	110.2
5. Democratic Republic of Congo	109.9
6. Afghanistan	109.3
7. Iraq	107.3
8. Central African Republic	106.4
9. Guinea	105.0
10. Pakistan	102.5
11. Haiti	101.6
12. Côte d'Ivoire	101.2
13. Kenya	100.7
14. Nigeria	100.2
15. Yemen	100.0
16. Burma/Myanmar	99.4
17. Ethiopia	98.8
18. East Timor	98.2
19. North Korea	97.8
20. Niger	97.8
21. Uganda	97.5
22. Guinea-Bissau	97.2
23. Burundi	96.7
24. Bangladesh	96.1
25. Sri Lanka	95.7

Source: Fund for Peace, 2010, "Failed States Index 2010" (http://www.fundforpeace.org/web/index.php?option=com_content&task=view&id=452&Itemid=900).

(Continued)

TABLE 2.3	Sustainable States, 2013
Rank and state	**Total score**
165. Iceland	29.8
166. Canada	27.9
167. Netherlands	27.9
168. Luxembourg	27.3
169. Australia	27.3
170. Austria	27.2
171. New Zealand	23.9
172. Denmark	22.9
173. Ireland	22.4
174. Switzerland	21.8
175. Sweden	20.9
176. Finland	19.3
177. Norway	18.7

Source: Fund for Peace, 2010, "Failed States Index 2010" (http://www
.fundforpeace.org/web/index.php?option=com_content&task=view&i
d=452&Itemid=900).

A second interesting question is, How can we really measure state strength? Take a look at the indicators page of the index: http://ffp.statesindex.org/indicators. The index measures those twelve indicators and then adds them up, weighting them all equally, to arrive at an overall score for each country. Do the indicators each measure an important element of state strength? Is it feasible to think we can measure the indicators and arrive at a number to represent each of them in each country? Does it make sense to weight all the indicators equally, or are some more important than others? If you think some are more important, which ones and why? Does your answer connect to any of the theories of state strength and weakness we discussed earlier?

Comparativists don't all agree on the answers to these questions, but we look at evidence and try to generate testable hypotheses for state strength, weakness, and failure in an effort to help states develop stronger institutions. We do this because the human consequences of state weakness—civil conflict, refugees, and human rights violations—and the consequences for the international system are severe.

Data link:
The Failed States
Index

provide at least the basic political goods citizens expect. Somalia and Afghanistan are only the best-known examples of this worst-case scenario. Even moderately strong states, such as described in our case studies of Mexico and Russia that follow, provide many political goods but may be quite weak in particular areas, harming legitimacy, political stability, or economic well-being. One of the most important reasons for studying comparative politics is to understand how and why political institutions work effectively to produce strong states that can maintain security, gain real legitimacy, and avoid the humanitarian costs and dangers of state weakness and failure.

COUNTRY AND CONCEPT
The Modern State

Country	Approximate year modern state established	Failed States Index, 2013		GDP per capita (ppp)	Government revenue as % of GDP	Corruption Perception Index, 2010 (0 = highly corrupt, 10 = highly clean)	Legitimacy (0 = least legitimate, 10 = most legitimate)
		Rank among 178 countries	Score (12 = lowest risk of state failure, 144 = highest risk of state failure)				
Brazil	1889	126	62.1	$12,000	35.3%	3.7	5.19
China	1949	66	80.9	$9,100	18.3%	3.5	6.58
Germany	1871	165	29.7	$39,100	40.8%	7.9	6.68
India	1947	79	77.5	$3,900	18.8%	3.3	4.46
Iran	1925	37	89.7	$13,100	6.1%	2.2	4.72
Japan	1867	156	36.1	$36,200	27.9%	7.8	5.62
Mexico	1924	97	73.1	$15,300	9.0%	3.1	3.55
Nigeria	1960	16	100.7	$2,700	5.6%	2.4	5.56
Russia	1917	80	77.1	$17,700	34.0%	2.1	2.27
United Kingdom	1707	160	33.2	$36,700	37.9%	7.6	6.68
United States	1787	159	33.5	$49,800	28.3%	7.1	6.82

Sources: Failed state data are from the Fund for Peace, 2010. Data on GDP per capita are from the CIA *World Factbook* (https://www.cia.gov/library/publications/the-world-factbook/index.html). Data on government revenue as percentage of GDP are from the Heritage Foundation's 2010 Index of Economic Freedom (http://www.heritage.org/index/ranking). Data on corruption are from Transparency International, 2010. Data on state legitimacy are from Bruce Gilley, "The Meaning and Measure of State Legitimacy: Results for 72 Countries," *European Journal of Political Research* 45, no. 3 (2006): 499–525 (doi:10.1111/j.1475-6765.2006.00307.x).

CASE STUDIES OF STATE FORMATION

We have chosen eleven countries to illustrate the trends, theories, and debates in comparative politics. We introduce all eleven below by describing the historical development of each state. Nations, citizenship, and political regimes are all exam-ined more fully in the following chapters, but we touch on these issues as well to provide a general political history here. We focus now primarily on the development of each state and its relative strength or weakness and present them from strongest to weakest as measured by the Failed States Index. The countries represent a diverse set of political and economic situations. Some are quite wealthy and provide signifi-cant political goods for their citizens; others are among the poorest countries on the planet. Together, they provide a full array of the realities of politics in the contem-porary world. The Country and Concept table above presents some basic informa-tion about our eleven case study states. The various measures of state strength in the table produce some surprises. Despite Iran's important international role and its moves toward acquiring nuclear weapons, by most measures it is a fairly weak state. Similarly, the external power of the United States does not translate into its being the strongest state in the world, though it is certainly one of the stronger ones. A measure of legitimacy that includes not just human rights but citizens' perceptions of the effectiveness of their government suggests that China's government may be more legitimate than many Western observers believe. Stronger states tend to have more revenue, though this varies because what the state does with its revenue is important as well.

The Strongest States

The strongest states among our case studies were all established as modern states in the eighteenth and nineteenth centuries, industrialized relatively early, and are among the world's wealthiest countries. In other ways, however, their origins lay in quite differ-ent circumstances, from the consolidation of independent monarchies in the United Kingdom and Germany to a negotiated agreement in the United States and a defensive strengthening against Western encroachment in Japan. Only one, the United States, began as a colony. In fact, all four were at least briefly colonial powers themselves. They all have firm control of their territory and strong militaries, though in the case of Germany territorial consolidation (or reconsolidation) has been quite recent (1990). All also have high levels of legitimacy based on liberal democracy, though questions persist about the ability of their political systems to continue to provide political goods adequately. They have relatively strong senses of national unity, though three of the four face significant questions about immigration and racial differences. That, along with the related issues of uneven economic development and potentially vio-lent groups internally (terrorists, among others), are their most common weaknesses. None is the very strongest according to the Failed States Index (see Table 2.2), but all are in the top thirty. Despite this, each still has elements of relative weakness: no state is perfectly strong.

GERMANY: THE FIRST MODERN WELFARE STATE

Germany, Europe's largest country, lies at the heart of the continent. This central position has made it important throughout European history. Indeed, with no clear natural boundaries between German-speaking and neighboring areas, German speakers spread across central Europe in the Middle Ages, resulting in major questions and battles over the extent of German sovereignty and territory. For centuries Germans were split into hundreds of small principalities, duchies, and the like, and political loyalty and identity were primarily local. Adding to this fragmentation, the formation of Protestantism by German monk Martin Luther beginning in 1521 created religious divisions that only exacerbated long-standing political divisions among the German people.

The first stirrings of a united Germany occurred after Napoleon's defeat in 1813. A new German Confederation arose, but it was only a loose association, dominated by Prussia, and centered in the city of Berlin. A unified Germany finally emerged under Otto von Bismarck, the chancellor (equivalent of a prime minister) of Prussia. Bismarck came to power in 1862 and set about expanding and uniting Germany under Prussian control. Between 1864 and 1870, he conquered lands populated by German speakers that were under "foreign" control. In 1871 a new, united Germany was proclaimed, with the Prussian king named as the German kaiser and Bismarck as the chancellor. This new Germany had a legislature

- **FAILED STATES INDEX**
  29.7 (165 of 178); weakest on "vengeance-seeking group grievance" (terrorism threat) and "uneven economic development"

- **TERRITORY**
  Widespread sense of national identity among German-speaking people, but consisted of many states until 1871; boundaries changed with wars until 1990; brief colonial empire prior to World War I

- **SOVEREIGNTY**
  Established over much of German-speaking people by 1871; divided by the Cold War, 1945–1990

East Berliners stand atop the Berlin Wall in 1989, shortly before it was brought down to reunite the divided German state. Reunification in 1990 meant the elimination of the separate and largely illegitimate East German state, whose territory was absorbed by the much stronger and more legitimate West German state. This was only the most recent change in the boundaries of the German state.

- **LEGITIMACY**
  Based on nationalism first; failed liberal democracy after World War I led to Nazi rule; divided state with liberal democratic and communist components until united under democratic constitution in 1990

- **BUREAUCRACY**
  First modern welfare state starting in late nineteenth century; extensive since World War II

Web link:
Interactive map on the consolidation of Prussia

and elections, but virtually all power was in the hands of Kaiser Wilhelm I and Bismarck.

The new German state became actively involved in the economy, pursuing rapid industrialization in an attempt to catch up with the economic might of Britain, then Europe's most powerful state. The primary opposition to Bismarck came out of this industrialization in the form of the Social Democratic Party (SDP), founded in 1875, which demanded greater workers' rights and democracy. Bismarck successfully resisted the party's efforts, both by brutal repression when necessary and by creating Europe's first social welfare programs. The latter included health insurance and old-age pensions; administering these programs also expanded the country's bureaucracy.

By 1900 Germany had become an industrial powerhouse with aspirations to become an empire. It colonized several territories in Africa before World War I. Germany's defeat in "the Great War" ended the country's first regime. As Allied forces moved on Berlin in 1918, the kaiser fled, and the leaders of the SDP proclaimed a democratic republic, shifting the basis for legitimacy from nationalism to democracy, but the subsequent democracy, known as the Weimar Republic, survived only fourteen years. Defeat in the war and subsequent reparations to the victorious Allies left the nation devastated and led to support for political extremists, including the growing Nazi Party. Adolf Hitler became chancellor in 1932 and effectively eliminated democracy a year later (see chapter 3). Hitler's defeat at the end of World War II led to Germany's territorial division. While the United States, Britain, and France united the areas of the country they controlled under one government, the Soviet Union refused to allow its sector to rejoin the rest. It became the German Democratic Republic (GDR), better known as East Germany, a communist state so closely controlled by the Soviet Union that its own sovereignty was quite limited. The rest became the Federal Republic of Germany (FRG), governed by the Basic Law (the equivalent of a constitution) that took effect in 1949. West Germany, as it came to be known, reemerged as a democratic and industrial powerhouse in Central Europe. It joined France in creating what would become the European Union.

Germany and the city of Berlin were to remain divided for nearly thirty years. Not until the fall of communism brought an end to the Cold War in 1989 were the country and city reunited. Nothing signified this more dramatically than the destruction of the Berlin Wall, which had split the German capital since 1961. By 1990 Germany had been reunified under the constitution of the former West Germany. This process was economically and politically difficult, requiring the integration of the much poorer East German population into the unified nation. Once the worst of its growing pains were behind it, a reunited German state led the way in transforming what had been the European Community into the European Union, giving up significant economic sovereignty to the larger body. This culminated in the creation of the euro currency and European Central Bank in 1999. Despite the recent difficulties over the role of the euro, the EU nonetheless represents a new phase in the development of states, one in which states for the first time voluntarily ceded elements of sovereignty to a larger body. While the financial crisis that began in 2008 took a significant toll, Germany emerged from it as even stronger compared with the rest of Europe, the clearly dominant economic player in the EU.

While Germany was founded on the basis of a cultural sense of nationalism based on speaking German (see chapter 4), it has seen significant immigration, mainly from Turkey and some other Muslim countries. This has posed a continuous challenge and significant debate over national identity and the integration of non-German and Muslim immigrants. This continuing conflict is reflected in its two weakest indicators on the Failed States Index: "vengeance-seeking group grievance" (based in part on concerns about terrorism in the country), and "uneven economic development" (based in part on economic differences between immigrants and others, though also on regional economic differences).

Video link:
Reporting on the fall of the Berlin Wall

Web link:
A difficult choice for Turks in Germany

Data link:
OECD, Better Life Index: Germany

CASE Summary

The modern German state emerged relatively late in Europe after uniting many of the widely dispersed German-speaking people. Its sovereignty was questioned and briefly eliminated under occupation, and its territory was divided by the Cold War. Nonetheless, the German state, under several different regimes, consciously and effectively created an industrial powerhouse in the heart of Europe that was also the first modern welfare state with an extensive modern bureaucracy. Democracy emerged twice, though disastrously the first time, and was only secure and universal throughout Germany after 1990. Today, the modern German state is widely considered to be one of the world's strongest, most legitimate, wealthiest, and most stable. This combination makes it the strongest state of our eleven cases as measured by the Failed States Index.

CASE Questions

1. Germany has had multiple types of governments and was even divided into two states for forty years, yet today it is one of the world's strongest states. What explains this unusual outcome of a tumultuous history?
2. Which single element of state strength that we identified earlier in the chapter is most influential in explaining the German case and why?

CASE Study

UNITED KINGDOM: THE LONG EVOLUTION OF A STRONG STATE

- **FAILED STATES INDEX** 33.2 (160 of 178); weakest on "sharp or severe economic decline" and "vengeance-seeking group grievance" (terrorism threat)

- **TERRITORY** Consolidated from three nations (England, Wales, and Scotland) by 1707; colonial empire from mid-nineteenth to mid-twentieth century

- **SOVEREIGNTY** Aided by island status; fully developed by 1707; partially yielded to European Union

The full union of England and Scotland under the Act of Union of 1707 officially established the Kingdom of Great Britain and marked the start of the modern state. A century later, with the addition of Ireland (a British colony), the United Kingdom (also called the U.K., Great Britain, or simply Britain) was established. With the independence of the Republic of Ireland, the name was officially changed to the United Kingdom of Great Britain and Northern Ireland in 1927. The origins of the state were laid well before 1707, though. The Norman invasion of 1066 created a new kingdom that initially included part of what is now northern France. The indigenous Anglo-Saxons saw the Norman invaders, who came to constitute the bulk of the nobility, as foreign oppressors. Over several centuries, however, the cultural and linguistic divisions between conqueror and conquered slowly disappeared, and a new language, English, emerged.

This state's territory expanded over the centuries. England and Wales (the western section of the island) were formally united in the Act of Union of 1542. Scotland and England were first united under a single crown when King James VI

Queen Elizabeth II on her way to give her annual address to Parliament. The queen remains the head of state and the key symbol of the United Kingdom's enduring statehood, though she no longer has any real power. Indeed, her speech was written by the elected government of Prime Minister David Cameron and handed to her to read. She represents the state and nation, but power resides in the elected Parliament.

of Scotland also became King James I of England. That union finally brought the entire island under a single state, created a single British parliament, and eliminated the separate Scottish and Welsh parliaments. Both Scotland and Wales came to be primarily English speaking, linguistically uniting the kingdom, though some cultural distinctions remain to this day, including a distinct Welsh language spoken by a minority.

The greatest threat to the monarchy's sovereignty came from religious wars between Protestants and Catholics. After King Henry VIII broke with the Catholic Church and established the Church of England (known as the Anglican Church in the United Kingdom and the Episcopal Church in the United States) in 1534, religious conflicts dominated politics for well over a century. This culminated in a civil war in the 1640s that brought to power a nonroyal, Protestant dictatorship under Oliver Cromwell. The monarchy was restored after about twenty years, only to be removed again, this time peacefully, by Parliament in the Glorious Revolution of 1688. After this, the doctrine of liberalism gained greater prominence, and slowly the two faiths learned to live under the same government. The Glorious Revolution began a long transition in the basis for legitimacy from the traditional monarchy to liberal democracy, which we detail in chapter 3.

Starting in the mid-eighteenth century, Britain became one of the first countries to begin industrializing. By the nineteenth century, rapid economic transformation helped Britain become the most powerful country in the world, enhancing and securing its external sovereignty and helping it create a global empire. That empire declined rapidly after World War II, by which time Britain had become a distant second power vis-à-vis the United States. World War II helped inspire a growing nationalist movement across Asia and Africa that resulted in nearly all British (and other) colonies gaining their independence by the 1960s.

Industrialization expanded the domestic strength of the state as well and helped create its modern bureaucracy, distinct from the monarch. Domestically, the sacrifices made to win World War II produced a consensus in favor of a more egalitarian society, leading to the creation shortly after the war of the British welfare state, further expanding the bureaucracy and enhancing legitimacy. Starting in the 1960s, the British state slowly yielded some sovereignty to what became the European Union (EU). Its embrace of the EU, however, has always been partial: it did not adopt the common currency, the euro, and the economic difficulties facing the EU since 2008 have reignited a significant debate over whether Britain should stay in the union at all.

Britain successfully molded a national identity out of English, Welsh, and Scottish identities, though the latter two reemerged and helped create "devolution"— the passing of some powers (such as over education)—to newly created Welsh and Scottish parliaments in 1998. The big exception to this is Northern Ireland, where

- **LEGITIMACY**
  Traditional legitimacy of monarchy with some limits since thirteenth century; slow transition to liberal and democratic legitimacy since 1688

- **BUREAUCRACY**
  Industrialization in nineteenth and twentieth centuries expanded democracy and modern bureaucracy; welfare state since World War II

Video link:
The Glorious Revolution

Data link:
The spread of industrialization

Data link:
Interactive immigration map of the UK

the relatively poor, Catholic majority long fought to join the Republic of Ireland but the wealthier Protestant minority, supported by the British, have kept it part of the United Kingdom. More recent questions of national identity have arisen, as in Germany, around the question of immigration, particularly of Muslims. Since World War II, the previously homogenous Britain has seen large-scale immigration from its former colonies in the Caribbean, Africa, and South Asia in particular, creating new categories of people such as "black Britons." A growing debate over the place and role of Muslim immigrants (in Britain, mostly from South Asia) has raised questions about national identity that inevitably affect legitimacy as well. Like Germany, this is reflected in relatively weak scores on relevant indicators on the Failed States Index.

Data link:
OECD Better Life Index: United Kingdom

CASE Summary

The modern British state developed over centuries of evolution and internal war but was finally united in 1707. Industrialization made it the most powerful state in the world by the nineteenth century. While it lost its empire and yielded some sovereignty to the EU in the twentieth century, Britain nonetheless remains a strong, modern state. No one questions its sovereign control of its territory (with the partial exception of Northern Ireland), and it maintains a functioning and legitimate democracy, which rules over an extensive bureaucracy that implements the state's decisions and oversees a fairly extensive welfare state. As in both Germany and the United States, questions surrounding immigration and identity provide some of the most significant remaining areas of state weakness.

CASE Questions

1. In contrast with the United States, the modern British state arose from a long, historical evolution. What impact has this history had on the modern state, and what differences does this create compared with the U.S. case?
2. What are the weakest elements of the British state, and what effects do these weaknesses have?

CASE Study

THE UNITED STATES: A CONSCIOUSLY CRAFTED STATE

A t first glance, the origin of the United States in a conference that brought together thirteen separate colonies appears most unusual. Few states were created so completely by design rather than by slow historical evolution. Prior to 1776, Britain's thirteen North American colonies were separate entities with significant cultural and political differences. Yet while the origin of the U.S. state was unusual, its early trials and tribulations, and questions about its very existence, were similar to those of many other postcolonial states.

North America's colonial history was not unlike that of South America, despite primarily British rather than Spanish and Portuguese conquest. The earliest settlers came looking for wealth; others followed looking for freedom to practice their religion, which is distinct from believing in or practicing freedom of religion. From early on, the economy of the southern colonies was based on large-scale plantation agriculture, which used extensive labor. Because British conquest decimated the Native American population through disease and displacement, this group was not available as a labor force. Indentured servants from Britain were soon augmented by African slaves with no rights and no possibility of gaining freedom. While most northern colonies allowed slavery, their economies did not depend on it.

Acting as representatives of poor and rich alike, the white, wealthy authors of the Declaration of Independence adopted the enlightened views then prevalent among European intellectuals. They envisioned a nation in which "all men are created equal and endowed by their Creator with certain inalienable rights." The

- **FAILED STATES INDEX**
  33.5 (159 of 178); weakest on "uneven economic development" and "vengeance-seeking group grievance" (terrorism threat)

- **TERRITORY**
  Expanded via purchase, invasion, and war across a continent

- **SOVEREIGNTY**
  Established via negotiation among thirteen colonies to create central government; challenged by Civil War over issue of slavery

- **LEGITIMACY**
  Constitution established liberal state under which democratic rights slowly extended over two hundred years to mass of citizenry

- **BUREAUCRACY**
  Small and corrupt until early twentieth century; progressive reforms created modern form, and modest welfare state added since World War II

The signing of the Declaration of Independence in 1776 was a unique event at the time: a state was being created by conscious design rather than emerging from political battles among rival monarchs. It would take much more work to draft a working form of government and a civil war to create a real sense of national unity. Many colonies would follow the example of the United States in later centuries, demanding independence and writing their own constitutions.

five-year war that followed achieved independence for the American colonies, but the first effort at creating a functioning state in 1781, the Articles of Confederation, fell into disarray within a few years, in part because of a lack of effective sovereignty. The Articles severely curtailed the national government's power, preserving for the separate thirteen states the right to approve all taxes and trade policies. This weakness led to the Second Continental Congress in 1787, which resulted in the U.S. Constitution, the document on which the state's legitimacy has depended for over two centuries. The Constitution laid out a plan for a stronger, more sovereign central government with powers to establish a coherent national economy and uniform foreign policy. States did retain significant areas of sovereignty, such as responsibility over policing, infrastructure, and education, creating one of the first examples of federalism, in which a state's power is divided among more than one level of government.

The Constitution also made clear that the political elite at the time had a very limited concept of "all men are created equal." The Framers certainly meant "men," since women had no political rights, but they did not mean "all." To secure the support of the southern states, slavery was preserved. By counting each slave as two-thirds of a person (but not giving slaves any rights), slaveholding states received more representation in Congress than their number of voters justified.

Under the aegis of white settlers, the United States dramatically expanded its territory at the expense of native populations and Mexico; industrialization produced a stronger economy; and the population of the new state continued to grow. Immigration and industrialization increased the size and power of the northern states relative to the southern ones, while a growing abolitionist movement questioned the continuing legitimacy of slavery, a position on which the new Republican Party took the strongest stand.

When the country elected Abraham Lincoln as its first Republican president in 1860, Southern leaders no longer recognized the federal government's legitimacy, leading to the Civil War, a four-year, failed effort by the South to preserve a slaveholding society. In the middle of the war, Lincoln signed the Emancipation Proclamation and freed the slaves in conquered Southern territories, gaining European support and augmenting the North's armies by enlisting freed slaves. African Americans, however, did not truly achieve full legal citizenship, including the right to vote, for another hundred years with the passage of the Civil Rights and Voting Rights Acts in 1964 and 1965, respectively. (A prior milestone in the expansion of democratic legitimacy was granting voting rights to [initially white] women in 1920.) The Failed States Index suggests that this racial legacy continues to weaken the state, lying behind what is by far its weakest indicator: "uneven economic development."

The United States became a global power with the second industrial revolution of the late nineteenth century. Cities grew dramatically as immigrants poured into urban areas to provide labor for rapidly expanding factories. This brought demands for changes in the state. The United States had been well known for and weakened

Video link:
The emancipation strategy

by corruption: political leaders at all levels regularly appointed their supporters to government jobs, often regardless of their qualifications. After a long period of such "machine politics," reformists lobbied for and successfully established a civil service under which most jobs in the bureaucracy would be permanent and based on some concept of merit, rather than on the whims of the next elected politician. The same reform movement ultimately produced a constitutional amendment that created the national income tax, which became the state's primary source of revenue. This began the state's modern bureaucracy.

Further expansion occurred with the New Deal in the 1930s, under which an expanded government helped provide jobs and old-age pensions to people in need as part of the effort to pull the country out of the Great Depression. The New Deal, followed by the Great Society programs of the 1960s, which sought to improve health care (Medicare and Medicaid) and reduce poverty (Aid to Families with Dependent Children, or AFDC, and food stamps), increased the size and reach of the U.S. state. Nonetheless, it remained quite a bit smaller than most of its European counterparts, a fact that you can see clearly by comparing the United Kingdom and United States in the "Government Revenue" column in the Country and Concept table on page 57.

Video link:
The New Deal

These new roles also strengthened the central government vis-à-vis the states. While the formal rules in the Constitution did not change, the central government's ability to fund popular programs run by the states gave it much greater power than it had possessed a century earlier. Federalism continues to divide sovereignty in the United States among the national (or federal) government and the fifty states, making the United States a more decentralized (and, critics contend, fragmented) state than most wealthy countries. Nonetheless, the state is far more centralized and involved in American lives than it was a century ago.

While the United States generally has firm external sovereignty via control of its territory and by far the most powerful military in the world, territorial boundaries still raise questions. Significant illegal immigration from neighboring Mexico along the world's longest border between a wealthy and a middle-income country shows the limits of sovereignty for even the most powerful state. As is the case with Germany, the country also continues to struggle with how immigrants are incorporated into the national identity (see chapter 4).

Web link:
Illegal immigration again rising in the U.S.

Data link:
OECD Better Life Index: United States

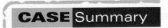

CASE Summary   The United States established its sovereignty in an unusually clear and explicit way, first by making a Declaration of Independence and then basing its legitimacy on a consciously crafted constitution. The new state's sovereignty was tested in the War of 1812 against its former colonizer and again in the Civil War, but it held. The state simultaneously expanded its territory dramatically via invasion of Native American lands, land purchases from European colonial powers, and war with neighboring Mexico. Its modern bureaucracy developed and expanded with industrialization and then the creation of a moderate welfare state. Today, it is the world's leading superpower externally, though internally the strength of its state is high but not the highest in the world (at least according to the Failed States Index). This is due in large part to continuing inequality among the population stemming from the legacy of slavery and immigration.

CASE Questions

1. The United States is unusual in that it is a state created by self-conscious design rather than historical evolution. What impact does that origin have on the strength of its state and the differences between it and other states?

2. What are the weakest elements of state strength in the United States, and what effects do these weaknesses have?

CASE Study

JAPAN: DETERMINED SOVEREIGNTY

Japan is one of the few places in the world that successfully avoided European colonization. It went on to become the first "non-Western" country to join the ranks of the world's wealthy and most powerful states. An island state, Japan has maintained its territorial sovereignty for centuries.

Japan reduced its monarchy to a largely symbolic role much earlier than European countries did. Following nearly a century wherein warring states competed for control, Tokugawa Ieyasu claimed the title of shogun in 1603 and fully established sovereignty over the entire territory. The new state came to be called the Tokugawa Bakufu, or shogunate, and was roughly similar to European feudal states, though more centralized than most. The ruling Tokugawa family did not hold all power but rather shared it with 260 landlords called *daimyo*. The third important class in medieval society, the samurai or warriors, were a "landless aristocracy."

Under the Tokugawa Shogunate (1603–1867), Japan virtually isolated itself from outside influence until U.S. warships under the command of Commodore Matthew Perry sailed into the harbor at Edo (present-day Tokyo) in 1853. A series of unfavorable treaties with the United States, France, and Britain produced immediate protests,

- **FAILED STATES INDEX 36.1 (156 of 178); weakest on "mounting demographic pressures" (aging population)**

- **TERRITORY Fully consolidated by 1603; colonial empire in Asia in late nineteenth and early twentieth centuries**

- **SOVEREIGNTY Feudal system with unusually strong center since 1603, with nearly complete isolation until modern state established in 1867**

led by the samurai, against what they saw as undue Western influence. By the early 1860s, a samurai alliance had formed in opposition to the shogunate. After a series of battles, the shogunate ceded power in October 1867, establishing what came to be known as the Meiji Restoration, so called because the new government claimed to be restoring the Emperor Meiji to his full powers. In truth, the new government was controlled by the samurai, who eliminated the feudal classes of both the shogun and *daimyo*.

The Meiji government went on to create the first truly modern state in Japan. Though unhappy with the earlier treaties with Western powers, the new government launched a series of modernizations, borrowing openly and heavily from the West, especially Western technology. The new state ultimately included a modern army and navy, the beginnings of compulsory education, and the establishment of a single school to train all government civil servants. Significantly, the new military had nearly complete autonomy, as no form of civilian control existed over it. This military helped Japan gain colonial control over Taiwan in the 1890s and Korea in 1905, briefly creating a Japanese empire. The Meiji government introduced the first written constitution in 1889, formally codifying state institutions, including the first parliament, albeit an extremely weak one. After a brief period of greater parliamentary power after World War I, General Tanaka Giichi became prime minister and reasserted military power at the expense of civilian leaders. This ushered in a period of growing Japanese imperialism. The military effectively intimidated all civilian political leaders and pushed the government toward a more aggressive foreign policy. This new approach led to Japan's invasion of China in 1931, its alliance with fascist Germany and Italy, and its attack on Pearl Harbor in 1941.

World War II ended for Japan with the United States dropping atomic bombs on Hiroshima and Nagasaki in August 1945. The Japanese surrender led to the country's full occupation by the United States. Under General Douglas MacArthur, the United

- **LEGITIMACY**
  Traditional but unusually weak monarchy since 1100s; monarch only symbolic since 1867; liberal democracy since 1950

- **BUREAUCRACY**
  Developed with industrialization prior to World War II; exceptionally powerful influence on state since World War II

Web link:
Sage Colleges Meiji era resources

Japan was the first non-Western state to create a fully modern economy. By first isolating itself from Western control and then borrowing Western technology, Japan's unusually strong state helped create what is now the world's third-largest economy, as evidenced by the neon lights and bustle of its famed Ginza Street in downtown Tokyo.

States completely demilitarized Japanese society and then wrote a new democratic constitution for the country. The document's provisions prohibited Japan from creating a military or ever engaging in war, although Japan ultimately did create a "self-defense" force that has since become the second-richest military in the world. In spite of the fact that one party has won all but two national elections since 1950, liberal democracy has fully replaced monarchy as the basis for the state's legitimacy, though the monarch remains as a symbol of the nation, as in the United Kingdom.

The bureaucracy became very powerful under Liberal Democratic Party (LDP) rule, working much more closely with Japanese businesses than did governments in most Western countries. Since 1990, however, Japan's unusually powerful bureaucracy has been rocked by a seeming inability to restart economic growth and a series of corruption scandals. Economic stagnation over the past two decades has combined with a rapidly aging population (Japan has one of the world's lowest birth rates and the world's highest life expectancy) to present seemingly intractable economic problems, reflected in "demographic pressures" being by far its weakest indicator on the Failed States Index. Nonetheless, nearly seventy years after its defeat in World War II, the country remains the third-largest economy in the world.

Data link:
Interactive population projections chart

Data link:
OECD Better life Index: Japan

CASE Summary

Japan is unusual among non-Western states because it effectively resisted Western colonization and then established a modern state that grew strong enough to allow interaction with the West while resisting incursion. The military ultimately took control of this state, created an empire, expanded industrialization, established a modern bureaucracy, and then lost power at the end of World War II. After five years of occupation, in which Japan's sovereignty was forfeited for the first time in four hundred years, Japan reemerged as a sovereign state fully in control of its traditional territory and with a new source of legitimacy: liberal democracy. Its earlier bureaucracy, though, survived the war and became an exceptionally powerful force. Today, despite significant economic problems, it remains one of the strongest states in the world.

CASE Questions

1. Japan is virtually unique in emerging early on as the world's strongest non-Western state. What best explains this unusual history?
2. How do the strengths and weaknesses of the Japanese state compare with the case studies of relatively strong Western states such as Germany, the United Kingdom, and the United States?

Moderately Strong States

The following five countries can be considered moderately strong (or weak) states. They have many of the functions of modern states in place and provide citizens many political goods. In various important ways, however, they are notably weaker than the strongest states we outlined earlier. This weakness often manifests itself in particular areas, including much higher levels of corruption, weaker rule of law, and more difficult intergroup conflicts. They are all middle-income countries, not nearly as wealthy as the strongest states but much wealthier than the poorest. Three of the five were created via colonial rule, so their very identities and names are relatively recent, though Russia and China date back much further. The modern state emerged in most of them in the early to mid-twentieth century, and was challenged by regional, cultural, or linguistic groups in several cases. Like Germany and Japan, most have seen multiple bases for legitimacy over the last century, though India, the largest and one of the most enduring democracies in the world, is an exception. Questions of legitimacy, then, are often very much alive in some of these countries. With relatively minor exceptions, they face no serious threats to their territory, despite sometimes seething discontent in particular regions. With only moderately strong bureaucracies, however, internal sovereignty is notably weaker than in the strongest states; the state simply does not have the capacity to deliver political goods nearly as uniformly. In some ways, some of the cases—particularly India, Brazil, and China—seem to be getting much stronger, but in other ways they and others are getting weaker. It is unclear whether stronger states will emerge in these cases or not, though that is certainly possible.

CASE Study

BRAZIL: A MODERATELY STRONG, AND NOW LEGITIMATE, MODERN STATE

Like most countries, Brazil's modern state was the product of European colonial rule. Prior to Portuguese colonization in 1500, its population was relatively small compared with much of the Americas. The Portuguese effectively subjugated the indigenous population, and colonial Brazil became a major producer

- **FAILED STATES INDEX** 62.1 (126 of 178); weakest on "demographic pressures" and "uneven economic development"

- **TERRITORY** Colonial creation; Portuguese half of South America

- **SOVEREIGNTY** Inherited peacefully at independence; legacy of weak central government vis-à-vis states and local elites

- **LEGITIMACY**
  Monarchy until 1889; limited democracy thereafter; legacy of military intervention claiming legitimacy based on modernization; now consolidated democracy

- **BUREAUCRACY**
  Expanded greatly since 1964 under state-guided development; high corruption

of sugarcane and other agricultural products, farmed largely with African slave labor. Indeed, Brazil had more slaves than any other colony in the Americas. A Portuguese, landowning elite emerged as the socially and economically dominant force in the colonial society.

In contrast with the Spanish colonies in South America, Brazil gained independence from Portugal as a single country, creating by far the largest territory in South America under one sovereign government. This was partly due to its unusual route to independence. In most of South America in the early nineteenth century, the landowning elite led rebellions against Spanish rule. In contrast, the Portuguese royal family actually fled to Brazil in 1808 to evade Napoleon's conquest of Portugal. In 1821 King João VI returned to Portugal after regaining his throne, leaving his son, Dom Pedro, in Brazil to rule on his behalf. A year later, Dom Pedro declared Brazil independent and declared himself emperor, with no real opposition from Portugal.

The new state's economy remained agricultural and used slave labor until the late nineteenth century, making Brazil the last slaveholding society in the world. Growing international and domestic pressure to end slavery led the elite to conclude wage labor would be more effective. Slavery was finally abolished in 1888. The same liberal ideas that led some Brazilian elites to oppose slavery also led them to oppose the empire and favor democracy instead. Just a year after the abolition of slavery, civilian and military reformers convinced key military leaders to overthrow the emperor in a bloodless coup and establish a republic.

The leaders of the new republic created Brazil's modern state, drafting a constitution that created a democratic system of government but gave voting rights to literate men only, restricting the voting population to 3.5 percent of the citizenry. This disenfranchised virtually all the former slaves, who were illiterate.

Brazilians celebrate the announcement that they would host the 2016 Olympics, which came not long after they found out that they would also host the 2014 World Cup. Both events symbolize Brazil's growing importance. Very strong economic growth in the new millennium and a stable, democratic state have made Brazil one of the ten largest economies in the world and a growing player on the world stage.

Economic influence was shifting to urban areas, but political control remained vested in the rural landowning elite. Known as *coroneis,* or "colonels," these individuals used their socioeconomic dominance to control the votes in their regions in a type of machine politics. Meanwhile, in the growing urban areas, **clientelism,** the exchange of material resources for political support, developed as the key means of mobilizing political support. As more urban dwellers became literate and gained the right to vote, elite politicians gained their support by providing direct benefits to them, such as jobs or government services to their neighborhoods. Clientelism and *coronelismo* (rule by *coroneis*) became ways to shore up political power in Brazil's first, partial democracy. Corruption and clientelist use of bureaucratic jobs as perks for supporters simultaneously bloated and undermined Brazil's young bureaucracy. Such corruption indicated a weak modern state.

A leading practitioner of clientelism, Getúlio Vargas, used it and military support to gain complete power and eliminate democracy in the 1930s. He created a new regime, the quasi-fascist *Estado Novo* (New State), that he ruled from 1937 to 1945. He significantly expanded the state's economic role and power, creating state-owned steel and oil industries, and expanded health and welfare systems to gain popular support (which also strengthened the state's bureaucracy). When the end of World War II discredited fascism, Vargas was forced to allow a return to democratic rule.

The New (democratic) Republic was plagued by economic problems and political instability. By the early 1960s, the elite and military saw growing militancy on the part of workers as perhaps the first stage in a communist revolution. In a preemptive strike, the military overthrew the elected government in 1964 with U.S. and considerable upper- and middle-class support. The military ruled until 1985, leading what we will term a "modernizing authoritarian" regime (see chapter 3), which produced very rapid economic growth and industrialization, further expanding the state's size and capabilities. By the late 1970s, growing inequality and a slowdown in economic growth led workers in the expanding industrial cities to organize illegal unions. Despite government efforts to stop them, these unions and followers of liberation theology in the Catholic Church led a growing movement for democracy, which ultimately forced the military to slowly shift power back to elected officials. Democratic governments have ruled since, firmly establishing liberal democracy as the basis for legitimacy. In the first decade of the new millennium, Brazil's democratic governments oversaw a new period of rapid economic growth that substantially reduced poverty and strengthened the state. This growth has made Brazil a major global economic player, via the informal "BRICS" (Brazil, Russia, India, China, South Africa) grouping.

clientelism
The exchange of material resources for political support

Video link:
The man behind Brazil's economic boom

Web link:
The Economist on corruption in Brazil

Data link:
OECD Better Life Index: Brazil

CASE Summary   While maintaining a large sovereign territory since independence, Brazil has faced repeated questions about the state's legitimacy. Various Brazilian leaders have responded by claiming legitimacy on the basis of charismatic appeals, clientelism, modernization, and democracy.

Brazil's new democracy now seems to be fully established. While the state has presided over rapid economic growth and reduced poverty, "uneven economic development" remains one of its biggest weaknesses. It also continues to be plagued by high levels of corruption, which at times undermine the rule of law and bureaucratic effectiveness, as well as a security apparatus that sometimes seems beyond civilian control and abuses human rights. It is nonetheless a moderately strong modern state, exercising effective control over its territory and people, enjoying democratic legitimacy, and having the largest economy in the Southern Hemisphere.

CASE Questions

1. Brazil is the strongest of our "moderately strong states." What are the main elements that make it significantly weaker than the "strong states" above?
2. What has been the role of democracy in strengthening or weakening the Brazilian state over the last century?

MEXICO: CHALLENGES TO INTERNAL SOVEREIGNTY

Prior to the Spanish conquest, the territory that is now Mexico hosted a series of powerful empires, from the Olmecs, who ruled as far back as 1400 BCE, to the Aztecs, who controlled much of the territory when conquistador Hernán Cortés landed his ships on the Yucatán Peninsula in 1519. In colonial times, Spain exploited Mexico for its gold and silver, but most important was the country's large, disciplined population, which provided valuable labor for the colonial regime. Because of this, Mexico did not become an important market for the African slave trade.

Mexico became a sovereign state with the War of Independence (1810–1821), but in the immediate aftermath found itself bitterly divided along regional (north–south) and ideological (liberal versus conservative) lines. Divisions manifested themselves in

- **FAILED STATES INDEX**
  73.1 (97 of 178); weakest on "uneven economic development" and "security apparatus" (drug cartels)

- **TERRITORY**
  Spanish colonial creation, half its original size following the Mexican-American War (1846-1848)

the successive military coups that rocked Mexico throughout much of the century, with strongmen (*caudillos*) constantly changing allegiances in support of one side or another. These conflicts resulted in a weak state and a limited capacity to develop a functioning bureaucracy.

The internal rifts also had a negative impact on Mexico's ability to defend its sovereignty, as evidenced by the Mexican-American War (1846–1848) and its immediate aftermath. The terms of the peace called for the sale of territories comprising much of what is now the American southwest to the United States, shrinking Mexican territory to under one-half of its original size.

The instability of the nineteenth century did eventually end, but at the cost of political freedoms. Porfirio Díaz, a *caudillo* who had mastered the art of consolidating power through bribery and intimidation, founded an authoritarian regime and ruled from 1876 until 1910, marking the longest tenure of any statesman in Mexican history. His rule, termed the *Porfiriato*, based its legitimacy on an ability to deliver political order and unprecedented economic growth. The Díaz regime's primary supporters were among the upper class and business elite. Its enemies were among the peasant class (*campesinos*), who lost land to foreign speculators only to find the state unresponsive to their grievances. When Díaz reneged on a promise to retire in 1910, anti-Díaz forces, supported by the rural poor, instigated the Mexican Revolution (1910–1920), which resulted in the regime's collapse. Despite Díaz's resignation in 1911, the revolution soon became a civil war, with various factions turning against the new government of Francisco Madero. Madero was unable to disarm fellow revolutionaries, notably the guerrillas led by General Francisco "Pancho" Villa in the north and the peasant armies of Emiliano Zapata in the south.

- **Sovereignty:** Achieved in War of Independence (1810–1821); recent challenges by southern guerrilla movement and northern drug cartels

- **LEGITIMACY** Nineteenth-century divisions (liberal versus conservative *caudillos*); revolution followed by twentieth-century semi-authoritarian state; twenty-first-century democracy

- **BUREAUCRACY** Developed with single-party domination over the twentieth century; part of ruling party's clientelist networks until 2000

Web link: Treaty of Guadeloupe Hidalgo, 1848, ceding Mexican territories to the United States

The two best-known leaders of the Mexican Revolution, Pancho Villa (center) and Emiliano Zapata (holding sombrero), pose with other revolutionary leaders. The Mexican Revolution (1910–1920) created the modern Mexican state but ultimately produced seventy-five years of rule by one party, the Institutional Revolutionary Party (PRI). In 2000 Mexico finally made a transition to a democratic form of government via free and fair elections. The long PRI rule created a moderately strong, if repressive, state that has made Mexico a growing player on the world stage.

Ultimately, Villa and Zapata were assassinated, and power was consolidated by an emerging, revolutionary elite. The modern Mexican state was established by President Plutarco Elías Calles (1924–1928), who created the longest-ruling political machine in Mexican history, a party that was eventually named the Partido Revolucionario Institucional (Institutional Revolutionary Party), or PRI. While the PRI embraced the revolution-era democratic constitution of 1917, in practice it formed a semi-authoritarian system that governed Mexico from 1929 to 2000. The party was able to maintain power through systemic corruption, bribery, and intimidation, as well as clientelism and effective voter mobilization tactics (see chapter 3).

The PRI's legitimacy rested mainly on its association with the values of the Mexican Revolution, especially land reform and the empowerment of the *campesinos*. As the state achieved a new level of stability, Mexico created a functioning bureaucracy that, while corrupt, made important strides in furthering literacy, access to health care, and overall economic development. It used oil wealth and trade with the United States to achieve significant industrialization, transforming Mexico into a middle-income country, though with sharp income and regional inequality.

Starting in the early 1980s, the party moved away from its traditional policies that protected the rural poor, adopting policies more favorable to a free-market economy with less government intervention. This led to a fissure within the party and the defection of the left flank under Cuauhtémoc Cárdenas (son of a legendary president who nationalized Mexico's oil industry in 1938). Cárdenas created a new party and ran for president in the 1988 elections, garnering an unprecedented 30 percent of the vote amid widespread claims of electoral fraud, which the PRI vehemently denied. The PRI's unending string of questionable electoral victories finally seemed to be taking a toll on its fragile legitimacy.

Mexico finally transitioned to democracy in 2000 with the bellwether election of Vicente Fox of the National Action Party as president, the first non-PRI president in over seventy years. This move from semi-authoritarianism to free democratic competition reflects changing notions of legitimacy, from clientelism to electoral democracy.

Despite its democratization, Mexico remains plagued by severe economic and regional disparities along with questions over the strength of the state. First, Mexico has experienced large-scale flight of labor to the United States. This has not only been a source of tension between Mexico and several U.S. states but is also symptomatic of the desperate economic situation faced by millions of Mexicans. In the south, farmers, especially those of indigenous origin, face economic dislocation. This led in the 1980s to the formation of the Zapatista Army of National Liberation (EZLN). Based in the southern state of Chiapas, the EZLN waged a guerrilla campaign in 1994 in the tradition of Zapata's fighters during the Mexican Revolution, though it has since reverted to more peaceful methods of demonstration.

Web link:
Election of
Vicente Fox, 2000

By far the most critical challenge to Mexican sovereignty today, however, comes in the north, where a war among rival drug cartels has killed over forty thousand people since 2007. While U.S. consumers have been supporting the border states' manufacturing, or *maquiladora,* economy, America has also been the prime market for the Mexican drug trade. This has raised further questions about the impact and direction of U.S.-Mexican interconnections. Endemic police corruption, lack of alternative economic opportunities, a supply of small arms from north of the border, and a large appetite for drugs there have all led to the degradation of government authority in the northern region. This has called into question the state's ability to keep a monopoly on legitimate violence for the first time since the end of the Mexican Revolution. A surge in economic growth starting in 2011, however, raised hopes that the Mexican state would grow stronger and overcome its most serious difficulties.

Audio link:
Mexico's crisis of disappearance

Data link:
OECD Better life Index: Mexico

CASE Summary

The long-ruling PRI created a modern state that effectively controlled authority and maintained sovereignty for three-quarters of a century. It consciously used an interventionist economic development strategy, funded mainly by oil production, to initiate industrialization. When forced to do so in the 1980s, it adapted to a more open free-market economy that included a great expansion of trade with the United States, its powerful northern neighbor. Economic success amid continuing poverty and declining legitimacy ultimately created a growing movement for democracy, which finally succeeded in peacefully ousting the PRI from power in 2000, changing the basis for the state's legitimacy. Today, Mexico faces challenges to its internal sovereignty in the south at the hands of an indigenous guerrilla group and, more threateningly, in the north at the hands of drug cartels who seem more powerful than the state's security forces. This important middle-income country has seen significant economic success in the last generation but is plagued by growing questions of internal sovereignty.

CASE Questions

1. Since the revolution a century ago, Mexico has been marked by exceptional political stability—the same regime ruled for nearly eighty years—yet it is only a moderately strong state. Why?
2. Which elements of state strength best explain the increasing strength of the Mexican state over the last twenty to thirty years?

CASE Study

RUSSIA: STRONG EXTERNAL SOVEREIGNTY WITH WEAK RULE OF LAW

- **FAILED STATES INDEX**
  77.1 (80 of 178); weakest on "security apparatus" and "human rights and rule of law"

- **TERRITORY**
  Multinational empire consolidated under tsar; communist state of USSR broken into fifteen countries in 1991, reducing Russia to pre-imperial borders

- **SOVEREIGNTY**
  Feudal state with unusually strong monarchy under tsar; modern state established by communist rule; postcommunist state weak but getting stronger; continuing challenges to central control from regions

The earliest state that is a direct ancestor of modern Russia was a relatively centralized premodern kingdom that emerged in Moscow in the fourteenth century. Ivan IV Vasilyevich (Ivan the Terrible) took the title "tsar" (emperor) in 1547 and greatly increased the monarch's power and reach by taking over vast swaths of territory to the east and west. By 1660 Russia was geographically the largest country in the world, a claim it has maintained ever since. The country became a vast, multinational empire in which more than one hundred languages were spoken, governed by a monarchy that would last until 1917.

The tsar was an absolutist ruler with even greater power than most monarchs in Europe. For example, Russian tsars owned all the land in Russia until 1785, when the gentry were finally allowed to own land. Over the centuries, an expanding bureaucracy emerged to administer the tsar's lands. Nonetheless, the Russian monarchy essentially had the attributes of an early modern absolutist state in terms of effective sovereignty and control over territory.

The biggest reform of the state and economy occurred in 1861, when the serfs were emancipated, meaning they were no longer legally required to remain on and work the land on which they were born. This allowed them to respond to rapid industrialization in the late nineteenth century, moving to the growing cities. Radical

Members of the pro-Kremlin youth movement Nashi rally in support of Vladimir Putin in front of the Kremlin and Saint Basil's Cathedral in Moscow. The new Russian state emerged from the collapse of the Soviet Union in 1991. After a decade as a very weak state, it became significantly stronger under Putin, to the detriment of democracy. Putin has increasingly identified himself with nationalist symbols from the Soviet and pre-Communist Russian state, both to project an image of strength and to gain greater legitimacy.

movements grew in these newly expanded cities, including groups demanding democracy and a growing Marxist movement. Tsar Alexander III was finally forced to agree to the creation of an elected legislature, the *Duma*, in 1905. He dissolved the body after only three months, however; Russia's first, very brief experiment with democracy was over.

Not long afterward, Russia was drawn into World War I, which proved economically disastrous. Because it was still primarily a poor and agricultural society, soldiers were sent to the front ill equipped and hungry, and as conditions worsened, mass desertions occurred. A crisis of legitimacy undermined the state's ability to maintain its territorial integrity and military force.

By the end of the war, the Bolsheviks, a communist group under Vladimir Ilyich Lenin, had gained popularity. The makings of another electoral democracy emerged in February 1917, only to be overtaken by a communist revolution that October. The communists assassinated the tsar and his family, after which many of the non-Russian areas of the empire declared themselves independent. It took the communist movement three years to fully recapture what had been the tsarist empire, more or less preserving prior Russian territory. A new government called the Union of Soviet Socialist Republics (USSR), or the Soviet Union (see chapter 3 for more details), was formed, a brutal but nonetheless modern state. The Communist Party created a dictatorial regime that it tightly controlled. A new basis for legitimacy was established in Communist rule, but most analysts believe the Communist regime's real legitimacy was fairly short-lived.

The Communists modernized Russia, but at tremendous human cost (estimates range as high as twenty million dead). Lenin's successor, Joseph Stalin, rapidly industrialized the country, taking resources and laborers from the countryside as needed. The state took complete control of all economic activity. The secret police dealt with anyone who opposed the state's methods, contributing to the formation of one of the most oppressive police states in history. Yet Stalin also created a superpower, which became the only serious rival to the United States after World War II. After his death, Soviet leaders reduced the degree of terror but maintained centralized control over an increasingly bureaucratic form of communism. The Communist bureaucracy controlled virtually all economic activity and was initially successful at rapid industrialization, but it could not keep pace with the West's economic growth. Recognizing the need for change, a new leadership under Mikhail Gorbachev began a process of reform in 1985 that soon resulted in the collapse of the Soviet state.

When elements of the Soviet military who were opposed to some of Gorbachev's reforms attempted a coup in August 1991, Boris Yeltsin, the leader of the Russian part of the Soviet federation and himself a Communist reformer, stood up to the tanks and proclaimed the end of Soviet rule. The military, faced with masses of people in the streets and with the eyes of the world on it, was forced to back down. By December,

- **LEGITIMACY**
  Traditional monarchy overthrown by communist revolution; democracy in 1990s; semi-authoritarian regime with strong nationalist appeal since

- **BUREAUCRACY**
  Extremely powerful under Communist Party rule, controlling economy; postcommunist weakening with growing corruption; perhaps strengthening since 2000

Web link:
"End of the Soviet Union"

Video link:
Putin and Russian nationalism

Data link:
OECD Better Life Index: Russia

Gorbachev had agreed to the dissolution of the Soviet state. The old tsarist empire split into fifteen separate states, with Russia the largest by far.

Today, Russia remains a very multi-ethnic state, with a federal system of government that gives some power, at least in theory, to the various regions, which are defined loosely along ethnic lines. After the dissolution of the Soviet regime, Russia gained a new claim to legitimacy, as an electoral democracy emerged in the 1990s. It was very fragile, however; the state became demonstrably weaker, as powerful mafias and super-rich "oligarchs" controlled most political power and economic wealth. Yeltsin's handpicked successor, Vladimir Putin (1999–2008, 2012–), reduced the level of democratic freedoms, and simultaneously strengthened the central state. Putin centralized power in the executive, strengthened the central state vis-à-vis regional governments, reduced crime, and restored order. In 2012 and 2013, he increasingly championed nationalism as a basis for legitimacy, most famously passing laws banning American adoption of Russian babies and "homosexual propaganda." Despite Putin's successful strengthening of the state, he has done so in ways that have undermined the rule of law and created a growing police state. He also still faces threats to Russia's territorial integrity in Chechnya, where a guerrilla movement continues to battle for independence.

CASE Summary

Russia has seen three dramatically different regimes, with a possible fourth emerging in the new millennium. Prior to the 1990s, the country had an exceptionally strong state that controlled most economic activity far more tightly than virtually any modern state does today. It also controlled a vast, multinational empire along its borders, one that was lost with the dissolution of the Soviet Union. The smaller but still vast Russian state continues to be plagued by ethnic and national differences, some of which have resulted in violent conflict. The various regimes' claims to legitimacy have been drastically different and have always been challenged. After a period of fairly extreme weakness in the 1990s, the state has become stronger in most areas in the new millennium, though it remains corrupt and has a weak rule of law.

CASE Questions

1. Russia has seen exceptionally dramatic swings in the claims to legitimacy of its different regimes. What impact might that have on the strength of its state?
2. What explains the unusual combination of great external sovereignty versus weaker internal strength in the Russian case?

CASE Study

INDIA: ENDURING DEMOCRACY IN A MODERATELY WEAK STATE

India is the world's largest democracy and one of the few postcolonial countries to maintain democratic rule for nearly all of its history. Arguably, it is also the world's most diverse country, with more than 250 different languages, five major religions, and a complex caste system that has crucial political implications. Its independence movement, led by the charismatic Mahatma Gandhi, was the first successful anticolonial effort of the post–World War II era and inspired many other anticolonial leaders to pursue independence.

The territory that is now India, Pakistan, and Bangladesh was once divided among many kingdoms, most of which were Hindu. Muslim invaders created the Moghul Empire in 1526, which dominated most of northern and central India and ruled over a mostly Hindu population, while the south remained under the control of local Hindu kings. Like other premodern rulers, both the Hindu kings and Muslim emperors had only loose sovereignty over daily life. At the local level, members of the elite caste, the Brahmin, governed.

By the middle of the 1700s, the British East India Company had established an informal empire over most of the territory, breaking Moghul rule and acting as a government. The Sepoy Rebellion in the Indian army in 1857 ended company rule,

- **FAILED STATES INDEX**
  77.5 (79 of 178); weakest on "vengeance-seeking group grievance" (Muslim-Hindu conflicts primarily) and "uneven economic development"

- **TERRITORY**
  Created by British colonial rule, though divided into India and Pakistan at independence

- **SOVEREIGNTY**
  Established with independence in 1947; dispute with Pakistan over control of Kashmir region

- **LEGITIMACY**
  Continuous liberal democracy; secular government questioned by Hindu nationalists and other religious movements

- **BUREAUCRACY**
  Created by British colonialism; central to economic policy; weakening due to external pressure for reform and growing corruption

An election official shows workers on a tea plantation how to use a new electronic voting system. While India's state is weakened by corruption, suffers from widespread religious and ethnic tensions, and remains extremely poor despite recent economic gains, it has endured as the world's largest democracy for more than six decades.

and the British government took direct control of its largest colony. As colonizers often did, the British required educated local people to fill the administrative offices of their colonial state. Creating an all-Indian civil service and military and the start of a modern bureaucracy helped create greater unity among the subcontinent's disparate regions, and newly educated Indians filled the offices of these new institutions. Unfortunately for the British, the first stirrings of nationalism would arise from this educated elite.

The Indian National Congress, which eventually became the Congress Party that has ruled India for most of its independent history, was founded by urban elites in 1885. Although its top leadership was primarily Hindu, the Congress operated on democratic and secular principles and claimed to represent all Indians. Gandhi transformed it into a mass nationalist movement starting in 1915. As the nationalist struggle continued through the 1920s and 1930s under Gandhi's leadership, India's Muslim leaders increasingly felt unrepresented in the organization, and by the end of the 1930s, some Muslim leaders were beginning to demand a separate Muslim state.

The push for independence succeeded after World War II. Muslim leaders, however, demanded and received from the British a separate Muslim state, Pakistan. In 1947 the simultaneous creation of the two states (against Gandhi's fierce opposition) resulted in the mass migration of millions of citizens, as Hindus moved from what was to be Pakistan into what would become India, and Muslims went in the other direction. At least a million people perished in violence associated with the massive migration, probably the largest in world history.

India thus gained independence under the rule of the Congress Party in a democratic and federal system. Besides economic development, the government's other great challenge was the demand for greater recognition by India's diverse ethnic and religious groups. Throughout the 1950s, leaders of local language groups demanded, and some received, states of their own within the federal system. The legitimacy of the democratic system as a whole was questioned by only a few groups, however, most of which were communist inspired.

When Indira Gandhi (no relation to Mahatma) gained leadership of the Congress Party and the country as prime minister in 1971, she increasingly centralized power in her own hands. In 1975 she declared a "state of emergency" that gave her the power to disband local governments and replace them with those loyal to her. This was the only period that threatened the survival of India's democracy. Her actions were met with increasing opposition, however, and she was forced to allow new democratic elections two years later, in which the Congress Party lost power for the first time in its history.

Indira Gandhi returned to power democratically in 1980s but was assassinated in 1984 by a member of one of India's many religious groups, the Sikhs; the assassin

Video link:
BBC: India and Pakistan partition

Web link:
Map of partition

was part of a growing movement for an independent Sikh state. While this movement was never successful, it was the first significant example of violent religious-political conflict since the partition of India and Pakistan. Since then, political battles have increased between Muslims and Hindu nationalists, both of whom reject the official secularism of the national government. Out of this has emerged a renewed Hindu nationalist party that won a national election and formed the government in 1996. India's official principles of secular government, though, have remained in place (see chapter 12).

Until the 1990s, India's economic development policies included a role for an active and growing state, including its colonially created bureaucracy that over the decades became less efficient and more corrupt. Since the mid-1990s, India has reduced the role of the state in the economy and has achieved much higher growth rates, carving out a major niche in the global economy in areas related to computer services and programming. It remains, however, a country with widespread malnutrition and the largest number of poor people in the world. While presiding over an expanding economy, the current government (again under Congress Party rule) faces continuing religious tensions, especially vis-à-vis the impoverished Muslim minority, many of whom seem to believe India's democracy is not for them.

Video link:
Gapminder/ TEDIndia Talk: "Asia's Rise: How and When"

Data link:
OECD country statistical profile: India

CASE Summary   Indian territory and sovereignty emerged out of colonial rule and the nationalist movement for independence. Most unusual for postcolonial states, its democracy has survived and seems legitimate in the eyes of the bulk of the population. Its state remains relatively weak, however, with this weakness manifested in continuing corruption, religious tensions, and poverty. India was famed for its strong bureaucracy after independence, but reforms to reduce the bureaucracy's role in economic policy and growing corruption have weakened it. In recent years, the state has presided over a growing economy, and many observers see elements of a potential economic superpower. India increasingly rivals its largest neighbor, China.

CASE Questions

1. What have been the effects of colonialism on the relative strength of the Indian state?
2. What are the weakest elements of the Indian state, and how do these differ from the strong states discussed earlier? What explains these differences?

CASE Study

CHINA: ECONOMIC LEGITIMACY OVER POLITICAL REFORM

- **FAILED STATES INDEX 80.9 (66 of 178); weakest on "human rights and rule of law" and "vengeance-seeking group grievance"**

- **TERRITORY**
  Established in ancient empire, though with changing boundaries; Communist rulers annexed disputed territory of Tibet

- **SOVEREIGNTY**
  Longest continuous sovereign entity in world history under empire; civil war in early twentieth century; sovereignty restored by Communist revolution in 1949 and start of modern state

China is the world's most populous country. It had the world's fastest growing economy in the 1990s, managed to avoid the recession of 2008–2009 entirely, and is widely recognized as the world's "oldest civilization." Although its modern state arose only in 1949 under Communist rule, the Chinese empire was first united in 221 BCE. While several dynasties came to power over the centuries and its exact boundaries shifted somewhat, the empire existed, more or less unified, until 1911. This makes it the longest continuously sovereign political entity in human history.

The empire's demise began in the mid-nineteenth century. While trade with the outside world had long existed, Britain, the United States, and other European imperial powers began demanding greater access to Chinese markets and trade in the 1840s. The Opium Wars from 1840 to 1864 resulted in a series of very unequal treaties that gave Western powers access to China as well as effective sovereignty over key areas of the country, even though the country was never formally colonized.

In reaction to increasing foreign control and economic decline, a series of revolts known as the Taiping Rebellion broke out in the 1850s, though the emperor ultimately regained control with the help of European forces that wanted to preserve their favorable treatment. The restoration of the empire brought relative stability, but only until the end of the century. What many saw as continued foreign domination and

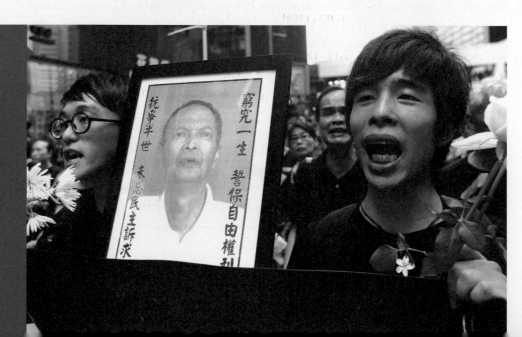

A protester carries a portrait of Chinese dissident Li Wangyang, who died under mysterious circumstances after taking part in the famous Tiananmen Square protest in 1989. The Chinese state has presided over the most successful period of economic growth in human history, but it has preserved its authoritarian regime. Can an increasingly wealthy and powerful state remain nondemocratic for the long term, in contrast with the pattern of European history?

economic stagnation produced growing discontent. Sun Yat-sen, an American-educated doctor and revolutionary leader, started a nationalist movement that proclaimed its opposition to the empire and to foreign imperialism. The first stirrings of this movement came in 1905, and by 1911 military uprisings signaled the empire's imminent collapse. On January 1, 1912, the empress resigned and the Republic of China was established.

The new nationalist government quickly became a dictatorship and ushered in more than a decade of chaos and war. Warlords gained control of various parts of the country as the Chinese state's sovereignty and territorial control crumbled. In the 1920s, the nationalists slowly regained control with the help of an alliance with a new political force, the Chinese Communist Party (CCP). The nationalists turned against the Communists after regaining power and their sovereignty was seriously compromised by reliance on warlords in some areas, the continuous threat of civil war with the CCP, and Japanese invasion. While the nationalists had regained control, they ruled a very weak state.

The CCP, under its new leader, Mao Zedong, moved to the countryside after the nationalists broke the alliance. Starting in the southeast, Mao put together a revolutionary movement that began an intermittent civil war with the government. In 1934–1935, Mao led the famous Long March, a six-thousand-mile trek by party supporters. The CCP then took effective control of the northwestern section of the country and began creating the prototype of its future Communist regime. The Japanese invasion of 1937 left the country's territory and sovereignty divided among the CCP, the nationalist government, and Japan. After the Japanese withdrawal at the end of World War II, the Communist revolution triumphed in 1949, despite U.S. military support for the nationalists, who fled to the island of Taiwan and formed a government there. Communist rule created the first truly unified modern Chinese state, but at horrific cost. The new government instituted massive land reform programs and campaigns against corruption, opium use, and other socially harmful practices. It also took control of the economy, creating a Soviet-style command economy with a massive bureaucracy, which attempted to industrialize the world's largest agrarian society. The result was the Great Leap Forward, an effort at rapid rural industrialization that led to a famine that killed at least twenty million people. Political purges sent many others to "re-education camps," prison, or execution. The Cultural Revolution from 1966 to 1976 was a period in which Mao mobilized his followers against what he saw as entrenched bureaucrats in his own party and state; his efforts created widespread political uncertainty, repression, and economic and social dislocation.

The Cultural Revolution ended with Mao's death in 1976. Deng Xiaoping, one of Mao's earliest comrades who had been removed from power during the Cultural Revolution, established his supremacy over the party and state in 1979. Deng initiated a series of slow but ultimately sweeping economic reforms that focused on allowing greater market forces in the economy and reducing the direct role of the

- **LEGITIMACY**
  Traditional empire; nationalist government came out of civil war; communist ideology until 1978; modernizing authoritarian state since then

- **BUREAUCRACY**
  Ancient Confucian system of merit; great expansion under Communist rule; growing problem of corruption

Web link:
The Taiping Rebellion, "The Land System of the Heavenly Kingdom"

Web link:
A panoramic view of China's cultural revolution

state. These reforms continue today, a thirty-five-year process of introducing a market economy that is still not complete. The result has been the fastest economic growth in the world that has moved millions of Chinese out of poverty, spurred a huge exodus from rural areas to cities, and allowed much greater inequality than existed under Mao.

Politically, Deng and his successors have resisted most efforts to achieve greater freedom and democracy. While the state's legitimacy is still officially based on communism, its pursuit of capitalist development has meant its real legitimacy is implicitly based on its ability to modernize the economy and provide wealth. Thus, China now has what we will call a modernizing authoritarian regime (see chapter 3). Many observers see a fundamental contradiction between allowing economic freedoms but denying political ones and argue that ultimately the CCP will have to allow much greater political freedom if its economic success is to continue. This, along with the social and environmental effects of extremely rapid economic growth, widespread corruption, and growing inequality, are the major weaknesses facing the Chinese state today.

Data link:
OECD country statistical profile: China

CASE Summary   China established its territory and sovereignty centuries ago, though both were severely challenged from the late nineteenth to mid-twentieth centuries. Out of that chaotic period emerged the world's second major communist regime, which created a modern, if brutal, state. The Communists regained full sovereignty, expanded the state's territory to include the still-disputed region of Tibet, and reestablished a strong bureaucracy that came to control the entire economy. The regime's legitimacy was based on communist doctrine, augmented by Mao's initial charisma, but clearly declined over the years. Since Mao's death, the regime has still officially proclaimed communism as its ideology, but in reality the regime now bases its legitimacy on its successful economic policy. The CCP has presided over a modern state that has achieved perhaps the most remarkable economic advance in human history. China has become the second-largest economy in the world and a potential economic and political superpower. It is still plagued, however, by problems of corruption, weak rule of law, and questions about its legitimacy in the absence of any significant political reform.

CASE Questions

1. What impact does the legacy of Mao's communist system have on the strength of the modern Chinese state today?
2. China boasts the oldest and most enduring premodern state in world history. What impact does this have on the strength of its modern state?

The Weakest States

The weakest states in the world appear to be quite fragile. The Failed States Index characterizes them with words such as *critical* and *in danger*. In many cases, their territorial integrity is at least threatened, if not outright violated. Even where they maintain official control, that control is often rather weak: their borders are porous, with huge black markets in people and goods. Corruption is rife throughout the state and many institutions therefore function only sporadically, leaving much of the population dependent on personal networks and clientelist ties to survive and try to prosper. They are by and large quite poor economies, with many dependent on the export of key primary commodities, making the resource curse a common problem. These states provide very limited political goods for their citizens, undermining legitimacy, whatever its basis. The weakest can accurately be characterized as "quasi-states," maintaining legal sovereignty and the access to the international system that entails, but only minimally achieving internal sovereignty. Our cases studies of Iran and Nigeria are two of the largest of these and stronger than many, but nonetheless illustrate the contours of extreme state weakness.

IRAN: CLAIMING LEGITIMACY VIA THEOCRACY

I ran is the modern descendant of the great ancient empire of Persia, and it has been heavily influenced by a series of invasions. The most important of these were the Arab invasion in the seventh century that brought Islam to the region and the Safavid invasion of 1501 that converted 90 percent of the population to the Shia version of Islam. The Safavids created the first of two empires that united the territory but relied on local elites to rule, especially in peripheral areas; neither created a fully modern state.

In the nineteenth century the empire's real power was drastically reduced by Russian and British imperialism. Like China, Iran was never formally colonized, but the government came to be extremely dependent upon and compliant with the Russians and British, granting them very favorable economic terms for key resources such as oil and depending on them for military support when needed. This era also saw the

- **FAILED STATES INDEX**
  89.7 (37 of 178); weakest on "legitimacy," "human rights and rule of law," and "factionalized elites"

- **TERRITORY**
  Solidified in nineteenth century; smaller than ancient kingdoms

- **SOVEREIGNTY**
  Never formally colonized, though heavily influenced by British and Russian imperialism

- **LEGITIMACY**
  Traditional monarchy until first modern state; modernizing authoritarian state under shah in twentieth century; Islamic theocracy since 1979

- **BUREAUCRACY**
  Expanded by shah's modernization policies; expanded social services under Islamic republic; continuing problem of corruption

modern, much reduced, borders of Iran clearly demarcated. European imperialism severely compromised Iran's sovereignty and reduced its territory, in spite of never officially colonizing the country. By the start of the twentieth century, popular discontent with this foreign influence led to street demonstrations from citizens demanding a new constitution. In 1906 the shah (the supreme ruler) allowed the creation of a democratic legislature, but the state remained weak, divided, and heavily influenced by Russia and Britain.

In the midst of this, Colonel Reza Khan led a coup d'état that overthrew the weakened empire and established what came to be known as the Pahlavi dynasty, ruled first by Reza Shah and then by his son, Mohammed Reza Pahlavi. The Pahlavis created the first truly modern state in Iran. During their rule from 1925 to 1979, they increased the size of the central army tenfold, dramatically expanded the bureaucracy, and gained full control over the provinces. The Pahlavis established a modernizing authoritarian state, expanding both the state and the economy, increasing agricultural and industrial production, and building tremendous infrastructure, with the government itself directly involved in most of these efforts. They continued to welcome extensive foreign investment, especially in the growing oil sector. They also centralized power in their hands; the elected legislature continued to exist with an elected prime minister at its helm, but its power was greatly reduced. When a left-leaning prime minister challenged continued foreign control of the oil industry in 1953, the shah, with active British and U.S. support, overthrew the prime minister and established a fully authoritarian state that eliminated all elected offices.

From the start, the 1953 coup was unpopular because many Iranians saw it as foreign inspired. Soon afterward, the shah launched a series of social and economic reforms to modernize, as he saw it, Iranian society, which further expanded the role and reach of the state and its bureaucracy. He staked his claim to legitimacy on these modernizations, which included land reform and secularization; the latter reduced the

Worshippers pray at a mosque in Tehran. The increasingly authoritarian regime in Iran bases its legitimacy on a version of Islamic theology that claims all state authority should be derived from religious law. Mosques are a major source of regime communication to followers and legitimacy for the clerics, who are the most powerful figures in the government.

role of Islamic law. An economic crisis in the late 1970s created growing opposition to his policies, which favored wealthier and urban over poorer and rural sectors of society. The opposition coalesced behind the leadership of an exiled Shiite spiritual leader, Ayatollah Ruhollah Khomeini. Protests spread through the streets and mosques, and local Islamic militias took over entire neighborhoods, leading to a general strike in 1978 and an antigovernment rally of more than two million people in December of that year. Facing this growing opposition, the shah went into what was supposed to be temporary exile in January 1979 but never returned, his legitimacy completely gone. A month later, Khomeini came back from exile to complete the Iranian revolution and establish the Islamic Republic of Iran, the first theocratic government in the modern era.

Audio link:
The Iranian Revolution

The Islamic Republic has gone through phases of greater openness to political debate and greater repression (see chapter 8), but it has endured and remains regionally powerful. While basing its claim to legitimacy firmly in theocracy, it includes limited elements of democratic rule that have had more influence at some times than others. Patronage from oil revenue and corruption are probably more important than elections in maintaining the government's authority. Questions remain, however, about its legitimacy, as seen in the massive street protests against the presidential election outcome in 2009. While politically quiescent since then, the country continues to seethe with opposition to the government, which responds with increasing repression. Its bid to become a nuclear power, or at least to acquire much greater nuclear capabilities, has recently made Iran the center of major global debate. While it is an important regional player and focus of global attention, over time the Islamic Republic has become a weaker and weaker state.

Data link:
UN data profile: Iran

CASE Summary   The Pahlavis established the first modern Iranian state, expanding its sovereignty internally and externally, and attempted to reduce the influence of Islam. The Ayatollah Khomeini, his followers, and his successors have re-Islamized the country, but within the confines of a modern (though corrupt) bureaucratic state whose territory and sovereignty are secure but whose legitimacy is less certain. The Islamic regime has expanded the social services the state provides and, therefore, the size and reach of the bureaucracy; it has also asserted international power and influence via threatened nuclearization, though severe questions over its legitimacy continue to weaken it.

CASE Questions

1. Iran and China share one aspect of their history: strong but informal Western influence in the nineteenth century. What impact did this have on the development of the modern states in the two countries? In what ways were those impacts similar and different?
2. What are the weakest elements of the Iranian state, and what affects do they have?

CASE Study

- **FAILED STATES INDEX
  100.7 (16 of 178);
  weakest on "legitimacy,"
  "vengeance-seeking
  group grievance,"
  "security apparatus,"
  and "factionalized elites"**

- **TERRITORY
  Created by colonial rule
  out of numerous large
  and small precolonial
  systems; divided by civil
  war, 1967–1970**

- **SOVEREIGNTY
  Gained with
  independence in 1960
  but threatened by recent
  demands for secession;
  weak internally**

- **LEGITIMACY
  Nationalist movement
  divided along ethnic and
  regional lines; limited
  legitimacy of postcolonial
  democratic government;
  six military coups; weak
  democracy since 1999**

NIGERIA: AN EXTREMELY WEAK STATE

Nigeria, like most African states, is a product of colonialism. It is by far the largest African country in terms of population (approximately one-seventh of all Africans are Nigerians) and a major oil producer. Approximately 250 languages are spoken within its borders because under colonial rule a huge number of separate societies were brought together under one state. Prior to colonial conquest in the late nineteenth century, the territory that is now Nigeria was home to numerous and varied societies. The northern half was primarily Muslim and ruled by Islamic emirs (religious rulers) based in twelve separate city-states. The southern half consisted of many societies, the two biggest of which were the Yoruba and Igbo. The Yoruba lived in a series of kingdoms, sometimes politically united and sometimes not, though they shared a common language and religion. The Igbo in the southwest also shared a common language and culture but were governed only at the most local level by councils of elders; they had no kings or chiefs.

The British conquest of what became Nigeria began around 1870. European powers, increasingly competing with one another economically and politically, decided to carve up the African continent in their own interests in what came to be known as the "scramble for Africa." The British united Nigeria as one colony in 1914. In northern Nigeria, they established indirect rule, the form of rule they would use throughout their African empire. Under indirect rule, the British, in theory, left precolonial kingdoms

Nigerians protest the removal of fuel subsidies and demand the end of corruption in 2012. While oil provides the state with massive revenues, it has promoted equally massive corruption, which has weakened the state and siphoned benefits from oil production away from the common people. Despite exporting large amounts of oil, Nigeria's impoverished majority cannot afford fuel without a government subsidy. A democracy has emerged over the last decade, but corruption and a lack of local benefits from oil revenues remain problems.

intact to be ruled by local leaders. In northern Nigeria, this meant ruling through the emirs, who in general accepted British oversight as long as they were left to run their internal affairs mostly as they pleased. In the south, kings and chiefs fulfilled this role where they existed, but where there were no chiefs the British simply invented them. British colonialism gave local rulers more power than they had before, in exchange for rulers' acquiescence in implementing unpopular policies such as forced labor and the collection of colonial taxes. This undermined the legitimacy of those who had been precolonial rulers and prevented newly invented rulers from gaining any legitimacy.

As in India, the colonial state required educated natives to help staff bureaucracies that provided essential services. Christian missionaries provided virtually all of the education for many decades. In the south Christianity and Western education expanded rapidly; southerners filled most of the positions in the colonial state. The northern emirs, on the other hand, convinced colonial authorities to keep Christian missionaries out in order to preserve Islam, on which their legitimacy was based. This meant that northerners received far less Western education. The north, already poorer than the south, fell behind in educational attainment and subsequent job opportunities. As the colonial state and bureaucracy expanded, especially after World War II, more and more southerners moved north to take up positions as clerks for the government. Their presence would prove explosive after independence.

The educated elite became the leadership of the nationalist movement after World War II. Given the history of divisions in the country, it is no surprise that this movement was split from the start. Northern leaders actually resisted independence for many years, fearing their region would lose out to the more educated southerners who had most of the government jobs. The educated southern elite, however, pushed hard for independence. The British finally negotiated a new government for an independent Nigeria that would be federal, with three regions corresponding to the three major ethnic groups, and political parties formed mainly along regional and ethnic lines.

As in virtually all African countries, the new government was quite fragile. In contrast with their approach in India, the British began introducing the institutions of British-style democracy just a few years before independence in Nigeria and most of their African colonies. Nigerians had no prior experience with electoral democracy and little reason to believe that it would be a superior system for them. In response to fraudulent elections and anti-Igbo violence, the army, led primarily by Igbo, overthrew the elected government in January 1966 in the first of six military coups. A countercoup six months later brought a new, northern-dominated government to power under General Yakubu Gowon, but the Igbo military leadership refused to accept it. In January 1967, under the leadership of General Chukwuemeka Ojukwu, they declared their region the independent state of Biafra. Not coincidentally, large-scale oil production had just begun, and the oil wells were in the area claimed as Biafra. A three-year civil war ensued that cost the lives of a million people, mostly due to starvation. The central government defeated the separatists in Biafra and reestablished a single state in 1970. Interrupted by only four years of elected rule, the military governed Nigeria

- **BUREAUCRACY**
  Colonial creation; suffers from extreme levels of corruption fuelled by oil wealth

Web link:
Map of linguistic groups of Nigeria

Web link:
Map of Nigeria's three federal regions

Web link:
Oil and corruption

until 1999. While all military leaders pledged to reduce corruption and improve development, in reality, oil revenue overwhelmed all other economic activity and fuelled both corruption and the desire of those in power to stay there. A weak state grew ever weaker and more corrupt. The military maintained control, even as the institutions of government became increasingly ineffective and their popularity plummeted.

In 1999 the military finally bowed to popular and international pressure and carried out the country's first free and fair election in twenty years. The newly elected president, former general Olusegun Obasanjo, launched a much publicized drive against corruption, the results of which have been modest. While many observers have questioned the integrity of all four elections under the new democracy, Nigeria's democracy nonetheless remains intact, with no threat of further military intervention. With corruption reduced but still quite significant, the provision of political goods, however, remains very limited. The democratic government has also faced growing religious tension in the northern states, many of which have adopted Islamic law. Most recently, a violent Islamist group, Boko Haram, has initiated a series of attacks on Christians across the country. In the oil-rich areas of the former Biafra, ethnic militias have demanded greater benefits for their people. Despite its natural resources and the fact that the most recent president, Goodluck Jonathan, comes from the region, the area's residents are among the poorest in the country. At its height in 2005 and 2006, this violence disrupted oil production and helped drive up world oil prices. In spite of these problems, in the last several years the country has seen significant economic growth, and for the first time in decades much of it is coming from non-oil sectors of the economy, perhaps promising new hope for Nigerians.

Web link:
Non-oil sectors boost growth in Nigeria

Data link:
UN data profile: Nigeria

CASE Summary

With the exception of the 1967–1970 civil war, the Nigerian state has maintained its sovereignty and territory, mostly under military rule. It continues to be extremely weak, however. The military's claims to legitimacy always involved promises to end corruption, restore economic growth, and return the country to democracy, but those promises were rarely fulfilled. The democratic government that has been in place since 1999 is a great improvement over previous regimes, but it has had only limited success in solving the deeply entrenched problems the country faces. While the state's territory is intact, its sovereignty is threatened by ethnic militia, it suffers from widespread corruption that undermines bureaucratic efficiency, and its legitimacy remains an open question. Ironically, the state's weakness results in part from its oil wealth, which has been a huge incentive for corruption.

CASE Questions

1. Nigeria and India are our only two case studies of states that were put together during colonialism from multiple premodern political entities (a common history in Africa and Asia). What impacts does this history have on the strength of the two states? In what ways were those impacts similar and different?

2. What are the weakest elements of the Nigerian state and what affects do they have?

CONCLUSION

The modern state is a political form that has been singularly successful. Arising nearly five hundred years ago, it has spread to every corner of the globe. In fact, the modern world demands that we all live in states. Strong states can provide the political goods that help improve citizens' lives, though nothing guarantees that they will. Although in the short term, state strength can also be used to oppress the citizenry, many political scientists argue that long-term strength must come from legitimacy and the effective provision of political goods. The characteristics of modern states—territory, sovereignty, legitimacy, and bureaucracy—combine to produce an exceptionally powerful ruling apparatus. In strong states, rulers command military force to prevent foreign attack and domestic rebellion, and they control a set of state organizations that can effectively influence society in myriad ways. When this all works well, it can give ruling elites legitimacy and therefore greater power. Weak states, on the other hand, lack the capacity, and often the will, to provide political goods. This threatens their legitimacy and often leaves them dependent on international support or key resources for their survival. While they may appear strong because they use a great deal of force against their own people, this is in fact often a sign of weakness: they have no other means of maintaining their rule. The weakest states are prone to collapse, becoming failed states, as violent opponents can challenge the state's monopoly on the use of force with relative ease.

This raises a long-standing question: How can weak states become stronger? The answer usually involves the creation of impersonal institutions and the rule of law. This can lead citizens to trust the state to act fairly and in the interest of all to the greatest extent possible, giving the state greater legitimacy and strength that it can use to provide political goods. The strongest modern states are virtually all democracies, which are based on such notions as treating all citizens equally and limiting what the state can do, though electoral democracy certainly is no guarantee of state strength.

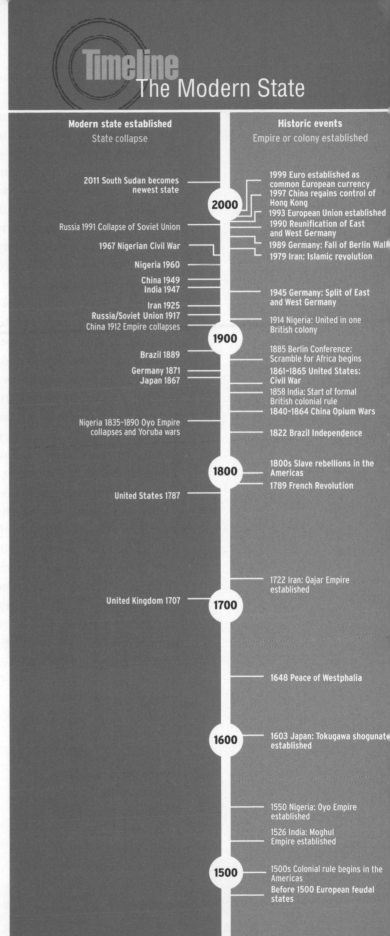

Timeline
The Modern State

Modern state established / State collapse	Historic events / Empire or colony established
	1999 Euro established as common European currency
2011 South Sudan becomes newest state	1997 China regains control of Hong Kong
2000	1993 European Union established
	1990 Reunification of East and West Germany
Russia 1991 Collapse of Soviet Union	1989 Germany: Fall of Berlin Wall
1967 Nigerian Civil War	1979 Iran: Islamic revolution
Nigeria 1960	
China 1949	
India 1947	1945 Germany: Split of East and West Germany
Iran 1925	
Russia/Soviet Union 1917	1914 Nigeria: United in one British colony
China 1912 Empire collapses	
1900	
Brazil 1889	1885 Berlin Conference: Scramble for Africa begins
Germany 1871	1861–1865 United States: Civil War
Japan 1867	1858 India: Start of formal British colonial rule
	1840–1864 China Opium Wars
Nigeria 1835–1890 Oyo Empire collapses and Yoruba wars	1822 Brazil Independence
1800	1800s Slave rebellions in the Americas
	1789 French Revolution
United States 1787	
	1722 Iran: Qajar Empire established
United Kingdom 1707 **1700**	
	1648 Peace of Westphalia
1600	1603 Japan: Tokugawa shogunate established
	1550 Nigeria: Oyo Empire established
	1526 India: Moghul Empire established
1500	1500s Colonial rule begins in the Americas
	Before 1500 European feudal states

The strongest states in Europe and elsewhere resulted from centuries of evolution in most cases, as ruling elites ultimately compromised to create more impersonal and powerful institutions that would allow greater economic growth and, therefore, resources for the state. Postcolonial states had very different historical origins, based on colonial conquest and carving out of territory rather than agreements among domestic elites and local conquest. With independence, these states took the modern form but not necessarily all of the modern content. They often lacked a strong sense of national unity based on a shared history. The international system, however, demands that they act like states, at least internationally. Their rulers therefore act accordingly, often gaining significant power in the process, even in relatively weak states. Lack of wealth, or wealth in the form of a resource curse, can also produce very weak states, often in combination with a problematic colonial legacy.

Political scientists have used various theoretical approaches to understand the modern state. Both Marxist and political culture theorists have long made arguments about how and why states develop. Marxists see them as reflecting the power of the ruling class of a particular epoch. Under capitalism, that ruling class is the bourgeoisie, and the liberal state in particular represents the bourgeoisie's interests. In postcolonial countries, weaker states reflect the weak, dependent nature of the ruling elite there. Cultural theorists argue that underlying values, in particular a strong sense of nationalism, are crucial to maintaining a strong state, which must be based on some shared sense of legitimacy. Without this, effective sovereignty will always be limited.

In recent years, rational-choice and institutionalist theories have become more prominent. The modern state, these theorists argue, emerged in response to the rational incentives of the emerging international state system, rewarding rulers who developed effective sovereignty, military force, and taxation. Once established, strong state institutions tend to reinforce themselves as long as they continue to function for the benefit of the elites whom they were created to serve, and provide adequate political goods to the citizenry. As these states demand more from citizens, they develop a rational interest in establishing some type of popular legitimacy, a subject we look at in much greater depth in the next chapter.

KEY CONCEPTS

absolutism (p. 46)

bureaucracy (p. 42)

charismatic legitimacy (p. 41)

clientelism (p. 73)

external sovereignty (p. 39)

failed state (p. 51)

feudal states (p. 45)

ideal type (p. 50)

internal sovereignty (p. 39)

legitimacy (p. 41)

quasi-states (p. 54)

rational-legal
    legitimacy (p. 42)

resource curse (p. 53)

sovereign (p. 39)

state (p. 36)

strong state (p. 51)

territory (p. 38)

traditional legitimacy (p. 41)

weak state (p. 51)

 Sharpen your skills with SAGE edge at **edge.sagepub.com/orvis3e.**
SAGE edge for students provides a personalized approach to help you accomplish your coursework goals in an easy-to-use learning environment.

WORKS CITED

Anderson, Perry. 1974. *Lineages of the Absolutist State.* London: New Left Books.

Fund for Peace. 2013. "Failed States Index 2013" (http://www.foreignpolicy.com/articles/2013/06/24/2013_failed_states_interactive_map).

Jackson, Robert H. *Quasi-States: Sovereignty, International Relations, and the Third World.* 1990. Cambridge Studies in International Relations No. 12. New York: Cambridge University Press.

Lange, Matthew. 2009. *Lineages of Despotism and Development: British Colonialism and State Power.* Chicago: University of Chicago Press.

North, Douglass Cecil, John Joseph Wallis, and Barry R. Weingast. 2009. *Violence and Social Orders: A Conceptual Framework for Interpreting Recorded Human History.* Cambridge, UK: Cambridge University Press.

Rotberg, Robert I., ed. 2004. *When States Fail: Causes and Consequences.* Princeton, NJ: Princeton University Press.

Weber, Max. 1970. "Politics as Vocation." In *From Max Weber: Essays in Sociology,* edited by H. H. Gaert and C. Wright Mills. London: Routledge and Kegan Paul.

RESOURCES FOR FURTHER STUDY

Jessop, Bob. 1990. *State Theory: Putting Capitalist States in Their Place.* Cambridge, UK: Polity Press.

Levi, Margaret. 2002. "The State of the Study of the State." In *Political Science: State of the Discipline,* edited by Ira Katznelson and Helen V. Milner, 33–55. New York: Norton.

Pierson, Christopher. 1996. *The Modern State.* New York: Routledge.

Poggi, Gianfranco. 1990. *The State: Its Nature, Development, and Prospects.* Cambridge, UK: Polity Press.

Tilly, Charles, ed. 1975. *The Formation of National States in Western Europe.* Studies in Political Development No. 8. Princeton, NJ: Princeton University Press.

WEB RESOURCES

Brookings Institution Index of State Weakness
(http://www.brookings.edu/research/reports/2008/02/weak-states-index)

Comparative Constitutions Project
(http://comparativeconstitutionsproject.org)

***Foreign Policy* and The Fund for Peace, Failed States Index 2010**
(http://www.foreignpolicy.com/articles/2013/06/24/2013_failed_states_interactive_map)

The Heritage Foundation, Index of Economic Freedom
(http://www.heritage.org/index/ranking)
International Crisis Group
(http://www.crisisgroup.org)
Organisation for Economic Co-operation and Development (OECD), Better Life Index
(http://www.oecdbetterlifeindex.org)
Organisation for Economic Co-operation and Development (OECD), Country Statistical Profiles
(http://www.oecd-ilibrary.org/economics/country-statistical-profiles-key-tables-from-oecd_20752288)
Transformation Index BTI
(http://www.bti-project.org/home)
Transparency International, Corruption Perception Index
(http://www.transparency.org/policy_research/surveys_indices/cpi)
United Nations
(http://www.un.org/en)
The World Bank, Worldwide Governance Indicators
(http://info.worldbank.org/governance/wgi/index.asp)

3

STATES, CITIZENS, AND REGIMES

KEY QUESTIONS

- How do different ideologies balance the rights of citizens with the state's ability to compel obedience?

- On what grounds do different regimes give citizens an opportunity to participate in politics? Who rules where citizens do not seem to have such an opportunity? Can this be justified?

- To what extent does ideology explain how different regimes are organized and justify themselves? What else helps explain how different kinds of regimes actually function?

- Do our case studies reveal patterns that suggest where different regime types emerge and why?

regime
A set of formal and informal political institutions that defines a type of government

The proper relationship between a state and its people, individually and collectively, is one of the most interesting and debated questions in political science. All successful modern states are able to compel their citizens to obey and to regulate many areas of their lives. No modern state can do this, however, without answering questions about the legitimate boundaries of such compulsion and regulation. States vary on how far and under what circumstances they can compel individuals and groups to obey those in authority, how extensively they can intervene in people's lives, and how and whether some areas of individual and collective life should not be subject to the state's power. These differences are embodied in what political scientists call regimes. The Country and Concept table on page 100 demonstrates the wide variety of regimes and the levels of freedom that they allow their citizens among just our eleven case studies.

This chapter examines variations in the relationships between states and citizens embedded in different regimes. A **regime** is a set of formal and informal political institutions that defines a type of government. Regimes are more enduring than governments but less enduring than states. Democratic regimes, for example, may persist through many individual governments. The United States elected its forty-fourth presidential government in 2008, yet its democratic regime has remained

The broom (to sweep away corruption) is the symbol of the new All Progressives Congress party in Nigeria. The new party was created by three opposition parties to challenge the ruling People's Democratic Party, which has controlled Nigeria since it became a democracy in 1999. Its continued rule threatens to undermine real competition in the relatively young democracy.

intact for over two centuries. Similarly, a modern state may persist though many regime changes from democratic to authoritarian or the other way around. The state—the existence of a bureaucracy, territory, and so on—is continuous, but its key political institutions can change. The Country and Concept table shows the great variation around the world in regime stability over the last century, from the single, continuous regimes of the United States and the United Kingdom to the eight regimes Nigeria has seen.

Each regime is based at least partially on a political ideology that is usually explicitly stated and often quite elaborately developed. Political ideologies, at their core, are about answering the question, What is the appropriate relationship between the state and its people? Ideologies make normative claims about who should be allowed to participate in politics, how they should participate, and how much power they should have. We will focus on major political ideologies that have been used to underpin regimes over the last century. As we discuss each ideology, we stress the way it conceives of the appropriate relationship between a state and the people over whom it claims sovereignty. We also examine the ways in which

COUNTRY AND CONCEPT
Modern Regimes

Country	Current regime	Year established	Number of regimes in 20th and 21st centuries	Freedom House score
Brazil	Liberal democracy	1989	5	Free
China	"Communist" modernizing authoritarian	1949: People's Republic established	3	Not free
Germany	Liberal democracy	1945: Federal Republic of Germany established 1991: Reunited with German Democratic Republic	4	Free
India	Liberal democracy	1947: Independence	2	Free
Iran	Theocracy	1979: Islamic Republic proclaimed	4	Not free
Japan	Liberal democracy	1947	2	Free
Mexico	Liberal democracy	2000: First free and fair election	3	Free
Nigeria	Democracy (though with neopatrimonial elements)	1999	8	Partly free
Russia	Semi-authoritarian	1993: Constitution promulgated	3	Not free
United Kingdom	Liberal democracy	1688: Glorious Revolution	1	Free
United States	Liberal democracy	1789	1	Free

regimes diverge from their ideological justifications because no regime operates exactly as its ideology claims.

CITIZENS AND CIVIL SOCIETY

Before we begin discussing any of this, however, it is helpful to understand a little bit more about the historical development of the "people" over whom modern states claim sovereignty. Ideas about how the people stand in relation to the state have evolved in tandem with the modern state described in chapter 2. At the most basic level, a **citizen** is a member of a political community or state. Notice that a citizen is more than

citizen
A member of a political community or state with certain rights and duties

an inhabitant within a state's borders. An inhabitant may be a member of a physical community, but a citizen inhabits a political community that places her in a relationship with the state. In the modern world, everyone needs to be "from" somewhere. It is almost inconceivable (although it does happen) to be a "man without a country." By this minimal definition, everyone is considered a citizen of some state.

The word *citizen,* however, is much more complex than this simple definition suggests. Up until about two or three hundred years ago, most Europeans would have thought of themselves as "subjects" of their monarchs, not citizens of states. Most people had little say in their relationship with the state; their side of that relationship consisted primarily of duty and obedience. The very nature of the absolutist state meant that few mechanisms existed to protect subjects and enable them to claim things as their "rights." If the king wanted your land or decided to throw you in jail as a possible conspirator, no court could or would overrule him.

This began to change with the transition to the modern state. As the state was separated from the person of the monarch and its apparatus was modernized, states gained both the ability and the need to make their people more than just subjects. The concept of sovereignty, like the state itself, was divorced from the person of the sovereign, and many European philosophers and political leaders began to toy with the idea that sovereignty could lie with the people as a whole (or some portion, such as male landowners) rather than with a sovereign monarch. This was an important step in the development of the concept of modern citizenship: citizens, unlike subjects, were inhabitants of states that claimed that sovereignty resided with the people. Thus, after the French Revolution overthrew the absolutist *ancien régime,* people addressed one another as "citizen."

Marianne is a key symbol of France, created during the French Revolution to represent liberty and reason. Here, she is depicted at the storming of the Bastille prison on July 14, 1789, a key event in the revolution, which helped usher in liberalism and the modern conception of citizenship in Europe.

Over time, as the modern state developed, people began to associate a complex set of rights with the concept of citizenship. In the mid-twentieth century, the philosopher T. H. Marshall (1963) usefully categorized the rights of citizenship into three areas: civil, political, and social. **Civil rights** guarantee individual freedom and equal, just, and fair treatment by the state. Examples include the right to equal treatment under the law, habeas corpus, and freedom of expression and worship. **Political rights** are those associated with political participation: the right to vote, form political associations, run for office, or otherwise participate in political activity. **Social rights** are those related to basic well-being and socioeconomic

civil rights
Those rights that guarantee individual freedom as well as equal, just, and fair treatment by the state

political rights
Those rights associated with active political participation, for example, to free association, voting, and running for office

social rights
Those rights related to basic well-being and socioeconomic equality

New citizens take the oath of citizenship in Canada. As citizens, rather than just residents, they will enjoy many civil, political, and social rights. Canadians have basically the same civil and political rights as Americans.

Web link:
CIVICUS, Enabling Civil Society Index

Web link:
CIVICUS 2013 Report on Civil Society

Video link:
Civil society at crossroads

equality, such as public education, pensions, or national health care. Marshall believed that modern citizenship included basic legal (civil) status in society and protection from the state as well as the right to actively participate in the political process. He argued that full citizenship also requires enough socioeconomic equality to make the civil and political equality of citizenship meaningful. Modern conceptions of citizenship go beyond just the focus on rights, however; others stress the participatory role of citizens in the political community, the obligations of citizenship, or citizenship as an identity. A citizen, then, is a member of a political community with certain rights, perhaps some obligations to the larger community as well, and ideally (for most theorists) an active participant in that community.

Participation, of course, typically happens in organized groups of one sort or another, what we call "civil society." Like citizenship, civil society in Europe developed in conjunction with the modern state. We defined civil society in chapter 1 as the sphere of organized, nongovernmental, nonviolent activity by groups larger than individual families or firms. Absolutist states would not have conceived of such a realm of society separate from the state itself, for what would this have meant? If a monarch could dispose of lands and goods, grant monopolies on tax collection, and determine which religion the realm would follow, what could "society" mean apart from that? The rise of religious pluralism and of modern, capitalist economies alongside the modern state meant that there were now areas of social life outside the immediate control of the state, and the gradual evolution of civil and political rights made it possible for individuals to organize themselves into new groups for all kinds of purposes, including political action.

This history should not be romanticized or thought of as a linear movement toward modern, democratic citizenship. Change was neither inevitable nor always positive. The same changes that gave us the modern state, however, also gave us the modern concept of the citizen and the modern concept of an independent civil society in which citizens could organize collectively for all sorts of purposes, from religious worship to charitable activity to political action.

Today, ideas of citizenship and civil society are connected to regime claims to legitimacy via the concept of "popular sovereignty." Recall that a claim to legitimacy is a key characteristic of modern states: all modern regimes make some claim to legitimacy, and most do so based on representing and speaking on behalf of "the people." Although it is a distinctly European and liberal democratic notion, the idea of popular sovereignty has deeply influenced all subsequent political ideologies. Even dictators claim to be working on behalf of the citizenry. They may claim that they must deny certain rights in the short term to benefit society as a whole in the long term (or, in the case of theocracy, that God has willed certain exceptions to citizens' rights), but they still lay some claim to working toward the well-being of the citizens.

Some argue that a "postnational" citizenship is now emerging as the latest chapter in this history, especially in the European Union (EU) (Lister and Pia 2008). We can see this in several major institutions around the world: the rights of citizenship are embedded in key UN documents, the International Criminal Court in the Hague exists to enforce those rights on behalf of the world community, the EU has a "social charter" that sets standards for treatment of citizens in all EU countries, and most EU members have a common immigration policy that allows people to travel freely within the union as if they were travelling in only one country. In terms of participation, as international organizations such as the World Trade Organization become more important, citizens are forming international groups to try to influence those policies. Keck and Sikkink (1998) called this phenomenon "transnational civil society." These new trends are undoubtedly important and likely to grow, but for now almost all citizenship in terms of core rights still resides within the nation-state. Even in the EU, one gains "European" citizenship only via citizenship in a member state.

Web link:
The rights of EU citizens

In practice, regimes vary enormously in their relationships to both citizens' rights and civil society. Virtually no country fully provides all three types of rights described by Marshall. Similarly, the manifestation of civil society ranges from flourishing, lively groups of independently organized citizens, like the many interest groups and political movements in the United States or Europe, to highly controlled or actively repressed groups, such as the government-controlled labor union in China. In short, modern citizens and civil society are much like the modern state: the ideas represent an ideal type but are not universally implemented in contemporary societies. By looking at regimes' political ideologies, we can learn how they attempt to justify and legitimize their various relationships with their citizens.

REGIMES, IDEOLOGIES, AND CITIZENS

Not all political ideologies have been embodied in regimes, but every regime has some sort of ideology that attempts to justify its existence in the eyes of its

Major Political Ideologies and Regime Types

LIBERAL DEMOCRACY

ORIGINS   Social contract theory. Legitimate governments form when free and independent individuals join in a contract to permit representatives to govern over them.

KEY IDEA   Individuals are free and autonomous, with natural rights.

Government must preserve the core liberties—life, liberty, and property—possessed by all free individuals.

CHARACTERISTICS   Representative democracy. Citizens have direct control, and leaders can be removed.

Separation of powers, federalism, and social citizenship supplement, but are not essential to, legitimate government.

WHO HAS POWER   Legislature.

COMMUNISM

ORIGINS   Marxism. Ruling class oppresses other classes, based on mode of production. Historical materialism means that material (economic) forces are the prime movers of history and politics.

KEY IDEA   Proletariat will lead socialist revolution. Socialist society after revolution will be ruled as a dictatorship of the proletariat over other classes; will eventually create classless, communist society in which class oppression ends.

CHARACTERISTICS   Lenin believed that the vanguard party can lead socialist revolution in interests of present and future proletariat. Vanguard party rules socialist society using democratic centralism and is justified in oppressing classes that oppose it.

WHO HAS POWER   Vanguard party now; proletariat later.

FASCISM

ORIGINS   Organic conception of society. Society is akin to a living organism rather than a set of disparate groups and individuals.

KEY IDEA   Rejects materialism and rationality; relies instead on "spiritual attitude."

The state creates the nation, a "higher personality"; intensely nationalistic.

Corporatism. The state recognizes only one entity to lead each group in society (for example, an official trade union).

CHARACTERISTICS   The state is at the head of the corporate body. It is all-embracing, and outside of it no human or spiritual values can exist. "Accepts the individual only in so far as his interests coincide with those of the State" (Benito Mussolini, 1935).

WHO HAS POWER   A supreme leader.

MODERNIZING AUTHORITARIANISM

ORIGINS End of colonialism and desire to develop; technocratic legitimacy.

KEY IDEA Modernization theory. Postcolonial societies must go through the same process to develop as the West did. Development requires national unity; democracy would interfere with unity.

CHARACTERISTICS Four institutional forms: one-party regimes, military regimes, bureaucratic-authoritarian regimes, and personalist regimes. Neopatrimonial authority is common.

WHO HAS POWER A modern elite—a relatively few, highly educated people—who are capable of modernizing or "developing" the country; the claim to rule based on special knowledge is technocratic legitimacy.

SEMI-AUTHORITARIANISM

ORIGINS Primarily failed transitions to democracy.

KEY IDEA Legitimacy is based on a combination of liberal democratic and modernizing authoritarian ideologies.

CHARACTERISTICS Allows limited freedoms of expression and association.

Allows limited political opposition to hold some elected offices but ensures ruling party/leader holds most power.

Informal institutions are often more important than formal institutions.

Contradictions exist between democratic and authoritarian elements.

WHO HAS POWER Ruling party.

THEOCRACY

ORIGINS Ancient religious beliefs.

KEY IDEA Rule is by divine inspiration or divine right.

CHARACTERISTICS Islamist version:

- *Islamism*. Islamic law, as revealed by God to the Prophet Mohammed, can and should provide the basis for government in Muslim communities.
- *Ijtihad*. The belief that Muslims should read and interpret the original Islamic texts for themselves, not simply follow traditional religious leaders and beliefs.
- *Sharia*. Muslim law should be the law of society for all Muslims.

WHO HAS POWER God is sovereign, not the people.

citizens and the world. Regimes are much more than just the legal and institutional embodiments of their ideologies, however. Although all regimes have formal rules and institutions that reflect, at least to some extent, their ideological claims to legitimacy, they also have informal rules and institutions, and these may conflict with their ideological claims. Informal institutions may be more important than formal ones; rulers may not actually believe the ideology they proclaim; or the realities of being in power, of trying to govern a complex society, may necessitate ideological modifications. As we noted in chapter 2, weak states in particular are characterized by relatively weak formal institutions. In these states, knowing the informal rules and institutions at work may be more important to understanding how their regimes actually function than knowing the formal institutions embodied in their constitutions.

The major regime types we detail in this chapter include some in which the official ideology and related formal institutions represent the most important elements of a regime, as well as others in which informal institutions are more important. Even where informal institutions predominate, though, ideologies are important. The major political ideologies have defined the terms of the most important political debates of the past century: liberal democracy versus communism versus fascism versus theocracy. (For a description of the major ideologies, see the "Major Political Ideologies and Regimes" box on page 104.) Most regimes have come to power in the name of one or another of the ideologies outlined below, and many have made serious efforts to rule along the lines prescribed by them. While liberal democracy is certainly not universally accepted, it has become powerful enough that all regimes, implicitly or explicitly, must respond to its claims; therefore, we turn to it first.

Liberal Democracy

Democracy means different things to different people: many people find it hard to define, yet they think they know it when they see it. The word literally means rule by the *demos,* or the people, but that doesn't tell us very much. In this book, we will follow the main convention in comparative politics and use a "minimal definition" of the term, typically referred to as *liberal democracy.* The two parts of the phrase are stated together so frequently that in many people's minds they have become one. The distinction between the two, however, is important to understanding both the development of liberal democracy and current debates over its expansion around the world, which we discuss in subsequent chapters.

Liberalism, the predecessor of liberal democracy, arose in the sixteenth and seventeenth centuries amidst the religious wars in England and the later revolution in France. The key liberal thinkers of the period created a model of political philosophy known as **social contract theory.** Although there are many variations, all social contract theories begin from the premise that legitimate governments are formed when free and autonomous individuals join in a contract to permit representatives to govern over them in their common interests. The originators of this idea, Thomas Hobbes and John Locke in England and the Baron de Montesquieu and Jean-Jacques Rousseau in France, started from a new and innovative assumption: all citizens should

social contract theory
Philosophical approach underlying liberalism that begins from the premise that legitimate governments are formed when free and independent individuals join in a contract to permit representatives to govern over them in their common interests

be considered free and equal. They theorized an original "state of nature" in which all men (and they meant men—women weren't included until much later) lived freely and equally with no one ruling over them. They argued that the only government that could be justified was one that men living in such a state of nature would freely choose.

Beginning with Locke, all social contract theorists ultimately came to the same basic conclusion about what such a freely chosen government would look like. Locke argued that in the state of nature, government would only arise if it helped preserve the core liberties of all free men: life, liberty, and property (a phrase Thomas Jefferson later adopted and modified into "life, liberty and the pursuit of happiness" in the Declaration of Independence). This became the central doctrine of liberalism: a regime is only justified if it preserves and protects the core liberties of autonomous, free, and equal individuals. A state can only infringe on these liberties in very particular circumstances, such as when an action is essential for the well-being of all or when a particular citizen has denied others their rights. Preservation of rights is essential and severely limits what governments can do.

Key Characteristics of Liberal Democracy The classical liberal doctrine on the preservation of rights justifies limited government to enhance individual freedoms, but it says nothing about how a government will come to power or make decisions. Liberals argued that men in a state of nature would desire a government over which they had some direct control, with leaders they could remove from office if necessary, as protection against a state trying to destroy basic liberties. The idea of representative democracy was thus born and justified. By voting, citizens would choose the government that would rule over them. Those chosen would be in office for a limited period, with some mechanism for removal if necessary.

With elected representatives, some type of legislature would be essential and central to government. This would be a body in which elected officials would debate and decide the important issues of the day. While kings and courts had long existed in Europe as the executive and judicial branches, liberals argued that the most important branch ought to be the legislative, the body of elected representatives of free and equal citizens. Montesquieu added the idea of giving each branch of government independent powers as a way to divide and thereby further limit the state overall. (This doctrine, adopted in the United States but not in the United Kingdom, is not essential to liberal democracy but is rather an extension of the liberal ideal of limited government.)

For all of their forward thinking about equality and limited government, most liberals still conceived of the citizens to which these concepts applied as male property owners only (one of the rare exceptions was the nineteenth-century philosopher John Stuart Mill). They argued that while everyone had some basic civil rights, only men who owned property were adequately mature, rational, and independent of the whims of others to be given the right to vote and participate in governing. Restricting full citizenship to this group meant that all citizens could be considered equal: different men held different amounts of property and had different abilities, but compared with the rest of society they were roughly similar. It was not long before groups not initially granted full citizenship, such as men without property, women, and racial minorities, began asking why they weren't considered as free and autonomous as anybody else. This question produced the largest political struggles of the nineteenth and twentieth centuries in Europe and the United States, struggles to fully democratize liberalism. As citizenship slowly expanded to include more and more groups, real inequality among citizens increasingly began to conflict with the proposition that "all men [and later, all people] are created equal."

Modern liberal democratic regimes arose from this history. Leaders in these regimes justify their actions by claiming to preserve and protect core civil and political liberties: freedom from government intervention in private lives (except under clearly defined and limited circumstances), freedom of religious practice, freedom of expression, freedom of association, and the rights to vote and hold office. Citizens in a liberal democracy use these freedoms to create civil society, though civil society's strength, organization, and daily relationship with the state vary from country to country (we discuss this in detail in chapter 7). All liberal democracies are characterized by some system of elections by which voters, now defined almost universally as all adult citizens (certain categories of citizens, however, are still excluded: one of the largest is ex-felons, prevented from voting in many U.S. states), choose key members of the government, who serve limited terms and may be removed. Some liberal democracies include other safeguards, such as separation of powers. Some include the provision of extensive government services to attempt to achieve something closer to equal social citizenship. The debate continues, of course, over how much power liberal freedoms actually give to the average citizen vis-à-vis the elite. Marxists, among others, argue that liberal rights to vote and join organizations do not give any real power to the average citizen. They and other elite theorists contend that elites such as major business leaders gain disproportionate influence in any "democracy" and influence government policy in their favor, often against the interests of average citizens, who have no real recourse in spite of the rights liberalism provides.

Political scientist Robert Dahl captured the essentials of the liberal democratic system of government by noting the eight key guarantees it provides: freedom of association, freedom of expression, the right to vote, broad citizen eligibility for public office, the right of political leaders to compete for support, alternative sources of information, free and fair elections, and institutions that make government policies depend on votes and other forms of citizen preferences. We include these in our working definition of **liberal democracy.**

Video link:
Liberal democracy and its limits

liberal democracy
A system of government that provides eight key guarantees, including freedoms to enable citizen participation in the political process and institutions that make government policies depend on votes and other forms of citizen preferences

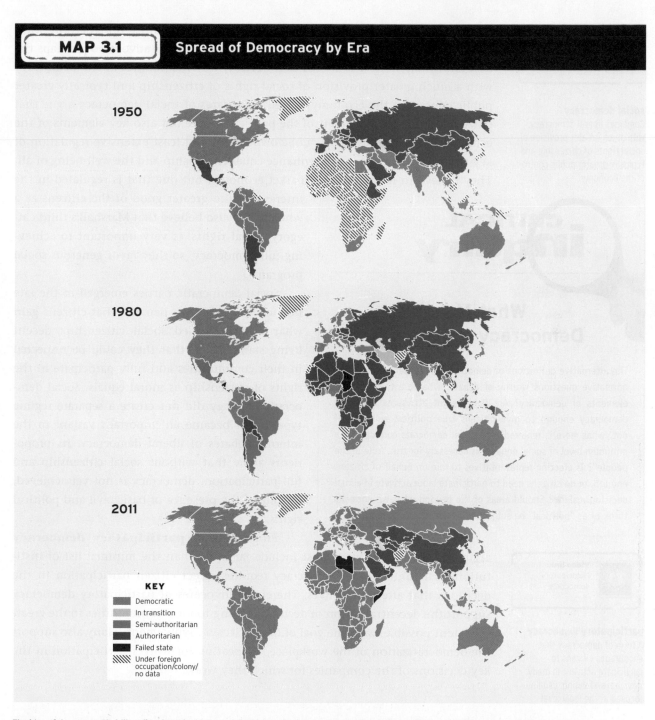

| MAP 3.1 | Spread of Democracy by Era |

1950

1980

2011

KEY

- Democratic
- In transition
- Semi-authoritarian
- Authoritarian
- Failed state
- Under foreign occupation/colony/ no data

The idea of democracy that liberalism launched has spread widely, especially in recent years. Between 1950 and 1980, most colonial rule came to an end, but democracy did not spread very far. By 2011, however, many more countries had become democratic, and many authoritarian regimes had become somewhat more open semi-authoritarian regimes that allowed some limited political competition, as we discuss later in this chapter. Only a relative handful of purely authoritarian regimes remain.

Source: Data from Polity IV Project: Political Regime Characteristics and Transitions, 1800–2009 (http://www.systemicpeace.org/polity/polity4.htm). The "Polity" variable employed, with the following coding by the authors: democracy (6–10); semi-authoritarian, (-5–5); authoritarian, (-10–-6).

social democracy
Combines liberal democracy
with much greater provision of
social rights of citizenship and
typically greater public control
of the economy

What Makes a Democracy a Democracy?

The alternative definitions of democracy raise a set of important normative questions worthy of debate: What are the essential elements of democracy? Are Dahl's eight attributes of liberal democracy enough to give citizens true political equality? If not, what more is required? Are social democrats correct that a minimum level of social equality is necessary for true "rule of the people"? Is electing representatives to rule on behalf of citizens enough, or do citizens need to participate more actively in actual decision making? Should areas of life beyond what we normally think of as "political" be subject to democratic control as well?

participatory democracy
A form of democracy that
encourages citizens to
participate actively, in many
ways beyond voting; usually
focused at the local level

Varieties of Democracy Liberal democracy is certainly not the only form of democracy that democratic theorists have imagined or advocated. Perhaps the best known alternative is **social democracy,** which combines liberal democracy with a much greater provision of social rights of citizenship and typically greater public control of the economy as well. Advocates of social democracy argue that citizens should not only control the political sphere but also key elements of the economic sphere. They favor public ownership or at least extensive regulation of key sectors of the economy to enhance equal citizenship and the well-being of all. They believe in maintaining a market economy, but one that is regulated in the interests of the greater good of the citizens as a whole. They also believe that Marshall's third category, social rights, is very important to achieving full democracy, so they favor generous social programs.

Social democratic parties emerged in the late nineteenth century to demand that citizens gain what Marshall called social citizenship: decent living standards so that they could be respected in their communities and fully participate in the rights of citizenship as moral equals. Social democratic ideology did not create a separate regime type, but it became an important variant in the internal debates of liberal democracy. Its proponents argue that without social citizenship and full participation, democracy is not yet achieved, in spite of the presence of basic civil and political rights.

Proponents of **participatory democracy** argue that real democracy must include far more than the minimal list of institutional guarantees. Real democracy requires direct citizen participation in the decisions that affect their lives. Therefore, advocates of participatory democracy support the decentralization of decision making to local communities to the greatest extent possible, with the goal of direct citizen involvement. Many also support the democratization of the workplace, advocating for worker participation in the key decisions of the companies for which they work.

UNITED KINGDOM: "CRADLE OF DEMOCRACY"

- **REGIME**
  First liberal democratic regime

- **CITIZEN AND STATE**
  Gradual but contentious expansion of citizens' rights in nineteenth and early twentieth centuries

- **CLAIM TO LEGITIMACY**
  Parliamentary sovereignty

- **RECENT TRENDS**
  Constitutional reforms in the new millennium, devolution and Supreme Court

Many of the most important developments in the history of liberal democracy occurred in the United Kingdom (UK), or England before it became the UK. The core ideas of limiting a sovereign's power and creating what was called a parliament (from the French word *parler*, meaning to talk) arose long before they were codified in the philosophy of Locke and others. The earliest important milestone was the Magna Carta, signed by King John in 1215 under pressure from feudal lords. It included the first right to trial by peers, guaranteed the freedom of the (Catholic) church from monarchical intervention, created an assembly of twenty-five barons (chosen by all the barons of England) that became the first parliament, and guaranteed nobles the right to be called together to discuss any significant new taxes. All of these rights and guarantees were strictly designed to preserve the dominance of the nobility, but they were a significant first step in limiting the monarch's individual power.

Four centuries later, religious divisions between Catholics and Protestants led to the English civil war that removed the king but ended in a dictatorship under Oliver Cromwell. Cromwell was eventually overthrown and the monarchy restored, but Locke developed his ideas largely in reaction to the deep religious divisions and violence of the civil war. The Glorious Revolution of 1688 saw Parliament's bloodless removal of King James II from the throne and the installation of a new king and queen, a dramatic expansion of parliamentary power over the monarch. The following year, Parliament passed a Bill of Rights that substantially expanded the rights of citizenship. From that point forward, Parliament gained increasing power vis-à-vis the monarchy, and the power of the prime minister—an individual appointed by the king but who worked closely with Parliament—grew significantly.

The growing power of the elected Parliament was significant, but political citizenship was still restricted primarily to men with substantial property holdings, who constituted less than 5 percent of the population. The nineteenth century saw significant challenges to this system: the franchise was extended first to the growing middle class in 1832 (though the electorate remained all male and grew only to about 7 percent of the population) and then to most adult males via reforms in 1867 and 1884. A movement for women's suffrage emerged by the mid-nineteenth century, but not until 1918 were

The modernistic Scottish Parliament building in Edinburgh (left) is a sharp contrast to the stately British Parliament building in London (right). Britain devolved certain powers to the newly created Scottish and Welsh Parliaments in 1997, a major change to Britain's liberal democratic regime. The ruling party in Scotland intends to hold a referendum in September 2014 on the question of declaring full independence from Great Britain.

women thirty years of age and older (later lowered to twenty-one) given the right to vote. None of this expansion of political citizenship occurred easily. Large-scale pressure from civil society was necessary to achieve each reform. Liberal rights expanded, but only when those without them demanded (vociferously, and sometimes violently) that they be included in full citizenship.

The British model of liberal democracy is unusual, in part because of its history. No equivalent of the American or French Revolution occurred to cause a definitive break from monarchy and the establishment of democracy. The development of the liberal democratic regime in Britain was much more gradual. No unified, written British constitution exists, though many of the elements of a constitution—the fundamental rules of how the regime works—are written down in various laws passed by Parliament. In the absence of a single constitution, British democracy is based on the concept of **parliamentary sovereignty,** which holds that Parliament is supreme in all matters. Members can write any law they choose via majority vote. Rights are preserved only by a collective consensus that Parliament should not reverse them. This is a great example of a powerful but *informal* political institution, a set of implicit rules and norms that are not violated even though in theory they could be. Political culture theorists would explain this institution by pointing to British cultural values. Institutionalists might suggest that the institution, established originally in the Bill of Rights of 1689, has served citizens' interests well and therefore is preserved. In any case, the system has continued to operate with only limited change for more than three centuries.

The two most important recent changes to Britain's democratic regime have addressed decentralization of power from Parliament to regional governments and the judiciary. In 1997 Prime Minister Tony Blair and his Labour Party government allowed devolution of some powers (such as over education and social services) to newly created Scottish and Welsh parliaments, which had ceased to exist when the two kingdoms were integrated into the United Kingdom centuries earlier. It was the biggest decentralization of power since the United Kingdom was created. Unlike the constitutionally guaranteed federalist system that grants powers to the states in the United States, devolution was voted on by the British Parliament, which in theory could vote to reverse it. Political pressure, however, is pushing in the other direction; the Scottish National Party, the governing party in Scotland, plans to hold a referendum in 2014 on the question of Scotland becoming a completely independent country. In 2005 the Blair

parliamentary sovereignty
Parliament is supreme in all matters; key example is the United Kingdom

government also created a freestanding Supreme Court as a final court of appeals, a job that had previously been done by the unelected House of Lords in Parliament. Though it lacks the power to reverse acts of Parliament that the U.S. Supreme Court has vis-à-vis Congress, its existence is another step in reducing the power of Britain's Parliament.

In the twentieth century, Britain's democracy also wrestled with the notion of social rights, for even after civil and political rights were made universal, socioeconomic inequality remained great. After World War II, based on a sense that all citizens had shared the sacrifices necessary to win the war and therefore should share in the rewards, the British government expanded its welfare state extensively. This included the National Health Service, which essentially made access to health care a universal right, plus other universal benefits such as an annual "child allowance" from the government for all parents raising children. New rules instituted in 2013 by the government of Prime Minister David Cameron ended the universality of the child allowance, restricting it primarily to parents with incomes of less than 50,000 British pounds (about $75,000). The debate over what should and should not be a social right in Britain's liberal democracy continues.

Web link: Debate about benefits in Great Britain

CASE Summary Britain's unusual liberal democracy has evolved slowly, and often contentiously, over centuries. Citizenship rights have expanded to include all adult citizens despite the absence of a single, written constitution. Parliamentary sovereignty gives Britain an unusually centralized form of democracy (which we explore in detail in chapter 6) but one that has preserved and expanded basic liberal rights for a very long time. Like all liberal democracies, Britain continues to debate how much the power of the central government ought to be limited and how universal social rights should be.

CASE Questions

1. What does the UK case teach us about the process of establishing and expanding liberal rights?
2. The UK's regime is unusual among liberal democracies in that it doesn't have a written constitution. Look back at the core tenets of liberal democracy: Does the UK regime seem to qualify fully as a liberal democracy? Why or why not?

Communism

The first and most influential ideological alternative to liberal democracy was communism, which became the basis for regimes in Russia, China, and a number of other countries. Karl Marx, the originator of communism, grounded his philosophy on what he called **historical materialism,** the assertion that material (economic) forces are the prime movers of history and politics. He believed that to understand politics, one must first understand the economic structure of a society and the economic interests that arise from it. As the material forces in the society—technology, raw materials, and

historical materialism
The assumption that material forces are the prime movers of history and politics; a key philosophical tenet of Marxism

the way they are combined to make goods—change, so too will the political, social, and ideological systems. Feudalism produced all-powerful lords and monarchs, with religious sanction from the church as the chief ideological justification, to keep the peasants in their place producing a surplus for the lords. The shift to capitalism produced liberalism, in which political power was no longer vested in the landed aristocracy but was instead given to all men of property. This allowed the rising bourgeoisie, the owners of capital, to gain political power. Capitalism requires labor that is paid a wage and can move from place to place (see chapter 5 for more on capitalism), so the feudal system that required peasants to stay on the land where they were born was abolished, and many peasants were forced off their land to work for a daily wage in cities.

Liberal democracy, according to Marx, is the political and ideological shell that allows capitalism to work and that serves the interests of the bourgeoisie, capitalism's ruling class. When Marx was developing his ideas, only men of property had full political rights in most countries. Even where those rights had expanded to others, as in the United States by the 1830s, Marx argued that this was only a charade. He called liberal rights "equal rights for unequal people," arguing that where workers did have the vote, it was virtually meaningless because those with wealth were the only ones with any real power. Civil society, he argued, was a realm dominated by capitalists as well, a sphere created to give capitalists independence from the state and a means by which they could control the state.

mode of production
In Marxist theory, the economic system in any given historical era; feudalism and capitalism in the last millennium in Europe

Marx saw the transition from one **mode of production** to another, such as from feudalism to capitalism, as a process of **social revolution.** He argued that all modes of production ultimately create contradictions they cannot overcome, leading to revolution. Capitalism, he believed, would be characterized by an ever greater division between the bourgeoisie and the proletariat, workers who must sell their labor for a wage to survive. Marx believed that as more and more wealth and power accrued in the hands of capitalists, the proletariat would become so poor that they would not be able to consume all of capitalism's products, creating an economic crisis that would usher in a new era of social revolution. Just as the liberal revolutions had been led by the bourgeoisie and had established liberal democracy, the next revolutions would be communist revolutions led by the proletariat—what Marx called the "specter haunting Europe" in *The Communist Manifesto* (1848/1888). Marx believed this revolution was inevitable and that it was the job of the communist movement to recognize when and where social revolutions were emerging and bring them to fruition to create a new and better society and political system.

social revolution
In Marxist theory, the transition from one mode of production to another; Marxist understanding of revolution

The communist society that Marx believed would emerge from these revolutions would abolish class distinctions and collectively own the means of production. All people (or at least men—Marx was no more feminist than most other nineteenth-century philosophers) would be paid the same amount for the same work, and everyone would have to work. This he saw as the first stage of communism, which he also called socialism. He was quite explicit about who would rule during this stage: the **dictatorship of the proletariat,** an absolute rule by workers as a class over all other classes. This dictatorship was not of one man but of the entire class, which would control and

dictatorship of the proletariat
In the first stage of communism in Marxist thought, characterized by absolute rule by workers as a class over all other classes

ultimately eliminate all other classes. Civil society distinct from this workers' state would no longer be needed. This was justified in Marx's view because all governments, including all liberal democracies, have been class dictatorships; liberal democracies are simply dictatorships of the bourgeoisie. As this socialist society developed, everyone eventually would become equal in the sense of all being part of the proletariat. At that point, the second, higher stage of communism would develop in which no state would be necessary because no class divisions would exist, and all dictatorships would end.

Marx did not write in detail about what this communist society and its government would look like, in part because he did not believe in prescription and speculation about the future. Philosophically, he believed that communism was both inevitable and the final stage of human historical evolution. Just as political systems and ideologies are the product of economic forces, Marx believed human nature was as well. With class division and exploitation eliminated, he believed that human nature itself would change from being self-interested and greedy under capitalism to being what he viewed as more fully human under communism. This would facilitate the creation of his ultimate and, he believed, inevitable goal of a communist utopia. Critics dispute this utopian goal and therefore the means to achieve it. Liberals reject the notion that any end, whether feasible or not, justifies violating the fundamental rights of any individual or group, as would occur under the dictatorship of the proletariat. They fear instead that a communist state would simply become a dictatorship of an individual or small group over all of society. Postmodern theorists have argued that Marxism, or any theory claiming certainty about the "laws" of human history, inevitably will result in a totalitarian state restricting all freedoms in the name of achieving an unreachable utopia. These themes are illustrated well in the history of communism in Russia.

CASE Study

RUSSIA: THE FIRST SELF-PROCLAIMED COMMUNIST REGIME

Marx was an active revolutionary for most of his life, but he did not live to see a communist revolution succeed. Based on his analysis of capitalism, he believed the revolution would start in the wealthiest and most advanced capitalist societies, such as the United Kingdom, Germany, and France. Russia at the

- **REGIME**
  Communist; totalitarian under Stalin; finally, bureaucratic socialism with battles for resources behind the scenes

- **CITIZEN AND STATE**
  Citizenship only for those who accepted the party's rule

- **CLAIM TO LEGITIMACY**
  Vanguard party ruling on behalf of proletariat

- **KEY INSTITUTIONS**
  Decision making in soviets, with final authority in politburo

- **CONTEXT**
Revolution in the "wrong country"

vanguard party
Vladimir Lenin's concept of a small party that claims legitimacy to rule based on its understanding of Marxist theory and its ability to represent the interests of the proletariat before they are a majority of the populace

Marx thought Russia was not ready for communism, but Vladimir Lenin (above) led a revolution there. He modified Marxist doctrine to adapt it to Russian circumstances and suggested that a vanguard party of committed revolutionaries could lead a precapitalist, agrarian nation into communism.

democratic centralism
The organization of a ruling party, primarily in communist regimes, in which lower organs of a party and state vote on issues and individuals to represent them at higher levels; the highest level makes final decisions that all must obey

turn of the twentieth century, however, was still primarily rural, with growing multinational investment controlled by foreigners and an unstable and oppressive political system. The liberal, bourgeois revolution, let alone the socialist one, had yet to happen there. In fact, late in his life Marx wrote to Russian revolutionaries, telling them to wait for the revolutions in the wealthier parts of Europe before pursuing their own socialist dreams.

Vladimir Lenin never met Marx; he did, however, read and admire his writings, and by the late nineteenth century, shortly after Marx's death, Lenin had become a committed communist revolutionary. As Russians writhed in the throes of World War I, a disastrous and unpopular war for them, Lenin led his forces to victory in the October Revolution of 1917 and created the first self-proclaimed Communist regime.

Lenin knew that according to Marx, Russia was not ripe for revolution, so to legitimize his regime, Lenin modified Marx's political theories. He argued that where capitalism had not developed sufficiently to produce the economic crisis and socialist revolution, a committed band of revolutionaries, a **vanguard party,** could still lead a revolution. This party would take power and rule on behalf of the proletariat until the country was fully industrialized and therefore fully proletarian. Socialism, the first stage of communism, would last longer than Marx had envisioned, but the revolution could occur sooner. Lenin also believed that once the revolution succeeded in Russia, the proletariat of the wealthier European countries would see the possibility of a proletarian regime and rise up to create their own. He fully expected the communist revolution to spread quickly across Europe and create a set of socialist regimes that would build communism together.

Once in power, and seeing that the revolution was not going to spread rapidly across Europe, Lenin had to figure out how the Soviet Union would survive as the lone socialist state. The dictatorship of the proletariat would, for the time being, be the dictatorship of the single vanguard party, which was justified in ruthlessly suppressing all opposition that represented other class interests, especially the nobility and bourgeoisie of prerevolutionary Russia. The party thus became the sole representative of the people, and the regime it created was based on Lenin's idea of **democratic centralism,** under which lower organs of the party and state would vote on issues and individuals to represent them at higher levels; ultimately individuals at the top level would make final, binding decisions. Once these decisions were made, all lower levels were expected to follow orders without question. In practice, those at the top controlled virtually all power, allowing only ideas and people they already had approved to rise through the hierarchy.

The regime consisted of a set of **soviets,** or legislative bodies, which made decisions at all levels. After gaining full control of the prerevolutionary Russian empire and some additional territories, the new regime and state were named the Union of Soviet Socialist Republics (USSR). Officially, the soviet was the decision-making body at each level of the regime, from the village to the province to the national state, but in reality each soviet was tightly controlled by the Communist Party, which was the only legal party to which any politically active person or official had to belong. At the top of the entire system was the **politburo,** the party's chief decision-making organ. This small, mostly male group collectively and secretly selected each new general secretary of the party. The general secretaries were the country's most powerful rulers, and most served in that position until death.

Lenin came to recognize by 1921 that while central state control of the government had merit, similar control of the economy was hurting production, especially in agriculture, the largest sector of the economy. Once again, ideological modification seemed essential. In response, he created the New Economic Policy, under which state control of the economy was partially loosened. Lenin died from a stroke at a relatively young age only three years later.

After a five-year succession struggle, Joseph Stalin came to power and radically reversed Lenin's economic policies. Stalin launched a plan to rapidly institute state control of the economy, taking ownership of virtually all land and extracting huge surpluses from agriculture to build industry. The result was rapid industrialization that transformed the Soviet Union from a poor agricultural country into an industrial powerhouse and superpower by World War II. Those who opposed Stalin's policies were ruthlessly suppressed; estimates of deaths under his reign range from two to twenty million. He created a **totalitarian regime** that he tightly controlled, eliminating all vestiges of civil society.

Stalin's successors, Nikita Khrushchev (1956–1964) and Leonid Brezhnev (1964–1982), reduced aspects of Stalin's reign of terror and created what became an oppressive but predictable communist system. Political scientists of the time debated extensively how centralized or pluralist this regime was. While it certainly was not pluralist in the democratic sense of the term, many observers argued that factions jockeyed for power and influence behind the scenes. Understanding how the regime actually functioned required far more than just understanding the Leninist beliefs on which it was founded. A new subfield of comparative politics emerged called "Kremlinology" in which experts looked for informal signs of who had real power. For instance, which officials were standing or sitting closest to the top leaders indicated who had the most influence at a particular moment. Behind the façade of democratic centralism and the complete absence of public debate, numerous factions battled to gain resources and power.

With Brezhnev's death, a new generation of leadership emerged in the person of Mikhail Gorbachev (1985–1991). Stalin's policies had rapidly industrialized the

soviets
Legislative bodies in the Communist regime of the Soviet Union

Video link: Khan Academy video on communism

politburo
The chief decision-making organ in a communist party; China's politburo is a key example

totalitarian regime
A regime that controls virtually all aspects of society and eliminates all vestiges of civil society; Germany under Hitler and the Soviet Union under Stalin are key examples

Video link: Russia Today, Russia remembers Stalin's purges

economy, but the inefficiencies of central state control had grown over time, and the wealth and productivity of the Soviet Union had declined compared with that of Western countries. To try to increase economic productivity and allow a modicum of open political debate, Gorbachev launched new economic and political policies called *perestroika* and *glasnost*, respectively. These policies initiated a cycle of events over which Gorbachev eventually lost control. In August 1991, after the military's failed attempt at a coup d'état that was intended to restore some of the old order, the Soviet Union began to crumble. In December 1991, the Soviet Union officially ceased to exist, and fifteen separate states, including Russia, emerged once the dust had settled. This began the difficult process of transition to democracy in Russia that we explore further in chapter 9.

CASE Summary

For seventy years, Russia's communist regime, based on the principles of Marx as modified by Lenin, claimed to be working on behalf of the proletariat. Regime members argued, however, that only highly trained and educated communists could use Marxist analysis to serve the proletariat's interests effectively. This claim to legitimacy justified repression of all public dissent. The regime thus restricted citizenship to those who accepted the party's wisdom and rule; those who opposed the party were traitors to the class that rightfully should rule. Civil society under Communist Party rule was completely eliminated, and the state, led by the party, controlled virtually all aspects of individuals' lives, including where they worked, the clubs and organizations to which they could belong, and the prices they paid at the cash register.

The Russian Communist Party set the basic model of communist rule that was copied, with some modifications, in China and elsewhere after World War II. Only China, Cuba, Vietnam, and North Korea still maintain a claim to communism, and only North Korea fully maintains the centralized economic system that was at the heart of the effort. Cuba has experimented with limited liberalization of the economy, and China and Vietnam have essentially allowed capitalism to emerge and, while still claiming to be communist, are in fact modernizing authoritarian regimes.

CASE Questions

1. No regime perfectly matches the ideology on which it is based. What are the most important ways in which the Soviet regime differed from Marxist ideology, and what explains those differences?
2. Can the problems that arose in the Soviet regime best be explained as the result of inherent flaws in Marxist ideology, flaws in Lenin's ideas, or flawed implementation of those ideas in this particular case?

Fascism

Fascism was the other major European alternative to liberal democracy in the early to mid-twentieth century. It was self-consciously both antiliberal and anticommunist. Fascist ideology espouses a conception of society being akin to a living organism rather than a set of disparate groups and individuals. The state is central to and dominant within this organic society; it regulates and ensures the smooth functioning of the organism, much as the brain does for the body. Italian fascist leader Benito Mussolini, in *Fascism: Doctrine and Institutions* (1933/1968), argued that "the State is all-embracing; outside of it no human or spiritual values can exist. . . . The Fascist State . . . interprets, develops, and potentiates the whole life of a people." He goes on to say that the state creates the nation (that is, the collective identity of the people), which is itself a "higher personality." Fascists are thus intensely nationalistic, but they conceive of the nation as created by and loyal to the state first and foremost. Unlike liberals, who emphasize individual freedom, fascists argue that the individual is and should be subsumed within the state. Mussolini, for example, said the fascist "accepts the individual only in so far as his interests coincide with those of the State, which stands for the conscience and the universal will of man as a historic entity." Thus, the interests of the state are justifiably dominant over both individual citizens and civil society. This state, in turn, is led by one man who becomes the supreme leader and head of the state, which itself is both the head and the spirit of the nation. He rules on behalf of the entire "body" of society so that it can function properly.

Fascist belief in society as an organic whole leads to the argument that society should not have competing organizations that could potentially work against one another. Fascists reject the liberal notion of civil society as a sphere of voluntary organizations independent of the state. Instead, just one organization, controlled by the state, should represent the interests of each component of society. This idea is known as **corporatism.** In fascist (and some other authoritarian) societies, the state creates one trade union to "represent" all workers—one business association, one farmers' association, one women's association, etc.—all tightly controlled by the state.

Fascists also reject Marxists' emphasis on materialism and economic life. Instead, Mussolini calls fascism "a spiritual attitude," describing a fascist life as "serious, austere, religious." Fascists reject much of the rationality that is the basis for all types of Western philosophy, appealing instead to spiritual principles and traditions of a nation as a living organism. Fascist doctrine sees life as a struggle and proclaims a life of action. It views each nation as a unique and historical force that must work to maximize its power and position in the world, and it accepts war as a part of this struggle for the glorification of the state, the nation, and the leader.

Fascists share the modern conception of citizenship in the sense of a direct relationship between citizens and a state. Like communists, however, they define citizens not as everyone legally in the state's territory but much more narrowly. Only those

corporatism
System of representation in which one organization represents each important sector of society; two subtypes are societal and state corporatism

loyal to the state can be citizens, and even these citizens do not have rights in the liberal sense of the concept. Since they have no existence outside of the state, the concept of individual rights preexisting or separate from the state is nonsensical. Citizens are left only with duties, which they fulfill as part of achieving a more complete life. Fascists, like communists, thus justify the complete elimination of civil society, but in contrast to communists, Mussolini openly admitted that the fascist state was and should be totalitarian. Liberals, of course, reject fascism because they start from the premise that the individual exists independently of society and the state. Marxists would accept the elimination of civil society and other restrictions of rights, but not in the name of the organic nation, which they view as detrimental to the real interest of the proletariat on whose behalf they claim to rule.

CASE Study

GERMANY: RISE OF THE NAZI PARTY AND A TOTALITARIAN STATE

F ascists generally glorify the nation, but they do not explicitly proclaim one nation as inherently superior to all others. They also do not define the nation as being of one racial or cultural group. Under the leadership of Adolf Hitler, Germany's National Socialists (Nazis), however, married fascism and racism to claim that the German nation, defined in racial terms as "Aryan," was superior to all others and deserved to rule over them.

- **REGIME**
  Naziism-merged fascism and racism; totalitarian, but with internal factions

- **CITIZEN AND STATE**
  Citizenship based on race/nationality and support for Nazi regime

- **CLAIM TO LEGITIMACY**
  National/racial grandeur and state as head of organic society

- **RECENT TRENDS**
  Naziism delegitimizes fascism, but "neofascists" still exist

Germany's economy was in dire straits in the 1920s, due in part to its defeat in World War I and the subsequent war reparations. The Great Depression that started in 1929 made things even worse. Blaming the mainstream parties in power for their increasingly difficult lives, German voters began shifting their allegiance to the "radical" parties: the Communists and Nazis. By the 1932 election, the Nazis had won 37 percent of the vote, the largest percentage of any party. Thus, Adolf Hitler did not grab power via a violent revolution or military coup; he was elected. Following the norms of Weimar's parliamentary democracy (see chapter 6 for an explanation of parliamentary democracy), Hitler became chancellor (the German equivalent of a prime minister), Germany's key leader of government. Because his party did not have a majority of seats in the Reichstag (the German legislature), he had to invite members of other parties to join his government to form a coalition. Members of the Nationalist

Party, the chief mainstream conservative party, sympathized with enough of Hitler's goals to agree to be his partners in government. They believed that, despite Hitler's antidemocratic rhetoric and writings, they could use their influence in the government to keep him in check. They were wrong.

Shortly after Hitler became chancellor in early 1933, the Reichstag burned to the ground. Hitler arrested a Communist activist and launched an anti-Communist campaign, claiming that a communist revolution threatened the nation. In reality, it is almost certain that the Nazis themselves burned the Reichstag to initiate their grab for total power. Hitler used the "emergency" to ban personal liberties, allowing him to arrest Communist members of the Reichstag as well as other opponents. After seeing what happened to the Communist legislators, members of the Reichstag, with Nazi Party militia surrounding the building, agreed to pass the Enabling Act that effectively eliminated the Reichstag's legislative powers, and a dictatorship was born. Hitler and his party immediately used this new law to ban all opposition political parties and replace all trade unions with the party-controlled German Labor Front, beginning the process of creating the totalitarian state that fascist doctrine calls for, including the complete elimination of an autonomous civil society. Pluralists, however, argue that even this totalitarian state had factions within it. Some members of the National Socialist Party took the socialist part seriously, favoring government control of the economy to build a stronger nation. Hitler, however, sided with business in the interest of rapid economic growth. Early in June 1934, he had "radical elements" in the party, who wanted to institute actual socialism, murdered during the "Night of the Long Knives." From then on, large industries worked relatively closely with the Nazis. They initially favored Hitler's elimination of trade unions and later benefited from heavy government investment in infrastructure and military production in the buildup to World War II. Just as was true behind the scenes in the Soviet Union, factions continued to exist within the Nazi regime, with fierce internal battles for power in various ministries. While the regime was as close as any has ever been to being fully totalitarian, factionalism nonetheless continued to exist.

Naziism combined fascism with racism, aimed primarily at Jews. The regime slowly and systematically implemented anti-Semitic policies, first encouraging boycotts of Jewish businesses and firing Jewish civil servants in 1933, then officially classifying people as Jewish and registering Germany's entire population by race in 1935. Jewish businesses were looted and burned during *Kristallnacht* ("Night of Broken Glass") in November 1937, and shortly thereafter, Jewish citizenship was eliminated

Fascists believed that the state was preeminent over society, so only one state-sanctioned organization should represent and speak for each group, whether workers, business, or youth. Here, Nazi leader Adolf Hitler poses with a member of the Nazi Youth, an organization the party used to socialize young people into loyalty to the regime.

and Jews were encouraged to emigrate from Germany to "purify" the state. The Holocaust did not begin in earnest until the start of World War II, when Jews could no longer flee in large numbers. By the end of the war approximately six million Jews had died at the hands of the Nazis and their allies across Europe. In addition to Jews and political opponents, the systematic killing included the sick and disabled who, according to the Nazis, could not contribute to the national good; homosexuals because they were considered "morally depraved"; members of various faiths other than the official, Nazified, German Evangelical Church because they were seen as denying the supremacy of fascism; and "gypsies" (Romanis) because they were seen as impure and flawed.

Web link:
Holocaust Museum: A Learning Site for Students

CASE Summary   Fascists came to power in the same era in Germany, Italy, Spain, and Portugal. Hitler created Nazi puppet regimes as well in the countries he conquered. Nazi rule followed the precepts of fascism, denying all individual rights in the name of the strength of the state and the glorification of the nation, defining citizenship in terms of who supported that effort, repressing opponents as necessary, and replacing an autonomous civil society with corporatist control. The Nazis, in contrast to most fascists, added explicit racism, especially vis-à-vis Jews, to their ideological justification.

The horror of Nazi rule, and fascist rule in general, delegitimized fascist ideology the world over. No regime proclaims itself as fascist today. While small fascist political movements and parties exist, none that claims the name has any significant political influence. Many observers, however, argue that fascist tendencies continue to threaten democracy in many countries. Parties that espouse a virulent nationalism, often defined on a cultural, racial, or religious basis and opposed to immigrants who they see as threats to the "soul of the nation," are frequently termed **neofascist.** These groups usually deny the label, however. The best-known example of neofascism is France's National Front, led originally by Jean-Marie Le Pen. Le Pen argued that the greatest danger facing France is the immigration of Muslims, mainly from North Africa. He claimed that Muslim immigration is destroying the French nation, and he called for policies that would reward white French women for having more babies and would severely restrict or even eliminate immigration. Shockwaves rippled through France and much of Europe in 2002, when Le Pen came in second in the presidential election. In early 2011, Marine Le Pen succeeded her father as head of the National Front and toned down some of his rhetoric to try to broaden the party's support. In the wake of the 2008–2009 global financial crisis, extreme right-wing, anti-immigrant parties that many see as neofascist made significant electoral gains in the Netherlands, Finland, Austria, Hungary, and Greece, and the National Front in France roughly equaled its 2002 share of the vote in the 2012 election. While fascism is dead, it is clear that neofascism is not.

neofascist
Description given to parties or political movements that espouse a virulent nationalism, often defined on a cultural or religious basis and opposed to immigrants as threats to national identity

CASE Questions

1. Based on the German case, what seems to explain the rise of fascist regimes? Can you tie your answers to this question to some of the theories of political behavior discussed in chapter 1?
2. How could we best determine if contemporary extreme right parties such as the National Front are "neofascist"? What core principles would we look for to determine this? If we did believe a particular party fits this label, what should we do about it in a liberal democracy?

Modernizing Authoritarianism

While no regime currently uses fascism as an acceptable claim to legitimacy, the argument that the needs of the state and nation must take precedence over liberalism's individual rights remains common. Many regimes that arose after the end of colonial rule could be termed modernizing authoritarian: their common claim to legitimacy was that they would modernize or "develop" their countries. Modernizing authoritarian regimes are not all based on a single and consciously elaborated ideology like the other types of regimes discussed in this chapter, but each nonetheless explicitly or implicitly appeals to a common set of precepts. Some have an elaborate ideological justification for their legitimacy; others do not. Many of these states are relatively weak, so the formal institutions based on their claim to legitimacy may reveal less about how they actually rule than their informal institutions. They all, however, share a set of core assumptions that underpin their official claim to legitimacy.

Core Assumptions The first of these assumptions is that development requires the leadership of a "modern elite." In societies with relatively few highly educated people, the assumption is that power should be in the hands of those who understand the modern world and how to advance within it. They should be the ones who rule, at least until their societies are "ready" for democracy.

This assumption is an appeal to **technocratic legitimacy,** a claim to rule based on knowledge that was part of **modernization theory.** This theory of development argued that in order to develop, postcolonial societies needed to go through the same process of modernization that the West had undergone. Modernization theorists argued that the modern elite—a "new type of enterprising men" in the words of Walt Rostow (1960), one of the pioneers of the theory and a founder of the American foreign aid program—would lead the development process. Modernization theorists assumed, as we noted in chapter 1, that democracy would arise along with economic development. The leaders of the modernizing authoritarian regimes, however, recognized the contradiction between democracy

technocratic legitimacy
A claim to rule based on knowledge or expertise

modernization theory
Theory of development that argues that postcolonial societies need to go through the same process that the West underwent in order to develop

and the idea that development requires the leadership of an educated elite. They believed that in a country in which a large percentage of the population was illiterate, democracy would not necessarily put the "right" people in power. In their eyes, this legitimized truncating democracy and limiting citizens' rights in favor of some form of authoritarian rule led by elites who claimed to have special leadership abilities based on their education.

The second common assumption of modernizing authoritarian regimes is that they can produce the benefits of "development." The word *development* means many things to many people, but in political discourse throughout the postcolonial world since the 1950s, it has meant moving in the direction of creating societies like those found in the West, at least economically, to bring very poor populations closer to the standard of living found in wealthier countries. For the poorest countries, this meant transforming poor, overwhelmingly agricultural societies into urbanized, industrialized societies with dramatically higher productivity and wealth. For middle-income countries, such as Brazil, development meant continuing the industrialization that had already started, "deepening" it from relatively low-technology to higher-technology and higher-productivity industries. All of this required the application of modern science and technology, which the educated and technocratic elite claimed to understand and be able to employ on behalf of the entire country. The goal, and the main justification for authoritarian rule, was development.

Web link:
Authoritarianism's new wave

Development also required national unity, the third assumption underpinning these regimes. Postcolonial elites argued that achieving the Herculean task of "catching up" to the West necessitated unusual measures. Their countries did not have time for lengthy debates about what policies to pursue. Instead, the modern elite should take control to move the country forward. Debate and democracy had to wait until the "big push" for development was completed, or at least well underway.

All of these assumptions have faced severe criticism. Liberals reject the notion that individual rights must be subsumed in an effort to achieve greater collective ends. They also question the assumption that democracy is necessarily so divisive that effective policymaking cannot occur. Marxists, as noted in chapter 1, argue that modernizing authoritarian regimes really represent neocolonialism. The local ruling class is working in its own interests, not those of the country as a whole and, furthermore, works on behalf of global capitalist forces, which influence policy behind the scenes and against the interests of the poor majority. Fascists, on the other hand, would likely be more sympathetic to many of the arguments of modernizing authoritarianism, in that the two doctrines share the notion that national greatness requires restricting individual rights.

Institutional Forms Modernizing authoritarianism has taken three distinct institutional forms: one-party regimes, military regimes, and personalist regimes. While they all share the key assumptions of the general model, each has different origins and somewhat different institutions (or lack thereof). **One-party regimes,** once common in Africa and Asia, were based on a single party gaining power after independence and systematically eliminating all opposition in the name of development and national unity. These regimes eliminated all effective opposition, but some, such as Kenya and Côte d'Ivoire, did achieve notable economic progress.

Military regimes took power via coups d'état, meaning military takeovers of government; they justified elimination of the previous government in terms of modernizing authoritarianism. Often citing prolonged economic stagnation or growing social unrest as their impetus, military leaders argued that they would "clean up the mess" of the prior government and get the country at least started down the road to development before returning it to civilian and democratic rule. Some military regimes were more serious in this intent and more economically successful; others seem to have used the assumptions of modernizing authoritarianism to justify their own hold on power, with little development taking place; our case study of Nigeria is a good example, which we will explore in more depth in chapter 8.

One of the most institutionalized types of military regimes is known as **bureaucratic-authoritarian regimes.** Argentine political scientist Guillermo O'Donnell (1979) coined the term, arguing that the military dictatorships that arose in many Latin American countries in the 1960s constituted a specific sub-regime type. They came to power in a particular economic context with the express purpose of furthering economic development. The industrialization that had taken place in the wealthier Latin American countries, such as Brazil and Argentina, had reached a limit, partly based on workers' demands for a greater share of the rewards. Militaries came to power in this context to repress workers' demands (in part via corporatism, similar to earlier fascist regimes) and to expand state-led investment in greater industrialization. Democratic governments, they argued, were incapable of doing this. Like all modernizing authoritarian regimes, repression of liberal rights was justified in the name of "development," which required a specific set of policies and type of regime in this particular context.

Personalist regimes usually arose as a result of either one-party rule or via military coup, but either way a central leader came to dominate. This leader not only eliminated all opposition but also weakened the state's institutions in order to centralize power in his own hands. Mobutu Sese Seko of Zaire (now the Democratic Republic of the Congo) and Ferdinand Marcos of the Philippines were classic examples of this type of leader. Personalist regimes justify their rule by using the assumptions of modernizing authoritarianism, and occasionally they have produced some economic successes. Personalist regimes typically centralize power for the benefit of the leader, however, achieving very little in the way of real development.

Modernizing authoritarian regimes arose primarily in postcolonial states, many of which are relatively weak states with weak formal institutions. Informal

one-party regime
A system of government in which a single party gains power, usually after independence in postcolonial states, and systematically eliminates all opposition

military regime
System of government in which military officers control power

bureaucratic-authoritarian regime
A regime characterized by institutionalized rule under a military government with a primary goal of economic development; coined by Guillermo O'Donnell to describe Latin American military regimes in the 1970s

personalist regime
System of government in which a central leader comes to dominate a state, typically not only eliminating all opposition but also weakening the state's institutions to centralize power in his own hands

Tanzania's One-Party Regime

From the 1960s until the 1980s, the African state of Tanzania was an interesting example of a modernizing authoritarian one-party regime. Julius Nyerere, the president from 1962 to 1985, has been called Africa's "philosopher-king," in part because he was unusually self-conscious and explicit in justifying his regime. He argued that political parties in Western democracies are based primarily on social class divisions and that since Africa had few and minor class divisions, there was no need for opposing parties. He suggested that in Africa, "when a village of a hundred people have sat and talked together until they agreed where a well should be dug they have practised democracy" (1966). He thereby justified a one-party state. His party, the Tanzanian African National Union (TANU), overwhelmingly won the country's first election on the eve of independence, and it didn't take much effort to change the constitution to legally eliminate the opposition.

In addition to his idea of "African democracy," Nyerere envisioned creating an "African socialism," dubbed *ujamaa* in Swahili. He argued that this would return the country to its precolonial origins, but with distinctly modern additions. The centerpiece of the effort was the creation of *ujamaa* villages in which Tanzanians would live and work communally. This arrangement would also facilitate the provision of more modern social services such as schools, health clinics, and clean water. While Nyerere justified *ujamaa* as a return to precolonial "traditions," it was in fact an example of a modernizing authoritarian regime in action. It distorted precolonial practices and postcolonial realities against the will of the people in the interests of "development." Nyerere's vision of precolonial Africa was historically inaccurate, and the rural majority had no interest in farming communally or moving into villages. Nyerere ultimately turned to force to create his vision; the state moved millions into new villages and tried to force communal labor. The results were disastrous for agricultural production and the country's economy, though the government was able to improve health care and education, achieving the amazing feat of nearly universal literacy in one of the world's poorest countries.

Nyerere's commitment to village democracy ultimately proved limited; public debate became more and more circumscribed over time. His twin goals of African democracy and African socialism were contradictory. The bulk of the population

Tanganyika African National Union (TANU) youth league members carry hoes in a parade in 1968. The youth league was an important element of the ruling party in Tanzania's modernizing authoritarian regime. The hoes symbolize agriculture, the backbone of the economy and key to the regime's claims to legitimacy based on "development."

didn't support Nyerere's vision of African socialism; had they been able to exercise full democratic rights, they would have voted against it. Throughout TANU's rule, however, the party did hold parliamentary elections once every five years, allowing two party-approved candidates to compete for each seat. Though the candidates could not question the ruling party's overall policies, they could and did compete over the question of who would best represent the area, so the elections were fair, if not free.

By 1985, Nyerere realized that his vision had produced a bankrupt country and that the key economic policies would have to change. He resigned the presidency voluntarily, only the third African president ever to do so, rather than implement a reversal of his vision. In the 1990s and following the trend across the continent (see chapter 9), Nyerere argued in favor of opening the country to multiparty democracy, saying the time for one-party rule was over. The country did allow full legal opposition, starting with the election of 1995, but TANU (renamed CCM, Chama Cha Mapinduzi, or Party of the Revolution) continues to rule against only token opposition.

institutions are therefore often quite important to understanding how these regimes function. Power in weak states becomes quite personalized, and the rule of law is inconsistent. These traits can characterize any of the forms of modernizing authoritarian regimes, though they are most prevalent in personalist regimes. Military and one-party regimes vary more in their level of formal institutionalization. They too can have very weak institutions in which the personal authority of key leaders matters more than the formal organization of power under the party or military as an institution.

Examining some of the weakest states, comparativists studying Africa have suggested that many regimes there are imbued with **neopatrimonial authority.** German sociologist Max Weber (1925/1978) defined "patrimonial" societies as those in which rule is based on reciprocal personal ties and favors, not bureaucratic institutions or formal laws. Many African regimes combine the trappings of modern, bureaucratic states with underlying informal patterns of patrimonial authority that work behind the scenes to determine real power; hence, the term *neopatrimonial*. Constitutions, laws, courts, and bureaucracies all exist, but power really derives mainly from personal loyalty, personal favors, and patronage. Patron-client relations are central in these regimes. Rulers maintain their power by distributing patronage to their followers, who are personally loyal to the rulers. Politics becomes a competition among key patrons for access to the state's resources that they then distribute to their supporters. Neopatrimonial authority in Africa and elsewhere can exist within military, one-party, or personalist regimes. Indeed, many scholars argue that new democracies in Africa, including in Nigeria, retain many elements of neopatrimonial rule; they may now have the formal institutions of electoral democracy, but power remains based primarily on personal access to the state (now via elections) and distribution of its resources as patronage.

The modernizing authoritarian regime type is different from the other regime types in that both its forms and the extent to which a particular government consciously elaborates the ideology can vary significantly. These regimes do share a common set of assumptions, at least some of which they use to legitimize their rule. They all make a central claim that democracy, citizens' rights, and civil society must be curtailed to provide development because development requires national unity and democracy would threaten that unity. While their formal institutions are derived from the precepts of modernizing authoritarianism, in many cases informal institutions are at least as important. While many of these regimes have given way to some type of democracy in recent years (see chapter 9), their institutional legacy remains strong, and certainly some modernizing authoritarian regimes continue to exist. Brazil under military rule from 1964 to 1985 was a classic case of this type of regime.

neopatrimonial authority
Power based on a combination of the trappings of modern, bureaucratic states with underlying informal institutions of clientelism that work behind the scenes; most common in Africa

CASE Study

BRAZIL: THE BUREAUCRATIC AUTHORITARIAN STATE, 1964–1985

- **REGIME**
  Bureaucratic-authoritarian

- **CITIZEN AND STATE**
  Repressive, but not as severe as many in Latin America at the time

- **CLAIM TO LEGITIMACY**
  Modernization and anticommunism

- **KEY INSTITUTIONS**
  Military presidency; limited civilian opposition in legislature

- **CONTEXT**
  State-led industrialization produces "Brazilian Miracle"

Brazil emerged from World War II as a semi-industrialized economy and returned to being a democracy, albeit a very unstable one. After the abrupt resignation of President Jânio Quadros, who had been elected in 1960, Vice President João Goulart stepped up to the presidency. Seen by workers and the poor as sympathetic to their cause, Goulart emboldened them to organize street protests to claim what they saw as their fair share of the fruits of development. These in turn led to rising concern from business owners, landowners, and other conservatives, who organized their own counterdemonstrations. It was not long before the Brazilian military, with quiet support from the United States, decided that the instability threatened the country's development. Military officials overthrew Goulart in a coup d'état in 1964.

The Brazilian military came to power at the height of the Cold War, just five years after Fidel Castro had led a communist revolution in Cuba. This meant that anticommunism was an important addition to the common justifications for modernizing authoritarian regimes. The military regime suppressed independent unions and returned the country to the corporatist model that had been in place during the earlier quasi-fascist regime. It then expanded industrialization via significant government investments in new industries, particularly in heavy industry such as auto manufacturing and airplanes. The regime explicitly claimed legitimacy on the basis of technocratic expertise and anticommunism, and brought many talented economists into the government to develop the new economic plan. It was a classic bureaucratic authoritarian regime. The result came to be known as the "Brazilian Miracle," a period of particularly rapid economic growth

Brazil's military regime was less violent than its infamous neighbors in Chile and Argentina of the same period, but violence was certainly used to repress dissent, and student and worker protests were often targets. In 1968 cavalry charged students gathered to protest the killing of a student by police in Rio de Janeiro.

that was at its zenith from 1967 to 1973. Despite this growth, however, much of the population remained mired in poverty.

The Brazilian military government certainly repressed its opponents as necessary to implement its economic model, though it was less repressive than were many Latin American military governments. It allowed elections for a national congress but restricted competition to only two legal parties: one that supported the government and one that was a legal opposition. The opposition, however, was limited in what it was allowed to say, the congress itself had quite limited powers, and the military resorted to electoral tampering to maintain government party control. Ultimate decision making remained with the top military leaders.

By the late 1970s, world oil shocks had contributed to an economic slowdown across the country. Independent unions once again formed, this time in open violation of the law. Strikes became more common and had greater impact than before, given the rapid industrialization of the past two decades; there were now more industrial workers, and their industries were more important to the economy. Trade unions and political activists in the Catholic Church became more active in civil society, playing a key role in starting a movement for democracy that eventually brought Brazil's modernizing authoritarian regime to an end in 1985, when the first civilian president since 1964 took office.

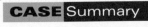

CASE Summary

Brazil's bureaucratic-authoritarian regime was one of the more conscious and committed modernizing authoritarian regimes and emerged in one of the stronger postcolonial states. It elaborated a clear ideological justification for what it did, focusing on the need to further economic development and fight communism. The military leaders saw themselves as a technocratic elite, and they hired civilian technocrats to augment their policy expertise. The elite believed democracy had to be suppressed because it would, at best, slow development and, at worst, lead to a communist takeover. The regime produced a period of rapid economic growth, but as that growth slowed in the late 1970s, regime legitimacy plummeted. The regime was ultimately forced to allow a return to democracy.

CASE Questions

1. What similarities and differences are there between the military regime in Brazil and fascist regimes in Europe earlier in the century?
2. Compare the Brazilian case with the box above on the one-party regime in Tanzania during the same era. What common elements and what differences do you see? Does it make sense to think of both of them as "modernizing authoritarian"?

Semi-Authoritarianism

semi-authoritarian regime
Type of hybrid regime in which formal opposition and some open political debate exist and elections are held; these processes are so flawed, however, that the regime cannot be considered truly democratic; also called *electoral authoritarian*

Since the end of the Cold War and the wave of democratizations that followed, modernizing authoritarian regimes have become far less common. A related but distinct regime type, however, has become more common: **semi-authoritarian regimes.** Comparativist Marina Ottaway coined the term *semi-authoritarianism* to characterize regimes that "allow little real competition for power . . . [but] leave enough political space for political parties and organizations of civil society to form, for an independent press to function to some extent, and for some political debate to take place" (2003, 3). These regimes are also sometimes referred to as "electoral authoritarian" regimes (Schedler 2006). In semi-authoritarian regimes, opposition parties are allowed to exist and win some elected offices, but the ruling party manipulates electoral rules and processes enough to ensure that it maintains virtually all effective power. Such regimes typically allow some limited freedom of expression as well, but they ensure that this also does not threaten the ruling party's grip on power.

Some scholars have referred to semi-authoritarian regimes as "hybrid regimes" because they seem to combine some democratic and some authoritarian elements. This is clear ideologically: they attempt to legitimize themselves using a combination of democratic and modernizing ideas. Unlike modernizing authoritarian regimes, they proclaim themselves democratic and point to democratic elements to justify this claim, in particular the presence of regularly scheduled elections (however flawed they are in practice). At the same time, semi-authoritarian regimes invoke ideas from modernizing authoritarianism as well, justifying limits on democracy as essential for national unity and development. This combination means that, as in modernizing authoritarian regimes, informal political institutions and practices are often as or more important in semi-authoritarian regimes than the formal institutions of rule.

Semi-authoritarian regimes have become far more common in the last twenty years. Indeed, they are probably the most common regime type in the new millennium (Brownlee 2007). This is undoubtedly due in part to the growing international acceptance of liberal democratic norms: in the post–Cold War and postcommunist world, it is no longer legitimate to proclaim a regime as purely authoritarian (of whatever ideology). Semi-authoritarian institutions—such as minimally competitive elections and a national legislature in which opposition parties are allowed to hold a few seats and, within limits, criticize the ruling party—provide a veneer of democratic legitimacy to regimes that in an earlier era might have been modernizing authoritarian. This is especially true in states that at least began a transition to democracy, typically in the 1990s. Full reversion to modernizing authoritarianism is unacceptable to the citizenry and the international community, and even the beginning of a transition to democracy usually unleashes popular pressure that the regime can better manage by allowing some limited opposition to exist, rather than repressing it entirely. Our case study of Russia is an example of this path to semi-authoritarian rule (see chapter 9). Mexico, however, shows that some semi-authoritarian regimes have been around much longer.

CASE Study

MEXICO: SEMI-AUTHORITARIANISM UNDER THE PRI

Mexico was home to one of the longest-lasting semi-authoritarian regimes anywhere. Between 1929 and 2000, Mexico's Institutional Revolution Party, or PRI (Partido Revolucionario Institucional), used control and support of labor, clientelism, electoral fraud, and repression to keep key federal and state offices in the party's hands. At the same time, the regime allowed and even encouraged the active participation of opposition parties, so long as they did not garner enough votes to pose a significant challenge to the PRI.

Ideologically, the regime claimed legitimacy partly on the basis of the legacy of the Mexican Revolution (1910–1920). While the revolution included many different leaders and groups with varying purposes, the bulk of its support came from its ideological promises to end the extreme inequality of nineteenth- and early-twentieth-century Mexico. Mexican revolutionaries were not communists, but the most popular leaders like Emiliano Zapata and "Pancho" Villa based their appeal on nationalism, land redistribution to the peasants, and better wages and conditions for urban workers. The PRI claimed it represented peasants, workers, and the downtrodden generally, and for a long time it maintained their loyalty and support. It mobilized that support, though, via clientelism and corporatism, and while it allowed

- **REGIME**
  Semi-authoritarian

- **CITIZEN AND STATE**
  Corporatism, clientelism, electoral fraud, and repression if necessary

- **CLAIM TO LEGITIMACY**
  Revolutionary nationalism and modernization

- **KEY INSTITUTIONS**
  Presidential power nearly unlimited for six years; regular elections and orderly succession

- **RECENT TRENDS**
  Transition to democracy, 1988–2000

Lázaro Cárdenas (1934–1940) was the most important and famous Mexican president during the era of the PRI's semi-authoritarian state. He set the "populist" policy course for the party, helping it to create a sense of legitimacy based on its provision of patronage to core constituencies, especially unionized workers and peasants. His political and economic framework stayed in place, with minor changes, until the 1980s debt crisis forced the PRI to shift to a more open-market economy. This was the beginning of the end of the PRI's political dominance.

official opposition to exist, the PRI made sure that it won virtually every election in the name of the revolution.

The PRI traces its origins to President Plutarco Elías Calles (1924–1928), who used the party organization as a vehicle for placing his handpicked successors in office starting in 1929. The party was a way for Calles to remain influential without running for office again, given the state's commitment to the revolutionary slogan of "No Reelection," meaning that officeholders could not be reelected to subsequent terms. The importance of "No Reelection" largely accounts for the party-centric, rather than personalist, semi-authoritarianism of twentieth-century Mexico.

The PRI's main electoral constituency has been referred to as a three-legged stool comprising laborers, peasants, and bureaucrats, though over time the party became more like a big tent that includes liberals, radicals, and even conservatives. This broad base increased the PRI's competitive edge and allowed it to poach potential rivals from opposition parties. Pitched battles did take place internally, and many historic presidential administrations emerged as a result of one wing of the party winning over its competition. Such was the case with Lázaro Cárdenas (1934–1940), whose radical faction ended Calles's tenure as party leader and began an era of left-wing reform. For the rest of the PRI's history, power and the presidency shifted from radical to more conservative factions via elections every six years, but the party's control was never in doubt.

During the long period of one-party domination, the president remained the central and most powerful figure within both the state and the party apparatus. The president appointed the official leaders of the party as well as all governors and senators. Despite the precedent set by earlier presidents such as Calles and Cárdenas, who remained influential even after leaving office, the PRI eventually developed a system in which a president would govern unencumbered for one term and then retire from public life altogether. This meant that at the end of every six-year presidential term (called the *sexenio*), a new leader, chosen by his predecessor, would step in and take over the reins of the country.

While this system of orderly succession did forestall the emergence of a personalist regime, it came at great cost: Mexican presidents were known to take advantage of their limited time in office and guaranteed safe retirement to engage in widespread graft, and they encouraged their close associates to do the same. In addition, outgoing presidents often escalated government spending at the end of their term to facilitate the election of their successor, which resulted in predictable cycles of inflation at the start of each *sexenio* (see chapter 5).

Despite its many problems, the semi-authoritarian regime remained in place thanks in part to robust control of and support from labor, among other groups. Under Cárdenas, labor's relationship with the regime grew to new heights, with the formation of the Mexican Labor Confederation, or CTM (Confederación de Trabajadores de Mexico). Under this corporatist arrangement, the CTM became the overwhelmingly powerful labor union in Mexico and went so far as to organize militias capable of checking the military's power. This close relationship with the regime meant that the

CTM, and a similar peasant union, mobilized support for the party in exchange for better working conditions and patronage.

Apart from managing corporatist networks, Mexico's regime reverted to clientelism, which at its most basic level took the form of vote buying. Most of the time, however, clientelist relationships were tied to supporting rural interests. Between the end of the revolution and the start of World War II, the state engaged in large-scale land reform. By the 1970s, clientelism was exercised through massive government spending on agricultural development projects. This helped guarantee a loyal rural constituency that to this day remains the electoral backbone of the PRI.

When corporatism and clientelism were not enough to ensure the outcome of a vote—especially in the face of the mobilization capabilities of opposition forces among conservative Catholic activists and leftist students in the universities—the ruling party resorted to electoral fraud. Favorite tactics included stuffing ballot boxes, moving polling locations at the last minute, having supporters vote multiple times, and, if necessary, altering the numbers once the votes had been tallied.

Always concerned about maintaining the veneer of democratic legitimacy, semi-authoritarian regimes such as Mexico's prefer to maintain control via clientelism and behind-the-scenes electoral fraud rather than outright violence. If necessary, though, the PRI was not above using force to guarantee its rule. The most infamous example of this came when the military opened fire on antigovernment student protesters on October 2, 1968—days before the start of the Mexico City Olympics. This became known as the Tlatelolco Massacre, named after the neighborhood where the killings took place. In addition to the deaths and injuries—with disputed figures ranging from a few dozen to several hundred—Tlatelolco is remembered because the media initially failed to report on the events. When they did, they downplayed their gravity. Though the media were never fully censored in the way one would expect in a fully authoritarian system, self-censorship was commonplace in Mexico, with private media consistently avoiding politically dangerous stories. This stance was due largely to lucrative government advertising and, sometimes, direct bribes of journalists.

Video link:
1968 massacre at Tlatelolco

These strategies allowed the PRI to win 98 percent of all mayoral and congressional elections between 1946 and 1973. By the late 1980s, though, opposition parties began to make inroads that could no longer be ignored. Part of this shift was probably due to urbanization and free-market reforms, which made traditional clientelism more difficult to maintain. In 1989 the conservative Partido Acción Nacional (PAN), or National Action Party, became the first opposition party to elect a governor. In 1988 Cuauhtémoc Cárdenas (son of former PRI president Lázaro Cárdenas) was part of a left-wing faction that defected from the PRI to form a new party in response to the government's increasingly market-oriented economic policies. Cárdenas ran for president and garnered 30 percent of the vote to the PRI's 52 percent (compare this with the 1976 election, in which the PRI trounced the opposition with 98.7 percent of the vote). To this day, many believe that Cárdenas, who claimed victory but was denied the presidency, was the actual winner at the polls.

Web link:
Favorite son, Cuauhtémoc Cárdenas

Given the tense political climate that emerged following the closely contested and controversial election, the ruling party was forced to introduce concrete steps toward providing electoral fairness and broader representation in government. The first free election took place in 1994, though voters opted for continuity and bureaucratic experience, and gave the election to Ernesto Zedillo of the PRI. Although the PRI kept the presidency, the days of one-party rule were numbered. A new, democratic, three-party system emerged in the country, and the PRI would have to compete alongside the others. In 2000 the election of the PAN's Vicente Fox finally broke the PRI's seventy-one-year monopoly on the presidency, ushering in a new era in Mexican politics. Unhappiness with the state of the economy, though, led Mexican voters in 2012 to put the PRI back in power under the leadership of new president Enrique Peña Nieto, but this time the party is in power freely and fairly in a democratic regime. We examine this transition to democracy in Mexico in detail in chapter 9.

CASE Summary

Though it existed long before the term was coined, the PRI created a classic semi-authoritarian regime. The party's dominance was unquestioned for sixty years. Throughout, however, it held elections for the presidency and the lower house of the legislature that allowed internal elite competition and rotation of power across factions within the party. Opposition parties won a handful of seats but never enough to threaten the regime. This system provided a veneer of democratic legitimacy, and the PRI pursued policies that kept many workers and peasants loyal to it for decades. At least implicit, however, was the claim that by maintaining power, the PRI was able to modernize the country; it did in fact achieve significant economic development (see chapter 5). This combination of claims to democratic and modernizing legitimacy under what was really authoritarian rule is the hallmark of semi-authoritarian regimes. Our case study of Russia in chapter 9 will provide a contemporary version of this regime type.

CASE Questions

1. Semi-authoritarian regimes typically base their legitimacy on a combination of nondemocratic and democratic claims. What were the most important bases of legitimacy for the PRI-led regime, and how democratic were these claims?

2. Understanding most regimes requires understanding both formal and informal institutions. How important were the two types of institutions in understanding the key elements of Mexico's regime? Do formal or informal institutions seem more important, and why?

Theocracy

Theocracy is rule by religious authorities. They rule on behalf of God and following His dictates. It's very unlikely that you would have found theocracy included in a text-book on comparative politics forty years ago. If it were mentioned at all, it would have been in connection with the "divine right of kings" of medieval and early modern Europe under which the monarchy was thought to represent God on Earth, sanctioned as such by the universal Catholic Church. Today, the prime example of theocracy is not Christian but Muslim. Like other kinds of regimes, the Muslim theocracy in Iran is based on a well-elaborated political ideology. Iran currently is the world's only true theocracy, but political movements aimed at achieving similar regimes exist through-out the Muslim world. Some other countries, such as Saudi Arabia, have monarchies that are closely tied to and in part legitimized by Islamic religious authority, but their primary basis for legitimacy is the monarchy itself. We focus on Islamic theocracy as an ideology and regime type not because it is the only conceivable kind of theocracy but because it is the only contemporary example of a theocratic regime and because theocratic political ideology is an important challenger to liberal democracy today.

The political ideology that has inspired such fear in much of the West and such admiration in some of the Muslim world is typically known as "Islamic fundamen-talism," a name that implies a set of ideas that is often quite different from what its adherents actually believe. The word *fundamentalist* implies "traditional" to many people, but nothing could be further from the truth in this case. "Traditional" Islamic beliefs, as developed over the centuries, hold that religious law ought to be the basis for government, but in practice local cultural traditions and rulers compromised these precepts significantly. In many countries in the twentieth century, traditional Muslim religious authorities compromised with modernity and the increasing secularization of the state by withdrawing from politics nearly completely and allowing secular, mod-ernizing authoritarian regimes to emerge. Indeed, many Islamists argue that the rise of a new, politicized Islamic movement over the past century is in large part a reaction to Western imperialism; it is not at all "traditional," but rather a reaction to twentieth-century events (Abu-Rabi 2010). Bassam Tibi (2011) says it involves "the invention of tradition" rather than the re-creation of an actual tradition.

Given this reality, most scholars prefer the term **Islamism** instead of *Islamic fun-damentalism*. While it has many variations, Islamism is generally defined as a belief that Islamic law, as revealed by Allah to the Prophet Mohammed, can and should provide the basis for government in Muslim communities, with little equivocation or compromise with other beliefs or laws. Islamism arose in the nineteenth and twentieth centuries with the goal of "purifying" Muslim society of the creeping influences of the West and secularism that traditional Muslim religious leaders had often been willing to accept. In line with this, most Islamists explicitly reject the Muslim concept of *taqlid*, the acceptance of all past legal and moral edicts of the traditional clergy, and instead

theocracy
Rule by religious authorities

Islamism
The belief that Islamic law, as revealed by God to the Prophet Mohammed, can and should provide the basis for government in Muslim communities with little equivocation or compromise

embrace *ijtihad,* the belief that Muslims should read and interpret the original Islamic texts for themselves. They base their ideology on their interpretation of the Quran and Sunnah, the two holiest books of Islam, and take as their primary model the seventh-century Muslim society and state created by Mohammed and his immediate followers. Islamists vary in the degree to which they are willing to compromise with aspects of the contemporary world. Not all, for instance, support stoning as punishment for adultery, but most adhere to a fairly strict belief in Muslim law, **sharia**. Past compromises by traditional clergy are therefore unacceptable.

Islamists believe that sovereignty rests with Allah, so they ultimately reject democracy and its idea of popular sovereignty. Some, however, such as the early Palestinian leader Taqi al-Din al-Nabhani (1905–1978), reserve a place for *shura,* which means "consultation with the people." He believed the Muslim state should be led by a caliph, a supreme religious and political leader, but that the caliph should be acceptable to the population as a whole and be advised by an elected council. Some religious authorities have since used this concept to argue in favor of allowing an ideologically limited civil society, one that stays within the bounds of Islamic practices, ideas, and law. Much debate has arisen over how compatible Islamism is with democracy (Tibi 2011), but those who argue the two can be combined base that argument on the concept of *shura.* Some Islamists, such as the Muslim Brotherhood in Egypt, are willing to go a step further and participate in democracy as a means of gaining power. Though banned under the long-ruling, semi-authoritarian regime of Hosni Mubarak, the Brotherhood nonetheless unofficially ran candidates as independents in Egypt's constricted elections. Once Mubarak was overthrown, the Brotherhood created a political party that became the dominant political force during the regime transition; its candidate, Mohamed Morsi, won the first presidential election, though was overthrown in a military coup in 2013. Other Islamists, including Sayyid Qutb, a key early leader of the Muslim Brotherhood, reject the notion of democracy altogether, maintaining that any compromise with democracy violates Allah's sovereignty. Our case study of Iran shows the tension between the sovereignty of Allah and the idea of *shura.*

As the electoral participation of some groups demonstrates, while all Islamists place great significance on *jihad,* not all advocate violence. **Jihad** means "struggle," and, although it is not one of the "five pillars" of the faith, it is an important concept in Islam. The Quran identifies three kinds of *jihad.* The first and most important is the individual's internal struggle to renounce evil and live faithfully by following proper religious practices. The second is the struggle of the individual to right evils and injustice within the *umma,* the Muslim community as a whole. The third and least important is protection, armed and violent if necessary, of the *umma.* The most radical Islamists argue that the *umma* is under attack externally from the West and internally via secularization and Westernization. For groups like al-Qaida, this view justifies violent opposition to these forces, both outside and within the *umma.* Furthermore, following *ijtihad,* these individuals reject the traditional teaching that violent *jihad* should only be carried out on the orders of high religious authorities. They argue

---

sharia
Muslim law

Web link:
"With Upheaval, How Large Is the Opening for Islam?"

jihad
Derived from an Arabic word for "struggle" and an important concept in Islam; the Quran identifies three kinds of *jihad*

instead that individuals, and religiously untrained leaders like Osama bin Laden, can discern for themselves when and where violent *jihad* is not only a justifiable option but a moral necessity.

Although Iran's Muslim regime is a recent development and the sole contemporary version of theocracy today is Islamic, theocracy is one of the oldest forms of government still in existence. Like all theocrats, Islamists believe in a government established according to their understanding of Allah's teaching, giving sovereignty not to "we the people" but rather to Allah. Followers vary widely in the methods they use to achieve Islamist regimes and in the details of what those regimes would look like. Some include quasi-democratic elements, such as consultation with some sort of legislative body, and some are willing to try to gain power via electoral democracy, give limited rights to citizens, and allow some civil society. All, however, would give great power to religious authorities to interpret and implement Allah's sovereignty on Earth. Critics reject this notion of sovereignty from God, and Marxists famously reject the concept of God altogether. Fascists might have some sympathy with the idea of a strong central ruler governing on behalf of all, but the goal for fascists would not be to follow God's will but to strengthen the nation. Islamist philosophers and ideologues have created many variants of Islamist regimes in the abstract, but only one has gained power and ruled for a sustained period: Iran's revolutionary Islamic government.

CASE Study

THE ISLAMIC REPUBLIC OF IRAN: THEOCRATIC STATE, 1979–

Islam in Iran is unusual in that the vast majority of the country's population and major religious authorities are Shiites, not Sunnis. In the seventh century, Islam split over the succession to the Prophet Mohammed. Those who became Shiite believe the Prophet's son-in-law, Imam Ali, was rightful heir to the leadership of the *umma* and that descendants of Imam Ali remain the only rightful religious authorities. Major Shiite religious authorities are chosen from among his heirs. Sunnis, who constitute approximately 85 percent of the world's Muslims, believe that any religiously educated person of appropriate stature and training can become a major leader of the *umma*, and they reject the claim that a particular bloodline should rule. Iran and Iraq are two of only four Muslim countries with Shiite majorities; Iran is nearly all Shiite.

- **REGIME**
  Theocracy, but tension between theocratic and democratic elements

- **CITIZEN AND STATE**
  Islamist faithful only; democratic space and participation vary over time

- **CLAIM TO LEGITIMACY**
  Sovereignty of Allah under Shiite Islam

- **KEY INSTITUTIONS**
  Supreme leader; secular president and limited parliament

- **RECENT TRENDS**
  Growing repression

Iranian President Hassan Rouhani (center) waves to supporters in front of a poster depicting the founder of the Islamic Republic, Ayatollah Ruhollah Khomeini. Rouhani's election in 2013 gave reformers hope that changes were coming, but the regime gives the supreme leader nearly unlimited power based on the claim that he is the chief representative of Allah's sovereignty, so it was not clear how many changes would be forthcoming.

The Islamic Republic in Iran nonetheless exemplifies the ideology and contradictions of Islamist theocracy more broadly.

Prior to 1979, Iran had a modernizing authoritarian regime under the leadership of the Pahlavi dynasty; father and then son ruled the country from 1925 to 1979. The dynasty, however, kept whatever benefits came out of this modernization for itself and its close supporters, and domestic opposition mounted. One of the country's major religious leaders, Ayatollah Ruhollah Khomeini, emerged as a major spokesperson and leader of this opposition. Jailed and later forced into exile in neighboring Iraq and then France, Khomeini was the symbol and most popular leader of the revolution that swept the shah from power in 1978–1979 (see chapter 9). His Islamist ideals became the basis for the new government.

Khomeini's most original contribution to Islamist doctrine was the concept of the supreme leader. He argued that one leader with enough religious authority and popular support should be the ultimate guide of the Islamic state, with the power to veto any law. Khomeini also believed, however, in consultation, or *shura*, and so was quite willing to allow the existence of an elected parliament, the Majlis, as long as its laws were subject to the approval of the supreme leader or other major clergy he might deputize to fulfill that function. Because of this, tensions between theocratic legitimacy, resting in clerical authority, and quasi-democratic elements such as elections have characterized the regime since its beginning. A new Iranian constitution was ratified by referendum in December 1979. It established Iran as an Islamic Republic that specifically followed Shiite doctrine and declared Allah as sovereign. The position of supreme leader was created, with Khomeini filling that role, and a Guardian Council of twelve clergy was formed as his main watchdogs over the government. The council must approve or veto every law the parliament passes, as well as approve all candidates for office. A directly elected president administers the government on a daily basis. While Khomeini preserved the pre-Islamic court system, *sharia* became the sole source of law and clergy head all major courts. Clergy also monitor all of the president's cabinet ministers who are in charge of the various departments of the government.

The regime is clearly theocratic, since supreme religious authorities can ultimately make or unmake any governmental decision. Some democratic elements have been allowed, however. Regular elections for president and parliament have been held on schedule since the regime's beginning (see chapter 8). Nonetheless, the Guardian Council can disapprove any candidate for office who is deemed not adequately committed to the goals of the Islamic revolution, which has meant the degree of openness of the elections has varied greatly. In the first parliamentary election in 1980, a large number of parties competed and entered parliament, and a "moderate" won the presidency. He claimed commitment to the revolution but also took a practical stance toward modifying Islam to meet the necessities of running a modern state. By 1983 Khomeini forced him and other moderates out of office and in 1986 banned all parties, arguing that they were divisive. Informally, he allowed factions to continue to exist, but the elimination of all parties kept opposition forces repressed.

Audio link:
"My Name Is Iran"

As real political options narrowed and the power of the Majlis vis-à-vis the Guardian Council declined, elections excited less interest and voter turnout dropped. A decade later, in the late 1990s, elections again became more exciting and popular affairs after the clergy once again allowed a moderate reformer, Mohammad Khatami, to run for president. Following his election, however, the clergy proceeded to frustrate virtually every reform effort he undertook and made sure that a candidate more loyal to them, Mahmoud Ahmadinejad, won the election of 2005. Ahmadinejad was reelected in what most observers believe to have been a fraudulent election in 2009, which was followed by massive street protests, several deaths, and thousands of arrests of regime opponents. In 2013 a somewhat more moderate candidate, Hassan Rouhani, was elected president, though he was far more deferential to the ruling clergy than Khatami a decade earlier had been.

Despite some periods of greater openness, citizen ability to voice opinions and engage in political activity has been quite limited. When allowed, a very active press has emerged, as it did right after the revolution and again in the late 1990s. Whenever this press begins to question the goals of the revolution beyond certain limits, however, religious authorities close it down, and a period of repression sets in. The Iranian theocracy limits civil society severely, especially when key religious authorities feel threatened with a potential loss of power. But the country has nonetheless seen growing pressure for change and a more active civil society than was present in many Middle Eastern countries, at least until the "Arab Spring" uprisings of 2011.

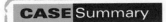

CASE Summary   Ayatollah Khomeini helped create the first true theocracy in the modern world. It follows Shiite Islamist principles and includes some democratic elements justified via the concept of *shura*. The power of those democratic elements, however, has varied over time. Khomeini's death allowed stronger reformist movements and politicians to emerge in the 1990s, ensconced in the democratic elements of the regime: the presidency and Majlis.

Conservative clergy used the religious institutions that the revolution created to frustrate reform and preserve what they saw as the pure path of the Islamist regime. As socioeconomic changes continue and Iranians increasingly use the Internet and other means of communication to access the outside world, theocracy survives, but it seems to rely increasingly on force to maintain control (see chapter 8).

CASE Questions

1. How important are democratic elements in Iran's theocratic regime? Compare these to the democratic elements in Mexico's semi-authoritarian regime: Which of the two seems to give greater power to democratic institutions such as elections?
2. Does it make sense to categorize the Iranian regime as theocratic, or should it be considered semi-authoritarian instead? Why do you answer as you do?

CONCLUSION

All political ideologies involve the question of the proper relationship between individual citizens and the state. Most citizens of established democracies probably consider liberal democracy's insistence on limited state power and citizens' rights, especially the right to participate in politics through voting, as the presumptive norm. Liberal democracy, however, is an outlier in this regard. Communism, fascism, modernizing authoritarianism, semi-authoritarianism, and theocracy all tilt the balance in varying degrees in favor of the state. Each finds some grounds for arguing that government should not rest in the hands of citizens or elected representatives alone. Most ideologies offer some sort of rationale for giving a select group, whether it's the working class, the fascist state itself, or a technocratic or religious elite, more say and limiting the participation of others. In these ideologies, real citizenship is thus restricted to members of the key party, those loyal to the nation, those capable of helping the country achieve development, or those who are part of the faithful. This was true for much of liberalism's history as well, of course, as male property owners were the sole citizens. Despite this history, all long-standing liberal regimes have been democratized over the last century as the formal rights of citizenship have expanded to include virtually all adults.

The question of who actually has power, though, may be less clear than formal ideological differences suggest. Pluralist theorists have argued that in almost all regimes, even some of the most totalitarian, factions exist. Elites clearly rule, but they do not rule in a fully united manner. They are divided into factions that vie for power, resources, and influence, often behind the facade of a united and repressive regime. And critics argue that elites often control real power in liberal democracies as well, despite widespread formal rights. Liberal equality of citizenship may exist legally, but it never exists in reality, even where fairly extensive social rights are practiced. The sharp distinctions between liberalism and its ideological alternatives may be less in practice than they are in theory.

Ideology offers what regimes hope is a compelling justification for their actions and often serves as a blueprint on which their formal institutions are based, but regimes rarely abide strictly by their ideologies. Democracies vary in their institutional structures, for instance, and even the most established ones have only relatively recently granted full citizenship rights to all adult citizens regardless of gender or race. Similarly, communist regimes modified Marx's ideal of rule by the proletariat in favor of Lenin's concept of rule by the vanguard party. Many modernizing authoritarian regimes have failed to meet their own goals of technocratic government and instead have lapsed into neopatrimonial or other forms of corrupt rule. Often, informal institutions and norms tied to culture and history explain more about how a regime actually works than the official ideology does, especially in weak states. In other instances, practical circumstances make leaders choose paths that diverge from their own stated ideology, as when Lenin espoused the New Economic Policy.

Because ideology alone does not explain how regimes arise and function, comparativists have used a wide array of theories to examine regimes. Political culture theorists, for instance, have argued that the first communist dictatorship emerged in Russia in part because of the long-standing authoritarian elements in Russian political culture, bred under centuries of tsarist rule. Marxists, of course, use their structural theory to explain the rise of particular regimes, arguing that ideology is simply a mask to justify class dictatorships of various sorts: liberal democracy emerged to serve the interests of the bourgeoisie and foster capitalism; modernizing authoritarian regimes further neocolonialism and the interests of both the budding capitalist elites in postcolonial societies and global corporations. Institutionalists, on the other hand, argue that what matters most is not just regimes' ideological blueprints but how well developed their formal institutions are and, therefore, how important informal institutions and practices are. Ideology is important to understanding regimes' claims to legitimacy, but understanding how they actually govern requires far more—a subject we investigate further in Part II of this book. First, though, we turn to another crucial issue for modern states: their relationship to identity groups.

KEY CONCEPTS

bureaucratic-authoritarian regime (p. 125)

citizen (p. 100)

civil rights (p. 101)

corporatism (p. 119)

democratic centralism (p. 116)

dictatorship of the proletariat (p. 114)

historical materialism (p. 113)

Islamism (p. 135)

jihad (p. 136)

liberal democracy (p. 108)

military regime (p. 125)

mode of production (p. 114)

modernization theory (p. 123)

neofascist (p. 122)

neopatrimonial authority (p. 127)

one-party regime (p. 125)

parliamentary sovereignty (p. 112)

participatory democracy (p. 110)

personalist regime (p. 125)

politburo (p. 117)

political rights (p. 101)

regime (p. 98)

semi-authoritarian regime (p. 130)

sharia (p. 136)

social contract theory (p. 106)

social democracy (p. 110)

social revolution (p. 114)

social rights (p. 101)

soviets (p. 117)

technocratic legitimacy (p. 123)

theocracy (p. 135)

totalitarian regime (p. 117)

vanguard party (p. 116)

Sharpen your skills with SAGE edge at **edge.sagepub.com/orvis3e.** **SAGE edge for students** provides a personalized approach to help you accomplish your coursework goals in an easy-to-use learning environment.

WORKS CITED

Abu-Rabi, Ibrahim M. 2010. "Editor's Introduction." In *The Contemporary Arab Reader on Political Islam*, edited by Ibrahim M. Abu-Rabi, vii–xxv. New York: Pluto Press.

Acemoglu, Daron, and James A. Robinson. 2006. *Economic Origins of Dictatorship and Democracy.* Cambridge, UK: Cambridge University Press.

Brownlee, Jason. 2007. *Authoritarianism in an Age of Democratization.* Cambridge, UK: Cambridge University Press.

Keck, Margaret E., and Kathryn Sikkink. 1998. *Activists beyond Borders: Advocacy Networks in International Politics.* Ithaca, NY: Cornell University Press.

Lister, Michael, and Emily Pia. 2008. *Citizenship in Contemporary Europe.* Edinburgh, UK: Edinburgh University Press.

Marshall, T. H. 1963. *Class, Citizenship, and Social Development: Essays.* Chicago: University of Chicago Press.

Marx, Karl, and Friedrich Engels. 1888. *The Communist Manifesto.* Translated by Samuel Moore with Friedrich Engels. London: William Reeves Bookseller. (Originally published as *Manifest der Kommunistischen Partei* in London in 1848.)

Moore, Barrington, Jr. 1966. *Social Origins of Dictatorship and Democracy: Lord and Peasant in the Making of the Modern World.* Boston: Beacon Press.

Mussolini, Benito. 1968. *Fascism: Doctrine and Institutions.* New York: Howard Fertig. (Originally delivered as address to National Cooperative Council, Italy, in 1933.)

Nyerere, Julius K. 1966. *Freedom and Unity: Uhuru Na Umoja; A Selection from Writings and Speeches, 1952–65.* London: Oxford University Press.

O'Donnell, Guillermo A. 1979. *Modernization and Bureaucratic-Authoritarianism: Studies in South American Politics.* Text ed. Berkeley: Institute of International Studies, University of California.

Ottaway, Marina. 2003. *Democracy Challenged: The Rise of Semi-Authoritarianism.* Washington, DC: Carnegie Endowment for International Peace.

Polity IV Project. 2010. "Political Regime Characteristics and Transitions, 1800–2009" (http://www.systemicpeace.org/polity/polity4.htm).

Rostow, W. W. 1960. *The Stages of Economic Growth: A Non-Communist Manifesto.* Cambridge, UK: Cambridge University Press.

Schedler, Andreas, ed. 2006. *Electoral Authoritarianism: The Dynamics of Unfree Competition*. Boulder, CO: Lynne Rienner.

———. 2009. "The Contingent Power of Authoritarian Elections." In *Democratization by Elections: A New Mode of Transition*, edited by Staffan I. Lindberg, 291–313. Baltimore, MD: Johns Hopkins University Press.

Tarrow, Sidney G. 1998. *Power in Movement: Social Movements and Contentious Politics*. New York: Cambridge University Press.

Tibi, Bassam. 2012. *Islamism and Islam*. New Haven, CT: Yale University Press.

Weber, Max. 1978. *Economy and Society*. Edited by Guenther Ross and Claus Wittich. Berkeley: University of California Press. (Originally published as *Wirtschaft und Gesellschaft* in Germany in 1925.)

RESOURCES FOR FURTHER STUDY

Dahl, Robert A. 1971. *Polyarchy: Participation and Opposition*. New Haven, CT: Yale University Press.

Esposito, John L. 1997. *Political Islam: Revolution, Radicalism, or Reform?* Boulder, CO: Lynne Rienner.

Held, David. 1996. *Models of Democracy*. 2nd ed. Stanford, CA: Stanford University Press.

Husain, Mir Zohair. 2003. *Global Islamic Politics*. 2nd ed. New York: Longman.

Marx, Karl, and Friedrich Engels. 1978. *The Marx-Engels Reader*. Edited by Robert C. Tucker. 2nd ed. New York: Norton.

McCann, James A., and Jorge I. Domínguez. 1998. "Mexicans React to Electoral Fraud and Political Corruption: An Assessment of Public Opinion and Voting Behavior." *Electoral Studies* 17 (4): 483–503. doi: 10.1016/S0261-3794(98)00026-2.

Mill, John Stuart. 1870. *The Subjection of Women*. New York: D. Appleton.

Pitcher, Anne, Mary H. Moran, and Michael Johnston. 2009. "Rethinking Patrimonialism and Neopatrimonialism in Africa." *African Studies Review* 52 (1): 125–156. doi:10.1353/arw.0.0163.

Roy, Olivier. 2004. *Globalized Islam: The Search for a New Ummah*. CERI Series in Comparative Politics and International Studies. New York: Columbia University Press.

Sargent, Lyman Tower. 1987. *Contemporary Political Ideologies: A Comparative Analysis*. 7th ed. Chicago: Dorsey Press.

Sherman, John W. 2000. "The Mexican 'Miracle' and Its Collapse." In *The Oxford History of Mexico*, edited by Michael C. Meyer and William H. Beezley, 537–568. Oxford, UK: Oxford University Press.

Suchlicki, Jaime. 2008. *Mexico: From Montezuma to the Rise of the PAN*. 3rd ed. Washington, DC: Potomac Books.

WEB RESOURCES

CIRI Human Rights Data Project
   (http://www.humanrightsdata.org)

Citizenship, Involvement, Democracy Survey
   (http://www.uscidsurvey.org)

DataGov, Governance Indicators Database
   (http://www.iadb.org/datagob)

Freedom House, Freedom in the World Survey
   (http://www.freedomhouse.org/report/freedom-world/freedom-world-2013)

4 STATES AND IDENTITY

KEY QUESTIONS

- How and why do identity groups form and become politically salient?

- How does the social construction of identity groups influence who has power in a state?

- What are the different political issues faced by different types of identity groups?

- Why does ethnic, religious, or racial diversity lead to violent conflict in some places but not in others?

- What lessons can be learned that might help prevent identity-based conflict in the future?

The great political battle of the second half of the twentieth century was between liberalism and communism, but nationalism won. Nationalist, ethnic, and religious movements seemed to be the main beneficiaries of the fall of communism, and they emerged as the greatest challenges to democracy. Since the end of the Cold War, an internationalist Islamist movement has gained strength in many countries, a number of countries in the former Soviet sphere have been wracked by ethnically based political battles, and full-scale genocide has occurred in Bosnia and Rwanda. From the battles to create new governments in Iraq and Afghanistan to secessionist struggles in Chechnya and ethnic conflict in Kyrgyzstan, "identity politics" has come to the fore.

Comparativists began examining political conflicts based on identity long before the post–Cold War surge in identity conflicts. The first major question we address is, Why do these identities emerge and become politically important in the first place? We also ask how race, ethnicity, and religion influence groups' access to power and how groups might share power to reduce conflict. Finally, we ask why ethnic, religious, or racial fragmentation leads to violence in some places but not in others.

We address identity politics in both this chapter and in chapter 12. In this chapter, we look at identity groups that have often challenged the very existence of modern states. In chapter 12, we will examine groups that

A Kyrgyz (left) and an Uzbek (right) man shake hands in 2010 during a time of violent ethnic conflict in Kyrgyzstan. Identity conflict cannot be understood simply by examining physical or cultural markers of difference between groups; rather, it is a result of complex social and political processes.

question and wish to change the terms of modern citizenship—the ways in which they are included and represented in modern states—but not the existence of the states themselves. As we noted in chapter 2, states and nations are intimately connected. Internationally, the state is seen as the representative and voice of the nation. Domestically, political leaders can gain legitimacy and power by proclaiming their nationalism and castigating their opponents as "traitors" to the nation. As modern states developed, many actively championed the creation of nations over which to rule. This process almost always involved attempts to homogenize a disparate populace. In some cases, this led to the exclusion of certain groups from the "nation." In others, reactions against the effort to create a homogeneous national identity led to the rise of nationalist, ethnic, racial, or religious movements that claimed an identity distinct from the "nation" that the state was proclaiming. These groups thus questioned the very existence of the state, or at least demanded some degree of political autonomy within it.

We noted in chapter 3 that groups based on some sense of common identity are only one of many kinds of political groups, but they often have a particularly intense

COUNTRY AND CONCEPT
Ethnicity, Race, and Religion

Country	Major language group	Largest ethnic/ racial group, % of population	Largest religions, % of population	Index of ethnic fractionalization*	Major modern, identity-based conflicts
Brazil	1 major (Portuguese)	White, 53.7%	Roman Catholic (nominal) 73.6%, Protestant 15.4%	0.5408	None
China	1 major (Mandarin), ~6-12 sublanguages (though categorization is controversial)	Han Chinese, 91.5%	Officially atheist, so percentages unknown. Current estimates are Taoist, Buddhist, and Christian 3-4%; Muslim 1-2%. Actual percentages likely much higher.	0.1538	Uyghur dispute, 1949– Tibetan dispute, 1959–
Germany	1 major (German), 7 minor	German, 91.5%	Protestant 34%, Roman Catholic 34%, Muslim 3.7%	0.1682	Nazi repression of Jews/ Holocaust, 1933-1945
India	1 major linguistic group (Hindi, 41%), with hundreds of other major and minor language groups and dialects	Hindi, 41%	Hindu 80.5%, Muslim 13.4%	0.4182	• India/Pakistan partition, 1947-1948 • Kashmir dispute, 1947– • Hindu-Muslim conflicts/riots, 1950–(intermittent) • Sikh independence movement, 1960s-1984
Iran	4 major (Persian, Pashto, Kurdish, and Balochi); more than 80 other varieties	Persian, 61%	Shiite Muslim 89%, Sunni Muslim 9%	0.6684	Islamic Revolution, 1978-1979
Japan	1 major (Japanese)	Japanese, 98.5%	Shinto 84% and Buddhist 71%	0.0119	None
Mexico	1 major (Spanish); several indigenous languages	Mestizo, 60%	Roman Catholic 83%	0.5418	Chiapas Rebellion, 1994–
Nigeria	6 major (English, Hausa, Yoruba, Igbo, Fulani, Ibibio); more than 500 total	Hausa and Fulani, 29%	Muslim (mostly Sunni) 50%, Christian 40%	0.8505	• Biafran civil war, 1967-1970 • Ogoni and related movements, 1993– • Muslim-Christian battles over *sharia*, 1999–(intermittent); *Boko Haram* Islamist group

Russia	1 major linguistic group (Russian), with more than 100 other major and minor languages	Russian, 79.8%	Russian Orthodox 15-20%, Muslim 10-15%	0.2452	• War of Transniestira, 1990-1992 • Chechen Wars, 1994-1996, 1999-
United Kingdom	1 (English), with more than 5 others, including Scots, Welsh, Gaelic	White British, 92.1%	Church of England 22.2%, all Christian 71.6%	0.1211	Northern Ireland nationalist movement, 1921-1998
United States	1 (English), but with 11% of the population speaking Spanish	White alone, 79.96%	Protestant 51.3%, Roman Catholic 23.9%	0.4901	• Civil War with slavery as key issue, 1861-1865 • Urban race riots, 1965-1968

Sources: Data are from most recent country census results, the *CIA World Factbook*, and the United Nations. Ethnic fragmentation data are from Alberto Alesina et al., "Fractionalization," *Journal of Economic Growth* 8, no. 2 (2003): 155-194.

*0 = perfectly homogeneous and 1 = highly fragmented.

hold on people's loyalties. Few people would risk their lives defending the Sierra Club or Chamber of Commerce, but everyone is expected to do so for their nation, and many would do so for their ethnic or religious group as well. Political mobilization of this intensity can lead to political violence. The potential for this ultimate political commitment means that states must and do care deeply about identity politics. All states seek to develop and gain legitimacy from some sense of identity, but the "wrong" identity can be the gravest threat a state can face.

The Country and Concept table on pages 146–147 portrays the linguistic, ethnic, racial, and religious diversity in our case study countries as well as the major conflicts that have arisen from that diversity. Our case studies run the gamut from one of the

Afrikaners enjoy a segregated beach in the 1950s in South Africa. Systems of racial segregation like apartheid in South Africa or Jim Crow in the United States require not just separation of races but careful construction of racial identity to clearly demarcate the races. Under apartheid, hundreds of people got their official racial classification changed each year.

most ethnically homogeneous societies in the world, Japan, to two of the most diverse, India and Nigeria. Some have seen frequent identity-based violent conflicts, while others have had none. What accounts for these differences?

THE DEBATE OVER IDENTITY

Many people view loyalty to their nation, ethnic group, or religion as natural, or even divinely ordained, but the intensity and political impact of this loyalty vary widely across countries and over time. While group membership of some sort may be "natural" to humans, a particularly intense political loyalty to the nation, ethnic group, or faith clearly is not, given how greatly it varies. The **political saliency**—the political impact and importance—of identity groups is created, not innate. Explaining this process is our first major task. Given the enduring importance of identity to politics, it's not surprising that social scientists have developed several different approaches to understanding how identities are formed and why they become politically salient. Theorists disagree over whether identity politics should be explained by focusing on the elite or society as a whole and whether rational self-interest or political culture is the primary motivating force. The three main approaches to explaining the rise of identity groups also have implications for how identity-based conflicts could be resolved.

The oldest approach is now commonly called **primordialism.** Primordialism provides the central assumptions of many people's understanding of group origins and differences, and it is implicit in the arguments of most nationalist, ethnic, and racial leaders. The purest primordialists believe exactly what we mentioned above: that identity groups are in some sense "natural" or God given, that they have existed since "time immemorial," and that they can be defined unambiguously by such clear criteria as kinship, language, culture, or phenotype (physical characteristics, including skin color, facial features, and hair). Based on these assumptions, many primordialists see conflict among groups as understandable, and perhaps even inevitable, given their innate differences. Resolving these conflicts, therefore, seems unlikely to primordialists; the best option is probably separate states for the "naturally" distinct and conflicting groups. Few social scientists are pure primordialists today; virtually all have been convinced that group identities change enough that the argument that they are somehow "natural" is insupportable. However, the approach still holds important popular and political influence.

A more nuanced primordial argument can be based on political culture or political psychology. Because cultural values and beliefs are deeply ingrained, they can be the basis for more or less immutable group identities. Religious tenets understood in this way served as the basis of an influential work by Samuel Huntington titled *The Clash of Civilizations* (1996/1997). Huntington argued that the world can be divided into seven or eight major "civilizations" based largely on religious identity, and that the major wars of the future will occur along the boundaries of these civilizations. Psychology, of course, is equally deep-seated. Roger Petersen (2002) argued that emotions like fear,

political saliency
The degree to which something is of political importance

primordialism
A theory of identity that sees identity groups as being in some sense "natural" or God given, as having existed since "time immemorial," and as defined unambiguously by such clear criteria as kinship, language, culture, or phenotype

Video link:
The myth of the clash of civilizations

hatred, and resentment can trigger ethnic conflict, typically set off by some structural change such as the abrupt end of communism in Eastern Europe.

The first major challenge to primordialism came from scholars who proposed a theory known as **instrumentalism.** Instrumentalists reject the idea that politically important identity groups originate from the deeply held, enduring characteristics emphasized by primordialists. Instrumentalism is instead a rational-choice theory focused on elites: rational and self-interested elites manipulate symbols and feelings of identity to mobilize a political following. Paul Brass, the first to put this view into words, argued that ethnic groups "are created and transformed by particular elites . . . [and t]his process invariably involves competition and conflict for political power, economic benefits, and social status between competing elite, class and leadership groups" (1991, 25). According to instrumentalists, without elite leadership and context, "primordial" identities have little political relevance, the "cultural givens" won't matter much, and people who possess common cultural traits may not even see themselves as part of a cohesive group. For instrumentalists, then, resolving identity conflicts is primarily a matter of finding ways to prevent elites from mobilizing political followings based on identity groups, or giving them incentives to work cooperatively to reduce conflict.

The most recent and currently dominant approach to understanding identity is **constructivism.** Like primordialism, it is partly based on political culture, but instead of accepting the primordialists' view of cultural identities as unchanging, constructivism uses the postmodern ideas of political culture outlined in chapter 1, emphasizing the shifting interpretation of symbols and stories. It also accepts much of the instrumentalists' focus on the malleability of identity but suggests the process is more complex because elites cannot manipulate identities in any way they please. In this sense, constructivism is a more pluralist and less elite theory. Constructivists argue that a complex process, usually referred to as **social construction,** creates identities. Societies collectively "construct" identities as a wide array of actors continually discuss the question of who "we" are.

According to constructivism, this discourse is crucial to defining identities, or "imagined communities" (Anderson 1991). Identity communities are "imagined" in the sense that they exist because people believe they do: people come to see themselves as parts of particular communities based on particular traits. These communities are not immutable, though they typically change relatively slowly. Furthermore, individuals are members of a number of different groups at the same time. Elites can attempt to mobilize people using the discourse and symbols of any one of several identities in a particular time and place, but they cannot create an identity that no one else has imagined; the ongoing social discourse provides the cultural material for and limits on elite manipulation.

This creation of social and cultural boundaries, even where no legal ones exist, is central to the social construction of identity. As a group defines who "we" are, it also creates boundaries that define who "they" are. To take the most obvious example, the

Video link: Samuel Huntington on *The Clash of Civilizations*

instrumentalism
A theory of identity politics that argues rational and self-interested elites manipulate symbols and feelings of identity to mobilize a political following

constructivism
A theory of identity group formation that argues that identities are created through a complex process usually referred to as social construction

social construction
Part of constructivist approach to identity, the process through which societies collectively "construct" identities as a wide array of actors continually discuss the question of who "we" are

Video link: A primer on social construction

concepts and identities of "man" and "woman" could not exist without each other. If humans were a species of only one sex, neither word would exist. The same is true, constructivists argue, for all types of identity.

Afrikaner identity in South Africa, for instance, emerged in the nineteenth century among the descendants of Dutch and French settlers in juxtaposition to both the indigenous black African population and the invasion of British colonists. The social construction of this particular identity inherently included and excluded, and who was included and excluded had crucial consequences for who ruled. When the Nationalist Party took power and instituted apartheid in 1948, it did so in the name of the Afrikaner nation; while Nationalists allowed British citizens full political rights, they kept power closely in Afrikaner hands and denied black South Africans any power whatsoever. Someone perceived as not part of a nation, as black South Africans were, had no significant social standing or political influence. Within a nation, if a powerful racial or ethnic group sees itself as superior, other groups may have difficulty asserting significant political power. The very terms by which identities are constructed can influence who has the most power.

Constructivists argue that identities and boundaries are created in part by the interpretation and reinterpretation of symbols and stories. Through families, the media, and the public education system in all countries, individuals develop a sense of identity as they learn the importance and meaning of key symbols and stories. The state always plays an important role in this process. As a government develops and implements educational curricula, it requires that children be taught the "national history," which can include only certain events interpreted in certain ways if the "facts" are to support a specific national identity. The end result of this only partly planned and always amorphous process is adherence to certain beliefs, values, symbols, and stories that come to constitute an identity: for example, a flag, a monarch, the struggle for independence, the fight for racial equality, and monuments to fallen heroes. Marc Howard Ross (2007), though not defining himself as a constructivist, made a similar point, arguing that what he called "psychocultural narratives and dramas" shape groups' identities and interests.

Some of the most important symbols in the social construction of identity involve gender. Notions of gender—and in particular symbols of what a "proper" woman is within a national, ethnic, religious, or racial group—are frequently key ways in which group boundaries are demarcated. Nira Yuval-Davis and Flora Anthias (1989) argued that women's identity is crucial to establishing other identity categories. By having babies, women literally reproduce the community. As the primary child care providers in almost all societies, they also pass on key cultural elements to the next generation. Finally, women serve as symbolic markers of community identity and boundaries. Anne McClintock (1991), for instance, showed how the idea of a "pure" Afrikaner woman helped solidify Afrikaner nationalism and separate it from other white South Africans in particular. A more recent example is the wearing of the Islamic veil, which has become an issue of debate both in Europe and in several Middle Eastern countries (see chapter 12). What women do, how they behave, and where and how they are seen can all be issues of identity. We discuss women's movements in chapter 12 because they focus primarily on redefining citizenship rather than the nation itself, but we must note here that when women question their existing roles, they threaten virtually all other communal identities that rely in part on particular gender roles and symbols to define themselves.

Constructivists often look beyond formal political solutions to try to reduce identity-based conflict. While instrumentalists are mainly concerned with affecting elite political behavior, constructivists often focus on trying to shift identity-based discourses over the longer term to create more inclusive identities and thereby reduce the sense of "us" versus "them" on which conflict is based. They may, for instance, suggest rethinking how the "national" history is taught to allow what they see as greater inclusion of different groups in the national narrative, giving people in those groups a greater sense of recognition and belonging. This can reduce stigmatization of those groups and thereby reduce possible future tension and conflicts. For instance, in the United States in the 1990s, historians influenced by constructivism suggested significant and controversial changes to the teaching of U.S. history in public schools to include more material on racial minorities' roles, in particular. Critics suggested this would undermine national unity by emphasizing differences, while supporters saw it as teaching a more inclusive national story that could help reduce long-standing racial tensions and misunderstandings.

Like most contemporary social scientists, in this text we adopt a primarily constructivist approach, as it seems to combine the best of past theories. It is clear that identities are not fixed, and, as we'll see below, their political saliency varies greatly, both across countries and over time. Elites certainly play an important role in the process of creating and politically mobilizing identity groups, but identities develop over too long a period and are too intensely felt to be subject to complete manipulation. Culture matters, not as a static entity but rather as a set of symbols and stories available for interpretation. Leaders of groups that are excluded from power can interpret the symbols and stories of identity categories to raise passions and challenge the status quo. State leaders typically work to reinforce a sense of national identity tied to support for the state and to find ways to accommodate other identities without threatening the strength and political legitimacy of the state itself.

IDENTITY-BASED POLITICAL MOBILIZATION AND VIOLENCE

Constructivism is the dominant theory trying to explain how identities form and become politically salient. It does not, however, fully explain why some identities become the basis for large-scale and effective political movements while others don't. Why are leaders of some national or ethnic groups able to mobilize mass followings, putting thousands of demonstrators in the streets proclaiming their groups' demands? Why are some of those efforts successful at achieving their goals and others are not?

Moving a step further, why do some of these movements ultimately employ violence while others remain peaceful?

Many theorists attempting to address these questions have looked at identity-based groups as just one subset of a broader category; they attempt to explain political mobilization of all types of political groups, not just those based on identity. The oldest theories are psychological. The best known is based on the concept of **relative deprivation,** a group or individual's belief that they are not getting their share of something of value relative to others in the society. If people come to identify this relative deprivation with an identity—their ethnicity, race, or religion, for example—it can prove a powerful motivator of action, or so early psychological theorists such as Ted Robert Gurr (1970) argued. Recently, Julian Wucherpfennig and colleagues (2012) argued that civil wars, once started, endure much longer if they involve ethnic groups that have been systematically excluded from power, implicitly suggesting that relative deprivation when felt along ethnic lines plays a role in prolonging violence, whether it explains the origins of that violence or not.

Most recent theorists have suggested that psychological motivations are inadequate at explaining why some identities ultimately become the basis for large-scale movements and others don't. Instrumentalists, of course, argued that leaders mobilize followings, implicitly making a very individualistic argument that leaders' ability explains why some identity-based movements are larger and more successful than others. More recent theory, though, has mostly focused on a combination of structure and process. Doug McAdams, Sidney Tarrow, and Charles Tilly (2001) argued that identity-based movements can be understood as part of what they termed **contentious politics,** which they defined as any interaction in which a group makes claims that conflict with others' interests, leading to coordinated efforts to secure those claims that in some way involve the state. They used their framework to analyze everything from social protests to civil war, but its origins lie in the study of social movements (which we examine in chapter 7). Key elements of their understanding of how movements succeed or fail include the organizational and other resources they and their opponents have, the various groups' perceptions of the political opportunities they face, and how they socially construct political identities. National, ethnic, racial, and religious identities are exceptionally powerful identities on which to base group mobilization. The contentious politics model tries to explain how powerful this mobilization is by examining the resources of the various groups involved, including the state, and the opportunities and threats they face, tracing the interactions of the various groups involved to understand the eventual outcome.

The contentious politics framework has become an influential tool comparativists use to examine political mobilization of all sorts, including mobilization based on identity. (We will discuss it again in chapter 7, when we examine social movements, and chapter 9, when we look at revolutions.) While it has proven useful to explain mobilization, however, it doesn't fully explain when and why nonviolent mobilization shifts to violence. Ethnic or national groups that turn to violence to pursue their ends

relative deprivation
A group or individual's belief that they are not getting their share of something of value relative to others in the society

contentious politics
Any interaction in which a group makes claims that conflict with others' interests, leading to coordinated efforts to secure those claims that in some way involve the state

make headlines, even though they represent a minority of all such movements. Most people find it easy to understand why people who feel their group is being repressed or deprived would march in the streets in protest; it's harder to understand why they would start killing people from other groups or take up arms against the government.

Comparativists have used numerous theories to grapple with this difficult question. Probably the oldest is the primordialist argument of "ancient hatreds": some groups of people have grievances dating back centuries, hatreds they pass from one generation to the next, and they will attack one another when they get the chance. As we've seen, though, primordialism ignores the historical variation and modern origins of most identities and fails to explain why violence breaks out at certain times and not others. A popular alternative is a rational-choice explanation based on the **security dilemma.** This is a situation in which two or more groups do not trust and may even fear one another and do not believe that institutional constraints will protect them, often because the state is weak. In that context, the fear of being attacked leads people to attack first, believing that doing so is necessary to protect themselves.

Another well-known approach was developed by economists (Collier and Hoeffler 2004; Collier, Hoeffler, and Rohner 2009) but has been very influential in political science. These economists sought to explain the outbreak of civil wars, whether tied to identity or not. Based on a large, quantitative examination of all civil wars since 1960, they argued that greed and opportunity were the key factors that led to violence. Where valuable resources such as minerals were available for groups to fight over and reap the rewards of, civil war was more likely, indicating greed is a major driving force. Civil war is also more likely in societies with large numbers of young men, available to join ethnic militia, and in societies with mountainous terrain in which rebels can hide, suggesting opportunity is also a major factor. In contrast, societies with greater ethnic fragmentation were not more likely to have civil wars, indicating these wars really weren't about identity politics at all, even if their leaders claimed that is what they were fighting over. Implicit in this model is an instrumentalist view of ethnically based civil war: leaders manipulate the right context to start wars.

Some political scientists have used the comparative method to present alternative arguments to the economists' quantitative approach. Monica Toft (2003) tried to explain violence in which the state is battling a communally based rebel group (as opposed to two or more nonstate groups battling one another). She argued that when both a geographically concentrated group and the state view the group's territory as essential and indivisible, violence is much more likely. A group that is geographically concentrated will have greater capability and legitimacy for demanding control over its own territory, while the state is likely to fear the precedent set by the successful rebellion and so is unwilling to bargain over it. Violence is often the result of this standoff.

In contrast, Roger Petersen (2002) combined structural and psychological explanations, hypothesizing that emotions are crucial mechanisms for translating the structural factors that create the possibility of violence into action. He posited three emotions that serve this purpose: fear, hatred, and resentment. Fear is a response to

security dilemma
A situation in which two or more groups do not trust and may even fear one another, and do not believe that institutional constraints will protect them, increasing the likelihood that violence will break out between them

situations like the security dilemma in which a group's primary motivation is safety. Hatred is a motivation when an opportunity arises for violence against a group that has been frequently attacked in the past. Resentment motivates violence after a sudden change in status hierarchies among ethnic groups. Each logically results in violence against a particular type of group; fear, for instance, targets violence at the group considered the biggest threat, while resentment targets violence at that highest-status group that can be effectively lowered via violence.

Perhaps the most difficult test of these theories in recent history is the genocide in Rwanda in 1994. In one hundred days, thousands of Hutu slaughtered 800,000 of their Tutsi compatriots in the worst genocide since the Holocaust. In most cases of genocide, including Rwanda, people had been living together more or less peacefully (though not without resentment and memories of past violence) when, seemingly overnight, large numbers of one group started slaughtering people in a different group. While many people view Africa as full of "ancient tribal" animosities, no situation shows the inaccuracy of this primordial argument better than Rwanda. Hutu and Tutsi spoke the same language, lived in the same communities and neighborhoods, had the same customs, followed the same religions, and had lived for centuries in the same kingdom. Cultural differences between them didn't exist. What did exist were several other elements commonly involved in political mobilization and violence: a potential battle over a key resource (land), a sense of relative deprivation, fear of attack in a situation of extreme political uncertainty, and an elite using a racist ideology to mobilize hatred of the "other" as part of an effort to build a strong state that it could control.

A soldier stands at a checkpoint in Rwanda in 1994. Like all genocides, Rwanda's was planned in advance and led by a militia created for the purpose. Roadside checkpoints were a key location where Hutu militia members found and killed Tutsi.

The Tutsi dominated the precolonial kingdom, but a Hutu-led government controlled the country from independence in 1960 to the genocide. Tutsi exiles who had long lived in neighboring Uganda invaded the country in 1990. By 1993 a cease-fire had been established, and democratic elections were planned. Elements on both sides, however, feared the results. Hutu leaders enjoyed the privileges of power and wanted to maintain them, and some Tutsi rebel leaders seemed unwilling to allow the majority (overwhelmingly Hutu) to rule, even via democratic means. A group of Hutu extremists in the government began propagating an anti-Tutsi ideology. They continuously told their followers that the Tutsi were trying to regain complete power, take away Hutu land, and kill them. In a very densely populated country dependent on agriculture, the threat to land ownership was particularly explosive. The Hutu extremists also created private militia of unemployed and desperate young Hutu men, and when the Hutu president's plane was shot down on April 6, 1994, the extremists and their armed militia swung into action. Barriers went up across streets all over the capital, and the militia began systematically executing "moderate" Hutu who might oppose the genocide (lists of the first to be killed had been prepared in advance), as well as any Tutsi they found. The extremist hate-radio directed much of the effort, telling the militia where Tutsi were hiding. Members of the militia demanded that other Hutu join them in identifying and killing Tutsi; those who refused would themselves be killed. The killing didn't stop until the Tutsi-led rebellion swept into the capital, took over the country, and stopped the genocide—but only after three-quarters of the entire Tutsi population had been killed. Instrumentalist leaders took advantage of a situation of fear (the security dilemma) and relative deprivation to mobilize people around a socially constructed identity tied to hatred of the opposing group. While crimes of this magnitude are still impossible to comprehend fully, we can see some patterns that help us find a rational explanation based on past theories.

We now turn to a more detailed examination of identity-based politics by looking at the following types of groups: those based on nation, ethnicity and religion, and race.

CRITICAL inquiry

Ethnic Fragmentation and Political Conflict

Scholars and policy makers have long argued that ethnic differences tend to produce violent political conflicts. Collier and Hoeffler (2009), however, claimed that ethnicity has little to do with conflict; it is simply a way to justify conflict and mobilize supporters. Map 4.1 provides measures of ethnic fragmentation and violent political conflict around the world. Comparing the two maps, what patterns do you see? Does it seem that countries with greater ethnic fragmentation also have a lot of violent political conflict? What hypotheses can you develop from the map to explain why political violence occurs more in some places than others? What do the maps suggest for the debate over what explains ethnically based violence?

NATIONS AND NATIONALISM

The nation remains a fundamental building block of the global political system. Each state claims to be the sole legitimate representative of a nation, and each nation claims a right to its own state. Despite this, clearly defining the word *nation* is no easy task. Writing over a century ago, French theorist Ernest Renan (1882), after trying to figure out which particular cultural characteristics produced nations in Europe, finally concluded that no single cultural feature was crucial. Instead,

> a nation is a soul, a spiritual principle. Two things, which are really only one, go to make up this soul or spiritual principle. One of these things lies in the past, the other in the present. The one is the possession in common of a rich heritage of memories; and the other is actual agreement, the desire to live together, and the will to continue to make the most of the joint inheritance.

MAP 4.1 Civil Wars and Ethnic Fragmentation

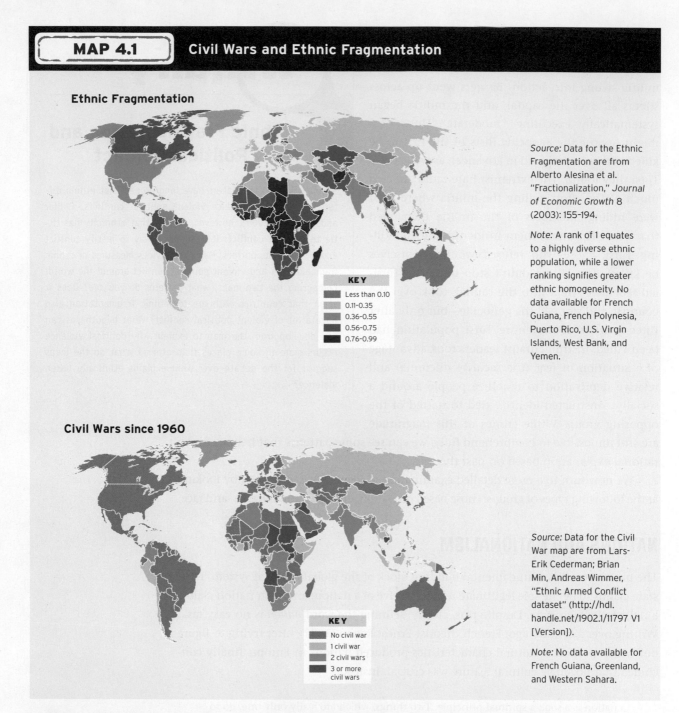

Ethnic Fragmentation

KEY
Less than 0.10
0.11–0.35
0.36–0.55
0.56–0.75
0.76–0.99

Source: Data for the Ethnic Fragmentation are from Alberto Alesina et al. "Fractionalization," *Journal of Economic Growth* 8 (2003): 155–194.

Note: A rank of 1 equates to a highly diverse ethnic population, while a lower ranking signifies greater ethnic homogeneity. No data available for French Guiana, French Polynesia, Puerto Rico, U.S. Virgin Islands, West Bank, and Yemen.

Civil Wars since 1960

KEY
No civil war
1 civil war
2 civil wars
3 or more civil wars

Source: Data for the Civil War map are from Lars-Erik Cederman; Brian Min, Andreas Wimmer, "Ethnic Armed Conflict dataset" (http://hdl.handle.net/1902.1/11797 V1 [Version]).

Note: No data available for French Guiana, Greenland, and Western Sahara.

A comparison of the level of ethnic fragmentation and the outbreak of civil wars around the world demonstrates that the relationship between ethnicity and violent conflict is more complicated than people usually assume. While some countries with the highest levels of ethnic fragmentation have suffered from multiple civil wars (such as Congo, Angola, and Nigeria), others have had none (Kenya, Kazakhstan, Canada).

The resemblance of Renan's deduction to contemporary notions of social construction is striking. A nation is an "imagined community," imagined through shared memories. All of those memories beyond the immediate experience of the individuals themselves are shared only because a group has learned to share them, in part through state-sponsored education.

The distinction between a nation and an ethnic group is less clear than that between a nation and a state. The Irish are members of a nation, but when they immigrate to the United States, they become, sooner or later, part of an "ethnic group." The Zulu in South Africa are an ethnic group, but the Palestinians, who are less culturally distinct from their neighbors (or at least from other Arabs) than are the Zulu from neighboring South African groups, are generally regarded as a nation. As Renan concluded long ago, no particular set of cultural markers fully distinguishes a nation from an ethnic group. The only clear definition ties back to the state. A **nation** is a group that proclaims itself a nation and has or seeks control of a state. This desire to be a nation and thus to control a national state is **nationalism.** Ethnic groups, on the other hand, do not think of themselves as nations and do not desire to control their own state as much as they want **autonomy** within a larger state.

Not surprisingly, most nationalist leaders are primordialists: each claims his nation has existed since the beginning of time as a mighty and proud people. As we saw in chapter 2, however, most scholars see nationalism as a fundamentally modern concept tied to the rise of the modern state and economy. The first European nations, such as France and England, were largely the products of preexisting states. Once nationalism emerged as an idea, though, political and intellectual elites started propagating a sense of national identity long before they controlled their own states, as the development of Germany demonstrates. In former colonies, nationalism emerged as a movement for independence from colonial oppressors. And once the creation of the state is accomplished, the process of developing a national identity continues. As Italian nationalist Massimo d'Azeglio declared shortly after the unification of Italy in the 1860s: "We have made Italy. Now we must make Italians."

A long debate exists over the origins of nationalism. Prior to the 1960s, most scholars were primordialists, assuming and asserting that nations stemmed from ancient cultural entities, just as nationalist leaders claimed. Since then, historical research has demonstrated that nations are modern entities, though this still leaves much to explain. Probably the most influential scholar, Ernest Gellner (1983), argued that the emergence of nations became necessary with industrialization. Rising industry required a large domestic market, which was facilitated by the rise of modern states, and a large workforce that was literate in the same language. States therefore created public education systems in a single vernacular language and actively propagated a sense of common identity to serve the needs of industry as well as to strengthen their own legitimacy. Marxist analysts argue that nationalism arose to facilitate capitalism, often in the "periphery" of the capitalist system where leaders needed a sense of national loyalty to gain legitimacy among workers who were hurt by capitalism (Nairn

nation
A group that proclaims itself a nation and has or seeks control of a state

nationalism
The desire to be a nation and thus to control a national state

autonomy
The ability and right of a group to partially govern itself within a larger state

Web link:
The Nationalism Project

Video link:
John Green on nationalism

1977). Benedict Anderson (1991) argued that the rise of printing led to the expansion of a written vernacular around which nationalism developed; the state leveraged this technology in the form of education, mapmaking, and censuses. While there are exceptions (Smith 1998), most scholars support the idea that nations are modern entities tied in some way to the development of the modern state and economy.

Nationalism has a complicated relationship with liberal democracy as well. At least until the mid-twentieth century, many nationalists saw themselves as carving democratic nations out of the remnants of feudal or colonial empires. Before "we, the people" can declare ourselves sovereign, "we" must have a sense of "us" as a "people": who is and is not included in "us" defines who has the rights of democratic citizenship. If "we" use particular cultural or physical characteristics to define "us," then we exclude as well as include people in our "nation." In this context, two distinct forms of nationalism have crucial implications. **Cultural nationalism** is national unity based on a common cultural characteristic, and those people who don't share that particular characteristic cannot be included in the nation. This definition poses obvious challenges for democracy, for how can those lacking the "national" characteristic be full citizens with democratic rights? For this reason, most observers see **civic nationalism** as more supportive of democracy. In civic nationalism, the sense of national unity and purpose is based on a set of commonly held political beliefs. Those who share the beliefs are part of the nation. In many cases, societies' sense of nationalism may be unclear because both types are present simultaneously. Americans, for instance, would certainly claim a civic nationalism based on the principles in the Declaration of Independence and Constitution. On the other hand, a recent survey showed that over 90 percent of Americans think that for a person to be a "true American" he must speak English; among Americans with the strongest sense of national identity, two-thirds believed that a "true American" has to be Christian and one-third believed a "true American" has to be white (Theiss-Morse 2009). Clearly, cultural (in this case religious and racial) nationalism also exists in the United States.

France and Germany provide a classic comparison of these different kinds of nationalism and their complicated relationship with democracy. The two countries also illustrate that even what are perceived to be strong and deeply rooted nations were, in fact, constructed, and relatively recently. As Rogers Brubaker put it, "For two centuries . . . France and Germany have been constructing, elaborating, and furnishing to other states distinctive, even antagonistic, models of nationhood and national self-understanding" (1992, 1). He went on to express how these two models illustrate the variation in the relationship between the state and the nation that we outlined above:

> In the French tradition, the nation has been conceived in relation to the institutions and territorial frame of the state. Revolutionary and Republican definitions of nationhood . . . reinforced what was already in the ancient regime an essentially political understanding of nationhood. . . . [T]he German understanding has been *Volk*-centered and differentialist. Since national feeling developed before the

cultural nationalism
National unity based on a common cultural characteristic wherein only those people who share that characteristic can be included in the nation

civic nationalism
A sense of national unity and purpose based on a set of commonly held political beliefs

nation-state, the German idea of the nation was not originally political. . . . This prepolitical German nation, this nation in search of a state, was conceived not as the bearer of universal political values, but as an organic cultural, linguistic, or racial community. . . . On this understanding, nationhood is an ethnocultural, not a political fact. (Brubaker 1992, 1)

These generalizations have regularly been contested within each country, however. French nationalism at first glance seems predominantly civic, but it has strong cultural elements; German nationalism is clearly cultural, but that notion has been continually challenged, especially since the Nazi era. France's absolutist state was instrumental in forging a unified concept of a French nation. The state expanded outward from Paris, incorporating neighboring regions that spoke various languages into a single political unit. The concept of nationalism did not fully enter French political discourse until the Revolution of 1789, long after the state was fully established and quite extensive. This allowed a civic and territorial nationalism to emerge, but French nationalism was culturally **assimilationist** from the start. Regional linguistic and cultural divisions were seen not as the democratic right of separate peoples but rather as unacceptable divisions in the unity of revolutionary and democratic France. This nationalist ideal fully developed under the Third Republic after 1870, when the country's first universal, public education system was created, consciously designed to instill a common version of the French language and a common set of democratic political values. By the end of the nineteenth century, France's citizenship laws were based on *jus soli,* or residence on the state's "soil," thus conferring citizenship on second-generation immigrants.

This primarily civic nationalism did not go without challenge, however. Throughout the nineteenth century, France's political right tried to create a strongly cultural and primordial nationalism that focused on an often quasi-racial definition of the "pure" France that excluded immigrants. The contemporary heir to the movement is the National Front (FN) led by Marine Le Pen. The FN advocates a shift from *jus soli* to *jus sanguinis*, citizenship based on blood rather than residence, a demand that reflects a primordial understanding of the nation. The National Front's efforts to redefine French nationality and citizenship in the direction of *jus sanguinis* have never succeeded, but the party's appeal has been substantial. Our case study of Germany presents quite a distinct picture from neighboring France but nonetheless shows the continuing tension between civic and cultural nationalism.

assimilationist
Characterized by a belief that immigrants or other members of minority cultural communities ought to adopt the culture of the majority population

jus soli
Literally, citizenship dependent on "soil," or residence within the national territory; for example, in France

jus sanguinis
Citizenship based on "blood" ties; for example, in Germany

A person poses with a French electoral card in 2009 to protest the government's decision to launch a debate on national identity. Critics argued that the debate was a way for the mainstream conservative government to appeal to supporters of the far-right, anti-immigrant National Front, a move that could stir up divisive national and racial sentiment in order to win votes.

NATIONALISM IN GERMANY

German nationalism long predates the modern German state. For centuries, German speakers lived side by side with Slavs and other ethnic groups while retaining their German language and culture. While a "primordial" language and culture existed, however, it took Napoleon's invasion in the early nineteenth century and the influence of the Romantic movement to foment modern German nationalism. Advocates of Romanticism envisioned the nation as an organic whole with a "distinct personality" (note the similarity to fascist ideas outlined in chapter 3). Intellectual elites shaped German nationalism by defining "Germany" in linguistic and cultural terms that juxtaposed German identity with the identities of the neighboring Slavs in the east and French in the west.

As outlined in chapter 2, Otto von Bismarck finally united much of what is now Germany in 1871. Like his contemporaries in France's Third Republic, he tried to use education to create greater cultural homogeneity in the new state, and he wrote citizenship laws based partly on *jus soli*. His new *Reich* (the German nation and its territory), however, still included large populations of linguistic minorities and excluded huge numbers of German speakers in Austria and eastern Europe. Continuing emigration of Germans to eastern Europe and immigration of non-Germans into the *Reich* led nationalists, such as the Pan-German League, to demand a revision of the citizenship laws in 1913. The new laws reflected the long-standing German cultural conceptualization of

- **ORIGINS**
  Nationalism precedes the modern state

- **TYPE**
  Cultural nationalism until recently

- **BASIS OF CITIZENSHIP**
  Jus sanguinis, until recent reform

- **CONTEXT**
  Turkish "guest workers" and continuing debate over who is "German"

A Turkish woman walks past a Turkish grocery store in an immigrant neighborhood in Berlin. Until 2000, Germany's *jus sanguinis* definition of citizenship meant that millions of Turkish residents and their German-born children were not citizens. Since then, more have gained citizenship, though a restrictive process means only a minority of longtime Turkish residents have become citizens so far.

the nation by basing citizenship strictly on *jus sanguinis,* legally codifying a cultural understanding of what it meant to be "German."

Nazi ideology developed out of German cultural nationalism, marrying it to explicit racism. The nation was thought of not only in cultural, but also racial, terms. The master Aryan race was superior to all others, and Adolf Hitler's regime stripped "non-Aryans" of citizenship rights, expelling or exterminating many, especially Jews. With the end of World War II, the Soviet Union expelled millions of ethnic Germans from eastern Europe, and others left voluntarily as Soviet control tightened. Citizenship in the new West Germany continued to reflect the concept of the cultural nation: all ethnic Germans were welcomed into West Germany and automatically granted citizenship. This open-arms policy was in stark contrast to the treatment of the growing number of non-German immigrants, who rarely gained citizenship no matter how many generations their ancestors had resided in Germany. Access to political power required being part of the German cultural nation.

The debate over who is and should be "German" continues today, especially in the context of growing immigration. The large numbers of Turks who immigrated to Germany in recent decades were initially welcomed to fulfill essential jobs. Following German national self-conception, these immigrants were known as *gastarbeiters,* or "guest workers"; they were to stay as long as they were employed and then return home. Today, more than two million ethnic Turks live in Germany, and many have raised children there. Until recently, however, very few could gain German citizenship because of Germany's *jus sanguinis* law. Starting in the 1980s, a movement demanding greater inclusion of immigrants had arisen, supported by labor unions and the new Green Party. In 2000 the government (then ruled by the Social Democrats and Greens) finally allowed German-born children of immigrants who had been in the country at least eight years to apply for citizenship, provided they could pass a German language test and renounced their prior citizenship. As a result, approximately 800,000 former Turkish citizens now have German citizenship. After an initial spurt, though, the number of immigrants successfully applying for citizenship dropped in half from 2000 to 2010. Turkish immigrants, in particular, did not want to give up their prior citizenship, and the German government rarely allowed them to become dual citizens. About two-thirds of Turkish residents remain noncitizens, then, despite the fact that many have lived in Germany for decades.

Video link:
Report on *Germany Does Away with Itself*

The revised citizenship law did not end the debate over the place of Turks in the German nation. Some argue it helped create a backlash against Muslim immigrants in particular. In 2010 a member of the board of the national bank, Thilo Sarrazin, wrote a book titled *Germany Does Away with Itself* that argued that Germany was becoming literally stupider and culturally weaker due to the presence of too many Muslim immigrants. This touched off a raging debate, and he was forced to resign, but a poll showed that as many as a third of Germans agreed with his sentiments and the book became a best seller. In May 2012, riots broke out in one city, pitting German nationalists who staged anti-Muslim rallies against Muslim immigrants upset at what they saw as disrespect for the Prophet Mohammed. Citizens of Turkish origin, though, have become more involved in politics, with a state governor appointing the first German cabinet minister of Turkish descent in 2010. Turkish political activists have also begun demanding the inclusion of Islam in religious education in public schools (in Germany, Christianity is regularly taught in public schools).

CASE Summary   The German case shows the underlying complexity of what may seem to be a very stable national identity. Germany long maintained a strictly cultural nationalism that left millions of immigrants and their children without political rights. A 2000 reform finally changed this, though citizenship is far from automatic. Neither civic nor cultural nationalism has become the unquestioned and universal conception of "we," at least not for very long. These political battles between contending visions of the national identity are fought in the realm of citizenship laws, meaning they have a direct bearing on who gains democratic rights and who does not.

CASE Questions

1. Most theorists of nationalism argue that it is a modern phenomenon rather than a relic of ancient history. In what ways is that true or not true in the German case?
2. What does the German (and French, in comparison) case suggest about the debate over whether civic or cultural nationalism is more beneficial in a democracy?

ETHNICITY AND RELIGION

As identity categories, ethnicity and religion share many characteristics. While religion is based on a set of beliefs and ethnicity on a perceived common culture or descent, ethnic and religious groups make similar political demands. Their different markers (beliefs versus culture) are not terribly important for understanding their political behavior. We turn to ethnicity first and then can apply much of what we learn to religion as well.

Ethnicity and Ethnic Conflict

Now that we have defined and illustrated what a nation is, defining an ethnic group becomes an easier task. An **ethnic group** is a group of people who see themselves as united by one or more cultural attributes or a sense of common history but do not see themselves as a nation seeking its own state. Like a nation and all other identity categories, ethnic identity is imagined: people's perceptions are what matter, not actual attributes or some "objective" interpretation of history. Ethnic groups may be based on very real cultural attributes, such as a common language, but even these

ethnic group
A group of people who see themselves as united by one or more cultural attributes or a sense of common history but do not see themselves as a nation seeking its own state

are subject to perception and change. In the former Yugoslavia, Serbs, Croats, and Bosniaks all spoke closely related versions of what was known as Serbo-Croatian. As ethnic conflict and then war emerged in the early 1990s, each group began claiming it spoke a distinct language—"Serbian," "Croatian," or "Bosnian"—and nationalists in all three groups began to emphasize the minor linguistic differences among them. People think of African "tribes" as modern remnants of ancient, unchanging groups, but the Nigerian case below shows how even there, ethnicity is socially constructed and quite modern. (See the "What's in a Name?" box on page 164 for a fuller discussion of "tribes" in Africa.)

If ethnic groups do not desire to have their own state, what do they want? Their political interests generally revolve around what Charles Taylor (1994) called the **politics of recognition.** All identity groups, including nations, want to be recognized. Ethnic groups usually desire recognition within the confines of a nation-state shared with other ethnic groups. This recognition may take the form of official state support of cultural events, school instruction in the local language, official recognition of the local language as one of the "national" languages, or inclusion of the ethnic group's history in the national history curriculum. If an ethnic group resides primarily in one area, it also may demand some type of regional autonomy, such as a federal system of government in which its leaders can control their own state or province. The issue of federalism became so contentious in India in the 1960s that the national government created a commission to examine it. The commission recommended the creation of a number of new states based on linguistic boundaries. For practical reasons, not all of India's hundreds of language areas could receive their own states, but the largest ones did.

In contrast to national identity, ethnicity is not always political. In the United States today, white ethnic identity has very little political content. Irish Americans may be proud of their heritage and identify culturally with Ireland, but few feel any common political interests based on that. This can change, of course: a century ago many Irish Americans felt their identity was tied very strongly to their political interests. A crucial question, then, is when and why ethnicity becomes politically salient. As instrumentalists point out, leadership can be a key catalyst. Because of the potential intensity of ethnic attachments, they are a tempting resource for ambitious politicians. A leader who can tie ethnic identity to political demands can gain tremendous support.

Constructivists point out, however, that leaders cannot do this at will. The context is almost always important. If a group believes those in power have discriminated against it economically, socially, or politically, members may see their political interests and ethnic identity as one and the same. Their history, which they may pass from parent to child, is one of discrimination at the hands of the powerful "other," leading to strong feelings of relative deprivation. On the other hand, sometimes relative wealth can lead to ethnic mobilization. If an ethnic group is based in a particular region that has a valuable resource such as oil, group members may feel that they should receive

politics of recognition
The demands for recognition and inclusion that have arisen since the 1960s in racial, religious, ethnic, gender, and other minority or socially marginalized groups

What's in a Name? Tribe, Ethnicity, and Nation

When Westerners think of Africans and Native Americans, they think of "tribes," but no one refers to the Basques in Spain or Scots in Britain as a tribe. Instead they are ethnic groups, linguistic groups, or "nations." We defined a nation as a group of people who have or want their own state. By that definition, Basques and Scots only partially qualify: some of them want their own state, but many simply want greater autonomy within Spain or Britain. In this sense, they are very similar to a good portion of the Zulu in South Africa. So why are the Zulu a tribe while the Scots and Basques are not?

The word *tribe* usually conjures up the image of a small, primitive group tied together by a common culture, language, kinship, and system of government based on a chief. People tend to understand tribes in primordialist and negative terms; that is, they are "traditional" groups that have survived into the modern world and therefore cause political problems. As our case study of Nigeria shows, nothing could be further from the truth. Modern African ethnic groups arose in their current form during the colonial era and only sometimes originated in precolonial identities or states. The Kalenjin of Kenya consist of eight separate groups speaking closely related languages that assumed a common ethnic identity only in

the 1950s, primarily via a popular radio program. To call the Kelenjin a "tribe," evoking the word's connotation of a small and primitive group, masks this history.

The real reason *tribe* is associated with Africans and Native Americans is rooted in eighteenth- and nineteenth-century racist assumptions. At least since Julius Caesar, *tribe* has implicitly meant a backward and inferior group of people. Caesar used *tribus* to refer to the "barbarian," blue-eyed blonds he conquered in northern Europe. Later, European slavers and colonists used it to classify people they saw as backward and inferior, and the term stuck. For an interesting discussion of the use of *tribe* in Africa, see Chris Lowe's 1997 article "Talking about 'Tribe': Moving from Stereotypes to Analysis" at www.africafocus.org/docs08/ethn0801.php. Contemporary scholars of Africa prefer the term *ethnic group* for people in Africa, Europe, or anywhere else who have an identity derived from some cultural characteristic but who are not a nation in the way scholars define that term. Many Native Americans, on the other hand, prefer the term *nation,* even though most of them do not seek complete sovereignty from the larger states in which they reside.

Web link:
Chris Lowe, "Talking about 'Tribe': Moving from Stereotypes to Analysis"

more benefits from what they see as "their" resource. The national government, on the other hand, will see the resource as belonging to the nation as a whole, to be controlled by the central government. This is a central issue in the ethnic and religious divisions in Iraq because the country's oil reserves are located in both Kurd and Shiite areas but not in Sunni areas. Sunni leaders, not surprisingly, want oil revenue fully controlled by the central government in Baghdad, not by regional governments.

A security dilemma can also lead to ethnic mobilization. With the fall of communism in eastern Europe and the former Soviet Union, many people felt great fear about the future. The old institutions had collapsed, and the new ones were untested. In this situation, it is relatively easy for a political leader to mobilize support with an ethnic or nationalist appeal that suggests that other groups will take advantage of the uncertain situation and try to dominate. A classic case is Serbian leader Slobodan Milošević, who proclaimed sympathy with the Serb minority in Kosovo in a famous speech in 1987, taking upon himself the mantle of Serb nationalism. Croatian and Bosnian Muslim leaders, fearful of Serb domination, soon responded in kind. The eventual result was war and genocide in which the three ethno-religious groups that had lived together relatively peacefully under Communist rule developed increasingly strident cultural nationalism and ultimately dismembered the country. The sudden creation of a security dilemma such as the collapse of communism can be what theorists of contentious politics call a key political opportunity. When combined with a capable leader who can mobilize enough material and organization resources, strong ethnic movements are likely to emerge.

Religion as Group Identity

We can apply most of what we have learned about ethnic groups to religious groups as well. A religious group identifies itself as having a particular set of characteristics centered on religious membership or beliefs. When membership alone is the criterion, the group is identified simply by nominal affiliation with the religion, regardless of actual practice or belief. The three major groups in the former Yugoslavia were defined primarily in this manner: Serbs are Orthodox Christian, Croats are Catholic, and Bosniaks are Muslim. As noted above, once tension and conflict began to emerge, leaders in each of the groups started to emphasize cultural distinctions. Ironically, because Communists had ruled the country since World War II, religious belief and practice were very low among all three groups prior to the conflict; religious affiliation was a marker of identity based on birth, not a matter of personal faith. As the conflict spread, religious observance increased within all three groups. Once people start shooting at you because of your religion, it starts to loom larger in your consciousness.

One might assume that religious group membership can be more inclusive and flexible than ethnicity, more like civic nationalism than cultural nationalism. Virtually all religions allow conversion to the faith, so while you may not be able to become Chechen, except perhaps through marriage, you can convert to Islam. In practice this may be more difficult than in theory, however, especially where religious identity has become a divisive cultural marker and a basis for political mobilization. It is unlikely that members of other groups will want to convert at this point, or be accepted if they did. Conversion is much more likely when the political salience of religious identity is relatively low.

The demands of religiously mobilized groups are comparable to those of ethnic groups: recognition and autonomy. For religious groups, recognition certainly involves the right to practice one's faith openly, but it might also include demands that the state officially recognize the religion in the form of state-sponsored religious holidays or recognize and perhaps fund religious schools. A desire for autonomy could be expressed as a demand for federalism if the religious group lives in a particular region. Within its own province, the group could then practice its religion and use the provincial government to support it. Demands for autonomy can also take the form of asking that religious leaders and organizations be granted legal control over marriage, death, and other personal matters.

Methods of Reducing Ethnic or Religious Conflict

Government leaders who want to remain in power and preserve peace must respond to or preempt the threat of politically mobilized ethnic or religious groups. One means of doing this, common in authoritarian governments, is simply to ban all public appeals to ethnicity, religion, or other "sectarian" identities. From the 1960s to the 1980s, Tanzania's one-party regime had internal elections that were actually competitive, but candidates were strictly forbidden from making any ethnic, regional, or religious appeals. Many a military leader has banned not only political parties but also all sorts of ethnically based groups and clubs.

Democracies typically take less draconian measures, trying to create institutions that recognize but limit conflict. Two broad approaches to this are the centripetal and consociational. The **centripetal approach,** championed most strongly by political scientist Donald Horowitz (1985), argues that ethnic or religious conflict can best be resolved by giving political leaders and parties incentives to moderate their demands in order to gain more votes. Particular types of electoral systems can encourage moderation by requiring winning candidates to gain votes over a broad geographic area. Also, rules for recognition of parties can require them to have representation and leadership across ethnic or religious lines. Our case study of Nigeria is a classic example of this approach.

Consociationalism (Lijphart 1977) doubts the likelihood of moderating groups' demands via centripetal means and instead assumes and accepts ethnically or religiously divided parties, granting each some share of power in the central government. Switzerland, Northern Ireland, and Belgium are examples of this system. Power sharing can be done formally, as in Lebanon where power is divided along religious lines: by agreement of all parties, the president is always a Christian, the prime minister a Sunni Muslim, and the Speaker of the parliament a Shiite Muslim. It can also be done more informally. The electoral system, for instance, can be designed to encourage the formation of parties based on key identities. The parties, once elected, can then work out power-sharing arrangements in some type of government of national unity. Typically, each major ethnic or religious party will have, in effect, a veto over major legislation, so all must agree before laws are passed. Consociationalism can be quite stable, but underlying tensions can surface, provoking repeated constitutional crises and government breakdown, as in Belgium from 2007 to 2011.

The best-known recent effort at consociationalism was the Belfast Agreement of 1998 that ended the religiously based conflict in Northern Ireland, one of the oldest communal conflicts in the world. The origins of the conflict date back to British colonial rule, when English and Scottish Protestant plantation owners oversaw a Gaelic, Catholic population. In the mid- to late nineteenth century, an Irish nationalist movement arose, and most of Ireland gained independence in 1920. The six northern counties, however, remained part of Great Britain, gaining only limited

centripetal approach
A means used by democracies to resolve ethnic conflict by giving political leaders and parties incentives to moderate their demands

consociationalism
A democratic system designed to ease ethnic tensions via recognizing the existence of specific groups and granting some share of power in the central government to each, usually codified in specific legal or constitutional guarantees to each group

A radical Protestant mural in 2007, nearly a decade after the Belfast agreement ended religious conflict in Northern Ireland. While the consociational agreement produced a new government and peace, popular sentiments on both sides remain a challenge.

local government under Protestant control. The nationalist movement, demanding that the northern counties be joined with the Irish Republic, continued its efforts throughout the twentieth century, and the conflict became particularly heated and violent starting in the late 1960s. By the early 1990s, it became clear to both sides that they could not achieve their core aims unilaterally. The nationalists recognized they could not militarily defeat the British, and the unionists (Protestants favoring continued union with Great Britain) acknowledged they could not continue to rule unilaterally without paying a steep price in terms of lives, political stability, and economic well-being.

This set the stage for the historic agreement creating a consociational solution that, while far from perfect, is holding to date. Under the agreement, Northern Ireland would remain part of Great Britain, and Ireland renounced its long-standing claim to the territory. Government would devolve, however, from direct rule from London to local rule in Northern Ireland based on a consociational system that created a form of power sharing. A new National Assembly would be elected based on a proportional electoral system known as the Single Transferrable Vote (STV), which ensured that nationalists and unionists would have seats in parliament equal to their share of the national vote (see chapter 7 for details on proportional electoral systems). A first minister and deputy first minister elected by the National Assembly share executive power. They must each win a majority vote of both the nationalist and unionist members of the National Assembly (every member, once elected, must declare herself to be officially unionist, nationalist, or other). Cabinet positions are then shared among all parties in the assembly based on their share of the total seats. In this way, both sides of the sectarian divide must support the government. Despite a promising start, compromise between the main parties remained elusive, and a government wasn't formed until 2007. Numerous efforts to forge cross-community relationships in civil society and integrate institutions such as schools have begun, but they have been far from successful so far. Indeed, in late 2012, forty days of Protestant rioting broke out in Belfast after the Catholic-controlled city council voted to limit the number of days the British flag would be flown over city hall. The riots were in part stoked by fears that higher Catholic birthrates would soon make Protestants a minority, shifting the balance of power in the consociational government. Despite these problems, the consociational system has succeeded in ending almost all of the violent conflict and establishing a government in which the former antagonists are sharing power peacefully, at least for now.

Both centripetal and consociational approaches can be combined with federalism (see chapter 6 for more details) as an additional means of limiting tension. Consociationalists argue for creating ethnically or religiously homogeneous states or provinces so that central governments can try to shift the focus of identity politics from the center to the regional governments. A group may not have much influence in the central government, but members may hold all of the offices in a specific province. Centripetalists, on the other hand, often argue for creating ethnically or religiously mixed states or provinces to encourage compromise within each one, moderating tensions. They also hope that subdivisions within what seem to be homogeneous states or provinces will emerge via local political competition, undermining broader group loyalty. Federalism with homogeneous states or provinces has been the most common means of resolving identity-based conflicts in the post–Cold War era.

Multi-ethnic and multi-religious states need not be conflictual, but they often are. The wrong context combined with ambitious leaders can produce deep-seated, potentially violent political battles. Authoritarian states often try to avoid such conflict by simply banning any expression of ethnicity or religion, but in the long run this approach is unlikely to work. Some degree of recognition, autonomy, or both is usually essential if a mobilized group is to find its place peacefully inside a larger state. Northern Ireland provides a consociational example of this, and our case study of Nigeria provides a centripetal one.

NIGERIA'S STRANGE HISTORY OF ETHNICITY AND RELIGION

- **ORIGINS**
  Colonial origins of ethnic identity

As outlined briefly in chapter 2, Nigeria is the quintessential colonial creation. People of many languages and faiths were brought together within its boundaries, where approximately four hundred languages are now spoken. Three groups emerged as numerically predominant: the Hausa in the north, the Yoruba in the west, and the Igbo in the east. We say "emerged" because that is exactly what happened. While many Nigerians perceive their ethnic identity in primordial terms, those identities were in fact socially constructed primarily in the twentieth century. The Hausa are a Muslim people sharing a common language who were governed in twelve separate city-states by Muslim emirs in the eighteenth and nineteenth centuries. Today, they constitute approximately 30 percent of Nigeria's population. The Yoruba shared a common language and a common indigenous religion, but for most of their precolonial history were divided among several kingdoms, which sometimes lived in peace but suffered prolonged warfare in the late precolonial period. Under colonial rule, most Yoruba converted to Christianity, though a large minority today are Muslim. The Yoruba constitute about 20 percent of Nigeria's current population. The Igbo, on the other hand, had no conception of themselves as a people prior to colonial rule. They lived in small, mostly independent villages ruled by councils of elders—a classic acephalous, or stateless, society. The word *Igbo* first appears in documents in the 1930s. Under colonial rule, members of this group converted to Christianity more quickly and completely than did the Yoruba or Hausa. By independence, they constituted 18 percent of Nigeria's population.

Despite their different origins, all three identities had emerged as ethnic groups by the end of colonial rule. Each came to perceive its collective interests as "tribal," defined by region and language. Indirect rule (described in chapter 2) played a part in this, as colonial chiefs became leaders over what the British, and the Nigerians, increasingly came to see as "tribes." Missionaries and anthropologists were crucial in the recognition of the Igbo and other stateless societies as distinct groups. As they wrote down "tribal histories" that told primordialist stories of ancient and noble traditions and political unity, and transcribed a common "Igbo" language, they codified that language and Igbo culture.

- **CONTEXT**
  Political power, resource battles, and civil war
  - Shift in political saliency from ethnicity to religion
  - Oil and ethnic conflict
- **TYPE**
  Centripetalism and federalism to manage ethnic conflict

Conflict over ethnicity and oil caused Igbo ethnic leaders to declare a separate country of "Biafra," leading to civil war in 1968. The war caused an estimated one million deaths (mostly from starvation) and millions of refugees. Oil and ethnicity are still a volatile mix in southeastern Nigeria.

For all three groups, internal political disagreements faded in the face of their common interests vis-à-vis the colonizer and, increasingly, one another. As members of these groups moved to the growing colonial cities to work, they encountered members of other groups and gained employment and other benefits from members of their own group who had moved to the urban areas before them. These migrants began to compete for jobs, with members of each group supporting their own, so separate patron-client networks developed within each group, establishing the importance of ethnicity to people's material well-being. Those who became Christian were the first to be educated in colonial schools and in the English language, which gave them an advantage in the job market. The Igbo in particular benefited from this; the Hausa, being Muslim and therefore receiving little Christian education, lost out. Military employment, however, required less education than most sectors of the economy, and the Hausa and other northerners found greater success in this arena. Southerners, and especially the Igbo, dominated in education, civil service, and private business, even outside their own region of the country.

The approach of independence in 1960 provided a context for solidifying ethnic and regional identity, and separate nationalist movements emerged in each of the three regions, each led by one of the three major ethnic groups. Budding national leaders mobilized followings on ethnic and regional bases, as instrumentalists would predict. Obafemi Awolowo rallied the Yoruba by creating a cultural organization, the Egbe Omo Oduduwa, or "the descendants of Oduduwa" (the mythical founder of the Yoruba people). Similarly, northern leaders used memories of the independent Muslim Sokoto caliphate of the nineteenth century to mobilize support for the Northern People's Congress. Leaders of the three groups and the British negotiated a federal system of government for the new state that gave some autonomy to each of the three regions. This meant that a coalition of two of the three would be required to form a national government. The newly independent government was fragile from the start. The three major parties, one representing each ethnic group, consolidated their power over the minorities in their own regions. The minorities, members of Nigeria's over three hundred much smaller ethnic groups, resented the political power of the larger groups and began demanding their own regions. By the 1990s, this pressure would result in the creation of thirty-six states out of the original three regions. Growing tensions between the central government and the regions, as well as friction among the three major parties, led to a chaotic and violent second election in 1964. The military stepped in with the nation's first coup d'état in 1966, led mainly by Igbo officers. Whatever the military's actual reason for taking power, the Yoruba and Hausa saw the coup and the subsequent elimination of federalism as an Igbo effort to grab total power. In response, widespread rioting broke out in northern cities. Hausa attacked Igbo working as civil servants and in business, and tens of thousands were killed.

This violence merged with a battle over a new resource, oil, located in the eastern region dominated by the Igbo. A second military coup six months after the first brought a northern military government to power that restored federalism, this time creating twelve states, giving some smaller ethnic groups their own states. The coup was also an attempt to keep control of oil revenues out of Igbo hands. After the second coup and further violence against Igbo in the north, the Igbo military leader of the eastern region declared the independence of a new country, Biafra, in 1967. The result was a three-year civil war (1967–1970), ultimately unsuccessful, in which more than a million people perished.

Because of their numerical strength overall and their predominance in the military, northerners have controlled most Nigerian governments. In the current Third Republic, inaugurated in 1999, leading northern politicians decided to support a Yoruba, who ruled with greater support from the north than from his own region from 1999 to 2007. His handpicked successor was a northerner, creating an informal agreement that the presidency would alternate between a northerner and southerner. The untimely death of the second president in 2010, however, meant his vice president, a southerner, took power, causing northerners to feel cheated out of their full presidential term. Each democratic constitution has tried to contain ethno-regional conflict through the use of federalism and centripetal rules governing how political parties could form. The 1979 constitution required all political parties to have representatives in all areas of the country; to win the presidency, a candidate had to win not just the most votes but also at least 25 percent of the vote in two-thirds of the nineteen states. Similar provisions in the 1999 constitution seem to have coincided with less ethnically tense politics at the national level.

The reduction in ethnic tension, however, is due in part to a shift of political saliency from ethnic to religious identity. With the rise of the global Islamist movement, identity politics began to shift subtly in Nigeria. The first local Islamist movement emerged in 1980, and religious tension continued to simmer throughout the 1990s. The 1999 constitution gave state governments the right to set their own legal systems. Newly elected governors in several northern states used this provision to rally a religious following by proclaiming Islamic *sharia* as state law. One reason for the popularity of this move was the weakness of the Nigerian state itself. The government seemed incapable of controlling crime, reviving the economy, or controlling growing ethnic militias in parts of the south. Given this uncertain context, both ethnic and religious identity appealed to many people as possible sources of security. Although in theory *sharia* can apply only to Muslims, and a secular legal system would remain for non-Muslims, Christian minorities in the north were nonetheless mobilized to oppose what they saw as the Islamization of their states. Increasing competition over land among ethnic groups, some Christian and others Muslim, also fueled this conflict. Implementation of *sharia,* though, has varied across and within individual states. In most places it is not enforced in Christian areas, and even in most Muslim areas punishments such as amputations are rarely enforced (Okpanachi 2011). This history has to some extent diffused the crisis around *sharia*'s initial adoption.

A violent Islamist movement came to the fore in 2003, *Boko Haram.* Its name means "Western education is sinful," and it is dedicated to the eradication of Western

Video link:
What do *Boko Haram* extremists want?

influence and the creation of an Islamist state in the north. Since 2009, it has expanded the scale of its attacks, targeting Christian churches, schools, and state institutions such as police stations and prisons. Over one thousand people have been killed. Many observers argue the weak Nigerian state has been incapable of effectively responding. Some of the response itself has involved excessive violence. In 2009 the military captured and executed (without a trial) the group's original leader, and in 2011 and again in 2013 the president imposed "states of emergency" that eliminated civil rights in northern states in order to fight the insurgency; none of these measures reduced the violence. In 2013 the military was widely reported to have gone on a rampage, indiscriminately killing hundreds of civilians in one village, in response to a *Boko Haram* attack that killed some soldiers. Nigerian political scientists Iro Aghedo and Oarhe Osumah (2012) argued that state weakness and poverty have produced a sense of personal insecurity and relative deprivation that has made it easy for *Boko Haram* to recruit new members from among young, unemployed men. On the other hand, they and other observers claimed the bulk of Nigeria's Muslims support neither *Boko Haram*'s violence nor the military response to it.

In the southeastern part of the country, local ethnic movements emerged in the mid-1990s around the issue of benefits from oil. Members of these movements, which contained both peaceful and violent elements, argued that all the oil revenue went to the central government and they were left with environmental devastation and poverty, in spite of living in the oil-rich region. The best known of these movements originated among the Ogoni, who were led by internationally known poet Ken Saro-Wiwa until his execution in 1995. He and his movement successfully linked Ogoni ethnic demands with environmental and oil revenue concerns in a locally powerful movement. With Saro-Wiwa's execution, the peaceful Ogoni movement declined and violent clashes became more common, mostly involving young men from the Ijaw ethnic group. In 2003 several oil producers suspended operations in Nigeria entirely until the country's military regained control of the situation. A 2009 cease-fire temporarily halted the violence, but the government's failure to follow through on reforms quickly enough meant it did not last long. In 2010 the largest violent group, the Movement for the Emancipation of the Niger Delta (MEND), detonated bombs in the capital at Nigeria's celebration of its fiftieth anniversary of independence; this was the first time the oil-fueled ethnic violence had spread beyond the oil-producing region itself.

CASE Summary   A number of lessons can be taken from the history of Nigerian ethnicity and religion. First, although they are socially constructed and usually quite modern, once ethnic and religious divisions are politicized, they become difficult to contain. Both military and civilian governments struggled with these forces, and at times their efforts at control exacerbated the problems rather than ameliorated them. Even seemingly logical solutions, such as creating more state governments and requiring that political parties have some degree of support across the country, had limited success because in the context of economic inequality, relative deprivation, political insecurity, and conflict over oil, political leaders were able to raise ethnic and religious support quite easily.

Second, the political saliency and focus of different identities can shift relatively quickly. In the 1960s, national political divisions were primarily a three-way split among the major ethnic groups and regions. Thirty years later, the major political division was along a two-way, north-south, Muslim-Christian divide. Ethnicity had not disappeared; it had simply become more localized. In areas of religious conflict over the use of *sharia* as state law, ethnic and religious divisions often overlapped at the local level. In the southeastern oil region, local ethnicity continued to be very powerful, and Yoruba and "Biafran" separatist movements still exist today, ready to gain more followers when the time is right. All of this has posed severe challenges for Nigeria's efforts at democracy. Ethnic conflict was a primary force frustrating the two prior attempts at democracy, and religious and ethnic tensions threaten to undermine the current democracy.

CASE Questions

1. What are the effects of Nigeria's colonial origins on its ethnic and religious conflicts?
2. Why have the Nigerian government's efforts to control ethnic conflict via centripetal policies had only limited success?
3. What might explain why the focus of greatest political conflict shifted from ethnicity to religion over time in Nigeria?

RACE

While the distinction between ethnic group and nation is relatively clear, the difference between ethnic group and race is much more ambiguous. In a particular context, it may seem obvious, but a consistent distinction is difficult to apply systematically. Following Stephen Cornell and Douglas Hartman (2007, 25), we define a **race** as "a group of human beings socially defined on the basis of physical characteristics." Most ethnic identities focus on cultural rather than physical characteristics, though many do see specific physical characteristics as markers of particular groups as well. Most racial groups are distinguished by physical characteristics, though they and others may also perceive cultural distinctions. The distinction between race and ethnicity, then, is not perfect, but this is probably the best we can do.

An interesting example of the interconnectedness of the terms comes from ethnic and racial categorizations in much of Latin America. In Latin American countries with substantial indigenous populations, such as Guatemala, indigenous people who keep

race
A group of people socially defined primarily on the basis of one or more perceived common physical characteristics

their traditional language, dress, and customs regard themselves as an ethnic group. The dominant groups in society, however, may regard these people in both ethnic and racial terms. This is made clear when a separate term (such as *ladino* in Guatemala) is reserved for persons of indigenous descent who adopt Spanish and no longer maintain indigenous customs. In this case, race and ethnicity are clearly intertwined and depend very much on whose opinion is being asked.

Perhaps more important than the actual definitions of race and ethnicity is the difference in these identities' origins and social construction. Ethnic identity usually originates at least partially in a group's self-assertion of its identity. While others may try to impose an identity on the group, most ethnic groups represent people who are themselves claiming an identity and the political demands that often go with that claim. Race, in contrast, originates in the imposition of a classification by others. Race in its modern sense began with Europeans' expansion around the globe and their encounter with markedly different peoples. Primarily to justify European domination and slavery, European explorers and, later, colonists classified the native populations of the lands they conquered as distinct and inferior races. Embedded within the very classification was an assertion of power (primarily Steven Lukes's third dimension of power outlined in chapter 1). This legacy continues today: almost every racial classification system marks current or quite recent differences in power along racial lines. Ethnicity can also represent starkly different positions in a power structure (as many have argued has been the case in Nigeria), but in many cases it does not (as in the case of German Americans or Italian Americans today). Ethnicity and race, then, usually differ in how they are marked (culture versus physical characteristics), their origins (self-assertion versus external imposition), and the degree of power differences embedded in their contemporary social construction.

For the concept of race, just as for that of nation and ethnicity, we emphasize perception. Genetically, members of racial groups, such as white and black Americans, have as much in common with one another as they do with members of their own groups: genetic variation is no greater across the two groups than it is within each. Races are constructed by focusing on particular differences, such as skin color, and ignoring the far more numerous similarities. Discussing sex, Sigmund Freud referred to this process as "the narcissism of minor differences," the process by which humans amplify the importance of very minor biological variations, such as X versus Y chromosomes or skin color.

Like all socially constructed categories of identity, racial identity varies across time and space, as the following case studies of the United States and Brazil demonstrate. While racial groups may seem absolutely fixed and "natural" to most people in a particular time and place, they are just as subject to change as national and ethnic identities. This is also true of political mobilization along racial lines. Theoretically, a racial identity need not be political in the sense of being a basis for common political goals, but given the power dynamic inherent in racial classification, a political element nearly always exists. Like ethnicity, whether this leads to political mobilization of a racial group depends on the ability of particular leaders to articulate a common agenda by using the symbols of racial identity and discrimination in a compelling way. A dominant or majority group, such as white Americans, typically will not see itself as pursuing a common political agenda, though members of other races may think otherwise. Groups in a minority or subordinate position are more likely to view their political interests as tied to their racial identity, in part because they face discrimination on that basis.

Politicized racial groups usually desire recognition and representation. Autonomy is a less common goal because racial groups usually do not share a distinct geographical home. Recognition usually means official governmental recognition of the race as a socially important group through such means as inclusion on a census form, the teaching of the group's historical role in the larger national history, and the celebration of its leaders and contribution to the nation's culture. In addition, racial groups desire representation in the sense of full formal and informal participation in their government and society. Thus, racial demands typically do not involve such mechanisms as federalism but instead focus on inclusion in public and private employment, political offices, and the educational system. Frequently, as in the United States, members of minority races may argue that past discrimination justifies some type of preferential system that works relatively rapidly to achieve representation equal to their share of the population. Mechanisms to do this might include numerical targets or goals for hiring, increased funding for training and education, or adjustments to the electoral system that make the election of racial minorities more likely. As the cases of the United States and Brazil show, racial politics can be just as intense as ethnic or national politics, so state leaders often see it as in their interests to respond, or at least appear to respond, to racial demands.

Web link:
The Enlightenment's race problem, and ours

CASE Study

RACIAL POLITICS IN THE UNITED STATES

On the night Barack Obama was elected the first African American president in U.S. history, he stood before a massive crowd in Chicago and said, "If there is anyone out there who still doubts that America is a place where all things are possible; who still wonders if the dream of our founders is alive in our time; who still

- ORIGINS
  Slavery, legal segregation, and the making of "white" America

- TYPE
  Demands for representation via black political responses to discrimination

- CONTEXT
  Immigration and social construction of new racial categories; and the meaning of Obama's election

questions the power of our democracy, tonight is your answer. . . . It's the answer spoken by young and old, rich and poor, Democrat and Republican, black, white, Latino, Asian, Native American, gay, straight, disabled and not disabled. . . ." He claimed a new era had begun. For months, Americans had been debating whether their country was "ready" to elect its first black president. Would it mean the end of the long national saga of racial animosity and segregation, or was it merely window dressing, the election of a black man who worked hard to appeal to whites and who would govern a country no less racist than before?

Obama's election is but the most recent major event in America's long racial history. While most Americans today see racial categories as self-evident and more or less fixed, nothing could be further from the truth. The three oldest racial categories in the United States are white, black/African American, and Native American. The white-Native conflict reduced Native populations nearly to extinction. The black population, on the other hand, grew substantially, and the white-black division became the one that had the greatest impact on American political history and national identity. This racial division was first defined legally to distinguish clearly between black slave and white citizen. The "one-drop" rule classified anyone with virtually any black heritage as black and therefore as a slave, ensuring that the offspring of slave women and white masters remained slaves and thus property. In the immediate aftermath of slavery, legal racial definitions remained important in underpinning the segregationist laws of the Jim Crow era. The famous *Plessy v. Ferguson* case of 1896 codified such postslavery racial definitions by classifying a person as "black" if the individual had one-eighth black ancestry. Like the one-drop rule before it, this definition served to keep the black population clearly identified and the black-white boundary as distinct as possible.

The black-white division, though, has not been the only racial question in U.S. history. The clear categorization of all European immigrants as white that is so accepted

An Obama campaign sign in 2012, part of the incumbent president's successful effort to capture the rapidly growing Hispanic vote. Obama's electoral success rested heavily on the creation of a multi-racial coalition of voters that was only 60 percent white.

today was by no means automatic. Writing in 1897 in *The Conservation of Races*, and reflecting the racial understanding of his time, the great black intellectual W. E. B. Du Bois listed the following races:

> the Slavs of eastern Europe, the Teutons of middle Europe, the English of Great Britain and America, the Romance nations of Southern and Western Europe, the Negroes of Africa and America, the Semitic people of Western Asia and Northern Africa, the Hindoos of Central Asia and the Mongolians of Eastern Asia.

The predominantly Anglo population of the United States in the late nineteenth century shared Du Bois's categorization, which meant they did not view immigrants from southern and eastern Europe as racial equals. This changed only with the slow assimilation of Irish, Italians, Poles, Jews, and others into the white majority. A study of this era and this process is aptly titled *How the Irish Became White* (Ignatiev 1995). Part of how they became white, the author argues, was proclaiming loudly their own racism against blacks, thus differentiating themselves from blacks and identifying instead with whites.

The ultimate success of these groups in claiming a place of equality within the white majority had significant effects. First, by the end of the twentieth century, no discernible differences in socioeconomic standing existed between members of these groups and the larger white population. Second, this assimilation process helped preserve a clear white majority in the country. Given the huge number of immigrants, had they ultimately been classified into the distinct races listed by Du Bois, today the country would have no clear racial majority. Third, white "ethnics," as they are sometimes called, may view their ethnic origin as a source of pride and cultural distinction, but it has virtually no impact on their political allegiance or behavior.

This is certainly not true, on the other hand, for African Americans and other blacks, whose racial identity has always profoundly affected their political activity. Du Bois (1897) wrote that the "American Negro" (his preferred term) suffered from a "double consciousness [in which o]ne ever feels this two-ness—an American, a Negro; two souls, two thoughts, two unreconciled strivings; two warring ideals in one dark body, whose dogged strength alone kept it from being torn asunder." The very history of racial terminology reflects the struggle of descendants of African slaves to assert a positive racial identity. *Colored* was the "polite" term among whites to identify blacks during the Jim Crow era, though, as statements from Du Bois to Martin Luther King show, many blacks preferred *Negro* to assert what they saw as a more positive image. In the late 1960s, *black* came to replace *Negro* via the "black power" movement, which was an attempt to unite around the most obvious sign of racial character, skin color, and proclaim "black is beautiful." In the 1980s, Jesse Jackson helped popularize *African American*, arguing that his people should have the same status as any other "hyphenated" immigrant group. In the new millennium, even that term has become contested. As unprecedented numbers of black Caribbean and African immigrants have arrived, the question of what term, if any, captures all Americans of African descent is still very much alive. Many Caribbean immigrants do not identify as "African American," while newly arrived Africans, and their American-born children, may be giving a whole new meaning to the term.

Throughout this terminological evolution, African Americans have been united and politically mobilized by their common experience of discrimination. Until at least the early 1960s, local laws throughout the United States kept most blacks restricted to impoverished ghettoes or isolated rural areas with limited access to social, economic, or political opportunities. They were, at best, second-class citizens. This situation produced two major branches of thinking about black identity, both of which have always involved important political positions and demands. From Frederick Douglass to Martin Luther King Jr. and Jesse Jackson, a liberal integrationist strand has focused primarily on proclaiming and demanding racial equality within the existing U.S. political and social system. King's core demands were the rights enshrined in the Declaration of Independence and the U.S. Constitution: a system that actually operates on the precept that "all men are created equal." The legal elements of this effort were achieved with the Civil Rights Act of 1964 and the Voting Rights Act of 1965, finally granting African Americans the complete rights of citizenship.

These laws did not fully eliminate the effects of past discrimination, however. In the last five decades, the efforts of leaders within the African American community have focused on programs to achieve full social and economic integration that will ensure equal representation of African Americans in the political system, the economy, and civil society. These efforts have included demands for (1) "affirmative action"—that is, programs in education, employment, and business that accommodate specific hiring policies directed toward minorities; (2) equal funding for educational opportunities; (3) greater funding for programs to improve conditions for the poor, who are disproportionately black and Hispanic; (4) changes in the electoral system to enhance the possibility that African Americans will be elected into public office; and (5) encouragement of African American voting and other forms of participation in the electoral process.

Running parallel to this first line of defining black identity is a black nationalist strand of thinking. Melanye Price (2009) identified four key elements of this ideology: (1) black self-determination in the sense of control over their own community institutions; (2) a clear plan for obtaining and maintaining their own financial, political, and intellectual resources for a self-sustaining community; (3) severing ties with whites that foster ideas of racial inferiority; and (4) a global view of black oppression and liberation. One of the earliest and most extreme manifestations of this ideology was promoted by Caribbean-born activist Marcus Garvey, who popularized the "back to Africa" movement in the early twentieth century. Based on the belief that blacks would never be accepted as full citizens in the United States, he proposed a large-scale immigration to a new, or renewed, homeland in Africa. This was the ultimate demand for autonomy rather than representation.

More recent black nationalists generally do not demand complete segregation from white America but greater black autonomy within it. Leaders of the "black power" movement of the 1960s went beyond proclaiming blacks' rightful place in U.S. society by emphasizing that fundamental change in the U.S. socioeconomic system was needed before racial equality could be achieved. Their actions aimed first at creating a more positive self-image among the black community rather than demanding immediate changes in white behavior or attitudes. Groups like the Black Panthers worked to improve the lives of poor blacks in urban areas, provided self-defense training and protection (from the police as well as from criminals), and educated blacks about the glories of their African past, all with little support from white society. Advocates of this approach argued that not until black power was achieved in this way could blacks ultimately force racist whites to move toward racial equality. Survey data from the 1990s showed that only about 15 percent of African Americans could be characterized as adherents of black nationalism (Price 2009).

Video link:
Malcolm X explains black nationalism

Blacks and whites, of course, are not the only racial groups in the United States. The people now called "Asian Americans" and "Hispanics" have been present since at least the mid-nineteenth century, and Mexicans lived in the Southwest long before it became part of the United States. The terms *Asian American, Hispanic,* and *Latino,* however, are of very recent origin. Immigrants from China, Japan, and other Asian countries, as well as residents of Mexican descent, identified themselves primarily by nationality until the mid-twentieth century. Chinese immigrants, for instance, thought of themselves as Chinese, and later Chinese American, but not as Asian American. Intellectual and political activists in these minority communities were influenced by the black power movement in the 1960s and began to conceive of themselves and their political demands in new ways. Rather than focusing on their separate countries of origin, leaders began to shift the focus of their identity to their common experiences in the United States. They argued that Chinese, Japanese, Filipino, and other immigrants faced common linguistic and racial hurdles and experiences in the United States, so they coined the term *Asian American* to unite them under one identity. This movement began with a student strike in San Francisco in 1968, as Japanese, Chinese, and Filipino students came together from separate ethnically defined organizations to form a new Asian American Political Alliance. Because Asian Americans still represent only about 4 percent of the national population, they have had limited political influence, particularly in major cities. Many Asians, however, have moved to suburbs, creating the first suburbs with large immigrant populations. With a concentrated population in these smaller cities, particularly on the West Coast, they have become more successful at gaining political office (Lai 2011).

Similarly, leaders of Mexican, Puerto Rican, Dominican, and other South and Central American groups in the 1960s began to use the more overarching term *Hispanic* to assert a common identity tied to their common language and experience of discrimination. Hispanics became the largest "minority" group in the country in 2000 and grew by an additional 43 percent by 2010. While most Americans probably think of Hispanic as a racial category, it is legally a linguistic category: Hispanics are defined as Spanish speakers or descendants of Spanish speakers. Officially, these individuals can be of any race. The U.S. Census, however, still has not come to reflect accurately the self-perception of Hispanic Americans. In the 2010 census, 53 percent of Hispanics identified themselves racially as white, but another 37 percent identified themselves as "some other race," indicating an unwillingness to accept any of the official U.S. racial categories. After 2000 the Census Bureau tried unsuccessfully to eliminate the category of "some other race" in an attempt to force Hispanics to choose among the existing racial categories, but political pressure by the Hispanic community successfully resisted this effort. A 2005–2006 survey of Hispanics found that fully 51 percent said that "Hispanic/Latino" is a racial category (Latino National Survey). While the construction of the category "Hispanic/Latino"—socially, politically, and legally—is still very fluid, a Hispanic/Latino racial identification may well emerge, becoming the newest addition to the construction of racial categories in the United States. The possible shift from a primarily linguistic to a racial identity reflects in part a shift of focus from a common cultural heritage to a common position in America's racial hierarchy. Hispanics, in any case, are becoming an important force in American electoral politics. Matt Barreto (2010) showed that Latino candidates successfully mobilize Latino voters to vote for them and increase Latino voter turnout in the process. Many analysts also saw the growing Latino/Hispanic vote as a significant element in President Obama's reelection in 2012.

Racial inequality in the United States remains considerable despite the political mobilization of racial groups in recent decades. Figures 4.1 and 4.2 show recent data for education and income for the largest racial groups. As these data make clear, while Asian Americans have equaled whites' income and surpassed whites' level of education, African Americans and Hispanics continue to suffer much lower levels of both. The ratio of white incomes to black and Hispanic incomes remained constant (white incomes are about twice black and Hispanic averages) between 1989 and 2010, while the disparity of wealth levels hit their highest level in 2010 (white wealth was over six times the average for blacks and Hispanics). The Great Recession increased this disparity by 50 percent (Lowry 2013). Asian Americans do not graduate from high school in as high a percentage as do whites, indicating something of a divided Asian American population, with many earning college degrees but quite a few not even finishing high school. School segregation actually increased from 1991 to 2004 across all racial categories, and residential segregation remains extensive. While residential segregation has declined since 1970 for African Americans, it has remained high, the highest for any racial group, and has actually increased for Latinos. Asian American residential segregation has declined and is only moderate—still significant, but well below the rates for African Americans and Latinos (Schmidt et al. 2010, 109–120).

Obama's rapid ascent raises new questions about political representation of racial minorities: Has their underrepresentation finally started to end, a half-century after the Voting Rights Act? It has certainly improved since then, but unevenly; no group is fully represented except whites, who are overrepresented, as the data in Figures 4.4 and 4.5 demonstrate. The House of Representatives in 2013 was notably closer to being representative than the Senate, but even in the House, Hispanics remain significantly underrepresented. African Americans have come close to parity in the House but had no representation in the Senate, to which only six African Americans have ever been elected (Barack Obama and Cory Booker were the most recent). A broad study by Schmidt et al. (2010) found that while levels of participation and representation have increased significantly for all racial minorities over the last generation, they remain outside the main ruling coalitions and therefore have been unable to get the policies they most strongly support, such as affirmative action and immigration reform, passed into law.

In this socioeconomic and political context, then, has the Obama candidacy and presidency had a major impact? Many African Americans, in particular, claim it has, saying they can now honestly tell their children (or at least their sons) that they can "become whatever they want to be." On the other hand, Obama has tried to avoid many racially contentious issues, and his presidency has had little effect on the data in Figures 4.1 through 4.5. Many celebrated Obama's strong showing among white voters. He won 2 percent more white votes than did the Democratic candidate in 2004, John Kerry, but his opponent still won 55 percent of white votes overall. Obama, however, won 95 percent of the African American vote and 67 percent of the Hispanic vote. Obama voters overall were about 60 percent white, compared with 90 percent white for his opponent. Obama also won in 2008 in the context of a severe recession and a very unpopular incumbent president of the opposite party. Political scientists Michael Lewis-Beck and colleagues created a statistical model based on past elections to predict what we might expect for an opposition victory in that context, and they found that Obama probably would have received about 5 percent more of the vote than he did, were racial bias not a factor. The researchers also noted that the Democratic congressional vote nationwide was several percentage points above Obama's total (Lewis-Beck, Tien, and Nadeau 2010). Michael Tessler and David Sears (2010) used extensive survey research to explain this outcome, showing that racial resentment—sentiments measured by survey data showing feelings of antipathy toward another race—among whites played a bigger role in the 2008 election than it had in any other election since the measurements began. Voters with high levels of racial resentment were much more likely than those with little or no racial resentment to support Hillary Clinton over Obama in the Democratic primary and John McCain (the Republican nominee) over Obama in the general election. Racial resentment was a more powerful predictor of voters' choice than almost any ideological interests. Tessler and Sears conclude that the presence of an African American candidate racialized American politics more than it had been for decades.

Since the election, the virulently anti-Obama "Tea Party" movement has arisen and gained great attention, especially when a few of its members yelled racial and homophobic epithets at black and gay members of Congress during the debate over health care. Surveys of Tea Party members in 2010 showed that whites who strongly supported the movement are significantly more likely to believe that African Americans have received too much attention and that they do not face serious discrimination anymore. Also, in the first two years of Obama's presidency, the number of antiblack hate crimes rose sharply. Pasek et al. (2012) used three extensive surveys to conclude

---

FIGURES 4.1–4.5   Racial Disparity in the United States

Figure 4.1 Percent Population with College Degree

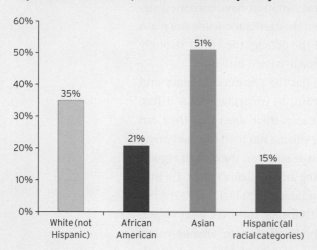

Figure 4.3 Racial Groups as Percentage of U.S. Population

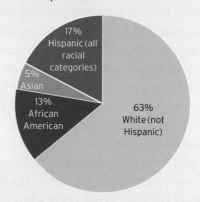

Figure 4.2 Median Household Income per Household Member, 2009 ($US)

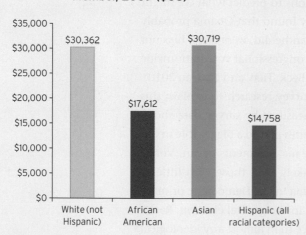

Figure 4.4 Racial Disparity in House of Representatives

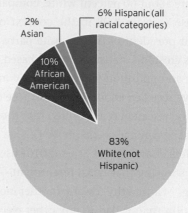

Figure 4.5 Racial Disparity in Senate

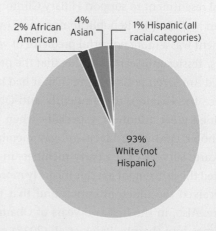

Sources: Income data are from the 2009 Census Population Survey, U.S. Census Bureau; education data for 2011 are from "Educational Attainment," U.S. Census Bureau (http://www.census.gov/hhes/socdemo/education/data/cps/historical/index.html); population data are from "State & County Quick Facts," U.S. Census Bureau (http://quickfacts.census.gov/qfd/states/00000.html); and political representation data are from "The United States Congress Quick Facts," ThisNation.com (http://www.thisnation.com/congress-facts.html) and "Membership of the 113th Congress: A Profile," Congressional Research Service (https://www.fas.org/sgp/crs/misc/R42964.pdf).

Note: There are 435 total seats in the U.S. House of Representatives and 100 seats in the Senate.

that white racial resentment increased slightly from 2008 to 2012, and antiblack attitudes lowered Obama's job approval ratings by 2 to 3 points and cost him 4 percentage points in the 2012 election. Obama's share of the white vote dropped from 43 percent in 2008 to 39 percent in 2012; 56 percent of his voters were white in 2012 (down 4 percent from 2008), compared with 89 percent for his opponent, Mitt Romney.

In the longer term, the Obama presidency, and Obama himself, raise bigger issues about the social construction of race and racial politics in the United States. Many observers have pointed to the growing racial diversity of the country, especially the rapidly growing Hispanic and Asian populations, and the increasing rates of racial intermarriage (something Obama himself symbolizes, as the son of a white woman and black man), to argue that the United States may finally be entering a "post-racial" era. Most scholars of race in the United States, however, dispute this. They point out that the bulk of intermarriage is within the growing Hispanic community and between Hispanics and members of other groups; black-white levels of intermarriage outside the Hispanic community have risen much more slowly. More generally, the country remains racially segregated in terms of residence, education, criminal justice, and income, especially between whites on the one hand and blacks and Hispanics on the other. Much evidence suggests that attitudes are not changing rapidly, either. Donald Kinder and Cindy Kam (2009) used extensive survey research to show that many whites and Asian Americans, in particular, continue to hold negative stereotypes about blacks and Hispanics. These attitudes, furthermore, have political implications: for instance, they lead whites to favor Social Security because they see it as benefitting elderly white people while opposing "welfare" because they see it as favoring blacks and Hispanics. Cara Wong (2010) showed that whites who identified blacks as part of their "community"—people to whom they felt somehow close—were significantly more likely to support policies they perceived to favor blacks, such as affirmative action, than whites who did not feel close to African Americans. No more than a quarter of whites, however, lived in such communities. Similar trends existed among African Americans, though a higher percentage of them lived in integrated communities.

Video link:
President Obama speaks about Trayvon Martin and racism

CASE Summary   The election of Barack Obama is clearly an event of great import, the biggest milestone in the fight for racial equality in the United States since the Voting Rights Act of 1965. The debate over whether the United States will overcome the power of inequalities and prejudices built into the country's socially constructed racial system will continue, however. American racial categories were constructed in a way that both reflected and reinforced the divisions of power based first on slavery and then on legal segregation. As segregation and discrimination have become more informal and (some argue) ambiguous, racial identities have as well, now being legally based on self-identification rather than governmental imposition. Immigration has long had an important role to play in the social construction of race in America, and the current era of Hispanic and Asian immigration is no exception.

A crucial question is whether recent immigrant groups, like their European predecessors a century ago, will assimilate into the white majority or remain distinct; the answer will play a major role in how Americans think about race and its political impact over the next century. As in many places around the world, the response of racially subordinate groups has varied from demanding full inclusion to greater autonomy or even separation, but the former has almost always won out over the latter. In our next case study, Brazil, race is socially constructed in quite different ways, resulting in very different racial political dynamics as well.

CASE Questions

1. How has the social construction of race in U.S. history influenced the political position of different racial groups in American democracy?
2. What are the possible long-term political impacts of rising Asian and Hispanic immigration to the United States, and why?
3. What impact has the Obama presidency had on American racial attitudes and racial politics?

- **ORIGINS**
  Slavery and ambiguous and complex definition of racial categories

- **CONTEXT**
  A policy of "whitening"; claims of a "racial democracy"; and difficulty creating a black political movement

- **POLICY ISSUE**
  Affirmative action and continued questions of "Who is black?"

RACE IN BRAZIL

A comparison of the United States and Brazil demonstrates in stark terms the variation and importance of racial identity and racial politics in different contexts. Like the United States, Brazil was a major slaveholding society. Indeed, Brazilian slavery was much more extensive and lasted longer. At the time of abolition in 1888, approximately half of Brazil's population was at least partially of African descent.

Despite very different conceptions of racial identity and politics, racial discrimination and inequality in Brazil are similar to what is found in the United States. The different conceptions of race, however, have made it much more difficult for a clear black racial consciousness to emerge in Brazil and effectively demand black recognition and representation. Only in the last thirty years has a sustained Afro-Brazilian political movement emerged and achieved some success in altering the country's racial policies.

The black-white dichotomy that characterizes U.S. racial history makes little sense to most Brazilians. Brazil contains literally dozens of informal racial categories and distinctions. Intermarriage between light-skinned and dark-skinned people has been and remains fairly common. More important, Brazil's social construction of race is nearly opposite to that of the United States. Racial identity is constructed not on the basis of descent but on the basis of physical features, with seven major categories from "white" (*branco*) to "black" (*preto*) and numerous minor ones. Throughout the twentieth century, Brazil proclaimed itself a racial democracy because no legal racial segregation had existed there since the end of slavery. Simultaneous with and contradictory to these claims, however, has been an explicit desire to "whiten" the population in a variety of ways.

The different ways race has been socially constructed in the United States and Brazil have their origins in differences in slavery. Slaves in Brazil, working in tropical conditions on plantations, tended to die younger than North American slaves. The system survived not by the biological reproduction of slaves but instead by the large-scale importation of new slaves to replace the dead. This meant that defining the children of slaves as slaves was not as economically important as it was in the United States. Combined with the fact that for a long time Portuguese immigrants to Brazil were overwhelmingly male, the result was the beginnings of a *pardo,* or mixed-race, group. Creating a clear "black-white" dichotomy was not as important as it was in the United States, so a multilayered system of racial classification corresponding loosely to Brazil's extensive racial intermarriage emerged instead.

With the declining economic importance of the northeastern plantations in the late nineteenth century and international pressure to end the last system of legalized slavery in the New World, Brazil achieved abolition peacefully. The growing industrialization of southern cities led many former slaves to move south, especially to Rio de Janeiro. The central government in Rio never imposed legal segregation of the sort found in the United States during the Jim Crow era, but it did pursue the policy of "whitening." This included encouraging and even subsidizing the immigration of European workers and completely banning black immigration. By 1920 half of the industrial workforce was composed of immigrants, and virtually all of them were from southern and eastern Europe. As in the United States, this large-scale immigration of people who came to be defined as "white" kept the black and *pardo* proportion of the population smaller than it would have been otherwise.

in CONTEXT

Race and Ethnicity in Latin America

Nearly 50 percent of Brazilians are of African descent, whereas only 1 percent are indigenous. In most Latin American countries, though, identity politics focuses on indigenous ethnicity. Survey data on race and ethnicity in Latin America are difficult to interpret, but the following data give some idea of the issues of race, ethnicity, and access to power and resources that concern the region.

- 29 percent (about 150 million people) of the population of Latin America and the Caribbean is of African descent; more than half of these live in Brazil.

- 8 percent (about 40 million people) of the region's population is indigenous and lives in every country except Uruguay.

- 400 indigenous languages are spoken in the region.

- Indigenous people comprise 30 to 50 percent of the populations of Bolivia, Ecuador, Guatemala, and Peru.

- Nearly 25 percent of all Latin American indigenous people live in Mexico, but they comprise only 10 percent of Mexico's population.

- Indigenous people are disproportionately poor; for example, while approximately 66 percent of all Guatemalans are poor, 90 percent of indigenous Guatemalans are.

Source: Mayra Buvinic and Jacqueline Mazza, with Ruthanne Deutsch, ed., *Social Inclusion and Economic Development in Latin America.* Washington, DC: Inter-American Development Bank, 2004.

Audio link:
Skin color still plays big role in ethnically diverse Brazil

Web link:
Race, class, and education in Brazil

Whitening in Brazil also included active encouragement of racial intermarriage to "improve" black genetics with white genes, and those few blacks or *pardos* who were able to crawl up the class ladder were also "whitened" in the process. Racial discrimination was milder for those with higher levels of education and wealth, leading to the common Brazilian phrase "money whitens." Brazil's white population, facing a country in which at least half of the population was of slave descent, actively encouraged the creation of intermediate racial categories as buffers between them and poor, uneducated blacks. Even the census was employed for this purpose. Over the years, the Brazilian government actively used it to encourage people to identify with some intermediate category instead of "black" or to deny the existence of race entirely by simply not asking any racial questions. The policy worked: the 1890 census recorded 44 percent of the population as "white"; the 1950 census put the figure at 62 percent. More recently, growing racial awareness has meant a shift in self-definition. For the first time, the 2010 census found that a minority—48 percent—of Brazilians identified as "white." Self-identifying as "black," however, remained low: only 7.6 percent identified that way, while 43 percent identified as "pardo."

The whitening policy also allowed what was called the "mulatto escape hatch." If education, intermarriage, and a better income could whiten people and improve their social status, why actively try to identify yourself as "black"? For this reason, most poor blacks viewed their difficulties in terms of class, not race, preferring to view themselves as poor, a condition they could escape, than as black, a condition they could never change. Bailey (2009), using several surveys from 1995 to 2002, found that most Brazilians' sense of racial group identity was weak, though they simultaneously recognized racial discrimination as a reality and problem in their society. In this context, political activists had a difficult time constructing and maintaining an Afro-Brazilian identity. In contrast to the United States during the same period, no significant black movement emerged in the 1950s and 1960s. A stronger black movement emerged with the new democracy in the 1990s, but the insistence of most groups in the movement that anyone who is not white should identify as "black" has limited its appeal.

The military government in power from 1964 to 1985 reinforced the policy of denying the importance of race. In response, the *Movimento Negro Unificado* (Unified Black Movement) became an active part of the struggle for democracy, but the group's long-term gains remained limited. Beginning in the 1980s, newly elected state governors, especially in the major urban areas like Rio de Janeiro, started to place some blacks in leadership positions. At the national level, however, the major political parties, even those on the left of the political spectrum, continued to focus on class issues and to downplay the importance of race, and very few self-identified blacks were elected to the National Congress.

Brazil is still a racially unequal society. Blacks and *pardos* have incomes that are only 60 percent of the average white income, are twice as likely to be illiterate, and live six years less on average. In 2008, 46 of 513 members of the National Congress were identified as being of African descent, but only 17 self-identified as "black." Most Brazilian politicians, whatever their background or skin color, still see little political gain from identifying as Afro-Brazilian.

The most dramatic recent change in Brazil's racial policies was the government's official endorsement of a quota-based affirmative action program in 2002. Fernando Henrique Cardoso, president from 1995 to 2003, actively encouraged a rethinking of Brazil's racial policy, helping to start the country's biggest debate on race in decades. Those who opposed affirmative action argued that it is impossible to determine who is truly "black" and therefore deserving of preferential treatment; proponents argued that all those who identify as "not white" face discrimination. Affirmative action has mainly occurred within Brazil's universities, where blacks and *pardos* have constituted a tiny fraction of the student body. As universities have implemented racially based admissions policies, they have faced difficult challenges determining who should qualify. Some have used independent panels to assess photos or interview candidates to determine which applicants should qualify for preferential admission. In one famous case, twin brothers received different classifications, one white and the other black (following Brazil's long-standing construction of race based on color, not descent). By

2009, forty-eight public universities and hundreds of (less prestigious in Brazil) private universities had adopted racial quotas; by 2011, black and *pardo* enrollments in private universities had increased more than 200 percent and in public universities by almost 25 percent. A study at the state university in Rio de Janeiro, the pioneer of the quota system, found that those admitted under quotas performed equally as well as the general student body (Andrea Cicalò 2008).

Despite success at expanding access to higher education, affirmative action set off a major debate. Some observers have argued that affirmative action may actually serve to encourage the creation of a stronger Afro-Brazilian identity and movement, as members of this group come to see themselves as the beneficiaries of the policy (Racusen 2010). Bailey (2009) found that when the possible benefits of affirmative action policies were mentioned in surveys, the percentage of respondents who said they were black increased substantially. Francis and Tannuri-Pianto (2012) similarly found that the quota system for admissions at the University of Brasilia increased dark-skinned recipients' willingness to identify as "black." Others worry that the policy will further divide the country racially. Many argue that the real problem is class, not race. In 2009 a Brazilian court ruled Rio de Janeiro's quota system unconstitutional on the grounds that it is a system of racial discrimination, but a landmark Supreme Court decision in April 2012 reversed that decision, accepting quotas as legitimate. That and growing popular support led the national government to pass a sweeping affirmative action bill in late 2012. It requires all federal universities to reserve half of their admission slots for graduates of public high schools, which are mostly attended by poorer students. In addition, those slots must represent the racial mix of the area in which each university is located. The law passed the Congress with only one dissenting vote, and opinion polls show it is supported by two-thirds of Brazilians. While this alone will not resolve all racial concerns or debates, it is a dramatic shift from a country that long held it was a "racial democracy" in which race did not matter.

Video link:
Brazil in black and white

CASE Summary   The social construction of race in Brazil is strikingly different from that in the United States. With the state not needing to demarcate a clear legal line between black and white, either during slavery or afterward, and with a long history of racial intermarriage, Brazilian racial classifications have been much more fluid and complex than the historical duality between black and white in the United States. Based on this, Brazilians have long argued that their country is a racial democracy and have consciously distanced themselves from the legalized segregation of the United States and South Africa under apartheid. But Brazil's discrimination has been simply different, not less. One of the authors noticed a classified ad in a Brazilian newspaper in the 1980s seeking an office receptionist that said the employer needed a "*moca da boa aparencia*"—literally a "good-looking girl." While that was striking to a postfeminist American, he later found out that the language was coded and really meant a "fair-skinned girl," even more striking to a post–civil rights American.

Indeed, the lack of stark racial divisions and legalized discrimination is a major explanation for the limited black political mobilization in Brazil. In spite of this, the country has now adopted the most sweeping affirmative action law in the Western hemisphere. This still does not fully resolve Brazil's long-standing question: Who is black?

CASE Questions

1. Why is the social construction of race in Brazil so different from what it is in the United States?
2. How has the social construction of race affected racial politics and representation in Brazil, and how does this compare with the U.S. case?

CONCLUSION

Identity politics is so common and explosive in part because the very construction of the groups often creates and reflects differences in political power. This is most common in the case of race, but it can be true for ethnic or national differences as well (and certainly for gender and sexual orientation, subjects we examine more closely in chapter 12). As identity categories are created, a sense of superior and inferior status is often embedded within them. European expansion created a white-dominated racial order within many countries and globally. For several centuries, European (white) society, culture, and political systems were seen by those in power as superior; others could gain access to power, if at all, by trying to become "white" (as in the United States and Brazil, in different ways) or at least by adopting and accepting white institutions and norms. The recent economic and political gains of people of color in many countries have altered this trend, though many analysts still see subtle ways in which white norms are held as superior, and in most countries whites remain socioeconomically advantaged in many ways.

As these examples suggest, how a group is defined influences what it may claim in order to gain or enhance its power: anything from specific legal protections like antidiscrimination laws or the right to school their children in a local language to regional autonomy, power-sharing arrangements, or national statehood. Similarly, actions taken in pursuit of redress of grievances may range from lobbying, voting, and constitutional reform to armed violence and secession. In countries with significant immigration, like the United States and Germany, new immigrants continually raise new issues: their racial or ethnic categorization must be clarified, and the ongoing construction of their categories will influence their place and political power in the broader "nation" they are attempting to join.

Each person belongs to various identity groups, but whether people act politically based on these group memberships depends on a variety of factors. First, the group in question must have a preexisting sense of itself: it must be an "imagined community" with both perceived historic ties and a forward-looking agenda. Second, it must have some felt grievance. Finally, groups seem to need political leadership, elites who can build on and strengthen the identity and link it to particular grievances and appropriate action. Instrumentalist theory uses a rational-choice approach to argue that elites can work with and strengthen a weakly felt sense of identity, as the creation of countries like Germany or Italy out of many smaller regional groups suggests, but the groups must have some shared and accepted basis for this to work, and the elites must also have adequate resources and political opportunities, as the "contentious politics" literature argues.

It is also useful to remember that the political salience of even strongly felt identities can change rather quickly. Nigeria and Sudan are both examples of this. In Nigeria, political conflict has shifted from a primarily ethnic to a primarily religious basis; in Sudan, the change has been in the opposite direction over roughly the same time period. The case of Nigeria also suggests the influence of globalization: local groups may be influenced by dominant global discourses as they begin to mobilize. Today, the resurgence of global Islamism provides a context that enhances the tendency of local groups to see their struggle in religious terms; for most of the twentieth century, in contrast, the dominant global discourse was about nationhood, encouraging local groups that saw themselves as culturally different to cast their struggles in ethnic or nationalist terms. Changes such as these show clearly that the primordialist argument, based on a very static political culture theory, has limited explanatory power.

Explaining why violence breaks out in identity-based conflicts is both crucial and difficult. Factors that explain the rise of identity movements, such as relative deprivation, can be used to explain the outbreak of violence as well, but that model leaves us with the question of why violence isn't more common than it is. Recent studies have focused on particular aspects of identity-based conflicts that seem to spur violence: irresolvable competing claims to territory perceived by one or more groups as a "homeland" (such as Israel and Palestine, Serbia and Kosovo); fear based on a domestic security dilemma, often in the context of a weak state or rapid political changes (the former Yugoslavia); and resentment based on long-standing feelings of mistreatment and exclusion from power (Rwanda). No single factor will probably ever explain why people seek to harm and kill others simply because they are defined as somehow "different," but we have now developed a fairly convincing list of the various factors embedded in the structure of the conflicts that lead identity-based competition to become violent.

The question, then, is, What can states do to prevent these conflicts? Because identity politics often threatens the very existence of states, governments have to care about the issues involved. The leaders of governments typically want to mobilize a national identity tied to the state, while simultaneously demobilizing all other identities. Sometimes, however, the very effort to create a unifying national identity spawns challenges from ethnic, religious, or other groups. National identities based on specific racial or ethnic groups inherently exclude some groups as they include others. As the excluded groups are politically mobilized, state leaders must try to find a way either to eliminate that mobilization (the typical authoritarian option) or contain it within the institutional boundaries of the existing political system through federalism or other power-sharing mechanisms (as democracies typically try to do). Power sharing of some type seems essential to keeping identity-based political competition within nonviolent bounds, but this is never easy. Political leaders often try to achieve this while yielding little in the way of real power or resources, as the case of Nigeria has shown over the years, which only causes opponents to demand more. And once a conflict has become violent, reducing tension and rebuilding trust afterward can be particularly difficult. Once mobilized, identity politics can thus be quite explosive.

KEY CONCEPTS

assimilationist (p. 159)

autonomy (p. 157)

centripetal approach (p. 166)

civic nationalism (p. 158)

consociationalism (p. 166)

constructivism (p. 149)

contentious politics (p. 152)

cultural nationalism (p. 158)

ethnic group (p. 162)

instrumentalism (p. 149)

jus sanguinis (p. 159)

jus soli (p. 159)

nation (p. 157)

nationalism (p. 157)

political saliency (p. 148)

politics of recognition (p. 163)

primordialism (p. 148)

race (p. 173)

relative deprivation (p. 152)

security dilemma (p. 153)

social construction (p. 149)

$SAGE edge™
for CQ Press

Sharpen your skills with SAGE edge at **edge.sagepub.com/orvis3e.** **SAGE edge for students** provides a personalized approach to help you accomplish your coursework goals in an easy-to-use learning environment.

WORKS CITED

Aghedo, Iro, and Oarhe Osumah. 2012. "The Boko Haram Uprising: How Should Nigeria Respond?" *Third World Quarterly:* 853–869.

Alesina, Alberto, Arnaud Devleeschauwer, William Easterly, Sergio Kurlat, and Romain Wacziarg. 2003. "Fractionalization." *Journal of Economic Growth* 8 (2): 155–194.

Anderson, Benedict. 1991. *Imagined Communities: Reflections on the Origin and Spread of Nationalism.* New York: Verso.

Bailey, Stanley R. 2009. *Legacies of Race: Identities, Attitudes, and Politics in Brazil.* Stanford, CA: Stanford University Press.

Barreto, Matt. 2010. *Ethnic Cues: The Role of Shared Ethnicity in Latino Political*

Participation. Ann Arbor: University of Michigan Press.

Brass, Paul R. 1991. *Ethnicity and Nationalism: Theory and Comparison*. Newbury Park, CA: Sage.

Brubaker, Rogers. 1992. *Citizenship and Nationhood in France and Germany*. Cambridge, MA: Harvard University Press.

Cicalò, Andrea Giuseppe. 2008. "What Do We Know about Quotas? Data and Considerations about the Implementation of the Quota System in the State University of Rio de Janeiro (UERJ)." *Universal Humanist* 65: 262–280 (http://www.sci elo.unal.edu.co/scielo.php?script=sci_art text&pid=S0120-48072008 000100012).

Collier, Paul, and Anke Hoeffler. 2004. "Greed and Grievance in Civil War." *Oxford Economic Papers* 56 (4): 563–595. doi:10.1093/oep/gpf064.

Collier, Paul, Anke Hoeffler, and Dominic Rohner. 2009. "Beyond Greed and Grievance: Feasibility and Civil War." *Oxford Economic Papers* 61 (1): 1–27. doi:10.1093/oep/gpn029.

Cornell, Stephen, and Douglas Hartmann. 2007. *Ethnicity and Race: Making Identities in a Changing World*. 2nd ed. Thousand Oaks, CA: Pine Forge Press.

Du Bois, W. E. B. 1897. *The Conservation of Races* (http://www.teachingamericanhistory .org/library/index.asp?document=1119).

Francis, Andrew M., and Maria Tannuri-Pianto. 2012. "Using Brazil's Racial Continuum to Examine the Short-Term Effects of Affirmative Action in Higher Education." *Journal of Human Resources* 47 (3): 754–784.

Gellner, Ernest. 1983. *Nations and Nationalism*. Oxford, UK: Blackwell.

Gurr, Ted Robert. 1970. *Why Men Rebel*. Princeton, NJ: Princeton University Press.

Horowitz, Donald L. 1985. *Ethnic Groups in Conflict*. Berkeley: University of California Press.

Huntington, Samuel P. 1997. *The Clash of Civilizations and the Remaking of World Order*. New York: Touchstone. Originally published in 1996 by Simon and Schuster.

Ignatiev, Noel. 1995. *How the Irish Became White*. New York: Routledge.

Kinder, Donald R., and Cindy D. Kam. 2009. *Us against Them: Ethnocentric Foundations of American Opinion*. Chicago: University of Chicago Press.

Lai, James S. 2011. *Asian American Political Action: Suburban Transformations*. Boulder, CO: Lynne Rienner.

Latino National Survey. University of Washington Institute for the Study of Ethnicity, Race and Sexuality (http://depts.washing ton.edu/uwiser/LNS.shtml).

Lewis-Beck, Michael S., Charles Tien, and Richard Nadeau. 2010. "Obama's Missed Landslide: A Racial Cost?" *PS: Political Science & Politics* (January): 69–76. doi:10.1017/S1049096509990618.

Lijphart, Arend. 1977. *Democracy in Plural Societies: A Comparative Exploration*. New Haven, CT: Yale University Press.

Lowe, Chris. 1997. "Talking about 'Tribe': Moving from Stereotypes to Analysis." With Tunde Brimah, Pearl-Alice Marsh, William Minter, and Monde Muyangwa (http://www.africaaction.org/talking-about-tribe.html).

Lowrey, Annie. 2013. "Wealth Gap among Races Has Widened since Recession," *New York Times*, April 28 (http://www .nytimes.com/2013/04/29/business/ racial-wealth-gap-widened-during-reces sion.html?emc=eta1).

Nairn, Tom. 1977. *The Break-Up of Britain: Crisis and Neo-Nationalism*. London: New Left Books.

Okpanachi, Eyene. 2011. "Religious and Legal Pluralism in Nigeria: Between Conflict and Compromise: Lessons on *Sharia* and Pluralism from Nigeria's Kaduna and Kebbi States." *Emory International Law Review*, 897–919.

Pasek, Josh, Jon A. Krosnick, and Trevor Tompson. 2012. *The Impact of Anti-Black Racism on Approval of Barack Obama's Job Performance and on Voting in the 2012 Presidential Election* (http://www.stanford .edu/dept/communication/faculty/kros nick/docs/2012/2012%20Voting%20 and%20Racism.pdf).

Petersen, Roger. 2002. *Understanding Ethnic Violence: Fear, Hatred, and Resentment in*

Twentieth-Century Eastern Europe. New York: Cambridge University Press.

Price, Melanye T. 2009. *Dreaming Blackness: Black Nationalism and African American Public Opinion.* New York: New York University Press.

Racusen, Seth. 2010. "Affirmative Action and Identity." In *Brazil's New Racial Politics,* edited by Bernd Reiter and Gladys Mitchell, 89–122. Boulder, CO: Lynne Rienner.

Renan, Ernest. 1882. *What Is a Nation?* (http://www.nationalismproject.org/what/renan.htm).

Ross, Marc Howard. 2007. *Cultural Contestation in Ethnic Conflict.* Cambridge, UK: Cambridge University Press.

Schmidt, Ronald, Sr., Yvette M. Alex-Assensoh, Andrew L. Aoki, and Rodney E. Hero. 2010. *Newcomers, Outsiders, and Insiders: Immigrants and American Racial Politics in the Early Twenty-first Century.* Ann Arbor: University of Michigan Press.

Smith, Anthony D. 1998. *Nationalism and Modernism.* New York: Routledge.

Taylor, Charles. 1994. "The Politics of Recognition." In *Multiculturalism: Examining the Politics of Recognition,* edited by Amy Gutmann, 25–74. Princeton, NJ: Princeton University Press.

Tessler, Michael, and David O. Sears. *Obama's Race: The 2008 Election and the Dream of a Post-Racial America.* Chicago: University of Chicago Press.

Theiss-Morse, Elizabeth. 2009. *Who Counts as an American? The Boundaries of National Identity.* Cambridge, UK: Cambridge University Press.

Toft, Monica. 2003. *The Geography of Ethnic Conflict: Identity, Interests, and Territory.* Princeton, NJ: Princeton University Press.

Wong, Cara J. 2010. *Boundaries of Obligation in American Politics: Geographic, National, and Racial Communities.* Cambridge, UK: Cambridge University Press.

Wucherpfennig, Julian, Nils W. Metternich, Lars-Erik Cederman, and Kristian Skrede Gleditsch. 2012. "Ethnicity, the State, and the Duration of Civil War." *World Politics:* 79–115.

Yuval-Davis, Nira, and Flora Anthias, eds. 1989. *Woman-Nation-State.* Consultant editor Jo Campling. Basingstoke, UK: Macmillan.

RESOURCES FOR FURTHER STUDY

Cordell, Karl, and Stefan Wolff, eds. 2011. *Routledge Handbook of Ethnic Conflict.* New York: Routledge.

Ghai, Yash P., ed. 2000. *Autonomy and Ethnicity: Negotiating Competing Claims in Multi-Ethnic States.* Cambridge, UK: Cambridge University Press.

Hobsbawm, Eric J. 1990. *Nations and Nationalism since 1780: Programme, Myth, Reality.* Cambridge, UK: Cambridge University Press.

Hutchinson, John, and Anthony D. Smith, eds. 2000. *Nationalism: Critical Concepts in Political Science,* Vol. IV. New York: Routledge.

Juergensmeyer, Mark. 1993. *The New Cold War? Religious Nationalism Confronts the Secular State.* Berkeley: University of California Press.

Kaufman, Stuart J. 2001. *Modern Hatreds: The Symbolic Politics of Ethnic War.* Ithaca, NY: Cornell University Press.

McAdam, Doug, Sidney Tarrow, and Charles Tilly. 2001. *Dynamics of Contention.* New York: Cambridge University Press.

Taras, Raymond, and Rajat Ganguly. 2002. *Understanding Ethnic Conflict: The International Dimension.* 2nd ed. New York: Longman.

Tilly, Charles, and Sidney Tarrow. 2007. *Contentious Politics.* Boulder, CO: Paradigm Publishers.

Van Deburg, William L., ed. 1997. *Modern Black Nationalism: From Marcus Garvey to Louis Farrakhan.* New York: New York University Press.

WEB RESOURCES

Conflict Analysis Resources, Royal Holloway, University of London
(http://www.rhul.ac.uk/economics/home.aspx)

Correlates of War
(http://www.correlatesofwar.org)

Fractionalization Data, The MacroData Guide
(http://www.nsd.uib.no/macrodataguide/set.html?id=16&sub=1)

The Religion and State Project, Bar Ilan University, Israel
(http://www.religionandstate.org)

Research Network on Gender Politics and the State
(http://libarts.wsu.edu/polisci/rngs)

United States Institute of Peace
(http://www.usip.org)

The World Bank, Data and Research
(http://econ.worldbank.org)

5 STATES AND MARKETS

KEY QUESTIONS

- How and why should states intervene in the market economy?

- In what ways do economic policies reflect the relative power of different groups in a society?

- How important are globalization and international organizations in determining the economic policies of individual countries?

- Why have some states intervened in the market economy more than others?

The "Great Recession" that began in the United States in 2007 and spread across the globe in 2008–2009 caused not only massive economic upheaval but major political changes as well. Between 2008 and 2012, governments changed hands in the United States (the presidency, at least), the United Kingdom, France, Ireland, Iceland, Spain, Portugal, Italy, Greece, and Japan, among other countries. And in all of those contests, the state of the economy was a major factor in the incumbent party's loss. As Bill Clinton's 1992 presidential campaign put it, "It's the economy, stupid!" Political leaders in democracies across the globe rise and fall on the basis of citizens' perceptions of the economy and their own economic well-being.

Market economies have become nearly universal since the end of the Cold War. In these economies, the state does not control the economy as the communist governments did in the past, but governments can and do intervene in the economy to try to encourage economic growth and influence how economic benefits are distributed. Therefore, the relationship between the state and the market and the debates surrounding it are crucial to understanding modern politics virtually everywhere. As the Country and Concept table (page 198) demonstrates, even though virtually all countries are now market economies, they have achieved widely varying levels of economic success. Different histories, positions in the global economy, and

Italians protest in October 2012 against "austerity" policies imposed by the Italian government in response to the country's debt crisis. The prime minister lost the subsequent election and it took weeks for a coalition of parties to put together a new government.

economic policies produce dramatically different levels of wealth, economic growth, unemployment, inequality, and poverty.

This chapter examines the fundamental economic concepts that will help us understand the enduring relationship between the state and the market and the long-standing debates over that relationship. We will return to these themes in chapter 10, where we look at contemporary economic challenges facing states in the era of globalization.

THE MARKET, CAPITALISM, AND THE STATE

A **market economy** is an economic system in which individuals and firms exchange goods and services in a largely unfettered manner. This includes not only the exchange of finished products but also inputs into the production process, including labor. To most people, this seems like a natural state of affairs, but until fairly recently it was the exception, not the norm. In many preindustrial societies, people subsisted on the fruits of their own labor and engaged in very limited trade. In feudal Europe, most people were legally bound to a particular lord and manor and could not exchange

market economy
An economic system in which individuals and firms exchange goods and services in a largely unfettered manner

COUNTRY AND CONCEPT
States and Markets

Country	Average GDP growth (annual %) 1980–2011[1]	Average unemployment (% of total labor force), 1980–2012[2]	Average inflation (% change), 1980–2013[3]	Absolute poverty, 2013 (% of population below $1.25 per day)	Inequality (Inequality-Adjusted Human Development Index), 2010[4]
Brazil	1.22	6.42	361.0	5.2	55.0
China	8.88	3.13	4.7	15.9	41.5
Germany	1.65	8.32	2.3	0.01	28.3
India	4.3	3.3	8.3	41.6	36.8
Iran	0.87	11.3	19.7	< 2.0	38.3
Japan	1.8	3.49	1.0	0.01	24.9
Mexico	0.97	3.74	29.0	4.0	51.6
Nigeria	1.12	N/A	20.0	64.4	42.9
Russia	0.81	8.46	85.8	< 2.0	43.7
United Kingdom	1.82	7.51	4.0	0.01	36.0
United States	1.59	6.38	3.6	0.01	40.8

[1] World Bank, GDP per capita growth (annual %) (http://data.worldbank.org/indicator/NY.GDP.PCAP.KD.ZG).

[2] World Bank, World Development Indicators, average total unemployment (% total labor force) (http://databank.worldbank.org/data/views/reports/tableview.aspx). Reliable unemployment data for Nigeria are not available because of the difficulties of measuring unemployment in an economy characterized by a large informal sector.

[3] International Monetary Fund, World Economic Outlook Database (http://www.imf.org/external/pubs/ft/weo/2013/01/weodata/index.aspx); Human Development Reports, "Multidimensional Poverty Index" (http://hdr.undp.org/en/media/HDR_2010_EN_Table5_reprint.pdf).

[4] Human Development Reports, "Inequality-Adjusted Human Development Index" (http://hdr.undp.org/en/media/HDR_2010_EN_Table3_reprint.pdf).

their labor for a wage anywhere they pleased. The creation of the modern market economy required that feudal bonds restricting labor be broken so that most people would become dependent on market exchanges. In modern industrial and postindustrial societies, virtually the entire population depends on earning a wage or receiving a share of profit via the market.

Capitalism

capitalism
The combination of a market economy with private property rights

Capitalism is not exactly the same thing as a market economy, though the terms are typically used interchangeably. Rather, capitalism is the combination of a market economy with private property rights. In theory, one can imagine a market economy without individual property rights. For example, collectively owned firms could be free to produce whatever they could for a profit in an unfettered market. Yugoslavia under the communist rule of Jozef Tito attempted but never fully implemented a modified version of such a system in the 1960s and 1970s.

Virtually all countries have some form of a capitalist economy today, although the degree to which the market is unfettered and the precise nature of private property rights vary widely. There is no absolute law in economics about how "free" market exchanges or private property must be for a capitalist economy to function. The debates over the extent to which the state should intervene to limit and shape market exchanges and property rights are at the core of many of the most important political issues around the globe. The end of the Cold War eliminated the communist **command economy**—an economic system in which most prices, property, and production are directly controlled by the state—as a viable political economic model, but it did not end the debate over what ought to be the relationship between the market and the state.

Because people tend to see the capitalist market economy as somehow natural, they also see it as existing independently of government. Nothing could be further from the truth. Command economies were ultimately of limited efficiency, but they proved that a state can exist for a long time without a market economy. Capitalism, on the other hand, cannot exist without the state. In a situation of anarchy—the absence of a state—the market would be severely limited; without state provision of security, property and contract rights, and money, exchange would be limited to bartering and would require extensive provision of private security forces. Mafias are examples of this kind of capitalism, which arises where states are weak or absent; they provide their own security and enforce their own contracts. While this structure can create some productive economic activity, the uncertainty of property rights and contracts, and the costs of private security, limit economic growth and create a society in which few would like to live. This points to the first of several *essential roles* the state must play in a capitalist economy: providing security. In addition to certain roles that are essential to capitalism, the modern state also often plays important roles that are not essential but are either *beneficial* or *politically generated*.

Essential Roles

The state's essential roles are providing security, establishing and enforcing property and contract rights, and creating and controlling currency. Most essential roles, and many of the beneficial ones as well, involve the provision of **public goods,** those goods or services that cannot or will not be provided via the market because their costs are too high or their benefits are too diffuse. National security is an excellent example of a public good. Individual provision of security is extremely expensive, and if any one company could pay for it, the benefits would accrue to everyone in the country anyway, not allowing the company to generate revenue sufficient to cover the costs. The state must provide this service if the market economy is to thrive.

command economy
An economic system in which most prices, property, and production are directly controlled by the state

public goods
Those goods or services that cannot or will not be provided via the market because their costs are too high or their benefits are too diffuse

Video link:
Defining public
goods

Protection of property and contract rights is also an essential state function in a market economy. Capitalism requires investing now with the expectation of future gains. Some uncertainty is always involved, but if potential investors have no means of ensuring that the future gains will accrue, no one will invest. Property rights protect not only property legally purchased in the market but also future property—the profits of current investment and productive activity. Similarly, profits require honest market exchanges: if a ton of cotton is promised for delivery at a set price, it must actually be delivered at that price. Details can vary significantly, but some legal guarantee that current and future property and exchanges will be protected is essential to achieving the productivity associated with modern market economies.

The modern state must also provide a currency to facilitate economic exchanges. States did not always print or control currency. Prior to the American Civil War, for instance, private banks printed most currency in the United States (hence the old-fashioned term *banknote*). When the state took over this process and created a uniform currency, exchanges across the entire country were eased. This happened transnationally as thirteen countries adopted the euro as the single currency of the European Union (EU) in 2004, greatly easing exchange across much of the continent.

Beneficial Roles

Several other roles the state commonly plays in the modern market economy are not absolutely essential, but most analysts consider them beneficial. These include providing infrastructure, education, and health care, and correcting market failures. The first three are all examples of public goods. Roads are a classic example of infrastructure as a public good. Private roads can and sometimes do exist, but governments build the bulk of all highway systems. Most of the time, it is too costly to build private roads. Public provision of a road network lowers the cost of transporting goods and people, which improves the efficiency and profitability of many sectors of the economy.

Similarly, most economists and business leaders see an educated populace as beneficial to economic efficiency. Workers who can read, write, and do arithmetic are far more productive than those who cannot. Companies could provide this education themselves, but because education is a lengthy process, because children learn many things more efficiently and effectively than do adults, and because workers can switch jobs and take their company-provided education with them, providing basic education is not a profitable endeavor and is therefore a nearly universal function of the state.

In most countries, the provision of basic health care is seen in similar terms. Obviously, a healthy workforce is more productive than an unhealthy one, and investment in health is most productive in the early stages of life; the economic benefits of high-quality prenatal and early childhood health care are far greater than the benefits of health care for the elderly. Most countries, therefore, consider health care a public good. At the very least, the government aggressively intervenes in the health care market to ensure that such care is provided to all.

Today, vigorous debates about the state's role in providing public goods and services continue in many countries. While virtually all agree that basic education is beneficial and ought to be provided by the state (the United Nations has officially endorsed education as a right for all), that still leaves a great deal open to dispute: How much secondary and higher education should the state provide? Should the government pay for all or most of a person's higher education, as is the case in most of Europe, or should the individual pay a substantial share, as in the United States? Health care is even more controversial. While most agree that a healthy workforce enhances a market economy, how to achieve such a healthy population is the subject of near-constant debate. These issues are analyzed in greater depth in chapter 11.

The fourth beneficial economic function of the modern state is intervention to correct market failure. **Market failure** occurs when markets fail to perform efficiently. The primary justification for a market is efficiency: a well-functioning market maximizes the efficient use of all available resources. Three common causes of market failure are **externalities** (transactions that do not include the full costs or benefits of production in the price), imperfect information, and monopolies in which one seller can set prices. Advocates of an unfettered market recognize market failures as something governments should try to correct, but exactly when such intervention is justified and how governments should respond remain controversial.

Market externalities occur when a cost or benefit of the production process is not fully included in the price of the final market transaction, thereby reducing efficiency. Environmental damage is a common externality. If a factory pollutes the air as it makes a product, costs are incurred at least by local residents. The factory owners, however, do not have to pay those costs as they make and sell their products, and the price charged customers doesn't include those costs. The factory will pollute more than it would if it and its customers had to pay the costs of that pollution. Many economists argue, therefore, that the state should intervene to make the producers and consumers of the product bear its full costs.

Markets can also only maximize efficiency when buyers and sellers know the full costs and benefits of their transactions. Economists call this having "perfect information." In our financially and technologically complex societies, market actors often lack perfect information. The financial collapse that caused the 2008–2009 recession resulted in part from a set of transactions in which consumers and investors did not fully know what they were purchasing. The first breakdown in information came as many Americans purchased homes during the housing boom earlier in the decade. Potential buyers were desperate to purchase as home prices rose rapidly. Some lenders, especially in the "hottest" markets, offered buyers variable-rate mortgages with payments and interest that were low in the short term but that increased dramatically later. Many buyers seemed not to understand how high the payments would go, and some lenders used aggressive or fraudulent techniques to sell mortgages to uncreditworthy buyers, seeking to earn loan-processing fees and interest in the short term and not caring whether the borrowers would be able to pay back the loans in the long term (a practice known as predatory lending).

market failure
Phenomenon that occurs when markets fail to perform efficiently or fail to perform according to other widely held social values

externality
A cost or benefit of the production process that is not fully included in the price of the final market transaction when the product is sold

The second set of transactions in which buyers lacked perfect information occurred on Wall Street, where major banks sold investments called "mortgage-backed securities" (MBS), which were basically bundles of these high-risk mortgages Theoretically, these investments helped to spread out the risks of these high-risk mortgages across many investors. Banks tried to reduce risk further by selling MBS investors a kind of insurance called credit default swaps (which are part of a broader investment category called derivatives), which would compensate them if the mortgage holders defaulted on their loans. However, the Wall Street banks selling these investments and the companies that rate the risks did not fully disclose or realize the level of risk in the mortgages, so investors did not fully understand the risks involved in their investments. Once housing prices began to fall significantly in 2008, the most heavily involved Wall Street banks, most notably Lehman Brothers, faced bankruptcy as their investors tried to sell the MBS as quickly as possible but found no buyers, so the value of those investments collapsed. Even worse, the banks had to pay off those investors who had bought credit default swaps. Bankruptcy ensued for some of the banks, and investors in the United States and around the world (often unknowingly via instruments like pension funds) faced a massive loss of wealth. The result was the biggest economic downturn since the Great Depression. The market failure embedded in this series of transactions in which buyers of all sorts lacked "perfect information" led to renewed debate over how much government regulation is necessary in the mortgage and financial markets.

The third common market failure is **monopoly**—the control of the entire supply of a valued good or service by one seller. In a market economy, competition among alternative suppliers is a key incentive for efficiency. Because monopolies eliminate this incentive, the state may intervene to prevent them. It may do so in three ways: by making the monopoly government owned and therefore (in theory) run in the

monopoly
The control of the entire supply of a valued good or service by one economic actor

A family is evicted from its home in Colorado in 2010. A financial crisis centered in high-risk home mortgages and Wall Street products derived from them started what became the Great Recession. Imperfect information among buyers of the mortgages and the Wall Street products helped produce this catastrophe.

interest of the general public, by regulating the monopoly to ensure that its prices are closer to what they would be in a competitive market, or by forcing the breakup of the monopoly into smaller, competing entities.

Some monopolies are considered **natural monopolies;** these occur in sectors of the economy in which competition would raise costs and reduce efficiency. Where a natural monopoly exists, it makes more sense to regulate or take control of it rather than force a breakup. A good example of a natural monopoly is the history of telephone service. A generation ago, every phone had to be hardwired into a land line, and all calls traveled over wires; this meant that competition would have required more than one company to run wires down the same street. This obviously would have been prohibitively expensive and inefficient. Britain, like many other countries, chose the first option to deal with this natural monopoly: it created the government-owned British Telephone company. The United States, by contrast, chose to heavily regulate a privately owned monopoly, and all services were provided by "Ma Bell" (as AT&T was nicknamed). By 1984, however, new ways to deliver voice and high-speed data transmission reduced the "natural" quality of the monopoly. A lawsuit led to the breakup of AT&T, spawning several local phone companies. With the advent of satellite and wireless technology, the natural monopoly evaporated; around the world, governments have privatized or deregulated phone services, and consumers now have a choice of providers.

natural monopoly
The control of the entire supply of valued goods or services by one economic actor in a sector of the economy in which competition would raise costs and reduce efficiency

Politically Generated Roles

All the economic functions of the state discussed to this point are economically required or at least beneficial to the market. The final category of state functions in a market economy are those that are politically generated by citizens demanding that a state take action. Most economists do not see these functions as essential or perhaps even beneficial to creating an efficient market, but states have taken on these roles because a large section of the populace has demanded them. Karl Polanyi argued in his 1944 book, *The Great Transformation,* that the rise of the modern industrial economy produced political demands to limit what many people saw as the negative effects of the market. This led to what is now termed the modern welfare state. Through the democratic process in European countries and the United States, in particular, citizens demanded protection from the market, and governments began to provide it to a greater or lesser extent. Primary examples of these politically generated state functions are government regulations requiring improved working conditions and policies that redistribute income.

Because these state interventions are the results of political demands, they remain very contentious and vary greatly from country to country. In wealthy industrial economies, modern working conditions, including a minimum wage, an eight-hour workday, and workers' health and safety standards, are largely the product of labor union demands. Yet, as the case studies at the end of this chapter show, labor policies in wealthy countries vary significantly, particularly in areas such as the length of the workweek, job security, the length of maternity leave, and the amount of paid vacation time that employers are required to give. In countries that have begun industrializing more recently, such as Brazil and China, labor unions are recent creations that have not had the opportunity to successfully champion the same reforms that are now taken for granted in countries that industrialized much earlier. Minimum wages may be low or nonexistent, workdays may be as long as twelve hours, and paid vacations are rare. This disparity between wealthier and poorer countries is at the core of the controversies surrounding globalization.

Similar controversy and variation exist around income redistribution policies. Typically referred to as "welfare" in the United States (though Social Security, which is not usually seen as "welfare," is also an income redistribution policy), these policies exist to mitigate the effects of unequal income distribution that markets generate. Markets can provide great economic efficiency and growth, but they have no rules for how wealth is distributed. As social and economic inequality expanded in the late nineteenth and early twentieth centuries, reformers began to demand that the state take action to help those who were gaining little or nothing in the market. For reasons we explore in the case studies at the end of this chapter, the extent to which the early industrializing countries in Europe and the United States pursued income redistribution and poverty amelioration varied considerably. As with proper and regulated working conditions, income redistribution policies barely exist at all in the poorest countries; the poorest people are left to survive in the market as best they can.

Overall, the symbiotic relationship between the modern state and the market economy provides a means to analyze state interventions in modern economic life. The state must carry out certain roles if capitalism is to survive and thrive. Political leaders know that much of their popularity rests on the ability to generate goods and services, jobs, and government revenue. In the modern economy, states pursue various policies and market interventions beyond those that are the bare essentials for the survival of capitalism. Some of these are widely recognized as beneficial to contemporary economies, though the details of how and how much to pursue them remain controversial. Other policies, however, are generated primarily by political demands emanating from society, especially in democracies. These policies remain the most controversial and vary the most from state to state, as we will see in the case studies at the end of this chapter and in chapters 10 and 11.

Data link:
Transformation Index's ranking of countries' progress on political and economic reform

KEY ECONOMIC DEBATES

Understanding political economy and the relationship between the state and the market requires the application of both political science and basic economics. Major economic theories lie behind the debates over how governments should intervene in the market. The first, central debate that must be understood is between Keynesian and monetarist theories of when, why, and how the state ought to attempt to guide

The Role of the State in the Market

Essential functions of the state	Beneficial functions of the state	Politically generated functions of the state
Provide national and personal security: Failure to do so produces anarchy or the creation of a mafia.	**Provide public goods:** These are goods or services not provided via the market because their costs are too high or their benefits are too diffuse, such as public education.	**Improve working conditions:** Examples include health and safety standards, eight-hour workday, minimum wage.
Protect property and contract rights: These are essential for investments to produce profits over time.	**Mitigate market failures:** These are interventions when the market fails to allocate resources efficiently. Examples include environmental regulations and law limiting monopolies.	**Redistribute income:** Examples include retirement benefits, unemployment compensation, welfare.
Provide a currency: Facilitates widespread exchange.		

the economy. Prior to the Great Depression, Western governments engaged in minimal intervention in the economy. Economists and government officials recognized that during economic downturns, unemployment rose and people suffered, but they believed that in the longer term, unemployment lowered wages until labor was cheap enough that businesses started to invest and employ people again, thus creating a new cycle of economic growth. Therefore, during economic downturns, government should do little but wait.

Keynesianism

John Maynard Keynes, after whom **Keynesian theory** is named, revolutionized economics after watching his native Britain enter the Great Depression in the 1930s. Keynes argued that the state could, and should, do more to manage economic crises. In an economic downturn like the Great Depression, the main problem was a lack of demand for goods and services, and he believed that through **fiscal policy,** or management of the government budget, government could revive demand and stimulate the economy. He suggested that the government could and should engage in **deficit spending;** that is, it should spend more than it collected in revenue to stimulate demand. To do this, it would borrow money. By creating new programs and hiring people, the government would put that money into people's hands; they in turn would start to buy other goods and services, and the economy would start to rebound. When the economic downturn was over, the government could pay off the debt it had taken on while deficit spending. This would slow demand in the economy, as too much

Keynesian theory
Named for British economist John Maynard Keynes, who argued that governments can manage the business cycles of capitalism via active fiscal policy, including deficit spending when necessary

fiscal policy
Government budgetary policy

deficit spending
Government spending more than is collected in revenue

demand can cause inflation. Keynes believed that in this way the state could manage the economy, smoothing out the cycle of economic expansion and contraction—known as the business cycle—that seemed inherent in unchecked capitalism. Done properly, such management might even achieve continuous full employment.

Keynesianism (and the onset of World War II) offered governments a way to help their economies out of the Depression, and most Western governments adopted it either explicitly or implicitly. The power of the economic theory alone, however, was not the only reason Keynesian policies became so popular. Deficit spending allowed elected politicians to create new programs to benefit their constituents without having to raise taxes to pay for them. The appeal for politicians facing reelection is obvious. In Europe, Keynesianism also gave social democratic parties economic justification for a significant expansion of social spending and welfare policies after World War II. This political logic led to frequent distortion of pure Keynesian policies—deficit spending continued in many countries even in times of economic growth in contradiction to Keynes's idea that when the economy improved, a government would pay off its debt.

By the 1970s, Keynesian policies came under sustained questioning, first by economists and then in the political arena. Due partly to the quadrupling of oil prices in 1973, most Western countries faced a new economic situation: stagflation, meaning simultaneous high inflation and high unemployment. Keynes's prescription of more government borrowing to reduce unemployment was seen as potentially disastrous in this situation because it was likely to produce more inflation.

Monetarism

monetarist theory
Economic theory that states only monetary policy can affect economic well-being in capitalist economies; rejects Keynesian policy, arguing instead for a reduced role for government in the economy

monetary policy
The amount of money a government prints and puts into circulation and the basic interest rates the government sets

In this context, an alternative economic theory, known as **monetarist theory,** gained popularity. American economist Milton Friedman developed the core ideas of the theory in the 1950s, but they were largely ignored for over a decade. Friedman and other monetarists argued that fiscal policy does not stimulate economic growth. Rather, government borrowing and deficit spending simply "crowd out" private-sector borrowing, impeding the ability of businesses to invest and thereby reducing long-term growth. The key to economic growth, Friedman argued, is **monetary policy:** the amount of money a government prints and puts into circulation and the basic interest rates the government sets. Inflation, monetarists argue, is caused chiefly by excessive government printing of money, and low growth is due in part to government borrowing. Defeating stagflation and restoring growth would therefore require reducing the amount of money in circulation, raising interest rates, and reducing deficit spending. Keynesians also believe monetary policy is important, but believe, like fiscal policy, it can be used to stimulate the economy when growth slows, thus minimizing the effects of any downturn. They argue that easing monetary policy—allowing more money to be put into circulation in an economy—can increase demand for goods and services and thereby spur growth. Monetarists, on the other hand, believe expanding the amount of money in the economy is likely to lead only to inflation; instead, monetary policy should generally keep the growth of money in the economy slow and steady, to prevent inflation.

Combined with deregulation and opening national economies to greater trade, monetarist theory became the theoretical justification for a move toward more free-market, business-friendly policies throughout the world starting in the 1970s that came to be known as **neoliberalism.** U.S. president Ronald Reagan and British prime minister Margaret Thatcher each put monetarist policies in place in the early 1980s. The economic boom that followed was seen as a vindication of monetarism and neoliberalism more broadly, which became the "conventional wisdom" in economic theory, at least until the recession of 2008–2009.

Keynesianism versus Monetarism: An Ongoing Debate

The 2008–2009 recession and its aftermath led to the most significant debate on economic policy in a generation. As the economy collapsed, most states, including the previously monetarist United States, first turned to Keynesian policy to try to restart economic growth; governments engaged in significant deficit spending to stimulate the economy. Monetarist restrictions on government spending collapsed in the face of the highest unemployment rates since the Great Depression and the political pressures that produced. As a slow recovery set in, however, governments on both sides of the Atlantic returned to greater fiscal austerity; fear of excessive debt became greater than desire for more short-term growth. Keynesian economists lambasted this move as happening far too early, pointing to similar policies in the mid-1930s that are believed to have lengthened the Great Depression. Monetarists, on the other hand, saw the move back in their direction as a wise reversal after the Keynesian panic of 2009. By 2012 and 2013, the debate remained unresolved. The U.S. and Japanese economies were continuing to grow slowly, while Europe returned to recession. European countries, led by Germany, pursued neoliberal policies of fiscal austerity (reducing government deficits and debts) and monetarist monetary policy, while the United States and Japan (starting in late 2012) both pursued greater deficit spending and easing of monetary policy, along Keynesian lines. By mid-2013, eurozone unemployment hit a new high of 12.2 percent, with youth (under twenty-five years of age) unemployment at 25 percent. Japanese and American growth produced domestic and international pressure on European governments to shift from their strict neoliberalism.

The recession also initiated a renewed debate about government regulation, especially of the financial sector. Monetarists/neoliberals believe market failure to be very rare, or even nonexistent. For instance, Alan Greenspan, chair of the U.S. Federal Reserve for most of the 1980s and 1990s, believed that private competition in the market for investments like mortgage-backed securities and credit default swaps would produce better security than would government rules. Investors could be counted on not to take on more risk than was prudent, meaning the government would be wasting money if it were constantly watching over their shoulders. Keynesians, on the other

neoliberalism
An economic theory related to monetarism that argues countries should reduce the role of government and open themselves to global trade to allow the market to allocate resources to maximize efficiency and thereby economic growth

hand, believe that market failure is fairly common, and therefore are generally willing to accept greater regulation. Many Keynesians believe this to be especially true of the financial sector, since they see it as unusually prone to irrational and inefficient booms and busts. The twentieth-century economic debate firmly underlies the twenty-first-century debate over both financial regulation and how to ensure economic growth over the long term.

Economic Development Debate

The monetarist-Keynesian debate also had an influential role in economic policy in the postcolonial world. Keynes was instrumental in the creation after World War II of the International Monetary Fund (IMF) and the World Bank, two key institutions of the postwar global economic system. By the early 1960s, both came to play an important role in the economic development of Africa, Asia, and Latin America. One basic assumption of the postwar global economic order was that free trade should be as widespread as possible. The economic argument in favor of this is known as **comparative advantage.** It holds that well-being will be maximized if each country uses its resources to produce whatever it produces relatively efficiently compared with other countries (i.e., it should produce the items that it can produce most efficiently compared with how well other countries produce them, even if it is not the most efficient at anything). It then trades with other countries for goods it does not produce, and all countries gain because they are using their resources as efficiently as possible. What this meant in practical terms was that the poor and agrarian countries of Asia, Africa, and Latin America would, for the foreseeable future, produce primarily agricultural products and raw materials. Their industries, where they existed, were quite new and therefore were not likely to compete successfully against the well-established industrial conglomerates of the wealthy countries.

   Leaders of these countries and the economists who supported them, however, were not willing to have their countries relegated to producing only agricultural products and raw materials. The new field of "development economics," then, came to be about how a state could intervene in the economy to stimulate rapid industrialization and growth. This meshed with the general Keynesian theory that the state could manage capitalism to enhance growth; in "developing countries," this management would simply take somewhat different forms than in industrialized countries. The central policy that developed out of these ideas was **import-substitution industrialization (ISI),** which stated that a developing nation should protect its new industries by placing restrictions on international trade, thus allowing its new industries to grow until they were strong enough to compete on the international market. By limiting the number of imported manufactured products or placing tariffs on them, postcolonial governments could encourage domestic and international investment in new industries in their countries. Most postcolonial countries pursued these policies, with the support of Western governments and the World Bank, from the 1950s to the 1970s.

comparative advantage
Theory of trade that argues that economic efficiency and well-being will be maximized if each country uses its resources to produce whatever it produces relatively well compared with other countries and then trades its own products with other countries for goods it does not produce

import-substitution industrialization (ISI)
Development policy popular in the 1950s-1970s that uses trade policy, monetary policy, and currency rates to encourage the creation of new industries to produce goods domestically that the country imported in the past

By the 1980s, ISI was becoming discredited, and neoliberals were advocating that developing countries should instead emulate the "East Asian miracle" by promoting export-led growth. In China, workers like these produce millions of pieces of clothing for export annually, helping spur the country's economic transformation over the last generation.

In many countries where new industries had not yet begun, governments even took on the role of business owner, creating wholly or partly government-owned industries that supplied the domestic market with key goods.

At first, ISI was relatively successful in creating new industries. Countries such as Brazil, Mexico, and Turkey saw very rapid economic growth throughout the 1950s and 1960s. By the 1970s, though, momentum was waning. Protecting industry from competition helped them get started, but in the long run it resulted in inefficient industries that could not compete on the international market. These industries and their employees, however, put political pressure on postcolonial governments to preserve the protections that they enjoyed. When oil prices quadrupled in 1973, countries that did not produce their own oil had to pay a lot more for oil and other key imports, but because their industries could not compete globally, the countries could not export enough goods to pay for the imports. These governments were forced to take out international loans to cover the resulting trade imbalance. When oil prices increased again in 1979, governments had to borrow even more money from international lenders. Some reached the brink of bankruptcy, and Mexico's declaration in 1982 that it was unable to meet its international debt obligations began a global "debt crisis," which ushered in a period of new economic policies in postcolonial countries.

The growing problems with ISI were emerging at the same time that economists and policy makers in the West were shifting from Keynesian to neoliberal ideas and becoming increasingly skeptical of the ability of governments to manage the market. The World Bank abruptly shifted its development agenda and prescriptions in 1980 and embraced a neoliberal development model. This shift was partly induced by the great economic success of a handful of East Asian countries that collectively came to be known as the "East Asian miracle." In contrast to most of the postcolonial world, these rapidly growing countries, most notably South Korea, Taiwan, Singapore, and the city of Hong Kong, either had never adopted ISI or had abandoned it early on in favor

Web link:
30 years since Mexico's default, Greece must break debt spiral

Web link:
30 years of neoliberalism since the Mexican debt crisis

of focusing on exporting in sectors in which they were competitive. Their success, especially in light of the problems ISI policies had begun to face, suggested to many policy makers that a new approach to development was needed.

The neoliberal model that emerged by 1980 shared monetarists' skepticism of state interventions in the market. Neoliberal economists argued that developing countries were no different from wealthy ones and, as such, they should follow the same basic monetarist policies. These economists compiled a package of policies that came to be known as **structural adjustment programs (SAPs).** These included directives to end government protection of industries and other restrictions on free trade, **privatize** (sell off) government-owned industries, and reduce fiscal deficits. SAPs required a drastically reduced government that would participate far less in the economy; this would allow comparative advantage and the market to signal how resources should be invested, which would maximize efficiency and economic growth.

structural adjustment programs (SAPs)
Development programs created in the 1980s; based on neoliberal principles of reduced government protection of industries, fiscal austerity, and privatization

privatize
To sell off government-owned assets to the private sector

The Successes and Failures of SAPs

The debt crisis that began in 1982 meant that many postcolonial governments had to ask the International Monetary Fund (IMF) for emergency financial assistance. Working in tandem, the IMF and World Bank demanded that the governments receiving assistance in the 1980s and 1990s implement SAPs, thus imposing this model on much of the postcolonial world. This was a slow process in many countries; the necessary steps were politically unpopular because they initially resulted in high inflation, increased unemployment, and drastic cuts in government services, including education and health care. The promise was that if a country could endure these short-term pains, the new policies would maximize efficiency and encourage new investment, thus producing economic growth in the long term.

Many analysts agree that SAPs were successful in certain cases, such as in Chile and several countries in Southeast Asia, but on the whole their effects were mixed. Comparing the first two maps in Map 5.1 provides one way to see the differential effects of this, in that SAPs began in 1980 and were largely ended by 2000. On the most common measure of development, gross domestic product (GDP) per capita, developing countries grew more quickly than wealthy countries from 1965 to 1980, indicating that development policies prior to SAPs were helping them "catch up" to earlier developers. In the 1980s and 1990s, however, they grew more slowly than wealthy countries, suggesting SAPs might have made things worse, or at least did not help them overcome other factors slowing their growth (Ocampo and Vos 2008, 10). Regional differences, however, were stark. On the one hand, East Asia grew at two to three times the world average over the period. On the other hand, Africa suffered economic contraction throughout the two decades, and Latin America contracted in the 1980s and saw very low growth of only 1.3 percent per year during

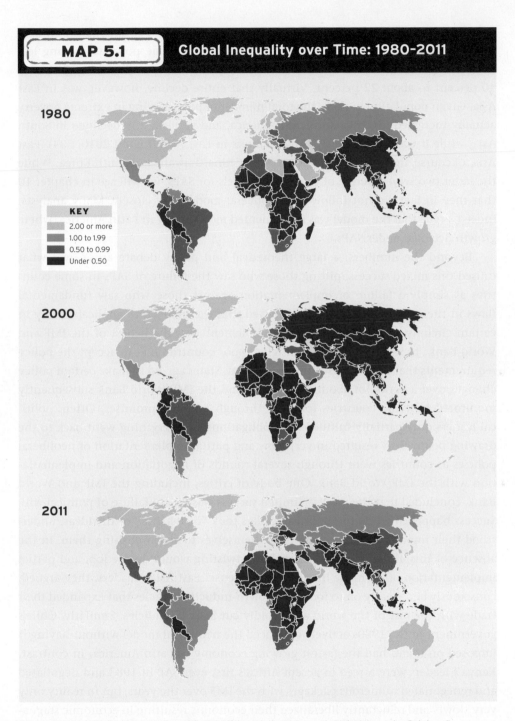

MAP 5.1 Global Inequality over Time: 1980-2011

1980

KEY
- 2.00 or more
- 1.00 to 1.99
- 0.50 to 0.99
- Under 0.50

2000

2011

Source: UN Department of Economic and Social Affairs, "National Accounts Main Aggregates Database" (http://unstats.un.org/unsd/snaama/selbasicFast.asp).

Note: The numbers in the legend measure each country's GDP expressed as a multiple of the average world GDP. Countries in yellow and green have GDPs above the average world GDP for the years shown. Countries in blue have GDPs that are below the average world GDP for the years shown. No data available for French Guiana and Western Sahara.

the 1990s (Round 2010, 330). Changes in poverty mirrored the changes in growth. The percentage of the world's population living in extreme poverty (earning less than one dollar per day) was cut in half over the two decades, from just over 40 percent to about 22 percent. Virtually that entire decline, however, was in East Asia. Given population growth, the total number of people living in extreme poverty actually increased in Africa and Latin America, and very slightly declined in South Asia, while it was cut by nearly three-quarters in East Asia (Round 2010, 334). East Asia, of course, includes the rapidly growing China, Taiwan, and South Korea. While the latter two served as one of the initial models for SAPs, we will see in chapter 10 that they in fact did not follow the neoliberal model very closely. Many analysts, indeed, argue that the model was implemented most closely in Latin America, where growth declined under SAPs.

Beyond the numbers, a large theoretical and policy debate arose over what caused this mixed success, pitting those who saw the failure of SAPs in some countries as simply a failure of implementation against those who saw fundamental flaws in the model and those who believed that the model was applicable only in certain circumstances. Most SAPs were implemented at the behest of the IMF and World Bank. To secure essential debt relief, poor countries had to accept the policy requirements that the two institutions imposed. States agreed to make certain policy changes over a period of about three years, and the IMF/World Bank subsequently monitored how the countries followed through on their promises. Often, political leaders only partially fulfilled their obligations, so everything went back to the drawing board. This resulted in very slow and partial implementation of neoliberal policies as countries went through several rounds of negotiation and implementation with the IMF/World Bank. One body of critics, including the IMF and World Bank, concluded that the model's limited success was due to failure of political will. Success happened when top political leaders took "ownership" of the ideas, understood their importance, and committed themselves to accomplishing them. In the absence of this, no amount of external arm-twisting would do the job, and partial implementation often made little economic sense. East Asian leaders, they argued, consciously chose early on to focus on growth-inducing policies that expanded their trade with the rest of the world and rapidly cut back ISI policies. Similarly, Chile's government in the 1980s actively embraced the neoliberal model without having it imposed on it and had the fastest growing economy in Latin America. In contrast, Kenya's leaders were forced to accept Africa's first ever SAP in 1983 and negotiated and renegotiated numerous packages with the IMF over the years, but in reality only very slowly and reluctantly liberalized their economy, resulting in economic stagnation for most of the 1980s and 1990s.

Other critics contended that the model should have taken political dynamics into account. Lack of implementation, they argued, came not just from lack of understanding and commitment but also from the rational actions of self-interested political leaders. This was particularly true in Africa, where neopatrimonial politics meant that leaders' political survival depended on their ability to provide supporters with patronage, something the reforms jeopardized. This was clearly the case in Kenya; the government used patronage regularly to reward supporters to maintain power and therefore dragged its feet on implementing SAPs that would reduce the government's resources. Related to this, institutionalists contended that markets only work well when embedded in strong institutions, such as clear property rights and contracts. The ultimate goal of the neoliberal model is to improve efficiency to encourage investment and thereby future growth. Weak states that have weak institutions, however, will never gain greater investment because investors cannot be certain their investments and future profits will be secure. The initial neoliberal model ignored this essential area entirely and so was successful only where key institutions were already relatively strong.

Another group of critics argued that SAPs worked only in certain circumstances. A leading theory for East Asian economic success is called the "flying geese" theory (Ozawa 2010). It argues that, like flocks of geese, when one economy in a region is successful, others can follow in its wake by producing goods that the newly wealthy country needs. In East Asia, the original "lead goose" was Japan, followed by South Korea and Taiwan, and later by China. Without a regional leader like Japan, the policies could produce few benefits in Africa. Related to this, some analysts argued that the neoliberal model suffered from a *fallacy of composition,* a term used in the study of logic to indicate that just because something is true in one case does not mean it will be true when applied to all cases. In relation to SAPs, it suggests that market-friendly policies designed to attract investment will succeed in some cases, probably the earliest ones and those with other attractions to investors. When the same policies are extended to all countries, however, there will not be enough investment capital available to respond. Furthermore, the earliest success cases will be likely to attract even more investment, leaving the latecomers empty-handed. Even if later or less attractive states pursue the "right" policies, they still may not see the investment necessary to spark economic growth.

A final school of critics argued that the neoliberal model undermines the real fundamentals of long-term development: infrastructure and human capital. They contended that states succeed at instigating economic development by providing key political goods that investors will need: infrastructure, especially efficient transportation and communications systems; and human capital, meaning an educated and healthy workforce. They pointed out that these were exactly the advantages with which East Asian countries, including China, began. SAPs demand fiscal austerity, typically meaning cuts to both. For countries with relatively little of either, these policies proved detrimental to economic growth.

Web link:
Structural adjustment programs

CRITICAL inquiry

Structural Adjustment Programs

SAPs were intended to correct economic imbalances in developing countries in order to encourage investment, renew economic growth, and thereby reduce poverty via a shift from the protectionism of ISI to more open economy and export-oriented growth. The IMF along with the World Bank were the major organizations that imposed SAPs on often reluctant governments around the world. Table 5.1 presents the number of IMF agreements between 1980 and 2000 (the era in which structural adjustment was pursued most actively) for a selection of countries. While this alone does not tell us everything we might want to know about how much individual countries pursued SAPs, it is an indication of the influence of the IMF's policies. The question is, Do these SAPs lead to better economic outcomes? The table also provides data on GDP per capita, trade, poverty, and infant mortality (the best measure of overall health). Based on this table, what trends do you see? Can you use the data to come to conclusions about who is correct in the debate over SAPs? Did they enhance economic growth and improve well-being in developing countries? Did they create even greater poverty, as their critics asserted? What other information would you like to have to answer these questions even better?

TABLE 5.1	Effect of SAPs on Development: Changes in Key Indicators, 1980-2000								
Country	# IMF agreements, 1980-2000	GDP per capita (constant dollars PPP), 1980	GDP per capita (constant dollars PPP), 2000	Trade surplus or deficit (current account balance, % of GDP) 1980*	Trade surplus or deficit (current account balance, % of GDP) 2000*	Absolute poverty level (poverty gap at $1.25 a day PPP, %) 1980	Absolute poverty level (poverty gap at $1.25 a day PPP, %) 2000	Infant mortality rate (per 1,000 live births) 1980	Infant mortality rate (per 1,000 live births) 2000
Argentina	7	10,075	10,282	−1.23	−3.15	0.0 (1986)	2.8	173	95
Ghana	9	993	1,067	−0.21	−6.56	18.0 (1988)	14.4 (1998)	95	64
Indonesia	2	1,323	2,623	3.36	4.84	21.4 (1984)	12.5 (1999)	76	38
Kenya	9	1,375	1,283	−10.72	−2.31	15.4 (1992)	16.9 (2005)	69	70
Mexico	5	10,238	11,853	−4.61	−2.78	3.0 (1984)	1.5	55	24
Nigeria	3	1,645	1,469	8.85	12.47	21.9 (1986)	28.7 (2004)	129	113
Pakistan	8	1,224	1,845	−3.19	−0.29	23.9 (1987)	6.3	111	76
Peru	4	6,083	5,543	−5.06	−2.90	3.0 (1986)	4.6	79	30
Philippines	6	2,827	2,697	−6.91	−2.75	10.3 (1985)	5.5	53	29
Tanzania	4	823 (1998)	868	−7.69	−4.30	29.7 (1992)	41.6	105	78
Zambia	5	1,532	1,028	−15.08	−18.34	40.0 (1991)	26.9 (1998)	98	91

* Positive numbers show exports are greater than imports and negative numbers show imports are greater than exports.

Source: Data are from International Monetary Fund (number of SAPs, changes to trade surplus and deficit) and World Bank (GDP per capita PPP, absolute poverty rate, infant mortality rate).

By the new millennium, the neoliberal consensus was shifting, at least somewhat, and critics were proposing significant policy modifications in light of the neoliberal model's limited success and the greater success of countries like China that seemed to pursue alternative models. While most economists and policy makers still argue in favor of the basics of market-friendly policies to encourage trade and investment, they also recognize the importance to developmental success of strong institutions, infrastructure, and human capital. The World Bank, in particular, now has active policies pursuing each of these goals. We discuss these trends further in chapter 10. First, though, the shift toward monetarism in the wealthy countries and neoliberal policies in the developing countries helped usher in what many argue was a new era in the history of the relationship between states and markets: globalization.

GLOBALIZATION: A NEW WORLD ORDER, OR DÉJÀ VU ALL OVER AGAIN?

There is no doubt that the 2008–2009 recession showed the negative elements of globalization clearly: a financial crisis based in the United States quickly spread around the world. Major European investors had stakes in the high-risk securities that collapsed on Wall Street, causing European banks to face possible bankruptcy and Cyprus, Greece, Ireland, Italy, Portugal, and Spain to come close to default. Export markets for developing economies like China and India plummeted, and a brief era of economic growth in Africa was nipped in the bud. These global effects all started with average people in places like Arizona and Florida buying homes with risky, variable-rate mortgages.

Globalization has become perhaps the most frequently used, and abused, term in political economy. It first gained prominence in the 1990s, and since then hundreds of books and countless articles have been written about it. It has cultural as well as

Key Economic Theories

	Keynesianism	Monetarism/Neoliberalism
Architect	John Maynard Keynes	Milton Friedman/World Bank/IMF
Role of governments	Governments should actively manage business cycles	Governments should play diminished role in economy; open economies to global trade
Key instruments	Fiscal policy, including deficit spending; regulation; looser monetary policy	Monetary policy; deregulation; privatization
Policy for developing countries	*Import-Substitution Industrialization (ISI)*: Trade restrictions to protect domestic industry	*Structural Adjustment Programs (SAPs)*: Open trade, privatization of industry, deficit reduction
Criticisms	Deficit spending reduces private investment and growth and causes inflation; regulation limits business success	Monetarist restrictions on government spending slow growth during recession; deregulation creates boom and bust; increases inequality

economic and political implications, but we will focus on the latter two in order to understand its effects on the relationship between the state and the market. That economic activity across borders has increased over the last generation is beyond question: between 1980 and 2010 trade as a share of global GDP increased from 30 percent to 56 percent, foreign direct investment more than quadrupled, and annual minutes of international phone calls from the United States went from two billion to seventy-five billion (Dadush and Dervis 2013).

globalization
A rapid increase in the flow of economic activity, technology, and communications around the globe, and the increased sharing of cultural symbols, political ideas, and movements across countries

Globalization has many definitions. We define it as a rapid increase in the flow of economic activity, technology, and communications around the globe. Three key questions have arisen about globalization: (1) Does it represent a brave new world in which the fundamental relationship between the state and the market has changed forever, or is it simply the latest phase in that relationship—something new and interesting but not fundamentally different? (2) What caused it in the first place? (3) What can and should be done about it, if anything?

A Brave New World?

Globalization's earliest adherents saw it as a portent of fundamental change. Japanese scholar Kenichi Ohmae, writing in 1995, argued that globalization would result in the "end of the nation-state." He focused on economic aspects of globalization, but others have broadened this general argument, claiming that the rapid flow of money, goods and services, ideas, and cultural symbols around the globe will eventually make the nation-state irrelevant. Regional, if not global, management will have to fill the role currently played by the state. The flow of ideas and culture will severely weaken national identity, as the Internet in particular will allow people to form identities not linked to territories and their immediate local communities. All of these changes ultimately will require political responses in the form of strengthened international organizations for global governance and a new global civil society to respond to global problems with global solutions.

Since the initial separation of the economic and political spheres in early modern Europe, capital's greatest weapon has been its mobility: business can usually threaten to move if it does not receive adequate treatment from a state. The state, in sharp contrast, is tied to a territory. Ohmae and other prophets of change are right that globalization has significantly increased capital mobility so that businesses can credibly threaten to leave a country much more easily now than they could a generation ago. This mobility has increased capital's power in relation to states. In trying to manage their economies, policy makers must be actively concerned about preserving the investments they have and attracting new ones, and with business able to move relatively easily, states increasingly must compete to attract it.

Similar changes in global finance—the flow of money around the world—also have weakened the state. Most countries now allow their currencies to be traded freely. Electronic communications have made currency transactions nearly instantaneous. For a government trying to pursue sound monetary policies through control of its money supply and interest rates, this new world of global currency flow can be problematic. The collapse of many Southeast Asian economies in 1997 was caused at least in part by currency speculators, traders who purchase a country's currency not to buy goods in that country but simply to try to buy it at a low valuation and sell it later at a higher valuation. When the speculators, led by international financier George Soros, found the Southeast Asian economies were weaker than they had believed, they began to sell the currencies rapidly. This led to a classic market panic in which virtually all international traders sold those currencies, causing immense economic loss and political instability in the region and, ultimately, in developing countries worldwide. States, especially in small and poor countries, must base monetary and fiscal policy not only on domestic concerns but also on how "global markets" might react. Greece learned this lesson in 2010; it faced bankruptcy because the global market thought its debt was too high and therefore charged it extremely high interest rates when the country wished to borrow. Ultimately, the European Union and IMF had to craft a "rescue package" of loans that required Greece to follow "austerity measures" similar to those the IMF imposes on developing countries. This resulted in several years of political turmoil as more than one government fell and demonstrations against the pain of austerity became commonplace. Italy and Cyprus soon followed. In Cyprus in 2013, the government faced a particular problem: it had to rescue its banking sector without alienating Russian investors who had deposited large sums in Cypriot banks. The initial solution was to tax its own people's savings instead, but the parliament and populace rejected that idea. The government was caught between the rock of pleasing a particular subset of international investors and the hard place of its domestic constituency.

Video link:
The Greek debt crisis explained

A protester in March 2013 urges the parliament in Cyprus to reject a deal her government had made with the EU to resolve its banking crisis. The plan raised taxes on ordinary Cypriots while protecting the bank deposits of wealthy Russians who used Cyprus's banks to store money outside their own country. Parliament ultimately rejected the deal, forcing a renegotiation that was at least slightly more favorable to Cypriot citizens.

The rapid flow of all sorts of economic transactions across state borders has no doubt shifted the relative power of capital and the state. States do still have an important role to play; however, their power varies significantly. Political scientist Geoffrey Garrett (1998) argued that European countries can maintain policies favoring labor unions and related groups if they provide long-term stability and predictability for business. The Great Recession raised questions about this argument, as many European governments felt the dramatic effects of international bond markets no longer having faith in them; the result was intense pressure to reduce social welfare spending and regulations protecting labor. Poor countries are in an even weaker position. Investments in Europe mostly involve hiring highly trained labor for which business is willing to pay more to ensure long-term stability. Businesses in Europe also have the advantage of the EU, a huge and wealthy market in which to sell products. El Salvador, by contrast, has none of these advantages. Investments there are in agriculture and "light manufacturing," which involve a large amount of cheap, unskilled, and easily replaceable labor. The Salvadoran government is in a significantly weaker bargaining position vis-à-vis likely international investors than is the German government.

In the new millennium, the scholarly consensus has moved away from Ohmae's view of globalization toward a more modest assessment of its effects. Certainly all of the trends described above exist, and most agree that globalization is likely to weaken the nation-state, but few now believe that globalization will destroy it. While the fundamental relationship between states and business has not been transformed into something entirely new, there has been a shift in their relative power. Any state interested in the economic well-being of its populace must negotiate the rapidly expanding global markets as well as possible, bargaining for the best "deal" for its people. Knowing how to do this effectively is not easy, as some of the case studies below illustrate.

Causes of Globalization

What factors facilitated this weakening of the state vis-à-vis capital? The causes of globalization are undoubtedly multiple, but two major answers to this question have competed for attention. The first one is that technology is the driving force of globalization. The costs of communication and transportation have dropped dramatically. Air travel, once a luxury good for the elite, is now a common practice for citizens of wealthy countries. Advances in containerization and just-in-time manufacturing have allowed more rapid and efficient shipment of goods. And, as we all know, the personal computer, the mobile phone, and the Internet have created instantaneous global communications capabilities while reducing costs. All of this has allowed businesses to expand across national borders at unprecedented rates. Those arguing that globalization does represent a new era point out that this communications and transportation revolution allows transnational corporations to coordinate complex production processes for both goods and services across multiple countries in a manner that is entirely new. Shoes may be designed in Portland, Oregon, but produced in Malaysia using Bangladeshi labor and material inputs from Vietnam and China, all coordinated by "just-in-time" manufacturing to deliver just the number of shoes that are likely to sell in your local shopping mall this month.

A second school of thought argues that while technology was necessary for globalization, government policies made globalization a reality. The shift to neoliberal economic policies that started around 1980 significantly reduced the role of most governments in regulating economic transactions, especially across their borders. The creation of the World Trade Organization (WTO) accelerated a process, started after World War II, of lowering tariffs on imports and exports. Removing government controls on exchange rates allowed money to travel around the world without limit, seeking the best return at the least risk. In most postcolonial countries, the IMF and World Bank imposed these policies on initially reluctant governments via SAPs.

It is difficult to disentangle technological and policy changes to find a single cause of globalization. The different answers, though, have important implications. If technology is the primary cause, then globalization is inevitable and irreversible. If policies play an important role as well, then globalization may be subject to change. Both technology and policy seem crucial to the ultimate outcome, and they are interrelated. As technological change opened new areas of potential profit for international businesses, the leaders of those businesses became a source of powerful political pressure to liberalize economic policies so that they could take advantage of the new opportunities. Once policy shifted in a more liberal direction, more businesses were able to benefit from the changes, demand increased for more new technology to facilitate global communications and transportation, and the political pressure in favor of liberalized economic policies expanded that much further. The presence of "foreign" companies became the norm in much of the world, blunting the political backlash that might have occurred. It is hard to imagine today that controversy would arise in the United States over this issue, as it did when Toyotas and Hondas first entered the mass market in the 1970s or when a Japanese firm briefly purchased Rockefeller Center in the 1980s. People throughout the world have become accustomed to purchasing consumer products from across the globe and working for corporations with headquarters eight time zones away.

Political Responses

The expanded global market and capital mobility also raise questions about the level at which political responses to economic problems can and should occur. As we noted above, individual states are still important, as they navigate global markets the best they can via their economic policies. More and more analysts argue, however, that new global problems require global political solutions. An obvious example is the ultimate global environmental problem: climate change. If pollution is an externality that should cause states to intervene in the market to protect the environment, then climate change is a global externality that only global agreement can remedy. Future generations, one way or another, will pay the costs of this externality that businesses and their consumers are not paying today, but no single state, even the largest and wealthiest, can solve the problem alone. Similarly, individual governments acting alone cannot solve the problem of poor states keeping their labor costs low and working conditions poor in an effort to attract foreign investment. Individual governments that change their policies will simply lose out to the competition. A uniform global policy on wages and working conditions, though extremely difficult to achieve, would be needed to reduce this competition.

Many groups in civil society are not waiting for states to implement globally coordinated policies on their own. Citizens' groups are actively organizing across borders to put pressure on governments or international bodies such as the WTO, the IMF, and the World Bank to enact global measures to address global problems. This effort burst into popular consciousness with the famed "battle for Seattle," a large and at times violent antiglobalization protest at the WTO meeting in Seattle in 1999. Ever since, WTO, IMF, and World Bank meetings have often been the sites of protests, but they are also the sites of tamer meetings of transnational NGOs working on development issues, some criticizing and some cooperating with the multilateral organizations. To the extent that nongovernmental groups are successful, individual states may again be weakened because, as citizens focus their political organization and pressure at the international level, they make individual states less relevant. Many core economic problems, including most discussed in this chapter, remain at the national level, however, particularly in large and wealthy countries. So while the state is weakened vis-à-vis capital, it is far from dead.

Globalization and the European Union

The creation of the European Union (EU), and especially the creation of its common currency, the euro, has raised fundamental questions about globalization and state sovereignty over economic policy. On the one hand, the EU's creation could be argued to limit globalization by creating a regional market as an alternative. On the other hand, EU member states have given up far more economic sovereignty to a transnational organization than have any other modern states.

Initially, EU member states did not really yield substantial sovereignty because each state retained an effective veto over Europe-wide policies. That changed with the Single European Act of 1987, which limited a single state's veto power; not even Germany, the biggest state, can veto decisions. Instead, several states must vote together to block a decision, which means that individual states have given up their individual sovereign right over key economic decisions. The next and biggest step was the Maastricht Treaty of 1992, which created the euro, controlled by a new European Central Bank (ECB). The seventeen states that have so far agreed to participate (the EU has twenty-seven members but only seventeen have adopted the euro so far) gave up their ability to control their own monetary policy and agreed to limits on their fiscal policy. Given the centrality of monetary policy to both Keynesian and monetarist economic management, these states have given up perhaps the most important economic policy tool they have. To "join" the euro, states had to pledge to bring their inflation and interest rates close to the European average and restrict their budget deficits to 3 percent of GDP and their public debt to 60 percent of GDP, policies that derive from monetarist theory. The European Central Bank controls the money supply and therefore monetary policy for these states. Crucially, however, each state continues to control its own fiscal policy; the disjuncture between monetary and fiscal policy, and limited EU power over the latter, was at the center of the "euro crisis" that began in 2009.

The Great Recession hit the EU and especially the euro extremely hard. Maintaining the limits on debt that were agreed upon when the euro was created has always been

MAP 5.2   The European Union

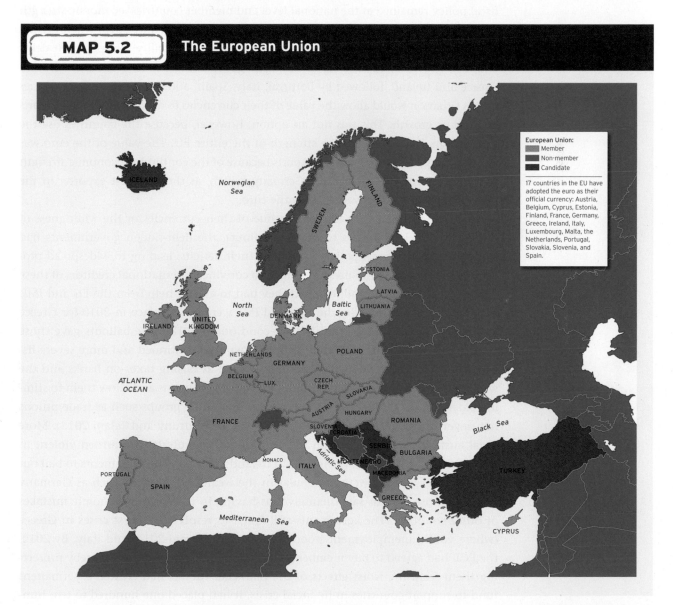

Source: Adapted from European Union (http://europa.eu/about-eu/countries/index_en.htm).

hard, even for the healthier economies such as Germany and France, both of which failed to meet the targets some years prior to the crisis. In the economic boom that preceded the crisis, several of the weaker economies ran up debts and deficits, using the strength of the euro to help them borrow money cheaply. Others, such as Spain and Ireland, had fiscal surpluses before the crisis, but the recession hit the countries' banking sector so hard that their tax revenue plummeted, creating a fiscal crisis. In some countries, such as Ireland and Cyprus, the banking sector constituted a huge share of the entire economy, setting off a severe recession when the financial crisis hit. The crisis revealed the problems created by EU control of monetary policy while fiscal policy remained at the national level and member countries' economic strength varied greatly. The full extent of the crisis was only revealed in 2010, when private international creditors began to doubt the weaker states' ability to repay their debts and, therefore, started refusing to buy their government bonds. The worst hit were Greece and Ireland, followed by Portugal, Italy, Spain, and Cyprus. Usually countries in this situation would allow the value of their currencies to drop to encourage exports and restart growth. This was not an option, however, because the countries use the euro and its value is tied to the strength of the entire EU. The value of the euro was not dropping fast enough to spur exports because of the continuing economic strength of the larger countries, especially Germany, which, as the strongest exporter in the region, had long been advantaged by the euro.

Without the ability to lower the value of their currencies or the willingness of the wealthier EU countries to provide bailouts, the debt-ridden governments had to institute severe fiscal policies to reduce their deficits, leading to widespread protests. Even these austerity measures failed to convince international creditors of these countries' economic soundness, and they had to ask for help from the EU and IMF. Bailout packages funded by the ECB and IMF were put in place in 2010 for Greece and Ireland, with Greece requiring a second one in 2011. The bailouts gave those countries new funds to back their debt but required continued and more severe fiscal austerity to reduce deficits. Alternatives such as raising taxes on banks and the wealthy across Europe to help fund the weaker governments and allow them to stimulate demand along Keynesian lines were proposed by groups such as trade unions but never seriously considered by the ECB or IMF (Cafruny and Talani 2013). More fiscal austerity led to further and more widespread protests that turned violent in Greece and toppled the governments in Ireland and Italy. The agreements to bail out the countries in crisis were unpopular in the wealthier countries such as Germany as well, whose citizens saw themselves as having to pay for the economic mistakes of other countries. The agreements still failed to resolve the worst crises in Greece (where youth unemployment stood at 62 percent in mid-2013) and Italy. By 2013, the ECB had agreed to buy member government bonds if necessary (thereby protecting them from the worst effects of the markets); the EU had created a permanent fund to support countries in financial crisis, it had placed one hundred to two hundred of the largest banks under direct supervision of the ECB to help ensure their integrity, and it had initiated policies to give stronger incentives to governments to stick to the official limits on their debts and deficits. All of this was an effort to reassure investors about the long-term stability of the euro. Critics contended, however, that even further measures to strengthen the union by moving toward a truly transnational fiscal policy may ultimately be needed (Cafruny and Talani 2013).

For the first time since the creation of the euro, the crisis produced open discussion (especially in Greece) about whether continuing to use the common currency was wise. Critics of the EU have long opposed the fiscal and monetary policies required to join the euro, seeing them as forcing every member country to follow the neoliberal economic orthodoxy that they see as undermining European social welfare policies. The crisis reinforced these arguments, calling into question the benefits that a single currency was supposed to provide while requiring even more unpopular fiscal policies. By 2013, the worst of the immediate financial crisis seemed over, though the economies of the countries hardest hit were still in deep recessions, with unemployment in some as high as 25 percent and predictions that they would not see renewed economic growth for a decade. The crisis had shown, however, the difficulty national governments have in dealing with global financial flows, even in the most integrated region of the world. Major structural reforms that Germany in particular called for, such as a stronger EU fiscal policy that would impose austerity on member governments if needed, were resisted by the populace in the weakest countries who were increasingly skeptical of the advantages of the EU and globalization more generally.

Video link:
EU leadership hardens its pro-austerity stance

Web link:
After austerity, what?

STATES AND MARKETS AROUND THE WORLD

As with any area of comparative politics, economic policies in the real world do not follow perfectly the various abstract economic models. Many factors not taken into account in economic theories influence government policies. These include broad political ideologies; the relative strengths of particular groups, especially business and labor; and international influences.

To illustrate real-world variation in the relationship of the market to the state, we look at five of our case study countries: three wealthy, industrialized democracies and two developing countries. Figures 5.1 to 5.6 provide an overview of key economic data for all five and offer some of the overall story of each country. The market-oriented model in the United States has produced great wealth, relatively good growth (until recently), and moderate unemployment and inflation, but relatively high inequality and poverty. Germany's social market economy struggled with low growth and high unemployment until fairly recently, though the country has controlled inflation very well and has far less inequality than the United States. Japan's developmental state achieved high growth prior to 1990 but has been in crisis since then, with growing unemployment and deflation and modest poverty and inequality. Mexico is a middle-income country that is much poorer than the United States, Germany, or Japan. It has achieved modest economic growth and unemployment and has recently reduced inflation significantly and improved growth, though it is also one of the most unequal

FIGURES 5.1–5.6   Economic Overview

Figure 5.1 GDP per Capita, 2012

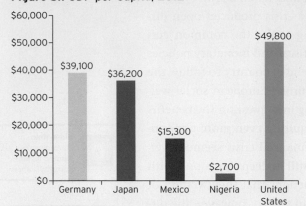

Figure 5.4 GDP Growth, 1980 to Present (%)

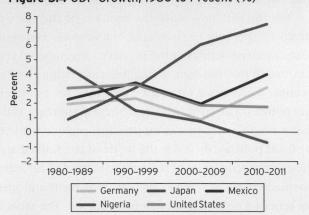

Figure 5.2 Inequality, GINI Index, 2012

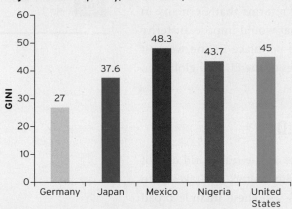

Figure 5.5 Unemployment Rate, 1990 to Present (%)

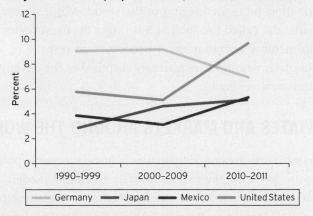

Figure 5.3 Population Living below National Poverty Line (%)

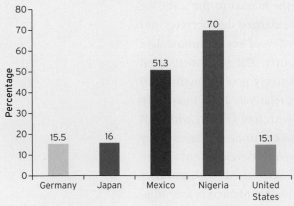

Figure 5.6 Inflation Rate, Consumer Price Index, 1980 to Present (%)

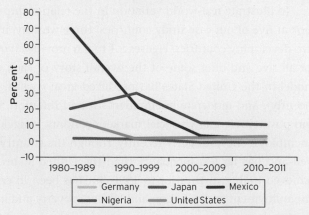

Sources: Data are from *CIA World Factbook*, Country Comparison: GDP Per Capita, 2012 estimates (https://www.cia.gov/library/publications/the-world-factbook/fields/2004.html#ni); The World Bank, Indicators, GDP growth (annual %) (http://data.worldbank.org/indicator/NY.GDP.MKTP.KD.ZG); International Labor Organization (http://laborsta.ilo.org). Data for the unemployment rate, average annual (% of labor force). Reliable unemployment data for Nigeria are not available because of the difficulties of measuring it in an economy characterized by a large informal sector. *CIA World Factbook*, "Distribution of Family Income—GINI Index" (https://www.cia.gov/library/publications/the-world-factbook/fields/2172.html#ni). *CIA World Factbook*, "Population below Poverty Line" (https://www.cia.gov/library/publications/the-world-factbook/fields/2046.html#ni).

economies in the world. Nigeria, by far the poorest of the five, is dependent on one crucial export, oil, reflected in its rising growth rates as the price of oil has risen. Despite its growth, it remains a very poor country and suffers from relatively high inflation, inequality, and very high poverty.

CASE Study

THE UNITED STATES: THE FREE-MARKET MODEL

- **ECONOMIC MODEL**
  Laissez-faire

- **ECONOMIC POLICY**
  Fluctuating between monetarist and Keynesian

- **GLOBALIZATION EFFECTS**
  Manufacturing job loss; financial sector gain

- **ECONOMIC MILESTONES**
  Great Depression and New Deal; 1970s stagflation

- **GREAT RECESSION**
  Origins; high unemployment and debt; relatively good recovery

The 2008–2009 "Great Recession" that began in the United States shook the foundations of the leading economic model in the world and led the government under newly elected president Barack Obama to engage in the largest Keynesian deficit spending in a generation to stimulate the economy. By the 2012 election, a fundamental debate over the proper role of government in the economy became the centerpiece of the campaign. The Republican Party, long a champion of limited government intervention, followed monetarist theory in insisting on reduced government deficits, which would require massive spending cuts rather than tax

The Great Recession began in the U.S. housing market as a classic "bubble" burst. Detroit, Michigan, a former industrial stronghold, was hit particularly hard. Here, the General Motors headquarters towers over debris from destroyed buildings. Job and population losses forced Detroit to declare bankruptcy, the largest city to do so in U.S. history.

increases because greater taxes would hurt business and therefore growth. Democrats countered with an Keynesian argument that in a recession the government needed to help stimulate the economy in the short term, and worry about deficit reduction only after growth is well underway.

The United States has long been the greatest exemplar of the free-market, or *laissez-faire,* model of economic development and capitalism. Compared with the governments of most wealthy countries, including Germany and Japan, the U.S. government has taken a hands-off approach to the economy for most of its history. Not until the Great Depression and the New Deal of the 1930s did the government begin to attempt to guide the economy to increase growth and employment and to redistribute income. From the New Deal through the 1960s, the government more or less followed Keynesian policies, but by the 1980s, it had shifted toward monetarism, moving back toward its historic reluctance to be involved in the economy. That monetarist focus came into question, though, since the start of the Great Recession.

The modern U.S. economy emerged in the late nineteenth and early twentieth centuries as rapid industrialization transformed the country from a primarily agricultural and rural society into a rapidly growing urban and industrial economy. The government's nearly complete lack of involvement in the economy up to that point had to change in response to this transformation. Its initial policies, however, were aimed primarily at ensuring that the market would remain as free as possible. The first time the government took on a major beneficial function other than building infrastructure and schools was in an effort to eliminate or regulate monopoly control of key sectors of the economy. This started with regulation of the railways and then expanded with the landmark Sherman Antitrust Act of 1890.

With industrialization also came the rise of labor unions. The government opposed the increasingly frequent strikes, the most famous of which were the Haymarket Riots of May 1886 in Chicago. Workers began the strike to demand an eight-hour workday, but within days it included 350,000 people nationwide. On May 4, it ended with a rally during which a bomb killed a police officer and the police killed dozens of unarmed

in CONTEXT

Central Banks

A central bank or some other monetary authority is a crucial institution of economic policy. Many central banks were started in part to create a unified national currency. In most wealthy countries today, central banks are independent institutions, supposedly free of political influence, that establish currency stability and monetary policy. The U.S. Federal Reserve System was a relative latecomer among wealthy countries at establishing a central bank, as the timeline demonstrates.

demonstrators. This event helped get May 1 declared "Labor Day" in most countries in honor of workers' struggles for labor rights. (Ironically, the United States is one of a very few countries that celebrate Labor Day on a different date.)

By the early twentieth century, the U.S. government recognized that it would need to broaden its role in the economy. In 1913 it created both the nation's first central bank, the Federal Reserve (the "Fed"), and the income and corporate tax systems. The Fed, modeled after the British and German central banks, was given a monopoly on printing legal currency and charged with regulating the nation's money supply. With growing industrialization, the government also recognized that taxes on trade, the primary source of government revenue in the nineteenth century, would no longer suffice. Since industry had come to generate the bulk of the nation's wealth and employment, the government began taxing business profits and personal incomes to provide a stronger revenue stream. Although the government began to play a larger role in the economy in this era, it remained focused on ensuring the smooth functioning of a free market by eliminating monopolies, opposing unions, providing a stable monetary system, and gaining government revenue from taxation of private economic activity.

This remained the model of U.S. economic policy until the Great Depression and the New Deal. The Great Depression, which produced 25 percent unemployment at its peak in 1933, shook the foundations of the nation's belief in the free market. During this time of rapidly rising union membership and radical political demands, Franklin Roosevelt won the presidency in 1932 with a promise of a "new deal." The fruition of this promise was an ambitious program of unprecedented government spending on public works projects that employed large numbers of workers to improve the nation's infrastructure. It also created a federally mandated eight-hour workday, collective bargaining rights for workers, a minimum wage, protection against unfair labor practices, federal subsidies for farmers, and federal income support for poor single mothers. With government acquiescence, union membership doubled between 1925 and 1941, reaching its peak in the 1960s.

Government social services also expanded, most importantly with the creation of the Social Security system. This began as a program to provide pensions to retired workers but was soon expanded to include pensions for their survivors and assistance for the disabled. Social Security has done more to reduce poverty in the United States than has any other government program before or since.

The New Deal era was one of unprecedented growth in government involvement in the economy, in employment creation, and in worker protection, as the

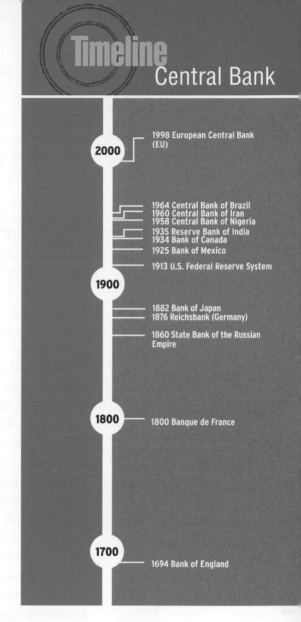

Timeline

Central Bank

2000 — 1998 European Central Bank (EU)

1964 Central Bank of Brazil
1960 Central Bank of Iran
1958 Central Bank of Nigeria
1935 Reserve Bank of India
1934 Bank of Canada
1925 Bank of Mexico
1913 U.S. Federal Reserve System

1900

1882 Bank of Japan
1876 Reichsbank (Germany)

1860 State Bank of the Russian Empire

1800 — 1800 Banque de France

1700 — 1694 Bank of England

government moved to take on more beneficial and politically generated functions. It was a period of more or less Keynesian economic policy in which the government actively worked to improve economic growth and expand employment. In the 1960s, Lyndon Johnson's administration initiated the "Great Society" to complete the goals of the New Deal. The pillars of this effort were the creation of Medicare, medical insurance for Social Security recipients; Aid to Families with Dependent Children (AFDC), a much-expanded welfare program for poor mothers; and Medicaid, health care for AFDC and other welfare recipients. These programs, along with the earlier Social Security system, helped reduce poverty from 25 percent of the population in 1955 to 11 percent by 1973. However, slower economic growth and waning political support subsequently led the government to reduce the real value of these antipoverty programs, contributing to a rise in the poverty rate to around 14 percent by the 1990s.

Sustained economic growth and Keynesian policies continued through the mid-1960s. By the late 1960s, continued deficit spending caused by the cost of the Vietnam War and the Great Society programs helped produce rising inflation. The quadrupling of world oil prices in 1973 further slowed economic growth and spurred more inflation, producing "stagflation" by the late 1970s that the government seemed incapable of reversing. Ronald Reagan won the presidency in 1980 on a platform that emphasized the need to reduce the size and scope of government by embracing monetarism's prescriptions for reduced government spending, accepting a "natural rate of unemployment," and freeing the market to restart growth. President Jimmy Carter had begun some deregulation of industry in the late 1970s, but Reagan expanded this effort substantially and reduced the power and reach of unions, whose membership had been declining throughout the 1970s. This trend has continued, with union membership now reduced to about what it was a century ago. Reagan also cut spending on social programs and cut taxes to spur economic growth. At the same time, the Federal Reserve embraced monetarist policies, raising interest rates and reining in the money supply to reduce inflation. This combination produced a severe recession between 1981 and 1983, but then sustained economic growth reemerged for the rest of the decade. Reagan reversed the Keynesian effort of the New Deal–Great Society period, marking the most dramatic shift in economic policy since the 1930s.

Reagan embraced monetarism, but his tax cuts and high military spending resulted in record budget deficits. President Bill Clinton and Congress finally eliminated these deficits in the 1990s. Though Clinton was a Democrat, like Johnson and Roosevelt, his economic policies continued the trend begun under Reagan, a Republican. Monetarism continued to be the accepted economic theory, and during the 1980s and 1990s the U.S. government methodically removed most of the restrictive New Deal–era regulations on banking. Economists and businesses alike expected these changes to increase efficiency and profitability throughout the banking and financial sectors without creating any undue risk, arguing that modern banking was fundamentally different than it had been during the Great Depression. President George W. Bush continued these monetarist policies after taking office in 2001, although following September 11, 2001, he increased military spending and cut taxes, which returned the nation to the budget deficits characteristic of the 1970s and 1980s.

Monetarist policies helped produce substantial economic expansion from 1983 to 2000, though growth slowed in the new millennium. They also produced greater inequality and poverty. The GINI Index, an overall measure of inequality, was at about 37 in the United States in the late 1940s. It dropped (meaning greater equality) to 35 by the late 1960s, but by 1994 it had risen to 42, where it has remained since. The Great Recession seems to have expanded inequality further. The richest 1 percent of all Americans "captured about 95 percent of the income gains since the recession ended," giving them about 20 percent of total income—one of the highest levels ever recorded (Lowrey 2013). As the Country and Concept table (page 198) shows, this is a much higher level of inequality than in other wealthy countries. In the late 1960s, the wealthiest fifth of the U.S. population had 40.6 percent of all income; by 2001, that figure had risen to 49.6 percent. The poorest fifth's share of income, on the other hand, dropped from 5.6 percent to 3.5 percent. From 1980 to 2011, the wealthiest 1 percent of the population saw its incomes increase an average of 115 percent, while the fiftieth percentile (the middle of the income distribution) saw its incomes increase by only an average of 11 percent. Inequality has affected social and economic mobility in the United States as well. A recent study comparing income differences between adults in the early 2000s and their parents in the 1960s found that one-third were upwardly mobile, one-third were downwardly mobile, and one-third remained roughly where their parents had been, and that the economic position into which people were born heavily influenced their future income (Isaacs 2007). Many European countries now have higher rates of social mobility than does the United States.

The Bush administration's first response to the Great Recession in 2008 was a tax rebate to every taxpaying household to stimulate the economy, essentially a Keynesian policy: using deficit spending to stimulate a sluggish economy. When the Wall Street firm Lehman Brothers went bankrupt in September 2008, however, the full-scale financial crisis began, showing that Bush's initial response was far from adequate. Banks virtually ceased all lending for several months, afraid that any loans they made would not be repaid. At the same time, the country became aware of the magnitude of the slump in housing prices, leading to foreclosures of high-risk mortgages, which in turn caused a rapid drop in the values of investments based on those mortgages. Without access to credit, businesses could not invest and began firing workers. The nation's GDP plunged 8.4 percent in the second half of the year, and unemployment rose from 4.9 to 10 percent by the end of 2009.

Video link:
Five years after Lehman Brothers' collapse

Once it was understood that the crisis was primarily in the housing and financial sectors, the Bush administration and Congress created the Troubled Asset Relief Program (TARP), under which the government agreed to purchase or guarantee bank-owned investments tied to the plummeting housing market in exchange for a substantial share of the banks' stock. The government, in effect, became a substantial owner of a number of American banks. The new Obama administration in 2009 implemented more "bailouts," as they came to be known, this time for the troubled auto industry. While the credit market remained very weak until the middle of the year, ultimately credit began to flow again, and the economy began to recover by the end of 2009. In spite of fears that the taxpayers would never get their money back, most major banks and auto companies repaid the government, repurchasing government-owned stock by mid-2010. The Obama administration also pushed through Congress an unprecedented stimulus plan of $787 billion in early 2009 in a clear attempt to use Keynesian policy to "jump-start" the economy.

In late 2010, continued high unemployment led both Congress and the Federal Reserve to take further stimulus measures. First, the Federal Reserve announced a policy of "quantitative easing," essentially printing new money and using it to buy $600 billion of U.S. Treasury bonds, thus effectively pumping that amount of money into the economy via the banking system. At the end of the year, the Obama administration and Congress compromised on a tax bill that preserved for all taxpayers the so-called "Bush tax cuts," which had been passed a decade earlier, reduced Social Security taxes for 2011, and extended unemployment benefits. The president and Congress paid for all of this by expanding the deficit.

The economic recovery, which saw the stock market rise dramatically from its low point in March 2009, did not provide much relief for the average person. Unemployment dropped but was still at 7.5 percent by mid-2013. The housing program did stabilize housing prices and slow the rate of foreclosures, though foreclosures continued at an unusually high rate. The stimulus package initially prevented deep cuts in state governments' budgets, but as the money ran out by 2011, states faced the prospect of massive budget cuts and had to lay off workers. By 2012, several American cities were literally declaring bankruptcy, unable to pay their bills. The bailout of the banks, widespread publicity about bank managers' high bonuses in spite of the recession, and the continuing high unemployment rates left many Americans angry that the government seemed to have saved Wall Street but had ignored "Main Street."

While the administration, Congress, and the Federal Reserve all seemed to agree (at least quietly) that further stimulus was needed in the short term, voters were deeply skeptical of its potential impact on their lives. The newly elected Republicans in the House of Representatives set out to reduce budget deficits substantially in 2011, locking horns with Democrats who still controlled the Senate and with President Obama; implicitly, this was a classic battle over which economic theory to pursue. This debate over fiscal policy came to a head in December 2012, when Congress finally passed a compromise on New Year's Eve that raised taxes on the wealthiest 1 percent to avoid automatic spending cuts that had been put in place two years earlier. This postponed those cuts only until March 2013, however, at which point, with no further compromise, they went into effect, cutting federal spending across the board. Moody Analytics and several other private-sector economic analysts argued that the spending cuts would reduce economic growth by 1.2 percent and keep unemployment about 0.5 percent higher than it would have been without the cuts (Calmes and Weisman 2013).

With the worst of the recession over (at least in the financial and housing sectors), the U.S. government turned its attention to measures designed to prevent future crises. After the Great Depression, the government had regulated banks rather strictly, treating commercial banks that people use on a daily basis differently than investment banks on Wall Street. In the 1990s, however, President Clinton and a Republican-dominated Congress, influenced by monetarist arguments, lifted many of those restrictions, allowing most banks to engage in many different activities. Simultaneously, investment bankers created new kinds of investments that the government regulated only lightly or not at all, including derivatives like the credit default swaps that would be part of the 2008–2009 financial crisis.

In the aftermath of the Great Recession, few economists or policy makers repudiated monetarist policies entirely, but many argued that the crisis had demonstrated the need for more regulation of the financial sector. Some wanted to prevent banks from getting "too big to fail," others wanted to re-create the earlier separation of commercial and investment banks, and still others simply argued that the investment products themselves needed closer government regulation. As is the case when monopolies arise, the state's interest in preserving a healthy and growing capitalist economy may require it to enact policies against the immediate interests of particular capitalists—in this case, major investment banks whose unchecked search for profits seemed to threaten the stability of the system as a whole. In July 2010, Congress passed and President Obama signed the largest financial regulatory bill since World War II. While it did not fully return banks to the pre-1980s regulations or limit their size, it instituted regulation of the derivatives markets; established a council to monitor the largest banks (those considered "too big to fail"); instituted regulations to ensure that if such banks do fail, their stockholders—rather than taxpayers—will pay the costs; and restricted banks from making speculative investments with their own money. Two years later, however, most of the laws' regulations had yet to be implemented; over 60 percent of regulation deadlines had been missed. This was in part due to the financial industry's active opposition to many regulations, including suing in federal court to prevent some of them from being enacted (Edwards 2013). It remained unclear how much financial regulation the government would achieve in the context of the American political system and *laissez-faire* economic history.

CASE Summary   The U.S. model of free-market growth is an exception, not the norm. Most other governments choose to intervene more substantially in market processes. For a long time, the United States preferred to limit government as much as possible to "essential" functions. It took a half-century of union effort to move the U.S. government to adopt some politically generated functions, including regulating working conditions and protecting workers against the economic effects of advancing age and disability. The mid-twentieth century saw a period of expanded government involvement in more politically generated roles, starting with the New Deal, but some of those policies have been reversed since the 1980s. Other New Deal–Great Society policies, notably Social Security and Medicare, have proven more popular and durable, despite monetarist demands for reduced government spending. The United States seems to have permanently embraced a somewhat expanded government role in the market, though the government remains far less invasive than the governments of almost all European countries. America's championing of unfettered markets, free trade, and globalization made it a symbol of a new era, but the Great Recession badly damaged that image. In the aftermath of that crisis, the Keynesian-monetarist debate was joined anew, deeply dividing the two major parties. U.S. policy became more Keynesian than European policy after the recession and U.S. recovery was better, but that did little to resolve the debate.

CASE Questions

1. The United States has shifted economic policy between monetarism and Keynesianism several times. Overall, which seems to be the most effective policy option, and why?
2. While the United States has long championed the "free-market model," the government has in fact intervened in the market in various ways. What are the main impetuses behind those interventions? Are they primarily essential, beneficial, or politically generated interventions?

CASE Study

social market economy
In Germany, a postwar economic system that combines a highly productive market economy with an extensive and generous welfare state, as well as unusually active involvement of both business and labor in economic policy

GERMANY: THE SOCIAL MARKET ECONOMY

Over the course of the twentieth century, Germany created a much-admired model of regulated capitalism known as the **social market economy**. This model combined a highly productive market economy that became the world's leading industrial exporter with an extensive and generous welfare state, as well as unusually active involvement of both business and labor associations in

German chancellor Angela Merkel casts her vote in parliament for the bailout of Cyprus, a fellow EU member. Germany emerged from the Great Recession as the strongest economy in Europe, and Merkel used that strength to impose tough austerity measures on European economies facing debt and financial crises.

setting and implementing economic policy. Productivity, wages, and job security were relatively high, and inequality was relatively low. Germany also led the way in creating the EU and then the euro. Globalization raised significant questions about the viability of the social market economy, as Germany faced continuing high unemployment in the 1990s and early years of the new millennium, much slower economic growth, difficulty financing its generous social welfare benefits, and trouble maintaining the strict limits on deficit spending that the euro requires. The country pursued several reforms in the new millennium that allowed it to remain one of the world's leading exporters, but arguably undermined parts of the social market economy model. While it was hit heavily by the recession of 2008–2009, it recovered more quickly than many other countries. Some analysts were once again talking about a "German miracle" because, despite a large drop in GDP, unemployment went up only slightly during the recession. This has left it the strongest economy in Europe, and playing a central role in trying to resolve the financial crisis affecting the weaker economies within the "euro zone." Critics, however, contend it still faces underlying problems that so far it is not resolving.

The modern German economy first developed under Otto von Bismarck in the 1860s and 1870s. Bismarck set out to build German national strength via economic growth, so he pursued policies that protected industry and produced rapid industrialization and urbanization to catch up with early industrializers like Britain and France. This came at the expense of workers, who faced horrific working conditions, social dislocation in the expanding cities, and low wages. These conditions helped produce the Social Democratic Party (SDP) in 1875 to work for socialism via nonviolent means. Bismarck, worried about the socialist threat, committed the state to some beneficial and politically generated market roles. He created extensive (for its time) social policy for workers while simultaneously outlawing socialist parties and labor unions. The new policies included the world's first national health insurance system, accident insurance, and old-age and widows' pensions subsidized by the federal government, all developed a half-century before similar policies in the United States. Working conditions, on the other hand, did not change. Basically, the program was a conscious effort

- **ECONOMIC MODEL**
  Social market economy

- **ECONOMIC POLICY**
  Monetarist

- **GLOBALIZATION EFFECTS**
  Neoliberal reforms

- **ECONOMIC MILESTONES**
  Reunification; growing unemployment; costs of social spending

- **GREAT RECESSION**
  Slowing growth; European leader

to continue industrialization via cheap labor while protecting workers from the worst situations they might face.

After Germany's loss in World War I and the establishment of the Weimar Republic, social welfare policies expanded further. The government broadened the insurance and pension systems in response to hyperinflation following the war. The influence of labor unions increased rapidly as their numbers increased, and by the mid-1920s, employers had agreed to establish an eight-hour workday and a forty-eight-hour workweek. Social expenditures leapt from 19 percent of government spending in 1919 to 40 percent by 1930, and wages rose as employers and unions agreed to mandatory collective bargaining (Crew 1998). In response to rapid inflation, many companies began paying what was termed a "social wage," a wage that was adjusted to account for the costs of supporting a family.

Adolf Hitler interrupted this process, but after his defeat, the new government of West Germany took up pretty much where things had left off and extended the social welfare system again. The Christian Democratic Union (CDU) under Konrad Adenauer governed West Germany from its first election in 1949 until 1966. Though a "conservative" party, the CDU officially coined the term *social market economy* and fully developed the model. Christian Democrats generally saw protection of workers as part of their Christian ideology. Granted, the SDP often wanted social spending to expand even more rapidly, but both major parties agreed with the basic premises of the system. The social market economy created a form of capitalism in which close relationships and interpenetration between the private and public sectors have shaped economic and social policies. The national government passes broad regulatory standards for various sectors of the economy, industries, and professions, but it allows state governments (*Länder*) to work with businesses to formulate detailed implementation plans. The *Länder* work closely with industrial organizations to implement local policies, and industries accept those policies rather willingly because they've had a role in their formulation.

Unions also have a role to play negotiating binding wage agreements with employers' associations, which all employers in a given sector must follow. Unions are also represented on the supervisory boards of all German firms with more than two thousand employees. This system, known as **codetermination,** was created in 1976 and gives unions power to influence employers' policies. One effect was that the unions came to understand what they must do to help achieve the high levels of productivity and product quality for which German firms have become famous. Codetermination creates an element of democracy within the management of business enterprises, though ultimately businesses are still privately owned and must answer to their stockholders and lenders, as in any other capitalist economy. The system has been modified and is now less extensive than it was initially, largely due to government responses to globalization, which we'll return to in chapter 10.

This economic model made Germany one of the most successful economies in the world from the end of World War II until the 1980s. No economy is perfect, but Germany enjoyed relatively rapid growth and became one of the world's wealthiest economies, with very low unemployment and inflation and exceptionally generous social welfare benefits. It also became one of the world's leading exporters of

codetermination
A system in Germany that requires unions to be represented on the supervisory boards of all German firms of more than two thousand employees

high-quality manufactured goods. All of this began to change, however, with the end of the Cold War and the acceleration of globalization, as can be seen in Figure 5.1 (page 224). Reunification required the economic absorption of the much poorer East Germany into the social market economy. Privatization of formerly government-owned industries in East Germany created massive unemployment. West Germans had to fund huge social programs, infrastructure construction, and job training programs as they worked to integrate the eastern economy into the western. The biggest single problem resulting from this process was unemployment, which had hovered around 1 percent for decades in West Germany but hit nearly 12 percent in reunified Germany by 1998 and stayed as high as 9 percent through 2005. After that, it began to drop significantly, as the country absorbed more East German workers and collective bargaining with unions changed to give firms more flexibility to reduce wages. In the former East Germany, the unemployment rate was still about 13 percent in 2009.

In addition to pioneering the social market economy, Germany has been a key leader in the European Union. The German central bank, the Bundesbank, had restricted German monetary policy to keep inflation low, and the new European bank is charged with doing the same. Germany's social policies long called for generous benefits to the growing numbers of unemployed, but membership in the EU requires it to maintain strict limits on government spending, a contradiction that led the country to be out of compliance with EU fiscal rules for a couple of years in the early 2000s.

The expenses of reunification and the institution of the euro as a common currency have produced the most significant political discord and electoral shifts in Germany since the end of the Nazi era. Germany voted out the CDU in 1998. That party, led by Helmut Kohl, had championed German reunification whatever the cost. The new SDP government under Gerhard Schröder introduced Agenda 2010, legislation that significantly lowered the protections and benefits the social market economy had provided. Agenda 2010 included reductions to health and unemployment benefits to reduce the government deficit and prod more people to work and greater flexibility in the labor market to allow employers to fire workers. But it also included a policy that encouraged employers to reduce workers' hours rather than firing them, with the government making up the difference. German voters once again expressed their displeasure with the reforms in 2005, narrowly but definitively voting Schröder and the SDP out and returning the CDU to power under Germany's first woman chancellor, Angela Merkel. The German economy shrank by 5 percent in 2009; this contraction was one of the hardest hits taken in Europe from the Great Recession. The global downturn affected the German financial sector because German banks were heavily invested in some of the risky securities that had caused the financial crisis. Exports, long the mainstay of German manufacturing, also dropped nearly 20 percent. Germany, however, bounced back rapidly, growing by 3.7 percent in 2010 and 3 percent in 2011.

Despite a long history of fiscal austerity, the German government initially turned to Keynesian stimulus to respond to the recession. After the stimulus, though, the government also passed a constitutional amendment requiring a balanced budget.

The stimulus plan and recession caused the government's budget deficit to soar to 4.5 percent of GDP by 2010, but by 2013 the balanced budget amendment and renewed growth had reduced it to around 1 percent, an exceptionally low number. Keynesian critics contend, however, that in the long run the requirement of a balanced budget will make needed public investment in energy, child care for the increasingly female workforce, and education impossible or very painful (Tooze 2012).

Web link:
Germany's perverse devotion to austerity

Remarkably, the recession only raised unemployment by about 1 percentage point, a far less dramatic drop than most countries saw. Indeed, since 2010, unemployment has been below 7 percent, its lowest level since 1992. The Agenda 2010 reforms that encouraged companies to reduce hours rather than fire workers are estimated to have saved as many as 500,000 jobs (Rattner 2011). Ultimately, though, the crisis began to hit Germany. Its European neighbors are its largest trading partners and as their economies declined, Germany inevitably felt the reverberations. While growth had returned in 2010, by late 2012 it had dropped to just above zero, where it stayed in early 2013.

CASE Summary

Germany's economic model is quite distinct from the free-market system of the United States; the difference can be traced all the way back to Germany's initial industrialization. Germany's industrialization was more similar to what came to be called developmentalism or import substitution industrialization than the U.S. model. While certainly capitalist, the social market economy includes much more extensive state intervention. In its heyday, government, business, and labor organizations worked closely together to guide the economy on a path of growth and near full employment while providing social services far more generous than those available in the United States. Globalization, the EU, and reunification called the model into question by the turn of the twenty-first century. The Agenda 2010 reforms have helped Germany start to adapt, with unemployment dropping substantially, but at the cost of significant alteration to the original economic model that made Germany famous. While reforms have helped Germany navigate the euro crisis more successfully than most of its neighbors, it's not clear that that success can be sustained, or that the current government policies have fully addressed the longer-term underlying problems, a subject we return to in chapter 10.

CASE Questions

1. Why was the social market economy such a success story from the 1960s to the 1980s? What changed to make it seem less successful, and what does that teach us about the prospects for more extensive government intervention in the economy in the future?

2. Compare the U.S. and German case studies. Why do you think the German government chose to intervene in the market so much more extensively than the U.S. government did?

CASE Study

JAPAN: THE DEVELOPMENTAL STATE AND ITS CRISIS

Japan was the first non-Western society to industrialize successfully and create a fully modern and wealthy economy. This process began under Japan's first modern state, the Meiji regime, which led the country from 1868 until World War II. But the country became fully developed only after World War II, when a distinct model of market-state relations emerged: the developmental state. Though it was interventionist like the German model, the Japanese model arose not from the demands of organized labor and fear of a socialist democratic party, but instead from the concerted effort of the government to achieve rapid economic growth and industrialization. The primary purpose of intervention under the Japanese model has been to guide key sectors of the economy to achieve maximum growth, and the developmental state made Japan the second-largest economy in the world by the 1980s. As Table 5.2 (page 241) shows, however, Japan has experienced persistent economic stagnation since 1990 and has instituted only limited reforms in the face of the vicissitudes of globalization. This has brought the developmental state model into question, both in Japan and around the world.

The Meiji Restoration of 1867 brought to power a new state determined to modernize the country. The government actively intervened in economic activity, directly

- **ECONOMIC MODEL**
  The developmental state

- **ECONOMIC POLICY**
  Keynesian; more monetarist since 1990 crisis

- **GLOBALIZATION EFFECTS**
  Decline of developmental state's ability to influence economy

- **ECONOMIC MILESTONES**
  1990 collapse and decade of stagnation and deflation

- **GREAT RECESSION**
  Renewed recession after brief growth; political upheaval and promises of bold reform

Recent Japanese college graduates at a ceremony welcoming them to their new jobs with Sumitomo Mitsui Banking Corporation, the bank at the heart of the Mitsui *kereitsu*. Mitsui was a long-standing *ziabatsu* prior to World War II that the U.S. occupation dismantled. It recreated itself as a *kereitsu* and was a major force in the rise of Japan to become the third-largest economy in the world.

investing not only in infrastructure but also in key industries. Once the government started an industry, it often sold it to private investors at bargain prices and actively encouraged industrial mergers to create larger and more internationally competitive firms. This produced a very concentrated business class, at the heart of which were the *zaibatsu*, three family-dominated industrial conglomerates that controlled key areas of the economy and had close relations with the government. In contrast to standard practice in capitalist economies, especially the United States, the government helped create business cartels in order to control specific sectors of the economy, and it helped create trade associations in order to coordinate development efforts among firms in the same industry.

After World War II, the United States dethroned not only the emperor but also the *zaibatsu*. While the Meiji government saw the conglomerates as part of a deliberate industrialization strategy, the United States objected to them on political and economic grounds. Politically, they were part of the fascist Japanese past and therefore needed to be replaced by a more "democratic" business class. Economically, they were antithetical to healthy competition in a market economy. The United States therefore wrote antimonopoly legislation into Japanese law that disbanded the *zaibatsu*. But a shortage of capital for investment forced the United States to allow Japanese banks to own stock in industrial companies and to allow the companies to own stock in one another. The capital shortage also led Japan's ministry of finance to allow twelve key banks to "overlend" money to companies, meaning that the banks were allowed to lend more money than they had, with government protection.

By the 1960s, the fully developed result of all this was the *keiretsu*: complex networks of firms that are owned separately but work together closely. Some are direct descendants of the *zaibatsu*. At the center of most *keiretsu* is a major bank, which lends money on favorable terms to its *keiretsu* members and typically sends representatives to work in the firms to which it has lent money to ensure that its loans are being used wisely. Firms in a *keiretsu* own stock in one another's companies and therefore give one another orders for products. "Vertical" *keiretsu* like Toyota and Nissan involve a major manufacturer tied to hundreds of favored suppliers. While ownership of capital is not as concentrated as it was under the Meiji regime, the system nonetheless encourages long-term relationships among firms and limits the ability of firms outside the *keiretsu*, including foreign firms, to do business.

developmental state
A state that seeks to create national strength by taking an active and conscious role in the development of specific sectors of the economy

What Chalmers Johnson (1982) termed the **developmental state** emerged along with the rise of the *keiretsu*. A developmental state does not seek just to establish the rules of the game for capitalism and encourage overall economic growth. It also consciously seeks to create national strength in particular economic areas, taking an active and conscious role in the development of specific sectors of the economy. The Japanese government did this via two key bureaucratic agencies, the Ministry of Finance (MOF) and the Ministry of International Trade and Industry (MITI). Until liberalization in the 1970s, the MOF had extensive influence over the banking sector via its control over interest rates and over the role of banks in the *keiretsu*. By guaranteeing the key banks loans, the MOF had substantial influence of where and how they lent.

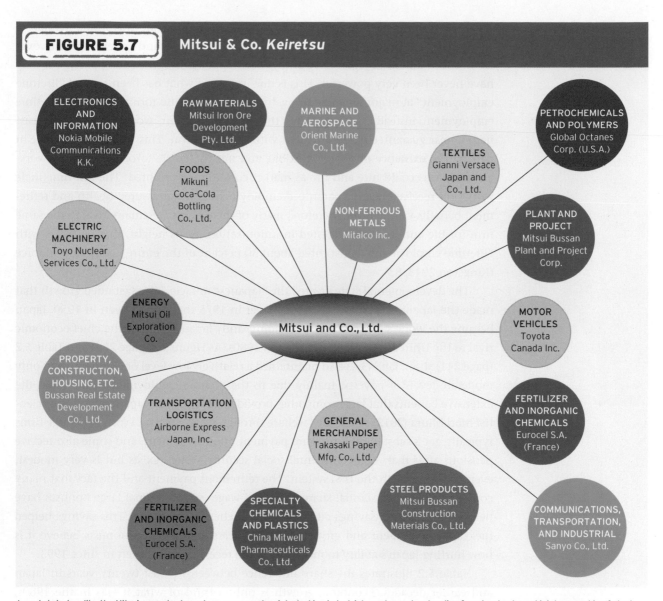

FIGURE 5.7   Mitsui & Co. *Keiretsu*

Mitsui and Co., Ltd.

ELECTRONICS AND INFORMATION
Nokia Mobile Communications K.K.

RAW MATERIALS
Mitsui Iron Ore Development Pty. Ltd.

MARINE AND AEROSPACE
Orient Marine Co., Ltd.

PETROCHEMICALS AND POLYMERS
Global Octanes Corp. (U.S.A.)

TEXTILES
Gianni Versace Japan and Co., Ltd.

FOODS
Mikuni Coca-Cola Bottling Co., Ltd.

NON-FERROUS METALS
Mitalco Inc.

PLANT AND PROJECT
Mitsui Bussan Plant and Project Corp.

ELECTRIC MACHINERY
Toyo Nuclear Services Co., Ltd.

ENERGY
Mitsui Oil Exploration Co.

MOTOR VEHICLES
Toyota Canada Inc.

PROPERTY, CONSTRUCTION, HOUSING, ETC.
Bussan Real Estate Development Co., Ltd.

TRANSPORTATION LOGISTICS
Airborne Express Japan, Inc.

GENERAL MERCHANDISE
Takasaki Paper Mfg. Co., Ltd.

FERTILIZER AND INORGANIC CHEMICALS
Eurocel S.A. (France)

FERTILIZER AND INORGANIC CHEMICALS
Eurocel S.A. (France)

SPECIALTY CHEMICALS AND PLASTICS
China Mitwell Pharmaceuticals Co., Ltd.

STEEL PRODUCTS
Mitsui Bussan Construction Materials Co., Ltd.

COMMUNICATIONS, TRANSPORTATION, AND INDUSTRIAL
Sanyo Co., Ltd.

Japan's *keiretsu*, like the Mitsui example shown here, are complex, interlocking industrial conglomerates. Lending from key banks and joint ownership of stock allow those in charge of the *keiretsu* to control most of the members of the group and keep outsiders from entering. They are not technically monopolies, but their highly integrated structures make it difficult for firms outside the *keiretsu* to compete.

Source: FundingUniverse.com, "Mitsui & Co., Ltd. History" (http://www.fundinguniverse.com/company-histories/mitsui-co-ltd-history).

MITI influenced industrial policies more specifically through extensive licensing of technology and "administrative guidance," the bureaucracy's practice of informally and successfully suggesting that an industry or firm pursue a particular endeavor. MITI was able to use this informal system to guide industrial growth because of the licensing, financial, and other powers it held over business and because of the close relationship that developed among key industries, bureaucracies, and the ruling party. Leaders in all three of these sectors would move from one to the other over the course of their careers; for instance, former bureaucrats frequently became members of parliament.

T. J. Pempel (2000) argued that Japan's development state was fundamentally a "conservative regime" in the sense that it favored business and governing elites over labor. Labor unions in Japan have always been opponents of the ruling party, but they have never been very powerful. This is due in part to what has been termed "lifetime employment" at major Japanese firms. In reality, there is no formal system of lifetime employment; instead, each member of the core, "permanent" workforce has (or at least had) a near guarantee of employment with the same firm. This was made possible in part by the existence of a large, flexible, and mostly female force of part-time workers that firms could hire and fire as market conditions warranted. The full-time male workforce received nearly guaranteed employment and was assured health and retirement benefits via the firm. Therefore, many of them chose to remain loyal to the same firm for life and were uninterested in unionization. At its height, these workers with "lifetime employment" constituted about 30 percent of the entire Japanese workforce (Kingston 2013, 83).

The developmental state created the "Japanese miracle," the sustained growth that made the Japanese economy six times larger in 1975 than it had been in 1950. Japan became the world's second-largest economy, and "Japan Inc." was the chief economic rival to the United States in the 1970s and 1980s. As Figure 5.2 (page 224) and Table 5.2 (page 241) show, Japan has also maintained a relatively low level of inequality and only moderate levels of poverty, mainly due to the lifetime employment system and the extensive benefits that large companies provide workers, what Japanese political scientist Mari Miura (2012) called the "welfare through work" system. Workers at large firms typically get a substantial lump-sum payment upon retirement, and some also receive pensions after that. A governmental social security system exists but is very modest, even compared with the U.S. system. The retirement payment and the fact that many companies pay a substantial share of annual wages via occasional large bonuses have helped make Japan's savings rate one of the highest in the world. This savings helped fuel rapid investment and growth in earlier years, but some economists believe it is now hurting Japan's ability to move out of the recession it has been in since 1993.

Table 5.2 illustrates the sharp difference between the last twenty years in Japan and earlier decades. Economic growth is only a third of what it was in the 1980s, unemployment has increased substantially, and prices are actually falling, a sign of serious economic stagnation or recession. The economic miracle ended in 1990; on the first business day of that year, real estate and stock prices, which had been climbing rapidly, plummeted and the bubble burst. There had been warning signs: productivity growth had been slowing since the 1970s, as had the government's ability to influence the direction of economic activity. Acquiescing to international pressure, the government had slowly begun to reduce its power to control flows of money and financing in the late 1970s. In the 1980s, the system of guaranteeing bank loans led Japanese corporations to take on excessive debt, which they invested in real estate and other unproductive areas. Because of deregulation, the MOF could do little to stop them. Simultaneously, the more successful Japanese companies such as Toyota and Nissan fully entered the age of globalization, investing elsewhere in the world so that

TABLE 5.2	Profile of Japan's Economy, 1970-2011				
State	**1970**	**1980**	**1990**	**2000**	**2011**
GDP growth (annual %)	10.7	2.8	5.2	2.9	−0.7
Social expenditures (total, as % of GDP)	..	10.3	11.2	16.1	22.4
Gross national savings (as % of nominal GDP)	..	..	33.2	27.5	22
Share of income or consumption, ratio of richest 20% to poorest 20%	..	..	4.3	3.4	3.4

Source: Data are from World Bank Indicators, OECD, UNDP Human Development Reports.

instead of exporting cars from Japan, they began building them in the United States and Europe. This reduced Japan's key source of growth: exports. All of this reduced the extent to which *keiretsu* members continued to coordinate their activity, as the corporate structure of the Japanese economy in the 1990s and 2000s moved perceptibly toward a more "American" model of vertically integrated, globally active corporations (Lincoln and Shimotani 2009).

When the bubble burst, the government had difficulty responding. It tried both Keynesian and monetarist policies, engaging in deficit spending and lowering official interest rates all the way to zero, but nothing seemed to revive economic growth. A key problem was massive bad bank debt from all the poorly invested loans. Government spending went to paying off the bad loans and bailing out the banks that had made them. Corporations cut their permanent workforces and shifted to more part-time workers, reducing worker benefits and real wages.

In April 2001, Junichiro Koizumi was swept into power as prime minister on promises to reform the system, but he faced entrenched business and bureaucratic interests that opposed his efforts. He intended to dismantle much of the developmental state by reducing regulation and government control over the economy but was only partially successful. Koizumi lowered deficit spending to reduce the size of the government, but, as Keynesian economics would predict, this hurt growth by reducing the demand for goods. After a long battle, he succeeded in privatizing the postal service savings system, which eliminated the bureaucracy's control over the giant savings system that it used to subsidize favored industries—a key mechanism of the developmental state.

Global economic growth and Koizumi's partial reforms helped restore positive but slow economic growth from 2003 to 2007, and also helped rein in the deflation (declining prices) that had plagued Japan for a decade. The reforms of the labor system—significantly weakening "lifetime employment"—also meant that up to a third of the labor force was now in temporary positions, many of which would be lost in the global recession in 2008–2009. The more flexible labor market increased both inequality and poverty, even before the global recession (Miura 2011). The recession destroyed the modest gains in economic growth that Koizumi's reforms had achieved. Japan was hit exceptionally hard by the recession because of its dependence on exports, particularly to the United States. In 2009 the Japanese economy shrank by more than 5 percent, and deflation worsened significantly. The government responded with a Keynesian economic stimulus that increased its already high fiscal deficit and once again reduced interest rates to zero. Modest economic growth returned in late 2009 and in 2010 hit 4 percent. The massive earthquake and tsunami in March 2011, however, cut growth to 0.4 percent for 2011. The earthquake, the fourth biggest in recorded history, killed twenty thousand people, displaced hundreds of thousands more, and resulted in an expensive cleanup of a damaged nuclear reactor; the total costs were estimated at $330 billion.

The economic crisis produced a seismic political change, as the long-ruling Liberal Democratic Party (LDP) was swept from power in November 2009. The new government came to office promising to reduce corruption and the bureaucracy's tight control over economic policy (see chapter 7), though its initial reform efforts were once again met by fierce opposition from entrenched interests. Internal divisions in the new ruling party and the crisis of the tsunami led the Japanese to see the new government as weak and ineffective. They returned the LDP to power in a landslide in December 2012. The new prime minister, Shinzo Abe, campaigned on a platform of classic Keynesian stimulus to restart economic growth. Shortly after taking office he initiated a large stimulus plan focused on building infrastructure that was equal to 2.6 percent of the country's GDP, bigger in relative terms than President Obama's stimulus plan in 2009. He also replaced the head of the central bank, demanding it allow higher inflation in order to spur economic growth, and agreed to join negotiations for a U.S.-initiated free trade agreement that would require Japan to open its economy to greater trade. The new leadership decided to try Keynesian expansionist policies in spite of the fact that Japan had the highest total debt of any major industrialized economy, a debt more than double the entire economy and higher than even Greece's. The initial result was expansionary fiscal and monetary policy in early 2013 that caused the Tokyo stock market to climb substantially and the value of the yen to drop by 20 percent, encouraging greater Japanese exports. Many analysts saw this new policy as the best hope Japan had seen in years for finally turning its economy around.

Video link:
Japan's debt
problem visualized

CASE Summary   Postwar Japan created a new model of political economy, called the developmental state, which proved spectacularly successful at transforming the country into a global power and one of the wealthiest countries in the world. Even more than in Germany, the state guided economic growth, encouraging what a more *laissez-faire* model would see as excessive collaboration among large conglomerates and between them and the government. The mechanisms through which the state achieved this, however, proved to have negative effects when faced with the pressure of globalization in the form of more open financial systems, global investment by Japanese companies, and speculative investment in real estate and stock markets. The Great Recession ended the first economic growth in over a decade, and the government changed hands twice. The new government bet on Keynesian over monetarist policies in 2013, in sharp contrast to policy in Europe in particular.

CASE Questions

1. Like Germany, Japan had a very successful economic model that fell on hard times in the 1990s. What changed to make the model less successful? How does this compare with the decline of Germany's social market economy model? Can we explain both using the same arguments, or are there factors unique to each that explain the decline?
2. What lessons does Japan's long struggle with stagnation have for other countries facing economic problems in the last few years, since the Great Recession?

CASE Study

MEXICO: FROM PROTECTIONISM TO NEOLIBERALISM

The Mexican economy has gone through several monumental transitions in its modern history—from the late nineteenth century, pro-business policies of the Porfirio Díaz regime to the postrevolution protectionism of the long-ruling PRI, which dominated the country for most of the twentieth century. A move toward neoliberalism began in the early 1980s, following a massive debt crisis and subsequent IMF-imposed structural adjustment programs. This neoliberal shift is underscored by the fact that Mexico today maintains the highest number of free-market trade agreements of any country in the world, a development that has clearly improved macroeconomic growth but has also led to increased income and regional inequality.

The prerevolutionary era of Porfirio Díaz gave Mexico a glimpse of large-scale economic growth, which remained at about 8 percent between 1884 and 1900. The Díaz regime embraced modernizing authoritarianism, which created vast wealth for the upper crust but left many behind. Existing social class distinctions only became more

- **ECONOMIC MODEL** ISI initially; shift to neoliberalism in 1980s–1990s
- **ECONOMIC POLICY** Keynesian to neoliberal
- **GLOBALIZATION EFFECTS** NAFTA and dependence on the United States
- **ECONOMIC MILESTONES** Debt crises of 1982 and 1994
- **GREAT RECESSION** Mirrors U.S. economy

pronounced with the influx of foreign direct investment. The rich simply got richer, while the poor remained poor.

Díaz fell from power in 1911 as a result of the Mexican Revolution. Emerging from the ashes of the revolution was a PRI-led regime that followed a model of corporatism and supported the broad, working-class and peasant constituency that had inspired Díaz's overthrow. Powerful political figures such as presidents Lázaro Cárdenas (1934–1940) and Luís Echeverría (1970–1976) became associated with a staunch, anti-elite populism. Under these leaders, oil nationalization, land redistribution, and ISI became the touted successes of the regime.

Such protectionist and clientelistic programs were in large part funded through Petróleos Mexicanos (PEMEX), the company that oversees all of Mexico's oil production. Though it was the world's sixth-largest oil producer at its peak, Mexico has seen its reserves decline while haphazard infrastructure development has limited PEMEX's ability to reap the full benefits of its oil fields. Some of the constraints on the oil sector came from the state's appetite for revenue to fund its public programs. In 1976 massive new oil reserves were discovered in the Gulf of Mexico, but the state's disproportionate increase in spending largely cancelled out many of the expected gains.

Major changes began during the transition between Presidents Echeverría and José López Portillo in 1976, when the Echeverría government allowed the value of the peso to be determined by the currency market rather than set by the government; the peso quickly lost 50 percent of its value. In many ways, the government had no choice but to devalue, since the currency's price had lost credibility in the eyes of the market, and capital began to flee. Mexico fell into crisis, and the international community intervened with loans, the first of several such interventions.

Mexico's 1982 debt crisis began with falling oil prices and massive, dollar-denominated debt. The United States pursued its own anti-inflationary policies at home, strengthening the dollar and causing the Mexican peso to fall sharply in relation to the U.S. currency. This made it much more expensive for Mexico to pay back its debt, putting the country in a state of near-insolvency. As this happened, capital began to flee the country in the billions of dollars. President López Portillo responded by nationalizing Mexico's banks, which remained state controlled until the 1990s. The crisis ushered in what became a global debt crisis, and it put the IMF and U.S. government in a position to demand fundamental changes in economic policy, creating what Mexicans refer to as the "lost decade" of economic decline.

The country's steady move toward a neoliberal economic model began in earnest during the presidency of Miguel de la

A Mexican farmer takes part in a 2008 protest against the removal of protection for Mexican-grown corn as a result of the North American Free Trade Agreement. NAFTA has arguably increased overall economic growth in Mexico but left it heavily dependent on the United States. Mexican farmers have been hit particularly hard by competition from (often subsidized) American farmers.

La Patria no se vende
Con la vida se defiende

Madrid (1982–1988), who significantly increased the government's reliance on technocrats to run the state. Foreign-educated experts, disconnected from the politics of the revolution and the PRI's populist heyday, controlled economic policy. By the time Carlos Salinas de Gortari (1988–1994)—a Harvard-educated technocrat himself—left office, Mexico's commitment to free-market economics was well established and strongly supported by the IMF and U.S. government. The country had joined the General Agreement on Tariffs and Trade (GATT) in 1986 and signed the North American Free Trade Agreement (NAFTA) in 1992. At the macroeconomic level, changes were visible. In the late ISI period (1970–1985), GDP growth averaged 4.5 percent per year in the best-performing Mexican states; this figure dropped to only 2.5 percent during the early free-market period (1985–1992). Studies show, however, that without NAFTA, growth would have been 4 to 5 percent lower by the year 2002. While NAFTA has increased productivity, however, it has had only marginal impact on employment. As Figure 5.1 demonstrates, unemployment has changed little in the past twenty years, and Mexico remains one of the most unequal societies in the world. Indeed, inequality increased as the wealthy benefitted from the new business opportunities neoliberal policies provided while the average wage dropped 40 percent over the 1980s and 1990s and the minimum wage dropped 70 percent. The neoliberal policies did reduce inflation dramatically and improved growth notably in the 1990s, though the economy slowed down in the new millennium.

The most noticeable effect of NAFTA has been Mexico's shift toward exports, which rose from 25 percent of GDP in 1985 to more than 82 percent in 1998. As the economy became more dependent on trade, however, regional disparities became more pronounced, with northern states most able to exploit their proximity to U.S. markets. The less-developed southern states have lagged behind. In the free-trade economy, cheap, state-subsidized corn from the United States has displaced traditional and less-developed agriculture meant for local consumption. This has resulted in billions of dollars in losses to local growers, negatively affecting already impoverished rural communities. Neoliberalism, however, has not ended state spending as a political tool. Toward the end of the twentieth century, currency devaluation and concurrent inflation became staples of the Mexican economy, given the unwritten rule that outgoing presidents would increase social welfare spending in order to increase the popularity of their handpicked successors. Even Presidents de la Madrid and Salinas did not hesitate to maintain high levels of deficit spending during periods of transition, and this practice brought about yet another catastrophe: the 1994 economic crisis.

The crisis, one of the most serious in Mexican history, was born out of a perfect storm. First, Salinas's social program "Solidarity" ran up the deficit significantly. Second, successor Ernesto Zedillo (1994–2000) allowed the peso to devalue against the dollar, sending the currency on another downward spiral. In addition, a series of political flashpoints—including an insurgency in the south led by the Zapatista Army of National Liberation, the assassination of presidential candidate Luís Donaldo Colosio in Tijuana, and the instigation of democratic competition in 1994—combined to cause investor panic. Only emergency loans from the United States and the International Monetary Fund (IMF) saved Mexico from financial ruin once again.

Today, Mexico continues to depend heavily on the United States; 80 percent of its exports go to the United States. Free trade between the two countries not only gives Mexican manufacturers access to the vast U.S. market, but NAFTA invites companies from all over the world to set up manufacturing plants, or *maquiladoras,* just south of the U.S.-Mexico border to take advantage of inexpensive labor and then export their goods north to the United States tariff-free, providing Mexico with needed foreign direct investment. Many Chinese and Korean firms, for instance, have opened plants in northern Mexico. After the 1990s boom in *maquila* manufacturing, the sector slowed down in the new millennium in the face of competition from even cheaper labor in China. As wage rates in China rose rapidly toward the end of the decade, however, manufacturing grew again along the U.S.-Mexican border.

The transition to a democratic government and election of the first non-PRI president in 2000 changed economic policy remarkably little. The new ruling party had always been in favor of free-market policies, so it did not change the neoliberal direction of the country. The dependence on exports to the United States meant that the 2008–2009 global recession hit Mexico very hard. Its GDP dropped by 6.5 percent in 2009, though as the United States began to recover so did Mexico. Growth returned to 5.6 percent in 2010, but it slowed again to 3.9 percent in 2011. Similarly, foreign investment was up significantly in 2010 and 2011, then slowed in 2012. The recession also meant higher levels of poverty and reduced migration to the United States as the U.S. job market for immigrants (legal and illegal) dried up. In the wake of the recession and continued concern about rampant drug-related violence, the PRI regained power in 2012, this time as a democratically elected party. The new president, Enrique Peña Nieto, promised major reforms to revive the economy. Just before he entered office, the Congress passed legislation substantially reducing labor market restrictions. Then Peña Nieto was able to negotiate a rare coalition of the three major political parties and quickly pass major reforms to both the education and telecommunications sectors. In September 2013, he announced a plan to increase tax collection from wealthy Mexicans in order to reduce dependence on oil revenues and to fund universal retirement pensions, unemployment insurance, and educational expansion. This, he argued, would also free up oil revenue to be reinvested in the oil industry and allow foreign investment in the oil sector, a very controversial proposal given the connection between Mexico's revolution and the national control of oil. If passed, these economic reforms would be the most important in Mexico in at least two decades.

By 2013, economic forecasters saw Mexico as an "up and coming" economy. Its growth rate had surpassed regional rival Brazil, and the new government promised reforms that would likely spur further foreign investment. Over the long term, though, the effects of Mexico's shift to neoliberalism remain unclear: during the ISI period (1940–1982) its average growth rate was 3.1 percent; since 1982 it has averaged about 1 percent. Cypher and Wise (2011) argued, following the logic of free trade and comparative advantage, that NAFTA has made Mexico primarily an exporter of cheap labor via *maquiladoras* and migration and has left it still heavily dependent on the United States.

Web link:
What an open oil sector in Mexico might look like

Data link:
Transformation Index, Mexico

CASE Summary

Mexico represents a classic case of the shift from ISI to neoliberal policies, with all of the benefits and costs that entails. ISI combined with oil revenue to create substantial growth until the 1970s, when growing debt and global economic problems undermined it. Mexico virtually declared bankruptcy and was forced to accept neoliberal policies in exchange for Western (especially U.S.) support. The neoliberal shift culminated with the signing of NAFTA, greatly expanding Mexico's manufactured exports to the United States. This has renewed growth via foreign investment but has also expanded inequality and increased dependence on Mexico's primary export market, the United States, leaving it especially vulnerable to global economic shocks like the 2008–2009 recession. If trade liberalization has created overall growth, however, the country's sharp inequalities have only increased with the emergence of neoliberal policies.

CASE Questions

1. Mexico is a classic case of the shift from ISI to neoliberal economic policies in developing countries. What have been the benefits and costs of neoliberal policy in Mexico? Weighing these costs and benefits, has the neoliberal model benefitted the country overall?
2. Nineteenth-century dictator Porfirio Díaz famously said, "Poor Mexico, so far from God and so close to the United States!" What have been the major effects of Mexico's modern economic relationship with the United States? Overall, has that relationship strengthened or weakened Mexico's economic development, and why?

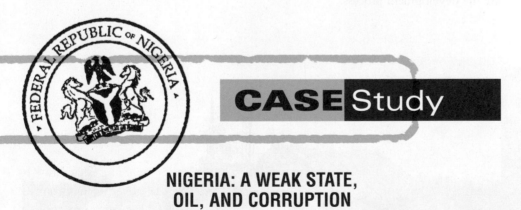

CASE Study

NIGERIA: A WEAK STATE, OIL, AND CORRUPTION

- **ECONOMIC MODEL**
  ISI; slow shift to neoliberal from 1983

- **ECONOMIC POLICY**
  Focused on oil revenue only

- **GLOBALIZATION EFFECTS**
  Oil dependency

- **ECONOMIC MILESTONES**
  Rising and falling oil prices; debt crisis; grand corruption

- **GREAT RECESSION**
  No recession because of oil prices

Like almost all African countries, Nigeria was a poor, agricultural country with little industry of any kind when it gained independence in 1960. As much as 98 percent of the population worked in agriculture, producing 65 percent of the country's GDP and 70 percent of its exports. Like other African states, its new government initially attempted to industrialize via ISI. By the mid-1970s, however, oil production and revenue had overwhelmed all other aspects of the economy and made the government dangerously dependent on the global oil market for political and economic survival. The huge influx of oil revenue and the active involvement of the government in the economy helped make Nigeria one of the most corrupt societies and governments in the world. Corruption and mismanagement combined to leave average Nigerians gaining virtually nothing from the country's massive oil wealth. The democratic governments in place since 1999 have managed to improve economic performance somewhat; not only has oil revenue increased due to higher prices, but for the first time in decades, non-oil growth has also increased in recent years.

The origins of Nigeria's economic problems, and the troubled relationship between the state and the market, lie in colonial rule. As was true throughout sub-Saharan Africa, colonial rulers in Nigeria allowed only particular economic opportunities to Africans. In Nigeria, peasant farmers were encouraged to produce food and export crops, and these became the backbone of an export economy based on cocoa, cotton, peanuts, and palm oil. Nigerians were not allowed any significant opportunity in industry, and foreign businesses controlled what little industry there was. Africans' sole route to economic advancement under colonial rule was education and employment in the colonial government. At independence, the educated elite was primarily employed in government and had virtually no involvement or expertise in private industry. They thus saw an expansion of the government's role in the economy as central both to national development and to their own interests. As we noted earlier, development economists at the time agreed with this approach, arguing that in the absence of an indigenous capitalist class, the state could beneficially intervene to initiate the development process.

Children paddle past an oil pipeline near their home in southeastern Nigeria. Nigeria suffers from a classic "resource curse," as dependence on oil has created corruption and massive environmental problems but done little to reduce the poverty that most Nigerians face.

The earliest manifestation of this model of state intervention in the interests of development came in the agricultural sector, in which the government had monopoly control over the domestic and international marketing of key crops. Of particular importance was control over export crops such as cocoa and cotton. The government bought export crops from Nigerian farmers at low prices and then sold them internationally at much higher prices. The difference became a key source of government revenue, essentially an unofficial but quite substantial tax on farmers. British colonial rulers created this system, and the newly elected independent government continued it. When world prices for key crops were relatively high, the system worked well. When those prices dropped in the late 1960s, however, farmers faced even lower prices, and protests and riots broke out in key agricultural areas.

Despite farmers' opposition to this unofficial tax, modernization theorists would argue that as long as the government used the revenue gained from agricultural exports to make productive investments in industry, its actions were justified. However, Nigeria's federal system of government made effective and efficient distribution of revenues very difficult. The bulk of the revenue from agriculture went to the regional governments, and each government used the revenue to build infrastructure and encourage industrialization. In the process, one regional government often duplicated the efforts of another. Export crop revenues also became an early source of corruption, further undermining efficient investment.

Given the lack of private Nigerian involvement in industry, the government, supported by aid donors and advisors, saw joint government investment with foreign companies as crucial to industrialization. In 1963 private Nigerian investment constituted only 10 percent of large-scale manufacturing, foreign capital controlled 68 percent, and the various governments controlled the remaining 22 percent. By the 1970s, the government had rapidly expanded its investment in large-scale industry. Most of the private Nigerian investors were themselves government officials or political leaders, so participation in the government and politics remained the key source of wealth.

Until the early 1970s, Nigeria's economic story of taxation of agricultural exports and state-led investment in industry was typical of Africa as a whole. Nigeria, however, possessed large oil reserves. In 1961, money from oil exports constituted less than 8 percent of government revenue; by 1974, that number hit 80 percent. Since then, Nigerian governments have invested virtually nothing in agriculture, which has declined from being the most important sector of the economy to one that continues to employ many people but produces very little. The country depends almost totally on oil exports for its well-being, but both military and democratically elected leaders have frequently misused oil wealth, and huge variations in world oil prices mean the country is at the mercy of a fickle international market.

The biggest economic change came with the quadrupling of world oil prices in 1973, which gave the Nigerian government a windfall from which it has yet to recover. The governments of the 1970s used the oil wealth to invest in large-scale infrastructure projects, borrowing money against future oil revenues to do so. When the oil market collapsed in the mid-1980s, the government was unable to pay back its loans and faced bankruptcy. Once again, it became a fairly typical African state, going to the IMF after 1983 to negotiate an SAP. The politically painful reductions in the government's size and activity that the IMF required were more than even the military governments could bear, and the process of instituting neoliberal policies was long and remains incomplete. Certainly, the government has reduced its involvement in industry (other than oil) and cut its size, but it has still only partially liberalized.

The central role of the state in the economy combined with huge oil revenues to create a situation ripe for corruption. Nigeria's worst ruler, Sani Abacha, is rumored to have stolen approximately $2 billion in government oil revenue in just five years while he was in power in the 1990s. By 2000, Transparency International ranked Nigeria as the world's most corrupt country. As in other parts of the postcolonial world, state intervention in the economy gave government officials many opportunities to grease palms and stuff their own pockets. Every law that required government approval for some economic activity created a point at which an official could ask for a bribe. The fact that government employment was the chief source of wealth contributed to this process. Ambitious young leaders went into government and politics not just to gain political power and to lead but also to make money.

Once again, the origins of the corruption problem lay in colonial rule. The colonial government was seen as a source of wealth and resources; it had no other legitimacy in the eyes of the people. The illegitimacy of the colonial government and the newness of democracy after independence meant that governmental institutions were weak, so people did not value them and were not interested in fighting to preserve them. Corruption, then, was easy to engage in for those who were interested. The more corruption grew, the less legitimacy state institutions had, and a vicious cycle ensued. A norm arose in which people expected government officials and politicians to provide something for them. Patron-client links and the provision of resources became nearly the sole means of maintaining political support. Thus, neopatrimonial forms of rule became common. Nigerian leaders took bribes and stole from government coffers both to feather their own nests and to provide resources to their supporters, who would reciprocate by granting political support to the leaders.

The democratic government that replaced military rule in 1999 initiated a series of anticorruption measures. An initial target was the return of the billions of dollars that Abacha had stolen, some of which the new government was able to get back from various European banks. In subsequent years, several major politicians in the new government also became targets of court cases. For the first time in Nigeria's history, political leaders faced criminal prosecution for stealing the country's wealth. In the run-up to the election in 2007, however, then-president Olusegun Obasanjo used the anticorruption agency to target and eliminate potential opponents. Still, the overall results of the anticorruption campaign have been positive: Nigeria improved in Transparency International's rankings from a score of 1.2 (dead last) in 2000 to 2.7 (139th out of174 countries) in 2012.

The new democratic government used its international support to gain financial aid and debt relief from Western donors, but in turn it was required to make substantial progress in moving its economic policies in a neoliberal direction. By 2006, the country's overall debt had dropped to less than one-tenth of what it had been two years earlier (Gillies 2007, 575). The government also brought inflation under control via tight monetary policy, stabilized government spending and the country's currency, and reduced various tariff barriers. Donors responded not only with debt relief but also with a massive increase in aid, from less than $200 million in 2000 to more than $6 billion in 2005. All this combined with rapidly increasing world oil prices to substantially improve Nigeria's global economic position. Economic growth has been relatively strong—around 5 percent in the new millennium—and non–oil sector growth was an impressive 9 percent from 2003 to 2009.

Nigeria's oil wealth allowed it to weather the Great Recession without an economic downturn. High oil prices kept its growth rate at a robust 7 percent in 2009, rising to 7.8 percent in 2010 before falling to 6.7 percent in 2011—still a high growth rate by global standards. Oil continues to cause multiple problems, however. Nigeria's nearly complete lack of productive oil refining means that, ironically, it must import most of its oil products. It has long used oil revenue to subsidize gas prices for the country's consumers; the subsidies have served as an important source of patronage for politicians and led to large fiscal deficits. In January 2012, with the encouragement of the IMF, the government ended the subsidies, setting off days of riots and ultimately a nationwide strike. The government backed down, reinstating the subsidies at half the level they had been before, which continues to cause fiscal problems. The government is short of revenue to pay for this and other services because of the massive corruption in the oil sector. President Goodluck Jonathan in 2012 commissioned a study of the oil sector that found a combination of domestic and international (by international oil companies) malfeasance had cost the government over $100 billion in the last decade, a figure that shocked the nation. The government continues to promise to pass a sweeping reform of the oil sector that has been discussed since 2008; if enacted, it could make the sector much more transparent to reduce corruption, deregulate gas prices, and partially privatize the national petroleum company to increase efficiency. Whether that actually happens depends on the details of the bill the legislature eventually passes and how faithfully it is implemented. In mid-2013, it remained in the parliament, with MPs battling over the effects of various policies on their home regions. Meanwhile, the poverty level has risen from 43 percent in 1985 to nearly 54 percent today.

Web link:
Ratings agency says Nigeria's economy is stable

Data link:
Transparency International Corruption Perceptions Index: Nigeria

Nigeria as an Oil Exporter

The Country and Concept table allows you to compare Nigeria with two other oil exporters, Iran and Russia, but it is also instructive to compare Nigeria with its partners in the Organization of the Petroleum Exporting Countries (OPEC). Nigeria has the largest population and one of the lowest GDPs in OPEC, making it among the poorest countries in the organization. A recent IMF report found that Nigeria and other sub-Saharan African oil exporters face much greater developmental challenges than exporters from other regions, including running out of oil sooner, lower oil reserves per capita, high oil dependence, and greater infrastructural and human development gaps. All the data below are for 2012.

	Nigeria	OPEC average
Population	163.3 million	34.6 million
Barrels of oil produced per day	1,974,800	2,510,133
Oil export revenue per capita (real $, billions)	$527	$2,331
GDP per capita	$1,443	$23,838
Proven crude oil reserves	37.2 billion barrels	99.9 billion barrels

Source: Organization of the Petroleum Exporting Countries, *Annual Statistical Bulletin 2012* (http://www.opec.org/opec_web/static_files_project/media/downloads/publications/ASB2012.pdf); World Bank.

CASE Summary

At least until the last few years, Nigeria has been a case study of development gone wrong. The largest country in Africa and blessed (or cursed) with abundant oil reserves, it remains one of the world's poorest countries. The development models pursued—both ISI and SAPs—were justified in terms of reigning theories of economic development in their respective eras, but neither led to significant development. Dependence on vacillating oil markets left the government in crisis when oil prices dropped. Weak institutions, political demands, and massive oil wealth when prices were high produced monumental levels of corruption that undermined virtually all development efforts and expanded debt. Neoliberal policies are designed to encourage investment, but, at least until recently, they achieved little in Nigeria outside the oil sector. In the absence of strong and coherent state institutions and a favorable global economic context, economic blueprints do not produce the expected results, though they are frequently used to justify the politically motivated actions of various leaders. The new millennium has been slightly kinder to Nigeria, however. The new democratic government has somewhat reduced corruption, successfully convinced foreign creditors to forgive debt, and achieved the first real growth outside the oil sector in decades.

CASE Questions

1. Given the problems oil wealth has caused Nigeria to date, how might the government go about creating policies that would start to use oil wealth more effectively for the benefit of the country?
2. One element in the debate over neoliberal development policies is the question of whether they will work in every country, and whether certain kinds of institutions must exist for them to work well. Comparing Mexico and Nigeria, what lessons can you draw regarding these questions? What do these two cases suggest about the likely success of neoliberal policies in different contexts?

CONCLUSION

With the extension of the market economy to nearly every corner of the globe, a universal set of issues exists involving the relationship between the market and the state. The state must perform certain tasks so that the market can function efficiently and in turn produce revenue for the state. The market is likely to generate greater wealth if the state is able to go beyond these essential functions by establishing policies to encourage investment and growth. Political pressure can lead to yet other policies, as organized groups in society demand particular state intervention in the market in their favor. Clear and consistent economic theories of how and why the state should intervene serve as intellectual guides for state actions. However, no government's policies follow these blueprints perfectly, as our case studies have shown.

The five case studies in this chapter demonstrate the great variation around the world in the relationship between the state and the market economy. The United States has long been the model of a free-market economy with limited state intervention, though as we have seen, even here the state has intervened and expanded over the past century to try to improve economic outcomes and limit negative market effects. Germany's social market economy represents the common European alternative. While there are variations from country to country, most of the wealthier countries of Europe guide and limit the market much more than the United States does, providing much more generous government support to those not "making it" in the market. Like most countries after the first wave of industrialization, Germany and Japan also used state intervention to guide investment into particular sectors. Postcolonial countries industrialized even later, leaving them today with a less secure position in the global market and with greater inequality. Where institutions are reasonably strong, as in Mexico, significant economic development has occurred even though great inequality, poverty, and at times instability persist. In weak states such as Nigeria, weak institutions make implementing any development policy difficult. This is especially true when a weak state possesses oil or other mineral wealth, which distorts economic and political incentives, spurs corruption, and makes development that benefits the bulk of the population even less likely.

Globalization has challenged all past economic models. Whether these models were successful or not in earlier decades, they now face rapidly moving capital that seems to limit their options and pushes them all in the direction of greater openness to the market. The Great Recession accelerated this process, as even the EU scrambled to bail out its weakest members. Even weaker nations seem to have less room to maneuver in an era when international forces are increasingly powerful vis-à-vis domestic ones. The ability of states to navigate the forces of globalization has profound implications for their citizens' well-being, a subject we return to at length in chapter 10.

Explaining the variation in state intervention in the market has long been a preoccupation of comparativists. Marxist analysts, whose theories of the dominance of the bourgeoisie are challenged by the existence of extensive welfare states such as Germany's, argue that the elite in capitalist societies sometimes sacrifice the short-term interests of particular businesses in order to preserve the system as a whole. Probably the most widely accepted explanation, however, is a pluralist one: countries with stronger workers' movements and unions have created the policies these groups favor. This immediately raises the question of why some countries developed stronger unions than others. Analysts comparing the United States with countries in Europe, in particular, have asked why U.S. unions are weaker and why no strong socialist party has emerged in the United States. One common explanation is the "frontier thesis," which cites the option of moving west as an escape valve that allowed workers to flee rather than organize and fight. Another is a racial thesis, which proposes that racial divisions within the American union movement kept it from gaining more strength. Both of these ideas point to differences in political culture as a potential explanation for variation in economic policies.

Weak unions are just one example of weak institutions, which institutionalists argue are the key to explaining the economic paths of different countries. They suggest that more than just group strength is involved in creating stronger welfare states in some countries than in others. The strength of institutions is also crucial, especially the strength of parties, unions, and business associations. The ability of stronger institutions in Germany to discipline their members produced a less confrontational environment that allowed stronger welfare policies to gain support. As globalization has weakened those institutions, German economic and social policy has shifted, largely toward a more market-oriented model. Strong bureaucratic institutions similarly help explain the rise of the developmental state in Japan. Globalization also made those institutions weaker over time, helping to undermine what was a widely admired model of economic growth.

While domestic groups of one sort or another are likely the main forces behind economic policy in wealthy and powerful countries, in poorer countries they seem distinctly less able to influence policies. In Nigeria, policies that in theory were designed to use the state to enhance national development instead favored the elite, who controlled key government machinery. As a result, the majority of the Nigerian population saw few benefits. In both Mexico and Nigeria, and throughout the postcolonial world, the ideas of development economists in the West have been very influential. Since the debt crisis of the early 1980s, structural adjustment policies imposed by the World Bank and the IMF have forced many countries to pursue policies that have had little domestic support. In many such countries, the government's annual budget must receive approval from IMF headquarters in Washington, D.C., before the elected government submits it to parliament for approval. Answering the question "Who rules?" may require looking beyond the confines of a country to the broader international community.

We will return to these debates in chapter 10, when we examine more contemporary issues surrounding globalization. First, though, we need to understand how different regimes and institutions function to channel political power, the primary subject of Part II of the book.

KEY CONCEPTS

capitalism (p. 198)

codetermination (p. 234)

command economy (p. 199)

comparative advantage (p. 208)

deficit spending (p. 205)

developmental state (p. 238)

externality (p. 201)

fiscal policy (p. 205)

globalization (p. 216)

import-substitution
industrialization (ISI) (p. 208)

Keynesian theory (p. 205)

market economy (p. 197)

market failure (p. 201)

monetarist theory (p. 206)

monetary policy (p. 206)

monopoly (p. 202)

natural monopoly (p. 203)

neoliberalism (p. 207)

privatize (p. 210)

public goods (p. 199)

social market economy (p. 232)

structural adjustment
programs (SAPs) (p. 210)

Sharpen your skills with SAGE edge at **edge.sagepub.com/orvis3e**. **SAGE edge for students** provides a personalized approach to help you accomplish your coursework goals in an easy-to-use learning environment.

WORKS CITED

Altman, Roger C. 2009. "Globalization in Retreat." *Foreign Affairs* 88 (4).

Cafruny, Alan W., and Leila Simona Talani. 2013. "The Crisis of the Eurozone." In *Exploring the Global Financial Crisis,* edited by Alan W. Cafruny and Herman M. Schwartz, 13–34. Boulder, CO: Lynne Rienner.

Calmes, Jackie, and Jonathan Weisman. 2013. "Economists See Deficit Emphasis as Impeding Recovery." *New York Times.* May 8, 2013 (http://www.nytimes.com/ 2013/05/09/us/deficit-reduction-is-seen-by-economists-as-impeding-recovery .html?emc=eta1&_r=0).

Crew, David F. 1998. *Germans on Welfare: From Weimar to Hitler.* New York: Oxford University Press.

Cypher, James M., and Raúl Delgado Wise. 2011. *Mexico's Economic Dilemma: The Developmental Failure of Neoliberalism.* New York: Rowman and Littlefield.

Dadush, Uri, and Kemal Derviş. 2013. "The Inequality Challenge." *Current History* 112, no. 750 (January): 13–19 (http://www .brookings.edu/research/articles/2013/01/ inequality-challenge-dervis).

Edwards, Haley Sweetland. 2013. "He Who Makes the Rules." *Washington Monthly.* March/April 2013 (http://www .washingtonmonthly.com/magazine/ march_april_2013/features/he_who_ makes_the_rules043315.php?page= all).

Garrett, Geoffrey. 1998. *Partisan Politics in the Global Economy.* Cambridge, UK: Cambridge University Press.

Gillies, Alexandra. 2007. "Obasanjo, the Donor Community and Reform Implementation in Nigeria." *The Round Table* 96 (392): 569–586. doi:10.1080/ 00358530701625992.

Isaacs, Julia B. 2007. *Economic Mobility of Families across Generations.* Washington, DC: The Pew Charitable Trusts (http:// www.brookings.edu/~/media/research/ files/papers/2007/11/generations%20 isaacs/11_generations_isaacs.pdf).

Johnson, Chalmers A. 1982. *MITI and the Japanese Miracle: The Growth of Industrial Policy, 1925–1975.* Stanford, CA: Stanford University Press.

Kingston, John. 2013. *Contemporary Japan: History, Politics, and Social Change since the 1980s.* 2nd ed. Malden, MA: John Wiley & Sons.

Lincoln, James, and Masahiro Shimotani. 2009. "Whither the *Keiretsu,* Japan's Business Networks? How Were They Structured? What Did They Do? Why Are They Gone?" Working Paper Series, Institute for Research on Labor and Employment, University of California, Berkeley (http://www.escholarship.org/ uc/item/00m7d34g).

Lowrey, Annie. 2013. "The Rich Get Richer through the Recovery." Economix. *New York Times,* September 10 (http://econo mix.blogs.nytimes.com/2013/09/10/ the-rich-get-richer-through-the-recovery/?ref=business&_r=0).

Miura, Mari. 2012. *Welfare through Work: Conservative Ideas, Partisan Dynamics, and Social Protection in Japan.* Ithaca, NY: Cornell University Press.

Ocampo, José Antonio, and Rob Vos. 2010. *Uneven Economic Development.* New York: Zed Books.

Ohmae, Kenichi. 1995. *The End of the Nation State: The Rise of Regional Economies.* New York: Simon and Schuster.

Pempel, T. J. 2000. *Regime Shift: Comparative Dynamics of the Japanese Political Economy.* Ithaca, NY: Cornell University Press.

Polanyi, Karl. 1944. *The Great Transformation.* New York: Farrar and Rinehart.

Rattner, Steven. 2011. "The Secrets of Germany's Success." *Foreign Affairs* 90 (4).

Round, Jeffrey. 2010. "Globalization, Growth, Inequality, and Poverty in Africa: A Macroeconomic Perspective." In *The Poor under Globalization in Asia, Latin America, and Africa*, edited by M. Nissanke and E. Thorbecke, 327–367. Oxford, UK: Oxford UniversityPress.

Siavelis, Peter M. 2007. "How New Is Bachelet's Chile?" *Current History* 106 (697): 70–76.

Tooze, Adam. 2012. "Germany's Unsustainable Growth." *Foreign Affairs* 91 (5).

Transparency International (http://www.transparency.org).

RESOURCES FOR FURTHER STUDY

Bates, Robert H. 2001. *Prosperity and Violence: The Political Economy of Development.* New York: W. W. Norton.

Friedman, Milton. 1962. *Capitalism and Freedom.* Chicago: University of Chicago Press.

Gilpin, Robert. 2000. *The Challenge of Global Capitalism.* Princeton, NJ: Princeton University Press.

Heilbroner, Robert L. 1985. *The Nature and Logic of Capitalism.* New York: W. W. Norton.

International Monetary Fund. 2007. *Regional Economic Outlook, Sub-Saharan Africa.* Washington, DC: International Monetary Fund (http://www.imf.org/external/pubs/ft/reo/2007/afr/eng/sreo1007.pdf).

Jameson, Kenneth P., and Charles K. Wilber. 1996. *The Political Economy of Development and Underdevelopment.* 6th ed. New York: McGraw-Hill.

Keynes, John Maynard. 1935. *The General Theory of Employment, Interest, and Money.* New York: Harcourt Brace.

The Levin Institute, The State University of New York. "Globalization 101: A Student's Guide to Globalization" (http://www.globalization101.org).

Organization of the Petroleum Exporting Countries. 2006. *OPEC Annual Statistical Bulletin 2006* (http://www.opec.org/opec_web/static_files_project/media/downloads/publications/ASB06.pdf).

Rapley, John. 2007. *Understanding Development: Theory and Practice in the Third World.* 3rd ed. Boulder, CO: Lynne Rienner.

Siebert, Horst. 2005. *The German Economy: Beyond the Social Market.* Princeton, NJ: Princeton University Press.

Woo-Cumings, Meredith, ed. 1999. *The Developmental State.* Ithaca, NY: Cornell University Press.

WEB RESOURCES

International Labour Organization, LABORSTA Internet
(http://laborsta.ilo.org)

International Monetary Fund, World Economic Outlook Database
(http://www.imf.org/external/pubs/ft/weo/2013/01/weodata/index.aspx)

Organisation for Economic Co-operation and Development (OECD), Stat Extracts
(http://stats.oecd.org)

UNDP Human Development Reports, International Human Development Indicators
(http://hdr.undp.org/en/statistics)

The World Bank, Economic Policy and External Debt
(http://data.worldbank.org/topic/economic-policy-and-external-debt)

6 GOVERNING INSTITUTIONS IN DEMOCRACIES

KEY QUESTIONS

- A democracy must limit the power of its executives to provide accountability. Which institutional choices best ensure accountability, and how?

- How much power should a minority have in a democracy? How do different democracies seek to guarantee that minorities are protected from possible majority tyranny? Do some institutional choices seem to guarantee this better than others?

- Do greater participation and representation of many voices in government result in less effective policymaking?

- How can we explain why an institution that works well in one setting might not work as well in another?

- What explains why particular democratic institutions arise in particular countries but not in others?

Americans are taught from a young age the importance of the three branches of government—executive, legislative, and judicial—and how essential their separate but equal status is for democracy. Understanding politics, however, requires far more than simply understanding the formal institutions of government. The social, cultural, and historical contexts in which those formal institutions exist can have significant bearing on how institutions function in practice. On paper, a president in one country may have similar powers as a president in another country, but what each can achieve might vary greatly in the two distinct contexts. The actual power of particular institutions often changes over time as well, as changing socioeconomic and cultural factors give greater resources to one or another institution, or a particular leader helps strengthen or weaken an institution. The first question we must ask, then, has to do with **institutionalization:** To what degree are a state's government processes and procedures established, predictable, and routinized? Comparativists look at how institutionalized the political institutions of a particular state are. This varies within and across all regimes. It is important to examine in democracies and even more important in authoritarian regimes, where it tends to vary more, as we'll see in chapter 8.

President Mwai Kibaki holds Kenya's new constitution, ratified in a popular referendum in August 2010. The new constitution changed Kenya's governing system from a British-style parliamentary system inherited fifty years earlier at independence to a U.S.-style presidential system. The big question is whether this would finally provide accountability and stronger rule of law in Kenya's fledgling democracy.

The study of institutions in democracies, which is the focus of this and the next chapter, raises other important questions for democratic theory and comparative politics. The first question involves who rules: Do certain institutional arrangements achieve greater **political accountability,** meaning the ability of the citizenry to directly or indirectly control political leaders and institutions?

Argentine political scientist Guillermo O'Donnell (1999) used the terms *vertical* and *horizontal accountability* to analyze the extent to which the power of key state institutions is under democratic control. **Vertical accountability** refers to the ability of individuals and groups in a society to hold state institutions accountable, whereas **horizontal accountability** refers to the ability of the state's institutions to hold one another accountable. The latter represents indirect control on the part of the citizenry, in that particular institutions implicitly act on behalf of the citizenry to limit the power of and thereby control other institutions or leaders. For instance, a legislature presumably should have enough power vis-à-vis the executive branch to limit what the executive can do, to ask him to justify his actions, and ultimately to punish

institutionalization
The degree to which government processes and procedures are established, predictable, and routinized

political accountability
The ability of the citizenry, directly or indirectly, to control political leaders and institutions

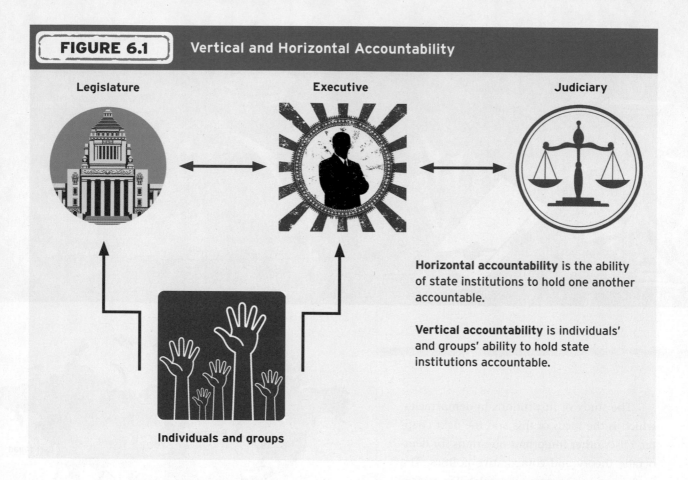

FIGURE 6.1   Vertical and Horizontal Accountability

Legislature   Executive   Judiciary

Horizontal accountability is the ability of state institutions to hold one another accountable.

Vertical accountability is individuals' and groups' ability to hold state institutions accountable.

Individuals and groups

vertical accountability
The ability of individuals and groups in a society to hold state institutions accountable

horizontal accountability
The ability of state institutions to hold one another accountable

executive
The branch of government that must exist in all modern states; the chief political power in a state and implements all laws

him if he acts in ways unacceptable to the state's constitution or majority opinion in the country. Similarly, the court system may have the power to rule legislative or executive actions unconstitutional, thus preserving the basic system of government against politicians' attempts to abrogate it.

This chapter focuses on horizontal accountability, as we examine the relative power of governing institutions in relation to one another. We examine vertical accountability in greater detail in the next chapter, looking at institutions of participation and representation.

Note that only one of the branches of government, the executive, is essential to a modern state as we defined it in chapter 2. Modern states are sovereign entities that administer territories and people; therefore, an executive power and accompanying bureaucracy are essential to their existence. The **executive** is the chief political power in a state. The position is filled through elections in a democracy and typically is embodied in the single most powerful office in the government, referred to as a president or prime minister in most countries. The modern state, however, also includes a bureaucracy, a large set of lesser officials whose function is to implement the laws of the state, as directed by the executive. We explore both executive powers and modern bureaucracies in this chapter.

The executive is essential, but as the idea of horizontal accountability suggests, a legislature with autonomy from the executive is an important institution of democratization, even if it is not crucial to the modern state itself. Similarly, a judiciary is essential for the state to punish crime and enforce property and contract rights, but it need not have a political role independent of the executive, although in a democracy this can be an important element of horizontal accountability. The process of democratization is in part a matter of creating mechanisms through which the power of the executive is limited. In democratic theory, the **legislature** makes the law, and the **judiciary** interprets it. The power and autonomy of each, however, vary significantly in practice.

legislature
Branch of government that makes the law in a democracy

judiciary
Branch of government that interprets the law and applies it to individual cases

Many political scientists believe that forces in the modern world are strengthening the executive branch. The contemporary state has more technically sophisticated functions to carry out than in earlier eras. Legislators often delegate the more technical decisions implied in particular laws to bureaucrats because the legislators lack the technical competence to make those decisions. Over the course of the twentieth century, this meant a general upward trend in the size and power of the bureaucracy that the executive branch leads, which makes issues of control of the executive even more paramount. Some political scientists also worry about limiting the role of the judiciary, seeing a "judicialization" of politics in which courts and judges replace elected officials as key decision makers.

A second crucial question in democracies is, How much power should be given to the majority that, at least in theory, rules? Democracy implies majority rule, but how much power the majority has over dissident minorities is a fundamental question. Some formal institutions give the representatives of the majority far greater power than do others. The United Kingdom and United States stand in sharp relief on this issue and illustrate the range of available options. As we discuss below, the British Parliament has the legal right to pass any legislation it pleases, which gives the majority party tremendous powers. In contrast, the U.S. Constitution divides and thereby limits power significantly. Even when the same party controls both houses of Congress and the presidency, that party's power is limited by the ability of the Supreme Court to declare laws unconstitutional and by the various powers reserved specifically for state governments. Both countries are democracies, but they address the question of how formal institutions should protect minorities quite differently.

A final key question is, What is the potential trade-off between popular participation in the government and representation of many viewpoints, on the one hand, and effective governance, on the other? If the institutions of a particular regime strongly limit one another and many different groups are represented in the decision-making process, do these factors limit the ability of the government to make effective policy? Comparativist Arend Lijphart (1999) examined this potential trade-off. He suggested that we think of democracies on a continuum from what he termed "majoritarian" to "consensus." **Majoritarian democracies** concentrate power in a single place and office; they have a single-party executive, executive dominance over the legislature, a single legislative branch, and constitutions that can be easily amended.

majoritarian democracy
A type of democratic system that concentrates power more tightly in a single-party executive with executive dominance over the legislature, a single legislative branch, and constitutions that can be easily amended

consensus democracy
A democratic system with multiparty executives in a coalition government, executive-legislative balance, bicameral legislatures, and rigid constitutions that are not easily amended

coalition government
Government in a parliamentary system in which at least two parties negotiate an agreement to rule together

Consensus democracies, in contrast, have multiparty executives called a **coalition government** (in which at least two parties negotiate an agreement to rule together), executive-legislative balance, bicameral legislatures (with two roughly equally powerful houses), and rigid constitutions that are not easily amended. If a trade-off exists between representation and effective policymaking, majoritarian systems ought to be more effective because they have much more concentrated power with fewer checks on it. They seem likely to produce less horizontal accountability, however, since they have few institutions to check the executive. G. Bingham Powell (2000) noted, though, that vertical accountability is likely to be greater in majoritarian systems because voters know exactly who is responsible for government policy. In consensus systems with coalition government and multiple participants in the policy-making process, on the other hand, responsibility is less clear.

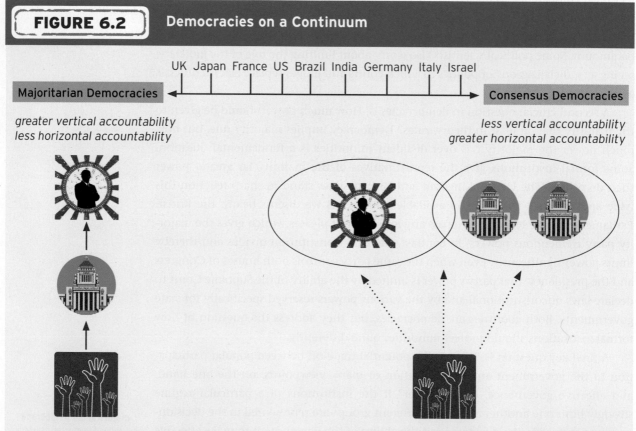

FIGURE 6.2   **Democracies on a Continuum**

UK Japan France US Brazil India Germany Italy Israel

Majoritarian Democracies ←————————————————→ **Consensus Democracies**

greater vertical accountability
less horizontal accountability

less vertical accountability
greater horizontal accountability

- Power is concentrated: fewer institutions to check executive power
- Single-party executive
- Executive dominance over legislature
- Single legislative branch
- Easily amended constitutions
- Key example = UK's Westminster

- Power and decision making are more dispersed
- Multiparty executives (coalition government)
- Executive-legislative balance
- Bicameral legislatures
- Hard-to-amend constitutions
- Key examples = coalition government in Israel or divided government in the US

COUNTRY AND CONCEPT
Snapshot of Governing Institutions

Country	Executive-legislative system	Judicial system		Federal system	Bureaucracy: corruption[1] (scale of 0-100, 100 = least corrupt)
		Type of legal system	Right of judicial review		
Brazil	Presidential	Code law	Yes	Symmetric federalism	43
China	NA	Code law	No	Unitary	39
Germany	Parliamentary	Code law	Yes	Symmetric federalism	79
India	Parliamentary	Common law	Yes	Asymmetric federalism	36
Iran	Semipresidential (authoritarian)	Islamic *sharia*	No	Unitary	28
Japan	Parliamentary	Code law	Yes	Unitary	74
Mexico	Presidential	Code law	Yes	Symmetric federalism	34
Nigeria	Presidential	Common law and *sharia*	Yes	Symmetric federalism	27
Russia	Semipresidential	Code law	Yes (but weak)	Asymmetric federalism	28
United Kingdom	Parliamentary	Common law	No	Unitary	74
United States	Presidential	Common law	Yes	Symmetric federalism	73

[1]Transparency International, Corruption Perceptions Index, 2012 (http://www.transparency.org/policy_research/surveys_indices/cpi).

Comparativist George Tsebelis (2002) studied limits on effective policymaking as well. He argued that a key distinction among political systems and institutions is the number of veto players they have. A **veto player** is an individual or collective actor whose agreement is essential to effect policy change. Veto players may exist on the basis of institutional positions defined by a constitution or via partisan battles and political support. Tsebelis further argued that the greater the number of veto players and the greater the ideological distance among them, the less likely policy change will be. We will see how both the arrangement of governing institutions (examined in this chapter) and institutions of participation and representation (examined in chapter 7) create veto players. We will examine the trade-offs among horizontal and vertical accountability, representation, and effective policymaking in both chapters.

veto player
An individual or collective actor whose agreement is essential for any policy change

The Country and Concept table shows the great variation in our case studies' governing institutions, even among those that are democracies. We begin with the relationship between the executive and legislative branches, which, more than anything else, distinguishes different kinds of democracies. We then examine the roles of the judiciary and the modern bureaucracy and their relationships to the executive and legislative branches. We also look at the question of federalism and the extent to which the overall power of the state is either centralized in national institutions or dispersed among subnational units of government; federalism can be another means of achieving accountability.

EXECUTIVES AND LEGISLATURES

head of state
The official, symbolic representative of a country, authorized to speak on its behalf and represent it, particularly in world affairs; usually a president or monarch

head of government
The key executive power in a state; usually a president or prime minister

The executive is indispensable to any state or regime and fulfills two very important roles. First, as **head of state,** the executive is the official, symbolic representative of a country, authorized to speak on its behalf and represent it, particularly in world affairs. Historically, heads of state were monarchs, who still exist as symbolic heads of state in a number of countries, including the United Kingdom and Japan. Second, as **head of government,** the executive's task is to implement the nation's laws and policies. The two parts of the executive function may be filled by one individual or two, but both are essential to any regime. Legislatures are less ubiquitous because authoritarian regimes can dispense with them. They are, however, crucial to democratic regimes because a legislature's very democratic function is to debate public policy and pass laws. We discuss the executive and legislature together because the relationship between them distinguishes three classic models of democratic government: parliamentarism, presidentialism, and semipresidentialism.

Parliamentarism: The Westminster Model

parliamentarism
A term denoting a parliamentary system of democracy in which the executive and legislative branches are fused via parliament's election of the chief executive

prime minister (PM)
The head of government in parliamentary and semipresidential systems

If you ask Americans to define democracy, many will start with the "separation of powers." The oldest model of modern democracy, however, does not separate the executive and legislature. Commonly known as the Westminster, or parliamentary, model, it originated in Britain. Lijphart called **parliamentarism** the purest form of his "majoritarian" model in which power is concentrated in one place, creating very few institutional veto players. The fusion of the executive and legislative branches provides for an exceptionally powerful executive. This fusion exists in the office of the **prime minister (PM)** (in Germany, the chancellor), whose relationship to the legislature is the key distinguishing feature of the model. The PM is not only the executive but also a member of the legislature. She is the leader of the majority party or leading coalition party in the legislature. The PM, then, is not elected directly to executive office but rather is named after the legislative election determines the dominant party in parliament. Citizens cast one vote for a party or individual, depending on the electoral system, to represent them in parliament; the majority in parliament then names the prime minister. In practice, when citizens vote for parliament, they know who the PM candidate for each party is, so their vote for their preferred **member of parliament (MP)** or party is indirectly a vote for that party's leader to serve as PM.

Formally, the PM serves at the pleasure of parliament. Should a parliamentary majority lose confidence in the PM, members can cast a **vote of no confidence** that forces the PM to resign. At that point, the leading party in parliament can choose a new leader who will become PM, or the resigning PM will ask the head of state to call new parliamentary elections. Parliamentary systems often do not have fixed terms of office, and while the parliament can oust a prime minister, a PM can similarly dissolve parliament and call for new elections. In Britain, for example, the maximum term allowed between elections is five years, but a PM can call earlier elections to take advantage of an electoral opportunity for her party, or the majority party can remove the PM if it loses confidence in her. In practice, votes of no confidence are usually called by the opposition in parliament and are only successful in removing the government about 5 percent of the time, but they provide the opposition a means to highlight the government's weaknesses and usually result in opposition gains in the next election (Williams 2011).

Parliamentary systems separate the two functions of the executive. They have a "nonexecutive head of state," who embodies and represents the country ceremonially. Countries lacking a hereditary monarchy typically replace the monarch in this function with an elected head of state who, somewhat confusingly to Americans, is often called the "president." In most cases, this president's role, like the queen's in Britain, is small and ceremonial. Countries tend to elect esteemed elder statesmen (or less often women) who gracefully perform the ceremonial role while leaving all important executive functions to the head of the government, the PM. When a PM is the leader of the party that holds a majority of the seats in parliament and that party votes regularly as a bloc (as is almost always the case in parliamentary systems), the PM is an extremely powerful executive. Whatever legislation she puts forth is almost automatically passed into law by the legislature. A prime minister is in a somewhat different position if her party does not have a clear majority in parliament. In this situation, the PM will head a coalition government, in which at least two parties negotiate an agreement to rule together. A vote of no confidence is far more likely in a coalition government because if one party in the coalition is unhappy with a PM's policies, it can leave the coalition, causing the coalition to lose its majority. Smaller parties in the coalition often become partisan veto players; the PM must ensure that she has their support before she can get her legislation through parliament, a process that can involve extensive negotiations.

The prime minister also appoints the other ministers (what Americans call "secretaries") to the cabinet, but given the close executive relationship with parliament, these individuals cannot be whomever the prime minister pleases. The cabinet, especially in a coalition, serves as a check on the PM. Cabinet ministers must also be MPs, and in a coalition government the prime minister must consult with the other parties in the coalition about the distribution of "portfolios" (cabinet seats). Normally, all

member of parliament (MP)
An elected member of the legislature in a parliamentary system

vote of no confidence
In parliamentary systems, a vote by parliament to remove a government (the prime minister and cabinet) from power

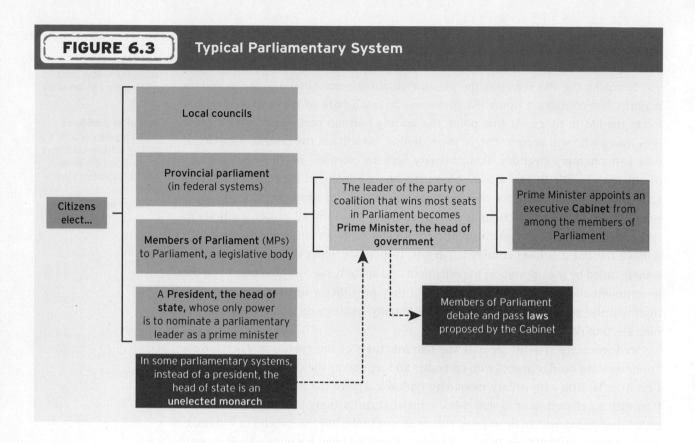

FIGURE 6.3   Typical Parliamentary System

Local councils

Provincial parliament
(in federal systems)

Citizens
elect…

Members of Parliament (MPs)
to Parliament, a legislative body

A **President, the head of
state,** whose only power
is to nominate a parliamentary
leader as a prime minister

In some parliamentary systems,
instead of a president, the
head of state is an
unelected monarch

The leader of the party or
coalition that wins most seats
in Parliament becomes
**Prime Minister, the head of
government**

Prime Minister appoints an
executive **Cabinet** from
among the members of
Parliament

Members of Parliament
debate and pass **laws**
proposed by the Cabinet

parties in the coalition, and certainly the biggest ones, get some representation in the cabinet. The cabinet, then, is often the site of the most important negotiations over policy. Whether all cabinet members are from the same party or from different parties in a coalition, once they have agreed to put forth a piece of legislation, it should pass through the legislature quite easily, as the classic case of Britain demonstrates. When no single party has a majority in parliament and therefore a coalition government is required, the process becomes more complex, as the example of Israel illustrates.

Because Israel is a country of numerous ideological, religious, and ethnic divisions, multiple parties compete in each election, and coalitions of parties must band together to form a government in its parliamentary system. The average government has lasted just twenty-five months. Israel's parliament, the *Knesset,* functions much like the British or any other parliament: a majority vote is required to elect a prime minister and form a government. The electoral system encourages the emergence and survival of many, small parties. Most elections feature as many as two dozen parties, with at least a dozen winning seats in parliament. While two or three major parties have always existed, most governments are a coalition of one major party, which provides the prime minister, and at least three others—sometimes as many as six—who also receive cabinet seats to ensure their support in parliament.

The 2013 election resulted in fourteen parties (some of which were actually coalitions of smaller parties) winning seats in parliament, with Prime Minister Binyamin

Netanyahu's Likud bloc winning the most—31 out of 120 seats. After the election, it took him six weeks to put together a working coalition government that included four parties in the cabinet. His government before the election included conservative religious parties that had long been in government, but they lost seats in the new election to a centrist party focused on domestic economic issues and a new party representing settlers in the West Bank, so Netanyahu included them in his new coalition and left the religious parties out. With an extremely ideologically diverse cabinet, the prime minister must negotiate policies continuously to keep the government together. Governmental dissolution and the instability that comes with it often lurk right around the corner.

Israel demonstrates what critics point to as a weakness of the parliamentary system: government instability. If no party can win a majority, a coalition government is essential. Thus, small parties with only a few seats in parliament can become crucial veto players. In sharp contrast to the majoritarian British system, in which one party almost always wins a majority of parliamentary seats and therefore governments are much more stable, the Israeli system often makes the prime minister a relatively weak chief executive and makes governments short-lived. The case of India also shows that how a parliamentary system actually functions depends very much on the historical, social, and cultural contexts in which it operates.

Web link:
The Economist on Israel's 2013 lection

CASE Study

PARLIAMENTARY RULE IN BRITAIN AND INDIA

Britain and India illustrate how similar governing institutions function differently in distinct social and political contexts. As a British colony, India adopted Britain's Westminster model almost completely, with the biggest institutional difference being that India is a federal system. Differences in the party systems and the socioeconomic and cultural contexts of the two countries, however, influence how the model functions in practice.

Britain's prime minister is often called the most powerful democratic executive in the world. The power of the office derives not just from its formal functions but also from the nature of Britain's parties and the strength of British institutions. Like the United States, Britain has two major parties (Labour and Conservative) that almost always alternate in power: one or the other wins a majority of legislative seats in virtually every election. This means that coalition governments are very rare (the coalition government elected in 2010 and led by Prime Minister David Cameron was the first

- **EXECUTIVE POWER**
  Depends on number and strength of parties; greater in Britain

- **LEGISLATIVE POWER**
  Greater than formal powers might suggest; parliament as "watchdog," even though government legislation almost always passes

- **ACCOUNTABILITY**
  Stronger vertical accountability but coalition governments likely to weaken it

- **VETO PLAYERS**
  Weak in Britain, with stronger and fewer parties

- **POLICYMAKING**
  Strong; coalition government weakens in India

- **RECENT TRENDS**
  PMs becoming more "presidential," but efforts to strengthen parliament via more committees and resources

since World War II). Unlike parties in the United States, British parties are highly disciplined in the legislature, meaning that MPs almost always vote in support of their party's position on legislation. This is partly an effect of the parliamentary system itself. Ambitious MPs want to become cabinet ministers, and the head of the party controls these positions; thus, MPs demonstrate loyalty to the party leadership. As head of the majority party, the PM can usually get legislation passed with ease. The system has very few veto players.

The British PM appoints approximately twenty cabinet ministers who run the individual departments of government and whom the PM is supposed to consult before making major decisions. By tradition, the PM's power is checked by the cabinet and the practice of collective responsibility, which means that all cabinet members must publicly support all government decisions. A cabinet member who cannot do so is expected to resign. Since cabinet members are themselves senior leaders of the majority party and MPs, collective responsibility constitutes an informal legislative agreement to policies prior to their formal introduction in Parliament.

Many argue that the cabinet's role has declined over the last generation and that PMs have begun to look more presidential. The two most important PMs of the last generation, Conservative Margaret Thatcher (1979–1990) and Labourite Tony Blair (1997–2007), centralized decision making in an inner circle of advisors and paid less attention to input from the cabinet as a whole. This practice reflected both their personalities as strong leaders and their popularity with the voting public. More than most PMs, they became charismatic figures in their own right, and their campaigns looked more like U.S. presidential campaigns, with a great deal more attention to the individual attributes of the party leader than is traditional in Britain. As long as these two powerful PMs were personally popular, they could pursue the policies they desired; their cabinets and parties went along because they also benefited from the popular support showered on the PM. As Thatcher's and Blair's popularity waned, however, both faced increasing resistance, showing that democratic control

Opposition leaders in India's parliament leave a meeting with the country's president in May 2013. India's parliamentary system, like Britain's, gives strong formal powers to the ruling party. The opposition has little opportunity to change or prevent the ruling party's legislation from becoming law, but they do have an important role publicly voicing criticism as they campaign to replace the ruling party in the next election.

still exists in the British system. Many observers saw the 2010 election as furthering the "presidentialization" of the British PM, though. For the first time, the campaign featured American-style televised debates among the three main contenders.

In Britain, a vote of no confidence is extremely rare. A more common means of removing unpopular PMs is for the majority party to replace them. When Thatcher lost popularity in the late 1980s but refused to change her policies or call a new election, Conservative MPs feared their party's future was sinking along with her popularity. They voted to replace her with John Major, who immediately became PM. Britain had a new chief executive without holding a general election, a perfectly legitimate step in a parliamentary system. Similarly, Tony Blair left office in 2007 without holding an election, retiring and handing power to the new Labour Party leader, Gordon Brown.

Given the growing power of the PM, what powers does Parliament have? In Britain's **bicameral legislature,** the lower house, the House of Commons, has virtually all legislative power. The older upper house, the House of Lords, consists of members known as "peers"; these are appointees of the PM and aristocrats who inherited their positions. (In 1999 the Blair government ended the institution of "hereditary peers," allowing only a small minority to remain in office until further reforms.) The only significant power held by the House of Lords for many years was to act as a final court of appeal for individual cases, and the Constitutional Reform Act of 2005 removed even that, creating a new Supreme Court as the final court of appeal. The Commons, though, retains considerable power. As noted above, even the most powerful PMs must take account of the views of their party's MPs in the Commons, especially if the PM's popularity is waning.

Parliament also serves an important watchdog function. The PM must attend Parliament weekly for Question Time, a very lively, televised debate among the major politicians of the day. During Question Time, the PM is expected to respond to queries from MPs and defend the government's policies. In addition, MPs have the right to question cabinet ministers about the activities of their departments, who must respond personally in Parliament, giving a public airing of issues of concern, large and small. The House of Commons recently created more committees that hold hearings on proposed legislation. In the British system, the fate of legislation introduced by the government (the cabinet) is rarely in doubt, but the committees allow MPs to investigate the implications of proposed laws, and at times the ruling party will allow legislation to be amended if committees identify problems. MPs have powerful incentives to vote with their party leaders in order to rise through the ranks to greater power.

Since the 1970s, however, MPs have voted against their party more frequently, though this dissent still constitutes less than 10 percent of all parliamentary votes. Voting against the party leadership is a way for MPs to express their disagreement with the leaders, often to garner greater support from their voters back home, but generally not a means of preventing government legislation from passing (Kam 2009). Occasionally, though, Parliament does refuse to support the PM, such as when Cameron asked for authorization to bomb the Syrian government in response

bicameral legislature
A legislature that has two houses

to its use of chemical weapons in September 2013. In most such cases, the PM has previously stated that his party's MPs are free to vote their conscience (rather than the party position) on a particularly important and divisive issue. Even with the recent changes, the British Parliament does not modify legislation nearly as much as the U.S. Congress does. Nonetheless, the executive branch must pay attention to the opinions of the majority-party MPs, and both houses of Parliament provide a forum for active, and at times closely watched, public debate. The prime minister's formal powers may allow him to ignore this legislative activity, but his political survival requires that he attend to it closely. Informally, therefore, Parliament remains an important check on even the most powerful PM.

Despite few formal differences, the role and power of the Indian prime minister and parliament are significantly different from the British model on which it was based. The divergence between the systems is due mainly to differences in the number of parties in the two countries. Like Britain and most parliamentary systems, India's MPs almost always vote with their party. Unlike Britain, India has multiple parties rather than just two. One party dominated the government for the first forty years after the nation's independence, but no party has since enjoyed such a majority. No single party has won a majority of seats in parliament in the last twenty years, necessitating coalition governments.

For four decades, one-party dominance meant that PMs were far less constrained than their British counterparts. The Indian National Congress (commonly called the Congress) ruled nearly continuously from 1947 to 1989. The country's first prime minister, Jawaharlal Nehru (1947–1964), was a hero of the nationalist movement for independence and a deeply popular and respected figure. His cabinet consisted of leaders of the major factions within the ruling party and served as the actual governing body, debating policy as a cabinet is expected to in a parliamentary system. Shortly after his death, his daughter, Indira Gandhi (1966–1977, 1980–1984), was selected to lead the Congress and therefore became PM. She desired independence from the faction leaders within the party. With this goal in mind, she achieved much greater centralized control of the Congress and, consequently, the government. The Congress Party lost its dominant position after 1989, and every government since has been a coalition of one large party and a number of smaller ones. This has profoundly changed the role of the PM. He remains the central executive and by far most important leader in the country, but all PMs since 1989 have had to compromise with other parties in order to form a government, and governments have often been unstable. This is clearly seen in the number of PMs India has had: in its first thirty years of independence (1947–1977), the country had only three PMs; in its second thirty years (1977–2007), it had twelve, only three of whom served full terms.

The rise of coalition government has made small parties who negotiate membership in these coalitions quite important. Not surprisingly, this has meant that parliament has become less effective (Pelizzo 2010), parliament passes fewer laws now than it did under the dominance of the Congress, and MPs spend far less time there. Parties are more important for their votes in putting together a coalition government than they are for their legislative activity, and most of the 544 MPs are focused more on their states than on the national government. Many of the small parties have little support outside a particular state, so the political fortunes of many MPs are tied to their role in state-level politics more than they are to the national parliament. These small parties, in fact, often decide to join coalition governments based on the parties' interests at the state level rather than any ideological affinity with the national government. Furthermore, some agree to support the coalition in parliament informally but refuse to become a formal part of it. This makes it easier for them to vote against the government in particular situations and blame the government for its failures without putting blame on themselves. As political malfeasance has increased in India, being an MP has also become a means of gaining access to corruption opportunities. Indian watchdog groups reported that as of 2013, nearly a third of sitting MPs had been charged with a crime of some sort and, on average, MPs running for reelection in 2009 were 300 percent richer than they had been before the last election in 2004. In 2011, four MPs were even charged with accepting bribes to vote a certain way on a vote of no confidence in the government.

For all of these reasons, many Indians have bemoaned the "decline of parliament" as an institution, but B. L. Shankar and Valerian Rodrigues (2011) argued that the shifts in parliament (with the exception of corruption) and greater party fragmentation reflect the changing nature of Indian society: more groups are now represented, MPs themselves are more diverse and therefore don't always agree, and MPs are increasingly focused on their local constituents—not necessarily bad things in a democracy. Coalition governments have also allowed the opposition in parliament to be more assertive. Under the single-party dominance of the Congress, opposition parties were reduced to protests such as walkouts of parliament. Now, parliamentary committees in India have become stronger. Opposition MPs have also started regularly introducing their own legislation, something relatively rare in parliamentary systems because without some government support, legislation has virtually no chance of being passed. Virtually unheard of in the era of Congress dominance, opposition bills are now quite regular, and some manage to pass with a coalition of small parties supporting them. Similarly, parliamentary debate now more regularly features opposition MPs.

Web link:
"India Ink" on chaos in Parliament

CASESummary The Westminster model in its purest form is the most centralized form of liberal democratic governing institutions. It is the classic case of Lijphart's majoritarian democracy, with few veto players. Whether the model operates this way in fact depends, though, on a number of factors. Most important is the number and strength of parties, which we discuss more fully in chapter 7. Britain has only two strong parties, so one has ruled unimpeded most of the time. Vertical accountability clearly exists, but horizontal accountability is limited. The Indian system under Congress party dominance was equally majoritarian.

Since 1989, however, coalition government in India has substantially increased the potential veto players, adding a degree of consensual democracy.

CASE Questions

1. Based on the United Kingdom and India, what factors are most important in explaining why parliamentary systems operate differently in different countries?
2. Lijphart saw the "Westminster model" as the most marjoritarian of all systems. Why do some parliamentary systems support his claim but others do not?

presidentialism
A term denoting a presidential system of democracy in which the executive and legislature are elected independently and have separate and independent powers

separation of powers
Constitutionally explicit division of power among the major branches of government

Presidential Systems: The Separation of Powers

Presidentialism needs little introduction for American students because the best known and most enduring example is the United States. In a presidential system, the roles of head of state and head of government are filled by the same person, who is given the title "president." The crucial, defining aspect of a presidential system, however, is not this fusion of executive roles. Rather, it is the concept of **separation of powers.** The American founders argued that the functions of the executive and legislative branches should be separate, and everything about any presidential system reflects this choice, no matter how the particulars of any specific constitution may differ. This means that the executive and legislative branches are elected separately in their own (though possibly concurrent) elections, and the president must be independently and directly (or nearly directly) elected. Regardless of the electoral or party system in place, this institutional feature gives presidential systems an element of consensual democracy: institutional veto players are built into the founding documents of the system.

Some countries elect a president by plurality; others use a two-round system to achieve an absolute majority. No matter how the elections are administered, the important thing is that the president's legitimacy as head of state and government derives from an electoral process in which the entire nation participates. Similarly, the legislature's legitimacy arises from the direct election of the representatives, who should

CRITICAL inquiry

Parliaments and Presidents

Map 6.1 shows how many parliamentary, presidential, and semi-presidential systems exist today and where they are located. What patterns do you see in terms of where different systems have been adopted? What might explain those patterns? Which theoretical arguments from chapter 1 can help you explain the patterns? Choose a country that you think might not fit the patterns you've noticed and do some background research to figure out why it's different. What does that tell you about why countries choose particular institutions and not others?

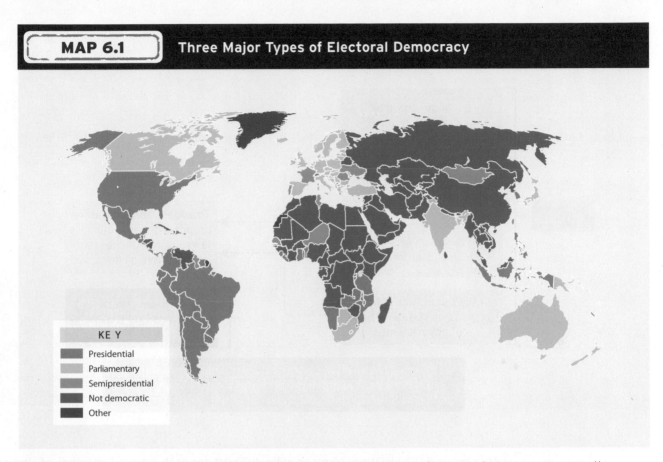

MAP 6.1   **Three Major Types of Electoral Democracy**

KEY

- Presidential
- Parliamentary
- Semipresidential
- Not democratic
- Other

Source: Data are from Freedom House, Freedom in the World 2013. (http://www.freedomhouse.org/report-types/freedom-world) and (http://en.wikipedia.org/wiki/File:Forms_of_government.svg). Modified by the authors.

therefore reflect the popular will. Even if the presidency and legislature are controlled by different parties, each is legitimized independently by the electoral process, and creating laws requires the agreement, in some way, of both the president and a majority in the legislature.

In contrast to parliamentary systems, presidents and their legislatures generally cannot interfere with one another's time in office. Presidents serve a fixed term, whether four years in the United States, Brazil, Chile, and Argentina; five years in Kenya; or six years in Mexico. During that fixed term, it is very difficult for a legislature to remove the president from office. Most countries make provision for some kind of impeachment process, but impeachment requires extraordinary measures and can only be justified in extreme circumstances. Barring this, no matter how much legislators disagree with the president or question his competence or policy, they cannot remove the executive from office. Similarly, legislators also have fixed terms.

Web link:
Presidential power

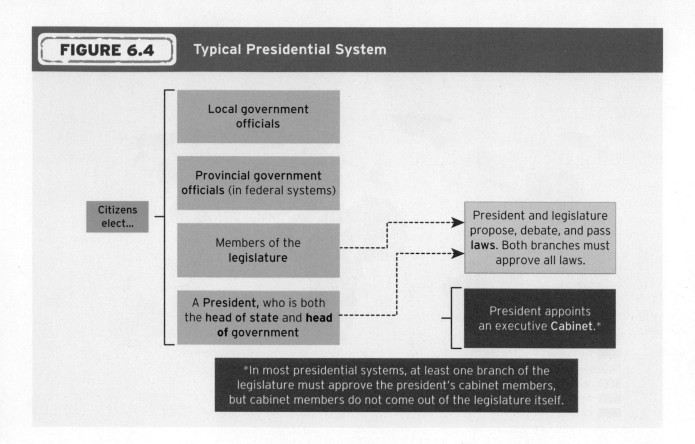

FIGURE 6.4   **Typical Presidential System**

Citizens elect...

- Local government officials
- **Provincial government officials** (in federal systems)
- Members of the **legislature** → **President and legislature** propose, debate, and pass **laws**. Both branches must approve all laws.
- A **President,** who is both the **head of state** and **head of** government → President appoints an executive **Cabinet.***

*In most presidential systems, at least one branch of the legislature must approve the president's cabinet members, but cabinet members do not come out of the legislature itself.

In a bicameral legislature, terms may be different for each house. Regardless of the details, a president may not tamper with a legislature's sessions by forcibly shortening or lengthening them.

Finally, the separation of powers is clear in the president's powers of appointment. Although presidents may need the consent of the legislature, they are largely free to appoint their own cabinet ministers or secretaries. They may, and in many cases (including the United States) must, appoint individuals who are not in the legislature. They may also appoint people from any party they wish. Their appointments need not reflect the composition of the legislature in any way. Once appointed and confirmed by the legislature, the officers serve at the president's pleasure, and the legislature can interfere only minimally with their activities. In practice, of course, most presidents try to appoint to their cabinet a group of people more or less representative of the major political factions in their party. The separation from the legislature, though, means they only do this to the extent they think is politically expedient, rather than being required to in order to form a government, as in a parliamentary system. Thus, the cabinet is typically a far less important decision-making body than in a parliamentary system. Also, because members of the legislature are not vying directly for cabinet appointments, the president has less control over them than a PM does, so the legislature becomes a more important and independent decision-making body. Ironically, this means that legislatures in presidential systems are typically more powerful than legislatures in parliamentary systems.

CASE Study

PRESIDENTIALISM IN THE UNITED STATES AND BRAZIL

Most countries in the Western Hemisphere have presidential systems, although the socioeconomic and political contexts of these systems vary widely, as the cases of the United States and Brazil show. While the formal rights and duties of each branch of government are somewhat different in the two systems, the informal power of the presidency varies even more because the office is set in very different political systems. In the United States, the office of the president was one of the more controversial parts of the Constitution when it was written. Many leaders, most notably Thomas Jefferson, feared that a single executive would inevitably become authoritarian, mimicking the British monarch from which the colonists had just won liberation. These fears might surprise contemporary Americans, for the office as originally designed was far more modest than what it has become. The president's main powers are (1) approving or vetoing legislation passed by Congress (Congress can override a veto with a two-thirds majority vote); (2) appointing cabinet secretaries and Supreme Court justices, other federal judges, and political appointees in the bureaucracy, subject to the Senate's approval; (3) serving as head of state and commander in chief of the armed forces; and (4) entering into treaties and declaring war, again subject to Senate approval.

On their own, these powers are modest by modern standards. The early presidents were certainly important, but they were not the central focus of national politics that the president has become today. Many of the most well-known presidents expanded the powers of the office. Ironically, this began with Thomas Jefferson,

- **EXECUTIVE POWER**
  Weak but growing over time; stronger with fewer parties, as in the United States

- **LEGISLATIVE POWER**
  Strong

- **ACCOUNTABILITY**
  Horizontal stronger

- **VETO PLAYERS**
  Built into system in legislature and executive

- **POLICYMAKING**
  Problems of gridlock in the United States and many weak parties in Brazil

- **RECENT TRENDS**
  Strengthening executive; greater gridlock in the United States; less in Brazil

Dilma Rousseff became Brazil's first woman president in 2010, replacing her mentor, the wildly popular Luis Inácio "Lula" da Silva. Although Brazil's president has great formal powers, she has severe limits on what she can accomplish because of the fragmented nature of Brazil's political parties and legislature.

who successfully proclaimed the right of the president to expand the country via the Louisiana Purchase. Starting with Andrew Jackson, the president became the de facto head of his party, giving him greater influence over Congress. In the twentieth century, Franklin Roosevelt created vast new social programs that increased the size and reach of the federal bureaucracy over which the president presides, and as the United States became a world superpower, the president's powers in foreign policy and war correspondingly gained importance as well.

The U.S. president ultimately has become the symbolic leader of the nation, the undisputed leader of his party, and both the chief initiator and implementer of legislation. The office has retained the symbolic legitimacy of all presidencies as the sole office for which every citizen votes, the embodiment of majority will, even though the individual selected by the Electoral College isn't always the individual who wins the most popular votes, as occurred in the 2000 presidential contest between Al Gore and George W. Bush. While legislation formally starts in Congress, in practice Congress looks to the president for major legislative initiatives; as the leader of his party who sits atop a vast technocratic bureaucracy, the president with his cabinet is in a better position politically and technically to formulate complicated legislation. Members of Congress initiate considerable legislation, but the most important legislation usually starts as a presidential initiative. The president's position as head of his party and chief fund-raiser also gives him great influence over legislators in his party. This is especially true when a president is popular: members of his party want to be closely associated with him and often yield to his desires to gain his support in the next election.

Individual legislators may vie for the president's approval, but the U.S. Congress as a body has substantial powers as well. Because legislators are independently elected, Congress jealously guards its autonomy from the executive branch. The U.S. House of Representatives and Senate have perhaps the most extensive and expensive staffs of any legislature in the world. Committees and subcommittees are crucial in investigating, amending, and passing legislation. Individual members have great freedom to introduce legislation compared with members of most national legislatures, and it's entirely possible that individual legislation will become law if it gains the support of the chairs of key committees or subcommittees. Most observers argue that the U.S. Congress is the most powerful legislature in the world, not only because it legislates on behalf of the most powerful country but because of its autonomy from the executive branch.

One direct result of the separation of powers is "gridlock," or the seeming inability to pass major legislation. This is a constant concern of contemporary American politics. The United States has only two major parties, but these parties are relatively weak; individual legislators are not beholden to party leaders, and they vote as they choose on each piece of legislation. This alone can occasionally produce gridlock, but stalemates are much more likely when one party controls the presidency and the other controls Congress, a common outcome of the U.S. presidential system. In this case, one of the president's main jobs has become trying to get his legislation passed, either by cajoling members of his own party to support him or by negotiating and compromising with the opposing party in Congress, especially when it is in the majority. The failure of this process produces gridlock.

When not trying to negotiate the maze of the legislative process, the U.S. president oversees a bureaucracy of thousands of people. Most are permanent civil servants, but several thousand at the top of the bureaucratic hierarchy serve at the president's pleasure. This gives the president great influence over the implementation of laws passed by Congress. Because no legislation can foresee every conceivable detail of implementation in today's technocratic society, the chief executive is given great latitude to enforce laws. For most of the nation's history, this power has been relatively uncontroversial; under President George W. Bush, however, this executive power became a subject of contention. Especially controversial were presidential "signing statements" that President Bush attached to more than one thousand provisions of legislation he signed into law. The precedent for such signing statements is quite old, but issuing signing statements only became frequent under Presidents Ronald Reagan and Bill Clinton in the 1980s and 1990s. The strongest of them, "constitutional signing statements," assert the president's authority not to enforce certain aspects of legislation because in his opinion they violate his constitutional powers. President Bush controversially asserted these rights via signing statements on legislation involving torture and treatment of prisoners of war. He contended that the legislation unduly restricted his ability to conduct war as commander in chief; his critics argued that Bush's signing statements unconstitutionally and unilaterally revoked parts of legislation with which he didn't agree, violating Congress's power to legislate. Despite criticizing Bush's action on the campaign trail, President Barack Obama had issued twenty signing statements by early 2013, in some cases reversing earlier Bush statements. Obama, on the other hand, has attempted to expand presidential power by aggressively issuing rules and regulations, especially during his second term. His frustration with a divided Congress that seemed unable to pass much legislation led him to adopt the slogan "We Can't Wait" to justify issuing executive orders on a wide array of policies. These included important policies regarding global warming as well as twenty-three new regulations designed to restrict gun access in the wake of the tragic shooting deaths at an elementary school in Newtown, Connecticut. These controversial assertions of powers by presidents of both parties are only the latest salvos in a two-hundred-year battle over the power of the U.S. presidency.

The fears of Thomas Jefferson were partly justified: the presidency of the United States is a very powerful office. On the one hand, the separation of powers in the presidential system, particularly in the context of relatively weak parties in the United States, limits what presidents can do. On the other hand, presidents' leadership of their party and control over foreign policy and thousands of key appointments give them far greater powers than many of the authors of the Constitution envisioned. This divided power in the context of a very old democracy with well-established

Web link:
Why the Obama administration has issued fewer signing statements

Video link:
Are signing statements an abuse of presidential power?

institutions and only two main parties produces a system that is often seen as slow to make policy, but the system is nonetheless well institutionalized, a crucial context for effective relations among the separate branches in a presidential system.

Presidentialism, however, can look very different when transplanted to different geographic, social, and institutional settings, as the example of Brazil shows. As in most of Latin America, Brazil's democratic regimes have always been presidential. The current system dates to a constitution approved in 1988. Brazil's president has more extensive formal powers than her U.S. counterpart, but a legislature with many weak political parties and the most decentralized federal system in the world make these powers substantially less effective than they appear on paper. Recent presidents, though, have managed to use incentives and growing discipline within the major parties to strengthen the presidency. Brazil's president is directly chosen in a two-round election: if no candidate wins an absolute majority on the first vote, a second vote takes place two weeks later between the top two candidates. Originally, the president could serve only a single five-year term. Constitutional amendments subsequently reduced the term to four years so it would coincide with legislative elections and allowed one reelection. The last two presidents, Fernando Henrique Cardoso and Luiz Inácio "Lula" da Silva, both were reelected to second terms. Presidents otherwise have the typical powers of the office in a presidential system: head of state and government, commander in chief of the armed forces, and appointment powers. In Brazil they also have several unusual powers: (1) the authority to issue "provisional decrees" (PDs), which become law for thirty days unless the National Congress approves them permanently; (2) a line-item veto, which allows a president to eliminate individual measures in a bill sent from the National Congress without vetoing the entire law; and (3) a monopoly over initiation of all legislation involving the budget.

Brazilian presidents must operate in a multiparty system with many fragmented parties. Because of Brazil's electoral system, politicians have little incentive to form broad, inclusive parties or to follow party leaders once they are in the National Congress. Both houses of Brazil's bicameral legislature, the Chamber of Deputies (the lower house) and the Senate (the upper house), include numerous parties. After the 2010 election, the Chamber of Deputies included twenty-two parties, the biggest of which—the president's party—had only 17 percent of the seats. The only way for presidents to get their legislation passed is to build coalitions among several parties. Indeed, in the last few elections, several parties have supported the two major presidential candidates, a result of preelection negotiations regarding sharing power after the election. After the election, the president appoints members of parties supporting her to the cabinet and other major offices, like a prime minister would in a parliamentary system. Indeed, Timothy Power (2010) termed the Brazilian case "coalitional presidentialism"; presidents essentially put together coalition governments like those in parliamentary systems, although the weakness of Brazil's parties means presidents still can have difficulty getting legislators to vote the way they want.

Presidents can also use the line-item veto to negotiate with individual legislators to gain their support for particular bills. As in the United States, Brazilian legislators engage in "pork-barrel" politics; that is, they seek to include specific spending projects for their home areas in the national budget. This is the contemporary continuation of a long Brazilian tradition of patronage politics in which elected officials bring home government resources as a primary means of gaining support. The president's line-item veto, however, allows the executive to decide which of these individual items to keep and which to eliminate, so she can exchange approval of a legislator's pet project for support on a crucial piece of legislation.

The first president directly elected under the 1988 constitution, whose party had only 3 percent of the seats in the Chamber of Deputies, ruled largely through PDs, issuing 150 of them in his first year in office. Often, when one expired, he would simply reissue it the next day, essentially making it last as long as he pleased. Brazil's Supreme Court never ruled against this practice, despite its dubious constitutionality. Subsequent presidents recognized the need to include the National Congress and used the various negotiation strategies to pass legislation. In 2001 the Brazilian Congress passed a reform to limit the president's ability to reissue PDs and to discourage their use altogether. Although the law severely limited reissuing PDs, their use actually increased. Cardoso doubled the rate of PDs he issued after the law passed, and his successor, Lula, increased them another 50 percent. The fractiousness of Congress encourages Brazilian presidents to make use of their unilateral power.

Overall, however, the powers of Brazil's president remain limited. Major presidential proposals often fail to pass the National Congress, and of those that do, virtually all are modified. Each piece of legislation requires extensive horse trading (or bargaining), not only with party leaders but also with individual legislators looking for favors. Early in Lula's first term, his administration combined not only cabinet seats and provision of "pork" to gain legislative victories, but added illegal payments to some legislators to gain their support, which erupted into a major corruption scandal that cost some of Lula's closest aides and several members of Congress their jobs. Pereira et al. (2011) argued that, while reprehensible, it was a logical extension of the situation in which the Brazilian president found himself: he had an ambitious legislative agenda and was not able to manipulate the legal means of bargaining adequately to get his proposals passed into law. Dilma Rousseff, elected to succeed Lula in 2010 and Brazil's first woman president, is, like Lula, from the Workers' Party (PT), which is the most united and ideologically driven party in the country. Although the PT's seats increased slightly in 2010, compromise with coalition partners is still key for Rousseff. Very slowly the Brazilian presidency and parties are becoming stronger institutions as the possibility of presidential reelection and limits on PDs give incentives for greater cooperation among the branches of government. Governance, though, remains a slow and difficult process in a presidential system with ineffectual and fragmented parties. Brazil's federalism also weakens the power of the presidency, a subject we will return to.

Web link:
Brazil's executive-legislative relations under the Dilma Coalition government

CASE Summary   The United States and Brazil both have certain inherent institutionalized veto players, a characteristic they share with all presidential systems. The bargaining necessary among branches of government, especially when they are controlled by differing parties, creates a degree of consensual democracy. How much this serves as a form of horizontal accountability depends very much on context. As in parliamentary systems, the number and strength of political parties matter; Brazil's fragmented legislature with many, weak parties produces numerous potential veto players. In the U.S. system, the president is more powerful, but again can be strongly checked by a Congress controlled by the opposing party. In both countries, the powers of the presidency have tended to increase, reflecting the continuing concerns about limited executive authority in modern democracies.

CASE Questions

1. Many comparativists argue that presidential systems are ineffective at making policy. Based on Brazil and the United States, what are the most important factors influencing how true that is?
2. The writers of the U.S. Constitution worried that executive power would become too great and erode democracy. Based on our two case studies, to what extent was that a valid concern?

Semipresidentialism: The Hybrid Compromise

semipresidentialism
A term denoting a semipresidential system of democracy in which executive power is divided between a directly elected president and a prime minister elected by a parliament

The third major executive-legislative system is the most recently created. **Semipresidentialism** splits executive power between an elected president and a prime minister. The president is elected directly by the citizens as in a presidential system and serves as the head of state, but she also has significant powers in running the government. The official head of government is the PM, who is the leader of the majority party or coalition in parliament, as in a parliamentary system. The PM is appointed by the president but must also obtain majority support in the parliament. Legislation requires the signature of the president, as well as support of the PM as head of the ruling party or coalition in parliament. The parliament can force the PM and cabinet to resign through a vote of no confidence. For semipresidentialism to be successful, the powers and duties of the president and PM as dual executives must be spelled out clearly in the constitution. For example, the president may be given power over military decisions (as in Sri Lanka) or foreign policy (as in Finland), whereas the prime minister typically concentrates on domestic policies. The specific division of powers varies greatly, however, and is not always clearly delineated.

The semipresidential system originated in France in the 1958 constitution establishing the Fifth Republic. Charles de Gaulle, a World War II hero and undisputed political leader of France at the time, envisioned the presidency as a stabilizing and powerful position, legitimated via national election. He assumed that the same party

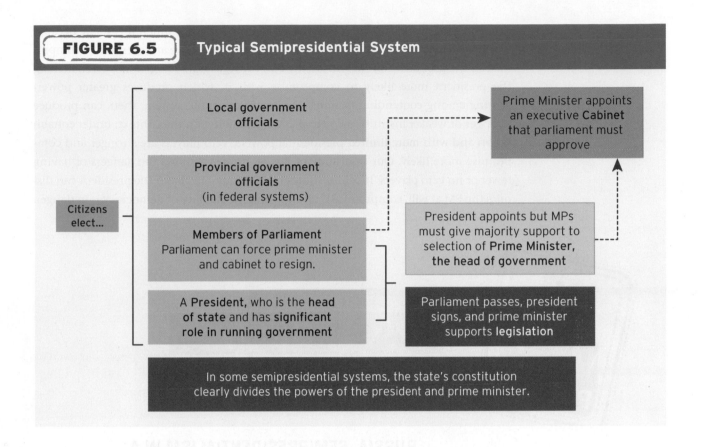

FIGURE 6.5 **Typical Semipresidential System**

Citizens elect...

Local government officials

Provincial government officials (in federal systems)

Members of Parliament
Parliament can force prime minister and cabinet to resign.

A **President,** who is the **head of state** and has **significant role in running government**

Prime Minister appoints an executive **Cabinet** that parliament must approve

President appoints but MPs must give majority support to selection of **Prime Minister, the head of government**

Parliament passes, president signs, and prime minister supports **legislation**

In some semipresidential systems, the state's constitution clearly divides the powers of the president and prime minister.

would win the presidency and a legislative majority. So long as it did, semipresidentialism gave the president, as head of the majority party who also appoints the PM, unparalleled power to govern.

This worked as intended until the 1980s, when for the first time the president was elected from one party and the majority of the legislature from another, a situation the French humorously call **cohabitation.** Under cohabitation, the president must compromise with the legislature by appointing a PM from the majority party in the legislature rather than from his own party. A compromise had to be worked out regarding the specific powers of the president and the PM, since the French constitution did not draw clear boundaries. In practice, the compromise has been that the president runs foreign policy while the PM and the legislature control domestic policy. Critics of semipresidentialism fear that it gives the president too much power, but cohabitation clearly limits those powers significantly. If a majority in the legislature is elected in opposition to the president, he is forced to accept the results and live with cohabitation and the limits it imposes. However, cohabitation can also produce gridlock and inability to legislate effectively, as in a purely presidential system.

In addition to cohabitation, a second crucial institutional question in semipresidential systems is whether the president has the power to remove the PM. Robert Elgie

cohabitation
Sharing of power between a president and prime minister from different parties in a semipresidential system

(2011) argued that if he does, the semipresidential system is much less stable because neither the president nor the majority in parliament will have an incentive to compromise. If the president cannot remove the PM, the legislature has greater power, making the president more likely to compromise with it, which produces greater power-sharing among contending factions. The semipresidential system, then, can produce stronger or weaker institutional veto players depending on the context: under cohabitation and with more limited presidential powers, veto players are stronger and compromise more likely. Our case study of Russia, however, shows the dangers of having fewer or no veto players; it demonstrates Elgie's argument that if the president can dismiss the PM at will, compromise is unlikely and the stability of democracy is in danger.

CASE Study

RUSSIA: SEMIPRESIDENTIALISM IN A NEW DEMOCRACY WITH WEAK INSTITUTIONS

- **EXECUTIVE POWER**
  Initially strong, now nearly unlimited; appoints and can remove PM

- **LEGISLATIVE POWER**
  Very weak; minimal appointment powers compared with most semipresidential systems; cabinet ministers do not need to be members of legislature

- **ACCOUNTABILITY**
  Minimal

- **VETO PLAYERS**
  None

- **POLICYMAKING**
  Strong, but centered almost entirely in executive

- **RECENT TRENDS**
  Under Putin, even further expansion of presidential powers

Russia is the largest country in the world with a semipresidential system, and it is certainly one of the most important. Its current government demonstrates the worst fears of the system's critics: that in a regime with weak institutions, a powerful presidency can be dangerous to democracy by allowing one official to achieve overwhelming power. This executive dominance is not inherent in all semipresidential systems, as France demonstrates, but Russia is a cautionary case of the problem of a strong presidency in a new democracy with weak institutions.

The Russian constitution adopted in 1993 created a semipresidential system with an exceptionally strong presidency. The president is directly elected to a six-year term (it was a four-year term until a 2012 constitutional amendment), with a maximum of two terms possible. He must be elected by an absolute majority: if no candidate wins a majority in the first election, a second is held between the top two candidates. The president appoints the prime minister with the approval of the parliament, the Duma, but if the Duma votes against the president's candidate for PM three times, it is automatically dissolved and new elections are called. This means that unless the president's opponents in the Duma think they will gain from an election, they will be very hesitant to oppose his nominee. The president also appoints all cabinet members,

Are two chief executives better than one? Dmitry Medvedev (right) was Vladimir Putin's prime minister and succeeded him as president in 2008. Putin then became Medvedev's prime minister, leading some observers to wonder who really was in charge. In 2012 Putin returned as president and Medvedev once again became a much weakened prime minister, as it became clear that Putin had retained the greatest power throughout.

who do not need approval by the Duma. Neither the PM nor the rest of the cabinet need to be members of the Duma, and the vast majority have not been. The Russian system, then, does not link the president and parliament via the PM and cabinet as fully as the original French model. This structure frees the president to appoint anyone he pleases to the cabinet, regardless of which party controls parliament. Furthermore, the president has direct control over several key ministries (Foreign Affairs, Defense, and Interior) and the Federal Security Service, the successor to the KGB; in these areas, his authority bypasses the PM and the cabinet altogether. Perhaps most important, the president can issue decrees that have the force of law and cannot be vetoed by the

in CONTEXT

Semipresidential Systems

Semipresidentialism spread rapidly in the 1990s with the wave of democratization in Africa and eastern Europe. Between 1990 and 1992, the number of semipresidential systems worldwide increased from ten to thirty-nine, and by 2010 there were fifty-two (Elgie 2011). Fifteen are former colonies of two semipresidential European countries, France and Portugal. Freedom House rated twenty-two semipresidentialist countries "free" in 2010, seventeen as partly free, and thirteen as not free.

Region	Number of semipresidential regimes	Free	Partly free	Not free
Africa	17	4	6	7
Americas	2	1	1	0
Asia	4	2	2	0
Europe*	24	15	5	4
Middle East	5	0	3	2

Sources: Data are from Robert Elgie, *Semi-Presidentialism: Sub-Types and Democratic Performance* (London: Oxford University Press, 2011), 24; Freedom House, Freedom in the World 2013 (http://www.freedomhouse.org/report-types/freedom-world).

Duma or challenged in court, which gives him the power to rule without legislative support. A constitutional amendment in 2000 also gave the president the power to appoint and dismiss all governors of Russia's eighty-nine regions (see the section on federalism below), who in turn appoint half of the members of the upper house of parliament. Election of governors was restored in 2012, but the law was then amended in 2013 to allow appointment in certain circumstances, returning significant power to the president. The Duma can vote no confidence in the prime minister but must do so twice to remove him from office. It can also impeach the president by a two-thirds vote, but it has only attempted to do so once, in 1999, and failed.

Russia's two major post-Communist presidents, Boris Yeltsin (1991–2000) and Vladimir Putin (2000–2008, 2012–), used the powers of the presidency quite differently. Yeltsin was the hero of the post-Communist revolution. He led the opposition to an attempted Soviet military coup in August 1991, which ultimately resulted in the demise of the Soviet Union. He also was the architect of the 1993 constitution. His rule, however, was chaotic. Because he was not a member of any political party, he was unable to marshal strong support for his reforms. For most of his presidency, his chief opposition was the former Communist Party, which had a plurality (but not a majority) of seats in the Duma. Yeltsin fought many battles with a hostile parliament and often enacted laws by decree. His war with parliament came to a head in 1999, when the Communists attempted to impeach him on charges of illegally prosecuting a war against the breakaway region of Chechnya and engaging in corruption. He appointed seven prime ministers over his tenure and more than two hundred cabinet ministers. His final prime minister was Putin, whom he anointed as his successor as president; Yeltsin actually resigned as president prior to the 2000 election in order to let Putin run as the incumbent.

Putin, a former KGB agent and leader, would prove to be a much stronger president than Yeltsin ever was, winning 53 percent of the vote in the first-round election in 2000. In the 2003 Duma election, his followers organized a new party, United Russia, which won control of parliament and proceeded to pass every major bill he submitted. He used his powers of decree and control over the prosecution of corruption to eliminate many of the "oligarchs" who had arisen under Yeltsin and come to control major sectors of the economy, replacing them with his supporters or taking direct state control of some companies. He also severely restricted nongovernment sources of media. After winning the 2004 election with more than 70 percent of the vote, he reformed the constitution to also gain effective control over the country's regional governments and, therefore, the upper house of the legislature. Facing a constitutional limit of two terms as president, Putin anointed Dmitry Medvedev as his successor, who was duly elected in May 2008. Putin himself became head of his ruling party in the Duma and PM and unofficially remained the chief leader of the country. Observers speculated as to whether Medvedev could use the great formal powers of the presidency to change Putin's policies. While Medvedev made numerous speeches suggesting he would fight corruption and move the country in a more democratic direction, no major policies ensued. As PM, Putin retained the personal loyalty of the majority of the Duma; no significant policy changes would occur without his support. Having created the vast formal powers of the presidency, Putin showed that his informal powers as the leader who had put virtually the entire political elite into office trumped even the powerful presidency, officially in Medvedev's hands.

After a term as prime minister, Putin was legally eligible to begin another term as president in 2012. He and Medvedev "agreed" to switch roles, with Putin running for and winning the presidency and Medvedev becoming prime minister again. This election, though, was not the overwhelming victory that the 2004 and 2008 elections had been; Putin won only 65 percent of the vote even though he had legally eliminated most serious opposition contenders, and the parliamentary majority of his party was reduced from 70 to 53 percent of the seats in the Duma. The election took place amidst large-scale opposition demonstrations, dismay that he was extending his time in office, and domestic and international charges of electoral fraud. Passing laws that massively increased penalties for unauthorized gatherings, Putin cracked down on opposition demonstrations against him, which were growing in Moscow in spring 2012. He adopted an increasingly strident nationalist ideology, proclaiming the greatness of Russia's past, rejecting Western democratic norms, and giving greater prominence to the Russian Orthodox Church.

Web link:
Robert Elgie
on Russian
semipresidentialism

CASE Summary   Putin used the already strong presidency in Russia's semipresidential system to amass great presidential and personal power in Russia's weakly institutionalized regime. His use of appointments, constitutional changes, control of the economy, and restrictions on political freedoms gave him so much unilateral control that most analysts argue Russia is no longer a true democracy but instead is a semi-authoritarian regime, which we examine in detail in chapter 9. The constitution, especially as amended by Putin, gives the president great powers; even if the legislature were controlled by an opposition party, its ability to act as a veto player would be limited, though not altogether absent. The Russian case, then, raises the worst fears about an excessively strong presidency in a semipresidential system that arises in the context of weak institutions in a new democracy. Formally, the system is designed to have elements of both vertical and horizontal accountability, but Putin's exercise of control over the electoral system to create a dominant ruling party with no effective opposition has nearly eliminated both.

CASE Questions

1. Some comparativists argue that the detailed logic of formal institutions is frequently not the most important element to understand in a political system. Instead, we ought to focus on how strong institutions are, regardless of how they are organized. What does our case study of Russia suggest about this argument?

2. In Russia, the semipresidential system clearly has not been very effective at enhancing accountability. Is this outcome inherent in semipresidential systems, or is it the result of specific factors in Russia?

COMPARING EXECUTIVE-LEGISLATIVE INSTITUTIONS

In comparing parliamentary, presidential, and semipresidential systems, comparativists ask three major questions: Which system is most democratic in the sense of providing greatest accountability? Which system is most effective at making public policy? Which system provides the greatest political stability for a democratic regime? All three systems provide vertical accountability in that major leaders are subject to electoral sanction by voters. The question is, How frequent and effective is this vertical accountability? Also, how much horizontal accountability exists? Lijphart (1999) argued that the more majoritarian systems provide less representation and accountability because power is so concentrated; on the other hand, concentration of power could well make policymaking easier. More consensual systems tend to be just the opposite: the distribution of power among major parties and institutions makes more robust horizontal accountability, often based on the presence of veto players, but may threaten effective policymaking.

Accountability

In all three types of executive-legislative systems, a trade-off often exists between vertical and horizontal accountability. In theory, the Westminster system, the most purely majoritarian system, is extremely democratic because it makes the legislature, the elected body of the people, supreme. In practice, the question of accountability is far more complex. First, much depends on the electoral system and number of parties. In multiparty systems such as contemporary India, parliamentarism may be more consensual, promoting negotiation, coalition building, and representation of a wide range of views in the cabinet. In a primarily two-party system like Britain's, however, in which one party almost always has a majority of parliamentary seats, the PM may be an unusually powerful executive because he is guaranteed legislative support. Some critics also argue that the modern world, particularly given the rise of television and other media, has strengthened the hand of the PM. Prime ministers are becoming similar to presidents—presidents who always have a legislative majority—and therefore vest too much power in the hands of a single individual. One the other hand, Powell (2000) argued this can provide greater vertical accountability: at election time citizens know whom to hold responsible for government policy.

Presidentialism seems to have greater horizontal accountability because of the separation of powers. The independent legislature can limit the president's prerogatives on a regular basis, and the individual elected members of the legislature are likely to have more influence on policymaking than under a parliamentary system. Again, how true this is depends in part on the nature of parties. A presidential system with strong parties that vote in lockstep and in which the president's party has a majority in the legislature will function much like a parliamentary system with a strong majority party. On the other hand, a presidential system with weaker parties (as in the United

States) or with a divided government (with the presidency and legislature controlled by different parties) provides for much greater horizontal accountability, though perhaps at the expense of effective policymaking. Many analysts claim the United States has faced this problem regularly in recent years.

Similarly, accountability in semipresidential systems depends on the strength and number of parties and the president's powers. If the president heads a strong party that controls a majority of the legislature, little horizontal accountability exists, though vertical accountability may be clearer. On the other hand, if a party opposed to the president controls the legislature, as under cohabitation in France in the 1980s, the president will have to compromise regularly with the prime minister. In this situation, horizontal accountability increases via more veto players.

Video link:
Indian MP argues that presidentialism would be better for India

Policymaking

Making public policy effectively in a democracy always requires compromise. A parliamentary system in which the PM's party controls a majority of the legislature is generally thought to be most effective at making policy precisely for the same reason critics say it is less democratic: there are no institutional constraints on the ruling party's actions. This allows it to decide what policies it wishes to pursue and make them law relatively quickly, compromising very little with opponents. Of course, the ruling party's members will ultimately face voters' judgment, but in the short term they face no formal constraints. Many observers contend this explains why PM Margaret Thatcher in the United Kingdom changed economic policies in a monetarist direction so much more successfully than did U.S. president Ronald Reagan, elected at about the same time and with a very similar ideology. Thatcher had a majority in Parliament who passed her proposals more or less without question, while Republican Reagan spent much of his term with a Democratic majority in Congress with whom he had to compromise.

In a parliamentary system with a coalition government, however, policymaking requires more compromises. For years, small parties representing ultra-Orthodox Jews were essential members of the cabinet in Israel's coalition governments. They used this power to bargain for passage of legislation exempting their sons from mandatory military service if they are studying the Torah. After the 2013 election, however, the prime minister managed to put together a coalition without them, and changes to the unpopular law were quickly passed.

In a review of the political science literature on this question, David Samuels (2007) concluded that overall, presidential systems are less likely to change the status quo via legislation, and when they do, change will take longer and be more expensive than in parliamentary systems. In semipresidential systems, much depends on whether the president, PM, and parliamentary majority are from the same party. If so, little compromise will likely be necessary. If one or more are from different parties, compromise is more essential and successful policymaking less likely. This, of course, makes short-term horizontal accountability stronger.

Video link:
Congressional gridlock in Congress over immigration

Stability

The biggest debate in recent years among comparativists examining these institutions has been over whether one system is more stable than another. Political scientist Juan Linz (1990) initiated the debate, arguing that presidentialism has many potential disadvantages. He saw the separation of powers as leading to what he called "dual legitimacy." Since both the legislature and the executive are independently and directly elected, each has legitimacy. Linz thought that since neither had a higher claim to legitimacy, there could be no democratic resolution of conflicts between them. He also argued that the direct election of the president could lead to chief executives with a "winner-take-all" mentality who would overemphasize their national mandate and be less willing to compromise; in this sense, he saw them as tending to be more majoritarian than consensual. Finally, Linz claimed that presidentialism is too inflexible: fixed terms mean that any serious problem for which a president might need to be removed—or even a president's death in office—could provoke a political crisis, as happened in Nigeria in 2010.

Following Linz, most scholarship has found that presidentialism is likely to be more crisis-prone and threatening to the survival of a new democracy than is parliamentarism (Samuels 2007). This is much more likely to be true, however, in a multiparty system, especially if the president does not have a working majority in the legislature. The smaller the size of the president's party and the greater the overall fragmentation of the legislature, the greater the likelihood of regime collapse in presidential systems (Samuels 2007). Linz's critics argue that presidential institutions themselves are not the problem. After extensive quantitative analysis, political scientist José Antonio Cheibub concluded that the society, not the institution, is the problem. Presidential systems "tend to exist in societies where democracies of any type are likely to be unstable" (2007, 3). All of these concerns are relatively muted in a more established democracy in which regime collapse does not seem to be a real possibility. In those cases, the fixed terms of the presidential system, some argue, provide greater continuity and stability, especially compared with some of the more fragmented parliamentary systems with many parties, like Italy or Israel.

Semipresidentialism, with its combination of a parliament and president, seems more difficult to analyze. On the one hand, Linz argued semipresidentialism poses the dangers of the strong presidency—dual legitimacy and unwillingness to compromise. On the other hand, the PM's dependence on parliament means that her cabinet will, if necessary, reflect a coalition of parties in a fractionalized system and allow a degree of flexibility not found in pure presidential systems. Empirical research has found that while the specific powers of the president in semipresidential systems are important (presidents should not be allowed to override the legislature or dismiss the PM), these systems are no less stable than parliamentary systems, even under cohabitation (Schleiter and Morgan-Jones 2009). Furthermore, voters in semipresidential systems are quite capable of assigning responsibility for policies to particular officials, in spite of the dual executive, making accountability clear, and semi-presidential systems seem just as capable of making policy decisions as other systems.

Executive-legislative institutions are at the heart of the biggest debates over how well democracies represent and govern their citizens. The effects of different institutional arrangements often appear reasonably clear in the abstract, but in practice the social, cultural, and political contexts make analysis much more complex. This complexity means that debates over democracies' varying effectiveness will continue to be a major subject of research in comparative politics for some time to come.

JUDICIARY

The judiciary is the least studied branch of government in comparative politics, which is unfortunate since it is becoming more important in many countries. On a daily basis, the job of the judiciary is to enforce a state's laws. Its more important political role, however, is to interpret those laws, especially the constitution. Most democracies have some version of **judicial review**, the authority of the judiciary to decide whether a specific law contradicts a country's constitution. Vested in unelected judges, this makes the court a veto player in the political system. It is clearly a potential means to limit majority rule and achieve horizontal accountability, but it also raises a fundamental question: Why should unelected officials have such power? How much power they actually have, though, depends not only on formal rules but also on the strength of the judiciary as an institution. New democracies have often had to build new judicial institutions, and the weakness of these has become a major concern in comparative politics. In this section, we discuss judicial review and its relationship to democracy, the judicialization of politics, and the question of judicial independence and institutional strength.

Dossiers await processing in Ecuadorean courts in 2011. Inefficient and poorly institutionalized judiciaries harm accountability and the rule of law in democracies. In Ecuador, the president declared a state of emergency in order to restructure the judiciary.

judicial review
The authority of the judiciary to decide whether a specific law contradicts a country's constitution

Judicial Review and the "Judicialization" of Politics

Two legal systems, common law and code law, emerged in modern Europe and spread to most of the world via colonialism (see Map 6.2). **Common law** developed in the United Kingdom and was adopted in most former British colonies, including the United States (it is sometimes referred to as Anglo-American law). Under common law, judges base decisions not only on their understanding of the written law but also on their understanding of past court cases. When a judge finds a law ambiguous,

common law
Legal system originating in Britain in which judges base decisions not only on their understanding of the written law but also on their understanding of past court cases; in contrast to code law

MAP 6.2   Code- versus Common-Law Countries

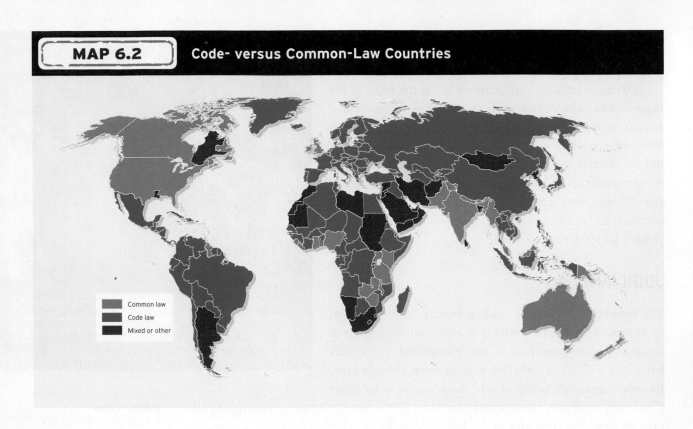

Common law
Code law
Mixed or other

---

stare decisis
Literally, "let the decision stand"; in common law, the practice of accepting the precedent of previous similar cases

code law
Legal system originating in ancient Roman law and modified by Napoleon Bonaparte in France in which judges may only follow the law as written and must ignore past decisions; in contrast to common law

he can write a ruling that tries to clarify it, and subsequent judges are obliged to use this ruling as precedent in deciding similar cases. This is known as the principle of ***stare decisis.***

Code law is most closely associated with the French emperor Napoleon Bonaparte, who codified it in what became known as the Napoleonic Code. (It is also known as Continental, or civil, law.) Under code law, which has its origins in ancient Roman law and was spread in modern Europe via Napoleon's conquests, judges may only follow the law as written, interpreting it as little as necessary to fit the case. Past decisions are irrelevant, as each judge must look only to the existing law. Like common law, code law spread globally via colonialism, especially to former French, Spanish, and Portuguese colonies.

The two systems logically led to different kinds of judicial review. Common-law countries, such as the United States, usually have decentralized judicial review: the same courts that handle everyday criminal cases can also rule on constitutional issues and can do so at any level. If a constitutional question begins in a lower court, it can be appealed upward, ultimately to the highest court. Code-law countries usually have centralized judicial review: a special court handles constitutional questions. Another important distinction is the question of who can initiate cases. Most common-law systems, including that of the United States, have concrete judicial review: only someone who has actually been negatively affected by the law in question can initiate a case. Most code-law systems have abstract judicial review; certain public officials or major political groups can call on the courts to make a constitutional ruling even before the law is fully in effect. The length of appointments to whatever court handles judicial review is also important. Some countries have lifetime appointments; others limit judges' terms.

The fundamental question about judicial review in a democracy is why judges, who are typically not elected and therefore not subject to vertical accountability, should be allowed to make decisions with major political consequences. Proponents argue that the difference in democratic legitimacy between judges and elected officials is far less sharply defined than is often assumed. First, legislatures and executives are never perfectly representative or accountable, so the difference between them and the judiciary may be less than it first appears. Second, the judiciary's horizontal accountability to executives and legislatures can be seen as an indirect source of democratic accountability. Judges are typically appointed by elected officials, so their stands on issues reflect the ideas of those officials and their constituents. Robert Dahl, one of the foremost scholars of democracy, argued in a widely read 1957 article that U.S. Supreme Court justices are part of political coalitions just as elected officials are and that they reflect the same political divisions that divide elected officials. Advocates of judicial review also argue that even if the judiciary is an imperfect democratic institution, it plays several crucial roles. It provides a check on executive and legislative power, serving as a mechanism of horizontal accountability. In the United States, many argue as well that judicial review exists to protect minority rights that might be trampled by a legislature or executive acting on majority opinion. In practice, however, most studies have shown that courts are more likely to rule in favor of those in power than on behalf of marginalized or oppressed minorities.

However one answers the questions raised by judicial review, it is certainly becoming more widespread, a process that Tate and Vallinder called the "judicialization" of politics. They argued that judicialization is "one of the most significant trends in late-twentieth and early-twenty-first-century government" (1995, 5). Taylor (2008) argued that this is happening not only because the judiciary has chosen to act as a veto player but also because other political actors increasingly use the judicial system to conduct their policy battles, making the judicial venue a "veto point."

Judicial Independence and Institutional Strength

Under any legal system, new or old, the judiciary must constitute a strong institution if it is to carry out its function properly in a system of horizontal accountability. Judicial review only matters in practice to the extent the key courts are willing and able to act independently of the other branches of government. This requires **judicial independence,** the belief and ability of judges to decide cases as they think

Web link:
Code law and common law

judicial independence
The belief and ability of judges to decide cases as they think appropriate, regardless of what other people, and especially politically powerful officials or institutions, desire

appropriate, regardless of what other politically powerful officials or institutions desire. Judicial systems that lack independence are weak institutions in which corruption is common; judges may accept bribes to decide cases in a particular way or refuse to rule against powerful individuals. This can affect everyday criminal and civil cases as well as constitutional questions. No particular formal procedure or power guarantees judicial independence, though Ferejohn and Pasquino (2003) found that the distinct constitutional courts common in code-law countries are particularly independent and effective.

What undoubtedly matters most to judicial independence, though, is informal factors that help make formal independence real in practice. Any number of factors can influence how much courts can actually practice the official powers granted them. Ferejohn, Rosenbluth, and Shipan (2007) argued that political fragmentation is key: countries with more fragmented political systems provide more political space for the judiciary to act independently. For instance, a presidential system's division of the executive and legislature raises the possibility of a divided government in which the judiciary may feel it can act more independently because the other branches disagree with one another. A parliamentary system with many parties that requires a coalition government can create a similar context for judicial independence. Judicial independence is less likely when courts do not feel they have the power to counter a strong majority consensus among elected officials.

A study of post-Communist countries found that even where judicial review is well established in the constitution, high courts use it rarely and warily, in part because they lack legitimacy and therefore do not believe themselves to be strong enough to withstand pressure from more powerful officials. Given that the judiciary lacks both military and financial resources, legitimacy is crucial to its institutional strength; without widespread support and acceptance on the part of other officials and the general populace, the judiciary has little power. Gibson, Caldeira, and Baird (1998) found that judiciaries typically gain legitimacy only over time as the populace comes to understand their role more fully and is satisfied with key court decisions. Leading judges are often acutely aware of this and act on cases in ways designed to enhance the institutional strength of the judiciary when the opportunity arises; judges' actions, no less than other political leaders', can at times be understood via rational-choice theory (Hirschl 2009). Diana Kapiszewski (2012) made a historical institutionalist argument that greater judicial ability to stand up to the executive successfully comes from informal institutions within the judiciary that gain it greater legitimacy and professionalization. These institutions arise in particular political contexts that give political leaders incentives to allow their initial development, and once created they tend to endure. As we will see in the case study of Brazil and in chapter 9, the institutional strength of the judiciary in new democracies, and therefore judicial independence, is often a problem.

CASE Study

THE JUDICIARY: BRAZIL

Brazil's relatively young democracy does not have one of the world's strongest judicial systems, but the judiciary has nonetheless achieved what many courts have not: a degree of judicial independence that has partially curbed executive and legislative power. Independence, however, has not necessarily brought legitimacy or effectiveness, and many observers argue that it has harmed policymaking while encouraging growing judicialization of the political process.

Judicial independence, judicial review in a code-law system, and moderate institutionalization have combined to produce Brazil's unusual situation. Brazil's 1988 constitution created a complex judicial system with constitutional protection for its autonomy in most personnel, budgetary, administrative, and disciplinary areas. The system is headed by the Supreme Federal Tribunal (STF), which hears constitutional cases. Under the STF is the Supreme Justice Tribunal, the court of final appeal for non-constitutional cases. Judges to these highest courts are appointed by the president with approval of the Senate (the upper house of the legislature).

Judges in the two levels of federal courts below these are appointed by the judiciary itself based on criteria of merit. Most serve life terms up to seventy years of age. As is typical in code-law countries, in addition to these constitutional and criminal courts,

- **CODE LAW**
  Special constitutional courts and abstract judicial review

- **JUDICIALIZATION**
  The constitutional court as veto point

- **INSTITUTIONALIZATION**
  Moderate-independence, but not complete legitimacy

The ceremonial opening of Brazil's Supreme Court in 2012. The Brazilian judiciary has become much stronger and more autonomous over the first two decades of the country's new democracy. It continues to suffer from an overwhelming number of cases, though, as political actors use it to try to reverse the outcomes of legislative battles, an example of the judicialization of politics.

separate codes and courts exist for labor disputes, military issues, and elections. This system is replicated in large part within each state of Brazil's federal system, resulting in a total of approximately 16,900 judges in hundreds of separate courts.

Initially, Brazil's top judges seemed hesitant to use their independence vis-à-vis the president. By 1992, though, the STF had gained confidence, and its rulings helped lead to the president's impeachment on corruption charges, a watershed event in the four-year-old democracy. The top courts have since ruled against a number of major political leaders on both constitutional questions and corruption charges, though in favor of the executive in other situations. Oliveira (2005) found that STF justices decided cases most frequently based on values of professionalism and expansion of the court's role vis-à-vis the other branches of the government; they were rarely submissive to political demands from elected leaders. Kapiszewski (2012) argued that this professionalism was based on a history of professionalizing the courts that dates back to the 1930s in Brazil, combined with the fact that the exceptionally fragmented National Congress meant presidents could not get judicial appointees approved if the appointees were seen as heavily partisan or ideological, so appointments of widely respected legal professionals became the norm. This independence enhanced horizontal accountability vis-à-vis the executive, but it also left few restraints on the judiciary. Carlos Santiso (2003) argued that while Brazil's judiciary serves an important function in horizontal accountability, its own lack of vertical accountability has become a major problem. Virtually all observers view the judiciary as slow, inefficient, and corrupt. Scandals involving judges have sometimes gone unpunished, many courts have a backlog of cases stretching out for years, and Brazilian judges are some of the most highly paid in the world. All of this has meant that "public contempt for the judiciary has reached unprecedented levels" (177).

Part of the problem with the huge number of cases is the system of code law and judicial review established in the constitution. Constitutional cases can come to the STF either on appeal from lower courts or directly from key political actors, including most government agencies, national business or labor organizations, state governments, and political parties. Until a 2004 reform, the STF processed as many as 100,000 cases per year, probably the highest number in the world. It even has a drive-up window for lawyers to file cases! Political leaders and groups have taken advantage of this situation to judicialize Brazilian politics. If they cannot win in a state legislature or at the federal level, they take a case to court, making a constitutional argument if possible. Just initiating a case can often bring significant publicity to a group's pet cause. Taylor (2008) found this tactic to be particularly common in policy areas in which there are concentrated costs to particular groups; they are very likely to make a constitutional challenge to try to protect themselves, even after losing the legislative battle. Brazil's independent judiciary has become a powerful veto point in Brazil's already fragmented political system.

Judicial independence has also made it difficult to clean up corruption or reform the parts of the system that almost everyone agrees aren't working. Brazil has long been one of the most unequal societies in the world, and stories abound of wealthy people bribing judges to ensure that court decisions go their way. The poor are more likely to be brought to court, more likely to be convicted, and more likely to be sentenced to long terms in Brazil's overcrowded and often violent prisons. So while Brazil's top court has become an important player in the national policy-making process, and a venue for other actors to pursue their policy goals, the judiciary as a whole remains only moderately institutionalized, and its continuing problems limit its legitimacy.

Web link:
Brazil's judiciary: not so swift justice

Judicial leaders have successfully fought against reforms of this system. In December 2004, to reduce the number of cases in the courts, the legislature passed some minimal reforms and created a National Judicial Council composed of both top judges and nominees outside the judiciary to oversee the budget and administration of the courts. The initial results of this reform were positive, cutting the number of cases almost in half (though that still left over fifty thousand cases at the court in 2008); further reforms that analysts viewed as likely to be beneficial were awaiting action in Congress, though agreement to move them forward seemed difficult to achieve.

CASE Summary The Brazilian case demonstrates how code law and abstract judicial review can put tremendous strain on the court system, particularly at the top, and encourage the judicialization of politics. Common-law countries, however, are not free of this problem; many in the United States see a similar trend of political actors using the courts to win battles they could not via the Congress. Judicial independence has been an important achievement in Brazil and has helped the country start to reduce widespread corruption, but it has not helped eliminate corruption within the judiciary itself. The judicialization of politics occurs via the court being a veto point where other actors can limit or reverse policy decisions that had majority legislative support. This raises the classic question of whether too many and too strong "checks and balances" (horizontal accountability) excessively limit governments' ability to govern. An additional arena in which this question emerges is the modern bureaucracy, to which we now turn.

CASE Questions

1. What does Brazil teach us about the question of whether the power of an unelected judiciary is justified in a democracy?
2. What does Brazil teach us about the trade-off between the benefits of the judiciary checking the other branches of government, on the one hand, and the role of the judiciary as a veto player or veto point, on the other?

BUREAUCRACY

Chapter 2 identified a bureaucracy as one of the key characteristics of a modern state. All states have an executive branch that includes a bureaucracy of some sort. The ideal modern bureaucracy consists of officials appointed on the basis of merit and expertise who implement policies lawfully, treat all citizens equally according to the relevant laws, and are held accountable by the elected head of the executive branch. This ideal is an important component in the full development of an effective modern state; as we noted in chapter 2, a state (whatever type of regime it has) will have greater capacity to rule its territory and people if it has an effective bureaucracy. A bureaucracy in this modern sense is also a key component of liberal democracy, as it recruits officials according to merit, administers policies according to law, treats citizens equally, and insulates bureaucratic officials from the personal and political desires of top leaders. On the other hand, bureaucracy can be a threat to democracy, so bureaucrats themselves must be held accountable. Who will prevent them from abusing their independence and autonomy? Because they are not elected, vertical accountability does not exist, meaning that horizontal accountability is very important.

Bureaucracy can limit the executive in a number of ways even as it enhances a state's capacity. Prior to modern reforms, bureaucratic positions in most societies were based on political patronage: leaders appointed all officials to suit the leaders' interests. (China was a major exception—Confucian ideas of merit in that country go back millennia.) Professionalization involved recruitment based on merit and a reduction of political patronage. It also came to mean that bureaucratic officials held technical expertise, on which political leaders often have to rely to make decisions in an increasingly complex world. Knowledge and expertise are key sources of bureaucrats' independent power. Modern bureaucracies developed into formal, hierarchical organizations in which career advancement, at least ideally, was based on performance and personal capability rather than on political connections.

Bureaucratic professionalization keeps the bureaucracy at least partially insulated from the whims of political leaders, but it raises the question of how the political leadership will hold the bureaucracy accountable. This can be understood as a **principal-agent problem.** The principal (the elected or appointed political leadership in the executive or legislative branches) assigns an agent (the bureaucrat) a task to carry out as the principal instructs; the problem is how the principal makes sure the agent carries out the task as assigned. Bureaucratic agents might well have strong incentives to deviate from their assigned tasks. Rational-choice theorists argue that bureaucrats, however professional, are as self-interested and rational as any other actors. Bureaucrats' preferences are usually to expand their sphere of influence and the size of their organization to enhance their own prestige and salary. This can expand the size of the bureaucracy, create inefficiencies, and distort the principals' purposes. Self-interest can also lead to corruption, if bureaucrats exchange favorable treatment of political leaders or ordinary citizens for bribes or other advantages.

principal-agent problem
A problem in which a principal hires an agent to perform a task but the agent's self-interest does not necessarily align with the principal's, so the agent may not carry out the task as assigned

Douglas Shulman, former commissioner of the Internal Revenue Service (IRS) (left), Lois Lerner, the director of the IRS's exempt organizations office (center), and Neal Wolin, deputy secretary of the U.S. Treasury (right) testify before a congressional committee in 2013 about the scandal involving the IRS's oversight of political groups tied to the Tea Party. One of the greatest problems facing political appointees such as Wolin is ensuring that civil servants like Lerner fulfill the current government's policies, a classic case of the principal-agent problem.

Numerous solutions to this problem have emerged over the years. In every state the political leadership of the executive branch selects a certain number of **political appointees** to head the bureaucracy. These appointees, starting at the top with cabinet ministers, serve at the pleasure of the president or prime minister and, among other things, are assigned the task of overseeing their respective segments of the bureaucracy. Different countries allow different numbers of political appointees: the United States typically allows six or eight for each significant department in the federal government, whereas two is more typical for each ministry in the United Kingdom. (The United States uses the term *department* to designate the major agencies of the government, whereas most of the world uses *ministry* to mean the same thing, harkening back to the religious influence on the early modern state.)

Political appointees' power over professional bureaucrats is limited by the legal means through which the latter are hired, paid, and earn career advancement; bureaucrats, however, must answer to political appointees within those legal limits. In democracies, legislators can write laws that are as specific as possible to limit bureaucrats' discretion. Whether they choose to do so, though, depends on a number of factors. If legislators trust bureaucrats or see them as sharing similar preferences, if they are not capable of writing detailed legislation, and if they can turn to the courts to control bureaucrats if necessary, then they are less likely to try to control bureaucratic behavior via detailed legislation (Huber and Shipan 2002). **Legislative oversight** is another key means of horizontal accountability; members of the legislature, usually in committees, oversee the bureaucracy by interviewing key leaders, examining budgets, and assessing how successfully a particular agency has carried out its mandate. Often, citizens use the judicial system to try to achieve accountability by taking individual officials or entire agencies to court, arguing that they have either failed to carry out their duties or have done so unlawfully.

None of these efforts to influence the bureaucracy works perfectly, in large part because principals never know exactly what their agents within a bureaucracy are doing, especially as technocratic knowledge becomes more important. For most of the

political appointees
Officials who serve at the pleasure of the president or prime minister and are assigned the task of overseeing their respective segments of the bureaucracy

legislative oversight
Members of the legislature, usually in committees, oversee the bureaucracy

twentieth century, governments relied heavily on professional socialization to maintain standards. They recruited people who had been trained to abide by key professional norms of neutrality and legality, and they believed they could count on most of these recruits to behave in the general "public" interest in alignment with their training. Some states, such as France and Japan, went so far as to recruit almost exclusively from one high-profile educational institution so that government bureaucrats garnered great prestige and professional status.

Rational-choice theorists, however, argued that training could not overcome the incentives and self-interest inherent in the bureaucracy, which tend to produce inefficiency and corruption. Following this line of argument, the **New Public Management (NPM)** movement arose. The movement first emerged in the United States and United Kingdom in the 1980s and was associated with President Ronald Reagan and Prime Minister Margaret Thatcher. NPM advocates contended that inherent inefficiencies meant that the bureaucracy required radical reforms to make it operate more like a market-based organization. Reforms included privatizing many government services so that they would be provided by the market, creating competition among agencies and subagencies within the bureaucracy to simulate a market, focusing on customer satisfaction (via client surveys, among other things), and flattening administrative hierarchies to encourage more team-based activity and creativity. The ideas of NPM became widely popular and were implemented in many wealthy democracies, though to varying degrees. Some countries, such as the United Kingdom and New Zealand, cut the size of their bureaucracies extensively via NPM, while others, including Germany and Japan, implemented it slowly and partially. While NPM reduced the size of government significantly in some countries, debate continues as to whether it improved bureaucratic performance in general.

Bureaucracy and Corruption

One of NPM's main targets was bureaucratic corruption. Where the state and its institutions are generally weak, reform requires not only making the bureaucracy more efficient but also strengthening it as an institution. When bureaucratic rules and norms are extremely weak, corruption and massive inefficiency are likely (O'Dwyer 2006). Political elites may be able to use a weak bureaucracy to pursue personal or financial interests of their own, citizens may be able to gain favors from the state via bribery, and bureaucrats themselves may steal from the state. Bribery and rent seeking are two primary types of corruption in bureaucracies. In the least institutionalized bureaucracies, citizens often have to bribe officials to get them to carry out the functions they are mandated to do. The principals—the political leadership—may not be interested in encouraging the bureaucracy to function effectively because they benefit from their own ability to purchase favors from bureaucrats. Alternatively, they may simply have lost all ability to control their agents in the bureaucracy, often because of very low

New Public Management (NPM)
Theory of reform of bureaucracies that argues for the privatizing of many government services, creating competition among agencies to simulate a market, focusing on customer satisfaction, and flattening administrative hierarchies

bureaucratic salaries. In the worst cases, officials seek bribes before they will carry out the most menial functions, such as issuing a driver's license or providing basic medicine. **Rent seeking** is the gaining of an advantage in a market without engaging in equally productive activity; it usually involves using government regulations to one's own benefit. In weakly institutionalized bureaucracies, for example, businesses may be able to bribe officials to grant them exclusive rights to import certain items, thereby reaping huge profits for little effort.

The rent-seeking model of corruption is based on a rational-choice theory of why corruption is greater in some countries than in others (see Map 6.3). Rational-choice theories, as always, focus on individual incentives, arguing that economic conditions are particularly important in explaining corruption: countries with more highly regulated economies and greater inequality are likely to be more corrupt. The former provides opportunities for corruption, as bureaucrats can demand bribes frequently; the latter means that average citizens have fewer resources to get what they want and therefore are more willing to pay bribes. Numerous other theories, however, have also sought to explain the puzzle of corruption.

rent seeking
Gaining an advantage in a market without engaging in equally productive activity; usually involves using government regulations for one's own benefit

Web link:
The true godfathers of Narcoland

MAP 6.3   Annual Corruption Scores, 2013

8.0 – 10
6.0 – 7.9
4.0 – 5.9
2.0 – 3.9
0 – 1.9
No data

Countries' scores on the Corruption Perceptions Index, in which 10 equals the least corruption and 1 the most, have been converted from the 100-point scale the CPI uses. The index is constructed by surveying business leaders and others who work in each country, asking them to identify how much corruption they perceive. In the most corrupt countries, bureaucratic rules are rarely followed, producing less equality under law and less efficiency in government.

Source: Transparency International Corruption Perceptions Index Scores, 2012 (http://www.transparency.org/policy_research/surveys_indices/cpi).

One of the oldest theories is based on political culture: corruption is greater where societies lack shared values about the importance of the public sphere, instead placing personal, family, or ethnic interests above those of the society as a whole. Others have noted that greater corruption is found in postcolonial societies; they contend that the lack of legitimacy of a postcolonial state that has no firm roots in the society leads citizens to believe one should gain whatever one can from the public sphere. Nigerian sociologist Peter Ekeh (1975) argued that in Africa, two "publics" exist: a "primordial public," which includes ethnic, religious, and community identities in which people feel reciprocal moral responsibility toward one another, and an amoral "civic public" involving the state, toward which people feel no obligation and therefore take from freely.

Video link:
Mexico's corruption

Much recent scholarship is institutionalist, focusing on the effects of political institutions in particular. The general consensus has been that in democracies with stronger parties and greater political competition, corruption is lower. Competition among institutions, such as in presidential and federal systems, is also seen as likely to reduce corruption by increasing horizontal accountability. Vineeta Yadav (2011) recently argued, however, that strong parties actually increase corruption. Based on case studies of Brazil and India as well as a much wider statistical analysis, she argued that stronger parties that control the legislative process actually encourage greater corruption because they need higher levels of cash for campaigns.

Michael Johnston (2005), one of the foremost scholars of corruption, combined theories based on economic factors and political institutions to argue that, rather than trying to predict the total amount of corruption, we need to understand its variation in different kinds of societies. He elaborated four models of different types of corruption, based on wealth level and the nature of the political system. Corruption in wealthy, established democracies is primarily based on "influence markets," in which corporations use access to politicians, usually via generous contributions to campaigns and parties, to gain preferential treatment from key bureaucracies, as in the case of Japan. In middle-income countries with newer and less well-institutionalized democracies, "elite cartels" emerge in which key political and business leaders form networks to gain control of the government and systematically use it to their joint political and financial benefit. In middle-income countries that just recently became democracies, institutions are even weaker and political competition more intense, uncertain, and personal; in these countries, "oligarchs and clans" scramble for spoils in the system. Our case study of Russia is a primary example. In the least institutionalized (and often poorest) states with personalized or neopatrimonial rule, corruption often takes the form of the "Official Mogul," a strongman who uses the resources of the state as he pleases to favor his political allies and punish his enemies, a situation that was common in much of Africa.

Video link:
Michael Johnston discusses corruption in the political system

The extent of the problem and the possible remedies for corruption vary, Johnston argued, across these four types of countries, though corruption is an important issue in all of them. Where it exists, even in modest proportions, it undermines the capacity

CRITICAL inquiry

Wealth, Corruption, and Democracy

The table below shows the levels of wealth, corruption, and democracy for a selection of countries around the world, including our eleven case studies. Michael Johnston argued that corruption isn't necessarily higher or lower in countries that are wealthier and more democratic, but different. Based on the table, what trends do you see? Are wealthier countries clearly less corrupt? Are democratic countries clearly less corrupt? Which of the two (wealth or democracy) seems most influential in determining the level of corruption? What do your answers suggest for Johnston's argument?

Corruption Perceptions Index		
Country	GDP per capita (current US $)*	CPI	Polity IV score
Norway	$98,080.91	85	10
United States	$48,111.97	73	10
Japan	$45,902.67	74	10
United Arab Emirates	$45,653.09	68	-8
Germany	$44,021.22	79	10
United Kingdom	$38,974.32	74	10
Czech Republic	$20,676.90	49	8
Chile	$14,394.46	72	10
Russia	$12,995.03	28	4
Brazil	$12,593.89	43	8
Mexico	$10,047.13	34	8

Country	GDP per capita (current US $)*	CPI	Polity IV score
Botswana	$8,532.62	65	8
Colombia	$7,104.03	36	7
China	$5,444.79	39	-7
Thailand	$4,972.37	37	7
Iran, Islamic Republic of	$4,525.95	28	-7
Indonesia	$3,494.60	32	8
Georgia	$3,202.53	52	6
Philippines	$2,369.70	34	8
India	$1,508.54	36	9
Nigeria	$1,501.72	27	4
Vietnam	$1,407.11	31	-7
Pakistan	$1,189.37	27	6
Kenya	$808.00	27	8
Rwanda	$582.56	53	-4
Mozambique	$533.31	31	5
Uganda	$487.11	29	-1
Niger	$374.45	33	6
Congo, Democratic Republic of the	$231.02	21	-4

Polity IV is a measure of how well institutionalized democracy is within a given country, with 10 being fully institutionalized democracy and -10 being fully institutionalized authoritarian regime.

Sources: GDP data are from the World Bank, GDP per Capita (current US $) (http://data.worldbank.org/indicator/NY.GDP.PCAP.CD/countries); CPI scores are from Transparency International, Corruption Perceptions Index, 2012 (http://cpi.transparency.org/cpi2012/results/#myAnchor1); Polity IV scores are from Polity IV, Case Format (http://www.systemicpeace.org/inscr/inscr.htm).

of the state, especially the bureaucracy, and the democratic ideal of equal citizenship. Japan demonstrates both the power and limits of bureaucracy and the complex issues that arise when bureaucracy weakens.

CASE Study

BUREAUCRATIC CONTROL AND CORRUPTION: JAPAN

All states have bureaucracies, but they have played a greater political role in some states than in others.

Japan is a case well known for a bureaucracy that played a pivotal role in its early economic and political development. The bureaucracy was almost the sole surviving institution after World War II and was intimately involved in setting economic policy in particular from the 1950s to the 1970s. Unfortunately, it has been weakened by corruption over the last thirty years that arguably has had a negative impact on economic well-being and the legitimacy of the country's democratic government more broadly.

The sweeping victory of the Democratic Party of Japan (DPJ) in 2009 (see chapter 7 for details) over the long-ruling Liberal Democratic Party (LDP) was the most important electoral outcome in Japan since World War II. One of the DPJ's major campaign promises was to reform the entrenched bureaucracy, seen by many Japanese as a source of unaccountable power that was preventing necessary reforms. The Japanese economy boomed for four decades after the war, thanks in part to Japan's long-standing tradition of a highly professionalized, elite bureaucracy that worked with business and elected leaders to create the famed "developmental state" (see chapter 5). Fears that the bureaucracy was becoming too powerful and corrupt, though, were realized in the revelations of the "recruit scandal" in 1988. Numerous scandals involving both bureaucrats and politicians have occurred since, but the power of the bureaucracy has been trimmed only partially.

- **BUREAUCRATIC STRENGTH**
  Strong under the developmental state, later reduced by globalization

- **CORRUPTION**
  "Iron triangles" and bureaucrats' political influence

- **REFORM**
  Limited effects of NPM; frustration of recent reform efforts

The scene at a harbor one hundred days after the tsunami that devastated parts of coastal Japan. The government was criticized, and the ruling party lost the subsequent election, for its failure to respond adequately to the crisis. Part of the problem was lack of coordination among various bureaucratic agencies, caused by reforms the government had put in place to try to reduce the bureaucracy's influence over policymaking.

The fact that the Japanese bureaucracy was the only major political institution to survive the post–World War II U.S. occupation largely intact gave it a tremendous advantage vis-à-vis other institutions in the new democracy. As in France, Japan's top bureaucrats are recruited primarily from one source: the law faculty at the University of Tokyo. From the 1950s through the 1970s, the unwritten rule was that the top graduates of that school would enter the elite corps of the bureaucracy to begin their ascent to the top. Bureaucrats' great prestige and potentially high income came from the common practice of *amakudari*, or the "descent from heaven," and rigid **iron triangles** among business, politicians, and key bureaucrats. Under *amakudari*, retiring civil servants gained lucrative positions in the businesses they previously regulated. Among other things, this gave bureaucrats an incentive to maintain favorable conditions for and relations with key corporations in their regulatory area. The term *iron triangle* was coined in reference to the United States, but the phenomenon is even stronger in Japan. Key bureaucrats, business leaders, and politicians cooperate to set policy to their mutual interest. In a classic example of the type of corruption Michael Johnston (2005) termed the "influence market," businesses give generous contributions to top politicians; in exchange, the politicians secure favorable treatment from key bureaucrats; and bureaucrats grant the favors because they will eventually be working in the businesses themselves.

The power of Japan's bureaucracy was unusual for a democracy: it controlled the key information and expertise needed to guide the growing economy and was a source of highly prestigious employment. The prime minister only made two or three political appointments in each ministry, for a total of fewer than fifty appointments (as compared with the several thousand that a U.S. president makes), giving him little executive oversight. Combined with little legislative oversight due to the iron triangles, the bureaucracy was left with great power vis-à-vis the other branches in Japan's democracy. At the height of its power, most major legislative initiatives began not with the prime minister or the legislature but rather in the relevant bureaucracy. Interestingly, this power did not result in the further growth of the bureaucracy. Though it retained great regulatory powers in the economy, the number of officials as a percentage of all employment was and remains the lowest among wealthy democracies, undoubtedly in part because of *amakudari*.

Admirers of the developmental state argued that this centralized and powerful bureaucracy played a positive role in Japan's economic success. Lack of oversight and the incentives of the iron triangle and *amakudari*, however, let corruption get out of control. While most Japanese knew that corruption was fairly common, they thought it did not affect the top echelons until major scandals broke out in the 1980s and 1990s. Combined with the economic stagnation of the 1990s, the scandals also diminished the prestige of the bureaucracy in general. At the height of the bureaucracy's power in the 1960s, forty-three top university graduates competed for each top bureaucratic position; by the 1990s only eleven did (Pempel 2000, 160). Business stagnation made *amakudari* more difficult, and the prestige of the bureaucracy plummeted.

iron triangle
Three-sided cooperative interaction among bureaucrats, legislators, and business leaders in a particular sector that serves the interests of all involved but keeps others out of the policy-making process

Changes to Japan's bureaucratic system have long been proposed but have seldom succeeded. Electoral reforms in 1993, a direct response to the worst scandals, seem to have had limited effect on the role of money in the election process (see chapter 7). The ideas of NPM filtered in from the United States and United Kingdom but also had relatively little impact. Neither Japanese bureaucrats nor politicians had significant interest in reforming a system from which they all benefited, and given the small size of Japan's bureaucracy, some of NPM's analysis clearly did not fit. A reformist prime minister, Junichiro Koizumi, entered office in 2001 with bold proposals for reform, but few became law (see chapter 5).

Longtime Japan analyst Karel van Wolferen (2010) argued that the DPJ government that came to power in 2009 tried to implement the most serious reform effort to date. Its key leaders wanted to fundamentally reduce the power of the bureaucracy vis-à-vis the PM and cabinet by building up the strength of elected offices. To that end, the first DPJ prime minister centralized key decision making in the cabinet and eliminated several important roles for senior bureaucrats, including what had been a crucial meeting of senior bureaucrats to coordinate policy across ministries, arguing that elected officials should make decisions and bureaucrats should implement them. He also instituted regular and important meetings of the elected cabinet, following the British model, which had not been the case before. This stark break with past practices and strong barrier between the elected officials and senior bureaucrats ultimately left key decision makers inadequately informed on important issues and bureaucrats feeling marginalized (Shinoda 2012).

In mid-2010 a new DPJ prime minister moved back to a policy of greater cooperation between elected officials and bureaucrats, including senior bureaucrats in some of the important policy-making meetings with elected officials. The government, however, proved inept in responding to the unprecedented crisis of the 2011 earthquake and tsunami, which killed twenty thousand people, displaced hundreds of thousands, and threatened nuclear catastrophe. Part of the problem was the various ministries' inability to coordinate policy, a result of the government having eliminated regular meetings among senior bureaucrats from different ministries (Shinoda 2012). The citizens' feeling that the government had not responded well to the crisis hurt its popularity further, forcing yet another prime ministerial resignation, and a third DPJ leader took over. He reversed almost all of the prior practices, reinstating bureaucrats' role in coordinating and setting policy in several areas. In spite of this, the Japanese public saw the government as incompetent, and the LDP swept back into power in the election of December 2012. The new government came to power with promises of using Keynesian policies to restart economic growth; some analysts feared this would mean a return to the old days of the "iron triangles" that would allocate government spending to their favorite pet projects. Early on, the new government seemed to be recreating virtually all of the key roles for bureaucrats that the DPJ had eliminated (Yakushiji 2013).

The relative power of the bureaucracy today remains in dispute. It is certainly more powerful than in most wealthy democracies, but globalization and deregulation have reduced its control of the economy (see chapter 5). In addition, it has become more internally divided, allowing more voices within and without to have an effect on key questions in Japanese politics. Even though recent reforms appear not to have had a major impact, the longer trend seems to point in the direction of at least somewhat greater accountability.

Web link:
Gail Marcus's blog
Nuke Power Talk

CASE Summary   As technocratic expertise becomes ever more important, major economic and social forces have pushed most countries in the direction of enhanced bureaucratic autonomy and power. This process can give rise to corruption, especially in countries with a historical legacy of strong bureaucracy such as Japan. Reform efforts to create greater horizontal accountability have been difficult to put into effect, even though models like NPM have long been available to draw on. Entrenched bureaucratic power, especially when supported by elected officials who benefit from it, can be very difficult to overcome, as the Japanese case demonstrates. Bureaucracy is an essential part of a functioning modern state and democratic regime, but maintaining control over it and limiting corruption remain constant concerns.

CASE Questions

1. Political scientists debate whether increasing bureaucratic power is inherent in our highly technological and complex era or is simply the result of inadequate political will and institutions with which to keep the bureaucracy in line. What does the Japanese case teach us about the answer to this debate?
2. Does Japan suggest that the design of political institutions or the nature of economic policies is more important in explaining the relative strength of the bureaucracy in a modern state?

FEDERALISM

So far, we have only considered governmental institutions at the national level. In every country, of course, they exist at lower levels as well, though their role and autonomy vis-à-vis the national government vary widely. The most important distinction is between unitary and federal systems. In **unitary systems** the central government has sole constitutional sovereignty and power, whereas in **federal systems** the central government shares constitutional sovereignty and power with subunits, such as states, provinces, or regions. Local governments exist in unitary systems, but they derive their

unitary systems
Political systems in which the central government has sole constitutional sovereignty and power; in contrast to a federal system

federal systems
Political systems in which a state's power is legally and constitutionally divided among more than one level of government; in contrast to a unitary system

powers from the central government, which can alter them as it pleases. In federal systems, some subnational governments have constitutionally derived powers separate from the central government that can only be changed via constitutional amendment.

The first modern federal system was the Dutch Republic of the United Provinces in what is now the Netherlands, but the best-known early example is the United States. Both states originally were contiguous units within larger empires that declared independence and banded together. In the case of the United States, separate and sovereign states—the original thirteen British colonies—came together to form a federation only after a looser union, a confederation, failed to produce a viable central state. Political scientist William Riker (1964) provided a now classic rational-choice explanation of how American federalism emerged, arguing that it resulted from a bargain among self-interested leaders of separate states who were motivated primarily by military concerns—protecting themselves from external threat.

Australia and Switzerland are other examples of federalism that arose from separate states that came together to form a new state. Most modern federations, however, came about in exactly the opposite way: through states trying to remain together, often after colonial rule, as our case study of India below demonstrates. In some cases, such as India, federations arose via democracy and implicit bargaining between regional elites and the central government. In other cases, such as Russia, authoritarian rulers imposed federalism to help them rule a vast, heterogeneous territory. As the Russian case study below indicates, imposed federalism seldom provides the stability or strong institutions of negotiated federalism.

Why Countries Adopt Federalism

Web link:
Forum of Federations' "Federalism by Country" list

While federal systems are a minority of the world's governments, they include most of its geographically largest countries. As the Country and Concepts table for this chapter (page 263) shows, among our case studies, all of the larger countries except China are federal systems. This is not accidental. Larger countries tend to adopt federal systems in part to provide some level of government closer to the populace than the national government.

A second purpose of federalism is to limit the power of the majority by decentralizing and dividing governmental power. Federal systems usually have bicameral legislatures, with the second (usually referred to as the upper) house representing the interests of the states or provinces. They also have some sort of judicial review to settle disputes between the levels of government. Both institutions limit the power of the executive and the majority controlling the lower (and usually more powerful) house of the legislature. Federal systems, then, typically institutionalize several veto players that do not exist in unitary systems.

Finally, as we mentioned in chapter 4, federalism is often a means to protect the interests of religious or ethnic minorities. When regional minority communities feel threatened by other groups' control of the national government, a federal system that creates separate states or provinces with clear ethnic or religious majorities can ease tensions. This explains why some relatively small states have chosen federal systems. Belgium, for instance, was created in 1830 as a buffer against potential French expansion. Federalism there is combined with consociationalism: the national cabinet and many other appointments must be split 50–50 between the two major language groups, the Flemish and Walloons; separate elections and parties exist for each group; and governments are virtually always a coalition of the two largest parties from each side. Despite its prolonged existence as a nation-state, regionalism in Belgium has always remained strong and seems to be increasing. In 2010 a Flemish nationalist party that calls for Flemish independence won an unprecedented 30 percent of the Flemish vote to become the largest party in the Belgian parliament. It took a world-record 541 days for the ethnically divided political parties in parliament to form a coalition government after the election.

Federalism and Accountability

A key determinant of the extent to which federalism limits majority power and provides accountability is the relative power and autonomy of the national and subnational governments. These factors, in turn, depend on the specific powers set out for each level of government in the constitution, the resources each level of government controls, and the composition and relative strength of the upper house in the legislature. The constitutions of all federal systems lay out the powers of both the central government and the states or provinces. Military, foreign, and monetary policies are always placed under the authority of the national level, as they are essential to the sovereignty of the modern state and a modern economy. States or provinces typically have power over education, transportation, and sometimes social services (at least partially). In more decentralized systems, like the United States and Brazil, states also have separate judicial systems that handle most criminal law.

The real power of each level of government, however, depends not only on formal powers ordained by the constitution but also on resources. Two key questions, and areas of political combat between the levels of government in any federal system, are how much each level of government can collect in taxes and how much each can spend. The power of taxation is particularly important, as it gives subnational units greater autonomy than they would have if they were wholly dependent on the central government for their revenue. In the most centralized unitary states, such as the United Kingdom and Ireland, the central government collects more than three-quarters of total government revenue; in the least centralized federal systems, such as Germany and Switzerland, the central government collects less than a third. Similarly, the central government in some unitary systems is responsible for around 60 percent of all expenditures, whereas in decentralized federal systems it is responsible for as little as 30 percent. During the twentieth century, revenue collection in federations became more centralized, reflecting the growing power of national governments over state or provincial ones.

The upper and weaker house of the legislature in a federal system is usually designed to represent the state or provincial governments, while the lower and more powerful house represents individual voters. The upper house's power and composition help determine the extent to which federalism limits majority rule. Its powers can be quite sweeping, as in the case of the U.S. Senate, which must approve all legislation, or much more limited, as in Germany's Bundesrat, which can only delay bills unless they directly relate to the *Länder.* Because states or provinces are typically of different sizes, smaller ones are often overrepresented in the upper house. In the U.S. Senate, every state has two seats: in 2010 the twenty least populous states had just under 10 percent of the U.S. population but elected 40 percent of the senators. Given that Senate legislation requires the approval of 60 percent of the body on important issues, the representatives of just over 10 percent of the population can stop legislation, an unusually severe restriction on majority rule. Population shifts to cities are causing the population gap between large and small states to increase and leaving small states increasingly rural and conservative and larger states increasingly urban and liberal, meaning the representation gap has partisan implications favoring conservatives. The ratio of representation of the smallest states to the largest in the U.S. Senate is about 66 to 1. The same ratio in the German Bundesrat is only 13 to 1; this ratio, combined with the weaker powers of the Bundesrat, shows clearly that German federalism does not restrict majority rule nearly as much as American federalism does.

The degree of institutionalization in federal systems is also important to accountability, especially at the local level. Examining Latin America, Edward Gibson (2013) argued that especially in poorer and more rural states or provinces, a federal system can preserve nondemocratic rule within a national democracy. As the large, federal Latin American countries such as Mexico, Argentina, and Brazil became democratic, some politically powerful "bosses" in particular states were able to use clientelism to maintain their rule largely unchallenged. In these cases, the new democratic institutions were not followed, so federalism allowed semi-authoritarian rule to continue at the state level, even though a democratic regime existed at the national level. Our case study of Russia is even more extreme: as democracy at the national level withered, federalism weakened with it.

Federalism and Minority Rights

Most federal systems today exist in heterogeneous societies; part of their purpose is to give some local autonomy to ethnic or religious minorities. While all of the issues outlined above apply to these federal systems, other factors also come into play in preserving ethnic minority autonomy. The United States is an example of a **symmetrical federal system:** all states have the same relationship with and rights in relation to the national government. In contrast, many federal systems in ethnically divided societies are **asymmetrical:** some states or provinces have special rights or powers that others do not. These special relationships are often negotiated individually between the leaders of a particular group and the central government, sometimes at the end of a civil war or under the threat of civil war or secession. A recent comparative study concluded that federal systems on the whole help to accommodate ethnic and religious divisions, resulting in less conflict than occurs in unitary systems with heterogeneous populations. However, the study also found that federal systems work best where there has not been a history of severe repression of one group over another; in such cases, even the best designed federal institutions may not be able to overcome the tensions and lack of trust between a regionally based group and the central government (Amoretti and Bermeo 2004).

Recent Trends in Federalism

In recent years, the once sharp division between federal and unitary systems has been blurring. The most decentralized federal systems have become somewhat more centralized as these federal governments have used their revenue power and constitutional authority to override state prerogatives in areas such as civil rights, education, and even the drinking age. (Since the 1980s, the U.S. federal government has enforced the mandatory minimum drinking age of twenty-one by denying transportation funding to states that refuse to abide by it; therefore, all states comply.) In unitary systems, such as the United Kingdom, some decentralization has taken place. This process is often termed **devolution** because it devolves power from the center to the regions or subnational units. A British parliamentary report commented that devolution differs from federalism because parliamentary sovereignty means that devolution of power is reversible. The "devolved" institutions in Scotland, Wales, and Northern Ireland remain subordinate to the British Parliament. Interestingly, Britain is an example of "asymmetrical devolution," since each region has its own set of devolved responsibilities (Leeke, Sear, and Gay 2003). In France, on the other hand, which had one of the most centralized unitary systems, new regional governments with limited powers were created in the 1980s in a symmetrical devolution.

All governments, both democratic and authoritarian, struggle with how much power to give subnational units of government and how much to retain in the center. In a democracy, this tension has crucial implications for the power of the majority and the preservation of minority rights, as the case studies of Brazil, India, and Russia demonstrate.

symmetrical federal system
A federal system in which all subnational governments (states or provinces) have the same relationship with and rights in relation to the national government

asymmetrical federal system
A federal system in which different subnational governments (states or provinces) have distinct relationships with and rights in relation to the national government

devolution
Partial decentralization of power from central government to subunits such as states or provinces, with subunits' power being dependent on central government and reversible

FEDERALISM: BRAZIL, INDIA, AND RUSSIA

- **CENTRAL VERSUS LOCAL CONTROL**
  Centralized India versus decentralized Brazil

- **SYMMETRY**
  Symmetrical federalism in Brazil versus asymmetrical in India and Russia

- **POLITICAL CONTEXT**
  Parties in India and semi-authoritarian rule in Russia more important than constitutional rules

- **INSTITUTIONALIZATION**
  Weak institutions and lack of democracy in Russia weakens federalism

Brazil, India, and Russia provide us with three distinct models of federalism: each represents differing degrees of centralization, symmetry, and institutionalization. Together, they demonstrate that how federalism works in practice depends more on political context and control over government revenue than on the

TABLE 6.1	Differences in Federalism: Brazil, India, and Russia		
	Brazil	**India**	**Russia**
Symmetry	Symmetric	Asymmetric	Asymmetric
Centralization	Decentralized; strong upper house in legislature representing states	Centralized; weak upper house in parliament representing states; national government may change state boundaries, dissolve state governments	Very centralized; "federalism" has very little substantive meaning; weak legislature, including upper house representing regions; central control of taxes
Role of ethnicity	Not based on ethnic or religious divisions	Ethnically and linguistically based federalism	Ethnic nationalism posed major recent challenge; ethnically defined regions
Power of states	Small states heavily overrepresented in Senate; they gain disproportionate share of revenue; state governors have much power	State-level parties gained greater influence for states via participation and bargaining in national-level coalition governments	Regional governors "undisputed bosses" at local level
Reforms	Reelection of governors in exchange for increased central power	Reduced ability of central government to dissolve state governments	Greater centralization; president appoints governors

formal powers granted in constitutions. Brazil is a case of exceptional decentralization that stringently limits what the majority in control of the national government can achieve; critics argue that the system was so decentralized that it harmed effective governance, at least until reforms in the 1990s. India, in contrast, is a much more centralized federal system in which the center, especially under the continuous rule of a dominant party, controls state governments rather tightly. Also in contrast to Brazil, India is an example of an asymmetrical federal system that arose in part to ameliorate and contain the effects of linguistic and religious diversity. Russian federalism is also asymmetrical, is formally centralized, and exists in part to contain ethnic differences, but it shows the limitations of federalism if federal institutions are weak and democracy threatened or eliminated.

Like the United States, Brazil is a case of decentralized, symmetric federalism. The power of states, and of their governors in particular, can severely limit national policymaking, though the balance between central and subnational power has ebbed and flowed over time. Brazil has twenty-six states, each with an elected governor and legislature. Federalism in the country dates back to Portuguese colonialism and has never been based on ethnic or racial divisions. Rather, at independence, local, landholding elites reacted against the empire's centralization by creating a very decentralized federal system that gave them great power at the local level, including constitutional guarantees to collect certain taxes. While authoritarian regimes centralized the system at times, the basic structure of federalism has survived through all of Brazil's regimes. The constitution of 1988 spells out the powers of the states in great detail. They are guaranteed a share

Russian president Vladimir Putin meets with the Ramzan Kadyrov, head of the Chechen Republic, one of the constituent units of Russia's federal system. The Russian army brutally crushed a Chechen rebellion; then Putin imposed Kadyrov as the republic's leader. Putin has greatly centralized power, reducing federalism to little more than a shell, as it was under Soviet rule.

of national tax revenue, continued taxing powers, control over their own state banks, and very little oversight from the federal government. The upper house in the federal legislature, the Senate, is composed of three senators from each state. Given the exceptionally unequal populations of the states, each vote for a senator in the least populous state is worth 144 votes in the most populous, a ratio more than double the disparity in the U.S. Senate. As in the United States, the Senate must pass all legislation, meaning that senators representing 13 percent of the population can block any legislation. Among other things, the power this provides the smaller and poorer states has resulted in their receiving far more than their per capita share of national revenue; the wealthier states have agreed to allow this to occur as long as they can maintain their own taxing powers.

Federalism

Federalism is an unusual institutional choice: only twenty-six countries have a federal system. Those twenty-six, however, account for over 40 percent of the world's population. In addition,

- seven are among the world's ten geographically largest countries and six are among the world's ten largest countries by population;

- seven of the world's ten largest electoral democracies by area are federal, as are five of the ten largest democracies by population;

- federal countries average 0.55 on an index of ethnic fractionalization, where 0 is perfect homogeneity and 1 is highly fragmented—the world average is 0.48; and

- five federal countries are geographically fragmented, composed of two or more islands or of a peninsula and at least one island.

Sources: Based on data from Forum of Federations 2011 (http://www.forumfed.org); Fearon 2003; and Freedom House 2007 (http://www.freedomhouse.org).

The greatest powers, however, are reserved for state governors. Brazilian politics has long revolved around the use of patronage to build a political following, and much of that patronage is in the hands of state governors. National political parties have always been quite weak, in part due to Brazil's electoral system; in reality, most parties are collections of separate state parties controlled via patronage by governors and other local elites. Brazil's primary problem in the 1990s—massive inflation and debt—was connected to the power and influence of these state governors. Much of the debt was held by banks owned and controlled by the twenty-six states, and governors used these banks as sources of patronage. They also had the power to force the federal government to bail out the banks if they got into financial difficulty. Thus, by the mid-1990s, Brazil's states were facing bankruptcy because of their irresponsible spending.

President Fernando Henrique Cardoso negotiated an agreement with the governors in the 1990s under which the federal government would bail out the states in exchange for the states privatizing the state banks. He combined this with a constitutional amendment that allows both the president and all governors to be reelected. Previously, like officials in most of Latin America, Brazil's executives could only serve one term, so governors used their one term to gain as much patronage from the state's resources as they could. The possibility of reelection gave them a longer-term stake in successful reform. Later, Cardoso also passed a law that limits the amount states can spend on salaries and employees (a key form of patronage) and prevents the federal government from bailing out the states in the future, effectively limiting governors' resources for patronage. Aaron Schneider portrayed the law as "the culmination of the long process of forming a new federal arrangement" (2007, 486), using fiscal rules to substantially increase the power of the national government vis-à-vis the states. Since these reforms, the power of state-level "political machines" that used clientelism to maintain power, as Gibson (2013) argued is common in Latin America, has been reduced substantially (Borges 2012). Brazilian federalism remains one of the most decentralized in the world, but over the past decade the pendulum has shifted noticeably back in the direction of centralization, facilitating more coherent policymaking at the national level.

As in Brazil, the origins of India's federalism lie in the colonial era. The British colonial government put modern India together from literally hundreds of separate states, ruling some areas directly and others via various agreements with local rulers. After independence, the new constitution recognized various categories of states and "union territories" with various powers. While most states today have the same basic powers, the central government has bargained with regional groups to create new states to enhance regional loyalty to the center. This has meant giving certain states greater autonomy and power than others. The designers of India's constitution specifically said they were not creating states along linguistic or ethnic lines, but over time that is primarily what has happened. A major commission in the 1950s led to the creation of new states drawn mostly along linguistic lines. In the northeast, six new states were eventually created along ethnic lines as well, and these have greater power and autonomy than do other states, including the freedom to respect local customary law and religious practices. While few new states have been created in recent years, the issue remains very much alive: from 2011 to 2013 protests broke out and several MPs resigned over their demand to create a new state out of a region of Andhra Pradesh in southern India.

India's constitution created an unusually centralized system of federalism. States do not write their own constitutions; each is under the authority of the same central constitution, which includes a parliamentary government with a chief minister who is the state-level equivalent of prime minister. The national government, however, has the right to create, eliminate, or change state boundaries as it pleases. It can also declare President's Rule in a particular state, under which the state government is dismissed and the prime minister in effect governs the state directly until he calls a new state election. The central government's greater taxing power, which has expanded over time, has given it great control over the policies of the states. In 1955–1956, Indian states could finance an average of 69 percent of their expenditures, with the rest coming from the national government; by 2000–2001, this was down to 49 percent (Rao and Singh 2005, 172). An upper house, the Rajya Sabha, exists to represent states but has no significant effect on legislation or the composition of the national government.

The extent to which this centralized constitutional arrangement has limited majority rule has varied over time, depending mainly on the party system. When the Indian National Congress (INC) was the sole dominant party and controlled the national government between 1947 and 1977, it had tremendous power. Prior to 1967, it controlled virtually all state governments, so they generally did the bidding of the central government, making federalism extremely weak. Once greater political competition at the state level emerged in the 1970s, Prime Ministers Indira (1966–1977;

1980–1984) and Rajiv (1984–1989) Gandhi used President's Rule for partisan purposes: they would have the president declare President's Rule in states controlled by opposition parties and then call and win new state elections. As we detail in chapter 7, since 1989 India's ethnically based federalism has helped create a number of state-level parties that dominate the politics in their states but have little influence or support elsewhere. Since 1989, India's national governments have always been coalitions between a major national party and several state-level parties. The state parties have used this situation to bargain with the national parties for greater state autonomy, protecting their states' interests vis-à-vis the central government better than the formal rules of the Indian constitution have. Also, a 1994 ruling by India's Supreme Court limited the ability of prime ministers to declare President's Rule. Recent changes in economic policy have also strengthened some state governments: greater market freedoms have allowed certain state governments to attract capital from around their world, enriching those states and their tax base vis-à-vis the national government. Thus, state governments seem to be achieving some degree of institutional autonomy, and horizontal accountability may be increasing vis-à-vis national institutions.

Despite the centralization of the system, India's federalism has managed to keep most ethnic and linguistic conflict within democratic bounds. Atul Kohli (2004) argued that India has used federalism to contain conflict when national leaders have been willing to compromise with regional groups and political institutions were strong. In the 1950s and 1960s, Prime Minister Jawaharlal Nehru used the creation of states to appease movements, such as the Tamils in the south, who demanded greater autonomy for their linguistic groups. In the 1970s and 1980s, Prime Ministers Indira and Rajiv Gandhi were less willing to compromise with regional forces, partly because they had less national political support, resulting in greater religious and ethnic conflict.

Although they have weakened over the past several decades, India's major political institutions remain strong enough for political leaders to make compromises that mean something. If state leaders can successfully bargain for certain powers, they have state institutions under their control that can make more or less effective use of those powers. Therefore, it is reasonable for them to assume that central authorities will adhere to the bargain struck, in contrast with our last case, Russia.

Russian federalism dates back to the expanding Russian Empire, but its more recent antecedent is federalism under the Soviet Union. Officially, the Soviets created the largest federal system in the world, consisting of fifteen separate Soviet "republics," of which Russia itself was only one; numerous smaller divisions also existed within the Russian Republic. Soviet federalism was elaborate, but absolute control by the Communist Party gave the republics and smaller political units no real autonomy. Local rulers, appointed by the central party, were able to run their governments more or less as personal fiefdoms, but they could not challenge or question central authority if a conflict between the center and the region arose. Federalism in any real sense cannot exist in an authoritarian system as centrally controlled as Soviet communism. The collapse of the Soviet Union resulted in the separation of the fifteen republics

Web link:
A challenge to
Indian federalism

into fifteen sovereign countries. The Russian Republic became a federation, though new and weak institutions have made it relatively ineffective in terms of horizontal accountability vis-à-vis the center.

Ethnic nationalism was a major challenge to post-Soviet Russia. The leaders of former Soviet "ethnic" homelands demanded various degrees of autonomy from Moscow after the Soviet Union collapsed. Most serious was Chechnya's demand for independence, which resulted in two wars between Russia and Chechen rebels in the 1990s. Today, it remains under Russian rule through the control of a Russian-backed government with little popular support and continued rebel opposition. While Chechnya was the only conflict to produce widespread violence, similar tensions across the country resulted in repeated efforts to amend federalism to recognize ethnically defined governments while preserving the Russian Federation as a whole. The Russian constitution of 1993 created an asymmetrical federal system with eighty-nine subnational units. The status of *republic* is given to areas deemed ethnically non-Russian. The titular ethnic group, however, constituted a majority of the population in only seven of the twenty-one republics. For example, in 2002 Karelians were only 9 percent of the population of the Karelia republic and Khakas only 12 percent of Khakassia. Republics have noticeably more power than do other federal units, including more power over state property and trade. The constitution, however, gives the greatest powers to the central government, reserving only a handful of powers for joint national-local control, and reserves no powers exclusively for subnational governments. The central government also has the greatest taxation powers: in 2001 it collected 85 percent of all revenue.

While the Russian constitution seems to have created a highly centralized system, its operation in practice in the 1990s has been termed "legal chaos" (Graney 2009, 205). Between 1993 and 1998, local demands led President Boris Yeltsin to sign separate bilateral treaties with more than half of the country's eighty-nine subnational governments. In the case of Tatarstan, the republic even gained the power to make separate treaties with foreign powers. Until 2004 each republic was governed by an elected president and elected legislatures; Kathryn Stoner-Weiss (2004) argued that these local officials "[are] the undisputed boss of any given region," suggesting local-level semi-authoritarian rule similar to what Gibson (2013) observed in Latin America. Vladimir Putin, Yeltsin's successor, came to power with a goal of centralizing power. Critics questioned the constitutionality of some of his early reforms, but they succeeded in bringing subnational governments and laws more in line with the central government's interests. In 2004 Putin moved to gut local autonomy nearly completely, introducing reforms that allowed him to appoint governors and up to half of the upper house of parliament, further centralizing what was already a centralized system of federalism.

President Medvedev briefly restored elections for governor in 2012, but after returning to power Putin passed a new law "allowing" federal units to request that he appoint a governor instead; as was expected, the first federal unit scheduled for an election, Dagestan, dutifully requested that Putin appoint a governor instead. Putin's reforms were part of his effort to transform Russia from a weak democracy to a semi-authoritarian state in which he and his allies had an effective monopoly on power. While this effort was quite successful, Obydenkova and Swenden (2013) argued that even in this context federalism places some limits on central authority. Ironically, with formal institutions so weak, the most autonomous regional leaders are those in the least democratic regions. Leaders who face no significant opposition rule regions with significant economic resources and have the support of local economic elites so they can bargain with central government authorities for greater autonomy and resources. For weaker local leaders, though, Russian federalism is a shell of what it once was, leaving them with little autonomy.

Russia's long history with federalism has been fraught with difficulty. Federalism under the chaotic democracy of the 1990s was institutionally weak and fragmented by an extreme asymmetry based on Yeltsin's individual deals with the republics and other subnational regions, but it was federalism nonetheless. As we noted earlier, it's difficult to have real federalism without democracy; even the semi-authoritarian rule of the sort Putin created requires enough centralization that any significant federalism is a threat that the ruling elite will seek to eliminate.

Web link:
A brief history of Russian federalism

CASE Summary

Federalism should include a number of institutionalized veto players, limiting majoritarian democracy and adding an element of horizontal accountability. Our three examples demonstrate that the extent to which this is true varies greatly and does not always depend on formal rules. Brazil and India are models of unusually decentralized and centralized systems, respectively. In Brazil, state governments and leaders were so powerful, at least until recent reforms, that they made national governing difficult. In India, by contrast, Congress Party domination and constitutional rules favoring the center made states quite weak. The party system in India, however, has had a role in decentralizing that power, as Congress has become dependent on state-level parties to stay in power. The evolution of federalism in both countries is an example of the bargaining relationship inherent in all federal systems; how much accountability exists and who can check whom depend on past bargains between governing units and their leaders. Russia, on the other hand, shows the extreme case, that of a central authority able to eliminate virtually all real elements of federal autonomy. This case shows that federalism at its core is a liberal system: to function at all, it must allow some autonomy from central authority.

CASE Questions

1. Comparing our three cases, what is the most important factor in understanding differences in how much accountability federalism provides?
2. What do our three cases suggest about the possible trade-off between accountability and effective policymaking in federal systems?

CONCLUSION

Political institutions clearly have an impact on who has the most power in a society and how they can exercise it. In strong institutions, the formal rules matter because on the whole they are obeyed. Rational-choice institutionalists argue that formal rules create a set of incentives to which political actors respond, incentives that can produce greater compromise or greater conflict in the political system as a whole.

A crucial question for a democracy is how the executive power of the state can be effectively limited. The first and most obvious answer is to subject the executive to vertical accountability via elections. That leaves great variation, though, focused mostly on horizontal accountability between elections: Does one set of governing institutions systematically hold executive power more accountable than other types of institutions? The answer in most cases depends not just on the formal governing institutions but on the broader political context in which they operate. The Westminster model seems to provide the weakest horizontal check on executive power, but only when the PM leads a cohesive majority party in parliament. And it arguably provides the clearest vertical accountability: voters know exactly who is responsible for government policy. Coalition governments, as India has had since 1989 and the United Kingdom since 2010, provide a nearly constant check on the PM, as she must secure coalition partners' agreement to make any significant policy. The judiciary in most democracies is specifically tasked with horizontal accountability via judicial review, but we've seen that courts must assert their independence carefully, given their lack of democratic legitimation via elections and lack of other resources on which to base their power. Japan shows us that even when the elected executive is held accountable, an entrenched bureaucracy may wield great and unelected power and successfully resist reforms to democratize it.

Besides accountability, a second great question in liberal democracy is how to protect minority rights. Accountability is to the majority, which can and often does trample the liberal rights of minorities. Does one set of institutions help preserve minority rights better than others? Most Americans would immediately think of the Supreme Court as fulfilling this role, but political science research indicates that the judiciary upholds the interests of the dominant majority at least as often as it does the minority, and that is likely to be even more true when the judiciary as an institution is relatively weak (Chinn 2006).

More consensual democracies in which a variety of viewpoints are represented within the major governing institutions and compromise is required to make decisions would seem to enhance minority rights. One form of this is federalism, which is often designed specifically to protect ethnic and regional minorities. How well this works depends on how much real power—determined not only by formal rules but by control of revenues—a federal system provides the national and regional governments. Again, the broader political context matters. For example, the strength of federalism in India has varied mainly due to changes in the party system.

A third major question for democracy involves the potential trade-off between representation and effective policymaking: Do some institutions provide more of one or the other, and does a clear optimum balance between them exist? Lijphart's consensual and majoritarian democratic models directly address this question. Majoritarian systems like the Westminster model, as well as tightly controlled policymaking such as exists under Japan's developmental state, ought to provide more effective policymaking at the expense of some immediate representation. Institutions that provide more horizontal accountability and require greater consensus, such as the U.S. or Brazilian presidential systems with weak parties and federalism, seem likely to slow down the policy-making process. Lijphart, though, argued that overall consensual models legislate nearly as effectively as majoritarian systems but add much greater representation. While Lijphart favored that balance, the debate is far from concluded. Political context matters here as well: the number and strength of political parties in office will affect how the institutions operate, as Indian history demonstrates—a subject we will examine in detail in the next chapter.

Looking comparatively, we can ask why the same institutions seem to work better in certain places than in others and why particular countries come to adopt particular institutions in the first place. Our cases suggest that wholesale change of institutions is difficult and unusual. Countries seem prone to follow what they know, as the examples of Britain's former colonies suggest. It is rare for a country to decide, as France did in 1958, that a complete change of institutions is in order, but countries transitioning to democracy face this choice as they write new constitutions. Cultural and historical institutional theories seem to explain best this continuity of institutions. Despite the elegant logic of rational-choice arguments about which works best, deeply held values, socialized into the population over time, tend to preserve existing institutions unless they prove exceptionally dysfunctional.

No clear answer to the question of why an institution works better in one place than another is obvious, though certainly social, political, and ethnic contexts matter greatly. A society that is deeply divided by ethnic difference and other past conflicts is likely to benefit from a more consensual set of institutions that requires compromise at every step of the way. A majoritarian system or powerful single office like a presidency is likely to breed distrust, as no political actor in the system is willing to trust the others with such great power. Excessive fragmentation across political parties and local governments, though, may make policymaking nearly impossible or even threaten the continued viability of the state as a whole.

The entire study of democratic institutions is also enmeshed in the theoretical debate between pluralists and elite theorists over who rules. It is about the trade-off between elite power, which might be more effective at making policy, and more dispersed power, which, while slowing down the policy-making process, provides greater representation and accountability. The debate is also about the extent to which pluralism is an accurate depiction of the dispersion of political power in a democracy and how institutions can assist in ensuring that it remains accurate.

KEY CONCEPTS

asymmetrical federal system (p. 309)	legislature (p. 261)
bicameral legislature (p. 269)	majoritarian democracy (p. 261)
coalition government (p. 262)	member of parliament (MP) (p. 265)
code law (p. 290)	New Public Management (NPM) (p. 298)
cohabitation (p. 281)	parliamentarism (p. 264)
common law (p. 289)	political accountability (p. 259)
consensus democracy (p. 262)	political appointees (p. 297)
devolution (p. 309)	presidentialism (p. 272)
executive (p. 260)	prime minister (PM) (p. 264)
federal systems (p. 305)	principal-agent problem (p. 296)
head of government (p. 264)	rent seeking (p. 299)
head of state (p. 264)	semipresidentialism (p. 280)
horizontal accountability (p. 259)	separation of powers (p. 272)
institutionalization (p. 258)	*stare decisis* (p. 290)
iron triangles (p. 303)	symmetrical federal system (p. 309)
judicial independence (p. 291)	unitary systems (p. 305)
judicial review (p. 289)	vertical accountability (p. 259)
judiciary (p. 261)	veto player (p. 263)
legislative oversight (p. 297)	vote of no confidence (p. 265)

Sharpen your skills with SAGE edge at **edge.sagepub.com/orvis3e.** **SAGE edge for students** provides a personalized approach to help you accomplish your coursework goals in an easy-to-use learning environment.

WORKS CITED

Amoretti, Ugo M., and Nancy Gina Bermeo, eds. 2004. *Federalism and Territorial Cleavages.* Baltimore, MD: Johns Hopkins University Press.

Bevir, Mark. 2010. *Democratic Governance.* Princeton, NJ: Princeton University Press.

Borges, André. 2011. "The Political Consequences of Center-Led Redistribution in Brazilian Federalism." *Latin American Research Review* 46 (3): 21–45.

Cheibub, José Antonio. 2007. *Presidentialism, Parliamentarism, and Democracy.* New York: Cambridge University Press.

Chinn, Stuart. 2006. "Democracy-Promoting Judicial Review in a Two-Party System: Dealing with Second-Order Preferences." *Polity* 38 (4): 478–500. doi:10.1057/palgrave.polity.2300071.

Dahl, Robert. 1957. "Decision-Making in a Democracy: The Supreme Court as a National Policy-Maker." *Journal of Public Law* 6: 279–294.

Diaz-Cayeros, Alberto. 2006. *Federalism, Fiscal Authority, and Centralization in Latin America.* Cambridge, UK: Cambridge University Press.

Ekeh, Peter P. 1975. "Colonialism and the Two Publics in Africa: A Theoretical Statement." *Comparative Studies in Society and History* 17 (1): 91–112. doi:10.1017/S0010417500007659.

Elgie, Robert. 2011. *Semi-Presidentialism: Sub-Types and Democratic Performance.* Oxford: Oxford University Press.

Fearon, James. 2003. "Ethnic and Cultural Diversity by Country." *Journal of Economic Growth* 8 (2): 195–222. doi:10.1023/A:1024419522867.

Ferejohn, John, and Pasquale Pasquino. 2003. "Rule of Democracy and Rule of Law." In *Democracy and the Rule of Law,* edited by José Maria Maravall and Adam Przeworski, 242–260. Cambridge, UK: Cambridge University Press.

Ferejohn, John, Frances Rosenbluth, and Charles Shipan. 2007. "Comparative Judicial Politics." In *The Oxford Handbook of Comparative Politics,* edited by Carles Boix and Susan Carol Stokes, 727–551. Oxford, UK: Oxford University Press.

Forum of Federations. 2011 (http://www.forumfed.org).

Freedom House. 2007. Democracies (http://www.freedomhouse.org).

Gibson, Edward L. 2013. *Boundary Control: Subnational Authoritarianism in Federal Democracies.* Cambridge, UK: Cambridge University Press.

Gibson, James L., Gregory A. Caldeira, and Vanessa A. Baird. 1998. "On the Legitimacy of National High Courts." *American Political Science Review* 92 (2): 343–358.

Graney, Katherine E. 2009. "Ethnicity and Identity." In *Understanding Contemporary Russia,* edited by Michael Bressler, 191–220. Boulder, CO: Lynne Rienner.

Hirschl, Ran. 2009. "The Judicialization of Politics." In *The Oxford Handbook of Political Science,* edited by Robert E. Goodin, 253–274. Oxford: Oxford University Press.

Huber, John D., and Charles R. Shipan. 2002. *Deliberate Discretion? The Institutional Foundations of Bureaucratic Autonomy.* Cambridge, UK: Cambridge University Press.

Johnston, Michael. 2005. *Syndromes of Corruption: Wealth, Power, and Democracy.* New York: Cambridge University Press.

Kam, Christopher J. 2009. *Party Discipline and Parliamentary Politics.* Cambridge, UK: Cambridge University Press.

Kapiszewski, Diana. 2012. *High Courts and Economic Governance in Argentina and Brazil.* Cambridge, UK: Cambridge University Press.

Kohli, Atul. 2004. "India: Federalism and the Accommodation of Ethnic Nationalism." In *Federalism and Territorial Cleavages,* edited by Ugo M. Amoretti and Nancy G. Bermeo, 281–300. Baltimore, MD: Johns Hopkins University Press.

Landfried, Christine. 1995. "Germany." In *The Global Expansion of Judicial Power,* edited by C. Neal Tate and Torbjörn Vallinder, 307–324. New York: New York University Press.

Leeke, Matthew, Chris Sear, and Oonagh Gay. 2003. *An Introduction to Devolution in the UK.* Research Paper 03/84, November 17. House of Commons Library (http://www.parliament.uk/documents/commons/lib/research/rp2003/rp03-084.pdf).

Lijphart, Arend. 1999. *Patterns of Democracy: Government Forms and Performance in Thirty-six Countries.* New Haven, CT: Yale University Press.

Linz, Juan José. 1990. "The Perils of Presidentialism." *Journal of Democracy* 1 (1): 51–69. doi:10.1353/jod.1990.0011.

Obydenkova, Anastassia, and Wilfried Swenden. 2013. "Autocracy-Sustaining versus Democratic Federalism: Explaining the Divergent Trajectories of Territorial Politics in Russia and Western Europe." *Territory, Politics, Governance* 1(1): 86–122 (http://www.tandfonline.com/doi/pdf/10.1080/21622671.2013.763733).

O'Donnell, Guillermo. 1999. "Horizontal Accountability in New Democracies." In *The Self-Restraining State: Power and*

Accountability in New Democracies, edited by Andreas Schedler, Larry Diamond, and Marc F. Plattner, 29–52. Boulder, CO: Lynne Rienner.

O'Dwyer, Conor. 2006. *Runaway State-Building: Patronage Politics and Democratic Development.* Baltimore, MD: Johns Hopkins University Press.

Oliveira, Vanessa Elias de Dados. 2005. "The Judiciary and Privatizations in Brazil: Is There a Judicialization of Politics? [Judiciario e privatizacoes no Brasil: Existe uma judicializacao da politica?]." *Dados* 48 (3): 559–587.

Pelizzo, Ricardo, 2010. "Fragmentation and Performance: the Indian Case." *Commonwealth and Comparative Politics* 48 (3): 261–280.

Pempel, T. J. 2000. *Regime Shift: Comparative Dynamics of the Japanese Political Economy.* Ithaca, NY: Cornell University Press.

Pereira, Carlos, Timothy J. Power, and Eric De Raile. 2011. "Presidentialism, Coalitions, and Accountability." In *Corruption and Democracy in Brazil: The Struggle for Accountability,* edited by Timothy J. Power and Matthew M. Taylor, 31–55. South Bend, IN: University of Notre Dame Press.

Powell, G. Bingham, Jr. 2000. *Elections as Instruments of Democracy: Majoritarian and Proportional Visions.* New Haven, CT: Yale University Press.

Power, Timothy J. 2010. "Optimism, Pessimism, and Coalitional Presidentialism: Debating the Institutional Design of Brazilian Democracy." *Bulletin of Latin American Research* 29 (1): 18–33.

Puddington, Arch. 2010. "Freedom in the World 2010: Erosion of Freedom Intensifies" (http://www.freedomhouse.org/).

Rao, M. Govinda, and Nirvikar Singh. 2005. *The Political Economy of Federalism in India.* Oxford, UK: Oxford University Press.

Riker, William. 1964. *Federalism: Origin, Operation, Significance.* Boston: Little, Brown.

Samuels, David. 2007. "Separation of Powers." In *The Oxford Handbook of Comparative Politics*, edited by Carles Boix and Susan Carol Stokes, 703–726. Oxford, UK: Oxford University Press.

Santiso, Carlos. 2003. "Economic Reform and Judicial Governance in Brazil: Balancing Independence with Accountability." *Democratization* 10 (4): 161–180. doi:10.1080/13510340312331294077.

Schleiter, Petra, and Edward Morgan-Jones. 2009. "Review Article: Citizens, Presidents and Assemblies: The Study of Semi-Presidentialism beyond Duverger and Linz." *British Journal of Political Science* 39: 871–892. doi:10.1017/S0007123409990159.

Schneider, Aaron. 2007. "Governance Reform and Institutional Change in Brazil: Federalism and Tax." *Commonwealth & Comparative Politics* 45 (4): 475–498. doi:10.1080/14662040701659928.

Shankar, B. L., and Valerian Rodrigues. 2011. *The Indian Parliament: A Democracy at Work.* New Delhi: Oxford University Press.

Shinoda, Tomohito. 2012. "Japan's Failed Experiment: The DPJ and Institutional Change for Political Leadership." *Asian Survey* 52 (5): 799–821.

Stoner-Weiss, Kathryn. 2004. "Russia: Managing Territorial Cleavages under Dual Transitions." In *Federalism and Territorial Cleavages,* edited by Ugo M. Amoretti and Nancy G. Bermeo, 301–326. Baltimore, MD: Johns Hopkins University Press.

Tate, C. Neal, and Torbjörn Vallinder. 1995. *The Global Expansion of Judicial Power.* New York: New York University Press.

Taylor, Matthew M. 2008. *Judging Policy: Courts and Policy Reform in Democratic Brazil.* Stanford, CA: Stanford University Press.

Transparency International. 2010. "Corruption Perceptions Index" (http://www.transparency.org/policy_research/surveys_indices/cpi).

Tsebelis, George. 2002. *Veto Players: How Political Institutions Work.* Princeton, NJ: Princeton University Press.

Vanberg, Georg. 2005. *The Politics of Constitutional Review in Germany*. Cambridge, UK: Cambridge University Press.

Williams, Laron K. 2011. "Unsuccessful Success? Failed No-Confidence Motions, Competence Signals, and Electoral Support." *Comparative Political Studies* 44 (11): 1474–1499.

Wolferen, Karel van. 2010. "Japan's Stumbling Revolution." *The Asia-Pacific Journal* (April 12) (http://japanfocus.org/-Karel_van-Wolferen/3341).

Yadav, Vineeta. 2011. *Political Parties, Business Groups, and Corruption in Developing Countries*. Oxford, UK: Oxford University Press.

Yakushiji, Katsuyuki. 2013. *Abe and the Triumph of the Old LDP* (http://www.tokyofoundation.org/en/articles/2013/abe-and-triumph-of-old-ldp).

RESOURCES FOR FURTHER STUDY

Cappelletti, Mauro, Paul J. Kollmer, and Joanne M. Olson. 1989. *The Judicial Process in Comparative Perspective*. Oxford, UK: Clarendon Press.

Frederickson, H. George, and Kevin B. Smith. 2003. *The Public Administration Theory Primer*. Boulder, CO: Westview Press.

Graber, Mark A. 2005. "Constructing Judicial Review." *Annual Review of Political Science* 8: 425–451. doi:10.1146/annurev.polisci.8.082103.104905.

Herron, Erik S., and Kirk A. Randazzo. 2003. "The Relationship between Independence and Judicial Review in Post-Communist Courts." *Journal of Politics* 65 (2): 422–438. doi:10.1111/1468-2508.t01-3-00007.

Mainwaring, Scott, and Matthew Soberg Shugart, eds. 1997. *Presidentialism and Democracy in Latin America*. New York: Cambridge University Press.

Mulgan, Aurelia George. 2002. *Japan's Failed Revolution: Koizumi and the Politics of Economic Reform*. Canberra, Australia: Asia Pacific Press.

Rosenbluth, Frances McCall, and Michael F. Thies. 2010. *Japan Transformed: Political Change and Economic Restructuring*. Princeton, NJ: Princeton University Press.

WEB RESOURCES

Binghamton University, The Institutions and Elections Project
(http://www2.binghamton.edu/political-science/institutions-and-elections-project.html)

International Institute for Democracy and Electoral Assistance (IDEA), Democracy and Development
(http://www.idea.int/development/index.cfm)

Transparency International
(http://www.transparency.org)

Unified Democracy Scores
(http://www.unified-democracy-scores.org/index.html)

University of Bern, Comparative Political Data Sets
(http://www.ipw.unibe.ch/content/team/klaus_armingeon/comparative_political_data_sets/index_ger.html)

7

INSTITUTIONS OF PARTICIPATION AND REPRESENTATION IN DEMOCRACIES

KEY QUESTIONS

- Do some types of institutions in democracies provide better overall representation of and influence for average citizens?
- How do institutions affect the representation of ethnic, gender, religious, and other groups?
- Why do people join political parties and participate in other kinds of political activity?
- How do different electoral and party systems affect political leaders' behavior?
- Are there clear patterns of when and where particular party and electoral systems develop?

This chapter examines the institutions that shape political participation and interest representation in democracies. Virtually all regimes allow some degree of participation and representation, if only to shore up their own legitimacy or at least the appearance of it. Regimes differ dramatically, however, in the degree to which they seek to control and limit participation and representation. Democratic regimes all claim to value and promote widespread participation and representation, but they differ significantly in regard to the "best" ways to promote citizen involvement and fair and accurate representation of interests. In general, democratic regimes face the problem of both stimulating and channeling participation and representation, whereas authoritarian regimes are more interested in constraining or co-opting them. Because participation and representation are vital to and hallmarks of democratic regimes, we discuss the relevant institutions in these regimes first. In chapter 8, we examine and compare the same kinds of institutions in authoritarian regimes.

Participation and representation clearly have major implications for answering the question, "Who rules?" Any democratic system worthy of the name ought to translate greater citizen participation into greater citizen power and influence, however imperfectly. Citizens in all democracies elect people to represent them, but democracies differ widely in how those people are elected and which citizens' voices are represented

A member of the "Occupy Movement" protests in Washington, D.C., in November 2011. The movement questioned whether the United States is still truly a democracy, given what they see as the undue influence of the political and economic elite, specifically the "top 1%" of income earners.

more fully. Different electoral systems embody different principles of representation and have different effects on accountability. We can demonstrate this by examining how well the systems represent those who seem likely to have less power in the society at large, such as women or racial or ethnic minorities. Given that these groups typically have fewer economic resources, do some systems of representation and participation allow them to have greater influence than do other systems? Elite theorists argue that modern electoral democracies in reality give limited power to those in more marginalized positions; elites dominate the national discourse, control major institutions, and influence voters more than voters influence who is in office. If true, this allocation of influence obviously undermines vertical accountability, a crucial element of democracy.

Another central question that immediately comes to mind regarding participation and representation is, Why do people participate in politics in the first place? We might imagine that the answers would be obvious: people want to have power or influence, to make a contribution to their community and nation, or to gain recognition and status. While all this is undoubtedly true for some political activists, rational-actor theorists

Video link:
Ron Paul, "The American Power Elite"

long ago explained that for most people most of the time, there is no rational reason to participate in political activity, including voting, because most people cannot significantly influence political outcomes. Expending time or money to work toward any political goal is irrational, given the huge number of citizens and the correspondingly small impact of each individual. This is an obvious problem in a democracy, and it is exacerbated by the fact that members of the elite, with their much greater direct access to key decision makers, have a greater incentive to participate and thus seem more likely to influence policy. Without any ameliorating circumstances, this would suggest that elite theory is correct: "democracies" are really elite controlled.

To overcome this dilemma, democratic institutions need to help resolve this **collective action problem**: individuals are unwilling to engage in a particular activity because of their rational belief that their individual actions will have little or no effect, yet when they all fail to act, all suffer adverse consequences (in the case of participation in democracy, losing control to the elite). If individuals participate in politics, they may be able to benefit collectively, but it is irrational for each individual to participate in the first place because his individual impact will be negligible. Understanding to what extent institutions overcome this problem is crucial to understanding how democratic any particular system is. A related question is, What influence do institutions—in this chapter, in particular, electoral and party systems—have on political leaders' behavior? What incentives do they give leaders? Do these incentives encourage leaders to promote more participation and representation, or less?

We will see that democracies vary greatly in terms of the three key institutions of representation and participation: elections, parties, and civil society. A glance at the Country and Concept table shows variation among our case study countries across all the institutions we will define and examine in this chapter. Can we explain these patterns? If certain types of institutions can better represent people than others, where and why have they developed, and can they be replicated elsewhere to the betterment of democracy overall?

Web link:
Occupy Wall
Street's webpage

collective action problem
Individuals being unwilling to engage in a particular activity because of their rational belief that their individual actions will have little or no effect, yet collectively suffering adverse consequences when all fail to act

FORMAL INSTITUTIONS: THE ELECTORAL SYSTEM

electoral systems
Formal, legal mechanisms that translate votes into control over political offices and shares of political power

Electoral systems are formal, legal mechanisms that translate votes into control over political offices and shares of political power. Different electoral systems provide distinct incentives to individual voters. They also influence political leaders' behavior and political parties' respective strengths and numbers, so they are crucial to understanding how individual parties function and what opportunities parties provide for citizen participation.

In almost all elections, enfranchised citizens vote for people who will represent them rather than voting directly on policy. This raises a key issue for electoral systems: How are votes aggregated and counted? Different systems are based on fundamentally different normative theories of what "good" representation looks like. One common choice is to represent people geographically; a country divides its territory

COUNTRY AND CONCEPT
Parties, Elections, and Civil Society

Country	Electoral system	Party system	Number of significant parties in legislature[1]	Interest-group system
Brazil	Open-list PR	Multiple	9	Pluralist
China	NA	One	1	State corporatist
Germany	Mixed PR	Two and a half	5	Neocorporatist
India	SMD/FPTP	Multiple	5 (in addition to dozens of minor parties)	Pluralist
Iran	Mixed SMD and multimember districts	None	0[2]	Weak
Japan	Mixed PR	Multiple	4	Pluralist
Mexico	Mixed PR	Multiple	3	Neocorporatist
Nigeria	SMD/FPTP	Dominant	3[3]	Weak
Russia	Mixed PR	Dominant	2	Weak
United Kingdom	SMD/FPTP	Two	3	Pluralist
United States	SMD/FPTP	Two	2	Pluralist

[1]Data on number of parties in legislatures are from *Political Handbook of the World, 2013* (Washington, DC: CQ Press, 2013).

[2]Although political parties are permitted under the constitution, none were recognized following the formal dissolution of the government-sponsored Islamic Republican Party in June 1987, despite Tehran's announcement in October 1988 that such groups would thenceforth be welcomed if they "demonstrated commitment to the Islamic system."

[3]Parties winning a significant number of seats in parliament in the 2007 elections and running viable presidential candidates in 2011 elections.

into geographic units, and each unit elects one or more representatives. This system assumes that citizens can best be represented via their membership in geographically defined communities. In contrast, some countries elect their legislatures nationally, or in very large districts. This system assumes that citizens' beliefs as espoused by parties or individual candidates, rather than geographical community, are most important for representation. In rare cases, democratic countries choose to represent specific groups within society rather than or in addition to geographic districts or parties. After an ethnic conflict, for instance, a country may decide it needs to provide special representation for ethnic minorities. Several countries have also legally reserved seats in parliament specifically for women to ensure that they are represented. Ultimately, electoral system choice depends on an answer to the questions, On what basis do we wish to be represented? and, With whom do we share our most important political interests or views?

In addition, electoral institutions often have important effects on governance because they affect the composition of legislatures and the executive branch. Familiar examples of gridlock in American politics or the legendary instability of Italian parliamentary regimes after World War II illustrate this dynamic. These problems do not result from presidential or parliamentary institutions, per se, but rather from the ways in which these institutions interact with the electoral system. Electoral systems help determine as well how majoritarian or consensual a particular democracy is. Systems that encourage many, fragmented parties are more consensual: they provide representation of diverse views in the legislature, but they may make effective government difficult because of the instability of coalition governments in parliamentary systems or the gridlock of different parties controlling the executive and legislative branches in presidential systems. Systems that encourage fewer parties tend to have the opposite effect and therefore are more majoritarian.

Single-Member Districts: "First-Past-the-Post" and Majoritarian Voting

single-member district (SMD)
Electoral system in which each geographic district elects a single representative to a legislature

plurality
The receipt of the most votes, but not necessarily a majority

"first-past-the-post" (FPTP)
An SMD system in which the candidate with a plurality of votes wins

Americans borrowed the **single-member district (SMD)** from Great Britain. In both countries, each geographic district elects a single representative. Two versions of SMD exist: plurality and majoritarian. In a **plurality** system, whoever gets the most votes, even if it's not a majority, wins the election. In a race with more than two contestants, the winner can be elected with a relatively low percentage of the vote total: 30 percent or so is not uncommon. This system is often called **"first-past-the-post" (FPTP)** because, as in a horse race, the single winner merely needs to edge out the next closest competitor. In a majoritarian system, the winner must gain an absolute majority of the votes (50 percent, plus one) rather than just a plurality. If no candidate wins an absolute majority, a second election takes place between the top two candidates to produce a winner. Because SMD systems produce one winner per district, they tend to be part of and support the majoritarian model of democracy; a single-party government is more likely to result, and each voter has a specific representative from his electoral district to hold accountable for government actions. Minority voices, however, are less likely to be represented.

Advocates of SMD systems argue they can give constituents a strong sense of identification with their representative. Even if you didn't vote for your representative and you disagree with her, she is still expected to work for you (as U.S. representatives often do by solving Social Security problems for constituents or writing letters of nomination to service academies). Your most vital needs and interests are assumed to have been aggregated into those of your district. Curtice and Shively (2009), however, examined this empirically and found no significant differences between SMD and other systems in terms of voters' level of contact with their representative, their knowledge of who their representative was, or their sense that their representative was representing them well.

Critics of the SMD system make two main arguments against it. First, many votes are "wasted," in the sense that the winning candidate does not represent the views of the voters who did not vote for him. This is especially true in systems with more than two viable parties. Perhaps only 30 or 35 percent of voters actually favored the winner, so the votes of the majority were arguably wasted. This may be one reason why voter participation tends to be lower in countries with SMD than elsewhere. Voters—especially those who prefer minor parties—may find voting a waste of time; the system doesn't encourage them to overcome the collective action problem. Supporters of SMD argue, however, that even voters who have not voted for their representative are represented via **virtual representation**: candidates from their party are elected in other districts and so their views are represented in the legislature, albeit not by their representative.

Second, this problem can be compounded by the under- or overrepresentation of particular parties. Consider a case in which a third party wins a significant share of the votes in many districts but a plurality in only one or two. The party would win a lot of votes but get only a couple of seats in the legislature. Conversely, if a large number of candidates from a particular party win by a very small plurality in their districts, that party's vote in the legislature will be inflated. The number of its representatives will suggest an overwhelming national consensus, when in fact the party may not have even won a majority of the vote nationwide. Figure 7.1 gives an example from Great

Virtual representation
When voters' views are represented indirectly in the legislature by their chosen party's candidates who have been elected in districts other than their own

Video link:
First past the pizza

British demonstrators demand that the country switch to a proportional representation electoral system. The long-standing SMD system advantages the two largest parties. British citizens ultimately voted in a referendum in 2011 to keep their old system.

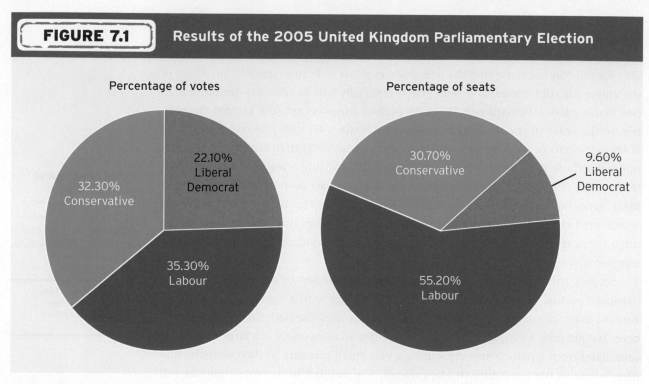

FIGURE 7.1 Results of the 2005 United Kingdom Parliamentary Election

Percentage of votes

- 22.10% Liberal Democrat
- 32.30% Conservative
- 35.30% Labour

Percentage of seats

- 30.70% Conservative
- 9.60% Liberal Democrat
- 55.20% Labour

Source: BBC (http://news.bbc.co.uk/2/hi/uk_news/politics/vote_2005/constituencies/default.stm).

Web link:
Electoral Reform webpage on FPTP

Video link:
John Cleese explains proportional representation

Britain's 2005 election, in which the two major parties, Labour and Conservative, won similar vote shares but very different numbers of seats, and the third party, the Liberal Democrats, won a far larger share of votes than parliamentary seats. Does this constitute a good representation of the voting public? According to proponents of FPTP, it does, but others argue that the voice of a large segment of the electorate is ignored. On the other hand, this makes the system majoritarian: it may promote efficient, stable policymaking by allowing decisive legislative action. This is one reason why some proponents prefer FPTP, despite its wasted votes, to the primary alternative, proportional representation.

Proportional Representation

proportional representation (PR)
Electoral system in which seats in a legislature are apportioned on a purely proportional basis, giving each party the share of seats that matches its share of the total vote

Proportional representation (PR) differs from SMD in almost every conceivable way. In PR, representatives are chosen nationally or in large electoral districts with multiple representatives for each district. Thus, either a national legislature is simply divided on a purely proportional basis, or multiple representatives for large districts are allocated proportionally according to the vote in each district. So, for instance, a party that gains 25 percent of the national vote receives a quarter (or very nearly a quarter) of the seats in the legislature. Most PR systems, though, include a minimal electoral threshold—for example, 3 or 5 percent of the vote—a party must cross to gain representation in parliament. Any parties that cross that threshold can be certain that they will be represented. As Figure 7.2 demonstrates for the 2010 Swedish parliamentary elections, a PR system translates each party's share of the votes into almost exactly the same share of legislative seats (in stark contrast to the FPTP system in Britain, as a quick comparison of Figures 7.1 and 7.2 shows). PR systems tend to be part of and support consensus models of democracy; multiple voices via multiple parties are likely to be represented in the legislature, and coalition government is a common outcome.

If voters are not choosing among individuals running for a single seat, whom or what are they voting for, and who ends up in the legislature? The answer reflects a very different view of representation from SMD, because in PR systems, the voter is usually voting for a party, not an individual. In **closed-list proportional representation** (the version of PR most dissimilar to SMD), each party presents a ranked list of candidates for all the seats in the legislature. Voters can see the list and know who the "top" candidates are, but when they vote, they actually vote for the party. If party X gets ten seats in the legislature, then the top ten candidates on the party list occupy those seats.

Another variant of PR is called **open-list proportional representation.** In this version, voters are presented with a list of candidates and vote for the candidate of their choice. When the votes are counted, each party receives a number of seats proportional to the total number of votes its candidates received. Those seats are then awarded to the top individual vote getters within the party.

PR assumes that voters primarily want the ideas and values embodied by their parties to be represented. Voters are represented by the party they support in the legislature, regardless of the geographic origins of individual legislators. PR has some obvious advantages over SMD. First, there are very few wasted votes, because even very small parties can gain some seats. To the extent that voters feel represented by a party, they can be assured that someone in the legislature is there to give voice to their views—although realistically, smaller parties can usually only impact policy via coalitions with larger parties. Second, perhaps because fewer votes are wasted, participation rates in PR countries are higher, as Figure 7.3 shows. Proponents of PR argue that elections under PR systems are therefore more democratic and more broadly representative, since larger percentages of voters participate and virtually all are guaranteed to have their views represented in the legislature. PR systems also tend to elect women and members of ethnic or racial minorities more frequently than SMD systems do, as party leaders often feel compelled (and in some countries are required by law) to include women or minority candidates on their party lists. However, as the following Critical Inquiry box suggests, it's not always clear if this is due to the PR system or other reasons, such as cultural mores in the countries that have PR systems.

Of course, the PR system has its critics, who point to the "indirect" nature of PR elections: voters don't really choose individual representatives, even in an open-list system. In large, multimember districts, the individual voter does not know that a certain

closed-list proportional representation
Electoral system in which each party presents a ranked list of candidates, voters vote for the party rather than for individual candidates, and each party awards the seats it wins to the candidates on its list in rank order

open-list proportional representation
Electoral system in which multiple candidates run in each district, voters vote for the individual candidate of their choice, and the candidates with the most votes in the party get the seats the party wins

FIGURE 7.2   Results of Sweden's 2010 Parliamentary Election

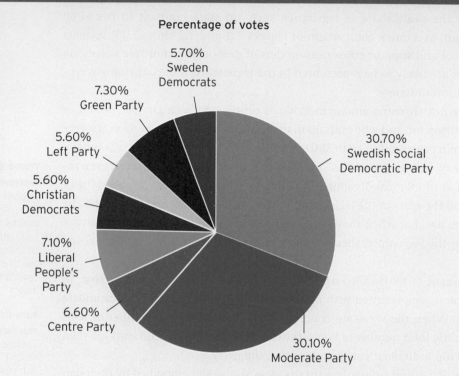

Percentage of votes

- 5.70% Sweden Democrats
- 7.30% Green Party
- 5.60% Left Party
- 5.60% Christian Democrats
- 7.10% Liberal People's Party
- 6.60% Centre Party
- 30.70% Swedish Social Democratic Party
- 30.10% Moderate Party

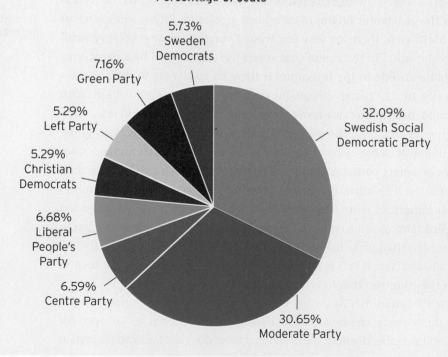

Percentage of seats

- 5.73% Sweden Democrats
- 7.16% Green Party
- 5.29% Left Party
- 5.29% Christian Democrats
- 6.68% Liberal People's Party
- 6.59% Centre Party
- 32.09% Swedish Social Democratic Party
- 30.65% Moderate Party

Source: Election Resources (http://electionresources.org/se/riksdag.php?election=2010).

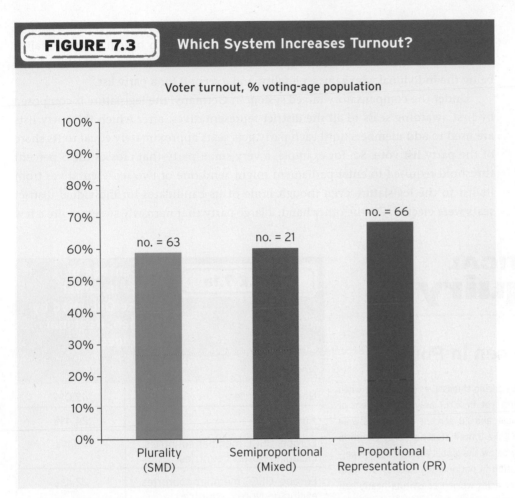

FIGURE 7.3 **Which System Increases Turnout?**

Voter turnout, % voting-age population

Source: Data are from International Institute for Democracy and Electoral Assistance, "What Affects Turnout?" Figure 25 (http://www.idea.int/vt/survey/voter_turnout8.cfm).

person is "her" unique representative. And in a closed-list system, party officials are the ultimate arbiters of a candidate's fate because they assign the ranking. Because of this, legislators are less likely to open local offices and focus on local issues (Shugart 2005). In addition, opponents of PR argue that having a broad range of parties in a legislature often has negative effects. Small parties, as noted above, often have little voice unless they join coalitions, but small extremist parties may gain inordinate power if they are able to negotiate key roles in ruling coalitions, as was long true for ultra-Orthodox religious parties in Israel. Coalitions can be hard to form in such a fragmented environment, and where they do form, they may be unstable. PR, therefore, is often criticized for producing governmental instability and ineffective, fragmented policymaking.

Web link: Netanyahu forms coalition with a nationalist party

Mixed, or Semiproportional, Systems

Given the plusses and minuses of SMD and PR, it is not surprising that some countries, including our case studies Germany and Japan, have chosen to combine the two. The

mixed, or semiproportional
An electoral system that combines single-member district representation with overall proportionality in allocation of legislative seats to parties; Germany is a key example

resulting hybrid is called a **mixed, or semiproportional,** system. A semiproportional system combines single-member district representation with overall proportionality. Voters cast two ballots: one for a representative from their district, with the winner being the individual who gains a plurality, and a second for a party list.

Under the compensatory mixed system in Germany, the legislature is composed by first awarding seats to all the district representatives, after which the party lists are used to add members until each party gets seats approximately equal to its share of the party list vote. So, for example, a very small party that crosses the 5 percent threshold required to enter parliament might send one or two representatives from its list to the legislature even though none of its candidates for individual district seats were elected. On the other hand, a large party that narrowly sweeps quite a few

CRITICAL inquiry

Women in Power

Americans are used to considering themselves progressive when it comes to women's rights, yet in 2013 only 17.8 percent of representatives in the House and 20 percent of senators were women. Those numbers put the United States seventy-eighth in the world in 2013, slightly below the global average of 20.8 percent for female representation in national legislatures. As Table 7.1b shows, in some democracies women constitute nearly half of the legislature, while others fare far worse than in the United States. What explains these disparities in how many women achieve power at the national level?

Table 7.1a suggests an initial hypothesis based on political culture, because regional breakdowns seem to suggest that it plays a role. An alternative hypothesis is that the election of women is a case in which institutions matter. Table 7.1b suggests that PR systems are more conducive to electing women than are SMD systems. Because closed PR systems (most PR systems are closed) require parties to submit lists of candidates, more women are nominated. A party may be under some pressure to include at least some women on its list, since an all-male (or even overwhelmingly male) list could provoke negative reaction. Some PR systems include a quota system: parties must include a certain percentage of women candidates on their lists. A third hypothesis is that the longer a country is democratic, the more women will gain office; democracy provides an opportunity for underrepresented and marginalized groups to gain more

TABLE 7.1a	Percentage of Seats in Lower House Occupied by Women, Regional Averages
Region	**% women**
Nordic countries	42.0%
Americas	24.4%
Europe, OSCE member countries, including Nordic countries	24.1%
Europe, OSCE member countries, excluding Nordic countries	22.4%
sub-Saharan Africa	21.2%
Asia	19.0%
Arab states	15.7%
Pacific	12.7%

Source: Data are from Interparliamentary Union, "Women in National Parliaments" (http://www.ipu.org/wmn-e/world.htm).

influence, and the longer democracy lasts the more likely it will be that such groups will gain influence.

Look at the tables carefully. Based on the data, which of the hypotheses seems to be the best explanation for how many women are elected to national legislatures? Why do you come to the conclusion you do on this question? What implications does your answer have for which electoral system is most democratic?

TABLE 7.1b	Women in World Legislatures		
Country	% women in lower house	Type of electoral system	Length of current regime in years
Sweden	44.7%	PR	95
Senegal	42.7%	Mixed	12
Finland	42.5%	PR	68
South Africa	42.3%	PR	18
Norway	39.6%	PR	67
Mozambique	39.2%	PR	18
Denmark	39.1%	PR	66
Costa Rica	38.6%	PR	93
Belgium	38.0%	PR	68
Argentina	37.4%	PR	29
Mexico	36.8%	Mixed	15
Spain	36.0%	Mixed	34
Serbia	33.2%	PR	6
Germany	32.9%	Mixed	22
Slovenia	32.2%	PR	21
New Zealand	32.2%	Mixed	135
Switzerland	29.0%	Mixed	164
Portugal	28.7%	PR	36
Italy	28.4%	PR	64
Austria	27.9%	PR	66
France	26.9%	SMD	43
Tunisia	26.7%	PR	0
El Salvador	26.2%	PR	28
Bolivia	25.4%	Mixed	30
Australia	24.7%	SMD	111
Canada	24.7%	SMD	124
Lithuania	24.5%	Mixed	21
Namibia	24.4%	PR	22
Poland	23.7%	PR	21
Latvia	23.0%	PR	21
Bulgaria	22.9%	PR	22
Philippines	22.9%	Mixed	25
United Kingdom	22.5%	SMD	132

Country	% women in lower house	Type of electoral system	Length of current regime in years
Malawi	22.3%	SMD	18
Czech Republic	22.0%	PR	19
Israel	21.7%	PR	64
Peru	21.5%	PR	11
Bosnia-Herzegovina	21.4%	PR	18
Moldova	19.8%	PR	21
Bangladesh	19.7%	SMD	3
Slovakia	18.7%	PR	19
Indonesia	18.6%	PR	13
United States	17.8%	SMD	203
Montenegro	17.3%	PR	6
Albania	15.7%	PR	15
South Korea	15.7%	Mixed	24
Ireland	15.1%	PR	91
Mongolia	14.9%	Mixed	20
Turkey	14.2%	PR	29
Chile	14.2%	Other	23
Guatemala	13.3%	PR	16
Niger	13.3%	Mixed	1
Romania	13.3%	Mixed	16
Paraguay	12.5%	PR	20
Sierra Leone	12.4%	SMD	10
Colombia	12.1%	PR	55
Uruguay	12.1%	PR	27
Georgia	12.0%	Mixed	21
Zambia	11.5%	SMD	11
India	11.0%	SMD	62
Ghana	10.9%	SMD	11
Cyprus	10.7%	PR	38
Ukraine	9.4%	Mixed	21
Hungary	8.8%	Mixed	22
Brazil	8.6%	PR	27
Panama	8.5%	Mixed	23
Benin	8.4%	PR	21
Botswana	7.9%	SMD	46
Japan	7.9%	Mixed	60

Source: Inter-Parliamentary Union, "Women in National Parliaments," World Classification Table (http://www.ipu.org/wmn-e/classif.htm). Based on figures for lower or single house.

seats might gain no more from its list when proportional representation is factored in. At the end of the day, the party composition of the legislature looks fairly similar to what it would have if it had been chosen based strictly on PR, but each district is also guaranteed its own, individual representative, as in a single-member system. In Japan, the noncompensatory mixed system reserves separate seats for representatives from the individual districts and from the party list vote. Parties get whatever the two seat totals happen to be, making Japan's system far less proportional than Germany's.

Mixed systems share some of the advantages of SMD and PR systems. Because they waste fewer votes, participation rates tend to be slightly higher, as in PR (see Figure 7.3), yet citizens are also guaranteed a personal representative to whom they can appeal. In addition, the single-district component of semiproportional systems tends to reinforce the dominance of a couple of large parties that find it easier to win a significant number of individual seats. Small parties also form and are represented, but the dominance of a couple of major parties facilitates coalition formation and stability.

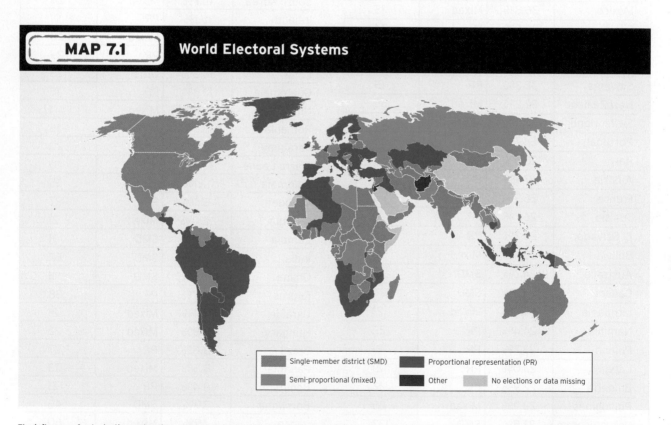

MAP 7.1   **World Electoral Systems**

Single-member district (SMD)   Proportional representation (PR)
Semi-proportional (mixed)   Other   No elections or data missing

The influence of colonization and region are clear in the distribution of electoral systems around the world. Former British and French colonies tend to have SMD systems, while the rest of continental Europe and its former colonies tend to have proportional systems.

Source: International Institute for Democracy and Electoral Assistance (http://www.idea.int/esd/world.cfm). Modified by the authors.

Single-member district systems give preference to representation based on geography, as opposed to the representation based on ideology that proportional representation systems favor. Geographical representation means that citizens can know specifically who "their" representative is and hold her accountable at election time. PR systems, on the other hand, represent ideological divisions in society. Given the importance of ideological beliefs in influencing how people vote in modern democracies, PR systems may represent important social divisions more effectively than SMD systems do. PR systems, however, do not give citizens a specific person who is "their" representative. SMD systems tend to produce a more majoritarian democracy, while PR systems tend to produce a more consensual one. Mixed systems fall in between the SMD and PR models. The type of representation is only one of the trade-offs that the choice of electoral system entails. An electoral system also has an important impact on two other formal institutions: political parties and party systems.

FORMAL INSTITUTIONS: POLITICAL PARTIES AND PARTY SYSTEMS

American political scientist E. E. Schattschneider wrote that "modern democracy is unthinkable save in terms of the parties" (1942/2009, 1). Political parties are associations that seek to formally control government. In democracies, parties seek to control the government via elections and are limited in what they can do once they gain control. They bring together individual citizens and a number of discrete interests into a coalition of broadly shared interests that potentially helps to overcome the collective action problem. The number of parties and their relative institutional strength constitute a **party system**. Parties perform important functions in any democracy, such as mobilizing citizens to participate in the political process, recruiting and training political elites, clarifying and simplifying voter choices, organizing governments, and providing opposition to the current government. Political scientists compare parties and party systems based on their ideologies, internal organization and strength, and the number of parties. These differences have important implications for where and how citizens can participate in a political system and the extent to which diverse interests are represented in a legislature.

party system
The number of parties and their relative institutional strength

Political Parties

Party organizations and their relationships to their members vary widely. Many parties in Europe began in the nineteenth century as cadre parties, collections of political elites who chose candidates and mobilized voters to support them. They had small memberships and often started among elected politicians who restricted membership to themselves and their closest elite supporters. With the universal franchise and full-scale industrialization, cadre parties became mass parties that recruited as many members as possible who participated actively in the party organization and expected to have some influence over it. Exactly how members are involved and how much influence they have, though, has varied from country to country and over time, as our case studies at the end of the chapter demonstrate. Most recently, many scholars of parties are concerned about a growing disconnect between parties and their members (and voters more generally) in Western countries.

All parties must mobilize citizens to support them, so how do they overcome the classic collective action problem of convincing the average citizen to participate? Most people would answer that citizens join parties because they agree with their ideas; in other words, for ideological reasons. This is often the case, but it is certainly not the only reason. People also join parties to gain direct material benefits. The party machines in early-twentieth-century U.S. cities, for example, offered preferential treatment to party members when allocating jobs or awarding business contracts with city governments. Most political scientists argue that material incentives for joining a party are more typical in new democracies in which parties are relatively weak and operate in relatively poor economies that provide citizens few economic opportunities. Joining a party can also come almost automatically from being a member of a particular group, as in the case of ethnically or religiously divided societies in which each group has its own party, or in the case of the Labour Party in Britain, which most union members automatically join via their union membership. Party membership itself can become a source of identification for particular families; new voters join and support the party their families "have always supported" without necessarily making a conscious choice.

The size of its membership and the reasons citizens join it are important in determining a party's institutional strength or weakness. The relationships among party members, political candidates, and campaign resources (mainly money) are also essential. Parties that have internal mechanisms through which registered members select candidates are likely to be stronger than those that select candidates via external processes, such as primaries in the United States. Candidates who are chosen by party members in an internal process like that used in Britain are likely to be very loyal to the interests and demands of the party members who formally select them and who provide the bulk of their campaign resources. Also, once elected, they are more likely to vote as a block in support of official party positions. In contrast, candidates in the United States raise most of their own campaign funds and gain their party's nomination via a primary election that is open to all registered voters in the party (or, in some states, to all voters regardless of party), not just formal party members who have paid dues and attended meetings. This means that candidates in the United States are much more independent of party leaders' demands, so they can act more independently once in office. U.S. parties are less unified and weaker than many of their European counterparts for this reason. A parliamentary system in which top party leaders can aspire to become cabinet members also strengthens parties, as MPs follow their party leaders' wishes in the hope of being selected for the cabinet.

When most people think of parties and their differences, though, the first thing that comes to mind is ideology. Klaus von Beyme (1985) created an influential categorization of European parties based on their origins and ideologies. The most important categories are liberal, conservative, socialist/social democratic, communist, Christian democratic, right-wing extremist, and the ecology movement. These reflect the social and economic changes that characterized nineteenth- and twentieth-century Europe. For example, conservative parties originated as cadre parties that were interested in defending the traditions and economic status of the landed elite against the liberals, who pressed for expanded rights for the bourgeoisie and the growth of market economies. Socialists and communists, meanwhile, tried to create mass parties to represent the interests of the emerging, but as yet disenfranchised, working class. Figure 7.4 explains each of von Beyme's categories in more detail.

The ideological divisions of the parties and loyalty to them, however, seem to be changing over the past generation. In the last twenty years, political scientists have noted, in particular, a decline of partisan loyalty toward the traditional parties that competed to govern wealthy democracies throughout the twentieth century. Declining party loyalty has resulted in lower voter turnout in most countries; increased electoral volatility (voters switch parties more frequently from one election to the next); more single-issue voting, especially on postmaterialist issues such as the environment or abortion; more new parties successfully entering the political arena; and greater focus on the personality of individual candidates rather than on parties. Most analysts see the decline of the traditional social divisions of class and religion on which major parties were based as part of the reason for the parties' decline. Beyond this, however, two schools of thought have emerged about what is happening and where it will lead. Russell Dalton and others saw a fundamental partisan *dealignment*, as voters and parties disconnect, probably for the long term. They argued that major parties used to serve two key functions: educating voters about political issues, and simplifying voters' choices. As voters have become more educated and media outlets have multiplied, they no longer need parties to educate them. The media changes have also prompted parties to campaign increasingly via national media rather than by mobilization of grassroots membership, and this has made it less important for them to maintain their membership base (Dalton and Wattenberg 2000).

Another school, more optimistically perhaps, sees a less permanent *realignment*; voters' preferences have changed and the traditional parties haven't kept up, but as parties change or new parties emerge, voters and parties will once again come into alignment. Inglehart's (1971) theory of postmaterialism (see chapter 1) is perhaps the most widely accepted explanation of realignment: the traditional economic divisions on which parties were based are no longer as important to voters. Others have argued that economic concerns are still important but that in postindustrial service economies and the age of globalization, those interests no longer fall neatly on either side of the "left-right" divide that long separated major parties (Iversen and Wren 1998; Rodrik 1997). In any case, as parties respond to these changes, they will capture voters' preferences better and Western democracies will enter a new era of partisan stability. Recently, Dalton (with two collaborators) shifted his earlier position (Dalton et al. 2011). Using a new dataset of multiple surveys in thirty-six democracies, they argued that

FIGURE 7.4 Von Beyme's Categorization of Political Parties

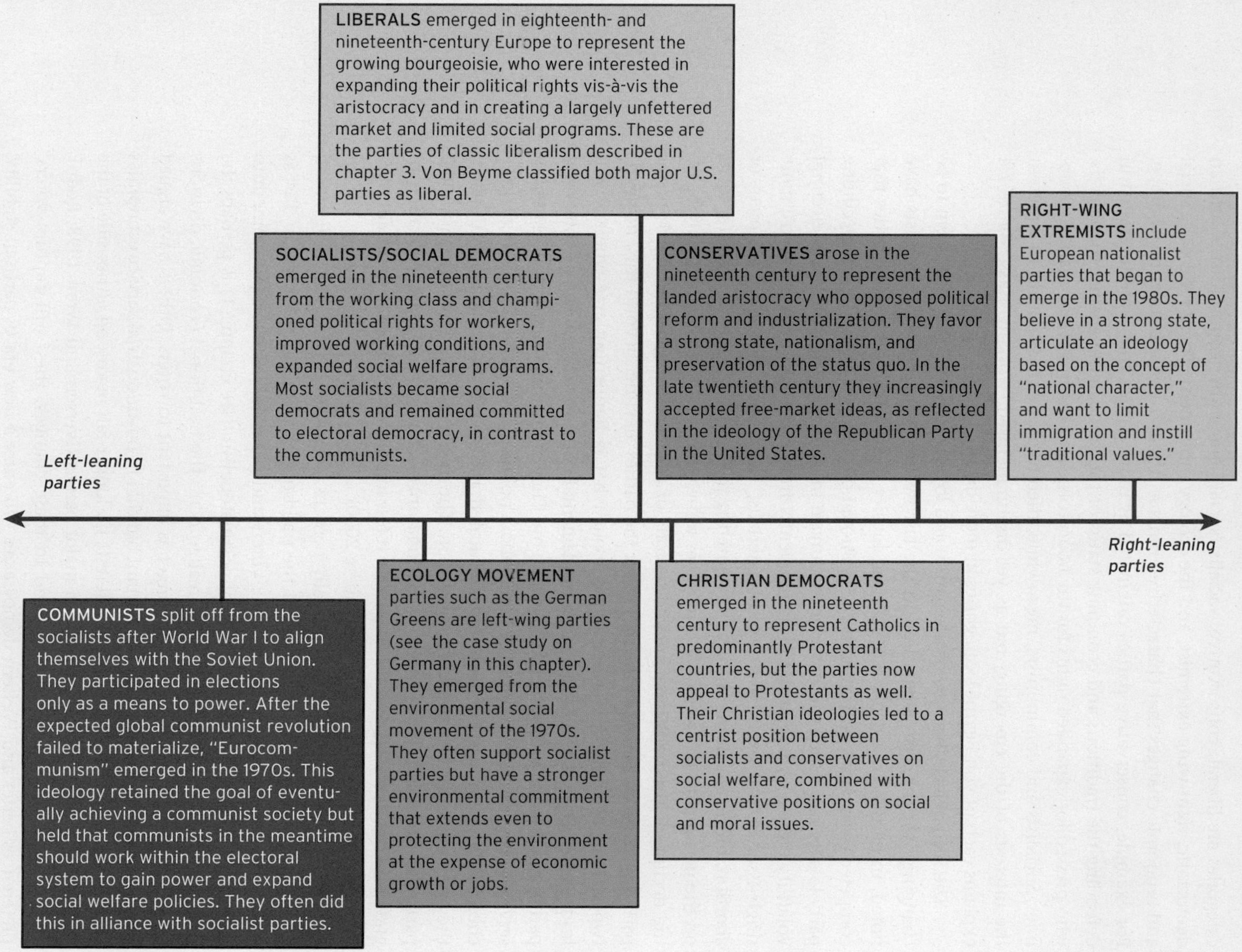

Left-leaning parties ← → *Right-leaning parties*

LIBERALS emerged in eighteenth- and nineteenth-century Europe to represent the growing bourgeoisie, who were interested in expanding their political rights vis-à-vis the aristocracy and in creating a largely unfettered market and limited social programs. These are the parties of classic liberalism described in chapter 3. Von Beyme classified both major U.S. parties as liberal.

SOCIALISTS/SOCIAL DEMOCRATS emerged in the nineteenth century from the working class and championed political rights for workers, improved working conditions, and expanded social welfare programs. Most socialists became social democrats and remained committed to electoral democracy, in contrast to the communists.

CONSERVATIVES arose in the nineteenth century to represent the landed aristocracy who opposed political reform and industrialization. They favor a strong state, nationalism, and preservation of the status quo. In the late twentieth century they increasingly accepted free-market ideas, as reflected in the ideology of the Republican Party in the United States.

RIGHT-WING EXTREMISTS include European nationalist parties that began to emerge in the 1980s. They believe in a strong state, articulate an ideology based on the concept of "national character," and want to limit immigration and instill "traditional values."

COMMUNISTS split off from the socialists after World War I to align themselves with the Soviet Union. They participated in elections only as a means to power. After the expected global communist revolution failed to materialize, "Eurocommunism" emerged in the 1970s. This ideology retained the goal of eventually achieving a communist society but held that communists in the meantime should work within the electoral system to gain power and expand social welfare policies. They often did this in alliance with socialist parties.

ECOLOGY MOVEMENT parties such as the German Greens are left-wing parties (see the case study on Germany in this chapter). They emerged from the environmental social movement of the 1970s. They often support socialist parties but have a stronger environmental commitment that extends even to protecting the environment at the expense of economic growth or jobs.

CHRISTIAN DEMOCRATS emerged in the nineteenth century to represent Catholics in predominantly Protestant countries, but the parties now appeal to Protestants as well. Their Christian ideologies led to a centrist position between socialists and conservatives on social welfare, combined with conservative positions on social and moral issues.

parties continue to serve important functions in mobilizing voters and representing their views reasonably accurately. Parties achieved this task by adapting to the new environment: using media more wisely, shifting sources of funding from membership dues to state subsidies, and maintaining party discipline within legislatures. They continue to be relevant in spite of the fact that only 10 percent of citizens across all thirty-six countries believe parties are interested in what ordinary people think.

Whatever the cause of the drop in partisan loyalty, parties have responded by changing how they conduct campaigns and how they relate to their members. In almost all countries, parties today have fewer members than in the past, though in many cases the members who remain have been given a greater role in choosing candidates and setting policies (Scarrow, Webb, and Farrell 2000). The ideological differences among parties have also tended to narrow over time, as parties can no longer rely on a core of committed partisan voters and must instead try to attract the growing number of uncommitted voters; these are mostly highly educated voters who tend to be in the ideological center. Many parties have therefore become what are termed "catch-all" parties. Overall, fragmentation and individualization of the electorate have weakened parties as institutions. Parties remain important legislatively, but they no longer command the loyalty of and represent core groups as clearly.

Political scientists Mark Blyth and Richard Katz (2005) took this argument one step further, creating an elite theory of contemporary parties. Using a political economy argument, they suggested that formerly catch-all parties are now becoming what they term "cartel parties." Catch-all parties, they argued, attracted voters by offering more and more government aid and services to them. By the late twentieth century, however, this strategy was meeting fiscal constraints, in part created by globalization. Governments were no longer able to expand social benefits continuously, so parties could no longer simply offer more to attract voters. They instead accepted neoliberal economic theories that argued for more limited government services (see chapter 5) and sold those to the electorate, lowering expectations about what was possible. At the same time, changes in media meant elections were won and lost based on access to large amounts of money for successful media campaigns. Mobilizing party members based on ideological passion and commitment was no longer necessary. Competition came to be about "managerial competence" rather than ideological differences or promises of benefits. In effect, major parties formed a cartel to maintain power, using media and money from the government to fund their own activities; all major parties implicitly came to agree on preserving the status quo. The only innovative policy alternatives in this context come from minor parties, which is perhaps one reason why their share of votes is increasing in most countries. SMD systems that keep minor parties out of power, then, would seem to be the most elitist under this theory.

The idea of declining partisan loyalty may seem odd to most Americans, who regularly see national politics as "too partisan." Compared with most European parties, however, American parties have always been less ideologically divided and more "catch-all" parties without a clear basis in a core social group, so they did not go through exactly the same history that European parties have. America's growing partisan division is often implicitly contrasted to an earlier era of bipartisan respect and cooperation. Political science research shows that greater partisan division has indeed arisen in the United States, but also that it is a return to long-standing patterns. The relative bipartisanship of the New Deal consensus from World War II through the 1970s was an anomaly in U.S. history. Furthermore, although the United States may be returning to greater partisanship, American parties are no more, and in many cases less, ideologically distant from one another than are European parties (Dalton et al., 132–137). Frances Lee (2009) argued that ideological division does not fully explain the partisan divisions and "gridlock" that characterize U.S. politics. Looking at the Senate, where the requirement of sixty votes to pass major legislation creates a significant veto player, Lee analyzed roll-call votes to argue that senators have a joint electoral interest in opposing one another, even when they do not disagree ideologically. This is especially true when parties can block an opposing president's goals and control the congressional agenda to assert their electoral message. American partisanship, she suggested, is as much about gaining electoral advantage as it is about real ideological differences. The U.S. case, then, may be less of an exception to the general trends discussed above than is at first apparent. It's entirely possible to argue, for instance, that Blyth and Katz's elite theory of "cartel parties" could apply to the United States.

Before these recent changes, the European ideologies that arose in the nineteenth and early twentieth centuries influenced parties throughout the world, though many countries have parties based on social divisions and ideas other than those derived in Europe. In Latin America, as in Europe, cadre parties emerged in the nineteenth century that pitted some type of conservative party favoring the landholding elite against liberals favoring reforms in the interest of industry and urbanization. Later, socialist parties championing workers' interests emerged as well. With industrialization, parties expanded their mass membership to some extent, though in many countries they remained rather weak due in part to authoritarian (usually military) interruptions to the democratic process. Military governments banned or severely limited the freedom of political parties and eliminated elections. Parties had to reemerge and rebuild whenever democracy was restored.

populism
A broad and charismatic appeal to poor people on the part of a leader to solve their problems directly via governmental largess; most common in Latin America in the early to mid-twentieth century

Populism developed in the mid-twentieth century as a distinct and powerful movement and ideological basis for parties in much of Latin America. Populists proclaimed a vaguely socialist ideology that promised direct government aid to poor people and gained support from urban workers. They also, however, were often close to the military and championed a strong sense of nationalism and a strong state, at times undermining democracy altogether in the name of state strength. President Juan Perón (1946–1955) of Argentina was probably the best-known Latin American populist. Their policies were often based on a form of clientelism—populist rulers rewarded urban supporters with government services and infrastructure—rather than a systematic shift toward a more socialist society.

Parties emerged as part of the nationalist movements in Asia and in Africa during colonial rule. These were mass parties from the start but often remained very weak, in part because they were so new. In addition, their primary ideology was anticolonialism

Argentine president Juan Perón, his wife, and top aides acknowledge supporters at a campaign rally in 1973. Perón was one of Latin America's best-known populists. Combining strong nationalism, provision of social services to the urban poor, and close ties with the military, populism was the dominant political force in Latin America in the mid-twentieth century.

because their members did not agree on much else. Many, in reality, were collections of disparate leaders, each with a following based on patronage and ethnic identity. After independence, many of these parties fragmented, inviting military intervention. Alternatively, one faction would gain control, create a one-party state, and eliminate democracy. Either outcome eliminated real party competition by destroying or emasculating most parties. These parties would eventually reemerge in the 1990s as very weak institutions in new democracies, a subject we turn to in chapter 9.

Party Systems

Individual parties exist in party systems, which are categorized by the number of parties and their relative strength. By definition, democratic party systems include at least two parties, but there is variation beyond that. At one extreme is the **dominant-party system,** in which multiple parties exist but the same party wins every election and governs continuously. In this system, free and (more or less) fair elections take place following the electoral rules of the country, but one party is popular enough to win every election. In South Africa, for instance, the African National Congress (ANC), Nelson Mandela's party that led the struggle for liberation from apartheid, has won all four elections easily. (It garnered just under 66 percent of the vote in the 2009 election.) Numerous opposition parties exist, have some seats in the legislature, and are allowed to compete openly in the elections, but the ANC remains overwhelmingly popular. The line can be thin between a dominant-party system and a semi-authoritarian regime; in the latter, a dominant party maintains power not only via its popularity but also via manipulation of the electoral system, control of government resources, and intimidation of other parties. We explore semi-authoritarianism in detail in chapter 8.

In a **two-party system,** only two parties are able to garner enough votes to win an election, though more may compete. The United States is a classic case of a two-party system: no third party has had significant representation in government since the Republicans emerged in the 1850s. Third parties, such as Ross Perot's Reform Party during the presidential campaigns of the 1990s, arise to compete in particular elections, but they never survive more than two elections as a political force of any significance.

dominant-party system
Party system in which multiple parties exist but the same one wins every election and governs continuously

two-party system
Party system in which only two parties are able to garner enough votes to win an election, though more may compete; the United Kingdom and United States are key examples

two-and-a-half-party system
Party system in which two large parties win the most votes but typically neither gains a majority; a third party (the "half" party) must join one of the major parties to form a legislative majority

multiparty systems
Party systems in which more than two parties could potentially win a national election and govern

In the oddly named **two-and-a-half-party system,** two large parties win the most votes, but typically neither gains a majority. Thus, a third party (the "half" party) must join one of the major parties to form a legislative majority. The classic case, at least until recently, was Germany.

Finally, **multiparty systems** are those in which more than two parties could potentially win a national election and govern. Some of these, such as Italy for most of its post–World War II history, are similar to the two-and-a-half-party system in that two of the parties are quite large. One of the large parties almost always wins the most votes but has to form a coalition with one or more of the smaller parties in order to gain a majority in parliament and govern. In still other multiparty systems, three or four relatively equal parties regularly contend for power, with a legislative majority always requiring a coalition of at least two of them.

How and why did these different party systems emerge and change over time in different countries? The main explanations are sociological and institutional. Sociological explanations posit that a party system reflects the society in which it emerges. Parties arise to represent the various interests of self-conscious groups in particular societies. In nineteenth-century Europe, two major conflicts emerged: an economic one between capital and labor and a religious one either between Protestants and Catholics or between church supporters and more secular voters. The economic conflict became universal as industrialization expanded. All countries eventually had some sort of party defending business interests (usually called "liberal") and a socialist or social democratic party championing workers' concerns. Religious divisions, on the other hand, existed in some places but not everywhere. For instance, Germany has a Christian Democratic Party that originally represented the Catholic minority and France does not because it is more religiously homogeneous. Where economic and religious divisions were politically salient, multiparty systems emerged; where only the economic division was important, two-party systems emerged.

Institutionalists, on the other hand, argue that the broader institutional setting, especially a country's electoral system, greatly shapes both the number and strength of parties. Political leaders will respond rationally to the institutional constraints they face by creating the types of parties that will help them gain power in the system in which they operate. One classic institutionalist argument is known as **Duverger's Law,** named after French political scientist Maurice Duverger. He contended that the logic of competition in SMD electoral systems results in the survival of only two parties in the long term. Multiple parties are unlikely to survive because all political parties must gain a plurality (or a majority, if required) in a particular district to win that district's legislative seat. The successful parties will be those whose members realize that their parties must have very broad appeal. Relying on a small, ideologically committed core group will yield no legislative seats. Parties without any legislative seats are less appealing to voters, who don't want to "waste" their vote. Over time, ambitious politicians realize that the way to electoral victory is through the already established major parties rather than the creation of new ones. Duverger's native France is one of the clearer examples of his law at work (see box).

In contrast, PR systems create an incentive for small, focused parties to emerge. The German environmental movement was able to create a successful Green Party

Duverger's Law
Institutionalist argument by French political scientist Maurice Duverger that SMD electoral systems will produce two major parties, eliminating smaller parties

because even with a narrow focus, the party could get enough votes to cross the minimum threshold and gain seats in parliament. Conversely, the United Kingdom does not have a strong Green Party because it could not compete for a meaningful number of seats with the Labour Party and the Conservatives. PR systems, then, tend to create more parties and parties that are more ideologically distinct than SMD systems.

Video link:
What is Duverger's Law?

The debate between sociological and institutional theories of party systems creates something of a "chicken and egg" question: Did political leaders create electoral systems to match the number and kinds of parties they led, or did the electoral systems provide incentives to create particular kinds of parties? The logic in both directions seems strong. In a society with multiple viable parties, party leaders seem likely to favor a proportional system if given the opportunity to choose. No one or two parties are dominant, so all would fear they would lose out in an SMD electoral system. Conversely, in a two-party system like that in the United Kingdom in the late nineteenth century, the two dominant parties would logically favor creating or preserving an SMD system, which strongly favors them over newer and smaller rivals.

Carles Boix (2007) presented a historical analysis to try to bring the two approaches together. He argued that in almost all of Europe, parties began as cadre parties—one liberal and one conservative—among the elite, with tiny electorates in SMD systems. Where religious divisions grew, religiously based parties challenged and sometimes split the two established parties. With the rise of the working class and its enfranchisement in the late nineteenth century, socialist parties emerged as well. Where SMD systems were well entrenched, such as in the United Kingdom, the socialists tended to displace one of the prior parties, and both the two-party and SMD systems survived. Where religious divisions had already split the two parties, or in newer democracies in the early twentieth century that did not have well-institutionalized electoral systems, the socialists and other smaller parties successfully demanded a proportional system. Amel Ahmed (2013) made a slightly different argument: both SMD and PR were products of efforts by conservative parties to contain workers' parties. Where conservative parties did not face a serious threat from a workers' party with socialist leanings, they would preserve SMD; where they faced a greater threat from workers, they created a PR system to accept but limit the electoral potential of the working class. Both systems were created to limit the threat of a working class majority dominating politics. Boix and Ahmed suggested that sociological and institutional forces influenced one another at particular historical points to create the twentieth-century party systems, which then remained relatively stable until the late-century decline of partisanship discussed earlier.

The debate between sociological and institutional understandings of party development also raises the question of whether the institutionalist argument about the effects of electoral systems on parties really reflects the logic of the institutions or the underlying society in which the institutions operate: Does SMD really lead to only two parties, or does that electoral system happen to exist in societies with only one major cleavage that would produce two parties no matter what electoral system you used? Comparativists Robert Moser and Ethan Scheiner (2012) found a way to examine this question by focusing on countries with semiproportional systems. By comparing election results for the SMD and PR seats within the same country, they were able to see the effects of the two different electoral systems in a single sociological context. Scientifically speaking, this allowed them to control for cultural and other variables, isolating the effects of the institutions. They found that SMD and PR systems had the effects institutionalists claim in long-established democracies such as those in western Europe. In newer democracies with less-institutionalized party systems, however, the electoral systems did not have any effect. In newer democracies, SMD did not tend to produce two parties because voters were not very strategic in their voting; for instance, they might have loyalty for a particular party because it represents their ethnic group and will not change that regardless of whether their party wins or not. Leaders of such parties know they can count on that support, so they have less incentive to compromise. In this situation, FPTP produces a winning candidate with only 20 to 30 percent of the vote in some cases because many candidates are competing but the number

France and the Shift toward a Two-Party System

France provides a classic case of Duverger's Law at work. Political instability plagued France's Third (1871–1940) and Fourth (1946–1958) Republics. Both suffered from constantly changing governing coalitions that typically lasted only a few months. The country under both regimes was deeply divided along ideological lines. Every election put numerous parties into parliament, producing unstable coalition governments. A crisis led to the creation in 1958 of the Fifth Republic, whose semipresidential system was designed to end the instability.

The prior republics had parliamentary governing structures with PR electoral systems, which facilitated the election of numerous parties into parliament. The constitution of the Fifth Republic created not only a semipresidential system but also an SMD two-round, majoritarian electoral system. For both legislative and presidential elections, a first-round election is open to all registered parties. If a candidate for a legislative district (or nationally, for the presidency) wins a majority of the votes in the first round, she is elected. If not, a runoff election is held two weeks later between the top two candidates in the first round, producing a majority winner. This allows all of France's numerous parties to contest the first-round election. When a second round takes place, the losing parties usually support the candidate who is ideologically closest to them.

This system has resulted in the creation of two "families" of ideologically similar parties, one on the left and one on the right, which are pledged to support each other in the second-round elections. In some cases, if they know a particular candidate is very strong in a district, other candidates within a party family might agree not to contest the first round to ensure the stronger candidate's victory. By the 1970s, each party family consisted of two significant parties, the Communists and the Socialists on the left and the Gaullists (political descendants of the Fifth Republic's founder, Charles de Gaulle) and Centrists on the right. Within each family, the two major parties were almost equally represented in the National Assembly, thus producing four major parties.

Further movement toward a more pure two-party system came in the 1980s and 1990s. The Communists became less popular with the end of the Cold War, and the Socialists won the presidency for the first time in 1981. By 1988, the Socialists held nearly 90 percent of the seats won by the left as a whole. On the right, the two main parties survived longer, but once the Gaullist Jacques Chirac became president in 1995, his movement also became dominant, gaining nearly 90 percent of the seats controlled by the right. By 2012, the two largest parties, the Socialists on the left and the Gaullists on the right, controlled 82 percent of the seats in the National Assembly, compared with only 56 percent in 1973. While the smaller parties continue to exist and gain some legislative seats, Duverger's Law has worked in his own country; the shift from PR to a majoritarian system has come close to producing a two-party system. This has provided much greater political stability than France had under earlier regimes, but some would argue that it has diminished representation of the country's ideologically diverse citizenry.

of parties does not drop over time. The ultimate question, perhaps, is whether the institutional logic will start having an effect over a longer time period as the democracies endure and parties become more institutionalized.

Parties and party systems have important implications for democratic rule. Recent trends suggest that the strength of the long-standing parties is declining in most countries. Parties may have less need than before for active members and be more focused on lowering citizen expectations and keeping themselves in power than on pursuing an ideological agenda. Does it matter whether citizens are more involved in the daily workings of the party, or is citizen approval or disapproval of party actions via the ballot box enough? Elite theorists point to declining partisan loyalty and grassroots activity as signs of growing elite control of modern democracies. Pluralists counter that ultimately voters still have the power to decide which party is in power.

The number of parties in a party system influences the type of parties that exist, the choices voters have, and the stability of governments. SMD tends to encourage two-party systems rather than the multiparty systems that are more likely under PR (at least in well-established democracies). In two-party systems, citizens must compromise with others within large parties before they elect representatives, rather than electing a representative of a relatively small and ideologically narrower party who will then compromise with representatives of other parties in the legislature. Most analysts have argued that an SMD system with only two (or relatively few) broad parties makes governing easier and policy more coherent. Multiparty systems, on the other hand, give more formal voice to diverse opinions in the legislature but can produce unstable coalition governments.

Recent work by Lorelei Moosbrugger (2012), however, questioned this idea. She argued that SMD systems with two parties actually have a more difficult time governing because politicians face greater threats from small and highly organized groups in those systems. She argued that small groups are able to act as veto players when they can identify who is responsible for policy and hold them accountable. SMD and two-party systems that produce a clear majority, especially in a parliamentary system, make it crystal clear who is responsible for policies. And the demands on politicians in SMD systems to appeal to a broad coalition of voters make them vulnerable to the threatened loss of even a small group in their electoral coalition. By threatening to vote against incumbents, small groups can veto policy changes they oppose, even if the policies have majority support of the general public. In PR systems with multiple parties, on the other hand, responsibility for policy is less clear and politicians need not get a majority of the vote, so they are less threatened by the loss of a particular, small group upset over one issue. She demonstrated using agricultural policy that farmers are able to prevent widely supported environment policies more effectively in SMD than in PR systems. By bringing organized interest groups into the analysis, she was able to conclude that the conventional wisdom about which type of party system is more effective at governing may be incorrect. We turn, then, to the important role of interest groups in modern democracies.

Web link:
Lorelei Moosbrugger
on Greek elections

CRITICAL inquiry

What Explains Government Effectiveness?

This chapter and the last have discussed at length the relationship between the type of political system and the effectiveness of policymaking. The data below allow us to examine this relationship ourselves. Table 7.2 lists a large set of electoral democracies. The first column is a measure of "government effectiveness" created by the World Bank. It assesses the quality of public services and the quality of policy formulation and implementation. The other columns identify key elements of the political systems: the electoral system, the executive/legislative system, and the number of "effective" political parties (a measure of the number and share of legislative seats of parties). Look closely at the table. Can you develop hypotheses for which elements of the political system produce more effective governance? Does a particular type of electoral system or executive-legislative system seem to be associated with more effective government? Do more parties or fewer create government effectiveness? Do you need to combine the variables to explain why some countries achieve more effective government than others? Finally, look at the list of countries and think about where they are in the world. Do other hypotheses emerge about government effectiveness that have nothing to do with the type of political system? What is your overall conclusion based on the table?

TABLE 7.2		Measures of Government Effectiveness		
Country	**Effectiveness***	**Electoral system**	**Executive/legislative system**	**Number of effective parliamentary parties**
Finland	2.25	PR	Parliamentary	5.83
New Zealand	1.93	Mixed	Parliamentary	2.98
Switzerland	1.89	Mixed	Presidential	5.57
Canada	1.85	SMD	Parliamentary	2.41
Netherlands	1.79	PR	Parliamentary	5.7
Norway	1.76	PR	Parliamentary	4.07
Liechtenstein	1.75	PR	Semipresidential	3.31
Australia	1.74	SMD	Parliamentary	2.92
Iceland	1.57	PR	Parliamentary	4.42
United Kingdom	1.55	SMD	Parliamentary	2.57
Germany	1.53	Mixed	Parliamentary	4.83
Ireland	1.42	PR	Parliamentary	3.52
United States	1.41	SMD	Presidential	1.97
France	1.36	SMD	Semipresidential	2.83

Country	Effectiveness*	Electoral system	Executive/legislative system	Number of effective parliamentary parties
Japan	1.35	Mixed	Parliamentary	2.45
Korea	1.23	Mixed	Presidential	2.28
Israel	1.20	PR	Parliamentary	7.28
Chile	1.17	Other	Presidential	5.64
Spain	1.02	Mixed	Parliamentary	2.6
Czech Republic	1.02	PR	Parliamentary	4.51
Portugal	0.97	PR	Semipresidential	2.93
Slovak Republic	0.86	PR	Parliamentary	2.85
Mauritius	0.76	SMD	Parliamentary	2.0
Hungary	0.71	Mixed	Parliamentary	2.0
Latvia	0.68	PR	Parliamentary	4.52
Lithuania	0.68	Mixed	Parliamentary	5.28
Poland	0.68	PR	Parliamentary	3.0
Uruguay	0.58	PR	Presidential	2.65
Croatia	0.55	PR	Parliamentary	2.59
Georgia	0.55	Mixed	Semipresidential	1.97
Botswana	0.53	SMD	Presidential	1.56
Greece	0.48	PR	Parliamentary	3.76
Italy	0.45	PR	Parliamentary	3.47
Turkey	0.41	PR	Parliamentary	2.34
South Africa	0.37	PR	Presidential	2.12
Costa Rica	0.35	PR	Presidential	3.9
Mexico	0.32	Mixed	Presidential	2.8
Jamaica	0.20	SMD	Parliamentary	1.8
Montenegro	0.10	PR	Parliamentary	3.18
Panama	0.10	Mixed	Presidential	3.66
Namibia	0.06	PR	Presidential	1.73
Tunisia	0.02	PR	Semipresidential	4.62

(Continued)

(Continued)

Country	Effectiveness*	Electoral system	Executive/legislative system	Number of effective parliamentary parties
Bulgaria	0.01	PR	Parliamentary	3.34
Brazil	-0.01	PR	Presidential	10.36
India	-0.03	SMD	Parliamentary	5.01
Ghana	-0.03	SMD	Presidential	2.04
El Salvador	-0.11	PR	Presidential	3.0
Macedonia, FYR	-0.11	PR	Parliamentary	2.91
Serbia	-0.15	PR	Parliamentary	4.87
Peru	-0.15	PR	Presidential	3.97
Argentina	-0.16	PR	Presidential	6.49
Albania	-0.20	PR	Parliamentary	2.6
Romania	-0.22	Mixed	Semipresidential	2.12
Indonesia	-0.24	PR	Presidential	6.13
Bolivia	-0.41	Mixed	Presidential	1.85
Senegal	-0.44	Mixed	Semipresidential	1.57
Benin	-0.46	PR	Presidential	8.83
Mozambique	-0.55	PR	Presidential	1.6
Moldova	-0.58	PR	Parliamentary	3.23
Niger	-0.67	Mixed	Semipresidential	4.64
Bosnia and Herzegovina	-0.76	PR	Parliamentary	7.67
Ukraine	-0.83	Mixed	Semipresidential	3.3
Paraguay	-0.83	PR	Presidential	3.43
Sierra Leone	-1.16	SMD	Presidential	1.9
Liberia	-1.21	SMD	Presidential	6.34

Sources: Government effectiveness data are from the World Bank, Worldwide Governance Indicators, "Government Effectiveness" (http://info .worldbank.org/governance/wgi/index.asp); data for the degree of institutionalization of democracy are from Polity IV (http://www.systemic peace.org/inscr/inscr.htm); data for number of effective parties are from Michael Gallagher, "Proportionality, Disproportionality, and Electoral Systems," *Electoral Studies* 10, no. 1 (1991): 33–51 (http://www.tcd.ie/Political_Science/staff/michael_gallagher/EISystems/Docs/ElectionIndices .pdf). These indices; data for electoral family are from IDEA (http://www.idea.int/uid/fieldview.cfm?id=156&themeContext=4).

*Estimate of governance (ranges from approximately -2.5 [weak] to 2.5 [strong] governance performance).

CIVIL SOCIETY

A great deal of participation and interest representation occurs in civil society, which is the sphere of organized citizen activity between the state and the individual family or firm that we discussed in chapter 3. As that chapter delineated, civil society arose in Europe with capitalism, industrialization, and democracy. Civil society and the organizations within it provide a space and mechanisms that citizens can use to influence government. As with parties, we ask questions about how well organizations in civil society enhance democracy: Are their internal rules democratic? Do they represent their constituents accurately? Do they gain undue influence? Do they have beliefs and foster policies that enhance democracy or harm it?

Our definition of civil society is a very broad one. It includes every conceivable organized activity that is not focused on individual self-interest and is not controlled by the government. Do all of these necessarily enhance democratic participation and representation? Does a parent-teacher organization or a local Little League matter to democracy? More troubling, does the Ku Klux Klan (KKK)? Is it a viable member of civil society? The KKK is clearly an organized group of citizens that provides a venue for participatory activities that could certainly be political in the sense of trying to influence governmental policy. Its core beliefs, however, violate the basic tenets of liberal democracy, so we could liken it to a political party that runs on a platform that questions the legitimacy of democracy (as the Islamic Front did in Algeria in the early 1990s). The beliefs of civil society organizations may well matter to how we assess their impact on democracy.

Their internal structure and the reasons their members join them can matter as well. These issues come up, in particular, with organizations focused on propagating ethnic or religious ideologies. Often, though certainly not always, membership in one of these organizations requires being born into the broader group that it represents. Ethnic and religious organizations are therefore typically different from groups in which individual citizens choose to come together based on a shared concern. Ethnic and religious groups also often view any internal dissent as a threat to the group's sense of identity, resulting in an undemocratic internal organizational structure. As more and more different kinds of countries become democratic, more and more varied types of civil society organizations arise, making the study of their impact on democracy increasingly important.

In most long-standing democracies, though, the term *civil society* typically connotes interest groups. These associations of individuals attempt to influence government, and most claim to represent clearly defined interests that their members share, such as protecting the environment, advancing civil rights, or representing various industries. They are formally organized, though their degree of institutionalization varies widely. They also are often regulated by the government and have to follow certain rules and procedures if they wish to be recognized as legitimate. Well-institutionalized interest groups are visible, have relatively large and active memberships, and have a significant

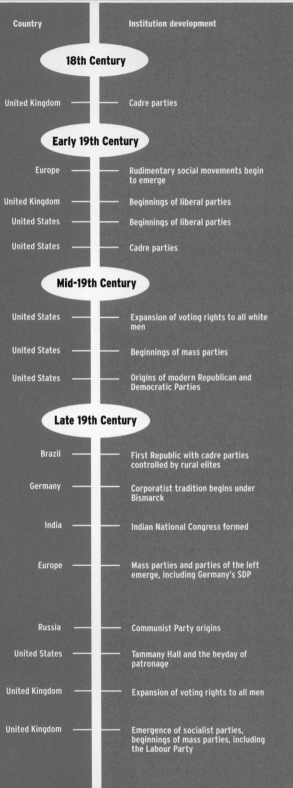

Country	Institution development
18th Century	
United Kingdom	Cadre parties
Early 19th Century	
Europe	Rudimentary social movements begin to emerge
United Kingdom	Beginnings of liberal parties
United States	Beginnings of liberal parties
United States	Cadre parties
Mid-19th Century	
United States	Expansion of voting rights to all white men
United States	Beginnings of mass parties
United States	Origins of modern Republican and Democratic Parties
Late 19th Century	
Brazil	First Republic with cadre parties controlled by rural elites
Germany	Corporatist tradition begins under Bismarck
India	Indian National Congress formed
Europe	Mass parties and parties of the left emerge, including Germany's SDP
Russia	Communist Party origins
United States	Tammany Hall and the heyday of patronage
United Kingdom	Expansion of voting rights to all men
United Kingdom	Emergence of socialist parties, beginnings of mass parties, including the Labour Party

(Continued)

voice on the issues in which they are interested. Less-institutionalized groups are less effective, and their legitimacy as representatives on various issues is often questioned. Similar to parties, interest groups bring together like-minded individuals to achieve a goal, but interest groups do not seek formal political power. If they are effective in carrying out their functions, the political system becomes more responsive and inclusive. Political scientists therefore investigate the internal organization of interest groups, the resources at their disposal, their overall institutional strength, and their relationships to the governments they try to influence.

Modern interest groups emerged in the nineteenth century alongside mass electoral democracy. Labor, business, and agriculture became the key "sectoral" categories of interest groups; that is, they represented the three key sectors of the economy. As the bulk of the citizenry became more involved in the political process, other interest groups emerged as well, including groups focused on expanding participation rights for women and racial minorities. In postcolonial countries, similar groups emerged. In Latin America, unions and business associations arose with the beginning of industrialization in the late nineteenth century. In Asia and Africa, trade unions developed under colonial rule as colonial subjects began to work for wages and started to organize. Unions became important in the nationalist struggles for independence in most countries. In ethnically and religiously divided societies, though, ethnic or religious organizations are often more politically important than unions or other sectoral groups. In these societies, the questions we ask above about which types of groups should be included in civil society loom large: Do strong ethnic group organizations that a citizen must be born into serve to strengthen democracy? With the spread of democracy since the end of the Cold War (see chapter 9), another set of important civil society organizations have emerged in new democracies: NGOs dedicated to enhancing development and democratic rights. Receiving the bulk of their funding from Western aid agencies, these groups sometimes have very prominent roles, even though it's often not clear how much popular support they have domestically. Thus, postcolonial countries, especially in Asia and Africa, often have civil societies in which ethnic groups and civically minded NGOs are more prominent than the traditional sectoral groups that are most prominent in Western societies. The question is, What effect, if any, does this difference have on democracies in the different societies?

Government–Interest Group Interaction: Two Models

No matter their origin or cause, the formal and informal relationships that interest groups have with government are crucial to how they operate and how effective they can be. The two major democratic models of government–interest group interaction are known as "corporatist" and "pluralist."

Interest-Group Pluralism We used the word *pluralist* in chapter 1 to describe one of the major theories that attempts to answer the question "Who rules?"; here, however, **interest-group pluralism** means a system in which many groups exist to represent particular interests and the government remains officially neutral among them. Under a pluralist system in this sense, many groups may exist to represent the same broad "interest," and all can try to gain influence. The government, at least in theory, is neutral and does not give preferential access and power to any one group or allow it to be the official representative of a particular interest. The United States is the primary model of this pluralist system. The Chamber of Commerce exists to represent business interests, but so does the National Association of Manufacturers, the National Association of Realtors, and myriad other groups. Washington, D.C., contains literally thousands of interest groups, sometimes dozens organized around

interest-group pluralism: Interest-group system in which many groups exist to represent particular interests and the government remains officially neutral among them; the United States is a key example

A boy practices target-shooting via a video game at the National Rifle Association's Youth Day in 2013. The NRA is one of the most powerful interest groups in the United States. The pluralist U.S. system gives interest groups exceptional access to legislators, in particular. Critics argue these "special interest groups" unduly influence policy and help create the "gridlock" familiar to Americans.

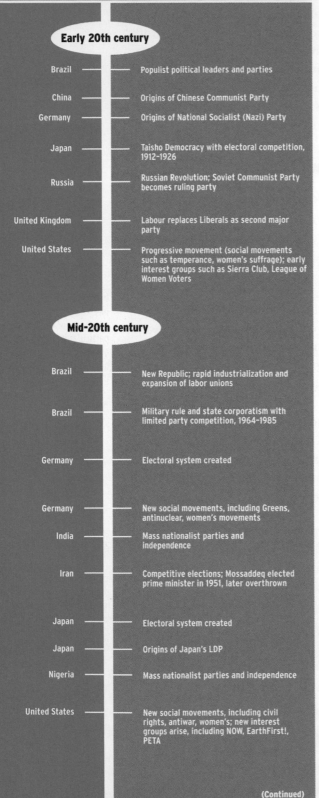

Brazil	Populist political leaders and parties
China	Origins of Chinese Communist Party
Germany	Origins of National Socialist (Nazi) Party
Japan	Taisho Democracy with electoral competition, 1912–1926
Russia	Russian Revolution; Soviet Communist Party becomes ruling party
United Kingdom	Labour replaces Liberals as second major party
United States	Progressive movement (social movements such as temperance, women's suffrage); early interest groups such as Sierra Club, League of Women Voters

Mid-20th century

Brazil	New Republic; rapid industrialization and expansion of labor unions
Brazil	Military rule and state corporatism with limited party competition, 1964–1985
Germany	Electoral system created
Germany	New social movements, including Greens, antinuclear, women's movements
India	Mass nationalist parties and independence
Iran	Competitive elections; Mossaddeq elected prime minister in 1951, later overthrown
Japan	Electoral system created
Japan	Origins of Japan's LDP
Nigeria	Mass nationalist parties and independence
United States	New social movements, including civil rights, antiwar, women's; new interest groups arise, including NOW, EarthFirst!, PETA

(Continued)

the same issue, all vying for influence over decision makers. This is repeated, on a smaller scale, in all fifty state capitals. The government of the day may listen more to one than another of these groups on a particular issue, but no official and enduring preference or access is given to one over others. Even when one large organization speaks on behalf of most of a sector of society—such as the AFL-CIO for labor—it is a loose confederation of groups whose individual organizational members can and do ignore positions and policies of the national confederation. Alternative groups have the right to organize as best they can. Figure 7.5 depicts this often confusing system, with multiple groups interacting directly with the government as well as forming various loose affiliations (such as the AFL-CIO) that also interact with the government.

Corporatism The major alternative to interest-group pluralism is corporatism. Unlike pluralism, which exists only in democracies, corporatism has more democratic (societal or neocorporatist) and less democratic (state corporatist) variants. We discuss the latter in chapter 8. **Neocorporatism,** also known as societal corporatism, is most common in northern Europe, where strong **peak associations** represent the major interests in society by bringing together numerous local groups, and government works closely with the peak associations to develop policy. Figure 7.5 depicts this more hierarchical system, in which government tends to interact with fewer, larger, and more highly institutionalized peak associations than under pluralism. Germany is a key example, examined in greater detail in the case study that follows. In a neocorporatist system, peak associations maintain their unity and institutional strength via internal mechanisms that ensure local organizations will abide by the decisions of the national body. By negotiating binding agreements with them, the state in effect recognizes the peak associations as the official representatives of their sectors. Unlike **state corporatism,** however, no individuals or groups are required to belong to these associations, and they maintain internal systems of democratic control. Dissatisfied members may try to change the association's policies or found alternative organizations, but most do not pursue the latter option because membership in the main body provides direct access to government.

Pluralism and Neocorporatism Compared Both pluralist and neocorporatist models have strengths and weaknesses. Pluralism allows greater local control and participation because any individual or group is free to start a new organization. National organizations have limited control over their local affiliates, so local members can work internally to move their local organization in whatever direction they wish. Because the state does not officially recognize any one group, there are fewer incentives for large organizations to maintain unity. This decentralization may limit the institutional strength and overall power of organizations in national politics. France is well known for its weak labor unions, for instance, in part because its two largest unions (one communist and one Catholic) are deeply divided over ideology.

Interest groups gain power vis-à-vis the state due to the resources they can bring to bear on the government. More centralized organizations have more resources and can legitimately claim to speak on behalf of more citizens. These factors increase their potential clout, although critics point out that no government treats each kind of group equally, at least in a market economy. Following the argument we laid out in chapter 5, business interests are crucial for the well-being of the economy; therefore, the government in any market economy, even in the most pluralist systems, will pay more attention to business interests than to others, no matter how effectively others organize. Critics of the pluralist model contend that business is still favored while other groups are weakened by their own divisions. They suggest that groups such as workers are better off under neocorporatist systems, in which they would be united in large, strong organizations that have a better chance of countering the always strong influence of business.

Because neocorporatist associations are so large and united, they typically have more direct influence on government than does any single national association in a pluralist system. The disincentives to creating new organizations, however, and the power that government recognition provides to the elite leadership of the peak associations, make neocorporatist associations seem less participatory. The incentives against starting alternative organizations are so strong that the vast majority of relevant constituents remain in the confines of already established entities rather than starting new ones, no matter how dissatisfied they may be. A crucial question in these systems, then, is the degree of democratic control *within* the peak associations. If the association has strong mechanisms of internal democracy, such as open elections for leadership positions and constituent participation in setting organizational policies, its leaders can legitimately claim to represent members' views. If the association does

neocorporatism
Also called societal corporatism; corporatism that evolves historically and voluntarily rather than being mandated by the state; Germany is a key example

peak associations
Organizations that bring together all interest groups in a particular sector to influence and negotiate agreements with the state; in the United States, an example is the AFL-CIO

state corporatism
Corporatism mandated by the state; common in fascist regimes

Web link:
Comparison of German and U.S. interest group interaction models

Late 20th/early 21st century

Brazil	Transition to multiparty democracy, 1985–1989
Brazil	Presidential victory of strong, programmatic party, the PT, in 2002
China	Emergence of very limited civil society under state corporatism
Germany	Reunification of East and West Germany, rise of Green Party, and expansion of number of parties from three to five
India	Rise of religious parties
India	End of Congress Party dominance, replaced by coalition governments from 1989 onward
India	Rise of lower-caste movements and parties
Iran	Elections, some with parties, under Islamic Republic, from 1980 onward
Japan	Electoral reform from SNTV to semiproportional system in 1993; watershed defeat of long-ruling LDP in 2009
Nigeria	Transition to multiparty democracy in 1999, though with seriously flawed elections; rise of dominant party, the PDP, by 2007
Russia	Fall of communism and birth of new parties, 1991
Russia	Reduction of party competition under Putin from 2000 onward; shift from mixed to PR electoral system in 2005
United Kingdom	Continued dominance of centrist, mass parties; first coalition government in sixty years after 2010 election
United States	Continued dominance of centrist, mass parties; growing electoral volatility from one party to the other

not, it may have significant access to government and influence, but it may not really represent its members' views.

Social Movements

Like political parties, established interest groups also may not change quickly enough to reflect changes in citizens' concerns in even the most pluralist systems. Well-established institutions provide powerful means for participation and representation, but because they are deeply entrenched, they tend to change slowly. When citizens perceive formal institutions as providing inadequate representation or opportunities for political participation, they may choose to participate in groups or activities outside of them. Such informal participation often occurs through **social movements.** Like interest groups, these are part of civil society, but unlike them, social movements have a loosely defined organizational structure and represent people who perceive themselves to be outside the bounds of formal institutions, seek major socioeconomic or political changes to the status quo, or employ noninstitutional forms of collective action.

What we now call social movements arose at least a century ago, but they have become much more common since the 1960s. In that decade in much of the Western world, growing numbers of citizens, particularly young "baby boomers," came to feel that their governments, political parties, and interest groups were not providing adequate forms of participation or representation. They viewed all major political institutions as organs of elite rule. Established interest groups were overwhelmingly controlled by white men. In response, new social movements arose challenging the status quo, including racial minorities, women, antiwar activists, and environmentalists. These groups have since been joined by many others, such as the antiglobalization movement that proclaimed itself to the world in 1999 in protests in Seattle, and the

FIGURE 7.5 Contrasting Models of State-Interest Group Interaction

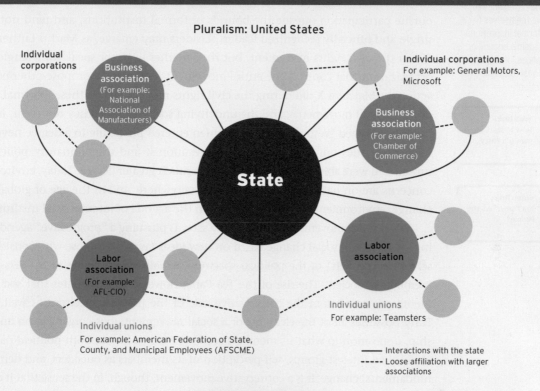

Pluralism: United States

Individual corporations

Business association
(For example: National Association of Manufacturers)

Individual corporations
For example: General Motors, Microsoft

Business association
(For example: Chamber of Commerce)

State

Labor association
(For example: AFL-CIO)

Labor association

Individual unions
For example: Teamsters

Individual unions
For example: American Federation of State, County, and Municipal Employees (AFSCME)

⎯⎯⎯ Interactions with the state
- - - - - Loose affiliation with larger associations

Neocorporatism: Germany

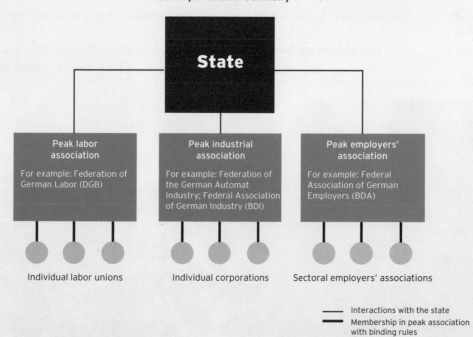

State

Peak labor association

For example: Federation of German Labor (DGB)

Peak industrial association

For example: Federation of the German Automat Industry; Federal Association of German Industry (BDI)

Peak employers' association

For example: Federal Association of German Employers (BDA)

Individual labor unions

Individual corporations

Sectoral employers' associations

⎯⎯⎯ Interactions with the state
▬▬▬ Membership in peak association with binding rules

social movements
Part of civil society; they have a loosely defined organizational structure and represent people who perceive themselves to be outside formal institutions, seek major socioeconomic or political changes, or employ noninstitutional forms of collective action

Web link:
How to start your own Tea Party

Video link:
Tea Party, "We the People"

Tea Party movement that arose across the United States in 2009 in opposition to what it saw as government encroachment on personal freedoms and the Constitution.

Social movements are distinct from interest groups in that they are more informal, pursue participation outside the bounds of formal institutions, and tend not to have single and officially recognized leaders. Leaders may emerge, as Martin Luther King Jr. did in the civil rights movement, but they neither lead nor speak for a single unified organization that controls the entire movement. Others may propose other courses of action, as Malcolm X did during the civil rights movement. Yet these informal, uncoordinated social movements, and the underlying social changes they represent, have profoundly changed Western societies. Women entered public life to a degree never before seen. Minorities united to get many segregationist and discriminatory policies overturned and were able to enter public life to a much greater degree. Today, environmental concerns are on national political agenda everywhere, and in the age of global climate change, environmentalists are putting it on the agenda of international institutions.

Most social movements are generally seen as pursuing a "progressive" agenda, meaning an agenda of social change based on new ideas favored by those who consider themselves on the "left" of the political spectrum, usually in the name of the less powerful members of society. The rise of the Tea Party, however, demonstrates that social movements can come from the conservative side of the political spectrum as well. The Tea Party possesses all of the elements of a social movement: loose organization and leadership, opposition to what its members see as the status quo in both political parties and established interest groups, self-perception of its members as outsiders, and demands for fundamental change. It is a conservative movement, though, in the sense that it calls for a return to an earlier era (based on what its members see as the original meaning of the U.S. Constitution). This would mean a rollback of many major policies of the last half-century.

Evolution of Social Movements As social movements have succeeded, sometimes they have changed. Some of their members have founded or joined formal

Members of the "Tea Party" movement protest at the U.S. Capitol in June 2013. Social movements typically form on the "left" or "progressive" side of issues, but the Tea Party is a social movement from the "right" or conservative side that has had a significant impact on U.S. politics since 2009.

interest groups, such as the National Organization of Women, or even political parties, such as the German Green Party. When successful social movements cross over into the sphere of formal institutions, new social movement groups often emerge to replace them with new and more challenging agendas. In the U.S. environmental movement, for example, the institutionalization of groups like Friends of the Earth as interest groups has left the role of social movements open to new challengers like EarthFirst! or 350.org. Sabine Lang (2013) argued the fate of many social movements has been what she and others have termed "NGOization." As social movements become more institutionalized, they become NGOs (nongovernmental organizations), developing organizational imperatives to find funding and hire professional staff. In the process, they adapt both their goals and strategies to work within institutionalized political systems rather than challenging those systems more directly, and, she argued, speak for rather than engage with the citizens whom they claim to represent.

Web link:
Environmental organization: 350.org

Social Movements and Democratic Participation Some political scientists see social movements as symptomatic of key problems with participation and representation in wealthy democracies in the last two decades. Robert Putnam, for example, decried a decline in **social capital**—that is, social networks and norms of reciprocity. He saw social capital as crucial to democracy and economic growth. Developed in the context of Italy and later applied to the United States in a widely read article and book, both titled *Bowling Alone* (2000), Putnam's argument was that even apparently "nonpolitical" organizations in civil society create social networks and mutual trust among members, which can be used for political action. The demise of traditional membership-based organizations such as local parent-teacher associations and, yes, bowling leagues, undermines the ability of citizens to trust and cooperate with one another, in turn hindering their ability to engage in collective action. Most research in this vein has focused on the United States, but scholars noted that since the 1970s, public opinion polls throughout Europe, North America, and Japan have shown a decline in levels of trust in virtually all political institutions. The extent to which this is true varies across countries, but the trend is similar everywhere. Some have argued that growing diversity in Western societies may be a common cause of reduced trust (Putnam 2007), though a recent cross-national study argued that segregation, not diversity, reduces trust and therefore social capital (Uslander 2012).

social capital
Social networks and norms of reciprocity that are important for a strong civil society

Many theorists have argued that mass communication—television, the Internet, mobile phones, and social networking technology—has had a role in reducing social capital and trust in political institutions. Others, though, question this. Pippa Norris (2002) argued that communication (and therefore representation) improves in countries with nearly universal access to television, telephones, and the Internet. The use of social-networking technology in the recent political mobilization in the Middle East, among other places, has led analysts to argue that the new technology may actually enhance participation rather than harm it. In wealthy countries, while levels of trust and membership in formal organizations have declined, involvement in political activities has not. It has, however, shifted to new and different organizations and

Audio link:
"Going Bowling": interview with Robert Putnam

forms, including social movements. Nicholas Lemann (1996), for instance, countered Putnam's thesis in *Bowling Alone* with the aptly titled article "Kicking in Groups," in which he highlighted increasing participation in youth soccer organizations. Citizens may participate in these new groups and perhaps influence government successfully, but they move relatively quickly among different issues and movements and may not develop strong ties with any particular group. The U.S. organization MoveOn! is an example; members are connected mainly via the Internet, and communication is almost exclusively via e-mail. These groups encourage electronic letter writing and petitions, phone call campaigns, and local demonstrations, despite the absence of formal local branches with official membership lists or regular meetings.

Rather than seeing social movements as a problem for democracy, theorists of contentious politics, which we defined in chapter 4 as a broad-based approach to understanding political movements of all sorts, see social movements as just one part of the broader category of contentious politics (McAdams, Tarrow, and Tilly 2001). Activists form groups and networks, as they come to understand their common interests, use resources at their disposal to try to achieve those interests, and seek political opportunities to engage the state—and global organizations as well in the era of globalization—to achieve the policies they seek. Contentious politics takes many forms, from grassroots organizations to global social movements, from petition writing to revolution. They see at least the nonviolent forms of contentious politics, including social movements, as a healthy and inevitable aspect of democracy.

As is often the case in comparative politics, there are no certain answers about these trends and what they mean. Nonetheless, the questions raised are profound. All agree that, in wealthy democracies at least, the ways in which people participate in local community groups and larger political institutions are changing significantly and that trust in political institutions has declined markedly. What effect does this have on the health of democracy? How much and what type of participation is necessary for a democracy to thrive? What kinds of institutional connections must exist between the political elite and the citizenry for the former to represent the interests of the latter? How much involvement and influence do average members need in political organizations—whether interest groups or parties—to ensure that those institutions represent their members well? Do new, less formal, and less stable forms of participation adequately replace mass-membership organizations such as trade unions and parties? Keep these questions in mind as we examine participation and representation in our case study countries.

PATRON-CLIENT RELATIONSHIPS

Another type of informal participation is undoubtedly the most widespread: patron-client relationships, meaning the direct provision of material support to individual voters in exchange for their support. Like all informal participation, patron-client relationships are most important where formal institutions are weakest or most restrictive. This means that patron-client relationships are usually most important in authoritarian regimes, but they certainly exist in democracies and are quite important in some, as the case studies on Japan and India demonstrate. Patron-client relationships sound undemocratic, or at least threatening to democracy. In the absence of other effective means of participation and representation, however, forming a relationship with a patron may be the best option available for having a voice and getting government help.

This form of participation is most common in a set of fairly clear contexts. Weak formal institutions are almost always part of this context but are rarely the only aspect. Poverty and/or inequality are frequently associated with extensive use of patron-client relationships as well. Poor people are more likely to need and accept material inducement in exchange for their political support, and a large income gap between patrons and their potential clients gives the patrons plenty of resources to pass out as "gifts" to clients. Some analysts also argue that political culture and norms play a role in this: societies in which gift giving and reciprocity between the elite and the average citizen are long-standing traditions are more likely to accept and practice these norms in the political arena. Patron-client relationships are particularly important in much of Africa. Extreme poverty and inequality in the context of weak government institutions mean that average citizens participate mostly by following a key patron. The patron's clients provide him (or, much more rarely, her) with political support, including votes, in exchange for material help when the client needs it. Even political parties are really just vehicles for key patrons to contest elections; when a patron changes parties, his clients move with him. Loyalty to the patron, not the party, is key. Patron-client relationships always include an element of domination and inequality. But in a context in which formal institutions do not provide the means for average citizens to overcome collective action problems and achieve meaningful participation and representation, becoming a client of a powerful patron may be the most beneficial form of participation available.

It is important to remember as well that patronage and patron-client relationships played an important part in the early growth of many political parties in countries we now consider quite democratic, including the United States. Material inducements are certainly one of the reasons people join and support political parties, as we noted above. Our case studies show that many, if not all, countries have or used to have some elements of patron-clientelism. In newly democratizing countries, patronage networks may carry over from nondemocratic to democratic regimes. Will they weaken with time, as seems to be the case in more established democracies? This is one of the comparative historical questions that political scientists try to answer.

CASE STUDIES IN PARTICIPATION AND REPRESENTATION

We now turn to an examination of participation and representation in several of the established democracies among our case studies. This will allow us to examine the interaction and overall effect of the electoral system, parties and the party system, civil society, and patron-client relationships on citizens' ability to participate and be represented. It will illustrate as well the questions and trade-offs addressed above.

THE UNITED KINGDOM: SMD/FPTP, TWO PARTIES, AND PLURALISM

The 2010 parliamentary election in Britain raised questions about whether the British political system was fundamentally changing. The election gave neither major party a majority of parliamentary seats, necessitating a coalition government for the first time since World War II. The Conservatives, who won the most seats, formed a coalition with the Liberal Democrats, the perennial third party. The election marked, perhaps, the culmination of a long transformation of Britain's party system, though it remains too early to tell if this will definitively be the case. The United Kingdom is (or at least was) a paradigmatic case of a two-party, SMD system with a pluralist interest group system. Of thirty-six long-established democracies, Britain ranked fourth on Arendt Lijphart's "index of interest-group pluralism," behind only Canada, Greece, and the United States (Lijphart 1999, 177). Given the nature of the parliamentary system, however, British interest groups focus their efforts heavily on the legislative branch, where most policymaking takes place. Britain has also witnessed the trends of declining partisan loyalty that have characterized wealthy democracies more broadly.

British parties began in the nineteenth century as cadre parties within Parliament, divided primarily over how much power they thought should be reserved for the long-ruling aristocracy. As the reforms of the later nineteenth century (see chapter 3) expanded the franchise, the two major parties, the Conservatives and the Liberals, slowly built mass parties to incorporate and appeal to the growing number of (male) voters. In 1900 trade unions and socialist societies founded the Labour Party. Throughout the world, parties

- **ELECTORAL SYSTEM**
  SMD and FPTP

- **PARTY SYSTEM**
  Two-party, but third-party survival, and declining support for major parties

- **CIVIL SOCIETY**
  Pluralist, but declining social capital and traditional interest groups

- **TRENDS AND REFORMS**
  Referendum to change the electoral system

Labour Party leader Gordon Brown (right), Conservative Party leader David Cameron (center), and Liberal Democrat Party leader Nick Clegg (left) in 2010. The Conservatives won the election that year and Cameron became prime minister, but in a coalition government with Clegg and the LDP, an unusual outcome for an SMD electoral system.

formed or evolved to represent workers as industrialization expanded, but only in Britain did labor unions successfully create their own party. By the 1920s, Labour had replaced the Liberals as the second major party and had led its first government. The Liberals survived as a third party, but until the 1970s they received a small fraction of the vote and only a handful of seats in Parliament. In terms of seats and votes, the United Kingdom for all intents and purposes had a two-party system. The SMD system that relies on simple FPTP to determine the winner of each election usually translates slim electoral victories into significant parliamentary seat majorities, as Figure 7.1 (p. 330) demonstrates for 2005, ensuring that one of the two dominant parties can form a single-party government.

As elsewhere in Europe, the major parties' share of the vote in Britain started to decline in the 1970s. Since 1974, the Liberal Party (renamed the Liberal Democratic Party in 1988) has won between 15 and 25 percent of the vote but always a much smaller share of seats, thanks to the FPTP electoral system. In 2010 neither major party was very popular in the context of the Great Recession. The British election was generally seen as the most "presidential" ever; among other things, it featured, for the first time, live televised debates among the three candidates for prime minister. In the first of these, Liberal Democrat leader Nick Clegg performed well, and the party's popularity grew. With the incumbent Labour PM, Gordon Brown, extremely unpopular, pundits began to speculate that Labour might even finish third for the first time in eighty years. That did not happen, but the electoral results (see Figure 7.6) denied the Conservatives a

Web link: Labour Party website

Web link: Liberal Democrats Party website

Web link: Conservative Party website

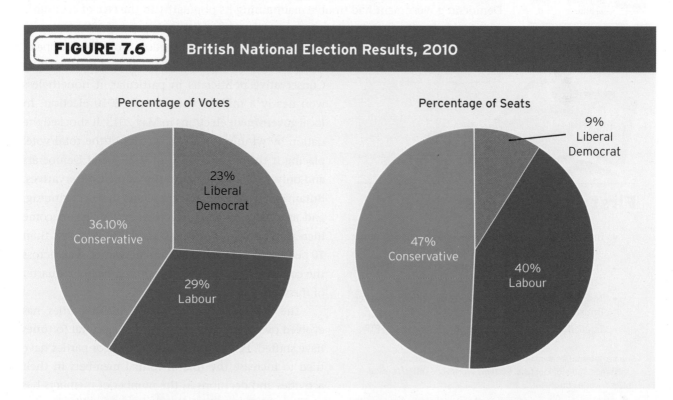

FIGURE 7.6   **British National Election Results, 2010**

Percentage of Votes

- 36.10% Conservative
- 23% Liberal Democrat
- 29% Labour

Percentage of Seats

- 9% Liberal Democrat
- 47% Conservative
- 40% Labour

Source: BBC (http://news.bbc.co.uk/2/shared/election2010/results).

majority of seats, setting up the coalition government. The two major parties' combined share of the vote fell to just over 65 percent, the lowest total in decades. The thirty-year slide of support for the two major parties finally went far enough to deny either party a parliamentary majority, even given the effects of FPTP.

Because the Liberal Democrats always win a significant percentage of the vote but a tiny share of seats in Parliament, they have long called for a PR system and demanded a referendum on changing the electoral system as their price for joining the coalition government in 2010. They compromised, however, with the Conservatives, agreeing to a referendum on instituting an "alternative vote" (AV) system instead of PR. AV is an SMD system in which voters rank all candidates rather than voting for just one. When the ballots are counted, the first-place votes for the candidate with the least votes in a district are reallocated to those voters' second-choice candidates. This continues until one candidate has gained a majority of the votes for the district. This system provides a single representative for each district who has the legitimacy of having won a majority of the votes, and it wastes fewer votes than does FPTP in a multiparty context. The Liberal Democrats believed it would encourage voters to rank their party first if they prefer it and one of the major parties second, knowing that if the LDP doesn't win, their vote will be transferred to their second choice. British voters, however, preferred to keep the FPTP system, defeating the 2011 referendum by a 2 to 1 margin.

The trend toward party fragmentation continued as the Conservative–Liberal Democrat government had trouble maintaining its popularity in the face of economic stagnation. The United Kingdom Independence Party (UKIP) began in 1993, dedicated to removing the United Kingdom from the European Union. Considered a "fringe" party and castigated by Conservative politicians in particular, it nonetheless won nearly a million votes in the 2010 election. In local government elections in May 2013, it shocked the nation by winning nearly a quarter of the total vote, placing it third, well ahead of the Liberal Democrats and only two points behind the ruling Conservatives. Britain's party fragmentation seems to be continuing, and as it does its FPTP electoral system has become increasingly disproportional: the UKIP won less than 10 percent of the local government council seats across the country, even though it captured nearly a quarter of the vote.

The internal organization of British parties has evolved over the years as the parties' electoral fortunes have shifted. Perhaps ironically, the major parties have tried to increase the role of formal members in their activities and decisions as the number of members has plummeted. Britain has no primary system like the one

Video link:
Is your cat confused about the alternative vote?

Web link:
United Kingdom Independence Party website

First Past the Post

- In 2010, fifty countries used "first-past-the-post" rules for their legislative elections
- These countries included the Bahamas, Canada, Jamaica, Kenya, Malaysia, Yemen, and Zambia
- The vast majority of countries using FPTP are former British colonies
- In 2010 no country in continental Europe used FPTP

Source: International Institute for Democracy and Electoral Assistance, Table of Electoral Systems Worldwide (http://www.idea .int/esd/world.cfm).

in the United States. Parties select their MP candidates for each constituency and present them to the voters. Like most European parties, sitting MPs had long controlled most real decision making in the Conservative Party. That changed after 1997, when a new party leader proposed direct election of the leader by all dues-paying party members. Candidates for individual seats are selected by dues-paying members in each constituency but are still subject to approval from national headquarters.

The Labour Party's initial organization was most unusual, having been created by unions rather than coming out of Parliament. Union members were automatically party members via their union membership, whatever their individual party preference. Initially, unions controlled 90 percent of the voting power in the party, so they could set the party platform and select the party leadership, but since the 1960s that has been trimmed substantially. Pressure from new social movements, whose activists wanted greater voice in the party, and more recently from party leaders (particularly Tony Blair) wanting to distance the party from the declining labor unions, led to fundamental reforms of the party's internal procedures. The party leader is now elected via an equal weighting of the votes of (1) paid-up individual members, (2) union members (who now must identify themselves as party members, rather than being automatically members based on their union membership), and (3) party MPs. Similarly, unions now only control half the votes at the annual convention, with individual members representing the other half. Like candidates from the Conservative Party, Labour candidates for parliamentary seats are chosen by local constituency members but then vetted by national headquarters. Combined, these reforms have reduced the influence of the unions vis-à-vis local activists and top party leaders. The ascendancy of social movement activists in the 1970s and 1980s pulled the party toward the left. In response, PM Tony Blair championed the most recent reforms in the 1990s to move the party toward the center of the political spectrum in order to gain support from middle-class voters, effecting a transformation of the party into what he called "New Labour." This strategy worked to give Labour its longest continuous stretch controlling the government (1997–2007) under Blair and his short-lived successor, Gordon Brown.

The most important players in Britain's pluralist interest group system have long been somewhat more centralized than are interest groups in most pluralist systems because the peak associations have greater control over their members. However, the system was never as centralized as corporatist systems, as our case study of Germany below shows. Business and labor are each represented by one major peak association: the Confederation of British Industry (CBI) for business and the Trades Union Congress (TUC) for labor. In the 1960s and 1970s, Labour Party governments even created quasi-corporatist arrangements in which the party consulted regularly and formally with both groups in an attempt to set wages and other economic policies. The limited ability of the groups to control their members, though, resulted in widespread strikes in the 1970s, culminating in the "winter of discontent" in 1978–1979 and Labour's electoral defeat in 1979 at the hands of Margaret Thatcher, the new Conservative leader. Thatcher immediately ended the corporatist arrangements and largely shunned not only the

Web link:
Confederation of
British Industry
website

Web link:
Trades Union
Congress website

TUC but also the CBI, preferring the advice and support of various conservative think tanks and ideological pressure groups.

Because decision making in Britain's parliamentary system is centralized in the cabinet, interest groups focus much more on lobbying the executive than the Parliament. Indeed, they lobby MPs primarily as a conduit to gain access to cabinet members. How much influence particular groups have, then, depends very much on which party is in power and which groups the prime minister, in particular, is willing to work with. Of course, all groups still have other means of influencing policy, such as petitioning, gaining media attention, contributing to campaigns, etc. Moosbrugger (2012) demonstrated that British interest groups can certainly have a powerful influence. The main farmers' union worked with relevant ministries to block several significant environmental policies that would hurt farmers economically, in spite of the fact that the vast majority of the British public favored the changes. British civil society has seen the same evolution that we noted earlier throughout Western societies: a decline in the support of traditional interest groups and the rise of new social movements. This was spurred in part by Thatcher's preference for working with smaller groups that shared her conservative ideology and her aggressive anti-union policies in the 1980s, which made organizing and striking much more difficult. Environmental, women's, antinuclear, and racial groups became important in the struggle for reorganization of the Labour Party in particular. The number of these groups has exploded since the 1960s. At the same time, the TUC in particular has declined as its membership base has contracted.

CASE Summary   While Britain has an FPTP electoral system and, as Duverger's Law would predict, a two-party system, there are indications that this may be changing. Due to both the origins and more recent internal battles of the Labour Party, a third party has always survived, though the electoral system prevented it from winning many seats. The 2010 election allowed it to enter government, though it's not clear if that result will repeat itself. The election, though, was part of a larger trend shared with other Western countries of declining support for the major parties, witnessed even more strongly in the 2013 local elections. A similar decline of traditional interest-group influence has occurred. What exactly this portends of the country's political system in the longer run remains uncertain.

CASE Questions

1. Britain's FPTP electoral system and party structure (particularly for the Labour Party) are unlike those in most European countries, yet it has faced several of the same trends that other European countries have faced. What might explain this?

2. What explains the survival of a viable, if small, third party in spite of Britain's FPTP electoral system? What does this suggest for the theoretical debate over sociological versus institutional explanations of the development and evolution of political parties?

DEUTSCHLAND BUNDESREPUBLIK

CASE Study

GERMANY:
TWO-AND-A-HALF-PARTY SYSTEM
AND NEOCORPORATISM UNDER THREAT

In the 2013 election, the two major parties in Germany gained only 67 percent of the vote, better than their share of the vote in 2009, which had been their lowest combined total ever. Chancellor Angela Merkel of the Christian Democratic Union (CDU/CSU) scored a personal victory, with her party receiving more votes than either major party had in years. Nonetheless, the decline of the long-dominant parties was clear, as were its causes: the declining significance of long-standing class and religious divisions in Europe and the partial unraveling of Germany's neocorporatist system. The 2013 election also may have heralded the demise of Germany's two-and-a-half-party system, as the "half" party, the Free Democrats (FDP) that had been the junior coalition party in most of Germany's post–World War II governments, fell so low that it failed for the first time in its history to gain representation in parliament. Two newer parties on the left continued to gain some seats, suggesting Germany has shifted definitively to a multiparty system.

Germany's democracy had been the paradigmatic example of the two-and-a-half-party system; an unusual, mixed electoral system; and a neocorporatist interest-group system. For much of its history, many political scientists saw the country as a model of effective policymaking in a democratic context. In recent decades, however, unusually strong social movements inspired by seemingly alienated citizens and by the economic effects of globalization have raised serious questions about both the effectiveness of the

- **ELECTORAL SYSTEM**
  Mixed proportional

- **PARTY SYSTEM**
  Two-and-a-half-party, becoming multiparty

- **CIVIL SOCIETY**
  Neocorporatist

- **TRENDS AND REFORMS**
  Weakening peak associations and neocorporatism; weakening support for major parties

The newly elected leaders of Germany's Green Party host a news conference in November 2012. The country's mixed PR electoral system helped make it possible for the German environmental movement to create its own party, which now has representation in parliament and was in a coalition government with the larger Social Democrat Party from 1998 to 2005.

German model and the adequacy of its institutions of participation and representation. Indeed, analysts have come to question whether both the two-and-a-half-party system and neocorporatism will survive.

The instability of Germany's first democracy, the Weimar Republic (1918–1933), profoundly influenced the post–World War II system the Allies helped create in West Germany. Parties were central to the new democracy and were explicitly recognized and regulated in the Basic Law, West Germany's constitution. The major parties that eventually developed were the Christian Democrats and the Social Democrats (SPD). The third or "half" party was the liberal Free Democrat Party, which lies ideologically between the two major parties. The mixed PR system encouraged the rise of this party system, but so did other factors. The conservative nationalists of the Weimar era were completely discredited by their association with Adolf Hitler, so no other conservative parties arose to challenge the CDU/CSU on the right. The German electoral system also requires that a party must receive 5 percent of the national vote to win seats in parliament, excluding the very smallest parties from power.

Initially, the CDU/CSU under Konrad Adenauer was the dominant party, ruling continuously from 1949 to 1969, usually with the support of the FDP. After the SPD moderated its ideology in 1959, giving up the official goal of nationalizing industry and accepting the basic parameters of Germany's social market economy (as described in chapter 5), its electoral appeal increased. By 1969 it had become the biggest party, forming a government with the FDP. Since then, power has shifted back and forth between the two major parties, almost always in coalition with the FDP or, more recently, with the Green Party. The two major parties increasingly became catch-all parties, competing for the most votes via expanded government programs but having limited ideological differences. The decline of the FDP, though, forced the two major parties into a coalition with each other after the 2005 election.

At the same time that the two-and-a-half-party system flourished, German neocorporatism reached its zenith. The German Trade Union Federation claimed to represent 85 percent of the unionized workforce. Via codetermination (see chapter 5) in the social market economy, its members constitute close to half of the board members of Germany's 482 largest firms. Business is represented by three peak associations, each representing different-sized firms. From the 1950s through the 1970s, these peak associations worked closely with the major political parties and the government to set wages and social policies. Most MPs on key committees were members of one of the peak associations, and many had worked professionally for them before entering parliament. SPD MPs often had strong union backgrounds, and CDU/CSU MPs had business connections, though labor and business associations had members in and maintained close contact with both parties.

Political scientists saw this model of stability and neocorporatism as a great success into the 1970s. Underlying it, however, were trends that would raise serious questions about key aspects of the system. Popular discontent became quite apparent by the late 1960s. A strong student movement arose that was opposed to the Vietnam War,

German rearmament, the consumer culture, and Germany's strong support for the United States in the Cold War. Growing unemployment affected would-be middle-class college students and working-class young adults alike. All of this discontent culminated in widespread protests in 1968, which the CDU/CSU government, with SPD support, effectively and forcefully put down. The demise of this movement led young political activists to pursue several different paths. Feminist, antinuclear and environmental groups became the most prominent of these "new social movements" in Germany. Some activists frustrated by the events of 1968 turned to violence, creating a series of small terrorist organizations that were responsible for a number of bombings in the early 1970s before the state ultimately defeated them.

Web link:
Social Democratic Party of Germany website

Web link:
Christian Democratic Union of Germany website

Web link:
Green Party Website

Other activists formed what came to be known as "civil action groups." These were small, local groups of usually not more than thirty people that were focused on petitioning local government on issues such as building new schools or cleaning up pollution. By 1979, 1.5 million Germans were participating in at least fifty thousand such groups. In the mid-1970s, some of the groups that focused primarily on the environment came together to form a national association. By 1980, members of this association formed a new party, the Green Party, and in 1983 it became the first new party since 1949 to break the 5 percent barrier and gain seats in parliament, reducing SPD support in particular. In 1998 it joined a coalition government with the SPD, creating what came to be called the "Red-Green Alliance" (*Red* referring to socialism), which ruled until 2005. The semiproportional system allowed the environmental movement to become a successful political party, though the activists who were most critical of the system were not necessarily happy with this outcome. This is an example of a classic trade-off between pure principles and compromise in the name of gaining influence or power.

The other major shift in the German party system came with the reunification with East Germany in 1990. The East German Communist state had a one-party regime, of course. A host of new parties emerged as this regime collapsed. The West German electoral system covered the entire reunited country, and initially, the major parties in the west reached out and worked with like-minded parties in the east to gain support there. Ultimately, they absorbed many of the eastern parties. The former ruling Communist Party recreated itself as the Party of Social Democracy (PDS) and positioned itself ideologically to the left of the SPD to champion in particular the poorer and heavily unemployed East Germans. Its association with the country's Communist past resulted in it gaining only 2.4 percent of the party vote in the first joint election in 1990, but it slowly expanded its appeal, winning 21 percent of the eastern vote by 1998. In 2007 it merged with some former members of the SPD to create the Left Party. It became the third-largest party in parliament after the 2013 election, winning 8.6 percent of the national vote.

Web link:
The Left Party website

At the same time that the new social movements, new parties, and reunification were altering the landscape of party politics, economic problems were threatening neocorporatism. The neocorporatist model in West Germany developed in the 1950s and reached its zenith in the 1970s after labor unions gained new power from a series of strikes, the union-aligned SPD took control of the government, and the codetermination laws were enacted. The ability of the peak associations to enforce collective wage agreements was key to this model. In the 1980s, these key associations began to weaken as unemployment rose. To encourage more employment, government and employers agreed to reduce the workweek to thirty-five hours in 1984, and in exchange the unions allowed greater flexibility in setting working conditions within firms. As control of working conditions became more localized, however, local unions had less reason to obey the dictates of the peak associations, weakening the peak associations' ability to negotiate on the behalf of all workers.

These trends accelerated in the 1990s as global competition heated up. Facing rising costs from exporters elsewhere in the world, smaller businesses began leaving the employers' association. Some business leaders began to campaign openly for a shift to a more neoliberal economic model. The decline of traditional manufacturing, meanwhile, caused union membership to plummet by four million during the decade. The peak associations for both business and labor were speaking for and able to enforce central agreements on a shrinking share of the private sector, further weakening neocorporatism.

Politicians responded to these trends by distancing themselves from the peak associations. Far fewer members of parliament from both parties were members of or worked in the key associations. In the face of these changes and continuing high unemployment, neither the CDU/CSU government prior to 1998 nor the SPD/Green government from 1998 to 2005 was able to negotiate new binding agreements with business and labor for fundamental reforms in the face of globalization. Both governments ultimately tried to impose these reforms unilaterally, without the support of the peak associations, and both failed to get them fully implemented and therefore lost power. The SPD government's attempt to reform the economy and welfare system in the first years of the new millennium alienated its traditional "left" and working-class voters. The result was the closely divided 2005 election that resulted in the grand coalition government. The new chancellor, Angela Merkel, was the leader of the CDU; she was also the first woman and first East German to lead the country. In the 2009 election, won by the CDU/CSU, the major parties' share of the total vote dropped to an all-time low of 57 percent, and voter turnout dropped substantially as well. As Figure 7.7 shows, the vote share of all three minor parties increased, with each surpassing 10 percent. Union members mostly still supported the SPD and religious voters supported the CDU/CSU, but economic changes and secularization meant there were fewer voters in both categories. In 2011 the Green Party reached a new milestone, winning control of the government in a *Land* (state) government for the first time, and came in second (ahead of the CDU/CSU) in another. Social changes had caused the decline of the two major parties' core bases of support (Zettl 2010). The major parties rebounded somewhat in the 2013 election, but primarily due to Merkel's personal popularity and the collapse of the FDP. Not shown in Figure 7.7 is the rise of a new party opposed to Germany's policies on the euro crisis, which almost gained enough votes to enter

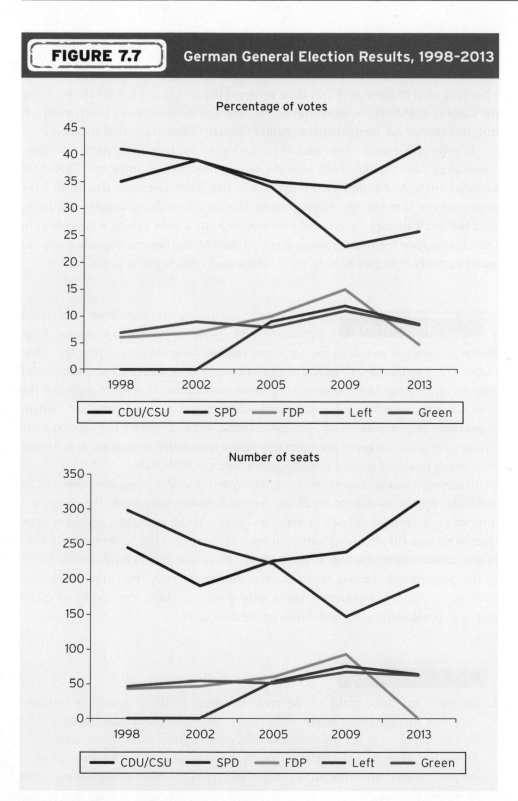

FIGURE 7.7   German General Election Results, 1998-2013

Percentage of votes

CDU/CSU — SPD — FDP — Left — Green

Number of seats

CDU/CSU — SPD — FDP — Left — Green

Source: Election Resources (http://electionresources.org/de).

parliament. These trends of declining older parties and the rise of several new ones have been strong enough that Thomas Poguntke (2012) argued that Germany's "two-and-a-half-party" system has fundamentally changed to a multiparty system similar to what Italy used to have, with two large parties vying for control but always requiring the support of at least one of several minor parties to form coalition governments. If true, this change has the potential to reduce Germany's famed political stability.

In spite of the longer-term decline in support of the two major parties, German voters were fairly content with how the government had handled the 2008–2009 financial crisis. At the time of the election in late 2009, Germany seemed to have weathered the storm better than had most countries, though subsequent policies to help bail out bankrupt Greece and preserve the euro system caused a large drop in Germans' support for Merkel's government. In 2013 Merkel became the only European leader in the Eurozone to be reelected since the euro crisis began in 2010.

CASE Summary   Globalization and European unification threatened Germany's neocorporatist system, weakening labor unions in particular as well as the union and business associations' ties with the major parties. Other social changes, such as the rise of new social movements and the decline of religious observance, have also eroded the major parties' bases of support, following the trends Dalton and others (e.g., Dalton and Wattenberg 2000) have noted for Western democracies generally. Germany's semiproportional electoral system has allowed these changes to result in the rise of significant new parties that influence elections. As in Britain, these trends produced unusual coalition governments in 2005–2009.

Germany's neocorporatist interest-group system has also come into question, as declining support for and power of the peak associations have made the corporatist institutions ever more difficult to maintain. In this sense, a pluralist system is more flexible because the decline of particular organizations does not necessitate a change in the institutions themselves, as no particular groups are given greater official access to the government. Despite its substantial differences with the United Kingdom, however, Germany's experiences again raise questions about the ability of major parties to govern effectively with broad national support.

CASE Questions

1. Germany has faced many of the same long-term trends as Britain in terms of declining strength of the largest parties and interest groups. In what ways are these changes different in the two countries, and what explains those differences?
2. Does Germany's mixed electoral system seem to give more representation to diverse groups than in Britain? Does this seem likely to make policymaking better or worse?

CASE Study

JAPAN: FROM DOMINANT-PARTY TO TWO-PARTY SYSTEM?

On August 30, 2009, the Democratic Party of Japan (DPJ) swept into power, winning 308 of the 480 seats in the lower and more powerful house of the Diet, Japan's parliament. It unseated the Liberal Democratic Party (LDP) that had ruled nearly continuously since 1955. Many analysts saw the 2009 election as the dawning of a new era in Japan. The election was the outcome of an electoral reform fifteen years earlier that had transformed Japan's electoral and party systems, spawning new parties and new political strategies. This fifteen-year history appeared to provide a textbook example of Duverger's Law at work, as a new electoral system seemed to transform Japan into a two-party system. The LDP's return to power in late 2012, though, raised questions about whether that transformation would really occur. Japanese democracy has had a rather weak civil society and limited participation, though that may be changing as well. Since the government liberalized its regulations over civil society, many new groups have sprung up and are demanding greater voice in the policy-making process.

The LDP dominated Japanese politics from the first election in 1955. Despite its name, it was a conservative party that supported the interests of business and economic growth. The party guided the creation of Japan's phenomenally successful development model, which we outlined in chapter 5, winning a majority of the legislative seats in every election to the Diet from 1955 to 1993 and always gaining a plurality (though, after 1963, rarely a majority) of the national vote. Its great economic success until 1990 allowed it to provide benefits to large segments of the population, including the rapidly growing urban middle class. It was a relatively weak party

- **ELECTORAL SYSTEM**
  Mixed

- **PARTY SYSTEM**
  Dominant-party system, shifting to two-party system?

- **CIVIL SOCIETY**
  Weak interest groups, but signs of growing strength

- **TRENDS AND REFORMS**
  Electoral reform from SNTV to mixed system; shift to two-party system?

Shinzo Abe, president of the Liberal Democratic Party (LDP), is elected prime minister by Japan's parliament, the Diet, in December 2012. Japan's mixed electoral system and a divided opposition gave the LDP a huge majority in the Diet because it won the vast majority of the SMD seats even though its share of the overall vote was only 35 percent.

Web link:
Liberal Democratic
Party of Japan
website

Web link:
Democratic Party
of Japan website

in terms of internal organization, with strong factions and weak central leadership, but the electoral system allowed those factions to share power and keep the party from splitting.

Japan's unusual single, nontransferable vote (SNTV) electoral system prior to 1993 was crucial to the LDP's success. SNTV has large, multimember districts, but each voter votes for only one candidate. The candidates who receive the most votes win. Each party, therefore, runs several candidates in each district, and the winning candidates often receive only 15 to 20 percent of the votes in their district. Like SMD, the system gave the winning party a larger share of seats in the legislature than its share of votes, so even as the LDP's popularity declined, it maintained majority control of the Diet. In addition, district lines were intentionally gerrymandered to overrepresent rural areas, the LDP's main support base.

The multimember districts under SNTV allowed several factions within the dominant party to run candidates and potentially win seats in each district. Most campaigns were mainly battles among the LDP factions rather than between the LDP and other parties. LDP factions were based not on ideology but rather on the loyal, patron-client networks within the party. In each district, a winning party had to run several candidates who would draw votes from different groups of voters so as not to dilute the support of each individual candidate. To gain the resources to compete not only against other parties but also against other candidates in the LDP, potential candidates would become loyal members of a faction. A patron who was a leading national party (and often government) official led each faction and provided campaign funds as well as patronage to his followers. To make sure no single candidate took too many votes away from the party's other candidates in the same district, each candidate also developed a local voter-mobilization machine, called *koenkai,* which consisted of area notables who could deliver votes. A candidate then promised the factional leader that he could use his *koenkai* to deliver a certain percentage of the vote in a district if the patron would provide campaign financing. Locally, a *koenkai* could transfer its loyalty from a retiring candidate to a new one, sometimes the original candidate's son. As in any other dominant-party systems, several small opposition parties continued to exist, but they never threatened the LDP's grip on power.

The 1990 economic crisis outlined in chapter 5 and growing corruption scandals inspired the 1994

SNTV

- The SNTV voting system used in Japan prior to 1993 is one of the world's rarest electoral systems
- Currently, only two countries use SNTV: Afghanistan and the Pitcairn Islands
- SNTV systems have the lowest average turnout of any electoral system: just 54 percent
- SNTV encourages better representation of minority parties and independent candidates than do simple SMD systems because SNTV elects multiple candidates in the same district

Source: International Institute for Democracy and Electoral Assistance, Table of Electoral Systems Worldwide (http://www.idea .int/esd/world.cfm).

reform of the electoral system. Patronage politics of the type practiced within the LDP is based on the exchange of loyalty for rewards. These rewards took the form of governmental largesse such as infrastructure improvements (and awarding the associated construction contracts to local supporters). Although this is common in many countries, Japanese politicians were also expected to attend local events, such as the weddings and funerals of their supporters, and provide generous gifts. Japanese elections, not surprisingly, became the most expensive in the world, in spite of the fact that candidates were not allowed to advertise on television and the length of campaigns was strictly limited. Patrons had to raise huge sums via corrupt deals that provided kickbacks from large businesses in exchange for government contracts or exemptions from the developmental state's regulations. As the economy and therefore the popularity of the LDP slipped, citizens and the media began to question this system, leading to the revelations of major corruption we discussed in chapter 6. The economic crisis was the final straw. Perceiving imminent electoral disaster, several major LDP leaders left the party in 1993 to form new opposition parties. Some formed a coalition government after the 1993 election that would briefly exclude the LDP from power for the first time since its founding.

The new government passed a fundamental reform of the electoral system, creating a mixed system in which 300 seats in the Diet would be elected in single-member districts and 180 would be elected via closed-list PR. A crucial difference between this new system and Germany's is that Japan's is noncompensatory, meaning that the SMD and PR votes are completely separate (though candidates can simultaneously run in both elections). Because there are far more SMD than PR seats, the system overall is more majoritarian than proportional. This is reinforced by the practice of both major parties awarding PR seats to candidates who perform well but do not win SMD seats. This gives candidates an incentive to campaign hard in an SMD election even if they have little chance of winning. Reformers believed this new system would reduce the role of money (and therefore corruption) in the electoral system, limit the power of the LDP, and lead to the emergence of a two-party system.

As Figure 7.8 demonstrates, until the 2012 election Japan seemed to be a model of the power of Duverger's Law. By the 2000 election, the DPJ had emerged as the primary opposition to the LDP. Smaller parties survived, but over the first five elections after the reform, the two largest parties' share of both votes and parliamentary seats rose, mainly due to the SMD seats. The difference between votes and seats in the SMD results demonstrates once again the disproportionality of the SMD system. At the district level, the trend is toward two candidates per district, and increasingly those contests are between the two largest parties (Reed 2005, 283). The DPJ's failure to revive the economy in the wake of the Great Recession and respond well to the devastating *tsunami* in 2011, however, caused it to fragment, as dozens of the party's MPs defected to other parties or created new ones; it suffered a huge loss in popularity. Forced to hold an early election in December 2012, it lost at the hands of the LDP, which regained majority control of the Diet and therefore the government.

Reed and colleagues (2012) argued that the 2012 election resulted in "the at least temporary disappearance of Japan's Duvergerian two-party system." The LDP landslide resulted not from the party's renewed popularity but from the collapse of the DPJ, which allowed a significant third party to arise and split the anti-LDP vote. Voter turnout in 2012 plummeted to 59 percent from 69 percent in 2009, and the vast majority of the abstentions were former DPJ voters who were alienated but did not support the LDP either. The LDP won only 2 more PR seats than it did in 2009, but the divided opposition vote allowed it to add a whopping 173 additional SMD seats (see Figure 7.8). The new third party, the Japan Restoration Party, was a regional party centered around the popular Osaka mayor. It and a couple of other small parties succeeded in dividing the opposition vote in the PR election, gaining a total of 71 PR seats, compared with only 17 in 2009, but gained very few SMD seats. Many voters were clearly alienated from the unpopular DPJ government but also not willing to support the LDP. They split the anti-LDP vote in a way that took PR seats away from the DPJ and gave them to smaller parties, but also handed the LDP massive numbers of SMD seats. Whether Duverger's Law will hold in Japan will depend on whether the newly split opposition remains divided in future elections. Even if this is the case, though, Japan's 2012 election demonstrated the crucial importance of electoral system choice in the difference in the parties' seat totals for the SMD and PR seats, and the disproportionality of the SMD system, especially in a multiparty context.

The electoral reform induced structural changes as well: all parties have become more centrally controlled. In 2001 Junichiro Koizumi became the first person to win the presidency of the LDP, and therefore the right to become prime minister, without the support of any of the major-party faction leaders. He instead appealed directly to the local voting members of the party, advocating a reformist agenda that attempted to solve the decade-old economic crisis. With the advent of the closed-list PR system, party endorsement became more important, enhancing party leaders' influence over local politicians in all parties. The combined effect of the rise of Koizumi and the end of multimember districts greatly reduced the power of factions within the LDP. They still matter for gaining certain party and bureaucratic posts but no longer dominate the electoral process as they once did. Politicians still have and use their *koenkai* to campaign and raise funds, but their share of total campaign expenditures has dropped relative to central party money, and the overall cost of campaigns has declined as well (Carlson 2007). Kabashima and Steel (2010) found that *koenkai* also became less important to voters; they increasingly shifted their attention during campaigns from local leaders to national media and the prime ministerial candidates. Using a historical institutionalist approach, though, Krauss and Pekkanen (2011) explained how the *koenkai* and other key party institutions were able to adapt to the new environment and survive, albeit with diminished influence.

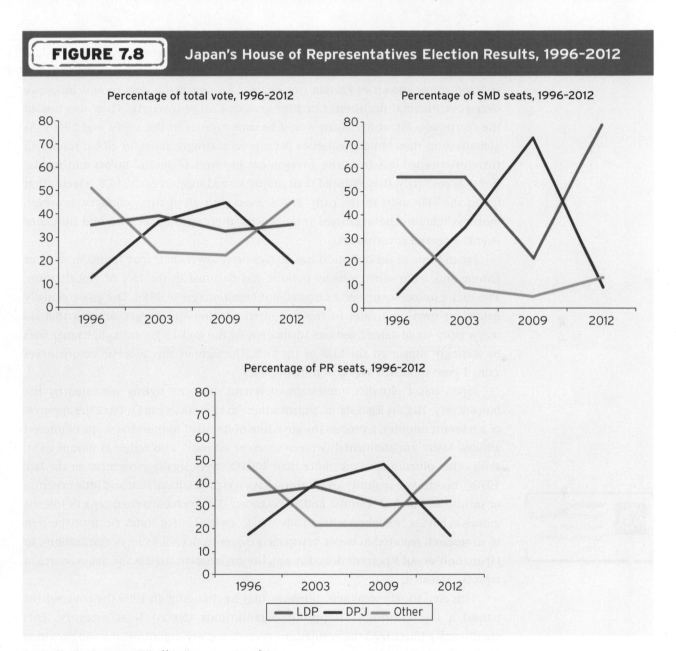

FIGURE 7.8 | Japan's House of Representatives Election Results, 1996-2012

Percentage of total vote, 1996-2012

Percentage of SMD seats, 1996-2012

Percentage of PR seats, 1996-2012

LDP — DPJ — Other

Source: Election Resources (http://electionresources.org/jp).

Political scientists have always considered Japan's civil society rather weak. Business was certainly very well represented and served during the period of LDP dominance. Most major business interests were represented in the *Keidanren*, a single organization closely associated with and supported by the ruling party in a neo-corporatist manner. At least as important, though, were the connections among key bureaucrats, major political leaders, and individual businesses. A major business interest, a relevant bureaucratic agency, and key members of the Diet would form an iron triangle. They allowed privileged business interests, especially the large conglomerates known as *keiretsu* (see chapter 5), personal access to and influence over governmental decisions, but they excluded other interests. They also fuelled the corruption for which Japan would become famous in the 1980s and 1990s. As globalization rose, larger businesses became increasingly active in global trade and therefore needed less from the government in terms of special favors and regulations. Accordingly, they reduced their unquestioned support of the LDP, a factor that led to the LDP splits in the early 1990s. Even with all of these changes, however, business remains the organized interest with the greatest access to and influence over the central government.

Japan's rate of unionization has always been lower than that found in most of Europe and, as in other wealthy nations, has declined in the face of globalization. Two major union organizations existed until their merger in 1989. The group actually fielded its own candidates in the first elections after the merger, arguing that no major party could defend workers adequately. By the mid-1990s, though, its members increasingly supported the LDP or the DPJ. Throughout this process, unions never gained great influence over government policy.

Japan has a pluralist interest-group system, but one tightly regulated by the bureaucracy. To gain legal status, organizations in civil society must have the approval of a relevant ministry, a process the government has used to limit the scope of interest groups. Many environmental, women's, senior citizens', and religious groups exist, as in other pluralist systems (more than 400,000 were legally recognized in the late 1990s), but the vast majority are local and have few professional staff and little expertise or influence. Political scientist Robert Pekkanen (2006) characterized Japan's interest groups as having "members without advocates." In the United States, nearly 40 percent of all research reported in major newspapers comes from civil society organizations; in Japan, only about 5 percent does. Instead, the government itself is the major source of reported research.

Web link:
Stanford University's JGuide page on Japanese interest groups

This civil society weakness, however, may be changing. In 1999 the government passed a law creating a nonprofit organizations (NPOs) legal category. This significantly liberalized the regulations on civil society organizations and provided tax breaks for financial support to many of them. More than forty thousand NPOs were officially recognized by 2011. The new law gives civil society organizations much greater autonomy from the government and the ruling party. Whether NPOs' new status gives Japan's civil society significantly greater autonomy and influence is yet to be determined. The majority of the new NPOs focus on social welfare issues that do not involve much direct "political" activity. Ogawa (2009) contended that the government's practice of actively encouraging volunteerism via NPOs is part of a broader neoliberal agenda of reducing the size of the state overall. NPOs, supported by unpaid volunteers, provide social services so that the state no longer needs to. Furthermore, volunteerism is encouraged in particular areas that are supportive of the state's needs but not in others that could be seen as oppositional or threatening. Martin (2011), on the other hand, saw the proliferation of groups as a sign that civil society and citizen engagement are increasing. Focusing on local women's groups, she found that since a decentralization gave local governments more power, citizens have engaged in more participatory activity such as referenda and demonstrations, belying the image of Japanese society (and women in particular) as passive. In the process, she argued, citizens have become less alienated from politics, a shift that she saw as a precursor to the 2009 DPJ electoral victory. Greater volunteer activity is certainly occurring, and with it presumably social capital is increasing, but whether this is creating a stronger civil society to represent Japanese citizens in the political realm is less clear.

Web link:
Japan NPO Center

Web link:
New Japan Women's Association

CASE Summary The 1994 electoral reform in Japan was one of the biggest systemic changes in established democracies of the last generation. While change has been slow, it is clearly having a profound impact on Japanese elections, parties, and the government in power. The trends suggest that participation is increasing; an opposition party finally held power for three years, coalition governments have become common, and civil society seems to be on the rise. As in our other case studies in this chapter, it is not clear that this trend has improved the ability of the government to formulate effective policies in the face of economic crisis. Japan's reforms, though, may provide an example of a successful change to an electoral system that has enhanced participation and representation.

CASE Questions

1. What does the complex history of the effects of electoral reform in Japan since 1994 teach us about Duverger's Law?
2. The recent rise of civil society in Japan has been primarily at the local level. Can such activity have a major impact on how well a democracy functions, or are national-level changes essential?

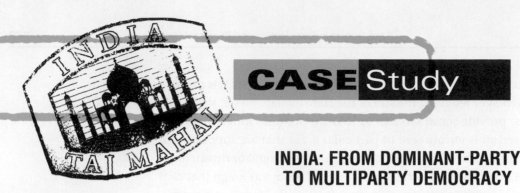

INDIA: FROM DOMINANT-PARTY TO MULTIPARTY DEMOCRACY

- **ELECTORAL SYSTEM** SMD/FPTP in a federal system

- **PARTY SYSTEM** Dominant party, 1947–1977; multiparty since

- **CIVIL SOCIETY** Language, caste, and religious groups more important than sectoral groups

- **TRENDS AND REFORMS** Shift to multiparty system and coalition government nationwide, but SMD produces two-party contests in many states

India, "the world's largest democracy," is a fascinating case study of democracy in a poor, exceptionally heterogeneous, postcolonial society. Critics initially argued that it was only partially democratic, with severe limits on real political alternatives or effective participation. The growth of multiple parties and coalition governments in recent years, along with the rise of interest groups and social movements representing the poorest segments of society, now suggest greater participation and representation. For three decades after independence, India had a dominant-party system similar to Japan's. The ruling party used broad-based support in an FPTP electoral system to win every election from 1947 to 1977. By the 1980s, though, the logic of FPTP combined with the sociological reality of a diverse India to produce two-party competition between a national and a state-based party within many states. At the national level, this ultimately produced a multiparty system that has required coalition governments since 1989. As in most postcolonial societies, the most politically influential groups in civil society are not business and labor, as they are in more industrialized societies, but instead identity-based groups.

The Indian National Congress party (commonly called the "Congress") led India to independence. The charismatic leaders Mahatma Gandhi and Jawaharlal Nehru created a party that dominated Indian politics for four decades. Nehru served as prime minister until his death and was succeeded two years later by his daughter, Indira Ghandi, who led the country from 1966 to 1984 (except for 1977–1980); she in turn was succeeded by her son, Rajiv, from 1984 to 1989. To achieve this dominance, Congress became a very broad-based party. While proclaiming a transformative ideology of social democracy, it mobilized support primarily via local Brahmin landowners, who effectively controlled the votes of millions of peasants. Because India uses an FPTP electoral system (adopted from its British colonizers), Congress never had to win an outright majority of the vote to control a majority of seats in parliament. In the first two decades, it polled between 45 and 47 percent of the national votes, a number that dropped to around 40 percent in later years.

As in any dominant-party system, the most important political battles were among factions within the ruling party. Like the LDP in Japan, Congress was a giant patronage machine, sharing the benefits of government in exchange for rural support via the local Brahmin elite, who became increasingly corrupt and less willing to follow dictates from the center. This was particularly true after Nehru's death, when Indira Gandhi centralized control of the party in an attempt to control factional battles, a move that local elites resented. This ultimately split the party, with her faction winning the crucial 1971 national election. Facing questions in court about the legitimacy of her election and growing resistance from powerful local Brahmin, she declared emergency rule in 1974, suspended most civil rights, threw political opponents in jail, and essentially ruled as a dictator for three years. This was the only interruption in India's democracy since independence. When forced to return to democracy three years later, Congress lost power for the first time since independence.

Opposition to Congress initially came from two ideological alternatives: communism and Hindu nationalism. The larger of two communist parties controlled two state governments for many years. It was sometimes part of a Congress-led coalition government at the national level and maintained a steady share of parliamentary seats until a precipitous drop in 2009. **Hindu nationalism** dates back to the late nineteenth century. Hindu nationalists call for a Hindu conception of the Indian nation, one based on the three pillars of geographical unity of all of India, racial descent from Aryan ancestors, and a common culture with Hindu roots (see chapter 12). In the 1980s, the Bharatiya Janata Party (BJP) emerged as the primary Hindu nationalist party and the largest rival to the Congress, with its greatest strength in the northern, Hindi-speaking region of the country, where both Hinduism and caste identities are strongest.

The first opposition victories over Congress came at the state level in 1967. In many states, elections became essentially two-party races between Congress and a local, state-level party that championed that state's interests (or the communist party in a couple of states). With the rise of the BJP in the 1980s and 1990s, the Hindu nationalists came to compete with state-level parties, especially in the north, to the exclusion of Congress. The importance of regional parties increased notably starting with the 1989 election; by 2009, they captured about 47 percent of the total vote. What emerged, then, was a system with two major national parties (Congress and the BJP) and numerous smaller parties, mostly at the state level. Each state party that competed against a national party successfully at the state level sent a handful of MPs to the national parliament. In the process, the total number of parties has exploded, from only 50 in 1952 to 342 in 2009 (Hasan 2010, 245). The number of "effective parties" in parliament increased from 4.8 in 1989 to 7.7 in 2009 (Palshikar 2013, 95).

Every election since 1989 has resulted in a coalition government, since neither of the major parties has been able to win a majority of parliamentary seats. Anti-Congress coalitions ruled from 1989 to 1991 and 1996 to 2004, while Congress won enough of the vote to form coalition governments from 1991 to 1996 and again since 2004. By the late 1990s, as political leaders realized coalitions were essential, they began forming them before elections, led by a national party and supported by numerous state-level allies, so that elections came to be contests among two major alliances and one or two smaller ones. Electoral losses were the result not only of receiving fewer votes but also of parties' shifting alliances. The alliances were based more on practical considerations, such as geographic interests and striking deals with the national parties, than on ideological affinities among coalition partners. Some analysts saw the Congress's widespread victory in the 2009 election as a reversal of this trend toward

Hindu nationalism
In India, a movement to define the country as primarily Hindu; the founding ideology of the BJP

Video link:
India's political
parties in crisis

party fragmentation and coalition government, but it primarily reflected the disproportionality of the SMD electoral system: Congress's share of the vote increased by only 2 percent, but it gained 61 additional parliamentary seats. It still won a total of only 206 of 543 seats and had to rule in coalition with the nine other parties in its electoral alliance. By the time several state elections took place in 2012, an increasingly unpopular Congress party suffered major losses to state-level parties, showing the latters' continued importance.

These fundamental political changes played themselves out at the same time major changes in Indian civil society were taking place. As in most postcolonial, primarily rural countries, the most important groups in civil society are not trade unions and business associations. Both certainly exist, but they are relatively weak. Most workers are in the informal sector and are typically not members of unions. They do organize, however, and in India women in the informal sector in particular have formed associations to demand greater social services from the state, rather than the traditional labor rights that typically interest unions (Agarwala 2013). An important farmers' movement is probably the strongest formal-sector organization. While these class-based groups certainly mattered, they were ultimately overshadowed in civil society by groups championing ethnic, religious, or caste interests. These groups came out of and appealed to the poor, rural majority but ultimately have come to speak for many urban citizens as well. Numerous movements arose around ethnic identity, based primarily on language. This was particularly true in the non-Hindi-speaking south of the country, where groups demanded greater recognition and autonomy in India's federal system. In the end, a major government commission created additional states, drawn largely along linguistic lines, to appease these groups (see chapter 6).

Web link:
Blog for South
Indian Farmer's
Movements

Movements based on religion proved much more explosive. A Sikh movement in the 1970s ultimately turned violent. The government defeated it, but a Sikh nationalist subsequently assassinated Prime Minister Indira Gandhi. The largest religious

Members of the Rashtriya Swayamsevak Sangh (RSS) at a rally in 2009. The RSS is a Hindu nationalist organization that supports the Bharatiya Janata Party (BJP). Critics argue the RSS is neofascist for its demands that India reject its long-standing secularism and embrace a more Hindu identity.

movement is Hindu nationalism. Muslims and Sikhs vociferously oppose Hindu nationalists' emphasis on the Hindu cultural heritage of all Indians. The primary organization of Hindu nationalists is the Rashtriya Swayamsevak Sangh (RSS), founded in 1925. It became a militaristic—many say neofascist—organization that trained young men for nationalist struggle, rejecting Mahatma Gandhi's nonviolence and his mobilization of the lower castes. After being fairly quiescent during the period of Congress dominance, the RSS reemerged strongly in the 1980s and founded the BJP. Its greatest cause became the destruction of a mosque and construction of a Hindu temple in its place in the northern city of Ayodhya. The mosque was built centuries ago on the site of the mythical birthplace of Lord Rama, one of Hinduism's most important deities. By 1990, the RSS had begun a march to the site with thousands of followers to destroy the mosque and begin building the temple. The government militarily repulsed the march, leading to violence across northern India in which hundreds of Hindus and Muslims died. Another march in 1992 was also put down, but only after RSS supporters had invaded the site and destroyed the mosque. The site remains in that condition to this day. Occasional violent conflicts between Hindus and Muslims have occurred ever since, as religion has replaced language as the most volatile basis of political divisions in India. In October 2010, a state high court ruled that the site would be shared among two Hindu groups and one Muslim group. All three groups appealed the ruling to the Indian Supreme Court, creating a complicated case still unresolved by mid-2013. The specter of the Ayodhya controversy emerged anew when the BJP nominated RSS member Narendra Modi as its 2014 candidate for prime minister. Modi was the chief minister of the state of Gujarat when India's worst religious violence this century took place there, as Hindus massacred Muslims after the latter attacked a train of Hindu pilgrims returning from Ayodhya. While he has never been formally charged, many believe Modi at minimum allowed the anti-Muslim pogrom to take place, and some believe he encouraged it.

Web link:
BBC Q&A on the Ayoda Temple dispute

The most common elements of Indian civil society, however, have been based on caste. The Indian caste system is an exceptionally complex social hierarchy that has changed dramatically over the past century. At an abstract level, virtually the entire society is divided into four large *varna,* or castes; in reality, there are literally thousands of *jati,* localized castes with more specific identities. Traditionally, most of the distinctions among castes were based on occupation, with certain castes performing certain types of work. Along with these economic distinctions came strict social practices, such as not eating dinner with, drinking from the same well as, or marrying a member of a caste beneath you. At the bottom of this hierarchy were the so-called untouchables, now known as *dalits.*

Technological change, increased access to education, urbanization, and employment/education quotas for lower castes have changed the economic basis for caste divisions. Brahmin landlords no longer control land as completely and thoroughly as they once did; many of the lower-caste occupations no longer exist; and growing numbers of people of all castes have moved to cities, taking up new occupations at various levels of education and compensation. Nonetheless, caste remains very important. A 1999 survey found that 42 percent of Brahmins worked in "white-collar" professional positions or owned large businesses, as opposed to only 17 percent of middle castes and 10 percent of *dalits.* Conversely, less than 4 percent of Brahmins worked as agricultural laborers, as opposed to 35 percent of *dalits.*

Although the Indian constitution legally banned "untouchability" at independence, the data show that *dalits'* position in society remains rather poor. They started associations in the colonial period, which developed rapidly after independence, and have expanded further since the 1980s. The colonial government started what Americans would call an "affirmative action" program (Indians refer to it as "positive discrimination") for *dalits,* which gives them preferential access to education and government employment. The Indian government substantially expanded these programs starting in the 1970s. *Dalit* groups have also successfully championed the reservation of parliamentary seats exclusively for *dalits* and "other backward castes and tribes"; these seats now constitute 120 of the nearly 600 seats in parliament. In Uttar Pradesh, a northern state, a party led by and championing *dalits* became the BJP's chief rival for control of the state in the 1990s. Developing these caste associations has involved shifting the social construction of caste identity. Traditionally, specific caste identities were very localized, and people mainly thought of themselves in relation to other local castes above and below them. Leaders of caste-based movements, associations, and parties have helped create a more "horizontal" understanding of caste, forging common identities among similar castes with different names in different locales. These movements created a new type of caste identity to which major parties had to respond if they wanted to win elections.

Video link:
The Untouchables

Identity-based groups, however, were not the only players in Indian civil society. Movements arose shortly after independence to champion a variety of environmental issues and women's concerns. These have been quite influential. Most recently, a social movement has arisen around the issue of battling the extensive corruption that plagues India. Symbolically led by Anna Hazare, movement members demanded that the government pass a bill creating an anticorruption agency designed in a way they believed would produce a real reduction in corruption. Hazare went on hunger strikes in April 2011 and August 2012 that captured national and international attention and brought out tens of thousands of protesters demanding passage of the anticorruption bill. The government yielded to his demands to end the fasts, but in mid-2013 it still had not passed the law and Hazare was again threatening a fast.

Hazare's mass movement, though, is not the most common form of civic activism in India today. Over the last two decades, Indian civil society has also witnessed the "NGOization" of many social movements as they have professionalized. In doing so, their demands have become less critical of the political and economic status quo and they have turned to the court system more often than protest to meet their demands, and succeeded primarily when the courts have agreed with them (Chandhoke 2011).

CASE Summary

Institutionalists would expect India's FPTP electoral system to create a two-party system. In India, however, great social and cultural diversity, a federal system, and FPTP have combined to produce numerous state-level two-party systems (following Duverger's Law). These forces have collectively created a multiparty national system, with two large national parties competing for power at the head of multiparty coalitions. Both major parties have lost support to the growing numbers of regional and state-level parties. This history is partly explained by the expansion of civil society, as excluded groups have organized and begun demanding greater access and participation. Unfortunately, some of these demands have taken violent forms, from some communist movements in the 1960s to the religious violence of the last decade. Much political organizing, however, has taken place within the nonviolent framework of India's electoral system.

India provides a case study of an electoral system in a very different context from the wealthy, Western democracies. A pluralist interest-group system also looks quite different in a country where the most important divisions are based not on industrialization but on region, ethnicity, caste, and religion. While often corrupt and sometimes violent, India's democracy has nonetheless kept interest groups and parties mostly operating within institutionalized bounds. It has also been a system in which participation and representation have expanded over the decades.

CASE Questions

1. What does the history of India's electoral and party systems teach us about the debate between institutional and sociological explanations of the evolution of political parties?

2. The "civic culture" argument we outlined in chapter 1 argued that democracy requires a certain type of culture to survive, one that characterizes the United Kingdom and the United States in particular. Comparing political participation in the Indian and the United Kingdom cases, what is your assessment of that argument?

CASE Study

BRAZIL: PARTIES AND CIVIL SOCIETY IN A YOUNG DEMOCRACY

Brazil has long been one of the world's most unequal societies. From the *coronelismo* of the nineteenth century to the populism of the more industrialized twentieth century, Brazil's elite has kept the masses under its control. Given this history, January 1, 2003, was not your average day for poor Brazilians. On that day, they celebrated the inauguration of President Luiz "Lula" Inácio da Silva, a trade-union leader who grew up in poverty with a fourth-grade education. The inauguration of the leader of the social democratic Workers Party (PT) seemed to herald the fruition of Brazil's new democracy. His party, born out of the workers' struggle to gain the right to form their own unions and end military rule, was a new type of political organization in the country's history. It had been created from the bottom up rather than from the top down. The popularity of his government's innovative social welfare program (see chapter 11) and rapid economic growth (see chapter 10) gave him approval ratings of 75 percent in 2010, prompting U.S. president Barack Obama to call him "the most popular politician in the world." It came as a shock, then, when massive demonstrations erupted three years later against the government of his handpicked successor, Dilma Rousseff. Participation burst dramatically beyond institutional boundaries as Brazilians expressed their extreme anger over a stagnant economy, massive corruption, and what they saw as the government's misplaced priorities.

- **ELECTORAL SYSTEM**
  Open-list PR
- **PARTY SYSTEM**
  Multiple and weak
- **CIVIL SOCIETY**
  Strong democracy movement; 2013 demonstrations
- **TRENDS AND REFORMS**
  Parties getting stronger

Protests like this one in Belo Horizonte broke out across Brazil in June 2013. Dismayed by the cost of new stadiums being built for the 2014 World Cup, corruption scandals, and a sudden slowing of economic growth, Brazilian civil society organized demonstrations that brought millions of people into the streets in over one hundred cities across the country. The protesters demanded an end to corruption and better schools and health care. The popularity of President Dilma Rouseff of the Workers Party plummeted. It wasn't clear that other politicians would reap benefits from the protests, though: Brazilians seemed jaded by all political parties and what they saw as a dysfunctional political system.

After twenty-five years of military rule, Brazil became a full democracy again in 1989. Its long but successful shedding of military rule was a classic transition to democracy. The 1988 constitution created the presidential system we outlined in chapter 6. The most interesting and controversial element of the new democratic constitution, however, was the electoral system that has helped produce the extremely fragmented party system we mentioned in chapter 6. Brazil uses an open-list PR system for the Chamber of Deputies, which is the lower and more powerful house of the National Congress. Each state is an electoral district that has a number of seats based loosely on its population. *Open-list* means that the individual candidates are listed on the ballot and voters can vote either for the party or an individual candidate. Within each district, a party gets a number of seats that is proportional to its total share of the vote, and then the individual candidates from that party who get the most votes get those seats.

This system gives candidates an incentive to garner as many individual votes as possible to place them as high as possible among their party's candidates. It provides no incentive for candidates within the same party to cooperate with one another. Given the long-standing role of patronage in Brazilian politics and the decentralized federal system, candidates understandably focus almost exclusively on local issues. Most are really representatives of particular areas or particular social groups, rather than party stalwarts. They are dependent on their own ability to mobilize supporters in their home areas and on important local leaders such as mayors and governors, but they are not dependent on national parties. Indeed, national parties are dependent on locally popular candidates to garner votes that add to the party's total tally in a state.

The obvious result is weak parties. In fact, parties were so weak that between 1989 and 1995, one-third of legislators switched parties while in office. With the exception of a few major parties, most parties (like most candidates) are really local. They represent one region or sometimes are just vehicles for a particular local candidate. The electoral system has no minimum threshold of votes a party must get to gain representation in the chamber, so a locally popular candidate with a tiny fraction of the national total may well end up in office. And yes, this produces many parties in the legislature. There were twenty-two after the 2010 election, though these were grouped into two broad coalitions: one supporting the PT-led government (which won a majority of seats—311 of 513) and one opposing it.

The degree and effect of this party weakness has been the subject of significant debate among scholars of Brazil. Initial assumptions in the 1990s were that such weak parties inhibited the system's ability to pass coherent legislation, thereby threatening the effectiveness of the new democracy. Legislators seemed to vote as they pleased, ignoring party leaders' positions and instructions. Political scientist Barry Ames (2001) suggested that when legislators did vote with their parties they did so not because of party loyalty but instead because they could gain patronage and resources for their home areas in exchange for their votes.

Research by Brazilian scholars Argelina Figueiredo and Fernando Limongi (2000), however, demonstrated that Brazil's parties were stronger than previously believed.

Figueiredo and Limongi's evidence showed that legislators voted with their parties to a higher degree than had been assumed, suggesting that party leaders were able to marshal their troops in favor of their preferred policies. More recent research (Santos 2008; Hagopian et al. 2009) suggested that legislators are increasingly voting as a bloc, that party switching has dropped to half of what it was in the early 1990s, and that electoral volatility (voters switching parties from one election to the next) is down. Frances Hagopian and colleagues (2009) used a rational-choice analysis of politicians' incentives to argue that changes in economic policies reduced the amount of government "pork" available to legislators. This has made politicians more dependent on parties' "brands" to secure office, which in turn has led them to support their party leadership more faithfully in legislative votes, stick to one party longer, and campaign on the party's platform. And though they are quite vague, the major Brazilian parties can loosely be grouped into "right," "center," and "left" parties (with several in each category). In recent elections, ideologically similar parties have formed coalitions to support the most popular candidates. The popularity of the last two presidents, Fernando Henrique Cardoso and Lula, undoubtedly helped spur coalitions, since parties want to support a winner if possible. In 2007 Brazil's top court imposed a rule that legislators could not switch parties after being elected and retain their seat; they argued that under the PR system, the seat they had belonged to the party, not the individual. Further reforms were proposed in Congress as well, including switching to a closed-list PR system, but all were soundly defeated. It seems increasingly clear that as weak as Brazilian parties were in the first few years of the new democracy, they have since gained some strength, even if they remain weak compared with parties in older democracies.

Another reason for somewhat stronger parties in recent years is the presence of the PT. Forged in the massive strikes of 1978–1979, the PT was a different kind of party from the start. From its first election in 1982, it refused to play by the rules of "politics as usual" in Brazil, insisting instead that it would recognize only those candidates whom it vetted as supporting its ideology. Because of its scathing critique of the corruption of the Brazilian political elite, it refused to cooperate with any other party, even others on "the left." It also refused to use patronage to gain political support. Its longtime leader, Lula, is a union leader who campaigned wearing blue jeans and using the working-class vernacular. He and the party, with their socialist policies and symbols, represented a grassroots critique of the entire Brazilian political elite.

The party's discipline and success by the 1990s led other parties to become somewhat more disciplined in imitation. Lula ran for president and came in second in the elections of 1989, 1994, and 1998, finally winning the presidency in 2002. In the end, the PT did have to make compromises to win. Most important, it dropped its opposition to forming coalitions, a crucial factor in Lula's eventual election. It also dropped its insistence on socialism as an economic policy and led a government that preserved most of the prior government's economic policies (see chapter 10). A scandal that emerged in 2005 involving the PT government bribing members of Congress to vote for its policies revealed that once in office it had also fallen into long-standing patterns of clientelism and patronage in order to rule.

Indeed, in spite of the growing strength of some of its parties, Brazil's patronage politics and weak institutions still make it a bastion of corruption, so much so that Transparency International's 1995 Corruption Perception Index gave it a score of 2.7 out of 10 (with 10 being the least corrupt), ranking it 37 out of 41 countries surveyed. By 2012, it had a score of 4.3 and a rank of 69 out of 174 countries. While improved, this still represents a significant corruption problem. In fact, some of the greater party-line voting in Congress was due to corruption. The scandal that erupted in 2005 when a member of Congress admitted that the PT government was paying legislators to support it ultimately implicated dozens of members of Congress, and Lula's chief of staff and several other top PT leaders were forced to resign. Indeed, by 2013, about a third of the sitting Congress was indicted on corruption charges of one sort or another, though Brazil's slow judiciary (see chapter 6) and rules protecting members of Congress meant that none had yet actually served time in jail.

The scandal became one of the issues behind the explosion of street demonstrations in June 2013. Brazil's civil society has long been active. It was instrumental in the transition to democracy; massive street protests were a regular part of the pressure that forced the military to leave power. Lula and his supporters helped create independent trade unions that broke the monopoly of state corporatism imposed by the military government; women's movements and Catholic organizations based around liberation theology also became active participants demanding democracy. Ironically, once achieved, democracy has led to concern about the effectiveness of participation. The country's exceptional social inequality, many argue, affects participation in the same way that it affects the rule of law: the poor, who are often black, are left out. The PT was innovative in trying to overcome this problem. Starting in the city of Porto Alegre under a PT government, the party has instituted a "participatory budgeting" (PB) system in which citizens in neighborhoods meet to set their priorities for the annual government budget. These groups elect representatives who meet at higher levels to produce a set of budget proposals for the city's officials to consider and enact. The system gives local citizens a voice and serves as a means of higher-level participation for more active citizens, who typically are members of local social movements or NGOs. The PB process has provided an avenue for greater participation for local civil society organizations (Avritzer 2009), though it's not clear that this was also effective at changing policy (Montero 2011). Once in power, the PT initially tried to institute national-level versions of participatory democracy, but these were ultimately criticized by participants as only advisory and having little real impact (Goldfrank 2011).

Lula presided over a period of exceptional economic growth and social innovations (see chapter 11) during which poverty was cut in half. An economic slowdown hit the country in 2011, however, just as it agreed to host both the 2014 World Cup and the 2016 Olympics. Inflation started creeping up as well, and when the government announced rate hikes to the crucial urban public transportation sector in June 2013, the demonstrations began. A group called "Free Fare" had campaigned since 2005 for reduced public transit fares; when it called a demonstration in São Paulo, the country's largest city, it was overwhelmed by thousands of people heeding the call to take to the streets in a peaceful protest. The police responded with force, and within a week, demonstrations of thousands—in some cases, hundreds of thousands—of people had spread to at least one hundred Brazilian cities. The protests were loosely organized and the demands defuse. Demonstrators' signs and speeches quickly moved from bus fares to demands that the government reduce corruption and spend less money on new soccer stadiums for the World Cup (a surprising demand in a country known for its rabid soccer fans). Instead, protestors called for better-funded public services, especially schools. Showing it clearly was a democracy, if a flawed one, the government responded with announcing reduced transit fares and more spending of oil revenues on schools, but the demonstrations continued, often at major soccer games. By Brazilian independence day in September, most reforms were stalled in the Brazilian Congress and smaller but still vociferous protests occurred in over a hundred cities across the country.

Alfred Montero (2011) argued that while Brazil's civil society includes numerous active groups, their effectiveness is limited. Long-standing clientelism continues to be the predominant relationship between political leaders and citizens, as the latter vote for local politicians who provide services and infrastructure, regardless of their party, ideology, or level of corruption. The weak parties created by the electoral system reinforce these tendencies. Thus, in spite of an active civil society, Brazil's citizens may not have much influence. Especially in poorer states, ruling parties centered on a long-standing leader, some from the military era, win large majorities, meaning competition is limited. In this context, the 2013 demonstrations may reflect growing frustration with participation that does not produce accountability.

CASE Summary   Brazil's still-young democracy is an example of a successful transition to democracy, though it certainly has continued problems. The institutions created in the 1988 constitution satisfied the various interests involved, although they perhaps did not create the most coherent political system imaginable. Most important are weak parties, which have made policymaking difficult and accountability limited. Party strength seems to be rising recently, though weak institutions and corruption remain serious problems. Participation is undoubtedly greater than at any time in Brazil's history, and the prominence of the PT has allowed poorer citizens more access to government than ever before. When economic growth was strong and poverty dropping, the government was quite popular. Once those trends leveled off, civil society mobilized millions in street demonstrations, though their long-term effects are uncertain.

KEY CONCEPTS

closed-list proportional
representation (p. 331)

collective action problem (p. 326)

dominant-party system (p. 343)

Duverger's Law (p. 344)

electoral systems (p. 326)

"first-past-the-post" (FPTP) (p. 328)

Hindu nationalism (p. 381)

interest-group pluralism (p. 353)

mixed, or semiproportional (p. 334)

multiparty systems (p. 344)

neocorporatism
(societal corporatism) (p. 354)

open-list proportional
representation (p. 331)

party system (p. 337)

peak associations (p. 354)

plurality (p. 328)

populism (p. 342)

proportional
representation (PR) (p. 330)

single-member district
(SMD) (p. 328)

social capital (p. 359)

social movements (p. 356)

state corporatism (p. 355)

two-and-a-half-party
system (p. 344)

two-party system (p. 343)

virtual representation (p. 329)

 Sharpen your skills with SAGE edge at **edge.sagepub.com/orvis3e.**
SAGE edge for students provides a personalized approach to help you accomplish your coursework goals in an easy-to-use learning environment.

WORKS CITED

Agarwala, Rina. 2013. *Informal Labor, Formal Politics, and Dignified Discontent in India.* Cambridge, UK: Cambridge University Press.

Ahmed, Amel. 2013. *Democracy and the Politics of Electoral System Choice: Engineering Electoral Dominance.* Cambridge, UK: Cambridge University Press.

Ames, Barry. 2001. *The Deadlock of Democracy in Brazil.* Ann Arbor: University of Michigan Press.

Avritzer, Leonardo. 2009. *Participatory Institutions in Democratic Brazil.* Baltimore, MD: Johns Hopkins University Press; Washington, DC: Woodrow Wilson Center Press.

Beyme, Klaus von. 1985. *Political Parties in Western Democracies.* Aldershot, UK: Gower.

Blyth, Mark, and Richard Katz. 2005. "From Catch-all Politics to Cartelisation: The Political Economy of the Cartel Party." *West European Politics* 28 (1): 33–60. doi: 10.1080/0140238042000297080.

Boix, Carles. 2007. "The Emergence of Parties and Party Systems." In *The Oxford Handbook of Comparative Politics,* edited by Carles Boix and Susan Carol Stokes. Oxford, UK: Oxford University Press.

Carlson, Matthew. 2007. *Money Politics in Japan: New Rules, Old Practices.* Boulder, CO: Lynne Rienner.

Chandhoke, Neera. 2011. "Civil Society in India." In *The Oxford Handbook of Civil Society*, edited by Michael Edwards, 171–182. Oxford, UK: Oxford University Press.

Curtice, John, and W. Phillips Shively. 2009. "Who Represents Us Best? One Member or Many?" In *The Comparative Study of Electoral Systems*, edited by Hans-Dieter Klingemann, 171–192. Oxford, UK: Oxford University Press.

Dalton, Russell J., David M. Farrell, and Ian McAllister. 2011. *Political Parties and Democratic Linkage: How Parties Organize Democracy*. Oxford, UK: Oxford University Press.

Dalton, Russell J., and Martin P. Wattenberg. 2000. *Parties without Partisans: Political Change in Advanced Industrial Democracies*. New York: Oxford University Press.

Duverger, Maurice. 1969. *Political Parties, Their Organization and Activity in the Modern State*. London: Methuen.

Figueiredo, Argelina Cheibub, and Fernando Limongi. 2000. "Presidential Power, Legislative Organization, and Party Behavior in Brazil." *Comparative Politics* 32 (2): 151–170.

Goldfrank, Benjamin. 2011. "The Left and Participatory Democracy: Brazil, Uruguay, and Venezuela." In *The Resurgence of the Latin American Left*, edited by Steven Levitsky and Kenneth M. Roberts, 162–183. Baltimore, MD: John Hopkins University Press.

Hagopian, Frances. 2005. "Chile and Brazil." In *Assessing the Quality of Democracy*, edited by Larry Diamond and Leonardo Morlino, 123–162. Baltimore, MD: Johns Hopkins University Press.

Hagopian, Frances, Carlos Vervasoni, and Juan Andrés Moraes. 2009. "From Patronage to Program: The Emergence of Party-Oriented Legislators in Brazil." *Comparative Political Studies* 42 (3): 360–391.

Hasan, Zoya. 2010. "Political Parties in India." In *The Oxford Companion to Politics in India*, edited by Niraja Gopal Jayal and Pratap Bhanu Mehta. Oxford, UK: Oxford University Press.

Inglehart, Ronald. 1971. "The Silent Revolution in Europe: Intergenerational Change in Post-Industrial Societies." *American Political Science Review* 65 (4): 991–1017. doi:10.1017/S0003055406392568.

Iversen, Torben, and Anne Wren. 1998. "Equality, Employment, and Budgetary Restraint: The Trilemma of the Service Economy." *World Politics* 50 (4): 507–546.

Kabashima, Ikuo, and Gill Steel. 2010. *Changing Politics in Japan*. Ithaca, NY: Cornell University Press.

Krauss, Ellis S., and Robert J. Pekkanen. 2011. *The Rise and Fall of Japan's LDP: Political Party Organizations as Historical Institutions*. Ithaca, NY: Cornell University Press.

Lang, Sabine. 2013. *NGOs, Civil Society, and the Public Sphere*. Cambridge, UK: Cambridge University Press.

Lee, Frances E. 2009. *Beyond Ideology: Politics, Principles, and Partisanship in the U.S. Senate*. Chicago: University of Chicago Press.

Lemann, Nicholas. 1996. "Kicking in Groups." *Atlantic Monthly* 277 (4): 22–26.

Lijphart, Arend. 1999. *Patterns of Democracy: Government Forms and Performance in Thirty-six Countries*. New Haven, CT: Yale University Press.

Martin, Sherry L. 2011. *Popular Democracy in Japan: How Gender and Community Are Changing Modern Electoral Politics*. Ithaca, NY: Cornell University Press.

McAdam, Doug, Sidney Tarrow, and Charles Tilly. 2001. *Dynamics of Contention*. New York: Cambridge University Press.

Montero, Alfred P. 2011. "Brazil: The Persistence of Oligarchy." In *The Quality of Democracy in Latin America*, edited by Daniel Levine and Jose Molina, 111–136. Boulder, CO: Lynne Rienner.

Moosbrugger, Lorelei K. 2012. *The Vulnerability Thesis: Interest Group Influence and Institutional Design*. New Haven, CT: Yale University Press.

Moser, Robert G., and Ethan Scheiner. 2012. *Electoral Systems and Political Context: How the Effects of Rules Vary across New and Established Democracies.* New York: Cambridge University Press.

Norris, Pippa. 2002. *Democratic Phoenix: Reinventing Political Activism.* New York: Cambridge University Press.

Ogawa, Akihiro. 2009. *The Failure of Civil Society? The Third Sector and the State in Contemporary Japan.* Albany, NY: SUNY Press.

Palshikar, Suhas. 2013. "Regional and Caste Parties." In *Routledge Handbook of Indian Politics,* edited by Atul Kohli and Prema Singh, 91–104. New York: Routledge.

Pekkanen, Robert. 2006. *Japan's Dual Civil Society: Members without Advocates.* Stanford, CA: Stanford University Press.

Poguntke, Thomas. 2012. "Towards a New Party System: The Vanishing Hold of the Catch-All Parties in Germany." *Party Politics* (October).

Powell, G. Bingham. 2000. *Elections as Instruments of Democracy: Majoritarian and Proportional Visions.* New Haven, CT: Yale University Press.

Putnam, Robert D. 2000. *Bowling Alone: The Collapse and Revival of American Community.* New York: Simon and Schuster.

———. 2007. "E Pluribus Unum: Diversity and Community in the Twenty-first Century: The 2006 Johan Skytte Prize Lecture." *Scandinavian Political Studies* 30(2): 137–174.

Reed, Steven R. 2005. "Japan: Haltingly Toward a Two-Party System." In *The Politics of Electoral Systems,* edited by Michael Gallagher and Paul Mitchell, 277–294. Oxford, UK: Oxford University Press.

Reed, Steven R., Ethan Scheiner, Daniel M. Smith, and Michael Thies. 2012. *The Japanese General Election of 2012: Sometimes, Lucky Is Better Than Popular.* December 27. The Monkey Cage (http://Themonkeycage.Org/2012/12/27/The-Japanese-General-Election-Of-2012-Sometimes-Lucky-Is-Better-Than-Popular/#Comments).

Rodrik, Dani. 1997. *Has Globalization Gone Too Far?* Washington, DC: Institute for International Economics.

Santos, Fabiano. 2008. "Brazilian Democracy and the Power of 'Old' Theories of Party Competition." *Brazilian Political Science Review* 2 (1): 57–76 (http://www.bpsr.org.br/english/arquivos/BPSR_v2_n3_jun2008_03.pdf).

Scarrow, Susan E., Paul Webb, and David M. Farrell. 2000. "From Social Integration to Electoral Contestation: The Changing Distribution of Power within Political Parties." In *Parties without Partisans: Political Change in Advanced Industrial Democracies,* edited by Russell J. Dalton and Martin P. Wattenberg, 129–153. New York: Oxford University Press.

Schattschneider, Elmer Eric. 2009. *Party Government.* 3rd ed. New Brunswick, NJ: Transaction. (Originally published 1942 in New York by Holt, Rinehart and Winston.)

Shugart, Matthew Soberg. 2005. "Comparative Electoral Systems Research: The Maturation of a Field and New Challenges Ahead." In *The Politics of Electoral Systems,* edited by Michael Gallagher and Paul Mitchell, 22–55. Oxford, UK: Oxford University Press.

Tocqueville, Alexis de. 1969. *Democracy in America.* Garden City, NY: Doubleday Anchor. (Originally published in two volumes in 1835 and 1840, respectively, in London by Saunders and Otley.)

Uslander, Eric M. 2012. *Segregation and Mistrust: Diversity, Isolation, and Social Cohesion.* New York: Cambridge University Press.

Zettl, Christian. 2010. *The German Federal Elections of 2009: The (Ultimate) Downfall of the German Volksparteien?* Paper prepared for the Political Science Association Conference. Newcastle-upon-Tyne, UK: Political Studies Association (http://www.psa.ac.uk/journals/pdf/5/2010/961_418.pdf).

RESOURCES FOR FURTHER STUDY

Aldrich, John H. 1995. *Why Parties? The Origin and Transformation of Political Parties in America*. Chicago: University of Chicago Press.

Art, David. 2011. *Inside the Radical Right: The Development of Anti-Immigrant Parties in Western Europe*. New York: Cambridge University Press.

Green, Michael J. 2010. "Japan's Confused Revolution." *Washington Quarterly* 33(1): 3–19. doi:10.1080/01636600903418637.

Levendusky, Matthew. 2009. *The Partisan Sort: How Liberals Became Democrats and Conservatives Became Republicans*. Chicago: University of Chicago Press.

Pharr, Susan J., and Robert D. Putnam, eds. 2000. *Disaffected Democracies: What's Troubling the Trilateral Countries?* Princeton, NJ: Princeton University Press.

Putnam, Robert D., ed. 2002. *Democracies in Flux: The Evolution of Social Capital in Contemporary Society*. New York: Oxford University Press.

Rosenbluth, Frances McCall, and Michael F. Thies. 2010. *Japan Transformed: Political Change and Economic Restructuring*. Princeton, NJ: Princeton University Press.

Skocpol, Theda. 2003. *Diminished Democracy: From Membership to Management in American Civic Life*. Norman: University of Oklahoma Press.

Thomas, Clive S. 2001. *Political Parties and Interest Groups: Shaping Democratic Governance*. Boulder, CO: Lynne Rienner.

Ware, Alan. 1996. *Political Parties and Party Systems*. New York: Oxford University Press.

Wren, Anne, and Kenneth M. McElwain. 2007. "Voters and Parties." In *The Oxford Handbook of Comparative Politics*, edited by Carles Boix and Susan Carol Stokes, 555–581. Oxford, UK: Oxford University Press.

WEB RESOURCES

Consortium for Elections and Political Process Strengthening (CEPPS), Election Guide
(http://www.electionguide.org)

Constituency-Level Elections Archive
(http://www.electiondataarchive.org)

Golder, Matt, "Democratic Electoral Systems around the World, 1946–2000"
(http://homepages.nyu.edu/~mrg217/elections.html)

Hyde, Susan, and Nikolay Marinov, "National Elections across Democracy and Autocracy"
(http://hyde.research.yale.edu/nelda/#)

International Institute for Democracy and Electoral Assistance (IDEA)
(http://www.idea.int)

Inter-Parliamentary Union, PARLINE Database on National Parliaments
(http://www.ipu.org/parline-e/parlinesearch.asp)

Johnson, Joel W., and Jessica S. Wallack, "Electoral Systems and the Personal Vote"
(http://thedata.harvard.edu/dvn/dv/jwjohnson/faces/study/StudyPage.xhtml?globalId=hdl:1902.1/17901)

University of California, San Diego, Lijphart Elections Archive
(http://libraries.ucsd.edu/locations/sshl/data-gov-info-gis/ssds/guides/lij)

AMERICA IS NOT FOR SALE!

8 AUTHORITARIAN INSTITUTIONS

KEY QUESTIONS

- Some authoritarian regimes disperse power more widely than others. How can comparativists determine "who rules" and what limits executive power in an authoritarian regime?

- Authoritarian regimes come in several different subtypes: military, one-party, theocratic, personalist, and semi-authoritarian. In what ways do differences across these subtypes explain differences in leaders' actions, levels of repression, and types of popular participation?

- Why are patron-client networks so prevalent and important in authoritarian regimes? In what types of authoritarian regimes do they seem most important, and what might explain this?

- Some authoritarian regimes allow at least some institutionalized limits on rulers' power. What explains where and why this happens, or doesn't happen?

The spread of democracy in the aftermath of the Cold War led some to believe that democratic rule was irreversible; dictators were historical relics, soon to be relegated to the "dustbin of history." Many Eastern European and African societies that threw off or severely challenged their authoritarian regimes, however, ended up creating new ones, albeit less repressive than their predecessors. Semi-authoritarian regimes, in which some opposition and participation were allowed but a key ruler or party firmly held onto power, became more common. In other cases, especially in the Middle East, the winds of democratic change did not blow strongly enough to seriously challenge authoritarian regimes until the sudden outburst of popular opposition in the "Arab Spring" of 2011. Abandoning the study of authoritarian regimes at the end of the Cold War was clearly premature, and in the new millennium comparativists have taken renewed interest in the subject. Authoritarian regimes have long outnumbered democracies. Indeed, only two of our case studies, the United States and the United Kingdom, have not had authoritarian regimes in the modern era. The Country and Concept table on page 400 shows how common and how varied authoritarian regimes are, just within our eleven case studies.

The answer to the question "Who rules?" seems like it ought to be particularly obvious in authoritarian regimes: the dictator does. In fact, discerning who really has power and how much power they have is not

Libyan leader Muammar el-Qaddafi (left) clasps hands with Syrian president Bashar Assad in 2008 in a sign of camaraderie between two personalist leaders. Both leaders faced civil war sparked by the "Arab Spring" in 2011. Qaddafi was overthrown and killed while Assad held onto power as the war dragged on in 2013.

always obvious. In chapter 3, we noted that in modernizing authoritarian regimes, neither ideology nor formal institutions necessarily explain who rules or how a particular regime functions. Authoritarian regimes tend to arise in relatively weak states that have weak formal institutions, and therefore informal institutions and processes are more important. This makes determining who has how much power particularly difficult.

The prevalence of important informal institutions in authoritarian regimes also makes explaining political behavior challenging. In chapter 3 we outlined several subtypes of authoritarian regimes based on their origins and formal institutions: one-party, military, personalist, theocratic, and semi-authoritarian. These subtypes clearly have somewhat different governing institutions, but given that formal institutions in authoritarian regimes tend to be weak, how much does this really explain? Are one-party regimes as a group different in distinctive ways from military regimes? Does one subtype always provide greater levels of institutionalized limits on executive power? Is one subtype always more repressive? It is clear as well that patron-client relationships and networks are important in virtually all authoritarian regimes. Why is this the case, and does this also vary across the subtypes of authoritarian regimes?

COUNTRY AND CONCEPT
Authoritarian Rule

Country	Twentieth-century authoritarian rule since independence (years)	Authoritarian regime type	Number of supreme leaders	Average length of leader's rule (years)	Cause of regime demise
Brazil	1930–1945	Modernizing authoritarian	1	15	Democratization
	1964–1985	Military	5	4	Democratization
China*	1927–1949	Modernizing authoritarian	1	22	Revolution
	1949–	Communist/modernizing authoritarian	5	13	NA
Germany	1871–1918	Modernizing authoritarian	2	23	War loss
	1933–1945	Fascist	1	12	War loss
India	None	–	–	–	–
Iran	1921–1979	Modernizing authoritarian	2	27	Revolution
	1979–	Theocratic	2	17	NA
Japan	1867–1945	Modernizing authoritarian	3	26	War loss
Mexico	1924–2000	Modernizing authoritarian	15	4.5	Democratization
Nigeria	1966–1979	Military	4	3	Democratization
	1983–1998	Military	3	5	Democratization
Russia	1917–1991	Communist	7	10	Democratization
	2000–	Semi-authoritarian	1	15	NA
United Kingdom	None	–	–	–	–
United States	None	–	–	–	–

*China's republic (1912–1927) never consolidated an effective state.

A key difference among authoritarian regimes that will help us answer these questions is the regimes' level of institutionalization, which we defined in chapter 6 as the degree to which government processes and procedures are established, predictable, and routinized. In the least-institutionalized personalist regimes, decisions truly can be made and implemented at the whim of the dictator. In other authoritarian regimes, the leader's power is still extensive, but it is somewhat curtailed by institutionalized checks. For example, the Brazilian military regime in the latter part of the twentieth century institutionalized a rotating presidency, with each branch of the military designating a president for an established term. Communist regimes have politburos and other mechanisms of high-level party consultation that may force some discussion and consensus building among the party elites. Trying to explain variations in institutionalized limits in authoritarian regimes is another important question that we examine in this chapter.

All modern states, including those with authoritarian regimes, have executive branches and bureaucracies and provide some sort of judiciary, though how much the judiciary is independent of the executive is a major question. Some authoritarian regimes also develop institutions such as legislatures and even hold elections to provide some degree, however small, of citizen participation, though not enough to threaten the power of the key rulers. We therefore examine the same sets of institutions in this chapter that we did in chapters 6 and 7 for democracies, but the distinct context and logic of authoritarian regimes require somewhat different foci and theoretical lenses to understand those institutions.

AUTHORITARIAN RULE AROUND THE WORLD

While not the promised land of universal democracy that some analysts thought it would be, the era after the end of the Cold War certainly had a significant effect on authoritarian regimes. Their numbers declined, particularly in the 1990s, and their institutions changed. The result was a decline in the number of purely authoritarian regimes and the rise of what we have termed semi-authoritarian regimes. With the expansion of democracy as a global ideal, more regimes attempted to legitimize their rule through the creation of elections and legislatures but kept those institutions limited enough to maintain authoritarian control overall. The ultimate control that authoritarian rulers—whether individuals, groups, or parties—preserve even in semi-authoritarian regimes means that we can analyze the latter with many of the same concepts we will use to analyze all authoritarian regimes, as we discuss below.

The total number of authoritarian regimes in the world peaked in the late 1970s, though the decline was much more rapid after the end of the Cold War. Authoritarian regimes ruled about 75 percent of all countries in the 1970s, but by 2008 that number was down to about 40 percent (Svolik 2012, 25). Furthermore, these numbers are based on a definition of an authoritarian regime as one that does not have either (1) free and competitive legislative elections or (2) a freely and competitively elected executive (via either direct or indirect election). Thus, many semi-authoritarian regimes are included. Map 8.1 shows this transformation around the world and over time.

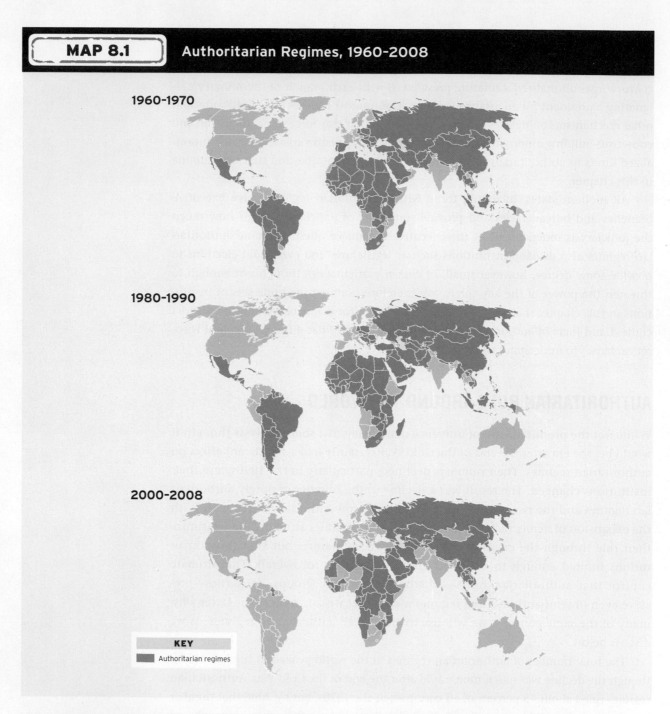

MAP 8.1 Authoritarian Regimes, 1960-2008

1960-1970

1980-1990

2000-2008

KEY
Authoritarian regimes

Shown on the maps are countries with authoritarian regimes lasting for at least two years during the decade covered. Since not all decades are included here, some countries with lasting authoritarian regimes are not shown. For instance, Serbia had an authoritarian regime from 1991 to 2000, which is not captured on the map. Civil wars are not counted as authoritarian regimes.

Source: Data for the map are derived from Milan W. Svolik, *The Politics of Authoritarian Rule* (Cambridge, UK: Cambridge University Press), 45–50. © Milan W. Svolik 2012.

The changing nature of the institutions in contemporary authoritarian and semi-authoritarian regimes is clear in Figures 8.1 and 8.2. Most dramatic is the precipitous drop (Figure 8.1) in single-party systems among authoritarian regimes at the end of the Cold War, which were replaced with multiple party systems. This clearly shows the sharp rise in semi-authoritarian regimes, the product of liberalization of older authoritarian regimes or (as we will discuss in chapter 9) failed transitions to democracy. Figure 8.2 demonstrates that these regimes now allow opposing parties some voice via legislatures as well. Over 80 percent of current regimes have elected legislatures of some sort, and about 60 percent allow multiple candidates per legislative seat, a good indicator of a semi-authoritarian regime. In about 40 percent, the ruling party controls less than three-quarters of the legislative seats, indicating it has allowed the opposition a significant (though still firmly minority) position. Today, most authoritarian regimes allow some sort of legislature and opposition parties to exist and participate in some form. The question we turn to next is why.

Web link:
The rise of competitive authoritarianism

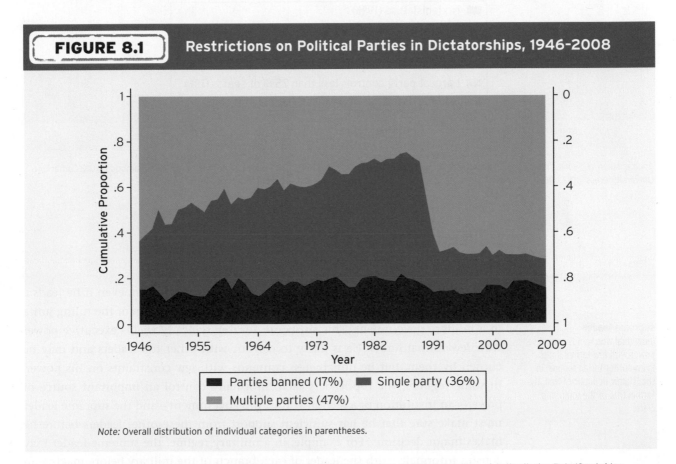

FIGURE 8.1 **Restrictions on Political Parties in Dictatorships, 1946–2008**

■ Parties banned (17%) ■ Single party (36%)
■ Multiple parties (47%)

Note: Overall distribution of individual categories in parentheses.

Source: Milan W. Svolik, "Figure 2.4, Restrictions on Political Parties in Dictatorships, 1946–2008," *The Politics of Authoritarian Rule* (Cambridge University Press), 35. © Milan W. Svolik 2012. Reprinted with the permission of Cambridge University Press.

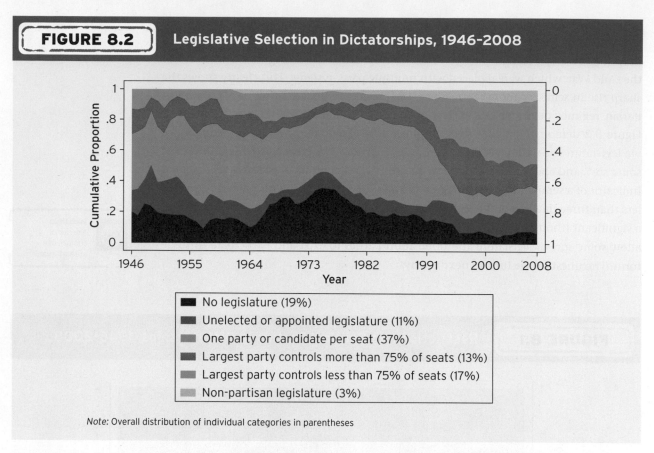

FIGURE 8.2   Legislative Selection in Dictatorships, 1946-2008

Legend:
- No legislature (19%)
- Unelected or appointed legislature (11%)
- One party or candidate per seat (37%)
- Largest party controls more than 75% of seats (13%)
- Largest party controls less than 75% of seats (17%)
- Non-partisan legislature (3%)

Note: Overall distribution of individual categories in parentheses

Source: Milan W. Svolik, "Figure 2.6, Legislative Selection In Dictatorships, 1946-2008," *The Politics of Authoritarian Rule* (Cambridge, UK: Cambridge University Press, 2012), 36. © Milan W. Svolik 2012. Reprinted with the permission of Cambridge University Press.

GOVERNING INSTITUTIONS IN AUTHORITARIAN REGIMES

supreme leader
Individual who wields executive power with few formal limits in an authoritarian regime; in the Islamic Republic of Iran, the formal title of the top ruling cleric

Virtually all authoritarian regimes recognize one supreme leader, even if he leads a larger ruling group, such as the politburo in a communist system or the ruling junta in a military government. This **supreme leader** typically wields executive power with few formal limits. He is likely to consult with other top leaders and may be chosen by them, but he nonetheless contends with few constraints on his power. In some regimes, the top leaders each informally control an important source of power—an institution or a faction within the government—and the supreme leader must make sure that he has sufficient support from these other leaders before he makes major decisions. For example, in a military regime, the supreme leader may consult informally with the leader of each branch of the military before making an important policy decision. In some more personalist regimes, even these informal limits may not exist.

All supreme leaders rule through some combination of repression, co-optation, and efforts at legitimation. *Repression* is the popular image that pops into people's minds when they think of dictators, but it is an expensive way to rule. Even the most ruthless dictator needs to find other means by which to ensure citizens' loyalties. *Co-optation* via material inducements and official positions (which often go hand in hand with corruption) is the most obvious alternative means of securing support. Most regimes also expend resources to try to instill loyalty in the citizenry to secure some actual *legitimacy*; if citizens believe in the regime, they will obey it without the costs of repression or co-optation. Communist parties use their well-developed ideology for this purpose to a greater extent than do most authoritarian regimes, but virtually all authoritarian regimes try to gain legitimacy in some way.

Security is certainly all regimes' top priority, and this is especially true for authoritarian regimes, which often have limited legitimacy. All types of authoritarian regimes, not just military ones, spend generously on military security, typically aimed more at internal than external threats. The loyalty of the military is, of course, crucial. One-party states either incorporate key military leaders into the party leadership or make sure that loyal party leaders have control of the military, or both. For example, after the 1979 revolution that overthrew Anastasio Somoza's personalist regime in Nicaragua, the new Sandinista regime insisted that the new military (which replaced the Somoza-created National Guard) remain under the control of the Sandinista army that had fought the revolution. The head of the army, Humberto Ortega, was not only a prominent Sandinista but was also the brother of Sandinista president Daniel Ortega. In personalist regimes, leaders often place close supporters, even family members, in key positions in charge of the country's security apparatus. In ethnically divided societies, they often place people of their own ethnic group, or even from their own hometown, within the security apparatus to ensure its loyalty. For instance, Saddam Hussein in Iraq put not only his fellow Sunni Arabs but also people from his home village in positions of authority in his extensive security apparatus. Personalist leaders also frequently create entirely new security organizations. Unable to rely on the loyalty of the existing military, they create personal, elite security forces that are loyal only to the executive, something both Hosni Mubarak in Egypt and Muammar el-Qaddafi in Libya did. If a president has access to enough resources, his personal security force might be better paid and armed than the national army. Many authoritarian rulers also create vast networks of spies, both civilian and military, whose job is to gather intelligence on regime opponents.

Ronald Wintrobe (1998) used a rational-choice approach to argue that all authoritarian leaders face what he termed the **dictator's dilemma**: because of the repression they practice, they lack accurate information on how much political support they actually have. Repression breeds fear, which in turn breeds misinformation; the greater the repression, the greater the dictator's dilemma. Uncertain of their position, dictators try to co-opt potential rivals by purchasing their loyalty. They can never be certain, however, of how much they need to spend to purchase the loyalty they require, so they tend to overspend, lavishing resources on key sectors from which they believe threats

Video link:
Milan Svolik on the Arab Spring

Web link:
Security forces interfere with Mubarak trial

dictator's dilemma
An authoritarian ruler's repression creates fear, which then breeds uncertainty about how much support the ruler has; in response, the ruler spends more resources than is rational to co-opt the opposition

may emanate. Various elements in the military often receive such attention. This is especially true in military regimes that came to power via coups d'état themselves. They are acutely aware that potential rivals within the military may well overthrow them. Milan Svolik (2012) argued also that authoritarian regimes that rely on the military for repression risk being overthrown by the military; the regime's reliance on the military gives the latter greater power and resources and therefore the ability to intervene. In ethnically divided societies, dictators may focus spending on their own ethnic group to maintain their core base of support. In a number of African authoritarian regimes in the 1970s and 1980s, you could tell who was in power by how well paved the roads were in different regions of the country. The current dictator would build infrastructure such as roads, schools, and hospitals mainly in his home area. As you drove from one region to another, you could literally see who ruled by the immediate and extreme change in the quality of the roads.

Another means of co-opting potential opponents is the creation of formal institutions such as legislatures and single ruling parties that provide lucrative government positions and access to patronage. Jennifer Gandhi (2008), however, argued that these institutions are more than just mechanisms of co-optation; they can actually provide a space in which policy compromise can occur: "Within these institutions, leaders of religious organizations, business and labor associations, and various other groups can express demands that do not appear as acts of public resistance to the regime. The dictator, in turn, uses legislatures and parties as a way to control dissent and to make concessions while appearing to be magnanimous rather than weak" (137). Gandhi demonstrated that regimes with legislatures and parties spend less money on the military and have greater respect for human rights, both of which are classic demands of opposition forces. This indicates that policy compromise is greater in authoritarian regimes with these formal institutions than in those without them.

Our case study of Brazil is an example of this dynamic. The military (in power from 1964 to 1985) recreated an elected legislature but limited participation to two parties, one officially supporting the regime and one officially opposing it. The opposition, however, was severely restricted in what it was allowed to say or do in the legislature, whose powers were fairly nominal in any case. Nevertheless, the legislature served as a forum in which the opposition party could voice its views and the government could respond. Many one-party states preserved legislatures as well, though these bodies consisted only of members of the ruling party. In Kenya in the 1960s and early 1970s, legislators were able to voice limited criticisms of the government, work on behalf of their constituents to gain resources for their home areas, and use their access to government to gain direct benefits for themselves and their closest associates via corruption. The parliament clearly served as a mechanism of co-optation and, occasionally, of limited policy discussion. When MPs criticized the dictator too much, though, they faced repression: several sitting MPs were detained and tortured in the mid-1970s when their criticisms of the regime became too strident, and the most popular member of their group was assassinated.

Some authoritarian regimes also allow for a degree of rule of law and autonomy for the judiciary, though this is always limited. Typically, judicial autonomy is permitted only in nonpolitical cases. Providing the political good of basic personal security to citizens who do not oppose the regime allows the regime to gain a degree of legitimacy. Allowing this type of limited judicial autonomy can also help top leaders gain information about how effectively their state functions on the ground, reducing the dictator's dilemma. Citizens can go to court to attempt to get local government to carry out its functions properly, revealing to leaders potential local problems. Authoritarian leaders, however, do not allow the rule of law to limit them in any fundamental way: when necessary, they are likely to use the judicial system to repress their opponents and remove judges to ensure that the leader's will is done. In many authoritarian regimes, the judiciary becomes quite corrupt as well. Regime leaders and other wealthy people often bribe judges to rule in their favor; once this begins, more and more people recognize what "justice" actually requires, and corruption expands.

All states, regardless of regime type, require a bureaucracy, and all leaders face the principal-agent problem we identified in chapter 6. In an authoritarian regime, though, the question is how strong and independent a bureaucracy the supreme leader wants. A less-institutionalized bureaucracy, while not serving citizens' interests well, may have distinct advantages to the leader in the form of patronage opportunities that it offers regime supporters. Bureaucratic positions provide opportunities for corruption. The top leaders can thus maintain loyalty by allowing officials to use their positions to their own benefit, weakening the institutions of the state but rewarding the loyalty of potential rivals. If this behavior is informally institutionalized, it can become somewhat predictable: lesser officials will remain loyal because they believe they can rise to higher and more rewarding positions, which can lead to somewhat predictable career paths within key institutions. In more personalist regimes, a similar process takes place, but in a less-institutionalized manner. The supreme leader alone appoints people to bureaucratic positions and may change these frequently to ensure that no official has too much connection with or influence over any one organization because that could ultimately threaten the ruler by creating an alternative power base. The box below that outlines the case of Mobutu Sese Seko in Zaire demonstrates this strategy.

As the Kenyan example above demonstrates, how well formal institutions serve as sites of co-optation and policy compromise depends in part on their level of institutionalization. Prior to the mid-1970s, Kenyan MPs had immunity from arrest or prosecution on the basis of their actions or statements in parliament. For the first decade of Kenya's one-party state, President Jomo Kenyatta respected parliamentary immunity. When he abrogated it in the 1970s, parliament's strength and importance were severely weakened. Its institutional strength did not recover until the advent of multiparty competition in the early 1990s.

Institutionalization requires institutions to function more or less as they are legally designed to do over an extended period of time. As institutions continue to function,

The "Politics of Survival" in Mobutu's Zaire

Zaire (now the Democratic Republic of the Congo) under the dictatorship of Gen. Mobutu Sese Seko (1965–1997) was a classic case of a corrupt, personalist regime in a weak state. Mobutu came to power via a U.S.-supported military coup in the midst of a civil war and created the formal structures of a one-party state, but his rule was very personalist. All power and all major decisions went through him, and personal loyalty and patronage were the key elements of political power. Over time he severely weakened virtually all state institutions by following the logic of what political scientist Joel Migdal (1988) termed "the politics of survival."

On the surface, personalist leaders like Mobutu appear all-powerful. In reality, they have limited power because they preside over weak institutions. One might think that they would try to strengthen the institutions to tighten their own grip on power. Migdal (1988) argued, to the contrary, that strengthening institutions can be extremely risky for the dictator; indeed, more often than not, a dictator in a weak state is driven to weaken institutions even further.

Strong institutions are certainly sources of power, but not necessarily for the supreme leader. He cannot directly control all of a state's institutions but must instead, like any national leader, rely on subordinates. Those subordinates who lead state agencies directly may well be the primary beneficiaries of the power that derives from strengthened institutions. An agency that can solve people's problems or provide valuable resources gains political support for those directly in charge of the agency, not necessarily for the supreme leader. These mid-level officials may become political rivals of the leader. Hence, leaders of weak states often undermine institutions via such practices as frequently shuffling subordinates so that none of them becomes entrenched in any one position and appointing people who are personally loyal to the leader but who may have little competence in their positions.

Mobutu was a master of this kind of politics. He ruled first and foremost by patronage, creating a regime that many referred to as a "kleptocracy," or rule by theft. A government appointment was a license to steal. He also shuffled personnel frequently. If he saw an important official as a rival, he would remove him and then return him to power shortly afterward. A famous case involved Nguza Karl-i-Bond. He was foreign minister and then head of the ruling party in the mid-1970s, but after being mentioned as a possible successor to Mobutu he was

A dirt street in a poor neighborhood of Kinshasa, Zaire's capital, at the end of Mobutu Sese Seko's rule. Mobutu's thirty-two-year reign destroyed both political institutions and infrastructure, as is typical for personalist rulers.

accused of treason in 1977, imprisoned, and tortured. A year later, Mobutu forgave him and restored him to the prominent office of state commissioner. Then, in 1981, Nguza fled into exile in Belgium, denounced Mobutu for his corruption and brutality, and even testified against him before the U.S. Congress. In 1986, however, Mobutu once again forgave him, and Nguza returned to Zaire to a hero's welcome; shortly afterward he was named to the prestigious position of ambassador to the United States in Washington, D.C. Examples like this proved to all that Mobutu could take people from a top position to prison and back again in the blink of an eye.

"The politics of survival" (along with generous Western support during the Cold War) kept Mobutu in power for three decades but weakened all institutions in Zaire. Even basic infrastructure declined as the state's resources and capabilities collapsed. When Mobutu's neighbor and ally, Rwandan president Juvénal Habyarimana, was facing an armed insurrection in the early 1990s, Mobutu is alleged to have told him, "Your problem is you built roads. They are coming down those roads to get you." Mobutu did not make that mistake: Zaire's road network deteriorated to almost nothing under his rule. Nonetheless, rebel forces eventually forced the aging Mobutu out of power after the end of the Cold War deprived him of his Western support.

they gain strength; actors become socialized into their functions and self-interested politicians will abide by institutional rules as long as they believe they can benefit from them. Functioning formal institutions can lead opposition leaders to accept the compromise of working within the institution rather than making more fundamental demands for change, to which the dictator would likely respond with repression. Stronger institutions can reduce conflict and lengthen the life of the regime. Indeed, Svolik (2012, 111) created a dataset of authoritarian regime longevity that showed that those with legislatures lasted much longer than those without.

Explaining Institutionalization in Authoritarian Regimes

This raises the question of why stronger institutions emerge in some authoritarian regimes and not in others. In some of the most personalist regimes, like Idi Amin's tyrannical regime in Uganda in the 1970s, the dictator eliminates virtually all institutions and rules on the basis of his often ruthless and paranoid whim. In others, like our case study of Brazil, an authoritarian regime abides by some institutional limits.

As with any big question in comparative politics, a number of answers have been offered over the years. Psychological theorists have examined the personality types of major authoritarian leaders such as Hitler, Stalin, and Mao, arguing that regimes reflect the personality of the supreme leader. Other scholars note that different types of authoritarian regimes are likely to result in different levels of institutionalization. A military that itself has strong institutionalized norms, such as the Brazilian military, is a hierarchical organization with a strong sense of identity and purpose. The strength of the military as an institution will be reflected in a relatively institutionalized form of military rule. Similarly, Communist parties might seem to be natural breeding grounds for more-institutionalized regimes. They have highly structured organizations, including politburos, committees, and cells, in addition to consultative and decision-making mechanisms. Both political culture theorists and historical institutionalists look to broader societal factors and history. An authoritarian regime in a country with some historical experience with democracy may well be more likely to adopt or recreate some limited formal institutions like a legislature. Citizens are accustomed to these institutions, and the regime leaders therefore believe they can gain legitimacy by at least appearing to adhere to these institutional norms.

Gandhi (2008) used a rational-choice institutionalist argument to explain why some authoritarian regimes allow legislatures and opposition parties: rational and successful dictators will understand what institutional concessions they must make, depending on their own and the opposition's strength. Where the opposition is united, formal institutions are more likely to arise. Where the regime controls extensive mineral wealth, giving it resources for greater patronage, institutions are less likely. Legislatures and opposition parties are also more likely, she argued, in civilian dictatorships than in either monarchies or military regimes. The latter have independent power bases—the monarchy in its family and traditional legitimacy and the military in its control of repression—that provide them greater power vis-à-vis the opposition and therefore less need for legislatures or opposition parties. She thus provided a rational-choice explanation for why authoritarian rulers would choose, as they have since the Cold War, to allow some opposition to form, shifting toward a semi-authoritarian regime.

More recently, Milan Svolik (2012) presented a different rational-choice argument, suggesting institutions arise not as an effort at co-optation or allowing policy compromise but as a result of the interactions between a dictator and his elite allies in a ruling coalition. Institutions are most likely to arise where a balance of power exists between a dictator and his closest allies. A dictator always worries about his allies overthrowing him, and his allies worry about the dictator assuming all power and creating a personalist regime that denies them a share of power. As a dictator tries to usurp more power for himself, his allies' only way to resist is a credible threat to overthrow him. The allies, however, face a collective action problem: any individual who commits to a rebellion to overthrow the dictator and is ultimately unsuccessful faces likely imprisonment or death. If the dictator is successful at initial moves to amass more personal power, his allies' credibility to resist him drops, and the collective action problem gets worse, meaning he can usurp even more power. The result of this process is a personalist dictatorship with no institutionalized limits on the dictator's power. If a balance of power exists between the dictator and his allies at the outset, however, the allies are more likely to be able to credibly threaten a rebellion against him and he is less likely to attempt to usurp power. Institutions such as legislatures and political parties with limited power can arise in this situation. The dictator's allies will want these institutions because they ensure regular interaction between themselves and the dictator, increasing their knowledge about his intentions, and they create formal rules that provide clear markers for them to use in assessing whether the dictator is trying to usurp more power. The dictator will agree to these restrictions because his allies possess a credible threat of overthrowing him.

Once created, these institutions are likely to extend the life of the regime, if not necessarily the individual ruler. Erica Frantz and Natasha Ezrow (2011) also focused on the interaction of a dictator and his closest allies. They examined the likelihood of individual leaders (as opposed to entire regimes) being overthrown and found that leaders of military and one-party regimes are more likely to be removed from office than are leaders of personalist regimes, but that when personalist leaders are overthrown, the entire regime is likely to collapse. This is because the supreme ruler's allies need to overcome their collective action problem and need access to military force to overthrow him. This is most likely in military regimes, where the ruler's allies are also military leaders who know one another well and obviously have access to force. Ruling parties help the top allies overcome their collective action problem as well, but they have less direct access to the military. When a leader is overthrown in these two regime types, however, the regime may well continue because the new ruler(s) comes from within the existing regime. Allies of personalist leaders have no

Web link:
What do legislatures in authoritarian regimes do?

institutional base in common and the rulers do not allow anyone who could be a threat to become an important ally; therefore, when personalist leaders are overthrown it is almost always at the hands of people outside the regime. As a result, the entire regime is likely to collapse.

The Problem of Succession

Weakly institutionalized authoritarian regimes are plagued by the question of succession. Electoral democracies provide a means of changing leadership on a regular basis; authoritarian regimes have no such procedure readily at hand. This means that each regime must create its own system for choosing new leaders. Again, the degree of institutionalization matters greatly. Communist regimes, for instance, generally choose new leaders from among key contenders within the politburo. While the exact process is usually hidden from the general public, both regime leaders and citizens know that should a leader die, resign, or be forced from office, a pool of successors is available and top party leaders will collectively choose one from among their own. The Country and Concept table on page 400 illustrates the institutionalization of succession in the Soviet regime; it had seven different leaders over seventy-four years, while many other authoritarian regimes fail to survive their founders' demise.

What Explains the Rise and Fall of Authoritarian Regimes?

We have now become familiar with several of the leading theories of why authoritarian rulers do or do not create institutions and allow some opposition to have a voice. Map 8.1 and Figures 8.1 and 8.2 on pages 402–404 showed us the broad patterns of when and where authoritarian regimes have arisen and disappeared and shifts in their use of particular institutions. Looking again at the map and figures, can the theories we've just discussed explain the patterns you see? What other hypotheses can you create that would explain the patterns you see in the map and figures?

Less-institutionalized regimes typically have no succession system. Personalist leaders often rule for life or until they are forced out of office. Many will groom a successor as they age, all the while working to make sure that the successor does not become a threat before the time to pass the baton arrives. In the most personalist regimes, the leader grooms his own son to be his successor. The Somoza dynasty in Nicaragua (1936–1979) began with Anastasio senior, who was succeeded by his son Luis, who in turn was succeeded by his brother, another Anastasio. This was also the case in the regimes of "Papa Doc" (1957–1971) and "Baby Doc" Duvalier (1971–1986) in Haiti. Baby Doc was only nineteen years old when his father died and he became head of state. Should a personalist ruler die without clearly identifying a successor, a battle among key elites can emerge that can cause the regime to crumble, often resulting in a military coup (or, in the past, external invasion) to reestablish order. Sometimes, as in the case of Nigeria, the death of a personalist ruler can be the opportunity for democracy to emerge anew. These various outcomes demonstrate that the lack of a succession process creates significant uncertainty and potential instability in less-institutionalized authoritarian regimes.

Audio link:
Succession: dictators and sons

Some authoritarian regimes do have modest institutionalized limits on executive power, but this is almost always a matter of very limited horizontal accountability among the elites and the institutions they lead. In the somewhat more open semi-authoritarian regimes, legal opposition and a legislature are allowed, but power is kept firmly in the hands of the key rulers. This can also provide some level of predictability in the political system: key policy changes may have some opposition input, and new leaders arise out of an opaque but at least vaguely understood process. None of this, however, means that average citizens have real representation or more than token opportunities for participation. Vertical accountability, the ability of the citizenry to hold leaders directly accountable, is extremely limited. We will take up this subject after examining three cases of governing institutions in authoritarian regimes.

CASE Study

CHINA: FROM COMMUNIST TO MODERNIZING AUTHORITARIAN RULE

- **REGIME TYPE**
  One-party, modernizing authoritarian

- **REPRESSION**
  Primarily aimed at major regime opponents

- **CO-OPTATION**
  Patronage and corruption opportunities within party and government

- **INSTITUTIONALIZATION**
  Greatly increased in top leadership, judiciary, civilian control of military

- **SUCCESSION**
  Regularized and signaled in advance from within ruling party elite

In November 2012, the Chinese Communist Party (CCP) held the biggest event on its calendar, the Party Congress, which happens once every five years. It anointed Xi Jinping as the new supreme leader, electing him general secretary of the party and head of the military commission; he was duly appointed president of the country a few months later. Xi's rise to the top was not a surprise; the prior Party Congress in 2007 clearly signaled Xi's position as the next leader by appointing him vice president, among other posts. The long process demonstrated the full maturation of an opaque but nonetheless predictable succession process that has emerged over the last two decades. It represents an institutionalization of the authoritarian regime that is part of the reason it has survived so long and so well. The Party Congress on the surface is all about uniformity, with nearly unanimous votes on every issue and leader. But the united face shown to the public is the product of months of jockeying among key leaders to get their people into top positions. Xi's ascension was a carefully orchestrated compromise between the two prior supreme leaders and their followers; his vice president is from the opposing faction. Institutionalization co-opts all major political elites to maintain unity.

President Hu Jintao and his successor, Xi Jinping, shake hands at the National People's Congress that appointed Xi president. China's exceptionally well-institutionalized authoritarian rule has, among other things, resolved the chronic problem of authoritarian regimes: succession. The succession from Hu to Xi was the third transfer of power within the ruling party since 1979.

China's communist regime has been in power since 1949 but has changed profoundly since Mao's death in 1976. Though communist in name, in practice China has become a modernizing authoritarian regime by successfully encouraging capitalist development while maintaining a firm one-party hold on political power via greater institutionalization and a mix of repression and co-optation. This is a far cry from the early days of the regime. Communist rule under Mao developed into a full-blown personality cult by the late 1960s. Mao's rule, especially during the Cultural Revolution (1966–1976), undermined most institutions; the regime was increasingly personalist and obedient to the whims of the aging Mao. The era is perhaps best captured by Chen Jo-hsi's short stories (1978), in which a young boy causes his parents great fear because he utters the phrase, "Chairman Mao is a rotten egg." His parents also keep comic books with images of Mao away from the boy, because should he draw in them and accidentally deface a picture of Mao, the family would be in serious political trouble. These may sound like exaggerated tales written to make a point, but the threat of being seen as unpatriotic for even the most innocuous of actions was very real.

Upon Mao's death, the new leader Deng Xiaoping (1978–1989) joined others in trying to reestablish order and stable governing institutions under the authority of the CCP. The leaders seem to have deliberately set out to create a more-institutionalized system of rule. These reforms were embodied in a new constitution in 1982, which was significantly amended in 1999. Authority remains vested first and foremost in the ruling party, which fuses executive and legislative functions. As Figure 8.3 shows, each key governing institution has a parallel party institution. The National Party Congress is the official decision-making body of the party, and the National People's Congress is the equivalent of the legislature. Both institutions are ostensibly elected by provincial and local bodies, but in reality the higher organs ensure that only candidates loyal to the ruling party are selected. Real power lies in the party's politburo and even more so in the smaller Politburo Standing Committee (PSC). The State Council and its Standing Committee are in effect the cabinet that actually runs the government, overseen by the politburo and PSC.

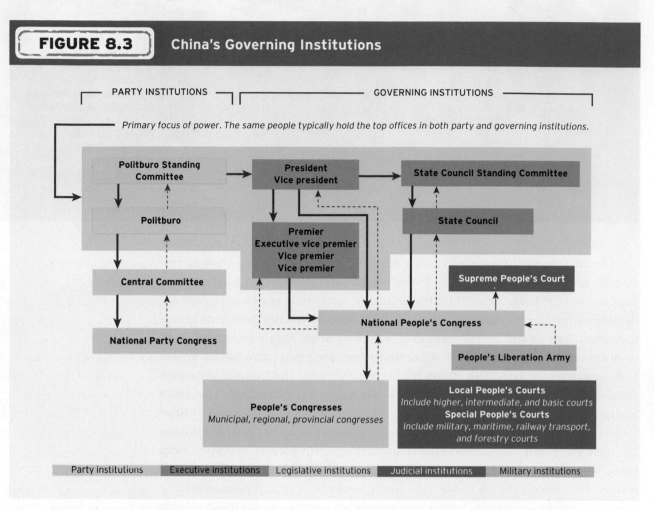

FIGURE 8.3 China's Governing Institutions

Note: Dashed arrows indicate formal selection process or direction of authority. Bold arrows indicate actual selection process or direction of authority.

Like all communist regimes, China has struggled with the relationship between the party and state institutions. Under Mao, membership in the top parallel institutions was nearly identical; today, overlapping membership continues but is by no means universal. The regime under recent leaders has tried to distinguish between the governing role of the State Council and the political oversight role of the politburo and the PSC. The ultimate authority of the party organs and their top leadership, however, remains unchallenged. There has always been one paramount leader who is simultaneously president, general secretary of the party, and chair of the Central Military Commission, though he does not rule alone. While the workings of the politburo and the PSC are secret, all reports suggest that today a great deal of open discussion occurs within these highest organs of power, and their members represent all major factions among the top elite.

Greater institutionalization is perhaps most apparent in leadership succession. Upon Mao's death in 1976, a two-year battle among factions ensued that created a period of great uncertainty. Ultimately, Deng and his allies emerged victorious, launching China on its current path. Deng anointed Jiang Zemin as his successor and systematically began transferring power to him in 1989, though the process took several years. In 2003 the transfer of power became regularized as Jiang chose Hu as his successor. Hu became general secretary of the party and president of the country, but Jiang tried to remain chair of the military commission. By 2005, though, he was forced to relinquish that post, regularizing the succession from one supreme leader to the next. Jiang continued to be influential, including having a substantial role in choosing the new politburo members in 2012, though there were signs that he was withdrawing from active politics with his protégé, Xi, now president. Generational change in the broader leadership has also come to be a hallmark of Party Congresses: the Central Committee elected at each Party Congress now routinely includes about 60 percent new members, with each Party Congress seeing a significant shift toward younger and more highly educated members (Shambaugh 2008, 153). China seems to have institutionalized a form of leadership succession both for the very top posts and more broadly that, while still opaque to outsiders, promises some predictability and stability. The new top leaders "emerge" among key contenders within the PSC and, once agreed upon, are formally anointed by the leadership and ratified by the Party Congress.

The Decline of Communism

Number of one-party communist states in 1975: sixteen

Albania	North Korea
Bulgaria	Poland
China	Romania
Cuba	South Yemen (People's Democratic
Czechoslovakia	Republic of Yemen)
East Germany	Soviet Union
Hungary	Vietnam
Laos	Yugoslavia
Mongolia	

Number of one-party communist states in 2013: five

China (in name only)	North Korea
Cuba	Vietnam (in name only)
Laos	

Source: Wikipedia (http://en.wikipedia.org/wiki/Single-party_state#Former_single-party_states/ and http://en.wikipedia.org/wiki/List_of_Communist_States).

Though the top leader has the fused power of all three important executive positions, he still does not rule alone. Chinese politics has always been characterized by internal factionalism. Mao and Deng had great power because of the respect they received as two of the revolutionary founders of the regime. Subsequent leaders must negotiate with other key leaders to gain support for their leadership and policies. With Hu's elevation to the top leadership, two major factions emerged: those with backgrounds in the party's youth league, through which Hu rose and who are supported by leaders from inland and poorer regions, and those from the wealthier, coastal areas, collectively known as the "Shanghai gang" (Li and White 2006). The two factions have split power very evenly since 2007 in terms of membership in the top decision-making organs. Li Cheng (2010) saw the factional balance serving as an informal system of checks and balances on the top rulers as they limit one another's power and, therefore, the power of the supreme leader. The succession of Hu to replace Jiang and

Xi (a member of the Shanghai faction) to replace Hu may also be establishing a norm of shifting the leadership between the factions.

In addition to the party leadership, the military has long been a crucial faction in Chinese politics but also has been subordinate to the civilian leadership of the party. The vast majority of the army, and certainly all of its top leaders, are ruling party members, trained to support the party and its ideals. Both Mao and Deng retained great military loyalty because of their personal roles during the revolution. Even Deng, however, had to appease the armed forces at times. For example, when the top commander in Beijing refused to use his troops to disperse the student demonstrators in Tiananmen Square in June 1989, Deng had to call a meeting of all seven regional commanders and persuade the other six to back the move before the army would act. After that, Deng initiated major reforms of the military that have significantly professionalized it as well as improved its funding. No military leaders have been in the top organs of the country's leadership since the 1990s, and while the military does have channels to let its voice be heard, it does so primarily in areas of direct relevance to it such as defense and foreign policy. The army remains an important faction behind the scenes, but for the moment the top leadership seems to have institutionalized effective civilian control over it, eliminating a potential threat to survival that is common in authoritarian regimes.

The judiciary has also seen significant institutionalization in the past two decades. Under Mao, virtually no criminal justice system existed; little in the way of codified law existed, and what law did exist was not followed with any regularity. Significant changes have occurred since 1980, though the Chinese legal system still does not include the basic rights familiar to Western citizens. The Supreme People's Court, the country's highest court, has the right to interpret the law and the constitution but not to overturn decisions of the National Congress. As always, the party remains supreme over all. Trials are now supposed to be open to the public, and most are, but the government still prevents the public from attending high-profile political cases. The trial of Bo Xilai on corruption charges in 2013 included the public release of edited transcripts, the highest level of transparency in a major political trial to date.

Civil law has been liberalized more extensively than criminal law, as the government has had to protect private property rights and contracts to attract foreign investment. A 1989 reform of administrative law greatly increased the ability of citizens to take local government agencies to court for not doing their job properly. An average of 100,000 such cases is filed annually, with a success rate estimated at 15 to 20 percent (Ginsburg 2008). A broad survey found rapidly growing use of and trust in courts among Chinese citizens in the new millennium, especially for handling civil disputes (Landry 2008). These changes appear to have helped the central government gather information on what is happening in local government, partially overcoming the dictator's dilemma that all authoritarian regimes face.

China has significantly institutionalized its regime, but the government is certainly still willing to use repression when necessary. Crackdowns against human rights activists and others became particularly severe leading up to the 2008 Olympics in Beijing. The government significantly increased security and restrictions in Tibet, a region whose populace desires greater autonomy or independence, after 500 monks protested continued Chinese rule. A similar response met protests by ethnic Uyghurs demanding greater freedoms and social services. The government has also fought a long-standing battle to limit access to the Internet to prevent citizens from posting or reading material that is too critical of the regime. In 2010 Google decided to quit operating in China because of restrictions on its search engine, as well as repeated cyberattacks on its computers that the company blamed on government agents. The government's response was to introduce a new law demanding that companies coop-erate even more fully with the regime's efforts to limit information. Fearing a public reaction to the 2011 uprisings in the Middle East, the government cracked down again on journalists and dissidents and censored Internet sites related to the uprising, includ-ing all references to the word *jasmine* because of the "Jasmine Revolution" in Tunisia. In 2013 the international NGO Reporters without Borders ranked China the seventh-worst country in the world on press freedom.

Video link:
Ai Weiwei: the Internet vs. the Chinese government

One of the biggest threats to the CCP does not come from protesters or dissidents but from within: corruption. With the rise of a market economy that is now paral-lel with and increasingly replacing the state sector, opportunities for corruption have multiplied rapidly. State and party officials are in positions to receive bribes because of their control over regulation of financial services, key licenses for business activities, land-use rights, infrastructure contracts, and government procurement. A new practice since the 1990s is *maiguan maiguan,* the buying and selling of government positions, especially at the local level in less-developed regions. In an extreme case, 265 local politicians in Heilongjiang Province, including the governor, were involved in the sale of government positions. Joseph Fewsmith (2013) argued that the CCP faces a classic principal-agent problem. The party leadership demands that local officials achieve eco-nomic growth while maintaining social stability. In the world's largest country, how-ever, much authority is left in the hands of local party leaders. As long as they "deliver" on the key items of growth and stability, they will please their superiors and earn promotions; otherwise, they are free to pursue their own interests. This has produced corruption, personalization of power in the hands of local leaders who control promo-tions, and an expansion of local government. When local citizens protest against inad-equate services (see below), social stability is threatened and higher authorities take notice. The party has attempted reforms such as greater local participation in leaders' appointment and promotion but none has been successful at overcoming the inherent principal-agent problem embedded in the party's top-down demands.

The party's Central Commission for Discipline Inspection is charged with ferret-ing out corruption within the party, and the Chinese leadership is emphasizing cor-ruption eradication more strongly than in the past. Pei (2007) reported that while 130,000 to 190,000 party members were disciplined between 1982 and 2007, only 6 percent were prosecuted, and only half of those have been convicted. In 2009 alone, however, 138,000 members were investigated and 5,000 punished in some way (Brown 2013). Nonetheless, the top leadership itself has long been beyond accountability, even though rumors of massive corruption among family members of the top elite are rampant. Some of this finally came out in the open in several major cases since 2010, most famously the downfall of Bo Xilai, a provincial party secretary and a rising star in the party. In 2012, one of Bo's top aides was accused of massive corruption and Bo's wife was ultimately implicated in a murder that Bo may well have been trying to cover up. His very public removal from office exposed high-level intrigue and corruption in the party like nothing had before. In a 2011 survey, Chinese citizens rated the government's success at combatting corruption to be the least effective of a host of public services, while simultaneously saying it was the most important. Over half of the respondents also said government officials are generally dishonest (Saich 2012). The anticorruption efforts, though, seem to be having some effect: in 1995 Transparency International ranked China as the fourth most corrupt country in the world, while in 2012 it was ranked eightieth, in the middle of the global spectrum. Nonetheless, corruption may well be the most serious institutional problem the regime faces. President Xi made it an early hallmark (at least rhetorically) of his term in office in 2013, launching a major anticorruption campaign.

CASE Summary   Modern China has transformed itself from a communist regime with strong personalist overtones under Mao into a modernizing authoritarian regime that has substantially institutionalized its rule. In the process, it has become much more stable and predictable, though it continues to use repression when necessary and faces a grave threat from corruption. Rising corruption, though, demonstrates that expending resources to co-opt potential opposition is an important survival strategy for the Chinese regime, just as it is for most authoritarian regimes. Despite these continuing problems, the regime has presided over the fastest-growing economy in the world and has found a solution to one of the chief problems of authoritarian rule: succession. Most observers believe these successes have given the regime significant legitimacy. The level and effect of participation, and the prospects of eventual democratization, remain questions that could undermine legitimacy, however, which we explore later in the chapter.

CASE Questions

1. What does China's succession system suggest about the relationship between personal power, succession, and regime survival in authoritarian regimes?
2. What does China's battle with corruption teach us about how well authoritarian regimes can reduce corruption, and what corruption's implications are for regime survival?

CASE Study

IRAN: THEOCRACY, SOME DEMOCRACY, GROWING MILITARY POWER?

The triumph of the Ayatollah Khomeini in 1979 in toppling the U.S.-supported regime of the shah of Iran and the subsequent Iranian hostage crisis were singular events in modern history. They ushered in the world's first modern theocracy—a new type of regime that the West greatly feared. Radical Islam had emerged as a new force in world politics. As reformist elements have tried to use the quasi-democratic institutions of the regime to move away from purely authoritarian rule, conservative clerics and government-supported militia have turned increasingly to repression, raising questions about how much influence the democratic elements really have.

The Islamic Republic of Iran created a unique set of political institutions that are based on the theocratic principles we outlined in chapter 3, but with significant participatory elements. The regime mixes appointed and elected offices to maintain the central control of the leading clergy while allowing some voice to other political forces, though within strict limits. Figure 8.4 provides an overview of these institutions. Elected officials are allowed to pass laws and voice some public criticism, but the authority of the Shiite clergy is final. So despite its unique institutions, the Iranian government rules like many other authoritarian regimes, through a combination of repression and co-optation but with a greater than usual effort to gain legitimacy. Also like other authoritarian regimes, it has and will again face the problem of the succession of its supreme leader. Similar to China, it also faces a question of whether it will become more democratic in the foreseeable future, as there is significant domestic pressure in that direction.

Khomeini's contribution to Islamic political thought is the position of supreme leader, which is always filled by a respected member of the clergy. He is both legal and spiritual guide of the country. First occupied by Khomeini himself and then (since Khomeini's death in 1989) by Ayatollah Ali Khamenei, the office has the power to appoint the heads of all the armed forces, the head of the judiciary, six of the twelve members of the all-important Guardian Council, and the leaders of Friday prayers at mosques. These powers mean that very little of significance can occur in Iran without at least the supreme leader's tacit consent. An Assembly of Experts composed entirely of clergy but that is popularly elected by citizens appoints the supreme leader and at least theoretically has the right to remove him, though so far it seems that the position has a lifetime term of office.

- **REGIME TYPE**
  Theocracy, but formal institutions combine theocratic and quasi-democratic elements

- **REPRESSION**
  Supreme leader able to eliminate political opposition when necessary via Guardian Council, Revolutionary Guard, and judiciary

- **CO-OPTATION**
  Patronage via Islamic foundations and Revolutionary Guard

- **INSTITUTIONALIZATION**
  Theocratic institutions always more powerful than quasi-democratic ones

- **SUCCESSION**
  Selection process for supreme leader amended to allow politically astute choice; president elected to four-year term

Iran's supreme leader Ayatollah Ali Khamenei waves to worshippers in 2005. Khamenei has increasingly centralized power in his hands, repressing virtually all political leaders who want to reform the Islamic Republic's governing structure or moderate its policies.

The supreme leader shares formal executive power with a directly elected president in a theocratic version of a semi-presidential system. The supreme leader has broader powers than the president and is the legal head of state. The elected president appoints a cabinet, which the parliament must approve and can remove, and runs the daily affairs of government. The president is selected via a majoritarian election and can serve two four-year terms, which the last four presidents have done. The dual executive creates the possibility of tension between the supreme leader and president similar to tensions between the president and prime minister under cohabitation in semipresidential systems. When an avowed reformist was president from 1997 to 2005, he clashed regularly with the supreme leader and the institutions like the Guardian Council that limited the president's power. When Mahmoud Ahmadinejad was elected president in 2005 and reelected in 2009 he had the supreme leader's support but lost it in 2011. Ahmadinejad was using increasingly secular nationalist rhetoric that threatened to go against the Islamist basis for the regime's legitimacy, and he had built up an independent base of support in the government via appointments of supporters to many positions. Ayatollah Khamenei ultimately opposed him, and the president's influence declined drastically. His supporters subsequently lost both the parliamentary election in 2012 and the presidential election in 2013. While analysts had wondered if Ahmadinejad's growing power would prove to be a real challenge to Khamenei, the episode demonstrated that the supreme leader remains truly supreme in Iran's power structure. The supreme leader's frustration with the dual executive became clear in late 2011, when he suggested the position of president ought to be replaced with a prime minister elected out of parliament—something he might pursue now that Ahmadinejad is out of office. After a moderate who is nonetheless sympathetic to the regime won the 2013 election, though, the supreme leader may be willing to let the presidency continue to exist.

As in other semipresidential systems, laws must be passed by the parliament and approved by the president. The Iranian system, however, strictly limits the freedom of these elected offices. The Guardian Council, consisting of six clergy appointed by the supreme leader and six lay leaders nominated by the head of the judiciary and approved by parliament, must also agree to all legislation. Given that all of its members are either appointed directly by the supreme leader or nominated by his appointed judiciary, the Council of Guardians is a bastion of conservatism and clerical authority that preserves the will of the supreme leader. It also must approve all candidates for election and has repeatedly banned candidates it has deemed unacceptable for

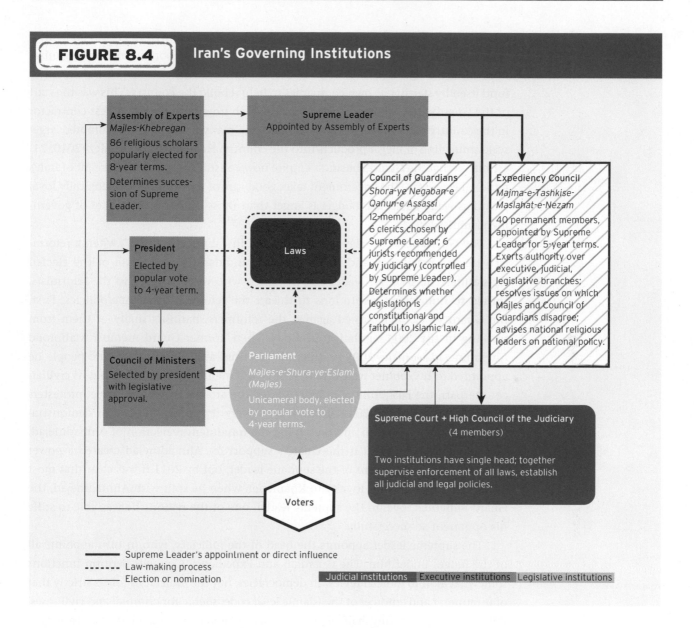

FIGURE 8.4 Iran's Governing Institutions

Assembly of Experts
Majles-Khebregan
86 religious scholars popularly elected for 8-year terms.
Determines succession of Supreme Leader.

Supreme Leader
Appointed by Assembly of Experts

Council of Guardians
Shora-ye Negaban-e Qanun-e Assassi
12-member board: 6 clerics chosen by Supreme Leader; 6 jurists recommended by judiciary (controlled by Supreme Leader). Determines whether legislation is constitutional and faithful to Islamic law.

Expediency Council
Majma-e-Tashkise-Maslahat-e-Nezam
40 permanent members, appointed by Supreme Leader for 5-year terms. Exerts authority over executive, judicial, legislative branches; resolves issues on which Majles and Council of Guardians disagree; advises national religious leaders on national policy.

President
Elected by popular vote to 4-year term.

Laws

Council of Ministers
Selected by president with legislative approval.

Parliament
Majles-e-Shura-ye-Eslami (Majles)
Unicameral body, elected by popular vote to 4-year terms.

Supreme Court + High Council of the Judiciary
(4 members)
Two institutions have single head; together supervise enforcement of all laws, establish all judicial and legal policies.

Voters

——— Supreme Leader's appointment or direct influence
- - - - - Law-making process
——— Election or nomination

Judicial institutions   Executive institutions   Legislative institutions

president, parliament, and local government councils. A second body, the Expediency Council, was added via constitutional amendment in 1989 to be an advisory body to the supreme leader. It has the power to resolve disputes between parliament and the Guardian Council, and its rulings are final. The supreme leader appoints all of its members, so it is an additional way for him to control elected officials.

The dual executive has control over the bureaucracy, judiciary, and armed forces. Like many authoritarian systems, Iran has more than one army. The Revolutionary Guard was formed as the armed wing of the revolution. Khomeini maintained it after the revolution because he didn't trust the regular national army, which was an institution of the prior regime. The Guard has become the most important military organization. After the Iran-Iraq War (1980–1988), the government encouraged the Guard to fund itself by starting its own companies to help rebuild the country. This was the start of the Guard's expanding business empire, which now includes the largest contractor in the country and numerous other companies in many fields, as well as rumored large-scale smuggling of illegal products into the country. Hen-Tov and Gonzalez (2010, 21) estimated that the Guard's business empire now constitutes at least 25 percent of Iran's national economy. The government takes good care of the large and ideologically loyal Guard as well—its annual budget is larger than those of all but a handful of government ministries.

The Guard began to play a more direct political role after 1997, when a reformist won the presidency and later reformist candidates took control of the elected legislature. The supreme leader and his allies, who were opposed to the reformists, turned to nonelected institutions to thwart the reform movement's policies. First, the Guardian Council turned against the reformers, banning many of them from running in the 2004 legislative elections. Then, former Guard member Mahmoud Ahmadinejad won the 2005 presidential election, and two-thirds of the people he appointed to his cabinet were also former Guard members. The Guard and its civilian counterpart, the Basij militia, infamously led the attacks against the street protesters after the disputed June 2009 election, effectively repressing the largest demonstrations since the revolution and preserving the fraudulent reelection of Ahmadinejad. Many analysts wondered if the Guard's support for Ahmadinejad created a power base that was independent of the supreme leader, but by 2011 it was clear that most of the Guard retained its loyalty to Khamenei; when he split with Ahmadinejad, the Guard remained loyal to the supreme leader, one of the reasons he was able to stifle his opponent so successfully.

The supreme leader appoints the head of the judiciary, who in turn appoints all of the judges under him. The Guardian and Expediency Councils perform functions somewhat akin to judicial review in democracies, but the judiciary's role is strictly that of interpreter and enforcer of the Islamic legal code, *sharia,* for criminal and civil cases. Other than nominating half of the Guardian Council, the judiciary has no formal political role. The supreme leader, though, has used it repeatedly to repress political opponents; numerous political activists, journalists, and students were prosecuted on charges such as treason after the 2009 demonstrations and sentenced to long prison terms.

In contrast to the absolute authority of the supreme leader, the autonomy and strength of the parliament (the *majlis*) are severely circumscribed, even though its formal powers look significant. In addition to passing all legislation, the *majlis* has approval authority over cabinet nominees and half the nominees to the Guardian Council, and it can investigate the executive's implementation of the law. It has used these powers repeatedly, exposing corruption in the bureaucracy and opposing many of Ahmadinejad's legislative initiatives after the split between the president and supreme leader. The power of the appointed clerics, however, always lurks behind the actions of the *majlis*. When the clerics disapprove of significant legislation, they don't hesitate to use their power to veto it via the Guardian Council and rewrite it in the Expediency Council. When the reformists gained control of the *majlis* in 2000, the Guardian Council vetoed virtually all of their significant reform legislation.

The Iranian regime, like virtually all authoritarian regimes, also uses patronage to maintain its control. The Iranian bureaucracy has expanded by as much as 50 percent under the theocratic regime. Because of Iran's massive oil revenue, government spending is a majority of the country's economy. This gives the top leadership significant patronage opportunities. Government and quasi-governmental foundations (called *bonyads*) have also become key venues through which the nation's oil wealth is shared with regime supporters. The revolutionary regime established Islamic foundations to provide aid to the populace during and immediately after the revolution. The foundations themselves often receive government funding, and some engage in commercial activity as well. One of the largest, the Imam Charity Committee, receives private donations in addition to the fourth-largest share of the government's annual budget. It is controlled by conservative supporters of the clergy, who use it to mobilize poor voters in favor of conservative candidates. The Revolutionary Guard also controls one of the largest *bonyads,* which provides income support to millions of people, giving the Guard its own independent basis for patronage. Some of these foundations and their leaders engage in outright corruption as well, stealing oil revenues and accepting bribes in return for access to key officials.

The importance of the supreme leader and his de facto life term leaves Iran with one of the classic problems of authoritarian rule: succession. Khomeini's popularity and power were based not only on the traditional legitimacy he enjoyed as a Grand Ayatollah, one of a handful of the highest religious authorities in Shiite Islam, but also on his charismatic legitimacy as the leader of the revolution. Khomeini and other leaders did not believe that any of the other Grand Ayatollahs could fully replace him as the supreme leader, so to avert a potential crisis, a constitutional amendment eliminated the requirement that the supreme leader come from only among their ranks. This allowed the regime to select then-president Ali Khamenei as the new supreme leader. He was only a midlevel cleric, and in fact was raised overnight to the rank of Ayatollah (still below Grand Ayatollah) in an effort to give him greater religious authority. Khomeini and his advisors chose someone who understood politics rather than an icon of religious authority. The other Grand Ayatollahs did not fight Khamenei's ascendance because they had become increasingly disillusioned with the regime; while initially in favor of the revolution, most had taken an increasingly traditionalist position during the 1980s, divorcing themselves from active politics. Still, lack of clerical support raised questions about Khamanei's legitimacy as supreme leader, which was one of the factors that led him to strengthen the power of the Revolutionary Guard, a military force loyal to him.

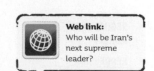

Web link:
Who will be Iran's next supreme leader?

CASE Summary

Iran's formal system of government combines theocratic institutions with quasi-democratic ones that are intended to provide some space for participation and for popular voices to be heard. The constitution, though, ensures that the supreme leader and the institutions he directly controls can dominate when they need to. They have used repression when necessary, patronage via the *bonyads*, and efforts to combine theocratic and democratic claims to legitimacy to remain in power. In the 1990s, the regime allowed reformist politicians who wanted to reduce strict adherence to Islam to gain elected office, but then it effectively blocked them from enacting significant changes. By 2005, the conservative clerical leadership and the increasingly powerful Revolutionary Guard had regained control. As the supreme leader became more dependent on the Guard in the new millennium, its power grew, leading some to see the regime as slowly, via informal means, making a transition from a theocracy to a military dictatorship. Major societal demands for greater democracy, however repressed, remain below the surface still, as was clear via the 2009 protests and the 2013 election of the candidate seen as politically most distant from the supreme leader. All this was despite the latter's open opposition, which we discuss in the case study on participation below.

CASE Questions

1. Recent trends have suggested that the quasi-democratic elements of Iran's governing institutions are relatively weak. Nonetheless, how might they help the top Iranian leadership overcome the "dictator's dilemma" that all authoritarian regimes face?

2. What does Iran's history suggest about the relative importance of repression, co-optation, and legitimacy for the survival of authoritarian regimes?

CASE Study

NIGERIA: WEAKENING INSTITUTIONS UNDER MILITARY RULE

- **REGIME TYPE**
  Military

- **REPRESSION**
  Directly by military; no legislature or parties

Nigeria's military ruled the country for a total of twenty-nine years (1966–1979 and 1983–1999) under seven military dictators. This history of recurring military intervention is outlined in the timeline on page 426. Nigerian military rule relied on a combination of repression, massive patronage, and attempts to gain legitimacy by promising a "return to democracy." Although some observers saw military rule as beneficial in the 1960s, coercion became more common as the economy declined, and the military regimes became more personalist. In the 1980s and 1990s, three successive leaders from the same regional military group consolidated their control over the government and its all-important oil revenues and used these revenues to engage in massive corruption and patronage to maintain their power. Over time, Nigerian institutions grew weaker so that by the 1990s the country was recognized as one of the most corrupt in the world.

Every Nigerian military government eliminated the country's legislature entirely; none attempted to use a legislature with even limited power to gain increased legitimacy. Instead, the military governments created executive councils to rule by decree, with the top leader taking the title of president, head, or chairman. Under the first long-serving leader, Gen. Yakubu Gowon (1967–1975), the council was somewhat consensual. As the military governments became more personalized over the years, however, the councils became mere rubber stamps for the key leaders. Military governments typically appointed a mix of military and civilian leaders as cabinet ministers, and civilian elites in business, academia, and politics repeatedly proved themselves willing to work with a military government in exchange for the perks and power that came with cabinet positions. Military leaders used these positions to co-opt both military and civilian elites; not surprisingly, as oil revenues and corruption grew, these positions became more lucrative and coveted. The "indigenization" decree of 1972 required Nigerian ownership of most business investment, opening up lucrative opportunities for both the civilian and military elites. Each of the military regimes used such rewards to buy off at least some of its potential civilian opposition as well as to ensure the loyalty of key military personnel.

- **CO-OPTATION**
  Oil wealth and federalism as patronage

- **INSTITUTIONALIZATION**
  Declining over time; increasingly personalist

- **SUCCESSION**
  Coup and counter-coup; return to democracy in 1999

Gen. Sani Abacha, Nigeria's most corrupt and brutal military leader, was in power from 1993 until his death in 1998. He used his control of the military to prevent a transition to democracy, despite widespread popular support for it. A transition finally happened shortly after his unexpected death.

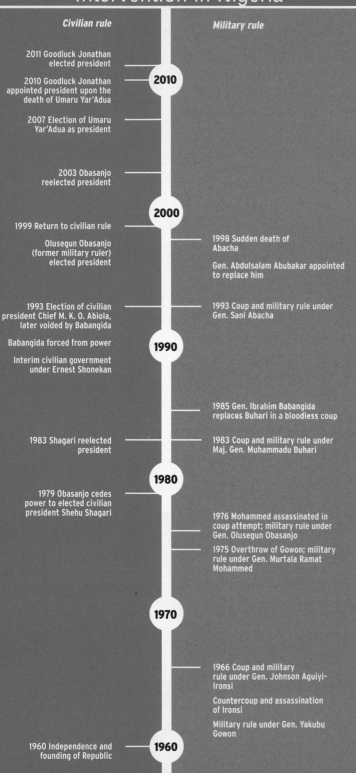

Timeline
History of Military Intervention in Nigeria

Civilian rule	Military rule

2010

2011 Goodluck Jonathan elected president

2010 Goodluck Jonathan appointed president upon the death of Umaru Yar'Adua

2007 Election of Umaru Yar'Adua as president

2003 Obasanjo reelected president

2000

1999 Return to civilian rule

Olusegun Obasanjo (former military ruler) elected president

1998 Sudden death of Abacha

Gen. Abdulsalam Abubakar appointed to replace him

1993 Election of civilian president Chief M. K. O. Abiola, later voided by Babangida

1993 Coup and military rule under Gen. Sani Abacha

Babangida forced from power

Interim civilian government under Ernest Shonekan

1990

1985 Gen. Ibrahim Babangida replaces Buhari in a bloodless coup

1983 Shagari reelected president

1983 Coup and military rule under Maj. Gen. Muhammadu Buhari

1980

1979 Obasanjo cedes power to elected civilian president Shehu Shagari

1976 Mohammed assassinated in coup attempt; military rule under Gen. Olusegun Obasanjo

1975 Overthrow of Gowon; military rule under Gen. Murtala Ramat Mohammed

1970

1966 Coup and military rule under Gen. Johnson Aguiyi-Ironsi

Countercoup and assassination of Ironsi

Military rule under Gen. Yakubu Gowon

1960 Independence and founding of Republic

1960

While the legislature was the only branch of government the military banned outright, it also severely weakened the bureaucracy, judiciary, and state governments. Up until Ibrahim Babangida's government in the late 1980s, top bureaucrats still maintained their permanent, professional status. Babangida, however, sharply reduced the distinction between top professional civil servants and political appointees, allowing him to use key civil service positions for patronage purposes. Growing corruption, as leaders throughout the system stole oil revenues, severely weakened the bureaucracy as an institution. As corruption became rife, civil servants no longer worked on the basis of clear rules and hierarchy. Instead, they increasingly gave jobs to their own clients, family, and friends; stole government funds for themselves; and engaged in nongovernmental businesses. All of this made clear bureaucratic control of the civil service impossible. Orders were not followed, functions were not properly carried out, and the bureaucracy lost all respect from the citizens, who had to bribe civil servants to get anything done.

Nigeria's military governments also severely weakened the judiciary. Civilian courts continued to exist, but military decrees were beyond any court's jurisdiction. Each military regime became more assertive than the one before in limiting individual rights, ignoring or undermining the courts, and repressing potential opposition. The first military leader declared that he wanted Nigeria to continue operating in a way that was "as normal as possible," so his and the next government interfered relatively little in daily governmental activities, including the judiciary. The later military governments, however, were another story. The Muhammadu Buhari government issued a series of decrees in 1984 and 1985 that severely undermined the judiciary, and military governments from that point on had the power to appoint and remove judges.

The Buhari and Babangida governments (1983–1985 and 1985–1993, respectively) rewarded compliant judges by promoting them and punished uncooperative judges by removing or at least not promoting them. In this environment, it is no surprise that the courts did not challenge the military regimes. Sani Abacha (1993–1998) went even further, entirely eliminating the jurisdictions of many courts, eliminating habeas corpus, and arresting hundreds of political opponents in 1994–1995.

Despite its control of the judiciary, the military created separate military tribunals to try opposition politicians, coup plotters, and leaders of local resistance movements such as the Ogoni movement discussed in chapter 4. With a weakened judiciary, individual rights had little protection. The Buhari government used tribunals to try people accused of corruption. The accused had little ability to defend themselves and often faced the death penalty. We mentioned the most famous case in chapter 4: the 1995 execution of poet and political activist Ken Saro-Wiwa. Saro-Wiwa was leader of the Movement for the Survival of the Ogoni People (MOSOP), which campaigned peacefully for the right of the Ogoni to benefit more from the oil produced on their land. Abacha, who was by far the most brutal of Nigeria's rulers, accused Saro-Wiwa and several other MOSOP leaders of killing several Ogoni traditional elders, a charge that all independent observers believe to be false. Saro-Wiwa and the others faced a military tribunal with no public access to the trial and were convicted and summarily executed, provoking international outrage.

Authoritarian Rule in Sub-Saharan Africa (SSA), 1970–2013

Number of SSA countries with one-party regimes

1970	1980	1990	2000	2013
16	27	28	2	1

Number of SSA countries with military regimes

1970	1980	1990	2000	2013
9	15	13	4	2

Level of freedom in SSA countries

Freedom rating	1976	2013
Free	3	11
Partly free	16	18
Not free	25	20

Source: Freedom House (2013), "Country Ratings and Status by Region" (http://www.freedomhouse.org/report-types/freedom-world).

Video link:
Ken Saro-Wiw: his last interview

Nigeria's military rulers used federalism to reward supporters, divide potential opponents, and manage ethnic political competition, all while centralizing control of federal institutions. In 1967 General Gowon replaced the three prior political regions with twelve states—six in the north and six in the south—in an effort to reduce the conflict that the division of the country into three large regions had caused (see chapter 4). This strategy worked to reduce conflict following the civil war (1967–1970), but it also began the process of centralization of power. The federal government became more powerful, and the new state governments were far less powerful than the governments of the larger regions had been. This shift of power to the central state was driven in part by rapidly rising oil revenues as world oil prices quadrupled in the early 1970s. More oil revenues meant the central government funded a growing share of states' budgets, strengthening the central government's power in Nigeria's federalist system.

Division into ever smaller states continued: Gowon added seven new states in the 1970s; General Babangida increased the total to thirty by 1991; and Abacha created six more, for a total of thirty-six, by 1998. State creation became a mechanism of patronage to reward supporters and divide opponents. Each new state required its own state government, which allowed for the local hiring of civil servants and for plum political positions to go to local government loyalists. State governors, who were military men, became famous for their corruption, using their state's share of oil revenue to feather their own nests and reward their own clients. Throughout, Nigeria maintained a symmetrical federal system, but one run by the military with power increasingly centralized.

The seven different military governments in Nigeria never succeeded in overcoming the problem of succession. No institutionalized succession process was ever established. Four were overthrown by counter-coups from within the military itself, two ended with the restoration of democracy (and one of these came about only after the sudden death of the dictator), and one ended with an aborted effort at a democratic transition (see the timeline on page 426). This demonstrates the fragility of regimes created by a military that itself was not very well institutionalized and therefore subject to greater and greater personalization.

CASESummary   Nigerian military governments began as relatively institutionalized regimes with a proclaimed goal of restoring democracy while preserving much of the daily functioning of the prior civilian government. Despite a rationale of returning to democracy soon, they made no attempt to create a legislature or allow political parties. Without these institutions, the military regimes became increasingly repressive, personalized, and less institutionalized. Speaking of the military dictator Ibrahim Babangida (1985–1993), Larry Diamond, one of the leading experts on Nigerian politics, said:

> Babangida degraded every institution he touched, and his fellow ruling officers followed his lead. Indeed, one of the most important legacies of Babangida's rule—with his lavish dispensation of cash, cars, contracts and kickbacks to the officer corps, as well as his license to use political appointments for personal accumulation—was the degradation of the military's own professionalism and institutional integrity, so that it increasingly became, like the politicians, a set of political actors, patrimonial ties, and factional alliances seeking after power, patronage, and wealth; another political party, but with an official monopoly on arms. (1997, 471)

As oil wealth grew rapidly starting in the early 1970s, corruption grew, giving military leaders an incentive to stay in power and a huge source of money for patronage. They used federalism as a form of patronage and increasingly undermined the institutional strength and autonomy of the judiciary and bureaucracy. Repression and patronage allowed the military to maintain power in the near absence of legitimacy until the death of dictator Sani Abacha in 1998, by which time internal and external pressure for change led to a transition to democracy, which we discuss in chapter 9.

CASE Questions

1. Can you use some of the theories of authoritarian rule we outlined earlier in the chapter to explain the decline of institutions over successive military regimes in Nigeria?
2. Was repression or co-optation more important in keeping the Nigerian military in power for so long?

ELECTIONS, PARTIES, AND CIVIL SOCIETY IN AUTHORITARIAN REGIMES

Elections, parties, and civil society are important to democracies in part because they help to overcome the collective action dilemma: they encourage participation and channel and promote democratic representation. It should not come as a great shock that authoritarian regimes are not particularly interested in overcoming the collective action problem. Many authoritarian regimes nonetheless create institutions that at least superficially resemble elections, parties, and interest groups, but these differ greatly from their more democratic counterparts, often in both form and function.

As we noted above, supreme leaders cannot rule by repression alone. They must care about gaining the support of potentially rival elites and, ideally, some legitimacy from the general populace. Many authoritarian regimes, both more and less institutionalized, use elaborate public displays of support to try to gain this legitimacy, a form of involuntary political participation. For example, they hold massive independence day celebrations, complete with throngs of cheering supporters and displays of military might to show their popularity and power. Participants typically have little choice but to participate and are often paid in some form. When Mexico's Partido Revolucionario Institucional (PRI) ruled as a semi-authoritarian regime, supporters would be trucked in from the countryside to rallies in the cities, where they would enjoy free food, drink, and entertainment. Referring to authoritarian regimes in Africa, Cameroonian scholar Achille Mbembe (1992) called such huge but empty displays the "banality of power." Svolik (2012), however, argued that these displays are not banal but serve a clear purpose: they arise after a personalist ruler has consolidated his power and serve as a warning to potential rivals who might think about rebelling against him.

In the most extreme cases of personalist rule, such public demonstrations become a **personality cult** that constantly glorifies the ruler and attempts to turn his every utterance into not only government fiat but also divine wisdom. Personality cults have arisen in an array of regimes, from communist North Korea under "Great Leader" Kim

personality cult
Phenomenon that occurs in the most extreme cases of personalist rule in which followers constantly glorify the ruler and attempt to turn his every utterance into not only government fiat but also divine wisdom

Il-Sung, to Zaire under Western-supporting dictator Mobutu Sese Seko, to "President for Life" Saparmurat Niyazov in post-Soviet Turkmenistan. Regimes with more elaborate ideological justification for their rule, such as communist and theocratic regimes, also make extensive use of their founding ideologies to try to gain popular legitimacy, as the case of Iran below demonstrates.

Elections and Parties

Beyond these massive demonstrations of support, most authoritarian regimes encourage carefully monitored and limited political participation. Even some one-party regimes that have held regular elections existed. Communist regimes usually allow direct elections at the most local level. The general electorate may get to participate in local block, neighborhood, or town elections, but then those representatives elect the next layer of representatives above them and so on up to the national parliamentary level. In addition, although nonparty candidates may be permitted at the local level, all candidates typically have to be cleared by the Communist Party before they can run. This system is consistent with the ideological perspective of communism because it permits popular participation while also preserving the guiding role of the Communist Party, the only legitimate representative of the people according to communist doctrine.

More common now are semi-authoritarian regimes in which a ruling party wins major elections easily, with some opposition parties winning a small share of power. The ruling party creates the system to ensure its continued rule. The more sophisticated and institutionalized systems do not usually require outright voter fraud for the ruling party to remain in power, though rulers will certainly engage in that too if necessary. Usually, the type of electoral system (typically a majoritarian one that favors the already large ruling party), gerrymandering constituency boundaries, vote buying, controlling access to the media, restricting civil liberties, using government resources for partisan purposes, and jailing opponents serve to keep the opposition under control. In Kenya in the 1990s, government civil servants openly campaigned for the ruling party during work hours, candidates handed potential voters gifts of cash or food, and opposition party rallies were denied permits or harassed by police. In Rwanda's 2010 presidential election, three opposition candidates ended up in jail by election day, allowing President Paul Kagame (in power since the genocide in 1994) to win 93 percent of the vote. In Mexico under the PRI's long rule, the government systematically spent money before each election to purchase political support in areas where the PRI needed votes (Magaloni 2006).

Given that authoritarian rulers can hold power without any opposition or elections at all, an obvious question is, Why do they bother creating these systems? A long-standing answer has been that such systems serve as a facade of democratic legitimacy, both domestically and internationally. The ascendancy of liberal democracy in the post–Cold War era makes this more important than it was earlier. Recently, scholars

Web link:
Global voices, bloggers on Rwanda's 2010 presidential elections

have come to believe that elections in authoritarian regimes serve other purposes as well. As we discussed above, Jennifer Gandhi (2008) argued that both legislatures and multiple parties co-opt the opposition and provide a space for some policy compromise. Using our case study of Mexico under the PRI as an example, Beatriz Magaloni (2006) argued that in addition to co-opting opposition within the system, elections provided the ruling party with information on who opposed it (helping overcome the dictator's dilemma), allowed power sharing among leaders within the ruling party, and deterred opponents by showing (via large election victories) the ruling party's ability to mobilize support. She suggested that elections in semi-authoritarian regimes demonstrate to elite opponents that the ruling party continues to enjoy significant support, thereby discouraging opponents from openly challenging the system. Authoritarian elections, then, do not threaten the regime but provide it with several clear benefits. The danger always exists, of course, that somehow the opposition will find a way to actually gain power. This is rare, and when it happens, the ruling party may openly "steal" the election via voter fraud to remain in power. This happened in Kenya in December 2007, setting off two months of ethnically based violence that killed 1,500 and displaced hundreds of thousands. In certain circumstances, however, such elections can be part of a transition from an authoritarian to a democratic regime, a subject we explore in the next chapter.

Video link:
Memories of violence haunt upcoming elections in Kenya

Authoritarian elections are coupled with very limited party systems. Most important and strongest is always the ruling party, whether in a one-party or semi-authoritarian system. Using a historical institutionalist perspective, Jason Brownlee (2007) argued that strong ruling parties emerge early in an authoritarian regime if the supreme leader is able to repress and co-opt potential opposition to create an elite coalition within the party. If he is unable to do this, a weak ruling party (or none at all) will develop, and the regime will be less stable and more likely to be overthrown. Svolik (2012) demonstrated statistically that since World War II, single-party authoritarian regimes have lasted much longer than regimes that either banned parties or allowed multiple parties (i.e., semi-authoritarian regimes). He argued that by requiring service to the party early in a potential leader's career and benefits (from top party positions) only later in a career, parties create "sunk" investments for politicians that will only pay off in the long term via loyalty to the regime. Combined with a party's control over a wide array of political and economic positions, this creates very strong incentives for would-be leaders to remain loyal to a regime rather than attempt to oppose it.

The ruling party is nearly always a vehicle for access to goods and jobs and thus a key mechanism for large-scale patronage. In Alfredo Stroessner's Paraguay, for instance, membership in the ruling Colorado Party was compulsory for government employees, and nearly a quarter of the population belonged to it. Mexico's PRI politicians operated on the basis of patronage, and citizens in rural regions in particular understood that votes for the PRI could result in material benefits for their communities. Similarly, membership in the Communist Party is usually a prerequisite for many jobs in any communist regime. Communist parties also promote political socialization of young people through party youth organizations and serve as ideological watchdogs for the leaders. Party cells exist in all government agencies, communities, and major organizations, such as state-run companies. While ruling parties in semi-authoritarian regimes do not fulfill all of these socialization and watchdog functions, they nonetheless provide real incentives that keep potential opponents within the system. The availability of institutionalized alternatives in the form of opposition parties, though, helps explain why Svolik (2012) found that regimes with multiple parties were not as long-lived as single-party regimes; the alternative parties provide a possibility of resistance to the regime that doesn't exist in single-party regimes.

Civil Society

Because participation must go through approved regime channels, civil society in authoritarian regimes is extremely circumscribed and repressed. Indeed, often it hardly exists at all. Communist regimes such as the Soviet Union and China at their height were totalitarian, as North Korea remains today. Totalitarian regimes completely eliminate civil society; the ruling party "represents" all interests that it believes deserve representation. Trade unions or youth or women's groups often nominally exist in communist countries, but these "mass organizations" are always part of the Communist Party. They cannot be said to be truly part of civil society, which by definition is autonomous from the state.

Noncommunist regimes often use state corporatism to control interest groups. Remember that corporatism is the idea that each component (or interest) in society should be represented by one organization. When a government legally mandates this, it is referred to as state corporatism because the state controls the interest groups and chooses the ones it wishes to recognize. A recent example was Mexico for most of the twentieth century under the PRI. The PRI claimed it was a revolutionary party representing the poor, and it recognized and included within the party a single labor organization, a single peasant association, and a single association for "popular groups"—small businesses, women's interests, and various others. These organizations were to represent their constituents within the party. Over time, however, they became increasingly corrupt and controlled by the elite at the top of the party hierarchy. The workers' organization, in particular, was very powerful within the party, and real wages rose for most of the PRI's long rule, even though the unions rarely contradict official party policies. In most of Asia and Africa, unions and other major interest groups arose with and were part of nationalist movements for independence. After independence, however, authoritarian regimes emasculated these organizations, often creating state corporatist systems in their place.

The emergence of social movements within authoritarian regimes is often one of the first signs of a democratic opening. In Latin America in the 1970s, labor-based social movements outside the confines of the official corporatist unions began challenging the status quo and ultimately forced authoritarian regimes to move toward democratization. Other social movements arose as well. Brazil, for instance, has active gay rights, Afro-Brazilian, and women's movements, many of which originated during the military regime. Indigenous movements also emerged in much of Latin America in the 1980s and 1990s, challenging authoritarian control of rural areas. With the spread of more electoral democracy since the end of the Cold War, interest groups and civil society more broadly have reemerged in most of these countries, but they face a legacy of weakness.

Patron-Client Relations

With civil society very weak and parties and elections mainly aimed at ensuring elite cohesion and regime survival, patron-client relations are often the primary means through which average citizens can participate in politics in authoritarian regimes. The weaker the formal institutions, the more this is likely to be true. Strong ruling parties and small but accepted opposition parties in semi-authoritarian regimes provide some institutionalized means of participation. In more personalist regimes, or regimes in which parties are weak institutions that command little loyalty, even these avenues are mostly cut off. By attaching themselves to a powerful patron, citizens can gain access to some resources, power, or influence. This occurs behind closed doors, of course, but as the patron gains power and position in the system, the clients gain also through special privileges and access to resources.

Such patron-client relationships are the primary means of political participation in virtually all sub-Saharan African countries. While myriad formal institutions exist, most citizens participate by attaching themselves to a patron. In Kenya's one-party regime (1963–1992), the ruling party consisted of ethnically and regionally based factions that were headed by major patrons. The system allowed very limited public political debate, so political leaders gained support by directing government resources toward their home areas and providing individual support to their myriad clients. Clients got jobs in government or influence in local politics by attaching themselves to patrons who could offer them these benefits.

Web link:
Inside Africa's politics of patronage

In the absence of other effective means of participation and representation, following a patron may be the best available option. A patron can represent a client's most immediate interests vis-à-vis the state. The problems in this type of system, though, are numerous. First, its informality means that no client is ever guaranteed anything. Each individual has a unique and largely private relationship with a patron, who will try to maintain the client's loyalty in the long term but who will not respond to every demand. Clients have no recourse unless an alternative patron is available. This is sometimes the case, but transferring loyalty is never easy or quick. Second, clientelism discourages citizens from organizing on the basis of collective interests. As long as citizens believe that following a personal patron is the most effective route to obtaining what they need from government, they have little incentive to organize collectively to change the government and its policies more broadly.

This is especially true in authoritarian regimes that violently repress any significant organized political activity.

Participation in authoritarian regimes is extremely limited. More-institutionalized regimes have allowed some formal participation, including elections with limited choices. With the spread of semi-authoritarian regimes in the last two decades, tightly controlled elections have become more common. Their main purpose, however, is elite cohesion and regime support. Citizens are rarely content with these limited choices in the long term because they give voters little real influence. Less-institutionalized regimes typically grant little or no opportunities for participation. Given this, many citizens "participate" on a daily basis simply to survive and prosper individually through the use of patron-client networks. This allows the leadership of a regime to use co-optation to maintain adequate support, or at least prevent outright rebellion.

Rebellion, however, can and does happen. Social movements often arise in these situations outside the limited formal boundaries of legal participation. Larger movements for change that bring an entire regime into question also can emerge and produce fundamental regime change, a subject we examine in the next chapter. But first, we look at participation in three authoritarian regimes in our case study countries.

CASE Study

CHINA: GROWING PARTICIPATION BUT NOT DEMOCRACY OR SEMI-AUTHORITARIAN RULE

- **ELECTIONS**
  Competitive local elections help overcome dictator's dilemma

- **PARTIES**
  Continued one-party rule but changing party membership; technocrats, entrepreneurs, and lawyers

- **CIVIL SOCIETY**
  Expansion but under state corporatism; growing local protests, labor unrest, online activism, and NGOs

China's rise as a global power has raised many important questions. For comparativists, probably the biggest involves political participation: Can China maintain its spectacular economic growth and growing global influence without allowing greater citizen participation and possibly a transition to democracy? As China has made its dramatic transformation from a truly communist regime to a modernizing authoritarian one it has begun to allow greater but still very limited forms of citizen input and participation. It has permitted almost all of this only at the local level, which may serve to strengthen the ruling party's grip on power rather than undermine it. It thus produces an enduring conundrum for theorists of authoritarian regimes and the dynamics of changes to those regimes.

China's Communist regime under Mao included ritualistic "participation" by the public in the form of token elections, but it also initiated spurts of greater participation as Mao attempted to overcome the inertia of bureaucratic control of his "revolution." For the average citizen, though, influencing government was much more informal and individual. CCP membership was the essential and only formal route into the political process beyond the most local level. Party membership was also the sole road ambitious citizens could travel to political, social, or economic success. Yet fewer than 10 percent of citizens were party members, which meant that most people who wanted to influence the government had to do so in informal ways. With the complete ban on any independent organizations, citizens had little ability to demand changes in government policy or to petition the government about issues of concern. As with most authoritarian regimes, patron-client linkages often took the place of institutionalized means of participation. In China, networks of personal supporters, including but not exclusively family, are known as *guanxi*. Before, during, and since the Mao era, the Chinese have used their *guanxi* to survive and attempt to prosper. At the height of the communist system, the state controlled virtually the entire economy, including the allocation of jobs, houses, and other services. Appearing loyal to the regime was crucial to one's success in the system, but *guanxi* helped a great deal as well. Relatives and friends in the system could help get you a better job or apartment or keep you out of trouble with local authorities. For the more ambitious, participation included becoming a member of and taking an active role in the local CCP apparatus in addition to using *guanxi* to help career advancement.

The rapid expansion of the market economy has forced the regime to open up the system of participation and representation at least slightly, making some political accommodations in terms of who can participate and how. This has involved co-opting new elites, allowing semicompetitive elections at the local level, and implementing elements of state corporatism to manage relations with the still limited civil society. One change has been the Communist Party itself. Throughout the Communist era, a debate raged over the role of "reds" and "experts." On one side were leaders, including

- **PATRON-CLIENT RELATIONSHIPS**
  Guanxi personal networks

- **LEGITIMATION**
  Based on growing *economy* and service provision

A candidate for a village committee stands in front of a blackboard displaying his vote total. The Chinese ruling party has allowed some competition in local-level elections, though how much real competition has happened varies from place to place.

Mao, who argued that those properly committed to revolutionary ideals (that is, loyal to Mao and the CCP) and from the proper "revolutionary classes" (the peasantry and proletariat) should constitute the core of the party and be given preference in participation. On the other side were those who favored party membership and participation for experts—that is, intellectuals, scientists, and engineers who, presumably, could help modernize the country. Since the country's opening to the world market, the CCP has shifted significantly in the direction of the experts. Farmers' and workers' share of party membership dropped from 63 percent in 1994 to 44 percent in 2003. Large numbers of scientists, engineers, and other intellectuals have joined the party. By 1997, technocrats made up about three-quarters of top Chinese leaders, a share that has since shrunk as they have been replaced by the two newest additions: lawyers and entrepreneurs. In 2001 the party leadership decided to allow private entrepreneurs into the party—this was the ultimate irony, including successful capitalists in the Communist Party (Dickson 2003). By 2011, an estimated 40 percent of Chinese entrepreneurs were party members. With the booming economy, it has become quite clear as well that party membership is highly correlated with wealth: "90 percent of China's millionaires are the children of high-ranking officials" (Saich 2013, 110).

The political implications of the changes are not clear. Given the development of liberalism in the West, we might expect that allowing intellectuals and especially entrepreneurs to enter the political system would expand democracy; the bourgeoisie, after all, was the class that helped create liberalism in Europe. Market economies, in precisely this way, are supposed to help produce and sustain liberal democracy. Political scientist Bruce Dickson (2003), however, surveyed China's new entrepreneurs and found that their political attitudes do not suggest they will help create greater democracy. In fact, they share the concerns of other party officials about limiting participation to the elite in order to maintain stability. Fewsmith (2013) reported that local business associations find it much easier to use connections and corruption to secure what they need from the state rather than champion the "rule of law." Chen and Lu (2011) surveyed middle-class citizens more broadly and found similar results: they did not have a particularly strong preference for democracy, and the more economically dependent they were on the state the less support they showed for democracy. The CCP so far seems to have opened up the party to the intellectual and business elite without risking its continued control.

Some observers see changes in the electoral laws as another attempt at co-opting potential opposition; others see it as the first real step in the direction of democracy. Following typically Communist practices, China long had direct elections for the most local level of government—village committees—but with only one party-approved candidate for each position. Over the course of the 1980s, the government revised the electoral law several times, first creating and then expanding the competitiveness of these local elections. Today, elections to committees are officially open to all. Candidates can be nominated by the party, other local organizations, or any group of ten citizens. Studies have shown that how this system actually works in practice varies greatly because local officials often severely limit the level of competition. Recent estimates are that the elections are actually competitive in about half of the country. Hundreds of thousands of candidates have lost village elections since 1999, and 48 percent of elected village officials are not Communist Party members (Landry, Davis, and Wang 2010, 766). One survey in the late 1990s found that more than half of voters had attended a campaign event and nearly 20 percent had participated in nominating a candidate (Shi 2006, 365). Electoral turnout has varied widely but in some places has been as high as 30 percent, a higher turnout than in most local elections in the United States. Several studies have shown that directly elected members of village committees are more responsive to villagers' concerns than are nonelected officials and that they more fairly allocate land, which is probably the most important task of village government (Kennedy 2010, 235). This incipient local democracy, however, has led to conflict and backlash. As freely elected local committees have pursued their interests, they have come into conflict with appointed party officials, which has led the party to reduce local committees' independence vis-à-vis party officials (Fewsmith 2013).

Video link:
Importance of rural village elections in China

Along with greater openness in local elections have come some of the problems that plague new democracies elsewhere: corruption, kinship-based politics, and sexism. Candidates in some village elections have engaged in vote buying—handing out gifts in exchange for votes. The candidates earn a return on this investment via corrupt land deals after they take office. Local village politics are often divided not by policy questions but by competition among local kinship groups for political control. And local elections have actually reduced the number of women in rural village committees, from 15 percent among party-appointed committees to less than 1 percent for elected ones. Even limited democracy allows local social mores and customs to have full expression in the political process, for better or for worse.

Civil society has expanded greatly over the past two decades, though it remains tightly circumscribed. Under full Communist rule, the party completely controlled all interest groups. The All-China Federation of Trade Unions (ACFTU), for instance, was the sole legal union, with mandatory branches in any enterprise with more than one hundred employees. The rapid expansion of private enterprises has made it difficult for the party to maintain its monopoly on union organization, but the ACFTU remains tightly controlled by and supportive of the government. A revised labor law enacted in 2008 made arbitration and court cases by workers easier. The number of such cases more than doubled, and in the most industrialized regions the system is overwhelmed with cases. Lee and Friedman (2009) argued that, as in other countries around the world, the opening of the economy to globalization has reduced workers' ability to secure the growing rights that the government has formally granted them. Forty percent of urban workers are part-time, casual, or temporary employees who have great difficulty demanding better treatment; nearly half of them report not receiving wages on time. In 2010, however, several major strikes erupted, most notably at Honda and Toyota plants. As the Chinese economy rebounded after the Great Recession, it became clear that its seemingly endless stream of cheap labor was running out: employers were starting to face labor shortages, and wages were rising in some areas, giving some workers the economic strength to strike and demand more. At the Honda plant in Foshan, workers unsuccessfully demanded the right to form their own independent union.

Citizens at all levels of society have become less dependent on the state, which in turn has less control over them. These increasingly independent citizens have taken the initiative to form various NGOs, which are focused mostly on local, material grievances such as housing, environmental, or working conditions. To control these organizations, the government has created a registration system for NGOs and approves only one organization of a particular type in each administrative area, in effect beginning a system of state corporatism. The state has also created its own organizations for the policy issues in which it is particularly interested; these are referred to by the Orwellian name government-organized nongovernmental organizations (GONGOs). An example is the China Family Planning Association, created to support China's one-child-per-family policy.

Video link:
NGOs in China: challenges and successes

Despite the restrictions the government puts on them, NGOs and interest groups have at times influenced the direction of government policy, though mostly at the local level. Local branches of the ACFTU have successfully supported workers' strikes on a number of occasions, and the national organization helped to get a five-day workweek approved. Lu Yiyi (2009) studied urban NGOs providing social services and found that despite financial and informational dependence on the state, the NGOs can achieve a degree of autonomy, in part through their personal relationships with local bureaucrats who can protect them from the more draconian demands of the state. Indeed, she found that GONGOs actually achieve greater autonomy than citizen-initiated NGOs. NGOs, of course, cannot voice any significant political criticisms of the regime as a whole. Hildebrandt (2013) argued that NGO leaders limit their own demands to what they find politically acceptable in a particular locale and issue area in order to preserve their organizations and have what impact they can. While civil society has clearly expanded dramatically, for all of these reasons it does not seem to have had the effect of pushing the country in the direction of democratization, as many theories of civil society typically suggest would occur in an authoritarian state.

The Chinese media, though tightly controlled, have expanded dramatically in the past generation. In the aftermath of economic reform, media outlets are mostly private and must be profitable. Government restrictions remain, however, and have tightened in some areas, especially in regard to the Internet. While criticisms of local officials' malfeasance are tolerated, political criticism of the regime is strictly prohibited. Daniela Stockman (2012) argued that, like the role of the courts, the media's criticism of local government helps the regime overcome the "dictator's dilemma" by providing it information about what is happening "on the ground." On the other hand, she finds that commercialization has not provided a greater diversity of political viewpoints in the media; indeed, citizens' opinions are more likely to be influenced in the direction of supporting the regime by unofficial media outlets than by the state-owned media.

This is because citizens trust unofficial sources more, but these sources still must report only news that stays within the bounds of the state's informal but tight censorship.

The biggest venue for criticism of the regime has been the Internet, and the government has created the so-called "Great Firewall of China" to prevent Internet users from accessing information on sensitive topics. The regime employs tens of thousands of cyberpolice and sophisticated security programs to constantly monitor Internet use. Nonetheless, Chinese "netizens" have created active online communities and techniques to evade censorship. The latter include new Chinese-language characters that can make it past filtering systems, websites based on foreign servers, and meetings held in secret chat rooms. Online activism has become a major source of criticism of the regime, most dramatically with the "Charter 08" manifesto that called for democracy (Yang 2009). The government responded to this in late 2012, passing new restrictions on online communications; most important, it required all Internet and cell phone users to register with their real names so that anonymous posts could be traced back to them.

Even though elections and civil society now offer opportunities for greater participation than in the past, pressure for more fundamental changes still exists. The most famous case is the Tiananmen Square protest in 1989. What started as a few hundred students mushroomed within a week to daily protests by 200,000 students. They demanded the government reevaluate the career of the reformist leader Hu Yaobang (who had just died), free jailed intellectual dissidents, publicly account for party leaders' finances, permit freedom of the press, and provide greater funding for education (note that they did not demand full democracy with competitive national elections, as is often asserted). The government eventually agreed to negotiate with the students but gave little ground. With student interest waning and many returning to class, a group of 3,000 began a hunger strike as a final effort to make their demands heard. This garnered massive public support, as more than a million Beijing residents turned out to defend the hunger strikers, who finally got some minor concessions from the government and, facing serious health consequences, decided to end the hunger strike. That night, the government declared martial law in the city and called in the army. At least a million citizens poured into the streets and erected barricades to try to prevent the army from entering, but it overcame the populace and moved into Tiananmen Square. In the middle of the night it opened fire on the remaining student dissidents, killing between 1,000 and 3,000 students and civilians. The military action sparked worldwide condemnation, but the regime survived.

More recently, the government cracked down on Falun Gong, a religious sect founded in 1997. It was legally registered as a religious organization, but in April 1999 the group organized a silent march of 10,000 followers in Beijing to protest a government article critical of the movement. After that, the government banned the organization and has since jailed thousands of its supporters. Large-scale protests in the outlying regions of Tibet and Xinjiang in 2008 met similar repression.

This history of repression has successfully eliminated most large-scale protests for the time being, but many local protests continue. An estimated 8,700 protests (what the

Chinese government calls "mass incidents") took place in 1993; by 2010, the number had risen to 180,000 (Fewsmith 2013, 26–27). A key organizational tool for protesters and petitioners is to get the ear of the central government via the media or dramatic acts, often referred to as "troublemaking." The central government is often more willing to make concessions to the protesters than is local government because the central authorities are more concerned about the overall legitimacy of the system. Using the contentious politics approach discussed in chapter 7, Xi Chen (2012) found that petitioners who included "troublemaking" were far more successful than those who did not. He argued, furthermore, that the Chinese state actively facilitated this form of protest as a means of allowing citizen input and pressure on local government that did not threaten the party's rule more broadly. Cai (2010) concluded that social groups in China are similar in many ways to social movements elsewhere; where they can amass their forces and use media exposure well, they can overcome opposition from local governments to force change. Success depends, of course, on the cost to the government of making the change; making demands whose costs are too high often leads to repression.

How far and how fast all of the political reforms will go is probably the major question that political scientists looking at China ask. Teresa Wright (2010) used a political economy approach to argue that the regime has been more successful than many assume at maintaining its legitimacy. China's economic policy, while creating much greater inequality than in the past, has nonetheless favored many segments of society. First and foremost, the regime has earned the support of budding entrepreneurs and professionals, who have gained great wealth under the reforms. In addition, workers in the private sector, and even workers in the declining state-owned sector who still have some social welfare protections from the state, fear that they would be worse off if the ruling party were no longer in power. Comparativist Tony Saich (2012) conducted surveys from 2003 to 2011 on satisfaction with government. In 2011 overall satisfaction with the central government stood at well over 80 percent, slightly down from 2009 but about where it has been across the decade. Respondents consistently reported higher levels of satisfaction with the central government than with local governments; satisfaction with the most local level of government, though, increased markedly from just over 40 percent in 2003 to over 60 percent in 2011. The still low level of satisfaction with local government may both reflect and explain the massive number of protests aimed locally. For a regime that has staked its legitimacy mainly on its ability to "modernize" the country, however, 80 percent approval ratings suggest a higher level of legitimacy than many outsiders might assume is the case. In 2012 and 2013, protests over the closing of a newspaper and ever worsening pollution raised questions about whether the regime was still maintaining its performance-based legitimacy (Wong 2013). China's new president, Xi Jinping, meanwhile, started a campaign within the party in 2013 to warn members about key ideas that would undermine the party's grip on power; at the top of the list were "constitutional democracy" and "universal human rights." Clearly, the current leadership has no intention of yielding to demands for democracy anytime soon.

CASE Summary

China has evolved from a communist to a modernizing authoritarian regime. As it has, it has adjusted its communist system of forced participation in a way that helps to legitimize the regime. The opening of the market economy has required the party to allow some greater participation, but it has nonetheless kept demands for fundamental reform effectively repressed. The co-opting of key elites into the ruling party, the creation of state corporatist regulation of civil society, and the use of repression when necessary have kept large-scale protest to a minimum since Tiananmen Square in 1989. Locally, reforms have been haphazard and only partially implemented, though the best evidence suggests that they have expanded over time. Semicompetitive elections have allowed some real participation at the local levels of government, but nothing on a larger scale. Democracy advocates within China and around the world hope that the initial expansion of participation will ultimately yield greater pressure toward real democratic reform, though that seems a long way off at this point.

CASE Questions

1. The Chinese government has allowed participation and criticism at the local level in various ways but repressed it firmly at the national level. Can you use the idea of the "dictator's dilemma" to explain this pattern of behavior?
2. China often seems to be pursuing a contradictory set of policies that alternatively allow and then repress participation. What does this mean for the possibility of democracy emerging over the long term?

CASE Study

IRAN: FROM PARTICIPATION AND REFORM TO RENEWED REPRESSION

On June 12, 2009, Iran's president Mahmoud Ahmadinejad faced reelection. Early on, he was predicted to win easily, but he fared poorly in a televised debate, and suddenly his opponents and their supporters believed he was vulnerable. Interest in the election skyrocketed, and predictions shifted to a possible

- **ELECTIONS**
  Presidential and legislative, but Guardian Council control of candidate selection

- **PARTIES**
  Banned for many years; allowed now, but very weak

- **CIVIL SOCIETY**
  Weak but growing until post-2005 repression; Green Movement of 2009

- **PATRON-CLIENT RELATIONSHIPS**
  Islamic foundations and Revolutionary Guards

- **LEGITIMATION**
  Tension between Islamist and democratic claims

Video link:
Iran's Green Movement

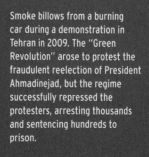

Web link:
Iran's presidential election

opposition victory. The morning after the election, the government announced the results with only two-thirds of the votes counted, claiming the president had won 62 percent of the vote, clearly a fraudulent outcome. The number-two candidate, reformist Mir-Hossein Mousavi, called on his supporters to protest, and within a day more than one million people marched through the streets of Tehran in the largest demonstration since the 1979 revolution. After weeks of demonstrations, the government finally and effectively cracked down, arresting as many as five thousand protesters, putting over one hundred on televised trials on what seemed like trumped-up charges, and allegedly torturing and raping some in prison. In the June 2013 presidential election, the supreme leader and Ahmadinejad were thwarted again, as the closest thing to a reformist candidate won. It was, however, a far cry from 2009: the victor, Hassan Rowhani, was seen as a moderate but nonetheless a regime insider who was unlikely to challenge the supreme leadership. Despite this, people poured into the streets to celebrate the election victory of the candidate who was most distant from the supreme leader, once again showing that Iranian voters were willing to use the democratic elements of Iran's theocracy to show their displeasure with the regime.

The dramatic events of 2009 were perhaps the zenith of a long battle between conservative supporters of the regime who wished to preserve the power of the clergy and Revolutionary Guard, and reformist elements who wanted to strengthen the quasi-democratic institutions, reduce the role of Islamic law, and more fully open the society to the world. Citizens demanding change have put reformers into office off and on over the history of the Islamic Republic, most notably during the Khatami presidency (1997–2005). The supreme leader and his allies, however, effectively blocked reformers' efforts and forced them out of office via Ahmadinejad's first election in 2005. The election of the moderate, Hassan Rowhani, as president in 2013 showed that the clerical leadership had been successful at repressing reformers; while

Smoke billows from a burning car during a demonstration in Tehran in 2009. The "Green Revolution" arose to protest the fraudulent reelection of President Ahmadinejad, but the regime successfully repressed the protesters, arresting thousands and sentencing hundreds to prison.

they celebrated Rowhani's victory, they recognized that the changes he might put in place would be modest.

Majlis elections in Iran are majoritarian in single-member districts. They are held every four years, and while none has been truly free and fair, the Guardian Council at times has allowed significant competition. The council is pivotal to the process because of its power to ban candidates from running, a power it has used increasingly to thwart reformers' efforts to gain power. In the 1997 presidential election, Mohammad Khatami, a reformist cleric, won a sweeping victory that many observers saw as the start of a major liberalization of the political system. Until 2000, however, conservatives in parliament were numerous enough to block major reforms. In the 2000 *majlis* election, the Guardian Council did not prevent reformist candidates from running because of Khatami's popularity, and reformists won an overwhelming victory, clinching 80 percent of the vote. The new *majlis* passed reforms involving greater freedoms of expression, women's rights, human rights in general, and market-oriented economic policies. The Guardian Council, however, vetoed many of these, arguing that they violated *sharia*. By the 2004 *majlis* election, the Guardian Council once again felt it was safe to clamp down. Thousands of reformist candidates were banned from the election, leading most to boycott it. Conservatives won the election, but turnout dropped from nearly 70 percent to 50 percent. Since then, the council has repeatedly banned reformist candidates, leading the major reformist party to boycott the 2012 *majlis* election altogether.

The 2013 presidential election once again showed the power of the Guardian Council to enforce the interests of the supreme leader. Forty candidates put their names forward, but the council approved only eight, six of whom were conservative supporters of the clerical leadership. Both President Ahmadinejad's preferred candidate and the leading reformist candidate, former president Hashemi Rafsanjani, were banned. As the campaign developed, Rafsanjani endorsed Rowhani as the closest thing to a true reformist candidate, and he won with just over 50 percent of the vote. The election showed both the continuing popular demand for change and the clerical leadership's ability to limit reformers' efforts.

Political parties are weak institutions in contemporary Iran, but given the severe restrictions on the power of elective offices, this is understandable. The prerevolutionary regime of the shah was modernizing authoritarian and rarely allowed significant participation, so the country has no major history of political parties. Despite the Islamic constitution's guarantee of a right to form parties, Khomeini banned them in 1987, claiming they produced unnecessary divisions. Reformist president Khatami successfully legalized parties again in 1998, which helped make the 2000 *majlis* election the most open and competitive ever. Khatami's reformist supporters coalesced into a party called the Khordad Front that won the huge victory that year. Parties continue to exist, but as loose coalitions around individual leaders, not as enduring organizations with which citizens identify. In spite of this weakness, the government banned the two leading reformist parties after the 2009 election.

Like political parties, civil society is not particularly strong in Iran, but the period of reformist ascendancy—1997 to 2004—saw an explosion of civil society activity when government restrictions were temporarily relaxed. Of particular note were media, women's, and student groups. Whenever the government has allowed it, the media have expanded rapidly. Leading up to the 2000 *majlis* election, many newspapers emerged, and an exceptionally open political debate occurred. Since that time, religious authorities have again repressed newspapers, closing them down for criticizing the government too harshly and drastically reducing public debate. Civil society groups once again emerged in the 2009 protests until they met with overwhelming repression. Since 2009, numerous political activists and journalists have been arrested and jailed, and key journalistic and legal associations were banned. The government created a new "cyberpolice force" to monitor the Internet and disrupt bloggers and social media sites critical of the regime, which were important in organizing the 2009 demonstrations. The government has also banned several organizations working to defend human rights in the country.

Women have become an important organized force over the last decade. Ironically, in terms of women's position in society, the Islamic regime may well have been more "modernizing" than the earlier modernizing authoritarian regime of the shah. Women now constitute 62 percent of university students, and a birth control policy has lowered childbearing and population growth rates dramatically. Conservative clergy have resisted changes to laws regarding divorce, clothing, and other issues associated with religious observance, but they have allowed significant socioeconomic changes in women's lives. These changes have fostered the growth of women's organizations calling for even further change, a topic we explore in chapter 12. All major politicians now court the women's vote during elections.

Video link: Fighting for women's rights in Iran

The Green Movement that emerged in response to the fraudulent 2009 election showed both the strength and weakness of Iran's incipient civil society. It brought at least a million people onto the streets of Tehran and reached beyond its middle-class base, but it did not have much effect in the countryside. Though initiated in response to an appeal from the losing candidate, it had no clear formal organization. A decentralized organizing system using Twitter and Facebook became the main means of communication, aided by public statements and occasional public appearances by reformist leaders. Protests continued for weeks and showed the youthful participants that change was possible, but the government successfully repressed them in spite of widespread international condemnation. Moussavi, the leading reformer, called for demonstrations again in February 2011 in support of the "Arab Spring" movements in Egypt and Tunisia. Tens of thousands of Iranians turned out, but the government responded with force, disbanding the demonstrations and arresting its leaders once again, in spite of the fact that the regime itself was in favor of the "Arab Spring." Four years after the huge demonstrations and in spite of the partial victory in the 2013 presidential election, the reform movement seems effectively crushed, at least until some new opening (most likely via a split within the regime) allows some political space for action.

Given the weak formal institutions of participation and the government's repeated repression of them, it is not surprising that patron-client networks are a crucial form of political activity as well as a key way to gain support for the government. Patron-client factions long predate the Islamic regime in Iran, and the regime has done little to eliminate them. Indeed, many scholars argue that such factions are essential to the regime's continued rule. The ruling elite consists of numerous patrons in key government or *bonyad* positions and informally leading a large number of clients who provide them with political support. These factions are crucial venues through which political participation occurs. Indeed, President Khatami's reforms in the late 1990s and early 2000s were aimed in part at strengthening civil society to weaken the patron-client networks that clerics and their supporters use as tools of co-optation. Under President Ahmadinejad, factions and networks of former Revolutionary Guards have expanded their power and position within the government dramatically.

Ideological factions exist as well, overlapping and at times crossing the existing factional divisions based on clientelism. David Menashri (2001), an Israeli expert on Iran, argued that shortly after Khomeini's death, three significant factions emerged among both clergy and secular politicians. Conservatives supported adherence to pure Islamist ideals in terms of personal life and moral values and opposed interaction with the West, but they generally supported a market economy and private property. Radicals agreed with conservatives on religious and moral purity, but they supported

Iran and the Middle East

In spite of its reputation as a "pariah state" in much of the West, Iran was about average in its region in terms of the level of freedom and social well-being enjoyed by its population, at least until the controversial 2009 election and its aftermath moved the country in a less democratic direction.

	Iran	Middle East/North Africa average*
Freedom House civil liberties score	6	5
Freedom House political rights score	6	5
Democracy Index 2008	2.83	3.54
Democracy Index 2013	1.98	3.73
Human Development Index 2013	0.742	0.652
Literacy rate	77%	82.61%

Sources: Data are from Freedom House (2013); *CIA World Factbook;* and Democracy Index 2012 (Economist Intelligence Unit) (http://www.eiu.com/public/thankyou_download.aspx?activity=reg&campaignid=demo2010).

Averages exclude North Africa. For Human Development Index, use "Arab States."

Khomeini's revolutionary rhetoric in favor of significant state intervention in the economy. Pragmatists, the third faction, were willing to moderate Islamic purity and open up more to the West as well as move in the direction of a market economy; these were the core of the reformists who supported President Khatami in the 1990s and the Green Movement in 2009. President Ahmadinejad became the chief radical, trying to enforce Islamic purity in social and cultural areas, but coupling that with populist economic policies that were initially popular with the impoverished and still win him some support.

Ahmadinejad was elected in 2005 with the support of a coalition of social conservatives and the poor, to whom he appealed with a populist campaign that promised more jobs, housing, and social spending. His ruling coalition quickly revealed significant internal contradictions. For instance, social conservatives in the *majlis* rejected some of his economic policies, such as using more oil money to fund social programs for the poor. On the other hand, despite his socially conservative rhetoric, Ahmadinejad limited his reversal of earlier social reforms, knowing that his youthful supporters would likely rebel if he reimposed too many social restrictions. He banned "Western and indecent music" from state-owned media but only partially restored restrictions on women's attire and other policies that social conservatives favor. As his rhetoric became more secular and nationalist after 2009, and the combination of international sanctions and his economic policies sent the economy spiraling downward, he lost the support of the conservatives, including the supreme leader. His coalition collapsed, and it had no candidate in the 2013 election. Rowhani's victory in that election has given pragmatist reformers some hope, though all indications are that reforms will be moderate at best.

CASE Summary

Iran is the only fully developed Islamic theocratic regime in the world today. This gives it an unusual ideological justification and, at least initially, gave it revolutionary and ideological legitimacy. After more than three decades, however, the regime shows attributes of many other authoritarian regimes in that it rules via repression, co-optation, and efforts at legitimation. The clerical elite have proven willing to repress opponents who step beyond what they are willing to tolerate. The 2009 crisis badly damaged the legitimacy of Iran's quasi-democratic institutions and raised questions about the future of any real participation or representation. The successful repression of that movement led many to believe the population had grown quiescent, if not supportive of the regime, but the surprise victory of the moderate candidate in the 2013 presidential election showed that Iran's people were still willing to support any movement for change, no matter how small and limited. While the population lacks organizational strength or a public voice in the face of severe repression, it may be waiting for an opening to reemerge even more forcefully.

CASE Questions

1. What does the history of the 2009 and 2013 presidential elections and Green Movement suggest about the possibility of democratic change in Iran in the near future?
2. Given the role of the Guardian Council in controlling candidates for elections when it so chooses, do the democratic elements of Iran's regime really make any difference to how it is ruled?

CASE Study

NIGERIA: DECLINING PARTICIPATION AMID INCREASINGLY PERSONALIST RULE

Each time a Nigerian military ruler took power, he claimed that he would remain in power only briefly and restore democracy soon. Perhaps for this reason, Nigerian military leaders never allowed even limited elections or a legislature to enhance their legitimacy. They did allow some political participation as part of a seemingly unending, Sisyphean process of "returning to democracy." Actual transitions to democratic rule, however, occurred only in 1979 and 1999. One of the primary ways the military tried to gain legitimacy was to create elaborate processes for writing new constitutions to prepare for a new democracy. Constituent assemblies were created in which politicians and leading members of civil society participated, and new procedures and electoral rules were drafted. The most open political activity took place within these assemblies, as old political alignments based on region and ethnicity informally emerged in the form of factions. While none of this fully fulfilled the functions that Jennifer Gandhi (2008) laid out for legislatures in authoritarian regimes, they did provide occasional space for actual political participation.

In the process of preparing for a return to democracy, the military government would eventually have to allow political parties to reemerge and begin campaigning, but they often restricted them in various ways. Babangida (in 1989–1993) rejected all thirteen parties that sought registration and instead created two and wrote their platforms himself. Abacha (in 1995) allowed five parties to be officially registered, but all of

- **ELECTIONS**
  None except during transitions to democracy

- **PARTIES**
  None except during transitions to democracy

- **CIVIL SOCIETY**
  Initially allowed to operate openly as a means to overcome dictator's dilemma but growing repression over time

- **PATRON-CLIENT RELATIONSHIPS**
  Growing corruption and oil revenue

- **LEGITIMATION**
  Promise of return to democracy

Adams Oshiomole, the president of the Nigeria Labour Congress, greets supporters near the end of the military dictatorship. The labor movement, along with other elements of civil society, was instrumental in forcing the military to relinquish power in 1999.

them were pledged to support him for the presidency. Such parties provided little real opportunity to voice opposition to the military regimes themselves.

Civil society fared better under Nigerian military rule than did political parties. In the 1970s, labor unions and professional associations continued to operate more or less as they had before, though this was in part because they did not challenge the regimes. The press also was unusually free for an authoritarian regime. All of this gave the military rulers some means of overcoming the dictator's dilemma because it allowed them to gather information on what people actually thought of their rule. The governments of the 1980s and 1990s, however, increasingly repressed civil society. When medical doctors went on strike to protest their working conditions and to express their general opposition to the government in 1984–1985, the government banned them. When the Nigerian Bar Association opposed the use of military tribunals, preventive detention, and other restrictions on the rule of law and human rights, and the Nigerian Union of Journalists defended its colleagues who had been jailed and detained in crackdowns on the press in the late 1980s and early 1990s, both faced repression. Even greater brutality and repression under dictator Sani Abacha in the 1990s inspired greater opposition, as several major democracy movements coalesced to oppose him. We examine these movements in greater detail in chapter 9.

Ethnic and religious associations also grew substantially in the 1990s. Nigerians increasingly saw the military rulers of the 1980s and 1990s (all of whom were Muslims from the north and associated with the Kaduna mafia, a group of military men named after the northern city in which many of the members maintained homes) as centralizing political power in the hands of one ethno-regional and religious group. Christians in the southern part of the country voiced strong opposition to Babangida's 1989 decision to have Nigeria join an international group called the Organization of the Islamic Conference (OIC). In religiously mixed areas, violent conflicts broke out in several cities in the late 1980s and early 1990s as tensions rose. As discussed in chapter 4, new and more fundamentalist Islamic movements began to emerge in the northern region.

Nigerian political scientist Julius Ihonvbere argued in the mid-1990s that Abacha's crackdown on all efforts to establish democracy led many political activists to resort to ethnic political mobilization, producing "more than at any other time in Nigeria's history, a hardening of regional positions" (1994, 218). Ken Saro-Wiwa and MOSOP became the best-known ethnically based movement, but many others arose as well. This legacy of growing religious and ethnic sentiment and organizations, some of which became violent, is one of the major obstacles to the stability of Nigeria's young democracy.

CASE Summary   Nigeria's military regimes became increasingly centralized, repressive, and corrupt over time. While those of the 1970s allowed civil society to survive more or less intact, later rulers centralized power in their own hands and eliminated virtually all institutionalized channels of dissent. Predictably, corruption became a way of life in such personalized regimes of weak institutions, and patron-client networks became the main form of political participation and economic survival. Nigerian political scientist Julius Ihonvbere reported that by the early 1990s, it was "impossible to survive or make progress in the country without (1) belonging to a particular religion; (2) having connections with top military officers, their spouses, or traditional rulers; (3) coming from particular sections of the country; and (4) getting involved directly in one form of corruption or another" (1994, 1). Civil society, rather than being a means of participation and influence within the authoritarian regime, focused solely on fundamental regime change as part of the democratization movement that was sweeping across Africa in the 1990s. The questions we take up in the next chapter are whether and how a new democracy can emerge from such a regime and, if so, what will be its prospects and problems.

CASE Questions

1. Nigerian military governments proscribed any type of formal participatory institutions such as elections and parties, while China has allowed some elections at the most local level and Iran has allowed national ones. Comparing the three regimes, what can you hypothesize about the relationship between allowing some elements of formal participation and the stability of authoritarian regimes?

2. Why did the Nigerian military rely purely on the promise of a "return to democracy" for legitimation?

CONCLUSION

By the dawn of the new millennium, it was clear that while democracy had expanded, authoritarianism was not about to disappear entirely. Since the end of the Cold War, semi-authoritarian rule has expanded, and more "closed" authoritarian rule that allows no formal opposition has been on the wane (with China clearly being the world's biggest exception to the trend). The differences between fully authoritarian and semi-authoritarian rule, though, aren't as great as they might at first appear. Understanding the opaque political dynamics of authoritarian and semi-authoritarian regimes will continue to be a concern for comparative politics for the foreseeable future.

On the face of it, dictators seem to control virtually everything in authoritarian regimes. The executive would seem to be all-powerful. As we've seen, though, this is often not the case, which makes figuring out who rules rather difficult. The key question is not just what formal institutions exist but how institutionalized they are. Ultimately, in authoritarian regimes the supreme leader or a small coterie of leaders (such as a politburo) has final authority to decide as they will. Ruling by fiat and repression alone, however, is both difficult and expensive. Holding a gun to every citizen's head, as well as maintaining the loyalty of those holding the guns, is not easy. All regimes, therefore, seek to gain some sort of legitimacy or at least to buy support via co-optation. A means to achieve both legitimacy and support is to limit the supreme leader's power in order to give others, especially key elites, some influence. Institutionalized and therefore predictable governing and limited participatory institutions can accomplish this. Examining those institutions and how strong they are can thus be a key means to understanding who really rules and how much influence they have. Even in the most personalist regimes with little institutionalization, patron-client relationships are important for co-opting opposition. More powerful individuals control more patronage, and on the other side, some clients are more powerful and thus more likely to have their requests attended to than others. Comparativists attempt the difficult task of understanding these informal networks and relationships to determine who rules in countries where institutions matter little.

Comparativists have long catalogued authoritarian regimes into various subtypes. It's clear, however, that certain commonalities exist in all authoritarian regimes. For instance, all dictators face the dictator's dilemma, though they attempt to solve it in different ways. All dictators also rule through some combination of repression, co-optation, and attempts at legitimation, but again in differing ways and amounts. Some of this variation is systematic across subtypes: different subtypes display consistent and distinct behavior. One-party and of course semi-authoritarian regimes provide opportunities for greater participation via formal institutions. Military regimes are less likely to do so, as political participation and open dissent are foreign to professional military culture. Following the logic of the dictator's dilemma, regimes that allow less participation are likely to require more repression and co-optation. Military regimes seem likely to use repression, given their inherent control of force. Personalist regimes that have weak institutions across the board focus mostly on co-optation via patronage, using repression as well but often in less institutionalized and therefore less effective ways. Such a personalist regime might have, for example, multiple and competing military agencies that are informally loyal to individual leaders rather than to the regime as a whole. The splits within the military in response to the 2011 uprising in Libya show the possible effects of this aspect of personalist rule.

The earliest theoretical approaches to understanding authoritarian regimes focused mainly on individual leaders or national cultures. Individual leaders are clearly crucial in such regimes, so scholars used psychological theories to understand their personal influences and motivations. Other scholars, looking beyond the individual, used political culture theories to argue why such regimes emerged in the first place and how they operated. Authoritarian regimes emerged in countries with political cultures that had authoritarian traits such as lack of interpersonal trust, lack of belief in core democratic principles, lack of popular interest in participation in politics, or a popular desire to follow a perceived "strong" leader. For example, the lack of any lengthy democratic experience in postcolonial Africa created regimes that eliminated virtually all democratic trappings.

More recently, scholars have used rational-actor or historical-institutionalist models to understand authoritarian regimes. Dictators face a common set of governing problems. To overcome these, they engage in a combination of repression, co-optation, and legitimation. This action pattern, rational-actor theorists argue, is determined by the dictators' and their opponents' or allies' rational responses to their conditions, the most important of which are the relative strengths of the actors and the resources at their disposal. Historical institutionalists agree with much of this, but assert that the creation of key institutions, such as strong ruling parties, happens at particular historical junctures and heavily influences regime strength and longevity; institutions cannot be created at any time the dictator comes to believe he needs them. As with many arguments in comparative politics, institutionalist theories are at the forefront of the debate today but have not definitively proven their case. We turn next to another set of difficult questions about regimes: why and how they change from one type to another via military coup, revolution, or democratization.

KEY CONCEPTS

dictator's dilemma (p. 405)   supreme leader (p. 404)
personality cult (p. 429)

 Sharpen your skills with SAGE edge at **edge.sagepub.com/orvis3e.**
SAGE edge for students provides a personalized approach to help you accomplish your coursework goals in an easy-to-use learning environment.

WORKS CITED

Boroumand, Ladan. 2009. "Civil Society's Choice." *Journal of Democracy* 20 (4): 16–20 (http://www.journalofdemocracy.org/articles/gratis/Boroumand-20-4.pdf).

Brown, Kerry. 2013. "The CCP and the One-Party State." In *Handbook of China's Governance and Domestic Politics,* edited by Chris Ogden, 3–11. New York: Routledge.

Brownlee, Jason. 2007. *Authoritarianism in an Age of Democratization.* Cambridge, UK: Cambridge University Press.

Cai, Yongshun. 2010. *Collective Resistance in China: Why Popular Protests Succeed or Fail.* Stanford, CA: Stanford University Press.

Chen, Jie, and Chunlong Lu. 2011. "Democratization and the Middle Class in China: The Middle Class's Attitudes toward Democracy." *Political Research Quarterly* 64 (September 2011): 705–719.

Chen, Jo-hsi. 1978. *The Execution of Mayor Yin and Other Stories from the Great Proletarian Cultural Revolution.* Bloomington: Indiana University Press.

Chen, Xi. 2012. *Social Protest and Contentious Authoritarianism in China.* Cambridge, UK: Cambridge University Press.

Diamond, Larry, 1997. "Postscript and Postmortem." In *Transition without End:*

Nigerian Politics and Civil Society under Babangida, edited by Larry Diamond, Anthony Kirk-Greene, and Oyeleye Oyediran, 465–484. Boulder, CO: Lynne Rienner.

Dickson, Bruce J. 2003. *Red Capitalists in China: The Party, Private Entrepreneurs, and Prospects for Political Change.* New York: Cambridge University Press.

Fewsmith, Joseph. 2013. *The Logic and Limits of Political Reform in China.* New York: Cambridge University Press.

Frantz, Erica, and Natasha Ezrow. 2011. *The Politics of Dictatorship: Institutions and Outcomes in Authoritarian Regimes.* Boulder, CO: Lynne Rienner.

Gandhi, Jennifer. 2008. *Political Institutions under Dictatorship.* Cambridge, UK: Cambridge University Press.

Ginsburg, Tom. 2008. "Administrative Law and the Judicial Control of Agents in Authoritarian Regimes." In *Rule by Law: The Politics of Courts in Authoritarian Regimes,* edited by Tom Ginsburg and Tamir Moustafa, 58–72. Cambridge, UK: Cambridge University Press.

Hen-Tov, Elliot, and Nathan Gonzalez. 2010. "The Militarization of Post-Khomeini Iran: Praetorianism 2.0." *Washington Quarterly* 34 (1): 45–59. doi: 10.1080/0163660X.2011.534962.

Hildebrandt, Timothy. 2013. *Social Organizations and the Authoritarian State in China.* Cambridge, UK: Cambridge University Press.

Ihonvbere, Julius Omozuanvbo. 1994. *Nigeria: The Politics of Adjustment and Democracy.* New Brunswick, NJ: Transaction.

Kennedy, John James. 2010. "Rural China: Reform and Resistance." In *Politics in China: An Introduction,* edited by William A. Joseph, 225–249. Oxford, UK: Oxford University Press.

Landry, Pierre F. 2008. "The Institutional Diffusion of Courts in China: Evidence from Survey Data." In *Rule by Law: The Politics of Courts in Authoritarian Regimes,* edited by Tom Ginsburg and Tamir Moustafa,

207–234. Cambridge, UK: Cambridge University Press.

Landry, Pierre F., Deborah Davis, and Shiru Wang. 2010. "Elections in Rural China: Competition without Parties." *Comparative Political Studies* 43 (6): 763–790. doi: 10.1177/0010414009359392.

Lee, Ching Kwan, and Eli Friedman. 2009. "The Labor Movement." *Journal of Democracy* 20 (3): 21–24.

Li, Cheng. 2010. "China's Communist Party-State: The Structure and Dynamics of Power." In *Politics in China: An Introduction,* edited by William A. Joseph, 165–191. Oxford, UK: Oxford University Press.

Li, Cheng, and Lynn White. 2006. "The Sixteenth Central Committee of the Chinese Communist Party: Emerging Patterns of Power Sharing." In *China's Deep Reform: Domestic Politics in Transition,* edited by Lowell Dittmer and Guoli Liu, 81–118. Lanham, MD: Rowman and Littlefield.

Lu, Yiyi. 2009. *Non-Governmental Organizations in China: The Rise of Dependent Autonomy.* New York: Routledge.

Magaloni, Beatriz. 2006. *Voting for Autocracy: Hegemonic Party Survival and Its Demise in Mexico.* Cambridge, UK: Cambridge University Press.

Mbembe, Achille. 1992. "Provisional Notes on the Postcolony." *Africa: Journal of the International African Institute* 62 (1): 3–37. doi: 10.2307/1160062.

Menashri, David. 2001. *Post-Revolutionary Politics in Iran: Religion, Society, and Power.* London: Frank Cass.

Migdal, Joel S. 1988. *Strong Societies and Weak States: State-Society Relations and State Capabilities in the Third World.* Princeton, NJ: Princeton University Press.

Pei, Minxin. 2007. *Corruption Threatens China's Future* (Policy Brief 55). Washington, DC (http://carnegieendowment.org/files/pb55_pei_china_corruption_final.pdf).

Saich, Tony. 2013. "Political Representation." In *Handbook of China's Governance and Domestic Politics,* edited by Chris Ogden, 109–119. New York: Routledge.

———. 2012. *The Quality of Governance in China: The Citizens' View.* Cambridge, MA: John F. Kennedy School of Government, Harvard University: Faculty Research Working Paper, RWP12-051 (November).

Shambaugh, David. 2008. *China's Communist Party: Atrophy and Adaptation.* Washington, DC: Woodrow Wilson Center Press.

Shi, Tianjian. 2006. "Village Committee Elections in China: Institutionalist Tactics for Democracy." In *China's Deep Reform: Domestic Politics in Transition,* edited by Lowell Dittmer and Guoli Liu, 353–380. Lanham, MD: Rowman and Littlefield.

Stockman, Daniela. 2012. *Media Commercialization and Authoritarian Rule in China.*

Cambridge, UK: Cambridge University Press.

Svolik, Milan W. 2012. *The Politics of Authoritarian Rule.* Cambridge, UK: Cambridge University Press.

Wintrobe, Ronald. 1998. *The Political Economy of Dictatorship.* Cambridge, UK: Cambridge University Press.

Wong, Edward. 2013. "In China, Widening Discontent among the Communist Party Faithful." *New York Times,* January 19 (http://www.nytimes.com/2013/01/20/world/asia/in-china-discontent-among-the-normally-faithful.html?emc=eta1).

Wright, Teresa. 2010. *Accepting Authoritarianism: State-Society Relations in China's Reform Era.* Stanford, CA: Stanford University Press.

Yang, Guobin. 2009. "Online Activism." *Journal of Democracy* 20 (3): 33–36. doi: 10.1353/jod.0.0094.

RESOURCES FOR FURTHER STUDY

Clapham, Christopher S. 1982. *Private Patronage and Public Power: Political Clientelism in the Modern State.* New York: St. Martin's Press.

Clapham, Christopher S., and George D. E. Philip, eds. 1985. *The Political Dilemmas of Military Regimes.* Totowa, NJ: Barnes and Noble.

Jahanbegloo, Ramin, ed. 2012. *Civil Society and Democracy in Iran.* New York: Lexington Books.

Mbembe, Achille. 2001. *On the Postcolony.* Berkeley: University of California Press.

McFaul, Michael. 2005. "Chinese Dreams, Persian Realities." *Journal of Democracy* 16 (4): 74–82. doi:10.1353/jod.2005.0068.

WEB RESOURCES

Quality of Government Institute, University of Gothenburg, The QoG Data
(http://www.qog.pol.gu.se/data)

World Bank, Database of Political Institutions
(http://go.worldbank.org/2EAGGLRZ40)

World Justice Project, Rule of Law Index
(http://www.worldjusticeproject.org/rule-of-law-index)

World Values Survey
(http://www.worldvaluessurvey.org)

9 REGIME CHANGE

KEY QUESTIONS

- Why does the military intervene in politics in certain countries and not in others?

- How can civilians maintain effective control over the military? When the military takes power, what explains how it rules and how much power, if any, it shares with civilians?

- Why do revolutions occur? What motivates leaders and their followers, and what determines whether they succeed or fail?

- What best explains why some new democracies survive while others revert to authoritarianism?

- Can a democracy survive in any country or does it require a certain type of society, culture, or economy?

Regime change is the high drama of comparative politics. Many of our most iconic political images are of regime change, from the "shot heard round the world" signaling the start of the American Revolution in 1776 to Nelson Mandela taking the oath of office in South Africa in 1994 to protesters in Tahrir Square in Egypt in 2011. They are images of popular and charismatic leaders backed by the mobilized masses demanding a better world. There can also be less positive images, though, like that of a general seizing power as tanks roll into the capital, as happened in Egypt in 2013. Comparativists analyze all of these events, whether positive or negative, as **regime change**, the process through which one regime is transformed into another.

Comparativists have long studied regime change. Initially focused on military coups d'état and social revolutions, since the 1980s we have concentrated primarily on what Samuel Huntington (1991) called the "third wave" of democratization. All types of regime change remain important, however, as the Country and Concept table on page 456 illustrates. While democratization has been the most widespread type of regime change in the last two decades, military coups have occurred in recent years in Guinea and Mali. The "Arab Spring," and the recent history of Egypt in particular, shows that it's often not clear in the short term what kind of regime change is taking place as

Hundreds of thousands of Egyptians watch fireworks set off to celebrate the military's ouster of President Mohamed Morsi on July 7, 2013. The military coup came two-and-a-half years after a political revolution that started a process of democratization. The tortuous route and uncertain outcome of Egypt's regime change is not unusual.

it happens. Understanding all three types remains essential.

The study of regime change raises several fundamental questions in comparative politics: Why do revolutions or military coups happen in some countries and not in others? When the military stages a coup, what explains how it rules and how much power, if any, it shares with civilians? Why does democratization succeed or fail? Can democracy survive in any country or in only certain types of countries, and why? We address all of these questions in our examination of regime change, starting with the historically most common type: military coups d'état.

regime change
The process through which one regime is transformed into another

THE MILITARY IN POLITICS: COUPS D'ÉTAT

Military force is central to the modern state. All states must have a military and maintain effective control over it to maintain sovereignty. Americans generally view the military as an organization that is firmly under civilian control and that should stay out of politics. In reality, no military is completely apolitical. When President Barack

COUNTRY AND CONCEPT
Regime Change and Outcome

Country	Date	Type of regime change (20th century)	Outcome: type of regime	Length of new regime (years)
Brazil	1930	Military coup	Neofascist	15
	1945	Democratization	Democracy	19
	1964	Military coup	Bureaucratic-authoritarian	21
	1985	Democratization	Democracy	28+
China	1911	Revolution from above	State collapse/warlord rule	16
	1949	Revolution from below	Communist	64+
Germany	1918	Democratization	Democracy	15
	1933	Fascist putsch	Fascist	12
	1950	Democratization	Democracy	63+
	1990	Democratization (end of East German state)	Democracy (expanded)	NA
India	1947	Democratization (end of colonial rule)	Democracy	66+
Iran	1921	Military coup	Modernizing authoritarian	58
	1979	Revolution from below	Theocratic	34+
Japan	1950	Democratization	Democracy	63+
Mexico	1920	Revolution	Semi-authoritarian	74
	1994	Democratization	Democracy	19+
Nigeria	1960	Democratization (end of colonial rule)	Democracy	6
	1966	Military coup	Personalist	13
	1979	Democratization	Democracy	4
	1983	Military coup	Personalist	16
	1999	Democratization	Democracy	14+
Russia	1917	Revolution from below	Communist	74
	1991	Democratization	Democracy	9
			Semi-authoritarian	13+
United Kingdom	None	NA	NA	NA
United States	None	NA	NA	NA

Obama decided that he wanted to get the U.S. military out of Iraq and reduce its presence in Afghanistan, various military leaders made it clear they disagreed with those decisions. When congressional committees consider the U.S. defense budget, they hold hearings and listen to the advice of top military leaders, among others. These are both examples of the military engaging in political activity. The key is that a regime with effective control over the military, whether democratic or authoritarian, keeps such activities within institutionalized limits: the military does not go beyond the bounds set by the civilian leadership. When it does, a constitutional or political crisis can arise. We now examine the most flagrant military intervention in politics, the **coup d'état**, in which the military forcibly removes the existing regime and establishes a new one.

> **coup d'état**
> When the military forcibly removes an existing regime and establishes a new one

When American students are asked why the military does not stage a coup in the United States, the first answer is usually that the Constitution prevents it. The elected president is commander in chief, and the military must obey him. But given that the Constitution is a piece of paper and the president is one unarmed person, whereas the U.S. military is arguably the most powerful force on the planet, there must be more to it than that. And there is. A civilian regime, whether democratic or authoritarian, goes to great lengths to ensure that the military is loyal to the regime's ideals and institutions. Civilian leaders try to inculcate the appropriate values in the military leadership, either professional values specific to the military or more general values that are supportive of the regime and that reflect the broader political culture. Well-established democracies train military leaders carefully in military academies, such as West Point in the United States or Sandhurst in Britain, to instill professional values that portray the military as prestigious and apolitical. Since military personnel come out of society as a whole, a strong system of political socialization throughout the society that ingrains respect for the major political institutions also helps to ensure that military leaders have those same values. Communist systems attempt to achieve the same ends via direct Communist Party involvement in the military, mandatory party membership for the military leadership, and, like democracies, political socialization in the broader society.

Less institutionalized authoritarian regimes often lack these types of generally effective and systematic mechanisms. Instead, they rely on the creation of multiple military institutions (as mentioned in chapter 8), so that no single one becomes too powerful, or on informal ties of loyalty such as ethnic affiliations between the ruler and military personnel. Many African personalist rulers created a well-equipped and well-paid presidential guard from the same ethnic group or region as the president, which was personally loyal to the president as an individual patron. The job of this presidential guard was, in part, to protect the president from his own army.

Why Do Military Coups Happen?

Military coups occur when all efforts to keep the military loyal to (or at least under the control of) the regime fail. Three major schools of thought attempt to explain why coups happen. In the 1960s, when coups became quite common in postcolonial countries, the dominant explanation focused not on the military itself but instead on the societies and political systems in which the coups occurred. Samuel Huntington, focusing on the weakness of institutions, contended that "the most important causes of military intervention in politics are not military . . . but the political and institutional structure of the society" (1968, 194). Samuel Finer, in his classic 1962 work *The Man on Horseback*, made a political-culture argument: countries with political cultures that do not highly value nonmilitary means of transferring power and civil society are more prone to coups. Weak institutions and corrupt rule under early postcolonial leaders created political instability and often violence. The military, these theorists argued, intervened to restore order when civilian leaders had weakened the civilian regime via corrupt and incompetent rule. Most of these early students of military coups were modernization theorists who argued that the military, with its training and hierarchical organization, was one of the few modern institutions in postcolonial societies. They believed that the military could rule in the national interest, reestablishing order and restarting development. This thinking was in line with the theories of modernizing authoritarianism prominent at the time (see chapter 3).

More recently, Africa scholar Chris Allen (1995) argued that military coups in Africa in the 1960s and 1970s happened in states in which civilian elites could not resolve the "clientelist crisis" that resulted from decolonization. He argued that African political parties mobilized voters via clientelism in the elections before and right after independence, as we discussed in chapter 7. The parties that won the first elections gained enormous advantages by gaining control of state expenditures to use as patronage; those who lost used whatever means they could to battle against the incumbent advantage. The losers appealed more strongly to ethnic loyalty and used violence as necessary to try to regain power. Politics became an unregulated "spoils" game of growing ethnic divisions, corruption, and violence. Some leaders managed to avoid the worst of this by negotiating agreements among key elites and thereby creating more stable, one-party regimes with a powerful central ruler who limited political competition (Tanzania and Kenya are classic examples). Regimes that could not achieve this spiraled into crisis, with military coups a common result (our case study of Nigeria is a prime example). While not sharing modernization theorists' belief in the positive aspects of military rule, Allen does concur with their understanding of coups as coming from failures of civilian leadership.

A second school of thought looked not at society but within military organizations themselves. These theorists argued that a military engages in a coup to advance its own institutional interests, such as getting larger budgets, higher pay, or better equipment (Huntington 1964; Janowitz 1964). When military leaders perceive civilian rulers as not adequately considering the military's needs, they may intervene, not in the national interest, but rather to improve their own position. They may also instigate a coup in response to what they perceive as unjustified civilian intervention in military matters, such as the appointment of top officers without the military's approval or the

Coups in Africa

All of the major explanations for military coups could apply to Africa, one of the continents that has been most prone to coups over the years. As Map 9.1 and the In Context box on page 460 show, however, some African countries and some decades have seen more coups than others. What trends do you see in terms of where and when coups have happened? Can you formulate multiple hypotheses to explain these trends? Do the data in the map and the In Context box support any of the theories we've outlined for why coups occur? How would you try to determine which hypothesis best explains why coups occurred when and where they have in Africa?

MAP 9.1   **Coups in Africa**

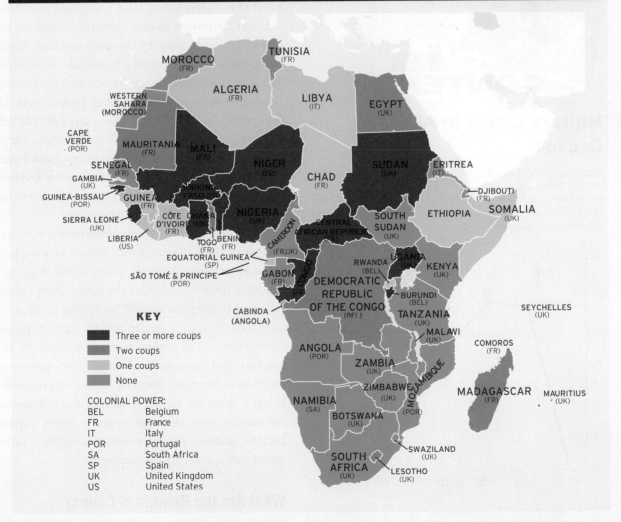

KEY

- Three or more coups
- Two coups
- One coups
- None

COLONIAL POWER:
BEL	Belgium
FR	France
IT	Italy
POR	Portugal
SA	South Africa
SP	Spain
UK	United Kingdom
US	United States

Source: Updated version of map in Peter J. Schraeder, *African Politics and Society: A Mosaic in Transformation,* 2nd ed. (New York: Thomson/Wadsworth, 2004), 203.

assignment of inappropriate duties. Military leaders may see a coup in these situations as a defense of their professional status vis-à-vis civilian leaders. In effect, the military in this theory is just another interest group clamoring for power and position within the government, but one with guns.

Samuel Decalo developed the third major explanation for coups by drawing on the ideas of neopatrimonialism. Focusing on Africa, he argued that the first two schools of thought misunderstood the nature of many African (and perhaps other postcolonial) militaries and therefore failed to recognize the true motivations for coups. The typical African military, he said, was "a coterie of distinct armed camps owing primary clientelist allegiance to a handful of mutually competitive officers of different ranks seething with a variety of corporate, ethnic and personal grievances" (1976, 14–15). He believed that prior theorists mistakenly viewed the military as a united and professional body concerned with either national interests or its own interests. Instead, he saw African armies as riven by the same regional, ethnic, and personal divisions that characterize neopatrimonial rule in general. Decalo argued that most coups occurred because particular military leaders wanted to gain power for their own interests, those of their ethnic group or region, or those of their faction within the military. Coups were about gaining a greater share of power and resources for the coup leaders and their clients, not about the interests of society as a whole or even "the military" as an institution.

As our case studies below demonstrate, it is often very difficult to discern which theory best explains a particular coup. Military leaders invariably claim that they intervened to save the nation from corruption and incompetence and, as always in modernizing authoritarian states, to provide unity to pursue development. The leaders portray the military as a modern and national institution that intervenes only out of necessity, but their subsequent rule often betrays them as having other motives. Knowing definitively why they intervened is often difficult because motives for intervention and their subsequent rule are not always connected.

What Are the Results of Coups?

Whatever the reasons behind coups, different kinds of militaries and different kinds of coups tend to

Web link:
List of coups
d'états

Video link:
Coups in
West Africa

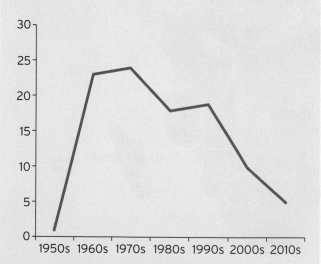

Military Coups in Africa by Decade

Nigeria's history of military coups and regimes from the 1960s into the 1990s was part of Africa's continuing pattern of coups and military rule in the region. Coups in the first decade of the twenty-first century were down 43 percent from the average of twenty-one coups per decade from the 1960s to the 1990s.

Source: George K. Kieh and Pita O. Agbese, *The Military and Politics in Africa: From Engagement to Democratic and Constitutional Control* (Aldershot, UK: Ashgate, 2002). Updated by the authors.

produce different kinds of military regimes. The factor that is probably of greatest importance in determining the kind of military regime is the institutional strength of the military itself, as we noted in chapter 8. A military that maintains a strongly hierarchical organization is less likely to produce a coup that is driven by individual or sectional interests. Rather, an institutionalized military might instigate a coup to try to create order out of political chaos or a coup that is in the narrow interests of the military as an institution. The military regime resulting from the coup is likely to be relatively institutionalized, predictable, and stable, if not necessarily legitimate. In addition, a coup carried out primarily in the interests of the military as an institution is likely to result in a shift of governmental resources toward military spending, which usually has deleterious economic effects overall. A more personal coup is likely to produce a more personalist regime that is far less institutionalized than other types of authoritarian regimes and is more subject to countercoups in the future.

CASE Study

COMPARING COUPS: BRAZIL AND NIGERIA

Brazil and Nigeria provide stark contrasts in the contexts of their coups, the nature of their militaries, and their postcoup regimes. They both demonstrate, however, the difficulty of explaining military coups. Political scientists have used both societal and institutional (within the military) arguments to explain Brazil's 1964 coup, which ushered in a bureaucratic-authoritarian state, a crucial milestone in the country's political and economic development. The Brazilian military was involved in politics since the founding of the republic in 1889. It was instrumental in the governments of the first decade and emerged again as central under the neofascist Estado Novo in the 1930s. Even during the country's democratic periods, the military has been politically influential. Elected officials regularly consulted with military leaders on a variety of policy issues, and the military leaders were quite willing to get involved in politics when they thought necessary, at least until the consolidation of Brazil's new democracy in the 1990s.

The origins of Brazil's 1964 coup can be traced to the creation of an elite military academy after World War II, the Escola Superior de Guerra (ESG), or Superior War College, which came to play an influential role in the Brazilian military and elite politics in

- **INSTITUTIONALIZATION** Brazil's military more institutionalized; Nigeria's less so

- **CAUSES OF COUPS** Societal versus military for Brazil; societal versus personal for Nigeria

João Goulart, Brazil's elected president who was overthrown by the country's military in 1964. Goulart's leftist policies and intervention in the military hierarchy helped provoke the U.S.-backed coup that initiated twenty years of military rule.

general. Its faculty developed what came to be known as the National Security Doctrine in the 1950s. This doctrine was then taught to ESG students, who were not only high-ranking military officers but also selected senior civilian officials. Essentially, it envisioned national security as including not just protection from foreign aggression but also economic development and prevention of domestic insurrection. At the height of the Cold War, the ESG military intellectuals saw domestic communist insurrection as a primary threat and strong economic development as essential to national security. The ESG's National Security Doctrine laid the intellectual roots for the 1964 coup and subsequent military regime.

In 1961 democratically elected president Jânio Quadros abruptly resigned and was succeeded by his vice president, João Goulart. Goulart was a leftist who seemed intent on reforming Brazil's very unequal society: strengthening labor unions, redistributing land, and providing greater benefits to the urban working classes. He clashed with both the military elite and the conservative majority in the National Congress, both of whom saw him as trying to move the country in the direction of socialism, and perhaps even communism. As Goulart failed to get his policies passed through the National Congress and faced growing opposition within the military, he became more populist. To try to gain greater military loyalty, he replaced several senior military officers who opposed him with others who were more supportive, thus dividing the military itself. Finally, in March 1964, he dramatically called for fundamental reforms that the conservative elite, both civilian and military, opposed. When junior navy officers revolted against their superiors, demanding the right to unionize, Goulart supported them.

The night after Goulart proclaimed his support for the naval officers, the military moved to take over the reins of government in a largely bloodless coup it dubbed the "Revolution." The regime it subsequently created was strongly institutionalized and based heavily on the National Security Doctrine. It attempted to keep a veneer of civilian rule by preserving most of the prior constitution, but it also issued Institutional Acts, which gave the military president the power to overrule the legislature and revoked many basic rights. Eventually, the party system was restricted to two tightly controlled parties, one that supported the regime and one that was allowed to oppose it within strict limits. When popular opposition from students, workers, and the rural poor arose, the military leadership did not hesitate to use force against them. Brazil's military government was far less brutal than many in Latin America at the time, but it nonetheless jailed and killed opponents when necessary.

Web link:
Telegram from the U.S. ambassador to Brazil, March 1964

Several explanations for the 1964 coup have been put forward. The best known is Guillermo O'Donnell's concept of the bureaucratic-authoritarian state. O'Donnell (1979) argued that the coup came about because of economic contradictions that the democratic government could not resolve. If capitalist industrialization was to continue, it required a repressive government to force it on an increasingly restless population. Industrialization and populism, the dominant way of mobilizing support in Brazil's democracy, had produced a growing working class that demanded a greater share of the benefits of economic growth. The elite realized that this would reduce the resources available for further investment. Additional industrialization would require investment in heavier industry, and that in turn would require lower wages. An elected government could not do this politically, so the military stepped in, under the auspices of its National Security Doctrine, to take the necessary steps.

Video link:
Anniversary of 1964
Brazil coup

Other analysts, however, have noted that the coup itself was caused just as much by Goulart's direct threat to the military hierarchy. By removing military officers who opposed him, and especially by supporting junior officers who wanted to unionize, Goulart was interfering with the autonomy of the military itself. Riordan Roett (1978) contended that the military remained divided over Goulart's economic policies but united in opposition to him because it saw him as undermining the autonomy of both the military and Congress. It is entirely possible, of course, that these two sets of factors (economic pressures plus threats to the autonomy of the military) dovetailed, coming together to give the military the incentive and justification to intervene and set Brazilian politics on a fundamentally different course.

Nigeria's military is very different from Brazil's because it is far weaker as an institution. Nevertheless, Nigeria's history of regime changes once again demonstrates the difficulty of understanding the motives for military coups. The country has had six successful coups (see the timeline in chapter 8) and at least two failed coup attempts. Without exception, each of the military leaders came to power promising to serve only in a

Military Coups in Latin America by Decade

Brazil's military coups and regimes (1930–1945 and 1964–1985) were part of a broader trend of coups and military rule in the region that has declined over time.

Source: Data are from *Political Handbook of the World 2011* (Washington, DC: CQ Press, 2012).

"corrective" capacity to end corruption, restore order, and revive the economy before handing power back to elected civilians. In reality, the military ruled for two very long periods (1966–1979 and 1983–1999) under multiple leaders and returned the country to democratic rule only after much domestic and international pressure. Analysts have identified both societal and individual motives behind the actions of Nigeria's military. We focus here primarily on two of the six coups: those that overthrew democratic governments.

The first two military interventions happened six months apart in 1966. Nigeria's First Republic, its initial postcolonial democracy, had very weak institutions and grew increasingly chaotic from independence in 1960 until 1966. The democratic government and subsequent military governments were riven by increasingly intense ethnic rivalries. Numerical advantage gave the northern region control of the government at independence. After the government manipulated two elections, citizens in the western region, who felt the northern-dominated government had stolen control of the country, turned violent. By late 1965, the national government had lost effective control of the western region, and general lawlessness was spreading throughout the country.

In January 1966, five army majors led a rebellion in an attempt to overthrow what they saw as an illegitimate national government. Most of the leaders, including Gen. Johnson T. U. Aguiyi-Ironsi, who ultimately took over as the military ruler, were ethnic Igbo from the eastern region. In carrying out the coup, they killed several important northern and western political and military figures but no eastern ones. Ironsi abolished all parties and ethnic associations, and soon declared the end of Nigeria's fractured federalism, creating a unitary state instead. Many analysts viewed Ironsi as genuinely interested in national well-being, but northerners saw the coup and Ironsi's elimination of federalism as an attempt by the eastern, Igbo military elite to centralize all power for themselves. Six months later, the northerners responded with a counter-coup that brought army chief of staff Yakubu Gowon to power. Gowon was backed by northern military leaders who were intent on removing what they saw as an "Igbo" government. He immediately recreated a federal system, with twelve states replacing the former three regions. Eastern military leaders rebelled, proclaiming themselves the leaders of the independent Republic of Biafra. A three-year civil war ensued. Gowon received much credit for winning the war and helping reconcile the nation afterward. As all of Nigeria's military leaders would do, he had from the start promised a return to democracy. By the mid-1970s, however, he and the military governors of the states were seen as increasingly corrupt, stealing from Nigeria's rapidly growing oil revenues and continually delaying the promised return to democracy. Ultimately, other northern military leaders overthrew him and returned the country to democracy in 1979.

That democracy would last until 1983, and in many ways, the events of that year can be seen as a repeat of those of 1965, though without the same ethnic conflict. The Second Republic government that was elected in 1979 and reelected in 1983 was again dominated by officials from the northern region, and by 1983 it was both corrupt and malfeasant. Nigeria's economy was declining as the level of corruption seemed to be skyrocketing and world oil prices were plummeting. Consequently, the 1983 election in which incumbent president Shehu Shagari was reelected was widely seen as fraudulent.

The coup weeks later came with little opposition. At first glance, one could say that the coup leaders were motivated by the weakness and chaos of the civilian regime. William Graf, a leading scholar of the era, argued differently (1988). In contrast to 1966, the coup leaders were not junior officers but rather the top military officials in the country, primarily from the north. This means that the coup was not ethnically motivated, in that both the perpetrators and the main victims were northerners. Graf went on to say that, instead, the main motivation for the coup was the desire of top officers to maintain their access to government resources and preserve the social status quo. He suggested that the top military officers took control because they saw the corruption of the civilian elite as excessive. The officers believed that corruption threatened to provoke an uprising within the military and perhaps within the broader society. Indeed, rumors abounded that junior officers, with a more radical interest in fundamentally changing the Nigerian regime, were about to stage a coup. In the subsequent regime (1983–1999), however, power remained in northern hands, among what Nigerians refer to as the "Kaduna mafia."

Web link:
In coup-prone Nigeria, two halves make a crisis

Nigeria's two coups that directly overthrew democratic rule can be explained by societal factors, which include the weakness of prior political institutions and increasing political and economic chaos. In both cases, the argument goes that the military stepped in to restore order in a situation in which stable democracy no longer existed. However, the leaders of the coups may have had other motives, and both faced subsequent countercoups. These brought to power northern military leaders who ruled for extended periods during which corruption grew and institutions weakened, as we discussed in chapter 8. Personal, ethnic, and regional interests in gaining power and resources seem at least as likely an explanation for the coups as the political problems the military allegedly stepped in to resolve.

CASE Summary   In both Brazil and Nigeria, understanding the precise motives for coups is difficult because while all coup leaders claim to intervene in the national interest, the subsequent governments, especially in the case of Nigeria, belie those intentions. Therefore, motives other than protecting the national interest seem at least equally plausible. The biggest difference between the two countries is probably the level of institutionalization of their militaries. Brazil's more institutionalized military entered politics with a clear ideology and was a strong enough institution to implement its vision, for better or worse, and it preserved some very limited civilian political participation in the process. Nigeria's far less institutionalized military reflected the country's ethnic and class conflicts, and it ruled in a far less institutionalized manner that ultimately undermined Nigeria's political institutions. It also engaged in at least as much corruption as the civilian officials it overthrew.

1. What does the comparison of military coups in Brazil and Nigeria teach us about the utility of the theories of why coups occur? Is one particular theory more convincing than the others in explaining coups in both countries? If not, why not?

2. What are the connections between why the coups happened in the two countries and the characteristics of the subsequent military regimes? (You might want to look back on the case studies of Nigeria in chapter 8 and Brazil in chapter 3 to help you answer this question.)

REVOLUTION

Military coups change governments and often regimes, while revolutions change the entire social order. Revolutions are rare and profound events that mark major turning points not only in the lives of the countries in which they occur but often in world history as well. On the continent of Africa alone there have been more than eighty military coups since 1960, whereas only a handful of revolutions have occurred elsewhere in the world.

As with so many terms in political science, scholars have debated endlessly how to define *revolution*. The important point for our purposes is to distinguish revolutions from other forms of regime change. We therefore define a **revolution** as a relatively rapid transformation of the political system and social structure; it results from the overthrow of the prior regime by mass participation in extralegal political action that is often, but not always, violent. The major revolutions in the modern era have happened in France (1789), Mexico (1910–1920), Russia (1917), China (1911–1949), Cuba (1959), Nicaragua (1979), Iran (1979), and the Eastern European satellite states of the Soviet Union—Bulgaria, Czechoslovakia, East Germany, Hungary, Poland, and Romania (1989–1990). More recently, the regime changes in Tunisia and Egypt in 2011 have often been referred to as revolutions. Whether they are or not, though, depends on their long-term outcomes. They certainly produced regime change, but whether they will fundamentally change the political and social structure of the countries seems less clear.

revolution
A relatively rapid transformation of the political system and social structure that results from the overthrow of the prior regime by mass participation in extralegal political action, which is often (but not always) violent

Web link:
List of revolutions

Types of Revolution

Political scientists distinguish among revolutions in several ways. One way is to classify them by the ideologies that inspire them: the liberal revolution of France, the communist revolutions of Russia and China, and the Islamic revolution of Iran. These ideological differences would seem to be crucial, yet most scholars of revolution argue just the opposite, that the ideological motivations and pronouncements of key leaders do not explain very much about revolutions. Typically, only the top leadership

Lech Walesa, the trade union leader who became the chief leader of the anticommunist movement in Poland, campaigns for president in 1989. The collapse of communism in eastern Europe from 1989 to 1991 is the most recent example of full revolutions: not only the regime but also the social and economic structures of society fundamentally changed. Some countries, like Poland, became fully democratic, while others did not; but they all profoundly changed via revolutions, the rarest form of regime change.

thoroughly understands and believes in the ideology in whose name the revolution is fought. Many participants have other motivations for joining the revolution, and specific political circumstances must exist for revolutions to succeed. Ideology helps more to explain the outcomes of revolutions in that the subsequent regimes, as we discussed in chapter 3, arise out of the ideological commitments of the revolutionary leadership. However, ideology usually does not tell us much about why the revolutions happened in the first place.

A common way that scholars distinguish among revolutions is to classify them as either **revolutions from above** or **revolutions from below.** The classic revolutions before the 1980s are the main cases on which theories of revolution are based, and these were all revolutions from below; that is, in each the mass uprising of the populace to overthrow the government was a central part of the process. Some scholars argued that the revolutions to end communism in Eastern Europe, in contrast, were primarily revolutions from above (Sanderson 2005). The end of communism was certainly a revolution in the sense that the fundamental social and economic structures of societies were transformed from communist to capitalist. Political changes were equally dramatic, though they varied more widely. Some countries created fully democratic regimes while others created new forms of authoritarian rule, though none of the new regimes was communist. While popular pressure was certainly involved in the process, communism fell in most countries primarily because the political elite within the system abandoned it, choosing instead to create new systems. The outcomes were often negotiated among political elites, each with the backing of a segment of the populace. In contrast to revolutions from below, massive and violent uprisings usually did not occur and were not necessary, and except for the ill-fated Soviet coup attempt of August 1991, the old regime was not able to strike back violently against the

revolutions from above
Revolutions in which the outcomes are negotiated among political elites, each with the backing of a segment of the populace

revolutions from below
Revolutions in which a mass uprising of the populace to overthrow the government plays a central role

Video link:
Burma's unlikely revolution from above

Video link:
The revolutions of
1989

revolutionary forces. These revolutions from above happened relatively peacefully and quickly. Several of them also produced liberal democracy, an outcome that no revolution from below has yet achieved.

Why Do Revolutions Happen?

As they have regarding military coups, comparativists have developed several theories to explain why revolutions occur and their likely outcomes. These theories focus on the economic structure of the old regime, psychological theories of the motivation to revolt, the resources and organization of the revolutionary movements, the structure and weakness of the old state institutions, and the process of modernization. The first theorist of revolution in the modern era was Karl Marx. As we explained briefly in chapter 3, Marx believed that social revolution was the necessary transition from one mode of production to another, and that the most important transition would be from capitalism to communism. Therefore, he thought the major revolutions of the future would be communist and would happen first in the wealthiest, most advanced capitalist countries. Events would show that he was clearly wrong about where, and therefore why, revolutions would occur. Most major revolutions from below since Marx's death have been communist-inspired, but they have not happened in wealthy capitalist societies or democracies. Instead, they have occurred in relatively poor countries with authoritarian regimes, most notably in Russia and China. On the other hand, most revolutions from above have not been inspired by communism but instead by the desire to put an end to communism.

Marx explained revolutions as the result of a particular historical situation. More recently, numerous scholars have viewed revolutions as part of the modernization process more generally. Samuel Huntington (1968) saw them as being most likely to occur after economic development has raised popular expectations and political demands, but state institutions have not developed adequately to respond to them. Steven Pincus (2007) argued more narrowly that state modernization is the key: revolutions are most likely when the old regime is attempting to modernize the state, which brings new groups into contact with the state and expands its activities. If, in this process, it becomes apparent that the state may lack a full monopoly on the use of violence, revolutionary leaders will try to take advantage of the situation. Perhaps the most influential modernization approach, though, was Barrington Moore's *Social Origins of Dictatorship and Democracy* (1966). Moore set out to answer not only why revolutions occur but also why democracies emerge in some places and dictatorships (sometimes via revolutions) in others. He focused on the transition from agricultural to industrial society, arguing that if the landed elite commercializes agriculture by removing the peasants from the land and hires labor instead, as happened in Britain, the landed elite would ultimately become part of the bourgeoisie and demand liberal rights, putting the country on the path to liberal democracy. In contrast, if the peasantry remained on the land into the modern era, as in Russia and China, they continued to be affected by the commercialization of agriculture in ways that harmed them. In response, they provided the basis for revolutionary communist movements.

Many scholars have searched for theories that try to explain revolutions more broadly, outside the context of particular historical periods. One group focused primarily on the motivations of the populace to participate, often using social-psychological theories. James Davies (1962) argued that revolution occurs at periods of rising expectations: people don't revolt when they are at their lowest point but rather when things have started to get better and they want more. Ted Robert Gurr (1970) contended that relative deprivation explains revolution because people revolt when they feel deprived relative to what they believe they deserve. Our case study of Brazil may be an example of this. While it hasn't seen a revolution, in June 2013 widespread protests broke out, with hundreds of thousands of people participating in cities across the country. The protests were targeted at the government for raising public transportation fares, corruption, and spending too much money building stadiums for the 2016 World Cup and not enough money on schools and other basic services. The protests broke out after years of a booming economy. The government had used that economic growth and stronger social welfare programs (see chapter 11) to cut poverty in half. Economic growth slowed dramatically, however, starting in 2011, perhaps dashing what had been rapidly rising expectations. This was likely one of the causes of the massive protests.

Was the American Revolution Really a Revolution?

The careful reader might note that we did not include the United States in our list of countries where major revolutions have occurred. This may come as a surprise to American students who are accustomed to thinking of the "American Revolution" as a pivotal historical event. It certainly was that, but whether it was a revolution in the sense that comparativists use the term has been subject to extensive debate. Barrington Moore (1966) argued that the real revolution in the United States was the Civil War, which ended slavery as an economic system and established the dominance of industrial capitalism. The crux of the debate is whether the American war for independence and the founding of a new republic fundamentally transformed not just political institutions but society as a whole. It was clearly the first nationalist war to throw off the yoke of colonial rule. It also clearly established an unprecedented republic based on liberal ideals that was a crucial milepost on the long road to liberal democracy. But was it a true revolution in the sense of creating fundamental social change?

One school of thought argues that the American War of Independence was led primarily by the colonial elite, who did not envision or implement a major redistribution of wealth. Granted, they eliminated British rule and created a new republic based on the republican ideal of equality of all citizens, but they defined citizens very consciously and deliberately as white male property owners. Wealth was actually distributed less equally after the war than it had been before, and, arguably, slavery was more entrenched (Wood 1992). Not only was slavery codified in the Constitution, but it expanded for several more decades. Indeed, the Constitution as a whole can be seen in part as an effort to limit the effects of egalitarianism in that it created an indirectly elected Senate to represent state governments rather than citizens and an indirectly elected president with the power to veto laws passed by the directly elected House of Representatives.

The chief proponent of the view that the "American revolution" really was a revolution is historian Gordon Wood. Wood argued that the American Revolution "was as radical and as revolutionary as any in history" (1992, 5). Though he readily conceded most of the points mentioned above, he argued that the egalitarian ideals of republicanism created not just a political but also a social

(Continued)

(Continued)

and cultural revolution during and after the war. Republican thought did not deny the existence of all forms of superiority but instead argued that superiority should not come from birth but from talent and reason. Some men (women were not included) would rise to the top as leaders of the new society based on their abilities, their hard work, and the willingness of others to elect them to positions of leadership. Government was therefore to serve the public interest in a way that a monarchy never did or could.

This egalitarian ideal spread throughout society, Wood contended, leading to further questions about the prerogatives of rank and privilege. He noted numerous changes to social and cultural norms, such as pressure to end many private clubs, the taking of the titles "Mr." and "Mrs." that were previously reserved for the landed gentry, and the shift from reserving the front pews in churches for select families in perpetuity to selling rights to those pews to the highest bidders. As the latter suggests, the revolution caused commerce to expand rapidly as well; wealth became even more unequally distributed, but many new men gained it. This revolution of ideas and in the way men treated other men (the treatment of women changed little, and wouldn't for well over a century) helped to create a new society never before seen in which inherited status was considered illegitimate and leadership and high status were to be based solely on merit and election.

In the long term, the American Revolution clearly had a profound effect, especially due to its notion of equal citizenship. As Wood rightly noted, its ramifications went far beyond what its original Founders intended. But most of the political and social elite before the War of Independence remained the elite after the war. As for the grand ideals of equality, they applied only within the very restricted realm of white, male property owners for another generation. As Crane Brinton (1965) noted in his classic study of revolutions, the American Revolution (which he included as one of his cases) is also quite peculiar in its evolution and result: no reign of terror occurred, as is so common in revolutions, and an authoritarian state did not ultimately result. This isn't to say that it's a bad thing that these events didn't happen, but their absence, along with the other points above, raises questions about whether the first war of independence against European colonialism was also a revolution.

Video link:
Really a
revolution?

A later school of thought, following the "contentious politics" framework we discussed in chapters 4 and 7, claimed that resources and political opportunity are required to produce a revolution, not just motivation. Adequate resources in the hands of revolutionary groups or a weak and therefore vulnerable state, or both, are necessary conditions, they argued, for successful revolutions to occur. Charles Tilly (1978) suggested that the directly political dimension of a potentially revolutionary situation is important because not only must there be grievances against the old regime, but also an organization that can mobilize those grievances into a powerful mass movement. Theda Skocpol (1979) noted that a crucial ingredient for successful revolutions is a state in crisis, often one that has been weakened by international events. She pointed to the effects of World War I on Russia as an example. A revolution can only happen where a state faces a severe crisis and lacks the resources to respond, creating a political opportunity. Combined with a mass uprising, this conjunction of events explains the major revolutions of the past as well as the infrequency of revolutions today, she argued. Jeff Goodwin (2001) also focused on the state but argued that certain types of states are prone to revolution: those with weak, neopatrimonial regimes that exclude major groups from a share of power. These regimes are not capable or willing to allow political opposition some role in politics, which forces them to turn to revolution as the only option for change, and the states' weakness means they cannot resist revolutions once started.

As with many areas of comparative politics, the theoretical debate over the cause of revolutions will undoubtedly continue. Some scholars see revolutions as products of particular historical epochs or transitional periods, which could help explain why there seem to be fewer of them now than in the past. Others see them as the result of forces and circumstances not tied to a particular era, such as rising expectations, contentious politics, or weak states. If they are correct, then revolutions are probably likely to occur again. Understanding which approach, then, is correct has significant implications for our ability to predict the future.

Revolution or Terrorism?

Revolutions and coups bring to mind an image of armed men taking over a state, perhaps killing innocent civilians in the process. A more contemporary image of politically instigated violence is terrorism. An important question in the new millennium is the difference, if any, between revolution and terrorism. Is a revolutionary a terrorist, and vice versa? Is *terrorist* just a new term for *revolutionary*? Both revolution and terrorism can be forms of **political violence**, the use of violence by nonstate actors for political ends. We include the term *nonstate* in this definition simply to distinguish political violence that is conducted by individuals or groups who are not acting on behalf of a state from war or other violent acts that are conducted by states. We make no assumption or argument here about the ethical superiority or justification of political violence vis-à-vis war, but we think it is useful to distinguish the terms analytically.

Despite the fact that they both involve political violence, revolutions and terrorism have fundamental differences. The most important distinction is between ends and means. Successful revolutions result in a fundamental transformation of a society. They are usually violent, but not always. Their end, or goal, distinguishes them from other types of political movements or political violence. **Terrorism**, on the other hand, is a means. It can be defined quite simply as political violence targeted at civilian noncombatants. Some revolutionaries have certainly used terrorism and some terrorists have been revolutionaries, but not all.

Revolutionaries by definition seek to overthrow an existing state. On the other hand, leading scholar of terrorism Martha Crenshaw (1981) long ago noted that terrorists usually have different purposes. The most common goal of an act of terrorism is to influence a broader audience, not the actual target of the violence. Revolutionaries aim at the state and attempt to overthrow it. Terrorists generally try to avoid the state and make no effort to overthrow it; they typically engage in acts of terrorism, whatever their long-term political goals, to inflict violence without directly confronting the state.

political violence
The use of violence by nonstate actors for political ends

terrorism
Political violence targeted at civilian noncombatants

(Continued)

(Continued)

Some terrorists may indeed pursue revolutionary aims, but many do not. Since 2001, the primary form of terrorism in the news is connected with radical Islamists, but many political groups, such as the Irish Republican Army (IRA) in Northern Ireland, have engaged in terrorism with national-ist, secessionist, or other secular aims that fall short of a full social revolution. Al-Qaida and related groups certainly seem to seek the establishment of a new type of society, though it is unclear how much they wish to take over existing states. Much of their ideology centers on the purification of the Islamic *umma*, the transnational Muslim religious community. Some groups, such as the Taliban when it was in power in Afghanistan, seem willing to mostly ignore the state rather than build a new one once they have destroyed the old. This is in marked contrast to revolutionaries, whose primary aim after the revolution is to build a new state. When an Islamist extremist attacks a Western target, it is often not completely clear whether he seeks to undermine the existing social order (in Western or Islamic coun-tries), to force the West (especially the United States) to change its foreign policy, or to encourage religious reform within exist-ing Islamic societies. The aims of such an extremist may or may not be "revolutionary" in the sense of how the term is used in comparative politics.

Comparativists and others have used a wide array of theo-ries to try to explain terrorism. This debate draws on many of the ideas such as contentious politics used previously to explain revolutions or social movements (see chapter 7). Scholars have argued that motivation for terrorism comes from psychological sources, relative deprivation or other types of alienation, structural inequalities, charismatic leaders, or ideological (including religious) beliefs. Others note that, like revolutions or social movements, terrorism requires resources and political opportunities to actually happen, regardless of individual motivations.

Terrorism, a concept that has been around for two hundred years, has become a "hot" new topic in international politics, but methods of understanding it have largely been based on long-standing theories in comparative politics.

What Are the Results of Revolution?

Aside from some of the former Communist countries of Eastern Europe, the general outcome of revolution has been fairly consistent: authoritarian rule and the creation of stronger states. Postrevolutionary governments have taken various forms, based in part on the ideological beliefs of their revolutionary leaders, but none has become an enduring democracy directly after the revolution. This was true even in France, where many of the revolution's leaders were liberals. Skocpol (1979) argued convincingly that all major revolutions, which were caused in part by the weakness of the *ancien régime,* ultimately created stronger states than had previously existed in those countries.

Scholars account for these outcomes by pointing out the extremely difficult politi-cal circumstances facing postrevolutionary governments. The entire regime and social structure have been overthrown, so new ones must be created. Massive violence out-side the control of the state is at the heart of most revolutions, and any new regime must recreate the state's monopoly on the use of force. Postrevolutionary societies are almost by definition deeply divided along ideological lines; the new leadership is com-mitted to a particular ideological blueprint of what the new regime and society should look like, while many followers do not fully share this commitment. All of these factors lead postrevolutionary leaders to brook little dissent and to view any opposition as a threat to the revolution. As our cases below demonstrate, the immediate postrevolu-tionary situation often includes a diversity of viewpoints, but those who do not share the vision of the key leadership are quickly eliminated, and with them go the prospects for democracy, at least in the short to medium term. As revolutionary leaders consolidate their power and eliminate their enemies, they create stronger states as well, at least in the short to medium term. Eventually, as the case of the Soviet Union attests, those states might weaken, but after the revolution is consolidated, the new state will be stronger than the old one was.

The exceptions to this rule are some of the postcommunist revolutions that were revolutions from above (for example, in the Czech Republic, Hungary, and Poland). The complete collapse of communism in the early 1990s led to a widespread perception in Eastern Europe that communist regimes were illegitimate; thus, postrevolutionary divisions in these cases were not nearly as great as in classic revolutions. The populaces were also not as mobilized, and the revolutions from above were largely nonviolent. All of these elements made the compromises necessary for democracy more possible, though the failure to establish democracy in some of the postcommunist countries, including parts of Yugoslavia, Romania, and the Central Asian republics, indicates that a democratic outcome was by no means guaranteed (Sanderson 2005).

REVOLUTION: CHINA AND IRAN

While political scientists have long debated the causes of revolutions, looking at actual revolutions suggests that they cannot be explained by any single factor. Several factors came together simultaneously to create the conditions for revolution in our case studies, and this perhaps explains why revolutions have been such rare events. The outcomes of these revolutions were similar in that they produced authoritarian regimes, but these regimes are quite distinct because they are based on the differing ideologies of the revolutionary leaders.

The revolution in China in 1949 resulted from a combination of a sense of relative deprivation on the part of the peasant majority, the creation of a political organization (the Communist Party) that could mobilize popular discontent, and an extremely weak state. The first Chinese revolution, which was largely a revolution from above, occurred in 1911 when the *ancien empire* finally fell. The peasantry, which constituted the great majority of the population, had long-standing grievances and a tradition of revolting against local landlords who became too repressive. During the late nineteenth and early twentieth centuries, though, the peasantry faced greater impoverishment than

- **SIMILARITIES**
  Relative deprivation, weakened state, and political opportunity cause revolutions

- **DIFFERENCES**
  Strength and unity of revolutionary political organization

Crowds in Beijing welcome Communist Party soldiers in January 1949. The Communist takeover led by the party and its leader, Mao Zedong (center picture on the banner), was a classic social revolution that created a regime that, while dramatically changed, remains in power today.

usual as the empire declined and lost control of much of its territory to Japanese and Western interests. A younger generation of elites increasingly questioned the traditions of and justifications for the old empire. In the first decade of the twentieth century, the Empress Dowager Cixi tried to respond to this growing disenchantment and rebellion with a series of reforms. Reformers, however, wanted far more radical change; many wholly rejected Confucian traditions and argued for a liberal society. Young military leaders in the provinces shared these sentiments and were the local leaders of the 1911 rebellion that created Sun Yat-sen's nationalist Republic of China.

The new republic failed to establish a democracy or hold the country together; regional warlords took over provinces and preyed on the local population while battling one another for territory. The plight of the peasantry only got worse. Chiang Kai-shek managed to reunite the country in 1927, but under a repressive authoritarian regime led by a group who referred to themselves as Nationalists. A new generation of people still clamored for change inspired by Western models, not only liberal ones but also communist. Members of the same young, educated elite who had championed nationalism and liberalism were the initial adherents of communism, with support from the newly established Soviet Union. The Communist Party became the principal military and political rival to the Nationalists in the 1920s. During the famous Long March (1934–1935), Mao Zedong gained control of the party and began implementing his major revision of Marxist revolutionary doctrine by focusing on the peasantry as a potentially revolutionary group.

At the end of the Long March, the Communists established themselves in Yenan in northern China, creating in effect a state within a state. They began implementing their new society, and for the first time in a century peasants saw their situation in life at least stabilize, if not improve. They became the backbone of Communist Party support. Mao also built up the party, welcoming intellectuals, elites, and peasants. It became the central authority in the "liberated" territory, an early version of the state he would create after 1949. The Communists' guerrilla tactics also proved effective against the Japanese occupiers during World War II and popular with the Chinese public, giving the Communists the mantle of defenders of the beleaguered nation.

After World War II, the final phase of the revolution broke out: a four-year civil war that the Communists won based on expanding support from the peasantry against Western-supported Nationalist forces. Communist victory ushered in a new state that completely changed Chinese society; a full social revolution from below had occurred. Like most revolutions, it resulted in an authoritarian state. Those who had supported the revolution but were not Communists, and even Communists who argued for alternatives to Mao's preferred policies, were quickly eliminated, making the People's Republic of China a full-scale dictatorship.

The 1949 revolution certainly was based on grievances among the peasantry, but success also required political resources—a mechanism through which local peasant grievances and revolts could be channeled into a broader movement—and the Communist Party became that mechanism. It successfully overthrew a regime that had been weak from its inception in 1911 and had been weakened further by its humiliation at the hands of the Japanese in World War II. Deprivation, state weakness, and political mobilization had to combine to produce the Chinese revolution.

The Iranian revolution of 1979 that created the Islamic Republic contrasted starkly with the Chinese Communist revolution in terms of ideology, but it emerged from roughly similar circumstances. A sense of relative deprivation arose among many segments of the population despite a growing economy; the old regime was weakened by at least the perception of a loss of international (especially U.S.) support; and a religious leader became the charismatic symbol of revolution. The movement, though symbolically led by the Ayatollah Khomeini, was not united under one organization like the Chinese Communist Party. After the revolution, therefore, numerous groups with differing ideologies competed for power. Khomeini and his religious followers simply proved to be the most popular and were able to outmaneuver other groups to assume complete control during the first year of the new regime.

The shah of Iran's government had seemed to be a classic case of a modernizing authoritarian regime during the 1960s and 1970s. The shah consciously sought to modernize society by encouraging foreign investment, greater mechanization of agriculture, access to higher education, and secularism. These policies, however, did not benefit everyone equally. Instead, they favored larger over smaller enterprises, foreign over domestic investors, and urban over rural interests. While economic growth and personal incomes rose noticeably on average, what the poor saw was the elite's conspicuous consumption, which they compared with their own very meager gains. The 1973 quadrupling of world oil prices brought Iran a glut of wealth but skewed its distribution even further. Modernization of agriculture drove rural migrants to the cities, and there they joined the long-standing *bazaari* groups (petty traders in Iran's traditional bazaars). *Bazaaris* felt threatened by modernization as well, as the shah encouraged Western shops and banks to open in Iran to cater to the growing urban middle class, thus reducing the *bazaaris'* market opportunities (Clawson and Rubin 2005).

Video link:
Communist takeover of China

Web link:
Fifty years of communism in China

The *bazaaris* and recent urban migrants, along with students and workers, became key supporters of the revolution. Opposition to the shah had survived underground ever since the early 1950s but was divided along ideological lines among nationalists who wanted greater democracy, Marxists, and religious groups. Secular intellectuals wrote anonymous letters and circulated pamphlets calling for the overthrow of the shah. The Islamic clergy opposed the shah's Westernization policies as a threat to Islam. Exiled radical cleric Ayatollah Khomeini increasingly became the chief symbol of opposition to the regime, and even though the opposition groups supported varying ideologies, they all united in opposition to the shah.

A perception that the shah's regime was weak was a crucial element in igniting the actual revolution. U.S. president Jimmy Carter enunciated a new foreign policy based on human rights and noted the shah's regime as one that did not adequately protect such rights. The United States had strongly supported the regime for decades, so even the hint of U.S. willingness to consider regime change inspired the opposition to act. In January 1978, the government wrote a newspaper article attacking Khomeini. The following day, theology students organized a large demonstration in protest in the holy city of Qom. The shah's police responded with violence, and at least seventy people were killed. The religious opposition, joined by students and the *bazaaris*, then used the traditional mourning gatherings for those killed to organize greater demonstrations. By September, a demonstration of more than a million people took place in Tehran, and the shah once again reacted with the use of force: more than five hundred people were killed. The government declared martial law shortly afterward, shutting down universities and newspapers. This only led to greater opposition as the urban working class joined the movement by organizing strikes, including in the country's crucial oil sector.

By December, the shah had tried to respond to the rising revolt by replacing his prime minister, but this was not nearly enough to satisfy the growing opposition. In January 1979, the new prime minister managed to get the shah to leave office "temporarily" and began dismantling his hated secret police. The opposition, though, demanded Khomeini's return from exile, a demand the government continued to resist until finally giving in on February 1. Khomeini immediately declared one of his supporters the "real Prime Minister," a claim the government rejected. The opposition mobilized its followers to invade prisons, police stations, and military bases on February 10 and 11 to take them over in the name of the revolution. After two bloody days in which hundreds more people were killed, the revolutionaries succeeded in gaining power.

Video link:
Iranian revolution, 1979

Unlike the Chinese revolution, however, no single political organization had control of the movement. Khomeini was the charismatic and symbolic leader, but one who also pledged to work with other forces. The revolutionary forces that came to power included religious groups that followed Khomeini, secular liberal nationalists who argued for democracy, and Marxists of various sorts. Over the course of the first year, however, Khomeini systematically put his supporters in charge of key institutions and called for an early referendum on the creation of an Islamic republic. The population overwhelming approved this move, and the new constitution discussed in chapter 8 was put in place. Over the next few years, Khomeini and his religious supporters increasingly repressed the other factions of the revolutionary movement to take firm control and create Iran's authoritarian theocracy.

CASE Summary   The revolutions in China and Iran both came out of societies in which a sense of relative deprivation was widespread and the state had been noticeably weakened. The Chinese people had seen massive social dislocation and economic decline for at least fifty years prior to the revolution, while Iranians had witnessed a growing economy that precipitated growing inequality. Both felt a sense of deprivation relative to what they thought they deserved. Both states were weakened and appeared vulnerable, though in China's case the decline of the state was much more severe. The political organization that took advantage of the revolutionary opportunity in China was much more united and organized than the mix of forces that overthrew the shah, resulting in a more united, but also more ruthless, postrevolutionary regime in China.

CASE Questions

1. We argued that relative deprivation, state weakness, and political opportunity caused the revolutions in China and Iran. Look back at our discussion of the causes of revolution. Can you use some of the other theories to explain these two cases as well? Which theory do you find ultimately most convincing, and why?
2. Look back in chapter 8 at the case studies of the authoritarian regimes that resulted from these two revolutions. What elements of the later regimes can you explain by understanding the process and causes of the revolutions that created them?

DEMOCRATIZATION

In 1972 Freedom House, a nongovernmental organization (NGO) that analyzes the level of political and civil rights in countries around the world, classified forty-four countries as "free," meaning that they were fully functioning liberal democracies. In 1990 the number of "free" countries rose to sixty-one, and in 2013 it had grown to ninety. The third wave of democratization (the first two waves having followed each of the world wars) was a dramatic process. It included the "People Power" movement that overthrew the corrupt and brutal dictator Ferdinand Marcos in the Philippines, the fall of the Berlin Wall in Germany, and the election of Nelson Mandela in South Africa. It seemed that the world's people were arising en masse to demand democratic rights. Figure 9.1 shows the impact of the third wave, as the percentage of fully authoritarian regimes plummeted starting in the late 1980s while the number of democracies and semi-authoritarian regimes increased markedly.

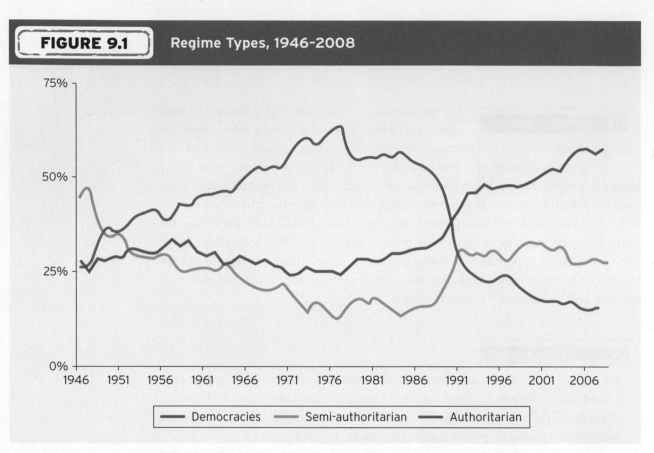

| FIGURE 9.1 | Regime Types, 1946-2008 |

Source: Fabrice Lehoucq, Figure 17.1, Regime Types, 1946-2008, "The Third and Fourth Waves of Democracy," in Jeffrey Haynes, ed., *Routledge Handbook of Democratization* (Routledge: New York, 2011), 274. Reprinted with permission of Taylor & Francis Books (UK).

Note: Semi-authoritarian regimes are regimes with scores between -5 and 5. Authoritarian regimes score between -10 and -6 and democracies rate between .6 and 10. The labels shown above have been modified from the original by the authors to conform to terminology used in this book. What was shown as "semidemocracy" in the original figure is referred to as semi-authoritarian in the above; "autocracy" is labeled here as "authoritarian."

Without a doubt, democracy expanded, but the image of global mass rebellion overwhelming dictators and establishing lasting democracy was, alas, overly simplistic. Furthermore, in the new millennium, progress has slowed or even reversed. Freedom House data indicated that 2013 was the seventh straight year in which the number of countries that became less free was greater than the number that became more free. Comparativists have tried to understand the expansion of democracy and its more recent stagnation by asking why countries become democratic, how they become democratic, what obstacles they face, how democratic they are, how likely they are to stay democratic, and how they can become more democratic.

Prior to the third wave, all but a handful of democracies were wealthy, Western countries. In the 1950s and 1960s, political scientists understandably followed the ideas of modernization, arguing that democracy could be sustained only in certain types of societies. Seymour Martin Lipset (1959) famously argued that democracies arise only in countries with reasonably wealthy economies and a large middle class that is educated and has its basic needs securely met. In these societies, political competition is not too intense and therefore compromise, an essential component of democracy, is easier. In *The Civic Culture* (1963, 1989), Gabriel Almond and Sidney Verba argued that democracy can thrive only in countries that have democratic political cultures (what they called "civic cultures") in which citizens value participation but are willing to defer to elected leaders enough to let them govern. Other scholars argued that political developments must occur in a particular sequence. For instance, a strong state and sense of national identity must emerge before a democracy can.

The Transition Paradigm

The third wave wreaked intellectual havoc on modernization theories as democracy began breaking out in all the "wrong" places. First southern European and then Latin American military dictatorships became democratic. Then the end of the Cold War unleashed a new round of democracy creation, first in the former Communist countries of Eastern Europe and then in Africa and parts of Asia. These were countries that were far too poor, that still faced questions about the strength of their state and national identity, and that seemed not to have democratic cultures, yet here they were writing constitutions, holding elections, and establishing democracies. Almost out of necessity, a new approach to the study of democratization emerged. Influenced by rational-choice theory, a new generation of democratization theorists argued that democracy could emerge in any country if the major political elites came to see it as a set of institutions that could serve their interests, whether they or their followers actually believed in democratic principles or not. Well-institutionalized democracy provides all major political actors with a degree of participation, protection from the worst forms of repression, and the possibility that they can gain power at some point. These features led self-interested political leaders to create democracies in countries that comparativists previously had seen as bound to be autocratic for years to come. While theorists did not dispute the idea that democracy would be easier to sustain in countries that were wealthier and had prior democratic experience, the new "transition paradigm" provided a model for how democracy was possible anywhere.

Basing their ideas mainly on the experiences of southern Europe and Latin America, democratization theorists argued that understanding elite dynamics and negotiations in times of crisis was crucial to explaining this new process of **transition to democracy.** They defined this as a regime change typically involving a negotiated process that removes an authoritarian regime and concludes with the founding election of a new, democratic regime. When an authoritarian regime faced a severe crisis of some sort—economic downturn or succession were common crises out of which democracy could emerge—its leadership would split internally into **hardliners** and **softliners.** The former would believe in repressing any opposition and preserving the status quo, while the latter would be willing to consider compromising

transition to democracy
A regime change typically involving a negotiated process that removes an authoritarian regime and concludes with a founding election of a new, democratic regime

hardliners
Leaders of an authoritarian regime who believe in repressing any opposition and preserving the status quo when faced with a demand for political liberalization or democratization

softliners
Leaders of an authoritarian regime who are willing to consider compromising with opponents as a means to survive demands for democratization

radicals
Leaders of democracy movements who wish to achieve immediate and complete democracy and are unwilling to compromise with the existing regime

moderates
Leaders of democracy movements who are willing to compromise with the authoritarian regime to gain partial democracy

political liberalization
The opening of the political system to greater participation; typically before a transition to democracy

pact
In a transition to democracy, a conscious agreement among the most important political actors in the authoritarian regime and those in civil society to establish a new form of government

founding election
The first democratic election in many years (or ever), marking the completion of a transition to democracy

with opponents as a means to survive the crisis. Simultaneously, the crisis would produce a surge in the activity of civil society, typically led by unions, religious authorities, or middle-class professionals who demanded fundamental political reforms. Civil society subsequently would often divide between **radicals,** who wanted immediate and complete democratization, and **moderates,** who were willing to compromise with the authoritarian government to make some gains. A successful transition to democracy would be most likely if the softliners in the regime and the moderates in civil society could each gain the upper hand over their internal opponents and then negotiate with one another to establish new rules of the game. Some form of democracy, though often with limits, would become a compromise on which both sides could agree (Huntington 1991).

Most theorists believe that an ideal process of transition to democracy begins with **political liberalization,** or the opening of the political system to greater participation. This would include legalizing opposition parties, lifting restrictions on the media, and guaranteeing basic human rights. The political opening would allow negotiations between leaders of the old regime and those of the rising civil society. Ideally, this would result in a **pact,** an explicit agreement among the most important political actors in the regime and civil society to establish a new form of government. The pact would ideally produce a new democratic constitution and be followed by a **founding election.** This would be the first democratic election in many years (or ever) and would mark the completion of the transition. Most theorists argued that the regime and civil society have to be of roughly equal strength for the transition process to produce a full democracy. If the regime, and especially the hardliners within it, were very strong, it would control the process, and any democracy that resulted from the transition would have significant limitations. In Chile, for instance, the military under dictator Augusto Pinochet wrote a democratic constitution that reserved seats in the Senate and control of the central bank for the army. On the other hand, if civil society, especially its more radical elements, were too strong, it would demand full democratization with no protection for members of the old regime, and the resulting hardliner backlash would crush the nascent democratization.

South Africa's transition to democratic rule in 1994 is a classic case of the transition process. The apartheid regime was besieged internally and externally in the 1980s. It faced widespread international sanctions and an increasingly violent and radical uprising on the streets of the black townships. It had tried modest liberalizations such as allowing mixed-race people some minimal political participation, but this was met with simply more resistance. Upon coming to power in 1990, President F. W. de Klerk shocked the nation and the world by quickly announcing that he was freeing Nelson Mandela from prison and lifting the ban on Mandela's party, the African National Congress. Faced with a crisis that he did not believe his government could contain, de Klerk became a softliner who, after secret negotiations before the public announcement, came to see Mandela as a moderate with whom he could negotiate.

Three years of negotiations for a new constitution ensued, with white hardliners and black radicals frequently and sometimes violently attacking the process and both parties involved. Ultimately, though, Mandela and de Klerk held majority support of their respective communities and agreed on a pact, a new constitution that was then ratified by the population. On April 27, 1994, Nelson Mandela was elected president, ending the world's last bastion of legal racial segregation. The ANC has ruled ever since, though, which has raised questions about how fully democratic the society has really become.

South Africa's successful transition was not completely surprising, in that it was a middle-income country; its level of socioeconomic development seemed to make democracy plausible. A much more surprising African success story was Ghana, a country with a history of military coups and a Gross National Income per capita of only $1,410 in 2013. As the third wave of democratization washed over Africa, Ghanaian military ruler Jerry Rawlings agreed to allow multiparty competition based on a new constitution that he and his aides wrote. It created a presidential system that gave the president great powers, and Rawlings won the subsequent election. Domestic and international electoral observers saw significant electoral fraud, and many feared Ghana's democracy might be stillborn. After that founding election, however, the electoral commission brought the major political leaders together to discuss what electoral rules they would use in the future. With the support of external aid, the leaders helped strengthen the national election commission itself, which helped the opposing leaders gain some trust in one another and in the political process in general. The greater fairness of the next election in 1996 reinforced this trust. While Ghana did not have a full pact, the major leaders did agree on a set of electoral rules that they came to accept and believe would work. In 2000 Rawlings was constitutionally barred from running for a third term. He did not resist leaving office, and without Rawlings leading the ticket his party lost the election; power changed hands from one elected leader to the next for the first time in Ghana's history. In 2008 Rawlings's party won the presidency again, by less than one-half of 1 percent of the vote. The losing party ultimately accepted the outcome of what was called Africa's closest election ever, and for the second time, power was peacefully transferred from one party to another. Ghana's democracy is certainly not perfect, but in contrast to our case study of Nigeria and many other African countries, democracy is functioning well; Freedom House has long rated it as fully "free."

These cases of successful transitions to democracy in countries that modernization theorists of the 1960s and 1970s would have thought could not be democratic show the power of the transition paradigm in understanding how new democracies can arise in some of the least expected places. Creating a democracy and sustaining it longer term, however, are two different things. While numerous transitions took place in the 1990s, many of them did not produce long-lasting democratic regimes. That became the next big question for students of democratization.

Video link:
Interview with Nelson Mandela

Video link:
Five lessons for nations in transition

The Arab Spring: Revolution, Democratization, or None of the Above?

As 2011 began, the world watched as seemingly out of nowhere tens of thousands of Tunisians took to the streets, demanding the ouster of the country's long-ruling president, Zine Ben Ali, in what came to be known as the Jasmine Revolution. As this revolt unfolded, Egyptians began flooding the main square in Cairo, demanding the ouster of their even longer-ruling president, Hosni Mubarak. In just six weeks, two of the oldest and seemingly most stable authoritarian regimes of the Arab world had fallen. Protests erupted shortly afterward in both Libya and Syria as well, but with very different outcomes. Rather than the relatively peaceful creation of new regimes, both suffered civil war. Libya's ended with the ouster of the old regime, while Syria's regime clung to power and the war raged on in mid-2013. Protests broke out in several other Arab countries as well, but none saw a regime change or war; instead, the old regime successfully repressed the protests. Many people refer to the Arab Spring as a "revolution," but was it that, or was it democratization, or did the return of the military to power in Egypt in July 2013 represent a military coup? And what explains the different trajectories regime change took in these different countries?

The regime change in Tunisia could certainly be considered a political revolution, in that a movement from within society forced fundamental regime change, but neither it nor the short-lived regime change in Egypt were full-scale revolutions in the sense of fundamentally changing not only the political but also the social and economic structures of society. While the top rulers and a handful of their closest associates were ousted and either fled the country (in Tunisia) or were arrested (in Egypt), much of the elite stayed, and some became active participants in the new order. Even in Libya, some members of the old regime and elite remained as part of the new order, though in a much more chaotic situation.

As of mid-2013, Tunisia had successfully held new elections that put in place a three-party coalition government led by a moderate Islamist party. A controversy over writing a new, permanent constitution created political paralysis, as the governing party insisted on staying in power until the constitution was completed while their opponents demanded it resign before the talks began. Freedom House gave it a rating of 3.5, or "partly free," though close to being "free." Egypt's transition was more difficult and certainly remained incomplete in 2013. Both parliamentary and presidential elections were held, but were subject to much dispute. The Muslim Brotherhood, an organization similar to the ruling party in Tunisia, dominated the elections and formed the new

Rebels fight in Sirte, Libya, in October 2011. The personalist nature of the Libyan regime is one of the reasons why the country faced civil war rather than democratization when the regime fell. While a new government was in place, militia such as these were still not fully under government authority by 2013.

government. The Supreme Constitutional Court, however, annulled the parliamentary election and forced the parliament to disband. In response, President Mohamed Morsi, a member of the Muslim Brotherhood, declared in November 2012 that he would rule by decree until the new constitution was fully implemented and new elections held. The Brotherhood's opponents ultimately walked out of the negotiations for a permanent constitution, which the government nonetheless completed and the citizenry ratified via a referendum. In 2012 Freedom House rated Egypt at 5.5, which is also "partly free" but not far from the "not free" category.

Following Morsi's declaration that he would rule by decree, opposition mounted and his legitimacy plummeted. Secular opponents led large-scale demonstrations against him in July 2013, demanding his ouster. Fearing a complete breakdown of order, or at least interested in protecting its vast economic holdings in the country, the military stepped in and removed Morsi, which most observers saw as a coup. The military appointed a civilian leadership to rule, but the key leaders soon resigned in protest to the military's continued, brutal crackdown in opposition to it. The military rulers claimed they wanted all parties, including the Muslim Brotherhood, to participate in the political process, but the Brotherhood refused to recognize the new government's legitimacy and demanded Morsi's return to power. The military arrested most top Brotherhood leaders and killed scores of protesting Brotherhood members, raising questions about its claims to include all political forces in a future regime. By late 2013, the military regime seemed increasingly entrenched and the prospects for any future democracy grim. If a democracy does emerge, the Muslim Brotherhood, the most popular political force in the country in 2011, will almost certainly not be allowed to participate.

What explains these different outcomes, both in terms of Egypt vis-à-vis Tunisia but also those two regime changes versus civil war or repression elsewhere? A key part of the answer lies in the heart of any state and regime: the military. Both Egypt's and Tunisia's authoritarian regimes were relatively institutionalized, with coherent militaries that had major stakes in the stability of the society and economy. In both cases, the old rulers gave up power not when the protesters went into the streets, but when the military decided to support the protesters to protect its own interests vis-à-vis the regimes' top leaders. A united military forced the old dictators out of office and took an active part in the transition to a new regime. Stepan (2012) argued that in Tunisia the exiled secular and Islamist opposition leaders had been meeting secretly in Europe for several years and therefore knew and trusted one another. This allowed them to negotiate a pact with the military that created the new regime relatively seamlessly, creating a PR electoral system that ensured all significant parties would be well represented in parliament. In Egypt, military leaders initially took full control and pushed through enough constitutional changes to hold elections but preserved significant control for themselves. The secular and Islamist forces had not worked together at all and did not trust one another or the military. The single-member district (SMD) elections gave the Muslim Brotherhood dominant power in the elected bodies, but the military still retained control of its own interests, and the judiciary—still full of the appointees from the old regime—ruled important elements of the new regime illegal. By 2013, the legitimacy of all political institutions was seriously questioned by at least some

major segments of the population, and a deep chasm had clearly developed between the Muslim Brotherhood and more secular political forces.

The regimes in Libya and Syria were both much more personalist and divided. When protests broke out in Libya the regime responded with repression, but in the eastern region, which had never supported the dictator Muammar el-Qaddafi, protesters took over the major city and essentially declared themselves free of the regime. The military, like society at large, was divided by regional and kinship loyalties. Qaddafi responded with military force, but elements of the divided military broke off and formed independent militia, igniting the civil war. With Western support, the militia eventually gained control of the entire country. A new government was put in place and elections held, but it remained extremely weak, in large part because many of the militia remained independent; the state had not fully restored its monopoly on the legitimate use of force. The Syrian regime responded forcefully to protesters as well, which led to the creation of independent militia and the start of the civil war. Syrian society was divided along sectarian lines and some military personnel broke with the regime but most did not, enabling the regime to hold out much longer than in Libya (and the West, for strategic reasons, chose not to intervene). In still other countries, such as Bahrain, the military held firm with the regime and united, and protests were crushed.

The Arab Spring produced different outcomes in different places in part because of the nature of the authoritarian regimes and particularly the militaries at the heart of them. The distinct paths taken by the transitions to new regimes in Tunisia and Egypt, though, demonstrated key elements of the transition paradigm, particularly the importance of a pact to establish a new order to which all major political forces could agree. By 2013, tensions certainly remained in Tunisia, particularly between Islamist extremists who continued to push for a more Islamist regime and more secular Tunisians, but the basic institutions of a new democratic regime were functioning. In Egypt and Libya, the transition outcome remained far from clear.

Video link:
On democratization in the Middle East

Video link:
Why Egypt is not a good example of democratization

Democratic Consolidation

democratic consolidation
The widespread acceptance of democracy as the permanent form of political activity; all significant political elites and their followers accept democratic rules and are confident everyone else does as well

Transition theorists developed the concept of **democratic consolidation** to help answer the question of the sustainability of democracy, but much dispute over the definition and utility of the concept has arisen. Intuitively, democratic consolidation is simply the idea that democracy has become widely accepted as the permanent form of political activity in a particular country. It has become "the only game in town," and all significant political elites and their followers accept democratic rules and are confident that everyone else does as well. This is important, because democracy requires faith that in the future, any significant party or group might gain power via an election. If some major political actors do not believe that, they might be tempted to use nondemocratic means to gain power, fearing that their opponents will not give them a chance to win via free and fair elections in the future.

Knowing when a country has reached the point of democratic consolidation, however, is quite difficult: How can we know whether all the actors in the country have accepted democracy unquestionably? Samuel Huntington (1991) argued that a country must pass the "two-turnover test" before we can consider it a consolidated democracy: one party must win the founding election, and then a different party must win a later election and replace the first party. By this strict standard, West Germany did not become a consolidated democracy until 1969, India until 1980, Japan until 1993, Mexico until 2012, and South Africa still does not qualify. Whatever measure is used, though, it's clear that many new democracies have not fully consolidated.

The failure of many new democracies to achieve consolidation has resulted in growing skepticism of the transition paradigm and a reexamination of the older modernization thesis regarding where democracy will thrive. Adam Przeworski and colleagues (2000) created a data set of 141 countries from 1950 to 1990, asking if greater socio-economic development predicts both whether countries have transitions to democracy and how long those new democracies survive. They found a strong statistical relationship between development and the sustainability of democracy, arguing that "democracy is almost certain to survive in countries with per capita incomes above \$4,000" (Przeworski et al. 2000, 273), but a very weak relationship between development and the likelihood that a country would have a transition. They concluded that in terms of predicting transitions, "modernization theory appears to have little, if any, explanatory power" (Przeworski et al. 2000, 137). Carles Boix and Susan Stokes (2003) challenged these findings. They used the same data but removed some countries from it: states during the Cold War that were tightly controlled by the Soviet Union and countries heavily dependent on oil wealth. They argued that both of these factors would prevent democracy from occurring and therefore should not be included in a test of modernization theory overall. Removing these countries from the data, they concluded that for the countries on which the theory focuses—poor and middle-income countries—development does indeed make transitions to democracy more likely.

A similar debate arose among those examining the effects of culture. Ronald Inglehart and Christian Welzel (2005) used data from a global survey of citizen beliefs to examine the effect of what they call "emancipative values" on democracy, values that emphasize freedom of expression and equality of opportunities. They showed that even controlling for earlier experience with democracy and prior economic development, countries with higher emancipative values in the early 1990s were much more likely to have stronger democracies after 2002. Hadenius and Teorell (2005), however, criticized Inglehart and Welzel's measure of democracy, arguing it combined a real measure of democracy (Freedom House scores) with an unrelated measure of corruption. Using only the Freedom House measures, Hadenius and Teorell found no relationship between emancipative values and levels of democracy. Clearly, the debate over modernization theory remains unresolved.

Web link:
The debate about emancipative values

Transition theorists look for evidence of democratic consolidation because they fear democratic breakdown—that is, a return to authoritarian rule. Relatively few countries that have completed a transition to democracy, however, have reverted to full-scale authoritarian rule. Some hold reasonably free and fair elections but do not abide by the full array of liberal rights and the rule of law, while others become semi-authoritarian regimes in which a ruling party rigs elections as necessary to stay in power. The growing number of semi-authoritarian regimes has led scholars to ask whether and when these regimes might give way to greater democracy. Levitsky and Way (2010) argued that whether these regimes move toward democracy, move away from it, or remain stable semi-authoritarian regimes depends on Western linkage (economic, political, and social ties and cross-border flows with the West) and leverage (vulnerability to Western pressure), as well as the strength of the state and ruling party vis-à-vis the opposition. Strong Western influence raises the costs of authoritarian crackdown since those regimes face greater external pressure and thus tends to move the regimes toward democracy. Strong states and ruling parties in the absence of Western influence, though, tend to produce more fully authoritarian regimes, as the opposition cannot counter the regime's power and external pressure is weak. Lindberg (2009) showed how in Africa, elections can shift the balance of power between the ruling party and opposition. Even quite limited elections allow the opposition to win some share of power and give dissidents within the ruling party a viable alternative and thus an incentive to defect to the opposition. When political leaders think an opposition coalition has a real chance to win, they become even more likely to join it, further strengthening its chances until a "tipping point" is reached at which a large opposition coalition emerges to win an election in spite of the incumbent's manipulation of the system (Van de Walle 2006).

The Quality of Democracy

For democracies that avoided a reversion to authoritarian or semi-authoritarian rule, the next logical consideration is the quality of democracy, including the extent of participation, the rule of law, and vertical and horizontal accountability. Attempts to measure each of these areas have portrayed the quality of democracy produced by the third wave as distinctly mixed (Roberts 2010; Levine and Molina 2011). Scholars have tried to explain the weaknesses in new democracies by looking at the effects of rapid

Video link:
Levine and Molina
on the quality of
democracy

economic reform, ethnic fragmentation, weak civil society, and weak or inappropriate political institutions. Many scholars assumed that ethnic fragmentation in particular is likely to harm the chances of democracy; they argued that ethnically divided societies have a weaker sense of national unity that often results in bitter political competition for control of the state and therefore threatens to go beyond democratic norms and institutions. A study by Steven Fish and Robin Brooks (2004) across approximately 160 countries, however, found no correlation between ethnic diversity and the strength of democracy.

Transition theorists have long worried that if democracy does not produce favorable policy outcomes quickly, a populace with limited attachment to core democratic values will reject it altogether. Many postcolonial countries going through transitions to democracy simultaneously went through neoliberal economic reform, which in the short term often causes economic decline before it brings benefits. In her 2003 book *Ordinary People in Extraordinary Times*, Nancy Bermeo examined the hypothesis that popular disenchantment undermines democracy, looking at the breakdown of democracy in Europe before World War II and in Latin America in the 1960s. She found that the populace as a whole did not reject democracy in times of economic crisis but instead key elites did. The military in Latin America, for instance, feared economic instability and put an end to democracy without widespread popular support for their action.

Weak political institutions and civil society can also lead to democratic breakdown and the rise of semi-authoritarian regimes. The transition process in sub-Saharan Africa has not fit the model derived from Latin America and southern Europe very well because African countries possess much weaker institutions and civil societies. Michael Bratton and Nicholas van de Walle (1997) argued that Africa's neopatrimonial regimes result in transitions in which political competition remains primarily about securing access to government resources for patronage. Pacts almost never happen because parties are little more than temporary vehicles for shifting coalitions of patrons trying to gain power, and parties neither have sufficient ideological disagreements nor are stable enough to provide the credible commitments that pacts require. In the absence of pacts, incumbents typically do not liberalize their regimes completely, instead holding elections that are only partially free and fair. More often than not, they win those elections, and even when the opposition wins, it is likely to pursue a semi-authoritarian regime in order to maintain its access to key resources. Freedom House ratings reflect this outcome: while almost all African countries have experienced at least an attempted transition, only eleven were rated as "free" in 2013, while twenty were "partly free" and eighteen were "not free."

Not only weak institutions but also inappropriate ones can harm new democracies and create semi-authoritarian regimes. New democracies are often deeply divided societies, either ideologically or ethnically. Juan Linz (1990) argued that the "perils of presidentialism" (see chapter 6) are particularly important in new democracies. Because new democracies are often deeply divided and competing elites do not fully trust one another or the new democratic institutions, consensus democracies with power-sharing mechanisms such as coalition government in parliament are likely to help preserve democracy. Others disagree, suggesting instead that presidential systems can provide both democratic legitimacy and stability by having a single head of state directly elected by a majority of the nation. Kapstein and Converse (2008) argued that the issue of whether a new democracy is presidential or parliamentary is less important than how effective the limits on the executive are. Steven Fish (2006) supported this argument, using a new data set that measured the strength of the legislative branch to show that a strong legislature is the most important institutional ingredient in

MAP 9.2 Democratic Institutionalization

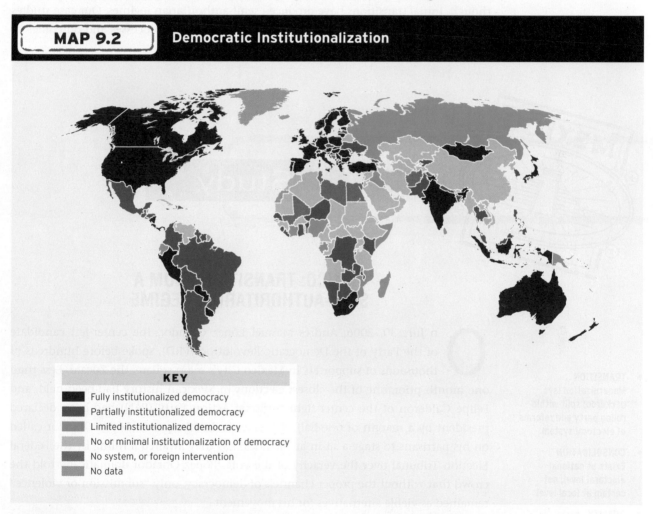

KEY

- Fully institutionalized democracy
- Partially institutionalized democracy
- Limited institutionalized democracy
- No or minimal institutionalization of democracy
- No system, or foreign intervention
- No data

Map 9.2 shows Polity IV institutionalized democracy scores for 2013. The Polity IV institutionalized democracy score measures the degree of institutionalization of democracy within a state, with 10 being the highest degree of institutionalization and 0 being the lowest. Democracy is conceived as three essential, interdependent elements: (1) institutions and procedures through which citizens can effectively express preferences for alternative policies and leaders, (2) institutionalized constraints on executive power, and (3) the guarantee of civil liberties to all citizens. Even this careful definition and data collection, though, demonstrate the difficulty of measuring democracy. Many analysts, for instance, would strongly question the conclusion that the Democratic Republic of the Congo is a "partially institutionalized democracy," given that it doesn't fully control its territory.

Source: Data are from Polity IV (http://www.systemicpeace.org/inscr/inscr.htm).

maintaining democracy, regardless of the kind of political system in place. On the other hand, Edward Gibson (2012) warned that even when national politics are democratized, "subnational authoritarianism" can survive as local leaders in federal systems are able to monopolize power, a problem we examine in our case study of Mexico below.

The 1990s were the halcyon days of democratization, when it seemed that democracy was spreading to nearly every corner of the globe. It has certainly spread significantly, with most Latin American countries making apparently long-term transformations toward consolidated democracy. Some Asian and African countries, as Ghana demonstrates, have also made successful transitions. In many other cases, though, initial transitions have produced semi-authoritarian regimes. Our case studies of Mexico, Russia, and Nigeria demonstrate the diverging processes and outcomes of the "transition era."

CASE Study

MEXICO: TRANSITION FROM A SEMI-AUTHORITARIAN REGIME

- **TRANSITION**
  Modernization lays backdrop; split within ruling party and reforms of electoral system

- **CONSOLIDATION**
  Exists at national electoral level; not certain at local level

- **QUALITY**
  Weak institutions, weak rule of law, corruption, drug-cartel violence, continuing clientelism

- **FREEDOM HOUSE RATING IN 2013: 3.0 = "partly free"**

On July 30, 2006, Andrés Manuel López Obrador, the center-left candidate of the Party of the Democratic Revolution (PRD), spoke before hundreds of thousands of supporters in Mexico City's main square, the Zócalo. Less than one month prior, one of the closest elections in Mexican history had been held, and Felipe Calderón of the center-right National Action Party (PAN) had been declared president by a margin of one-half of 1 percent. In his speech, López Obrador called on his partisans to stage a sit-in at the Zócalo as they awaited a ruling by the Federal Election Tribunal over the veracity of the vote. López Obrador dramatically told the crowd that without the proper channels of democracy, only "submission or violence" remained as viable alternatives for his movement.

Ultimately, the tribunal held Calderón to be the legitimate victor, but the summer of 2006 was a difficult test for Mexico's young democracy. Between the years 1929 and 2000, the PRI's semi-authoritarian regime (see chapter 3) made one-party rule a fact of life in Mexico, and this had been the only post-PRI election ever held. The contention surrounding Calderón's victory now threatened to plunge the country into disarray. But this never materialized, as the majority of the public soon turned its back on López

Enrique Peña Nieto, left, stands with outgoing president Felipe Calderón at Peña Nieto's inauguration in December 2012. Peña Nieto's victory returned the PRI, Mexico's ruling party during the semi-authoritarian regime, back to power, but this time via a fully democratic election. The transfer of power from the PRI to Calderón's PAN in 2000 and then back to the PRI in 2012 meant Mexico passed the "two-turnover test," a sign of democratic consolidation.

Obrador, preferring to accept the official results as declared by Mexico's democratic institutions. In response to the crisis, Congress passed electoral reforms that further leveled the playing field between the incumbent party and challengers, and in 2012 the PRI itself regained the presidency in an election that was not nearly as controversial as the prior one. In terms of credible national elections and the two-turnover test, Mexico is a consolidated democracy; in other ways, though, challenges remain.

Modernization theorists might have expected Mexico to democratize as early as the 1950s, but Sebastián Garrido de Sierra (2011) argued that three factors combined to delay democratization until well into the 1990s. First, prior to electoral reforms in the 1990s, Mexican elites did not have viable avenues to defect and form an opposition. Second, urbanization by the 1990s finally moved enough Mexicans away from the reach of the PRI's rural clientelistic networks and into areas where other forms of political mobilization were more easily achieved. Last but not least, a historic split in the leadership of the PRI created the necessary impetus for opposition.

The seeds of change, though, were sown much earlier. The PRI had maintained its authoritarian rule via large-scale clientelism, using state resources as patronage; repression when needed; and some legitimacy, mostly based on the relative success of the economy and the party's efforts to distribute wealth more widely than many governments do. As far back as 1968, the PRI began to lose legitimacy after the Tlatelolco massacre, which led to hundreds of deaths, mostly of students protesting against the government. A series of economic crises and downturns in the 1970s and 1980s further undermined the PRI's claims to legitimacy. After the biggest one, the 1982 debt crisis, the PRI began to shift toward neoliberal economic policies (see chapter 5) that undermined their sources of patronage and hurt the incomes of poor and rural people, two of their key constituents. The economic downturn also spurred activity in civil society questioning the government's policies and working to help those hurt by them. The spark that led to visible political change was a split in the ruling party. The shift to neoliberal policies created divisions between PRI leaders loyal to the party's traditional claims to egalitarianism and newer leaders who favored neoliberalism. When one of the latter was chosen as the presidential candidate in 1988, Cuauhtémoc Cárdenas, a PRI insider, revolted and ran as an opposition candidate. Son of the legendary president Lázaro Cárdenas, who famously nationalized the country's oil industry in the 1930s, Cuauhtémoc was heir to his father's political reputation and thus was able to galvanize leftist segments in the PRI to join his cause.

The 1988 election became among the most contested in Mexican history, with PRI candidate Carlos Salinas de Gortari officially garnering just over 50 percent of the vote, Cárdenas 31 percent, and conservative PAN candidate Manuel Clouthier 17 percent. Cárdenas denounced the election as a fraud and claimed to be the legitimate victor—something millions of Mexicans believe to this day. Given the dark reputation of the PRI, it ultimately didn't matter whether this claim was true—the PRI's legitimacy suffered a significant blow.

Several important developments took place following the 1988 vote as the PRI tried to reform the system to restore some legitimacy, and opposition forces took advantage of the ruling party's weakness. First, constitutional changes gave birth to the IFE (Instituto Federal Electoral, or Federal Electoral Institute) and the TRIFE (Tribunal Federal Electoral, or Federal Electoral Tribunal). The IFE was established as an independent body tasked with administering federal elections, while the TRIFE was a subsidiary of the judiciary tasked with resolving electoral disputes. (It was the TRIFE that ultimately validated Calderón's victory in 2006.) Second, the media shed many of its self-imposed limits on expression. Newspapers and television stations began taking an increasingly fair approach to political coverage, exposing the country's leaders to criticism and even ridicule. Third, Cárdenas formed the PRD in 1989 as a permanent home for disaffected PRI activists who sought both further democracy and a greater commitment to the radical heritage the PRI had once claimed. The PRD helped turn Mexico into the three-party system it is today.

Finally, the long-established but previously weak opposition party, the PAN, also became an increasingly powerful force. The PAN began to attract a larger following, and for the first time since its founding in 1939, it won a statewide office in 1989, capturing a governorship. The PRI allowed the PAN victories as part of an implicit pact between the two parties. The pro-business PAN agreed with the PRI's neoliberal policies and both wanted to limit the success of the more critical PRD. The PRI allowed the PAN to win some elections in exchange for the PAN's acceptance of President Salinas's questionable 1988 election and support of neoliberalism (Hamilton 2011, 146–149). The ruling party compromised with the moderate PAN in an effort to keep the more radical PRD out of power, following the logic of the transition paradigm outlined above.

By the time of the 1994 election, political contestation was open enough that the PRI's Ernesto Zedillo is now considered to be the first democratically elected president of Mexico. But Zedillo's election and therefore government still faced serious questions of legitimacy. The government had reacted harshly to the Zapatista uprising that began in January 1994 in the southern state of Chiapas. The Zapatistas demanded greater rights for indigenous Mexicans and opposed the official start of NAFTA. Later in the year, the country faced yet another economic crisis that ultimately provoked a collapse of the country's currency. Zedillo ran for office only after the death of Luis Donaldo Colosio, the original PRI candidate. Colosio was brutally gunned down while campaigning in Tijuana; Zedillo, then Colosio's campaign manager, was chosen to replace him. While a lone gunman was captured after the murder, many suspected that Zedillo or others in the PRI had a hand in it (Pérez Silva 2004). Although Zedillo won on the basis of his moderate tone and technocratic legitimacy, Colosio's murder reinforced the view that the highest political circles in the country were criminal in nature.

Web link:
The 1994 elections: still neither fully free nor fair

Zedillo's government never overcame the economic crisis it inherited, even though it pursued further electoral reforms to try to rebuild its legitimacy. In 1997 the PRI lost control of the National Congress for the first time in its history. Although the PRI held its first openly contested primary in 2000, its monopoly over the presidency had finally also reached its limit. Change came with the election of conservative Vicente Fox Quesada, a member of the PAN, as president. Fox, a former president of Coca-Cola of Mexico and governor of Guanajuato, won with around 43 percent of the vote, vis-à-vis 36 percent for the PRI's candidate and 17 percent for Cuauhtémoc Cárdenas.

The election of Vicente Fox brought wild, unrealistic hopes about what democracy would mean for Mexico, and Fox himself did little to tamp down expectations. At one point, he infamously claimed that as president he would resolve the government's dispute with Zapatista rebels in the south "in fifteen minutes." This was one of many election promises that fell short of their mark, as Mexico experienced increasing inequality, greater criminal violence, and general political gridlock, making the Fox presidency among the least popular in recent Mexican history. Ironically, one of Fox's biggest difficulties was negotiating with members of Congress to pass legislation, a necessity now that Congress was no longer subservient to the president but instead represented a wider array of Mexican political forces. The ability of Congress to limit the president's power and the strength of three, ideologically distinct parties is one of the strongest elements of Mexico's young democracy.

Audio link:
A modern Mexico?

Other aspects of Mexico's democracy, however, remain fragile. Claudio Holzner (2011) pointed to weak institutions as the core problem that in turn produces weak rule of law, continuing clientelism, continuing corruption, local-level authoritarianism, and near loss of sovereignty to drug lords in some states. Clientelism and corruption allow the wealthy to continue to enjoy disproportionate political power. Drug gangs became so powerful in some states that the police were entirely corrupted and drug lords financed their own candidates for governor, mayor, and other offices. The PAN government after 2006 tried to battle the drug lords with increased military intervention, which produced tens of thousands of deaths but did not reduce drug gangs' power. Even in states without significant drug gangs, some local leaders from the PRI era

Freedom House Scores: Mexico and Latin America

Mexico's transition to democracy was a belated part of a broader move toward democracy across Latin America. In 1990 Mexico lagged behind its regional neighbors in terms of democracy, but the transition in 2000 meant it had caught up. Growing problems with the quality of its democracy by 2013, though, once again meant it lagged behind other democracies in the region.

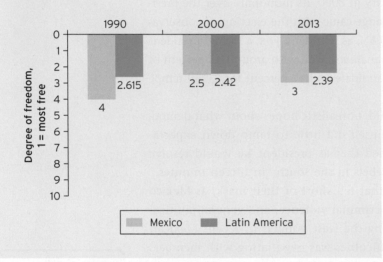

were able to use control of state resources as patronage to preserve "subnational authoritarian" rule. This is tied to increasing corruption: the country fell from 57th place in the Corruption Perceptions Index in 2008 to 105th place in 2012. Since 2011, however, a series of public scandals and judicial charges have come forward against former governors, usually after they lose an election to an opposing party, which is happening more frequently as opposition parties are able to use the electoral system to overcome entrenched rulers. Thus, while national politics increasingly appear to represent a consolidated democracy, the quality of that democracy, especially at the local level, is far from ideal.

By the 2012 campaign, Mexico had not fully recovered from the effects of the global recession: economic growth was slow, unemployment high, and poverty increasing. Calderón's use of the military to battle drug gangs increased the death rate dramatically but was seen as achieving little. In this context, Mexicans voted the PRI candidate, Enrique Peña Nieto, into office as president. No party questioned seriously the legitimacy of the election, an improvement over 2006. The return of the PRI to power, however, raised questions about Mexican democracy. The PRI continued to enjoy semi-authoritarian control of a number of state governments via entrenched and corrupt governors, and it had disproportionate support from the country's two major television networks. It proclaimed itself committed to democracy and did not have majority control of Congress, so it required support from one other party to pass legislation. The latter provides some horizontal accountability, though analysts doubted that the former ruling party would initiate any reforms to strengthen Mexico's democracy over its six years at the helm. It was not clear that the Mexican populace would demand further reforms either: in 2011 only 40 percent believed democracy to be the best form of government, and the percentage of the population that said democracy was working well was the lowest in all of Latin America (Flores-Macías 2013, 137).

CASE Summary Mexico has completed a transition to democracy that few doubt. Consolidation, in the sense of all major actors (save the drug cartels) accepting the democratic process as "the only game in town," seems well established, and the country passed the "two-turnover test" in 2012. Modernization certainly may have provided the backdrop that helped this democracy come into being, but economic crisis, loss of the ruling party's legitimacy, and related changes within the elite in the 1980s and 1990s were necessary to make it happen when it did. This democracy, though, is plagued by the problems of a still-weak state, the most important of which are endemic corruption and drug-related violence that seem beyond the state's ability (or desire) to stop. Gaining control over these problems will likely be essential to the long-term health of Mexicans' hard-won democracy.

CASE Questions

1. Given the discrepancy between national electoral politics and local politics, can we say that Mexico has truly become a consolidated democracy? What evidence is most important in answering this question?
2. Does Mexico suggest that modernization theory or the "transition paradigm" is correct in terms of where and when democratization is likely to occur?

CASE Study

RUSSIA: TRANSITION TO A SEMI-AUTHORITARIAN REGIME

As Russian president Boris Yeltsin climbed atop a tank in Moscow to stop a coup attempt in August 1991, it seemed that freedom was on the rise in Russia. The coup was the last-gasp effort of hardliners in the old Communist regime of the Soviet Union. The reforms of softliner Soviet president Mikhail Gorbachev in the late 1980s had significantly opened the Soviet political system and economy, but demands for far greater reforms were in the air. With Gorbachev on vacation, elements in the military tried to roll the tanks into Moscow to restore the old system

- **TRANSITION**
  Initially to democracy with weak institutions, then to semi-authoritarian regime

- **CONSOLIDATION**
  None

- **QUALITY OF DEMOCRACY**
  Weak legislature and parties in 1990s; not a democracy since 2000

- **FREEDOM HOUSE RATING IN 2013: 5.5 = "not free"**

Opposition activists Gennady Gudkov and Ilya Ponomarev lead a protest in Moscow in September 2012. Thousands demonstrated against strongman Vladimir Putin's return to the presidency and, more generally, the growing authoritarianism of the regime. Despite the protests, Putin's control remained unchallenged a year later.

and prevent the reconfiguration of the Soviet Union as a smaller, more decentralized federation. It was a classic case of hardliners within the regime trying to repress political liberalization. Popular and international opposition, led by Yeltsin, forced the military to back down. By December, the Soviet Union was dissolved. Fifteen new countries emerged, with Russia being by far the biggest and most important, and each was expected to transition to democracy. The world's number-two superpower appeared to be starting an unprecedented transition from a Communist regime to one that was democratic and capitalist.

Russia's transition, however, has not been to democracy but instead to semi-authoritarian rule. This has been a result of the effects of partial and poorly institutionalized economic reform, weak political institutions, an exceptionally strong presidency, and the perverse effects of Russia's abundant natural resources. The full effects of this shift to semi-authoritarian rule would be clear only after Vladimir Putin, Russia's second president, consolidated his rule in the first few years of the new millennium. While he abided by the constitutional limit of two terms as president, he handpicked his successor, who dutifully chose Putin for the number-two position of prime minister. In 2012 Putin once again ran and won the presidency in an election many saw as fraudulent. He could hold onto power, though, at least another two terms, to 2024.

Russia's transition started long before Putin rose to power. Gorbachev's most dramatic reform was ending the Communist Party's claim to absolute power in February 1990. This was followed in March by Russia's legislative elections, and Yeltsin's election as president a year later. At the time, Russia was still just one of fifteen constituent republics of the Soviet Union, and these were the first elections to include non-Communist candidates since the Communist revolution. The military backlash destroyed the possibility of a negotiated pact and led to the dissolution of the Soviet Union. The provincial Russian institutions then became those of the newly independent state, with Yeltsin as president. The transition from a state-controlled to a market economy began immediately and was very difficult, making the new government unpopular early on. Yeltsin claimed that the benefits of the new capitalist economy would be widespread, but the immediate effect was a dramatic increase in prices that left Russians with little means of support; especially hard-hit were those who relied on government pensions. More often than not, former Communist factory managers became the owners of newly privatized businesses. To the average worker, it looked like not much had changed, until the owners had to fire much of the bloated workforce to compete in the new market economy. The economy shrank 14.5 percent, and inflation ballooned to more than 1,500 percent in 1992. Unemployment tripled from 1992 to 1998. A few spectacularly successful businessmen, especially in Russia's huge oil sector, emerged to control vast swaths of the economy. Key allies of Yeltsin, they formed a group that came to be known as the "family," and in effect ran the economy and the government.

The early years of an independent Russia were as chaotic and difficult politically as they were economically. While the elected legislature included non-Communist members, the Communist Party still held a majority of seats. Yeltsin feared holding new elections because of the unpopularity of the economic changes. Faced with an increasingly hostile parliament, he ruled primarily by decree. He proposed the creation of the semipresidential system with an exceptionally strong presidency that we outlined in chapter 6. The legislature refused to ratify his ideas, leading him to disband it in September 1993. Legislators barricaded themselves in the parliament building, determined not to leave and voting to impeach Yeltsin. After a weeklong standoff, Yeltsin called in the army to lay siege to the parliament building, forcibly ending the Soviet-era parliament. Once again, a moment when a negotiated pact might have been possible ended instead with violence. Yeltsin subsequently held a referendum on the constitution, which passed by a narrow margin, and an election for a new legislature. In spite of these successes, he still faced opposition to many of his reforms and continued to rule by decree without legislative support. Citizens also blamed him for the unpopular, brutal, and ineffective war in the breakaway region of Chechnya. He narrowly won reelection in 1996, but neither his popularity nor the economy ever fully recovered.

A primary reason why Yeltsin lacked support in the legislature was that he refused to join a political party, trying instead to appear "above" partisan politics. His refusal to participate, in addition to the very weak powers of the Duma, resulted in the creation of weak parties. The mixed electoral system (similar to Germany's) in the 1993 constitution was part of the problem. Half the Duma's seats were elected via closed-list proportional representation (PR) and the other half via single-member districts. Unlike in Germany, few parties could compete effectively in both types of elections; the few national parties won most of the PR seats, and independent candidates with no party affiliation but strong local bases of support won many of the SMD seats. Power resided overwhelmingly in the executive branch, in any case. Therefore, most parties were of limited consequence, rising and falling with the popularity and shifting allegiances of major politicians. Across four elections from 1993 to 2005, anywhere from twelve to seventeen parties were in parliament, and fewer than half of them in one parliament continued to exist and hold seats in the next one. Ironically, the biggest exception is the Communist Party, which has the clearest ideology and is reputed to include 500,000 members. To date, it is also the largest force in the Duma that is not allied with the executive.

Political scientists Hans Oversloot and Ruben Verheul (2006) argued that the most important party in Russia is the "party of power, the party that those around the president create to win as many seats as they can in the *duma,* insuring support for the president's proposals." This party has changed from one election to the next; it was called Russia's Choice in 1993, Our Home Is Russia in 1995, Unity in 1999, and United Russia since 2003. Putin chose to help foster his party of power, United Russia, to a degree Yeltsin never did. He used his greater popularity (throughout his first two terms, his popular approval ratings rarely dipped below 70 percent) and his control over patronage to ensure that United Russia won handily. Since 2003, United Russia has easily dominated the Duma, meaning the Duma has rubber-stamped everything Putin has proposed.

In constructing a semi-authoritarian regime, Putin significantly centralized power in the executive and eliminated most vestiges of real democracy. In addition to increasing the powers of the presidency vis-à-vis the regions, he harassed and closed down most independent media, undermined independent civil society groups with new regulations, and broke the informal power of the oligarchs who had arisen under Yeltsin. He replaced Yeltsin's "family" with a group of former agents of the Federal Security Bureau (FSB), the successor to the KGB where he had spent most of his career. Members of this group sit in key ministries and agencies throughout the executive branch, have been appointed as governors, and control many important companies (Hesli 2007).

Putin also changed the electoral system. Under the mixed electoral system, his most significant opposition came from independent MPs elected in the single-member districts, so he changed the electoral system to a purely closed-list PR system to eliminate independent candidates. This reduced the number of parties from forty in 2003 to fourteen in 2008. If real electoral competition existed, this could be seen as enhancing democracy, since fewer and larger parties give voters clearer and more credible options. But in the context of Putin building his party of power, repressing civil society and the media, and using oil wealth as patronage to buy off opponents, the drop in the number of parties was simply part of a broader process of centralizing control. In 2013, however, Putin reversed course, recreating the mixed system, though with a 5 percent threshold to keep out smaller parties. With overwhelming control of the Duma, allowing a few independent candidates would no longer pose a challenge to his authority.

Constitutionally barred from running for a third term as president, Putin announced he would be a candidate for prime minister. He handpicked Dmitry Medvedev, a relatively obscure bureaucrat without a major political following, to succeed him as president. While some observers believed that Medvedev had a stronger commitment to the rule of law than did Putin, little changed during his presidency. Prime Minister Putin clearly remained the dominant political figure, controlling both Medvedev and parliament. Much speculation revolved around who would run for president at the end of Medvedev's term. Would Putin allow him to serve a second term, or would he return to the presidency himself? The answer came in September 2011, when Putin and Medvedev jointly announced that they would again switch jobs.

The announcement was met by general public dismay. Putin had used economic growth (based on high oil revenues) and improved security to gain much popular support through 2009 (Rose et al. 2011), but economic decline had damaged that by 2011.

The parliamentary elections in December 2011 included widespread fraud, some of it captured on video and posted on the Internet. After years of relative quiescence, Russian civil society awoke; protests of tens of thousands of people demanding fairer elections took place repeatedly from December 2011 to March 2012. The regime successfully resisted the protesters' demands, however, and Putin was duly elected (again, partly via fraudulent elections) president in March 2012. He quickly instituted new laws that dramatically increased the penalties for unauthorized demonstrations, put greater legal restrictions on NGOs, and reversed slight liberalizations Medvedev had made to Russian federalism (see chapter 6). He also increased his use of Russian nationalism to gain sup-

Freedom House Scores: Russia and Central Europe

In the aftermath of communism in central Europe, democracy spread rapidly, as seen in the region's improved freedom house scores. Russia, though, reversed course in the new millennium as Putin consolidated a semi-authoritarian regime.

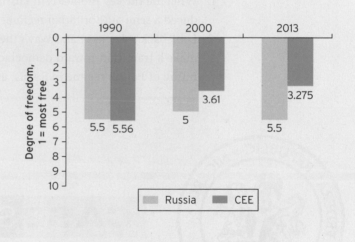

port, sharpening his opposition to the West in foreign policy and aligning himself more tightly with the Russian Orthodox Church. Putin's tactics included passing laws limiting Western adoption of Russian orphans, stigmatizing homosexuality by criminalizing providing information about it to children, and penalizing with jail terms anyone who "offends religious feelings." He even turned against close allies of Medvedev who were seen as too "liberal" and sympathetic to the opposition, bringing criminal charges against some and forcing others into exile. The legitimacy of Russia's semi-authoritarian regime had rested on its ability to deliver economic improvements; without that, Putin turned to nationalism and greater repression to maintain his control.

Video link:
The dictator's learning curve

Video link:
Putin's 2008 election

Putin's rule fully transformed Russia from a weak but fledgling democracy to a semi-authoritarian regime. Yeltsin and his supporters chose to establish a weak legislature to enable a strong presidency; the result has been the weak parties and the dynamics described above. Limited economic reform and massive oil production led to large-scale corruption and gave the executive the ability to co-opt much opposition via distributing patronage. Putin justified his actions in terms of building a strong state, improving the economy, and increasing security. His successes made him popular in spite of his undermining democracy for much of the first decade of the new millennium, but once economic growth dropped, so did his support. The protests against the 2012 election show that many Russians still desire at least a freer and fairer electoral system, but Putin and his United Russia party seem firmly in control.

CASE Questions

1. What are the key problems in Russia's transition to democracy that ultimately produced a semi-authoritarian regime?
2. Look back at Levitsky and Way's theory of when a semi-authoritarian regime might make a transition toward democracy (page 485). What would they predict for the future of Putin's regime in Russia, and why?

CASE Study

- **TRANSITION**
  Led by civil society; electoral democracy, but with dominant party system

- **CONSOLIDATION**
  Tension over regional, ethnic, and religious political rivalries, but civilian control of the military

- **QUALITY**
  Electoral fraud and corruption, but strengthened judiciary and limits on presidential power

NIGERIA: NEOPATRIMONIAL TRANSITION

Nigeria held its fourth consecutive multiparty election and inaugurated a third elected president in April 2011. Just four years earlier, the country changed presidents via an election for the first time in the country's history, though the same party has won every election since the democratic transition in 1999. Domestic and international observers saw the 2007 election as deeply flawed, neither free nor fair; the prior president's party and his handpicked successor won an overwhelming victory at all levels of government. Each of three successive national elections (1999, 2003, and 2007) was further from democratic norms than the one that preceded it. Given that history, the fact that the 2011 election was improved over 2007 gave some hope that the deterioration of Nigeria's young democracy might be reversing. Though the latest election seemed hopeful, a dominant-party system had emerged that limited democratic competition, a violent Islamist movement threatened sovereignty in the north, and corruption remained a serious problem. These problems are not uncommon in transitions to democracy in countries with enduring neopatrimonial forms of authority. In the context of a dominant-party system, a split in the ruling party in 2013 may augur well for the future, in that it raises the possibility of greater electoral competition.

The election of 1999 marked Nigeria's second return to democratic rule. The first created the Second Republic in 1979, which ended in a military coup in 1983 (see chapter 8) amid claims that elected leaders had expanded corruption and stolen the election. A failed transition in 1993, in which the military dictator annulled the presidential election because his candidate did not win, gave rise to a vociferous democracy movement. As in much of Africa, democratic transition in Nigeria began with grassroots protests. The 1999 democratic constitution and elections were the ultimate result. The constitution was modeled almost exactly after the 1979 one and created a presidential system with a first-past-the-post electoral system very similar to that of the United States.

The annulment of that long-awaited election in 1993 motivated many new groups to join the democracy effort; in 1994 they formed the National Democratic Coalition (NADECO), which included former politicians, union members, students, and human rights campaigners. NADECO's breadth allowed it to put greater pressure than ever before on Nigeria's military government. In its first campaign, "Babangida Must Go," it demanded that military dictator Ibrahim Babangida be replaced by the rightful winner of the election. Babangida did go but was replaced by the even more repressive and corrupt dictator, Sani Abacha. The real transition began only after Abacha's death in 1998. His successor recognized how discredited the military had become under Abacha's rule and immediately agreed to a transition. The subsequent elections in 1999 were far from perfect, but most observers deemed them minimally adequate to start Nigeria's new democracy. The military elite put together what became the ruling party, the People's Democratic Party (PDP), and chose the military dictator who had shepherded the 1979 transition, retired Gen. Olusegun Obasanjo, as its presidential candidate. Obasanjo was credited with having revived democracy in 1979 and having actively opposed Abacha, spending part of the 1990s in jail. He also had become something of an elder statesman in Africa, with wide international respect. Furthermore, in Nigeria's ethnically and religiously divided society, he benefited from being a Yoruba from the southwest. The long dominance

• **FREEDOM HOUSE RATING IN 2013**
4.5 = "partly free"

Nigeria's three presidents since the return of democracy in 1999: Olusegun Obasanjo (left; 1999–2007), Umaru Yar'Adua (right; 2007–2010), and Goodluck Jonathan (center; 2010–) stand together in 2007. When Obasanjo was prevented from running for a third term, he handpicked Yar'Adua as his successor. Yar'Adua's death in office in 2010 elevated Jonathan, who consolidated power and won the 2011 election. Elections marred by widespread irregularities and the continued rule of the same party since the transition have raised serious questions about the quality and sustainability of Nigeria's democracy.

in CONTEXT

Freedom House Scores: Nigeria and Africa

Nigeria's mixed record of democratization is not unusual for Africa. While Freedom House rates it slightly below average for sub-Saharan Africa, the difference is not substantial. After the initial wave of transitions in the early 1990s, improvements to democracy in the region have been slow and difficult to achieve. A handful of countries such as Ghana have created fully "free" democracies, but most regime change has resulted in semi-authoritarian regimes.

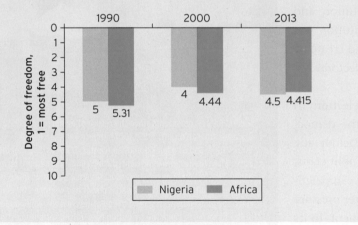

of northerners under military rule led all Nigerians to recognize that it was time for a president from the country's southern region.

So the Kaduna mafia, a group of Muslim military leaders from the north that has controlled most of Nigeria's governments, picked as its candidate a southerner whom it trusted and who was a former general himself. Ironically, Obasanjo won handily in most of the country but not in his home area among the Yoruba, who saw him as having sold out to northern military interests. By the 2003 election, Obasanjo and his party won more easily than in 1999. The only significant opposition came from a party led by northern leaders who were unhappy with Obasanjo. Its presidential candidate was Muhammadu Buhari, another former military dictator. He and Obasanjo's handpicked successor, Umaru Yar'Adua, were the two major presidential candidates in 2007 as well. Yar'Adua won 72 percent of the vote, and the PDP won a similar majority in the legislature. Though many parties existed, by 2007 only two had a real shot at gaining power, and the ruling party scored an overwhelming victory, though partly via fraudulent means.

As the 2011 election approached, the PDP continued to be dominant, with the most closely watched campaign being the primary election for the party's presidential nomination. In the legislative election, however, the party actually lost some seats, though it retained a slim majority overall. Its presidential candidate, incumbent president Goodluck Jonathan, won as well, though its victory was significantly smaller than in 2007. Even with this reduced victory, it still seemed that the country was moving toward a dominant-party system. In 2013, however, the PDP split as a former vice president and seven state governors stormed out of the party convention, objecting to the fact that their candidates were not given key party positions. Most of those who left are from the north and oppose President Jonathan's planned reelection bid in 2015. They announced the creation of the "new PDP." In response, Jonathan fired several cabinet ministers from their states. Whether this new party can become a significant rival to the PDP or those in power will be able to use fraudulent methods to prevent that from happening will determine whether a dominant-party system is consolidated in Nigeria or not.

Political parties in Nigeria are not strong institutions with loyal supporters based on party ideology and symbols; instead, they are based mainly on the support of key Big Men and their use of patronage. The neopatrimonialism that characterized military rule has continued under the new democracy. In 1999 a rule that required parties to gain the support of 5 percent of the voters in three-quarters of the states resulted in there being only three parties on the ballot. By 2003, the Supreme Court had invalidated this limit, and dozens of parties registered, "but most parties consisted primarily of the office staff at the national headquarters . . . and were typically centered on a Big Man who was funding the operations and running for president" (Kew 2004, 147). By 2010, sixty-two parties were officially registered, though only a handful were of widespread significance. Whether the "new PDP" can overcome such weaknesses will be important to the future of Nigeria's democracy.

Elections are institutionally weak as well. In 2003 the elections were free and fair in about one-third of Nigeria's states, "dubious" in another third, and completely fraudulent in the final third (Kew 2004). By 2007, observers for Human Rights Watch reported that "the elections were marred by extraordinary displays of rigging and the intimidation of voters in many areas throughout Nigeria" (Rawlence and Albin-Lackey 2007, 497). In quite a few states, no elections took place at all: officials simply made up results in favor of the ruling party. Voter turnout was grossly inflated in many states in which the ruling party won, and observers saw officials openly stuffing ballot boxes in a number of cases.

After assuming the presidency in 2010, Jonathan promised to improve the electoral process and appointed a well-known democracy advocate and scholar to head the electoral commission. Most observers credited the electoral commission with having substantially improved the credibility of the 2011 elections. Sporadic violence, long a part of Nigerian elections, continued to be a problem, however. In the northern state of Madiguri, a radical Islamist sect set off bombs shortly before the election, and rebels in the oil-producing delta region also used violence to disrupt the process.

While institutions of participation are extremely weak, Nigeria's experiment with democracy has produced some examples of institutionalization that have seemed to strengthen democracy. Civilian control of the military has been key. Military leaders of the Kaduna mafia backed Obasanjo for president in 1999 because they assumed that they could control him after he took office. After becoming president, however, he quickly removed the most politically active northern generals and replaced them with less politically active and more southern officers. Several years later, when Yar-Adua's prolonged illness left him incapacitated and the country's government very uncertain for nearly three months, rumors of military intervention were rife, but the armed forces remained in their barracks. While it is difficult to make predictions, given Nigeria's

Video link:
New parallel PDP

Video link:
Two-party system will deepen Nigeria's democracy

history of military coups, the Third Republic seems to have established civilian control over the military, a first in Nigerian history. Indeed, some observers believe that the reason elections have become so hotly contested and fraudulent is that the stakes are so high. No one expects military intervention, so election is the sole means of gaining political power.

A second institution that has been strengthened is the Supreme Court. The new constitution created a National Judicial Council that has helped insulate the judiciary from pressures from elected officials. The Supreme Court has made several important rulings that demonstrated its autonomy. In the area of federal versus state control over oil revenues, it ruled in some key cases in favor of the oil-producing states and in others in favor of the federal government, indicating a certain degree of autonomy from political pressure from either side. On the eve of the 2007 presidential election, it also ruled that Obasanjo's estranged vice president, whom the president had tried to prevent from running, could stand in the election, ruling against the sitting president. After the faulty 2007 election, the courts also ruled several gubernatorial victories invalid and required new elections. On the other hand, a deeply divided high court narrowly ruled that Yar'Adua's presidential victory was legitimate, a conclusion doubted by virtually all impartial observers. The opposition candidates, though, chose to accept the ruling, preventing a more prolonged crisis for the country's still-fragile democracy.

Perhaps the two most important tests of institutional strength for Nigerian democracy went against incumbent presidents, indicating some institutionalization of limits on personal rule. The first came when President Obasanjo launched a campaign to revoke the two-term limit for the presidency. Amending the constitution to allow Obasanjo a third term required Senate approval. Reportedly, he and his supporters were trying to bribe senators to vote in favor of the amendment with offers as high as $750,000. It became crystal clear, though, that the population overwhelmingly opposed the move, and the Senate voted it down despite all the pressure and inducements Obasanjo brought to bear. Some observers also argue that many of the elite quietly opposed Obasanjo as well. In a patronage-based system with oil revenue available, the presidency is very powerful and lucrative. The political elite do not want one individual to remain in office too long so that other leaders and groups have a chance to gain its benefits.

The second major institutional challenge began in 2009, when President Yar'Adua became gravely ill and left the country for treatment in Saudi Arabia. An incapacitated president is supposed to turn over his powers to his vice president, but Yar'Adua refused. His wife and closest aides did not let any Nigerians see him and released no information about his health. For two months, the country was without even an acting president. Amid growing domestic and international pressure to clarify the situation, Yar'Adua gave a radio interview in which he said in a weak voice that he hoped to return to work soon. The National Assembly took that as a public statement that he was incapacitated and appointed Vice President Jonathan as acting president. Once again, the sitting president and his closest aides were rebuffed in an illegitimate attempt to retain power. A couple of months later, after returning to Nigeria, Yar'Adua finally died, and Jonathan assumed the full powers of the presidency.

Establishing a stable federal order in Nigeria has long been a contentious process, and it continues to be under the new democracy. The biggest issue is control of revenue from the oil that is located in a handful of southeastern states. Currently, the oil-producing states get 13 percent of the oil revenue generated in their state. Nonetheless, their people remain among the poorest in the country, in part because of massive corruption in the state governments. In recent years, unfortunately, some of the movements demanding a greater share of the oil wealth have become armed gangs for hire to the highest bidder. They often serve as the violent wing of campaign teams. The nation was shocked when bombs exploded in the capital during the celebration of the fiftieth anniversary of its independence, killing at least sixteen people. The Movement for the Emancipation of the Niger Delta (MEND) took credit for the attacks; it was the first time the violence from the oil-producing region had hit the capital, and the event was deeply embarrassing for President Jonathan, who hails from the region himself. While the amnesty offered to armed rebels in the oil areas has reduced the level of violence since 2009, the underlying issues of environmental problems, inequality, and unemployment in the region remain.

The *sharia* controversy we described in chapter 4 is also part of the federalism question in Nigeria. The 1999 constitution allows states to set their own legal codes within national law, and Nigeria has long allowed dual civil law codes based on religion. The twelve northern states that have implemented *sharia* have expanded its use to criminal law as well, setting off confrontations with Christian minorities in several of these states and opposition from the south in general. Long-standing northern and Muslim control of national politics has left southerners and Christians fearful of any further Islamic movements. Because of federalism, each state's version of *sharia* is slightly different; some states apply some Muslim laws to non-Muslims and other states don't, while some include the harshest penalties such as stoning and others don't. So far, national courts have neither revoked states' rights to implement *sharia* nor insisted on a uniform version across all states. Of even greater concern in the north is the increased activity of Boko Haram, a violent Islamist group that has killed hundreds and poses a serious threat to Nigeria's internal sovereignty in the northeastern part of the country.

Ethnic and regional political rivalries continue to dominate Nigerian democracy. The informal understanding in 1999 that the presidency should alternate between a northerner and a southerner (hence from Obasanjo to Yar'Adua) became an official policy of the ruling party. Yar'Adua's death and Jonathan's ascension to the presidency inadvertently violated this principle in that Yar'Adua only completed part of his term and was replaced by Jonathan, a southerner. Initially, northern party leaders resisted the idea that Jonathan would be allowed to run for a full term of office in 2011. After extensive behind-the-scenes campaigning, which allegedly included funneling oil money to key governors to gain their support, the ruling party allowed him to stand for office, effectively ending the policy of alternating the presidency between north and south. Jonathan faced serious primary challenges within the party, though, from several major northern leaders. Northerners felt strongly that they had a right to see a northern leader returned to office to complete what they presumed would be Yar'Adua's two terms in office; Buhari, the major opposition candidate, gained support because of this. This issue lay behind the split in the ruling party in 2013; Jonathan's apparent intention to run for reelection reinforced the end of the north-south alternation of the presidency, provoking several important northern leaders to create the "new PDP."

All of these institutional problems are related to the overall weakness of the state. The country continues to be one of the most corrupt in the world, though it has made improvements. Transparency International's 1999 Corruption Perception Index ranked Nigeria as the second most corrupt country in the world, with a score of 1.6. In 2012 it was number 139 of 174 countries, with a score of 2.7, showing modest but noticeable improvement. This is due in part to an anticorruption drive Obasanjo launched that received great praise in its early years. Unfortunately, it seems that the ruling party under both Obasanjo and Jonathan has been willing to use the anticorruption efforts for political purposes, targeting charges at their opponents while protecting their supporters. Jonathan appointed a new head of the Central Bank who won praise for removing some corrupt officials, but how much change the new president would really achieve, and how much change he wanted, remained unclear. Continued corruption has made all state institutions weak, harmed the ability of the electoral commission to conduct proper elections, prevented people in the oil-producing states from benefiting from their oil, and led northerners to turn to *sharia* in the hope that it will be less corrupt and more just than secular courts.

Web link:
The consolidation of democracy in Nigeria

CASE Summary The Nigerian case demonstrates the potential to establish democracy in a poor country, as well as the severe problems that can arise when politics are based on neopatrimonialism. The competition for office becomes all-consuming and often violent, undermining democratic norms of the "free and fair" choice of candidates. Corruption continues throughout the country with only slight improvement, weakening all state institutions and popular faith in democracy. Yet the fragile democratic regime in Nigeria seems to have brought the military under control, and a coup seems less likely than at any time since 1966. A few other key institutions—term limits and judicial independence—have been strengthened as well. In 2011 even the much criticized electoral process seemed to improve at least slightly. Advocates of democracy in countries like Nigeria hope that these institutional gains will be the basis for further improvement and the slow establishment of a consolidated and relatively high-quality democracy, though that seems quite far off in Nigeria.

> **CASE** Questions
>
> 1. Comparing all three of our case studies of democratization, what effects do weak institutions have on the democratization process? Are the effects similar in all three countries? Which of the three suffered the greatest effects of weak institutions, and why?
> 2. Nigeria's transition juxtaposes some very serious problems against some notable successes in creating democratic limits on the executive. Given this, what do you think are the most important changes that would likely improve the quality of its democracy?

CONCLUSION

Regime change is a difficult process to understand and predict. By definition, it lies outside the realm of "normal" politics. Instead, it is a period of intense politicization and rapidly unfolding events. This makes it an exceptionally fascinating area of comparative politics to study, and many comparativists have. Many questions remain, however. Distinguishing one type of regime change from another is not always easy, at least until well after the process is complete. While we have distinct theories explaining coups, revolutions, and democratization, the processes can merge into one another, as the Arab Spring has shown most recently.

Regime change affects who rules, but not only in the direction that might be expected. At least in theory, democratization produces regimes in which citizens rule. How true that is, of course, depends on how complete the transition is and the quality of the democracy that emerges. Not infrequently, though, a democracy does not emerge at all. Similarly, a seemingly united revolutionary front in the interests of the people can result in leaders imposing their own vision on society, at least initially, and demobilizing popular participation in the new regime. In politics, those who fight for change do not necessarily get what they seek. The military holds the guns on which the state and regime rely and therefore can intervene directly if it chooses, putting themselves in power. But militaries, even highly institutionalized ones, are not designed to rule. Every military regime relies on civilian support to some extent, especially within the state itself. In some instances, such as under Brazil's bureaucratic-authoritarian regime, the military relies even more on civilians, inviting those who are sympathetic to it to actively participate in governing, even at the highest levels.

The often chaotic process of regime change continues to limit comparativists' predictive powers. Some cases, such as Ghana, defy the odds, producing democracy where theorists would least expect it. Consolidating a new democracy is an extremely challenging process. Partly for this reason, comparativists for years believed that democracy would only survive in very specific kinds of countries. That position was challenged by the "transition" paradigm, which argued that democracy could survive anywhere.

More careful recent scholarship suggests that while democracy can arise anywhere, its chances of survival are definitely higher in favorable cultural and economic contexts. The process can be easily undermined by institutional breakdowns of all sorts. An increasingly common result of these breakdowns, especially in the former Soviet Union and much of Africa, seems to be semi-authoritarian regimes, whose future will have a major impact on the future of democracy around the world.

Revolutions are much more rare, meaning a particular set of circumstances must account for them, but it is not always easy to determine what those circumstances are. A weakened old regime and state seem essential, as strong states can resist revolution no matter how many people are involved. A strong revolutionary organization that unites and mobilizes people's grievances also seems vital. Revolutions are known by their leaders' ideologies, but that does not always explain the motivations of the masses supporting them. The masses are often motivated by the failure of the old regime as well as a sense of relative deprivation, whether due to declining economic circumstances or rising expectations that have not been met.

Military coups are the most common and quickest form of regime change. When civilian efforts to socialize and thereby control the military fail, troops seize the capital for a variety of reasons. These can range from the military's sense that the nation needs to be "rescued," to the military's own interests as an organization, to the more particular interests of individual leaders or groups within the military. Which explanation is most useful often depends on the nature of the military itself, especially its degree of institutionalization, and is often far from obvious. Military intervention does not always lead to military rule either, as the case of Tunisia in particular demonstrates.

Regime change is such a large and important topic that virtually all major theories of comparative politics have been used to explain it. Political-culture theorists long argued that attributes of particular cultures set the stage for particular kinds of regime change. Ideology clearly has a role to play in explaining revolutions, or at least in explaining the revolutionary leaders' motivations, but it is of limited help in explaining mass involvement. Influenced by rational-choice theory, the transition paradigm argues that neither culture nor ideology is particularly important in understanding when a transition will occur; transitions take place when political elites see the acceptance of democratic institutions to be in their rational self-interest. While the first transition theorists seemed to believe that new democracies would survive as long as all major elites continue to view the institutions of democracy as operating to their collective benefit, modernization theorists have responded, with growing evidence, that either culture or a structural condition—such as economic development—is necessary to preserve democracy in the long run.

Comparative politics today focuses much more on democratization than on military coups or revolutions. We suggest, however, that the latter two types of regime change remain important topics of investigation. Military coups have certainly continued to occur in this era of democratization; a coup took place in Mali, a neighbor of Ghana that was also seen as having a successful transition to democracy, in March

2012. And studying revolutions teaches us much about how people are mobilized into political activity of all types. The dramatic regime changes in Egypt and Tunisia in 2011 may not qualify as revolutions by the standard comparative politics definition, but they may not be straightforward processes of democratization either, as Egypt in 2013 demonstrated. They challenge scholarly analysis to try to understand the full implications of these recent examples of regime change.

KEY CONCEPTS

coup d'état (p. 457)

democratic consolidation (p. 484)

founding election (p. 480)

hardliners (p. 479)

moderates (p. 480)

pact (p. 480)

political liberalization (p. 480)

political violence (p. 471)

radicals (p. 480)

regime change (p. 454)

revolution (p. 466)

revolutions from above (p. 467)

revolutions from below (p. 467)

softliners (p. 479)

terrorism (p. 471)

transition to democracy (p. 479)

for CQ Press

Sharpen your skills with SAGE edge at **edge.sagepub.com/orvis3e.** **SAGE edge for students** provides a personalized approach to help you accomplish your coursework goals in an easy-to-use learning environment.

WORKS CITED

Allen, Chris. 1995. "Understanding African Politics." *Review of African Political Economy* 22 (65): 301–320.

Almond, Gabriel A., and Sidney Verba. 1963. *The Civic Culture: Political Attitudes and Democracy in Five Nations.* Princeton, NJ: Princeton University Press.

———. 1989. *The Civic Culture Revisited.* Newbury Park, CA: Sage.

Bermeo, Nancy Gina. 2003. *Ordinary People in Extraordinary Times: The Citizenry and the Breakdown of Democracy.* Princeton, NJ: Princeton University Press.

Boix, Carles, and Susan Carol Stokes. 2003. "Endogenous Democratization." *World Politics* 55 (4): 517–549. doi:10.1353/wp.2003.0019.

Bratton, Michael, and Nicholas van de Walle. 1997. *Democratic Experiments in Africa: Regime Transitions in Comparative Perspective.* New York: Cambridge University Press.

Brinton, Crane. 1965. *The Anatomy of Revolution.* New York: Vintage Books.

Clawson, Patrick, and Michael Rubin. 2005. *Eternal Iran: Continuity and Chaos.* New York: Palgrave Macmillan.

Crenshaw, Martha. 1981. "The Causes of Terrorism." *Comparative Politics* 13 (4): 379–399.

Davies, James C. 1962. "Toward a Theory of Revolution." *American Sociological Review* 27 (1): 5–19.

Decalo, Samuel. 1976. *Coups and Army Rule in Africa.* New Haven, CT: Yale University Press.

Finer, Samuel E. 1962. *The Man on Horseback: The Role of the Military in Politics.* New York: Praeger.

Fish, M. Steven. 2006. "Stronger Legislatures, Stronger Democracies." *Journal of Democracy* 17 (1): 5–20. doi:10.1353/jod.2006.0008.

Fish, M. Steven, and Robin S. Brooks. 2004. "Does Diversity Hurt Democracy?" *Journal of Democracy* 15 (1): 154–166. doi:10.1353/jod.2004.0009.

Flores-Macías, Gustavo. 2013. "Mexico's 2012 Elections: The Return of the PRI." *Journal of Democracy* 24 (1): 128–141.

Freedom House. "Freedom in the World" (http://www.freedomhouse.org/template.cfm?page=15).

Garrido de Sierra, Sebastián. 2011. "Eroded Unity and Clientele Migration: An Alternative Explanation of Mexico's Democratic Transition." Paper presented at the annual meeting of the Midwest Political Science Association, Chicago, March–April.

Gibson, Edward L. 2012. *Boundary Control: Subnational Authoritarianism in Federal Democracies.* Cambridge, UK: Cambridge University Press.

Goodwin, Jeff. 2001. *No Other Way Out: States and Revolutionary Movements, 1945–1991.* Cambridge, UK: Cambridge University Press.

Graf, William. 1988. *The Nigerian State: Political Economy, State Class, and Political System in the Post-Colonial Era.* London: J. Currey; Portsmouth, NH: Heinemann.

Gurr, Ted Robert. 1970. *Why Men Rebel.* Princeton, NJ: Princeton University Press.

Hadenius, Axel, and Jan Teorell. 2005. "Cultural and Economic Prerequisites of Democracy: Reassessing Recent Evidence." *Studies in Comparative International Development* 39 (4): 87–106.

Hamilton, Nora. 2011. *Mexico: Political, Social, and Economic Evolution.* Oxford, UK: Oxford University Press.

Hesli, Vicki L. 2007. *Government and Politics in Russia and the Post-Soviet Region.* Boston: Houghton Mifflin.

Holzner, Claudio A. 2011. "Mexico: Weak State, Weak Democracy." In *The Quality of Democracy in Latin America,* edited by Daniel H. Levine and José E. Molina, 83–110. Boulder, CO: Lynne Rienner.

Huntington, Samuel P. 1964. *The Soldier and the State: The Theory and Politics of Civil-Military Relations.* New York: Random House.

———. 1968. *Political Order in Changing Societies.* New Haven, CT: Yale University Press.

———. 1991. *The Third Wave: Democratization in the Late Twentieth Century.* Norman: University of Oklahoma Press.

Inglehart, Ronald, and Christian Welzel. 2005. *Modernization, Cultural Change, and Democracy: The Human Development Sequence.* New York: Cambridge University Press.

Janowitz, Morris. 1964. *The Military in the Political Development of New Nations: An Essay in Comparative Analysis.* Chicago: University of Chicago Press.

Kapstein, Ethan B., and Nathan Converse. 2008. "Why Democracies Fail." *Journal of Democracy* 19 (4): 57–68. doi:10.1353/jod.0.0031.

Kew, Darren. 2004. "The 2003 Elections: Hardly Credible, but Acceptable." In *Crafting the New Nigeria,* edited by Robert I. Rotberg, 139–173. Boulder, CO: Lynne Rienner.

Kieh, George Klay, and Pita Ogaba Agbese. 2002. *The Military and Politics in Africa: From Engagement to Democratic and Constitutional Control.* Aldershot, UK: Ashgate.

Levine, Daniel H., and José E. Molina, eds. 2011. *The Quality of Democracy in Latin America.* Boulder, CO: Lynne Rienner.

Levitsky, Steve, and Lucan Way. 2010. *Competitive Authoritarianism: Hybrid Regimes after the Cold War.* New York: Cambridge University Press.

Lindberg, Staffan I. 2009. "The Power of Elections in Africa Revisited." In *Democratization by Elections: A New Mode of Transition,* edited by Staffan I. Lindberg, 25–46. Baltimore, MD: Johns Hopkins University Press.

Linz, Juan. 1990. "The Perils of Presidentialism." *Journal of Democracy* 1 (1): 51–69. doi:10.1353/jod.1990.0011.

Lipset, Seymour Martin. 1959. "Some Social Requisites of Democracy: Economic Development and Political Legitimacy." *American Political Science Review* 53 (1): 69–105. doi:10.2307/1951731.

Moore, Barrington. 1966. *Social Origins of Dictatorship and Democracy: Lord and Peasant in the Making of the Modern World.* Boston: Beacon Press.

O'Donnell, Guillermo A. 1979. *Modernization and Bureaucratic-Authoritarianism: Studies in South American Politics.* Berkeley: Institute of International Studies, University of California Press.

Oversloot, Hans, and Ruben Verheul. 2006. "Managing Democracy: Political Parties and the State in Russia." *Journal of Communist Studies and Transition Politics* 22 (3): 383–405. doi:10.1080/13523270600855795.

Pérez Silva, Ciro. 2004. *"Colosio Fernández Dirige Sospechas contra Salinas." La Jornada,* February 11. (http://www.jornada.unam.mx/2004/02/11/008n1pol.php).

Pincus, Steven. 2007. "Rethinking Revolutions: A Neo-Tocquevillian Perspective." In *The Oxford Handbook of Comparative Politics,* edited by Carles Boix and Susan Carol Stokes, 397–415. Oxford, UK: Oxford University Press.

Przeworski, Adam, Michael E. Alvarez, José Antonio Cheibub, and Fernando Limongi. 2000. *Democracy and Development: Political Institutions and Well-Being in the World, 1950–1990.* Cambridge, UK: Cambridge University Press.

Rawlence, Ben, and Chris Albin-Lackey. 2007. "Briefing: Nigeria's 2007 General Elections; Democracy in Retreat." *African Affairs* 106 (424): 497–506. doi:10.1093/afraf/adm039.

Roberts, Andrew. 2010. *The Quality of Democracy in Eastern Europe: Public Preferences and Policy Reforms.* New York: Cambridge University Press.

Roett, Riordan. 1978. *Brazil: Politics in a Patrimonial Society,* rev. ed. New York: Praeger.

Rose, Richard, William Mishler, and Neil Munro. 2011. *Popular Support for an Undemocratic Regime: The Changing Views of Russians.* New York: Cambridge University Press.

Sanderson, Stephen K. 2005. *Revolutions: A Worldwide Introduction to Political and Social Change.* Boulder, CO: Paradigm.

Skocpol, Theda. 1979. *States and Social Revolutions: A Comparative Analysis of France, Russia, and China.* New York: Cambridge University Press.

Stepan, Alfred. 2012. "Tunisia's Transition and the Twin Tolerations." *Journal of Democracy* 23 (2): 89–103.

Tilly, Charles. 1978. *From Mobilization to Revolution.* New York: McGraw-Hill.

Van de Walle, Nicolas. 2006. "Tipping Games: When Do Opposition Parties Coalesce?" In *Electoral Authoritarianism: The Dynamics of Unfree Competition,* edited by Andreas Shedler, 77–92. Boulder, CO: Lynne Rienner.

Wood, Gordon. 1992. *The Radicalism of the American Revolution.* New York: Knopf.

RESOURCES FOR FURTHER STUDY

Ackerman, Peter, and Jack Duvall. 2000. *A Force More Powerful: A Century of Nonviolent Conflict.* New York: St. Martin's Press.

Casper, Gretchen. 1995. *Fragile Democracies: The Legacies of Authoritarian Rule.* Pittsburgh, PA: University of Pittsburgh Press.

Dahl, Robert. 1971. *Polyarchy: Participation and Opposition.* New Haven, CT: Yale University Press.

Diamond, Larry, and Leonardo Morlino. 2005. *Assessing the Quality of Democracy.* Baltimore, MD: Johns Hopkins University Press.

Fish, M. Steven. 2005. *Democracy Derailed in Russia: The Failure of Open Politics.* New York: Cambridge University Press.

Haggard, Stephan, and Robert R. Kaufman. 1995. *The Political Economy of Democratic Transitions.* Princeton, NJ: Princeton University Press.

Morgenstern, Scott, and Benito Nacif, eds. 2002. *Legislative Politics in Latin America.* New York: Cambridge University Press.

O'Donnell, Guillermo. 1999. "Horizontal Accountability in New Democracies." In *The Self-Restraining State: Power and Accountability in New Democracies,* edited by Andreas Schedler, Larry Diamond, and Marc F. Plattner, 29–51. London: Lynne Rienner.

O'Donnell, Guillermo A., and Phillipe Schmitter. 1986. *Transitions from Authoritarian Rule: Tentative Conclusions about Uncertain Democracies.* Baltimore, MD: Johns Hopkins University Press.

Pinkney, Robert. 2003. *Democracy in the Third World.* Boulder, CO: Lynne Rienner.

Przeworski, Adam. 1991. *Democracy and the Market: Political and Economic Reforms in Eastern Europe and Latin America.* Cambridge, UK: Cambridge University Press.

Reynolds, Andrew. 2002. *The Architecture of Democracy: Constitutional Design, Conflict Management, and Democracy.* New York: Oxford University Press.

Schedler, Andreas. 2006. *Electoral Authoritarianism: The Dynamics of Unfree Competition.* Boulder, CO: Lynne Rienner.

Van Inwegen, Patrick. 2011. *Understanding Revolution.* Boulder, CO: Lynne Rienner.

Webb, Paul, and Stephen White, eds. 2007. *Party Politics in New Democracies.* Oxford, UK: Oxford University Press.

Wegren, Stephen K., and Dale R. Herspring, eds. 2010. *After Putin's Russia: Past Imperfect, Future Uncertain.* New York: Rowman and Littlefield.

Zakaria, Fareed. 2003. *The Future of Freedom: Illiberal Democracy at Home and Abroad.* New York: W. W. Norton.

WEB RESOURCES

Bueno de Mesquita, Bruce, Alastair Smith, Randolph Severson, and James Morrow, "The Logic of Political Survival Data Source"
(http://www.nyu.edu/gsas/dept/politics/data/bdm2s2/Logic.htm)

Global Integrity, 2009, Global Integrity Index
(http://report.globalintegrity.org/globalIndex.cfm)

Polity IV Project, 2011, "Political Regime Characteristics and Transitions, 1800–2009"
(http://www.systemicpeace.org/polity/polity4.htm)

Unified Democracy Scores
(http://www.unified-democracy-scores.org)

10 GLOBALIZATION, ECONOMIC SOVEREIGNTY, AND DEVELOPMENT

KEY QUESTIONS

- Do states continue to have effective economic sovereignty, or does globalization force them to adopt certain economic policies?

- What explains the ability of states to pursue successful development policies in the context of globalization?

- In what ways has globalization affected states' ability to respond effectively to economic crises?

- Why have some countries moved to liberalize their economies in the face of globalization more than others?

- What types of regimes are able to pursue more effective economic policies, and why?

The two biggest economic crises since the Great Depression began a decade apart, in 1997 and 2007. Both involved financial crises that started in largely unregulated financial markets in one part of the globe and then spread rapidly, affecting countries around the world. Both showed the potential negative effects of globalization and the limits it can put on individual states' ability to control their economies. The first crisis started when the government of Thailand was forced to "float" its currency, the baht. The Thai economy had been booming, along with those of the rest of the countries that were part of what was known as the "East Asian Miracle." International capital poured into Thailand, factories opened, and the real estate market soared. Much of this activity, however, went through unregulated banks in a relatively weak state, which may be why international investors began to doubt the stability and long-term prospects of the Thai economy. The famous venture capitalist George Soros was one of the first to sell his Thai currency, and as more investors sold, the Thai government no longer could afford to trade dollars for the baht at the set value. Running out of money, the government had to adjust the rate downward, lowering the baht's value against the dollar and other currencies. To beat the odds, investors sold their currencies rapidly, getting out of the currency market the way people get out of a stock market when they think it's about to crash. As investors pulled out, real

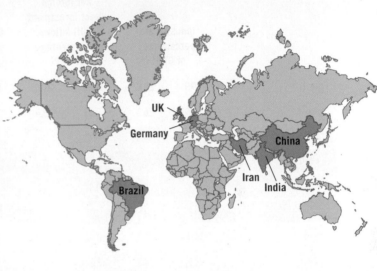

A trader at the close of the New York Stock Exchange on October 6, 2008. The credit crisis triggered a tumble in stocks that left the Dow below 10,000 for the first time in four years.

estate prices and company profits collapsed. Economies that had been booming went into steep decline, and unemployment soared. The economic contagion spread rapidly from Thailand to Indonesia, Malaysia, the Philippines, and South Korea, and later to other developing economies like Brazil and Russia.

The second crisis started in the booming U.S. housing market and the financial market in mortgage-backed securities and derivatives that were tied to it (see chapter 5). Beginning in the heart of the world's largest economy, it spread even more rapidly, hitting hardest in countries whose banks were heavily exposed to the market in U.S. mortgage-backed securities. In contrast to the East Asian crisis, in the Great Recession of 2008–2009, the wealthy economies declined the most and had the hardest time recovering, while the rapidly developing economies of China, India, and Brazil fell less and recovered sooner. In both cases, though, the crises spread rapidly through the global financial system, leaving individual states scrambling to respond effectively and raising questions about their economic sovereignty.

Globalization has clearly raised major questions about economic policy in both wealthy and poorer countries. As we discussed in chapter 5, the biggest of these are the "Who rules?" questions related to whether or not the state still matters. Are states still

COUNTRY AND CONCEPT
Globalization, Economic Sovereignty, and Development

Country	Industry as percentage of GDP[1]		Net foreign direct investment (FDI) inflows as percentage of GDP[2]		Exports of goods and services as percentage of GDP		Imports of goods and services as percentage of GDP		Portfolio investment equity as percentage of GDP	
	1995	2012	1995	2012	1995	2012	1995	2012	1995	2009*
Brazil	36.7	26.3	0.63	3.4	9.5	13	9	14	0.36	2.36
China	47.2	45.3	4.92	3.1	20.9	31	19	27	0.00	0.56
Germany	32.1	28	0.48	0.8	23.5	52	23	46	0.48	0.35
India	28.1	26.1	0.60	1.7	12.2	24	12	32	0.45	1.61
Iran	34.2	37.6	0.02	0.8	13.1	39	13	39*	0.00	–
Japan	34.4	26.3	0.00	0.00	7.8	15	8	16	0.96	0.25
Mexico	27.9	34.2	3.32	1.1	30.4	34	28	36	0.18	0.48
Nigeria	46.7	43	3.84	3.6	42.2	40	42	36	0.00	0.3
Russia	37	36	0.52	2.6	25.9	29	26	22	0.01	0.27
United Kingdom	32	21	1.88	2.3	28.8	32	28	34	0.70	3.52
United States	26.3	19.2	0.79	1.3	12.3	14	12	18	0.22	1.14

* Data are from 2009, the latest year for which data are available.

[1]Data on industry as percentage of GDP are from *CIA World Factbook* (https://www.cia.gov/library/publications/the-world-factbook/fields/2012.html#br).

[2]Data on stock of FDI, imports and exports of goods and services as a percentage of GDP, and portfolio investment equity are from the World Bank. FDI data are available at http://data.worldbank.org/indicator/BX.KLT.DINV.WD.GD.ZS; exports data are available at http://data.worldbank.org/indicator/NE.EXP.GNFS.ZS; imports data are available at http://data.worldbank.org/indicator/NE.IMP.GNFS.ZS/; and portfolio investment data are available at http://data.worldbank.org/indicator/BM.KLT.DINV.GD.ZS.

sovereign over their economies? Does globalization force different regimes and societies with different values to follow the same economic policies that are dictated by the need to attract global capital? Modern states, whatever the regime type, are expected to guide economic growth; even the most venal want leverage over the economy so they can benefit from it. Economic growth provides revenue to a state and legitimacy to a regime. How does globalization affect states' abilities to gain these benefits? To the extent states still matter, what explains whether a particular set of policies can steer an economy beneficially, and what explains which states are able to adopt these policies?

One thing is certain: globalization has helped produce dramatically different levels of economic development around the world. The "Country and Concept" table demonstrates this for our case-study countries. First, it shows the level of industrialization among our case-study countries, demonstrating that the wealthiest are now accurately termed *postindustrial*. It also shows key aspects of globalization: **foreign direct investment (FDI)**, foreign investment in directly productive activity; **trade**, exports and imports of goods and services; and **international capital flows**, the movement of money across national borders. In most countries, all three areas show marked increases. The greatest increases, though, are in the final column, portfolio investment equity, which partially measures the effects of international capital flows. These have expanded dramatically in almost all countries. The virtual elimination of barriers to moving money across borders and improvement in global communications have resulted in more than $1 trillion crossing international borders daily.

This chapter examines the impact of these trends on both economic well-being and states' abilities to respond effectively and maintain their economic sovereignty. We turn first to the wealthy countries. For them, the biggest issues are how to respond to the movement of manufacturing out of their countries and whether they can continue to maintain the level of social spending their citizens have come to expect, especially in Europe.

Video link:
What is FDI? The example of Malaysia

foreign direct investment (FDI)
Investment from abroad in productive activity in another country

trade
The flow of goods and services across national borders

international capital flows
Movements of capital in the form of money across international borders

Video link:
What is foreign trade?

WEALTHY COUNTRIES: GLOBALIZATION AND ECONOMIC SOVEREIGNTY

In the first globalization debate in the wealthy countries of Europe, North America, and Australasia (Australia, New Zealand, and Japan), the situation was not referred to as *globalization,* a word that had not yet come into vogue in the 1970s. It was about *deindustrialization,* especially in the United States. The countries that had long been known as "advanced industrial democracies" discovered that they were rapidly losing their industry; their economies were making a transition to "postindustrial" society in which the service sector, high-technology endeavors, and research and design were replacing manufacturing as the core of the economy. In retrospect, this was the start of a wave of globalization that began in earnest in the 1970s.

As transportation and communication improved and liberal trade policies allowed industries to take advantage of lower production costs in developing countries, corporations began moving manufacturing plants out of wealthy countries and exporting products back to their home markets. Hundreds of thousands of workers, long reliant on relatively well-paying and secure jobs in such industries as automobile manufacturing and steel, faced unemployment and bleak prospects. They had to seek retraining in newly emerging fields or take lower-paying, unskilled positions in sectors such as retail, where they often had to work multiple jobs for longer hours. Managers, meanwhile, reaped increasing salaries as their companies profited and expanded. The result in most countries has been growing inequality.

The abstract logic of globalization's effects on wealthy countries, then, seems pretty clear. As capital becomes more mobile and can flow around the globe, even wealthy governments must do what they can to attract it. They must maintain macroeconomic stability by keeping inflation low, which requires restraining government spending and the money supply (following the monetarist principles we outlined in chapter 5). They must keep corporate taxes low so that businesses will want to invest, but if taxes are low, then spending must be low as well, meaning that social welfare programs also have to be restrained. They must ensure that labor is flexible and relatively compliant and do what they can to keep labor unions from making too many demands, because rigid contracts and rules that guarantee jobs or benefits for long periods discourage investment. And, of course, they must keep tariffs and other barriers to the entry and exit of capital at a minimum.

According to this perspective, which Colin Hay (2004) called **hyperglobalization**, globalization tends to produce a **convergence** among the policies of wealthy countries. The distinctions among liberal market economies (e.g., the United States), European welfare states (e.g., Germany), and developmentalist states (e.g., Japan), as well as partisan differences over economic policy within each country, tend to disappear as all of these governments are forced to conform to the logic of attracting global capital. In the new millennium, however, growing numbers of scholars have questioned this argument, noting that while changes are certainly occurring in the general direction Hay predicted, they are not happening very rapidly and are strikingly different in different countries. Many comparativists use institutionalist arguments to suggest that, at least for wealthy countries, national economic sovereignty will continue to exist: countries can and are choosing unique means to respond to globalization's demands. While globalization applies pressure toward convergence, long-established political and economic institutions in specific countries heavily influence how these countries can and will respond, with different effects on their long-term economic well-being.

Varieties of Capitalism Approach

The most influential school of thought that questions hyperglobalization is known as the **varieties of capitalism (VOC)** approach. It focuses primarily on business firms and how they are governed in terms of their interactions with government, one another, workers, and sources of finance such as banks and stock markets. Proponents of this approach distinguish between two broad types of economies among wealthy capitalist countries: liberal market economies (LMEs) and coordinated market economies (CMEs).

Liberal Market Economies (LMEs)
Liberal market economies (LMEs), such as the United States and the United Kingdom, rely more heavily on market relationships, meaning that firms interact with other firms and secure sources of finance

---

hyperglobalization
Thesis that globalization is so powerful that it will overwhelm the power of nation-states, forcing convergence of economic policies

convergence
Argument that globalization will force similar economic and social policies across all countries

Web link:
Interactive map: spread of globalization

varieties of capitalism (VOC)
School of thought analyzing wealthy market economies that focuses primarily on business firms and how they are governed; divides such economies into LMEs and CMEs and argues that globalization will not produce convergence between them

liberal market economies (LMEs)
In the varieties of capitalism approach, countries that rely heavily on market relationships to govern economic activity; the United States and United Kingdom are key examples

through purely market-based transactions. They know little about one another's inner workings, which leads them to focus primarily on short-term profits to enhance stock prices, a key source of finance. Such firms' relationship to workers is also primarily via open markets: rates of unionization are low and labor laws are flexible, allowing firms to hire and fire employees with ease. The government's role in such economies is relatively minimal and is focused simply on ensuring that market relationships function properly through, for instance, fairly stringent antimonopoly laws and rules governing stock exchanges that guarantee that all buyers are privy to the same information.

Coordinated Market Economies (CMEs) Coordinated market economies (CMEs), by contrast, involve more conscious coordination among firms, financiers, unions, and government. Many firms and banks hold large amounts of stock in one another's operations, which gives them inside information on how the others operate. This, in turn, encourages firms to coordinate their activities and establish long-term relationships in terms of finance and buying inputs. Firms are able to focus on longer-term initiatives because financiers have inside information about the potential for long-term gains. CMEs tend to have stronger unions and higher levels of unionization, and worker training is focused within sectors of the economy and within related firms. The government is involved in negotiating agreements among firms and between firms and unions, and it allows or even encourages the close relationships that might be termed *insider trading* or quasi-monopoly situations in an LME. Germany is a prime example of a CME. Japan's developmentalist state is usually classified as a CME as well, though with a smaller role for unions than is found in European CMEs.

Implications Peter Hall and David Soskice (2001), who created the VOC approach, coined the term **comparative institutional advantage**, as opposed to the standard comparative (economic) advantage, to help explain how these different kinds of economies respond to the pressures of globalization. They argued that the various institutionalized relationships in each kind of economy are complementary: the institutions work together to provide greater benefits than any single institution could alone. It is difficult, they argued, to change one particular institution, such as corporate finance, without changing many others. Consequently, firms have interests in maintaining the institutions in which they operate, and they will be reluctant to change them in response to globalization. Firms in CMEs benefit from the various institutions that help them coordinate their activities, train their workers, and secure the services of employees over the long term. A more rigid labor market that does not make it as easy for workers to move from firm to firm, for instance, complements a training system in which firms invest in educating their workers for specific tasks. If workers could quickly move from job to job, the firms would lose the benefits of their training investment. In LMEs, by contrast, more flexible labor markets give firms little incentive to train employees. Workers and the public education system therefore invest in more general skills that workers can transfer from firm to firm, meaning that firms don't have to invest directly in employee training.

coordinated market economies (CMEs)
In the varieties of capitalism approach, capitalist economies in which firms, financiers, unions, and government consciously coordinate their actions via interlocking ownership and participation; Germany and Japan are key examples

comparative institutional advantage
Idea in the varieties of capitalism school of thought that different kinds of capitalist systems have different institutional advantages that they usually will try to maintain, resulting in different responses to external economic pressures

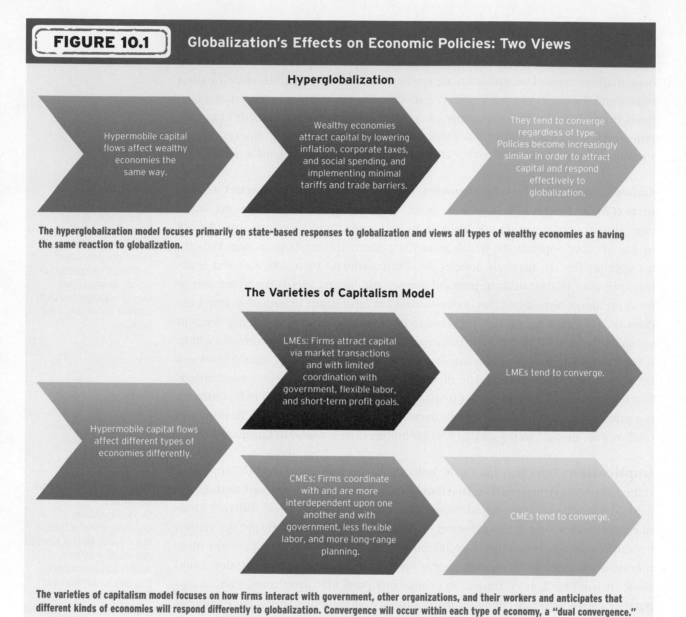

FIGURE 10.1 Globalization's Effects on Economic Policies: Two Views

Hyperglobalization

Hypermobile capital flows affect wealthy economies the same way.

Wealthy economies attract capital by lowering inflation, corporate taxes, and social spending, and implementing minimal tariffs and trade barriers.

They tend to converge regardless of type. Policies become increasingly similar in order to attract capital and respond effectively to globalization.

The hyperglobalization model focuses primarily on state-based responses to globalization and views all types of wealthy economies as having the same reaction to globalization.

The Varieties of Capitalism Model

Hypermobile capital flows affect different types of economies differently.

LMEs: Firms attract capital via market transactions and with limited coordination with government, flexible labor, and short-term profit goals.

LMEs tend to converge.

CMEs: Firms coordinate with and are more interdependent upon one another and with government, less flexible labor, and more long-range planning.

CMEs tend to converge.

The varieties of capitalism model focuses on how firms interact with government, other organizations, and their workers and anticipates that different kinds of economies will respond differently to globalization. Convergence will occur within each type of economy, a "dual convergence."

The comparative institutional advantage of LMEs is in their flexible market relationships. In response to globalization, they tend to strengthen market mechanisms even more. Governments work to decrease union influence, provide broad-based education for an ever more flexible workforce, and increase the variety and efficiency of open-market sources of finance such as stock markets. LMEs, advocates argue, are more adept at making radical innovations in response to new opportunities. Management and workers all have few reasons for caution, as their long-term futures are not tied to a specific firm.

The comparative institutional advantage of CMEs is in their ability to adjust but maintain their coordination mechanisms in response to globalization. Firms do not abandon countries with CMEs because doing so would cause them to give up the institutional advantages they have there, advantages in which they have long invested. CMEs are better at marginal innovation than at radical innovation because they can and must coordinate activities across a number of firms and sectors, including training workers in specific skills. Management and workers have incentives to make marginal changes to improve the performance of the firms in which they have a long-term interest. CMEs tend to be more innovative in older industries, such as pharmaceuticals, than in newer industries, such as high-tech sectors. Indeed, firms in CMEs tend to transfer their branches that engage in more radical innovations to LMEs, where they benefit from the comparative institutional advantages that LMEs offer.

The logic of the VOC approach also suggests that LMEs and CMEs are likely to pursue distinct fiscal and welfare policies. At first glance, it might seem that CMEs, with their high levels of government involvement in coordinating the economy, would be likely to pursue more interventionist, Keynesian fiscal policies, but VOC theorists argue exactly the opposite. Because CMEs have built in ways to stabilize the labor market to maintain employment, they are less likely to need or want to pursue fiscal stimulation. LMEs, on the other hand, have far more flexible labor markets; therefore, unemployment is likely to go up more quickly in a recession, and their governments will need to pursue more Keynesian stimulation to reduce unemployment.

Convergence theorists argue that governments will have to cut spending on social welfare as they cut taxes to attract global capital, whereas scholars using the VOC approach argue that in CMEs, business often supports social spending. Much of this spending provides workers with security, which helps them stay with a particular firm without fear of losing their jobs. Since large businesses in CMEs benefit from social spending, they tolerate higher taxes and spending. LMEs, on the other hand, operate much as convergence theorists speculate they "should." Greater labor market flexibility does not provide the same incentives found in CMEs, and firms are less willing to tolerate the high taxes necessary to maintain high spending, so social spending drops more precipitously in the face of globalization.

Responses to Globalization The Great Recession, of course, raised major questions for the VOC approach to understanding wealthy economies in the face of globalization. Every wealthy country felt the recession's effects quickly and dramatically. Is convergence in fact happening, despite the differences in types of advanced capitalist systems? Prior to the crisis, Hall and Gingerich (2009) tested the VOC approach with a series of extensive statistical techniques. They found that the patterns outlined by the approach held up empirically. Each type of economy (LME and CME) can be discerned by a set of complementary practices across a variety of statistical measures. Comparative institutional advantage holds up as well, in the sense that countries that more closely conform to one of the two models achieved higher growth rates. Countries with more mixed systems, and therefore less reinforcing comparative institutional advantages, grew more slowly. Across a variety of measures, however, they also found that most wealthy economies are moving in the direction the forces of globalization would suggest: protection of labor is down, social spending is down, and flexibility has increased. Hall and Gingerich point out, though, that the differences between LMEs and CMEs persist; while both types of economies have moved in the same direction, CMEs remain quite distinct from LMEs.

Kathleen Thelen (2012), however, argued that while coordination may be continuing, it is not necessarily resulting in the same outcomes. In particular, she noted that inequality is increasing in some CMEs but not in others. She suggested that VOC scholars have often conflated coordination and egalitarianism and that CMEs can preserve the former (as indicated by Hall and Gingerich's finding above) without the latter. Understanding the differences among CMEs requires understanding changes in the economies since the distinction between CMEs and LMEs first arose. Of particular importance were the rise of the service sector and decline of manufacturing and the entry of women into the labor force. Workers in the service sector do not require the specific skills that are needed in manufacturing but instead need more general skills. This makes coordination less crucial and more general education more important. In some CMEs, especially in Scandinavia, women were encouraged to enter the workforce early, and the extensive social welfare system (see chapter 11) created a large public sector as well. These workers did not demand, and business was not interested in providing, sector-specific skills, but they did need extensive training to respond to an increasingly flexible labor market. Coordination has been reduced, but relative social equality has been maintained. In other CMEs, including our case study of Germany, women did not enter the workforce as early. As manufacturing shrank as a share of the economy, the service sector demanded more flexible labor. Service-sector workers and women were not part of the coordinated system that benefitted manufacturing and were not powerful enough to demand changes; coordination in the CME continued, but its scope shrank as it applied to fewer and fewer workers. Those workers continued to benefit, but workers in the newer sectors—who are disproportionately women and immigrants—did not, so inequality increased. Thus, CMEs as a group have not responded in identical ways to the forces of economic change and globalization.

Video link:
Kathleen Thelen on varieties of capitalism

Scholars have also found little evidence that CMEs and LMEs pursued distinct fiscal policies or other responses to the Great Recession. Amable and Azizi (2011) examined fiscal policies over a twenty-year period prior to the recession and found no evidence that LMEs follow more expansionary policies during downturns, as the VOC approach suggests. Indeed, they found the opposite to be true and suggested that the skilled workers in manufacturing who are at the heart of CMEs have more difficulty finding new jobs than do other workers, so they demand Keynesian policies to keep unemployment down. Pontusson and Raess (2012) looked at fiscal policy in response to the Great Recession and argued that there is no discernible difference in how major, wealthy countries responded; all initially pursued Keynesian policies to stimulate the economy, then reduced those. While the amount of stimulus varied, CMEs and LMEs did not pursue distinctly different policies. Other scholars, while agreeing that globalization is not forcing homogeneity on all countries, have criticized the simple dichotomy between CMEs and LMEs, arguing that in various areas of economic policy it is clear that more nuanced differences exist among countries, especially within the CME category (Morgan and Whitley 2012). Nancy Bermeo and Jonas Pontusson (2012), while not rejecting the VOC approach entirely, noted that the longer-term effects of globalization produced a narrower range of responses to the Great Recession than to prior crises. In particular, deindustrialization, the decline of labor unions, and the rise of the financial sector in most wealthy countries meant it was difficult to mobilize workers to demand protection for particular industries (the auto industry was the only exception to this) to reduce unemployment more rapidly, as happened in some countries in the past. While this effect was strongest in LMEs, it existed in many CMEs as well.

The logic of globalization seems clear. Capital's greater mobility ought to give it greater power vis-à-vis immobile states and less-mobile workers. Virtually all scholars agree that this has happened to some extent over the past thirty to forty years, but the changes may not have been as dramatic as the hyperglobalization thesis asserted. VOC theorists argue that notable differences in how capitalism operates remain clear. Common trends toward greater openness to the market, however, seem equally clear. Our case studies of the United Kingdom and Germany are paradigmatic examples of an LME and CME economy. The United Kingdom demonstrates how an LME responds by instituting more "market-friendly" policies in the face of crises, aided by its majoritarian parliamentary system that makes enacting large policy changes relatively easy. Germany also demonstrates significant reform in the direction of an LME, but it still remains a CME, and one that has responded rather effectively to the Great Recession.

CASE Study

UNITED KINGDOM: RADICAL REFORM IN A LIBERAL MARKET ECONOMY

The United Kingdom and the United States are the classic examples of LMEs for scholars using the varieties of capitalism approach. Prior to the 1980s, however, the United Kingdom had exceptionally large and active trade unions, and since World War II, the country has had a far more extensive welfare state than the United States. While its social spending is below that of most European countries, it is

- **TYPE OF ECONOMY**
  LME

- **REFORM EFFORTS**
  Reforms as predicted by LME model; reduced power of trade unions, privatization of state-owned companies; some reduction in social spending

A banner held by demonstrators opposed to the British government's cuts to health care and social services. Fiscal austerity was the central principle of the Conservative government's response to continuing recession since the Great Recession.

- **RESPONSE TO GREAT RECESSION**
  First stimulus under Labour government, then austerity under Conservative government; very little recovery

- **EFFECTS OF POLITICAL SYSTEM**
  Majoritarian parliamentary system facilitated dramatic economic reforms

well above that of the United States. Twice in the last generation, the United Kingdom has pursued some of the most radical economic reforms of any major Western country, first in the 1980s under Prime Minister Margaret Thatcher and again beginning in 2010 under newly elected prime minister David Cameron. Thatcher's government profoundly reduced the role of the state in key areas via privatization of state assets, and it reduced the power of unions, as the varieties of capitalism approach would predict an LME would do in the face of globalization. Thatcher did not significantly reduce overall social spending, however. Cameron's more recent efforts zeroed in on spending and the budget deficit, introducing dramatic reductions to both, again as would be expected in an LME facing a severe financial crisis.

The 1970s were a period of unparalleled economic crisis in the United Kingdom. Rising oil prices and global recession hit the country particularly hard, reducing growth and increasing inflation. Both Conservative and Labour governments tried but failed to improve the economy. As inflation grew, unions demanded that wage increases keep up, which fueled more inflation. About half of the British labor force belonged to a union, an unusually high level even by European standards. The government tried voluntary agreements like those common in a corporatist system to get unions to restrain their demands and thereby slow inflation. Unfortunately, the peak labor association, the Trade Unions Congress (TUC), did not have the power over its members that unions in corporatist systems do, and local unions repeatedly ignored the voluntary restraints negotiated by the TUC leadership. In an LME such as the United Kingdom, neither unions nor businesses have a history of or an incentive to negotiate lasting agreements to moderate wage increases, so the result was a growing number of strikes. These culminated in the "winter of discontent" in 1978–1979, when the Labour government lost control and massive strikes occurred.

Out of this crisis rose a new manifestation of the Conservative Party, which Thatcher led to victory in the 1979 election. She won on promises of implementing a completely new approach to economic policy, unions, and the welfare state, along the same lines as the approach adopted by Ronald Reagan, who was elected U.S. president a year later. Her first target was the power of unions, which she sought to reduce to create a more flexible labor force, in line with the LME model. She passed legislation that made it far more difficult for unions to strike, culminating in a standoff with the National Mineworkers Union in 1984–1985 over a strike against the state-owned coal companies. Thatcher ultimately defeated the union, symbolizing the end of an era of union strength in the United Kingdom. By 1995, union membership had dropped from half of all employees when Thatcher was elected to only a third of all employees. As the LME model suggests, when facing global economic pressure, LMEs look to reduce labor costs and increase flexibility to compete more effectively. This is precisely what Thatcher did.

The second area of major reform under Thatcher was privatization of state-owned assets. Since World War II, the British state, especially under Labour governments, had taken ownership of numerous large companies, including utilities, mining, auto manufacturers, and airlines. Many of these were far from profitable when Thatcher took power. She began selling off the state-owned companies to private investors, ultimately privatizing 120 corporations. Some became profitable private-sector companies; others simply went bankrupt. One immediate effect was increased unemployment as the unprofitable companies laid off workers in large numbers; unemployment rose from an average of 4.2 percent in the late 1970s to 9.5 percent in the 1980s (Huber and Stephens 2001, A11).

Thatcher's most popular policy was not the privatization of state-owned companies but rather the sale of state-owned housing. After World War II, the British government had dedicated itself to building public housing for the working class. By the 1970s, the vast majority of the working class—typically union and Labour Party members—paid subsidized rents to live in publicly owned houses or apartments. Thatcher sold more than a million housing units, mostly single-family homes, mostly to the current tenants. This created a dramatically expanded class of homeowners who were no longer tenants of the state. Most political analysts argued that it also transformed many of these individuals from Labour voters into Conservative voters and helped Thatcher win two unprecedented landslide reelections.

Prime Minister Thatcher came to power a committed monetarist, advocating a reduced government with lower budget deficits and tight monetary policy to eliminate inflation. In the early 1980s, her government successfully reduced inflation by reducing the money supply and budget deficit. This deepened the ongoing recession but made clear that fighting inflation was Thatcher's top priority. She also shifted the source of taxation, reducing individual and corporate income taxes and compensating by raising Britain's national sales tax (the value-added tax, or VAT). The net result was an increased tax burden on lower-income groups and a lower burden on the wealthy. She was less successful in changing fiscal policy, failing to reduce significantly the overall size of the government's budget and social spending. She set out to radically reform Britain's welfare state, which centered on what the British call "social security," government payments to the poor, unemployed, disabled, and others who are unable to make a minimally adequate income in the market. She reduced the real value of social security payments and insisted that the unemployed seek work while collecting benefits. She also proposed dramatic changes to Britain's universal health system, the National Health Service (NHS), but the system's popularity prevented her from implementing most of these proposals (see chapter 11). In the end, her only revolutionary change to Britain's welfare system was the dramatic reduction in public housing. Later, the Labour government under Tony Blair (1997–2007) actually instituted the first work requirement for welfare benefits, and the new coalition government led by the Conservatives in 2010 increased these requirements, ultimately fulfilling some of Thatcher's long-held goals.

Web link:
Did Thatcher transform Britain's economy?

Video link:
What did Margaret Thatcher do for Britain's economy?

Despite the fact that social spending did not drop, inequality increased more in Britain under Thatcher than in any other wealthy country: the share of the population living on less than half of the average national income increased from 9 to 25 percent under Thatcher and has since dropped only slightly (Ginsburg 2001, 186). Regional inequality increased a great deal as well. Many of the unprofitable state-owned companies and older manufacturing firms were in the northern half of the country. Deindustrialization combined with Thatcher's reforms to hurt that region severely, causing increased unemployment and poverty, while the southern part of the country, especially London, became one of the wealthiest regions in Europe.

Thatcher's reforms reshaped the British economy by making it a purer LME. The reforms were particularly dramatic not only because of the crisis the country faced at the time but also because Britain's majoritarian parliamentary system allows a government great power to reorient policy. The comparison with Ronald Reagan in the United States is interesting in this regard. Elected just a year later and holding the same ideas as Thatcher, Reagan was not able to make nearly as sweeping reforms. While he pursued a similarly successful monetary policy to defeat inflation and reduced the power of unions (though not as significantly as Thatcher), Reagan instituted no changes as substantial as Thatcher's privatization. The U.S. presidential system, in which an independent Congress is often controlled by the opposition party, combined with a federal system that reserves considerable power for the states, limited what Reagan could accomplish.

Subsequent British governments have not fundamentally changed Thatcher's policies. The Labour government under Tony Blair (1997–2007) and Gordon Brown (2007–2010) took its most dramatic action immediately after coming into office: it gave autonomy to the Bank of England to set monetary policy, much as the Federal Reserve does in the United States. In the past, the PM and the cabinet had controlled monetary policy, so giving the bank autonomy clearly signaled that the new Labour government would value macroeconomic stability at least as much as its Conservative predecessors. The Labour government presided over a period of unprecedented economic well-being from 1997 to 2007, until the financial crisis of 2008–2009. GDP growth, averaging 2.6 percent annually, was well above that of other European countries; inflation averaged only 1.5 percent; the deficit was kept low; and Britain was the favored location for foreign investment in Europe (Faucher-King and Le Galès 2010). After 2002, the government invested more heavily in education and job training in a successful effort to lower the unemployment rate, which dropped to only 5.5 percent. A successful anti-child-poverty policy removed over one million children from poverty between 2005 and 2007, though overall inequality was reduced only slightly. Labour, however, did not reverse the policies that had weakened trade unions or the basic monetarist orientation of British macroeconomic policy, thus preserving the fundamentals of the British LME.

The exceptional British economic success up to 2007 was based in part on growing financial, stock, and real estate markets, all of which were heavily hit by the global financial crisis. The economy shrank nearly 5 percent in 2009, and unemployment hit 8 percent (up from 4.5 percent a couple of years earlier). As in most Western economies, sluggish growth resumed in 2010, though unemployment dropped only slightly. Gordon Brown's Labour government initially responded similarly to the U.S. government, first with large infusions of cash to ailing banks and then with a stimulus program, primarily via tax cuts, that dramatically increased the government deficit. The failure of these measures to have a significant short-term effect led to a Labour rout in the May 2010 election, which brought an unusual Conservative-led coalition government to power (see chapter 7). The new government quickly reversed course on economic policy, arguing that the government's growing debt threatened to undermine Britain's financial standing in the global economy, as was happening to both Greece and Ireland. The government's first budget introduced in October 2010 instituted draconian cuts in spending, averaging 19 percent. The goal was to reduce the budget deficit from 11 percent of GDP in 2010 to under 3 percent in 2015. The government also raised the retirement age, required those on long-term unemployment benefits to seek work actively, and capped those benefits at one year. Protests erupted several times after the announcement of the new budget, primarily among university students reacting against major tuition increases. The only sectors spared the ax were the National Health Service (see chapter 11) and primary and secondary education. A year later, though, the government increased austerity further, including raising the value-added tax, the biggest tax average citizens pay, to reduce the deficit. In mid-2013, it announced even more austerity, including ending automatic pay increases for civil servants and further cuts to social security recipients, though it promised new spending on infrastructure to try to stimulate the economy.

The effects of austerity by mid-2013 were less than the government had hoped. Indeed, in 2012 the economy slipped into a second recession. In 2013 it avoided a third recession by achieving growth slightly above zero. Unemployment was at 7.8 percent, only slightly below its peak in 2009, and inequality seemed to be increasing. Slow growth constrained tax revenues so the government budget deficit remained stubbornly high, at 7.7 percent of GDP. Inflation, however, was at 3 percent, so the Bank of England was reluctant to pursue more economic stimulation for fear of increasing inflation. The new policies clearly followed the standard path of an LME facing a globalization-induced crisis in that they reduced the size of the government to restore financial order and encourage renewed business investment. Britain's majoritarian parliamentary system allowed the new government to pursue these policies with little compromise, making them among the most dramatic responses to growing deficits anywhere in the world.

CASE Summary

Faced with crises induced by global economic forces, British economic policy responded mostly in a manner predicted by the LME model. First, Britain reduced the power of unions and privatized many state assets, and then it cut government spending and debt to encourage new investment. Thatcher's reforms resulted in a more flexible labor market with more competitive wages in which a higher percentage of employees worked at part-time jobs and far fewer were unionized. Britain's corporate ownership system, like that of the United States, remained dominated by large pension and insurance funds that were interested in short-term profitability. This strategy is typical of an LME, and with a more flexible labor market, it allowed British companies to enter new markets aggressively and relatively successfully. The initial result was a booming economy accompanied by growing inequality, but one that was highly exposed to the very global markets most severely affected by the financial crisis of 2008–2009. The primary exception to the LME model was fiscal policy, both the limited changes under Thatcher and the extreme austerity more recently. VOC theorists argued that LME countries in economic crisis have to pursue fiscal stimulus in the face of high unemployment and limited welfare benefits, but Britain's Conservative government has so far resisted that pressure, in spite of declining popularity. While Britain remains a highly competitive LME that has reformed to succeed in the globalization era, its prospects are uncertain as it tries to recover from the downside of its success: exposure to the global crisis.

CASE Questions

1. Britain provides one of the most dramatic examples of reform in an LME. Overall, does its experience suggest the LME model is a viable path to negotiate the globalized economy?

2. What explains the major exception to the LME model in Britain: its fiscal policy? What implications does this have for the utility of the LME model to help us understand contemporary wealthy capitalist countries?

Web link:
The unwisdom
of elites

CASE Study

GERMANY: STRUGGLING TO REFORM A COORDINATED MARKET ECONOMY

By the late 1990s, political pundits had shifted away from portraying the German social market economy as a singular success story of "high everything"—high productivity, high-quality goods, high wages, high taxes, high benefits—and toward portraying it as the "sick man of Europe" that was unable to reform in the face of new economic realities. Following the hyperglobalization thesis, they argued that Germany needed to change its economic model to prosper under globalization. Scholars using the varieties of capitalism approach question this conventional wisdom, however. To them, Germany is a classic case of a CME whose institutions, though modified, continue to function to its comparative institutional advantage. Significant changes in corporate finance, labor market flexibility, and welfare policies, however, have clearly been in the direction of an LME. It was particularly hard-hit by the 2008–2009 recession, in part because of changes in the financial sector. But its ability to rebound relatively quickly and to keep unemployment from increasing substantially indicated to many scholars that reforms had made the German model flexible enough to withstand the latest shocks from globalization. While having modified its policies, Germany still maintains a distinctively CME model that has weathered the latest crisis relatively well, though other crises loom ahead.

- **TYPE OF ECONOMY**
  CME

- **REFORM EFFORTS**
  Changes in corporate finance, reduced neocorporatist wage agreements, greater labor market flexibility

- **RESPONSE TO GREAT RECESSION**
  Relatively successful, continuing problems of large debt and aging population

- **EFFECTS OF POLITICAL SYSTEM**
  Reforms modest due to high number of veto players

Employees of Amazon in Germany hold a sign reading *Tarifvertrag* (labor contract) during a strike in July 2013. Greater labor flexibility has reduced worker protections as Germany's CME has adjusted to global pressures, including investments by American firms used to a more flexible labor market.

While German policies have clearly moved in the direction of the LME model, the question is how fundamental these changes are. Cox (2002) argued that most reforms have been "tinkering" rather than "transformative," but Streeck (2009) suggested that the cumulative changes across an array of economic sectors demonstrate that fundamental changes are in process. Streeck argued, though, that those changes are neither caused by globalization nor will they lead to Germany's transformation into an LME. Instead, he suggested that the changes are primarily due to contradictions within the German model itself, that they will continue in the direction of liberalization, but they will replicate neither the old CME nor an LME. The international market perhaps provided greater opportunity for these changes to occur, but was not the driving force. The key changes Streeck pointed to are in (1) corporate finance; (2) collective bargaining between employers and unions, which threatens to undermine the corporatist agreements that have kept wages high and labor unrest minimal; and (3) Germany's elaborate social welfare programs in response to chronic deficits. These factors have combined to significantly liberalize Germany's CME, though they have not completely transformed it.

Globalization has had its biggest impact in Germany's corporate finance system. While German practices have certainly not adhered completely to the LME model, German businesses have taken advantage of globalization in ways that have altered the coordination within Germany's CME. With the rise of new global financial opportunities, large German businesses and the German government have pushed for financial reform, including legal reforms to open the stock market up to global investors and the listing of German firms on global markets. Manufacturers have looked to these changes as providing new sources of finance, and banks see them as new areas of profit. The net effect from 1996 to 2002 was a reduction of over 50 percent in the share of firms' capital that was controlled by the banks that lent them money (Streeck 2009, 80). German firms instead rely increasingly on sales of stock to global investors as a primary means of obtaining financing. This means that German firms, like firms in LMEs, have had to become more concerned about anonymous shareholders' short-term interests in profits. Codetermination, unions' participation in corporate management (see chapter 5), still exists, but it has been reduced significantly due to increased concern for shareholders' short-term returns.

For banks, globalization provided new profit opportunities but exposure to high risk as well. German banks began investing heavily in securities, including mortgage-backed securities and derivatives based on the risky U.S. mortgages that were the source of the Great Recession. These investments provided significant profits, but the banks suffered severe losses when the bubble burst in 2008. The German government responded by creating a fund that troubled banks could voluntarily draw on, as well as essentially nationalizing the banks in the worst trouble. The government subsequently passed legislation that tightened up regulations to limit the practices that had gotten the banks into trouble in the first place and to increase the assets that banks were required to keep on hand in case of a crisis (Hardie and Howarth 2009).

Globalization has also affected wages and collective bargaining between employers and unions in Germany, though key elements of neocorporatism (see chapter 5) remain and have helped Germany weather the Great Recession relatively well. Germany's neocorporatist model was always based on peak associations of employers and unions being able to make and stick to wage agreements. These agreements kept wages high while providing stability and predictability. Globalization, though, has created divisions among German companies. The largest have invested significantly outside of Germany. In key sectors, notably pharmaceuticals, the most successful firms have noted the institutional advantages of LMEs such as the United States and have relocated (or sold) their more innovative components to those economies, leaving the less innovative areas, such as chemicals and metal working, in Germany. In doing so, they have created globally linked production processes that are very sensitive to disruption. Because of this, they have become more willing to agree to high wages to avoid strikes or lockouts. Smaller businesses, which lack international investment and are often in direct competition with manufacturers in other countries, cannot afford these higher wages, and they increasingly ignore agreements set between unions and the largest employers. Unions respond with more strikes at the local level against the smaller firms. The result has been a fragmentation of the neocorporatist agreements that used to govern wages. In 1995, 53 percent of all workplaces had wage agreements negotiated by industry-wide collective bargaining; by 2006 this had dropped to 37 percent (Streeck and Hassel 2003, 112; Streeck 2009, 39). Greater flexibility has also allowed firms to increase their use of temporary workers, who are not covered by any agreements and therefore have little job security. These trends coincided with the steep decline in membership in employers' associations and unions that we discussed in chapter 7.

High unemployment was long the Achilles' heel of the German economy (see Figure 10.2), but it dropped substantially in the first decade of the new millennium, from a high of nearly 12 percent in the late 1990s to below 8 percent just before the recession in 2008. The recession itself only increased unemployment by 1 percent, a phenomenon that some analysts dubbed a new "German Miracle." The greater flexibility in bargaining conditions at the level of the individual firm had a role in this success. Businesses were able to lower real wages throughout the decade of the 2000s, which facilitated the rise in employment. When the recession hit, the social market economy tradition of working cooperatively with unions allowed many employers to negotiate with their unions to accept cuts in wages and hours to avoid layoffs. The government gave incentives for this with its *Kurzarbeit* (short time) program, which subsidizes agreements that retain workers at reduced hours rather than firing them.

As we noted in chapter 5, Germany initially responded to the Great Recession as most Western countries did, with a stimulus plan. Germany's consisted mainly of fortifying its banks' financial position, stimulating the auto industry via a "cash for clunkers" program, and funding the *Kurzarbeit* program. As the budget deficit grew,

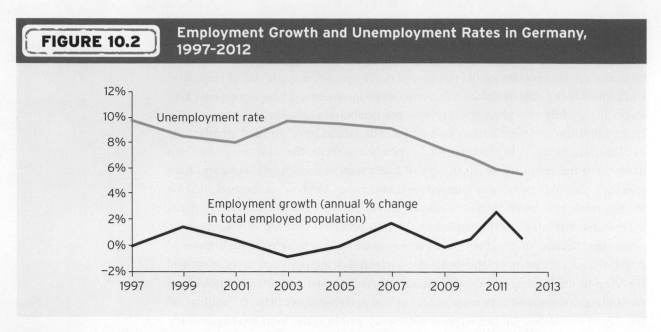

FIGURE 10.2 Employment Growth and Unemployment Rates in Germany, 1997-2012

Sources: Statistiches Bundesamt, Wiesbaden, 2011, and Eurostat (http://stats.oecd.org/Index.aspx?QueryId=38898 and http://appsso.eurostat.ec.europa .eu/nui/show.do?dataset=une_rt_a&lang=en).

though, it returned to its traditional stance of fiscal austerity, arguing that all of the EU should do the same. With its export markets rebounding and unemployment remaining low due to the *Kurzarbeit* program, the initial effects of the recession were short-lived. Growth returned in 2010 and 2011, but the country, along with most of Europe, returned to recession in 2012. By 2013, slight positive growth was restored. Fiscal austerity and declining demand for Germany's exports as economies like China and India began to slow down turned what looked like a healthy recovery into a second recession. Throughout, however, German unemployment continued to drop, hitting only 5.3 percent in mid-2013, and its fiscal deficit dropped below 1 percent by 2012.

One problem plaguing almost all wealthy countries even before the Great Recession is aging populations: fewer workers must pay for the social welfare benefits of more retirees. In Germany, the problem is particularly acute. By 2060, Germany's population is predicted to shrink by 20 percent and its workforce by 27 percent. Across the 1980s and 1990s, the government enacted reforms to the country's extensive welfare system to ease financial constraints (see chapter 11). While these efforts reduced spending increases from what they might have been, they were not enough to reduce Germany's relatively high public debt, which went from about 40 percent of GDP in 1994 to over 80 percent in 2011 (Streeck 2009, 69). Similarly, tax reforms that favored business were gradually enacted. From 1985 to 1995, corporate taxes' share of all taxes was cut in half, with most of the revenue loss compensated for by increases in taxes on workers (Daly

Web link: What Germany offers the world

Web link: Where factory apprenticeship is latest model from Germany

2001, 88). In the first decade of the new millennium, corporate taxes fell a further 22 percent, while personal income taxes dropped only 1.5 percent, thus shifting the burden even further from business to individuals. The combined result has been some increase in inequality in the new millennium, which we discuss further in chapter 11.

A number of analysts have noted that the relatively slow pace of reform in the German system is partly due to the nature of the country's political institutions. Germany's bicameral legislature and federal system give unusually strong powers to the legislature's upper house (not unlike the powers of the U.S. Senate), which has often been controlled by opposition parties. Any law that affects the state governments (meaning most laws) must pass the upper house as well as the lower house. Thus, the system has a large number of veto players. As early as the mid-1990s, Germany's third party, the pro-business FDP, was calling for fundamental reforms of the economic system. These were opposed by one or the other of the

Government and Growth in the EU

The government in Germany and in the EU as a whole consistently takes in a larger share of economic production as taxes than does the United States (see chart A). Many economists predict that this will hurt economic growth in Germany and the EU. Chart B, however, shows that the EU grew faster than the United States at the dawn of the new millennium, though the United States started to recover from the Great Recession sooner.

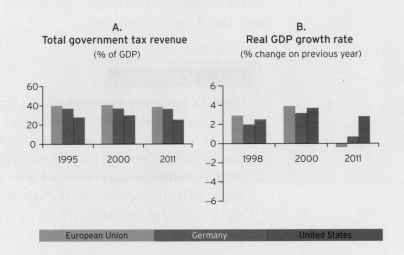

Sources: All data are from OECD and EUROSTAT (http://stats.oecd.org/Index. aspx?QueryId=21699); (http://epp.eurostat.ec.europa.eu/statistics_explained/images/f/f3/1_Total_tax_revenue_in_the_EU-27_and_euro_area_as_a_percentage_of_GDP.PNG); (http://epp.eurostat.ec.europa.eu/tgm/table.do?tab=table&init=1&plugin=1&language=en&pcode=tec00115).

major parties, as well as by unions and even some business interests that were content to preserve the status quo. Opponents were able to use one house or the other, as well as Germany's strong civil society, to resist radical reforms.

CASE Summary In its core activity of high-quality manufacturing, Germany's CME seems to be holding its own in a globalizing world, though analysts forecast different long-term trends. Germany has reformed its economic model in the direction of greater liberalization in both finance and labor. The main elements of the CME remain in place, but with reduced overall effects on the economy. Reforms reduced wages, social welfare benefits, and workers' bargaining positions, but they arguably helped Germany survive the Great Recession with only limited impact on employment. Both the Christian democratic government of Helmut Kohl (1982–1998) and the social democratic government of Gerhard Schröder (1998–2005) attempted for years to forge agreements on pensions, unemployment, and tax reform, but neither government was successful, and both ultimately instituted unilateral moves to achieve some reform. Germany's political system has enough veto players that negotiated agreements have become nearly impossible. Fiscal austerity since the Great Recession, as would be predicted in a CME, initially seemed to allow renewed growth but then helped produce a second recession. Like all of Europe, Germany's economy was stagnating by 2013, though it remained the best on the continent, especially in terms of employment. While there are major long-term economic questions on the horizon, in the short term the crisis left Germany stronger vis-à-vis its EU partners than at any time in its history.

CASE Questions

1. Germany has clearly instigated reforms that have moved it some distance away from the pure CME model and toward the LME model. How fundamental do these changes seem to be? Do they suggest the varieties of capitalism approach is still applicable, or is Germany a case in which globalization is forcing convergence?
2. Did the reforms Germany undertook prior to the Great Recession make it easier or harder for it to navigate its way through the crisis? Did some reforms help and others hurt, and if so, in what ways?

DEVELOPMENT AND GLOBALIZATION

Globalization has clearly affected the ways in which wealthy and powerful states guide their economies. While most political scientists no longer subscribe to the hyperglobalization thesis that the state is now irrelevant, virtually all recognize that states have had to alter their economic and social policies in response to pressures from rapidly expanding global market forces. If this is true for even the relatively powerful and wealthy states, could the hyperglobalization thesis apply to much poorer and less powerful states? Have they in effect lost economic sovereignty to the global market, or do its effects vary among them as well? If they do retain some economic sovereignty, what alternative strategies have they pursued, and which have done more to improve the lives of their citizens and reduce poverty?

For poor countries, their relationship with globalization is intimately connected with the goal of "development." The development debate we outlined in chapter 5—from import-substitution industrialization (ISI) to structural adjustment programs (SAP)—preceded the contemporary globalization debate, but both address the same key question: How can states in developing countries use economic policies to help them navigate the global economy in ways that are most beneficial to their people? Most important, how can they maximize economic growth and reduce poverty? If we can determine which policies are most beneficial, we can also ask, What types of regimes are most willing to and capable of pursuing those policies?

As we noted in chapter 5, great regional variation exists in economic growth and poverty reduction over the last several decades. Virtually all governments have followed neoliberal policies to some degree, opening their economies to the global market, but the results have not been consistent. Figure 10.3 compares each region's Economic Globalization Index score—a measure of economies' interactions with the global market—to growth rates and poverty rates since 1981. All regions have become more globalized over time, and the gap between the wealthier regions (Europe, East Asia, and Latin America) and the poorer regions (South Asia and Africa) has increased slightly. Economic growth and poverty reduction vary dramatically by region, but the connection to globalization is unclear. Africa, the poorest region, has had the highest level of globalization (driven in part by trade in minerals). Greater globalization has not systematically produced greater growth, though it appears to be loosely associated with poverty reduction. The rate of poverty reduction, though, varies dramatically by region even though change in the level of globalization does not. The question is, What has caused these trends, and what can be done to improve the effects of globalization in the countries that are falling behind?

What Role Can and Should the State Play in Development?

The reigning conventional wisdom about development policies for the past generation has been neoliberalism: the state should allow the market to operate more or less unfettered, following the logic of comparative advantage. Regardless of local circumstances, a free market maximizes the efficiency with which resources are used and therefore improves economic well-being overall.

Since the early 1990s, however, scholars and practitioners have been raising a growing number of questions about this model. The World Bank, in particular, has articulated an agenda of "good governance," arguing that states need to have more of a role in reform than the neoliberal model allows. Focusing on the alleviation of poverty, the World Bank argues that states need greater capacity to achieve key goals. First, they need to effectively and efficiently provide the key requisites for capitalist development that we outlined in chapter 5: security, property rights, contract enforcement, and infrastructure. Second, they need to enhance human capital and development potential via providing essential health and education services to the poor. Virtually all major Western development agencies continue to support the basic principle that states should not distort markets (as they did under ISI), but many now believe that the state does have a role to play in simultaneously attracting capital and alleviating poverty.

Data link:
World Bank governance indicators

FIGURE 10.3   The Effects of Economic Globalization

Economic globalization[1]

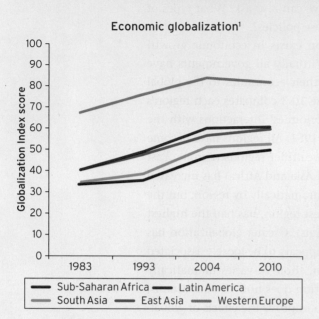

Legend: Sub-Saharan Africa — Latin America — South Asia — East Asia — Western Europe

Extreme poverty, % of population

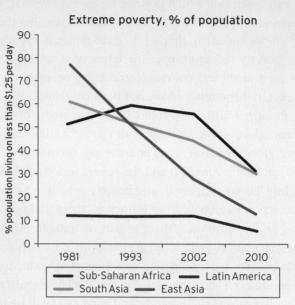

Legend: Sub-Saharan Africa — Latin America — South Asia — East Asia

Growth of GDP per capita, % per year

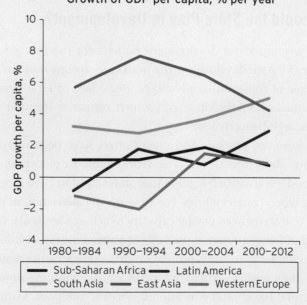

Legend: Sub-Saharan Africa — Latin America — South Asia — East Asia — Western Europe

Sources: Data for the Globalization Index are from the KOF Index of Globalization, "Economic Globalization" data (http://globalization.kof.ethz.ch/query). Data on GDP growth and extreme poverty are from the World Bank (http://data.worldbank.org).

[1]Composite of data on openness to and flows of trade, foreign direct investment, and portfolio investment.

The global financial crises of 1997–1998 and 2008–2009 also reduced neoliberalism's appeal. After the 1997–1998 crisis in booming Southeast Asia, critics argued the problem was rapid flow of investment in and out of countries that were open to the global economy, following neoliberal prescriptions. This suggested the need for mechanisms to slow down the speed at which these transactions could occur and to guide investors into longer-term investments rather than short-term currency speculation. Similarly, the risky investments that led to the Great Recession in 2008–2009 occurred in deregulated financial markets in the United States, leading governments around the world to increase the role of the state in financial regulation at least a little.

Given these critiques, it's not surprising that some alternatives have arisen. The World Bank itself has modified its policies to encourage a greater role for the state, as discussed above. Several more significant alternatives, though, have also gained popularity. One is derived originally from the Japanese developmental state model. It has been most prominent in a number of successful Asian developing economies. In Latin America, a leftist alternative to parts of the neoliberal model has arisen over the past decade in a number of countries, including our case study of Brazil. Finally, in response to the failure to reduce poverty in the poorest countries—what Paul Collier (2007) called "the bottom billion"—policy alternatives involving large investments via aid have gained currency. All of these alternatives accept many of the core neoliberal recommendations for macroeconomic policies but go beyond those to suggest a significantly greater role for the state, and in some cases external aid donors, in the economy. They believe that global market forces cannot be ignored but also that even the poorest states can and must play a significant role in harnessing those forces for the benefit of their citizens.

The Developmental State We outlined the key elements of the developmental state in our examination of Japan in chapter 5. The model was adopted and modified by a number of other Asian countries, starting with South Korea, and was a model for similar, though usually less successful, efforts elsewhere in the world. Developmental states consciously intervene in the market via an aggressive industrial policy: a policy aimed at strengthening particular industries. In contrast to the earlier ISI model, though, developmental states encouraged **export-oriented growth (EOG)**, growth via exports of goods and services, usually starting with light manufactures such as textiles. They tried to "pick winners," subsidizing and protecting new industries but demanding high performance from them and opening them up to global competition as soon as possible. The key aim was not to provide manufactured goods for the domestic market, as under ISI, but manufactured exports for wealthier countries. Light manufacturing is typically labor-intensive, so the new investments employed large numbers of people; Asian developmental states, in particular, used EOG to take advantage of their comparative advantage in large amounts of cheap labor.

While developmental states intervened in the economy, subsidizing and guiding investments into particular areas rather than letting the market fully determine

Web link:
Structural reform in Russia

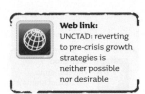

Web link:
UNCTAD: reverting to pre-crisis growth strategies is neither possible nor desirable

export-oriented growth (EOG)
Development policy based on encouraging economic growth via exports of goods and services, usually starting with light manufacturing such as textiles

investment patterns, they usually followed neoliberal fiscal and monetary policy, keeping inflation low and their currencies stable and realistically valued vis-à-vis others, thus encouraging investment and exports. Their successes were also based on the fact that their high-quality education systems had produced a highly literate and therefore productive workforce. Another key component of their success was a strong state, one in which economic bureaucracies were insulated from short-term political pressures so that they could pursue consistent, long-term policies. Several major analysts determined that this was a key factor for other states that wanted to pursue similar policies; weaker states that succumbed to short-term domestic pressures were far less successful (Haggard and Kaufman 1995).

The Asian economic miracle that was produced primarily by developmental states has been the biggest development success story of the last generation. A famous comparison is between South Korea and Ghana in West Africa. Upon Ghana's independence in 1957, it and South Korea had nearly identical per capita incomes and economies. Both were poor and mostly agricultural. Today, however, South Korea is a member of the OECD (Organisation for Economic Co-operation and Development), the club of the world's wealthiest countries. It had a per capita gross national income (GNI) of $22,670 in 2012, compared with Ghana's $1,550. This kind of performance lies behind the data in Figure 10.3 above. Such rapid growth almost always produces greater inequality, as some people get much richer and others are left behind. Growth in the early developmental states such as South Korea and Taiwan, however, was combined with reduced inequality. This was largely due to earlier policies that supported rural areas; reforms gave peasant farmers more equal access to land, universal education, and good infrastructure, facilitating their participation in economic growth. Labor-intensive manufacturing also helped reduce inequality, as it employed large numbers of people at relatively equal wages.

Web link:
The economic paradox of Ghana's poverty

Hyundai automobiles await export to South Africa. South Korea's phenomenal economic growth has been based on exports, making some of the country's biggest companies into household names around the world. The economic success of South Korea's "developmental state" raises a key development question: Can countries elsewhere in the world duplicate the model and its success?

The 1997–1998 financial crisis shook the foundations of the developmental state model. The massive loss of wealth in Asia ultimately brought down the government of longtime Indonesian dictator Suharto and threatened the political stability of other countries as well. The crisis originated in and centered on the "Little Tigers" of Thailand, Indonesia, Malaysia, and the Philippines—developmental states that followed the earlier examples like South Korea and have become middle-income countries today. The crisis produced recession and instability for many middle-income countries, in particular, though a decade later, the "Little Tigers" had recovered and were growing substantially again. In spite of this recovery, the Asian crisis and response to it profoundly affected the globalization and development debate. The crisis revealed that the developmental states' regulation of the financial sector in particular was very weak. Banks took on unsecured international loans and lent money for dubious investments, often to companies with which they had close, even familial, ties. When the crisis hit, the banks rapidly sank into bankruptcy since their creditors could not repay them and, in turn, they could not repay their own international loans. Neoliberals argued that in spite of East Asia's rapid success, the state's role was not as beneficial as had been assumed. Many began to argue that economic growth would have been even more rapid without state credit and subsidies to key industries. As we noted above, though, critics of neoliberalism made the opposite argument: lack of controls of the flow of money across borders allowed the speculative boom and subsequent bust.

The developmental state has been the most successful developmental model of the last generation, but it seems difficult to imitate in contexts other than where it began. Even in Asia, countries like Thailand and the Philippines, while achieving significant success and becoming middle-income countries, have not duplicated the success of South Korea or Taiwan. Moreover, our case study of China, the greatest success of all, only partly duplicates the developmental state. Nonetheless, the model has helped East and Southeast Asia benefit more from globalization than any other region, especially in the postcolonial world. While the leading exemplars of the model felt significant effects from the 1997–1998 and 2008–2009 crises, they nonetheless have achieved substantial overall economic growth and poverty reduction via engagement with the world market.

Web link:
The perils of premature deindustrialization

The "Pink Tide" in Latin America The neoliberal model and the IMF probably influenced Latin America more than any other region. The debt crisis that began in Mexico in August 1982 and quickly spread to Brazil and Argentina paved the way for the first SAPs, and the 1980s became known as the "lost decade" in Latin America because of the severe economic downturn that followed the debt crisis. Countries initiated market-oriented reforms at different rates, but all implemented such reforms eventually. By the mid-1990s, most Latin American countries had engaged in extensive privatization of state-owned activities, reduction of trade barriers, and fiscal restraint. Neoliberal reform, though, did not produce notable improvement in growth or reduction in poverty. Not surprisingly, this produced a political backlash. Citizens

Web link:
Pink tide rising

in Argentina, Bolivia, Ecuador, Brazil, and Venezuela elected leftist critics of neoliberal reforms in the new millennium, creating what many have called Latin America's "pink tide" (Wylde 2012). These new governing parties and coalitions have implemented policies that, while not rejecting all of neoliberalism, have significantly modified it. Analysts have referred to this as the "new developmentalism" (Bresser-Pereira 2009) or the creation of a new "developmental regime" (Wylde 2012).

Despite some success stories such as Chile, overall the neoliberal model in Latin America did not achieve significant growth or reduce either poverty or inequality by the end of the 1990s. Furthermore, the region suffered through a series of financial crises that many blamed on neoliberalism. The first major crisis happened in Mexico in 1994 and required a major inflow of cash from the U.S. government. Brazil's currency and stock markets were hit by the contagion from East Asia in 1998, though not as severely as in Asia itself. Argentina, which had the highest growth in the region in the 1990s, experienced a spectacular financial crash in 2001–2002. In 2002 the Argentine economy shrank by more than 10 percent, and the country went through four presidents within a few weeks as economic crisis produced political chaos. The 2008–2009 global financial crisis was thus only the latest in a long string. It resulted in an economic contraction of nearly 3 percent per capita in 2009, but the region rebounded relatively quickly and experienced 4.5 percent per capita growth in 2010.

The "pink tide" was a response to this difficult history. The "leftist" governments elected around the turn of the new millennium varied widely. Some, such as Argentina and Brazil, have preserved the major macroeconomic foundations of neoliberalism but have attempted to implement greater social programs aimed at the poor. Others, most famously that of Hugo Chávez in Venezuela, have intervened in the economy in ways that more seriously challenge the market model, including by heavily subsidizing certain sectors, such as food and fuel, and nationalizing some key industries, especially minerals. Most of the "pink tide" governments, though, preserved most neoliberal macroeconomic policies: they maintained more or less balanced budgets, kept inflation low, and made sure the economy was open to trade and investment. Some analysts have argued that these governments are essentially "social democratic": accepting the core elements of the market economy but expanding social welfare policies similar to many European countries. Christopher Wylde (2012), though, argued they are closer to developmental states, in the sense that most have accepted neoliberal macroeconomic policies and continued openness to the global economy but have used the state to encourage investment in certain key areas. The policies have worked reasonably well. Neoliberals feared that the "pink tide" would undermine what they saw as the gains of neoliberalism, including fiscal austerity and controlled inflation. In fact, through 2007, the "leftist" governments as a whole had achieved slightly higher growth rates and greater fiscal surpluses than other Latin American governments. The leftist governments did have higher inflation rates, but the difference was small (Moreno-Brid and Paunovic 2010). Growth for the entire region was robust prior to the Great Recession, averaging 5 to 6 percent per year, including in countries with "leftist" governments. Coupling this with expanded social services has resulted in the biggest reduction in poverty in generations in some countries, including our case studies of Brazil and Mexico.

The "pink tide" in Latin America is not as clear-cut a developmental model as the developmental state, but it nonetheless represents a significant challenge to neoliberalism. At least while global market forces were favorable, these governments were able to maintain neoliberal macroeconomic policies and openness to the global economy while simultaneously reducing poverty in some countries and using the state to guide investment via expansion of infrastructure in others. Some, such as Bolivia and Venezuela, took more direct government control of key sectors, with varied results (more beneficial in Bolivia than under Chávez in Venezuela). Whether globalization will allow this model to continue, though, under less auspicious circumstances since the Great Recession, remains to be seen, as our case study of Brazil below illustrates.

The "Bottom Billion" Economist Paul Collier (2007) coined the term *the bottom billion* to refer to the population of the poorest countries on Earth, those he believed were being left behind by globalization. While globalization and good development policies were increasing incomes and reducing poverty spectacularly in some places (China and Asia more generally) and more slowly in others (Latin America), in a minority of countries, mostly in Africa, they were doing neither. The key question he and many other analysts have asked is, Why? Being poor and heavily indebted, many of these countries were forced to implement neoliberal policies via structural adjustment programs mandated by the World Bank and the IMF in the 1980s and 1990s. The results, however, were even more disappointing than in most Latin American countries, as African economic data attest. Of 186 countries on the United Nations' Human Development Index in 2012, 23 of the bottom 25 were African. By the new millennium, the continent had become the poster child of economic failure in the age of globalization and the subject of growing attention from global development agencies, charitable foundations, and even rock stars. The failure of globalization and neoliberal policies to create growth and reduce poverty in the poorest countries, concentrated in Africa, produced the biggest development debate of the new millennium, about both the causes of this failure and what to do about it.

As noted earlier, the World Bank and others began advocating for developing stronger state institutions and human capital. Following an institutionalist approach, they argued that the absence of strong, market-friendly institutions is the problem. The core of the Asian developmental state model is strong economic institutions, such as key government bureaucracies, which encourage high levels of investment. In many poor states, institutionalists argue, neopatrimonial forms of authority and corruption harm investment and markets by exacting implicit taxes at all levels and distributing the revenue gained via patron-client networks and by weakening the rule of law. The World Bank now focuses heavily on "governance," a state's ability to implement policy fairly and well. This approach prescribes the creation of effective and efficient governing institutions that help provide strong rule of law, political stability, and key public goods such as infrastructure, education, and health care. Without these the risks for investment are too high, so even proper neoliberal policies will not induce domestic or foreign capitalists to invest.

Other analysts, such as Jeffrey Sachs, argued that specific conditions limit growth in the poorest countries. Sachs (2005) pointed to geography, disease, and climate as key issues in Africa in particular. Low population densities, few good ports, long distances to major consumer markets, many landlocked countries, and the ravages of tropical diseases all reduce Africa's growth potential in the absence of major foreign assistance. Given this, Sachs called for a massive inflow of aid, arguing that a large enough volume targeted the right way could end African poverty in our lifetime. This approach led to the creation of the United Nations' **Millennium Development Goals (MDGs)**, a set of targets to reduce poverty and hunger, improve education and health, improve the status of women, and achieve environmental sustainability, all fueled by a call for a large increase in aid. Collier (2007) argued for a more nuanced approach, suggesting that different countries were poor from differing reasons. Some faced a problem of bad governance, as argued above, while others faced a resource curse or debilitating political conflict; each problem, he argued, requires focus on that issue, with aid playing a part but targeted specifically to that problem.

Another form of aid to the poorest countries in the new millennium has been forgiveness of past debts. By 2005, a growing movement had convinced Western governments that the poorest countries needed relief from their debt burden, most of which had been contracted and stolen by dictators during the 1970s and 1980s. SAPs were intended to restart economic growth, which would have allowed the countries to pay off their debts, but the growth never happened, so the debt simply increased. This led the World Bank and IMF to create the Heavily Indebted Poor Country (HIPC) initiative, which forgave past debts of poor (mostly African) countries in exchange for new economic reforms (following pragmatic neoliberalism). By 2007, this had substantially reduced the poorest countries' overall debt, meaning they could use more of their export earnings to invest in future development.

But critics such as William Easterly (2006) and Dambisa Moyo (2009) have pointed to the fact that Africa has a long history as the world's largest aid recipient and yet has failed to achieve substantial development. Easterly argued that the result of misguided efforts such as Sachs's will be that "the rich have markets" while "the poor have bureaucrats." The former, he suggested, is the only way to achieve growth; the latter will waste and distort resources and leave Africans more impoverished and dependent on Western support. Moyo pointed to microfinance and the global bond markets as better means to achieve development than debt relief and continued dependence on aid. She argued that if poor countries had to use global bond markets to finance investment the way wealthier countries do, they would be forced to implement better policies along neoliberal lines, and these would foster growth. Stephen Kaplan (2013) found evidence in Latin America to support the disciplining effect of the global bond market: countries that relied more heavily on bonds to finance development maintained stronger fiscal austerity than countries that relied more heavily on loans; he did not

Web link:
Millennium Development Goals

Millennium Development Goals (MDGs)
Targets established by the United Nations to reduce poverty and hunger, improve education and health, improve the status of women, and achieve environmental sustainability

Web link:
The Millennium Development Goals 2013 Report

Web link:
Millennium Villages Project: stories

examine, however, if this had any effect on economic growth and well-being. The punishing discipline of the international bond market (the same discipline that Greece has faced in recent years) would create the incentives governments in poor countries require to develop both stronger institutions and better policies. Foreign aid will never achieve this discipline (as the HIPC debt forgiveness demonstrates) and therefore, Moyo suggests, will keep poor countries dependent and poor.

As this debate was unfolding, some analysts, including a number of African leaders, began to talk of an "African Renaissance." Overall economic growth improved significantly, averaging nearly 5 percent from 2000 to 2007. The global financial crisis did not hit Africa as hard as it did elsewhere, in part because of Africa's limited integration into the global economy. Growth slowed in 2009 to 1.6 percent, rebounded to 4.5 percent in 2010, and remained at that level in 2012. The population living in absolute poverty across the continent dropped from 51 percent in 2005 to 39 percent in 2012 (African Development Bank Group 2013). Much of this was fuelled, however, by rising prices for Africa's raw materials, especially oil. Clearly, some notable improvement has occurred, undoubtedly due to a combination of debt relief, improved economic policies, stronger governing institutions, and high commodity prices. Whether improvement can be sustained over the long term will determine whether Africa can finally begin to see the benefits of globalization, or whether the "bottom billion" will remain so.

Regime Type and Development Success

Whichever developmental model seems most effective at navigating globalization to achieve growth and reduce poverty, a subsequent question is, What type of government is most likely to pursue beneficial policies? The classic question in this area has been, Do democracies or dictatorships produce better economic development? Most theorists initially asserted that democracy provides incentives for politicians to pursue policies that will gain them support so they can win elections, and citizens will demand good economic policy. On the other hand, some of the primary development success stories such as South Korea, Taiwan, and China achieved much of their success under authoritarian regimes. Pundits and policy makers used this as evidence to argue that pushing democracy on a poor country too soon will produce neither healthy democracy nor economic development. Many argue that strong states need to be created, as well as healthy economies, before democracy is viable.

Web link:
Chinese leader's economic plan tests goal to fortify party power

Those arguing that democracy enhances growth and reduces poverty focus mostly on accountability, stability, and the rule of law. They hold that democracies provide greater popular accountability, so citizens will demand that their governments pursue beneficial economic policies. Once consolidated, democracy also enhances political stability; while changes of governmental leaders still occur, elections regularize the process so change does not threaten the ability of investors to predict future returns, and the investment that is the basis of growth will continue to flow. Finally, democracies better protect the rule of law, including the property rights and contracts that are essential elements of capitalist growth (see chapter 5). In contrast, dictatorships are less account-able, are more prone to unpredictable instability like coups d'état or revolutions, and do not protect the rule of law from the whims of the ruling elite.

Opponents of this view hypothesize that democracy impedes growth because democratic governments must follow political demands that favor consumption over investment. Long-term economic growth depends on investment, which can only happen if some of society's resources are not consumed. Democracies, this school of thought argues, have to bow to the will of the citizens, and citizens typically want more consumption now and are unwilling to invest and wait for future benefits. This is especially true in poorer societies, critics believe, where more impoverished people understandably demand consumption now. Furthermore, in democracies with weak institutions and weak political parties, these demands are based on patronage, giving political leaders an incentive to control as many resources as possible. This has the effect of expanding the role of the state, harming the business climate, and again, dis-couraging investment. Dictatorships, the argument goes, can resist pressure for greater consumption by repressing citizens' demands and can follow more consistent policies over time, as the East Asian success stories demonstrate.

Despite this extensive debate, empirical findings, many using quite sophisticated statistical techniques, have been rather ambiguous. Przeworski et al. (2000) and Yi Feng (2003) analyzed the relationship between regime type and economic growth, taking into account numerous economic factors that influence growth in an effort to isolate the independent effect of regime type. Przeworski et al. demonstrated overall that democracies and dictatorships achieve the same levels of growth, and this is true for both wealthier and poorer countries. Feng also found that democracy has little effect on growth but that this is due to two contradictory results: the direct effect of the level of democracy on growth is slightly negative (i.e., democracy harms growth), but democracy enhances growth indirectly by creating greater political stability. Still, the net result is near zero.

Democracy alone, however, may not be the determining variable in achieving growth and reducing poverty. The type of democracy and other aspects of the state may matter as well. Lijphart (1999) has long argued that consensual democracies produce greater well-being because the compromise they require forces leaders to distribute resources more equitably and provides greater stability, encouraging investment and growth. Huber and Stephens (2012) found that democracy encouraged the creation of the left-leaning parties in Latin America's "pink tide"; those parties produced more egalitarian social policy, which in turn improved human capital and therefore is likely to improve development. Flores-Macias (2012) presented a similar but more nuanced argument that the "pink tide" governments that have pursued stable macroeconomic policies that have aided growth, like our case study of Brazil, were characterized by relatively institutionalized party systems. Stronger party systems deter outsiders from entering the system and give leaders and parties incentives to maintain stability. "Pink tide" governments with weaker party systems, such as Venezuela, pursued more erratic and less beneficial policies. Anne Pitcher (2012) similarly argued that in Africa strong parties and quality of democracy lead to better policies and processes of privatization, a key element of neoliberal reform. Finally, others claimed that the coalition of forces in power is the crucial determinant. Mosley et al. (2012) found that if the elite splits in a democracy, often due to a particular crisis, and one segment of it is astute enough to try to co-opt the poor to help them prevail politically, they will pursue more pro-poor policies. This is not automatic in a democracy, though. The elite in a democracy in a very unequal society may well be able to maintain power, as elite theorists argue, with minimal attention to the bulk of the voters. Similarly, in ethnically divided democracies in which most people vote for "their" ethnic leaders, elites will face little pressure to pursue pro-poor policies because doing so will not affect their ability to garner votes—only ethnicity matters.

A major new study by Pippa Norris (2012), on the other hand, argued that the state's bureaucratic capacity, not the characteristics of the particular democracy, is the missing explanatory factor. Like previous studies, she found no clear relationship between democracy and economic growth or other developmental goals. When she added the state's bureaucratic capacity to her statistical model, however, both it and democracy were important in explaining success. She concluded that we need to distinguish between what she called "bureaucratic democracies" with high capacity to implement policies and "patronage democracies" lacking such capacity. Similarly, "bureaucratic autocracies" are more successful than "patronage autocracies," though not as successful as "bureaucratic democracies." Figure 10.4 provides the growth rates of each regime type. Even when controlling for many other factors that affect growth, democracy and state capacity, when considered together, make a difference. These distinctions within both democracies and autocracies, she argued, explain the ambiguous results of prior studies that focused on regime type alone.

Video link:
Effect of state capacity on economic growth

The mixed record of achievement in the age of globalization has led most development theorists and policy makers to adjust the original neoliberal model that championed hyperglobalization, modifying it to recreate a role for the state. Exactly what role, however, remains a major debate, and it's far from clear that any model can be applied everywhere. The greatest consensus is probably that a relatively strong state helps; it can implement policies more effectively, monitor cross-border activities more efficiently, and therefore is more likely to be able to provide the greatest benefits for its citizens. As we discussed in chapters 2 and 8, however, a strong state does not require or even necessarily benefit from an authoritarian regime. While there are examples of authoritarian regimes creating spectacular growth and poverty reduction, their record overall is quite erratic. Authoritarian regimes include some of the most successful, like our case study of China, and some of the worst, like Robert Mugabe's Zimbabwe. Democracy alone, however, does not seem to be a panacea, either. Combined with a strong state, though, it seems likely to help; at least that is the conclusion of much of the best evidence we currently have available.

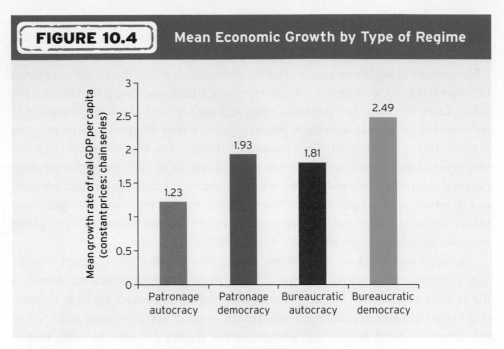

FIGURE 10.4   Mean Economic Growth by Type of Regime

Source: Pippa Norris, Figure 5.1, "Mean Economic Growth by Type of Regime," *Making Democratic Governance Work: How Regimes Shape Prosperity, Welfare, and Peace* (Cambridge, UK: Cambridge University Press, 2012), 115. Copyright © 2012 Pippa Norris. Reprinted with the permission of Cambridge University Press.

Globalization clearly limits what states can do; virtually all successful development efforts of the past two decades have included more or less neoliberal monetary and fiscal policies. Countries like Venezuela and Zimbabwe demonstrate what happens to those that veer far from neoliberal macroeconomic policies. Nonetheless, even developing states have some room to maneuver. We examine the detailed contours of these trends in four of our case studies.

CASE Study

CHINA: AN EMERGING POWERHOUSE

- **TYPE OF ECONOMY**
  Developmental state,
  with modifications

China's economic development has been unparalleled since the country's initial entrance into the world market. Its economy has taken more people out of poverty faster than any other in history. Since economic reforms began shifting the country away from the communist-planned economy in 1978, the population in absolute poverty (living on less than $1 per day) has dropped from about 60 percent to 10 percent, and GDP per capita has increased sixfold. Economic growth has averaged between 8 and 10 percent for thirty years and went above 10 percent in 2005–2007. (Exact data on long-term economic growth in China are disputed due to faulty data collection. The official figure for 1978–1998 was 9.7 percent per year, but the World Bank estimates the actual figure at 8.4 percent.) China even weathered the global financial crisis of 2008–2009 exceptionally well, experiencing reduced growth but no actual recession; growth rebounded quickly in spite of China's dependence on exports to Western markets that were all in severe recession. By mid-2013, though, growth had slowed somewhat and economic analysts began fearing that the world's biggest "growth engine" was finally starting to stall. China's development path, while certainly not identical to the earlier developmental state model, nonetheless shares some of its key elements: a strong authoritarian state that guided policy via gradual opening to the world, conscious favoring of certain sectors of the economy at certain times, pursuit of EOG, and the benefits of being in the East Asian region.

China's reforms emerged gradually, starting in 1978. The process continues, and remains incomplete, thirty-five years later. The first reforms were focused inward and on agriculture. The "household responsibility system" converted many of China's collective farms into family-leased and operated enterprises in which families could dispose of their surplus production on the open market, giving them an incentive to be more productive. In six years (1978–1984), virtually all farming households had converted to this system, agricultural production was growing at an unprecedented rate of 7 percent per year, and per capita rural incomes increased by more than 50 percent. In rural areas, township and village enterprises (TVEs), mostly owned by local governments, were given even greater freedom to produce what they could for a profit. Their production rose fivefold between 1983 and 1988 (Qian 2006, 235–237).

- **DEVELOPMENT OUTCOMES**
  World's greatest economic growth and poverty reduction

- **RESPONSE TO GREAT RECESSION**
  Stimulus plan focusing on infrastructure; continued growth

- **RECENT REFORM EFFORTS**
  Expanding private sector but continued role for state-owned industries

- **CONTINUING PROBLEMS**
  Growing inequality, labor unrest, aging population, environmental concerns

Workers lay tracks for a high-speed railway in Guangdong province in July 2013. Massive infrastructure spending was the Chinese government's main response to the Great Recession, stimulating demand and expanding transportation links for the rapidly expanding economy.

At the same time, the government gradually began to open to the market, domestically and internationally. It created a "dual-track" market system in 1984 under which state-owned enterprises (SOEs) continued to sell their products at official state prices up to their official state production quota but were free to sell their surplus at whatever market price they could get. Prior to reform, the government had set all retail prices. Over time, a larger and larger share of products were sold at market prices, reaching 95 percent by 1999. Throughout the 1990s, the government gradually but systematically lowered tariffs on imports and loosened restrictions on companies' rights to both import and export, a process that culminated in China's joining the World Trade Organization (WTO) in 2001. The result has been an explosion of international trade for the country: it increased fivefold between 1996 and 2005, with three-quarters of that expansion occurring after China joined the WTO (Qin 2007, 721).

In 1995 the government announced the start of privatization, selling off the vast majority of SOEs to private investors. The process resulted in the laying off of at least twenty million workers from 1995 to 1997, but the growing economy was able to employ many of them and the government created a pension system for the unemployed so layoffs did not cause widespread unrest (Qian 2006, 243; Frazier 2010). A decade later, the private sector constituted 70 percent of the economy and the state-owned sector only 30 percent. It's not clear, however, that the government intends to eliminate SOEs entirely. They remain important players in major sectors of the economy such as energy and steel. Indeed, in 2009, in the midst of the global financial crisis, SOEs' share of the economy actually increased slightly for the first time in a generation. The government's large stimulus package that helped the economy rebound quickly was channeled largely into infrastructure built mainly by SOEs. Government-owned energy companies have aggressively sought out contracts to extract raw materials, especially oil, around the world.

Banking is also an important sector that continues to have substantial government control. Early in the reform process, the government created a central bank and separated it from four other government-owned banks that would serve to finance investment in the SOEs. The government used these banks to direct large-scale investment in key areas such as energy, steel, and natural resources. By 1998, these banks faced significant losses due to bad loans, instigating a reform process that has reduced the number of bad loans over time, though the government still uses these banks to make loans they think are of political or economic importance, regardless of immediate profitability. The growing private sector finances most of its investment via its own burgeoning profits and some via the increasing number of international banks in the country (Knight and Ding 2013). The government uses direct control over key economic sectors, especially natural resources and banking, to guide investment into key areas, similar to what earlier developmental states had done.

The role of the state in creating institutionalized incentives for greater efficiency and production has been crucial to China's economic success. A World Bank study (Winters and Yusuf 2007) argued that the institutionalization of Chinese Communist

Party (CCP) rule that we delineated in chapter 8 was essential. Local officials and would-be entrepreneurs needed to trust that the central government would follow through on its commitments to allow profits to stay within local enterprises and continue support for the growing market. Given the history of Mao's capricious rule, it was not obvious at the dawn of Deng Xiaoping's era that the government would stick to its new commitments. The CCP gained credibility by institutionalizing its rule, assuring local party leaders and government officials that they would be promoted based on clear criteria tied in part to the success of their local enterprises and economies. As the system worked successfully over the first decade, it gained greater credibility. When China invited increasing foreign investment in the 1990s, greater institutionalization led investors to believe that continued political stability was likely. At the same time, the government began large-scale spending on infrastructure expansion and improvements, facilitating and showing its financial commitment to both domestic and foreign private investment.

China's economic success, measured in terms of economic growth, per capita income, and poverty reduction, is spectacular. This does not mean, however, that no problems exist. China has long faced global pressure, especially from the United States, to revalue its currency, the renminbi. It tied the value of the renminbi to the U.S. dollar early in the reform process and has periodically raised its value relative to the dollar, but the state has never allowed the currency's value to be determined solely by the market. This and a large amount of foreign currency from exports allowed China to weather the Asian financial crisis in 1997–1998 and the global crisis a decade later relatively easily. The government came under renewed pressure to raise the value of its currency during the global financial crisis, especially in 2010 as Chinese growth took off again while U.S. and European growth remained sluggish. U.S. and European governments wanted China to allow the value of its currency to rise to make Western exports more affordable for Chinese companies and consumers. The government responded with very slight revaluations in 2010 and promises to do more, promises similar to those it has made in the past and not fully implemented.

Web link:
China seems set to loosen hold on its currency

Domestically, China has experienced what most countries in the early stages of rapid industrialization do: growing inequality. This is in marked contrast to several of the "East Asian Tigers," notably South Korea and Taiwan, which simultaneously grew and became more equal. Inequality in China within rural areas, within urban areas, between urban and rural areas, and between provinces has grown substantially over the past thirty years. China's overall inequality as measured by the GINI Index was 0.49 in 2012, modestly higher than that of the United States, which is a sharp increase from the communist era. Since the early 1990s, the urban-rural gap has grown considerably, as foreign investment and manufacturing in coastal cities have exploded. Even though virtually all households have gained from the expanding economy, the wealthiest 20 percent have gained far more than their poorer neighbors, and the booming coastal regions have become much wealthier than the distant interior provinces, which remain largely rural and poor. One result has been the massive migration to the coastal cities of workers in search of jobs, and while the state has long tried to regulate this movement, it has been only partially successful. Privatization and migration from the countryside have produced considerable urban unemployment in recent years.

Under Jiang Zemin, the government recognized these problems and officially shifted focus from maximizing growth to providing greater social services, mainly in the form of pensions for unemployed and retired workers. These covered nearly half the workforce by 2005. Pensions provided a way to try to keep social and political peace by providing income to workers who were dislocated by the massive economic changes. In 2010 the government passed a comprehensive Social Insurance Law that is designed to guarantee all citizens a right to a pension, medical insurance, employment injury insurance, unemployment insurance, and maternity insurance—a policy that will undoubtedly take years to implement fully.

The government also revised the national labor law in 2008 to respond to growing worker unrest. The new law gave full-time workers rights to longer and more secure contracts and streamlined the arbitration process through which workers could demand better wages and working conditions. It stopped short, though, of allowing workers to form their own unions, preserving the monopoly of the official union in the country's state corporatist system. These changes backfired in many ways. Passage of the new law gave workers greater awareness of their rights, and cases flooded the courts. By 2010, the fastest-growing cities were facing a growing shortage of cheap labor. Worker protests and strikes expanded, most notably with a strike at a major Honda automobile plant, where workers demanded the right to form their own union. While the government successfully resisted that demand, wages did increase in some places, and the tight labor market continues. Despite conscious government policies to ameliorate the worst effects of the economic transformation on Chinese workers, growing labor unrest seems likely to remain a problem for the foreseeable future.

Web link:
Two sides to labor in China

The global financial crisis of 2008–2009 seemed mainly to augment China's role in the world. Like other "emerging markets," China recovered from the crisis much more quickly than the United States and Europe. It surpassed Japan in 2010 to become the second-largest economy in the world. While growth slowed to 8.7 percent (still a very high rate compared with world averages), it rebounded in 2010 to 9.1 percent. Part of this success is credited to the government's very large stimulus program in 2009, which invested heavily in infrastructure, including renewable energy and improved road and rail networks. Growth slowed by 2013 to 7.7 percent, however, still high by world standards but the lowest in China in over a decade. Manufacturing and exports, the heart of the economy, seemed to be slowing particularly quickly, and a boom in urban real estate markets had turned into a collapsing market in many cities. It was unclear how long China's success would last, but the new government under President Xi Jinping announced major plans to spur new growth. One was a plan to expand the market economy, eventually relaxing government control of interest rates and the currency's exchange rate. To start this, the government announced it was eliminating the floor on interest rates banks could charge on loans, freeing them to compete for business by lowering rates. Other much more important changes, though, are unlikely to be completed until later in the decade (Barboza and Buckley 2013). Eliminating restrictions on interest rates banks pay depositors is particularly important. For many years, restrictions on those rates have meant Chinese savers have lost money on their savings, lowering their income and ability to consume—and greater consumption is a key to spreading the benefits of economic growth more widely (Pettis 2013).

Even more ambitiously, the government announced a plan to move 250 million people from rural areas to newly built cities by 2025. More people in urban areas will demand more purchased goods, which will stimulate growth. In the short term, building the cities provides further government-funded stimulus to the economy. Rural residents who will be forced to move are to be compensated for their land and even receive an annual dividend after that. This will provide them some income to gain a foothold in the newly built towns and spend money, stimulating demand further. Initial efforts, though, have produced mixed results, as corruption in some areas left the forced migrants with little or no compensation and few job prospects (Johnson 2013). Whatever the long-term effects, the effort will be by far the biggest planned urbanization in human history.

Data link:
Transformation Index, China

CASE Summary   China's growth has been phenomenal. Opening itself to market forces has created the largest increase in wealth and decrease in poverty the world has ever seen. Growth did not result, however, from a rapid conversion to the neoliberal economic model. China's approach was much closer to the developmental state model, consciously choosing sectors in which to invest over time, using state financing to guide investment, and focusing increasingly on export growth. An increasingly institutionalized state provided investors with assurances that they would be able to keep their profits. The state also invested in expanding public infrastructure and continued the Communist Party's policy of educating the populace. The country also benefited from its massive size and population, which gave it a huge labor force to draw upon and a vast domestic market to attract investors. Being in East Asia helped as well, since Japan, Hong Kong (which Britain returned to China in 1997), and Taiwan are major investors in mainland China and significant buyers of Chinese exports. The Great Recession initially affected China only slightly, but by 2013 the continuing stagnation in Europe and the United States seemed to be taking a heavier toll. The new government responded with announcements of breathtaking new initiatives that, if fully implemented, will have profound effects and may spur growth anew. China certainly faces problems in the future that could slow its growth or create political instability, notably growing inequality, worker unrest, an aging population, and massive environmental problems (which we examine in chapter 11). Despite these problems, though, it is a singular success in the annals of development and globalization.

CASE Questions

1. In what ways is the Chinese case a good exemplar of the developmental state model? How is it similar to the basic model, and how does it differ?
2. What are the lessons of China's success for other poor countries as they try to develop and navigate globalization? Which elements of its model seem to be replicable and which elements seem not to be, and why?

CASE Study

INDIA: DEVELOPMENT AND DEMOCRACY

- **TYPE OF ECONOMY**
  Elements of developmental state, but partial

- **DEVELOPMENT OUTCOMES**
  Rapid growth in new millennium; limited poverty reduction

- **RESPONSE TO GREAT RECESSION**
  Initial stimulus and growth, then collapse and high inflation

- **RECENT REFORM EFFORTS**
  SEZs and new social programs aimed at the poor

- **CONTINUING PROBLEMS**
  Largest population in poverty and the most malnutrition in the world

In a reversal of the typical pattern of globalization, India's giant software company, Infosys, invested $250 million in 2007 to purchase a Polish call center, whose staff can speak and work with clients in half a dozen European languages. Infosys also owns call centers in Mexico and China to serve regional clients in their languages. Bangalore, site of Infosys's headquarters, has become a major global hub for information technology, especially software development and call centers. Infosys is the high-visibility element of India's recent broader success in dealing with globalization; the country's overall economic growth rate surpassed 7 percent in 2003 and 9 percent in 2005, averaging a very strong 6.4 percent from 1996 to 2009. In 2006–2007, Indian companies spent nearly $13 billion buying companies elsewhere in the world. Widely seen to be "on the move," India has become an increasingly important player in world economic affairs and the second Asian giant to rise via globalization. Yet it is also home to the largest number of poor people in the world, with nearly one-quarter of its population being undernourished. India's development and continuing problems stem from a significant 1991 policy shift toward engagement in the global economy, though its success is based on foundations laid much earlier. As with other developing economies, the 2008–2009 global recession did not hit India nearly as hard as it did wealthier countries. India's growth slowed briefly but rebounded to more than 7 percent by 2010, only to fall substantially in 2012–2013 amid fears that India's development model was sputtering. India's improved growth but sudden, recent slowdown demonstrate the possibilities and perils of economic reforms achieved by a democracy.

Indian workers cut grass by hand at Allahabad University in Uttar Pradesh, one of India's poorest states. India's economy has grown rapidly in the new millennium, but it remains the country with the largest number of poor people in the world.

During its first three decades of independence, India pursued a classic policy of planned ISI. While the economy was based on the market, it was highly regulated, both internally and externally. A number of major industrial sectors were reserved exclusively for government investment and control. Doing business required so many governmental forms and licenses that the system came to be known as the "permit, license, quota Raj." The extensive regulations reflected standard development theory in the ISI period, but they also provided numerous sources of patronage for the dominant Congress Party and its supporters. The program produced substantial, albeit inefficient, industrial investment. While progress was made, growth remained sluggish, rarely surpassing about 3 percent per year. This led some observers to refer to a "Hindu rate of growth" that would never exceed about 3.5 percent—a cultural argument to explain limited economic success.

Political dynamics in India's democracy affected economic policies in a major way in the 1970s and 1980s. The Congress Party's fall from power under Indira Gandhi in 1977 (see chapter 7) ushered in a period of increased political competition that forced the Congress governments in the 1980s to shift economic gears. Many observers trace India's current high level of growth to the 1991 liberalization of the economy, but comparativist Atul Kohli (2004, 2007) argued that the country's economic success is based on earlier changes that were only partially liberal. Around 1980, elites within the ruling party and bureaucracy, influenced in part by the shift in global development thinking at the time, came to the conclusion that development policies needed to be much more pro-business to achieve economic growth. The government sharply curtailed limits on the size of private business and the sectors in which it could invest, reduced business taxes, liberalized the stock market, passed laws to limit the ability of unions to strike, and made new public investments in infrastructure. The result was a doubling of growth rates in the 1980s to about 5.5 percent. Kohli argued that while these policies only partially followed the new neoliberal development model, they were very pro–domestic business. In a modest and gradual way, they paralleled those of the developmental states of East Asia, especially targeted policies designed to encourage growth in the computer sector (Evans 1995).

More dramatic liberalization began in 1991 in response to economic crisis. The growth of the 1980s had been partly fueled by debt, both public and private. It had to go hat in hand to the IMF in 1991 to secure emergency funding to avoid bankruptcy. The coalition government (led by the Congress) that came to power during this emergency used it to justify greater liberalization. The pro-business policies of the 1980s expanded, and the government implemented new policies to lower restrictions on imports, foreign exchange, and foreign investment. It also promised to reduce the size of the public sector and the fiscal deficit, privatize state-owned companies, and reform labor laws to further favor business. While these measures helped secure IMF support and were initially received favorably by the population, once the immediate crisis was over, opposition emerged. Farmers feared a reduction in their government subsidies, government bureaucrats resisted the reduction in their power that a more open market would entail, and advocates for the poor feared that the needy would fare even worse in a more open market. Business groups divided over the reforms. Older businesses in what was called the "Bombay Club" opposed opening to the global market, fearing that they wouldn't be able to compete, whereas new businesses in the export-oriented engineering and computing sectors formed a new association that favored liberalization (Sinha 2010). Rob Jenkins (2011) showed that democratic pressures continue in India's development process. In 2005 the government launched a major initiative to create hundreds of "special economic zones" (SEZs) in which far fewer restrictions would apply to foreign firms investing in export production. SEZs were an important early part of EOG in many countries, including China. Citizens who have lost land to the SEZ development, however, have mobilized to restrict it, raising doubts about its long-term durability. The result of these political forces in India's democracy has been significant but partial reform that continues to unfold.

On the economic front, the reforms of the early 1990s did not really change growth rates. After the economy recovered from the 1991 crisis, growth resumed at about the same 6 percent rate of the 1980s. The composition of growth, though, changed substantially (Kohli 2007). To reduce the fiscal deficit, the government had curtailed public investment, while the reforms encouraged greater private investment, both domestic and international. The greatest growth has come not in manufacturing but rather in services, including computing services. In 2007 India had two-thirds of the global market in offshore information technology services. Foreign direct investment increased from under $10 billion annually in the 1990s to about $90 billion in 2008, and trade went from 15 percent of the economy in 1990 to 40 percent by 2008. Compared with the most open economies of the world, India remains only partially globalized. Tariffs on imports were still at 22 percent in 2006, and only about one-quarter of the economy was involved in trade at the beginning of the new millennium (Kohli 2007, 105). The promised reforms of drastically reducing government's role by privatizing state-owned companies (including banks) and reforming labor laws never happened. Reform has been significant, albeit gradual, due in part to the politically contentious effects of those changes.

India's growth increased in the new millennium, averaging 8 to 9 percent for the five years prior to the Great Recession. The country certainly felt the recession, though growth remained above 5 percent and rebounded to over 7 percent by 2010. The government responded, as did most governments, with a Keynesian-style stimulus plan in early 2009 that invested heavily in infrastructure (long seen as a weak spot by domestic and international analysts) and that significantly increased deficit spending. Renewed growth by 2010 and increasing oil prices (which India must import) produced increased inflation and growing concern about the burgeoning government deficit. Growth shot up to 9.1 percent in 2010 but plummeted to only 1.9 percent in 2012, and the government feared further stimulus would worsen inflation too much. Growth is down in part because of substantially reduced investment, as investors fear political pressure against investment in areas such as mines and await further reforms to provide greater guarantees of security (Sridharan 2013). In mid-2013, the value of India's currency plummeted 20 percent versus the U.S. dollar, the biggest drop of any currency in the world, creating further inflationary pressure. The burst of rapid growth in the new millennium may have come to an end, at least until further reforms and/or renewed global growth occur.

Despite India's impressive growth record since 1980, poverty remains a serious problem, and inequality has grown. This is not to say that growth has not significantly lowered poverty, which stood at more than 50 percent in the 1970s but had dropped to under 30 percent by 2010. Since the onset of the 1991 liberalization, sixty million people have moved out of poverty, although India still has the largest number of poor people in the world. Forty-three percent of children under age five were malnourished in 2000, 68 percent of adults were literate in 2008 (up from 48 percent in 1990), and fifty-three out of every one thousand babies died in infancy (down from ninety-four in 1990) (Adams 2002; World Bank 1993; Kapur 2010). Economists Jagdish Bhagwati and Arvind Panagariya (2013) noted that the poverty reduction achieved by each percentage increase in GDP has been significantly lower in India than in the East Asian developmental states, including China. They argued that the concentration of growth and investment on relatively high-skill sectors like telecommunications and computing has not provided nearly as many jobs for the poor as the focus on lighter manufacturing like textiles has elsewhere. Indeed, they noted that in spite of the great growth over the past decade, the percentage of people employed in agriculture has not dropped noticeably; population growth has equaled the growth of nonagricultural employment. Small firms dominate the light-manufacturing sector in India, achieving lower productivity and generating less employment than in China, where large firms predominate. Funding social policies to reduce poverty, though often proclaimed to be important by the government, has also been quite limited (Harriss 2011). Two of the best known programs promise to provide 180 days of paid work to one member of each rural household per year and an extensive program providing subsidized food and

Web link:
India lags emerging economies in inclusive growth

Web link:
India's transformation is incomplete

Data link:
Transformation Index, India

cooking oil to poor families. Corruption, however, is estimated to reduce the benefits that the poor receive from these programs by as much as 70 percent (Yardley 2013).

A great deal of progress has occurred, but much remains to be done. Many of the poor remain in the agricultural sector. After rapid growth during the Green Revolution in the 1960s, agriculture has grown at a much slower rate than the rest of the economy since liberalization. It has also been regionally concentrated. The highly productive areas, notably the Punjab state on the Pakistani border, have seen tremendous growth in agriculture, while other states have stagnated. The same pattern appears for over-all growth and poverty. A few states have grown very rapidly and reduced poverty quite significantly, even as several others have seen little change. Some, most notably Kerala, have experienced only moderate growth but have invested heavily in social services, achieving very high literacy rates, low population growth, and high-quality health care. While these states have not seen the same growth as the wealthier states, their residents live better than most Indians because of committed public investments (Adams 2002).

CASE Summary

India's recent opening to the global market has made it a major player in key sectors such as software and other technology services, but the agricultural sector has stagnated. Reforms have reversed decades of ISI policies and heavy government intervention in the economy that produced much slower growth. New economic activity has been regionally uneven, however, so high levels of poverty remain in poorer areas and overall inequality is increasing. By favoring domestic business in ways that loosely emulate the East Asian development model and then opening further to global markets, the Indian government produced an expanding economy that increased income per capita from $355 in 1990 to $1,530 in 2012 while reducing overall poverty substantially. The Great Recession, higher global oil prices, and limits on further reform, however, have raised questions about the rate at which the world's largest democracy can grow, or should.

CASE Questions

1. In what ways do India's development policies replicate the developmental state, and in what ways do they not? What have been the implications of these differences between India's history and the developmental state model? What lessons can be learned from this analysis for other countries?

2. What are the implications of the Indian case for the debate over the relationship between democracy and economic development that we outlined earlier in the chapter?

CASE Study

BRAZIL: DOES GLOBALIZATION ALLOW A DIFFERENT PATH?

When working-class hero "Lula" and his Workers Party (PT) won the 2002 presidential election in Brazil, the poor celebrated it as the victory of one of their own who promised to provide them with a better life, while the rich worried that the economy would be ruined. Both have been proved partially wrong. Lula was one of the first "pink tide" leaders in South America and was one of the more moderate members of that group. His presidency did not reverse the core of Brazil's economic policy, which has been primarily neoliberal since the early 1990s. The new government did, however, institute major new social programs aimed at poverty reduction, and by its second term had achieved faster economic growth. Together, these resulted in Lula at least partially realizing his promises to substantially reduce poverty. Lula was the most popular president in the country's history as he handed off power to his handpicked successor, Dilma Rousseff, in January 2011. Since then, though, growth rates have slowed, a major corruption scandal (possibly involving Lula) has unfolded, and huge demonstrations against corruption, poor public services, and the money being spent on stadiums for the World Cup broke across the country in mid-2013. Does globalization really allow a different path for the "pink tide"?

- **TYPE OF ECONOMY**
  Primarily neoliberal, but with "pink tide" social policies

- **DEVELOPMENT OUTCOMES**
  Defeat of inflation via neoliberal policies in the 1990s; social spending and poverty reduction; rapid growth until 2011

- **RESPONSE TO GREAT RECESSION**
  Initial stimulus and growth, but then collapse and high inflation

- **RECENT REFORM EFFORTS**
  Promises to invest in education and health

- **CONTINUING PROBLEMS**
  High interest rates and inflation; commodity dependence

Demonstrators carry a banner reading "We want hospitals with FIFA standards" during a protest in June 2013. The massive demonstrations erupted over the price of public transportation, inadequate social services, corruption, and the cost of building new stadiums to "FIFA standards" for the 2014 World Cup.

Brazil's twentieth-century economic history is similar to Mexico's (see chapter 5). Brazil implemented one of the more successful ISI policies until the 1982 debt crisis, when it began a long, slow, and painful transition to neoliberal policies. Under the neofascist Estado Novo (1937–1945), the first state-owned companies were created, and the state used state corporatism to keep workers' wages low to attract investment. The military coup in 1964 produced a modernizing authoritarian regime that intensified ISI, rapidly expanded the state's involvement in the economy by creating more state-owned companies in heavy industry, built more infrastructure, and repressed unions further. The results from 1967 to 1973 came to be known as the "Brazilian Miracle," during which the economy grew at a rate of 9 to 10 percent per year. This completed the country's transition from an agricultural to an industrial economy, but it also produced much greater inequality.

By the onset of the 1982 debt crisis, Brazil had become the world's biggest debtor. It negotiated several agreements over the next decade with the United States and the major banks to which it owed money. These agreements reduced some of the debt in exchange for promises of policy changes in line with the neoliberal model advocated by the IMF. With the transition to democracy underway in the 1980s, however, change to the state's role in the economy was relatively slow. Until the early 1990s, Brazil followed a mix of policies—often termed "heterodox" because they followed no clear economic model—that had only modest success in reorienting the economy.

In 1992 Fernando Henrique Cardoso became finance minister. Cardoso and a team of economists created what came to be called the *"Real* Plan" to battle inflation. It followed orthodox neoliberal economic theory, including greater fiscal discipline via increased taxes and reduced spending; a tighter monetary policy via high interest rates; and a new currency (named the *real*) that was loosely tied to the value of the U.S. dollar. The *Real* Plan was spectacularly successful. Annual inflation went from 2,407 percent in 1994 to 11 percent in 1996. This success helped Cardoso get elected president in 1994 and thus continue his economic reforms. Due to the effects of the Asian financial crisis of 1998, however, Brazil had to accept a bailout package from the IMF that came with stringent demands for fiscal reform. In the mid-1990s, economic growth had hit 5 percent, but the crisis reduced it to nearly zero in 1998–1999.

By 2002, Cardoso's economic policies were widely unpopular, despite his success at ending inflation eight years earlier. Greater opening to the world economy produced a greater concentration of assets in both the industrial and large-scale agricultural sectors. Profits increased relative to wages, and unemployment increased from less than 5 percent in the 1980s to nearly 10 percent twenty years later (Baer 2008, 369–380). The Workers' Party (PT) had long championed a move toward a more socialist economic policy, though PT leaders often left "socialism" vaguely defined. During the 2002 presidential campaign, domestic and international business leaders feared a PT government, so investment slowed and foreign capital dried up in anticipation of what might come. To ease these concerns, the PT wrote a manifesto stating that "social development," focused on reducing poverty and inequality, was crucial to the party but that it would be coupled with orthodox economic policies to keep inflation low and the government budget in surplus. In part to convince business that he could be trusted, once in office Lula kept interest rates high and the budget deficit low, leaving him little money to spend on new social programs. A leading scholar of the Brazilian economy, Werner Baer, argued that Lula's government faced a "core dilemma": "the pursuit of a macroeconomic policy orthodox enough to win the approval of the international financial community and the achievement of a greater socioeconomic equality" (2008, 167).

Lula tried to do these two things sequentially by first securing economic stability and business confidence and then focusing on social programs. Baer suggested, however, that a fundamental incompatibility would persist: Brazil's orthodox policies to ensure international investor confidence in an open economy would prevent large amounts of social spending on

in CONTEXT

Brazilian Economic Growth

Before 1980, the Brazilian economic miracle produced higher economic growth rates than in much of the world. The "lost decades" of the 1980s and 1990s for both Brazil and Latin America as a whole destroyed growth, but they were followed by renewal in the new millennium.

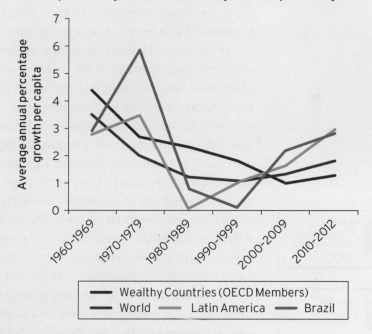

Per capita GDP growth rates (average annual percentages)

Legend:
- Wealthy Countries (OECD Members)
- World
- Latin America
- Brazil

Source: Data are from the World Bank, Annual GDP Growth Rate, per capita (http://data.worldbank.org/indicator/NY.GDP.PCAP.KD.ZG).

the poor. Lula's first term (2003–2006) seemed to bear this prediction out, but his second term (2007–2010) saw substantial gains for the working class and poor, as the government achieved both new social programs (see chapter 11) and increased growth and employment. By 2010, unemployment dropped from 9 percent to under 6 percent, and poverty was cut roughly in half by 2007. Both inequality and poverty dropped consistently from 2001 on, leading Brazil to meet the MDG of reducing poverty by half ten years ahead of the UN target date. Barros et al. (2010) found that this exceptional performance was due to greater regional spread of economic growth, improvements in education, higher minimum wages, and Lula's social programs.

Web link:
How President Lula changed Brazil

As in most "emerging markets," the Great Recession initially did not hit Brazil as hard as it did wealthier countries. The robust growth rate of 5 to 6 percent in the two years before the recession plummeted to 0.2 percent in 2009 but rebounded strongly to 7.5 percent in 2010, accompanied by a substantial decline in unemployment. Lula's government responded to the recession with a stimulus package that focused on building infrastructure, raising the minimum wage to stimulate domestic demand, and expanding credit via public lending institutions. By the end of 2010, the main economic concern was the possibility of an "overheated" economy—one growing so fast that inflation was already over 5 percent. Soon, though, other concerns emerged. Growth slowed dramatically, hitting only 1 percent in 2012, and inflation continued at 5 to 6 percent. Most analysts point to falling prices for key exports as the cause of Brazil's decline. Its exceptional growth over the previous decade relied heavily on selling commodities, especially to China, which became its biggest trading partner. The government kept interest rates high to battle inflation, which limited growth as well.

While unemployment stayed at a relatively low 6 percent, the sudden slowdown and continuing inflation set the context for what is probably a classic case of relative deprivation based on rising expectations. A protest against increased bus fares in June 2013 quickly morphed into demonstrations in one hundred cities, bringing over a million Brazilians into the street. They demanded not only lower fares for transportation, but less corruption, less spending on stadiums for the 2014 World Cup, and more investment in health and education. In spite of responding with promises of lower bus fares, using oil revenue to fund more social services, and political reform, President Rousseff's popularity plummeted as the much-admired PT development model seemed to fall apart with breathtaking speed. Ruchir Sharma (2012) argued that Brazil's model suffers from too high interest rates and currency value, too cumbersome of a business environment, and too much spending on social services. In effect, he argued that economist Baer's (2008) predictions at the outset of Lula's presidency were right: the PT's model was unworkable. By reducing poverty via social spending it increased demand, which increased inflationary pressure and limited its ability to stimulate growth. As soon as commodity prices fell, the contradictions in the model appeared. This analysis, however, set off a major debate in which many other analysts disputed him.

Web link:
A slow economy makes Brazilians long for Lula

Data link:
Transformation Index, Brazil

CASE Summary   Lula came to power as one of the more moderate members of the "pink tide." While he initiated commendable social programs (see chapter 11), maintaining international investor confidence required economic policies that initially gave him few resources to redistribute. High growth, however, allowed the PT government to fund social programs as the years went by, substantially reducing poverty. This growth, though, depended in part on high commodity prices, and when the global market shifted, largely because of slower growth in China and Europe, Brazil's model came into question. The PT, the party that claimed it was the champion of the poor, faced massive demonstrations in the streets.

It was not clear exactly how it could maneuver to restart growth while keeping inflation limited and not allowing poverty to rise again. A new commodity, oil, might come to the rescue: in 2007 Brazil discovered a large offshore oil field that, when fully developed in twenty-five years, will make it one of the top five oil exporters in the world. Oil, though, is often a very mixed blessing, as our case study of Iran demonstrates.

CASE Questions

1. What are the implications of the Brazilian case for Latin America's "pink tide"? In the face of globalization, does even a large developing country like Brazil have the ability to chart its own development policy, or does globalization limit it too much?

2. What does a comparison of the Brazilian and Indian cases teach us about the debate over the effect of democracy on economic development? What important differences and similarities do you see between these two democratic cases in terms of how and why democracy affects development?

CASE Study

IRAN: STRUGGLING WITH THE BLESSINGS OF OIL

When most Americans think of Iran, they think of its Islamist regime, U.S. sanctions against it, and its attempts to attain nuclear weapons. Economically, though, oil production and exportation is the country's most important global role. Oil wealth provides the vast majority of the country's exports and the state's revenue, and the leadership uses the latter to enhance its legitimacy. But these revenues have not necessarily encouraged wise use of resources. The Islamist regime uses oil revenue, channeled through Islamist charities and its own paramilitary groups, to provide a wide array of subsidies to the population. Thus, the government continues to control a major swath of the economy. Reformist governments in the late 1990s and early 2000s made some strides toward reducing the role of government and improving efficiency, but this has been partially reversed more recently.

- **TYPE OF ECONOMY**
  Oil dependent

- **DEVELOPMENT OUTCOMES**
  Good growth until 2011; some poverty reduction

- **RESPONSE TO GREAT RECESSION**
  Dependence on oil revenue

- **RECENT REFORM EFFORTS**
  Subsidy cuts; at least temporarily reduced dependence on oil

- **CONTINUING PROBLEMS**
  High inflation and unemployment; sanctions; political pressure for subsidies

An Iranian man shops in a supermarket in Tehran. Western sanctions and weak economic policies produced high inflation, a tumbling currency, and shortages of goods in Iran. The economic situation was the main reason Iranians elected a man they saw as a pragmatic moderate as president in 2013.

The country continues to rely heavily on the often fickle world oil market and to suffer from growing international sanctions over the nuclear dispute.

Iran's theocratic regime has not shielded it from the impact of globalization and the problems it brings to middle-income countries, but the revolution and oil have heavily influenced Iran's specific trajectory. The revolutionary government nationalized many economic assets in 1980, including large private companies and banks. They became state-owned enterprises (SOEs), and property confiscated from the shah's family and close associates funded the new Islamic foundations (*bonyads*), which became a key part of revolutionary rule. The eight-year Iran-Iraq War in the 1980s pummeled the economy, which shrank nearly 1.3 percent per capita per year over the decade. The 1990s saw some improvement, but this was accompanied by annual inflation of more than 20 percent and growing unemployment, which reached 16 percent by 2000. Throughout both decades, the country remained critically dependent on oil, which accounted for more than 80 percent of exports and anywhere from one-third to two-thirds of government revenue, depending on world oil prices.

The heavily state-controlled economy resembled the ISI policies of decades earlier in other middle-income countries. The Iranian government, though, intervened more extensively than did governments in many other countries. Government-controlled banks set interest rates uniformly, trade barriers were high, and the government set foreign exchange rates. The government budget provided large subsidies to the *bonyads* and to the SOEs as well, and lack of fiscal discipline played a major role in the high rates of inflation. Government subsidies and protection gave SOEs little incentive to operate efficiently: their losses from 1994 to 1999 equaled nearly 3 percent of the country's GDP (Alizadeh 2003, 273). The subsidies channeled through the *bonyads* and the Revolutionary Guard constituted 27 percent of the economy in 2008–2009; they essentially channel oil revenue to regime supporters to maintain their loyalty.

Facing growing economic problems, in the late 1990s the government under reformist president Mohammad Khatami attempted the first significant liberalization of the economy, a belated response to global trends and pressures. Iran's theocratic government even took advice from the bastion of Western economic imperialism, the IMF, in setting new policies. The most dramatic reforms included the implementation of a floating exchange rate, the sale of some government-controlled banks to the private sector (the government gave up controlling interest rates in the mid-1990s), reduction of import and export barriers, and privatization of SOEs. The latter has been slow and partial, in part due to fear of increasing already high unemployment (Amuzegar 2005). Overall, the reforms increased growth in the new millennium to around 5 percent per year and reduced inflation to less than 15 percent, but unemployment and poverty levels remained largely unchanged. Mahmoud Ahmadinejad was elected president in 2005 on a pledge to reduce corruption and redistribute resources to the poor. These policies were a return to the revolution's promise of social justice, and they made Ahmadinejad's election not unlike Lula's rise to power in Brazil. Ahmadinejad's first two years in office saw significantly increased public spending, buoyed by rapidly rising oil prices. It also saw higher inflation, however, and the lives of the poor were not changed much. Economic growth, fuelled by rising oil prices, reached nearly 8 percent before the global financial crisis.

While the direct effects of the crisis were relatively slight in economically isolated Iran, the country was nonetheless heavily affected by declining world oil prices. Oil export revenue fell 24 percent in 2009, and overall growth dropped to only 1.5 percent. Rising oil prices in late 2010 undoubtedly fed more revenue to the government, highlighting its continued dependence on a fickle global market. In response to the crisis, President Ahmadinejad, in spite of his rhetoric in favor of continuing subsidies, began to cut them; his hand was forced by the rapidly growing budget deficit. Past efforts to reduce subsidies had led to widespread protests and reversals of the cuts, but in late 2010 the government allowed gasoline prices to quadruple. This move was met with little visible protest, perhaps because of the severe crackdown on protests after the 2009 election (see chapter 8). Nonetheless, many analysts argued that subsidies needed to be cut further, and the government budget was still in deficit. Increased international sanctions starting in 2011 and stagnant oil prices affected the economy heavily. Growth dropped to zero by 2012, and as President Ahmadinejad handed power over to newly elected president Hassan Rouhani, inflation was estimated at over 40 percent and unemployment at around 25 percent. Perhaps the one silver lining of the Western sanctions is that Iran's dependence on oil revenue has finally begun to drop; Iran has starting processing more oil into other products, and nonoil exports paid for 60 percent of imports, more than double the percentage of a decade earlier. The sanctions, nonetheless, were causing increasing economic pain, which many analysts saw as the main impetus behind Rouhani's efforts to open up to the West and restart negotiations over Iran's nuclear program, in the hope of ending the sanctions entirely.

Audio link:
Iran's leaders send sobering message

Web link:
Iran's economy boosted by Rouhani's reformist approach

Data link:
Transformation Index, Iran

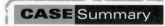

CASE Summary   Despite its massive oil revenue, Iran's theocracy has faced many of the same challenges that other middle-income countries in a global economy have navigated. Its attempt at state control of major assets resulted in inefficiency, inflation, and unemployment, though the regime has successfully lowered poverty levels. More market-oriented reforms were only partially successful, both in terms of changing policy and improving the economy. The global financial crisis resulted in a temporary drop in oil prices, sending the Iranian government's budget into a tailspin that finally forced the government to begin to remove some subsidies. Political supporters of the regime in the *bonyads* and Revolutionary Guards, however, continue to control a large share of the economy, and reducing their role further will be politically difficult. International sanctions increased their bite in recent years, leaving the economy in dire straits by 2013. Throughout the upheavals of revolution, expanding state control, partial liberalization, and sanctions, Iran has remained as dependent on oil as it was under the shah, and that dependence seems likely to hinder further reform.

CASE Questions

1. How different does oil make the Iranian case from other middle-income countries? What implications does Iran's history with oil have for Brazil's future as a rising oil producer? Will the very different type of regime in Brazil make a big difference to this question?
2. Iran's Islamist regime has long proclaimed a goal of not being influenced by the West and pursuing "Islamist" policies regardless of international opinions. To what extent has it been able to do this? Does regime type make a difference to how much a regime can influence the effects of globalization?

CONCLUSION

Globalization has certainly changed the context in which sovereign states, whether rich or poor, make economic policy. The increasingly open global economy pushes all states away from the use of time-honored economic policies that had limited the market, such as taxes, tariffs, and exchange rate controls. In addition, states are under increasing pressure to pursue policies that will keep inflation and state spending low and labor flexible.

As our case studies suggest, however, states have not all responded to globalization in the same way. Economic sovereignty, while clearly reduced, still exists. Among the wealthy countries, LMEs have intensified their openness to the market to varying degrees, whereas CMEs have moved in that direction much more slowly while preserving some aspects of their distinct model. Poorer countries are much more susceptible to the vicissitudes of the global market, as the repeated financial crises in these countries suggest, but these states are not powerless. They can play an important role in creating a context that fosters growth, human development, and effective responses to crises. The effects of the Great Recession, though, may show the limits of this; from India to Brazil to Iran, governments are struggling to overcome the lingering effects of the crisis.

Why have some states been more successful in the era of globalization than others? A key explanation is wealth. Despite challenges, wealthy countries have benefitted more from globalization than they have been hurt by it. The gap between the wealthiest and the poorest has increased, and the varieties of capitalism paradigm shows that wealthy countries continue to enjoy a significant degree of autonomy. Poorer countries have virtually all moved in the general direction of economic liberalization, but whether this has been a blessing is not always clear. Various analysts have argued that geography, resource endowment, distance from markets, government policies, and regime type all have a role in explaining why some countries, particularly "the bottom billion," continue to struggle in the face of globalization, while others thrive.

Neoliberal policies have often not reduced poverty and have sometimes led to repeated financial crises. In this context, several alternative models have arisen. While pursuit of export-oriented growth in East Asia has generated strong growth and reduced poverty, the developmental state model is based on a strong state that not all countries have. Latin America's "pink tide" governments have some similarities with the East Asian development states, but the former prioritized social spending and poverty reduction more than the latter. In "the bottom billion," the debate is over whether the mostly weaker states are able to pursue beneficial developmental goals at all, or instead should either pursue an even purer form of neoliberalism, absent foreign aid, or should be provided a massive influx of aid to overcome their inherent problems.

The Great Recession was only the latest in a series of economic crises in the era of globalization. Each has shaken the foundation of one or another economic development model and has raised questions about who weathers a crisis best and why. The latest crisis has shown perhaps more clearly than ever the force of the global market in limiting states' responses to crises. The crisis produced rapidly rising debt in several European countries, which ultimately were forced to seek bailouts from the EU and IMF. Initial stimulus packages in many countries gave way to fiscal austerity to appease international markets. While most middle-income and poor countries were not as dramatically affected initially, five years after the crisis the continuing stagnation in the global economy raised questions even in China about how long high growth and poverty reduction could continue. Growing numbers of countries faced stagnation, accompanied by demonstrators in the streets demanding change. The fortunes of the "pink tide," in particular, seemed to raise questions about how much economic sovereignty even relatively large middle-income countries like Brazil could achieve in the face of globalization. A key question in both wealthy and poor countries is how effectively a state can intervene in the market in the era of globalization to pursue goals such as greater equality, health, and the environment—subjects to which we now turn in chapter 11.

KEY CONCEPTS

comparative institutional
     advantage (p. 517)

convergence (p. 516)

coordinated market economies
     (CMEs) (p. 517)

export-oriented growth (EOG) (p. 535)

foreign direct investment (FDI) (p. 515)

hyperglobalization (p. 516)

international capital flows (p. 515)

liberal market economies (LMEs) (p. 516)

Millennium Development Goals
     (MDGs) (p. 540)

trade (p. 515)

varieties of capitalism (VOC) (p. 516)

 Sharpen your skills with SAGE edge at **edge.sagepub.com/orvis3e.**
SAGE edge for students provides a personalized approach to help
you accomplish your coursework goals in an easy-to-use learning
environment.

WORKS CITED

Adams, John. 2002. "India's Economic Growth: How Fast? How Wide? How Deep?" *India Review* 1 (2): 1–28.

African Development Bank Group. 2013. Annual Development Effectiveness Review 2013: Toward Sustainable Growth for Africa. Tunis, Tunisia, July.

Alizadeh, Parvin. 2003. "Iran's Quandary: Economic Reforms and the 'Structural Trap.'" *Brown Journal of World Affairs* 9 (2): 267–281.

Amable, Bruno, and Karim Azizi. 2011. *Varieties of Capitalism and Varieties of Macroeconomic Policy: Are Some Economies More Procyclical Than Others?* Max Planck Institute for the Study of Societies, Discussion Paper 11/6.

Amuzegar, Jahangir. 2005. "Iran's Third Development Plan: An Appraisal." *Middle East Policy* 12 (3): 46–63. doi: 10.1111/j.1061-1924.2005.00212.x.

Baer, Werner. 2008. *The Brazilian Economy: Growth and Development.* 6th ed. Boulder, CO: Lynne Rienner.

Barboza, David, and Chris Buckley. 2013. "China Plans to Reduce the State's Role in the Economy." *New York Times,* May 24 (http://www.nytimes.com/2013/05/25/business/global/beijing-signals-a-shift-on-economic-policy.html?emc=eta1).

Barros, Ricardo, Mirela de Carvalho, Samuel Franco, and Rosane Mendonça. 2010. "Markets, the State, and the Dynamics of Inequality in Brazil." In *Declining Inequality in Latin America: A Decade of Progress?,* edited by Luis F. López-Calva and Nora Lustig, 134–174. New York: United Nations Development Programme; Washington, DC: Brookings Institution Press.

Bermeo, Nancy, and Jonas Pontusson. 2012. "Coping with Crisis: An Introduction." In *Coping with Crisis: Government Reactions to the Great Recession,* edited by Nancy Bermeo and Jonas Pontusson, 1–32. New York: Russell Sage Foundation.

Bhagwati, Jagdish, and Arvind Panagariya. 2013. "Introduction." In *Reforms and Economic Transformation in India,* edited by Jagdish Bhagwati and Arvind Panagariya, 1–12. Oxford, UK: Oxford University Press.

Bresser-Pereira, Luiz Carlos. 2009. *Developing Brazil: Overcoming the Failure of the Washington Consensus*. Boulder, CO: Lynne Rienner.

Collier, Paul. 2007. *The Bottom Billion: Why the Poorest Countries Are Failing and What Can Be Done about It*. Oxford, UK: Oxford University Press.

Cox, Robert Henry. 2002. "Reforming the German Welfare State: Why Germany Is Slower Than Its Neighbors." *German Policy Studies* 2 (1): 174–196.

Daly, Mary. 2001. "Globalization and the Bismarckian Welfare States." In *Globalization and European Welfare States: Challenges and Change*, edited by Robert Sykes, Bruno Palier, and Pauline M. Prior (with Jo Campling), 79–102. New York: Palgrave.

Easterly, William. 2006. *The White Man's Burden: Why the West's Efforts to Aid the Rest Have Done So Much Ill and So Little Good*. New York: Penguin Press.

Evans, Peter B. 1995. *Embedded Autonomy: States and Industrial Transformation*. Princeton, NJ: Princeton University Press.

Faucher-King, Florence, and Patrick Le Galès. 2010. *The New Labour Experiment: Change and Reform under Blair and Brown*. Stanford, CA: Stanford University Press.

Feng, Yi. 2003. *Democracy, Governance, and Economic Performance: Theory and Evidence*. Cambridge, MA: MIT Press.

Flores-Macias, Gustavo A. 2012. *After Neoliberalism: The Left and Economic Reforms in Latin America*. Oxford, UK: Oxford University Press.

Ginsburg, Norman. 2001. "Globalization and the Liberal Welfare States." In *Globalization and European Welfare States: Challenges and Change*, edited by Robert Sykes, Bruno Palier, and Pauline M. Prior (with Jo Campling), 173–192. New York: Palgrave.

Haggard, Stephan, and Robert R. Kaufman. 1995. *The Political Economy of Democratic Transitions*. Princeton, NJ: Princeton University Press.

Hall, Peter Andrew, and Daniel Gingerich. 2009. "Varieties of Capitalism and Institutional Complementarities in the Political Economy: An Empirical Analysis." *British Journal of Political Science* 39 (3): 449–482. doi:10.1017/S0007123409000672.

Hall, Peter Andrew, and David W. Soskice, eds. 2001. *Varieties of Capitalism: The Institutional Foundations of Comparative Advantage*. Oxford, UK: Oxford University Press.

Hardie, Iain, and David Howarth. 2009. "*Die Krise* but Not *La Crise*? The Financial Crisis and the Transformation of German and French Banking Systems." *JCMS: Journal of Common Market Studies* 47 (5): 1017–1039. doi:10.1111/j.1468-5965.2009.02033.x.

Harriss, John. 2011. "How Far Have India's Economic Reforms Been Guided by Compassion and Justice? Social Policy in the Neoliberal Era." In *Understanding India's New Political Economy: The Great Transformation?*, edited by Sanjay Ruparella, Sanjay Reddy, John Harriss, and Stuart Corbridge, 127–140. New York: Routledge.

Hay, Colin. 2004. "Common Trajectories, Variable Paces, Divergent Outcomes: Models of European Capitalism under Conditions of Complex Economic Interdependence." *Review of International Political Economy* 11 (2): 231–262. doi:10.1080/09692290420001672796.

Huber, Evelyne, and John D. Stephens. 2001. *Development and Crisis of the Welfare State: Parties and Policies in Global Markets*. Chicago: University of Chicago Press.

———. 2012. *Democracy and the Left: Social Policy and Inequality in Latin America*. Chicago: University of Chicago Press.

Jenkins, Rob. 2011. "The Politics of India's Special Economic Zones." In *Understanding India's New Political Economy: The Great Transformation?*, edited by Sanjay Ruparella, Sanjay Reddy, John Harriss, and Stuart Corbridge, 49–65. New York: Routledge.

Johnson, Ian. 2013. "China's Great Uprooting: Moving 250 Million into Cities." *New York Times*, June 15 (http://www.nytimes.com/2013/06/16/world/asia/chinas-great-uprooting-moving-250-million-into-cities.html?emc=eta1).

Kaplan, Stephen B. 2013. *Globalization and Austerity Politics in Latin America.* Cambridge, UK: Cambridge University Press.

Kapur, Devesh. 2010. "The Political Economy of the State." In *The Oxford Companion to Politics in India*, edited by Niraja Gopal Jayal and Pratap Bhanu Mehta, 443–458. Oxford, UK: Oxford University Press.

Karshenas, Massoud, and Hassan Hakimian. 2005. "Oil, Economic Diversification, and the Democratic Process in Iran." *Iranian Studies* 38 (1): 67–490. doi:10.1080/0021086042000336546.

———. 2007. "State, Business, and Economic Growth in India." *Studies in Comparative International Development* 42 (1–2): 87–114. doi:10.1007/s12116-007-9001-9.

Knight, John, and Sai Ding. 2013. *China's Remarkable Economic Growth.* Oxford, UK: Oxford University Press.

Kohli, Atul. 2004. State-Directed Development: Political Power and Industrialization in the Global Periphery. Cambridge, UK: Cambridge University Press.

———. 2007. "State, Business, and Economic Growth in India." *Studies in Comparative International Development* 42 (1–2): 87–114. doi:10.1007/s12116-007-9001-9.

Lijphart, Arend. 1999. *Patterns of Democracy: Government Forms and Performance in Thirty-six Countries.* New Haven, CT: Yale University Press.

Moreno-Brid, Juan Carlos, and Igor Paunovic. 2010. "Macroeconomic Policies of the New Left: Rhetoric and Reality." In *Latin America's Left Turns: Politics, Policies, and Trajectories of Change*, edited by Maxwell A. Cameron and Eric Hershberg, 193–232. Boulder, CO: Lynne Rienner.

Morgan, Glenn, and Richard Whitley. 2012. *Capitalisms and Capitalism in the Twenty-first Century.* Oxford, UK: Oxford University Press.

Mosley, Paul, with Blessing Chiripanhura, Jena Grugel, and Ben Thirkell-White. 2012. *The Politics of Poverty Reduction.* Oxford, UK: Oxford University Press.

Moyo, Dambisa. 2009. *Dead Aid: Why Aid Is Not Working and How There Is a Better Way for Africa.* New York: Farrar, Straus and Giroux.

Norris, Pippa. 2012. *Making Democratic Governance Work: How Regimes Shape Prosperity, Welfare, and Peace.* Cambridge, UK: Cambridge University Press.

Ozawa, Terutomo. 2010. "Asia's Labour-Driven Growth, Flying Geese Style: Types of Trade, FDI, and Institutions Matter for the Poor." In *The Poor under Globalization in Asia, Latin America, and Africa*, edited by Machiko Nissanke and Erik Thorbecke, 87–115. Oxford, UK: Oxford University Press.

Pettis, Michael. 2013. *China Does Not Need to Grow at 7.5 Percent.* Washington, DC: Carnegie Endowment for International Peace (http://carnegieendowment.org/2013/07/18/china-does-not-need-to-grow-at-7.5-percent/gfyo).

Pitcher, M. Anne. 2012. *Party Politics and Economic Reform in Africa's Democracies.* Cambridge, UK: Cambridge University Press.

Pontusson, Jonas, and Damian Raess. 2012. "How (and Why) Is This Time Different? The Politics of Economic Crisis in Western Europe and the United States." *Annual Review of Political Science* 15: 13–33.

Przeworski, Adam, Michael Alvarez, José Cheibub, and Fernando Limongi. 2000. *Democracy and Development.* Cambridge, UK: Cambridge University Press.

Qian, Yingyi. 2006. "The Process of China's Market Transition, 1978–1998: The Evolutionary, Historical, and Comparative Perspectives." In *China's Deep Reform: Domestic Politics in Transition*, edited by Lowell Dittmer and Guoili Liu, 229–250. Lanham, MD: Rowman and Littlefield.

Qin, Julia. 2007. "Trade, Investment, and Beyond: The Impact of WTO Accession on China's Legal System." *China Quarterly* 191: 720–741.

Round, Jeffrey. 2010. "Globalization, Growth, Inequality, and Poverty in Africa: A Macroeconomic Perspective." In *The Poor under Globalization in Asia, Latin America, and Africa*, edited by M. Nissanke and E. Thorbecke, 327–367. Oxford, UK: Oxford University Press.

Sachs, Jeffrey D. 2005. *The End of Poverty: Economic Possibilities for Our Time.* New York: Penguin Books.

Sharma, Ruchir. 2012. "Bearish on Brazil." *Foreign Affairs* 91 (3). May/June.

Sinha, Aseema. 2010. "Business and Politics in Changing India: Continuities, Transformations, and Patterns." In *The Oxford Companion to Politics in India*, edited by Niraja Gopal Jayal and Pratap Bhanu Mehta, 459–476. Oxford, UK: Oxford University Press.

Sridharan, Eswaran. 2013. "Drift and Confusion Reign in Indian Politics." *Current History* 112 (753): 123–129.

Streeck, Wolfgang. 2009. *Re-forming Capitalism: Institutional Change in the German Political Economy.* Oxford, UK: Oxford University Press.

Streeck, Wolfgang, and Anke Hassel. 2003. "The Crumbling Pillars of Social Partnership." *West European Politics* 26 (4): 101–124. doi:10.1080/01402380312331280708.

Thelen, Kathleen. 2012. "Varieties of Capitalism: Trajectories of Liberalization and the New Politics of Social Solidarity." *Annual Review of Political Science* 15: 137–159.

United Nations: Economic Commission for Latin America and the Caribbean (ECLAC). 2010. *Preliminary Overview of the Economies of Latin America and the Caribbean 2010* (http://www.eclac.org/cgi-bin/getProd.asp?xml=/publicaciones/xml/4/41974/P41974.xml).

Van de Walle, Nicolas. 2001. *African Economies and the Politics of Permanent Crisis, 1979–1999.* Cambridge, UK: Cambridge University Press.

Winters, L. Alan, and Shahid Yusuf, eds. 2007. *Dancing with Giants: China, India, and the Global Economy.* Washington, DC: World Bank.

World Bank. 1993. *The East Asian Miracle: Economic Growth and Public Policy.* New York: Oxford University Press.

Wylde, Christopher. 2012. *Latin America after Neoliberalism: Developmental Regimes in Post-Crisis States.* New York: Palgrave Macmillan.

Yardley, Jim. 2013. "Ahead of Elections, India's Cabinet Approves Food Security Program." *New York Times*, July 4 (http://india.blogs.nytimes.com/2013/07/04/indias-cabinet-passes-food-security-law).

RESOURCES FOR FURTHER STUDY

Cameron, Maxwell A., and Eric Hershberg, eds. 2010. *Latin America's Left Turns: Politics, Policies, and Trajectories of Change.* Boulder, CO: Lynne Rienner.

Ferreira, Francisco H. G., and Michael Walton. 2005. *Equity and Development.* Washington, DC: World Bank.

Garrett, Geoffrey. 1998. *Partisan Politics in the Global Economy.* Cambridge, UK: Cambridge University Press.

Jha, Prem Shankar. 2002. *The Perilous Road to the Market: The Political Economy of Reform in Russia, India, and China.* London: Pluto Press.

Jones, R. J. Barry. 2000. *The World Turned Upside Down? Globalization and the Future of the State*. Manchester, UK: Manchester University Press.

Kohli, Atul, Chung-in Moon, and Georg Sørensen, eds. 2003. *States, Markets, and Just Growth: Development in the Twenty-first Century*. New York: United Nations University Press.

MacIntyre, Andrew, T. J. Pempel, and John Ravenhill, eds. 2008. *Crisis as Catalyst: Asia's Dynamic Political Economy*. Ithaca, NY: Cornell University Press.

Nissanke, Machiko, and Erik Thorbecke, eds. 2010. *The Poor under Globalization in Asia, Latin America, and Africa*. Oxford, UK: Oxford University Press.

Rothstein, Bo, and Sven Steinmo, eds. 2002. *Restructuring the Welfare State: Political Institutions and Policy Change*. New York: Palgrave Macmillan.

Sykes, Robert, Bruno Palier, and Pauline M. Prior (with Jo Campling), eds. 2001. *Globalization and European Welfare States: Challenges and Change*. New York: Palgrave.

WEB RESOURCES

CountryWatch
(http://www.countrywatch.com)

European Commission, Eurostat: Your Key to European Statistics
(http://epp.eurostat.ec.europa.eu)

KOF Index of Globalization
(http://globalization.kof.ethz.ch). Based on data from Axel Dreher, "Does Globalization Affect Growth? Evidence from a New Index of Globalization," *Applied Economics* 38, no. 10 (2006): 1091–1110; updated in Axel Dreher, Noel Gaston, and Pim Martens, *Measuring Globalisation: Gauging Its Consequences* (New York: Springer, 2008).

Luxembourg Income Study
(http://www.lisproject.org)

Organisation for Economic Co-operation and Development (OECD), OECD Statistics
(http://www.oecd-ilibrary.org/statistics)

UN Millennium Project, Millennium Villages: A New Approach to Fighting Poverty
(http://www.unmillenniumproject.org/mv/mv_closer.htm)

United Nations University, World Institute for Development Economics Research, World Income Inequality Database
(http://www.wider.unu.edu/research/Database)

World Bank, Economic Policy and External Debt
(http://data.worldbank.org/topic/economic-policy-and-external-debt)

11 PUBLIC POLICIES WHEN MARKETS FAIL
Welfare, Health, and the Environment

KEY QUESTIONS

- What do policy outcomes tell us about who has effective representation and power in a political system?

- Why do states intervene in the market via social, health, and environmental policies?

- Why have many governments pursued significant reforms to welfare states in the era of globalization?

- Why have states found it so difficult to reform health policy and control costs?

- Where and why did more effective welfare and health systems emerge, and can the most effective ones be replicated in other countries?

As globalization spreads the market economy, the issues raised in chapters 5 and 10 about the relationship between the state and the market loom ever larger. The long-standing debate over how much governments ought to intervene in the market in an effort to maximize citizens' well-being continues unabated. This chapter addresses three key areas that have long been subjects of debate in virtually every country: welfare, health care, and the environment. The common thread among them is the call for government to intervene in response to market failure.

We defined market failure in economic terms in chapter 5: markets fail when they do not maximize efficiency, most commonly because of externalities, monopolies, or imperfect information. Environmental damage is a classic example of a market failure to allocate resources efficiently. Markets can also fail, however, in the sense that they don't achieve the results a society collectively desires. In this chapter, therefore, we broaden the definition of market failure to a more general understanding that markets fail when they do not perform according to widely held social values. For instance, markets do not necessarily reduce inequality or end poverty, even though the alleviation of both is often a widely held social value. Governments develop what Americans call "welfare"

policies to respond to market failures to distribute wealth in socially acceptable ways.

Markets respond to individuals or companies with resources (money or commodities) that can be exchanged for other resources; because poor people have fewer resources they receive less from the unfettered market. Economists speak of "effective demand" in a market, meaning demand backed with money. Very little effective demand for food exists during a famine in a very poor country; gov-

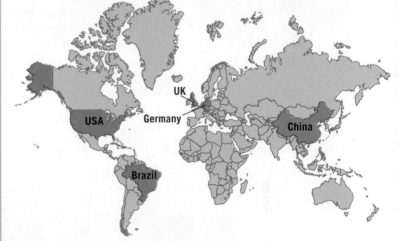

ernment and international intervention in the form of emergency food aid is justified because of the social value of keeping people from starving to death. Similarly, poor, uninsured individuals who are very sick may have no effective demand for health care, so the market will provide none, but governments might choose to intervene to restore their health based on a value of preserving and extending life for all citizens.

Government interventions of this type raise a host of interesting questions because they pit various groups of citizens against one another. The policy outcomes often tell us much about the classic "Who rules?" question: Who is better represented, and thus has power? They also raise major questions focused on why government intervenes

COUNTRY AND CONCEPT
Welfare, Health, and the Environment

Country	Welfare system	Life expectancy	Infant mortality rate (deaths per 1,000 births)	Health care system	Public expenditure on health (% of total expenditure on health)	Per capita total expenditures on health (U.S. dollars, PPP)	Annual CO_2 emissions (million metric tons of CO_2)	Per capita CO_2 emissions (tons)
Brazil	Liberal	74	20	NHS, plus much private financing and some private insurance	45.7	1,121	475	2.18
China	Liberal welfare state emerging: social insurance for pensions and unemployment; means-tested programs for others in urban areas	76	15	NHI emerging, plus much private financing and some private insurance	55.9	278	8,715	4.91
Germany	Christian democratic	81	4	NHI	75.9	4,875	748	10.06
India	Minimal: small means-tested programs, such as food subsidies and rural employment	65	47	NHS, plus much private insurance, direct financing, and NGO provision of health services	31.0	59	1,725	1.31
Iran	Mixed: social insurance for retirees; state-funded means-tested programs; Islamic charity via *bonyads* (Islamic foundations)	73	40	NHI	39.7	346	624	7.76
Japan	Employment-based, with additional means-tested government programs	83	2	NHI	80	3,958	1,180	9.54

Mexico	Liberal welfare state	75	16	NHS, plus much private insurance and direct financing	49.4	620	462	4.04
Nigeria	None	53	73	NHS, plus much private financing and NGO provision of health services	36.7	80	75	0.45
Russia	Social insurance for pensions; other benefits targeted to particular groups (in kind until 2007, cash since)	69	7	NHI	59.7	807	1,788	12.29
United Kingdom	Liberal	80	5	NHS	82.7	3,495	496	9.38
United States	Liberal	79	6	Market-based insurance	45.9	8,233	5,490	19.18

Sources: Life expectancy data are from World Health Organization (http://apps.who.int/gho/data/node.main.688?lang=en). Infant mortality data are from *CIA World Factbook* (https://www.cia.gov/library/publications/the-world-factbook/fields/2091.html#br). Health care spending data are from the World Bank for the most recent year available (http://data.worldbank.org/indicator/SH.XPD.PUBL). Per capita total expenditures on health care data are from the World Bank (http://data.worldbank.org/indicator/SH.XPD.PCAP/countries). CO_2 annual emissions data are from International Energy Agency (http://www.eia.gov/cfapps/ipdbproject/iedindex3.cfm?tid=90&pid=44&aid=8). Per capita emissions data are from the World Bank (http://data.worldbank.org/indicator/EN.ATM.CO2E.PC).

in the first place. In recent years, governments in all wealthy countries have reformed welfare policies substantially and tried, with limited success, to reform health care policies as well. Why have these trends been so widespread over the past twenty to thirty years, and why have some states been more successful than others at achieving reforms? The Country and Concept table shows the great variation in these policy areas across our case study countries. Welfare systems vary from quite extensive to nonexistent, with dramatically different effects on the level of poverty. Key health care indicators like life expectancy and infant mortality vary dramatically as well. The wealthy countries achieve roughly similar health outcomes but at very different costs, while poor countries' health fares far worse. Looking at the most important environmental concern, carbon dioxide emissions that cause global warming, our case studies include the two biggest polluters in the world—the United States and China—and others that, while likely to suffer the effects of global warming, are only a miniscule part of the problem. The case studies will allow us to examine these policy options and outcomes in widely varying circumstances.

"WELFARE": SOCIAL POLICY IN COMPARATIVE PERSPECTIVE

Most Americans think of welfare as a government handout to poor people. Being "on welfare" is something virtually all Americans want to avoid, as a certain moral opprobrium seems to go with it. Partly because of this, and partly because different countries relieve poverty in different ways, scholars of public policy prefer the term **social policy** to welfare. Social policy's primary goals are to reduce poverty and income inequality and to stabilize individual or family income. Most people view a market that leaves people in abject poverty, unable to meet their most basic needs, as violating important values. Similarly, when markets produce inequality that goes beyond some particular point (the acceptable level varies widely), many people argue that it should be reversed. Markets also inherently produce instability: in the absence of government intervention, capitalism tends to be associated with boom and bust cycles that result in economic insecurity, especially due to unemployment. Reducing this insecurity has been one of the main impetuses behind modern welfare states.

Various philosophical and practical reasons justify social policies. On purely humanitarian grounds, citizens and governments might wish to alleviate the suffering of the poor. States might also be concerned about social and political stability: high endemic poverty rates and economic instability often are seen as threats to the status quo, including a state's legitimacy, and poverty is associated with higher levels of crime almost everywhere. Keynesians argue as well that policies to reduce poverty and stabilize incomes are economically beneficial for society as a whole because they help increase purchasing power, which stimulates market demand.

Opponents of social policy disagree, criticizing it primarily for producing perverse incentives. Markets maximize efficiency in part by inducing people to be productive by working for wages, salaries, or profits. Neoliberal opponents of social policy argue that providing income or other resources for people whether they are working or not gives them a disincentive to work, which reduces efficiency, productivity, and overall wealth. Critics also argue that financing social policy via taxes discourages work and productivity because higher taxes reduce incentives to work and make a profit.

In liberal democracies, the debate over social policy also raises a fundamental question over the trade-off between citizens' equality and autonomy. According to liberalism, citizens are supposed to be equal and autonomous individuals, yet in a market economy, it's difficult to achieve both. Citizens are never truly socioeconomically equal. As we saw in chapter 3, T. H. Marshall (1963) argued that social rights are the third pillar of citizenship because without some degree of socioeconomic equality, citizens cannot be political equals. Following this line of thought, when the market fails to create an adequate degree of equality, governments should intervene to preserve equal citizenship. On the other hand, in market economies, market participation is a primary means of achieving autonomy. The founders of liberalism believed only male property owners could be citizens because they were the only ones who were truly

social policy
Policy focused on reducing poverty and income inequality and stabilizing individual or family income

autonomous; women and nonproperty owners were too economically dependent on others to act effectively as autonomous citizens. All liberal democracies have modified this position, but the fundamental concern remains. Many citizens view only those who participate in the market—whether by owning capital or working for a wage—as fully autonomous. Welfare policies that provide income from nonmarket sources can then be seen as problematic. Traditional liberals argue that social policy undermines equal and autonomous citizenship by creating two classes of citizens: those who earn their income in the market and those who depend on the government (funded by the rest of the citizens). This argument typically makes an exception for family membership: an adult who depends on other family members who participate in the market is implicitly granted full autonomy and citizenship. Social democrats argue, to the contrary, that citizens should be granted full autonomy regardless of their source of income and that social policies that keep income inequality and poverty below certain levels are essential to preserving truly equal citizenship. Different kinds of welfare states are in part based on different values in this debate.

Web link:
Who deserves welfare in India?

Web link:
Switzerland's proposal to pay people for being alive

Types of Social Policy

Whatever their justification, social policies can be categorized into four distinct types: universal entitlements, social insurance, means-tested public assistance, and tax expenditures. **Universal entitlements** are benefits that governments provide to all citizens more or less equally, usually funded through general taxation. The only major example in the United States is public education. All communities in the United States must provide access to public education for all school-age residents without exception, making it a universal benefit. Many European countries provide child or family allowances as universal entitlements: all families with children receive a cash benefit to help raise the children. Universal entitlements by nature do not raise questions about equal and autonomous citizenship, even when individual citizens may choose not to take advantage of them. No one questions the equal citizenship of public versus private school graduates in the United States, or those who do not have children and therefore don't get child allowances in the Netherlands. Critics, on the other hand, argue that universal entitlements are wasteful because much of the money goes to relatively wealthy people who do not need the benefits.

universal entitlements
Benefits that governments provide to all citizens more or less equally, usually funded through general taxation; in the United States, public education is an example

Web link:
Politics of universal entitlements

Web link:
The state of the 4-year-olds

Social insurance provides benefits to categories of people who have contributed to a (usually mandatory) public insurance fund. The prime examples in the United States are Social Security, disability benefits, and unemployment insurance. In most cases, both workers and their employers must contribute to the funds. Workers can then benefit from the fund when they need it: after retirement, when temporarily unemployed, or when disabled. Because only those who contribute can gain benefits, fewer questions arise about the beneficiaries deserving their benefits, even though there is usually only a very general relationship between the size of a person's contribution and the amount of his benefit. The average American retiree, for instance,

social insurance
Provides benefits to categories of people who have contributed to a (usually mandatory) public insurance fund; typically used to provide retirement pensions

Web link:
Obama's preschool proposal is a magical fantasy

earns substantially more in Social Security benefits than the total of his lifetime contributions with interest, but that gap has never raised questions of equal citizenship. In addition, by covering entire large groups of people—all workers or the spouses of all workers—social insurance is not seen as undermining equal citizenship because it covers things nearly everyone expects (retirement) or hopes to avoid (unemployment).

Means-tested public assistance

Social programs that provide benefits to individuals who fall below a specific income level; TANF is an example in the United States

Means-tested public assistance is what most Americans think of as "welfare." The Supplemental Nutrition Assistance Program (SNAP; also commonly known as "food stamps"), subsidized public housing, and Temporary Assistance to Needy Families (TANF) are examples in the United States. These are programs that individuals qualify for when they fall below a specific income level. Some countries impose additional requirements for public assistance, such as work requirements or time limits, but income level is the defining characteristic. Means-tested programs target assistance at the poor in contrast to the broader distribution of universal entitlements or social insurance, so they may be the most efficient means of poverty relief. Their disadvantage, though, is their impact on recipients' status as equal and autonomous citizens. Because only those below a certain income level can benefit, and benefits are typically financed from general taxation, recipients may be seen as somehow less deserving or not fully equal with other citizens who are paying taxes and not receiving benefits.

tax expenditures

Targeted tax breaks for specific groups of citizens or activities designed to achieve social policy goals

All three types of social policy discussed so far involve direct government spending. **Tax expenditures**, targeted tax breaks for specific groups of citizens or activities, have only been included as part of social policy fairly recently. To most people, tax breaks—not collecting taxes from someone—seem different from government spending. The net effect of the two, however, is quite similar. When the government selectively lowers the tax someone would otherwise pay, it is increasing that person's disposable income. A tax break for a particular activity, such as purchasing a home or investing in a retirement pension, subsidizes particular activities that the government presumably believes to be socially beneficial. By giving tax breaks for employees' and employers' contributions to health insurance and retirement pensions, for instance, the U.S. government is subsidizing those activities. A tax break for low-income people has the same effect as the same amount of social spending targeted at that group.

Tax expenditures are an important part of social policy, especially in the United States. They can be restricted to lower-income people or provided much more widely, with different effects on reducing poverty and inequality. In the United States, for instance, the Earned Income Tax Credit (EITC) aimed at lower-income families has become one of the largest poverty-reduction programs in the country, larger in fact than TANF, the program most Americans think of as "welfare." The tax deduction for interest paid on home mortgages, on the other hand, subsidizes all but the most expensive home purchases; it is a social policy designed to encourage home ownership (presumably improving standards of living and economic security) that provides greater benefits to the middle and upper classes than to the poor.

Different types of social programs are often associated with particular kinds of benefits or groups of recipients. Workers are often covered by social insurance, for instance, while public housing is typically means tested. What is true for tax expenditures, however, is true for all types of social programs; any of them could be used for any type of benefit. For instance, unemployment insurance is fairly restricted in the United States, benefiting only long-term employees and usually for only six to nine months after a worker becomes unemployed; elsewhere, similar programs are more extensive and less distinct from what Americans call "welfare." Preschool is a universal entitlement in France but is means tested via the Head Start program in the United States. Retirement benefits also could be means tested so that when older people no longer earn a market-based income, only those below a certain income level would qualify for benefits. Indeed, this has been one policy suggested in the United States as a way to reduce the long-term cost of the Social Security program. This would target retirement benefits more efficiently at reducing poverty but might raise questions of equal citizenship common to means-tested programs, questions that retirees currently don't face.

Types of Welfare States

Governments combine social programs in different ways and with different levels of generosity, creating distinctive **welfare states**. The Country and Concept table (pages 572–573) gives some idea of the wide variety of combinations states use. Evelyne Huber and John Stephens (2001), modifying the pioneering work of Gøsta Esping-Andersen (1990), classified wealthy countries into three main types of welfare states: social democratic, Christian democratic, and liberal. **Social democratic welfare states** strongly emphasize universal entitlements to achieve greater social equality and promote equal citizenship. Governments typically provide universal entitlements in a wide array of areas, including paid maternity leave, preschool, child allowances, basic retirement pensions, and job training. They use high rates of general taxation to fund their generous social benefits and typically redistribute more income (taxing the wealthy more and giving equal universal entitlements to all) than do other welfare states. Social insurance programs, such as employment-based retirement pensions, also exist, but these usually just supplement the universal entitlements. The primary examples of social democratic welfare states are the Scandinavian countries.

Christian democratic welfare states primarily emphasize income stabilization to mitigate the effects of market-induced income insecurity. Their most common type of social program, therefore, is social insurance, which is designed to replace a relatively high percentage of a family's market-based income when it is disrupted through unemployment, disability, or something similar. Benefits are usually tied to contributions, and financing is mainly through employer and employee payroll taxes rather than general taxation. This means that redistribution is not as broad as under social democratic welfare states. Most Christian democratic welfare states also feature corporatist models of economic governance; that is, social insurance programs tend to be administered by and through sectoral-based organizations such as unions, though under the state's guidance. We explore a prime example, Germany, in detail below.

welfare states
Distinct systems of social policies that arose after World War II in wealthy market economies, including social democratic welfare states, Christian democratic welfare states, and liberal welfare states

social democratic welfare states
States whose social policies strongly emphasize universal entitlements to achieve greater social equality and promote equal citizenship; Sweden is key example

Christian democratic welfare states
States whose social policies are based on the nuclear family with a male breadwinner, designed primarily to achieve income stabilization to mitigate the effects of market-induced income insecurity; Germany is key example

Sweden's Welfare State

Sweden's generous, redistributive social welfare state is a long-standing model of "the middle way" between capitalism and socialism. The Swedish Social Democratic Party was in power continuously from 1932 to 2006, except for two brief periods. The party instituted the first elements of a welfare state in the 1920s. From the start, it established basic services such as unemployment benefits and retirement pensions as universal social rights of citizenship. In the late 1950s, the party added extra benefits above and beyond the flat-rate universal ones. These were tied to earnings and replaced as much as 90 percent of workers' wages when they were unemployed, disabled, or retired. In the 1970s, the government expanded services designed to induce women into the workforce and support them once they are employed, including the world's most generous maternity and sick leave policies.

The state combined these benefits with very high tax rates on income (60 percent of the economy at their peak in the 1970s), but it used low corporate tax rates to encourage investment in export industries and had one of the most open trade policies in the world. At its height in the 1970s, Sweden was the world's second-wealthiest country, with robust growth, strong export levels by brand-name companies such as Volvo, virtually no unemployment, and the world's most generous social services. Even after reforms in the 1990s, Sweden's social services and taxes remain among the world's highest. Unemployment benefits still cover about 80 percent of wages and have virtually no time limit. Parental leave provides sixteen months of paid leave at any time during the first eight years of a child's life at 80 percent of full salary. Parents get ten paid "contact days" per year to spend time in their children's schools as volunteers, up to sixty days of benefits per year to care for sick children, and access to a daycare system that enrolls 75 percent of preschoolers, with more than 80 percent of the cost funded by the state (Olsen 2007, 147–151). To pay for this, government revenue remains more than half of the entire economy (compared with a little more than a third for the United States). In addition, more than 30 percent of all employees work in the public sector.

Sweden's model faced a crisis in the early 1990s. Declining industry and growing outsourcing of business combined with the bursting of a housing bubble (not unlike conditions in the United States in 2008) and demographic changes to increase unemployment, inflation, and the government's debt. When the Social Democrats lost the 1991 election, the newly elected Moderate Party government passed what was seen at the time as the most sweeping tax reform in the Western world, with the top income tax rate dropping from 80 to 50 percent and the marginal rate on corporate taxes from 57 to 30 percent (Huber and Stephens 2001, 242). Returning to power in 1994, the Social Democrats expanded the reforms, tying retirement pensions to levels of unemployment and economic growth, dividing the cost of pensions equally between employer and employee (previously, employers paid for virtually all of the benefits), and reducing unemployment benefits from 90 to 80 percent of income. Unions successfully resisted an attempt to impose a three-year limit on such benefits (nine months is typical in the United States).

Prior to the 2008–2009 recession, Sweden's growth had returned to normal levels. While the size and scope of the government had shrunk, inequality had increased only slightly, and poverty remained very low. Unemployment dropped as well, to about 8 percent, but remains one of the country's biggest problems. The global recession hit the country hard because it relies heavily on exports; its economy declined by nearly 5 percent in 2009, though it grew by nearly 7 percent in 2011, only to fall back to close to zero by 2013. The government's success helped the ruling Moderate Party win reelection in late 2010, the first time a party other than the Social Democrats had been reelected in over eighty years. Sweden's voters have consistently supported their extensive welfare state, indicating a widely held set of values that supports extensive government intervention to reduce poverty, inequality, and economic insecurity. The country's reliance on universal entitlements means extensive social policies do not seem to raise significant questions about equal citizenship.

Video link:
Sweden's march toward capitalism

Liberal welfare states focus on ensuring that all who can work and gain their income in the market do so; they are more concerned about preserving individual autonomy via market participation than reducing poverty or inequality. They emphasize means-tested public assistance, targeting very specific groups of recipients for benefits. A great deal of government effort often goes into assessing who is truly deserving of support, which usually boils down to determining who is truly unable to work for a wage. The emphasis on ensuring that only the truly deserving receive benefits often means that some poor people don't get assistance, and the desire to provide incentives for people to work can mean that benefits do not raise people out of poverty. But not all programs are means tested in these countries; retirement benefits are typically provided via social insurance. The United States, which we turn to below, is a prime example of this type of welfare state.

Explaining the Development and Evolution of Welfare States

Comparativists have used cultural, institutional, and structural arguments to explain the origins and evolution of the different types of welfare states. Cultural arguments have looked at differences in long-standing values. Anglo-American countries, they argue, have stronger liberal traditions emphasizing the importance of the individual and individual autonomy, which cause them to be more reluctant to engage in extensive government spending to help people via policy. Numerous surveys have shown, for instance, that despite upward social mobility being about the same in the United States and Europe, Americans are much more likely than Europeans to believe that people can work their way out of poverty if they really want to (Alesina and Glaeser 2004, 11–12).

Religious beliefs may also influence welfare states: countries more influenced by Protestantism, especially Calvinism, see wealth as morally superior and have less sympathy for the poor, whereas countries with more Catholics are more generous due to their belief in preserving social and family stability. A final cultural explanation argues that racial divisions and immigration history matter. Alberto Alesina and Edward Glaeser (2004) argued that this partly explains the striking difference in the generosity of social spending in the United States and Europe. Surveys show that people (not only Americans) are less sympathetic to those of different races, and in the United States many whites incorrectly perceive the poor as being mostly black or Hispanic. As a result, Americans are relatively unwilling to support policies to assist them. As immigration has diversified many European countries, similar phenomena may be arising there as well.

Huber and Stephens (2001) combined a structural argument focusing on the political organization of social classes with an institutionalist argument to explain the rise of distinct types of welfare states, as well as their relative levels of generosity. They argued that welfare states primarily reflect the strength and political orientation of the working and lower-middle classes. In countries where these classes were able to organize into strong labor unions and powerful social democratic parties, social democratic welfare states emerged that emphasize wealth redistribution and gender equality. Countries with more Catholics and stronger Christian democratic parties that appealed successfully to

liberal welfare states
States whose social policies focus on ensuring that all who can do so gain their income in the market; more concerned about preserving individual autonomy than reducing poverty or inequality; the United States is a key example

Web link:
How to conceptualize the welfare state

working and lower-middle classes saw the emergence of Christian democratic welfare states that emphasize social and family stability rather than resource redistribution and women's participation in the workplace. Where the working classes were not strong enough to organize to gain political power, liberal welfare states emerged that provide minimal support only for those who are truly unable to work. They combine this with an institutionalist argument: regimes with fewer veto players developed more extensive welfare states. Federal systems, for instance, tend to produce less extensive social policies, as do presidential systems. Feminist scholars have made similar arguments about the political origins of distinct welfare states but have focused on women's movements: where they were stronger earlier, universal benefits that need not go through a male breadwinner and policies that support women entering the workforce, such as child allowances and universal child care, developed the most (Sainsbury 2013).

The pressures of globalization initially led scholars to argue, following the hyperglobalization thesis, that the distinctions among types of welfare states would tend to disappear; global economic forces would pressure all welfare states toward the liberal model of reduced benefits. As we suggested in chapter 10, though, few countries have fundamentally altered their social policies. Indeed, social expenditures as a share of wealthy countries' economies and government budgets have increased over the past three decades. Institutionalist theorists (Pierson 1996) argued that the welfare state created institutions and their beneficiaries, which then constituted powerful coalitions blocking reform.

The aggregate data, however, hide important reforms. Upward pressure on social expenditures comes primarily from demographic changes in wealthy countries: as populations age, fewer workers must somehow pay the benefits for larger dependent populations, particularly the elderly. The rise of the service sector and global demands for more flexible labor have led to shifts in unemployment benefits that create greater incentives to get the unemployed back to work and invest more money in retraining workers. While

TABLE 11.1　Comparison of Welfare State Outcomes

	Social expenditure as % of GDP				GDP growth %		
	1980	1995	2006	2011	1981–1990	1991–2000	2001–2010
Social democratic welfare states	22.2	28.1	25.4	27.43	2.48	2.64	1.53
Christian democratic welfare states	20.6	23.6	26	26.57	2.27	2.1	1.23
Liberal welfare states	15.2	17.8	17.6	21.38	2.86	3.06	2

Sources: Data for social expenditures are from OECD (http://stats.oecd.org/Index.aspx?QueryId=4549#); data for GDP growth, unemployment, and women's labor participation are from the World Bank (http://data.worldbank.org/indicator/NY.GDP.MKTP.KD.ZG/countries?display=default), (http://data.worldbank.org/indicator/SL.UEM.TOTL.ZS/countries?display=default), and (http://data.worldbank.org/indicator/SL.TLF.CACT.FE.ZS).

only a few countries have fundamentally changed policies (as the United Kingdom did under Prime Minister Margaret Thatcher in the 1980s), most have reduced benefits to lower the costs of the programs. Governments have raised the minimum age at which people can retire, reduced the length of unemployment benefits and the percentage of salary that is replaced, raised employee contributions to social insurance programs, and removed guarantees of benefits so that they can reduce them in the future if necessary (Bonoli, George, and Taylor-Gooby 2000). Particular benefits in many countries have dropped substantially, even though fundamental reforms of entire welfare states have been quite rare.

Silja Häusermann (2010), focusing specifically on Christian democratic welfare states, argued that they have been able to achieve significant reforms without fundamentally changing because of the shift to postindustrial society that globalization has helped bring about. The growing number of part-time and female workers were not benefitting fully from the Christian democratic welfare state, which emphasizes income stability for unionized male breadwinners in older industries. Politicians have been able to put together new coalitions of support for moderate reforms by reducing benefits to older, unionized, male workers while providing new benefits, like more flexible pension coverage and greater child care, to the mostly female workers in service industries. The result, Häusermann argued, has been substantial reform but not complete reversal or retrenchment to the point of shifting to a liberal welfare state model. Globalization has, in a sense, forced change, but change has been filtered through shifting political institutions and coalitions.

Web link:
The Dutch rethink the welfare state

Comparing Welfare States

The different types of welfare states initially created significantly different societies in terms of how much of the national income passes through government coffers and

Unemployment as percentage of civilian labor force			Women's labor force participation (% women in labor force)			
1981-1990	1991-2000	2001-2010	1980	1994	2006	2011
4.52	8.21	5.82	69.3	72.2	60	59.2
7.35	7.5	6.41	47.2	58.2	50.5	52.87
10.67	8.93	6.13	53.8	63	57	56.9

TABLE 11.2	Social Expenditure, in Percentage of GDP, 2009	
	Gross public social expenditures	Net publicly mandated social expenditures
	2009	2009
Social democratic welfare states	28.2	24.2
Christian democratic welfare states	28.3	27.3
Liberal welfare states	21.5	25.7

Source: OECD (2013).

how much is redistributed from the rich to the poor. Tables 11.1 and 11.2 provide data comparing the three types of welfare states. Social democratic welfare states used to take the biggest share of the national economy as government revenue to provide extensive social services, reflected in their high social expenditures. In recent years, however, the Christian democratic systems have spent more as the costs of their extensive income-maintenance programs for the unemployed and elderly have risen rapidly, while the liberal welfare states spend significantly less.

The extensive social policies of the social democratic and Christian democratic welfare states did not lower economic growth significantly at their height in the 1980s, though liberal welfare states seem to be growing faster recently. Similarly, more generous welfare states actually achieved lower levels of unemployment until recent years. These economic data suggest that while states have been able to maintain different levels of social policy in the face of globalization, the more generous ones may be paying a price in recent years in terms of economic growth and employment.

Figure 11.1 shows that all three types of welfare states distribute enough income to lower poverty substantially, but the reductions are greatest in social democratic states, followed by Christian democratic states; the liberal welfare states tolerate much more poverty and inequality among their citizens. Note, however, that poverty has gone down only in Christian democratic states, and inequality has increased at least slightly in all three types of welfare states. Table 11.1 demonstrates differences as well in terms of gender inequality, at least as measured by participation in the paid labor force. Social democratic welfare states facilitated greater female participation via such policies as universal child allowances, paid maternity leave, and subsidized preschool. Liberal welfare states, with their emphasis on work, achieve higher female participation rates than do Christian democratic states, which built their welfare state around the male breadwinner.

Table 11.2 shows that when we compare gross (meaning just government expenditures) and net (taking into account taxes recipients of social expenditures pay back to the government) we see a different picture. Looking at this new measure of social expenditure, a group of scholars (Garfinkel, Rainwater, and Smeeding 2010; Alber and Gilbert 2010) have argued recently that the three models of the welfare state are

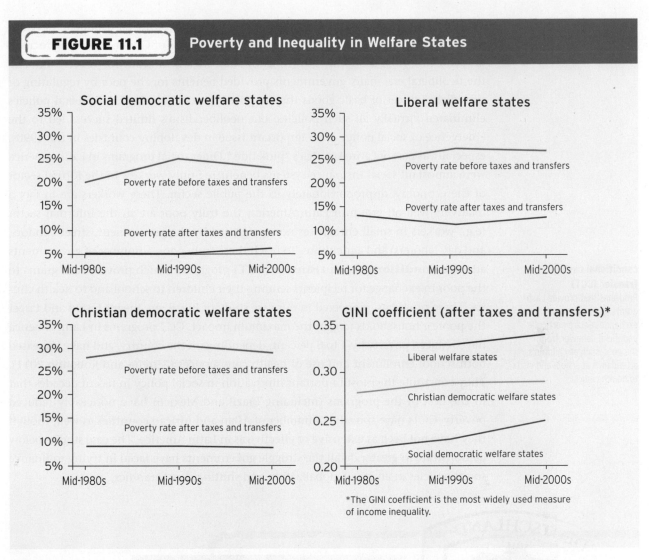

FIGURE 11.1 Poverty and Inequality in Welfare States

Source: OECD StatExtracts (http://stats.oecd.org/Index.aspx). Calculated using the classifications of the three welfare states (liberal welfare state, Christian democratic welfare state, social democratic welfare state) as defined in Evelyne Huber and John D. Stephens, *Development and Crisis of the Welfare State* (Chicago: University of Chicago Press, 2001).

not as distinct as has been suggested. While Sweden spends generously on universal programs, for instance, it also has high taxes on consumption (e.g., sales tax), so some of the spending on the poor comes back to the government in taxes. The United States, on the other hand, has very low social spending but much higher tax expenditures targeted at low-income people. Including all of these effects in the data shows that while social democratic systems spend more government money directly, liberal welfare states actually have higher net (including taxes) expenditures. The latter, though, do not reduce inequality or poverty nearly as effectively as the other two systems. Including taxes in the equation, they "expend" a lot of money on social policy but not in a way that systematically redistributes it from the wealthy to the poor.

Web link:
Who spends more on social welfare?

Web link:
The U.S. welfare state in comparison

Poorer Countries and Social Policy In poorer countries, neoliberal development strategies, bolstered now by the spectacular success of China, have long focused on achieving high economic growth as the best means of reducing poverty. Prior to the neoliberal era, many governments provided benefits for the poor by regulating or subsidizing prices of basic goods they required, particularly food. Neoliberal policies eliminated virtually all such policies, but neoliberalism's limited success led to the emergence of social policy as an important issue in developing countries in the 1990s, especially as part of Latin America's "pink tide." Older social programs in Latin America were almost all social insurance systems benefitting only workers in the formal sector of the economy, disproportionately in the public sector. These workers are in fact a relatively well-off group in Latin America; the truly poor are in the informal sector (e.g., workers in small enterprises not recognized by the government, street vendors, and day laborers) and agriculture. To reach these truly poor, a number of governments adopted **conditional cash transfer (CCT)** programs, which provide cash grants to the poor in exchange for recipients sending their children to school and to health clinics. These programs, pioneered in our case study of Brazil, are means tested and target the poorest households to gain the maximum impact. CCT programs in Latin America have reduced poverty by 4 to 8 percent, depending on the country, and have increased both school enrollment and use of health care services (Ferreira and Robolino 2011). They constitute the most important innovation in social policy in recent decades that in the best of the programs (including Brazil and Mexico) have noticeably reduced poverty. CCTs have spread to a number of Asian and African countries as well, though they have not been as extensive or effective as in Latin America. The case studies below demonstrate in greater detail the struggle governments have faced in trying to finance social policies in an era of globalization and shifting demographics.

conditional cash transfer (CCT)
Programs that provide cash grants to the poor and in exchange require particular beneficial behavior from the poor, such as children's attendance at school and visits to health clinics

CASE Study

GERMANY: REFORMING THE CHRISTIAN DEMOCRATIC WELFARE STATE

- **TYPE OF WELFARE STATE**
  Christian democratic

- **RECENT PROBLEMS**
  Growing pressure from aging population and need for more flexible labor market

Otto von Bismarck created the world's first social insurance program in Germany in 1883. Most of the country's modern Christian democratic welfare state was not put into place until 1949, but it still relies primarily on social insurance. Programs are paid for mainly by roughly equal employer and employee contributions. Following Germany's corporatist model, the system is run by nongovernmental organizations overseen by employer and employee associations, with the state providing the legal framework and regulations. In the golden era during which the economy was growing rapidly, the system provided relatively generous benefits and was self-financing. Structural changes, including reunification of West and East Germany, lower economic growth, higher unemployment, and an aging population have since brought severe financial constraints to the system, producing seemingly continuous reform efforts. Before 2003, reforms by governments of both major parties only slightly reduced the generosity of the system; that year, both parties supported a more fundamental change to unemployment benefits, which many argue is moving the system toward a liberal welfare state, though the other pillars of the system remain largely unchanged and social spending remains unusually high (Siebert 2005).

Prior to these recent reforms, the core social insurance system provided nearly complete income replacement in case of illness, at least 60 percent of an unemployed worker's salary for up to thirty-two months, and a retirement pension that averaged 70 percent of wages. These benefits continue to constitute the great majority of German social spending. Those unemployed for periods longer than three years received unemployment assistance at about 53 percent of their most recent salary, with no time limit. Others who had never worked a full year still received social assistance, a means-tested system that indefinitely provided enough support to keep them above the poverty line. Originally, the system assumed a male breadwinner could support his wife and children. As women entered the workforce, they supported reforms to make the system less focused on male breadwinners. In 1986 child benefits were added, including direct payments to and tax breaks for parents and government-paid contributions into social insurance to provide benefits for parents to take time off of work to care for young children. In the 1970s, maternity benefits of fourteen weeks that covered the full income of many women were added.

- **REFORMS**
  Hartz IV in 2003; major change to unemployment benefit; shift toward liberal welfare state?

Demonstrators in Berlin in November 2005 protest the Hartz IV reforms, the most significant change to the German welfare state since World War II. Despite the protests, the coalition government passed the reform, justifying it in part by the need to be globally competitive. In the long term, it will reduce both the amount and length of unemployment/welfare benefits, moving Germany's Christian democratic welfare state some distance toward a more liberal welfare state model.

The German Welfare State

Germany devotes an unusually large share of its economy to social spending, though not as much as Sweden. Both countries spend more and reduce poverty more than does the United States.

	Germany	Sweden	United States
Gross public social expenditures in 2009 (% of GDP)	27.8	29.8	19.2
Net (after taxes) publicly mandated social expenditures in 2009 (% of GDP)	27.5	26.1	28.9
Poverty rate (pre-tax and transfer) in 2010 (% of population)	32.3	27.8	28.4
Poverty rate (post-tax and transfer) in 2010 (% of population)	8.8	9.1	17.4

Sources: Public Social Expenditure, OECD (http://www.oecd-ilibrary.org/sites/factbook-2013-en/11/04/01/index.html?contentType=&itemId=/content/chapter/factbook-2013-88-en&containerItemId=/content/serial/18147364&accessItemIds=&mimeType=text/htm); OECD, "Income Distribution and Poverty" (http://www.oecd.org/statistics/datalab/income-distribution-poverty.htm).

An aging population and growing unemployment imposed financial constraints. The reform debate began in 1982 with the conservative CDU government focused on strengthening child benefits but otherwise reducing spending by increasing employer and employee contributions. Then German reunification in 1990 dramatically increased the costs of the system: unemployment rates skyrocketed in the former East Germany, and massive transfers of funds from the former West Germany were essential to pay social insurance benefits to these workers. The CDU government again sought reforms, making modest reductions to retirement pensions, but only via abandoning the traditional German neocorporatist policy-making process of consulting with business and labor associations before writing legislation. Even these modest reforms were unpopular enough that they were a major issue in the 1998 election, in which German voters ended sixteen years of CDU rule.

While the SDP criticized the CDU for making the system less generous, once in power the Social Democrats produced even more substantial reforms. In 2003 the SDP/Green government passed what became known as the Hartz reforms. The most controversial part, known as "Hartz IV," fundamentally changed a key element of Germany's welfare state. Rather than allowing workers to collect full unemployment insurance (set as a percentage of a worker's wage) indefinitely, the government limited it to twelve months, after which an unemployed worker would be placed on "Unemployment Benefit II," which was set at a fixed level (not connected to past earnings). Germany in effect switched benefits for the long-term unemployed from a social insurance system of income stability to a means-tested benefit more typical of a liberal welfare state. Also, unemployed workers were required to accept jobs at only 80 percent of their prior wage levels, rather than being allowed to wait for positions equivalent to their previous ones (Vail 2004), and retirement pensions have been reduced, from 70 percent of retirees' wages in the 1980s to what will eventually be only about 45 percent. The Hartz IV reforms sparked massive protests, but the government refused to back down. Leading "leftists" in the SDP responded by forming a new party before the 2005 election, which was a key reason the SDP lost the election (see chapter 7).

In 2010 Germany's Constitutional Court ruled the Unemployment Benefit II was beneath what was necessary for the dignity of the unemployed and their full participation in the society (in essence, calling for Marshall's "social rights"). In response, the government increased the benefit, but only slightly, by eight euro (about eleven U.S. dollars) per month as of 2012. After years of effort, a fundamental reform of the German welfare state was enacted that moved a key pillar of its system toward a liberal welfare state model. The reform is credited with helping to lower the unemployment rate, though critics note that this is because it forced people to take jobs at lower wages; indeed, Germany is the only country in Europe in which inequality of wages has increased over the last decade. The German poverty rate also rose to 11 percent, going from below to above the OECD average.

Audio link:
Germany's painful unemployment fix

Video link:
Jobless in Germany

While Hartz IV did not reform all aspects of the Christian democratic welfare state, it significantly modified one of the main elements of the system to reduce costs and create a more flexible labor market, all in line with the pressures of globalization.

CASE Summary The primary goal of the Christian democratic welfare state in Germany was to ensure income stability throughout a person's life. Once securely in the workforce, or dependent on someone who was, citizens could count on relative stability, at a minimum of half of their prior salary. This system was far more generous than liberal welfare states but redistributed less income than did social democratic ones. Mounting male unemployment, an aging population, and reunification put great pressure on this system. Lack of workers meant the insurance on which the system was based was underfunded, and growing numbers of part-time and female workers were left out. Even the Social Democrats decided they had to modify the system. The government reduced retirement and unemployment benefits, and the unemployment system now guarantees income stability for only one year; permanent support is only at a level just above the poverty line.

On the other hand, in response to the changing demographics of the labor force, the government expanded participation in the system to include more women, part-time workers, and the self-employed. In the long run, the hope is that these changes will reduce overall social spending, which in 2003 was at 27 percent of gross domestic product (GDP), well above the Organisation for Economic Co-operation and Development's (OECD) average of 21 percent. By 2011 it had dropped to 25.2 percent. The cost of these changes, though, is growing inequality and poverty. The new system makes Germany's Christian democratic welfare state notably more similar to a liberal welfare state, but the In Context box shows clearly that differences remain between Christian democratic Germany, the liberal United States, and social democratic Sweden.

CASE Questions

1. What does the history of reforms to the German welfare state teach us about the debate over the effects of globalization on social policy? Is the hyperglobalization thesis correct, or do important national distinctions still matter?
2. What values underlie Germany's Christian democratic welfare state, and do these seem to have changed fundamentally in the last decade?

CASE Study

THE UNITED STATES: REFORMING THE LIBERAL WELFARE STATE

- **TYPE OF WELFARE STATE**
  Liberal

- **RECENT PROBLEMS**
  Growing poverty, unemployment, and inequality

- **REFORMS**
  1996 reform ended entitlement to benefits and required work; tax credit and "food stamps" expanded and are now larger than cash benefit program

The In Context box on page 586 shows that based on income earned in the market alone, the United States has a smaller percentage of people living in poverty than Germany or Sweden, but taxes and government social programs lower the poverty rate by only about 7 percentage points in the United States compared with 20 or more in the European cases. The end result is much less poverty in Germany and Sweden than in the American liberal welfare state. The U.S. welfare state arguably emphasizes incentives to keep people employed, at whatever job and wage level, more than any other country. Aside from Social Security, the large social insurance system for the elderly, most U.S. social programs are means tested or tax expenditures, and are restricted to certain categories of recipients. The United States is one of only three countries in the world (the other two are Papua New Guinea and Swaziland) that guarantee no national paid maternity leave. Since 1996, poor people can still receive some income support for a maximum of five years, but they no longer have a legal entitlement to it beyond that unless they are disabled. The Earned Income Tax Credit (EITC), a tax expenditure program, is now larger than Temporary Assistance to Needy Families (TANF), the main means-tested spending program (and what most Americans think of as "welfare"). The federal system also sets only minimum standards and allows

Children attend a Head Start program in Hillsboro, Oregon. Publicly funded prekindergarten programs have expanded rapidly in recent years in the United States, funded mostly by state governments. The country's liberal welfare state provides only limited free or subsidized preschool, in contrast to the much more generous funding of these programs in most European welfare states.

state governments significant flexibility in implementing the main social programs, so benefits vary widely across states.

Most social policy in the United States began in the Great Depression as part of President Franklin D. Roosevelt's New Deal. The Social Security Act of 1935 established the system and remains the country's primary social program. This social insurance retirement program is similar to Germany's: pensions are tied to individuals' previous earnings and are financed by mandatory employer and employee contributions. Social Security is the country's most successful antipoverty program, and while not as generous as most European pension systems, it nonetheless dramatically reduced poverty among the elderly. Combined with Medicare, the health care plan for the elderly (see the Health Policy section below), it reduced American inequality by nearly 10 percent in 2000. (In contrast, "public assistance"—what most Americans think of as "welfare"—reduced American inequality by only 0.4 percent.) Prior to Social Security, the elderly had one of the highest rates of poverty, but now they have one of the lowest. President Lyndon Johnson's War on Poverty in the 1960s produced the second major expansion of American social policy. It augmented Social Security with Medicare, a health insurance program for the elderly. In addition, Aid to Families with Dependent Children became the main means-tested entitlement benefit for the poor, with each state legally obligated to indefinitely provide a minimum level of support, primarily to single mothers with resident children. Medicaid was created to fund health services for AFDC recipients, and the Food Stamps program provided vouchers for food purchases by poor families. By 1975, the poverty rate hit a low of about 12 percent of the population, half of what it had been in 1960.

In spite of notable success in reducing poverty, the programs were not widely accepted. Whereas Social Security was regarded as an earned benefit, AFDC was controversial from the outset. Critics argued that its structure of indefinite, per-child payments to families headed by women created perverse incentives for the poor to divorce or have children out of wedlock, have more children, and become dependent on government payments. Benefit levels also varied widely from state to state, with some states providing as much as five times what others did. In spite of the concerns of permanent "welfare dependence" and incentives to have more children, in reality, half of AFDC recipients received benefits for fewer than four years, and the average household size of recipients dropped from 4.0 in 1969 to 2.9 in 1992, meaning an average of only 1.9 children per mother, below the national average of 2.1 (Cammisa 1998, 10–17). Nonetheless, the perception of a perverse incentive structure persisted.

Reform proposals began as early as the late 1960s, but they grew significantly in the 1980s under President Ronald Reagan. Reagan's 1980 campaign was based in part on fundamentally changing the welfare system, though with a Democratic-controlled Congress, he never succeeded in changing social policy substantially. Indeed, when faced with a financial crisis in Social Security, Reagan led a bipartisan effort to increase the mandatory payroll tax to restore solvency without substantially cutting benefits. President Bill Clinton got elected as a "New Democrat" in 1992 on a platform that included a promise to "end welfare as we know it," and when the Republicans swept into control of Congress in 1994, they made a similar pledge, setting the stage for major reform. Two years later, Congress, with Republican support and mostly Democratic opposition, passed and President Clinton signed the most important reform of social policy since the 1960s. The legislation ended AFDC as an entitlement to poor, single mothers and replaced it with a new program, Temporary Assistance for Needy Families (TANF). TANF eliminated the bias against households with fathers, limited recipients to two years of continuous benefits and five years over a lifetime, required virtually all able-bodied recipients to work to keep their benefits, and allowed them to keep a significant share of those benefits after they began working.

Supporters of the reform believed it would reduce welfare dependence, encourage individuals to work, and lower poverty. Critics claimed it meted out harsh punishment to the poor, who would be cut off without the possibility of finding work that would lead them out of poverty. Numerous studies of the program's effects have been carried out without definitive conclusions. Part of the problem is that many factors besides social policy, the most important being overall economic growth, affect poverty and employment rates. TANF was introduced during a period of rapid economic growth. Poverty and the number of AFDC recipients actually had started falling two years before TANF was enacted because of strong growth, so it is difficult to judge TANF's impact.

Video link:
The American welfare state

What is clear is that the number of people receiving benefits fell sharply, from an average of more than five million households in 1994 to fewer than two million by 2005. Most of those leaving the rolls got jobs in the year they left the program, but only a minority worked the entire year. Most still work at part-time, low-paying jobs with no long-term job security. Overall incomes among poor households increased through 2000, though the poverty rate dropped only slightly (Grogger and Karoly 2005; Slack et al. 2007). Since 2000, as economic growth has slowed, TANF rolls have continued to shrink, though the number of recipients working has also started to fall and poverty levels have risen. The Great Recession increased the official U.S. measure of poverty (different from and lower than the internationally recognized rate in the In Context box above) to about 16 percent of all Americans, the highest level in decades. In response, TANF roles increased for the first time by 2010, before dropping slightly in 2011. Overall, since the reform, the percentage of poor single mothers (the main beneficiaries of the program) receiving AFDC/TANF and not working dropped by about half (from over 40 to about 20 percent) by 2009, and the percentage working and not receiving welfare doubled (from about a quarter to nearly half). More troubling, though, was the fact that the percentage of poor single mothers neither working nor receiving welfare also doubled (from about 15 to nearly 35 percent) (Lower-Basch 2011). When TANF was created in the 1996 reform, sixty-eight out of every one hundred families in poverty received its benefits; by 2011 that had dropped to twenty-seven out of every one hundred families in poverty (Center on Budget and Policy Priorities 2012). Welfare reform has moved many poor people away from dependence on the government, but it has neither substantially improved their income nor reduced the nation's poverty rate, which remains by far the highest among wealthy countries.

Web link:
Welfare reform is leaving more in deep poverty

At the same time as "welfare" reform, other income-support policies expanded. The EITC, a major tax expenditure that aims to benefit the "working poor," has been the fastest-growing social program in the country since 1990. By 2009, the U.S. government spent four times more on EITC than TANF. Congress passed a major expansion of it shortly before the 1996 welfare reform, raising the amount of the benefit and expanding the number of those eligible. In 2011 census data showed it lifted 5.7 million people out of poverty. Similarly, the funding and number of recipients of "food stamps," officially the Supplemental Nutrition Assistance Program (SNAP), fell during the 1990s but increased substantially in the first decade of the new millennium. In 2011 it moved an estimated 4.7 million people out of poverty. SNAP responded much more dramatically to the Great Recession in the United States than did TANF, with the number of beneficiaries rising and falling in nearly perfect parallel with unemployment levels from 2009 to 2012.

These contradictory trends in American welfare policy mirror debates over how generous the country's social policy really is. For decades, analysts compared government social spending and found the United States lagging far behind just about all European countries. This appears to be changing, though. In 2012 total U.S. social expenditures hit 20 percent of GDP, compared with the OECD average of only 21.9 percent. Net social expenditures (which include the effects of taxation of benefits and tax expenditure), narrow the gap even further: the U.S. figure for 2007 was 18.9 percent, compared with an OECD average of 20.2 percent (OECD 2011). Taking into account all of these factors, Christopher Howard (2007) argued that the American welfare state is much more extensive than commonly assumed but is still not very effective at reducing poverty or inequality. It channels a lot of money toward education and tax expenditures, which benefit far more people than just the poor, and the high cost of health care (see U.S. case study on health policy) means that a large share of social spending goes to health rather than reducing poverty.

Web link:
America's misguided approach to social welfare

Web link:
The welfare state: myth and measurement

Web link:
The surprisingly large U.S. welfare state

CASE Summary

The American liberal welfare state has accepted entitlement to permanent benefits only for the elderly and the disabled. All other spending programs are means tested, and the best known, TANF, is strictly limited in terms of how long people can use it and what they must do to get it. Indeed, tax expenditures have come to constitute a much bigger share of overall social policy than the standard "welfare" programs. Both creating and reforming social policy take place in the United States only at times of unusual crisis or consensus: the Great Depression, the tumultuous 1960s, and the politically volatile 1990s. The decentralized American system, with its weak political parties, means that major changes can occur only in unusual circumstances. The American federal system also means that social policy on the ground, in terms of who benefits and how much, varies greatly from state to state. The United States tolerates much higher levels of poverty and inequality than other wealthy countries in exchange for encouraging participation in the workforce at whatever level of remuneration possible.

CASE Questions

1. What does the U.S. reform effort suggest about which type of social policy is most efficient at reducing poverty?
2. Comparing the United States and Germany, how much of a difference is there now between the Christian democratic and liberal welfare state models?

CASE Study

BRAZIL: STARTING A WELFARE STATE IN A DEVELOPING ECONOMY

- **TYPE OF WELFARE STATE**
  Liberal (emerging)

- **RECENT PROBLEMS**
  Pension spending favors middle class; slowing economic growth

At his first presidential inauguration in 2002, former metalworker Luiz "Lula" Inácio da Silva famously declared, "If, by the end of my term of office, every Brazilian has food to eat three times a day, I shall have fulfilled my mission in life" (Hall 2006, 690). When he handed power to his handpicked successor in 2010, there were still hungry Brazilians, but the nation's poverty rate had dropped from nearly 49 percent to under 29 percent, and inequality had declined by 17 percent, one of the most impressive drops in history. Rapid economic growth and raising the minimum wage were important elements in these achievements, but so was Lula's "signature" success, the CCT program called Bolsa Família.

Despite being the largest economy in South America and one of the fastest growing in the new millennium, Brazil has long been home to great poverty and inequality. In the last two decades, however, the country expanded its pension system for the elderly and created Latin America's first CCT program, which ultimately reached over a quarter of the population, representing a new and important effort at alleviating poverty. As it has industrialized, the country has faced the same set of social policy options as wealthier states, but it has done so with far fewer resources and less effective bureaucratic institutions to implement policy. In this context, it is moving in the direction of creating a liberal welfare state focused primarily on means-tested programs in practice, in spite of lofty language in the constitution and recent legislation that suggests it will provide universal benefits.

For most of the country's history, Brazilian economic policy focused on achieving growth, while it became one of the most unequal societies in the world. As in many countries, the first systematic government social policy focused on the elderly. Until the 1990s, the pension system covered a small percentage of the population: civil servants, whose pensions were paid for by the government, and formal sector private employees, whose pensions came from mandatory contributions. This left out the large share of the population that works in the informal sector: most agricultural workers and those in quasilegal businesses that are not officially recognized and don't pay taxes. The new constitution established a right to a minimum income for all elderly people. In response, the government expanded existing pension programs and created new ones for those not already covered. One program covers anyone over a certain age who can prove past employment in the agricultural sector. The other offers means-tested benefits to any elderly person in a household with a monthly income less than one-half the minimum wage. While slightly less than half the population contributes to the pension system, 90 percent of the elderly now receive benefits from the combined programs, financed from general taxation. The result has been a near elimination of poverty among the elderly (Lavinas 2006, 110).

The biggest criticism of this pension system is its inequality. Lula's first and largest reform was to the pension system for civil servants. He argued that the generous benefits went to mostly middle-class civil servants (a small proportion of the population) and that reducing the program's cost would free up resources for the

• **REFORMS**
Expansion of pensions to eliminate poverty among the elderly; pioneer CCT program

A Brazilian woman holds her Bolsa Família card. The program has become the largest social program of its kind in Latin America. Along with rapid economic growth, it has helped move millions out of poverty and reduced Brazil's high levels of inequality.

poor. His eventual reform increased the retirement age, required middle-income civil servants to contribute to their pension system, and reduced its generosity. In the long run, these changes are predicted to save the government a great deal of money, though pensions remain by far the largest social policy in the country.

Lula's pledge to end hunger led to the creation of his signature program, Bolsa Família (Family Grant), early in his first term. The program provides food and cash grants, targeting poor and "very poor" households. The largest single component of Bolsa Família is Bolsa Escola (School Grant), which provides grants to poor parents who guarantee they will send their children to school and utilize children's health services. Local social service councils oversee implementation of the program, an attempt to reduce corrupt and political selection of recipient households. Anthony Hall (2006) reported that these measures have been successful where implemented, but the councils only function in two-thirds of municipalities. In the rest, the mayor's office is typically involved in recipient selection, with benefits often going to the mayor's political supporters. Both the World Bank and the Inter-American Development Bank support Bolsa Família, providing about one-quarter of its funding. Overall, it has been relatively successful, reaching forty-six million people by 2010, about one-quarter of the population (Baer 2008, 402; World Bank 2010). By the 2010 presidential election to choose Lula's successor, the program was so popular that both major candidates pledged to expand it. In 2011 President Dilma Rousseff announced a major expansion of the program, which in two years reached an additional 2.8 million recipients.

Despite the program's success, criticisms and concerns have certainly arisen. Some fear that it will create a "culture of dependency" because it has no time limits on benefits. On the other hand, some critics argue that far more expansive policies are needed, including transferring assets (especially land) to the poor and providing guaranteed and universal benefits. In fact, a leader of Lula's Workers' Party (PT) led a successful effort to have Brazil's National Congress pass a law in January 2004 that provides a universal entitlement to a minimum income for all residents. The law, however, has no time limit by which this new social right must be implemented (Lavinas 2006). Bolsa Família and expanded pensions for the elderly remain the only programs aimed at reducing poverty. Brazil's robust economic growth helped these programs to achieve unusual poverty reduction, but the universal right to a minimum income is some distance from realization.

Web link:
In Brazil social welfare programs worked

CASE Summary   Bolsa Família, the largest antipoverty program in Latin America, is a major innovation in the development of the welfare state in developing countries; thirteen Latin American countries had CCT programs in place by 2009. The World Bank, in spite of its past support for neoliberal development policies, now supports CCT programs as effective at alleviating poverty. Bolsa Família has substantially reduced poverty and inequality, though in a context of strong economic growth. How well the program can battle poverty in the face of slower growth remains to be seen.

> **CASE** Questions
>
> 1. In what ways does Brazil seem to be moving toward a liberal welfare state? Do you see elements of other types of welfare states in Brazil's system?
> 2. Look back at the debate in chapter 10 about how to help develop "the bottom billion." What does the striking success of CCT programs suggest about that debate? Can their success in middle-income countries like Brazil be extended to "the bottom billion"? Why or why not?

Social policy emerged as countries industrialized and became relatively wealthy; poverty was no longer the norm. Many citizens came to see continued poverty as unacceptable. For the poorest countries, such as Nigeria, poverty remains the norm, and no real social policy exists (save social insurance for a tiny fraction of workers, mostly in the public sector). Citizens of middle-income countries like Brazil, however, are beginning to ask the same questions as citizens of wealthy countries: How can social policy help reduce poverty?

Our next area of government intervention, health care, is characterized by greater value consensus around the world about the importance of extensive government involvement, though exceptions do exist to this consensus, especially in the United States.

HEALTH CARE AND HEALTH POLICY

Much of the world has adopted the idea that health care is a social right of all citizens. Wealthy countries have the resources to attempt to realize this right via interventions in the health care market, but most others lack the resources to make it a reality. A few countries, including the United States, do not embrace health as a social right but nonetheless claim the provision of the best health care possible to the largest number of people as a legitimate political and social goal.

Health Care and Market Failure

Social values are not the only reason for policy intervention in health care markets, however. Market failure takes distinct forms in health care that are based on specific characteristics of the health care market. The key problems are very high risk and poor consumer information, both of which produce inefficiency and misallocation of resources. High risk is the biggest factor driving the dynamics of the health care market and government intervention in it. People will do almost anything—pay any price or undergo any procedure—to restore their health when it is seriously threatened. On the other hand, healthy people don't need much medical care beyond annual checkups and preventative care. Those who lack the resources to pay for care when sick may face severe harm or even death. Insurance is the typical solution to high-risk markets.

It spreads risks across many people. Paying smaller, regular premiums more or less fixes the cost for each individual in the insurance pool, so catastrophic illness does not mean catastrophic bills. This principle also underlies homeowner's or auto insurance. Governments or private companies can provide insurance as long as a relatively large group of people with diverse risks pool their resources to cover emergencies as necessary.

Although insurance is a potential market-based solution to high risk, it creates its own potential market failure: **moral hazard**. Moral hazard occurs when parties to a transaction behave differently than they otherwise would because they believe they won't have to pay the full costs of their actions. In health insurance, this results from the gap between paying a fixed premium for health care and the costs of the care itself. If insurance covers the full cost of the care, patients have no incentive to economize because their costs (the insurance premium) will not change regardless of how much health care they use. Moreover, many insurance systems pay medical providers for each procedure, giving providers an incentive to oversupply procedures just as the patient has an incentive to overuse them. The obvious results are excessive medical procedures and rising costs. Governments intervene in health care in part to attempt to limit the effects of the moral hazard inherent in an insurance system.

Another market failure, poor information, compounds the problem of overuse. Patients generally rely on medical professionals to know what procedures or drugs are needed to get well. Even highly educated patients usually agree to their doctor's recommended treatment, especially if they are insured and face little direct cost. In the extreme case, a completely unregulated market with poor information can produce the iconic image of nineteenth-century American medical quackery, the "snake-oil salesman," a charlatan selling false remedies to desperate people. To avoid this, virtually all governments regulate both pharmaceuticals and medical practitioners.

Health Care Systems

Wealthy countries have developed three distinct types of health care systems to address these problems. These have served as models for poorer countries as well, though poor countries are severely limited by lack of resources. The earliest and still most common system in wealthy countries is **national health insurance (NHI)**. In an NHI system, the government mandates that virtually all citizens have insurance. NHI countries typically allow and encourage multiple, private insurance providers, while the government provides access to insurance to the self-employed or unemployed who do not have access via family members. Since the government mandates the insurance, it also regulates the system, setting or at least limiting premiums and payments to medical providers. In many NHI systems, access to health care is not specific to a particular employer, so workers can keep their insurance when they switch jobs. Germany pioneered this system in the late nineteenth century and continues to use it today, as do many other European countries and Japan. Few poor countries attempt to implement

moral hazard
Occurs when parties to a transaction behave in a particular way because they believe they will not have to pay the full costs of their actions

national health insurance (NHI)
A health care system in which the government mandates that virtually all citizens must have insurance

NHI because many of their citizens simply cannot afford insurance, although some do use a limited form of it for wealthier segments of the population, such as civil servants or employees of large corporations.

A **national health system (NHS)** is the second most common type of health care system in wealthy countries and the most common type worldwide. Frequently called a **single-payer system**, NHS is a government-financed and managed system. The government creates a system into which all citizens pay, either through a separate insurance payment (like Medicare in the United States) or via general taxation. The classic example of this type of system is in the United Kingdom, which established its NHS after World War II. In most NHS countries, the majority of medical professionals gain their income directly from the government, which implicitly controls the cost of medical care via payments for procedures, equipment, and drugs. Most poor countries have an NHS through which the government provides most medical care via hospitals and local clinics and in which doctors are direct government employees. With limited resources in poor countries, however, clinics and doctors are few, and many people lack access to or must wait long periods for what is often low-quality care.

The third system, a **market-based private insurance system**, is the least common. Although NHI and NHS countries typically permit some private insurance as a supplement for those who can afford it, the United States, Turkey, and Mexico are the only OECD countries that rely on private insurance for the bulk of their health care. In the United States, citizens typically gain insurance through their employment, and medical care is provided mostly by for-profit entities such as private clinics and hospitals. Government programs often exist in market-based systems to cover specific groups without private insurance, such as the poor, the unemployed, and the self-employed. Market-based systems, though, do not guarantee access to health care to all citizens, and even in the wealthiest of these countries, a sizeable minority lacks any insurance.

national health system (NHS)/single-payer system
A government-financed and managed health care system into which all citizens pay, either through a separate insurance payment or via general taxation, and through which they gain medical care

Video link:
What is single-payer health care?

market-based private insurance system
Health care system that relies on private insurance for the bulk of the population

Common Problems

Almost all countries face a common set of problems regardless of the system they use. The most evident are rising costs (especially in wealthy countries), lack of access to care, and growing public health concerns. Because of the need to contain costs, all countries and systems make decisions about how to ration care: who will get it, when, and how much.

Controlling Costs Wealthier countries are most concerned about cost, because as wealth increases, health care costs rise faster than incomes. This is because wealthier people demand more and better care, and improved but often expensive technology emerges to help provide that care. Wealthier countries also have relatively low birth rates and high life expectancies, so the proportion of the population that is elderly increases over time and needs more health care. In 2011 health expenditures in OECD countries varied from a high of 17.7 percent of GDP in the United States to a low of

Health Care in Wealthy Countries, 2011

Different health care systems in our case study countries have significant differences. Costs, in particular, vary dramatically, while outcomes are similar. Access to doctors, hospitals, and technology depends on how each country chooses to spend its health budget.

	Germany	United Kingdom	United States	OECD average
Costs				
Health care expenditures per capita ($), 2011	$4,875	$3,609	$8,608	$5,457
Health care expenditures as percentage of GDP, 2011	11.1	9.3	17.9	12.6
Public share of total health expenditures, 2009	77	84	48	72
Physicians' remuneration (ratio to average wage), 2009	3.3	4.2	3.7	NA
Outcomes				
Life expectancy at birth (years), 2011	81	80	79	80
Infant mortality rates (per 1,000 population), 2011	4	5	6	NA
Childhood measles vaccination rate, 2011	96	93	92.3	92
Access				
Practicing physicians (per 1,000 population), 2009	3.7	2.7	2.4	2.6
Acute care hospital beds (per 1,000 population), 2009	8.2	3	3	3.9
Access to doctor or nurse (% waiting longer than 6 days), 2009	16	8	19	NA
Wait times for elective surgery (% waiting longer than 4 months), 2008	0	21	7	NA

Sources: OECD (2011a); Access to specialists: Commonwealth Fund (2008).

5.9 percent in Estonia. From 2000 to 2009, expenditures grew at an annual average of 4 percent, well above overall economic growth. People in almost all wealthy countries use more and more of their income for health care, regardless of the system in place.

Wealthy countries use several means to try to control costs. A key factor is the size of insurance pools. Larger and more diverse pools of people lower costs because a larger number of healthy people (especially young adults) cover the costs of those (often the elderly) who use health care more heavily, thereby lowering premiums for everyone. NHS and NHI systems that group many or all of a country's citizens into one insurance pool gain a cost-saving advantage. In market-based systems, on the other hand, the risk pools are much smaller (usually the employees of a particular company), so costs tend to be higher. Governments in these countries spend less tax revenue on health care than do other governments, but citizens may spend more on health care overall via private insurance premiums and direct fees. The United States, which depends heavily on private insurance and has very low government expenditures on health care, has by far the highest overall health costs, both in terms of dollars spent per capita and as a share of GDP (compare the wealthy countries in the Country and Concept table on pages 572–573).

Data link:
Health care at a glance

Other cost-saving measures focus on limiting the effects of moral hazard. For example, paying doctors on a capitation, or per patient, basis rather than for each procedure creates an incentive to limit unnecessary procedures. Critics, however, argue that this gives providers an incentive to underprescribe, which endangers patients' well-being. A second strategy, "gatekeepers," can limit patients' demands for expensive treatments. Typically, a general practitioner serves as a gatekeeper who must give approval before patients can consult specialists in order to limit unnecessary trips to expensive specialists and procedures. Health maintenance organizations (HMOs) in the United States used both capitation and gatekeepers extensively in the 1990s to try to lower health care costs. A third approach is to require patients to make copayments, small fees that cover part of the cost of each service. Copayments change patients' incentives by making them pay more out of pocket rather than just fixed monthly insurance premiums or taxes. If kept to moderate amounts, copayments can theoretically discourage unnecessary or frivolous procedures; if set too high, however, they may discourage poorer patients from getting medically necessary care.

Clearly, a trade-off exists between cost containment and achieving a healthy population. Meeting all demands for health care instantly might produce the healthiest possible population, but it would be prohibitively expensive and would aggravate moral hazard. No society ever does this; instead, all choose to ration health care in some way, though many people may not perceive it as rationing. NHS countries can control costs most directly simply by limiting the overall health care budget, the payments to medical providers, purchases of new equipment, and/or drug prices. The result can be relatively low-cost but sometimes limited care. Limits typically take the form of patients waiting for certain procedures rather than getting them on demand. An NHS country must ration care by setting priorities on which services to provide more quickly and which, such as elective surgery, to delay. Waiting lines are longer in systems, including Britain's, that simply have fewer doctors per capita, another cost-saving measure. NHI countries can set insurance premiums and medical payments as well; they usually don't do so as universally as NHS countries, though Germany has experimented with greater regulation in recent years. Some countries, including the United States (the only wealthy country in this category), provide insurance only to a segment of the population, who thereby have access to fairly extensive care; those without insurance have very limited or no access to care. This is another way to ration.

The data in the In Context box (page 598) suggest that the form of rationing does not make a substantial difference to achieving a healthy population among wealthy countries, though it does have a significant effect on costs. Those with the lowest costs, such as Britain, do not have significantly lower health outcomes overall, measured by key data such as infant mortality or life expectancy. For poorer countries, where the main problem is not cost containment but availability of resources, lower costs do seem related to lower-quality health, as the Country and Concept table (pages 572–573) shows.

Access to Health Care Access is a much greater problem than rising costs for the very poorest countries, where limited resources mean much smaller numbers of doctors, hospitals, and clinics per capita. Even though individuals may be nominally covered by a government health plan, they cannot access health care if facilities and providers are not available. While many have NHS systems, as the Country and Concept table demonstrates, most health care funding still comes from private financing, often direct payments to providers without even the benefit of insurance. As a result of limited access and costs too high for the poor majority, preventable and easily treatable diseases continue to shorten life spans and cause debilitation and loss of income and productivity in much of the world. The problem of access in wealthy countries with NHS or NHI systems has been virtually eliminated; those systems provide insurance coverage for everyone, and medical facilities and doctors are plentiful. The only access problem typically is waiting times for some procedures. In market-based systems in wealthy countries, on the other hand, access is not universal: those without health insurance have only very limited access to care because they can't afford to pay for it.

Public Health The third major common problem is public health concerns. These are common to all countries but vary greatly. In the poorest countries, access to enough food and clean water remains a public health issue. Without access to clean water, populations continue to be plagued by a variety of contagious diseases. Furthermore, malnourishment exacerbates the effects of water-borne contagions, as immune systems are weak and resistance low. The health effects in terms of core indicators such as infant mortality and life expectancy are clear in the Country and Concept table (pages 572–573) compare the data for wealthy countries such as the United States, the United Kingdom, or Japan with poorer countries such as India or Nigeria.

CRITICAL inquiry

Comparing Health Care Systems

Wealthy countries present us with three distinct models of how to provide health care: NHS, NHI, and market-based. The table below provides some key data on access and cost of health care along with basic health outcomes for all three health care systems. Comparing the three, which do you think is the best overall model of health care? What are the principles or goals on which you base your assessment? Looking at the data, why do you come to the conclusions you do?

	NHS	NHI	Market-based
Costs			
Health care expenditures per capita	$3,179	$3,691	$4,573
Health care expenditures as share of GDP	9.87	10.63	12.9
Outcomes			
Life expectancy at birth	81	81.43	78.3
Infant mortality	4.2	3.27	7.2
Life expectancy at age 65	21.47	22.43	20
Access			
Medical doctors (per 1,000 population)	2.93	3.03	1.7
MRIS (per one million population)	8.43	19.67	25.9*

Source: All data are from OECD (2011a).

Note: All data are for 2009. Countries in the sample are, for NHS: New Zealand, Spain, and the United Kingdom; for NHI: France, Germany, and Japan; for market-based systems: Chile and the United States.

*United States only; data not available for Chile.

The wealthiest countries face a different kind of malnutrition: obesity. The highest rates of obesity in the OECD are in the United States and Mexico, and now include more than 30 percent of the population. Obesity rates are rising in almost all wealthy countries: food is inexpensive compared with our incomes, so we overconsume it.

Other public health issues resulting from affluence—alcohol and tobacco consumption—have seen positive change recently. Rates of alcohol use in the OECD declined by 9 percent from 1980 to 2009, while rates of tobacco use declined by about 18 percent from 1999 to 2009. Active public health education programs, along with legal limits and higher taxes on alcohol and tobacco consumption, reaped impressive results in many wealthy countries. Unfortunately, alcohol and tobacco consumption rates are increasing in many poorer countries, as their populations become wealthier and as alcohol and tobacco producers actively market in developing countries to compensate for shrinking consumption in their traditional markets.

Finally, globalization has produced a new set of public health concerns that cross borders as physical interaction among populations increases. These include the expansion of sexually transmitted diseases (especially HIV/AIDS) and insect-borne diseases such as Lyme disease, West Nile virus, and malaria. Increased importation and exportation of products and international travel have also led to the global spread of such conditions as salmonella, foot-and-mouth disease, and SARS. The spread of diseases to new populations lowers overall well-being and raises health care costs. Contagious disease is best dealt with via preventative measures such as education campaigns, infrastructure projects, free condoms, and control of insect populations, all of which are public goods and therefore inherently government responsibilities. With increasing globalization, what happens in one country increasingly affects others, meaning that health care policy makers in one country might be well advised to assist the citizens of other countries as well as their own.

GERMANY: PIONEER OF MODERN HEALTH POLICY

- **SYSTEM**
  NHI

- **MAJOR BENEFITS**
  Universal access and wide choice

- **MAJOR PROBLEMS**
  Growing costs

- **REFORMS**
  Aimed at lowering costs via incentives and maintaining equity of access

As noted earlier, Germany's Otto von Bismarck created the first modern, national health insurance system in 1883. Germany's NHI system is corporatist in both organization and management, relying heavily on professional and patient associations to implement it under the overall regulation of the state. It provides very generous benefits, including dental, hospital, and preventative care and even rehabilitative health spa treatments, primarily through a network of sickness funds financed by payroll taxes shared by employers and employees. Cost control has been a major issue (though less so than in the United States) and has prompted a series of reforms to limit costs, increase competition, and shift costs to users. As the In

A patient provides ten euros (about thirteen dollars) and his national insurance card to pay for a visit to a doctor's office. Modest copays have become a means of cutting down costs in Germany's NHI system.

Context box (page 598) shows, Germany has achieved average to above-average health outcomes as compared with other wealthy countries at below-average costs.

The sickness funds are nonprofit organizations run by boards of employers and employees. They are connected to employer, profession, or locale and are autonomous from the government in setting most of their policies and prices, though the services they must offer are uniform across the country. They negotiate services and payments with regional physician associations; doctors who wish to participate in the system (about 95 percent of them do) must be members of their regional association and abide by the negotiated agreements. All but the wealthiest Germans must belong to a sickness fund; in this way, Germany has long achieved universal coverage. The unemployed must belong to a fund as well, the costs of which are covered by federal and local governments. The wealthiest individuals may opt out of the system and purchase private insurance, though more than 90 percent of the population uses the sickness fund system. Residents can also purchase supplemental insurance to give them greater choice in where and how they are treated, and about 10 percent of sickness fund members do so (Adolino and Blake 2001, 225; Green and Irvine 2001, 57).

Employment determined which fund most Germans joined until a 1997 reform allowed citizens to choose their sickness fund and change it annually, introducing competition among funds. This reduced the number of sickness funds from 1,200 in 1985 to under 200 by 2010, as competition has pushed most out of the market (Green and Irvine 2001, 57; *The Economist* 2010). Nonetheless, German patients have exceptional levels of choice among sickness funds and, once they've selected a fund, among doctors. Despite nearly universal coverage, equity has been a continuous concern, especially for the Social Democratic Party. Some sickness funds have unusually high numbers of poor and unhealthy members, meaning their costs are well above the national average. A 1992 reform attempted to resolve this by creating a compensation system in which money is transferred from wealthier to poorer sickness funds. As costs have risen in recent years, relatively young, healthy, and wealthy people have increasingly opted out of the system altogether, taking the lowest-cost members out of the sickness funds and thereby raising premiums for everyone else. Reforms in 2007 for the first time mandated that all citizens have insurance, but the wealthy can still purchase private insurance instead of joining a sickness fund.

Cost containment has long been a major issue in the German system. The key relationship is between the sickness funds and the regional associations of physicians who negotiate agreements over payments to physicians. The first major reform of the system in 1977 established a classic corporatist solution: national negotiations among the sickness funds, physicians' associations, and the government to set targets for annual expenditure growth. In 1986 a binding cap on expenditures was established, negotiated each year between the sickness funds and physicians' associations. Finally, in 2007, as costs continued to rise, a more fundamental change in health care financing created a single nationwide premium schedule tied to workers' incomes. The new national fund distributes the premiums plus general tax revenue to sickness funds on a per capita basis, adjusting for the wealth and health of the membership of each fund. Individual sickness funds can give rebates to their members if they can provide services at a cost lower than what they receive from the national fund, or they can charge members additional premiums if necessary. This policy is designed to encourage efficiency as the funds compete for members. The 1997 reform allowing patients to choose which sickness fund to join allowed this competition, which should lower costs and create larger pools in each fund since the number of funds has dropped by three-quarters. Over the years, the government has also increased copayments to give patients incentives to economize on care.

Despite these reforms, cost remains a major concern for Germans in the new century. An aging population and expensive technological innovations continue to increase the cost of health care. Germany's extraordinarily high number of doctors and hospital beds per capita (see the In Context box, page 598) give patients tremendous choice, but they also cost a great deal. In the face of the global recession, Angela Merkel's Christian Democrat–Free Democrat coalition government passed yet another controversial reform in November 2010. It raised the insurance premiums from 14.9 to 15.5 percent of wages, with most of the increase paid for by employees. More controversially, it allowed future increases that will be paid fully by employees and can be flat fees, rather than a percentage of income; future increases will therefore hit poorer Germans more than wealthier ones. To try to control rising drug costs, the 2010 reform also required pharmaceutical companies to negotiate prices with insurance funds for new drugs; failure to do so will result in the government setting prices. Overall, the long series of reforms has meant that patients' share of total costs has more than doubled since 1991, providers have new incentives to economize on the number and type of procedures they prescribe, and growing reports suggest some patients are not receiving services in order to keep costs down (Gerlinger 2010).

CASE Summary

Germany has long been a model of the NHI system, but it continues to struggle with rising costs. Reform efforts remained within the corporatist tradition and the German Christian democratic welfare state until the most recent reforms, which have fundamentally altered financing by creating a uniform national premium schedule and shifting costs onto workers. Germany, like all wealthy countries, will continue to struggle with a health care sector that consumes an ever larger share of national income, though Germans have a system that achieves unusually high levels of care coupled with widespread patient choice and universal coverage. This is in sharp contrast to the United Kingdom's NHS, which controls costs quite effectively but, as the In Context box demonstrates, does so by limiting access more than in the United States or Germany.

CASE Questions

1. What does the German NHI system teach us about the costs and benefits of the NHI model?
2. What further reforms might help Germany control costs?

UNITED KINGDOM: REFORMING THE NHS

In March 2012, the British Parliament passed what many called the biggest change to British health care since the creation of the NHS after World War II. Pushed by Conservative prime minister David Cameron, the reforms were designed to instill more market-like competition in the system to increase efficiency. They passed only after a year of exceptionally acrimonious public debate. Like Germany, the United Kingdom was a pioneer of health care, creating the

- **SYSTEM**
  NHS

- **MAJOR BENEFITS**
  Universal access and low cost

- **MAJOR PROBLEMS**
  Quality of service, waiting times, and growing costs

- **REFORMS**
  Instill market mechanisms to increase competition and efficiency

Health care workers deliver a petition with ten thousand signatures to Prime Minister David Cameron opposing his proposed changes to Britain's popular NHS. The firestorm of opposition was so great that Cameron took the unusual step of delaying parliamentary approval of the plan for a year while modifications were made.

earliest and most universal NHS based on four key principles: universal services, comprehensive services, free to the patient, and financed by general tax revenue. With minor exceptions, the NHS has worked that way ever since, though both Conservative and Labour governments have made significant reforms in the last twenty years. Britain achieves health outcomes that are about average for wealthy countries at relatively low costs. As the In Context box (page 598) shows, it accomplishes this in part by having fewer doctors and hospital beds and, most important, by rationing nonessential care via long waits (though wait times for simply seeing a primary care doctor or nurse are quite low). The 2008–2009 recession, which hit Britain particularly hard, was one of the reasons why the Conservative-LDP coalition government introduced a sweeping plan to create incentives to improve efficiency and lower costs further.

The NHS traditionally functioned like one giant managed care system: it signed contracts with general practitioners (GPs) in each region of the country to deliver primary services to patients. Each region served as one large insurance pool, with an average of about half a million patients. GPs are paid on a combination of fee-for-service and capitation basis, and British patients can sign up with the GP of their choice, usually in their neighborhood, who provides basic care and functions as a gatekeeper, referring them to a specialist or hospital as needed. The NHS regional and district health authorities receive national government revenue to provide hospital and specialist services, and most services (except for some pharmaceuticals) are free to the patient at the point of service, having been paid for by general taxes. Waiting times for seeing GPs are very low, but waiting times for specialists and nonemergency hospital stays are among the world's highest.

No one can opt out of the NHS, since it's funded by general taxes, but patients can purchase private supplemental insurance that allows them to see private doctors and get hospital services without the long waits of the public system. As Britons have grown wealthier and have demanded more health care, a growing number supplement NHS coverage with private insurance. Patients can use the NHS for routine illnesses and private insurance for procedures that have long waiting lines in the NHS.

Britain has been less concerned about rising costs than other wealthy countries, at least until recently. While costs have risen substantially, they remain below average. The NHS allows the national government to control costs directly: it simply sets the annual overall budget, thereby limiting the system to a certain expenditure level. In the mid-1990s, Britain spent barely half of what the United States did as a share of its GDP. As part of reform efforts to improve the system, the Labour government (1997–2010) significantly increased health care spending, resulting in Britain partially closing the gap in terms of money spent and doctors available, as reflected in the In Context table (page 598). Despite the United Kingdom's ability to control costs, health care reform has been a major political issue since the 1980s. The NHS has always been and remains very popular with British citizens, but there are those unhappy with the long wait times for certain procedures and lower-quality care, both by-products of cost-control structures.

The NHS as originally structured had no internal incentives for efficiency. The Conservative government under Margaret Thatcher initiated a reform in 1990 that introduced elements of competition to increase efficiency. The idea was never popular, but Thatcher used her majority in Britain's parliamentary system to pass the reform anyway. It created large purchasers and sellers of health care. GPs with large practices (five thousand patients or more) were given their own budget by the NHS, which they used to purchase specialist and hospital services for their patients. Those who negotiated better deals would be likely to get more patients and earn more money. Similarly, hospitals gained the ability to manage their own affairs. Rather than being run by the regional health authorities, hospitals would sell their services to GPs. Hospitals were still public entities but could increase their revenue by providing the best services at the lowest cost.

The results of this bold experiment were mixed. Wait times dropped and there were signs of improved efficiency, but the benefits mainly went to patients of the GPs with the largest practices in the wealthiest areas. The Conservative government also kept overall funding low, so improvements in wait times and quality of care were not dramatic. Indeed, unhappiness with the state of the NHS was one reason the Labour Party under Tony Blair swept into office in 1997. In a series of reforms, the Labour government modified rather than eliminated the new system. The main reform was to strengthen regional associations, which would purchase services for patients. This kept an element of competition but eliminated the different deals GPs in the same area provided their patients. The Blair government also increased funding to hire more doctors and reduce wait times in hospitals, raising costs substantially.

Cameron's 2012 reforms reversed course again, moving even further in the direction of competition than Thatcher's policies two decades earlier. The new system replaced the regional authorities with groups of GPs who handle 80 percent of the NHS budget to purchase services for their patients. Most controversially, they are free to use that tax money to purchase services from NHS or private hospitals and specialists. NHS hospitals and specialists became independent units, required to break even via selling their services to the GP consortia. Those that lose money will presumably be sold to private operators or closed. The goal is to use competition to spur greater efficiency.

Reaction to the initial proposals was so negative that the government took the unusual step of "pausing" movement of the bill through Parliament in order to consult more with citizens and medical professionals through several commissions. Many citizens and medical personnel feared that the reform will ultimately allow a full privatization of the system and that it will create inequities, as patients in healthier and wealthier areas will ultimately obtain better care. The Cameron government and its supporters claim that the reforms will reduce administrative costs by one-third and instill greater efficiency throughout the system. At the time of passage, only 12 percent of GPs said they thought the reform would "noticeably" improve care, while 83 percent believed it would increase rationing.

CASE Summary In contrast to corporatist and federal Germany, Britain's NHS is a unitary and centralized system of health care. It has always been one of the country's most popular government programs, and it has allowed the government to keep costs relatively low, but at the expense of quality and timeliness of service, or so its critics claim. Britain's majoritarian system has allowed recent governments of both parties to enact significant reforms more easily than either Germany or the United States. These reforms have focused on reorganization to encourage improved efficiency and quality of service. The Labour government coupled this with sharply increased spending to provide Britons with health care quality closer to that of other European countries. In contrast, the Conservative/LDP government passed reforms to increase competition and the role of the private sector and to drive costs down. Even with this reform, however, British health care will continue to be funded by general taxation and be free or nearly so at the point of service. The United States, in contrast, remains the only wealthy system in the world with a primarily private health system that, as the In Context box (page 598) shows, achieves slightly below-average outcomes at much higher than average costs.

CASE Questions

1. Comparing the German and British health care systems, what are the primary benefits and costs of each? Which, overall, seems superior, and why?
2. Why has Britain passed more significant reforms to its system over the years than Germany has? Is it because the British system needs more changes, or for other reasons?

CASE Study

U.S. HEALTH POLICY: TRIALS AND TRIBULATIONS OF THE MARKET MODEL

On March 23, 2010, President Barack Obama signed the largest reform of the market-based health care system in the United States at least since the creation of Medicare and Medicaid in 1965. Its chief goals were to expand insurance coverage to 95 percent of the population and reduce overall costs, primarily by the government's (1) mandating that nearly all citizens get insurance; (2) helping create statewide markets for those without employment-based insurance so they could purchase insurance at reasonable prices, with subsidies as needed; and (3) increasing regulation of private insurers. The national debate over the reform was long and exceptionally divisive. Opponents on the right argued it represented an unprecedented expansion of government into the lives of citizens, while opponents on the left argued that failure to create a true NHS would mean the country would achieve neither universal coverage nor significant cost control. On the eve of its implementation three years later, only about half of the public supported the plan.

The United States spends more on health care—both as a dollar amount and as a share of its total economy—than any other country in the world. In 2011 health spending hit an all-time high of 17.7 percent of the entire economy. The data in the In Context box (page 598) suggest these large expenditures produce health outcomes comparable to, albeit slightly below, those in other wealthy countries. The United States possesses considerably more medical technology than most countries, but this

- **SYSTEM**
  Market-based, supplemented by government programs for the elderly and the poorest

- **MAJOR BENEFITS**
  Good access for those insured; high level of services

- **MAJOR PROBLEMS**
  Highest costs in the world; limited access, particularly for those not insured

- **REFORMS**
  2010 reform to expand coverage and perhaps bring down costs

President Barack Obama signs the health care reform bill on March 23, 2010. The reform, the biggest since the creation of Medicare and Medicaid in 1965, promises to increase insurance coverage to 95 percent of Americans while reducing costs. Even after its passage and initial steps of implementation, the public was evenly divided on its benefits, and opponents were challenging it in the courts and in voting booths.

has not produced better health. More than 60 percent of the U.S. population is covered by employment-based private insurance, with another 25 percent covered by government programs for particular categories of people. The remaining 15 percent or so have no health insurance and rely on their own resources or free care from mobile clinics, community outreach programs, or hospital emergency rooms, which are required by law to provide aid to anyone who walks in, though many do not. The uninsured have very limited access to care. Most are near poverty but are not recipients of government welfare benefits, work part-time jobs that do not provide insurance benefits, or are self-employed. They are the primary intended beneficiaries of the 2010 reform.

The American private insurance system became widespread during World War II. After the war, the government encouraged it via tax incentives: health benefits are not taxable income. The system gives advantages to large employers and their employees because each employer negotiates insurance rates as a company; larger companies have bigger risk pools and therefore can get lower premiums and better coverage. The authors of this textbook, for instance, had the best health coverage of their lives when they were very low-paid teaching assistants in graduate school. Their salaries were near the poverty level, but because they taught at a state university, they were state employees and received the generous benefits a very large employer (the entire state government) provided. Now, they have much higher salaries working at small liberal arts colleges, but not nearly as generous health benefits from employers of only a few hundred employees.

Web link:
As hospital costs soar, single stitch tops $500

Extensive U.S. government health programs only began in 1965 with the creation of Medicare (for the elderly and disabled) and Medicaid (for the very poorest, mostly TANF recipients). In 1997 the State Children's Health Insurance Program (SCHIP) was created to provide insurance for poor or low-income children. The combination of SCHIP and an expansion of Medicaid coverage reduced the percentage of low-income children who were uninsured from 22.3 percent in 1997 to 14.9 percent in 2005 (CBO 2007, 8). Overall, even before the 2010 reform, government spending on health was more than 40 percent of total health spending (though that was the second-lowest level in the OECD). Most of this spending went to the expensive Medicare program for the elderly. Health cost increases reached an alarming rate of nearly 20 percent per year in the late 1980s, leading even large corporations to start demanding some type of intervention to bring costs under control. The issue thus became a major part of the 1992 presidential campaign. After his election, President Bill Clinton proposed a plan that would have set up funds similar to Germany's sickness funds across the country and encouraged them to compete for clients among employers. Coverage would be mandatory and could travel with the employee from one job to the next, and those not employed would be covered by various federal programs and still be part of the funds. Facing fierce opposition from the insurance industry, the reform never passed Congress.

In the absence of national policy reform, employers (the primary purchasers of insurance packages) began reforming the existing system to lower costs via a rapid switch from fee-for-service insurance to HMOs, which try to hold costs down by capitation and gatekeeper rules. The share of privately insured Americans in fee-for-service plans dropped from 70 percent in 1988 to 14 percent in 1998. As a result, annual cost increases dropped from 18 percent in 1990 to less than 4 percent by 1996, removing health care costs as a significant political concern as the country entered the new millennium (Graig 1999, 22–35). By 2006, though, cost increases were rising again, hitting 17.2 percent. In the 2008 presidential election, rising costs had once again put health care on the national political agenda.

Obama entered office with a promise, strongly supported by his party—which controlled both houses of Congress—to achieve universal health insurance coverage. Labor unions had long championed creating an NHS. This radical reform, however, did not have majority support even within the Democratic Party, and the private insurance industry and Republicans vigorously opposed it. Many Democrats wanted instead to create what came to be called a "public option"—one health insurance choice among many—that could be achieved by opening up the federal government's insurance plan for its own employees, Medicare, or Medicaid to the broader public. Obama's initial proposal included a public option that would be open only to those not insured through their employers, preserving all existing private insurance as is. Ultimately, even this limited public option proved to be one of the most controversial elements of the plan and was eliminated.

The health reform that Obama and Congress adopted is projected to provide coverage eventually for about 95 percent of the population (up from the current 85 percent). It does this by mandating that all people but exceptional "hardship" cases must obtain health insurance and providing subsidies to premiums for low-income people. In October 2013 insurance "exchanges" opened in each state that are available to all those who don't have insurance through their employers. Private insurance companies offer plans in these exchanges that must meet certain minimum federal standards of service coverage. The exchanges create large pools of previously uninsured or under-insured people, allowing them to obtain much cheaper coverage than they each could individually. Medium and large employers will have to offer minimal health insurance to their employees; those that don't will pay a fine that will help pay for the subsidies for the uninsured. The reform also includes substantial regulation of insurance companies, preventing them from denying insurance to those with preexisting medical conditions or revoking it from the already ill, restrictions to which the insurance industry readily agreed in exchange for access to an additional 10 percent of the population as clients in the new exchanges. To make sure young and healthy people obtain insurance and thereby improve the overall insurance pool, the reform also allowed young adults to remain on their parents' insurance until age twenty-six.

The reform is intended to control costs first by forcing nearly everyone, including young and healthy people who are often uninsured, to pay into the system. This will create larger and more diverse pools that should reduce average costs. Fewer uninsured people should also reduce the very expensive but unnecessary use of hospital emergency rooms on which the uninsured have long relied for basic care. The most expensive insurance plans, dubbed "Cadillac plans," will eventually be taxed to discourage excessive use of the health system. By 2013, this had led 17 percent of all employers to reduce the costs (and undoubtedly the benefits as well) of their health care plans to avoid the tax. Cost control, of course, was aided by the Great Recession, which resulted in the much lower increases in health care spending in the United States (costs rose only 3.9 percent in 2011), though patients' out-of-pocket expenses continued to climb.

Implementation of the plan was itself steeped in controversy. Opponents believed the federal mandate to purchase insurance represented an unconstitutional intrusion in citizens' lives. While the government has long been able to "regulate commerce," opponents argued it could not mandate that citizens purchase a particular item, including health care. In a 5–4 vote, the Supreme Court ultimately held up this central provision of the plan as constitutional, but ruled that state governments did not have to agree to the expansion of the Medicaid program that would pay part of the subsidies for insuring lower-income people. About half the states, almost all of them controlled by Republicans, refused to expand Medicaid even though for the first several years the federal government would pay for it. Ironically, this will mean that while people slightly above the poverty line will receive subsidies in the form of tax credits to help them purchase health insurance, the poorest in states that refuse to expand Medicaid will not receive any subsidy at all. The states refusing to expand Medicaid contain 60 percent of the country's black population and 60 percent of the working poor without health insurance; initial projections were that eight million poor Americans would remain without insurance, mostly because of states' refusal to expand Medicaid (Tavernise and Gebeloff 2013). Most of these states also refused to create health exchanges, forcing the federal government to set them up in those states. Several states also passed legislation preventing any state government cooperation with the federal government as it created the exchanges, hampering implementation significantly. In October 2013, as the new exchanges opened, Republicans in the House of Representatives forced the federal government to shut down by refusing to pass a budget, demanding that the new health law be postponed for a year before they would support the budget. While that effort failed, the federal insurance exchanges required in all states that did not create their own failed to work properly over their first few months of operation, though the state-created ones worked much better.

While opponents claimed that the government couldn't afford the new health plan, the Congressional Budget Office estimated that it will actually save the government money over a decade. What is less clear is whether the cost controls will be adequate to reduce the very high overall (private and public) U.S. health costs. The plan was designed to have minimal effect on the already insured. Judith Feder and Donald Moran (2007), however, argued that until political leaders accept the fact that universal coverage combined with cost containment will require greater limits on the already insured, no fundamental reform will be possible. The implementation of the Obama plan over the next decade will determine whether or not they were right.

Web link:
Obama tries to dig out of his big Obamacare hole

Audio link:
How the Affordable Care Act pays for insurance subsidies

Video link:
Why are American health care costs so high?

CASE Summary

The American political system's openness and weak parties have made significant health care reform difficult. Obama and Democrats in Congress finally passed a substantial reform in 2010, but one that does not shift very far from the free-market model. Many analysts point to American political culture as an explanation for why the country has been so opposed to a universal health care system: Americans generally distrust "big government" and anything that can be labeled "socialist," making major government interventions in the economy relatively rare. The insurance industry and highly paid (by global standards) medical profession have also been powerful voices in preserving the market-based system. Medicare, Medicaid, and SCHIP have expanded coverage, though they have not achieved the universal coverage found in other wealthy countries. They also have done little to rein in costs, which remain by far the highest in the world. The great question of the next decade is whether the 2010 reform can finally bring costs down closer to the level in other wealthy nations, or whether more fundamental reforms will be necessary.

CASE Questions

1. Health care reform has been controversial in all three of our case studies. How can you explain the ability of each government to pass reform into law? Is it easier to do in one of the three countries, and if so, why? Are there particular contexts in which reform is more or less likely to occur?
2. Comparing all three of our cases, which has the superior health care system, and why?

Like social policy, distinct health care models have arisen in wealthy countries, providing different levels of government involvement in trying to ensure that all citizens have access to adequate health care. No society can afford to provide every type of care instantly to everyone who demands it. Within this limit, the "bottom line" of any health care system is, presumably, to produce the healthiest possible population at the lowest possible cost. Based on this formula, both NHI and NHS systems seem to fare better than purely market-based ones, probably because of the unique aspects of the health care market we discussed above. All wealthy countries, though, face a common set of problems, regardless of what type of system they have: rising costs due to an aging population and demand for more and better care, perverse incentives for both consumers and producers of health care that make it difficult to maximize efficiency, and growing public health problems associated with wealth such as obesity and heart disease. These structural problems have made health care reform a particularly divisive political issue, bringing down governments or realigning legislative majorities in all three of our case studies.

ENVIRONMENTAL PROBLEMS AND POLICY

Global warming (climate change) is only the latest and largest environmental problem confronting governments around the world. The modern environmental movement and environmental policies developed in the 1960s and 1970s. Environmental problems became a significant policy issue later than either health care or welfare, perhaps in part because the environment, in contrast to the other two, is a classic postmaterialist concern. Environmental preservation tends to become a more widespread social value as wealth rises and material interests are met. Early industrializers in Europe and the United States weren't very concerned about environmental degradation until the 1960s (with the exception of preservation of public land, which began much earlier), when people began to look at the effects of long-term pollution from the new context of economic security. Today, increasing wealth and security in some more recently industrialized countries also seem to be stimulating interest in clean air, water, and other environmental concerns. Globalization simply has added a new dimension to the problem.

The Environment and Market Failure

Environmental damage is an exceptionally clear case of market failure in the form of externalities. No form of pollution is without cost. When a factory pollutes a river with sewage, people downstream get sick and need costly health care while fish and other aquatic life die, raising the cost of fishing and reducing ecosystem diversity. Vehicle exhaust produces cancer-causing smog that results in millions of dollars of health care costs annually, and most people consider clean air and water beneficial, so they pay an implicit cost any time it is fouled. Polluters rarely pay the cost of their own pollution in an unfettered market: commodities cost less than they would if their true environmental costs were internalized in the production process. The market therefore devotes more resources to those undervalued products than it ought to, creating inefficiency. Meanwhile, other people bear the costs of the pollution produced, a classic externality.

Many environmental goods are inherently public and often free. Unregulated use of free goods like air, water, or public land can lead to the **tragedy of the commons**. This is an old idea. If free public grazing land exists in a farming area, all farmers will use it to graze their herds, and none will have an incentive to preserve it for future use; collectively, they will likely overgraze the land and destroy it so that they all lose out in the end. In wealthy industrial countries, a more current example is clean air, a completely "common" good we all breathe and pollute. Without a collective effort to limit use and abuse, no individual has the incentive or ability to preserve it, so it's likely to be overused. The free market grossly undervalues (at zero cost) a valuable public good.

National governments have been grappling with market interventions to compensate for environmental externalities, trying to avoid the tragedy of the commons, for

tragedy of the commons
No individual has the incentive or ability to preserve a common, shared good that is free, so without collective effort, it is likely to be overused and perhaps ultimately destroyed

Video link:
The tragedy of the commons

most of the last hundred years. Recently, globalization has raised new, international challenges in this process. Globalization has spread not only industrialization but also environmental damage. Industrialization always increases the pollution of previously agrarian societies. In addition, many observers fear that the dynamics of global competition will produce a "race to the bottom," as countries use lax environmental rules to attract foreign capital. Many argue that wealthy countries are not only outsourcing factories and jobs but pollution as well. For example, the quality of the air and water around Pittsburgh has dramatically improved as the city's steel industry has declined, while China, now the world's largest steel producer, faces a rapidly growing pollution problem. Our case study of Nigeria is another example: the southeastern region is dotted with nearly 1,500 oil wells, which for many years provided an estimated 40 percent of U.S. oil imports. Environmentally damaging oil spills are more common there than in most oil-producing areas: estimates suggest as much oil is spilled annually in Nigeria as was spilled by the disastrous Exxon *Valdez* oil spill in Alaska in 1989. Citizens of one of the poorest regions of a poor country thus pay a large share of the environmental costs of U.S. oil consumption. Opponents of the race-to-the-bottom thesis argue that postmaterialist values will be key: as globalization helps produce wealth, it will help lower pollution because wealth and environmental concerns seem to increase in tandem. Analyzing the World Values Survey, however, Dunlap and York (2012) found little correlation between wealth and environmental concerns; citizens of poor nations expressed somewhat different but just as strong (and sometimes stronger) concern for the environment as citizens of wealthier countries. Whichever argument proves more accurate in the long term, rapidly industrializing countries now face dramatically expanding environmental problems. This is clearest in Asia, as our case study of China shows.

Also tied to globalization are what many term "third-generation" environmental problems: these problems are global and therefore require global responses. Air and water pollution have always crossed borders, but this new concern is distinct. The source of the pollution matters little because the effects are truly global. The major example is global climate change. Burning fossil fuels—full of previously trapped carbon—have pumped excess carbon into the atmosphere. Virtually all scientists now agree that this has increased the entire planet's ambient temperature by an estimated 0.7°C (1.3°F) since the dawn of the industrial age in the nineteenth century, and the pace is accelerating. The 2007 *United Nations Human Development Report* (UNHDR) focused on climate change, recommending that the world endeavor to keep the temperature increase in the twenty-first century to no more than 2°C (UNDP 2007, 7). Current projections, if no changes are made, go as high as a 5°C rise (UNDP 2007, 3, 7). A new report in 2013 argued that to keep the increase to 2°C or less, total carbon emissions must be restricted to no more than a trillion ton, a level currently projected to be reached around 2040 (IPCC 2013). Temperature increases of a few degrees may not sound like much, especially if you live where the winters are long and cold, but it is greater than the change from the last ice age to our present climate. The effects would be catastrophic: rising sea levels would flood coastal areas around the world, and severe drought would afflict many areas—especially in the tropics, which are already relatively poor.

Developing countries have long struggled to achieve sustainable development: economic development that can continue over the long term. Development always involves increased use of resources, but if nonrenewable resources are being used quickly, development won't be sustainable. As demand for food and land increases, for instance, farmers and ranchers clear forested areas throughout the tropics. This gives them nutrient-rich soil on which to grow crops and graze cattle, as well as valuable wood to sell on the global market, but tropical rainforest soils are thin and are quickly depleted when put to agricultural use. After a few years, new land must be cleared as the old is exhausted. The result is rapidly disappearing forests and development that is unsustainable in the long run. Deforestation also increases global warming because trees absorb and retain carbon. Farmers' and ranchers' rational response to growing global demand for agricultural products, then, has created unsustainable development and more global warming. Globalization-induced pollution of air and water and rapid use of nonrenewable resources make the goal of sustainable development ever more challenging for many poor countries.

Risk and Uncertainty

While most analysts agree that environmental damage is an externality that must be addressed, a vociferous debate thrives on the uncertainty nearly always present in environmental issues. Scientists can rarely tell us exactly what a particular form or amount of pollution will do. As with health problems, the best we can do is predict *likely* outcomes. The top climate scientists in the world won the Nobel Peace Prize for their 2007 Intergovernmental Panel on Climate Change Report, but even their most certain predictions were termed "very likely" (90 percent certainty) or "likely" (66 percent certainty) outcomes of climate change. Similarly, we know that air pollution causes lung cancer, but we can't predict with absolute certainty how many cases it will cause, let alone which individuals will be affected. Environmental policy everywhere has to be based on **risk assessment** and **risk management**. Risk assessment tells us what the risks of damaging outcomes are, and risk management is policy used to keep those risks to acceptable levels. The costs of reducing risks must be weighed against the potential (but always uncertain) benefits.

Much of the debate, of course, is over what level of risk is "acceptable." In recent years, the European Union (EU) and its member states have employed the **precautionary principle**, which emphasizes risk avoidance even when the science predicting the risk is uncertain. This principle lies behind the EU ban on genetically modified organisms (GMOs) in food. With limited scientific evidence on whether GMOs are harmful or benign, the EU errs on the side of caution, banning them until the science is clarified. The United States, especially under the administration of George W. Bush, erred more toward reducing the costs of environmental fixes. For example, the United

risk assessment
Analysis of what the risks of damaging outcomes are in a particular situation

risk management
Policy used to keep risks to acceptable levels

precautionary principle
A policy that emphasizes risk avoidance even when the science predicting a risk is uncertain

States currently allows extensive use of GMOs in the absence of greater scientific evidence of harm.

How do governments respond when they decide that environmental damage is an unacceptable risk? Several approaches exist. The oldest is known as **command and control policies**, which involve direct government regulation. These were the first type of policies most wealthy countries enacted in the 1970s. Based on assessments of health and other risks, a government simply sets a level of pollution no one is allowed to surpass, or requires companies to pay a penalty if they do. Businesses must reduce production or find ways to produce the same goods with less pollution. At least in the short term, this policy is likely to raise production costs partially through internalizing the costs of pollution control. Command and control policies require governments to set very specific limits on many pollutants from many sources and to inspect possible polluters to ensure they are following the regulations. Both of these tasks are expensive, leading many analysts to argue for what they see as more efficient means of pollution control in the form of incentive systems.

The best-known incentive system is the **cap and trade system**, in which a government sets an overall limit on how much of a pollutant is acceptable from an entire industry or country and issues vouchers to each company that give it the right to a certain number of units of pollution. The individual companies are then free to trade these vouchers. Companies that face high costs to reduce their pollution levels will be interested in buying additional pollution rights, while those that can more cheaply invest in new and cleaner technology will sell their rights. In theory, pollution is reduced in the most efficient way possible and at the least cost. Government agencies must still determine the overall cap on pollution, but the market allocates that pollution.

Critics point out that cap and trade can result in high levels of pollution at particular sources. If you live downriver from the factory that purchased a large number of pollution rights, your water will be particularly polluted, while the water in other locations gets cleaner. This problem can be corrected by setting a maximum allowable level of pollution rights for any single source, limiting the market in pollution rights to ensure people in particular spots do not pay the costs for the rest of the country's cleaner air and water. Simply taxing pollution directly is another way to provide an incentive to reduce it without dictating specific levels from specific sources. Both cap and trade and taxation systems require the government to set an overall cap or tax at a level that will reduce pollution by the desired amount. While perhaps less complicated than specifying pollution levels from each source, this is still a complex and uncertain task.

Tax or cap and trade systems attempt to set a direct cost on pollution, forcing polluters to internalize an externality. A similar goal is embedded in policies to control use of what otherwise could be free goods, such as public land and the minerals under it, to avoid the tragedy of the commons. User fees on public land exist to limit use of it for ranching and other activities so that the overuse inherent in free public goods

Web link:
The debate about genetically modified food labeling

command and control policies
Pollution control system in which a government directly regulates the specific amount of pollution each polluting entity is allowed

cap and trade system
Market-based pollution control system in which the government sets an overall limit on how much of a pollutant is acceptable and issues vouchers to pollute to each company, which companies are then free to trade

does not occur. Similarly, governments can charge for access to minerals, including oil. Given that minerals and fossil fuels are nonrenewable, their depletion contains an intergenerational externality: future generations will pay the price of finding alternatives to the finite resources current generations use. Many economists argue that this justifies government intervention to tax mineral extraction, raising the internal cost of mineral production. In practice, many governments, including the United States, pursue exactly the opposite strategy, subsidizing mineral exploration and development in order to maximize production and lower consumer costs in the present. Cheaper minerals and fuels spur economic growth, which all legitimate states strive to achieve. Oil production, in particular, is also seen as a matter of national security, as each state tries to reduce its dependence on other states for this most crucial of commodities. Subsidizing this activity, however, encourages rather than discourages the tragedy of the commons in nonrenewable resources.

Climate Change The complexity of environmental regulation is magnified at the international level, but the policy options are similar. Global warming became a well-known concern in the 1980s, but the first significant international effort to respond to it was signed at the major international environmental conference in Rio de Janeiro in 1992, and this was only a voluntary agreement for countries to adopt goals of reducing their carbon output. Growing scientific consensus and continued negotiations led to the signing of the Kyoto Protocol in 1997, which included mandated targets for developed countries: they would reduce their carbon emissions by an average of 5 percent below their 1990 levels by 2012. It provided no mandates on developing countries, however, which led the United States, the world's largest carbon producer at the time, to reject it.

A major successor to the Kyoto Protocol was to be approved in Copenhagen in 2009. Once again, a binding treaty that included all countries—including the two biggest producers of greenhouse gases, China and the United States—failed to materialize. In its place, a nonbinding accord was produced in which countries pledged to adopt voluntary measures that would keep twenty-first-century warming to no more than the targeted 2°C. In fact, the International Energy Agency examined the promises the individual countries made and concluded that following them would likely produce a temperature rise of 3.5°C; only the most dramatic and least likely policy changes would result in meeting the 2°C target. The 2012 follow-up conference in Doha, Qatar, again failed to reach a new comprehensive agreement but instead extended the life of the Kyoto Protocol to 2020; its binding requirements, however, only covered 15 percent of global carbon emissions because of the refusal of the United States and several other wealthy countries to participate, and the absence of binding agreements on large, developing countries like China and India.

Much of the controversy over climate change is a battle between developed and developing countries. Figure 11.2 and Maps 11.1 to 11.3 illustrate what this debate is about. Figure 11.2 shows that since the dawn of the industrial era, the wealthy,

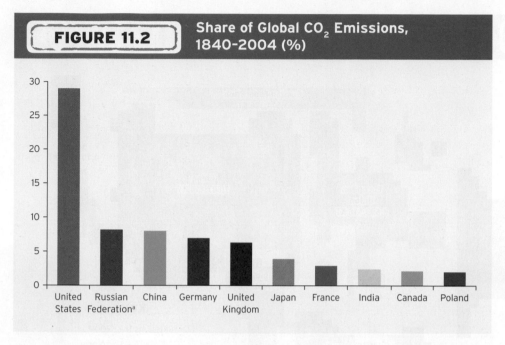

FIGURE 11.2 **Share of Global CO$_2$ Emissions, 1840–2004 (%)**

Source: Figure 1.4, UN Human Development Report, 2007/2008, "Fighting Climate Change: Human Solidarity in a Divided World," 41 (http://hdr.undp.org/en/media/HDR_20072008_EN_Complete.pdf).

a. Includes a share of USSR emissions proportional to the Russian Federation's current share of CS emissions.

Western countries have produced the great bulk of carbon emissions over the long term. Because these gases do not dissipate, wealthy countries have produced the vast majority of the total greenhouse gases to date. The United States alone is estimated to account for nearly 30 percent of the total since 1840 (UNDP 2007, 40). Map 11.1, however, shows that while wealthy countries remain major carbon producers now, a few rapidly industrializing countries account for a significant share of CO$_2$ emissions as well, especially China, the world's biggest producer currently. Map 11.2 demonstrates, on the other hand, that in per capita terms, the wealthy countries still produce far more than even China, let alone other developing countries. Each American produces far more carbon annually than each Chinese does. Finally, comparing Maps 11.1 and 11.3 shows that the countries that produce the least carbon are the most vulnerable to the effects of climate change.

These data make the battle lines of the debate clear. The wealthy countries, led by the United States, argue that we cannot reduce global warming without all of the biggest polluters, including China and India, agreeing to curb their emissions significantly. The developing countries, led by China, counter that the wealthier countries are the main source of the total excess carbon in the atmosphere and that each individual in wealthy countries produces far more carbon that each individual Chinese or Indian does. Therefore, the wealthy countries have an obligation to reduce emissions the most. Moreover, denying countries now industrializing the right to pollute will

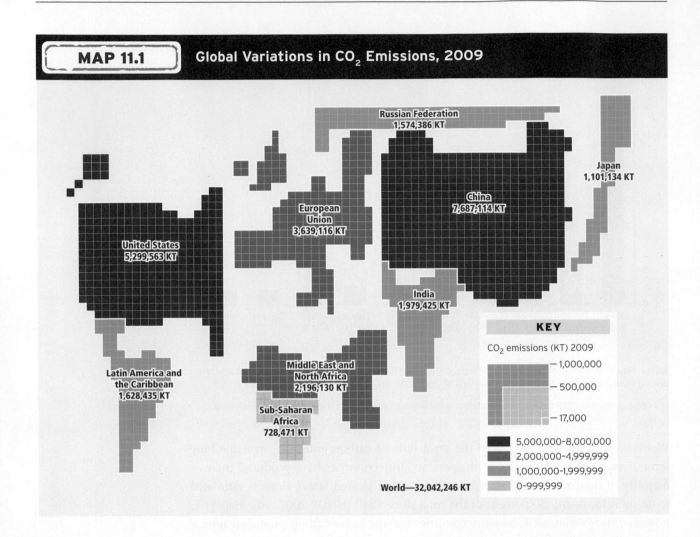

MAP 11.1   **Global Variations in CO$_2$ Emissions, 2009**

Russian Federation
1,574,386 KT

Japan
1,101,134 KT

China
7,687,114 KT

European
Union
3,639,116 KT

United States
5,299,563 KT

India
1,979,425 KT

Latin America and
the Caribbean
1,628,435 KT

Middle East and
North Africa
2,196,130 KT

Sub-Saharan
Africa
728,471 KT

KEY

CO$_2$ emissions (KT) 2009

— 1,000,000

— 500,000

— 17,000

5,000,000–8,000,000
2,000,000–4,999,999
1,000,000–1,999,999
0–999,999

World—32,042,246 KT

doom them to inferior status forever. The wealthy countries benefitted from unlimited carbon pollution while they were industrializing, for which the entire world will pay the price, and it is unethical to ask countries now industrializing to curb their development prematurely. Furthermore, the poorest countries argue that they have not caused the problem but will suffer the greatest effects, making a moral claim on the major polluters to reduce pollution and pay for mitigation of climate change's worst effects.

Given this structure of interests, numerous formulas for how to share the cost of reducing carbon emissions have been developed. Wealthy countries argue for *grandfathering*, the basis for the Kyoto Protocol, under which all countries reduce their emissions relative to a baseline year, so their past emissions are "grandfathered" in. The *historical responsibility* approach favored by some poorer countries, on the other hand, argues that wealthy countries should compensate the rest of the world for the carbon emissions they have already produced. The most common proposal from

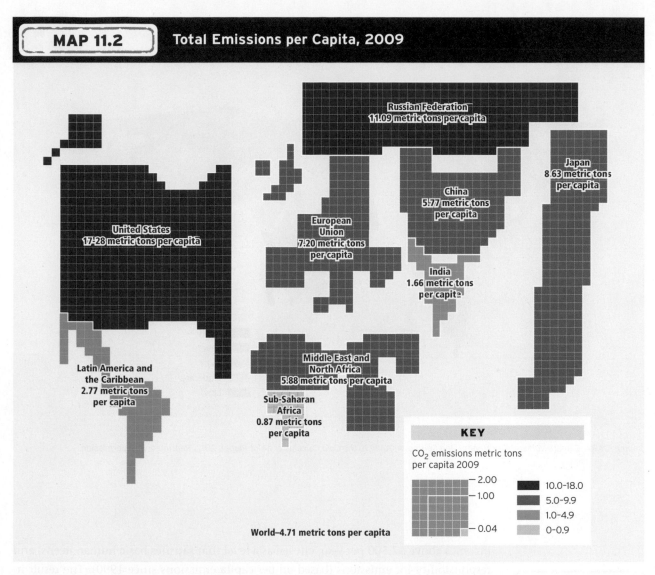

MAP 11.2   **Total Emissions per Capita, 2009**

Russian Federation
11.09 metric tons per capita

Japan
8.63 metric tons per capita

China
5.77 metric tons per capita

European Union
7.20 metric tons per capita

United States
17.28 metric tons per capita

India
1.66 metric tons per capita

Middle East and North Africa
5.88 metric tons per capita

Latin America and the Caribbean
2.77 metric tons per capita

Sub-Saharan Africa
0.87 metric tons per capita

KEY

CO_2 emissions metric tons per capita 2009

— 2.00
— 1.00
— 0.04

10.0–18.0	
5.0–9.9	
1.0–4.9	
0–0.9	

World–4.71 metric tons per capita

Source: Data for Maps 11.1 and 11.2 are from the World Bank (http://data.worldbank.org/indicator/EN.ATM.CO2E.PC) and (http://data.worldbank.org/indicator/EN.ATM.CO2E.KT).

poorer countries is a *per capita contraction and convergence* principle: every person on the planet would be given the same rights to emissions, which would be reduced over time to lower overall emissions. Countries that exceed their rights would have to reduce their total and/or purchase excess rights from other countries; those with surplus rights could sell them. While not making up for the full historical legacy, this would place much greater burden on wealthier countries (Parks and Roberts 2009). Paul Baer et al. (2009) argued for what they term Greenhouse Development Rights based on countries' capacity to pay (defined as the percentage of their population with

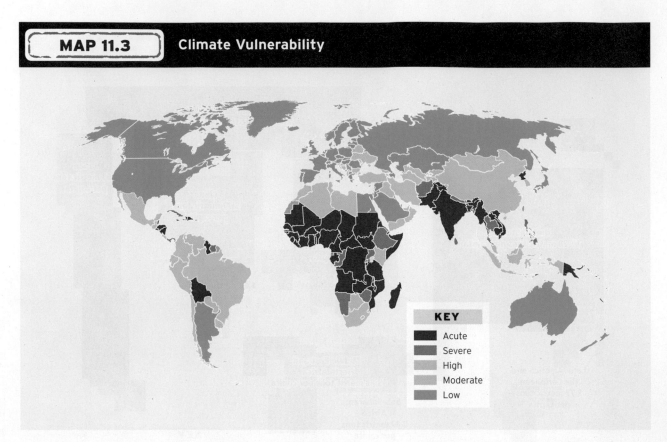

MAP 11.3   **Climate Vulnerability**

KEY

- Acute
- Severe
- High
- Moderate
- Low

Source: DARA, *Climate Vulnerability Monitor, 2nd Edition: A Guide to the Cold Calculus of a Hot Planet,* 2012. Reprinted with permission.

Web link:
Greenhouse
Development
Rights

incomes above $7,500 per year, chosen as a level that satisfies basic human needs) and responsibility for emissions (based on per capita emissions since 1990). The result in 2009 places about two-thirds of the burden on the wealthy countries, of which the United States would pay 27 percent, while China would be responsible for about 15 percent (Global Development Rights 2013).

Whoever pays the cost, no international consensus exists on exactly which policy mechanisms should be used to reduce greenhouse gases. The United National Development Programme (UNDP) 2007 report on climate change suggested a carbon tax or a cap and trade system to reduce emissions. The EU already instituted its own cap and trade system, which operates as one market across all EU members, as a means of complying with the Kyoto Protocol. It initially was too generous in the cap it set, leading to a surplus of emissions rights (that no one needed) and a drop in their prices. In 2008 the cap was significantly lowered, the trading prices quadrupled, and carbon emissions were reduced the following year. It is estimated to have reduced emissions at participating facilities (utilities, factories, etc.) by 2 to 5 percent (Ellerman et al. 2010). Kyoto also allows companies and countries to gain emission credits by investing in projects that reduce emissions elsewhere in the world. Because many factories in the developing world use older technology, it's cheaper to reduce emissions there than in wealthy countries. Given that global climate change is just that—global—it doesn't matter where emissions are reduced. A rapidly growing market has emerged that now includes several thousand emissions reduction projects globally, with over half of them located in China. The EU system and Kyoto have created the beginning of what could become a truly global market for greenhouse gas emissions, if a comprehensive agreement to cap them globally is eventually reached.

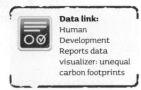

Data link: Human Development Reports data visualizer: unequal carbon footprints

In the absence of a successful multilateral agreement to create a truly global system to reduce greenhouse gas emissions, numerous smaller-scale efforts have arisen. Matthew Hoffmann (2011) argued that the failure of Copenhagen could be a turning point: smaller-scale efforts may become the center of what he called "experimental climate governance." The efforts involve everything from networks of activists cataloging carbon production and its reduction to networks of cities agreeing to reduce their carbon footprint to groups of U.S. states creating cap and trade systems on carbon emissions. The efforts share a belief that market-oriented solutions are possible. How effective these efforts can be, even though they have grown rapidly in the new millennium, remains an open question. Leaders of Europe's energy-intensive industries complain that they cannot compete internationally because they face carbon constraints that their competitors elsewhere, including in the United States and China, do not. A logical response to this could be to move industrial production from countries with carbon limits to countries without limits, which could actually increase overall carbon emissions because the products of those industries would be shipped back to their consumer markets. The question this raises is whether it's possible to reduce carbon emissions adequately without a truly global system.

Of the three policy areas we discuss in this chapter, the environment is the easiest area in which to justify government intervention in markets. Environmental damage is clearly an externality that should be internalized for efficient allocation of resources and long-term sustainability. This has become particularly clear and urgent in the face of global climate change, which threatens to wreak havoc on the lives of millions in the relatively near future. A number of clear policy choices exist as well. Their implementation, however, has been limited and slow. Different policies internalize costs in different ways, resulting in different people paying those costs. Both within individual countries and on a global scale, individual polluters and national governments strive to minimize the costs they will have to pay. Our case studies of perhaps the two countries that are most crucial to the debate—the United States and China—illustrate the conflicts well.

CASE Study

THE UNITED STATES: PIONEER THAT LOST ITS WAY?

April 22, 1970, the first Earth Day, marked the coming of age of the environmental movement in the United States. The now annual event emerged out of the fervor of the 1960s and represented a strikingly broad consensus in the country: environmental problems were important, and the government should do something about them. From 1965 to 1970, the number of people saying the quality of their air and water was a serious issue went from less than a third of the population to nearly three-quarters. In May 1969, only 1 percent of people mentioned pollution as one of the "most important" problems facing the country, but by May 1971 that number had risen to 25 percent (Layzer 2006, 33). A decade of rapid expansion of the government's role in protecting the environment made the United States a pioneer in the field. The decentralized U.S. political system and shifting ideological trends in the country, however, meant that further progress was mixed. Indeed, by the twenty-first century, the United States had become one of the chief obstacles to a comprehensive, binding treaty to reduce the greenhouse gases that cause global warming. The country had gone from environmental policy pioneer to environmental policy problem.

The major U.S. environmental policy that predates 1970 was the protection of public lands for recreational and ecological purposes, from the creation of the national park system in the early 1900s to the preservation of pristine wilderness areas starting in 1964. Landmark legislation of the early 1970s included the creation of the Environmental Protection Agency (EPA), the Clean Air Act (1970), the

The oil from this Shell Oil open pit mine in Alberta, Canada, would travel through the proposed Keystone XL pipeline across the United States to New Orleans. Opposition to the pipeline and concern about global warming led President Obama to declare he would only approve the pipeline if it did not significantly add to carbon emissions.

Clean Water Act (1972), and the Endangered Species Act (1973). In one area, this progress continued in the 1980s, as President Ronald Reagan, generally an opponent of environmental policy, helped champion the Montreal Protocol of 1987, which eliminated the use of ozone-depleting chemicals. It is projected to restore the ozone layer to its pre-1980 level by the middle of the twenty-first century. These were all command and control policies, setting specific regulations for allowable levels of pollution from individual sources and protecting specific species and plots of land. Coming from a broad bipartisan consensus, they established the United States as a pioneer in environmental protection, generally seen as being well ahead of most European countries.

Reagan's election in 1980 began a reversal of this environmental trend. His neoliberal economic ideology led him to argue for a reduced government role in the environment. He significantly reduced funding to the EPA and other environmental agencies and appointed opponents of government intervention to key environmental posts. These officials rewrote regulations to reduce their impact on business. By mid-decade, Congress began resisting some of these policies. The most significant congressional reversal was the Superfund Act (1986), which required that thousands of toxic waste sites be cleaned up. A later milestone was a major amendment to the Clean Air Act in 1990, which for the first time included a cap and trade system focused on one particular pollutant: sulfur dioxide, a key ingredient in acid rain. The system has significantly reduced this pollutant nationwide, at an estimated cost of only half what a similar reduction under the older command and control model would have incurred (Freeman 2006, 206).

The 1980s also saw the emergence of a new element in U.S. environmental activism in the form of the **environmental justice movement.** It began in 1982, in Warren County, the poorest county in North Carolina, in which 65 percent of residents were African American (three times the state average). When a waste disposal company proposed locating a toxic waste facility in the county, the residents organized demonstrations, and the environmental justice movement began. Focused on environmental damage in particular locales, members argued that poor and, especially, black or Hispanic neighborhoods are much more likely to be sites for polluting industries and toxic waste depositories. The movement has grown significantly since then, and it laid out a clear set of principles at a major conference in 1991. While research results depend on how the researchers define "neighborhood" or "community," it seems that across the United States, black and Hispanic citizens are more likely to live in areas where air and water pollution exceed legal limits and where toxic chemicals are produced or stored (Ringquist 2006).

Bill Clinton's election in 1992 with noted environmentalist Al Gore as his vice president gave environmental advocates hope that the policies of the Reagan/Bush years would be reversed. By the end of the decade, however, environmentalists had mixed assessments of the Clinton administration, noting some significant successes but

environmental justice movement
A movement focused on exposing and fighting against racial and class inequalities in exposure to pollution, started in the United States in 1982

also major failings. A key issue was global warming. Both Republican and Democratic presidents had agreed to voluntary reductions in greenhouse gas emissions, but they continued to resist mandatory targets, including the Kyoto Protocol. President George W. Bush repudiated the treaty entirely and pursued an energy policy that provided greater incentives for fossil fuel exploration and development. The United States is estimated to spend about $100 billion per year—half the world's total—on fossil fuel subsidies, encouraging rapid use and therefore depletion of these nonrenewable resources and promoting global climate change (Hempel 2006, 305). The most recent element of this is new technology that makes mining shale oil and hydrofracking for natural gas economically feasible, both of which are expanding rapidly in the United States and Canada, reducing U.S. oil imports significantly. Critics contend that this increased mining will lower fossil fuels' costs and increase their consumption, thereby putting more carbon in the atmosphere. Supporters of the new technology argue that compared to the alternatives, particularly coal, the new techniques will reduce carbon emissions overall. A major environmental issue arose in 2012 when the government proposed the building of a pipeline from Canada to the Gulf of Mexico to transport shale oil from Canada. After more than a year of debate and controversy, the Obama administration announced in 2013 that it would only approve the pipeline if it did not significantly add to the problem of carbon pollution.

Barack Obama came to office having pledged to enact fundamentally new energy and climate change policies. He committed his administration to full involvement in negotiating a replacement for the failed Kyoto Protocol and personally helped negotiate the rather weak resolution that emerged from the Copenhagen conference in 2009, after a binding treaty once again failed to gain support. Domestically, the administration proposed and the House of Representatives passed legislation to create a cap and trade system to reduce greenhouse gases by 17 percent by 2020 and over 80 percent by midcentury, but Republican (and some Democratic) opposition in the Senate blocked the measure. This led the administration to pursue EPA regulation of greenhouse gases, which the agency in 2009 ruled substantially harmed health and therefore could be regulated legally under the Clean Air Act. That act, however, requires reduced emissions only on new and renovated utilities, so the EPA's long-term impact is uncertain. Industry tried to challenge the EPA's right to regulate greenhouse gases, but the Supreme Court ruled in 2007, and reaffirmed in a 2011 case, that the EPA does have the right to regulate those gases under the Clean Air Act. In 2013 Obama made a major speech asserting greater urgency regarding climate change, but actual regulations that would reduce carbon production remained several years off.

Despite what environmentalists see as setbacks, U.S. policy has produced a much cleaner environment, though not all areas have seen success. The greatest success has

Video link:
The Clean Air Act's legacy

Web link:
Clean Air Act

been with air pollution. Since the first Earth Day in 1970, production of the six key ingredients of air pollution has dropped by 60 percent in spite of significant population growth and even greater economic growth. The only exceptions were a slight increase in nitrous oxide (a secondary ingredient in acid rain) and carbon dioxide, the key greenhouse gas. Acid rain, regulated by a cap and trade system, has dropped substantially as well. Surveys of water quality at the turn of the century indicated that 61 percent of rivers and 55 percent of lakes met acceptable standards for clean water, though destruction of wetlands by development continues at about fifty-eight thousand acres per year (Kraft and Vig 2006, 21–24; Yarett 2010). On the other hand, the number of species on the endangered list has quadrupled, energy use per person has not changed and is much higher than in most other wealthy countries, and the average amount of garbage per person has increased 38 percent despite a quintupling of recycling.

CASE Summary

The American political system makes it particularly easy for groups to get legislation vetoed. Rational-choice scholars have noted that environmental legislation, in particular, often provides diffuse benefits to many people and high costs for a few (typically businesses), so the latter are often able and highly motivated to block such legislation. Environmental legislation succeeds only at times of generally high concern among the broader public, which leads legislators to override the veto efforts of a few key players. As a result, U.S. policy has a stop-and-go character, with occasional great advances followed by periods of reversal or stagnation. Some legislation, such as fossil fuel subsidies, works in reverse: it provides huge benefits to particular actors and diffuse costs (via taxes to pay the subsidies) to the general population. These types of policies have endured in the U.S. system despite what most economists see as their clear encouragement of externalities and therefore inefficiency and environmental damage. The U.S. political system produced both the pioneering legislation of a generation ago and the limits on action more recently, especially regarding global climate change.

CASE Questions

1. Why has the United States shifted from a pioneer of environmentalism to an opponent of most global climate change efforts?
2. Do domestic or international factors better explain the United States' reluctance to support binding agreements on reducing carbon emissions?

CASE Study

CHINA: SEARCHING FOR SUSTAINABLE DEVELOPMENT

- **LONG-STANDING ISSUES**
  Rapid economic growth produces massive environmental problems; government prioritized growth over environmental protection

- **TYPES OF INTERVENTION**
  Command and control; recently, experimental market-based incentives for local governments to prioritize environmental protection more

- **RECENT TRENDS**
  Increased emphasis on environmental policy since 2002

- **OVERALL SUCCESS**
  Still massive pollution problems: air, water, and greenhouse gases

As the 2008 Summer Olympics approached, commentators around the world began to question whether Beijing could really host the games adequately, not because of a lack of infrastructure or resources but because of the quality of the air the athletes would be breathing. Even after the government instituted a policy to remove half of Beijing's 3.3 million vehicles from highways, banned 300,000 aging vehicles found to be especially heavy polluters, encouraged commuters to return to using the bicycles once so ubiquitous across the country, opened three new subway lines, and set up numerous new bus lines, some athletes still bowed out of competition in China, citing fears of asthma attacks and physical stress (Associated Press 2008a, 2008b).

China's environmental degradation and problems are breathtaking, no pun intended. Besides urban air pollution, 30 percent of the nation's water is unfit for human or agricultural use, almost 90 percent of the country's grasslands and forests are suffering degradation, and the Yellow River now dries up before it reaches the ocean, becoming an open sewer (Morton 2006, 64–65; Ho and Vermeer 2006). Severe soil erosion and desertification have doubled since the 1970s and are degrading an area the size of New Jersey each year (Economy 2010, 66). The result of all of this is skyrocketing health problems: air pollution in northern China is estimated to have caused 1.2 million premature deaths in 2010, lowering life expectancy by five years vis-à-vis the less polluted southern China, and cancer rates increased by 30 percent over the past thirty years. In Beijing, where the most polluted days reach forty times the internationally

A long-distance race participant wears a mask to protect himself from the smog as he runs past the National Stadium built for the 2008 Summer Olympics in Beijing. China's rapid industrialization has produced dramatic environmental problems, including many of the most polluted cities in the world. Chinese authorities took numerous measures, such as banning some vehicles and shutting down factories, to clean the air for the Olympics.

recommended maximum level of air particulates, residents regularly wear facemasks to protect them from air pollution. Those who can afford to, choose apartments and schools partly based on the quality of the air filtration system they use. Facing mounting public pressure on the issue, the government announced a major new command and control initiative in September 2013 that will set upper limits on air particulate levels in major cities, ban the most heavily polluting vehicles by 2015, and slightly reduce the nation's dependence on coal. How well this will be implemented, though, remains uncertain.

The 2013 law is the latest in a series of moves since 2002 by the Chinese leadership, as it has made a significant commitment to environmental protection. In 2008 it elevated the main environmental protection agency to a full cabinet ministry and doubled funding for the environment. The Chinese government has passed an impressive array of environmental laws and signed numerous international environmental treaties, but protecting the environment still is in conflict with the country's rapid economic growth, and the laws are weakly enforced at the local level.

The Ministry of Environmental Protection (MEP) is the key agency governing environmental protection in China, and while it has had energetic leaders and been a bureaucratic advocate for the environment, it has had limited ability to enforce China's environmental laws. It is dependent on Environmental Protection Bureaus (EPBs) controlled by local governments for most of its funding and staff. Local government leaders are rewarded in China's system primarily for their ability to further rapid economic growth, so they have had virtually no incentive to slow growth in favor of protecting the environment. Consequently, the effectiveness of environmental policies varies greatly. In some major cities, such as Shanghai and Guangzhou, leaders have become more committed to environmental concerns, due to pressure by strong environmental NGOs and because they have the resources to fund better policies. Shanghai, for instance, has committed 3 percent of its GDP to environmental protection, more than double the national average (Chan, Lee, and Chan 2008, 297; Economy 2010, 123). Even the doubling of China's national environmental budget falls well below the 2 percent of GDP that most scholars see as essential for it to reverse its most severe environmental problems (Wu 2009).

Most early environmental policies were command and control, though in the last decade MEP has begun to experiment with market-based policies as well. The two major command and control policies have long been fining excessive polluting from individual sources, such as factories, and requiring environmental impact assessments (EIAs) for new industrial projects. The fines, however, are quite small, so even when the laws are enforced, many firms find it cost-effective to pay the fines and keep polluting. The local EPBs often collude in this because they gain their revenue from the fines, so if they really succeeded at reducing pollution, their revenue would decline. In this context, the EIAs had little effect for many years, though recent trends suggest that may be changing. In 2005 the government began a highly publicized process of rejecting greater numbers of projects on environmental grounds. In what came to be known as "environmental storms," it suspended 30 projects in early 2005, and by August 2008 it had rejected over 400 more. The Great Recession, though, seems to have partially reversed this. To expedite construction projects that were part of the government's successful economic stimulus plan, the MEP created a "green passage" policy that gave quick approval to 150 major projects; provincial authorities radically reduced the time they took to approve EIAs as well (Johnson 2008, 97–99; Wu 2009, 280; Economy 2010, 78).

An initial market-based experiment was the 2006 introduction of the concept of a "green GDP" in several major cities, in which an estimate for the cost of environmental damage is subtracted from the cities' annual GDP increase. The intent was to introduce a measure by which local government officials could be held accountable: the central government could use this measure, instead of simple GDP growth, as the chief means of evaluating local officials' performance. The data showed that environmental damage cost 3 percent of the cities' total GDP, though many believed the real figure should be much higher. The central government initially announced that it would expand this green GDP to the entire country the following year, but local governments successfully resisted the plan, and there has been no follow-through on the experiment (Johnson 2008, 95–97). MEP continued calculating a national Green GDP, however, stating in 2010 that environmental damage represented 3.8 percent of total GDP. Despite this progressive measure, the MEP is charged with monitoring the pollution level of 300,000 factories and other pollution sources, and has only a few hundred employees directly working for it, a daunting task.

Concern about the environment among Chinese citizens was evident as far back as the 1970s, but it has taken an organized form only since the mid-1990s, as the government has allowed some NGOs to function. The first two environmental NGOs were created in 1994 and 1996, and by 2008 more than 3,500 were officially registered with the government. Most are urban based, and as many as half are student organizations. This trend is reflected in local protests as well: in 2005 there were 51,000 environmental protests across the country, an increase of 30 percent over the previous year. The government often tolerates environmental NGOs and local-level protests, because top officials see them as pushing recalcitrant local officials to enforce environmental policies better while doing little harm on the national level. Indeed, the government has started its own environmental government-organized nongovernmental organizations (GONGOs) as well. In 2012, three days of massive demonstrations ultimately stopped the construction of a petrochemical plant in a coastal city that the local government strongly supported. In Beijing the same year, an online movement successfully convinced the government to begin announcing when air pollution levels exceed acceptable limits, so that citizens can stay indoors to protect themselves.

Internationally, China is best known for its successful opposition to any mandatory limits on production of greenhouse gases for developing countries. Despite being one of the main obstacles to a binding agreement at the Copenhagen negotiations in 2009, the Chinese government committed itself to cut its carbon intensity—carbon dioxide emissions per unit of GDP—by 40 to 45 percent by 2020. As part of this effort, it has achieved greater energy efficiency over the past several years. It nearly met the goal of a 20 percent reduction in energy intensity set in the five-year plan that ended in 2011. The MEP's final report on that plan also noted that it had reduced pollutants in surface water by 32 percent and sulfur dioxide emissions by 19 percent. It nonetheless called the overall environmental situation "very grave" (Johnson 2011). The plan for 2011–2015 set a goal of reducing carbon intensity by 17 percent, which puts China on pace to achieve its Copenhagen goals (though on the low end of the acceptable range).

Web link:
Clean air drive in China likely to take a long time

Video link:
Chinese citizens losing patience with air pollution

CASE Summary China's rapid industrialization and massive size have made it one of the largest polluters in the world, though on a per capita basis it remains a modest one. After decades of nearly complete neglect of environmental protection, the leadership in the new millennium has significantly raised the official emphasis on doing better. Its efforts are supported by a rapidly growing network of local and national environmental groups, but while progress has clearly been made, the fundamental conflict between rapid economic growth and environmental protection remains unresolved. The MEP has become stronger but is still relatively weak vis-à-vis local governments. Fundamental changes of direction, such as the idea of the green GDP or changing key performance incentives for local officials, continue to be resisted. As the largest producer of greenhouse gases and with a rapidly growing economy, China's environmental policies have become crucial not only to its own well-being but to that of the planet as a whole.

CASE Questions

1. China, perhaps more than any other country, illustrates the issues involved in the relationship between globalization and the environment. What lessons does our case study provide on this topic?
2. How might greater democracy affect environmental protection in China? What impact, positive or negative, does the authoritarian nature of the regime have on environmental policy?

Pollution is a classic example of market failure, and it has now gone global. In an attempt to internalize the external costs of pollution, governments initially intervened by imposing specific limits on pollution to create cleaner air, water, and land. More recently, market-based policies have emerged that promise to achieve similar results at lower costs. With intervention, the costs of various production processes shift, with some people bearing those costs and others benefiting, which leads to major political battles in every country. Climate change is only the latest, and biggest, of these environmental battles. It has the added problem, and perhaps potential benefit, of being truly global, requiring a global solution that has little to do with locale. But it raises the same question as all environmental issues: Who will pay the costs of internalizing major externalities?

CONCLUSION

The outcomes of policy battles can tell us much about "Who rules." Policy outcomes reflect the relative strength of various groups in a given political system. More extensive welfare states, especially prior to the 1990s in Europe, likely reflect the greater power of workers and unions in those countries, in contrast to the United States. European countries for the most part have reduced welfare benefits in recent decades, though, suggesting that workers' power is declining relative to other forces, domestic and international. In poorer countries, the poor who would benefit most from social welfare and health care interventions seem to lack significant power, as those countries pursue few such policies, either because the governments are not interested or because they lack the resources. Innovative social policies in Brazil and elsewhere in Latin America, though, suggest that in a democratic setting, it is possible for the poor to overcome these problems at least partially and gain greater benefits.

Environmental policies, which usually assign clear costs and benefits to particular groups, perhaps demonstrate relative power most directly. Self-interested actors, whoever they are, are likely to resist paying the costs of environmental improvement, at least until a broader consensus emerges that change is essential for all to survive. For most environmental issues, including climate change, the least powerful player in the game is probably future generations, who lack any political clout now. They may well end up paying the greatest costs for internalizing externalities in the long run.

State intervention in each of the three policy areas has its own rationale, but in all three, market failure of some sort offers a reason for the state to modify pure market outcomes. States don't intervene solely because they recognize market failures, however. Normative and political motivations also need to be present. Markets can create powerful veto players, which can only be overcome via collective action and/or consensus on the part of broader and usually more diffuse actors who believe they will benefit from intervention. For instance, the Great Depression in the United States helped bring the value of reducing poverty to the fore and led to the birth of the welfare state, while in Britain it was the post–World War II consensus on rebuilding a new and more equitable society that produced social and health policy. Similarly, wealthy industrial countries have led the way in environmental intervention, reflecting a classic postmaterialist value. Middle-income and rapidly industrializing countries may be attempting to join the bandwagon, but in the very poorest countries, it is difficult to argue convincingly that resources are something to be conserved rather than depleted to meet immediate human needs.

Globalization, too, has had an impact on policies in all countries. If hyperglobalization theorists are correct, then wealthy states will converge toward more market-based policies, and poorer countries, rather than choosing among models, will be forced to do the same. On social policy, our cases show a persistence of diverse models but a trend toward at least limited reform in the direction of a more liberal welfare state. Across all three types of welfare states, for instance, workers and the poor have seen social policy benefits reduced, work requirements and limits on social assistance increased, and their contributions to social insurance systems increased.

Reform in health policy seems to be more difficult. Globalization, increasing wealth, and an aging population make reform of health policy particularly urgent and difficult. While significant changes occurred after about 2005 in our case study countries, they do not represent wholesale shifts from the long-standing systems in each country. Health care systems create their own institutionalized interests that resist change, from medical practitioners' support of the NHS in the United Kingdom and NHI in Germany to American insurance companies' opposition to a single-payer model. Health care, perhaps because it affects everyone, including relatively wealthy and powerful players, seems particularly difficult to reform.

In general, wealth seems to raise the prospect that countries can and will act effectively on value consensus in these three policy areas, but we need to explain significant variation among wealthy countries as well. The most widespread explanation of why some governments intervene more extensively than others is implicitly pluralist: in some countries, poorer groups have organized better and have more power, and policy reflects this. Institutions can matter as well, though. They create veto players that can be particularly powerful at blocking policy change, toward either more or less intervention. Germany's federal system and less centralized parliament, for instance, seem to make policy change there more incremental than in the more majoritarian United Kingdom. This cuts both ways, of course: the United Kingdom has not only created major interventionist policies like the NHS but also made some of the most dramatic reforms of both welfare and health policies. Reforms are also influenced by the differing effects of similar global and social pressures in different countries: an aging population, women's entrance into the workforce, immigration, and the economic pressure of globalization.

Judging which set of policies is most "successful" in each of the three issue areas must in part be based on normative values, especially in social policy. If reducing poverty is the key goal, social democratic welfare states seem to be best; if ensuring people are employed is most important, though, a liberal welfare state may seem to be better. In health policy, what is "best" may be a little clearer. If the key criterion is gaining the most health at the least cost, it seems clear that market-based systems fare poorly, and well-established economic arguments explain why. Judging which is better between the NHS and NHI models, however, depends more on values. The NHS seems to be able to keep costs lower, but the NHI provides better services and choice. Judging environmental policy success also depends on values: How much do we value clean air and water? How much do we value the well-being of future generations versus our own right now? In terms of economic theory, environmental policy seems the easiest area in which to justify government intervention, but how much and how it should be done depend very much on larger value questions, including about who should pay how much of the costs and when.

Finally, truly global health and environmental problems, especially, may require new types of global policy solutions. States may increasingly have to interact with one another to hammer out effective and feasible policy solutions to problems, implementing these solutions across borders. The normative, political, and economic issues associated with working out such new global policies will be significant, as the example of climate change suggests, but global problems will increasingly demand states' attention in the twenty-first century.

KEY CONCEPTS

cap and trade system (p. 617)

Christian democratic welfare
    states (p. 577)

command and control policies (p. 617)

conditional cash transfer (CCT) (p. 584)

environmental justice
    movement (p. 625)

liberal welfare states (p. 579)

market-based private insurance
    system (p. 597)

means-tested public assistance (p. 576)

moral hazard (p. 596)

national health insurance (NHI) (p. 596)

national health system (NHS) (p. 597)

precautionary principle (p. 616)

risk assessment (p. 616)

risk management (p. 616)

single-payer system (p. 597)

social democratic welfare
    states (p. 577)

social insurance (p. 575)

social policy (p. 574)

tax expenditures (p. 576)

tragedy of the commons (p. 614)

universal entitlements (p. 575)

welfare states (p. 577)

 Sharpen your skills with SAGE edge at **edge.sagepub.com/orvis3e.** **SAGE edge for students** provides a personalized approach to help you accomplish your coursework goals in an easy-to-use learning environment.

WORKS CITED

Adolino, Jessica R., and Charles H. Blake. 2001. *Comparing Public Policies: Issues and Choices in Six Industrialized Countries.* Washington, DC: CQ Press.

Alber, Jens, and Neil Gilbert, eds. 2010. *United in Diversity? Comparing Social Models in Europe and America.* Oxford, UK: Oxford University Press.

Alesina, Alberto, and Edward L. Glaeser. 2004. *Fighting Poverty in the U.S. and Europe: A World of Difference.* Oxford, UK: Oxford University Press.

Associated Press. 2008a. "Beijing to Take Half of All Government Cars off the Road." *USA Today*, June 23 (http://www.usatoday.com/news/world/environment/2008-06-23-china-cars_N.htm).

Associated Press. 2008b. "Beijing Traffic Cut to Help Clear Air for Olympics." CNN/IBNLive.com, July 21 (http://ibnlive.in.com/news/beijing-traffic-cut-to-help-clear-air-for-olympics/69238-2.html).

Baer, Paul, Glenn Fieldman, Tom Athanasiou, and Sivan Kartha. 2009. "Greenhouse Development Rights: Towards an Equitable Framework for Global Climate Policy." In *The Politics of Climate Change: Environmental Dynamics in International Affairs,* edited by Paul Harris, 192–212. New York: Routledge.

Baer, Werner. 2008. *The Brazilian Economy: Growth and Development.* 6th ed. Boulder, CO: Lynne Rienner.

Bonoli, Giuliano, Vic George, and Peter Taylor-Gooby. 2000. *European Welfare Futures: Towards a Theory of Retrenchment.* Cambridge, UK, and Malden, MA: Polity Press and Blackwell.

Cammisa, Anne Marie. 1998. *From Rhetoric to Reform? Welfare Policy in American Politics.* Boulder, CO: Westview Press.

CBO (Congressional Budget Office). 2007. *The State Children's Health Insurance Program.* Washington, DC: Government Printing Office.

Center on Budget and Policy Priorities. 2012. *Policy Basics: An Introduction to TANF* (http://www.cbpp.org/cms/?fa=view&id=936).

Chan, Gerald, Pak K. Lee, and Lai-Ha Chan. 2008. "China's Environmental Governance: The Domestic-International Nexus." *Third World Quarterly* 29 (2): 291–314. doi:10.1080/01436590701806863.

Commonwealth Fund. 2008. *Commonwealth Fund International Health Policy Survey of Sicker Adults* (http://www.commonwealthfund.org/Content/Surveys/2008/2008-Commonwealth-Fund-International-Health-Policy-Survey-of-Sicker-Adults.aspx).

Dunlap, Riley E., and Richard York. 2012. "The Globalization of Environmental Concern." In *Comparative Environmental Politics: Theory, Practice, and Prospects,* edited by Paul F. Steinberg and Stacy D. VanDeveer, 89–112. Cambridge, MA: MIT Press.

The Economist. 2010. "Dr. Rösler's Difficult Prescription: The Hard Case of Reforming German Health Care." April 29 (http://www.economist.com/node/16015443?story_id=16015443).

Economy, Elizabeth C. 2010. *The River Runs Black: The Environmental Challenge to China's Future.* 2nd ed. Ithaca, NY: Cornell University Press.

Ellerman, A. Denny, Frank J. Convery, and Christian de Perthius. 2010. *Pricing Carbon: The European Union Emissions Trading Scheme.* Cambridge, UK: Cambridge University Press.

Esping-Andersen, Gøsta. 1990. *The Three Worlds of Welfare Capitalism.* Princeton, NJ: Princeton University Press.

Feder, Judith, and Donald W. Moran. 2007. "Cost Containment and the Politics of Health Care Reform." In *Restoring Fiscal Sanity 2007: The Health Spending Challenge,* edited by Alice M. Rivlin and Joseph R. Antos. Washington, DC: Brookings Institution Press.

Ferreira, Francisco H. G., and David A. Robalino. 2011. "Social Protection in Latin America: Achievements and Limitations." In *The Oxford Handbook of Latin American Economics,* edited by José Antonio Ocampo and Jaime Ros, 836–862. Oxford, UK: Oxford University Press.

Freeman, A. Myrick, III. 2006. "Economics, Incentives, and Environmental Policy." In *Environmental Policy: New Directions for the Twenty-first Century,* 6th ed., edited by Norman J. Vig and Michael E. Kraft, 193–214. Washington, DC: CQ Press.

Garfinkel, Irwin, Lee Rainwater, and Timothy Smeeding. 2010. *Wealth and Welfare States: Is America a Laggard or Leader?* Oxford, UK: Oxford University Press.

Gerlinger, Thomas. 2010. "Health Care Reform in Germany." *German Policy Studies/Politikfeldanalyse* 6 (1): 107–142.

Global Development Rights. 2013 (www.gdrights.org/calculator).

Graig, Laurene A. 1999. *Health of Nations: An International Perspective on U.S. Health Care Reform*. 3rd ed. Washington, DC: CQ Press.

Green, David G., and Benedict Irvine. 2001. *Health Care in France and Germany: Lessons for the UK*. London: Institute for the Study of Civil Society.

Grogger, Jeffrey, and Lynn A. Karoly. 2005. *Welfare Reform: Effects of a Decade of Change*. Cambridge, MA: Harvard University Press.

Hall, Anthony. 2006. "From Fome Zero to Bolsa Família: Social Policies and Poverty Alleviation under Lula." *Journal of Latin American Studies* 38 (4): 689–709.

Häusermann, Silja. 2010. *The Politics of Welfare State Reform in Continental Europe: Modernization in Hard Times*. Cambridge, UK: Cambridge University Press.

Hempel, Lamont C. 2006. "Climate Policy on the Installment Plan." In *Environmental Policy: New Directions for the Twenty-first Century*, 6th ed., edited by Norman J. Vig and Michael E. Kraft, 288–331. Washington, DC: CQ Press.

Ho, Peter, and Eduard B. Vermeer. 2006. "China's Limits to Growth? The Difference between Absolute, Relative, and Precautionary Limits." *Development and Change* 37 (1): 255–271. doi: 10.1111/j.0012-155X.2006.00477.x.

Hoffmann, Matthew J. 2011. *Climate Governance at the Crossroads: Experimenting with a Global Response after Kyoto*. Oxford, UK: Oxford University Press.

Howard, Christopher. 2007. *The Welfare State Nobody Knows: Debunking Myths about U.S. Social Policy*. Princeton, NJ: Princeton University Press.

Huber, Evelyne, and John D. Stephens. 2001. *Development and Crisis of the Welfare State: Parties and Policies in Global Markets*. Chicago: University of Chicago Press.

IPCC (Intergovernmental Panel on Climate Change). 2013. *Climate Change 2013: The Physical Science Basis* (http://www.ipcc.ch).

Johnson, Ian. 2011. "China Faces 'Very Grave' Environmental Situation, Officials Say." *New York Times*, June 3.

Johnson, Thomas R. 2008. "New Opportunities, Same Constraints: Environmental Protection and China's New Development Path." *Politics* 28 (2): 93–102. doi: 10.1111/j.1467-9256.2008.00316.x.

Kraft, Michael E., and Norman J. Vig. 2006. "Environmental Policy from the 1970s to the Twenty-first Century." In *Environmental Policy: New Directions for the Twenty-first Century*, 6th ed., edited by Norman J. Vig and Michael E. Kraft, 1–33. Washington, DC: CQ Press.

Lavinas, Lena. 2006. "From Means-Test Schemes to Basic Income in Brazil: Exceptionality and Paradox." *International Social Security Review* 59 (3): 103–125. doi: 10.1111/j.1468-246X.2006.00249.x.

Layzer, Judith A. 2006. *The Environmental Case: Translating Values into Policy*. 2nd ed. Washington, DC: CQ Press.

Lower-Basch, Elizabeth. 2011. "Cash Assistance since Welfare Reform." *TANF Policy Brief*, January 21. Washington, DC: CLASP (http://www.clasp.org/admin/site/publications/files/CashAssistance.pdf).

Marshall, T. H. 1963. *Class, Citizenship, and Social Development: Essays*. Chicago: University of Chicago Press.

McGuire, James W. 2010. *Wealth, Health, and Democracy in East Asia and Latin America*. Cambridge, UK: Cambridge University Press.

Morton, Katherine. 2006. "Surviving an Environmental Crisis: Can China Adapt?" *Brown Journal of World Affairs* 13 (1): 63–75.

OECD (Organisation for Economic Co-operation and Development). 2008. *OECD*

Factbook 2008: Economic, Environmental, and Social Statistics. Rev. ed. Paris: OECD.

———. 2011a. "Health at a Glance 2011" (http://www.oecd.org/health/health-systems/49105858.pdf).

———. 2011b. "Social Expenditure Database" (http://www.oecd.org/document/9/0,3746,en_2649_33933_38141385_1_1_1_1,00.html).

Olsen, Gregg M. 2007. "Toward Global Welfare State Convergence? Family Policy and Health Care in Sweden, Canada, and the United States." *Journal of Sociology and Social Welfare* 34 (2): 143–164.

Parks, Bradley C., and J. Timmons Roberts. 2009. "Inequality and the Global Climate Regime: Breaking the North-South Impasse." In *The Politics of Climate Change: Environmental Dynamics in International Affairs,* edited by Paul Harris, 164–191. New York: Routledge.

Pierson, Paul. 1996. "The New Politics of the Welfare State." *World Politics* 48 (2): 143–179. doi:10.1353/wp.1996.0004.

Ringquist, Evan J. 2006. "Environmental Justice: Normative Concerns, Empirical Evidence, and Government Action." In *Environmental Policy: New Directions for the Twenty-first Century,* 6th ed., edited by Norman J. Vig and Michael E. Kraft, 239–263. Washington, DC: CQ Press.

Sainsbury, Diane. 2013. "Gender, Care, and Welfare." In *The Oxford Handbook of Gender and Politics,* edited by Georgina Waylen, Karen Celis, Johanna Kantola, and S. Laurel Weldon, 313–336. Oxford, UK: Oxford University Press.

Sen, Amartya. 1999. *Development as Freedom.* New York: Knopf.

Siebert, Horst. 2005. *The German Economy: Beyond the Social Market.* Princeton, NJ: Princeton University Press.

Slack, Kristin Shook, Katherine A. Magnuson, Lawrence M. Berger, Joan Yoo, Rebekah Levine Coley, Rachel Dunifon, Amy Dworsky, et al. 2007. "Family Economic Well-Being Following the 1996 Welfare Reform: Trend Data from Five Nonexperimental Panel Studies." *Children and Youth Services Review* 29 (6): 698–720.

Smeeding, Timothy. 2005. "Government Programs and Social Outcomes: The United States in Comparative Perspective." Luxembourg Income Study Working Paper Series, Working Paper No. 426 (http://www.lisproject.org/publications/liswps/426.pdf).

Tavernise, Sabrina, and Robert Gebeloff. 2013. "Millions of Poor Are Left Uncovered by Health Law." *New York Times.* October 3 (http://www.nytimes.com/2013/10/03/health/millions-of-poor-are-left-uncovered-by-health-law.html?emc=eta1&_r=0).

UNDP (United Nations Development Programme). 2007. *Human Development Report 2007/2008: Fighting Climate Change; Human Solidarity in a Divided World.* New York: Palgrave Macmillan (http://hdr.undp.org/en/reports/global/hdr2007-8).

Vail, Mark I. 2004. "The Myth of the Frozen Welfare State and the Dynamics of Contemporary French and German Social-Protection Reform." *French Politics* 2 (2): 151–183.

World Bank. 2010. "Lifting Families out of Poverty in Brazil—Bolsa Família Program" (http://web.worldbank.org/WBSITE/EXTERNAL/NEWS/0,,contentMDK:20754490~menuPK:141310~pagePK:34370~piPK:34424~theSitePK:4607,00.html).

Wu, Joshua Su-Ya. 2009. "The State of China's Environmental Governance after the 17th Party Congress." *East Asia* 26 (4): 265–284. doi:10.1007/s12140-009-9089-9.

Yarett, Ian. 2010. "Has Anything Gotten Better since That First Earth Day?" *Newsweek,* April 26, 56.

RESOURCES FOR FURTHER STUDY

Brady, David. 2009. *Rich Democracies, Poor People: How Politics Explain Poverty*. Oxford, UK: Oxford University Press.

Donaldson, Cam, and Karen Gerard. 2005. *Economics of Health Care Financing: The Visible Hand*. New York: Palgrave Macmillan.

Goodin, Robert E., Bruce Headey, Ruud Muffels, and Henk-Jan Dirven. 1999. *The Real Worlds of Welfare Capitalism*. Cambridge, UK: Cambridge University Press.

Huber, Evelyne, and John D. Stephens. 2012. *Democracy and the Left: Social Policy and Inequality in Latin America*. Chicago: University of Chicago Press.

Jacobs, Lawrence R., and Theda Skocpol. 2010. *Health Care Reform and American Politics: What Everyone Needs to Know*. Oxford, UK: Oxford University Press.

———. 2011. "Society at a Glance 2011—OECD Social Indicators" (http://www .oecd.org/document/40/0,3746,en_2649 _37419_47507368_1_1_1_37419,00.html).

Schreuder, Yda. 2009. *The Corporate Greenhouse: Climate Change Policy in a Globalizing World*. New York: Zed Books.

WEB RESOURCES

American Human Development Project, "The Measure of America 2010–2011: Mapping Risks and Resilience"
(http://www.measureofamerica.org/the-measure-of-america-2010-2011-book)

Council on Environmental Quality, U.S. Department of Energy
(http://energy.gov/nepa/council-environmental-quality)

Organisation for Economic Co-operation and Development (OECD)
(http://www.oecd.org)

United Nations Statistics Division, Environment
(http://unstats.un.org/unsd/environment/default.htm)

U.S. Census Bureau, International Statistics
(http://www.census.gov/compendia/statab/cats/international_statistics.html)

World Health Organization, Global Health Observatory
(http://www.who.int/gho/en)

12
POLICIES AND
POLITICS OF
INCLUSION AND
CLASHING VALUES

12 POLICIES AND POLITICS OF INCLUSION AND CLASHING VALUES

KEY QUESTIONS

- When values and identities such as religion and gender clash, what does the outcome tell us about who rules?

- How do culture and institutions shape the particular demands of identity groups?

- How does globalization influence group demands for recognition and inclusion?

- What might explain why different types of secularism have developed in different countries?

- How have differences in secularism affected religious conflict and state responses to challenges from religious groups for inclusion?

Over the past fifty years, numerous groups have demanded greater inclusion in their societies and in the political process, raising a host of new policy issues. These groups include the ethnic, racial, and religious groups we discussed in chapter 4 as well as groups demanding changes to policies toward gender and sexual orientation. In many countries, these have been part of the new social movements we mentioned in chapter 7. The common element among these groups is the fundamental questions they raise about equal citizenship, particularly about individual versus group rights in democracies. States throughout the world have created new policies to try to address these concerns, and globalization has meant that even states with very little open political space or only weak demands for change have nonetheless felt pressure to address at least some of these issues.

These groups and debates raise a number of new questions in comparative politics. First, what can the policy outcomes of these debates tell us about who rules? Who seems to have most power in these policy areas? Why do particular groups make the demands they do, and why do governments respond as they do to those demands? Variation in social context and in governmental policies in these areas is certainly great, as the Country and Concept table demonstrates for our case studies. Levels of religiosity, gender equality, and acceptance of homosexuality vary widely across our

eleven cases, producing distinct dynamics that we explore throughout the chapter.

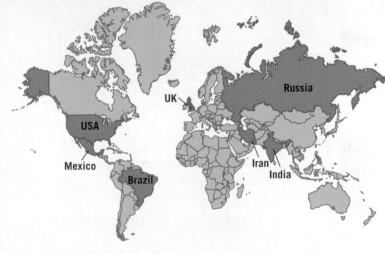

THE DEBATE OVER INCLUSION AND GROUP RIGHTS

The policy debates that these questions raise return us to issues we examined in prior chapters. Chapter 4 argued that identity-based groups desire some combination of recognition, autonomy, representation, and participation. In this chapter, we add improved social status to this list. The groups that have made these demands do so in part to achieve what we examined in chapter 3—equal citizenship—and they see better social status as part of that. Their demands for inclusion raise questions about what equal citizenship should look like. Formally or informally excluding particular groups of citizens from the political sphere threatens this fundamental democratic value. Including them, however, can cause clashes with other groups with equally strong and opposing values. While few people or governments question the legitimacy of equal treatment of all citizens regardless of ethnic or racial identity, doing the same for women, homosexuals, or transgender individuals often conflicts with deeply held religious beliefs or long-standing cultural practices. Even when the

COUNTRY AND CONCEPT
Policies and Politics of Inclusion and Clashing Values

Country	RELIGION			GENDER	
	Freedom of religion constitutionally guaranteed?*	% of respondents who say, "I am a religious person"†	Gender Inequality Index 2012 (0 = least gender disparity; 1 = greatest gender disparity)‡	Ratio of estimated female to male earned income**	Ratio of female to male adult literacy**
Brazil	Yes. ICRF score: 3	88.0	0.447	0.60	1.00
China	Yes, but very little actual freedom of religion exists, and the government tries to control religious institutions and practice. ICRF score: 1	21.8	0.213	0.68	0.91
Germany	Yes, but some small religious groups have lodged complaints about discrimination, persecution of "sects," and unfair taxation policy. ICRF score: 2.5	42.9	0.075	0.59	1.00
India	Yes, but minority Muslim and Christian populations complain of discrimination. ICRF score: 2.5	77.9	0.610	0.32	0.65
Iran	No. Islam declared official religion. ICRF score: 1	83.7	0.496	0.32	0.87
Japan	Yes. Religious corporations monitored by Ministry of Education in wake of Aum Shinrikyo attacks. ICRF ranking: 3	24.2	0.131	0.45	1.00
Mexico	Yes, but restrictions on role of churches, such as no public support for religious schools, no clergy can serve in public office, and no property ownership. Some discrimination at local level against non-Catholics. ICRF score: 2.5	75.4	0.382	0.42	0.77
Nigeria	Yes, but in practice many parts of Nigeria under *sharia*. ICRF score: 2.5	–	–	0.42	0.77
Russia	Yes, but only certain religions afforded full legal status. ICRF score: 1.5	73.6	0.312	0.64	1.00
United Kingdom	No constitution, but customary legal protection against religious discrimination. ICRF score: 4.5	48.7	0.205	0.67	1.00
United States	Yes. ICRF score: 4.5	72.1	0.256	0.62	1.00

*Information is from the International Coalition for Religious Freedom (http://www.religiousfreedom.com).

†World Values Survey data (http://www.worldvaluessurvey.org). Scores are based on a 5-point scale, with 1 being least religious freedom and 5 being most freedom.

‡The UN's Gender Inequality Index is a composite indicator that captures gender inequality in five key areas: maternal mortality, adolescent fertility, seats in national parliament, population with at least secondary education, and labor force participation rate. It ranges from 0, which indicates that women and men fare equally, to 1, which indicates that women fare as poorly as possible in all measured dimensions.

§GDI, the UN's Gender Development Index, is a composite index that measures human development in the same dimensions as the Human Development Index (HDI) while adjusting for gender inequality in those basic dimensions. These dimensions are a long and healthy life, access to

SEXUALITY

Laws against homosexuality[††]	Status of gay marriage	% of respondents who say that "homosexuality is never justifiable"[‡‡]	% of respondents who say that "homosexuality is always justifiable"[‡‡]
No.	Legal as of 2013.	31.8	9.6
No.	Not legal.	78.1	1.5
No. Some laws against discrimination; some states have constitutional protections.	Not legal, but registered partnership exists.	10.5	27.1
No. Same-sex intercourse decriminalized in 2009.	No laws allowing or prohibiting same-sex marriage, and widespread reports that such marriages occur.	63.7	9.3
Yes, punishable by prison term or possibly death.	Not legal.	82.3	1.3
No. Some laws against discrimination exist.	Not legal.	24.2	9.1
No. Some laws against discrimination exist.	Not legal nationwide, but allowed in Mexico City and the state of Quintana Roo.	34.4	13.4
Yes. In areas governed by *sharia*, punishable by death.	Not legal.	–	–
No. Some laws against discrimination exist, but law banning "homosexual propaganda" passed in 2013.	Not legal.	66.4	4.5
No. Laws against discrimination exist.	Legal.	20.3	21.7
No. Some discrimination legal.	Legal in 13 states and the District of Columbia, but banned in 35 states.	32.5	14.8

knowledge, and a decent standard of living. These basic dimensions are measured separately for females and males in the GDI by life expectancy at birth; adult literacy and combined gross enrollment in primary, secondary, and tertiary level education; and estimated earned income per capita in PPP US$, respectively. See UN *Human Development Report 2009*, Table J (http://hdr.undp.org/en/media/HDR_2009_EN_Table_J.pdf).

**Data are from UN *Human Development Report 2009* (http://hdrstats.undp.org/en/indicators/130.html).

[††]Data are from Daniel Ottosson, "LGBT World Legal Wrap Up Survey," May 2010. Available at http://old.ilga.org/Statehomophobia/ILGA_State_Sponsored_Homophobia_2010.pdf. See also http://www.ilga.org/statehomophobia/LGBcriminallaws-Daniel_Ottoson.pdf.

[‡‡]Response to World Values Survey question: "Please tell me for each of the following statements whether you think it can always be justified, never be justified, or something in between?"

principle of equal citizenship is not questioned, major controversies arise over what the state must and can do to help ensure equal status and what "equal treatment" means.

The Demands of Identity Groups

The first demand identity groups usually make is for recognition. They want the state and the rest of society to recognize them as distinct groups with distinct and legitimate concerns. They usually seek legal rights at least equal to other citizens. While the last vestige of legalized racial discrimination was eliminated with the end of apartheid in South Africa in 1994, legal discrimination against women, especially in areas of property ownership and family law, remains fairly common, and legal discrimination against homosexuals is the norm in most of the world.

Members of ethnic or religious groups also sometimes seek autonomy to control their own affairs, either in a particular region where they are in the majority or over areas of their lives influenced by cultural traditions or religious beliefs, such as family law and property rights.

A third demand that virtually all groups make is for representation and full participation in the political process. This is initially a simple legal matter of ensuring basic political rights, but it often becomes more complicated and controversial as groups question whether they are truly being allowed to participate on an equal footing with other citizens and whether institutional changes are necessary for them to achieve that equality.

A final demand we add in this chapter is for better social status. Virtually all groups that mobilize to make demands for inclusion on the basis of identity begin in a socially marginalized position: they are typically poorer and less educated than the average citizen and may be socially segregated as well. Harkening back to T. H. Marshall's (1963) ideas of the social rights of citizenship (see chapter 3), they argue that they need better education and economic positions and greater respect from and acceptance in society as a whole. How to achieve those improvements has proven quite controversial in many countries.

Equal citizenship is not the only value involved in policies of inclusion. Demands for inclusion often produce confrontations among competing values. Historically, demands for racial or ethnic equality gave rise to such conflicts: many white supporters of apartheid in South Africa and Jim Crow laws in the southern United States believed that racial mixing would threaten the well-being of society as a whole. In the contemporary world, most such conflicts are between religious or cultural beliefs, on the one hand, and claims for equality across genders or sexual orientations on the other. Recent controversies over gay marriage are just the latest in a long history of clashes of deeply held values.

POLITICS OF INCLUSION AND THE MODERN STATE

The questions these policies raise are so profound and so central to liberal democracy that numerous political philosophers have developed arguments centered on which policies of inclusion should be pursued and why. Most of this debate has taken place in the context of democratic theory: normative theories about how democracy ought to work. It has clear implications, though, for any modern state, since all modern states grapple with the demands of mobilized groups asking for greater inclusion. At the heart of the debate is the question of individual versus group rights. Liberal democracy in its classic formulation is based on individual rights and the equal treatment of all citizens. As we saw in chapter 3, it took the better part of two centuries to implement this idea in basic legal terms before getting to the contemporary debates liberal regimes face over what true inclusion means.

Arguments for Group Rights

Some theorists argue, however, that individual rights, no matter how fully respected, will never allow full inclusion of culturally distinct or socially marginalized groups. Social or cultural differences mean that legal equality alone cannot facilitate real inclusion for these groups. More must be done, usually in the form of rights for or preferential policies that target the distinct needs and weak social position of particular groups. Theorists making these arguments support policies of several types: (1) recognizing and actively supporting the preservation of distinct cultures; (2) granting some degree of governing autonomy to particular groups; (3) reforming representative institutions such as electoral systems and political parties to enhance or guarantee participation and officeholding for members of particular groups; and (4) actively intervening to improve the socioeconomic status of distinct groups, usually via government intervention in the market. Opponents argue that such "special" group rights or preferences undermine the norm of equal citizenship, serve to perpetuate a group's distinct and therefore unequal position, and threaten the common identity and bonds on which citizenship and national identity are based.

Two of the most prominent advocates of group rights and preferences are political theorists Will Kymlicka (1995) and Iris Marion Young (2000). Both argued from within the tradition of liberal democratic theory, but they suggested that in certain circumstances group rights are not only justified but also essential to achieve full inclusion of all citizens. Kymlicka claimed that minority cultures must be recognized and granted certain collective rights because the individual autonomy on which liberal democracy is based entails freedom to choose among various options in life, and those options can only be understood within the context of a particular culture. Culture gives individuals the means to understand the world and their role in it, providing them with the means to choose how to act and what to believe. For this reason, among others, people deeply value their cultures and are justified in doing so.

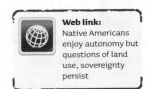

Web link:
Native Americans enjoy autonomy but questions of land use, sovereignty persist

Kymlicka contended that collective rights for minority cultures are justified "to limit the economic or political power exercised by the larger society over the group, to ensure that the resources and institutions on which the minority depends are not vulnerable to majority decisions" (1995, 7). This is particularly true for minority groups that are part of preexisting cultures incorporated into larger states, such as Native

Americans in the United States; these groups not only deserve protection within the larger society but also, if they wish, some degree of autonomy to preserve their culture. Even for immigrants and other minority groups, though, Kymlicka favored cultural support and protection, arguing that most people find it very difficult to cross cultural barriers fully and so, without recognition and protection of their distinct cultures, they will not be able to participate completely in the larger society and make the choices on which democratic citizenship depends.

Kymlicka and coauthor Wayne Norman (2000) argued for **multicultural integration** rather than assimilation. The latter, as practiced in the United States and elsewhere, has the goal of eventually integrating immigrants' cultures into the larger culture of the whole society. Conversely, multicultural integration

> does not have the intent or expectation of eliminating other cultural differences between subgroups in the state. Rather, it accepts that ethnocultural identities matter to citizens, will endure over time, and must be recognized and accommodated within [political] institutions. The hope is that citizens from different backgrounds can all recognize themselves, and feel at home, within such institutions. (14)

Kymlicka and Norman drew inspiration from the **communitarian** philosophical tradition, which argues that humans are inherently social and political animals and therefore can only function well in strongly bonded communities. Public policy, therefore, should not be neutral toward communities, including cultural ones, but should actively work to strengthen them. Communitarians argue that liberals fail to recognize that citizens are bearers not only of rights but also of responsibilities to the larger community on which they depend. Some communitarians have been accused of being willing to forsake some individual rights, especially freedom of expression and gender equality, in favor of strengthening communities. Kymlicka and Norman, though, were clear that only cultural practices that do not violate fundamental liberal rights should be allowed and encouraged via multicultural integration.

Young (2000) offered a different approach to justifying group rights. She focused not on identity and culture but rather on what she termed "structural social groups," or groups of people who share a structural position and therefore similar experience in social and political institutions. A structural position can be based on economic position, physical attributes, or a variety of other factors. Structural groups can therefore overlap with cultural groups but are not the same thing. She argued that collective rights or preferences for such groups are justified in the interests of justice and greater democracy. Democracy, she suggested, should have as one of its primary goals the seeking of justice. This is a form of what is termed **deliberative democracy**—that is, democracy that asks citizens not only to assume their rights and minimally participate through voting but also to engage actively in democratic discussion in the effort to build a better society.

Deliberative democracy, Young argued, is enhanced and justice is more likely to be attained when all important social perspectives are included in the discussion. She further argued that groups in structurally marginalized positions are typically not

multicultural integration
Accepts that ethnocultural identities matter to citizens, will endure over time, and must be recognized and accommodated within political institutions; in contrast to assimilation

communitarianism
Philosophical tradition supporting the argument that humans are inherently social and political animals and thus can only function well in strongly bonded communities

Video link:
What kind of democracy do we want?

deliberative democracy
Democracy that asks citizens not only to assume their rights and minimally participate through voting but also to engage actively in democratic discussion in the effort to build a better society

included unless governments intervene to ensure that they are. Her goal was inclusive democracy:

> Inclusion ought not to mean simply the formal and abstract equality of all members of the polity of citizens. It means explicitly acknowledging social differentiations and divisions and encouraging differently situated groups to give voice to their needs, interests, and perspectives. (2000, 119)

Young's version of deliberative democracy draws on feminist theory. Modern feminism began philosophically to examine women and their structurally marginalized position but over time came to recognize that other groups were in similar structurally marginalized positions. Feminists concluded that policy needed to take those positions into account for true equality to be achieved. Not only legal equality but the recognition of and appropriate response to differences across groups are essential.

Young's position leads her to favor adjusting political discussion and debate to recognize and value the forms of communication that marginalized groups, such as women or speakers of different languages, are often more comfortable using. She also suggested that if a history of discrimination or current practices prevents members of marginalized social groups from being elected or appointed to political positions, some reform is warranted. This could take the form of rules for how parties select candidates, reserved legislative seats for particular groups, reserved positions on appointed boards for particular groups, or the drawing of electoral districts to increase the likelihood that members of particular groups will be elected.

Arguments against Group Rights

Critics of group rights make several arguments in response to Kymlicka, Young, and others. The classic liberal position is that only individuals can have rights and all individuals should have them equally. This implies support for government policies of nondiscrimination, but it does not justify giving distinct rights or preferences to members of particular groups or treating them differently in any other way. Once legal equality is achieved, individuals are and should be free to pursue political participation as they desire and are able. The state should not intervene in any way in response to either cultural or social differences, which, even if acknowledged to exist, are beyond the state's rightful purview.

Indeed, proponents of civic nationalism (see chapter 4) fear that group rights will undermine political stability and democracy, both of which, they argue, require a common identity, a shared set of values, or both. Nationalism underlies the development of the modern state and of democracy, and each state is given international legitimacy as a representative of "a people." A sense of commonality, then, is essential to domestic and international legitimacy for all states. Civic nationalists see group rights and preferences as divisive and fear that acknowledging and accommodating them will preserve differences rather than encourage commonality. This in turn will ultimately

Video link:
The disuniting of America

Web link:
Roosevelt bars the hyphenated

undermine political stability and make democratic discussion difficult because of a lack of common values.

A third, but similar, strand of criticism of group rights comes from proponents of deliberative democracy who suggest that the goal of democratic discussion should not be the representation of particular interests and bargaining among them but instead should be the achievement of a collectively defined common good. Giving special rights or preferences to particular groups will encourage them to pursue their own interests, and others will respond in kind, diverting attention from the common good.

Finally, all liberal theorists ask, To what extent can and should group rights be supported if those groups pursue goals contrary to a state's liberal ideals? Should a religious group that explicitly opposes equal rights for men and women not only be allowed to participate in the political process but be given specific preferences?

These theoretical arguments lie behind the many concrete policy debates that face contemporary states. These debates take different forms in different societies, depending on which groups have demanded inclusion, how they have done so, and the nature of the regime. While many of the overtly political goals of representation and participation seem relevant only in democracies, even leaders in authoritarian regimes face pressure to include members of marginalized groups in positions of authority. We examine the most controversial contemporary debates in this chapter: those involving religion, gender, and sexual orientation.

RELIGION: RECOGNITION, AUTONOMY, AND THE SECULAR STATE

Religion is both the oldest and, in a sense, newest basis for questions of inclusion and clashing values. As we noted in chapter 3, religious divisions within Christianity in early modern Europe led to civil wars and the emergence of liberalism. Eventually, secular states became universal in Western societies, which, at least in theory, relocated religion into the private sphere. The secular state reached its zenith after World War II and the onset of independence of numerous secular states across Africa and Asia. In the past generation, however, and with renewed emphasis since the terrorist attacks of September 11, 2001, religion has again become a major issue in almost all societies. As we noted in chapter 4, religious groups typically seek recognition and autonomy first and foremost.

The vast majority of the world's states are officially secular, with most of the exceptions being in the Middle East. Secularism, however, takes many different forms in principle, and its implementation does not always match those principles. The key relationship is between the state and organized religious groups such as churches and religious associations. In liberal democracies, few question the right of citizens to practice any religion they choose in the private sphere (with the possible exception of religious practices that break other kinds of laws, such as those against drug use or polygamy). In most societies, religious groups may organize, build houses of worship, and do charitable work as they desire. Controversies arise over what role, if any, the state should play in this process and what role, if any, the religious groups should play in secular politics and policy.

The Different Forms of Secularism

Several approaches to secularism exist today. These approaches reflect the broader debate over multiculturalism and group rights. Some argue that the state should be absolutely neutral toward all religious practice that does not violate basic liberal principles: individuals should be free to pursue their religious beliefs but should receive no assistance or support from the state to do so, no matter who they are. Others argue that the state should recognize and in certain situations support or protect religious groups, especially those that are minorities or marginalized. Following the ideas of multicultural integration, they see a need for certain group rights aimed at particular religious groups in order to enhance both their autonomy and their ability to participate fully in the broader society.

The version of secularism most familiar to Americans we might call the **neutral state model**: the state should be neutral about, but not opposed to, religion. Religious perspectives in secular politics are treated the same as any other perspectives, with the state (at least in theory) being a neutral arbiter that does not choose sides in the debate. This form of secularism stems from the earliest days of the United States, when thirteen colonies with different predominant branches of Christianity (in many cases, officially recognized by the individual colonial governments) had to find a way to live together. The English civil war just over a century earlier illustrated the price paid by a state that was not neutral. Recent controversies in the United States have therefore involved actions that seem to question this neutrality, such as posting the Ten Commandments in courtrooms or public school classrooms, or requiring children to pray in school or learn about creationism in addition to or instead of the theory of evolution. Other controversies implicate the state in actively supporting religion, such as government funding for religious groups' charitable work; abstinence programs in schools in lieu of sex education courses; or incentives for individuals to marry rather than have sexual relations, and possibly children, out of wedlock.

neutral state model
A model of secularism wherein the state is neutral about, but not opposed to, religion

Audio link:
Supreme Court case puts public prayer back in the spotlight

A more absolute version of secularism the French call *laïcité*. It developed in societies whose political origins lay in a battle to separate the state from a single, dominant religion. France, Turkey, and our case study of Mexico are all examples of this. The French and Mexican revolutions and the establishment of the modern state in Turkey after the demise of the Ottoman Empire each involved the creation of a secular republic independent of the politically powerful Catholic Church in France and Mexico and the Islamic caliphate in Turkey. The result was a secularism advocating that religion should play no part in the public realm. The state is not neutral toward religions but rather is actively opposed to religion having any role in the public sphere. Private religious practice remains acceptable, as long as it is kept private. Religious references in political discourse, while not illegal in most cases, are nonetheless considered

laïcité
A model of secularism advocating that religion should play no part in the public realm

Islamic Headscarves in France and Turkey

France is at least nominally largely Christian, but it is home to the largest Muslim population in Europe, most of whom are immigrants from North Africa. The population of Turkey is nearly all Muslim. Both countries have faced considerable controversy over young women wearing Islamic headscarves to school. The issue aroused such passion in part because each state's sense of national identity includes its particular conception of secularism; any questioning of it threatens national identity itself.

In October 1989, the principal of a junior high school in a Paris suburb expelled three Muslim girls for wearing the *hijab,* the Muslim headscarf, in school. This immediately became a major national controversy that pitted defenders of *laïcité* and feminists, who viewed the headscarf as a form of oppression, against defenders of religious freedom and multicultural understanding. The government ultimately determined that religious symbols could be worn in schools unless "by their nature . . . or by their ostentatious or protesting character . . . [they] disturb the order or normal functioning of public services" (Fetzer and Soper 2005, 79). Given the vagueness of this language, dozens of Muslim girls were expelled from school, so the controversy continued. In 2003 Conservative president Jacques Chirac finally appointed a commission on *laïcité* that recommended completely banning the wearing of all "conspicuous religious symbols" in schools. After heated debate, the French parliament passed this into law in 2004, and since then, more Muslim girls have been banned from school for wearing the *hijab.* Critics contend that the law is an anti-Muslim attack on religious freedom, since students have long worn small crosses and yarmulkes to school without incident. Supporters argue that the law is essential to the preservation of a secular republic under the threat of encroaching Islamist ideology and to the preservation of French gender equality.

More recently, the *burqa,* the full-body and full-face covering worn by some Muslim women, has also become controversial. In 2010 parliament passed a ban on wearing the *burqa* in public places because it saw the garb as contradicting the French ideals of *laïcité,* equality between the sexes, and *fraternité* (brotherhood), allowing an exception only for places of worship. Most Muslims argued against the ban, saying it would further marginalize them from mainstream French life. Critics also noted that fewer than two thousand women in the entire country regularly wear the *burqa;* they suggested that the campaign was more about political leaders appealing to nationalist sentiments to gain political support, and

"Islamophobia," than it was about an actual policy problem. This move came as several other European countries passed similar bans, the Swiss passed a referendum prohibiting the building of mosques with minarets, and the United States vociferously debated whether to allow the opening of an Islamic education center and mosque near the former World Trade Center site in New York City.

In Turkey, as in France, secularism is tied deeply to national identity. Kemal Atatürk founded the modern Turkish state after World War I based on an explicit campaign to modernize and Westernize the country, in part by eliminating the role of Islam in the former seat of the Muslim caliphate and Ottoman Empire. Whenever Muslim parties that called for Turkey to recognize its place in the Muslim Middle East gained too much power, they were banned or the military carried out a coup. The Muslim headscarf on women, though, was not banned in universities and government offices until 1981, and the ban wasn't regularly enforced until after the military forced an Islamist government out of power in 1998.

A new Islamist party, the Justice and Development Party (JDP), arose in 2001, led by the popular, charismatic mayor of Istanbul, Tayyip Erdoğan. In contrast to past Islamist parties, the JDP modified the call for an end to Westernization. While preserving its embrace of Islamic principles on social issues, it also supported globalization, economic modernization tied to the West, and Turkey's application to join the European Union. This garnered it greater support than prior Islamic parties; it won the 2002 national election and has been the ruling party since.

The JDP came to power promising to allow women to wear headscarves more widely, including in universities, but it did not pass legislation to that effect until February 2008. The secular elite reacted swiftly. Millions of secularists held pro-ban demonstrations, and the Constitutional Court ruled in June 2008 that the new law was unconstitutional. The public prosecutor filed a case asking the Constitutional Court to ban the JDP and seventy of its top leaders for violating Turkey's secular principles. In 2009, however, the court ruled in favor of the party, and it remained in power. After winning a referendum in 2010 to amend the constitution, the JDP government felt it had the political strength to stop enforcing the ban on headscarves in universities. While it has not changed the constitution further, women are now allowed to wear headscarves at universities. Furthermore, the prime minister stated in 2013 that the state would allow female public officials and civil servants to wear headscarves, though the constitutionality of that is a point of contention and could result in a court ruling in the future. In 2013, women MPs were allowed to wear headscarves in parliament for the first time.

Because American conceptions of secularism involve neutrality on the part of the state but not restrictions on the public display of religion, Americans often find it odd that a simple headscarf would provoke a major political crisis on two continents. The huge controversy over locating an Islamic center near the site of the former World Trade Center, though, should give Americans some feel for the powerful emotions that can be unleashed by religious symbols. French and Turkish secularism have long envisioned a strictly secular public sphere, a vision that rising Islamic sentiment is challenging. Both states have reacted by restricting women's ability to wear clothing that symbolizes their Islamic faith, though by 2013 Turkey was moving toward fewer restrictions while France was moving toward more. As we noted in chapter 4, what women do and wear often become symbolic markers of national identity. A similar debate emerged after the 2011 "Jasmine revolution" in Tunisia. The long-banned Islamist party quickly emerged as a powerful political force, and women increasingly donned headscarves in what had been the most secular Arab state, raising concerns among secularists that the revolution would result in a religious "takeover" of government.

inappropriate. In practice, not all of these societies have enforced this doctrine strictly; in France, for instance, the state supports many Catholic schools as long as they follow secular state educational guidelines. In Turkey, the state is more actively involved in actually controlling various aspects of religious practice among Sunni Muslims, who make up the vast majority of the population. Controversies arise in this type of secularism when a religious group seeks an independent public role for its religious beliefs, as the case of Islamic girls wearing veils in France and Turkey demonstrates.

A third variant of secularism Alfred Stepan (2011) termed **positive accommodation**. It sees the state as neutral among but willing to support religions that it recognizes as important elements in civil society. Our case study of Germany is the classic model of this type. Following its corporatist tradition, Germany since the end of World War II has officially recognized various Judeo-Christian faiths, the leaders of which register with the government to gain recognition. The state even collects a tax on their behalf to help fund them, and they help administer some of Germany's extensive welfare programs. Controversies in this type of secular state involve deciding which religious groups gain recognition and how they have to be organized to do so. Most Sunni Islamic sects, for instance, are nonhierarchical, which means that each mosque is independent. This has raised questions in Germany about if and how the state should recognize Muslim groups the way it has Judeo-Christian ones. (Several pilot programs have been instituted in recent years to address this situation.)

A model related to "positive accommodation" is the established religion model of Scandinavia and our case study of Britain. In relatively religiously homogeneous societies such as these, the state has long recognized an official church. In modern, secular democracies, however, this recognition has become largely symbolic, in that other religions are not actively discriminated against. Like under positive accommodation, the state might fund religious schools, for instance, but not exclusively those of the established church. As our case study of Britain below demonstrates, the questions under this model are similar to those under positive accommodation: Under what

Video link:
French
headscarf ban

positive accommodation
A model of secularism wherein the state is neutral among but willing to support religions that it recognizes as important elements in civil society

Web link:
Germany moves to recognize Islam

circumstances are religions recognized and accommodated? The established religion model, of course, also has nondemocratic versions, such as in Saudi Arabia, where the regime's legitimacy is tied closely to its support of a particular version of Islam, and key clerics play important roles in establishing laws on personal behavior that follow their interpretation of *sharia*.

These models of secularism arose first in Europe and North America, but most postcolonial states are also officially secular, while making various accommodations for religions. On the whole, perhaps the biggest difference between African and Asian states, in particular, and European states is that the former are much more religious, as the Country and Concept table (pages 642–643) indicates for most of our case study countries. Stepan (2011) argued that in our case study of India, among others, a new model of secularism has arisen, what he termed the "respect all, positive accommodation, principled distance" model. The state in multi-religious societies under this model attempts to respect and give autonomy to all major religions but also includes an element of "positive accommodation" in terms of state funding of religions. Philosophically, it closely resembles Kymlicka's multicultural integration in the sense that particular groups may be given particular rights in the interests of both social harmony and their inclusion in the broader society. As our case study of India below demonstrates, that can be a difficult process in practice.

Web link:
An interview about religion and democracy

Challenges to the Secular State

Religious groups worldwide have challenged the secular state in all its forms. In seeking recognition and autonomy, they are typically interested in gaining official status in countries where that is important, including the teaching of their religion in public schools, establishing and gaining support for their own parochial schools, gaining legal recognition of their religious holidays, using religious symbols and ideas in the public sphere, and being allowed to practice their own religious law in personal and family matters. Some of these simply require the state to include a new religious group in policies it already pursues toward other religious groups. Other groups, though, want more. They ask that the state be less secular in one way or another, or that it set policies preferential to their religion over others.

Europe has been the site of some of the most vociferous debates over demands from religious groups. Increasing Muslim immigration has made the place of Islam in these primarily secular and historically Christian societies a major issue in policy circles and in comparative politics. Islam now constitutes the third-largest religion in Europe after Catholicism and Protestantism, and as Muslims have settled in the region, their demands for the right to build mosques that look like the mosques in the countries from which they came, to establish Muslim schools, to have women wear veils in public, to have their religious holidays celebrated as official holidays, and to include their religious teachings in secular school curricula have echoed across the continent.

European states have responded in various ways to these demands, and Muslim groups seem to have been more successful in some countries than in others. Social movement theorists have tried to explain these differences by looking at the resources and political opportunities the new Muslim groups have at their disposal. Resource mobilization theorists suggest that Muslim groups are often decentralized and financially weak, meaning that most have had limited success at convincing European states to change their policies. Those that are somewhat wealthier and more hierarchically organized have been more successful. Political opportunity theorists argue the difference depends on what openings different European governments allow. For instance, in Germany far fewer Muslims are given citizenship than in Britain, so British Muslims have the opportunity to have greater influence. Similarly, the more centralized political system and parties in France mean Muslims have had to focus on national-level politics, whereas in Britain local government is a more important political arena and Muslims have been able to win some policy battles at the local level.

Joel Fetzer and Christopher Soper (2005) argued that the most important explanation of all, however, is the legacy of past church-state relations. Germany's formal recognition of several religious groups has led Muslims there to ask for the same, to become part of the system, and to organize themselves in a manner that allows the German state to recognize them. Germany's long-standing church-state relationships have shaped not only the government's response to the Muslims but also what Muslim groups have requested. Similarly, the presence of the official Church of England and the tradition of teaching religion in both religious and secular schools have meant that Britain has been willing to include the study of Islam in its secular school curriculum and has been more willing to fund Muslim schools than has France.

Religious demands have provoked debates far beyond Europe, however. We investigate some of them in three quite distinct case studies of secular states: the United Kingdom, India, and Mexico.

CASE Study

UNITED KINGDOM: RELIGIOUS CHALLENGE TO MULTICULTURALISM

London is one of the most racially, culturally, and religiously diverse places on Earth. After centuries of relative homogeneity, since World War II and decolonization Britain has been the recipient of large-scale immigration from its former colonies in the Caribbean, South Asia, and Africa. The 1960s gave witness to

- **TYPE OF SECULARISM**
  Established church; multiculturalism as official policy

- **MAJOR RELIGIOUS GROUPS**
  Muslims, primarily from South Asia

- **MAJOR RELIGIOUS ISSUES**
  Recognition and state funding of Islamic schools; antiterrorism laws

multiculturalism
The belief that different cultures in a society ought to be respected; in the United Kingdom, the policy governing how the state treats racial and religious minorities

Conservative member of Parliament (MP) Enoch Powell's thinly veiled racist call for the end of immigration to preserve the white Briton heritage and well-being, on the one hand, and the adoption of an official policy of **multiculturalism**, on the other. Britain's multiculturalism policy

> encouraged cultural groups to create their own organizational structures, to safeguard their customs and religious practices as they saw fit, and to introduce an awareness of and celebration for Britain's cultural pluralism into the state education system. (Fetzer and Soper 2005, 30)

Until very recently, however, this policy was focused almost exclusively on race and culture, not religion. Antidiscrimination laws on the basis of race became national policy in the 1960s, but not until December 2003 did the government make discrimination on the basis of religion illegal. Since the 1980s, British Muslims have increasingly sought inclusion as a religious group, and their goals have included recognition, support, and some degree of autonomy. They have sought greater inclusion of their religion in school curricula, funding for their own schools, and rights to practice their faith publicly without discrimination.

Britain's unusual immigration history produced the challenges it faces today in dealing with religious diversity. From 1948 to 1962, citizens of the Commonwealth (the former British colonies) could immigrate to Britain and automatically gain rights equal to those of British citizens. Starting in 1962, it became more difficult for Commonwealth citizens to immigrate, based on explicit fears that too many nonwhite immigrants were arriving, but the migrants already in the country retained the right to bring their families to join them, which many did. By far the largest number of these came from South Asia, and many of them were Muslim.

Muslims now represent about 5 percent of Britain's population and have founded more than one thousand mosques and many educational associations. Muslims

Muslim men break the fast on the last day of Ramadan in August 2013. Some estimate that there are more observant Muslims in the country than there are observant members of the Church of England. Muslims' growing demands for recognition, especially in the educational sphere, and concerns about terrorism, have created major controversies in multicultural Britain.

remain socially and economically marginalized in several ways, however. The number of Muslims in British prisons has tripled since 1997; they constitute about 13 percent of the nation's prisoners, nearly three times their share of the overall population. Residential segregation continues to predominate in most British cities, and Bangladeshis and Pakistanis, who constitute three-quarters of Britain's Muslims, are the poorest demographic group in the country. Their children also perform more poorly in school than do other groups. In 2013 a series of four bombings of mosques raised questions about growing anti-Muslim sentiment.

Britain's policy of multiculturalism originally focused on race. By the 1980s, a "black" political movement had grown that attempted to group all people who were not white under one political and racial umbrella. While this new identity was popular among people of Caribbean descent, far fewer South Asians accepted it; many began to identify more with their religion than their racial or cultural heritage. The event that made clear to all that religion, not race, was becoming the most important identity for Britain's Muslims was the controversy over Salman Rushdie's novel *The Satanic Verses*. Rushdie is a British, Pakistani novelist who was already well known in literary circles when he published his controversial novel in 1988. Many religious Muslims of various sects were offended by the novel's portrayal of the Prophet Mohammed and his family, and Iran's Ayatollah Ruhollah Khomeini, among other leaders, issued a *fatwa* (religious ruling) condemning Rushdie. Large-scale protests broke out across Britain, and numerous Muslim organizations united to demand that the book be banned. This produced a major political backlash in the name of free speech that a large number of non-Muslim blacks readily joined. Many Muslims concluded from the experience that their interests diverged from those of the black community, even though virtually all British Muslims are also racial minorities.

Muslim organizations were well established long before the Rushdie affair, however: the first umbrella organization, the Union of Muslim Organizations, began in the 1970s, and the Council of Mosques was established in the 1980s. The political prominence of such organizations grew substantially in the 1990s, as Muslims came to identify with their religion more than with their ethnicity or race. Surveys show that British Muslims are more closely identified with their religion than Muslims in much of the rest of Europe: 80 percent think of themselves as Muslims first and British second and are worried about the decline of religious values in Britain. This did not mean, however, that they support an Islamist ideology that questions the legitimacy of the secular state. To the contrary, most of Britain's Muslims follow the Hanafi school of Sunni Islam, which respects the *ulema* (clerics) and *sharia* but also the sovereignty of the secular state. They generally have a favorable view of their government and are actually more trusting of it than are British Christians (Allen and Wike 2009, 155–156; Maxwell 2010). Individually, Muslims are very active politically. Most are British citizens, and in Britain immigrants from the Commonwealth have the right to vote. Indeed, Muslims vote at higher percentages than do white Britons. Given that most

Web link:
A tale of two mayors

Web link:
British Muslims and local democracy: after Bradford

Web link:
Taking part: Muslim participation in contemporary governance

Muslims live in urban areas (40 percent in London alone), many have been elected to local urban offices. In 2010, eight Muslims were elected MPs, including the first three women Muslim MPs and two from the Conservative Party (almost all have been Labour MPs). That is still barely more than 1 percent of the Parliament, however, far below full representation for 5 percent of the population.

Participation, though, has not produced complete satisfaction of all their demands. Muslim associations seek recognition and the right to religious equality. A key area of dispute has been education. The Church of England (also called the Anglican Church in the United Kingdom or the Episcopal Church in the United States) is by law the country's official church and faith. This means relatively little now, but it has left an important institutional legacy in church-state relations. The British education system, even in public schools, includes religious instruction. Historically, this meant the teaching of Anglican beliefs. The Anglican Church runs many state-funded schools, especially at the primary level. They are required to teach the same national curriculum as nonreligious state schools. Muslim parents placed their children in these highly regarded church schools, but they increasingly resented the Christian elements of the education. Since the 1980s, the government has encouraged local school authorities to include religious instruction that reflects the school's community. This has meant including Islamic instruction in areas with heavy Muslim populations, though this process has been long and slow, requiring significant agitation by Muslims at the local level. Local *ulema* have been actively involved in urging and assisting schools to incorporate Islamic education (Fetzer and Soper 2005).

The heavily secular nature of British education, however, has become a growing concern to many Muslims, who responded by creating a movement to found separate Muslim schools. The movement began in the 1970s, and by 2010 there were 151 Islamic schools across the country (Fetzer and Soper 2005, 44). In the late 1980s, a few of these started petitioning the government for funding parallel to that received by Christian and Jewish schools. After initial resistance, the Labour Party government officially approved the United Kingdom's first state funding for Muslim schools in 1997; by 2010, 11 Muslim schools had received state funding (out of 7,000 state-funded religious schools in the country). These institutions must comply with the established national curriculum just like all other religious schools.

Like all religious groups, British Muslim organizations have worked to achieve government recognition in various areas of everyday life. They were less successful in areas other than education until quite recently. This is reflected in the fact that not until the 2001 census were people asked what their religious affiliation was; prior to that, estimates of Muslims and Hindus were based on the census's racial and ethnic information. Discrimination in employment on the basis of religion was made illegal in 2003, and then only because EU provisions required it. In October 2007, the Equality and Human Rights Commission was created, with a mandate to work "to eliminate discrimination, reduce inequality, protect human rights and to build good relations" on the basis of not only race, gender, and disability but also "age, sexual orientation and religion or belief, as well as human rights" (Local Government Improvement and Development 2011). In 2013, the issue of Muslim women wearing full-face veils arose in Britain when a college tried to ban them.

This new recognition of religion as an important category for inclusive citizenship comes in the shadow of the September 11, 2001, attacks in the United States and the July 7, 2005, London subway bombings carried out by British-born Muslims. Responding to both, the Labour government enacted terrorism acts that give the state much greater latitude to investigate and detain, without charges, citizens or foreigners suspected of being or assisting terrorists. Many British Muslims felt threatened by these new laws. Indeed, between September 2001 and September 2004, 664 people had been held in detention without being charged or given a trial, almost all of them Muslim (Modood 2006, 46–47). The Conservative–Liberal Democrat government that came to power in 2010 modified the antiterrorism laws in 2011, reducing detention to the previous fourteen-day maximum and softening other restrictions as well.

The terrorist bombings and debate over Islamic schools have brought to the fore new questions regarding Britain's official "multiculturalism." Critics contend the policy reinforces segregation rather than integration by encouraging ethnic and religious groups to focus on their distinct identities. Critics point to the Netherlands, which has reversed what was a strongly stated multicultural policy. Prime Minister Cameron (2010–) has questioned whether multiculturalism as a policy goal should continue at all. Uberoi and Modood (2013), however, argued that these debates and pressures do not represent a wholesale repudiation of the policy but a rethinking of it. They claimed that British political leaders of both major parties are actively trying to create a more inclusive definition of "Britishness" that is a multicultural form of civic nationalism. The debate over how multicultural British policy should be seems likely to continue.

CASE Summary Since the 1980s British Muslims have become a significant political force. They have used Britain's multiculturalism policy, which long ignored religion, to include Islam in school curricula and to gain state funding for some Muslim schools. Individually, many have become active participants in the political process as well. Nonetheless, British Muslims remain overrepresented in prisons, underrepresented in Parliament, poorer, less educated, and residentially segregated. In this context, a minority of young Muslim Britons have become alienated and attracted to more radical versions of Islam, a problem that will continue to challenge the British government as it attempts, belatedly, to recognize and work to include Muslims as full citizens. The great majority of British Muslims believe in nonviolent versions of Islam, and they condemned terrorism even as they protested Britain's participation in the invasions of Afghanistan and Iraq. They are both British and Muslim, a relatively new and complex identity category that British society still struggles to understand, accept, and accommodate.

CASE Questions

1. What does the British case teach us about how religious groups can be successful at achieving political demands? Is it because of the resources at their disposal, political opportunities, or the nature of the preexisting relationship between the state and religious groups?

2. What does the British case teach us about why and how politicized identity groups form? Why did South Asian immigrants to Britain ultimately identify more with their religious than their cultural heritage?

CASE Study

INDIA: SECULARISM IN A RELIGIOUS AND RELIGIOUSLY PLURAL SOCIETY

On February 27, 2002, a train full of Hindus returning from a pilgrimage to a disputed Hindu temple unexpectedly stopped in a small town in Gujarat, a western state in India and the birthplace of Mahatma Gandhi. A Muslim mob set the train on fire, killing fifty-eight passengers. In response, Hindu nationalists called for a massive protest, which the state government supported. The protest quickly became a rampage against Muslims and their businesses; as many as 2,000 Muslims were killed and 150,000 displaced, and for three days the police did nothing to stop the violence.

This was only part of the most recent round of major religious violence in India, the world's largest and officially secular democracy. Religious divisions led to the partition of India and Pakistan at independence, which left India with a population that is more than 80 percent Hindu but that has numerous religious minorities, including a Muslim minority that is about 13 percent of the population. After partition, religion was not a major division in India's secular democracy for two decades, but since the 1970s it has become increasingly important. India has seen major debates over what exactly secularism should mean, especially in the area of personal law governing marriage, divorce, and inheritance. These debates have pitted the idea of equal citizenship for all individuals against the idea of community rights to practice a religion and observe specific religious laws.

- **TYPE OF SECULARISM**
  Respect all, positive accommodation, principled distance

- **MAJOR RELIGIOUS GROUPS**
  Growing Hindu-Muslim disputes and tensions

- **MAJOR RELIGIOUS ISSUES**
  Religious autonomy versus uniform laws; Ayodhya mosque/temple controversy

India's "respect all, positive accommodation, principled distance" model has arisen from three ideas of secularism that have competed throughout India's history: the state as modernizer working to reduce the influence of all religions, the state as neutral arbiter among religions, and the state as protector of religious minorities against the Hindu majority. Much of the top leadership of the nationalist movement, the educated elite, saw religion as backward and standing in the way of modernization. For them, secularism meant that the state should work to reduce the influence of religion in public life, encouraging instead an equal and secular citizenship and national identity. Most recognized, however, the reality that the country was very religiously observant and religiously diverse. Ultimately, the constitutional statutes regarding the place of religion in the operation of the state were based on the idea of equal respect for all religions. For the most part, religious organizations were left the authority to mind their own affairs, though within limits. Article 26 of the country's constitution "provides freedom to manage religious affairs, subject to public order, morality and health," and Article 25

A Hindu *sadhu* (holy man) stands near Indian troops outside the Hindu temple in Ayodhya on October 2, 2010. A dispute over Muslim versus Hindu control of the contested site has resulted in some of the worst religiously based violence since independence. In 2010 the Supreme Court ruled that control of the site should be divided, but it's not clear that will end the controversy, or the violence.

> provides for freedom of conscience and free profession, practice and propagation of religion subject to public order, morality, and health. It confers on the state the right to regulate or restrict any economic, financial, political, or other secular activity which may be associated with religious practice. (Rao 2006, 53–54)

These clauses seem to grant religious groups autonomy to practice their faiths but also grant the state the ability to limit these practices when it deems necessary, an ambiguous stance that has led to decades of dispute.

Not surprisingly, these principles have been put into practice in varying ways over the years. The state does not allow religious education in publicly financed schools, but it does allow and even aids religious schools that have religious curricula. Given the decentralized nature of both Hinduism and Islam, the government has also intervened at times to facilitate interactions among religious organizations of the same faith or has informally recognized certain groups as representing these religions. The southern state of Tamil Nadu, for instance, helps administer Hindu temples and their large endowments, with prominent members of the government on the boards of directors of the temples as well. These temples own half a million acres of prime agricultural land and manage great wealth, making the happiness of their membership politically important.

Personal law came to be the most controversial religious question in India, especially involving Muslims. Uncertainty over Islamic law led to the creation of the All India Muslim Personal Law Board (AIMPLB) in 1973 to oversee the implementation of *sharia* in personal law. By the 1980s, it had established itself as the unofficial voice of the Muslim community on personal law, but its position soon came into dispute. In 2000 it issued what it hoped would be a definitive treatise giving a detailed version of proper *sharia* personal law, but that failed to quell growing questions about the board's position. Critics within the Muslim community argued that the board had become beholden to a particular version of Islam and therefore did not represent the larger community (Jones 2010). By 2005 the board had split, and two additional boards had been created, the All India Shia (Shiite) Personal Law Board and the All India Muslim Women's Personal Law Board, the latter an Islamic feminist effort to interpret *sharia* in ways that expand rights for women. As in other cases where the state recognizes and gives autonomy to a religious group, who is the official arbiter of the group's traditions and beliefs is an important and often contested question.

The constitution's ambiguous position of granting autonomy to religious groups to follow their own personal law while simultaneously promising to work toward an eventual "uniform civil code" is at the heart of growing legal disputes. At independence, a debate was already underway over a Hindu Code Bill that would reform Hindu law to outlaw polygamy for Hindus and grant women greater rights to divorce and inheritance. Legislation in 1955 finally gave limited rights to Hindu women, including banning polygamy for Hindus, but it still prevented women from inheriting agricultural land, the most important form of wealth in the country. While only a partial victory for women's rights, the act nonetheless established the principle that Hindu law was subject to secular legal principles. The latter did not, however, govern Muslim law, leaving a disjointed legal framework that remains to this day (Harel-Shalev 2013).

The biggest battle over personal law and religion occurred in 1986. Shah Bano, a seventy-three-year-old Muslim woman divorced from her husband of more than fifty years, went to court to seek financial support from him because a law in the criminal code, which applies to all citizens regardless of religion, requires husbands to provide for their former wives. Under Muslim law, however, a husband is not usually obligated to support his wife for more than three months after divorce. The case went all the way to the Supreme Court, which ruled that the state's criminal code overrides Muslim personal law and, therefore, Shah Bano's husband had to support her. This seemingly innocuous personal case led to large-scale protest and intense political drama. The AIMPLB launched a campaign against the ruling that included a demonstration of half a million people in Bombay, numerous conferences attended by tens of thousands of people, and even a thirty-five-thousand-strong women's protest. In response, secular liberals, reformist Muslims, and women's movements launched counterdemonstrations and demanded further reforms directed toward fulfilling the constitution's promise of a uniform civil code.

The case pitted individual equal rights of citizenship directly against communal rights of religious law and practice. After some hesitation, the Congress Party government chose to support communal rights, introducing the Muslim Women's (Protection of Rights on Divorce) Bill in parliament in February 1986. The vociferous parliamentary debate, framed mainly in terms of the rights of a religious minority versus universal equal rights, was closely watched across the country. The bill ultimately passed; the communal rights of the religious minority had won out. Ironically, in the new millennium, courts have interpreted its provisions in ways that favor Muslim women, giving them greater benefits after divorce (Basu 2008).

Web link:
Shah Bano case: Muslim women's rights

Video link:
Shah Bano case gives hope to Muslim women

The Shah Bano case occurred in the context of rising religiously inspired participation in electoral politics. Although a small minority, Muslims in India participate actively in party politics. Where they constitute a sizable group, they often support a Muslim-identified party, which can win elections as long as Muslims make up around a third of the electorate. Where they are a smaller minority, they choose a secular party they hope will support their interests, though Hindu politicians usually lead such parties. While it was dominant, the ruling Congress Party received the most Muslim votes. Since the Congress's decline in the late 1980s, Muslims also have supported state-level and ethnic parties. This participation, though, has not resulted in equal representation or socioeconomic status in Indian society. A 2006 government commission on the status of Muslims found that they remain underrepresented in most levels of government and have poverty and education rates similar to *dalits*, the so-called "untouchables" (Harel-Shalev 2013).

Growing Muslim movements are in part a reaction to the growth of Hindu nationalism and its party, the Bharatiya Janata Party (BJP) (see chapter 7), which was the ruling party from 1999 to 2004. The BJP's ideology, *Hindutva*, is based on a claim that Hinduism lies at the core of Indian national history and identity. Most Hindu nationalists do not claim that Muslims have no rights in India, but they do argue that Muslims and others must recognize the cultural influence and centrality of Hinduism to true Indian nationalism. The party actively opposes what it sees as "appeasement" of Muslims and other religious minorities and instead calls for a uniform civil code and the end of quotas reserving educational and civil service positions for Muslims or other minorities (an Indian form of affirmative action). Hindu nationalists reject official secularism, arguing it is a Western import of little relevance to deeply religious India: "According to the BJP, India will emerge as a strong nation only when it becomes a cohesive *Hindu Rashtra,* a Hindu nation-state" (Rao 2006, 76). At the state level, BJP governments have actively worked to rewrite Indian textbooks to remove what they see as bias in favor of the Muslim role in the country's history. While in power at the national level, however, the party moderated its views substantially and did not pursue the uniform civil code. Despite this partial moderation, the Hindu nationalists have caused significant fear and opposition among Muslims.

Since the start of the U.S.-led war in Afghanistan, fears of Islamic militancy have risen in India. The disputed northern region of Kashmir has long been a flashpoint. The Kashmiri movement was originally a regionally based drive for autonomy or independence from both India and Pakistan, rejecting both Hindu and Muslim domination.

India's continued refusal to allow a referendum on Kashmir's independence, however, has led the movement in an increasingly religious direction, with the active support of neighboring Pakistan. Terrorist bombs that destroyed a Mumbai hotel and killed hundreds in 2008 raised tensions further, though in response, Muslims led a major demonstration against terrorism. Howard Spodek (2010) argued that while violent Muslim militancy certainly exists in India, it is unlikely to achieve a widespread following; India's democracy continues to allow Muslim participation, and its economic success is reducing the young, unemployed population that is typically subject to militant recruitment. A potentially violent conflict was avoided when an appeals court ruling in 2010 divided ownership of the disputed temple site in Ayodhya (from which the Hindu pilgrims were returning when attacked in 2002) between Hindus and Muslims, and no major reaction occurred. In early 2011, the country's Supreme Court stayed the appeals court ruling, however, pending its own decision. By 2013, the Court was still considering the case while Hindu activists again began mobilizing people to demonstrate to demand the building of a Hindu temple on the disputed site.

Video link:
Supreme Court criticizes Ayodhya verdict

CASE Summary India's battle over secularism and the role of religion raises the classic questions about equal citizenship and clashing values that have arisen in the West, but in very different circumstances. Faced with a religious and religiously divided population, the founders of India's democracy agreed to a secular state but defined that state via the unusual "respect all, positive accommodation, principled distance" principle. Recognizing religious groups' autonomy to follow their own laws, however, has pitted communal rights against individual rights of equal citizenship. The state has come to treat Hindus and Muslims differently in this arena, granting much greater autonomy to the Muslim minority. Much of this debate has involved, as is so often the case, questions about women's rights within the religious community. Despite the goals of the country's first leaders, the state's official secular stance does not seem to be reducing the role of religion. Indeed, religious movements seem stronger now than at any time since independence. These movements among Hindu and Muslim groups (as well as other small religious groups such as Sikhs) have raised serious challenges to Indian secularism, the survival of which some see as threatened.

CASE Questions

1. Why has personal law involving things like marriage and divorce become such a contentious subject in Indian politics? What does this teach us about how religion becomes politicized?

2. Indian policy on religion is ambiguous: on the one hand, it attempts to grant religious groups autonomy, while on the other hand it strives to create uniform laws for all. Why has India not been able to resolve this ambiguity, and how might it best do so in the future?

CASE Study

MEXICO: ANTICLERICALISM IN A CATHOLIC COUNTRY

M exico is a predominantly Christian country, with over 90 percent of its population self-described as Catholic. Despite the overwhelming influence of the church, however, the country has a long-running tradition of French-style *laïcité*, or *laicismo* in Spanish. The Mexican state under the seventy-one-year rule of the PRI always maintained an uneasy relationship with the Catholic Church, in large part owing to the anticlerical tradition of the party's radical wing, which itself had roots in nineteenth-century battles over the influence of the church. The story of Mexico serves as an important example of a highly religious society that has grappled with a policy of strict church-state separation.

Anticlericalism in Mexico originated in large part from the *laïcité* that emerged out of the French Revolution. The Mexican War of Independence of 1810 was led by an alliance of convenience between liberal activists and conservatives. For liberals, the church became a major target, as it represented the connection to the elite of the old (colonial) regime, much as it had to French revolutionaries just decades prior. In the 1830s, the government began a series of reforms, including the secularization of education; the breaking of financial ties with the church; and, most alarming to the

- **TYPE OF SECULARISM**
  Laicismo

- **MAJOR RELIGIOUS GROUPS**
  Catholic Church versus secularists

- **MAJOR RELIGIOUS ISSUES:**
  Role of the Catholic Church in public affairs

Actors perform the Passion of the Christ in Ciudad Juárez, on April 2, 2010. Mexico has long had a complicated relationship with the Catholic Church. While the overwhelming majority of Mexicans are Catholic and fairly religious, the state since the revolution has been secular and usually anticlerical, with policies similar to the French *laïcité*.

conservatives, the expropriation of church land. A coup in response to these reforms reversed many of them, but the seesawing between religious sentiments and radical secularism continued for decades.

In 1859 radical liberals launched a successful attack against the conservative government and pushed to marginalize the church in several ways. They nationalized church property and sold it at auction; closed down monasteries; and created a civil service system to infringe on the church's traditional role of cataloguing births, marriages, and deaths. The new government thus established a clear separation between church and state, which remains a pillar of the Mexican political system. By the time of the Mexican Revolution of 1910, anticlericalism ran strong among the commanders, many of whom viewed religion as an oppressive instrument of elite landowners.

The 1917 constitution helped set in place many of the radical views that emerged from the revolution. Like the Indian constitution, Mexico's constitution portrays an ambiguous vision of secularism. Early on, the constitution employs the kind of secular language found in the First Amendment of the U.S. Constitution, in that "Congress may not dictate laws that establish or prohibit any religion" (Article 3, 1917 Constitution). But later on the document is more reminiscent of the French and Turkish models of *laïcité*. It mentions "the historic principle of the separation of the state and the churches" (Article 130), and goes on to state that "ministers of cults [i.e., priests] will not be able to carry out public duties. As citizens, they will have the right to vote, but not to be voted in" (Article 130, Sec. D). In addition, clergy were banned from holding public religious services, publishing religious literature, or opposing "the laws of the country or its institutions" (Article 130, Sec. E).

By the time the postrevolutionary regime consolidated power under Plutarco Elías Calles (1924 to 1928), divisions between the radical victors of the revolution and the church had intensified. In 1926, in response to political attacks from conservatives, Calles deported around two hundred members of the clergy, closed all religious schools, and halted all religious services. Christians rebelled, igniting the Cristero War (1926–1929). The National Action Party (PAN), which took the presidency in 2000 in the first transfer of power away from the PRI in seventy-one years, was founded in 1939 against this backdrop of state-led anticlericalism. It became associated with conservative values and has traditionally been seen as close to the church.

In conjunction with democratization in the 1990s, the Mexican state began to embrace a more tolerant stance toward religion in general, though the principles of *laicismo* remain part of the debate. In many ways, the inheritors of *laicismo* are members of the Party of the Democratic Revolution (PRD), which since its founding in 1989 has attracted many disaffected radical PRI members. In Mexico City, where abortion is legal in the first twelve weeks of pregnancy, the PRD has been dominant since the late 1990s. In 2009 the party was the driving force behind the legalization of gay marriage in the capital. The Catholic Church fought these reforms, but the Supreme Court ruled abortion to be a matter for the states to decide and the gay marriage law to be constitutional.

Web link:
Mexico inches toward closer church ties

The church itself and PAN politicians have become more assertive in introducing religion into the public sphere under Mexico's democracy. In the conservative state of Guanajuato, the church has tried to push for the public funding of Catholic education. In 2012 the national church faced strong criticism for issuing a "guideline" for the national election, urging the faithful to support the "right to life," implicitly opposing both abortion and gay marriage. While it did not break Mexican law against the church's taking political action, critics contended it broke the spirit of the law. While both PAN presidents—Vicente Fox and Felipe Calderón—did not venture far in their criticism of *laicismo,* Fox caused great controversy when he kissed the ring of the pope, and Calderón openly discussed his faith while president. Several PAN mayors have publicly invited God to take control of their cities, provoking further fears of the erosion of *laicismo.*

Despite the strong influence of the Catholic Church, Mexicans have become accustomed to the lay state. For example, a survey conducted by a progressive Catholic organization found that 91 percent of Catholic Mexicans were in favor of access to contraception, and 96 percent felt that access should be provided free of charge by the government—positions inconsistent with traditional church doctrine. Even the more pro-Catholic PAN has been coy about taking on church-state separation directly.

Web link:
Mexico's separation of church and state

CASE Summary

Mexico's long-standing anticlericalism is reminiscent of Turkey and France, with whom it shares a history of a political founding based in part on opposition to an established religion. While Mexicans by and large remain religious people, the church has not played the role it has in many Latin American countries. In the nineteenth century, as was true in much of Europe, divisions between conservatives supporting the church and liberals wanting to reduce its power were central to national politics. The revolution established *laicismo* as the law of the land. The church and its supporters have at times battled to regain a greater role for the church, and in the context of the new democracy the state has become more tolerant of religion. Nonetheless, laicismo appears to be firmly planted in Mexico, at least for the foreseeable future.

CASE Questions

1. What are the advantages and disadvantages of Mexico's policy of *laicismo* compared with the U.S. model of state neutrality vis-à-vis religious groups?
2. As religions become more prominent in newly democratized Mexico, should *laicismo* remain official policy, or are there grounds for a change to a different relationship between church and state?

Secularism has long been seen as a part of modernity and therefore the modern state. Religion and religious divisions, however, are becoming more, not less, relevant to modern politics. Officially secular states find it nearly impossible to be truly neutral among religions, and religious minorities argue the state should not be completely neutral but instead work to protect their threatened interests. Doing so in the name of cultural respect raises fundamental questions about values, often pitting individual rights as understood by liberals against group rights aimed at cultural preservation. These debates have affected Western states, many of which seemed headed toward complete secularization just a few decades ago, as well as more religious postcolonial states and societies. As is so often the case, these battles about the place of religion and religious values centrally involve the role of women and women's rights, a subject to which we now turn.

GENDER: THE CONTINUING STRUGGLE FOR EQUAL SOCIAL STATUS, REPRESENTATION, AND PARTICIPATION

The women's movement and changes in women's position, activity, and status have been the most dramatic social and political revolution of the last generation, especially in wealthy countries. The number of women in the workforce in wealthy countries, in professional positions, and in higher education has skyrocketed since the 1960s. Jeane Kirkpatrick wrote in the early 1970s in her classic study of the United States, *Political Woman*:

> Half a century after the ratification of the nineteenth amendment, no woman has been nominated to be president or vice president, no woman has served on the Supreme Court. Today, there is no woman in the cabinet, no woman in the Senate, no woman serving as governor of a major state, no woman mayor of a major city, no woman in the top leadership of either major party. (1974, 3)

With the exception of presidential nomination by a major party (and Hillary Rodham Clinton came close in 2008), all that has changed. While women still make up a small percentage of each of the offices Kirkpatrick mentions, they are present in noticeable numbers, and many other countries outstrip the United States in percentage of women in high offices.

While movements for women's rights and equality arose and fell in various countries over the last several centuries, the contemporary women's movement in the West emerged from the tumultuous 1960s. At the time, women's rights and feminism were seen as exclusively Western concerns of little relevance to the rest of the world, especially the poorest countries. In many postcolonial countries, though, the women's movement has expanded greatly since the 1980s, often in conjunction with the democratization process we discussed in chapter 9. This expansion was marked by major United Nations conferences on women in 1985 in Nairobi, Kenya, and in 1995 in Beijing, China. Women in many postcolonial societies struggle to gain equal legal status with men in areas of family law, a victory now mostly won in wealthier countries. Also, like women in wealthier countries, they demand greater social status and a more extensive role in the political process.

The women's movement and feminist theory have raised fundamental political questions. We noted in chapter 4 that gender is an unusual identity category in part because women themselves often are used as markers of identity. Particular notions of gender roles frequently help define what it means to be a member of a particular nation, ethnic group, race, or religion, so when women challenge traditional gender roles, they implicitly challenge the validity of other identity groups to which they belong. Women who demand recognition of gender as a distinct category of concern have thus come into conflict not only with nationalists in the West but also with postcolonial nationalists who demanded national unity to throw off colonial rule, male revolutionary leaders who demanded unity to achieve the revolution, and leaders of racial or ethnic groups who demanded unity to overcome oppression. Women's movements and feminist theory can also conflict with the goals of multiculturalism: recognition of group rights along cultural lines may entail acceptance of cultural practices that feminists argue harm women. Thus, feminism has threatened all other groups at one time or another.

Differing Feminist Agendas

As they challenged other groups, feminists also debated among themselves what their full agenda ought to be. This debate mirrors the broader debate on multiculturalism and group rights. Liberal feminists, like proponents of liberal equality more generally, focus on gaining equal rights with men as their main goal, and they tend not to challenge social or political norms beyond that, accepting existing political and economic systems but demanding equal treatment within them. Many feminist theorists, though, demand more than just equal treatment in legal, political, and economic contexts. Like other proponents of group rights, most have come to believe that major social and political institutions need to change if women are to make full use of legal equality. Carole Pateman (1988), for instance, questioned the terms of equal citizenship itself, contending that citizenship as typically conceived is inherently male and patriarchal, with its greatest expression being military service. Echoing the ideas of Iris Young on including all voices in democracy, Pateman argued for a new conception of citizenship that values women's lived experience—one that places motherhood, for instance, on the same moral level as military service. Women in racial or ethnic minorities and in the Global South, on the other hand, have criticized the global women's movement as being too focused on concerns exclusive to white women in wealthy countries, arguing successfully over the last two decades for an expansion of feminist theory and political demands to recognize the distinct needs of women of color and poor women.

Objectives and Outcomes

Shifting the Boundaries of the Public and Private Spheres Women's demands for inclusion have raised a fundamental question about what is and ought to be "public" and "private." Liberal political debate is restricted to what is deemed public, with private matters left to the individual, family, and religious institutions. Each society defines for itself, however, what is public and what is private, and the women's movement has successfully pressured many societies to redefine these boundaries to make formerly private concerns into public ones. In most societies, including those in the West, men's treatment of their wives was a private concern: verbal, physical, and sexual abuse, as long as it did not go as far as murder (and sometimes even when it did), was typically ignored and considered a private, family matter. The women's movement has changed this in many societies by arguing that abusive relationships within the private sphere of the family violate fundamental rights and impede women's ability to participate fully in the public sphere. Women's demands continue to question and at times shift the public/private boundary in many societies, especially in areas of legal status and relationships within families.

Web link:
Women's human
rights: a fact sheet

Social, Legal, and Economic Status In many societies, women have gained recognition as a group with legitimate concerns and basic political rights equal to men; they are allowed to vote and, at least in theory, hold elective office. Their social and legal status, however, is less uniformly equal to men's. Women's groups worldwide have sought greater access for women to education and participation in the labor force at all levels, and while women have not achieved full parity, they have made tremendous gains in a wide variety of societies. Many people in the West have an image of Western women as having achieved nearly equal status with men while women in postcolonial countries continue to be mired in oppression. In fact, in many postcolonial countries, this image no longer applies. The gender gap in educational access and attainment has narrowed substantially in most Latin American and African countries and in some Asian ones as well over the last two decades, although, as is true everywhere, professional status and labor force participation rates lag behind education. The Country and Concept table (pages 642–643) provides several measures of gender equality for our case study countries, showing that some postcolonial societies are not that much more unequal in gender terms than are wealthier countries, while Map 12.1 displays gender inequality rankings around the world.

Data link:
The UN's Gender
Inequality Index

Concerns about achieving greater social and economic status have led women to demand reproductive rights and state support for childbearing and child rearing. Because women bear children and in all societies continue to do the bulk of child rearing, improvement in these areas is essential to improving their social status. Women's movements have successfully championed the spread of access to contraception in much of the world, and birth rates have fallen significantly in most countries over the

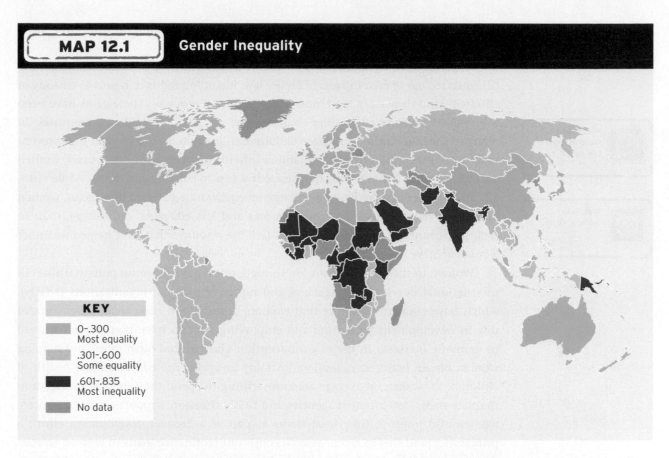

Source: Gender Inequality Index 2012, International Human Development Indicators, United Nations Development Programme (http://hdr.undp.org/opendata).

last generation. Legalized abortion remains a controversial subject, with women successfully leading efforts in many societies to support it even as moral objections, often from other women, keep it illegal in quite a few others. Women in approximately sixty countries currently have access to legal abortion.

Women, especially in wealthier countries, have also demanded greater state support for childbearing and child rearing to facilitate their participation in the labor force. Support has included paid and unpaid maternity leave, paid and unpaid paternity leave (for fathers to help with child rearing), and access to affordable and high-quality childcare. State responses to these demands have broadly mirrored the types of welfare states outlined in chapter 11. Social democratic welfare states provide more generous maternity leave and greater access to childcare, and women's labor force participation is highest in these societies. Christian democratic welfare states are generous, but their ruling philosophy remains based primarily on the male-head-of-household model, and these societies have lower labor force participation rates for women. Liberal welfare states, though providing relatively ungenerous benefits, are in the middle on women's labor force participation, reflecting the emphasis of these states on work over social assistance.

A key target of women's groups worldwide has been the achievement of legal status equal to that of men in areas of family law, including rights in regard to custody of children, land ownership, and inheritance of family property. These gains have been achieved in virtually all wealthy countries but not in all postcolonial countries. In many of the latter, women still face various legal inequities vis-à-vis men that prevent them from independently owning land or inheriting property; in some cases, women are even restricted from having independent access to banking and travel. While virtually all countries have active women's movements working toward these goals, women in most developing societies remain poorer and less educated, on average, than in wealthier countries, so their movements lack the resources that have helped wealthier women achieve many gains.

Women in the poorest countries, though, often have powerful potential allies in international development agencies and nongovernmental organizations (NGOs), which have come to recognize that women, especially in rural areas, play a crucial role in development. Educating and employing women have been shown to lead to dramatic increases in use of contraception and reduced birth rates, and helping women obtain better incomes demonstrably improves the education and health of children, as women on average are more willing to spend their income on children than are men. Development agencies and NGOs therefore support efforts to educate women and improve their legal status as part of a broader development effort; a primary form of this in recent years has been microfinance loans to women to start their own small businesses. As with the broader women's movement, external efforts such as these have raised numerous debates. Women activists in postcolonial societies often argue that Western development agencies and NGOs, however sympathetic to the cause they might be, do not fully understand the perspectives or needs of the women they are trying to help. Donor agencies' and NGOs' priorities can distort domestic groups' goals because the latter must follow the direction of those providing them with financial support. That said, it is nonetheless clear that the women's movement has expanded globally over the last generation and that numerous aid agencies and NGOs are actively working to champion what they perceive to be women's interests.

Political Representation Women's movements have also focused on improving the representation and participation of women in the political process, even in countries that are not fully democratic. As we noted in chapter 7, proportional representation (PR) electoral systems tend to produce higher numbers of women representatives, as do multimember district systems. Jane Mansbridge (2000) argued that "descriptive representation"—representation by people who look like you and have similar life experiences—is particularly important when social inequality results in particular groups of citizens not trusting their elected representatives who hail from

Web link:
National Women's
Law Center

Web link:
Women Watch

a different group, communication among members of different groups might be difficult, or unforeseen issues arise between elections. For instance, gender inequality may make many women not trust or feel comfortable communicating honestly with their male representatives. Furthermore, when a new issue arises that did not exist at the time of the last election, citizens may want representatives from their social group who have had similar experiences to make decisions that will reflect their perspectives. Most feminists believe that greater descriptive representation will thus produce greater substantive representation: the effective representation of identified women's issues and concerns. For all these reasons, women's movements have worked to improve the percentage of women in political office.

While women have definitely gained ground in parliaments around the world, they remain just 20.9 percent of the total members of parliament worldwide (see Map 12.2), and only twelve women were heads of state in 2013. Parliamentary representation varies widely but not systematically by region; a number of postcolonial states have higher percentages of female representatives than do the United States or some European countries. Indeed, tiny Rwanda in central Africa has the highest proportion of women legislators in the world, at 56 percent; it and Andorra are the only countries above 50 percent. The relatively slow process of change has led women's movements in many countries to champion the creation of quotas for women's legislative participation. These take three forms: (1) political parties, in closed-list PR systems, voluntarily impose their own internal quota for women on their lists of candidates; (2) laws require that women constitute a certain percentage of all parties' candidates; or (3) laws reserve a certain number of legislative seats for women, elected in a separate vote from the rest of the legislature. Quotas are typically set at anywhere from 25 to 50 percent of the total seats or candidates. While only ten states had any type of quota before 1980, over one hundred had them by 2010. The majority of these, however, have been voluntarily adopted within parties.

Krook (2009) argued that quotas are implemented most successfully where they fit with other major political institutions; if they contradict other aspects of the political system, they are unlikely to have a major impact. Because party quotas are for the number of candidates, they do not guarantee women a particular number of legislative seats; how well the rest of the political system supports women candidates is therefore important. Aili Mari Tripp and Alice Kang (2008) concluded from a large statistical analysis that quotas, especially reserved seats and voluntary party quotas, and use of PR electoral systems have a greater effect on the number of women in legislatures than economic development, religion, or other commonly used explanations for why women gain seats. Quotas also are associated with greater substantive representation of women's issues; women elected to legislatures via quotas report feeling more obligated to work on behalf of women's issues than do women elected without quotas, who often want to downplay women's issues in the interests of appearing to be "serious" legislators and appeal to male voters (Krook and Schwindt-Bayer 2013, 565).

Data link:
Women in national parliaments

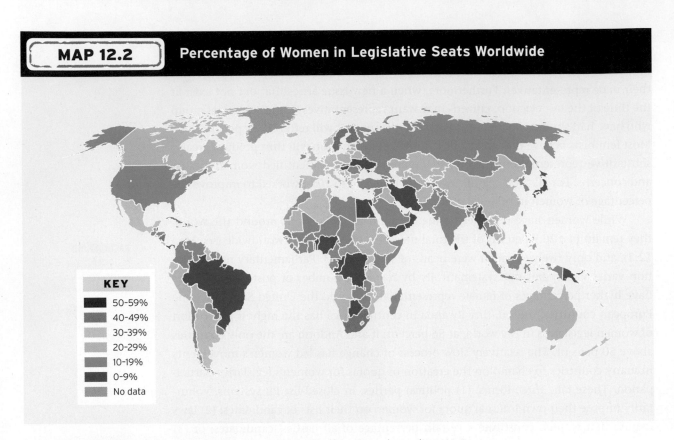

MAP 12.2   **Percentage of Women in Legislative Seats Worldwide**

KEY

- 50–59%
- 40–49%
- 30–39%
- 20–29%
- 10–19%
- 0–9%
- No data

Source: Inter-Parliamentary Union, Women in National Parliaments (http://www.ipu.org/wmn-e/world.htm).

Note: Percentages are for lower and single houses only. Data for upper houses, where available, can be found at the source website above. South Africa's estimate does not include the thirty-six special rotating delegates appointed on an ad hoc basis; all percentages given are therefore calculated on the basis of the fifty-four permanent seats.

Data link:
The Quota Project

Web link:
Are quotas for women in politics a good idea?

Video link:
India: quotas help women enter men's world of politics

The success of quotas, especially those mandated by law (more typical in Asia and Africa than in Europe), raises the key questions in the debate over multiculturalism and inclusion in democracies. Supporters of simple liberal equality argue that women are free to vote and run for office and if they are elected are free to serve. Any type of quota violates the principle of equal citizenship for all. Supporters of quotas, on the other hand, argue for the group right of descriptive representation, following Iris Young's argument that democracies need to ensure that the voices of marginalized groups are included in policy discussions. Does requiring that women are a certain percentage of candidates or MPs violate the liberal principles of equal citizenship, or is it a necessary measure to enhance those principles in the face of long-standing social pressures and norms that have kept women out of political office?

Even in countries where women have achieved substantial gains, they have not achieved full parity with men. Nowhere are women fully equal with men in terms of professional status, wages, or political representation. We examine these issues in two countries that have faced significant changes in the last twenty years, countries that most people do not think of as having important women's movements: Russia and Iran. These countries demonstrate the ubiquity of the global women's movement and the questions it has raised.

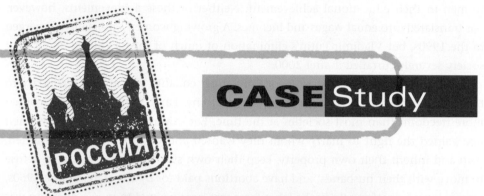

CASE Study

RUSSIA: WOMEN THROUGH SOCIAL AND POLITICAL TRANSFORMATION

Russian women have lived through dramatic and at times traumatic social, economic, and political change since the end of the Cold War. The state and regime under which many of them grew up imploded, an older state (Russia) was recreated, the state's social and economic systems were transformed almost entirely, and a new regime (some would argue two regimes) emerged. The Soviet Union left an unusual legacy for women's role in society. Soviet women were heavily involved in the labor force and highly educated before their contemporaries in the West or postcolonial societies, and the Soviet Union at times attempted to counter traditional cultural norms about gender roles, though with mixed results. Yet Soviet women had no

- **BACKGROUND**
  In Soviet era, social status relatively good but no political participation

- **CONTEMPORARY ISSUES**
  Transition to market economy lowered women's employment and wages; fewer women in legislature; resurgence of traditional attitudes about gender roles

- **WOMEN'S MOVEMENT**
  Active in 1990s curtailed by Putin's semi-authoritarian rule

- **GENDER INEQUALITY INDEX**
  0.312–48 of 147 in 2012

Supporters of the feminist punk band Pussy Riot demonstrate outside the band's court trial in 2012. The group's lyrics demanding women's and gay rights, and opposing Russian president Putin, resulted in members' arrest after a controversial performance in a Russian Orthodox cathedral. Two were given jail sentences for "hooliganism," while some others fled the country.

Web link:
Russian women in
search of a cause

Web link:
Russian women's
rights rally broken
up

history of autonomous political action, in spite of some formal "representation" in the centralized Soviet political system. In the new Russia, women have nearly complete legal rights in all areas, but in practice these are often not enforced. They continue to face cultural and social constraints to their full participation in society and politics, but they remain nearly equal to men in their participation in the economy and superior to men in their educational achievement. Neither of these achievements, however, has translated into equal wages and incomes. A growing women's movement emerged in the 1990s, but Vladimir Putin's elimination of much of Russia's autonomous civil society severely curtailed it after 2000.

The Soviet Union's claim to favor full gender equality was always secondary to the needs of building a stronger state and economy. Early Soviet laws gave women more freedoms than most societies at the time. For example, by the 1920s, women had gained the right to marry whom they wanted and divorce when they wanted, own and inherit their own property, keep their own surnames after marriage, refuse to move with their husbands, and have abortions paid for by the state. By the 1960s, women's participation rate in the labor force was nearly equal to men's, abortion was legal and widely available, and women were rapidly catching up with men in the educational system.

The state, however, faced a demographic dilemma, which only grew worse after the end of Communism: it encouraged women to participate in the labor force to increase production, but at the same time Russian women were having fewer babies. Indeed, abortion rates in Russia were and remain among the highest in the world, estimated as high as 60 percent of all pregnancies. In 2011 the government passed modest restrictions on abortion, limiting it to the first twelve weeks of pregnancy unless a woman could not afford a child, in which case it is allowed up to twenty-two weeks, although it rejected calls from the Russian Orthodox Church to require husbands' consent to abortions. To counter this fertility decline, the Soviet government instituted generous and widely available childcare as early as the 1920s and later added generous maternity leave: a total of 112 days at full pay. With fewer workers needed and the birth rate continuing to fall in the late 1980s, the Communist state in its last years shifted to an even more traditional attitude. In the words of Mikhail Gorbachev, the Soviet Union's last Communist leader:

> Over the years . . . we failed to pay attention to women's specific rights and needs arising from their role as mother and home-maker, and their indispensable educational function as regards children. . . . Women no longer have enough time to perform their everyday duties at home—housework, the upbringing of children and the creation of a good family atmosphere. . . . We are now holding heated debates . . . about the question of what we should do to make it possible for women to return to their purely womanly mission. (quoted in Racioppi and See 1995, 824)

This would be a harbinger of things to come in terms of cultural attitudes, though not of actual shifts in the work done by women.

The transition to a market economy after the dissolution of the Soviet state produced dramatic economic decline for most of the 1990s. Men and women alike suffered from this, but most observers see women as having lost more. Women's full legal rights were preserved in the new 1993 constitution, but economic and cultural change nonetheless harmed women's position. Women continued to equal men in their participation rates in employment, and both suffered unemployment at about the same rates in the 1990s. Men, however, gained new jobs more quickly. In the early 2000s, as the economy began to rebound, men and women benefited about equally. Women's wages, however, have always been and remain below men's: they were on average 70 percent of men's at the end of the Communist era, and by 2009 this number had dropped to 65 percent despite women's higher education levels. Women receive lower wages and are in less prestigious positions even in fields in which they predominate, such as education and public service. The biggest cause of the wage gap, though, is the shift of women out of high-paying sectors, such as finance and industry, since the end of the Soviet era (Roschin and Zubarevich 2005, 7–17). A 2010 UN report found that 71 percent of all professionally employed women were working in sectors in which the average wage was below the national average (Baskakova and Soboleva 2010).

The transition to a market economy has also affected other aspects of women's working and personal lives. Women increasingly end up in part-time employment, which further lowers their income relative to that of men. They are also overrepresented among Russia's poor, in part due to the large numbers of impoverished and elderly widows, as Russian women's life expectancy is twelve years longer than men's, one of the largest gaps in the world. (The reasons for this gap are the subject of much debate; the factors include much higher male rates of tuberculosis, industrial accidents, suicide, and alcohol and drug abuse.) Women seem to suffer more from psychological problems as well.

The Soviet system of state-sponsored preschools shrank dramatically as funding dried up in the 1990s. In the late Soviet era, as many as 84 percent of children three years of age and older were in childcare institutions; by 2000, that number had fallen to only 47 percent. Families, including extended families, have been forced to make up the difference. The Soviet Union's relatively generous maternity leave policies were preserved and even extended, and a "parental leave" for either parent was instituted as well, to be used until a child reaches eighteen months of age, though it only provided $17 per month in the 1990s, when the poverty level was about $200 (Teplova 2007).

By 2007, the Russian government was once again concerned about low birth rates, so it began offering financial rewards to mothers of second and third (and more) children. By 2012, these benefits were worth $12,000; while that was not enough to allow mothers (or fathers) to quit working for a wage, it did provide a significant boost to income that encourages home purchases or saving for children's education. Like women in the United States and elsewhere, Russian women continue to perform most household work and childcare. In the mid-1990s, they were employed an average of thirty-eight hours per week, compared with forty-three hours for men, but women also did an average of thirty hours per week of household chores and childcare, whereas men did only fourteen hours per week (Roschin and Zubarevich 2005, 20).

Russian women did not sit idly by in the face of these challenges. An active women's movement arose in the early 1990s, supported by Western donors interested in developing Russia's new civil society. The Soviet Union had allowed only state-controlled women's organizations to exist; no autonomous civil society groups had been permitted until the reforms of the late 1980s. New women's organizations mushroomed in the early 1990s, with two thousand registered by the end of the decade. Many of these were small and poorly funded groups that did not survive long, but a few became important centers for gathering information and publicizing issues of concern to women. The most prominent of these groups began under the leadership of highly educated, professional women. A division emerged within the movement between those who had been members of the official state-sponsored organizations of the Soviet era and focused on making practical gains in women's immediate well-being, and self-consciously feminist groups that were critical of the former Soviet organizations and sought extensive changes in social and cultural attitudes toward women (Racioppi and See 1995). While the women's movement gained strength in the early 1990s, by the end of the decade, internal divisions and a lack of resources had noticeably weakened it. Under President Putin it declined further, as did most autonomous organizations in Russian civil society. Johnson and Saarinen (2013) found that Putin's crackdown, including making foreign funding of NGOs illegal, cut in half one of the most prominent success stories of the 1990s women's movement: the creation of women's crisis centers around the country. Those run by NGOs independent of the state shrank particularly dramatically, and those that survived curtailed open political activity and explicitly feminist rhetoric.

Even at its height in the 1990s, the movement had limited success placing women in decision-making positions. The powerless Soviet legislature had a quota that ensured one-third of its members were women. This quota was eliminated at the time of the first competitive election for the Russian (as opposed to Soviet) parliament in 1990, resulting in only 5.4 percent of its members being women. The successor to the official Soviet women's organization, the Union of Women of Russia, formed a political party, Women of Russia, to contest the 1993 legislative elections. The party succeeded in raising women's numbers in the lower house of parliament: women constituted 13.6 percent of all members (higher than in the United States at the time), a significant accomplishment given the context. By the next election in 1995, however, many women were disillusioned with the party's failure to provide any concrete benefits, and it failed to gain the 5 percent of votes necessary to be allotted seats in the parliament. The total representation of women in that parliament fell to 10 percent, with a further decline to less than 8 percent in the 1999 election. This trend was reversed in elections in the new millennium: by 2013 (in the far less powerful legislature) 13.6 percent of the members of the lower house were female, tying Russia for ninety-eighth place with Swaziland on a global list (Inter-Parliamentary Union 2013).

Despite possessing full legal rights, Russian women continue to face attitudinal barriers to full participation in society. Social attitudes about women's roles have become more traditional since the end of Communist rule. While a majority of both men and women expect women to work for a wage and accept women's participation in the paid workforce, and a majority of women want a fulfilling career, a majority of both genders also think that the man should be the primary breadwinner in the family. A 2002 study found the persistence of many traditional stereotypes of ideal male characteristics: strength, intelligence, and the provision of material security; ideal female characteristics were appearance, loving children, and housekeeping skills (White 2005, 431). These attitudes are apparently reflected in the economy as well: women have reported discrimination in hiring by men who prefer them to stay in the home, as well as incidents in which they were forced by employers to sign contracts promising not to get married or have children because businesses fear having to pay maternity leave. Putin's government has used particularly "masculine" rhetoric and images to glorify him and his role in the nation and has increased both nationalist and traditional Orthodox religious rhetoric tied to traditional gender norms (Johnson and Saarinen 2013).

Video link:
Russia marks International Women's Day

CASE Summary   While the new Russian state has preserved full legal rights and fairly extensive benefits for women, including maternity leave, it has done little to counter the underlying attitudes and norms that continue to limit the progress of women. In spite of limited government action, women's overall position seems to have improved in the new millennium: its score on the UNDP's Gender Equality Index (a measure of reproductive rights, empowerment, and employment) improved from 0.425 in 2000 to 0.312 by 2012, not far behind the U.S. rating of 0.256. Overall, the state, though, provides little support for ending discrimination against women. A recent United Nations report summed up the situation:

> There have been two distinct phases of policy formulation and implementation [about women's issues in Russia]. The first stage, in the 1990s, gave an appearance of activity, but tended to be limited to words. . . . [In] the second phase, dating from the turn of the Millennium, the state has given up both declarations and actions. Gender issues have effectively dropped out of the Government's socioeconomic priorities. (Bobylev 2005, 60)

Putin's crackdown on women's organizations along with the rest of civil society and his complete control of the legislature suggests that little will change in the foreseeable future.

CASE Questions

1. What do the circumstances of post-Communist Russia mean for women and women's movements there? What opportunities and obstacles do they face that are different from women in Western or other countries?

2. Thinking back to the debate over individual and group rights, which argument in that debate seems most useful in trying to help Russian women now and in the future?

IRAN: SOCIAL GAINS, POLITICAL AND CULTURAL RESTRICTIONS, AND ISLAMIC FEMINISM

- **BACKGROUND**
  "Modernization" under the shah; greater restriction under the Islamic Republic

- **CONTEMPORARY ISSUES**
  Contradiction between social and economic gains and restrictive laws

- **WOMEN'S MOVEMENT**
  Mixes secular and Islamic women; active participation in 2009 antiregime protests

- **GENDER INEQUALITY INDEX**
  0.496–104 of 147 in 2012

In 2003 Iranian human rights lawyer and feminist activist Shirin Ebadi won the Nobel Peace Prize amidst great adulation from much of the world but condemnation from the Iranian government. Four years later, the government responded to a new wave of women's activity against discrimination with a new crackdown on public morality, especially women's public appearance. "Chastity police" arrested hundreds and harassed thousands of Iranians, mostly women, for not abiding by a particular interpretation of Islamic teachings about what women can do and how they can appear in public. These events were part of a long-standing dispute over women's rights in Iran. While the Iranian government certainly does not treat women equally in cultural and political areas, it has nonetheless allowed and often even encouraged significant social and economic gains. This has created a contradiction, as educated and employed women demand greater equality and the government continues to deny it. The women's movement leading this effort includes not only secular feminists opposed to the Islamic regime but also Islamic feminists who argue for an interpretation of Shiite Islamic teachings that grants greater gender equality than the Islamic Republic so far will accept.

Under the shah's modernization program of the 1960s and 1970s, women were encouraged to reject their traditional roles and appearance in order to "modernize" along Western lines. The effort had a much more significant effect in urban than rural areas. Like the rest of the shah's policies, though, it increasingly came to be seen as

Iranian women wait in line to vote in the 2013 presidential election. Women under the Islamic Republic have made massive gains in education and control over reproduction (lower fertility and more access to contraception) but continue to lag in employment and access to political power. While large numbers of women's NGOs operate within the country, very few women are in major leadership positions in government.

imposed by a dictator doing the West's bidding, and women were active participants in the 1978–1979 revolution that created the Islamic Republic. The revolutionary process itself brought women into the political arena in unprecedented numbers.

As the Islamist clerics under the Ayatollah Khomeini consolidated their power in 1979–1980, however, one of their first acts was to reverse the shah's Family Protection Law, which had Westernized much of the country's family law. The new regime eliminated women's right to divorce while giving men nearly an unlimited right to leave their wives; required women to wear the *hijab,* the Islamic veil, in public; forced women out of the legal profession and restricted them from several other professions; banned contraception; and segregated the education system. Many women who had been active in the revolution felt betrayed and protested these changes, including hundreds of thousands who took to the streets in March 1979 to protest mandatory veiling, but their protests proved fruitless.

During the 1980s most of the social gains women had made since the 1960s were at least partially reversed: women's employment levels dropped, their political participation was minimal (only 4 women out of 270 MPs were elected to the first parliament after the revolution), and without access to contraception they bore more children. The absence of men during the Iran-Iraq War (1980–1988), however, gave women an opportunity to enter school at all levels to an unprecedented degree, which the government encouraged as part of a literacy campaign. Indeed, gender segregation of schools increased girls' enrollment, as conservative parents were more willing to send their daughters to all-female schools. Any critical political activity was still severely repressed, but women found new paths to enter the public arena and education system.

In the early 1990s, the various restrictions put on women's economic roles came into direct conflict with the government's economic liberalization program. Spurred by a renewed women's movement and facing economic necessity, the government partially reversed various laws restricting the advancement of women. Over the course of the decade, most restrictions on what women could study and where they could work were eliminated, and the government reintroduced and actively supported contraception and mandated maternity leave. Women were also allowed to reenter the legal profession in any position except that of courtroom judge. Fertility rates dropped, women advanced through the educational system, female literacy increased dramatically, more women chose not to marry, and the age of women's first marriage increased (Bahramitash and Kazemipour 2006). The reformist government under President Mohammad Khatami (1997–2005) accelerated these trends with an explicit policy of furthering women's position in society.

By the new millennium, the results of these actions were quite significant. From the revolution to 2002, women's life expectancy increased from fifty-eight to seventy-two years, their literacy rate increased from 31 to 69 percent, the share of women still single in their early twenties increased from 21 to 54 percent, their fertility rate dropped from an average of 6.5 live births to 2.7, the gap between men and women in age of marriage and level of education dropped dramatically, and women's share of seats in public universities rose to 60 percent (Bahramitash and Kazemipour 2006). The rapid gains, in fact, led to a conservative backlash in the new millennium that put quotas on the number of women allowed in certain fields of study and at universities away from their homes (Aryan 2012). Women's improved status did not translate into large gains in employment, however. Women continue to be employed at much lower rates than men and tend to work in lower-paid sectors, especially the government and universities. They constitute only 2 percent of all top political, decision-making, and managerial positions (Nejadbahram 2012, 82–84). Many women and men argue that women pursue education in such high numbers in part because few economic alternatives are open to them (Rezai-Rashti and Moghadam 2011). Universities appealed to young women also because they were places where they could get away from restrictions imposed on them at home and in the larger society. Nonetheless, women's dramatic educational advances created huge social changes, and ultimately were supported by most families, who were willing to support their daughters' educational goals (Aryan 2012).

Among other outcomes of these social changes, Iran's divorce rate skyrocketed in the new millennium, tripling from 2000 to 2010 despite laws making divorce extremely difficult for women. One in seven marriages now ends in divorce. Women frequently waive their right to financial support under Islamic law in order to gain their husband's agreement to divorce. Anthropologist Pardis Mahdavi (2009) studied sexual relationships in contemporary Iran and reported she never met a woman who was "happily married" but did find very high levels of extramarital affairs, instigated by both wives and husbands.

As these dramatic social and economic changes were taking place, an active women's movement reemerged that involved both secular and Islamic feminists. The latter asserted their right to interpret the holy texts (*ijtihad*) and argued that Islam actually emphasizes gender equality. They used the Prophet Mohammad's wives

Women in Iran and the Middle East

Improvements in the status of women in Iran since the late 1980s have made it roughly equal with the average of other Middle Eastern states on a variety of measures of women's well-being and equality, below average on political representation, but well ahead of the regional average in reduced fertility rate and women's education.

	Gender Inequality Index (2012)	Gender-empowerment measure (2010)	Fertility rate (births per woman, 2010-2015)	Ratio of female to male income (2009)	Percentage female adult literacy rate (2007)	Percentage female population with at least secondary education (2012)	Percentage female seats in parliament (2012)
Iran	0.496	0.331	1.7	0.32	77.2	62.1	3.1
Middle East	0.555	0.43	2.6	0.3	75.5	31.8	13

Sources: United Nations Development Report 2007/2008 and 2009/2010; Gender Inequality Index data for 2012 (http://hdr.undp.org/en/statistics/data and UNDP Gender Indices), (http://hdr.undp.org/en/statistics/indices/gdi_gem), (http://hdr.undp.org/en/statistics/gii).

and daughters as examples of women actively involved in the public sphere. They argued that

> true Islam . . . combined equality of opportunity for men and women to develop their talents and capacities and to participate in all aspects of social life, because it acknowledged women's maternal instinct and their essential role within the family. (Paidar 1995, 241)

These feminists rejected what they saw as Western society's sexual objectification of women and the individualistic assumptions of much Western feminism, but they nonetheless argued for a place of equality within Iran's Islamic society.

As the broader reform movement grew in the 1990s (see chapter 8), the women's movement became more active. This was clear in the growing role of women's NGOs. Their number increased from none in 1995 to 480 by 2004, and they were very active in providing services and education for women, especially in urban areas (Koolaee 2012, 140). Women also have started numerous publications whenever press restrictions are partially eased, the best known of which has been *Zanan* (*Women*), which became a major forum for both secular and Islamist women to present their arguments. Inspired in part by Shirin Ebadi's Nobel Prize, the women's movement proclaimed itself publicly at its first major demonstration at Tehran University in 2005, demanding constitutional changes to end gender discrimination. Despite police harassment, some five thousand women managed to attend. Subsequently, the movement began the Campaign for One Million Signatures to change the constitution (Hoodfar and Sadeghi 2009). Under the increased repression of the Ahmadinejad government, the movement was divided over how overtly political it should be, but nonetheless the campaign was perhaps the largest civil society activity at the time.

Despite severe cultural and legal restrictions on women, the Islamic constitution gave them full rights to participate in politics, except for being barred from holding the office of the president. Prior to 1991, only women who were clearly identified as Islamists had been elected to the parliament. In that year's election, secular women activists were added to their ranks, and women's numbers peaked in the 1996 election at fourteen MPs, who formed the first women's caucus in the parliament. When the Guardian Council prevented reformist candidates from running for parliament in 2000, however, the number of women MPs dropped and has never recovered. In 2013 only nine women (out of 290 MPs) served in parliament. From the start of the Islamic Republic, most of the small number of women MPs worked actively in support of achieving greater equality for women. In the area of family law, women were granted slightly more rights to divorce, including the indexing of the traditional payment a man must make to his wife when divorcing her to take inflation into account, and greater rights over guardianship of children, which came with child allowances from the government. Such legal victories, though, have remained relatively rare and minor. Since 2000, many women MPs are members of conservative political forces that are favored by the supreme leader and do not push from women's rights reforms as much as earlier women MPs did.

At the height of the reformist movement under President Mohammad Khatami (1997–2005) the government reduced the severity of the cultural restrictions on women's public actions. It did not enforce the rules about veiling and public segregation of the sexes with the zeal of earlier or subsequent governments. The election of President Mahmoud Ahmadinejad ended the Khatami-led reform effort. Ahmadinejad's renewed efforts to restrict women and segregate them in public included not only the crackdown since 2007 but also banning numerous women's (and other dissident) publications and websites and expanding the gender segregation of public amenities, including buses, taxis, and even telephone booths. More than one city built women-only parks behind high walls within which women could enjoy being outdoors and exercise without being veiled. In 2012 and 2013, parliament proposed laws that restrict women from travelling internationally without their husband's or father's approval (similar to laws in Saudi Arabia) and banned women from studying seventy-seven fields, mostly in sciences and engineering, in state universities (the ban does not affect Iran's two hundred private universities).

This crackdown, however, did not eliminate the women's movement. A women's coalition formed during the 2009 campaign and demanded to know each presidential candidate's position on key women's issues, a level of engagement women had not achieved before in presidential elections. Women were also active participants in the massive protests that followed the rigged elections. Victoria Tahmasebi-Birgani (2010), a participant in the demonstrations, argued that both secular and Islamist women were involved not only to demand democracy but to demand greater gender equality, as they now see the two as inseparable.

Video link:
Fighting for women's rights in Iran

Web link:
Kurdish men for equality

Newly elected president Hassan Rohani said during his 2013 campaign that he believed men and women should be treated equally and promised to create a Ministry of Women's Affairs. He initially disappointed women activists, though, when he appointed only one woman to his cabinet, which he did only after protests against his initial cabinet list, which included no women.

CASE Summary
Economic needs and the women's movement have combined to achieve significant social, educational, and economic gains for women, though success has been far less in the legal, political, and cultural spheres. These changes have had a profound effect on Iranian families in terms of frequency and age of marriage, number of children, and frequency of divorce. An active women's movement continues. The movement includes both secular and Islamic women. The 2009 protests in which it actively participated and the government's response to those protests, however, show that women still have much to achieve.

CASE Questions

1. What does the contradiction in Iran between significant socioeconomic and educational advance, on the one hand, and severe political and cultural restrictions, on the other, teach us about which areas are most important for the advancement of gender equality? Does it suggest one area should be the primary target for change first?

2. What would the various theories on multiculturalism that we discussed at the start of the chapter argue about the Iranian case? Would any of them justify some of the policies toward women in the name of respecting religious belief and cultural differences? Why or why not?

The women's movement has fundamentally questioned and challenged conventional liberal notions of modern citizenship as well as all other forms of identity. It has been the most successful domestic and international social movement of the last half-century, changing mores and policies in many countries. Our case studies and much other evidence point to a broad trend of women achieving great gains in the educational sphere that have translated only partially into gains in the economic sphere. While women are working for wages far more frequently than they used to in virtually every country, they work for less money and in less prestigious positions than men. Similarly, while they have made substantial gains in political power in many countries, especially in parts of Europe, they are nowhere equal to men in the political sphere. These continued shortcomings raise fundamental questions about whether our understanding of citizenship, common social attitudes, and major institutions have to change before women will achieve equal citizenship in its broadest conception. In addition to raising all these questions, the feminist movement has been intimately connected with the rise of the "gay rights movement," to which we now turn.

SEXUAL ORIENTATION: ASSIMILATION OR LIBERATION?

What is commonly known as the "gay rights movement," the demand for inclusion in full citizenship for people of all sexual orientations, challenges social norms at least as much or more than the women's movement. The movement for equality based on sexual orientation faces a unique set of challenges compared with the other movements discussed in this chapter and in chapter 4. Its primary demand has been for public recognition; once this is achieved, other demands include full legal equality and open representation and participation in the political process. Recognition is especially central to the movement because homosexual activity has been hidden throughout most of human history. Homosexuals are able to hide their identity in a way women or minorities typically cannot. Throughout history and around the world, people have engaged in homosexual activity but have hidden it because of social and political discrimination and criminalization. In this context, being publicly recognized and "coming out" as gay or lesbian is the first crucial political act and demand. Literal recognition, in the sense of no longer having to hide, is essential.

Who Is Included in the Movement

A major debate within the gay rights movement has long been how to identify the group(s) and whom to include. The matter of definition is not simple. Indeed, the term *homosexual* itself first appeared in print only in 1869. Prior to that, people were well aware of the fact that individuals of the same sex had sexual relations, but this was thought of as a practice, not as a category of people or an identity. Given the strong social and financial pressure to marry in virtually all societies, much homosexual activity took place and continues to take place among individuals married to members of the opposite sex. Only in the last century have people come to think of themselves as homosexuals and, more recently, as "gay" or "lesbian."

But even with this social construction of an identity category, the name and exact boundaries of the group and movement have shifted over time. Originally referred to as "homosexual," by the late 1960s the group had adopted the term "gay and lesbian" in some countries, in part because "homosexual" had been a term used by psychiatrists to classify the practice as a mental disorder. By the 1980s, though, it was becoming clear that not all people who were not heterosexual identified themselves as gay or lesbian. Sex research has long shown that sexual preferences do not fit into absolute categories but rather extend along a continuum, from sole preference for the opposite sex on one end and for the same sex on the other and a range of variation in between. Eventually, the categories "bisexual" and "transgender," the latter meaning people who do not identify clearly with either major gender, were added to produce "lesbian, gay, bisexual, and transgender" (LGBT), the most common current designation in the United States. Recently, some activists and theorists have adopted the word *queer*, formerly considered derogatory, as an affirmative term to include the entire LGBT group or sometimes as an addition to the label, as in LGBTQ.

Assimilationist versus Liberationist Approach

In addition to these definitional debates, the LGBT community has debated the terms on which it should try to gain inclusion. Like the women's movement, members are divided over the extent to which they should simply seek equal rights within the existing system or seek to transform the norms of the system. Those who favor an assimilationist approach seek equal civil and political rights but generally are willing to adopt the cultural norms of mainstream, heterosexual society: for instance, they favor same-sex marriage, the expansion of a heterosexual institution to include them. The **liberationist** approach, on the other hand, seeks to transform sexual and gender norms, not simply to gain equal rights with heterosexuals but also to liberate everyone to express whatever sexual orientation and gender identity they wish; the goal is to gain social acceptance and respect for all regardless of their conformity to preexisting norms or institutions. Those favoring a liberationist approach question the importance of same-sex marriage because they question the entire idea of marriage as a patriarchal, heterosexual institution that they would like the freedom to move beyond. They certainly favor equal rights, but they seek much greater change than that, calling for a new "sexual citizenship" (Bell and Binnie 2000). This debate mirrors the broader debate about multiculturalism and group rights. Some liberationists portray a "gay culture" that deserves autonomy and respect along the lines of multicultural integration, while the more mainstream part of the movement takes a more traditional liberal stance of demanding equality for all. Iris Young (2000) would see inclusion of gay voices of all types, and paying particular attention to the most marginalized in the liberationist wing of the movement, as crucial for achieving full democracy and citizenship for all.

In terms of rights, members of the LGBT group are unusual in the sense that they secured basic political rights as individuals long before civil rights; that is, as individuals

liberationist
Member of the LGBT movement who seeks to transform sexual and gender norms so that all may gain social acceptance and respect regardless of their conformity to preexisting norms or institutions

CRITICAL INQUIRY

The World Values Survey: Attitudes toward Women, Religion, and Homosexuality

This chapter treats claims for inclusion by religious groups, women, and gays and lesbians separately, though we note that they share many similarities and can be understood using the same philosophical debate. The Critical Inquiry table provides data from the World Values Survey of attitudes toward all three groups and a few other key variables for a selection of countries. What patterns can you see in the data? Do attitudes for all three areas go together? Why or why not? What hypotheses can you generate to explain the patterns you find? Can you tie these hypotheses to some of the theories that explain political behavior that we've examined throughout the book?

	Importance of religion (% responding "very" and "rather important")	Membership in church (% active members)	Trust people of another religion (%)*	Importance of democracy (%)**	Men deserve jobs more than women (%)	Men make better political leaders (% responding "agree" and "strongly agree")	Homosexuality justified (% responding justified or very justified)***	Don't want homosexuals as neighbors (%)***
Argentina	65.4	17	62.8	87.1	27.7	32.2	45.6	23.7
Brazil	91	50.5	50.3	73.2	23	31.7	26.5	26.1
Colombia	NA	24.5	37	67.5	NA	29.3	27.1	53.5
Chile	73.4	23	37	67.8	30.2	49.3	39.2	39.1
Burkina Faso	96.5	24.4	55.4	65.8	52.3	62.5	5.7	81.6
Ghana	97.9	72.1	52.8	91.4	53.6	78.2	5.4	79.3
Rwanda	95.8	53	67.2	86.3	25.3	51.6	3.4	63.3
South Africa	90.5	51.1	63.4	81.1	37.1	50.6	16.7	45.9
Germany	33.9	12.9	42.8	88.8	17.8	18.8	60.3	17.3
France	40.9	4.4	77.7	77.6	18.1	24.7	59.5	34.1
United Kingdom	40.7	19.2	80.9	79.3	16.2	19.7	50.4	18.8
United States	71.6	37.9	79.5	76.4	6.8	24.7	31.2	26
Egypt	99.6	0.9	39.2	86.8	89.1	92.5	NA	NA
Iran	94.7	20.1	NA	64.6	69.4	78.7	4	93.4
Iraq	99.4	NA	NA	NA	83.9	90.2	NA	NA
Morocco	98.5	1.5	22.5	82.4	50.8	58.4	NA	NA
India	80.7	21.9	45.3	46.4	51.4	63	23.5	45.2
Indonesia	98.8	38.1	39.9	75.9	55.4	60.9	2.9	69.8
Japan	19.6	4.4	NA	76.9	27.1	43.9	42	NA

Source: World Values Survey (http://www.wvsevsdb.com/wvs/WVSAnalizeQuestion.jsp).

*Percentage combines answers "trust completely" and "trust a little" in the survey.

**Percentage combines answers 8-10 from the survey, where the survey used a scale of 1-10, with 1 being "not at all important" and 10 being "absolutely important."

***World Values Survey notes that questions having to do with homosexuality were not asked in some countries for "cultural reasons."

they could vote or run for office like any other citizen, as long as they kept their sexual orientation private. As a group, though, they were unwelcome until quite recently in all societies. They could not proclaim their identity publicly in most countries because of laws criminalizing their behavior. Repeal of such laws therefore became one of the movement's first priorities. Beyond decriminalization of their behavior, they have worked for passage of antidiscrimination laws that prevent government, employers, educators, and adoption agencies from discriminating on the basis of sexual orientation. Those who favor same-sex marriage do so in part because they see the right to marry as part of equal civil rights since in all societies, marital status comes with legal benefits, such as taxation, inheritance, employment benefits, and control over major health decisions. The movement's political success remains greater than its success in the area of civil rights in a number of countries. While active gay rights movements engage in the political process in wealthy democracies without restraint, in most countries they have still not achieved equal civil rights in terms of antidiscrimination laws, marriage, and related areas.

STATE RESPONSES TO THE LGBT MOVEMENT

States have responded to these movements in various ways, as Map 12.3 demonstrates. Some have not only decriminalized homosexual activity but have legalized same-sex marriage; others have severe penalties for any homosexual activity. In many countries, homosexual activity is no longer criminal, though it is still socially ostracized. On the whole, the movements have clearly been more active and influential in wealthier countries. In well-established democracies, LGBT movements have been able to use their political rights to demand full civil rights, but with only partial success. The biggest issue of recent years has been same-sex marriage. A handful of states have granted complete rights to marry, starting with the Netherlands in 2001 and by 2013 including fifteen countries, as shown on Map 12.3. In the United States, by 2013, sixteen states (constituting 30 percent of the U.S. population) had legalized gay marriage and nine others had recognized some sort of civil union for same-sex couples. Most of the rest of the U.S. states, however, have explicitly banned same-sex marriage in their constitutions. Proponents of same-sex marriage argue it is a matter of equal civil rights for all. Opponents disagree based on religious beliefs or on the argument that heterosexual marriage is a key building block of social order and should be preserved as such. In contrast to many of the debates over inclusion, in this case those arguing for the status quo do so on the basis of preserving particular group rights (religious justifications for heterosexual marriages), while those seeking change argue for treating all individuals equally.

Web link:
International Gay, Lesbian, Bisexual, Trans and Intersex Association

Fewer postcolonial societies have active LGBT movements. Higher levels of religiosity and cultural traditions in many of these societies mean greater social opposition to public proclamation of homosexuality, as Map 12.3 and the Country and Concept table (pages 642–643) demonstrate. In a growing number of postcolonial countries, however, active gay rights movements have arisen. Indeed, South Africa became the

Web link:
Gay rights around the world

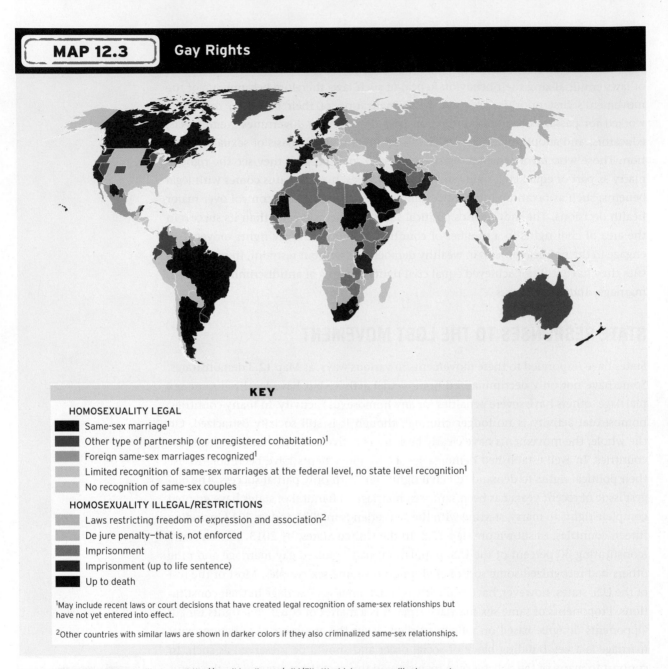

MAP 12.3	Gay Rights

KEY

HOMOSEXUALITY LEGAL

◼ Same-sex marriage[1]

◼ Other type of partnership (or unregistered cohabitation)[1]

◼ Foreign same-sex marriages recognized[1]

◼ Limited recognition of same-sex marriages at the federal level, no state level recognition[1]

◼ No recognition of same-sex couples

HOMOSEXUALITY ILLEGAL/RESTRICTIONS

◼ Laws restricting freedom of expression and association[2]

◼ De jure penalty—that is, not enforced

◼ Imprisonment

◼ Imprisonment (up to life sentence)

◼ Up to death

[1]May include recent laws or court decisions that have created legal recognition of same-sex relationships but have not yet entered into effect.

[2]Other countries with similar laws are shown in darker colors if they also criminalized same-sex relationships.

Source: Wikipedia, Homosexuality Laws (http://en.wikipedia.org/wiki/File:World_homosexuality_laws.svg).

first country in the world to include sexual orientation in its constitution as a category protected from discrimination. In 2005 a South African court interpreted this to apply to marriage, making it also one of the first countries to legalize gay marriage. Fledgling LGBT movements elsewhere in Africa, however, such as in Zimbabwe, Kenya, and Uganda, face much greater popular and legal resistance, and in many

African and Middle Eastern countries, homosexual activity remains explicitly illegal. One of our two case studies, Brazil, is an example of a postcolonial society with an active LGBT movement that has had some notable policy successes, including legalizing gay marriage in 2013. We compare it with the United States, the country that has been at the forefront of the LGBT movement for a generation now, though the U.S. government has not responded with pro-LGBT policies as quickly as have a number of other governments.

THE UNITED STATES: BIRTHPLACE OF A MOVEMENT, BUT LIMITED POLICY CHANGE

The modern gay rights movement was born in New York City in 1969 at the famous Stonewall riots. New York police raided a popular gay bar, the Stonewall Inn, on June 28, setting off five days of sometimes violent defense of the bar and attacks on the police. While a small gay rights movement had existed since the 1950s, the Stonewall event led to its rapid expansion across the country and then around the world. The movement has had greater success at the state and local level than at the national level in the American federal system, resulting in a patchwork of laws and rights across the country. This limited success has been due in part to the growth of an equally active anti–gay rights movement centered in conservative religious groups, with greater strength in some areas of the country than in others.

The first gay rights movement was the Mattachine Society, founded in Los Angeles in 1951. Known as the "homophile" movement, its main goals were to unify homosexuals, raise their and others' consciousness of their existence and numbers, and lessen discrimination against them. The movement quickly divided over assimilationist versus liberationist strategies, with the former becoming dominant

- **BACKGROUND**
  Early movement very small and assimilationist; Stonewall riots create "gay rights" movement in 1969

- **TYPE OF MOVEMENT**
  Primarily assimilationist, though with liberationist elements

- **SUCCESSES**
  Legalization of homosexual activity; full participation in military; active political participation

- **CONTINUING CHALLENGES**
  Employment discrimination and same-sex marriage

throughout the 1960s. While branches opened in a number of major cities and the movement won a couple of important court cases on discrimination in employment, it remained a small effort. William Eskridge described the effects of Stonewall on this fledgling movement:

> Literally overnight, the Stonewall riots transformed the homophile movement of several dozen homosexuals into a *gay liberation movement* populated by thousands of lesbians, gay men, and bisexuals who formed hundreds of organizations demanding radical changes. (1999, 99)

A month after Stonewall, the Gay Liberation Front was formed. Soon thereafter a more assimilationist Gay Activist Alliance emerged, once again reflecting division in the movement.

By the 1980s, this social movement had grown exponentially, with the assimilationist forces forming several major interest groups, including the Human Rights Campaign (HRC), the National Gay and Lesbian Task Force (NGLTF), and the Lambda Defense and Legal Education Fund. These and other groups lobbied Congress and state legislatures for legal changes, pursued court cases, and funded gay candidates for office as well as straight candidates who supported their cause. The HIV/AIDS crisis, which disproportionately affected gay men in its early years, gave new impetus to a more social movement orientation among activists. Believing that neither the government nor the mainstream gay rights groups were adequately addressing the epidemic, new groups emerged and demanded greater attention as well as greater freedom to express their sexuality publicly. The best known of the HIV/AIDS groups was the AIDS Coalition to Unleash Power (ACT UP), formed in 1987. It and other groups fought for greater funding for AIDS research and drugs and initiated the practice of occasional marches on Washington, D.C., the first of which was held in 1979, to demand broader gay rights in general. ACT UP also sought to recruit racial minority members, whose absence from the broader movement (similar to their absence from the early women's movement) had been notable and a source of criticism and weakness.

The LGBT movement, both the assimilationist and liberationist strands, has become a significant component of American civil society and political activity, as has opposition to it. The movement has successfully elected a growing number of openly LGBT candidates to office at all levels of the American political system. In an extensive quantitative and qualitative study of descriptive representation of the LGBT community at the state level, Haider-Markel (2010) found that LGBT candidates are just as likely to get elected as straight candidates but that they choose to run only in districts with constituents who are likely to be sympathetic to them. He also found that a higher percentage of LGBT state legislators made it more likely that "gay rights" legislation would be initiated and passed, though the LGBT legislators themselves were not always the chief sponsors of the legislation. Often, they instead played a role they termed "educating" straight legislators about the importance of LGBT issues. The most important factor in passage of gay rights legislation, however, was not the number of LBGT legislators but the general attitudes of the states' voters toward gay rights issues, leading Haider-Markel to recommend that the movement continue to focus on changing broad societal attitudes.

Members' success in establishing themselves as a political force, however, has not been matched with complete success in achieving their policy objectives. Legal battles have become a major area of policy action. The first Supreme Court decision of note ruled in favor of the Mattachine Society's right to transmit its magazine through the mail; the U.S. Post Office had banned its distribution via the mail on the grounds of obscenity, even though it was simply a news magazine addressing gay issues. LGBT activists believed the Supreme Court had set the stage for a federal repeal of all sodomy laws in the 1965 *Griswold v. Connecticut* decision, which legalized the use of contraception by married adults on the grounds of a "right to privacy" implicit in the Constitution (a right later used to legalize abortion in *Roe v. Wade* in 1973). In 1986 the Court heard *Bowers v. Hardwick,* in which a Georgia man had been arrested in his own bedroom for having sex with another man. In a 5–4 decision, the Supreme Court ruled that the right to privacy did not apply, in part because no long-standing tradition of respecting privacy in the case of homosexual relations existed. Finally, in the 2003 case of *Lawrence v. Texas,* the Court ruled 6–3 that sodomy laws were unconstitutional for violating the right to due process, explicitly reversing its 1986 decision.

Web link:
Some states still have sodomy laws

Another area of success, after a protracted battle, is the right of members of the LGBT community to serve openly in the military. When President Bill Clinton came to office, the movement thought—based on statements made during his campaign—that it had a champion for its concerns, and he was the first president to meet with leadership from the major groups in the White House. Nonetheless, facing opposition from Congress and the military, Clinton created the "don't ask, don't tell" policy instead of allowing gay men and lesbians to serve openly. Under the new policy, the military no longer inquired about sexual orientation but also gay soldiers could not reveal their orientation. Discharges based on sexual orientation totaled over 17,000 before its

repeal. In September 2010, a federal judge in California ruled that the policy violated the Equal Protection and First Amendment rights of service members. At the same time, the U.S. military leadership, after an extensive survey of its members, concluded that allowing gays and lesbians to serve openly would not jeopardize military readiness and therefore national security. With a court ruling against "don't ask, don't tell" and the military undermining the main argument in its favor—national security— Congress passed, and on December 22, 2010, President Barack Obama signed, a bill that repealed the law. Gays and lesbians now serve openly in the U.S. military, as they do in many other militaries.

Other legislative and legal battles have not been as successful. While nearly half the states have laws protecting against employment discrimination on the basis of sexual orientation and another twelve on the basis of gender identity, the federal government has never passed a law prohibiting private-sector discrimination nationwide, even though federal employees themselves have this protection. Legislators first introduced such legislation in 1974. Currently titled the Employment Non-Discrimination Act (ENDA), the bill has continuously been introduced but has not passed in Congress. Its latest version includes protection not only on the basis of sexual orientation but also gender identity, including transgendered people.

The biggest current issue in the United States and much of the wealthy world is legalization of same-sex marriage. The mainstream, assimilationist organizations in the American movement have fought for this right in terms of American civil rights laws, arguing that restricting marriage to a man and a woman is discriminatory. The first court case to question a state's refusal to grant a same-sex couple a marriage license was in 1993 in Hawaii, but it ultimately resulted in the state passing a constitutional amendment banning same-sex marriage and passing a law allowing civil unions. The case produced a nationwide campaign against same-sex marriage, which led to twenty-nine state laws and constitutional amendments explicitly restricting marriage to a union between a man and a woman and a federal law, the Defense of Marriage Act (DOMA), passed by Congress and signed by President Clinton in 1996, doing the same.

The movement for legalizing same-sex marriage gained great momentum in the new millennium. Massachusetts became the first state to allow gay marriage in May 2004; and by 2013, sixteen states and the District of Columbia had followed suit. In the 2012 election, Maine and Maryland became the first states to legalize gay marriage via the ballot box rather than the courts or state legislature. In 2012 President Obama became the first president or major presidential candidate to declare himself in favor of legalizing gay marriage; he was also the first president to mention gay rights and gay marriage in an inaugural address in January 2013. Later that year, probably the most important Supreme Court cases on gay rights to date were decided simultaneously. The Court ruled that DOMA was unconstitutional, giving legally married gay couples (in states that allow same-sex marriage) the same federal benefits as straight married couples. In the second case, the Court ruled it did not have jurisdiction to overturn an appellate court ruling that legalized gay marriage in California. The ruling applied only to California, however; the Court declined to rule on whether gay marriage should be legal across the country. This left gay marriage legal in sixteen states but specifically prohibited in thirty-five others. In combination with the end of DOMA, this has resulted in a patchwork of legal situations for gay couples. For instance, same-sex spouses can get spousal Social Security benefits if they live in a state where same-sex marriage is legal but not if they live in a state where it is illegal. Clearly, this legal and political battle is not over.

Web link:
Freedom to Marry
website

Many analysts saw these rapid changes as reflecting changing attitudes toward gays and gay marriage in the population as a whole. Polls found that in 2008 only about 45 percent of Americans supported gay marriage, but by 2012 that number had jumped to nearly 55 percent. Similarly, the number of people reporting that they had a family member or friend who was gay jumped from 45 to 60 percent (likely reflecting more people "coming out" as gay). Regional variation in this, reflecting variation in state laws on the subject, was strong, however (CNN/ORC Poll 2012).

CASE Summary   The United States was the birthplace of the LGBT movement and continues to have one of the most active movements in the world. Strong opposition from Christian conservatives, a stronger political force in the United States than in other wealthy countries, and the decentralized, federal system have resulted in the movement achieving only partial success, however. Though successful at ending criminalization of homosexual conduct and discrimination in the military, the movement has achieved only partial success in ending employment discrimination and restrictions on same-sex marriage. These battles, however, are far from over. Opinion polls show the nation divided on the issue of same-sex marriage but with a growing majority in support, and younger Americans are much more supportive than older ones, giving the movement hope that change will come eventually.

CASE Questions

1. What does the case of the gay rights movement in the United States teach us about how and why new social movements become more effective? Which tactics, resources, or political opportunities helped the movement gain significantly more support in the new millennium?

2. What does the importance of the same-sex marriage debate in the United States suggest about the debate about multiculturalism and group rights with which we began this chapter? Do the demands being made and policies being adopted suggest a move toward multicultural integration, simple liberal equality, or a growing deliberative democracy in which gay voices are given greater respect?

CASE Study

BRAZIL: LGBT RIGHTS IN A NEW DEMOCRACY

São Paulo, Brazil's largest city, annually hosts what is reputed to be the biggest gay pride parade and biggest annual LGBT gathering on the planet. Although Brazil is the world's largest predominantly Catholic country, it has a long history and reputation of being relatively open about sexuality in general. It has long had a well-established LGBT community, but it only developed an open political movement with the transition to democracy in the late 1970s. Like the movement in the United States, the Brazilian movement went through years of controversy over how to define itself. It has succeeded in getting policies that are more inclusive of LGBT rights than most states, especially in comparison to most postcolonial states, but its aims are by no means completely met. The movement continues to work to achieve policies to eliminate discrimination on the basis of sexual orientation and to reduce violence against members of the LGBT community. It achieved a milestone success, however, when a Brazilian court ordered the legalization of same-sex marriage in 2013.

The first explicit Brazilian gay rights group, Grupo Somos (We Are Group), formed in São Paulo in 1979. It was preceded in the 1960s by mostly apolitical homophile groups like those in the United States before Stonewall. Grupo Somos emerged at the same time that major pressure on the military regime for political

A lesbian couple displays their wedding rings after getting married in the city of Campinas, Brazil, in 2013. The Brazilian Supreme Court had ruled shortly before that denying gays and lesbians the right to marry violated the constitutional ban against discrimination. Brazil is the third and by far the largest Latin American country to legalize gay marriage, after Argentina and Uruguay.

opening of the country began (see chapter 9). By the early 1980s, about twenty mostly male gay rights groups existed, but many of these did not survive more than a few years and were plagued by divisions over the inclusion of lesbians and transvestites. Both of the latter formed separate organizations at various points. Until 1992, the major annual meeting of the movement was called the Brazilian Meeting of Homosexuals; in 1993 this became the Brazilian Meeting of Lesbians and Homosexuals; in 1998 the Brazilian Meeting of Lesbians, Gays, and Transgenders. Finally, in 2005 the Brazilian Association of Lesbians, Gays, and Transvestites was founded, bringing all the major groups under one umbrella. (In Brazil the movement is known usually by the label GLT rather than LGBT, and *T* includes the active transvestite community but not a "transgender"-identified group, a category not widely accepted there.)

The movement's growth, despite its divisions, has been impressive. The leadership of the union-based Workers' Party (PT) (see chapter 7) rhetorically embraced gay rights activists and their cause at the first party convention in 1981, though opposition from some Catholic activists in the party continued. The AIDS crisis first hurt and then strengthened the movement in the 1980s. Initially, AIDS hit the gay male population the hardest, as it did in the United States. As awareness grew, however, infection rates among gay men dropped significantly. Simultaneously, and partly as a result of active pressure from the movement, Brazil developed an AIDS prevention and treatment policy that became a global model of success. Many AIDS NGOs with ties to the gay rights movement arose in the 1980s. By the 1990s, the World Bank and other international donors were funding some GLT groups that were helping to implement the National AIDS Program. Several hundred gay rights groups now constitute the overall movement. In 2006 Juan Marsiaj noted that "the size and diversity of the Brazilian GLT movement make it the largest and one of the strongest of its kind in Latin America" (172).

In 1823 Brazil became one of the first countries in the world to eliminate anti-sodomy laws. While homosexual activity is not illegal, the law only partially enforces antidiscrimination. The gay rights movement worked hard to get "sexual orientation" included in the 1988 constitution's antidiscrimination clause but was unsuccessful. A national antidiscrimination law focusing on discrimination by commercial enterprises and government offices passed the Congress in 2000. By 2003, three states and more than seventy municipalities, including the country's two largest cities, had passed some type of antidiscrimination law. A law to outlaw all forms of discrimination on the basis of sexual orientation and gender identity passed one house of Congress in 2006 and has the ruling party's support, but it never passed the second house.

In contrast to the United States, the federal government controls marriage law in Brazil. The PT introduced a bill in the National Congress in 1995 to legalize civil unions nationwide, but it never passed. Court cases have expanded the rights of same-sex couples, however. The Constitution's antidiscrimination clause does not list "sexual orientation" specifically but does mention "and other forms of discrimination." Using this clause, the federal high court ruled in 2000 that same-sex partners in a "stable union" should be treated as married couples in the social security and public pension systems. In 2008 the movement's hopes increased further when President Luiz Inácio "Lula" da Silva of the PT said publicly he would do all he could to see that a hate crimes law against homophobia and a civil union law were enacted. Once again, the courts took the lead, legalizing civil unions in 2011 and same-sex marriage in 2013.

Web link:
Brazilian gay unions must be registered as marriages

Brazil's GLT community has actively engaged in the PT, which became the governing party in 2002. In 1992 a gay and lesbian group was officially formed within the party to pressure elected members to support GLT causes. The PT government, responding to pressure from the GLT movement, launched the National Conference for Lesbians, Gay Men, Bisexuals, Transvestites and Transsexuals, the first government-sponsored conference of its kind in the world. A year later the government announced a groundbreaking plan to eventually end all forms of discrimination against the GLT community.

In spite of these developments, harassment of gay citizens remains a major concern and common occurrence, and Congress still has not passed a law fully criminalizing such behavior. Antigay violence is unusually widespread in Brazil, and it increased by nearly 50 percent in 2013. This demonstrates that while there is growing acceptance of Brazil's GLT community, opposition continues to exist. In 2013 a member of Congress who is an evangelical minister was elected chair of a key congressional committee and introduced a bill that would allow psychologists to treat homosexuality as a pathology, but the bill failed to pass and a poll showed that 84 percent of Brazilians believed he should step down from his position.

CASE Summary   The GLT community in Brazil enjoys significantly greater rights than it did during the 1980s and more than those allowed to LGBT communities in many countries. Arguably, it has been at least as successful as the U.S. movement that helped inspire it. The transition to democracy, which emphasized expanded rights for all, even though "sexual orientation" was explicitly rejected for inclusion in the new constitution, established a political context in which Brazilian policy has shifted significantly. This culminated in the legalization of same-sex marriage in 2013. In terms of recognition, the first and most important goal of the LGBT movement, Brazil has achieved a great deal. The GLT community is widely known and celebrated, especially via São Paulo's gargantuan gay pride parade. Opposition from both traditionalist Catholic and evangelical Protestant movements continues, but all indications are that the Brazilian political system has expanded its definition of equal citizenship to include GLT members in such a way as to effect permanent change.

CASE Questions

1. What differences do you see in how gay rights have advanced in the United States and Brazil? What explains these differences: differences in the political systems, the cultures, or the gay rights movements themselves?
2. How do the gay rights movements in these two cases compare with the women's movements in Russia and Iran? What similarities do you see in how and why groups organize and achieve success, or not?

The LGBT movement has raised, if anything, more profound challenges to conventional social mores and institutions than the women's movement has. Sexual orientation is unique as an identity category due to the ability of homosexual and bisexual individuals to "hide" their identity relatively easily. This has meant that as individuals they have long had basic political rights for which women, racial, and other identity groups often had to fight. As a group, however, they were repressed and forced to hide until quite recently. They remain the group least frequently given recognition, respect, and rights by states around the world. Like feminists, gay rights activists raise fundamental questions about core institutions such as marriage, not only who ought to be included but also how it should be defined and whether it should exist. Some simply want inclusion in existing institutions, but others want more fundamental institutional and attitudinal changes. Our case studies are two countries that have had unusually active movements, yet their policies continue to allow certain areas of discrimination based on sexual orientation. This is in part because the goals of the movement conflict with deeply held values based on cultural or religious traditions that accept group membership and behavior only within the bounds of heterosexual practice. In this sense, the LGBT movement raises the same questions about citizenship and inclusion that we have discussed throughout this chapter.

CONCLUSION

Identity groups always pose challenges to the modern state. As we saw in chapter 4, under some circumstances ethnicity, race, or religion can challenge the very conception of a nation. At other times, religion, like gender and sexuality, poses a different kind of challenge to modern states as they address issues of inclusiveness and equal citizenship. In liberal democracies, such challenges cut to the heart of one of the defining characteristics of the regime. Demands for inclusive citizenship can also raise challenges when they clash with the demands of other identity groups. States must then resolve the question of which groups' demands to meet. This can be particularly difficult when, for instance, women or LGBT groups demand individual civil rights in the name of equality, while a religious, ethnic, or other minority group claims a conflicting right to respect for its cultural practices.

The outcomes of protracted and intense political battles always reveal something about who rules in a particular political system. Policy outcomes, at least in part, reflect the relative power of different political forces. In the political disputes we examined in this chapter, a dominant group protecting the status quo exists in almost all cases. Lack of identity-based conflict may indeed reflect nearly complete domination by that group, as the "second face of power" (see chapter 1) would suggest. Where questions about the inclusion of minority or marginalized identity groups have become politically salient, those groups have at least gained enough power to raise their demands. Their success demonstrates growing power; continuing limitations on their demands equally demonstrate limits on their power. On that basis, women, especially in wealthier countries, seem to have achieved greater power than LGBT groups. The power of religious minorities varies more around the world; Muslim traditionalists in India seem to have enough power to keep control over personal law, an important issue to them, while Muslims in France have met with far less success in their ability to assert their religious identity publicly.

As the comparison of Muslims in India and in France suggests, culture and institutions can play an important role in explaining what demands are raised, how they are raised, and how successful they are. As our cases suggest, many factors are at work in this process. First, it is important to recognize that the demands of similar groups in different countries are not always the same. Cultural context, at least in the short term, can have an important role in explaining these differences. For instance, our cases show that not all women's groups have adopted Western feminist demands or rationales for women's rights. Thus, states are responding to different sets of demands from the start.

Second, the institutional context in which identity groups make demands also matters. Institutions create the avenues through which groups approach the state, sometimes shaping groups' demands. Does a group approach the state at the local or national level? Through protests, votes, or lawsuits? On which particular issues? All of these questions are deeply affected by the institutional context, as cases from gay rights in the United States to Muslim rights in the United Kingdom suggest.

Many aspects of the groups themselves may play a key role in their success or failure. Most important, a critical mass of people must recognize themselves as part of a group with common interests vis-à-vis the state. At that point, their ability to mobilize resources, to frame a persuasive argument, and to exploit political opportunities can be crucial to their success. As several of our examples suggest, from religious Muslims in Turkey to LGBT groups in the United States, their mobilization may also encourage the countermobilization of groups with conflicting values. Struggles for recognition, whether they involve demands for equal citizenship or communal rights or both, are usually protracted and difficult.

More and more groups throughout the world appear to be demanding inclusion, recognition, and individual or communal rights, suggesting that globalization may be playing a role as well. Cultural and ideological aspects of globalization seem to be particularly important, starting with the rhetorical dominance of liberal democracy. As we've stressed throughout the book, the dominance of democratic discourse makes it important for virtually all states to justify their actions in terms of citizenship, and this provides an opening and a basis on which groups can demand inclusion and recognition. In addition, the wave of democratization in the 1990s has opened political space for identity groups around the world. Indeed, women's movements and other identity-based movements were part of the social movement cohort that helped push the tide of democratization forward in the first place.

Globalization also has given more impetus to the construction of identity movements, whether via globalized examples and inspiration or via assertions of local identity against the forces of global homogenization. The movement of people across borders and especially postcolonial immigration has raised questions about inclusiveness and the definition of citizenship in long-established democracies. Media also certainly play a role, as news of identity group mobilizations in one place travels quickly and may spark similar organizing elsewhere. For this reason, people often speak of a wave of "global feminisms" of different types beginning in the 1970s. Although groups throughout the world developed feminist goals and tactics to suit their particular circumstances, news and ideas from other countries encouraged women everywhere to organize for their own agendas.

The trend toward greater mobilization around issues of identity is strong right now, but as always in comparative politics, we cannot assume that what is true today will be true tomorrow. We do believe that identity will continue to be a key challenge to the politics of nation-states, and particularly liberal democracies, and these challenges are likely to arise in other places if more countries expand their openness to global ideas and increase the scope of their civil societies. In the future, however, new conflicts and new political trends will arise, and students of comparative politics will be challenged to document and explain the patterns, sources, and outcomes of future political conflicts.

KEY CONCEPTS

communitarianism (p. 646)

deliberative democracy (p. 646)

laïcité (p. 649)

liberationist (p. 685)

multicultural integration (p. 646)

multiculturalism (p. 654)

neutral state model (p. 649)

positive accommodation (p. 651)

Sharpen your skills with SAGE edge at **edge.sagepub.com/orvis3e.** **SAGE edge for students** provides a personalized approach to help you accomplish your coursework goals in an easy-to-use learning environment.

WORKS CITED

Allen, Jodie T., and Richard Wike. 2009. "How Europe and Its Muslim Populations See Each Other." In *Muslims in Western Politics*, edited by Abdulkader H. Sinno, 137–160. Bloomington: Indiana University Press.

Aryan, Khadijeh. 2012. "The Boom in Women's Education." In *Women, Power, and Politics in 21st Century Iran*, edited by Tara Povey and Elaheh Rostami-Povey, 35–52. Burlington, VT: Ashgate Publishing Company.

Bahramitash, Roksana, and Shahla Kazemi-pour. 2006. "Myths and Realities of the Impact of Islam on Women: Changing Marital Status in Iran." *Critique: Critical Middle Eastern Studies* 15 (2): 111–128.

Baskakova, Marina E., and Irina V. Soboleva. 2010. "Promoting Gender Equality and Empowerment of Women." In *National Human Development Report in the Russian Federation 2010: Millennium Development Goals in Russia; Looking into the Future,* edited by Sergeĭ Nikolaevich Bobylev, 48–62. Moscow, Russia: United Nations Development Programme (http://www.undp.ru/nhdr2010/National_Human_Development_Report_in_the_RF_2010_ENG.pdf).

Basu, Srimati. 2008. "Separate and Unequal: Muslim Women and Un-uniform Family Law in India." *International Feminist Journal of Politics* 10 (4): 495–517. doi: 10.1080/14616740802393890.

Bell, David, and Jon Binnie. 2000. *The Sexual Citizen: Queer Politics and Beyond.* Cambridge, UK, and Malden, MA: Polity Press and Blackwell.

Bobylev, Sergeĭ Nikolaevich. 2005. *Human Development Report 2005—Russian Federation: Russia in 2015; Development Goals and Policy Priorities.* Moscow, Russia: United Nations Development Programme.

CNN/ORC Poll. 2012. May 29–31 (http://i2.cdn.turner.com/cnn/2012/images/06/06/rel5e.pdf).

Equality and Human Rights Commission (UK). "About Us" (http://www.equalityhumanrights.com/about-us).

Eskridge, William N., Jr. 1999. *Gaylaw: Challenging the Apartheid of the Closet.* Cambridge, MA: Harvard University Press.

Fetzer, Joel S., and J. Christopher Soper. 2005. *Muslims and the State in Britain, France, and Germany.* Cambridge, UK: Cambridge University Press.

Haider-Markel, Donald P. 2010. *Out and Running: Gay and Lesbian Candidates, Elections, and Policy Representation.* Washington, DC: Georgetown University Press.

Harel-Shalev, Ayelet. 2013. "Policy Analysis beyond Personal Law: Muslim Women's Rights in India." *Politics & Policy* 41: 384–419. doi:10.1111/polp.12016.

Hoodfar, Homa, and Fatemeh Sadeghi. 2009. "Against All Odds: The Women's Movement in the Islamic Republic of Iran." *Development* 52 (2): 215–223. doi: 10.1057/dev.2009.19.

Inter-Parliamentary Union. 2013. *Women in National Parliaments* (http://www.ipu.org/wmn-e/classif.htm).

Johnson, Janet Elise, and Aino Saarinen. 2013. "Twenty-First Century Feminisms under Repression: Gender Regime Change and the Women's Crisis Center Movement in Russia." *Signs* 38 (3): 543–567.

Jones, Justin. 2010. "'Signs of Churning': Muslim Personal Law and Public Contestation in Twenty-first Century India." *Modern Asian Studies* 44 (1): 175–200. doi: 10.1017/S0026749X09990114.

Kirkpatrick, Jeane J. 1974. *Political Woman.* New York: Basic Books.

Koolaee, Elaheh. 2012. "Women in the Parliament." In *Women, Power, and Politics in 21st Century Iran*, edited by Tara Povey and Elaheh Rostami-Povey, 137–151. Burlington, VT: Ashgate.

Krook, Mona Lena. 2009. *Quotas for Women in Politics: Gender and Candidate Selection Reform Worldwide.* New York: Oxford University Press.

Krook, Mona Lena, and Leslie Schwindt-Bayer. 2013. "Electoral Institutions." In *The Oxford Handbook of Gender and Politics,* edited by Georgina Waylen, Karen Celis, Johanna Kantola, and S. Laurel Weldon, 554–578. Oxford, UK: Oxford University Press.

Kymlicka, Will. 1995. *Multicultural Citizenship: A Liberal Theory of Minority Rights.* Oxford, UK: Clarendon Press.

Kymlicka, Will, and Wayne Norman, eds. 2000. *Citizenship in Diverse Societies.* Oxford, UK: Oxford University Press.

Local Government Improvement and Development. 2011. "Equality and Human Rights Commission" (http://www.idea.gov.uk/idk/core/page.do?pageId=9277949).

Mahdavi, Pardis. 2009. *Passionate Uprisings: Iran's Sexual Revolution.* Stanford, CA: Stanford University Press.

Mansbridge, Jane. 2000. "What Does a Representative Do? Descriptive Representation in Communicative Settings of Distrust, Uncrystallized Interests, and Historically Denigrated Status." In *Citizenship in Diverse Societies,* edited by Will Kymlicka and Wayne Norman, 99–123. Oxford, UK: Oxford University Press.

Marshall, T. H. 1963. *Class, Citizenship, and Social Development: Essays.* Chicago: University of Chicago Press.

Marsiaj, Juan P. 2006. "Social Movements and Political Parties: Gays, Lesbians, and *Travestis* and the Struggle for Inclusion in Brazil." *Canadian Journal of Latin American and Caribbean Studies* 31 (62): 167–198.

Maxwell, Rahsaan. 2010. "Trust in Government among British Muslims: The Importance of Migration Status." *Political Behavior* 32 (1): 89–109. doi:10.1007/s11109-009-9093-1.

Modood, Tariq. 2006. "British Muslims and the Politics of Multiculturalism." In *Multiculturalism, Muslims, and Citizenship: A European Approach,* edited by Tariq Modood, Ann Triandafyllidou, and Ricard Zapata-Barrero, 37–56. New York: Routledge.

Nejadbahram, Zahra. 2012. "Women and Employment." In *Women, Power, and Politics in 21st Century Iran,* edited by Tara Povey and Elaheh Rostami-Povey, 73–89. Burlington, VT: Ashgate.

Paidar, Parvin. 1995. *Women and the Political Process in Twentieth-Century Iran.* Cambridge, UK: Cambridge University Press.

Pateman, Carole. 1988. *The Sexual Contract.* Stanford, CA: Stanford University Press.

Racioppi, Linda, and Katherine O'Sullivan See. 1995. "Organizing Women before and after the Fall: Women's Politics in the Soviet Union and Post-Soviet Russia." *Signs* 20 (4): 818–850.

Rao, Badrinath. 2006. "The Variant Meanings of Secularism in India: Notes toward Conceptual Clarifications." *Journal of Church and State* 48 (1): 47–81. doi:10.1093/jcs/48.1.47.

Rezai-Rashti, Goli, and Valentine Moghadam. 2011. "Women and Higher Education in Iran: What Are the Implications for Employment and the 'Marriage Market'?" *International Review of Education* 57 (3/4): 419–441.

Roschin, S. Yu, and N. V. Zubarevich. 2005. "Gender Equality and Extension of Women Rights in Russia in the Context of Millennium Development Goals." Moscow, Russia: United Nations Development Programme (http://www.undp.ru/Gender_MDG_eng.pdf).

Spodek, Howard. 2010. "In the Hindutva Laboratory: Pogroms and Politics in Gujarat, 2002." *Modern Asian Studies* XVIV (2): 349–399. March.

Stepan, Alfred. 2011. "The Multiple Secularisms of Modern Democratic and Non-Democratic Regimes." In *Rethinking*

Secularism, edited by Craig Calhoun, Mark Juergensmeyer, and Jonathan van Antwerpen, 114–144. Oxford, UK: Oxford University Press.

Tahmasebi-Birgani, Victoria. 2010. "Green Women of Iran: The Role of the Women's Movement during and after Iran's Presidential Election of 2009." *Constellations* 17 (1): 78–86. doi:10.1111/j.1467-8675.2009.00576.x.

Teplova, Tatyana. 2007. "Welfare State Transformation, Childcare, and Women's Work in Russia." *Social Politics* 14 (3): 284–322. doi: 10.1093/sp/jxm016.

Tripp, Aili Mari, and Alice Kang. 2008. "The Global Impact of Quotas: On the Fast Track to Increased Female Legislative Representation." *Comparative Political Studies* 41 (3): 338–361. doi: 10.1177/0010414006297342.

Uberoi, Varun, and Tariqu Modood. 2013. "Inclusive Britishness: A Multiculturalist Advance." *Political Studies* 61 (1): 23–41.

White, Anne. 2005. "Gender Roles in Contemporary Russia: Attitudes and Expectations among Women Students." *Europe-Asia Studies* 57 (3): 429–455. doi: 10.1080/09668130500073449.

Young, Iris Marion. 2000. *Inclusion and Democracy.* Oxford, UK: Oxford University Press.

RESOURCES FOR FURTHER STUDY

Hunter, Shireen T., ed. 2002. *Islam, Europe's Second Religion: The New Social, Cultural, and Political Landscape.* Westport, CT: Praeger.

Joppke, Christian, and John Torpey. 2013. *Legal Integration of Islam: A Transatlantic Comparison.* Cambridge, MA: Harvard University Press.

Lovenduski, Joni, ed. 2005. *State Feminism and Political Representation.* Cambridge, UK: Cambridge University Press.

Mazur, Amy G. 2002. *Theorizing Feminist Policy.* Oxford, UK: Oxford University Press.

Parekh, Bhikhu C. 2000. *Rethinking Multiculturalism: Cultural Diversity and Political Theory.* Cambridge, MA: Harvard University Press.

Sinno, Abdulkader H., ed. 2009. *Muslims in Western Politics.* Bloomington: Indiana University Press.

WEB RESOURCES

Center for American Women and Politics
   (http://www.cawp.rutgers.edu)
International Lesbian, Gay, Bisexual, Trans and Intersex Association
   (http://ilga.org)
Quota Project
   (http://www.quotaproject.org)
Servicemembers Legal Defense Network
   (http://www.sldn.org/templates/index.html)
UNDP Human Development Reports, Gender Inequality Index
   (http://hdr.undp.org/en/statistics/gii)
World Values Survey
   (http://www.worldvaluessurvey.org)

Glossary

absolutism Rule by a single monarch who claims complete, exclusive power and sovereignty over a territory and its people (chapter 2)

assimilationist Someone who believes immigrants or other members of minority cultural communities ought to adopt the culture of the majority population (chapter 4)

asymmetrical federal system Division of constitutionally assigned power to national and subnational governments, with different subnational governments (states or provinces) having distinct relationships with and rights in relation to the national government (chapter 6)

authoritarian regime A regime lacking democratic characteristics, ruled by a single leader or small group of leaders (chapter 1)

autonomy Ability and right of a minority group to partially govern itself within a larger state (chapter 4)

bicameral legislature A legislature that has two houses (chapter 6)

bourgeoisie The class that owns capital; according to Marxism, the ruling elite in all capitalist societies (chapter 1)

bureaucracy A large set of appointed officials whose function is to implement the laws of the state, as directed by the executive (chapter 2)

bureaucratic-authoritarian regime A regime characterized by institutionalized rule under a military government with a primary goal of economic development; coined by Guillermo O'Donnell to describe Latin American military regimes in the 1970s (chapter 3)

cap and trade system Market-based pollution control system in which the government sets an overall limit on how much of a pollutant is acceptable from an entire industry or country and issues vouchers to pollute to each company; individual companies are then free to trade these vouchers (chapter 11)

capitalism The combination of a market economy with private property rights (chapter 5)

centripetal approach A means used by democracies to resolve ethnic conflict by giving political leaders and parties incentives to moderate their demands (chapter 4)

charismatic legitimacy The right to rule based on personal virtue, heroism, sanctity, or other extraordinary characteristics; one of Max Weber's three versions of legitimacy (chapter 2)

Christian democratic welfare states States whose social policies are based on the nuclear family with male breadwinner, designed primarily to achieve income stabilization to mitigate the effects of market-induced income insecurity; Germany is a key example (chapter 11)

citizen A member of a political community or state with certain rights and duties (chapter 3)

civic culture Political culture in which citizens hold values and beliefs that support democracy, including active participation in politics but also enough deference to the leadership to let it govern effectively (chapter 1)

civic nationalism A sense of national unity and purpose based on a set of commonly held political beliefs (chapter 4)

civil rights The first of T. H. Marshall's rights of citizenship; those rights that guarantee individual freedom as well as equal, just, and fair treatment by the state (chapter 3)

civil society The sphere of organized, nonviolent activity by groups smaller and less inclusive than the state or government, but larger than the family or individual firm (chapter 1)

clientelism The exchange of material resources for political support (chapter 2)

closed-list proportional representation Electoral system in which each party presents a ranked list of candidates for all the seats in the legislature; voters can see the list and know who the "top" candidates are, but they vote for the party, and each party is awarded legislative seats based on their percentage of the total vote and awards those seats to the candidates on its list in the order in which they are listed (chapter 7)

coalition government Government in a parliamentary system in which at least two parties negotiate an agreement to rule together (chapter 6)

code law Legal system originating in ancient Roman law and modified by Napoleon Bonaparte in France, in which judges may only follow the law as written, interpreting it as little as necessary to fit the case; past decisions are irrelevant, as each judge must look only to the existing law; in contrast to common law (chapter 6)

codetermination In Germany unions are represented on the supervisory boards of all firms of more than 2,000 employees (chapter 5)

cohabitation Sharing of power between a president and prime minister from different parties in a semipresidential system (chapter 6)

collective action problem The unwillingness of individuals to undertake political action because of the rational belief that their individual action will have little or no effect; a problem democratic regimes must overcome via parties and interest groups (chapter 7)

command and control policies Pollution control system in which a government directly regulates the specific amount of pollution each polluting entity is allowed (chapter 11)

command economy An economic system in which most prices, property, and production are directly controlled by the state (chapter 5)

common law Legal system originating in Britain in which judges base decisions not only on their understanding of the written law but also on their understanding of past court cases; in contrast to code law (chapter 6)

communitarianism Philosophical tradition supporting the argument that humans are inherently social and political animals and thus can only function well in strongly bonded communities (chapter 12)

comparative advantage Theory of trade that argues that economic efficiency and well-being will be maximized if each country uses its resources to produce whatever it produces relatively well compared to other countries and then trades what it has produced with other countries for goods it does not produce (chapter 5)

comparative institutional advantage Idea in the "varieties of capitalism" school of thought that argues that different kinds of capitalist systems have different institutional advantages that they usually will try to maintain, resulting in different responses to external economic pressures (chapter 10)

comparative method The means by which scholars try to mimic laboratory conditions by careful selection of cases (chapter 1)

comparative politics One of the major subfields of political science, in which the primary focus is on comparing power and decision making across countries (chapter 1)

conditional cash transfer (CCT) Programs that provide cash grants to the poor and in exchange require particular beneficial behavior from the poor, such as children's attendance at school and visits to health clinics (chapter 11)

consensus democracy A democratic system with multiparty executives in a coalition government, executive-legislative balance, a bicameral legislature, and a rigid constitution not easily amended (chapter 6)

consociationalism A democratic system designed to ease communal tensions via the principles of recognizing the existence of specific groups and granting some share of power in the central government to each, usually codified in specific legal or constitutional guarantees to each group (chapter 4)

constructivism A theory of identity-group formation that argues identities are created through a complex process usually referred to as social construction; societies collectively "construct" identities as a wide array of actors continually discusses the question of who "we" are, identity groups are not frozen in time but change relatively slowly, and each individual can be part of more than one group (chapter 4)

contentious politics Any interaction in which a group makes claims that conflict with others' interests, leading to coordinated efforts to secure those claims that in some way involve the state (chapter 4)

convergence Argument that globalization will force similar economic and social policies to be adopted across all countries (chapter 10)

coordinated market economies (CMEs) In the varieties of capitalism approach, capitalist economies in which firms, financiers, unions, and government consciously coordinate their actions via interlocking ownership and participation; Germany and Japan are examples (chapter 10)

corporatism Interest group system in which one organization represents each sector of society; originally from the Catholic belief in society as an organic whole; two subtypes are societal and state corporatism (chapter 3)

coup d'état Military takeover of a government (chapter 9)

cultural nationalism National unity based on a common cultural characteristic; those people who don't share that particular cultural characteristic cannot be included in the nation (chapter 4)

deficit spending Government spending exceeds what is collected in revenue (chapter 5)

deliberative democracy Democracy that asks citizens not only to assume their rights and minimally participate through voting but also to engage actively in democratic discussion in the effort to build a better society (chapter 12)

democracy A regime in which citizens have basic rights of open association and expression and the ability to change the government through some sort of electoral process (chapter 1)

democratic centralism The organization of a ruling party, primarily in communist regimes, in which lower organs of a party and state vote on issues and individuals to represent them at higher levels, ultimately reaching the top level, which makes final, binding decisions that all must then obey without question; key organizational innovation of Vladimir Lenin, leader of the Russian Communist Party (chapter 3)

democratic consolidation The idea that democracy has become widely accepted as the permanent form of political activity in a particular country, and all significant political elites and their followers accept democratic rules and are confident everyone else does as well (chapter 9)

developmental state A state that seeks to create national strength by taking an active and conscious role in the development of specific sectors of the economy (chapter 5)

devolution Partial decentralization of power from central government to subunits such as states or provinces, with subunits' power being dependent on central government and reversible (chapter 6)

dictator's dilemma An authoritarian ruler's repression creates fear, which then breeds uncertainty about how much support the ruler has; in response, the ruler spends more resources than is rational on co-opting the opposition (chapter 8)

dictatorship of the proletariat The first stage of communism in Marxist thought, characterized by absolute rule by workers as a class over all other classes (chapter 3)

dominant-party system Party system in which multiple parties and free and fair elections exist but one party wins every election and governs continuously (chapter 7)

Duverger's Law French political scientist Maurice Duverger argued that "first-past-the-post" electoral systems will produce two major parties, eliminating smaller parties (chapter 7)

electoral systems Formal, legal mechanisms that translate votes into control over political offices and shares of political power (chapter 7)

elite theory Theory that all societies are ruled by a small group that has effective control over virtually all power; contrast to pluralist theory (chapter 1)

empirical theory An argument explaining what actually occurs; empirical theorists first notice and describe a pattern and then attempt to explain what causes it (chapter 1)

environmental justice movement A movement focused on exposing and fighting against racial and class inequalities in exposure to pollution, started in the United States in 1982 (chapter 11)

ethnic group A group of people who see themselves as united by one or more cultural attributes or a sense of common history but do not see themselves as a nation seeking their own state (chapter 4)

executive The branch of government that must exist in all modern states; it is the chief political power in a state and implements all laws (chapter 6)

export-oriented growth (EOG) Development policy based on encouraging economic growth via exports of goods and services, usually starting with light manufacturing such as textiles (chapter 10)

externality A cost or benefit of the production process that is not fully included in the price of the final market transaction when the product is sold (chapter 5)

external sovereignty Sovereignty relative to outside powers that is legally recognized in international law (chapter 2)

failed state A state that is so weak that it loses effective sovereignty over part or all of its territory (chapter 2)

federalism A system in which a state's power is legally and constitutionally divided among more than one level of government; in contrast to a unitary system (chapter 2)

federal systems Political systems in which a state's power is legally and constitutionally divided among more than one level of government; in contrast to a unitary system (chapter 6)

feudal states Premodern states in Europe in which power in a territory was divided among multiple and overlapping lords claiming sovereignty (chapter 2)

first dimension of power The ability of one person or group to get another person or group to do something it otherwise would not do (chapter 1)

"first-past-the-post" (FPTP) Electoral system in which individual candidates are elected in single-member districts; the candidate with the most votes, but not necessarily a majority, wins (chapter 7)

fiscal policy Government budgetary policy (chapter 5)

foreign direct investment (FDI) Investment from abroad in productive activity in another country (chapter 10)

founding election The first democratic election in many years (or ever), marking the completion of a transition to democracy (chapter 9)

globalization A rapid increase in the flow of cultural symbols, political ideas and movements, economic activity, technology, and communications around the globe (chapter 5)

hardliners Leaders in an authoritarian regime who believe in repressing any opposition and preserving the status quo when faced with a demand for political liberalization or democratization (chapter 9)

head of government The key executive power in a state; usually a president or prime minister (chapter 6)

head of state The official, symbolic representative of a country, authorized to speak on its behalf and represent it, particularly in world affairs; usually a president or monarch (chapter 6)

Hindu nationalism In India, a movement to define the country as primarily Hindu; the founding ideology of the BJP party (chapter 7)

historical institutionalists Theorists who believe institutions explain political behavior, shape individuals' political preferences and their perceptions of their self-interests, evolve historically in particular countries, and change relatively slowly (chapter 1)

historical materialism The assumption that material forces are the prime movers of history and politics; a key philosophical tenet of Marxism (chapter 3)

horizontal accountability The ability of state institutions to hold one another accountable (chapter 6)

hyperglobalization Thesis that globalization is so powerful, it will overwhelm the power of nation-states, forcing convergence of economic policies (chapter 10)

ideal type Term used by Max Weber for a model of the purest version that a thing might be (chapter 2)

ideological hegemony The ruling class's ability to spread a set of ideas justifying and perpetuating its political dominance (chapter 1)

import-substitution industrialization (ISI) Development policy popular in the 1950s–1970s that uses trade policy, monetary policy, and currency rates to encourage the creation of new industries to produce goods domestically that the country imported in the past (chapter 5)

institutionalism An approach to explaining politics that argues that political institutions are crucial to understanding political behavior (chapter 1)

institutionalization The degree to which government processes and procedures are established, predictable, and routinized (chapter 6)

instrumentalism An elite theory of identity politics: rational and self-interested elites manipulate symbols and feelings of identity to mobilize a political following (chapter 4)

interest-group pluralism An interest group system in which many groups exist to represent particular interests and the government remains officially neutral among them; the United States is a key example (chapter 7)

internal sovereignty The sole authority within a territory capable of making and enforcing laws and policies; an essential element of a modern state (chapter 2)

international capital flows Movements of capital in the form of money across international borders (chapter 10)

international relations The study of politics among national governments and beyond national boundaries (chapter 1)

iron triangles Three-sided cooperative interaction among bureaucrats, legislators, and business leaders in a particular sector that serves the interest of all involved but keeps others out of the policy-making process (chapter 6)

Islamism The belief that Islamic law, as revealed by God to the Prophet Mohammed, can and should provide the basis for government in Muslim communities, with little equivocation or compromise (chapter 3)

jihad Derived from an Arabic word for "struggle"; an important concept in Islam; the Quran identifies three kinds of *jihad*: internal struggle to live faithfully, struggle to resist evil and right injustice, and struggle to protect the Muslim community (chapter 3)

judicial independence The belief and ability of judges to decide cases as they think appropriate, regardless of what other people, especially politically powerful officials or institutions, desire (chapter 6)

judicial review The right of the judiciary to decide whether a specific law contradicts a country's constitution (chapter 6)

judiciary Branch of government that interprets the law and applies it to individual cases (chapter 6)

jus sanguinis Citizenship based on "blood" ties; Germany is a key example (chapter 4)

jus soli Literally, citizenship dependent on "soil," or residence within the national territory; France is a key example (chapter 4)

Keynesian theory Named for British economist John Maynard Keynes, who argued that governments can reduce the "boom and bust" cycles of capitalism via active fiscal policy, including deficit spending when necessary (chapter 5)

laïcité A model of secularism advocating that religion should play no part in the public realm (chapter 12)

legislative oversight Members of the legislature, usually in key committees, oversee the working of the bureaucracy by interviewing key leaders, examining budgets, and assessing how successfully a particular agency has carried out its mandate (chapter 6)

legislature Branch of government that makes the law in a democracy (chapter 6)

legitimacy The recognized right to rule (chapter 2)

liberal democracy A system of government that provides eight key guarantees: freedom of association, freedom of expression, the right to vote, broad citizen eligibility for public office, the right of political leaders

to compete for support, alternative sources of information, free and fair elections, and institutions that make government policies depend on votes and other forms of citizen preferences (chapter 3)

liberal market economies (LMEs) In the varieties of capitalism approach, countries that rely heavily on market relationships to govern economic activity, meaning that firms interact with other firms and secure sources of finance through purely market-based transactions; the United States and United Kingdom are key examples (chapter 10)

liberal welfare states States whose social policies focus on ensuring that all who can do so gain their income in the market; more concerned with preserving individual autonomy via market participation than with reducing poverty or inequality; the United States is a key example (chapter 11)

liberationist Member of the LGBT movement who seeks to transform sexual and gender norms, not simply to gain equal rights with heterosexuals but also to liberate all persons to express whatever sexual orientation and gender identity they wish in order to gain social acceptance and respect for all regardless of their conformity to preexisting norms or institutions (chapter 12)

majoritarian democracy A type of democratic system that concentrates power relatively tightly in a single-party executive, with executive dominance over the legislature, a single legislative branch, and constitutions that can be easily amended (chapter 6)

market-based private insurance system Health care system that relies on private insurance for the bulk of the population; the United States is a key example (chapter 11)

market economy An economic system in which individuals and firms exchange goods and services in a largely unfettered manner (chapter 5)

market failure Phenomenon that occurs when markets fail to perform efficiently or they fail to perform according to other widely held social values; often caused by externalities, high risk, or imperfect information (chapter 5)

Marxism Structuralist argument that says economic structures largely determine political behavior; the philosophical underpinning of communism (chapter 1)

means-tested public assistance Social programs that provide benefits to individuals who fall below a specific income level; TANF is an example in the United States (chapter 11)

member of parliament (MP) An elected member of the legislature in a parliamentary system (chapter 6)

military regime System of government in which military officers control power (chapter 3)

Millennium Development Goals (MDGs) Targets established by the United Nations to reduce poverty and hunger, improve education and health, improve the status of women, and achieve environmental sustainability (chapter 10)

mixed representation system Also called a semiproportional representation system; an electoral system that combines single-member district representation with overall proportionality in allocation of legislative seats to parties; Germany is a key example (chapter 7)

mode of production In Marxist theory, the economic system in any given historical era; feudalism and capitalism in the last millennium in Europe (chapter 3)

moderates Leaders of democracy movements who are willing to compromise with the authoritarian regime to make some gains toward democracy, even if partial (chapter 9)

modernists Theorists of political culture who believe that clear sets of attitudes, values, and beliefs can be identified in each country that change very rarely and explain much about politics there (chapter 1)

modernization The transformation from poor agrarian to wealthy industrial societies, usually seen as the process of postcolonial societies becoming more like societies in the West (chapter 1)

modernization theory Theory of development that argues that postcolonial societies need to go through the same process that the West underwent in order to develop (chapter 3)

monetarist theory Economic theory that only monetary policy can affect economic well-being in capitalist economies; rejects Keynesian idea of using fiscal policy to regulate economy, arguing instead for reduced role for government (chapter 5)

monetary policy The amount of money a government prints and puts into circulation and the basic interest rates the government sets (chapter 5)

monopoly The control of the entire supply of a valued good or service by one economic actor (chapter 5)

moral hazard Occurs when parties to a transaction behave in a particular way because they believe they will not have to pay the full costs of their actions (chapter 11)

most different systems design A common approach of the comparative method that looks at countries that differ in many ways but are similar in terms of the particular political process or outcome in which the research is interested (chapter 1)

most similar systems design A common approach of the comparative method that selects cases that are alike in a number of ways but differ on a key question under examination; often used by comparativists who focus exclusively on one region of the world (chapter 1)

multicultural integration Accepts that ethnocultural identities matter to citizens, will endure over time, and must be recognized and accommodated within political institutions; in contrast to assimilation (chapter 12)

multiculturalism In general, the belief that different cultures in a society ought to be respected; in the United Kingdom, the policy governing how the state treats racial and religious minorities (chapter 12)

multiparty systems Party systems in which more than two parties could potentially win a national election and govern (chapter 7)

nation A group that proclaims itself a nation and has or seeks control of a state (chapter 4)

national health insurance (NHI) A health care system in which the government mandates that virtually all citizens must have insurance; Germany is a key example (chapter 11)

national health system (NHS) A government-financed and managed health care system, often called a single-payer system; the government creates a system into which all citizens pay, either through a separate insurance payment or via general taxation, and through which they gain medical care; the United Kingdom is a key example (chapter 11)

nationalism The desire to be a nation and thus to control a national state (chapter 4)

natural monopolies The control of the entire supply of valued goods or services by one economic actor in sectors of the economy in which competition would raise costs and reduce efficiency (chapter 5)

neocolonialism Relationship between postcolonial societies and their former colonizers in which leaders benefit politically and economically by helping outside businesses and states maintain access to the former colonies' wealth and come to serve the interests of the former colonizers and corporations more than they serve their own people (chapter 1)

neocorporatism Also called societal corporatism; corporatism that evolves historically and voluntarily rather than being mandated by the state; Germany is a key example (chapter 7)

neofascist Description given to parties or political movements that espouse a virulent nationalism, often defined on a cultural or religious basis and opposed to immigrants as threats to national identity (chapter 3)

neoliberalism Development theory supporting structural adjustment programs; argues that developing countries should reduce the role of government and open themselves to global trade to allow the market to allocate resources to maximize efficiency and thereby economic growth (chapter 5)

neopatrimonial authority Power based on a combination of the trappings of modern, bureaucratic states with underlying informal institutions of clientelism that work behind the scenes; most common in Africa (chapter 3)

neutral state model A model of secularism wherein the state is neutral about, but not opposed to, religion (chapter 12)

New Public Management (NPM) Theory of reform of bureaucracies that argues for the privatizing of many government services so that they are provided by the market, creating competition among agencies and subagencies within the bureaucracy to simulate a market, focusing on customer satisfaction (via client surveys, among other things), and flattening administrative hierarchies to encourage more team-based activity and creativity (chapter 6)

normative theory An argument explaining what ought to occur rather than what does occur; contrast with empirical theory (chapter 1)

one-party regime A system of government in which a single party gains power, usually after independence in postcolonial states, and systematically eliminates all opposition in the name of development and national unity (chapter 3)

open-list proportional representation Electoral system with multiple candidates in each district; voters are presented with a list of all candidates and vote for the individual candidate of their choice; each party receives a number of legislative seats based on the total number of votes cast for all candidates from that party, and candidates with the most votes in the party get those seats; Brazil is a key example (chapter 7)

pact In a transition to democracy, a conscious agreement among the most important political actors in the authoritarian regime and in civil society to establish a new form of government (chapter 9)

parliamentarism A term for a parliamentary system of democracy (chapter 6)

parliamentary sovereignty Parliament is supreme in all matters; key example is the United Kingdom (chapter 3)

participatory democracy A form of democracy that encourages citizens to participate actively, in many ways beyond voting; usually focused at the local level (chapter 3)

party system The number of parties and each one's respective strength as an institution (chapter 7)

patriarchy Rule by men (chapter 1)

patron-client relationships Top leaders (patrons) mobilize political support by providing resources to their followers (clients) in exchange for political loyalty (chapter 1)

peak associations Organizations that bring together all interest groups in a particular sector to influence and negotiate agreements with the state; in the United States, an example is the AFL-CIO (chapter 7)

personalist regime System of government in which a central leader comes to dominate a state, typically not only eliminating all opposition but also weakening the state's institutions to centralize power in his hands (chapter 3)

personality cult Occurs in the most extreme cases of personalist rule; followers constantly glorify the ruler and attempt to turn his every utterance into not only government fiat but also divine wisdom; Mao Zedong in China was a key example (chapter 8)

pluralist theory Explanation of who has power that argues that society is divided into various political groups and power is dispersed among these groups so that no group has complete or permanent power; contrast to elite theory (chapter 1)

plurality The receipt of the most votes but not a majority (chapter 7)

politburo The chief decision-making organ in a communist party; China's politburo is a key example (chapter 3)

political accountability The ability of the citizenry, directly or indirectly, to control political leaders and institutions (chapter 6)

political actor Any person or group engaged in political behavior (chapter 1)

political appointees Officials who serve at the pleasure of the president or prime minister and, among other things, are assigned the task of overseeing their respective segments of the bureaucracy (chapter 6)

political culture A set of widely held attitudes, values, beliefs, and symbols about politics (chapter 1)

political development The processes through which modern nations and states arise and how political institutions and regimes evolve and the study of these processes (chapter 1)

political discourse The ways in which people speak and write about politics; postmodern theorists argue it influences political attitudes, identity, and actions (chapter 1)

political economy The study of the interaction between political and economic phenomena (chapter 1)

political ideology A systematic set of beliefs about how a political system ought to be structured (chapter 1)

political institution A set of rules, norms, or standard operating procedures that is widely recognized and accepted by the society and that structures and constrains political actions (chapter 1)

political liberalization The opening of the political system to greater participation; typically before a transition to democracy (chapter 9)

political rights The second of T. H. Marshall's rights of citizenship; those rights associated with active political participation: right to association, expression, voting, and running for office (chapter 3)

political saliency The degree to which something is of political importance (chapter 4)

political science The systematic study of politics and power (chapter 1)

political socialization The process through which people, especially young people, learn about politics and are taught a society's common political values and beliefs (chapter 1)

political violence The use of violence by nonstate actors for political ends (chapter 9)

politics The process by which human communities make collective decisions (chapter 1)

politics of recognition The demands for recognition and inclusion that have arisen since the 1960s in racial, religious, ethnic, gender, and other minority or socially marginalized groups (chapter 4)

populism A broad and charismatic appeal to poor people on the part of a leader to solve their problems directly via governmental largess; most common in Latin America in the early to mid-twentieth century (chapter 7)

positive accommodation A model of secularism wherein the state is neutral among but willing to support religions that it recognizes as important elements in civil society (chapter 12)

postmaterialist Set of values in a society in which most citizens are economically secure enough to move beyond immediate economic (materialist) concerns to "quality of life" issues like human rights, civil rights, women's rights, environmentalism, and moral values (chapter 1)

postmodernist An approach that sees cultures not as sets of fixed and clearly defined values but rather as sets of symbols subject to interpretation (chapter 1)

precautionary principle A policy that emphasizes risk avoidance even when the science predicting a risk is uncertain (chapter 11)

presidentialism A term denoting a presidential system of democracy (chapter 6)

prime minister (PM) The head of government in parliamentary and semipresidential systems (chapter 6)

primordialism A theory of identity that sees identity groups as in some sense "natural" or God given, having existed since "time immemorial," and able to be defined unambiguously by such clear criteria as kinship, language, culture, or phenotype (chapter 4)

principal-agent problem A problem common in any hierarchical situation in which a superior (principal) hires someone (agent) to perform a task but the agent's self-interests do not necessarily align with the principal's, so the problem is how the principal makes sure the agent carries out the task as assigned; in politics, common when the elected or appointed political leadership in the executive or legislative branches assigns a bureaucrat a task to implement laws in a particular way (chapter 6)

privatize Sell off public assets to the private sector (chapter 5)

proletariat A term in Marxist theory for the class of free wage laborers who own no capital and must sell their labor to survive; communist parties claim to work on the proletariat's behalf (chapter 1)

proportional representation (PR) Electoral system in which seats in a legislature are apportioned on a purely proportional basis, giving each party the share of seats that matches its share of the total vote (chapter 7)

psychological theories Explanations of political behavior based on psychological analysis of political actors' motives (chapter 1)

public goods Those goods or services that cannot or will not be provided via the market because their costs are too high or their benefits too diffuse (chapter 5)

quantitative statistical techniques Research method used for large-scale studies that reduces evidence to sets of numbers that statistical methods can analyze to systematically compare a huge number of cases (chapter 1)

quasi-states States that have legal sovereignty and international recognition but lack almost all the domestic attributes of a functioning modern state (chapter 2)

race A people who see itself as a group based primarily on one or more perceived common physical characteristics and common history (chapter 4)

radicals In democratic transitions, members of civil society who wish to achieve immediate and complete democracy and are unwilling to compromise with the existing regime (chapter 9)

rational choice institutionalists Institutionalist theorists who follow the assumptions of rational choice theory and argue that institutions are the products of the interaction and bargaining of rational actors (chapter 1)

rational choice theory Explanation of political behavior that assumes that individuals are rational beings who bring a set of self-defined preferences and adequate knowledge and ability to pursue those preferences to the political arena; these assumptions are then used to model political behavior in particular contexts (chapter 1)

rational-legal legitimacy The right of leaders to rule based on their selection according to an accepted set of laws, standards, or procedures; one of Max Weber's three versions of legitimacy (chapter 2)

regime A set of fundamental rules and institutions that govern political activity (chapter 3)

regime change The process through which one regime is transformed into another (chapter 9)

relative deprivation A belief that a group or individual is not getting its share of something of value relative to others in the society or relative to members' own expectations (chapter 4)

rent seeking Gaining an advantage in a market without engaging in equally productive activity; usually involves using government regulations to one's own benefit (chapter 6)

research methods Systematic processes used to ensure that the study of a specific item or situation is as objective and unbiased as possible (chapter 1)

resource curse Occurs when a state relies on a key resource for almost all of its revenue, allowing it to ignore its citizens and resulting in a weak state (chapter 2)

revolution A relatively rapid transformation of the political system and social structure that results from the overthrow of the prior regime by mass participation in extra-legal political action, which is often (but not always) violent (chapter 9)

revolutions from above Revolutions in which the outcomes are often negotiated among political elites, each with the backing of a segment of the populace (chapter 9)

revolutions from below Revolutions that involve the mass uprising of the populace to overthrow the government as a central part of the process (chapter 9)

risk assessment Analysis of what the risks of damaging outcomes are in a particular situation (chapter 11)

risk management Policy used to keep risks to acceptable levels (chapter 11)

ruling class An elite who possess adequate resources to control a regime; in Marxist theory, the class that controls key sources of wealth in a given epoch (chapter 1)

second dimension of power The ability not only to make people do something but to keep them from doing something (chapter 1)

security dilemma A situation in which two or more groups do not trust one another, fear one another, and do not believe that institutional constraints will protect them (chapter 4)

semi-authoritarian regime A type of hybrid regime in which formal opposition and some open political debate exist and elections are held to select the executive and legislative branches but in which the ruling party controls electoral outcomes and the regime cannot be considered democratic in any real sense; also called competitive authoritarian and electoral authoritarian (chapter 3)

semipresidentialism A political system in which executive power is divided between a directly elected president and a prime minister elected by a parliament; Russia and France are key examples (chapter 6)

semiproportional representation system See *mixed representation system* (chapter 7)

separation of powers Constitutionally explicit division of power among the major branches of government (chapter 6)

sharia Muslim law (chapter 3)

single case study Research method that examines a particular political phenomenon in just one country or community and can generate ideas for theories or test theories developed from different cases (chapter 1)

single-member district (SMD) Electoral system in which each geographic district elects a single representative to a legislature (chapter 7)

single-payer system See *national health system (NHS)* (chapter 11)

social capital Social networks and norms of reciprocity important for a strong civil society (chapter 7)

social classes In Marxist theory, groups of people with the same relationship to the means of production; more generally, groups of people with similar occupations, wealth, or income (chapter 1)

social construction Part of constructivist approach to identity; process through which societies collectively "construct" identities as a wide array of actors continually discusses the question of who "we" are (chapter 4)

social contract theory Philosophical approach underlying liberalism that begins from the premise that legitimate governments are formed when free and independent individuals join in a contract to permit representatives to govern over them in their common interests (chapter 3)

social democracy Combines liberal democracy with much greater provision of social rights of citizenship and typically greater public control of the economy (chapter 3)

social democratic welfare states States whose social policies strongly emphasize universal entitlements to achieve greater social equality and promote equal citizenship; Sweden is a prime example (chapter 11)

social insurance Provides benefits to categories of people who have contributed to a (usually mandatory) public insurance fund; typically used to provide retirement pensions (chapter 11)

social market economy In Germany, postwar economic system that combines a highly productive market economy with an extensive and generous welfare state and unusually active involvement of both business and labor associations in setting and implementing economic policy (chapter 5)

social movements Part of civil society; have a loosely defined organizational structure and represent people who have been outside the bounds of formal institutions, seek major socioeconomic or political changes to the status quo, or employ noninstitutional forms of collective action (chapter 7)

social policy Policy focused on reducing poverty and income inequality and stabilizing individual or family income (chapter 11)

social revolution In Marxist theory, the transition from one mode of production to another; Marxist understanding of revolution (chapter 3)

social rights The third of T. H. Marshall's rights of citizenship; those rights related to basic well-being and socioeconomic equality (chapter 3)

societal corporatism See *neocorporatism* (chapter 7)

softliners In democratic transitions, members of the authoritarian regime willing to consider compromising with opponents as a means to survive demands for democratization (chapter 9)

sovereign Quality of a state in which it is legally recognized by the family of states as the sole legitimate governing authority within its territory and as the legal equal of other states (chapter 2)

soviets Legislative bodies in the communist regime of the Soviet Union (chapter 3)

stare decisis Literally, "let the decision stand"; in common law, the practice of accepting the precedent of previous similar cases (chapter 6)

state A set of ongoing institutions that develops and administers laws and generates and implements public policies in a specific territory (chapter 2)

state corporatism Corporatism mandated by the state; common in fascist regimes (chapter 7)

strong state A state that is generally capable of providing adequate political goods to its citizens (chapter 2)

structural adjustment programs (SAPs) Development programs created by the World Bank and International Monetary Fund beginning in the 1980s; based on neoliberalism (chapter 5)

structuralism Approach to explaining politics that argues that political behavior is at least influenced and limited, and perhaps even determined, by broader structures in a society such as class divisions or enduring institutions (chapter 1)

subcultures Groups that hold partially different beliefs and values from those of the main political culture of a country (chapter 1)

supreme leader Individual who wields executive power with few formal limits in an authoritarian regime; in the Islamic Republic of Iran, the formal title of the top ruling cleric (chapter 8)

symmetrical federal system Division of constitutionally assigned power to national and subnational governments with all subnational governments (states or provinces) having the same relationship with and rights in relation to the national government (chapter 6)

tax expenditures Targeted tax breaks for specific groups of citizens or activities designed to achieve social policy goals (chapter 11)

technocratic legitimacy A claim to rule based on knowledge or expertise (chapter 3)

territory An area with clearly defined borders to which a state lays claim (chapter 2)

terrorism Political violence targeted at civilian noncombatants (chapter 9)

theocracy Rule by religious authorities (chapter 3)

theory An abstract argument that provides a systematic explanation of some phenomena (chapter 1)

third dimension of power The ability to shape or determine individual or group political demands by causing people to think about political issues in ways that are contrary to their own interests (chapter 1)

totalitarian regime A regime that controls virtually all aspects of society and eliminates all vestiges of civil society; Germany under Hitler and the Soviet Union under Stalin were key examples (chapter 3)

trade The flow of goods and services across national borders (chapter 10)

traditional legitimacy The right to rule based on a society's long-standing patterns and practices; one of Max Weber's three versions of legitimacy (chapter 2)

tragedy of the commons No individual has the incentive or ability to preserve a common, shared good that is free, so without collective effort, it is likely to be overused and perhaps ultimately destroyed (chapter 11)

transition to democracy A type of regime change typically involving a negotiated process that removes an authoritarian regime and concludes with a founding election for a new, democratic regime (chapter 9)

two-and-a-half-party system Party system in which two large parties win the most votes but typically neither gains a majority, thus requiring a third (the "half" party) to join one of the major parties to form a legislative majority; Germany is key example (chapter 7)

two-party system Party system in which only two parties are able to garner enough votes to win an election, though more may compete; the United Kingdom and United States are key examples (chapter 7)

typology A classification of some set of phenomena into distinct types for purposes of analysis (chapter 1)

unitary systems Political systems in which the central government has sole constitutional sovereignty and power; contrast with federal systems (chapter 6)

universal entitlements Benefits that governments provide to all citizens more or less equally, usually funded through general taxation; in the United States, public education is an example (chapter 11)

vanguard party Vladimir Lenin's concept of a small party that claims legitimacy to rule based on its understanding of Marxist theory and its ability to represent the interests of the proletariat before they are a majority of the populace (chapter 3)

varieties of capitalism (VOC) School of thought analyzing wealthy market economies that focuses primarily on business firms and how they are governed in terms of their interactions with government, each other, workers, and sources of finance; divides such economies into liberal market economies (LMEs) and coordinated market economies (CMEs) and argues that globalization will not produce convergence between them (chapter 10)

vertical accountability The ability of individuals and groups in a society to hold state institutions accountable (chapter 6)

veto player An individual or collective actor, such as a legislature or interest group, whose agreement is essential for any policy change (chapter 6)

virtual representation When voters' views are represented indirectly in the legislature by their chosen party's candidates who have been elected in districts other than their own (chapter 7)

vote of no confidence In parliamentary systems, parliament voting to remove a government (the prime minister and cabinet) from power (chapter 6)

weak state State that cannot provide adequate political goods to its population (chapter 2)

welfare states Distinct systems of social policies that arose after World War II in wealthy market economies, including social democratic welfare states, Christian democratic welfare states, and liberal welfare states (chapter 11)

Index

Page numbers with *b, f, m,* or *t* indicate boxes, figures, maps, and tables, respectively. Italicized page numbers indicate photographs.

Photo Credits

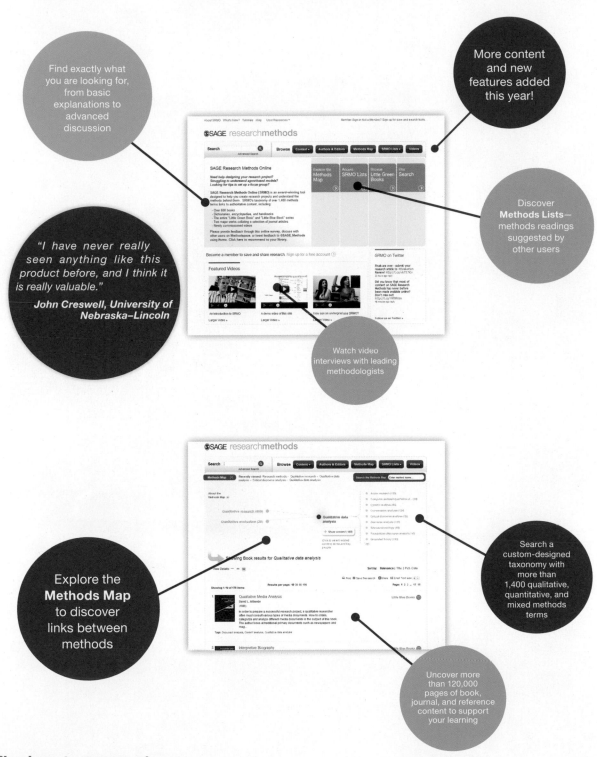

⊘SAGE researchmethods

The essential online tool for researchers from the world's leading methods publisher

Find exactly what you are looking for, from basic explanations to advanced discussion

More content and new features added this year!

"I have never really seen anything like this product before, and I think it is really valuable."

John Creswell, University of Nebraska–Lincoln

Discover **Methods Lists**— methods readings suggested by other users

Watch video interviews with leading methodologists

Explore the **Methods Map** to discover links between methods

Search a custom-designed taxonomy with more than 1,400 qualitative, quantitative, and mixed methods terms

Uncover more than 120,000 pages of book, journal, and reference content to support your learning

Find out more at
www.sageresearchmethods.com